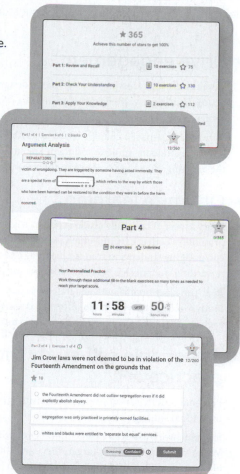

DRIVE GREATER ENGAGEMENT AND LEARNING WITH

OXFORD insight study guide

Every new print or electronic copy of this text comes with access to Oxford Insight Study Guide, a powerful, personalized learning tool designed to optimize your students' learning.

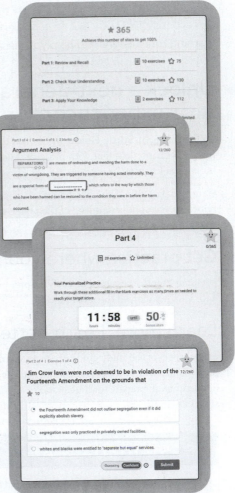

▶ Drive engagement

Developed with a learning-science-based design, **Oxford Insight Study Guide** actively engages students in a review of course content while encouraging effective reading and study habits.

Gamified, fast-paced chapter-based assessment activities reinforce students' understanding of key content that supports the learning objectives covered in their reading.

▶ Optimize learning

Every aspect of the study guide experience is designed to promote effective learning, emphasizing recall over recognition, encouraging students to read for meaning and context, and rewarding students for behaviors like spacing their study sessions.

Real-time, actionable data generated by student activity in the Study Guide helps you make informed decisions and ensure that each student is best supported along their unique learning path.

▶ Assignable self-study with personal practice

Personal Practice sessions prioritize material with which individual students need the most help.

Students work towards a target number of points in each chapter. When students reach the target, they earn 100% for the chapter, allowing them to build their knowledge and prepare for higher-stakes assessment in a low-stakes environment.

GET STARTED TODAY

For optimal effectiveness and flexibility, **Oxford Insight Study Guide** can be delivered through your school's learning management system or Oxford Learning Cloud. Contact your Oxford University Press representative or visit **oxfordinsight.oup.com** to learn more about integrating **Oxford Insight Study Guide** into your course.

Living Ethics

Living Ethics

An Introduction with Readings

2nd Edition

Russ Shafer-Landau
University of Wisconsin at Madison

New York   Oxford

OXFORD UNIVERSITY PRESS

Oxford University Press is a department of the University of Oxford.
It furthers the University's objective of excellence in research, scholarship,
and education by publishing worldwide. Oxford is a registered trademark of
Oxford University Press in the UK and certain other countries.

Published in the United States of America by Oxford University Press
198 Madison Avenue, New York, NY 10016, United States of America.

For titles covered by Section 112 of the US Higher Education
Opportunity Act, please visit www.oup.com/us/he for the latest
information about pricing and alternate formats.

Library of Congress Control Number: 2021943496

9 8 7 6 5 4 3 2 1

Printed by LSC Communications, United States of America

To Robert Miller, friend and editor

BRIEF CONTENTS

CONTENTS

PREFACE

ABOUT THIS BOOK

The book you have in your hands offers one-stop shopping for those who are interested in learning about moral philosophy. It includes a lot of material that I have written, as well as numerous readings selected from a wide array of classic and contemporary works. There's an overview of the terrain (Chapter 1) and a primer on how to engage in moral reasoning (Chapter 2), followed by a substantial introduction to ethical theory (Chapters 3–11, the remainder of Part 1).

Abstract questions of moral theory are fascinating—I've spent the bulk of my career thinking about them—but it's just as interesting to drill down into the philosophical details that surround contemporary moral issues. That's the focus of Part 2 (Chapters 12–23), which covers a dozen of these issues. The material in this part provides important background for serious reflection on these issues, and supplements that with a handful of representative readings: as advertised, an introduction. It should be just enough to whet your appetite for more, but not enough to leave you confident that you've plumbed the depths of any of the issues included here.

In Part 1, my aim is to reveal the attractions of the theories under consideration, and then to introduce some of the sticking points that have led critics to shy away from enthusiastic endorsement. As you'll soon discover, each of these theories is based on a deeply plausible idea about the nature of morality. You'll also find, however, that when these ideas are developed into coherent theories, they almost inevitably come into conflict with other ideas we hold

dear. Though the bulk of Part 1 is given over to my writing about the various ethical theories we encounter, each of the chapters (3–11) devoted to ethical theories also contains classic primary source material that enables you to get a sense of what the originators of these theories were up to.

In Part 2, we consider twelve topics of major ethical importance. Each of the dozen chapters of this part has a similar structure. There is substantial introductory material, followed by a selection of topical readings. In each chapter, we begin with a section entitled *Just the Facts*. This section presents relevant factual material, providing necessary background for our ethical investigations. As it's been for ages, many moral disagreements are founded on false beliefs; our moral outlooks are improved to the extent that we winnow out such mistakes and base our moral views firmly on solid evidence.

Arming oneself with the facts is a vital first step in forming a well-considered moral outlook. But more is needed. In the second section of each chapter, entitled *Argument Analysis*, I reconstruct and critically assess a battery of arguments on the topics of the chapter. In some cases I am pretty opinionated—in my view, a number of popular arguments on these topics do not survive close scrutiny. With most of these arguments, though, I try to be even-handed, indicating their strengths and weaknesses. My interest isn't in converting you to my way of thinking. Indeed, in many cases I am still trying to make up my own mind about these issues, and don't yet have an opinion to convert you to even if I wanted to!

Each chapter in Part 2 also contains a helpful grouping of *Essential Concepts*—key terms that are placed in **bold** on first mention in the text—along with their definitions. These are also collected at the end of the book in a Glossary, for ease of reference. Technical terms from outside of philosophy, as well as jargon from within it, can sometimes serve as barriers to the uninitiated. I don't like that. I've tried to identify all such unfamiliar terms and to be very clear about their meaning, so that these terms don't represent stumbling blocks. My aim is for you to become comfortable with these terms and concepts, so that you can appreciate what's going on at every step and eventually come to your own considered views about these matters.

Each of these chapters also contains a brief *Stat Shot*—a revealing set of statistics about the chapter's subject matter—as well as *Cases for Critical Thinking*. These are exercises designed to invite deeper reflection on issues related to our chosen topics. Often taken from the headlines, these brief case studies are designed to bring into sharp relief a set of practical and theoretical problems for your further consideration.

My hope is that all of this introductory material is interesting in its own right. But it is also meant to be useful, by providing the needed background to engage directly with the many readings that conclude each chapter. These selections are the work of authors who represent a wide spectrum of ethical standpoints. Enjoy!

NEW TO THE SECOND EDITION

While there have been small improvements made to Part 1 of this book, the bulk of the changes appear in Part 2. There is a new section on Privacy, which includes four new readings, and an additional eighteen readings across the remaining topics. Because we sadly don't have unlimited space, this has meant saying goodbye to many selections from the first edition. These include the following:

Mary Midgley	Trying Out One's New Sword
Tom Regan	The Case for Animal Rights
Mary Anne Warren	Difficulties with the Strong Animal Rights Position
R. G. Frey	Moral Standing, the Value of Lives, and Speciesism
Eric Posner and Cass Sunstein	Climate Change Justice
Peter Singer	Justifying Voluntary Euthanasia
Robert Nozick	The Entitlement Theory of Justice
Harry Frankfurt	Equality as a Moral Ideal
Michael Huemer	Is There a Right to Immigrate?
David Miller	Immigration: The Case for Limits
Angelo Corlett	Reparations to Native Americans?
Tommie Shelby	Justice, Deviance, and the Dark Ghetto
Michael Walzer	Terrorism: A Critique of Excuses
Virginia Held	Terrorism and War
Lionel McPherson	Is Terrorism Distinctively Wrong?
Stephen Nathanson	Can Terrorism Be Morally Justified?
Roberta Millstein	GMOs? Not So Fast
Gary Comstock	Ethics and Genetically Modified Foods
Maggie Gallagher	Normal Marriage
Raja Halwani	Virtue Ethics, Casual Sex, and Objectification
Nicholas Dixon	Alcohol and Rape

The good news is that the new material promises to be even more interesting and exciting. The new selections include two articles that were commissioned especially for this book—one written by Diane Jeske, on cultural relativism, and another by Javier Hidalgo, on open borders and immigration. The remaining twenty selections include the following:

Rosalind Hursthouse	Virtue Ethics and the Treatment of Animals
Lori Gruen	Experimenting with Animals
Peter Carruthers	Against the Moral Standing of Animals
John Broome	The Public and Private Morality of Climate Change
John Harris	The Survival Lottery
T.M. Scanlon	Why Does Inequality Matter?
Jason Brennan	International Aid: Not the Cure You Were Hoping for
Christopher Heath Wellman	Refugees and the Right to Control Immigration
Martin Luther King, Jr.	Letter from Birmingham City Jail
Michelle Alexander	The New Jim Crow
James Rachels	Why Privacy Is Important
Anita Allen	What Must We Hide: The Ethics of Privacy and the Ethos of Disclosure
James Stacey Taylor	In Praise of Big Brother: Why We Should Stop Worrying and Learn to Love Big Government
Peter Singer	Visible Man
Nick Bostrom	Transhumanist Values
Dan Wikler	Paternalism in the Age of Cognitive Enhancement
Robin West	The Harms of Consensual Sex
Tom Dougherty	Sex, Lies, and Consent
Elizabeth Brake	Is "Loving More" Better? The Values of Polyamory

INSTRUCTOR'S MANUAL AND STUDENT RESOURCES

Keshav Singh, Ben Schwan, Emma Prendergast, and David Bachyrycz prepared this book's very substantial on-line resources; once you've had a look, I expect you'll agree that they have done a superb job. The Oxford Learning Link (OLL) designed to support this book offers students free access to self-quizzes on book chapters and readings by distinguished philosophers, flashcards, and practice essay questions, as well as the e-book. In addition, the OLL also houses a password-protected Instructor's Manual, Respondus and Learning Management System (LMS)-compatible test banks, and PowerPoint lecture presentations. The manual itself has a "pen and paper" test bank of multiple-choice and essay questions, key terms, web links to sites of further interest, and case studies with accompanying discussion questions. For more information, please visit www.oup.com/he/shafer-landau-le2e.

All new print and digital copies of *Living Ethics*, Second Edition include access to the Oxford Insight Study Guide, a data-driven, personalized digital learning tool that reinforces key concepts from the text and encourages effective reading and study habits. Developed with a learning-science-based design, Oxford Insight Study Guide engages students in an active and highly dynamic review of chapter content, empowering them to critically assess their own understanding of course material. Real-time, actionable data generated by student activity in the tool helps instructors ensure that each student is best supported along their unique learning path. Learn more at oxfordinsight.oup.com.

LMS cartridges are available in formats compatible with any LMS in use at your college or university and include the following:

- The Instructor's Manual and Computerized Test Bank
- Lecture PowerPoints
- All student resources, including self-quizzes, flashcards, and practice essay questions

For more information, please contact your Oxford University Press representative or call 1-800-280-0280.

ACKNOWLEDGMENTS

The first edition of this book was many years in the making, and I want to thank my former editor, Robert Miller (now retired), for prompting me to undertake this project. Over the course of his career, Robert transformed the world of philosophy textbooks—he is the master, from whom all others must learn. Assistant editor Alyssa Palazzo and senior development editor Meg Botteon helped in innumerable ways; they have been a genuine pleasure to work with and are models of true professionalism. My fantastic research assistant, Eric Sampson, did yeoman's work in preparing much of the companion material in Part 2. I feel very grateful to have been able to work with such a stellar support team.

I would also like to thank Keshav Singh, Justin Morton, and Alex Pho for their help with a few chapters in Part 2. Thanks, too, to my UW colleagues Dan Hausman, Harry Brighouse, Paul Kelleher, and Rob Streiffer for pointing me in the direction of some interesting readings. Finally, I'd like to express my gratitude to the fine philosophers whose reviews helped to shape this book in so many ways:

Marcia Andrejevich, Ivy Tech Community College
Golam Azam, Northern Michigan University
Thomas Bontly, University of Connecticut
Jeffrey Brown, University of Northern Colorado
David Burris, Arizona Western College
Antonio Capuano, Auburn University
Jennifer Caseldine-Bracht, Manchester University
Teresa Celada, Wheaton College
Michael Dahnke, College of Staten Island
Michael Emerson, Northwest Michigan College
Bob Fischer, Texas State University
Gary Francione, Rutgers School of Law
Kyle Fritz, Florida State University
Jeffrey Fry, Ball State University
George Gittinger, Northwest Vista College
Elliot Goodine, Guilford Technical Community College
Mark Greene, University of Delaware
Charles Hinkley, Northwest Vista College
Curtis Lane, Long Beach City College
John Macready, Collin College
Michael Norton, University of Arkansas Little Rock
David O'Connor, Seton Hall University
Clare Palmer, Texas A & M University
Michael Robinson, College of Western Idaho
R. Allen Shotwell, Ivy Tech Community College
Owen Smiley, Front Range Community College
James Stacey Taylor, The College of New Jersey
Joshua Tepley, Saint Anselm College
Amy Timko, California State University Stanislaus
Christine Wieseler, Skidmore College
Sandy Woodson, Colorado School of Mines

I've tried to make this book as good as it can be. But I'm sure it can be better. If you have ideas for how this book might be improved, I'd be delighted to hear about them. The best way to get in touch is by email: russshaferlandau@gmail.com.

1

Moral Theory

CHAPTER I

What Is Morality?

Before investing yourself in the study of an academic subject, it would be useful to first have some idea of what you are getting yourself into. One way—sometimes the best—to gain such an understanding is by considering a definition. When you open your trigonometry text or chemistry handbook, you'll likely be given, very early on, a definition of the area you are about to study. So, as a responsible author, I would seem to have a duty now to present you with a definition of *morality*.

I'd certainly like to. But I can't. There is no widely agreed-on definition of *morality*. The absence of a definition does not leave us entirely in the dark, however. (After all, no one has yet been able to offer informative definitions of *literature*, or *life*, or *art*, and yet we know a great deal about those things.) Indeed, we can get a good sense of our subject matter by doing these four things:

1. Being clear about the difference between conventional and critical morality
2. Distinguishing the different branches of moral philosophy and their central questions
3. Identifying starting points for moral thinking
4. Contrasting morality with other normative systems, including religious ones

Let's get to work!

A. CONVENTIONAL AND CRITICAL MORALITY

Suppose you take a sociology or an anthropology course, and you get to a unit on the morality of the cultures you've been studying. You'll likely focus on the patterns of behavior to be found in the cultures, their accepted ideas about right and wrong, and the sorts of character traits that these cultures find admirable. These are the elements of what we can call **conventional morality**—the system of widely accepted rules and principles, created by and for human beings, that members of a culture or society use to govern their own lives and to assess the actions and the motivations of others. The elements of conventional morality can be known by any astute social observer, since gaining such knowledge is a matter of appreciating what most people in a society or culture actually take to be right or wrong.

Conventional morality can differ from society to society. The conventional morality of Saudi Arabia forbids women from publicly contradicting their husbands or brothers, while Denmark's conventional morality allows this. People in the United States would think it immoral to leave a restaurant without tipping a good waiter or bartender, while such behavior in many other societies is perfectly OK.

When I write about morality in this book, I am *not* referring to conventional morality. I am assuming that some social standards—even those that are long-standing and very popular—can be morally mistaken. (We'll examine this assumption in Chapter 3.B.) After all, the set of traditional principles that are widely shared within a culture or society are the result of human decisions, agreements, and practices, all of which are sometimes based on misunderstandings, irrationality, bias, or superstition. So when I talk about morality from this point on, I will be referring to moral standards that are not rooted in widespread endorsement, but rather are independent of conventional morality and can be used to critically evaluate its merits.

It's possible, of course, that conventional morality is all there is. But this would be a very surprising discovery. Most of us assume, as I will do, that the popularity of a moral view is not a guarantee of its truth. We could be wrong on this point, but until we have a chance to consider the matter in detail, I think it best to assume that conventional morality can sometimes be mistaken. If so, then there may be some independent, **critical morality** that (1) does not have its origin in social agreements; (2) is untainted by mistaken beliefs, irrationality, or popular prejudices; and (3) can serve as the true standard for determining when conventional morality has got it right and when it has fallen into error. That is the morality whose nature we are going to explore in this book.

B. THE BRANCHES OF MORAL PHILOSOPHY

As I'm sure you know, there are *lots* of moral questions. So it might help to impose some organization on them. This will enable us to see the basic contours of moral philosophy and also to better appreciate the fundamental questions in each part of the field you are about to study.

There are three core areas of moral philosophy:

1. **Value theory**: What is the good life? What is worth pursuing for its own sake? How do we improve our lot in life? What is happiness, and is it the very same thing as well-being?
2. **Normative ethics**: What are our fundamental moral duties? What makes right actions right? Which character traits count as virtues, which as vices, and why? Who should our role models be? Do the ends always justify the means, or are there certain types of action that should never be done under any circumstances?
3. **Metaethics**: What is the status of moral claims and advice? Can ethical theories, moral principles, or specific moral verdicts be true? If so, what makes them true? Can we gain moral wisdom? If so, how? Do we always have good reason to do our moral duty?

The issues that take up the second half of this book—matters such as abortion, economic justice, animal rights, and so on—are for the most part best seen as belonging to normative ethics. In past, philosophers used to group all such issues under the heading of "applied ethics." The thought—a very natural one, I believe—was that in order to make progress in solving moral problems, one first needs to determine which normative ethical theory is correct. One can then *apply* that theory to the facts at hand and crank out a correct verdict about the morality of the issues.

But, as you'll see when you get to the readings in the Moral Problems part of this book, many philosophers have opted to take a different path. They have thought it possible to resolve moral issues without first deciding on the correct moral theory. You might be skeptical about this—after all, how can we know whether the death penalty, for instance, is morally acceptable if we don't know what the fundamental moral rule is? Hold on to those doubts (if you have them), and then be sure to bring them to your readings in Part 2. Perhaps you'll be surprised at the progress we can make on those issues, even in the absence of a decided view about the ultimate principle of morality. Or you might instead find yourself returning to the material in Part 1, more convinced than ever that we need to first determine which moral theory is correct, before trying to resolve the moral issues of the day.

C. MORAL STARTING POINTS

One of the puzzles about moral thinking is knowing where to begin. Some skeptics about morality deny that there are any proper starting points for ethical reflection. They believe that moral reasoning is simply a way of rationalizing our biases and gut feelings. This outlook encourages us to be lax in moral argument and, worse, supports an attitude that no moral views are any better than others. While this sort of skepticism might be true, we shouldn't regard it as the default view of ethics. We should accept it only as a last resort.

In the meantime, let's consider some fairly plausible ethical assumptions, claims that can get us started in our moral thinking. The point of the exercise is to soften you up to the idea that we are not just spinning our wheels when thinking morally. There are reasonable constraints that can guide us when thinking about how to live. Here are some of them:

- *Neither the law nor tradition is immune from moral criticism.* The law does not have the final word on what is right and wrong. Neither does tradition. Actions that are legal, or customary, are sometimes morally mistaken.
- *Everyone is morally fallible.* Everyone has some mistaken ethical views, and no human being is wholly wise when it comes to moral matters.
- *Friendship is valuable.* Having friends is a good thing. Friendships add value to your life. You are better off when there are people you care deeply about, and who care deeply about you.
- *We are not obligated to do the impossible.* Morality can demand only so much of us. Moral standards that are impossible to meet are illegitimate. Morality must respect our limitations.
- *Children bear less moral responsibility than adults.* Moral responsibility assumes an ability on our part to understand options, to make decisions in an informed way, and to let our decisions guide our behavior. The fewer of these abilities you have, the less blameworthy you are for any harm you might cause.
- *Justice is a very important moral good.* Any moral theory that treats justice as irrelevant is deeply suspect. It is important that we get what we deserve, and that we are treated fairly.

- *Deliberately hurting other people requires justification.* The default position in ethics is this: do no harm. It is sometimes morally acceptable to harm others, but there must be an excellent reason for doing so or else the harmful behavior is unjustified.
- *Equals ought to be treated equally.* People who are alike in all relevant respects should get similar treatment. When this fails to happen—when racist or sexist policies are enacted, for instance—then something has gone wrong.
- *Self-interest isn't the only ethical consideration.* How well-off we are is important. But it isn't the only thing of moral importance. Morality sometimes calls on us to set aside our own interests for the sake of others.
- *Agony is bad.* Excruciating physical or emotional pain is bad. It may sometimes be appropriate to cause such extreme suffering, but doing so requires a very powerful justification.
- *Might doesn't make right.* People in power can get away with lots of things that the rest of us can't. That doesn't justify what they do. That a person can escape punishment is one thing—whether his actions are morally acceptable is another.
- *Free and informed requests prevent rights violations.* If, with eyes wide open and no one twisting your arm, you ask someone to do something for you, and she does it, then your rights have not been violated—even if you end up hurt as a result.

There are a number of points to make about these claims.

First, this short list isn't meant to be exhaustive. It could be made much longer.

Second, I am not claiming that the items on this list are beyond criticism. I am saying only that each one is very plausible. Hard thinking might weaken our confidence in some cases. The point, though, is that without such scrutiny, it is perfectly reasonable to begin our moral thinking with the items on this list.

Third, many of these claims require interpretation in order to apply them in a satisfying way. When we say, for instance, that equals ought to be treated equally, we leave all of the interesting questions open. (What makes people equals? Can we treat people equally without treating them in precisely the same way? And so on.)

Not only do we have a variety of plausible starting points for our ethical investigations; we also have a number of obviously poor beginnings for moral thinking. A morality that celebrates genocide, torture, treachery, sadism, hostility, and slavery is, depending on how you look at it, either no morality at all or a deeply failed one. Any morality worth the name will place *some* importance on justice, fairness, kindness, and reasonableness. Just how much importance, and how to balance things in cases of conflict—that is where the real philosophy gets done.

D. MORALITY AND OTHER NORMATIVE SYSTEMS

We can also better understand morality by contrasting its principles with those of other **normative systems**. Each of these represents a set of standards for how we ought to behave, ideals to aim for, rules that we should not break.

There are many such systems, but let's restrict our focus to four of the most important of them: those that govern the law, etiquette, self-interest, and tradition. The fact that a law tells us to do something does not settle the question of whether morality gives its stamp of approval. Some immoral acts (like cheating on a spouse) are not illegal. And some illegal acts (like voicing criticism of a dictator) are not immoral. Certainly, many laws require what morality requires and forbid what morality forbids. But the fit is hardly perfect, and that shows that morality is something different from the law. That a legislature passed a bill is not enough to show that the bill is morally acceptable.

We see the same imperfect fit when it comes to standards of etiquette. Forks are supposed to be set to the left of a plate, but it isn't immoral to set them on the right. Good manners are not the same thing as morally good conduct. Morality sometimes requires us *not* to be polite or gracious, as when someone threatens your children or happily tells you a racist joke. So the standards of etiquette can depart from those of morality.

The same is true when it comes to the standards of self-interest. Think of all of the people who have gotten ahead in life by betraying others, lying about their past, breaking the rules that others are following. It's an unhappy thought, but a very commonsensical one: you sometimes can improve your lot in life by acting immorally. And those who behave virtuously are sometimes punished, rather than rewarded, for it. Whistle blowers who reveal a company's or a government official's corruption are often attacked for their efforts, sued to the point of bankruptcy, and targeted for their courageous behavior. Though the relation between self-interest and morality is contested, it is a plausible starting point to assume that morality can sometimes require us to sacrifice our well-being, and that we can sometimes improve our lot in life by acting unethically. Unless this is shown to be mistaken—something that would require a lot of complex moral thinking, if it could be done at all—we are right to think that the standards of morality are not the very same as those of self-interest. (We will see a challenge to this view when considering *ethical egoism* in Chapter 3.A.)

Finally, morality is also distinct from tradition. That a practice has been around a long time does not automatically make it moral. Morality sometimes requires a break with the past, as it did when people called for the abolition of slavery or for allowing women to vote. And some nontraditional, highly innovative practices may be morally excellent. The longevity of a practice is not a foolproof test of its morality.

E. MORALITY AND RELIGION

Because many people look to religion for moral guidance, it is important to understand the relation between morality and religion, and to explain why, in the pages to follow, I will not be relying on religious commitments to present and assess the views under discussion.

Many people have the following thought: if God does not exist, then morality is a sham. The only legitimate source of morality is God's commands. On this view, **atheism**—the belief that God does not exist—spells the doom of morality.

The underlying idea seems to be this: because morality is a set of **norms** (i.e., standards that we ought to live up to), there must be someone with the authority to create them. Without God, there is no one but we human beings to make up the moral law. And we lack the needed authority to do the work. Our say-so doesn't make things right; our disapproval cannot make things wrong. We are limited in understanding and bound to make mistakes. A morality built upon our imperfections would lack credibility.

This vision of God's role in morality—as its ultimate author, the one who makes up the moral code—rests on a crucial assumption: that morality must be created by someone. Personal confession: I don't understand why this assumption is appealing. But that may be just one of my many limitations. In any event, those who do like the view I've just sketched will find themselves embracing the **divine command theory**:

> An act is morally required just because it is commanded by God, and immoral just because God forbids it.

I think that this is the natural, default view for a religious believer when thinking of God's relation to morality. But this view is not without its problems.

There are two of them. The first is obvious. The divine command theory makes morality depend on God's commands. Yet God may not exist. For the moment, though, let's just assume that God does exist, and see what follows.

To appreciate the second problem, imagine the point at which God is choosing a morality for us. God contemplates the nature of rape, torture, and treachery. What does He see? Being **omniscient** (all-knowing), God sees such actions for what they are. Crucially, He sees nothing wrong with them. They are, at this point, morally neutral. Nothing, as yet, is right or wrong.

But God did, at some point, make a decision. He forbade rape, theft, and most kinds of killing. If the divine command theory is correct, then He didn't forbid them because they were immoral. Did God have reasons for His decisions, or not?

If the divine command theory is true, then there is trouble either way. If God lacks reasons for His commands—if there is no solid basis supporting His decisions to prohibit certain things and require others—then God's decisions are arbitrary. It would be as if God were creating morality by a coin toss. But that is surely implausible. That sort of God would be arbitrary, and thus imperfect.

So a perfect God must have had excellent reasons for laying down the moral law as He did. But then it seems that these reasons, and not God's commands, are what make actions right or wrong. Actions are not right *because* God commands them. Whatever reasons support God's choices also explain why actions have the moral status they do.

Suppose, for instance, that God really did forbid us from torturing others, and that God had very good reasons for doing so. Although we can't presume to know God's thoughts, let's just assume for now that God based His decision on the fact that torture is extremely painful, humiliating, and an attack on a defenseless person. Assuming that these are the relevant reasons, then these reasons are enough to explain why torture is immoral. Torture is wrong *because* it is extremely painful, humiliating, and so on.

God's condemnation does not turn a morally neutral action into an immoral one. Rather, God recognizes what is already bad about torture. There is something in the very nature of torture that makes it morally suspect. To avoid portraying God as arbitrary, we must assume that He issues commands based on the best possible reasons. And here are the best possible reasons: God sees that an action such as torture is immoral, sees, with perfect understanding, that such things as kindness and compassion are good, and then issues the divine commands on the basis of this flawless insight. This picture preserves God's omniscience and integrity. But it comes at the expense of the divine command theory, and God's authorship of the moral law.

And after all, what is the alternative? If there is nothing intrinsically wrong with rape or theft, then God could just as well have required that we do such things. He could have forbidden that we be generous or thoughtful. But this makes a mockery of morality, and of our view of God as morally perfect.

This point is expressed by

The Divine Perfection Argument

1. If the divine command theory is true, then a morally perfect God could have created a flawless morality that required us to rape, steal, and kill, and forbade us from any acts of kindness or generosity.
2. A morally perfect God could not have issued such commands—anyone who did so would be morally imperfect.

Therefore,

3. The divine command theory is false.

The first premise is certainly true. The divine command theory says that God's choices wholly determine morality, and that nothing determines God's choices. And the second premise is highly plausible. A moral code that required such horrific acts, and forbade such good ones, could not be authored by someone worthy of love and worship, someone fit to serve as a model of moral perfection.

Now suppose that God exists but is *not* the author of the moral law. God could still play a crucial role in morality—not by being its inventor, but by being its infallible reporter, and our expert guide. God knows everything—including every single detail of the moral law. And if God is all-loving, then God will want to share some of that wisdom with us. How will He do it? By means of revelation, either personal and direct (say, by talking to you or giving you signs of certain kinds), or by indirect means (say, by inspiring the authors of a bible).

God doesn't have to be the author of morality in order to play a vital role in teaching us how to live. We can see this by considering an analogy. Imagine a perfectly accurate thermometer. If we wanted to know the temperature, we'd look to this device. But the thermometer is not creating the temperature. It is recording it in an error-free way. If we reject the divine command theory, then God is playing a similar role regarding morality. He is not creating the moral law. He is telling us what it is, in a way that is never mistaken.

There are some worries, of course. Here are some worth considering:

- Those who are not religious will need to look elsewhere for moral guidance.
- And they may be right to do so, because God may not exist.

Even if God exists, there are still two serious problems for those who seek divine guidance:

- We must select a source of religious wisdom from among many choices.
- We must know how to interpret that source.

These two problems can be illustrated by working through the popular

Argument from Religious Authority

1. If the Bible prohibits abortion, then abortion is immoral.
2. The Bible prohibits abortion.

Therefore,

3. Abortion is immoral.

The first premise asserts the moral authority of the Bible. But which bible? Different religions offer us different sacred texts, whose details sometimes contradict one another. So we must choose.

There is presumably one right choice and many wrong ones. The odds are stacked against us.

Premise 1 is plausible only if God has authored the Bible, or dictated its terms. Religious believers therefore have to make a case that this is so. They must justify the claims that God exists, that God has communicated with humanity, and that their favorite bible is the one that contains God's wisdom. It won't be easy to do this.

If God is all-powerful, then He could provide some extremely clear, undeniable evidence to settle these matters, evidence that would convince agnostics, atheists, and members of competing religions. But God has thus far chosen not to do this. That makes defense of premise 1 especially tricky.

And the challenges don't end there. Even if **theists**—those who believe that God exists—can adequately defend the first premise, and so justify the selection of their preferred bible, there is the further matter of how to interpret the sacred text. Neither the Hebrew nor the Christian scriptures, for instance, ever explicitly *mentions* abortion, much less prohibits it. Thus, even if you wanted to adopt a literal reading of those scriptures, problems will arise. There will be many important topics (such as abortion) that are never mentioned in the crucial text. Those that are mentioned may receive contradictory treatments (consider, as an early example, the literally incompatible creation stories of Genesis chapters 1 and 2). There may also be morally troubling advice on offer (think of the passages in Leviticus that permit slavery and the subordination of women, or those that require killing adulterers and disrespectful children).

Yet if we move away from a literal reading, we are faced with countless possibilities for interpreting the biblical texts. Believers must choose among them, and justify their choice in the face of a wide number of conflicting approaches. A defense of premise 2 is, therefore, no easy matter.

A final difficulty comes when having to balance the demands of a sacred text with the layers of tradition that form a crucial part of any living religion.

When your interpretation of a religious document conflicts with long-standing religious practice, or the advice of generations of religious authorities, which should win out? Consider as an example the famous eye-for-an- eye principle, which seems to be clearly required by God in the Hebrew scriptures (Exodus 21:23; Leviticus 24:20; Deuteronomy 20:21). Yet Jewish communities and their religious leaders have, for at least two millennia, read the decree in an imaginative, nonliteral way, softening its implications for wrongdoers and extending the principle to apply to cases where it cannot be taken literally. Does the text take priority over traditional practice and religious authority? Or is it the other way around? Believers must have a plausible view about how to settle such conflicts. Without one, their take on what God really wants for us may be very wide of the mark.

To summarize: those who seek divine guidance in trying to lead a moral life may succeed. But several conditions must be met. It must be the case that (1) God exists, and that we can be justified in believing this. (2) Theists must be justified in selecting a particular source of religious and moral wisdom, such as the Koran, the Book of Mormon, or the Christian scriptures. Theists must also (3) defend specific interpretations of those sources. Finally, when an interpretation conflicts with tradition, religious believers must (4) successfully argue for the priority of one over the other.

This is a daunting list. Yet philosophy is full of such lists, and the difficulty of a project is not, by itself, proof of its failure. Religious believers have their work cut out for them, no doubt of it. But then so does everyone else.

In the rest of the book, I do not make use of specifically religious claims. There are two reasons for this. First, we have seen the many challenges to the assumption that morality is based on religion, and it is worthwhile seeing how far we can get without having to rely on that assumption. Second, there is important precedent among religious philosophers for thinking that God gave us reason and understanding in order to make the fundamental truths of morality available to everyone. After all, a caring God would want even nonbelievers to understand the immorality of rape and genocide, and to appreciate the goodness of generosity and loving kindness.

F. CONCLUSION

Although it has proven difficult to come up with a sharp definition of *morality*, we can take several steps to help us get a better understanding of what we'll be focusing on for the remainder of this book. There is first of all the distinction between conventional and critical morality, where the former includes the moral views and practices that are actually accepted by a society or culture, and the latter represents moral standards that are free of the errors that sometimes infect conventional morality. Understanding the three branches of moral philosophy—value theory, normative ethics, and metaethics—can also help us to focus on our target. Identifying a set of plausible starting points for moral thinking can do the same. We can also come to appreciate what morality is by seeing what it is not—here, the contrast with other normative systems, such as the law, etiquette, self-interest, and tradition, may be helpful. Finally, while many people look to religion for moral guidance, there are some problems with doing so on the basis of the divine command theory, and there are, in any event, several hurdles that theists need to overcome in order to assure themselves that such reliance is appropriate.

ESSENTIAL CONCEPTS

Atheism: the view that God does not exist.
Conventional morality: the system of widely accepted rules and principles that members of a culture or society use to govern their own lives and to assess the actions and the motivations of others.
Critical morality: a set of moral norms that (1) does not have its origin in social agreements; (2) is untainted by mistaken beliefs, irrationality, or popular prejudices; and (3) can serve as the true standard for determining when conventional morality has got it right and when it has fallen into error.
Divine command theory: the view that an act is morally required just because it is commanded by God, and that it is immoral just because God forbids it.
Normative system: a set of norms; that is, a set of standards that specify how we ought to behave, ideals to aim for, and rules that we should not break.
Norms: standards that we ought to live up to.
Omniscient: all-knowing.
Theists: those who believe that God exists.

DISCUSSION QUESTIONS

1. Can you think of a good definition of *morality*?
2. What are some elements of conventional morality that you think are morally mistaken? Be sure to provide the reasons that support your verdict.
3. Do you agree with all of the starting points for moral thinking that were provided in section 1.C? If not, explain why. Can you think of any other plausible starting points?
4. Many people think that the standards of self-interest and morality can conflict. Do you agree? What reasons do you have for your response?
5. Critically assess the Divine Perfection argument. Do you think that it succeeds? Why or why not?

CHAPTER 2

Moral Reasoning

Moral reasoning, like all reasoning, involves at least two things: a set of reasons, and a conclusion that these reasons are meant to support. When you put these two things together, you have what philosophers call an **argument**. This isn't a matter of bickering or angrily exchanging words. An argument is simply any chain of thought in which reasons (philosophers call these **premises**) are offered in support of a particular conclusion. Watch for such words as *therefore*, *hence*, *thus*, or *so*—a claim that follows these words is usually the conclusion of an argument someone is offering you.

Not all arguments are equally good. This is as true in ethics as it is science, mathematics, or politics. It is easy to mistake one's way when it comes to ethical thinking. We can land at the wrong conclusion (by endorsing child abuse, for instance). We can also arrive at the right one by means of terrible reasoning. We must do our best to avoid both of these mistakes.

In other words, our moral thinking should have two complementary goals—getting it right, and being able to back up our views with flawless reasoning. We want the truth, both in the starting assumptions we bring to an issue and in the conclusions we eventually arrive at. But we also want to make sure that our views are supported by excellent reasons. And this provides two tests for good moral reasoning: (1) we must avoid false beliefs, and (2) the logic of our moral thinking must be rigorous and error-free.

There is no surefire test for determining when a belief is true or false. This goes for all beliefs, not just moral ones. Many people are firmly convinced by beliefs that turn out to be false; indeed, this probably describes you, me, and everyone we know. Of course we aren't aware of which of our beliefs are false, or else we'd change them. Still, none of us is omniscient. We all have our blind spots and intellectual limitations.

This isn't meant to be a counsel of despair. Though each of us is likely to have at least a few false beliefs, we also have lots of true ones. And while there is no surefire test to sort the true from the false, we can always seek to support our views by means of evidence and argument.

Importantly, it is possible to develop moral arguments that fail, even though every single one of their premises is true. The failure is of the second sort mentioned earlier: a failure of logic. Since logical reasoning is a key to successful reasoning, let's take some time to consider some of the basic elements of logic.

A. VALIDITY AND SOUNDNESS

Consider this argument:

1. Heroin is a drug.
2. Selling heroin is illegal.

Therefore,

3. Heroin use is immoral.

This is a moral argument. It is a set of reasons designed to support a moral conclusion. Both of the premises are true. But they do not adequately support the conclusion, since one can accept them while consistently rejecting this conclusion. Perhaps the use of illegal drugs such as heroin really is immoral. But we need a further reason to think so—we would need, for instance, the additional claim that all drug use is immoral.

The argument in its present form is a poor one. But not because it relies on false claims. Rather, the argument's logical structure is to blame. The logic of an argument is a matter of how its premises are related to its conclusion. In the best arguments, the truth of the premises guarantees the truth of the conclusion. This is the feature known as **logical validity**.

The heroin argument lacks this feature, and so is invalid. The truth of the argument's premises does not guarantee the truth of its conclusion—indeed, the conclusion may be false.

Since the best arguments are logically valid, we will want to make sure that our own arguments meet this condition. But how can we do that? How can we tell a valid from an invalid argument, one that is logically perfect from one that is logically shaky?

There is a simple, three-part test:

1. Identify all of an argument's premises.
2. Imagine that all of them are true (even if you know that some are false).
3. Then ask yourself this question: supposing that all of the premises were true, could the conclusion be false? *If yes*, the argument is invalid. The premises do not guarantee the conclusion. *If no*, the argument is valid. The premises offer perfect logical support for the conclusion.

Validity is a matter of how well an argument's premises support its conclusion. To test for this, we must assume that all of an argument's premises are true. We then ask whether the conclusion must therefore be true. If so, the argument is valid. If not, not.

Note that an argument's validity is a matter of the argument's structure. It has nothing to do with the *actual* truth or falsity of an argument's premises or conclusion. Indeed, *valid arguments may contain false premises and false conclusions.*

To help clarify the idea, consider the following argument. Suppose you are a bit shaky on your US history, and I am trying to convince you that John Quincy Adams was the ninth

president of the United States. I offer you the following line of reasoning:

1. John Quincy Adams was either the eighth or the ninth US president.
2. John Quincy Adams was not the eighth US president.

Therefore,

3. John Quincy Adams was the ninth US president.

In one way, this reasoning is impeccable. It is logically flawless. This is a valid argument. If all premises of this argument were true, then the conclusion would have to be true. It is impossible for 1 and 2 to be true and 3 to be false. It passes our test for logical validity with flying colors.

But the argument is still a bad one—not because of any logical error, but because it has a false premise (number 1; Quincy Adams was the sixth US president) and a false conclusion. The truth of an argument's premises is one thing; its logical status is another.

The lesson here is that truth isn't everything; neither is logic. We need them both. What we want in philosophy, as in all other areas of inquiry, are arguments that have two features: (1) they are logically watertight (valid), and (2) all of their premises are true. These arguments exhibit **soundness**, and for that reason are known as *sound* arguments.

Sound arguments are the gold standard of good reasoning. And it's easy to see why. They are logically valid. So if all of their premises are true, their conclusion must be true as well. And by definition, sound arguments contain only true premises. So their conclusions are true. If you can tell that an argument is valid, and also know that each premise is correct, then you can also know that the conclusion is true. That is what we are after.

You're now in a position to avoid a rookie mistake: referring to arguments as true or false. Premises can be true or false. Conclusions can be true or false. Arguments, though, are neither. Arguments are valid or invalid, sound or unsound.

I started this section by claiming that not all moral arguments are equally good. We're now able to see why. Some arguments rely on false premises. Others rely on invalid reasoning. Still others—the worst of the lot—commit both kinds of error. When developing your own arguments to support your moral views, it pays to keep both types of error in mind, so that you can be alert to avoiding these mistakes.

B. NECESSARY AND SUFFICIENT CONDITIONS

Logic is a huge field, and we are going to touch only the tip of the iceberg. In my experience, however, there are just a few key ideas that you need to master in order to be in a position to construct valid arguments and to determine whether those you are considering really do have a good logical structure.

One of the key ideas in logic is that of a **sufficient condition**. A sufficient condition is a guarantee. If X is a sufficient condition of Y, then X suffices for Y; X is enough for Y; X guarantees Y. If X is true, then Y is true; if X is the case, then Y is the case. In most classrooms, getting a 95 percent average is a sufficient condition of receiving an A. Being a human is a sufficient condition of being a mammal. Having a child is a sufficient condition of being a parent.

The importance of this will become clear in a moment. But first, consider another key logic concept: that of a **necessary condition**. Necessary conditions are requirements. If X is a necessary condition of Y, then X is needed for Y; X is a prerequisite of Y; X is required for Y. Y can be true only if X is true; Y can occur only if X does. Having some money is a necessary condition of being a millionaire; having a brain is a necessary condition of being a philosopher; for some, having one's morning caffeine is a necessary condition of being able to function properly.

Both sufficient and necessary conditions are conditions *of* or *for* something else. It doesn't make sense to speak of something as a sufficient or necessary condition, full stop. This becomes clear when you abandon the technical talk and just think of a guarantee or a requirement. If someone told you that this was a guarantee, or that was a requirement, you'd naturally ask: a guarantee *of what*? What is it a requirement *for*?

OK, why is any of this important? Here's one reason. One of the big goals of ethical thinking is to try to identify a good, wide-ranging test of what's morally right (or wrong). One way to think about such a test is to view it as a statement of conditions that are *both necessary and sufficient* for being morally right (or wrong). A claim that supplies necessary and sufficient conditions is called a **biconditional**, because it incorporates two conditions. A shorthand way to state biconditionals is to use this phrase: if and only if. To take a familiar example: someone is a bachelor if and only if he is an unmarried male. This says that being an unmarried male is both sufficient and necessary for being a bachelor: *if* someone is an unmarried male, then he's a bachelor, and he's a bachelor *only if* he's an unmarried male.

Think of this as a kind of fill-in-the-blank exercise. In moral philosophy, we want sufficient conditions for being morally right. So: if _____ (fill in your sufficient condition), then an act is morally right. Now make sure that however you filled in that blank is also a necessary condition: An act is morally right only if _____. The very same thing needs to fill in both blanks. So: an act is morally right if and only if _____. If you can fill in that blank in a way that withstands scrutiny, you will have done something truly great. You will have identified conditions that guarantee the moral rightness of an act, and that are also required for the act to be right.

Here's why we are on the lookout for conditions that are both necessary and sufficient for the morality of actions. Suppose your friend tells you: an act is wrong *only if* it causes pain. Notice what's going on here. Your friend is saying that an action's causing pain is a necessary condition of its being wrong; causing pain is a requirement of acting wrongly. I doubt your friend is right about this—there seem to be cases where people have acted immorally but no one has suffered as a result—but suppose my doubts are mistaken. Now this same friend tells you of a case where Tina has caused Tommy pain. Do you have enough information to know whether Tina's act is right or wrong? You don't. Sometimes it's morally OK to cause others pain; even if causing pain is a requirement of immoral action, it is *not* a sufficient condition, a guarantee, of immoral behavior.

Compare: a person is alive only if she has a heart; having a heart is a necessary condition of a person's being alive. Suppose I tell you that the person over there has a heart. Do you now know whether that person is alive? You don't. The person could be a corpse. Having a heart isn't a sufficient condition of being alive.

So you might think: fine, necessary conditions aren't all that helpful; it's sufficient conditions that are really important. Yet you're usually going to want something more than a sufficient condition, too. After all, I could tell you that betraying a vulnerable child just for kicks is sufficient for your action to be wrong; *if* you engage in such betrayal, then you're acting wrongly. I think this is true. But how often do you encounter such cases? This sufficient condition doesn't provide a good general test for moral wrongness, because most situations don't involve such betrayals. You're looking for a test that applies across the board and that can help you with the moral difficulties you're actually facing. That requires that you identify conditions that are both necessary and sufficient for moral rightness (or wrongness, depending on what you're trying to figure out).

C. VALID ARGUMENT FORMS

Necessary and sufficient conditions are important not just because of the role they play in constructing a general test for the morality of actions. They are central to understanding why some classic forms of valid argumentation work as they do.

There are lots of ways to construct logically valid arguments—and, as a quick review of our public culture reveals, a lot of ways to construct invalid arguments! (More on these in the next section.) Insofar as you care about supporting your ideas with solid reasoning, you'll want to avoid the latter and devote yourself to the former. We can't review every kind of logical argument, but we can do a quick survey of the ones that will take center stage in this book. After a chapter or two, you'll become quite familiar with them and will hopefully be in a position to construct such valid arguments on your own. Ideally, you'll incorporate true premises into those arguments, yielding the best kind of reasoning, and applying it to moral issues of great significance.

For the remainder of this chapter, I'm going to explain things by using variables—symbols that can be replaced by lots of different items of the same kind. If you're like me, and you see variables, you start to freeze up. Don't worry, all will be well. In particular, I'm going to use Ps and Qs as my variables; these stand in for any declarative sentence at all. Whenever you see 'P' or 'Q', feel free to replace it with whatever declarative sentence you like, no matter how short or long, no matter how plausible or crazy. It won't make any difference to the points we're about to discuss.

There are three argument forms that I'll be using over and over. They have fancy Latin names that you just need to memorize—sorry. The first is called **modus ponens**, and it takes the following form:

1. If P, then Q.
2. P.

Therefore,

3. Q.

As I mentioned earlier, 'P' and 'Q' are just meant to stand in for any declarative sentence. Try it out with any sentences you like, from something totally commonplace to something outrageous. The key thing is that no matter what sentences you substitute for 'P' and 'Q'—no matter whether they are true or false, related to each other or not—you are going to end up with a logically valid argument.

Here are two examples to soften you up:

1. If humans have rights, then you have rights.
2. Humans have rights.

Therefore,

3. You have rights.

1. If you have rights, then pencils have rights.
2. You have rights.

Therefore,

3. Pencils have rights.

The first one looks pretty good, yes? Its logic is impeccable: if premises 1 and 2 are true, the conclusion, 3, has to be true. The argument is not just valid; it is also sound, as all of its premises (1 and 2) are true. This guarantees that the conclusion is true.

The second argument probably looks fishy to you. But its logic is also flawless: if premises 1 and 2 were true, its conclusion would have to be true. Recall the test for validity: imagine that all premises are true, even if you know they aren't. Then ask whether the conclusion would have to be true. The answer here is *yes*; that indicates that this second argument is valid. But of course it is unsound—not all of its premises are true. Premise 1 is false, as is its conclusion.

Every instance of modus ponens reasoning is logically valid. That might seem an unsupportable claim. After all, there are billions of ways to fill in 'P' and 'Q' in the formula—how could we know that every single one will yield a valid argument?

To answer that question, I need to introduce another technical term, one that may be familiar to you from middle school grammar lessons: a **conditional**. A conditional is just an 'if-then' sentence. The first premises in both of the arguments we just considered are conditionals. A conditional has two parts, the 'if' part and the 'then' part. These, too, have names that you may recall from sixth or seventh grade. The 'if' clause is called the **antecedent** (literally: that which comes before); the 'then' clause is called the **consequent** (literally: that which comes after).

Now reread that last paragraph. I know there have been a lot of technical terms thrown at you all at once. But we'll use these repeatedly, so it pays to really get them ingrained. And we need to rely on these terms to understand exactly why every instance of a modus ponens argument is logically perfect.

Here's the explanation. Look at the first premise of a modus ponens argument. It is a conditional. It has two parts, its antecedent and its consequent. A conditional contains two crucial bits of information. The first is this: its antecedent is a sufficient condition of its consequent. In simpler terms: the 'if' clause is a guarantee of the 'then' clause. In a modus ponens argument, the second premise says that the guarantee is in place. The antecedent, which guarantees the consequent, is true. It follows that the consequent, which has been guaranteed, is true as well.

Think about this for a minute. In a conditional, you are stating that if one thing holds (I've arbitrarily labeled it 'P', but you could call it anything you want), then another thing (Q) will hold as well. In the conditional premise of a modus ponens argument, you are saying that the antecedent guarantees the consequent, that P guarantees Q. When you proceed, via premise 2, to affirm P, you say that the guarantee is secure. It follows logically that Q—the thing guaranteed by P—is also secure. This is why every modus ponens argument is logically valid.

Here is another type of argument that is always logically valid: it's called **modus tollens**.

A modus tollens argument has the following form:

1. If P, then Q.
2. Q is false.

Therefore,

3. P is false.

Note that modus tollens arguments start out just like modus ponens arguments do—with a conditional. Now here's where things get a little bit unexpected. I said earlier that there are two crucial bits of information contained in a conditional. The first, already mentioned, is that its antecedent is a sufficient condition of its consequent. Perhaps this seemed obvious to you. But the second bit of information rarely strikes people as obvious. When I took logic for the first time, I kept bumping up against it—I didn't find it intuitive at all. The second piece of information contained in a conditional is this: its consequent is a necessary condition of its antecedent. Sticking with our talk of Ps and Qs, the second bit of information says that Q is a necessary condition of P; P is true *only if* Q is true; P's truth requires Q's truth; Q's truth is necessary for P's truth.

So when I say, for instance, "If humans have rights, then you have rights," I am conveying two things. First, that humans have rights guarantees that you have rights. But second, and perhaps less obviously (it certainly seems less obvious to me), I am also relaying this information: humans have rights only if you have rights, too.

This second bit of information is crucial to seeing why every instance of modus tollens is logically valid. In a modus tollens argument, the conditional tells you that the consequent is a requirement for the antecedent. The second premise says that this requirement fails to hold. So the antecedent can't hold, either.

Perhaps a simpler way to see this is by introducing a principle that logicians take for granted but that we ordinary folk can find it hard to see.

The principle says that the following two statements are logically equivalent:

1. If P, then Q.
2. P only if Q.

In other words, whenever you write a conditional in the first way, you could also write it the second way (and vice versa), and the truth (or falsity) of the conditional would not change. Since it's true that *if* (P) humans have rights, *then* (Q) you have rights, it's also true that (P) humans have rights *only if* (Q) you have rights. Since it's false that *if* (P) you have rights, *then* (Q) pencils have rights, it's also false that (P) you have rights *only if* (Q) pencils have rights.

So we can see that modus tollens arguments can also be written in this way:

1. P only if Q.
2. Q is false.

Therefore,

3. P is false.

Maybe this makes the validity of all modus tollens arguments more intuitive. Written this way, it's clearer that the consequent, Q, is a necessary condition of the antecedent, P. The second premise says that Q, which is needed for P, is false. So P is false as well. And this is so no matter what 'P' and 'Q' stand for.

We're now in a position to show how to test for the truth of a conditional, which is going to be very important in the rest of the book, since so many of the arguments presented there take the form of a modus ponens or modus tollens argument. Here's the test: try to come up with a case in which the conditional's antecedent is true, but the consequent is not. If you can identify such a case, then the conditional isn't true. That's because the antecedent is supposed to guarantee the consequent; if you can come up with a case in which it fails to do so, then the conditional is false. It's also because the consequent is meant to be a necessary condition of the antecedent; if there is a case in which the antecedent holds even though the consequent doesn't, that shows that the consequent isn't, after all, a requirement of the antecedent. And so the conditional is false.

The **hypothetical syllogism** is a third type of argument whose instances are always valid. A hypothetical syllogism takes this form:

1. If P, then Q.
2. If Q, then R.

Therefore,

3. If P, then R.

Though I've written this with just two premises, a hypothetical syllogism can have three or more premises, so long as each additional one is a conditional that takes the consequent of the previous conditional and makes it the antecedent of the next.

Here's why every single hypothetical syllogism is valid. Focus on the first bit of information contained within a conditional: its antecedent guarantees its consequent. So, in the first premise, P guarantees Q. In the second premise, Q guarantees R. If one thing guarantees a second thing, and the second guarantees a third, then the first guarantees the third—the guarantee flows from the initial antecedent to the final consequent. A hypothetical syllogism basically represents a chain of guarantees, with the initial "hypothesis" (hence the name of this argument) guaranteeing the last link in the chain of conditionals.

There is a *lot* more logic one could learn about. But this is all you need to know in order to succeed with the material in this book.

D. FALLACIES

A **fallacy** is a mistake in reasoning. A formal fallacy is a kind of argument all of whose instances are logically invalid. In other words, no argument that commits a formal fallacy is *ever* logically valid. Informal fallacies are other kinds of mistaken patterns in reasoning. Here, as earlier, I'll need to be selective—whole courses and textbooks are devoted to the nature of logical (and illogical) reasoning. I'll draw your attention to a few of the more common mistakes we make in our reasoning, with the hope that being alerted to them will enable you to purify your reasoning and avoid these errors when engaging in your own critical reflections.

Let's first take a look at a couple of classic formal fallacies. Here's an example of one of them. Suppose your friend tells you that if God exists, then abortion is immoral. But she proceeds to claim that God doesn't exist. So, she concludes, abortion is morally OK. Or suppose that someone makes you the following offer: if you buy this item now, then you'll get 50 percent off. So you think: well, if I don't buy it now, then I'm not going to get that discount. Both of these lines of thought are **fallacious** (i.e., commit a fallacy). They are instances of the **fallacy of denying the antecedent**. This occurs when one reasons as follows:

1. If P, then Q.
2. P is false.

Therefore,

3. Q is false.

The fallacy gets its name from the action taking place in premise 2—denying the antecedent of the conditional in premise 1. The problem is that when you assert a conditional and then deny its antecedent, you have given *no* basis for denying the consequent. To see this, recall what the antecedent does: it serves as a sufficient condition, a guarantee, of the consequent. Premise 2 says that this guarantee doesn't hold. What follows? *Nothing.* That's because there can be many sufficient conditions for something. Suppose I tell you, correctly, that if someone is currently riding a bike, then he is alive. But I'm not riding a bike. Therefore . . . I'm dead? Not so fast. There are many sufficient conditions of being alive: riding a bike, reading an ethics textbook, having a conversation, eating breakfast, listening to music, and millions of other possibilities. The fact that someone fails to fulfill one of these sufficient conditions for being alive gives us no basis at all for thinking that he's dead.

To cement this thought, consider another example of denying the antecedent: if I'm a millionaire, then I have at least ten dollars. (True.) I'm not a millionaire. (True.) Therefore, I don't have ten dollars. (False.) This is a terrible argument, right? All premises are true; the conclusion is false; therefore, this argument cannot be valid. Note, though, that it has exactly the same logical form as the argument about God and abortion, and the argument about receiving a discount. Each of these arguments fails—they are all fallacious—though it is sometimes difficult to see this, especially if you find its conclusion attractive.

Another formal fallacy is known as the **fallacy of affirming the consequent**. This also begins with a conditional. And then, as the name implies, one affirms its consequent (i.e., states that it is true). One then concludes that its antecedent is true: if P, then Q; Q is true; therefore, P is true.

Consider: if life is meaningful, then God exists; God *does* exist; therefore, life is meaningful. Or: if God exists, then morality is objective; morality *is* objective; therefore, God exists. Many people have found these arguments persuasive. But they are fallacious. We can see this if we compare them to other arguments with the very same logical structure. Suppose I tell you that if I'm a millionaire, then I have ten dollars. (True.) I have ten dollars. (True.) Therefore, I'm a millionaire (sadly, false—if only it were that easy!) Or: if you're a famous ex-president, then you're a person. You're a person. Therefore, you're a famous ex-president. Again, both of these premises are true; the conclusion is false; therefore, this argument is invalid. Yet this argument and the one before have the very same logical structure as the two arguments that opened this paragraph. All four of those arguments are invalid.

The reason is simple. Think of the second crucial bit of information contained in a conditional—namely, that the consequent is a necessary condition, a requirement, of the antecedent. If Q is needed for P, you can't determine that P is the case just by determining that Q is the case. That's because there can be many necessary conditions for something. You need a lot of things to build a house, for instance—there are many necessary conditions that have to be met. You can't tell if a house has been built just by knowing that one of these conditions has been fulfilled. If there are many requirements for P, then you're in no position to know whether P is the case just because you know that one of its requirements is met. That's why affirming the consequent is a fallacy.

Let's turn now to some informal fallacies. One of these is the **ad hominem fallacy**, which occurs when you try to undermine a position by attacking the person who is advancing it. Politicians (and their supporters) do this all the time. "His views on immigration can't be trusted; after all, he's Latino." "She's rich, so don't believe a word she says about how to improve the economy." "He's a hypocrite; he didn't live up to his ideals, so his ideals must be bankrupt." These are all instances of bad reasoning. The truth is one thing; a person's motives, status, inherited traits, group membership, or character is another. The wisdom of an immigration or economic policy depends on the facts about these complicated matters, and not at all on the character or circumstances of the person who is defending them. Even bad people speak the truth sometimes. Even good people make mistakes. Greedy people can end up defending wise economic policies. And terrible immigration policies can be defended by those whose compassionate motives have misled them on this occasion.

A familiar type of ad hominem fallacy occurs when people discover that others have behaved hypocritically. If a person fails to live up to her ideals, then this shows that she lacks integrity. It says nothing, however, about the merit of those ideals. After all, a person might preach generosity and kindness, all the while betraying these values in her personal life. Such hypocrisy does *nothing* to undermine these values, though it says a lot about her character. The truth of a position is one thing; the person advancing it is another. If you want to determine whether her claims are correct, then you need to focus on the evidence for or against her position, rather than on the content of her character.

Another informal fallacy involves **appeals to irrelevant emotions**. This occurs when someone tries to convince you of a claim by playing on your emotions, rather than by offering facts and evidence that bear on the truth of the claim. Many different emotions can be targeted. Marketers are experts in appealing to *jealousy*, *envy*, and *insecurity* when trying to sell something depicted as exclusive or prestigious or elite—you don't want to be left behind, do you? Had you done some research, however, you would have discovered in many cases that the advertised products were no better, and perhaps even worse, than more ordinary ones. Politicians and pundits often appeal to *anger* or *fear* when arguing to close borders against would-be immigrants. Rather than citing relevant facts about the actual costs and benefits of more welcoming immigration policies, many who seek to limit immigration present inflammatory images or biased claims designed to evoke emotions of fear and anger that will prompt opposition to such policies.

Almost any emotion can be manipulated. We need to remember this, since emotions play powerful roles in our moral thinking. And some of these are illuminating, rather than distorting. We are often alerted to morally relevant facts by having an emotional experience, as when someone's suffering elicits our compassion, or a gross injustice provokes our outrage. The essential point is not to place a ban on emotions in our moral reflections, but rather to recognize that many appeals to emotions will distract us from appreciating the relevant facts.

Another informal fallacy is the **appeal to authority**, which involves relying on authority figures to substantiate a position outside of their area of expertise. There is nothing wrong with trusting a doctor's advice when trying to recover from a broken ankle, because that's within the scope of the doctor's expertise. But suppose that someone tries to get you to adopt a pro-choice position by claiming that 80 percent of the doctors in the United States favor abortion rights. That's an example of this fallacy. A medical degree does not make someone a moral expert. Even if most doctors are pro-choice, that is not itself any evidence that a pro-choice position is morally correct. The same fallacy occurs whenever a parent tries to justify his political views by saying, "I'm the grown-up here, so what I say goes." As we all know, being a grown-up doesn't make someone infallible. Parents may want to silence their children, or just end a discussion and move on, but one doesn't acquire political wisdom just by raising a child.

The **straw man fallacy** depicts an opponent's position in a way that makes it easy to refute, thereby diverting attention from the real position being advanced. This occurs when someone avoids engaging with the best arguments for a position one opposes, and instead substitutes an obviously terrible argument for the one that has actually been offered. The terrible argument is the straw man—something that can be easily demolished. But it is a basic principle of good reasoning that one should *charitably* interpret the views of those one disagrees with. Rather than construing their beliefs in the worst possible way, one should instead seek to identify the most plausible version of their position, and then critically engage with that. It is easy to score cheap points by painting someone's argument as ridiculous, especially when a critic replaces the real argument with a substitute that can be easily torn apart. While this sort of move may win a politician some votes, or a radio personality more listeners, it blocks reasoned inquiry, rather than offering a path to understanding.

The **appeal to ignorance**, known officially by its Latin name *ignoratio elenchi*, can take one of two forms. The first one, which we'll consider in this paragraph, occurs when one thinks that a claim is true because it hasn't been proven false. The basic idea is this: you don't know (hence the ignorance) that my claim is false. Therefore, it's true. The problem is that the absence of contrary evidence—the absence of good reason to doubt my claim—is not itself reason to believe my claim. Suppose I believe that there is an even number of stars in the universe. You can't prove me wrong. But that's no reason to think I'm right! Yet this is the same form of reasoning used by those who argue that the death penalty must be an effective deterrent, because it hasn't been proven to be useless. Or that plants and trees are conscious, because it hasn't been proven that they're not.

The second form that an appeal to ignorance can take is the mirror image of the first. This occurs when one thinks that a claim is false because it hasn't been proven true. Here, if we don't know that your claim is true, we just assume that it's false. Like the close cousin discussed in the previous paragraph, this form of reasoning is also fallacious. Some people assert, for instance, that scientists haven't proven that climate change is caused by increased fossil fuel consumption; therefore, it's false that such consumption is causing climate change. Set aside the contested question of whether climate scientists have or have not proven this link. Even if they haven't, this reasoning is fallacious. We can see this by applying it to a variation of an earlier example. I can't prove that there is an even number of stars in the universe. But you'd be making an obvious error if you concluded that there must be an odd number of stars out there! Likewise, even if we are ignorant of whether humans have caused climate change, this ignorance does not license us in claiming that they haven't.

The last of the informal fallacies that we'll consider is the **hasty generalization**, which occurs when someone illicitly draws a general lesson from only a small handful of cases. Consider the smear, popular in some circles, that all Muslims are terrorists. It's certainly true that *some* Muslims are terrorists. But so too are some Jews, some Christians, some Buddhists, some Hindus, and some atheists. It's obviously implausible to claim that all Christians or Jews are terrorists, even if one's attention is drawn especially to those who are. Some Americans commit acts of terror. That is no basis for thinking that all Americans are terrorists. The sort of fallacy at play here is common and easy to fall into—we naturally think that a few salient examples represent broader trends or even universal truths. But good reasoning requires that we survey a large and representative sampling of cases before making such sweeping claims.

E. CONCLUSION

Moral reasoning is a matter of creating and assessing arguments for some moral claim. Arguments are built from premises, designed to support a conclusion. The truth or falsity of the premises is one thing; the logical support they offer to a conclusion is another. Arguments can be poor despite having only true premises, because those premises can fail to logically support their conclusions. And arguments can be logically flawless—valid—even though their premises are false, leaving us no basis for believing their conclusions. The gold standard of moral reasoning is a sound argument—a valid argument all of whose premises are true.

Modus ponens, modus tollens, and hypothetical syllogism arguments are invariably valid. No matter whether their premises are actually true or false, every instance of these argument types is logically valid. In order to understand why this is so, one needs to grasp the notion of a necessary condition (a requirement) and a sufficient condition (a guarantee). Biconditionals are statements of conditions that are at once necessary and sufficient for something. If you are especially intrepid, you'll spend some time thinking about the biconditionals that correctly specify the necessary and sufficient conditions for the moral concepts you're most interested in, while avoiding all of the fallacies that we have just discussed. Good luck!

ESSENTIAL CONCEPTS

Ad hominem fallacy: trying to undermine the truth of a position by attacking the person who is advancing it.

Antecedent: the 'if' clause of a conditional; the clause that specifies a sufficient condition of the conditional's consequent.

Appeal to authority: an informal fallacy that involves relying on authority figures to substantiate a position outside of their area of expertise.

Appeal to ignorance: an informal fallacy, also known as *ignoratio elenchi*, that can take one of two forms. In the first, one believes a claim to be true because it hasn't been proven false. In the second, one believes that a claim is false because it hasn't been proven true.

Appeal to irrelevant emotions: an effort to convince you of a claim by playing on your emotions, rather than by offering facts and evidence that bear on the truth of the claim.

Argument: a chain of thought in which reasons are offered in support of a particular conclusion.

Biconditional: a claim that supplies a condition that is both necessary and sufficient for something; an 'if and only if' sentence.

Conditional: an 'if-then' sentence.

Consequent: the 'then' clause of a conditional; it specifies a necessary condition of the conditional's antecedent.

Fallacious: the feature of exhibiting or having committed a fallacy.

Fallacy: a kind of poor reasoning. A formal fallacy is an argument form all of whose instances are invalid. Informal fallacies are other kinds of mistakes in reasoning.

Fallacy of affirming the consequent: any argument of the form: if P, then Q; Q is true; therefore, P is true.

Fallacy of denying the antecedent: any argument of the form: if P, then Q; P is false; therefore, Q is false.

Hasty generalization: illicitly drawing a general lesson from only a small handful of cases.

Hypothetical syllogism: An argument of the form: if P, then Q; if Q, then R; therefore, if P, then R.

Logical validity: the feature of an argument that guarantees the truth of its conclusion, on the assumption that its premises are true.

Modus ponens: An argument of the form: if P, then Q; P; therefore, Q.

Modus tollens: An argument of the form: if P, then Q; Q is false; therefore, P is false.

Necessary condition: a requirement, a prerequisite, a precondition.

Premises: the reasons within an argument that, taken together, are meant to support the argument's conclusion.

Soundness: the feature that arguments have when they are logically valid and all of their premises are true.

Straw man fallacy: a form of reasoning that depicts a position in a way that makes it easy to refute, thereby diverting attention from the real position being advanced.

Sufficient condition: a guarantee.

DISCUSSION QUESTIONS

Consider these sample arguments. Some are valid and some are invalid. Reveal the logical structure of each argument by presenting it in terms of Ps and Qs and then explain why each argument is valid or invalid.

A1. The sun is a star.
  2. The earth is a planet.

Therefore,

  3. The earth is 93 million miles from the sun.

B1. If Hillary Clinton is president, then Bill Clinton is vice president.
  2. Hillary Clinton is president.

Therefore,

3. Bill Clinton is vice president.

C1. If water at sea level boils at 212 degrees F, then water at sea level boils at 100 degrees C.
2. Water at sea level boils at 212 degrees F.

Therefore,

3. Water at sea level boils at 100 degrees C.

D1. Either God exists or life has no meaning.
2. God doesn't exist.

Therefore,

3. Life has no meaning.

E1. If there is an afterlife, then it is wise to be moral.
2. There is no afterlife.

Therefore,

3. It isn't wise to be moral.

F1. If I am riding a bike, then I am alive.
2. I am not riding a bike.

Therefore,

3. I am not alive.

G1. If fetuses are human beings, then abortion is immoral.
2. Abortion is immoral.

Therefore,

3. Fetuses are human beings.

H1. If I am a millionaire, then I can afford to buy a new TV.
2. I can afford to buy a new TV.

Therefore,

3. I am a millionaire.

I1. If euthanasia is legalized, then this will reduce the overall amount of misery in society.
2. If euthanasia reduces the overall amount of misery in a society, then it is morally acceptable.

Therefore,

3. If euthanasia is legalized, then it is morally acceptable.

J1. If animals have rights, then it is wrong to eat them.
2. It isn't wrong to eat animals.

Therefore,

3. Animals don't have rights.

K1. Anti-drug laws are morally legitimate only if paternalistic laws are morally acceptable.
2. Paternalistic laws are morally unacceptable.

Therefore,

3. Anti-drug laws are not morally legitimate.

L1. If societies disagree about moral issues, then there is no objective morality.
2. Societies agree about moral issues.

Therefore,

3. There is an objective morality.

M1. The death penalty is justified only if it gives criminals their just deserts.
2. The death penalty gives criminals their just deserts.

Therefore,

3. The death penalty for murderers is justified.

N1. If you want to succeed in your moral reasoning, then you have to master the details of this chapter.
2. If you have to master the details of this chapter, then you should ask your instructor for help if you don't understand any aspect of it.

Therefore,

3. If you want to succeed in your moral reasoning, then you should ask your

instructor for help if you don't understand any aspect of this chapter.

Review the following fallacious arguments and identify the informal fallacy committed by each.

O. The death penalty is an excellent deterrent of crime; after all, sociologists haven't been able to prove that it isn't.

P. Some philosophers argue that we are morally required to give away most of our earnings to the needy, even if it means devoting less money to our loved ones. But in times of family emergency, these philosophers will always end up spending money to care for their family members. That shows that the rest of us aren't morally required to give away most of our earnings to the needy.

Q. Some corporations have voluntarily taken steps to reduce their emission of greenhouse gases. So we don't need to impose any regulations in order to mitigate the effects of climate change.

R. How would you feel if someone killed a member of your family? Angry, right? That shows that the death penalty is morally justified.

S. Two politicians are engaged in a debate.

First politician: We should not spend billions of dollars building a border wall; the money saved could be better spent on other types of immigration enforcement.
Second politician: That might make you feel good, but I can't support giving illegal immigrants all the rights and protections of ordinary US citizens.

T. Abortion is immoral. How do I know that? Because my priest says so. How do I know I can trust my priest's opinions on this matter? Because my church tells me so.

CHAPTER 3

Skepticism about Morality

There are many skeptical worries that can arise about morality. In this chapter we consider three of the most important of these doubts. The first of these—**ethical egoism**—says that we have no basic obligations to others; the only moral duty we have is to ourselves. The second source of doubt is **relativism**, which denies the objectivity of ethics and views moral rules as human creations, as binding (or not) as the rules of games. The third is known as **error theory**—the view that morality is make-believe, that moral claims are never true, that moral knowledge is impossible. My aim here is to clearly identify these sources of skepticism and to reveal why people have been attracted to them—while also explaining why the arguments for these doubts may not be as compelling as they appear.

A. EGOISM

Some people—not many—hold that your only moral duty is to yourself. As they see it, the supreme moral principle requires you to maximize your own self-interest. You are allowed to help others, but only if doing so is going to benefit you in the long run. This view is known as ethical egoism.

If ethical egoism is true, then morality isn't anything like we think it is. We assume that morality requires us to be generous, compassionate, and benevolent. We think it counsels us to avoid selfishness and self-centeredness. We think it requires some kind of impartiality, a recognition that we are not fundamentally more important than others. And we believe that it sometimes requires us to sacrifice our own interests for those of others who are needier or more deserving. Ethical egoism rejects all of these common assumptions.

There are three familiar considerations that people sometimes offer in support of ethical egoism. Here is one offered by Ayn Rand (1905–1982), whose writings on behalf of ethical egoism have been very influential in contemporary culture.[1] Call it

The Self-Reliance Argument

1. The most effective way of making everyone better off is for each person to mind his own business and tend only to his own needs.
2. We ought to take the most effective path to making everyone better off.
3. Therefore, we each ought to mind our own business and tend only to our own needs.

There are two problems with this argument. Its first premise is false. And its second premise is one that egoists cannot accept.

The first premise is false, because those who are in need of help would not be better off if others were to neglect them. If you are suffering a heart attack and I know CPR and am the only one able to help, then you are definitely *worse* off, not better, if I decide to leave you alone and go on my way.

Nor is complete self-reliance even a good general policy. It might be better if everyone were self-reliant than if everyone were

---

1. Her novels *The Fountainhead* (1943) and *Atlas Shrugged* (1957) have sold millions; for a more explicit presentation of her philosophical views, one might try *The Virtue of Selfishness* (1964).

constantly sticking his nose into other people's business. But these are surely not our only two options. There is a middle path that allows a lot of room for self-interest but also demands a degree of self-sacrifice, especially when we can offer great help to others at very little cost to ourselves. Everyone would be better off if people helped others to some extent, rather than if people offered help only when doing so served self-interest.

Further, the argument's emphasis (in premise 2) on our doing what will improve everyone's well-being is not something that the egoist can accept. For ethical egoists, the ultimate moral duty is to maximize personal benefit. There is no moral requirement to make everyone better off. The egoist allows people to help others, or to have a care for the general good, but only when doing so will maximize their own self-interest. And not otherwise.

Here is another popular argument, also given by Rand, for severely limiting our duties to others. Call this the *Libertarian Argument.* Libertarians claim that our moral duties to help other people have only two sources: consent and reparation. In other words, any duty to aid another person stems either from our voluntarily agreeing to accept that duty (i.e., our consent), or from our having violated someone's rights, and so owing a duty to repair the wrong we have done. But if I do not consent to help other people, and have done them no wrong, then I have no duty to help them.

This is a fascinating argument, and there is a lot one might say about it. Indeed, I think that it poses one of the most fundamental challenges in political philosophy. Yet we can avoid a look into its details, because even if the argument is sound, it cannot support ethical egoism.

The basic explanation for this is that egoists cannot accept the argument's central claim. Egoists deny that there are two ultimate sources of moral duty (consent and reparation). In fact, egoists deny that *either* of these is a source of moral duty. For them, self-interest is the only

source of our moral duties. We must fulfill our voluntary agreements, or repair the damage we've done, only when doing so is in our best interest. *When it is not, we have no moral duty.*

The Libertarian Argument tells us, for instance, that if we promise to volunteer at a local hospital, or consent to the details of a home sale, then we should follow through. However, if doing so fails to make us better off, then egoism says that we have no duty to stick to our agreements. Indeed, egoism *forbids* us from holding up our end of the deal. Libertarians would require that we keep our word. Since egoism and libertarianism often give such conflicting advice, egoism cannot gain support from libertarianism.

A third source of support for ethical egoism comes from a theory known as **psychological egoism**—the view that our sole motivation is the pursuit of self-interest. If this theory is true, then **altruism**—the direct desire to benefit others for their own sake, without any ulterior motive—does not exist. Here is

The Argument from Psychological Egoism

1. If psychological egoism is true, then we can't be altruistic.
2. If we can't be altruistic, then it can't be our duty to be altruistic.
3. Therefore, if psychological egoism is true, then it can't be our duty to be altruistic.
4. Psychological egoism is true.
5. Therefore, it can't be our duty to be altruistic.

That conclusion isn't exactly ethical egoism, but it's very close. So long as we assume that we have some duties, then those duties must be egoistic, since they can't be altruistic. And that's what ethical egoism says.

Premise 1 is true by definition. No matter whether you like or hate psychological egoism, you should accept this premise. Premise 2 is also very plausible. If we can't be altruistic, then it can't be our duty to be altruistic. Why? Because we are not required to do the impossible—morality might be pretty demanding at times, but it can't be *that* demanding. The initial conclusion, 3, follows logically from 1 and 2, so if they are true, as they certainly seem to be, then 3 must be true as well.

That leaves only premise 4, which asserts the truth of psychological egoism. But psychological egoism, though it can seem the only clear-eyed and sensible view of human motivation, is actually not that plausible. After all, there are many reports of people jumping into freezing waters or blazing automobiles in order to save complete strangers. Perhaps some of them were motivated by a desire for fame or a reward. But *all* of them? The evidence is strongly opposed to such a drastic claim.

All the evidence we have about how humans are motivated takes two forms: testimony (how people describe their own motivations) and behavior (how they act). Millions of people will say that they are sometimes—not always, and perhaps not even usually—motivated directly to help others for their own sake. And millions of people actually do help others. Surely some of this evidence is misleading: some people convince themselves of their altruistic motivations when in fact, deep down, they are really looking out for themselves. But why discount *all* of this evidence? If you are committed in advance to denying the possibility that anyone's testimony or behavior can count as good evidence for altruism, then your commitment to psychological egoism is a matter of blind faith rather than serious attention to the evidence.

Psychological egoists have of course offered some support for their view. There is, first,

The Argument from Our Strongest Desires

1. Whenever you do something, you are motivated by your strongest desire.
2. Whenever you are motivated by your strongest desire, you are pursuing your self-interest.

3. Therefore, whenever you do something, you are pursuing your self-interest.

Let us grant for the moment that premise 1 of the argument is true. So we always do what we most want to do. But *that doesn't yet show that our strongest desires are always for personal gain.* That is precisely what has to be proven. Premise 2 of this argument is **begging the question**—it assumes the truth of the conclusion that it is meant to support. It is preaching to the converted. It is not a neutral thesis that can appeal to both fans and opponents of psychological egoism. Premise 2 assumes that just because a desire is mine, it must have a certain object—me and my self-interest. But *whose* desire it is, and *what* the desire is for—these seem to be completely separate issues. Why couldn't my desire be aimed at your welfare? Or the well-being of a friend, or my country, or even a stranger?

Here is another argument:

The Argument from Expected Benefit

1. Whenever you do something, you expect to be better off as a result.
2. If you expect to be better off as a result of your actions, then you are aiming to promote your self-interest.
3. Therefore, whenever you do something, you are aiming to promote your self-interest.

I have my doubts about this argument. Premise 1 seems to ignore the existence of pessimists. And even optimists sometimes expect to suffer for their actions. Consider a person who thinks she can get away with a convenient lie but admits the truth anyway, knowing the misery that's in store for her as a result. Or imagine an employee late for an important appointment who increases his delay by helping a stranger cross a dangerous street. He doesn't anticipate any reward for his good deed, and knows that this delay is only going to stoke his boss's anger. Both cases seem to be counterexamples to the claim that our actions are always accompanied by an expectation of personal benefit.

For now, let's assume that my doubts are mistaken and that premise 1 is secure. Even so, the second premise—the one that says that if you expect a benefit, then that is your aim—is very implausible.

The problem is that it looks like the egoist is begging the question again. Think about those who enjoy volunteer work. Such people may well expect to gain something from their activities. Volunteers often report feelings of deep satisfaction from their efforts. But this doesn't show that their motives are self-interested.

The egoist might rely on a general principle to establish premise 2:

(G) Whenever you expect your action to result in X, then your aim is to get X.

But (G) is false. Whenever I lecture to a large audience, I expect some people to fall asleep. Believe me, that is not my goal. If I ever had the chance to play against a professional tennis player, I'd expect to lose. But it wouldn't be my aim to do so. My goal would be to enjoy the experience and to learn a thing or two. If a student fails to prepare for an exam, she may expect to receive a poor grade. It hardly follows that she is trying for one. The bottom line is that even if premise 1 of the Argument from Expected Benefit can withstand the earlier criticisms, premise 2 begs the question. We don't have good reason to find this argument compelling.

It seems that we have strong counterexamples to psychological egoism in the form of those who have taken great risks to oppose oppressive regimes. Many of these people claim that their conscience wouldn't let them do otherwise— had they taken the safe path, they wouldn't be able to live with themselves. In their eyes, to give in to evil is to tarnish oneself. Many people speak of the terrible guilt they'd feel if they did nothing to fight against injustice.

Egoists insist that even these people are wholly self-interested. They are opposing injustice in order to make sure that they can sleep well at night, that they can be free of crippling guilt. Having a clean conscience is a benefit. And so such people are acting from self-interested motives.

It is important to see why this sort of reasoning does not work. If a person is truly good, she will certainly be troubled at the thought of doing wrong. But that does not prove that her actions are motivated by a desire for a guilt-free conscience. Indeed, if she did not care about others, then she wouldn't lose a wink of sleep at the thought of their misery. Those who suffer pangs of guilt from having harmed others, or having missed a chance to help them, are precisely those who care about other people.

There appear to be many people who are altruistically motivated, and who show this by their expressions of care for those they love. Consider the mother who gives away the last of her food to save her only child. This seems like the essence of altruism. And yet the egoist might say that the mother is really looking out for herself, by trying to avoid a terrible personal loss, for she would be devastated at witnessing the death of her child. By helping her child, the mother is thereby helping herself.

Much of what was just said is true. But this cannot be good news for the egoist, since the details of this little story imply that egoism is false. For most parents, their own well-being crucially depends on that of their children. And so, when parents tend to the needs of their children, they are usually helping themselves in the bargain. But this doesn't show that parents are motivated by self-interest when they offer such help. As we've seen, even if people expect to gain by helping others, that doesn't prove that their aim is to acquire such benefit. Further, if a parent suffers at the thought of her child's misery, then that is evidence of altruism, not egoism. Those who care only for themselves do not suffer when thinking of the misery of others.

B. RELATIVISM

Each of us has our doubts about morality. Most of these reflect our occasional puzzlement about what's right and wrong—we aren't sure, for in-stance, whether it is ever okay to lie or to break a deathbed promise.

But there is another kind of doubt, one that can undermine all of our confidence in morality. This sort of puzzlement is not about the content of morality—what it requires or allows—but about its status. The worry, specifically, is that there are no **objective moral standards**. Such standards are those that apply to everyone, even if people don't believe that they do, even if people are indifferent to them, and even if obey-ing them fails to satisfy anyone's desires. Moral claims are objectively true whenever they ac-curately tell us what these objective moral stan-dards are or what they require of us.

Ethical relativism denies that there are any objective moral standards. Relativists are not entirely skeptical, though. They do believe that some moral standards are correct, and that these determine which moral claims are true and which are false. Many are true. People sometimes get it right in ethics, and they do that when their beliefs agree with the correct moral standards.

But these standards are never *objectively* correct. Rather, these standards are correct only *relative to* each society. A moral standard is cor-rect just because a society is deeply committed to it. That means that the standards that are ap-propriate for some people may not be appropri-ate for others. There are no objective, universal moral principles that form an eternal blueprint to guide us through life. Morality is a *human construct*—we make it up—and like the law, or like standards of taste, there is no uniquely cor-rect set of rules to follow.

Relativism says that *an act is morally ac-ceptable just because it is allowed by the guid-ing ideals of the society in which it is performed, and immoral just because it is forbidden by those ideals*. People find relativism attractive for a va-riety of reasons. One such source comes from the idea that morality is made especially for humans. Before humans entered the picture,

there was no such thing as morality. And once our planet heats up to intolerable levels, or the big asteroid hits, our species will vanish, and morality will be extinguished along with us. Moral requirements don't apply to snakes or cockroaches or blue jays, and relativism can easily explain why—morality is a set of rules that humans invented for their own use; these animals lack the brainpower to create or obey such rules. On this view, morality is made by and for human beings.

This leads to a second attraction—relativ-ism provides a straightforward, scientifically respectable account of morality. There is noth-ing mysterious about its decrees—morality is a code that reflects cultural taste, nothing more (or less).

And this in turn leads to a third source of appeal—the ease with which relativists can ex-plain the possibility of moral knowledge. For relativists, moral knowledge comes from having your finger on the pulse of society. That is all that's needed to know right from wrong.

Fourth, relativism is egalitarian in ways that many people find deeply attractive. According to relativism, we are unable to judge one culture's moral code as morally superior (or inferior) to another's, and this has seemed to many like a refreshing kind of equality in the moral sphere.

Finally, many embrace relativism because they believe that it offers strong support for a policy of tolerance. If each culture's moral code is neither superior nor inferior to another's, then it seems that we must tolerate cross-cultural dif-ferences, rather than insisting that we are right and they are wrong, or, as is sometimes done, backing up such insistence with force.

But this line of thinking is deeply mis-taken. If a culture's deepest values support intolerance—and this is certainly the case for many, perhaps most, cultures—then for those in such a society, being tolerant is *immoral*. According to relativism, tolerance is valuable if, but only if, one's society has a deep commitment to its importance. The problem here is obvious: tolerance is most needed just where it is valued the least. If relativism is correct, then there is nothing morally wrong about silencing minority views or killing those who hope to expand the rights of minorities if that is what the culture stands for. Relativism is thus a very weak basis on which to support the value of tolerance.

There are other concerns. Relativism implies that a culture's fundamental moral code is **infallible**—incapable of being mistaken. Relativists believe that whatever a society holds most dear is morally right. If relativism is true, then a society's ultimate moral principles can be based on prejudice, ignorance, superficial thinking, or brainwashing, *and still be correct.* According to relativism, the origins of our basic moral beliefs are irrelevant. No matter how we came by them, the relativist claims that our ultimate moral beliefs cannot be mistaken.

But social codes are sometimes based on principles of slavery, of warlike aggression, of religious bigotry or ethnic oppression. Cultural relativism would turn these core ideals into ironclad moral duties, making cooperation with slavery, sexism, and racism the moral duty of all citizens of those societies. The **iconoclast**—the person deeply opposed to conventional wisdom—would, by definition, always be morally mistaken. And yet it seems to make sense to ask whether the basic principles of one's society are morally acceptable. If relativism is correct, however, such questioning shows that you don't really understand what morality is all about.

Relativism also has trouble accounting for moral progress in our moral beliefs. This occurs when more of them are true and, in particular, when our most fundamental beliefs change for the better. The gradual reduction in racist and sexist attitudes in the United States seems to represent this sort of moral progress, for instance. The problem for relativism is that if a society's deepest beliefs are true by definition, then they *cannot* change for the better. They can

change, of course. But no such change would mark a moral improvement.

A final problem for relativism arises when it tries to account for moral disagreement. Relativism says that *a moral judgment is true just because it correctly describes what a society really stands for.* For instance, if different societies disagree about the appropriate political status of women, then members of each society are speaking the truth when they assert (or deny) female moral equality. But they can't all be right. The statement that women are deserving of full political equality cannot be simultaneously true and false.

Relativists can escape this problem in familiar ways. They will claim that moral judgments are true only relative to social agreements. On this line of thinking, moral judgments are just like legal ones. It isn't contradictory to say that smoking marijuana, for instance, is both legal and illegal, so long as we qualify things to note that it is legal in some areas and illegal in others.

Relativists will say that all of our moral claims have to be understood by reference to social agreements. When you say that meat eating is right, and your Hindu friend from Calcutta says that it is wrong, what is really being said is this:

> You: Meat eating is accepted by my social customs.
> Your friend: Meat eating is forbidden by my social customs.

And again, both of these claims can be true. The contradiction disappears. There is no single judgment that is both true and false.

But then the existence of cross-cultural moral disagreement also disappears. If all we do when making moral judgments is to issue sociological reports about what our society stands for, then cross-cultural moral disagreement vanishes. We are no longer talking about (for example) meat eating, abortion, or drug use.

We are talking about how our society feels about such things.

But it doesn't seem as if that is what serious moral debate is all about. For instance, it appears possible to note that one's society approves of making wives domestic slaves and yet to disagree with the morality of that policy. But that's not so if relativism is to escape the contradiction problem.

So the cultural relativist faces a dilemma. If moral claims are taken literally, then relativism generates contradiction. If moral claims are instead veiled reports of cultural commitments, then contradictions disappear, but cross-cultural disagreement becomes impossible.

Indeed, the cultural relativist may be unable to escape contradiction after all. People who are members of subcultures—smaller cultural groups located within larger ones—often face a familiar problem. They are forced to choose between allegiance to the larger society and to their particular subculture. They are members of at least two societies, and when their ethical codes conflict, these unfortunate people are faced with contradictory moral advice.

We could solve this problem if we could figure out which society's code is more important. But relativism doesn't allow us to do that. By its lights, no society's moral code is morally any better than another's. We might be tempted to let the conflicted individuals decide and say that the social code that takes priority is the one that they prefer. But this would undermine cultural relativism, since such a move would make the morality of their actions depend on personal choice, rather than cultural opinion.

Indeed, when your views and society's views clash, why think that society is always right? If morality is created by humans, then it is hard to justify the claim that moral wisdom always lies with the masses rather than with individuals. The majority may have the power to force the minority to do as it says. But might doesn't make right.

C. ERROR THEORY

Did you ever have the feeling, deep down, that morality is a sham? That it's just a set of traditional rules inherited from ancestors who based it on ignorance, superstition, and fear? Perhaps it's only a convenient fiction, with no underlying authority at all.

The error theory of morality is built upon these doubts. It is defined by three essential claims:

1. *There are no moral features in this world.* Nothing is morally good or bad, right or wrong, virtuous or vicious. A careful inventory of the world's contents will reveal all sorts of scientific qualities: being symmetrical, being a liquid, being two feet long, carbon-based, spherical, and so on. But the list will contain no moral features.

2. *No moral judgments are true.* Why not? Simple: there is nothing for them to be true *of*. There are no moral facts. And so no moral claims can be accurate, since there are no moral facts for them to record.

3. *Our sincere moral judgments try, and always fail, to describe the moral features of things.* Thus we always lapse into error when thinking in moral terms. We are trying to describe the moral qualities of things when we make moral judgments. But since nothing has any moral qualities, all of our moral claims are mistaken. Hence the error.

It follows that:

4. *There is no moral knowledge.* Knowledge requires truth. If there is no moral truth, there can be no moral knowledge.

Error theorists are not launching some small-scale attack on morality. They are not criticizing our current views on, say, welfare policy or capital punishment, and trying to replace them with better ones. Rather, as they see it, *all* moral views are equally bankrupt. There is some very deep mistake that everyone committed to morality is making. The error theorist promises to reveal that mistake and to expose the real truth: morality is nothing but a fiction.

Moral error theorists can vindicate their view only if they can show that there is some fatal flaw at the heart of morality. And that depends on what the fundamental error of morality is supposed to be. In principle, we can develop any number of error theories, depending on which basic error morality is supposed to commit. But in practice, there really has been only one candidate.

All error theorists have agreed that the core mistake that undermines morality is its assumption that there are objective moral standards that supply each of us with **categorical reasons**—reasons that apply to us regardless of whether acting on them will get us what we want. If this central assumption is mistaken, then the entire enterprise of morality is bankrupt.

There are two substantial points that error theorists must convince us of. First, they must show that buying into morality really does assume a commitment to moral objectivity and categorical reasons. That will be news to many—to relativists, for instance. If morality does not, in fact, rely on these assumptions, then the error theorist's criticisms will fail.

But suppose that the coherence of our moral thinking and practice does indeed depend on the twin assumptions that morality is objective and that it provides us with categorical reasons. This reveals the second point that error theorists must convince us of: they must show that at least one of these assumptions is false.

Perhaps they can do that. Though we can't consider all of the arguments that have been offered against the objectivity of moral standards, we do have time to examine the strongest of them.

One classic argument against moral objectivity takes its cue from a simple observation: there is a lot more disagreement in ethics than there is in science. And there is a ready explanation for this. Scientists are trying to understand the nature of objective reality, whereas in ethics, there is no objective reality to be discovered. When it comes to morality, we are merely expressing our personal opinions, ones that have been obviously shaped by the time and place in which we've been raised. Different upbringings, different moral outlooks. But scientists the world over can agree on a wide set of truths, no matter their religious or cultural backgrounds.

This line of thought is nicely summarized by

The Argument from Disagreement

1. If well-informed, open-minded, rational people persistently disagree about some claim, then that claim is not objectively true.
2. Well-informed, open-minded, rational people persistently disagree about all moral claims.
3. Therefore, no moral claim is objectively true.

Perhaps premise 2 is too strong. Maybe there are some moral claims that every smart, rational, open-minded person accepts. But without a lot more investigation, it would be premature to assume that this is so.

What is clearly true is that for any moral claim—even one you find to be simply obvious—there will always be someone else who thinks that it is false. But that doesn't show that premise 2 is true, since such people may not be well informed, or open-minded, or rational.

Indeed, moral disagreement might well be a product of sloppy reasoning, of mistaken nonmoral beliefs, of having a personal stake in the outcome, or of a general prejudice. What if we were able to correct for these sources of error? Imagine people who were absolutely on top of *all* of the details, say, of affirmative action policies, who were free of personal bias and other prejudices, and who were able to reason flawlessly. Perhaps they'd all agree about whether affirmative action is morally acceptable.

Perhaps. But I share the skeptic's concerns here and am not sure that even perfectly ideal reasoners would agree about every moral issue. So let's accept, at least for the moment, that premise 2 is true. What of premise 1?

That premise must be false. There are counterexamples galore. Brilliant physicists disagree about whether the fundamental elements of matter are subatomic strings; eminent archaeologists disagree about how to interpret the remains discovered at ancient sites; the finest philosophers continue to debate whether God exists. And yet there are objective truths in each area. There are objective truths about the fundamental nature of the physical world, about the nature of various prehistoric tribes, about whether there is or isn't a God. Gaining knowledge of these truths can be hard, and perhaps, in some cases, impossible. But our beliefs on these matters must answer to an objective reality. Our views don't make physical or archaeological or philosophical claims true; the facts are what they are, independently of what we think of them.

There is another reason to doubt premise 1: this premise is itself the subject of deep disagreement. Really smart people still argue about whether it is true. And so, if such disagreement is enough to undermine objective truth, then the premise, by its own lights, can't be objectively true! And it certainly isn't "relatively" true—that is, true just because I, or my society, believe in it. The premise, then, is false.

So deep disagreement, even among the best minds, is not enough to show that skepticism in an area is correct. As a result, the many disagreements we see in ethics are perfectly compatible with its objectivity.

Another classic argument against the objectivity of morality stems from this thought: morality is a sham if God does not exist. The idea seems to be this: the only way morality could rest on solid foundations is by being authored by God.

Some **atheists**—those who believe that God does not exist—have taken up this line of thinking and turned it into the following:

The Argument from Atheism

1. Morality can be objective only if God exists.

2. God does not exist.

3. Therefore, morality cannot be objective.

I'm going to make things much easier on myself by leaving that second premise alone. If it's false, and God exists, then the argument crumbles. But let's just assume for now that there is no God. Then what?

Well, if premise 1 is true, and objective morality really does depend on God, then morality isn't objective after all. Many people think that 1 is true. They reason as follows. Moral laws, like other laws, must have an author. But if the laws are objective, then (by definition) no human being can be their author. So who is? Three guesses.

This reasoning has always been very popular. But it is mistaken. It rests on this key assumption: *laws require lawmakers*. Suppose this assumption is true. It then follows that objective laws need lawmakers, too. But human beings cannot play this role, since objective truths are true independently of human opinion. That leaves only God to do the work.

But if atheism is true, then the crucial assumption is false. Laws would not require lawmakers. Atheists believe that there are objective laws—of logic, physics, genetics, statistics, and so on. And yet if God does not exist, these laws have no author. We discovered these laws. We invented the words to describe the laws. But they are not true because we believe or want them to be. Their truth is objective, not subjective. If atheists are correct, no one authored such laws.

Thus if atheism is true, objective laws do not require lawmakers. So, for all we know, objective moral laws do not require a lawmaker, either.

Atheists might say, though, that *moral* laws require lawmakers, even though other laws do not. But why single out morality like that? Until atheists can provide an explanation for holding moral laws to a different standard from other objective laws, they are best advised to allow that moral laws do not require an author, either.

The Argument from Atheism is thus unpersuasive. It will obviously do nothing to convince religious believers, since it just assumes (in premise 2) that they are wrong. But even if atheists are correct, and God does not exist, premise 1 is highly doubtful, because its best support is flawed. That support comes from the assumption that laws require lawmakers—an assumption that atheists themselves should not accept.

A third worry about objective morality is based on the idea that science is our exclusive path to understanding reality. And scientists never have to include moral features in their explanations of molecular structure, biological adaptations, heat transfer—or anything else. We no longer believe in ghosts or leprechauns because science cannot confirm their existence. Perhaps we should do the same with objective moral standards.

We can summarize this line of thinking in

The Argument from the Scientific Test of Reality

1. If science cannot verify the existence of X, then the best evidence tells us that X does not exist.
2. Science cannot verify the existence of objective moral standards.
3. Therefore, the best evidence tells us that objective moral standards do not exist.

This argument reflects a basic commitment to the idea that the supernatural does not exist, and that everything in the world can ultimately be explained by science. Since scientific investigation does not tell us whether actions are moral or immoral, good or evil, this seems to leave objective morality out in the cold.

Although there is a lot of controversy in philosophical circles about premise 2, I find it very plausible. Science tells us how things are. Science does not tell us how things ought to be. Science describes; morality prescribes. I just don't see how science could verify the existence of objective moral standards. I may be wrong about this, of course, but if I am, then this argument collapses right away: premise 2 would be false. But let's assume for now that premise 2 is secure.

What of premise 1? Is science the exclusive measure of reality? I have my doubts. Science has its limits. It is out of its depth when trying to tell us about our ultimate purpose, the basic goals we ought to aim for, the fundamental standards we should live by. Science can tell us a lot. But it can't tell us everything.

There is some reason to deny that science really does have the final word on *everything*. Consider this:

(T) A claim is true only if science can verify it.

(T) can't be true. For science cannot verify it. (T) is not a scientific statement. We cannot test its truth by analyzing what we see, hear, taste, feel, or smell. We cannot mathematically test it. There are no lab experiments that will confirm it.

Since (T) is false, it follows that there are some truths that science cannot confirm. Perhaps moral ones are among them.

Now consider this principle:

(B) You are justified in believing a claim only if science can confirm it.

(B) is also problematic, since science cannot confirm it. Only philosophy can do that. If we take (B) at face value, then by its own lights we cannot be justified in thinking that it is true. So we are not justified in thinking that science is the source of *all* truths.

This line of reply does not prove that objective moral values exist. But if successful, it does show that science cannot have the final say about everything. This means that at least some nonscientific claims are true, and perhaps highly credible. Moral claims may be among them.

Even if these arguments against objective morality fail, error theorists have a final argument that might do the trick. The argument relies on the familiar thought that all moral duties come prepackaged with a special power. They automatically supply people with reasons to obey them. And it doesn't matter what we care about. If it's really your duty to repay that loan or help your aged grandparents, then you've got an excellent reason to do so—even if doing these things fulfills none of your desires.

That's unusual. My reasons for writing this book, using my treadmill, or listening to music all depend on what matters to me. Most reasons are like this. The reasons that come from morality, however, are categorical. They apply to us regardless of what we care about.

Many philosophers cannot see how categorical reasons are possible. Their puzzlement has given rise to a powerful argument against the objectivity of morality:

The Argument from Categorical Reasons

1. If there are objective moral duties, then there are categorical reasons to obey them.
2. There are no categorical reasons.
3. Therefore, there are no objective moral duties.

This argument has convinced some very smart philosophers. And they may be right to be convinced. But there are two lines of response, each of which has been taken up by a large number of other philosophers. Since the argument is logically perfect, those who believe in objective morality will have to reject either the first premise or the second.

The first strategy is to challenge premise 1. This approach denies that objective moral duties must supply us with reasons for action. It may be that some people have no reason to do what morality requires of them. Whether there are objective moral standards is one thing; whether they supply us with reasons to obey them is another. The answer to the first question may be *yes*, even if the answer to the second is a disappointing *no*. If this line of thinking is right, then we will have to abandon the age-old hope of showing that everyone has reason to be moral.

The second strategy stands by premise 1, but rejects premise 2. On such a view, objective moral duties really exist, and they really do provide categorical reasons. There are reasons to behave morally, even if that good behavior doesn't get us what we want.

We can support such a view by appealing to compelling examples. Suppose you are hiking along a cliff path and notice a stranger who is absent-mindedly walking from the opposite direction. You see that he's about to take a wrong step and plunge to his death. There is a reason to yell to him and alert him of the danger. And that reason applies to you even if you don't care a bit about the man or about the pats on the back you'll receive when the story gets out. There is something to be said on behalf of your warning him, something that favors it, that justifies it, that makes it a legitimate thing to do. These are just different ways of saying the same thing: there is an excellent reason for you to save that stranger's life, even if doing so won't get you anything you care about.

I don't pretend that my analysis of this argument, or the earlier ones against objective morality, is conclusive. Philosophers have devoted thousands of pages to these arguments, and it would be arrogant to suppose that I could settle these matters in so short a span. Still, I do hope to have shown that things are more complicated here than one might have thought, and that anyone tempted to skepticism about morality will have to do *a lot* more work in order to justify their doubts.

D. CONCLUSION

There are many sources of concern about whether morality is all it's cracked up to be. These are not superficial worries, to the effect that one or another of our moral views may be mistaken, or that we are bound to make moral mistakes every now and then. The skeptical doubts discussed in this chapter go to the heart of the moral enterprise.

If ethical egoism is correct, then the story that we tell each other about what morality requires of us is all wrong. This form of egoism dictates that morality is all about the pursuit of self-interest. Perhaps the strongest argument for this view depends on the truth of psychological egoism, which poses its own threat to morality. If we cannot be altruistic, then we can't be required to be. But as we have seen, though psychological egoism can seem like the cynical truth about human motivation, the arguments offered in its support are quite weak.

Relativists direct their criticism to the thought that morality could be objective. As they see it, morality is a human creation, possessed of the same status as the law or etiquette. But the arguments for relativism are, in the end, less impressive than they have been taken to be, and there are some quite serious problems that emerge if we assume that relativism is true.

Error theorists regard morality as a convenient fiction. But the strongest of the critical arguments that target objective morality and categorical reasons are, at best, inconclusive, as there are plausible replies to each of those criticisms. This does not guarantee that morality is in good order. But our discussion has shown that skepticism about morality should not be our default position. Any such skepticism must be earned by providing a *very* compelling argument. It's not yet clear whether any such argument exists.

ESSENTIAL CONCEPTS

Altruism: the motivation to benefit others for their own sake.

Atheists: those who believe that God does not exist.

Begging the question: assuming the truth of the conclusion that one's argument is meant to support.

Categorical reasons: reasons that apply to us regardless of whether acting on them will get us what we want.

Error theory: the view that says that (1) there are no moral features in this world; (2) no moral judgments are true; (3) our sincere moral judgments try, and always fail, to describe the moral features of things; and, as a result, (4) there is no moral knowledge.

Ethical egoism: the ethical theory that says that an action is morally right if and only if it maximizes one's self-interest.

Iconoclast: a person whose views are deeply opposed to conventional wisdom.

Infallible: incapable of making a mistake.

Objective moral standards: those that apply to everyone, even if people don't believe that they do, even if people are indifferent to them, and even if obeying them fails to satisfy anyone's desires.

Psychological egoism: the psychological theory that says that the ultimate motivation behind every human action is the pursuit of self-interest.

Relativism: the view that there are no objective moral standards, and that all correct moral standards hold only relative to each person or each society.

DISCUSSION QUESTIONS

1. How do psychological egoists explain extreme acts of self-sacrifice, such as falling on a grenade for one's fellow soldiers? Do you find their explanation of such phenomena compelling?

2. Suppose that people always do what they most want to do. Is that enough to show that psychological egoism is true? Why or why not?

3. If someone expects to benefit from an action, does that show that she is trying to advance her self-interest? Why or why not?

4. Can ethical relativism make sense of the idea of moral progress? Does moral progress really exist?

5. Can actions be performed in more than one society at a time? If so, and if relativism is true, how might this lead to contradiction? Can relativists escape this problem? Why or why not?

6. What do error theorists typically claim is the "error" at the heart of our moral practice? Is the assumption that they identify really essential to our moral thought? If so, do you agree that it is an error?

7. What is the best explanation of the existence of widespread disagreement in ethics? Does the existence of disagreement suggest a lack of objective moral truth?

8. If ethics is not a science, and moral facts are fundamentally different from scientific ones, would this threaten the objectivity of morality? If so, how?

9. A character in Dostoevsky's *The Brothers Karamazov* said that "if God is dead, then everything is permitted." Do you find such a claim plausible or implausible? What reasons support your view?

10. What are categorical reasons? Do any categorical reasons exist? If not, does this undermine the claim that morality is objective?

READINGS

Cultural Relativism

Diane Jeske

We often hesitate before judging members of another culture whose moral views seem to differ greatly from our own. This hesitation has been supported by at least two forms of cultural relativism. The first assesses others by reference to the standards of a speaker's own culture. When you say, for instance, that female circumcision is wrong, your judgment is correct just in case members of your own culture disapprove of that practice. The second sort of relativism—the one that author Diane Jeske focuses on—makes the morality of actions depend on the standards of the culture that the action is performed in. In that case, your judgment that this practice is wrong would be true if you were judging a person who performed that action in the United States, but false if your judgment focused on the actions of those in various parts of Africa.

Cultural relativism implies that no action has a moral nature in itself. Moral standards, like those of the law or etiquette, may legitimately differ from culture to culture. The idea that actions are properly judged only relative to the local standards where they are performed has seemed to make good sense of how people can disagree about the morality of actions. It has also seemed to support a policy of tolerance and open-mindedness about cultural practices that differs from our own. But as Jeske argues, careful examination shows both of these claims to be problematic.

Jeske has us imagine Thomas Jefferson claiming that slavery is morally OK, while we deny that. It seems that we have a disagreement here. But we don't, if cultural relativism is true. If we're focused on whether slavery in eighteenth-century America is acceptable, then if cultural relativism is true, we'd have to agree with Jefferson. If we're instead focused on whether slavery is acceptable in contemporary American, Jefferson would have to agree with us. There would be no basis for disagreement, once we saw what the local standards really said about slavery.

When it comes to tolerance, cultural relativism tells us that the standards of the culture in which an act is performed are the ones that determine the action's morality. As we know, however, many cultures deeply endorse discrimination that targets members of various groups. If cultural relativism is true, then such discrimination is morally acceptable—in fact, opposing such discrimination would be immoral, since attempts to create greater equality would violate the existing standards of that culture. Cultural relativism endorses intolerance in cultures that stand behind discrimination and oppression, and endorses tolerance only in cultures that celebrate it. Jeske claims that cultural relativism therefore fails to offer a solid basis for supporting tolerance.

In the southern United States prior to the Civil War, the law considered many people of African descent to be property. A large majority of white people, rich and poor, in those southern states regarded the practice of African slavery as morally justified, and any form of abolitionist activity as morally wrong. Many of the revered figures of the early Republic, including Madison, Washington, and Jefferson, were slave-holders. The reverence of these figures continues in our contemporary world, a world that strongly condemns racism of any form. Many people will morally judge a person in 2020 who makes a racist joke more harshly than they will morally condemn Jefferson for having been a slave-holder.

Female circumcision is still widely practiced in parts of Africa, the Middle East, and Asia, with more than 200 million women alive today in 30 countries having been circumcised. Most forms of female circumcision have serious and irrevocable impacts on the physical, particularly reproductive, health and psychological and sexual well-being of the women who undergo the operation, which is usually carried out, without anesthesia, on girls under the age of 16. While people in the communities that circumcise their daughters morally condemn a failure to do so, those who live in countries such as the US, the UK, and Canada judge the practice to be morally wrong. However, many people in these latter countries will hesitate to morally judge those in, say, remote villages of Africa, who have their daughters circumcised.

These cases provide examples of the ways in which cultural practices have varied across cultures. They also illustrate the ways in which people in different cultures disagree in the moral judgments they make of such practices. With respect to non-moral matters (e.g. whether there is life on other planets, or whether the diversity of species is a result of evolution), when two people disagree, we simply assume that either one or both of them is wrong about the matter at hand. But many people are uncomfortable with such an approach to moral disagreement, and that discomfort in many cases results from the fact that moral disagreement is seen as a function of the persons at issue being from different cultures. Hence, we are reluctant to judge those in other cultures according to the same moral standards we use to judge members of our own culture.

After all, we are encouraged to celebrate diversity and tolerance. In particular, we are encouraged to celebrate diversity in and toleration of cultural practices that differ from our own. But practices such as female circumcision and slavery have a long history in and are regarded as having an important function in the cultures in which they are or have been found. Given our commitment to diversity and tolerance, then, we find ourselves hesitating in making moral judgments in such cases. Ought we to judge people in other cultures according to the same standards we use with respect to those in our own culture, or ought we to judge them according to different criteria?

One natural approach to these questions is to regard moral judgment as nothing more than a matter of how people feel about various practices. Around here, now, we reject and disapprove of both female circumcision and slavery, and so we say of those practices that they are morally wrong. But in other times or places, people have accepted and approved of female circumcision or slavery, and so they say of those practices that they are morally right. This is the approach taken by those who support the theory known as cultural *relativism*.

In this chapter we consider how best to understand cultural relativism so as to accommodate the way in which many people are tempted to talk about moral disagreement across cultures (section I). We will then consider whether acceptance of cultural relativism is the only or best way to handle our hesitancy in judging members of other cultures in the same way in which we judge members of our own culture and whether it provides the best explanation of moral disagreement across cultures (section II). We will also evaluate whether our commitment to diversity and tolerance is best served by or even compatible with a commitment to cultural relativism (section III). Finally, we will see that matters about culture and disagreement are perhaps not as straightforward as they initially seem (section IV).

I. RELATIVITY AND MORAL JUDGMENT

A familiar response to members of other cultures engaging in practices of which we disapprove is to say "that is the right thing *for them* to do even if it is not the right thing *for us* to do." It is certainly wrong *for me* to hold slaves, but, it might be said, that does not imply that it was wrong *for Thomas Jefferson* to hold slaves. Claims of this form suggest the view that moral judgment is in some way relative to an individual's cultural placement: it would be wrong *of me* to have my daughter circumcised, but it is not wrong *for women in certain African communities* to have their daughters circumcised.

Relativity in judgment is a phenomenon with which we are familiar outside of the domain of morality. Consider the following exchange between me and my brother: Me: "White chocolate is delicious." My brother: "White chocolate is not delicious. It is disgusting!" At first, it looks like my brother is contradicting me, and that he and I are engaged in a disagreement about the nature of white chocolate. But it takes very little reflection to see that that is not the case. Almost nobody thinks that there is some property, *being delicious*, that white chocolate either has or doesn't have, and that one of us has made a mistake as to whether white chocolate has that property. Rather, my saying "White chocolate is delicious" is another way for me to say something like "I really enjoy the taste of white chocolate." My brother, then, is saying that he does not enjoy the taste of white chocolate. After we have restated our claims, we can see that not only are we not disagreeing with one another, we are not even really talking about the same thing: I am talking about what I like, while my brother is talking about what he likes.

When I declared that white chocolate is delicious, my brother might have responded, "Well, maybe *for you* it's delicious, but it certainly isn't *for me*," just as someone might say of the woman in the remote African village who has her daughter circumcised, "Well, it was the right thing *for her* to do." So some philosophers and non-philosophers have proposed that judgments about an action's being right or wrong are like judgments that some food is delicious: just as "being delicious" is not a property of any food considered in itself, so "being right/wrong" is not a property of any action considered in itself.

There are two importantly different versions of cultural relativism. One renders the truth or falsity (what philosophers call the truth value) of a moral judgment relative to the *speaker's* culture. The other version relativizes the truth values of moral judgments to the culture of the person whose action is being morally assessed. Let's begin with a more formal statement of the first form of the view:

> **Cultural Relativism with Speaker-Relativity**: For person S to judge that person T's action is right (wrong) is for S to judge that members of S's culture approve (disapprove) of T's action.

When a friend and I are talking about forcing women to wear head coverings in public, we will say to each other, "That is wrong!" and take ourselves to have made a true claim. But if we were to note that members of Hassidic Jewish communities claim that it is not wrong to force women to wear head coverings in public, we might at least hesitate to judge that person to have said something false. Cultural relativism with speaker-relativity can make sense of this: the claim is true when made by me or my friend (21st century secular American academics), but false when made by a Hassidic Jew, because the truth value of a moral judgment is relative to the attitudes of the members of the speaker's culture.

So, according to the version of cultural relativism that makes the truth value of moral judgments relative to the attitudes of the speaker's culture, the standard by which any person is to judge the actions of anyone else are the standards of the person making the judgment. But that does not allow us to say of people in other cultures, "that's right *for them* even though it's not right *for us*." According to cultural relativism with speaker-relativity, when I make moral judgments, what is right for the members of my culture is right for everyone, and what is wrong for the members of my culture is wrong for everyone. In order to avoid this result, we can adopt:

> **Cultural Relativism with Agent-Relativity**: For person S to judge that person T's action is right (wrong) is for S to judge that members of T's culture approve (disapprove) of T's action.

Consider the case of Thomas Jefferson's being a slave-holder. When I judge that Thomas Jefferson's having been a slave-holder is wrong, according to cultural relativism with speaker-relativity, what I have said is true, because people in my culture disapprove of slave-holding. However, according to cultural relativism with agent-relativity, that judgment is false, because Thomas Jefferson's culture (white Americans in the southern states in the 1700s and 1800s) did not disapprove of slavery. So cultural relativism with agent-relativity allows us to make sense of saying, of slave-holding and Thomas Jefferson, "it was not wrong *for him*": what we are saying, according to this version of cultural relativism, is that people in Jefferson's culture did not disapprove of slave-holding.

Cultural relativism with agent-relativity accommodates and explains both of the features of moral judgment that we discussed in the introduction. First, if we accept cultural relativism with agent-relativity, we can see why we ought to be hesitant about making negative moral judgments about people in other cultures for engaging in practices that we, here and now, reject: to engage in moral judgment about a person's action is to assess whether her performing such an action is approved or disapproved of by members of *her* culture. According to this view, while it is certainly wrong *for me* to have *my daughter* circumcised, it is not wrong *for members of various African societies* to have *their daughters* circumcised. What is wrong for us here and now is not necessarily wrong for other people in other times or places.

Second, cultural relativism with agent-relativity makes sense of moral disagreement without forcing us to say that someone must be wrong when such disagreement occurs. Moral disagreement, like disagreement about whether white chocolate is delicious, is only apparent disagreement. When I say that it is wrong to hold slaves, while Thomas Jefferson (at least in the latter years of his life) said that it is not wrong to hold slaves, it looks as if we are disagreeing with one another, that the truth of my claim implies the falsity of his (and vice versa). But that appearance is misleading, according to cultural relativism with agent-relativity. For on that view, a claim such as "it is wrong to hold slaves" is importantly incomplete: in order to assign a truth value to the judgment, we have to know when and where the slave-holding is taking place. If I clarify by saying that I mean slavery is wrong for people in my culture, then my judgment is true. But if I am saying that slavery is wrong for members of Jefferson's culture, then my judgment is false. Once we understand that in making moral judgments we are really just talking about how an agent's culture regards her actions, we can recognize that what looks like disagreement across cultures is really just a matter of people in different cultures having different attitudes to various practices.

So cultural relativism (from here on, whenever I refer to cultural relativism I will be talking about the version with agent-relativity) seems to capture some aspects of our moral thought and discourse. But does it do so in the most plausible way? Do we need to relativize moral judgment to cultures in order to do so?

II. KNOWLEDGE AND THE RELATIVITY OF JUDGMENT

Cultural relativists defend their view by appealing to the ways in which they handle two aspects of our moral thought and discourse: (i) the fact that we tend to judge people in other cultures differently from how we judge members of our own culture, and (ii) the fact that moral disagreement is common across cultures. But there are other ways of accounting for these two features of our moral practice that do not require us to assume the truth of cultural relativism.

II.i Making Moral Judgments Relative to Culture

Consider the following case: Alfred is a physician in the 18th century, when it was widely believed that blood-letting was the medically appropriate treatment for an array of illnesses. Physicians would open a vein and allow a significant amount of blood to drain from a patient's body. We now know that blood-letting will not only not cure disease but that it will make the patient weaker and less well-equipped to fight her illness. If a physician today tried to utilize blood-letting to treat a serious illness such as cancer, we would judge him as acting immorally and would hold him responsible for any harm caused to his patient. However, we would not judge Alfred in the same way. In fact, we might say of Alfred's opening his patient's vein, "it was the right thing *for him* to do."

Why do we judge that what was right for Alfred to do in this case is different from what it is right for a contemporary physician, Abigail, to do? The obvious answer is that Alfred is working in a context in which it is reasonable for him to believe that blood-letting will aid his patient: it is the accepted go-to treatment, and all of the respected experts and textbooks endorse that treatment. Abigail, however, knows, or at least ought to know, that blood-letting will have adverse effects on her patient, because the practice is rejected by all of the relevant experts and textbooks. So our differing judgments of Alfred and of Abigail are the result of our differing judgments about what beliefs it is reasonable for each to have and to act on.

So let us reconsider our case of a community in which girls are circumcised. One reason for finding cultural relativism plausible is that it allows us to say that what is right for parents in this community is different from what is right for parents in our communities as a result of differing cultural attitudes toward the practice of female circumcision. But our case of Alfred and Abigail offers us another possibility as to why we might judge that what is right for an agent is relative to her cultural placement. That possibility involves an appeal to differences in background, non-moral knowledge. Our own moral rejection of the practice of female circumcision is to a

large extent a result of a recognition of the ways in which the practice harms women. But in many of the communities in which the practice is approved, people have false views about the effects of circumcising girls and young women: some believe that circumcision makes child birth easier, and some believe that the clitoris, which is usually removed as a part of the circumcision operation, poses serious and potentially lethal dangers to the men who have intercourse with uncircumcised women, and to the infants they give birth to. If these false beliefs were true, then we would probably have quite different moral views about female circumcision, given that our views about the potential harms and benefits to the people involved underlie our moral views about the rightness or wrongness of circumcision. So we might think that if members of communities that practice circumcision believe it to be beneficial to all involved, then we should not view them as acting wrongly, just as we do not judge Alfred to have acted wrongly, given his belief that he is doing what is best for his patients.

We can notice, however, that an agent's beliefs, no matter how sincerely held, are not always enough to cause us to judge her actions to be right. For example, many people still hold racist beliefs; very likely, some of those people sincerely believe that members of certain other races are emotionally or intellectually stunted or exceptionally dangerous. Now, if there were some race such that members of that race were, in the vast majority of cases, dangerous, then we would be justified in treating members of that race as a threat. Nonetheless, we do not say of contemporary racists that their racist actions are right. That's because we do not think that contemporary racists are justified in viewing members of other races in this way: racist thinking has been debunked quite decisively. Further, it seems that those who still have racist beliefs ought to know that their beliefs are false: they have access to all of the same data as the rest of us here and now, and have, in most cases, sufficient education to evaluate that data rationally. In most cases, such people are guided by illicit motives, such as a need to feel superior, and this leads them to deceive themselves into holding racist beliefs. Such people choose not to examine evidence that could undermine the beliefs that support their self-image, and they are culpable for making such a choice.

Consider again the case of Thomas Jefferson, slave-holder. Some people are inclined to say that it was right for him to hold slaves, but not all are willing to do so. After all, there were plenty of abolitionists whom Jefferson knew personally, and his younger self had advocated on behalf of the slaves and denounced the institution of slavery. In his later years, his views shifted, and they shifted, it seemed, the more financially dependent upon slavery Jefferson became. As we learn these facts about Jefferson, our willingness to say that it was right for him to hold slaves at least starts to waver, if not to disappear entirely. He starts to look less like Alfred and more like the contemporary racists who have self-interested reasons that motivate them to accept racist ideology.

Our moral beliefs are often a function of our non-moral beliefs. For example, our beliefs about how doctors ought to respond to their patients are a function of our beliefs about what sorts of treatments will best promote the patient's physical well-being. Our beliefs about the wrongness of African slavery are, at least in part, a function of our belief that slave-owners had mistaken non-moral views about the emotional and intellectual capacities of the people they enslaved. We morally reject female circumcision because we reject the beliefs about the harms it causes that its practitioners use to justify it. But we also recognize that what a person is justified in believing is to a large extent a function of her time and culture. Thus, moral judgment ought to be sensitive to the culture of the agent being evaluated, because that culture is relevant to what it is rational for that agent to believe. But the case of Thomas Jefferson shows that we need to be sensitive to the *particular* facts about the *particular* person we are evaluating. After all, there is a sense in which Jefferson and a poor, uneducated white Southerner belonged to the same culture, but it is quite clear that what it was rational for Jefferson to believe was, in many cases, quite different from what it was rational for the poor, uneducated person to believe. So particularities of background knowledge may do a better job of accommodating

some of our judgments about agents in other times or places than does an appeal to mere cultural placement.

II.ii Explaining Moral Disagreement

In the previous section, we saw that our tendency to relativize our moral judgments to an agent's culture can be explained by an appeal to cultural differences with respect to background, non-moral beliefs. This disagreement with respect to non-moral beliefs can, of course, also explain cultural divergence with respect to moral judgment as well. If our moral beliefs are often a function of our non-moral beliefs, then divergence with respect to the latter will cause divergence with respect to the former. For example, in the 19th century court case *Bradwell v Illinois*, it was held that it was legitimate to prevent women from practicing law. One of several reasons given was that every defendant deserved a good defense, and women, given their inferior intellectual capabilities and emotional instability, would not provide such a defense. We now believe that women are just as capable as men of being effective lawyers; if we did not, we would also be more likely to sympathize with barring women from the legal profession.

In fact, this explanation of moral disagreement might seem preferable to the way in which cultural relativism handles disagreement. As we saw in section I, the cultural relativist thinks that it will often turn out that there actually isn't any disagreement. When I claim that slavery is wrong, we need to specify where and when the slave-holding takes place. It is true that slavery is wrong for me, but it is false that slavery is wrong for Jefferson. So when Jefferson says that slavery is not wrong, if he is talking about his holding of slaves, then he is not, contrary to appearances, disagreeing with me. So if we think that there is genuine disagreement between me and Jefferson, then we would need to reject cultural relativism.

Let us now consider how cultural relativism handles diversity and toleration.

III. MULTICULTURALISM AND ETHICAL THEORY

We live in a world where we are encouraged to be tolerant of and to attempt to preserve cultural diversity. We condemn those in previous times who invaded other lands and tried to force indigenous persons to conform to the conquerors' own ways of life. Of course, much of this drive to colonize resulted from greed and a desire to dominate, but there were also those who sincerely believed that the indigenous persons lived in morally disreputable ways and needed to be brought to the moral light that the colonizers believed that they possessed. As a result, many ways of life were destroyed and entire peoples deprived of their cultural traditions—and, sometimes, of their very existence. Our response now is to view the colonizers as smug, arrogant people driven by a belief that there was only one correct way to live—their own.

Rejection of this sort of arrogance has motivated many of those who accept cultural relativism. If cultural relativism is true, then the conquerors are simply wrong to claim that there is one true moral code that transcends cultures—morality, according to the cultural relativist, is nothing over and above the attitudes of people in the agent's culture. So, when Westerners encountered other peoples who had different sorts of (for example) modes of dress or marital and family arrangements, their negative moral judgments of such people were just false: they were failing to judge those cultural practices relative to the attitudes of the people in those cultures. While it would be wrong for a British missionary woman in the 1800s to wander around in public in nothing more than a skirt made of animal skin or grasses, it was not wrong for women in certain African or Pacific Islander cultures to do so. Thus, it seems that cultural relativism discourages the sort of judgmental arrogance that has so often led (and continues to lead) to intolerance.

Before we embrace cultural relativism, however, there are a few questions that we need to address: (1) Do we believe that toleration ought to extend to all cultural practices? (2) Does denial of cultural relativism encourage the sort of smug arrogance that cultural relativists denounce? (3) Does cultural relativism actually support tolerance of diversity?

Let's begin with (1): Do we believe that toleration ought to extend to all cultural practices? The obvious answer is that of course we do not. African slavery in the American south was a deeply entrenched feature of the life of white culture in the southern states, as was the white supremacist world view that undergirded it. After the American Civil War, the lynching of black people (mainly men) became a cultural ritual in which entire communities participated: this ritual reinforced the culture of white supremacy in southern states. But slavery and lynching and other institutions supporting white supremacy caused, and continue to cause, immense amounts of harm to black Americans. Today we are struggling with the aftermaths of slavery and lynching, and we firmly believe that such practices ought to be condemned in the harshest terms.

We can notice that there is a vast difference between cultural practices such as slavery and those concerning how one dresses. Slavery was a practice that caused great harm to a vast number of people. Whether a woman is expected to bare or not to bare her breasts in public is quite different. Whereas the latter really does seem to be nothing more than a matter of cultural expectation and history, the former does not. Often, those who went to other lands and criticized and attempted to change aspects of the cultures that they encountered failed to give adequate consideration to the needs and conditions of people in those cultures. For example, what is regarded as appropriate dress is often a function of climate and of available materials. Marital and child-care arrangements are sometimes a function of the size of a community and the need to reproduce and to care for children in ways compatible with meeting the community's goal of survival. But slavery such as it was practiced in the American south was simply a way for a class of people (white land-owners) to benefit from the labor of others (people of African descent) in the most profitable manner possible. Understanding the motivations for cultural practices can reveal a great difference between those such as slavery and those such as smoking peyote: it is the difference between the motivation of benefitting oneself at the expense of others versus merely creating rituals that bind a group together or benefit the group as a whole, given existing conditions.

It is not always a straightforward matter to figure out which category a given cultural practice falls into. For many cultures that practice female circumcision, it is viewed as a rite of passage that helps to integrate girls into the community. But it is also an undeniable fact that the practice serves the function of denigrating the sexual autonomy and well-being of women in order to protect male control over lineage and other forms of property. In this respect, then, female circumcision is like slavery in being a practice that benefits one class of society at the cost of great harm to another. Toleration of such a practice would seem to be a form of complicity with exploitation and pain. Thus, such toleration does not seem at all admirable.

Let's move on to (2): Does denial of cultural relativism encourage the sort of smug arrogance that cultural relativists denounce? It might seem that if we commit ourselves to a moral code that transcends cultural attitudes and that can be used as a basis of criticism of existing moral codes, then we will proceed to criticize any cultural practice that does not meet our own standards, and will then regard ourselves as justified in using coercive force to change the ways of life of other peoples. Adherence to a culture-independent moral code, then, seems to encourage colonialism, violence, and other forms of intolerance that demean and harm those who are different from us.

However, these sorts of responses to other cultures are not the result of acceptance of a culture-independent moral code on its own. They are the result of acceptance of such a code coupled with either of the following assumptions: (i) that one's code is entirely and obviously correct, or (ii) that a judgment that a person or persons is acting wrongly justifies coercive interference.

But both assumptions are unjustified. First, one can accept that there is a culture-independent moral code without assuming that one's own culture's way of life completely accords with that moral code. There were, for example, white southerners even in Jefferson's day who regarded slavery as highly immoral and who worked to abolish it.

To be a good person, one needs to approach conventional practices, in one's own culture as well as in other cultures, with an open mind and a critical eye. Cultural practices are often a result of class interests and self-deception, and are often sustained through propaganda motivated by greed and other vices. Every person, in every culture, needs to recognize that they can learn from the different ways in which other cultures live and that their own cultural practices ought not to be accepted uncritically.

We also need to remind ourselves of the fact, discussed in the previous section, that moral truth is dependent on non-moral truth in important ways. So when we see people in other cultures doing things in ways that seem wrong to us, we need to stop and ask whether, in fact, those ways might actually be appropriate responses to the different circumstances in which those people find themselves. In past ages Inuit peoples in Greenland would sometimes kill infants whose fathers died. This seems morally horrific to us, until we remember that Greenlanders used to live always on the brink of starvation and that their survival depended upon successful hunting by male members of the group. If an infant had no father to hunt for it, then it would have to be fed by the efforts of other men who had their own families to sustain. The Greenlanders had to sacrifice someone given their circumstances, and so they chose to sacrifice those who presented a burden without being able to simultaneously contribute to the group's survival. Whether or not we agree with the choices they made, we can certainly see how complicated and heart-breaking their situation was, and how we ourselves, in their circumstances, might make the very same choice.

Finally, the second assumption above is just false. Even if we decide that a practice like female circumcision is wrong, even given the circumstances of the communities in which it is practiced, it does not follow that it is right for us to intervene, and it certainly does not follow that we are justified in intervening in a violent manner. If female circumcision is wrong, it is wrong because it causes so much harm to so many women and girls. So our response ought to involve trying to figure out how to end that harm. What sort of intervention would be best in the long run? Harsh criticism, for example, sometimes just produces a defensive reaction, and violence often just causes yet more suffering. Sometimes, unfortunately, our best response is no response. The wrongness of others' actions is never sufficient, in itself, to render our intervention right.

So denial of cultural relativism does not necessarily generate smug arrogance. Further, acceptance of it may well be compatible with smug arrogance and intolerance. Consider (3): Does cultural relativism actually support tolerance of diversity? Recall our British missionaries encountering cultures in which women appeared in public with bare breasts. The missionaries responded with deep disapproval, which reflected the dominant attitude in their own culture. In trying to change the ways in which the indigenous women dressed, the missionaries were acting in ways approved of by their own culture, and so (according to cultural relativism) were acting morally. If we accept cultural relativism, the following two claims are entirely compatible with one another: (i) S, in baring her breasts, is doing what it is right for her to do, and (ii) It is right for T to attempt to prevent S from baring her breasts. S's culture may approve of her appearing in public with bare breasts, and T's culture may approve of her trying to prevent S from appearing in public with bare breasts.

According to the cultural relativist, what is right for me to do is determined by the attitudes of my culture. So if my culture approves of conquering by violence and then colonizing other cultures, then it is right for me to be a violent, colonizing conqueror. If my culture disapproves of tolerance of diversity, then it is wrong of me to be tolerant and accepting. White southerners disapproved of abolitionist activity, so if I were a white woman in 1830s Alabama, it would be wrong for me to work to end slavery. If Black Lives Matter activists are correct in saying that our culture is one of white supremacy, then it is wrong for us who are members of this culture to strive for racial equality. One cannot have a culture-independent commitment to tolerance and equality if one is a cultural relativist, because cultural relativists reject any culture-independent moral truths. Two conclusions follow directly. First, rejection of cultural relativism does not entail intolerance. Second, acceptance of cultural relativism is, under certain circumstances, incompatible with tolerance.

IV. HOW MUCH MORAL DISAGREEMENT IS THERE?

Suppose that we were in discussion with an American slave-holder from 1850s South Carolina who claims that African slavery is morally justified. How would he attempt to defend his view? He would claim that black persons are not capable of caring for themselves, that slavery really does benefit his slaves, that emancipating black people would result in a serious danger to society, etc. Of course, we would respond that he is just wrong: black people are as capable as white people, slavery is no benefit to the enslaved, and that emancipation would bring about no serious dangers (except for those caused by disgruntled ex-slave-holders).

What is significant is that, if the slave-holder were to genuinely attempt to defend his moral position, he would not claim that harm to the slaves is just irrelevant, or that greed on the part of white slave-holders is a perfectly acceptable justification for the institution of slavery. He would recognize, just as we do, that moral justification ultimately requires showing how human well-being is promoted by a given action or practice. He would also recognize that moral justification cannot involve a mere appeal to how much money slavery will bring him. Similarly, in defending female circumcision, a member of a culture that approves of it would try to show how it promotes goods such as family stability and how it actually is better for the health of all involved. The point is that even in what appear to be extreme disagreements, there is usually some common ground, some agreement about the nature of moral justification and about what sorts of considerations are morally relevant. If we are open-minded and willing to listen to each other, we can hope to find that common ground and to see what exactly it is we are disagreeing about. That does not mean that we will always be able to resolve that disagreement, but it offers us a place to begin.

Diane Jeske: Cultural Relativism

1. Imagine what appears to be a moral disagreement between a slaveholder and abolitionist. How does cultural relativism with speaker relativity analyze this exchange? Does relativism with agent relativity do any better?

2. Cultural relativism implies that the correct moral standards are those endorsed by collectives of actual people, with their various intellectual and emotional limitations. Is this a limitation or an attraction of relativism? State the reasons behind your reply.

3. If cultural relativism is true, then we know whether a given action is right or wrong so long as we are familiar with the standards of the society in which it is performed. Is this a plausible view of how to gain moral knowledge? Why or why not?

4. Jeske argues that Thomas Jefferson can be rightly criticized for holding slaves, even though most members of his culture endorsed slavery. What is her basis for thinking this? Is her position plausible?

5. Many people endorse cultural relativism because they believe that it is needed to support the value of tolerance. Jeske gives some reasons to doubt this rationale. Do you think that her critique is plausible? Why or why not?

The Subjectivity of Values
J. L. Mackie

J. L. Mackie (1917–1981), who taught for many years at Oxford University, regarded all ethical views as bankrupt. In this excerpt from his book *Ethics: Inventing Right and Wrong* (1977), Mackie outlines the basic ideas and the central motivating arguments for his *error theory*—the view that all positive moral claims are mistaken. All moral talk, as Mackie sees it, is based on a false assumption: that there are objective moral values. This fundamental error infects the entire system of morality. The foundations are corrupt, and so the entire moral edifice must come tumbling down.

Mackie offers a number of important arguments to substantiate his critique of morality. The argument from relativity claims that the extent of moral disagreement is best explained by the claim that there are no objective values. The argument from queerness contends that objective moral values would be objectionably different from any other kind of thing in the universe, possessed of strange powers that are best rejected. Mackie concludes with his account of why so many people, for so long, have fallen into error by succumbing to the temptation to think of morality as objective.

MORAL SCEPTICISM

There are no objective values. This is a bald statement of the thesis of this chapter, but before arguing for it I shall try to clarify and restrict it in ways that may meet some objections and prevent some misunderstanding. . . .

The claim that values are not objective, are not part of the fabric of the world, is meant to include not only moral goodness, which might be most naturally equated with moral value, but also other things that could be more loosely called moral values or disvalues—rightness and wrongness, duty, obligation, an action's being rotten and contemptible, and so on. It also includes nonmoral values, notably aesthetic ones, beauty and various kinds of artistic merit. I shall not discuss these explicitly, but clearly much the same considerations apply to aesthetic and to moral values, and there would be at least some initial implausibility in a view that gave the one a different status from the other. . . .

The claim to objectivity, however ingrained in our language and thought, is not self-validating. It can and should be questioned. But the denial of objective values will have to be put forward not as the result of an analytic approach, but as an 'error theory,' a theory that although most people in making moral judgements implicitly claim, among other things, to be pointing to something objectively prescriptive, these claims are all false. It is this that makes the name 'moral scepticism' appropriate.

But since this is an error theory, since it goes against assumptions ingrained in our thought and built into some of the ways in which language is used, since it conflicts with what is sometimes called common sense, it needs very solid support. It is not something we can accept lightly or casually and then quietly pass on. If we are to adopt this view, we must argue explicitly for it. Traditionally it has been supported by arguments of two main kinds, which I shall call the argument from relativity and the argument from queerness. . . .

THE ARGUMENT FROM RELATIVITY

The argument from relativity has as its premiss the well-known variation in moral codes from one society to another and from one period to another,
and also the differences in moral beliefs between different groups and classes within a complex community. Such variation is in itself merely a truth of descriptive morality, a fact of anthropology which entails neither first order nor second order ethical views. Yet it may indirectly support second order subjectivism: radical differences between first order moral judgements make it difficult to treat those judgements as apprehensions of objective truths. But it is not the mere occurrence of disagreements that tells against the objectivity of values. Disagreement on questions in history or biology or cosmology does not show that there are no objective issues in these fields for investigators to disagree about. But such scientific disagreement results from speculative inferences or explanatory hypotheses based on inadequate evidence, and it is hardly plausible to interpret moral disagreement in the same way. Disagreement about moral codes seems to reflect people's adherence to and participation in different ways of life. The causal connection seems to be mainly that way round: it is that people approve of monogamy because they participate in a monogamous way of life rather than that they participate in a monogamous way of life because they approve of monogamy. Of course, the standards may be an idealization of the way of life from which they arise: the monogamy in which people participate may be less complete, less rigid, than that of which it leads them to approve. This is not to say that moral judgements are purely conventional. Of course there have been and are moral heretics and moral reformers, people who have turned against the established rules and practices of their own communities for moral reasons, and often for moral reasons that we would endorse. But this can usually be understood as the extension, in ways which, though new and unconventional, seemed to them to be required for consistency, of rules to which they already adhered as arising out of an existing way of life. In short, the argument from relativity has some force simply because the actual variations in the moral codes are more readily explained by the hypothesis that they reflect ways of life than by the hypothesis that they express perceptions, most of them seriously inadequate and badly distorted, of objective values.

But there is a well-known counter to this argument from relativity, namely to say that the items for which objective validity is in the first place to be claimed are not specific moral rules or codes but very general basic principles which are recognized at least implicitly to some extent in all society—such principles as provide the foundations of what Sidgwick has called different methods of ethics: the principle of universalizability, perhaps, or the rule that one ought to conform to the specific rules of any way of life in which one takes part, from which one profits, and on which one relies, or some utilitarian principle of doing what tends, or seems likely, to promote the general happiness. It is easy to show that such general principles, married with differing concrete circumstances, different existing social patterns or different preferences, will beget different specific moral rules; and there is some plausibility in the claim that the specific rules thus generated will vary from community to community or from group to group in close agreement with the actual variations in accepted codes.

The argument from relativity can be only partly countered in this way. To take this line the moral objectivist has to say that it is only in these principles that the objective moral character attaches immediately to its descriptively specified ground or subject: other moral judgements are objectively valid or true, but only derivatively and contingently—if things had been otherwise, quite different sorts of actions would have been right. And despite the prominence in recent philosophical ethics of universalization, utilitarian principles, and the like, these are very far from constituting the whole of what is actually affirmed as basic in ordinary moral thought. Much of this is concerned rather with what Hare calls 'ideals' or, less kindly, 'fanaticism.' That is, people judge that some things are good or right, and others are bad or wrong, not because—or at any rate not only because—they exemplify some general principle for which widespread implicit acceptance could be claimed, but because something about those things arouses certain responses immediately in them, though they would arouse radically and irresolvably different responses in others. 'Moral sense' or 'intuition' is an initially more plausible description of what supplies many of our basic moral judgements than 'reason.' With regard to all these starting points of moral thinking the argument from relativity remains in full force.

THE ARGUMENT FROM QUEERNESS

Even more important, however, and certainly more generally applicable, is the argument from queerness. This has two parts, one metaphysical, the other epistemological. If there were objective values, then they would be entities or qualities or relations of a very strange sort, utterly different from anything else in the universe. Correspondingly, if we were aware of them, it would have to be by some special faculty of moral perception or intuition, utterly different from our ordinary ways of knowing everything else. These points were recognized by Moore when he spoke of non-natural qualities, and by the intuitionists in their talk about a 'faculty of moral intuition.' Intuitionism has long been out of favour, and it is indeed easy to point out its implausibilities. What is not so often stressed, but is more important, is that the central thesis of intuitionism is one to which any objectivist view of values is in the end committed: intuitionism merely makes unpalatably plain what other forms of objectivism wrap up. Of course the suggestion that moral judgements are made or moral problems solved by just sitting down and having an ethical intuition is a travesty of actual moral thinking. But, however complex the real process, it will require (if it is to yield authoritatively prescriptive conclusions) some input of this distinctive sort, either premises or forms of argument or both. When we ask the awkward question, how we can be aware of this authoritative prescriptivity, of the truth of these distinctively ethical premises or of the cogency of this distinctively ethical pattern of reasoning, none of our ordinary accounts of sensory perception or introspection or the framing and confirming of explanatory hypotheses or inference or logical construction or conceptual analysis, or any combination of these, will provide a satisfactory answer; 'a special sort of intuition' is a lame answer, but it is the one to which the clear-headed objectivist is compelled to resort.

Indeed, the best move for the moral objectivist is not to evade this issue, but to look for companions in guilt. For example, Richard Price argues that it is not moral knowledge alone that such an empiricism as those of Locke and Hume is unable to account for, but also our knowledge and even our ideas of essence, number, identity, diversity, solidity, inertia, substance, the necessary existence and infinite extension of time and space, necessity and possibility in general, power, and causation. If the understanding, which Price defines as the faculty within us that discerns truth, is also a source of new simple ideas of so many other sorts, may it not also be a power of immediately perceiving right and wrong, which yet are real characters of actions?

This is an important counter to the argument from queerness. The only adequate reply to it would be to show how, on empiricist foundations, we can construct an account of the ideas and beliefs and knowledge that we have of all these matters. I cannot even begin to do that here, though I have undertaken some parts of the task elsewhere. I can only state my belief that satisfactory accounts of most of these can be given in empirical terms. If some supposed metaphysical necessities or essences resist such treatment, then they too should be included, along with objective values, among the targets of the argument from queerness.

This queerness does not consist simply in the fact that ethical statements are 'unverifiable.' Although logical positivism with its verifiability theory of descriptive meaning gave an impetus to non-cognitive accounts of ethics, it is not only logical positivists but also empiricists of a much more liberal sort who should find objective values hard to accommodate. Indeed, I would not only reject the verifiability principle but also deny the conclusion commonly drawn from it, that moral judgements lack descriptive meaning. The assertion that there are objective values or intrinsically prescriptive entities or features of some kind, which ordinary moral judgements presuppose, is, I hold, not meaningless but false.

Plato's Forms give a dramatic picture of what objective values would have to be. The Form of the Good is such that knowledge of it provides the knower with both a direction and an overriding motive; something's being good both tells the person who knows this to pursue it and makes him pursue it. An objective good would be sought by anyone who was acquainted with it, not because of any contingent fact that this person, or every person, is so constituted that he desires this end, but just because the end has to-be-pursuedness somehow built into it. Similarly, if there were objective principles of right and wrong, any wrong (possible) course of action would have not-to-be-doneness somehow built into it. Or we should have something like Clarke's necessary relations of fitness between situations and actions, so that a situation would have a demand for such-and-such an action somehow built into it.

The need for an argument of this sort can be brought out by reflection on Hume's argument that 'reason'—in which at this stage he includes all sorts of knowing as well as reasoning—can never be an 'influencing motive of the will.' Someone might object that Hume has argued unfairly from the lack of influencing power (not contingent upon desires) in ordinary objects of knowledge and ordinary reasoning, and might maintain that values differ from natural objects precisely in their power, when known, automatically to influence the will. To this Hume could, and would need to, reply that this objection involves the postulating of value-entities or value-features of quite a different order from anything else with which we are acquainted, and of a corresponding faculty with which to detect them. That is, he would have to supplement his explicit argument with what I have called the argument from queerness.

Another way of bringing out this queerness is to ask, about anything that is supposed to have some objective moral quality, how this is linked with its natural features. What is the connection between the natural fact that an action is a piece of deliberate cruelty—say, causing pain just for fun—and the moral fact that it is wrong? It cannot be an entailment, a logical or semantic necessity. Yet it is not merely that the two features occur together. The wrongness must somehow be 'consequential' or 'supervenient'; it is wrong because it is a piece of deliberate cruelty. But just what *in the world* is signified by this 'because'? And how do we know the relation that it signifies, if this is something more than such actions being socially condemned, and condemned by us too, perhaps through our having absorbed attitudes from our social environment?

It is not even sufficient to postulate a faculty which 'sees' the wrongness: something must be postulated which can see at once the natural features that constitute the cruelty, and the wrongness, and the mysterious consequential link between the two. Alternatively, the intuition required might be the perception that wrongness is a higher order property belonging to certain natural properties; but what is this belonging of properties to other properties, and how can we discern it? How much simpler and more comprehensible the situation would be if we could replace the moral quality with some sort of subjective response which could be causally related to the detection of the natural features on which the supposed quality is said to be consequential.

It may be thought that the argument from queerness is given an unfair start if we thus relate it to what are admittedly among the wilder products of philosophical fancy—Platonic Forms, non-natural qualities, self-evident relations of fitness, faculties of intuition, and the like. Is it equally forceful if applied to the terms in which everyday moral judgements are more likely to be expressed—though still, as has been argued in the original work, with a claim to objectivity—'you must do this,' 'you can't do that,' 'obligation,' 'unjust,' 'rotten,' 'disgraceful,' 'mean,' or talk about good reasons for or against possible actions? Admittedly not; but that is because the objective prescriptivity, the element a claim for whose authoritativeness is embedded in ordinary moral thought and language, is not yet isolated in these forms of speech, but is presented along with relations to desires and feelings, reasoning about the means to desired ends, interpersonal demands, the injustice which consists in the violation of what are in the context the accepted standards of merit, the psychological constituents of meanness, and so on. There is nothing queer about any of these, and under cover of them the claim for moral authority may pass unnoticed. But if I am right in arguing that it is ordinarily there, and is therefore very likely to be incorporated almost automatically in philosophical accounts of ethics which systematize our ordinary thought even in such apparently innocent terms as these, it needs to be examined, and for this purpose it needs to be isolated and exposed as it is by the less cautious philosophical reconstructions.

PATTERNS OF OBJECTIFICATION

Considerations of these kinds suggest that it is in the end less paradoxical to reject than to retain the common-sense belief in the objectivity of moral values, provided that we can explain how this belief, if it is false, has become established and is so resistant to criticisms. This proviso is not difficult to satisfy.

On a subjectivist view, the supposedly objective values will be based in fact upon attitudes which the person has who takes himself to be recognizing and responding to those values. If we admit what Hume calls the mind's 'propensity to spread itself on external objects,' we can understand the supposed objectivity of moral qualities as arising from what we can call the projection or objectification of moral attitudes. This would be analogous to what is called the 'pathetic fallacy,' the tendency to read our feelings into their objects. If a fungus, say, fills us with disgust, we may be inclined to ascribe to the fungus itself a non-natural quality of foulness. But in moral contexts there is more than this propensity at work. Moral attitudes themselves are at least partly social in origin: socially established—and socially necessary—patterns of behaviour put pressure on individuals, and each individual tends to internalize these pressures and to join in requiring these patterns of behaviour of himself and of others. The attitudes that are objectified into moral values have indeed an external source, though not the one assigned to them by the belief in their absolute authority. Moreover, there are motives that would support objectification. We need morality to regulate interpersonal relations, to control some of the ways in which people behave towards one another, often in opposition to contrary inclinations. We therefore want our moral judgements to be authoritative for other agents as well as for ourselves: objective validity would give them the authority required. Aesthetic values are logically in the same position as moral ones; much the same metaphysical and epistemological considerations apply to them. But aesthetic values are less strongly objectified than moral ones; their subjective status, and an 'error theory' with regard to such claims to objectivity as are incorporated in aesthetic judgements, will be more readily accepted, just because the motives for their objectification are less compelling.

But it would be misleading to think of the objectification of moral values as primarily the projection of feelings, as in the pathetic fallacy. More important are wants and demands. As Hobbes says, "whatsoever is the object of any man's Appetite or Desire, that is it, which he for his part calleth *Good*"; and certainly both the adjective 'good' and the noun 'goods' are used in non-moral contexts of things because they are such as to satisfy desires. We get the notion of something's being objectively good, or having intrinsic value, by reversing the direction of dependence here, by making the desire depend upon the goodness, instead of the goodness on the desire. And this is aided by the fact that the desired thing will indeed have features that make it desired, that enable it to arouse a desire or that make it such as to satisfy some desire that is already there. It is fairly easy to confuse the way in which a thing's desirability is indeed objective with its having in our sense objective value. The fact that the word 'good' serves as one of our main moral terms is a trace of this pattern of objectification. . . .

J. L. Mackie: The Subjectivity of Values

1. Why does Mackie refer to his view as an "error theory"? What is the "error" that Mackie takes himself to be pointing out?
2. Mackie cites widespread disagreement about morality as evidence for his view that there are no objective moral values. Yet he admits that the existence of scientific disagreement does not suggest that there are no objective scientific truths. Why does Mackie think that ethics is different from science in this regard? Do you think he is right about this?
3. One might object to Mackie's argument from disagreement by noting that some moral prohibitions (against killing innocent people, against adultery, etc.) are widely shared across cultures. Does this show that there is something wrong with the argument from disagreement? How do you think Mackie would respond to such an objection?
4. Mackie claims that objective values, if they existed, would be entities "of a very strange sort, utterly different from anything else in the universe." What feature of moral values would make them so strange? Do you agree with Mackie that the "queerness" of moral properties is a good reason to deny their existence?
5. Mackie suggests that his view is "simpler and more comprehensible" than accepting objective values. In what ways is his view simpler? Is this a good reason to reject the existence of objective values?
6. Mackie thinks that for his error theory to succeed, he must explain how people come to think that there are objective moral values in the first place. How does he attempt to do so? Do you think he is successful?

CHAPTER 4

The Good Life

If you are like me, and like everyone else I know, you've spent a fair bit of time thinking about how your life can go better. You may be doing pretty well already, or may be very badly off, or somewhere in between. But there is always room for improvement.

To know how our lives can be better, we first need to know how they can be good. In other words, we need a standard that will tell us when our lives are going well for us. That standard will help us determine our level of *well-being*, or *welfare*.

Many things can improve our well-being: chocolate, sturdy shoes, vaccinations, a reasonable amount of money. These things pave the way to a better life—they help to make it possible, and may, in some cases, even be indispensable to it. Philosophers call such things **instrumental goods**, things that are valuable because of the good things they bring about.

If there are instrumental goods, then there must be something they are good *for*, something whose value does not depend on being a means to anything else that is good. Such a thing is worth pursuing for its own sake; it is valuable in its own right, even if it brings nothing else in its wake. Philosophers call such things **intrinsically valuable**. Instrumental values are things that are good precisely because they help to bring about things that are intrinsically valuable.

When asking about what makes a life go better for us, we will of course want to know which things are instrumentally valuable, so we can get our hands on them. But when we take a philosophical step back and ask *why* (for instance) going to the dentist, or making money,

makes us better off, we will need to have some grasp of what is intrinsically good for us—something whose presence, *all by itself*, makes us better off. What might that be?

A. HEDONISM

The most popular answer is just what you'd expect: happiness. On this view, a good life is a happy life. This means something pretty specific. It means that happiness is necessary for a good life; a life without happiness cannot be a good life. It also means that happiness is sufficient for a good life: When you are happy, your life is going well. The happier you are, the better your life is going for you. And the unhappier you are, the worse off you are.

There is a name for this kind of view: **hedonism**. The term comes from the Greek word *hédoné*, which means "pleasure." According to hedonists, a life is good to the extent that it is filled with pleasure and is free of pain.

Hedonism has many attractions. First off, it allows that there are a variety of ways to live a good life, because there are many paths to happiness. Because the sources of happiness vary quite widely, and happiness is the key to a good life, there are many ways to live a good life.

Second, hedonists provide each of us with a substantial say in what the good life looks like. What makes us happy is largely a matter of personal choice. As a result, we each get plenty of input into what makes our lives go well.

In one sense, however, hedonism does not allow us to have the final say about what is good for us. If hedonism is true, then happiness improves our lives, whether we think so or not.

According to hedonists, those who deny that happiness is the sole thing that is intrinsically good for us are wrong, no matter how sincere their denial. In this way, hedonism follows a middle path between approaches to the good life that dictate a one-size-fits-all model and those that allow each person to decide for herself exactly what is valuable.

Third, the claim that happiness is intrinsically beneficial seems about as obvious as anything in ethics. And the value of everything else seems easily explained by showing how it leads to happiness. If hedonism is true, then happiness directly improves one's welfare, and sadness directly undermines it. Just about everyone believes that. Indeed, how could we even argue for something as basic as this? This is where thinking in this area *starts*. Perhaps no claim about well-being is more fundamental than the one that insists on the importance of experiencing happiness and avoiding misery.

Fourth, hedonism can justify the many rules for living a good life, while at the same time explaining why there are exceptions to these rules. Almost all of us are better off if we manage to be free of manipulation, disabling illness, enslavement, constant worry, unwanted attention, treachery, and physical brutality. Remove these burdens, and you immediately improve the quality of life. The hedonist's explanation is simple and plausible: in almost every case, eliminating these things reduces our misery.

Hedonism can also explain why there are exceptions to these rules. Some people—not many—enjoy being humiliated or manipulated. For them, we must put these experiences on the positive side of the ledger. Hedonism thus explains why it is so hard to come up with universal, iron-clad rules for improving our lives. Such rules hold only for the most part, because increasing our welfare is a matter of becoming happier, and some people find happiness in extremely unusual ways. Hedonism honors both the standard and the uncommon sources of happiness; no matter how you come by it, happiness (and only happiness) directly makes you better off.

Unsurprisingly, hedonism has also come in for criticism. The first concern is that we can sometimes get pleasure from doing terrible things. But when such enjoyment comes at someone else's expense, it hardly seems a good thing, much less the best thing. This gives rise to

The Argument from Evil Pleasures

1. If hedonism is true, then happiness that comes from evil deeds is as good as happiness that comes from kind and decent actions.
2. Happiness that comes from evil deeds is *not* as good as happiness that comes from kind and decent actions.
3. Therefore, hedonism is false.

This argument fails, and it's instructive to see why. There is a confusion contained within it, and it's one that is easy to fall prey to.

When we say that happiness that comes from one source is as good as happiness from any other source, we might mean that each is *morally equivalent* to the other. When we read premise 2 and nod our heads approvingly, this is probably what we have in mind.

But this is not what hedonists have in mind. They don't think that each episode of happiness is as morally good as every other. Rather, they think that the same amount of happiness, no matter its source, is *equally beneficial*. According to hedonism, happiness gained from evil deeds can improve our lives just as much as happiness that comes from virtue. In this sense, happiness derived from evil deeds *is* as good as happiness that comes from virtue—each can contribute to our well-being just as much as the other. Hedonists therefore reject premise 2.

And aren't they right to do so? Think about why the happiness of the wicked is so upsetting. Isn't it precisely because happiness benefits them, and we hate to see the wicked prosper? If happiness doesn't make us better off, why is it so awful when the wicked enjoy the harms they cause? And for those who share my vengeful streak: Why is it gratifying to see the wicked suffer? Because misery always cuts into our well-being, and we think it right that the wicked pay for their crimes. Hedonism makes perfect sense of these feelings.

A second criticism is that people's happiness sometimes rests on a false belief, which seems to undercut the value of the happiness. Imagine a woman who is happy in her marriage, partly because she trusts her husband and believes that he has been completely faithful. Suppose her belief is true. Now imagine another woman who is as happy as the first, and for the same reasons. But in this case, her belief is false—her husband has been cheating on her without her knowledge. It seems that the first woman's life is going better for her. And yet these two women are equally happy.

This story provides us with the basis of

The Argument from False Happiness

1. If hedonism is true, then our lives go well to the extent that we are happy.
2. It's not the case that our lives go well to the extent that we are happy; those whose happiness is based on false beliefs have worse lives than those whose happiness is based on true beliefs, even if both lives are equally happy.
3. Therefore, hedonism is false.

Hedonists accept the first premise, and so must deny the second.

But it is harder to do so here, when it comes to false beliefs. The late Harvard philosopher Robert Nozick tried to show this, in a thought experiment involving an "experience machine."[1] Imagine that there is an amazing virtual reality machine that lets you simulate any experience you like. Suppose you program it for a lifetime of the very best experiences. Once you plug in, you

think that you are in the real world, and have no memory of life outside the machine. Your entire life from then on is lived in the machine, and you are as happy as can be, believing yourself to be doing all of the things you truly enjoy.

Compare this with a case in which someone actually does the things and enjoys the experiences that the plugged-in person only imagines. It seems clear that the second life—the real one—is more desirable. Yet both lives contain the same amount of happiness.

This is meant to show that happiness is not the sole element of well-being. A good life is one that is happy, yes, but not only that. Our happiness must be based in reality. A pleasant life of illusion is less good for you than an equally pleasant life based on real achievement and true beliefs.

A third criticism starts with the assumption that one of the other things we want from life is to make our own choices about it. We resent it when other people manipulate us, even if they mean well. Sometimes we even prefer the definite prospect of sadness to a more pleasant life that is forced upon us without our consent. In short, we want **autonomy**—the power to guide our life through our own free choices. We want it even though acting autonomously sometimes costs us our happiness. We make free choices that lead to damaged relationships, financial disaster, and missed opportunities. Still, we need only imagine a life without autonomy to see what a tragedy it would be. That sort of life is one in which one is, at best, manipulated, and at worst, enslaved or completely brainwashed.

Here we have the makings of another argument against hedonism. Call this

The Argument from Autonomy

1. If hedonism is true, then autonomy contributes to a good life only insofar as it makes us happy.
2. Autonomy sometimes directly contributes to a good life, even when it fails to make us happy.
3. Therefore, hedonism is false.

---

1. See the reading at the end of this chapter.

The first premise is clearly true. The central claim of hedonism is that happiness is the only thing, in itself, that makes us better off. All other things (e.g., autonomy, virtue, true knowledge) improve our lives only to the extent that they make us happier.

So everything hinges on the second premise. It seems plausible. When we consider the lives of those who have been deprived of their autonomy, we see the absence of a great value, something that, by itself, appears to make a life a better one. Given a choice between drug-induced contentment and plotting our own risky course through life, we prefer the latter path. We want our lives to be authentic, to reflect our own values, rather than those imposed on us from the outside—even if we are not always happier as a result. Hedonism cannot account for that.

Perhaps happiness is not, after all, the key to our well-being. Let's now consider an alternative approach—one that tells us that getting what you want is the measure of a good life.

B. DESIRE SATISFACTION THEORY

The **desire satisfaction theory** of human welfare tells us that your life goes well for you to the extent that you get what you want. At the other end of the spectrum, your life goes badly just when your desires are frustrated. More precisely, something is intrinsically good for you *if* it satisfies your desires, *only if* it satisfies your desires, and *because* it satisfies your desires. Something is instrumentally good for you if, only if, and because it helps you to fulfill your desires.

There is a lot to like about this theory. The first of its benefits is that it explains why there are many models of a good life, rather than just a single one. What makes my life good may be very different from what does the trick for you, because you and I may not want the same things. Our deepest desires determine what counts as life's improvements or failures. On this line of thinking, *nothing*—not health, love, knowledge, or virtue—is an essential ingredient in making everyone's life better off. Whether our lives have been improved depends entirely on whether our desires have been fulfilled.

Second, if the desire theory is right, then each of us has the final say on what makes our life go well, because it's our own desires that determine how well we are faring. Further, no one gets to dictate which basic desires we should have. That is a personal matter. There is no universal standard for appropriate desires: to each his own. This view gives us a huge amount of freedom to choose our own vision of the good life. The only limitation here is that the good life must consist of satisfied desires. But what these desires are *for*—that is entirely up to you.

A third benefit of the desire satisfaction theory is that it entirely avoids the difficulties associated with objective theories of human welfare. Such theories claim that what directly contributes to a good life is fixed independently of your desires and your opinions about what is important.

There are lots of objective theories of welfare. Some theories, for instance, insist that the more knowledge you have, the better your life is going for you—even if you don't care very much about obtaining knowledge. Other theories insist that virtue is required for a good life, no matter how you feel about virtue's importance. Hedonists claim that happiness is intrinsically valuable—even if, very unusually, you don't care about being happy.

Desire theorists reject *all* objective theories of welfare. In doing so, they spare themselves the huge controversies that surround the defense of objective values. It is really difficult to argue for such values. That's because, for any contender, we can always ask a simple question: how can something make my life better if I don't want it, and don't want what it can get me? Sure, *if* you want to be a star athlete or a world-class musician, then daily practice will improve your life. But if you have no such dreams, and don't care about anything that such practice can get you, then *how could* it be good for you? That's a very hard question. Desire theorists never have to answer it.

Fourth, the theory can easily explain the close connection between our well-being and our motivations. To see this, consider

The Motivation Argument

1. If something is intrinsically good for you, then it will satisfy your desires.
2. If something will satisfy your desires, then you will be motivated (at least to some extent) to get it—so long as you know what you want and know how to get it.
3. Therefore, if something is intrinsically good for you, then you will be motivated (at least to some extent) to get it—so long as you know what you want and know how to get it.

The first premise states a central claim of the desire theory. The second premise seems clearly true, once we understand that desires motivate us to do things. And the argument is valid, so if both premises are true, then the conclusion must be true. Indeed, desire theorists regard this conclusion as an important truth, and think that it is a major strike against objective theories that they cannot allow for it.

A fifth benefit is that the desire theory provides a straightforward answer to one of life's eternal questions: how can I know what is good for me? The answer is simple: be clear about what you want. Then make sure you know how to get it.

These five attractions help to explain why the desire satisfaction theory is so popular. But (you guessed it) there are also a number of difficulties that this theory faces, and some of them are serious enough to force us to revise the view, and possibly even to reject it.

To appreciate these worries, let's remind ourselves of the two central claims of the desire theory:

(A) Something is intrinsically good for us only if it fulfills our desires; something is instrumentally good for us only if it helps us to fulfill our desires.

(B) If something fulfills our desires, then it is intrinsically good for us; if something helps to fulfill our desires, then it is instrumentally good for us.

(A) tells us that something must (help to) satisfy our desires in order to be beneficial; desire satisfaction is *necessary* for becoming better off. (B) tells us that satisfying our desires is enough to make us better off; desire satisfaction is *sufficient* for becoming better off. Let's begin by considering (A), and then move to a discussion of (B).

We can test (A) by seeing whether we can come up with an example in which something benefits us, even though it doesn't satisfy or help to satisfy any of our desires. If there are any such examples, then (A) is false. There do seem to be such examples. Three spring to mind.

The first is that of pleasant surprises. These are cases in which you are getting a benefit that you didn't want or hope for. Imagine something that never appeared on your radar screen—say, a windfall tax rebate, an unexpectedly kind remark, or the flattering interest of a charming stranger. It makes sense to say that you're a bit better off as a result of such things, even though they didn't satisfy any of your desires. Of course, now that you've experienced such things, you may well want more of them. But that's because they have made your life better already. And they did that without answering to any of your pre-existing desires.

The second case is that of small children. We can benefit children in a number of ways, even though we don't give them what they want and don't help them get what they want. A parent benefits her five-year-old by teaching him to read, for instance, even though the child doesn't want to read and doesn't know enough about the benefits of literacy to find them appealing.

The third case is suicide prevention. Those who are deeply sad or depressed may decide that they would be better off dead. They are often wrong about that. Suppose we prevent them from doing away with themselves. This may only frustrate their deepest wishes. And yet they may be better off as a result.

In each of these cases, we can improve the lives of people without getting them what they want or helping them to do so. They may, later on, approve of our actions and be pleased that we acted as we did. But this after-the-fact approval is something very different from desire satisfaction. Indeed, it seems that the later approval is evidence that we benefited them, even though we did not do anything that served their desires at the time. And that is evidence that (A) is mistaken.

If (B) is true, then we are better off whenever our desires are satisfied. There are many reasons to doubt this. First, we sometimes want something for its own sake, but our desire is based on a false belief. When we make mistakes like this, it is hard to see that getting what we want really improves our lives. Suppose you want to hurt someone for having insulted you, when he did no such thing. You aren't any better off if you mistreat the poor guy.

From now on, then, we should understand the desire theory to insist that it is only *informed* desires whose satisfaction will improve our lives. Fulfilling desires based on false beliefs may not improve our welfare. So the real thesis under consideration will be

> (C)vIf something fulfills our *informed* desires (i.e., those not based on false beliefs), then that thing is intrinsically good for us; if it helps us to fulfill our informed desires, then it is instrumentally good for us.

But this seems subject to a new problem. All of us want some things that seem entirely unrelated to us. Our desires are directed, say, at the interests of strangers, or at no interests at all. (Perhaps I want there to be an even number of planets, and now that Pluto has been banned from the club, I've finally gotten my wish.) In such cases, we can get what we want, even though it is hard to see how our lives are improved as a result.

Even when we focus on desires about our own life, we encounter potential problems. Suppose that you want something for yourself, and your desire isn't based on any false beliefs. And you get what you want. If (C) is true, this guarantees some improvement in your life.

But consider a young musician who has staked his hopes on becoming famous some day. And that day comes—but all he feels is disappointment, emptiness, boredom, or depression. It's hard to believe that desire satisfaction was sufficient in such a case for improving his life.

Another problem for the theory arises from cases in which I get what I want, but never realize this. I never know that my goal has been met. It doesn't seem that I am any better off in such a situation. Imagine a person deeply committed to finding a cure for a terrible disease. After years of hard work, she makes a discovery that will eventually—long after her death—result in a cure. But she goes to her grave never realizing this. She thinks her efforts have been wasted. Her success does not seem to mark any improvement in her life.

Another problem arises when we get what we want, but there is something problematic about our desires themselves. Some parents have raised their children to believe themselves unworthy of love, or incapable of real accomplishment. Some societies continue to treat the women among them as second-class citizens (if citizens at all). Women in such societies are told from the earliest age that any political or professional hopes are unnatural and beyond their reach.

It's easy to take such messages to heart. If you are told from the cradle that your greatest ambition should be to serve your master, then you may well end up with no desire any stronger than that. If desire fulfillment is the measure of a good life, then such lives can be very good indeed.

That doesn't seem right. For instance, it is tempting to think that a slave cannot live a very good life, regardless of whether her desires are fulfilled. And that is because she is unfree. But desire theorists reject the idea that there is anything intrinsically valuable about freedom. Nothing is important in its own right—not intellectual or artistic achievement, not freedom, not pleasure—unless one desires it. If it has been drilled into your head that it is foolish to seek freedom, or that education is unnecessary for "your kind," then a reasonable response may well be to abandon hope for any such things. Better to have goals you can achieve than to set yourself up for constant disappointment.

And yet what kind of life is that? The desire theorist seems forced to say that it may be among the best. The lower your expectations, the easier they are to satisfy. As a result, those who set their sights very low may have a greater number of satisfied desires than those with more challenging goals. But this hardly seems to make for a better life.

C. CONCLUSION

Hedonism has always had its fans. And, as we have seen, there are many good reasons for its popularity. It explains why there are many paths to a good life. It strikes a balance between a view that imposes just one blueprint of a good life and a view that allows anything to be valuable so long as you think it is. Hedonism accounts for why the rules of a good life allow for exceptions. And yet hedonism is not problem-free. It is committed to judging happiness based on false beliefs as beneficial as happiness that isn't. And hedonists cannot allow for the intrinsic value of autonomy.

There are a number of reasons to think that the good life consists in our getting what we want. But there are also some serious problems with this suggestion. Most of the problems boil down to this: the desire theorist cannot recognize that any desires are intrinsically better than any others. If your heart is set on repeatedly counting to nine, or on saying the word *putty* until you die, then (on this view) succeeding in such tasks yields a life as good as can be for you.

But a promising youth may have a death wish; an oppressed slave may want only to serve her master; a decent but self-loathing man may most want to be publicly humiliated. We can imagine these desires fulfilled, and yet the resulting lives appear to be impoverished, rather than enviable. Indeed, we regard such people as unfortunate precisely because of what they want—their desires are not fit to be satisfied, because they fail to aim for worthy ends.

To say such a thing, however, is to side with the objectivist, and to reject an essential element of the desire theory. For the desire theorist, nothing but satisfied desires makes us better off, and there are no objective standards that elevate some basic desires over others. If getting what you want is not the be-all and end-all of a good life, then there must be some objective standards to determine what is good or bad for us. Exercise: find out what they are.

ESSENTIAL CONCEPTS

Autonomy: the power to guide our life through our own free choices.

Desire satisfaction theory: the view that something is intrinsically good for you *if* it satisfies your desires, *only if* it satisfies your desires, and *because* it satisfies your desires.

Hedonism: the view that a life is good to the extent that it is filled with pleasure and is free of pain.

Instrumental goods: things that are valuable because of the good things they bring about.

Intrinsically valuable: worth pursuing for its own sake; valuable in its own right.

DISCUSSION QUESTIONS

1. What is the difference between intrinsic value and instrumental value?
2. Can you think of any case in which experiencing pleasure fails to contribute to a person's well-being? If so, consider what a hedonist might say in order to undermine such a case.
3. If you had a chance to get into the "experience machine" for the rest of your life, would you do it? Why might the idea of the experience machine pose a challenge for hedonism?
4. What are "evil pleasures" and why do they seem to be a problem for hedonism?

5. What is autonomy? Can hedonism account for the value of autonomy? Defend your answer.

6. Many people think that there is just one path to the good life. Do you agree? If so, what argument(s) can you give to someone who thinks otherwise?

7. Many people find the desire satisfaction theory attractive on the grounds that it leaves what counts as a good life "up to us." To what extent are our desires "up to us"? Can we really choose whether we want something or not?

8. The desire satisfaction theory tells us that our lives go better so long as we get what we want—no matter what we want. Can you think of any examples where this isn't so?

READINGS

Hedonism

John Stuart Mill

John Stuart Mill (1806–1873) was one of the great hedonistic thinkers. In this excerpt from his long pamphlet *Utilitarianism* (1863), Mill defends his complex version of hedonism. Sensitive to criticisms that it counsels us to pursue a life of brutish pleasure, Mill distinguishes between "higher" and "lower" pleasures and claims, famously, that it is "better to be Socrates dissatisfied, than a fool satisfied." He also offers here his much-discussed "proof" of hedonism, by drawing a parallel between the evidence we have for something's being visible (that all of us see it) and something's being desirable (that all of us desire it). He also argues for the claim that we do and can desire nothing but pleasure, and he uses this conjecture as a way of defending the view that pleasure is the only thing that is always worth pursuing for its own sake.

The creed which accepts, as the foundation of morals, Utility, or the Greatest-happiness Principle, holds that actions are right in proportion as they tend to promote happiness, wrong as they tend to produce the reverse of happiness. By happiness is intended pleasure and the absence of pain; by unhappiness, pain and the privation of pleasure. To give a clear view of the moral standard set up by the theory, much more requires to be said; in particular, what things it includes in the ideas of pain and pleasure, and to what extent this is left an open question. But these supplementary explanations do not affect the theory of life on which this theory of morality is grounded,—namely, that pleasure, and freedom from pain, are the only things desirable as ends; and that all desirable things (which are as numerous in the utilitarian as in any other scheme) are desirable either for the pleasure inherent in themselves, or as means to the promotion of pleasure and the prevention of pain.

Now, such a theory of life excites in many minds, and among them in some of the most estimable in feeling and purpose, inveterate dislike. To suppose that life has (as they express it) no higher end than pleasure,—no better and nobler object of desire and pursuit,—they designate as utterly mean and groveling; as a doctrine worthy only of swine, to whom the followers of Epicurus were, at a very early period, contemptuously likened: and modern holders of the doctrine are occasionally made the subject of equally polite comparisons by its German, French, and English assailants.

When thus attacked, the Epicureans have always answered, that it is not they, but their accusers, who represent human nature in a degrading light, since the accusation supposes human beings to be capable of no pleasures except those of which swine are capable. If this supposition were true, the charge could not be gainsaid, but would then be no longer an imputation; for, if the sources of pleasure were precisely the same to human beings and to swine, the rule of life which is good enough for the one would be good enough for the other. The comparison of the Epicurean life to that of beasts is felt as degrading, precisely because a beast's pleasures do not satisfy a human being's conceptions of happiness. Human beings have faculties more elevated than the animal appetites; and, when once made conscious of them, do not regard any thing as happiness which does not include their gratification. I do not, indeed, consider the Epicureans to have been by any means faultless in drawing out their scheme of consequences from the utilitarian principle. To do this in any sufficient manner, many Stoic as well as Christian elements require to be included. But there is no known Epicurean theory of life which does not assign to the pleasures of the intellect, of the feeling and imagination, and of the moral sentiments, a much higher value as pleasures than to those of mere sensation. It must be admitted, however, that utilitarian writers in general have placed the superiority of mental over bodily pleasures chiefly in the greater permanency, safety, uncostliness, &c., of the former,—that is, in their circumstantial advantages rather than in their intrinsic nature. And, on all these points, utilitarians have fully proved their case; but they might have taken the other, and, as it may be called, higher ground, with entire consistency. It is quite compatible with the principle of utility to recognize the fact, that some *kinds* of pleasure are more desirable and more valuable than others. It would be absurd, that while, in estimating all other things, quality is considered as well as quantity, the estimation of pleasures should be supposed to depend on quantity alone.

If I am asked what I mean by difference of quality in pleasures, or what makes one pleasure more valuable than another, merely as a pleasure, except its being greater in amount, there is but one possible answer. Of two pleasures, if there be one to which all or almost all who have experience of both give a decided preference, irrespective of any feeling of moral obligation to prefer it, that is the more desirable pleasure. If one of the two is, by those who are competently acquainted with both, placed so far above the other that they prefer it, even though knowing it to be attended with a greater amount of discontent, and would not resign it for any quantity of the other pleasure which their nature is capable of, we are justified in ascribing to the preferred enjoyment a superiority in quality, so far out-weighing quantity, as to render it, in comparison, of small account.

Now, it is an unquestionable fact, that those who are equally acquainted with and equally capable of appreciating and enjoying both do give a most marked preference to the manner of existence which employs their higher faculties. Few human creatures would consent to be changed into any of the lower animals, for a promise of the fullest allowance of a beast's pleasures: no intelligent human being would consent to be a fool, no instructed person would be an ignoramus, no person of feeling and conscience would be selfish and base, even though they should be persuaded that the fool, the dunce, or the rascal is better satisfied with his lot than they are with theirs. They would not resign what they possess more than he for the most complete satisfaction of all the desires which they have in common with him. If they ever fancy they would, it is only in cases of unhappiness so extreme, that, to escape from it, they would exchange their lot for almost any other, however undesirable in their own eyes. A being of higher faculties requires more to make him happy, is capable probably of more acute suffering, and certainly accessible to it at more points, than one of an inferior type; but, in spite of these liabilities, he can never really wish to sink into what he feels to be a lower grade of existence. We may give what explanation we please of this unwillingness; we may attribute it to pride, a name which is given indiscriminately to some of the most and to some of the least estimable feelings of which mankind are capable; we may refer it to the love of liberty and personal independence,—an appeal to which was with the Stoics one of the most effective means for the inculcation of it; to the love of power, or to the love of excitement, both of which do really enter into and contribute to it: but its most appropriate appellation is a sense of dignity, which all human beings possess in one form or other, and in some, though by no means in exact, proportion to their higher faculties, and which is so essential a part of the happiness of those in whom it is strong, that nothing which conflicts with it could be, otherwise than momentarily, an object of desire to them. Whoever supposes that this preference takes place at a sacrifice of happiness; that the superior being, in any thing like equal circumstances, is not happier than the inferior—confounds the two very different ideas of happiness and content. It is indisputable, that the being whose capacities of enjoyment are low has the greatest chance of having them fully satisfied; and a highly endowed being will always feel that any happiness which he can look for, as the world is constituted, is imperfect. But he can learn to bear its imperfections, if they are at all bearable; and they will not make him envy the being who is indeed unconscious of the imperfections, but only because he feels not at all the good which those imperfections qualify. It is better to be a human being dissatisfied, than a pig satisfied; better to be Socrates dissatisfied, than a fool satisfied. And if the fool or the pig are of a different opinion, it is because they only know their own side of the question. The other party to the comparison knows both sides.

It may be objected, that many who are capable of the higher pleasures, occasionally, under the influence of temptation, postpone them to the lower. But this is quite compatible with a full appreciation of the intrinsic superiority of the higher. Men often, from infirmity of character, make their election for the nearer good, though they know it to be the less valuable, and this no less when the choice is between two bodily pleasures than when it is between bodily and mental. They pursue sensual indulgences to the injury of health, though perfectly aware that health is the greater good. It may be further objected, that many who begin with youthful enthusiasm for everything noble, as they advance in years sink into indolence and selfishness. But I do not believe that those who undergo this very common change voluntarily choose the lower description of pleasures in preference to the higher. I believe, that, before they devote themselves exclusively to the one, they have already become incapable of the other. Capacity for the nobler feelings is in most natures a very tender plant, easily killed, not only by hostile influences, but by mere want of sustenance; and, in the majority of young persons, it speedily dies away if the occupations to which their position in life has devoted them, and the society into which it has thrown them, are not favorable to keeping that higher capacity in exercise. Men lose their high aspirations as they lose their intellectual tastes, because they have not time or opportunity for indulging them; and they addict themselves to inferior pleasures, not because they deliberately prefer them, but because they are either the only ones to which they have access, or the only ones which they are any longer capable of enjoying. It may be questioned whether any one, who has remained equally susceptible to both classes of pleasures, ever knowingly and calmly preferred the lower; though many in all ages have broken down in an ineffectual attempt to combine both.

From this verdict of the only competent judges, I apprehend there can be no appeal. On a question, which is the best worth having of two pleasures, or which of two modes of existence is the most grateful to the feelings, apart from its moral attributes and from its consequences, the judgment of those who are qualified by knowledge of both, or, if they differ, that of the majority among them, must be admitted as final. And there needs be the less hesitation to accept this judgment respecting the quality of pleasures, since there is no other tribunal to be referred to even on the question of quantity. What means are there of determining which is the acutest of two pains, or the intensest of two pleasurable sensations, except the general suffrage of those who are familiar with both? Neither pains nor pleasures are homogeneous, and pain is always heterogeneous with pleasure. What is there to decide whether a particular pleasure is worth purchasing at the cost of particular pain, except the feelings and judgment of the experienced? When, therefore, those feelings and judgment declare the pleasures derived from the higher faculties to be preferable *in kind*, apart from the question of intensity, to those of which the animal nature, disjoined from the higher faculties, is susceptible, they are entitled on this subject to the same regard. . . .

It has already been remarked, that questions of ultimate ends do not admit of proof, in the ordinary acceptation of the term. To be incapable of proof by reasoning is common to all first principles; to the first premises of our knowledge, as well as to those of our conduct. But the former, being matters of fact, may be the subject of a direct appeal to the faculties which judge of fact—namely, our senses, and our internal consciousness. Can an appeal be made to the same faculties on questions of practical ends? Or by what other faculty is cognisance taken of them?

Questions about ends are, in other words, questions of what things are desirable. The utilitarian doctrine is, that happiness is desirable, and the only thing desirable, as an end; all other things being only desirable as means to that end. What ought to be required of this doctrine—what conditions is it requisite that the doctrine should fulfil—to make good its claim to be believed?

The only proof capable of being given that an object is visible, is that people actually see it. The only proof that a sound is audible, is that people hear it: and so of the other sources of our experience. In like manner, I apprehend, the sole evidence it is possible to produce that anything is desirable, is that people do actually desire it. If the end which the utilitarian doctrine proposes to itself were not, in theory and in practice, acknowledged to be an end, nothing could ever convince any person that it was so. No reason can be given why the general happiness is desirable, except that each person, so far as he believes it to be attainable, desires his own happiness. This, however, being a fact, we have not only all the proof which the case admits of, but all which it is possible to require, that happiness is a good: that each person's happiness is a good to that person, and the general happiness, therefore, a good to the aggregate of all persons. Happiness has made out its title as one of the ends of conduct, and consequently one of the criteria of morality.

But it has not, by this alone, proved itself to be the sole criterion. To do that, it would seem, by the same rule, necessary to show, not only that people desire happiness, but that they never desire anything else. Now it is palpable that they do desire things which, in common language, are decidedly distinguished from happiness. They desire, for example, virtue, and the absence of vice, no less really than pleasure and the absence of pain. The desire of virtue is not as universal, but it is as authentic a fact, as the desire of happiness. And hence the opponents of the utilitarian standard deem that they have a right to infer that there are other ends of human action besides happiness, and that happiness is not the standard of approbation and disapprobation.

But does the utilitarian doctrine deny that people desire virtue, or maintain that virtue is not a thing to be desired? The very reverse. It maintains not only that virtue is to be desired, but that it is to be desired disinterestedly, for itself. Whatever may be the opinion of utilitarian moralists as to the original conditions by which virtue is made virtue; however they may believe (as they do) that actions and dispositions are only virtuous because they promote another end than virtue; yet this being granted, and it having been decided, from considerations of this description, what is virtuous, they not only place virtue at the very head of the things which are good as means to the ultimate end, but they also recognise as a psychological fact the possibility of its being, to the individual, a good in itself, without looking to any end beyond it; and hold, that the mind is not in a right state, not in a state conformable to Utility, not in the state most conducive to the general happiness, unless it does love virtue in this manner—as a thing desirable in itself, even although, in the individual instance, it should not produce those other desirable consequences which it tends to produce, and on account of which it is held to be virtue. This opinion is not, in the smallest degree, a departure from the Happiness principle.

The ingredients of happiness are very various, and each of them is desirable in itself, and not merely when considered as swelling an aggregate. The principle of utility does not mean that any given pleasure, as music, for instance, or any given exemption from pain, as for example health, is to be looked upon as means to a collective something termed happiness, and to be desired on that account. They are desired and desirable in and for themselves; besides being means, they are a part of the end. Virtue, according to the utilitarian doctrine, is not naturally and originally part of the end, but it is capable of becoming so; and in those who love it disinterestedly it has become so, and is desired and cherished, not as a means to happiness, but as a part of their happiness.

To illustrate this farther, we may remember that virtue is not the only thing, originally a means, and which if it were not a means to anything else, would be and remain indifferent, but which by association with what it is a means to, comes to be desired for itself, and that too with the utmost intensity. What, for example, shall we say of the love of money? There is nothing originally more desirable about money than about any heap of glittering pebbles. Its worth is solely that of the things which it will buy; the desires for other things than itself, which it is a means of gratifying. Yet the love of money is not only one of the strongest moving forces of human life, but money is, in many cases, desired in and for itself; the desire to possess it is often stronger than the desire to use it, and goes on increasing when all the desires which point to ends beyond it, to be compassed by it, are falling off. It may, then, be said truly, that money is desired not for the sake of an end, but as part of the end. From being a means to happiness, it has come to be itself a principal ingredient of the individual's conception of happiness. The same may be said of the majority of the great objects of human life—power, for example, or fame; except that to each of these there is a certain amount of immediate pleasure annexed, which has at least the semblance of being naturally inherent in them; a thing which cannot be said of money. Still, however, the strongest natural attraction, both of power and of fame, is the immense aid they give to the attainment of our other wishes; and it is the strong association thus generated between them and all our

objects of desire, which gives to the direct desire of them the intensity it often assumes, so as in some characters to surpass in strength all other desires. In these cases the means have become a part of the end, and a more important part of it than any of the things which they are means to. What was once desired as an instrument for the attainment of happiness, has come to be desired for its own sake. In being desired for its own sake it is, however, desired as part of happiness. The person is made, or thinks he would be made, happy by its mere possession; and is made unhappy by failure to obtain it. The desire of it is not a different thing from the desire of happiness, any more than the love of music, or the desire of health. They are included in happiness. They are some of the elements of which the desire of happiness is made up. Happiness is not an abstract idea, but a concrete whole; and these are some of its parts. And the utilitarian standard sanctions and approves their being so. Life would be a poor thing, very ill provided with sources of happiness, if there were not this provision of nature, by which things originally indifferent, but conducive to, or otherwise associated with, the satisfaction of our primitive desires, become in themselves sources of pleasure more valuable than the primitive pleasures, both in permanency, in the space of human existence that they are capable of covering, and even in intensity.

Virtue, according to the utilitarian conception, is a good of this description. There was no original desire of it, or motive to it, save its conduciveness to pleasure, and especially to protection from pain. But through the association thus formed, it may be felt a good in itself, and desired as such with as great intensity as any other good; and with this difference between it and the love of money, of power, or of fame, that all of these may, and often do, render the individual noxious to the other members of the society to which he belongs, whereas there is nothing which makes him so much a blessing to them as the cultivation of the disinterested love of virtue. And consequently, the utilitarian standard, while it tolerates and approves those other acquired desires, up to the point beyond which they would be more injurious to the general happiness than promotive of it, enjoins and requires the cultivation of the love of virtue up to the greatest strength possible, as being above all things important to the general happiness.

It results from the preceding considerations, that there is in reality nothing desired except happiness. Whatever is desired otherwise than as a means to some end beyond itself, and ultimately to happiness, is desired as itself a part of happiness, and is not desired for itself until it has become so. Those who desire virtue for its own sake, desire it either because the consciousness of it is a pleasure, or because the consciousness of being without it is a pain, or for both reasons united; as in truth the pleasure and pain seldom exist separately, but almost always together, the same person feeling pleasure in the degree of virtue attained, and pain in not having attained more. If one of these gave him no pleasure, and the other no pain, he would not love or desire virtue, or would desire it only for the other benefits which it might produce to himself or to persons whom he cared for. We have now, then, an answer to the question, of what sort of proof the principle of utility is susceptible. If the opinion which I have now stated is psychologically true—if human nature is so constituted as to desire nothing which is not either a part of happiness or a means of happiness, we can have no other proof, and we require no other, that these are the only things desirable. If so, happiness is the sole end of human action, and the promotion of it the test by which to judge of all human conduct; from whence it necessarily follows that it must be the criterion of morality, since a part is included in the whole. . . .

John Stuart Mill: Hedonism

1. Mill claims that "Pleasure, and freedom from pain, are the only things desirable as ends." Are there any examples that can challenge this claim?

2. What does Mill propose as a standard to determine which kinds of pleasure are more valuable than others? Is this a plausible standard?

3. Mill states that it is "Better to be Socrates dissatisfied, than a fool satisfied." What reasons does he give for thinking this?

4. In order to show that an object is visible, it is enough to show that people actually see it. Mill claims, similarly, "The sole evidence it is possible to produce that anything is desirable, is that people do actually desire it." Are visibility and desirability similar in this way?

5. Mill claims that "Each person's happiness is a good to that person." He then concludes from this that "the general happiness" is therefore "a good to the aggregate of all persons." Is this a good argument?

6. According to Mill, "The ingredients of happiness are very various, and each of them is desirable in itself." Does this contradict his earlier claim, given in question 1?

7. At the beginning of this selection, Mill says that pleasure and the absence of pain are the only things desirable as ends. Toward the end he claims that "Happiness is the sole end of human action." Are happiness and pleasure the same thing?

The Experience Machine

Robert Nozick

In this brief selection from his book *Anarchy, State, and Utopia* (1974), the late Harvard philosopher Robert Nozick (1938–2002) invites us to contemplate a life in which we are placed within a very sophisticated machine that is capable of simulating whatever experiences we find most valuable. Such a life, Nozick argues, cannot be the best life for us, because it fails to make contact with reality. This is meant to show that the good life is not entirely a function of the quality of our inner experiences. Since hedonism measures our well-being in precisely this way, hedonism, says Nozick, must be mistaken.

. . . Suppose there were an experience machine that would give you any experience you desired. Super-duper neuropsychologists could stimulate your brain so that you would think and feel you were writing a great novel, or making a friend, or reading an interesting book. All the time you would be floating in a tank, with electrodes attached to your brain. Should you plug into this machine for life, preprogramming your life's experiences? If you are worried about missing out on desirable experiences, we can suppose that business enterprises have researched thoroughly the lives of many others. You can pick and choose from their large library or smorgasbord of such experiences, selecting your life's experiences for, say, the next two years. After two years have passed, you will have ten minutes or ten hours out of the tank, to select the experiences of your *next* two years. Of course, while in the tank you won't know that you're there; you'll think it's all actually happening. Others can also plug in to have the experiences they want, so there's no need to stay unplugged to serve them. (Ignore problems such as who will service the machines if everybody plugs in.) Would you plug in? *What else can matter to us, other than how our lives feel from the inside*? Nor should you refrain because of the few moments of distress between the moment you've decided and the moment

you're plugged. What's a few moments of distress compared to a lifetime of bliss (if that's what you choose), and why feel any distress at all if your decision *is* the best one?

What does matter to us in addition to our experiences? First, we want to *do* certain things, and not just have the experience of doing them. In the case of certain experiences, it is only because first we want to do the actions that we want the experiences of doing them or thinking we've done them. (But *why* do we want to do the activities rather than merely to experience them?) A second reason for not plugging in is that we want to *be* a certain way, to be a certain sort of person. Someone floating in a tank is an indeterminate blob. There is no answer to the question of what a person is like who has long been in the tank. Is he courageous, kind, intelligent, witty, loving? It's not merely that it's difficult to tell; there's no way he is. Plugging into the machine is a kind of suicide. It will seem to some, trapped by a picture, that nothing about what we are like can matter except as it gets reflected in our experiences. But should it be surprising that what *we are* is important to us? Why should we be concerned only with how our time is filled, but not with what we are?

Thirdly, plugging into an experience machine limits us to a man-made reality, to a world no deeper or more important than that which people can construct. There is no *actual* contact with any deeper reality, though the experience of it can be simulated. Many persons desire to leave themselves open to

---

From Robert Nozick, *Anarchy, State, and Utopia* (New York: Basic Books 1974), pp. 42–45.

such contact and to a plumbing of deeper significance.[1] This clarifies the intensity of the conflict over psychoactive drugs, which some view as mere local experience machines, and others view as avenues to a deeper reality; what some view as equivalent to surrender to the experience machine, others view as following one of the reasons *not* to surrender!

We learn that something matters to us in addition to experience by imagining an experience machine and then realizing that we would not use it. We can continue to imagine a sequence of machines each designed to fill lacks suggested for the earlier machines. For example, since the experience machine doesn't meet our desire to *be* a certain way, imagine a transformation machine which transforms us into whatever sort of person we'd like to be (compatible with our staying us). Surely one would not use the transformation machine to become as one would wish, and thereupon plug into the experience machine![2] So something matters in addition to one's

---

1. Traditional religious views differ on the *point* of contact with a transcendent reality. Some say that contact yields eternal bliss or Nirvana, but they have not distinguished this sufficiently from merely a *very* long run on the experience machine. Others think it is intrinsically desirable to do the will of a higher being which created us all, though presumably no one would think this if we discovered we had been created as an object of amusement by some superpowerful child from another galaxy or dimension. Still others imagine an eventual merging with a higher reality, leaving unclear its desirability, or where that merging leaves *us*.

2. Some wouldn't use the transformation machine at all; it seems like *cheating*. But the one-time use of the transformation machine would not remove all challenges; there would still be obstacles for the new us to overcome, a new plateau from which to strive even higher. And is this plateau any the less earned or deserved than that provided by genetic endowment and early childhood environment? But if the transformation machine could be used indefinitely often, so that we could accomplish anything by pushing a button to transform ourselves into someone who could do it easily, there would remain no limits we *need* to strain against or try to transcend. Would there be anything left *to do*? Do some theological views place God outside of time because an omniscient omnipotent being couldn't fill up his days?

experiences *and* what one is like. Nor is the reason merely that one's experiences are unconnected with what one is like. For the experience machine might be limited to provide only experiences possible to the sort of person plugged in. Is it that we want to make a difference in the world? Consider then the result machine, which produces in the world any result you would produce and injects your vector input into any joint activity. We shall not pursue here the fascinating details of these or other machines. What is most disturbing about them is their living of our lives for us. Is it misguided to search for *particular* additional functions beyond the competence of machines to do for us? Perhaps what we desire is to live (an active verb) ourselves, in contact with reality. (And this, machines cannot do *for* us.) Without elaborating on the implications of this, which I believe connect surprisingly with issues about free will and causal accounts of knowledge, we need merely note the intricacy of the question of what matters *for people* other than their experiences. Until one finds a satisfactory answer, and determines that this answer does not *also* apply to animals, one cannot reasonably claim that only the felt experiences of animals limit what we may do to them.

Robert Nozick: The Experience Machine

1. Nozick suggests that most people would choose not to plug in to an "experience machine" if given the opportunity. Would you plug in? Why or why not?

2. Hedonists such as Epicurus and Mill claim that pleasure is the only thing worth pursuing for its own sake. If some people would choose not to plug in to the experience machine, does this show that hedonism is false?

3. One reason Nozick gives for not getting into the experience machine is that "We want to *do* certain things, and not just have the experience of doing them." Do some activities have value independent of the experiences they produce? If so, what is an example of such an activity?

4. Nozick claims that "Plugging into the machine is a kind of suicide." What does he mean by this? Do you think he is right?

CHAPTER 5

Consequentialism

Here we begin our extensive investigation into normative ethical theory, the area of philosophy that tries to identify the fundamental principles of morality. First up: **consequentialism**, a family of theories that places the emphasis on the consequences of our actions as the way to determine whether they are right or wrong.

A. THE NATURE OF CONSEQUENTIALISM

Consequentialism says that *an action is morally required just because it produces the best overall results*. Economists have coined a special word for this feature—being **optimific**. But how can we determine whether an act is optimific (i.e., whether it yields the best results)? It won't always be an easy thing to do in practice. But in theory, it's pretty straightforward. There are five steps to this process:

1. First, identify what is **intrinsically good**—valuable in and of itself, and worth having for its own sake. Familiar candidates include happiness, autonomy, knowledge, and virtue.
2. Next, identify what is intrinsically bad (i.e., bad all by itself). Examples might include physical pain, mental anguish, sadistic impulses, and the betrayal of innocents.
3. Then determine all of your options. Which actions are open to you at the moment?
4. For each option, determine the value of its results. How much of what is intrinsically good will each action bring about? How much of what is intrinsically bad?
5. Finally, pick the action that yields the greatest net balance of good over bad.

That is the optimific choice. That is your moral duty. Doing anything else is immoral.

We can develop dozens of different versions of consequentialism, depending on which things we regard as intrinsically valuable. The many consequentialist alternatives include, for instance, views that state that acts are right if and only if they yield the greatest improvement in environmental health, or best advance the cause of world peace, or do more than any other action to increase the amount of knowledge in the world. Each of these is a version of consequentialism.

Thus consequentialism isn't just a single theory, but is rather a family of theories, united by their agreement that results are what matter in ethics. We can't discuss every member of the family here, so I will restrict my attention, for the most part, to its most prominent version—**act utilitarianism**.

According to act utilitarianism, well-being is the only thing that is intrinsically valuable. And faring poorly is the only thing that is intrinsically bad. Thus this view states that *an action is morally required if and only if it does more to improve overall well-being than any other action you could have done in the circumstances*. Philosophers call this ultimate moral standard the **principle of utility**. The focus, importantly, is on maximizing the *overall* amount of well-being in the world—not just yours, not just mine, but that of everyone affected by our actions. When we fail to maximize good results, we act wrongly, even if we had the best intentions. Though good intentions may earn us praise, they are, according to utilitarians, irrelevant to an action's morality.

B. THE ATTRACTIONS OF UTILITARIANISM

Utilitarianism has garnered a lot of followers, not only among philosophers but also, especially, among economists and politicians. Let's consider some of its major selling points here, before turning our attention to some of its potential drawbacks.

Utilitarianism is a doctrine of impartiality, and this is one of its great strengths. It tells us that the welfare of each person is equally morally valuable. Whether rich or poor, white or black, male or female, religious or not, your well-being is just as important as anyone else's. Everyone's well-being counts, and everyone's well-being counts equally.

A second attraction is utilitarianism's ability to justify our basic moral beliefs. Consider the things we regard, deep down, as seriously immoral: slavery, rape, humiliating defenseless people, killing innocent victims. Each of these clearly tends to do more harm than good. Utilitarianism condemns such acts. So do we.

Now consider the things we strongly believe to be morally right: helping the poor, keeping promises, telling the truth, bravely facing danger. Such actions are highly beneficial. Utilitarianism commends them. So do we.

A third benefit of utilitarianism is its ability to provide advice about how to resolve moral conflicts. Because it has just a single ultimate rule—maximize well-being—it can offer concrete guidance where it is most needed.

Consider this familiar moral puzzle. I overhear some nasty gossip about my friend. She later asks me whether people have been spreading rumors about her. I know that she is extremely sensitive, and that if I answer honestly, it will send her into a downward spiral for several days. I also know that the source of this gossip is someone who actually likes my friend, and was

acting impulsively and out of character. She's probably feeling bad about it already, and probably won't repeat this unkindness.

Of course, we need to know a lot more about the situation before we can be confident about a recommendation, but if we just stick with the details given here, the utilitarian will advise me not to reveal what I have heard. Honesty may be the best *policy*, but that doesn't mean that full disclosure is always called for. When we consider our options, utilitarians tell us to pick the one that increases overall well-being. Telling the truth won't always do that.

Utilitarianism is also a doctrine that provides great moral flexibility—a fourth benefit. For utilitarians, no moral rule (other than the principle of utility) is absolute. An **absolute rule** is one that is not to be violated under any conditions. According to utilitarianism, it is morally okay to violate any rule—even one that prohibits cannibalism, or torture, or the killing of innocents—if doing so will raise overall well-being.

Most of us think that moral rules must allow some exceptions. But where to draw the line? How do we know whether to follow a moral rule or to break it? Utilitarianism gives us an answer. Morality is not a free-for-all. It is not a case of "anything goes." We ordinarily do best when we obey the familiar moral rules (don't steal, lie, kill, etc.). But there are times when we must stray from the conventional path in order to improve overall welfare. When we do this, we do right—even if it means breaking the traditional moral rules.

A fifth benefit of utilitarianism is its insistence that every person is a member of the **moral community**. To be a member of the moral community is to be important in your own right. It is to be owed a certain amount of respect. Membership in the moral community imposes a duty on everyone else to take one's needs seriously, for one's own sake.

Importantly, utilitarians also argue that nonhuman animals are members of the moral community. The reasoning behind their inclusion is recorded in a famous slogan by the pioneering utilitarian Jeremy Bentham (1748–1832): "the question is not, Can they *reason*? nor, Can they *talk*? but, Can they *suffer*?"[1] According to utilitarians, animals are important in their own right. Their importance does not depend on whether we happen to care about them. And the utilitarian explanation of this is very plausible: animals count because they can suffer.

Just to be clear, utilitarians allow that it is sometimes okay to harm members of the moral community. There are many cases in which maximizing overall well-being comes at a price. For instance, it may be acceptable to conduct certain intensely painful animal experiments, provided that they bring about very beneficial results. The point here is that, from the utilitarian perspective, we are not allowed to ignore the suffering of others. It doesn't matter whether the victims are human beings or not.

C. SOME DIFFICULTIES FOR UTILITARIANISM

One problem for utilitarianism is that it seems like a very demanding theory, in two respects. A plausible moral theory is one that most of us can live by. But asking us to be constantly benevolent, never taking more than a moment or two for ourselves—how many of us can be so altruistic? If no one but a saint can meet its standards, then utilitarianism is in deep trouble.

Utilitarians would agree with this. They do *not* believe that we must always be strategizing about how to improve the world. The reason is simple. People motivated in this way usually fail to achieve their goal.

The idea is that those who are always trying to get the best outcome are often bound to miss it. This isn't as strange as it sounds. Think of people whose sole purpose in life is to be as happy as they can be. Such people are rarely very happy. Constantly striving for this goal only makes it more elusive.

Utilitarians insist that we distinguish between a **decision procedure** and a **standard of rightness**. A decision procedure is just what it sounds like—a method for reliably guiding our decisions, so that when we use it well, we make decisions as we ought to. A standard of rightness tells us the conditions that make actions morally right.

Utilitarianism is, above all, a standard of rightness. It says that an action is right if and only if it is optimific. Importantly, a standard of rightness need not be a good decision procedure. Indeed, most consequentialists think that their standard of rightness—the principle of utility—fails as a decision procedure. Unless we find ourselves in very unusual circumstances, we should *not* be asking ourselves whether the act we are about to do is optimific.

The reasons given earlier explain this. Using the principle of utility as a decision procedure would probably *decrease* the amount of good we do in the world. That's because we would probably spend too much time deliberating or second-guessing our motivations, thereby reducing our chances of doing good. Whenever that is so, utilitarians require that we use something other than the principle of utility to guide our deliberations and motivations.

But mightn't utilitarianism demand too much of us in the way of self-sacrifice? Even if we needn't always deliberate with an eye to doing what is optimific, and even if we needn't always have a saint's motivations, we really must act so as to achieve optimific results. Whenever we fail, we are behaving immorally. That is bound to strike most people as excessive.

It appears that a consistently utilitarian lifestyle would be one of great and constant self-sacrifice. Anytime you can do more good for others than you can for yourself, you are required to do so. If you are like most readers of this book—in no danger of starvation, able to afford a night out, a new pair of jeans, a vacation every so often—then utilitarianism calls on you to do a great deal more for others than you are probably doing.

---

1. Jeremy Bentham, *Introduction to the Principles of Morals and Legislation* (1781), ch. 17.

If I have a choice between spending $1,000 on a beach vacation and sending that money to UNICEF (the United Nations Children's Fund), it's an easy call. UNICEF literature claims that $1,000 can provide 100 families with a basic water kit for use during emergencies, immunize 1,000 children against polio, or provide enough woolen blankets to cover 250 children during winter-weather emergencies. I'd be unhappy if I had to give up my vacation. But my unhappiness pales in comparison to the suffering of those whose lives could be saved if I spent my money on them, rather than myself. If utilitarianism is correct, then no more vacations for me (or you, probably).

There is an important lesson here: utilitarianism cannot make room for **supererogation**— action that is "above and beyond the call of duty." Such behavior is admirable and praiseworthy, but is not required. A classic case of supererogation is that of a bystander dashing into a burning building in order to rescue strangers trapped inside. Utilitarians must deny that even this is a case of supererogation, because they deny that *any* actions are above and beyond the call of duty. Our moral duty is to do the very best we can do. If, among all of the options available to you at the time, dashing into the building is going to minimize harm, then this is what you must do. Attempting the rescue isn't optional. It is your duty.

Another worry about utilitarianism, ironically, is its attachment to impartiality. The impartiality required by utilitarianism really is a substantial benefit of the theory. The happiness of a celebrity or a billionaire is no more important than that of a homeless person or a refugee. From the moral point of view, everyone counts equally; no one's interests are more important than anyone else's.

Yet there is also something worrying about impartiality, since morality sometimes seems to recommend *partiality*. It seems right, for instance, that I care about my children more than your children, that I care more for friends than

strangers, more for my fellow citizens than those living halfway around the world. And it also seems right to translate my care into action. If I have saved a bit of money, and it could either pay for my son's minor surgery or relieve the greater suffering of famine victims, most of us will think it at least permissible to pay the surgeon. But to do that is to be partial to the interests of my son. Utilitarianism does not allow that. It rejects the idea that a person, just because he is my son, my dear friend, or my fellow citizen, is more deserving of my help and attention.

Utilitarians can argue that there are many situations in which we should give preference to our near and dear—not because they deserve it or are more important than strangers, but because that is what is most beneficial. They could argue, for instance, that the results of sending my money overseas would actually be worse than relieving my son's suffering. Utilitarians will remind us that we must consider all consequences, not just short-term ones. If I were to sacrifice my son's interests so readily, he would feel hurt, and less secure in my love for him. These feelings are bad in themselves and would probably cause further harm in the long run. By contrast, famine victims who don't even know me won't feel slighted by my passing them over so that I can care for my son's needs. So if we take a sufficiently broad view of things, we can see that being partial to the interests of family and friends is usually optimific after all.

This sort of reasoning is sometimes correct. When all is said and done, we often get better results when focusing on family, friends, and fellow citizens. But not always. After all, in the tale just told, the long-term result of my not sending famine aid is that some people actually die, whereas my son, though in pain and perhaps resentful of my sending the money abroad, would still be very much alive. From an impartial point of view, the death of famine victims is surely worse than my son's medical problems. When minimizing harm means giving one's time or money to strangers, utilitarianism requires that we do so—even if that means sacrificing the important needs of friends and family.

This emphasis on impartiality leads to another problem. We are to count everyone's well-being equally. But suppose that nearly everyone in a society has a deep-seated prejudice against a small minority group. And suppose, further, that they use this prejudice to defend a policy of enslavement. Depending on the circumstances, it could be that utilitarianism *requires* slavery in this society.

When deciding the matter, we must take all of the harms to the slaves into account. But we must also consider the benefits to their oppressors. Everyone's interests count equally. Rich or poor, white or black, male or female. So far, so good. But also: ignorant or wise, just or unjust, kind or malicious—everyone's interests count, equally. If enough people are sufficiently mean and ignorant, then utilitarianism can require that we allow the sufferings they cause. Though such cases are not likely to occur that frequently, they can. And when they do, utilitarianism sides with the oppressors. That is a serious problem for any moral theory.

Perhaps the greatest problem for utilitarianism can be simply put: we must maximize well-being, but sometimes we can do this only by committing some serious injustice. Moral theories should not permit, much less require, that we act unjustly. Therefore, there is something deeply wrong about utilitarianism.

To do justice is to respect rights; to commit injustice is to violate rights. If it is ever optimific to violate rights, then utilitarianism requires us to do so.

Consider an example from wartime: **vicarious punishment**, which targets innocent people as a way to deter the guilty. Such a tactic often backfires. But it can sometimes be extremely effective. You might stop terrorists from their dirty work by abducting and threatening to torture their relatives. You might prevent guerilla attacks by killing the residents of the villages that shelter them. Though the torture

and deliberate killing of innocent civilians certainly infringes their rights, the utilitarian will require that it be done if it prevents even greater harm.

Cases of vicarious punishment are cases in which people do not deserve to be harmed. There are also many examples in which people do deserve some sort of penalty or punishment, but it is not optimific to give them their just deserts. Think of situations in which a student rightly receives a failing grade and appeals for a better one. Sometimes it really would be most beneficial to give the student the grade he wants, rather than the grade he has earned. Perhaps a job or a scholarship is on the line. If the benefits outweigh the costs, utilitarianism requires that the professor change the grade.

There are more serious cases. After World War II, US officials determined that it was beneficial to allow many Nazi scientists to escape punishment, so long as they agreed to share their weapons intelligence. Prosecutors sometimes let acknowledged murderers go free, if the killers testify against the crime bosses who once hired them. Political leaders with blood on their hands are often allowed to retire peacefully, so as to avoid the civil strife that would result were they prosecuted for their crimes. If utilitarianism is correct, then we must minimize harm—even if doing so means letting the guilty escape justice.

For as long as utilitarianism has been around, its fans have had to deal with the objection that it shortchanges justice. They have had ample time to develop replies. Let's consider these replies by framing each of them as a response to

The Argument from Injustice

1. The correct moral theory will never require us to commit serious injustices.
2. Utilitarianism sometimes requires us to commit serious injustices.
3. Therefore, utilitarianism is not the correct moral theory.

There are four replies that are especially important. The first is that justice is also intrinsically valuable. It might sound puzzling, but those who make this first reply accept this argument in every respect. Utilitarianism cannot allow for the independent importance of justice, and that disqualifies it from being a good moral theory. Strictly speaking, then, utilitarianism is false. But if we make a small change to the doctrine, then all will be well.

A defining feature of utilitarianism is its view that well-being is the only thing that is intrinsically valuable. Suppose we amend that, and say that justice is also important in its own right. So we should maximize well-being *and* maximize justice in the world. That will solve the difficulty.

Or will it? If we are to maximize happiness and justice, what happens when we can't do both? Which should we give priority to?

We could say: always give priority to justice. But this isn't very plausible. Suppose that there has been gridlock in the state legislature. For months, lawmakers have been unable to pass a spending bill. Finally, a compromise package comes to the floor. If it doesn't get passed, there is no telling when another spending package will be voted on. In the meantime, government will shut down, and tens of thousands of people will not receive paychecks, medical assistance, or welfare support. Furthermore, the spending bill looks *terrific*. It solves a great number of the state's problems, gives aid to the neediest, and sponsors projects that will do genuine good for most communities. There is only one problem: it includes a clause that unfairly denies a small community the agricultural subsidies that the governor had promised it. Still, given the alternatives, a legislator should definitely vote for the spending bill, even though this means a minor injustice. As a general matter, if the stakes are extremely high, and the injustice very small, then it *may* be right to perpetrate injustice.

Rather than always giving priority to justice, we might instead always give priority to well-being. But then we are right back to the original theory, and so have made no progress in solving the problem of injustice.

What seems right to say is this: sometimes it's best to prefer well-being to justice, and sometimes not. But without any principle to sort this out, we don't really have a coherent theory at all.

In the face of this problem, some utilitarians opt for a second reply, and claim that injustice is never optimific. This amounts to denying premise 2. Those who favor this second reply say that if we carefully consider all of the results of unfair actions, we will see that those actions aren't really optimific. A policy of vicarious punishment, for instance, may work in the short run. But it will cause such anger among the target population that an even greater number of them will join the opposition. And that will mean more innocent bloodshed over time.

Such a calculation is certainly true in many cases. But it is unwarranted optimism to suppose that things will always work out so fortunately. Sometimes, for instance, terror movements do lose support when the surrounding civilian population is forced to take the hit. Injustice can sometimes prevent great harm. It can, on occasion, also produce great benefits. We can't tell the many stories of the criminals who have gotten away with it, because their happiness depends on their crimes remaining secret. In some of these cases, there is substantial benefit and little or no harm. Utilitarianism must approve of such actions.

A third reply to the problem of justice denies premise 1 of the Argument from Injustice. Those who offer this reply allow that well-being and justice sometimes conflict. But when they do, it is justice, and not well-being, that must take a backseat. Justice is only a part, not the whole, of morality. Of course it is important to respect people's rights, but that is because doing so is usually optimific. When it isn't, rights must be sacrificed. So premise 1 of the Argument from Injustice is false.

Utilitarians who defend this strategy know that their recommendations will sometimes clash with conventional wisdom. But as we have seen, this is not a fatal flaw. Received opinion is not the final word in ethics. Utilitarianism began its life as a radical doctrine. That legacy remains.

Utilitarians can claim that our deepest moral convictions, including those that require us to do justice, reflect a utilitarian framework. We are socialized to tell the truth, protect the weak, keep our promises, and so on, *because doing so tends to be optimific*. But when it is not, utilitarians ask us to look at morality's ultimate standard, and to set aside our ordinary scruples in favor of the principle of utility.

Most of us agree that justice can sometimes be outweighed by other moral concerns. If, in a previous example, a legislator must authorize a minor injustice in order to pass an immensely beneficial spending bill, then morality gives the go-ahead. If you can administer CPR to a stricken passerby, and so save his life, then it is worth committing a minor injustice to do so. So justice may sometimes be sacrificed. But when? Utilitarians have an answer: whenever the results of doing so are optimific. If you don't like that answer, you need to supply a better principle that tells us when injustice is, and is not, permitted.

A fourth reply enables us to develop a closely related moral theory that deserves special mention here, because it promises to handle a number of objections to utilitarianism, while keeping much of its spirit. This is **rule consequentialism**—the view that *an action is morally right just because it is required by an* **optimific social rule**.

Which social rules are optimific? They are the rules that lead to optimific results when (nearly) everyone in a society accepts and follows the rule.

The basic idea is this. Rather than determine an action's morality by asking about its results, we ask instead about whether the action conforms to a moral rule. This is a familiar model in ethics. Most moral theories operate this way. What distinguishes them from one another is their different claims about what makes something a moral rule. Rule consequentialists have a specific view about this. The moral rules are the optimific social rules.

To know whether a rule is an optimific social rule, follow these three steps:

1. Carefully describe the rule.
2. Imagine what a society would be like if just about everyone in it endorsed the rule.
3. Then ask this question: will that society be better off with this rule than with any competing rule?

If the answer to this question is *yes*, then this rule is an optimific social rule. If the answer is *no*, then it isn't an optimific social rule, and so is not a genuine moral rule.

Rule consequentialism will probably instruct professors to give their students the grades they deserve, rather than those they would like to have. It will condemn the actions of thieves, even if they don't get caught and their victims suffer in only minor ways. It will likely prohibit such practices as vicarious punishment. When we focus on what is optimific as a general policy, we repeatedly get advice that agrees with our notions of justice. Even rule consequentialists who reject the intrinsic value of justice, and insist that well-being is the only thing of ultimate value, will almost always defend policies that are just. That's because in the long run, and as a general matter, just *policies* maximize well-being, even if, in isolated cases, just *actions* do not.

Rule consequentialism also solves other problems with act utilitarianism. It supports our belief that morality permits a certain degree of partiality, because policies that allow us to give preference to friends, loved ones, and fellow citizens will very often be highly beneficial.

Rule consequentialism can also say that certain actions are simply forbidden, even if they will sometimes achieve very good results. For instance, even if it would be optimific here and now to torture a prisoner, there may well be an optimific rule that forbids political torture. In most cases and over the long run, societies that ban torture may be much better off, in terms of both happiness and justice, than those that allow their officials to torture prisoners. If that is so, then torture is immoral—even if, in unusual cases, it yields real benefits.

So rule consequentialism has a lot going for it. And yet very few philosophers accept it. The reason was given over fifty years ago, by a prominent Australian philosopher, J. J. C. Smart.[2] In defending act utilitarianism, Smart accused rule consequentialists of irrational rule worship. That charge has stuck.

The basic worry is simple. Rule consequentialists demand that we obey moral rules, *even when we know that breaking them would yield better results*. But that is irrational, since in these cases, consequentialists know in advance that their ultimate goal (making the world the best place it can be) will not be fulfilled. It is irrational to knowingly defeat your own goals. Rule consequentialists do this whenever they issue a recommendation that differs from act utilitarianism.

Act utilitarianism demands that we always to do what is optimific. So, by definition, whenever rule consequentialists give us different advice, we are required to act in a way that fails to yield the best results. Rule consequentialists would forbid torture and embezzlement and vicarious punishment—even when specific instances of such action would be most beneficial.

This is self-defeating, since a consequentialist's ultimate aim is to produce the best possible results.

No matter what your ultimate goal is, the rules that *generally* achieve that goal will sometimes fail to do so. If you know that you are in one of those exceptional situations, then why follow the rule? Suppose that justice, not happiness, is the ultimate value. Suppose, too, that justice would be best served if everyone were to follow a certain rule, such as one that prohibits tampering with evidence. But why follow that rule if you know that this time, unusually, breaking the rule will yield the most justice?

If the ultimate purpose of morality is to make the world a better place, then it is irrational to knowingly behave in ways that fail to do this. And yet that is what rule consequentialism sometimes requires. That is why most consequentialists have rejected it.

D. CONCLUSION

Consequentialism is a perennial favorite with moral philosophers. Its emphasis on impartiality, its moral flexibility, its inclusion of non-human animals within the moral community, its orientation to the future, and its emphasis on results have great appeal for many ethical thinkers.

But we have also seen that there are worries for consequentialism, and these are not easily solved. We usually admire impartiality but sometimes think that partiality is what morality demands. Consequentialism can require a degree of self-sacrifice that strikes many people as extreme. And it sometimes calls on us to commit injustice. We reviewed the four most prominent replies to this concern, but we saw that each of them encountered difficulties. It's natural, then, to turn our attention next to a view that places primary importance on doing justice: the moral theory of Immanuel Kant.

2. See J. J. C. Smart, "Extreme and Restricted Utilitarianism," *Philosophical Quarterly* 6 (1956): 344–354.

ESSENTIAL CONCEPTS

Absolute rule: a rule that may never permissibly be broken.

Act utilitarianism: the moral theory that says that an action is morally required just because it does more to improve overall well-being than any other action you could have done in the circumstances.

Consequentialism: the family of moral theories that say that an action or a policy is morally required just because it produces the best overall results.

Decision procedure: a method for reliably guiding our decisions, so that when we use it well, we make decisions as we ought to.

Intrinsically good: valuable in and of itself, and worth having for its own sake

Moral community: that group of individuals who are morally important in their own right and, as such, are owed a certain amount of respect. Membership in the moral community imposes a duty on everyone else to take one's needs seriously, for one's own sake.

Optimific: producing the best results.

Optimific social rule: a social rule which, if nearly everyone accepted it, would yield better results than any competing social rule.

Principle of utility: the central doctrine of act utilitarianism.

Rule consequentialism: the view that an action is morally right just because it is required by an optimific social rule.

Standard of rightness: a principle that tells us the conditions under which actions are morally right.

Supererogation: action that is "above and beyond the call of duty."

Vicarious punishment: punishment that targets innocent people as a way to deter the guilty.

DISCUSSION QUESTIONS

1. Most utilitarians think that sometimes people are not to blame for performing actions that are very wrong, and that sometimes people should not be praised for doing the right thing. Why do they think this? Do you agree?

2. Utilitarians reject the existence of absolute moral rules (other than the principle of utility). Do you think that there are any absolute moral rules? If so, what are they, and how can their absolute status be defended against the utilitarian view that the ends justify the means?

3. Is there any way of measuring how much happiness is brought about by an action? Do we have any method for comparing the happiness of two different people? If the answer to these questions is "no," is this a problem for utilitarianism?

4. Critics claim that utilitarianism demands that we be saintly in our motivations. Explain this criticism and then discuss why you find it (im)plausible.

5. If utilitarianism is correct, then we may be morally required to undertake substantial sacrifice for others. What limits on such sacrifice does the utilitarian favor? Are these limits acceptable?

6. Utilitarianism requires us to be impartial. What does this amount to? In what sense does utilitarianism require that we treat all people equally? Is this a positive or a negative feature of the theory?

7. Which utilitarian reply to the Argument from Injustice do you think is the most promising? Do you think that this reply is ultimately successful? Defend your answer.

READING

Utilitarianism

John Stuart Mill

Though written over a hundred and fifty years ago in the form of a long pamphlet, Mill's *Utilitarianism* is the most influential presentation of the doctrine yet to appear. In this excerpt from its second chapter, Mill identifies the essential core of the moral theory, namely, its Greatest Happiness Principle: "actions are right in proportion as they tend to promote happiness, wrong as they tend to produce the reverse of happiness." Mill is keen to say that one's own happiness is no more important than another's—the utilitarian creed insists that a virtuous person will be concerned with the general happiness and align her own interests with those of the larger population to the extent possible.

The discussion here takes the form of replies to a series of objections; along the way, Mill takes the opportunity to identify positive attractions of the view. One objection is that utilitarianism demands too much of us by requiring that we always be motivated to promote the greater good. Mill replies by denying this and distinguishing between the standard of right action—the Greatest Happiness Principle—and the standard by which we assess people's motives and character. An act that yields only avoidable harm is wrong, even though the person who did it tried hard to do good. In such a case we need not blame the person, even though he acted immorally. Mill claims that only a small handful of people are in a position to do good on a large scale; as a result, most of us would do best not to ordinarily have the Greatest Happiness Principle as our primary motivation.

Indeed, rather than always ask ourselves which of our options will produce the greatest happiness, Mill thinks that we should rely on a battery of familiar moral rules to guide our actions and in most cases don't even need to reflect much in order to know which of our actions is the right one. We will do more good by relying on these familiar rules (e.g., don't lie, don't kill others, keep your promises) than on frequent, direct calculations of utility. But these rules are themselves justified because following them usually leads to increases in happiness or decreases in unhappiness. Further, these rules will sometimes conflict; when they do, Mill touts as a significant advantage of utilitarianism that its Greatest Happiness Principle provides a principled basis for determining how to resolve such conflicts.

The creed which accepts as the foundation of morals, Utility, or the Greatest Happiness Principle, holds that actions are right in proportion as they tend to promote happiness, wrong as they tend to produce the reverse of happiness. By happiness is intended pleasure, and the absence of pain; by unhappiness, pain, and the privation of pleasure. To give a clear view of the moral standard set up by the theory, much more requires to be said; in particular, what things it includes in the ideas of pain and pleasure; and to what extent this is left an open question. But these supplementary explanations do not affect

From John Stuart Mill, *Utilitarianism* (1861).

the theory of life on which this theory of morality is grounded—namely, that pleasure, and freedom from pain, are the only things desirable as ends; and that all desirable things (which are as numerous in the utilitarian as in any other scheme) are desirable either for the pleasure inherent in themselves, or as means to the promotion of pleasure and the prevention of pain. . . .

[T]he happiness which forms the utilitarian standard of what is right in conduct, is not the agent's own happiness, but that of all concerned. As between his own happiness and that of others, utilitarianism requires him to be as strictly impartial as a disinterested and benevolent spectator. In the golden rule of Jesus of Nazareth, we read the complete spirit of the ethics of utility. To do as you would be done by, and to love your neighbour as yourself, constitute the ideal perfection of utilitarian morality. As the means of making the nearest approach to this ideal, utility would enjoin, first, that laws and social arrangements should place the happiness, or (as speaking practically it may be called) the interest, of every individual, as nearly as possible in harmony with the interest of the whole; and secondly, that education and opinion, which have so vast a power over human character, should so use that power as to establish in the mind of every individual an indissoluble association between his own happiness and the good of the whole; especially between his own happiness and the practice of such modes of conduct, negative and positive, as regard for the universal happiness prescribes; so that not only may he be unable to conceive the possibility of happiness to himself, consistently with conduct opposed to the general good, but also that a direct impulse to promote the general good may be in every individual one of the habitual motives of action, and the sentiments connected therewith may fill a large and prominent place in every human being's sentient existence. If the impugners of the utilitarian morality represented it to their own minds in this, its true character, I know not what recommendation possessed by any other morality they could possibly affirm to be wanting to it; what more beautiful or more exalted developments of human nature any other ethical system can be supposed to foster, or what springs of action, not accessible to

the utilitarian, such systems rely on for giving effect to their mandates.

The objectors to utilitarianism cannot always be charged with representing it in a discreditable light. On the contrary, those among them who entertain anything like a just idea of its disinterested character, sometimes find fault with its standard as being too high for humanity. They say it is exacting too much to require that people shall always act from the inducement of promoting the general interests of society. But this is to mistake the very meaning of a standard of morals, and confound the rule of action with the motive of it. It is the business of ethics to tell us what are our duties, or by what test we may know them; but no system of ethics requires that the sole motive of all we do shall be a feeling of duty; on the contrary, ninety-nine hundredths of all our actions are done from other motives, and rightly so done, if the rule of duty does not condemn them. It is the more unjust to utilitarianism that this particular misapprehension should be made a ground of objection to it, inasmuch as utilitarian moralists have gone beyond almost all others in affirming that the motive has nothing to do with the morality of the action, though much with the worth of the agent. He who saves a fellow creature from drowning does what is morally right, whether his motive be duty, or the hope of being paid for his trouble; he who betrays the friend that trusts him, is guilty of a crime, even if his object be to serve another friend to whom he is under greater obligations.

But to speak only of actions done from the motive of duty, and in direct obedience to principle: it is a misapprehension of the utilitarian mode of thought, to conceive it as implying that people should fix their minds upon so wide a generality as the world, or society at large. The great majority of good actions are intended not for the benefit of the world, but for that of individuals, of which the good of the world is made up; and the thoughts of the most virtuous man need not on these occasions travel beyond the particular persons concerned, except so far as is necessary to assure himself that in benefiting them he is not violating the rights, that is, the legitimate and authorised expectations, of any one else. The multiplication of happiness is, according to the utilitarian ethics, the object of virtue:

the occasions on which any person (except one in a thousand) has it in his power to do this on an extended scale, in other words to be a public benefactor, are but exceptional; and on these occasions alone is he called on to consider public utility; in every other case, private utility, the interest or happiness of some few persons, is all he has to attend to. Those alone the influence of whose actions extends to society in general, need concern themselves habitually about so large an object. In the case of abstinences indeed—of things which people forbear to do from moral considerations, though the consequences in the particular case might be beneficial—it would be unworthy of an intelligent agent not to be consciously aware that the action is of a class which, if practised generally, would be generally injurious, and that this is the ground of the obligation to abstain from it. The amount of regard for the public interest implied in this recognition is no greater than is demanded by every system of morals, for they all enjoin to abstain from whatever is manifestly pernicious to society.

The same considerations dispose of another reproach against the doctrine of utility, founded on a still grosser misconception of the purpose of a standard of morality, and of the very meaning of the words right and wrong. It is often affirmed that utilitarianism renders men cold and unsympathising; that it chills their moral feelings towards individuals; that it makes them regard only the dry and hard consideration of the consequences of actions, not taking into their moral estimate the qualities from which those actions emanate. If the assertion means that they do not allow their judgment respecting the rightness or wrongness of an action to be influenced by their opinion of the qualities of the person who does it, this is a complaint not against utilitarianism, but against having any standard of morality at all; for certainly no known ethical standard decides an action to be good or bad because it is done by a good or a bad man, still less because done by an amiable, a brave, or a benevolent man, or the contrary. These considerations are relevant, not to the estimation of actions, but of persons; and there is nothing in the utilitarian theory inconsistent with the fact that there are other things which interest us in persons besides the rightness and wrongness of their actions. The Stoics, indeed, with the paradoxical misuse of language which was part of their system, and by which they strove to raise themselves above all concern about anything but virtue, were fond of saying that he who has that has everything; that he, and only he, is rich, is beautiful, is a king. But no claim of this description is made for the virtuous man by the utilitarian doctrine. Utilitarians are quite aware that there are other desirable possessions and qualities besides virtue, and are perfectly willing to allow to all of them their full worth. They are also aware that a right action does not necessarily indicate a virtuous character, and that actions which are blamable, often proceed from qualities entitled to praise. When this is apparent in any particular case, it modifies their estimation, not certainly of the act, but of the agent. I grant that they are, notwithstanding, of opinion, that in the long run the best proof of a good character is good actions; and resolutely refuse to consider any mental disposition as good, of which the predominant tendency is to produce bad conduct. This makes them unpopular with many people; but it is an unpopularity which they must share with every one who regards the distinction between right and wrong in a serious light; and the reproach is not one which a conscientious utilitarian need be anxious to repel.

If no more be meant by the objection than that many utilitarians look on the morality of actions, as measured by the utilitarian standard, with too exclusive a regard, and do not lay sufficient stress upon the other beauties of character which go towards making a human being lovable or admirable, this may be admitted. Utilitarians who have cultivated their moral feelings, but not their sympathies nor their artistic perceptions, do fall into this mistake; and so do all other moralists under the same conditions. What can be said in excuse for other moralists is equally available for them, namely, that, if there is to be any error, it is better that it should be on that side. As a matter of fact, we may affirm that among utilitarians as among adherents of other systems, there is every imaginable degree of rigidity and of laxity in the application of their standard: some are even puritanically rigorous, while others are as indulgent as can possibly be desired by sinner or by sentimentalist. But on the whole, a doctrine which brings prominently forward the interest that mankind have in the repression and prevention of conduct which violates the moral law, is likely to be inferior to no other in turning the sanctions of opinion against such violations. It is true, the question, What does violate the moral law? is one on which those who recognise different standards of morality are likely now and then to differ. But difference of opinion on moral questions was not first introduced into the world by utilitarianism, while that doctrine does supply, if not always an easy, at all events a tangible and intelligible mode of deciding such differences.

It may not be superfluous to notice a few more of the common misapprehensions of utilitarian ethics. . . . We not uncommonly hear the doctrine of utility inveighed against as a godless doctrine. If it be necessary to say anything at all against so mere an assumption, we may say that the question depends upon what idea we have formed of the moral character of the Deity. If it be a true belief that God desires, above all things, the happiness of his creatures, and that this was his purpose in their creation, utility is not only not a godless doctrine, but more profoundly religious than any other. If it be meant that utilitarianism does not recognise the revealed will of God as the supreme law of morals, I answer, that a utilitarian who believes in the perfect goodness and wisdom of God, necessarily believes that whatever God has thought fit to reveal on the subject of morals, must fulfil the requirements of utility in a supreme degree. But others besides utilitarians have been of opinion that the Christian revelation was intended, and is fitted, to inform the hearts and minds of mankind with a spirit which should enable them to find for themselves what is right, and incline them to do it when found, rather than to tell them, except in a very general way, what it is; and that we need a doctrine of ethics, carefully followed out, to interpret to us the will of God. Whether this opinion is correct or not, it is superfluous here to discuss; since whatever aid religion, either natural or revealed, can afford to ethical investigation, is as open to the utilitarian moralist as to any other. He can use it as the testimony of God to the usefulness or hurtfulness of any given course of action, by as good a right as others can use it for the indication of a transcendental law, having no connection with usefulness or with happiness.

Again, Utility is often summarily stigmatised as an immoral doctrine by giving it the name of Expediency, and taking advantage of the popular use of that term to contrast it with Principle. But the Expedient, in the sense in which it is opposed to the Right, generally means that which is expedient for the particular interest of the agent himself; as when a minister sacrifices the interests of his country to keep himself in place. When it means anything better than this, it means that which is expedient for some immediate object, some temporary purpose, but which violates a rule whose observance is expedient in a much higher degree. The Expedient, in this sense, instead of being the same thing with the useful, is a branch of the hurtful. Thus, it would often be expedient, for the purpose of getting over some momentary embarrassment, or attaining some object immediately useful to ourselves or others, to tell a lie. But inasmuch as the cultivation in ourselves of a sensitive feeling on the subject of veracity, is one of the most useful, and the enfeeblement of that feeling one of the most hurtful, things to which our conduct can be instrumental; and inasmuch as any, even unintentional, deviation from truth, does that much towards weakening the trustworthiness of human assertion, which is not only the principal support of all present social well-being, but the insufficiency of which does more than any one thing that can be named to keep back civilisation, virtue, everything on which human happiness on the largest scale depends; we feel that the violation, for a present advantage, of a rule of such transcendant expediency, is not expedient, and that he who, for the sake of a convenience to himself or to some other individual, does what depends on him to deprive mankind of the good, and inflict upon them the evil, involved in the greater or less reliance which they can place in each other's word, acts the part of one of their worst enemies. Yet that even this rule, sacred as it is, admits of possible exceptions, is acknowledged by all moralists; the chief of which is when the withholding of some fact (as of information from a malefactor, or of bad news from a person dangerously ill) would save an individual (especially an individual other than oneself) from great and unmerited evil, and when the withholding can only be effected by denial. But in order that the exception may not extend itself beyond the need, and may have the least possible effect in weakening reliance on veracity, it ought to be recognised, and, if possible, its limits defined; and if the principle of utility is good for anything, it must be good for weighing these conflicting utilities against one another, and marking out the region within which one or the other preponderates.

Again, defenders of utility often find themselves called upon to reply to such objections as this—that there is not time, previous to action, for calculating and weighing the effects of any line of conduct on the general happiness. This is exactly as if any one were to say that it is impossible to guide our conduct by Christianity, because there is not time, on every occasion on which anything has to be done, to read through the Old and New Testaments. The answer to the objection is, that there has been ample time, namely, the whole past duration of the human species. During all that time, mankind have been learning by experience the tendencies of actions; on which experience all the prudence, as well as all the morality of life, are dependent. People talk as if the commencement of this course of experience had hitherto been put off, and as if, at the moment when some man feels tempted to meddle with the property or life of another, he had to begin considering for the first time whether murder and theft are injurious to human happiness. Even then I do not think that he would find the question very puzzling; but, at all events, the matter is now done to his hand.

It is truly a whimsical supposition that, if mankind were agreed in considering utility to be the test of morality, they would remain without any agreement as to what is useful, and would take no measures for having their notions on the subject taught to the young, and enforced by law and opinion. There is no difficulty in proving any ethical standard whatever to work ill, if we suppose universal idiocy to be conjoined with it; but on any hypothesis short of that, mankind must by this time have acquired positive beliefs as to the effects of some actions on their happiness; and the beliefs which have thus come down are the rules of morality for the multitude, and for the philosopher until he has succeeded in finding better. That philosophers might easily do this, even now, on many subjects; that the received code of ethics is by no means of divine right; and that mankind have still much to learn as to the effects of actions on the general happiness, I admit, or rather, earnestly maintain. The corollaries from the principle of utility, like the precepts of every practical art, admit of indefinite improvement, and, in a progressive state of the human mind, their improvement is perpetually going on.

But to consider the rules of morality as improvable, is one thing; to pass over the intermediate generalisations entirely, and endeavour to test each individual action directly by the first principle, is another. It is a strange notion that the acknowledgment of a first principle is inconsistent with the admission of secondary ones. To inform a traveller respecting the place of his ultimate destination, is not to forbid the use of landmarks and direction-posts on the way. The proposition that happiness is the end and aim of morality, does not mean that no road ought to be laid down to that goal, or that persons going thither should not be advised to take one direction rather than another. Men really ought to leave off talking a kind of nonsense on this subject, which they would neither talk nor listen to on other matters of practical concernment. Nobody argues that the art of navigation is not founded on astronomy, because sailors cannot wait to calculate the Nautical Almanack. Being rational creatures, they go to sea with it ready calculated; and all rational creatures go out upon the sea of life with their minds made up on the common questions of right and wrong, as well as on many of the far more difficult questions of wise and foolish. And this, as long as foresight is a human quality, it is to be presumed they will continue to do. Whatever we adopt as the fundamental principle of morality, we require subordinate principles to apply it by; the impossibility of doing without them, being common to all systems, can afford no argument against any one in particular; but gravely to argue as if no such secondary principles could be had, and as if mankind had remained till now, and always must remain, without drawing any general conclusions from the experience of human life, is as high a pitch, I think, as absurdity has ever reached in philosophical controversy.

The remainder of the stock arguments against utilitarianism mostly consist in laying to its charge the common infirmities of human nature, and the general difficulties which embarrass conscientious persons in shaping their course through life. We are told that a utilitarian will be apt to make his own particular case an exception to moral rules, and, when under temptation, will see a utility in the breach of a rule, greater than he will see in its observance. But is utility the only creed which is able to furnish us with excuses for evil doing, and means of cheating our own conscience? They are afforded in abundance by all doctrines which recognise as a fact in morals the existence of conflicting considerations; which all doctrines do, that have been believed by sane persons. It is not the fault of any creed, but of the complicated nature of human affairs, that rules of conduct cannot be so framed as to require no exceptions, and that hardly any kind of action can safely be laid down as either always obligatory or always condemnable. There is no ethical creed which does not temper the rigidity of its laws, by giving a certain latitude, under the moral responsibility of the agent, for accommodation to peculiarities of circumstances; and under every creed, at the opening thus made, self-deception and dishonest casuistry get in. There exists no moral system under which there do not arise unequivocal cases of conflicting obligation. These are the real difficulties, the knotty points both in the theory of ethics, and in the conscientious guidance of personal conduct. They are overcome practically, with greater or with less success, according to the intellect and virtue of the individual; but it can hardly be pretended that any one will be the less qualified for dealing with them, from possessing an ultimate standard to which conflicting rights and duties can be referred. If utility is the ultimate source of moral obligations, utility may be invoked to decide between them when their demands are incompatible. Though the application of the standard may be difficult, it is better than none at all: while in other systems,

the moral laws all claiming independent authority, there is no common umpire entitled to interfere between them; their claims to precedence one over another rest on little better than sophistry, and unless determined, as they generally are, by the unacknowledged influence of considerations of utility, afford a free scope for the action of personal desires and partialities. We must remember that only in these cases of conflict between secondary principles is it requisite that first principles should be appealed to. There is no case of moral obligation in which some secondary principle is not involved; and if only one, there can seldom be any real doubt which one it is, in the mind of any person by whom the principle itself is recognised.

John Stuart Mill: Utilitarianism

1. Utilitarianism claims that my happiness is no more important than yours. This kind of impartiality seems highly appealing. But this also appears to prohibit us from giving ourselves or our family priority over the interests of others. Is this appearance correct? Can utilitarianism allow for partiality to oneself or one's family?

2. Mill claims that virtuous people will rarely have the Greatest Happiness Principle in mind when acting. Why does he say this? Is his claim plausible? And is it what a utilitarian really should say?

3. Mill believes that the motives that prompt an action are irrelevant to that action's morality. Is this claim plausible? Why or why not?

4. Many critics of utilitarianism claim that the theory requires that we sacrifice too much for others. Mill counters by saying that only a very few people are in a position to do much good for many others; as a result, most of us are not required to focus our efforts in ways that require significant self-sacrifice. Is Mill's view too rosy, especially now that we are so easily able to learn of how unfortunate others are and are easily able to give to charities that can help improve the lives of those who are less well off than we are?

5. Some have argued that utilitarianism is a godless doctrine. What is Mill's reply to this? Do you find it plausible?

CHAPTER 6

Kantian Ethics

Imagine a person who reasons as follows: I should keep my money rather than pay it out in taxes, because if I keep it, I'll be able to afford a wonderful vacation for myself and my family. And no one is actually going to suffer if I pocket the money, since it's only a few thousand dollars that we're talking about. There's no way that money could bring as much happiness in the government's hands as it could in mine.

Suppose he is right about that. He spends the money on his vacation. He and his family have a terrific time. He is never caught.

Still, he has done something wrong. So has the person who cheats on her exams and gets away with it. So has the person who gleefully speeds down the emergency lane and escapes the traffic jam that the rest of us are stuck in. So has the person whose campaign of dirty tricks has gotten him securely into office.

Despite any good results that may come from their actions, these people did wrong—or so we think. And the explanation of their immorality is simple. What they did was unfair. They took advantage of the system. They broke the rules that work to everyone's benefit. They violated the rights of others. No matter how much personal gain such actions bring, they are still wrong, because they are unfair and unjust.

Immanuel Kant (1724–1804) thought this way, and was very likely the most brilliant philosopher ever to have done so. He remains perhaps the most important voice of opposition to utilitarianism, and to its claim that the ultimate point of morality is to improve well-being rather than do justice.

A. CONSISTENCY AND FAIRNESS

There is a natural way to understand what is wrong with the actions in the examples just given. In each case, people are making exceptions of themselves. Their success depends on violating rules that most other people are following. This is a kind of inconsistency—of playing by one set of rules while insisting that others obey a different set.

People are inconsistent to the extent that they treat similar cases differently. Tax cheats or dirty politicians are in the same boat as the rest of us. There's nothing special about them, or their situation, that exempts them from the rules that everyone must follow. That you can get away with making an exception of yourself doesn't mean that it is right to do so.

Our deep opposition to unfairness, and the resulting importance we attach to consistency, are revealed in two very popular tests of morality. Each takes the form of a question:

1. What if everyone did that?
2. How would you like it if I did that to you?

When we ask such questions—in the face of a bully, a liar, or a double-crosser—we are trying to get the person to see that he is acting unfairly, making an exception of himself, living by a set of rules that work only because others are not doing what he is doing. These basic moral challenges are designed to point out the inconsistency, and so the immorality, of that person's behavior.

Consider the first question: what if everyone did that? This question is really shorthand for the following test: *if disastrous results would occur if everyone did X, then X is immoral.* If everyone used the emergency lanes in traffic jams, then ambulances and fire trucks would often fail to provide needed help, leaving many to die. If everyone cheated on their taxes, society would crumble. If every candidate resorted to dirty tricks, then the entire political system would become corrupted. The test works easily and well for these cases.

But the test fails for other cases, and so it cannot serve as a reliable way to learn the morality of actions. Consider a common argument against homosexual sex: if everyone did that, disaster would soon follow, for the human race would quickly die out. Even if this were true, that wouldn't show that homosexual sex is immoral. Why not? Well, consider those who have decided to remain celibate—perhaps they are priests, or committed lifelong bachelors who believe that one shouldn't have sex without being married. What if everyone did *that*—in other words, refrained from having sex? The same results would follow. But that doesn't show that celibacy is immoral.

What about the other test, the one that asks: How would you like it if I did that to you? This is a direct application of the **Golden Rule**, which tells you to treat others as you would like to be treated. The Golden Rule is the classic test of morality. Clearly, it is meant to be a test of consistency. If you wouldn't want to be slandered or exploited, then don't do such things to others. If you do them anyway, you are acting inconsistently, hence unfairly, and therefore immorally.

The Golden Rule seems to work well for these cases and many others. Still, the Golden Rule cannot be correct. Kant himself identified the basic reason for this. The Golden Rule makes morality depend on a person's desires. Most of us don't like to be hit. And so the Golden Rule forbids us from hitting others. Good. But what about masochists who enjoy being hit? The Golden Rule allows them to go around hitting others. Bad. The morality of hitting people shouldn't depend on whether you like to take a beating every now and then.

Consider a related problem, that of the fanatic. Fanatics are principled people. It's just that their principles are ones that we find frightening and revolting. Some fanatics are so wedded to their cause, so strong-willed and self-disciplined, that they would accept the suffering that they want to impose on their victims, were the role of victim and persecutor reversed. True, few Nazis, for instance, would really accept a march to the gas chamber were they to discover their Jewish ancestry. Most Nazis, like most fanatics generally, are opportunists of bad faith, ones with very limited empathy and only a feeble ability to imagine themselves in someone else's place. If roles really were reversed, they'd much more likely beg for mercy and abandon their genocidal principles. But some would not. There are true believers out there who are willing to suffer any harm in the name of their chosen cause. The Golden Rule licenses their extremism because it makes the morality of an action depend entirely on what you want and what you are willing to put up with.

Because the Golden Rule sometimes gives the wrong answer to moral questions, it cannot be the ultimate test of morality. Something else must explain why it works, when it does. Kant thought he had the answer.

B. THE PRINCIPLE OF UNIVERSALIZABILITY

Kant, like most of us, felt the appeal of the two tests just discussed. He agreed that common sense is deeply committed to the importance of fairness and consistency, something that these two tests were trying, but not quite succeeding, in capturing. His aim was to identify the ultimate principle of morality, one that would explain the attraction of the two tests while correcting for their shortcomings.

He thought he had found it in the following standard, the **principle of universalizability**:

> An act is morally acceptable if, and only if, its maxim is universalizable.

To understand what this means, we need to understand two things: what a **maxim** is, and what it is for a maxim to be **universalizable**.

A maxim is simply the principle of action you give yourself when you are about to do something. For instance, if you send a regular check to Oxfam, your maxim might be: contribute $50 per month to Oxfam to help reduce hunger. A maxim has two parts. It states what you are about to do, and why you are about to do it. You dictate your own maxims. These are the rules you live by.

Kant thought that every action has a maxim. Of course we don't always formulate these maxims clearly to ourselves prior to acting, but at some level, whenever we act, we intend to do something, and we have a reason for doing it. A maxim is nothing but a record of that intention and its underlying reason. Maxims are what we cite when we try to explain to others why we act as we do.

If we lack a maxim, then we aren't really acting at all. We could be moving our bodies, as we do when we sneeze or roll across the bed in our sleep. But the absence of a maxim in these cases shows that these are mere bodily movements, rather than genuine actions.

Kant thought that an action's rightness depends on its maxim. And this leads directly to a very important point. For Kant, the morality of our actions has nothing to do with results. It has everything to do with our intentions and reasons for action, those that are contained in the principles we live by. This is a clear break with consequentialism.

Indeed, we can imagine two people doing the same thing, but for different reasons. That means that they will have different maxims. And even if their actions bring about identical results, one of the actions may be right and the other wrong, since only one of the maxims may be morally acceptable. This is something that act consequentialists cannot accept.

It might be, for instance, that I keep my promises to you because I think it's right to do

so. But I might instead keep my promises because I want you to like me so much that you leave your fortune to me in your will. Assume that these different reasons don't change the results of keeping my promises. Then the utilitarian thinks that each case of promise keeping is equally good. But since my maxim is different in these cases, Kant thinks that the morality of these actions might be different. It all depends, as we'll shortly see, on whether their maxims are universalizable.

Many people agree with Kant's view that the morality of our actions depends not on their results, but on our maxims. This supports our thought that those who set out to do evil are acting immorally, even if, through sheer chance, they manage to do good. It also justifies the claim that people who live by noble principles are acting morally, even when some unforeseeable accident intervenes, and their action brings only bad results.

So the morality of actions depends on their maxims. But how, precisely? Not every maxim is going to be a good one. We need a way to sort out the good maxims from the bad. That's where universalizability comes in.

How can we tell whether a maxim is universalizable? Here is a three-part test:

1. Formulate your maxim clearly—state what you intend to do and why you intend to do it.
2. Imagine a world in which everyone supports and acts on your maxim.
3. Then ask: Can the goal of my action be achieved in such a world?

If the answer to this last question is *yes*, then the maxim is universalizable, and the action is morally acceptable. If the answer is *no*, then the maxim is not universalizable, and the action it calls for is immoral.

This should strike a familiar note. The test of a maxim's universalizability clearly echoes the rule consequentialist's test for optimific social rules (see Chapter 5.C) and the *what if everyone did that?* test discussed earlier. Indeed, Kant has us ask a version of that question in the second step of this three-part test. But unlike these other tests, Kant doesn't ask about whether people would be much better off in the imagined world, or about whether disaster would strike there. Instead, he asks about whether we could achieve our goals in that world. But what is so important about that?

The importance, for Kant, is that this three-part test serves as the real way to determine whether we are being consistent and fair. If our maxim is universalizable, then we are pursuing actions for reasons that everyone could stand behind. We are not making exceptions of ourselves. Our goals are ones that everyone *could* support, even if, in the real world, some are dead set against them. We are asking whether our aims could be achieved if everyone shared them. If they can be, this shows that we are living by fair rules. Were we making an exception of ourselves, our maxims wouldn't be universalizable.

Consider the tax cheat again. The only reason he can get what he is aiming for (a lovely vacation) is because enough others are not adopting his maxim. The same goes for the careless driver who speeds down the emergency lane. The morality of these actions doesn't depend on their results, but on their maxims. And those maxims are not universalizable. So those actions are immoral, as Kant says, and as we believe.

C. HYPOTHETICAL AND CATEGORICAL IMPERATIVES

Kant claimed that when we act on a maxim that can't be universalized, we are contradicting ourselves. We are being inconsistent. We are assuming that it is acceptable to act in a certain way, even though our purposes could not be achieved if others acted in that very same way. When we make an exception of ourselves, we are acting as if we were more important than anyone else, and going on as if we were exempt from rules that others must obey. But we are not more important than others, and we are not exempt from these requirements.

It follows that when we behave immorally, we are reasoning badly. We are making mistaken assumptions—that we are more important than other people, that the rules applying to them do not apply to us. Those mistakes, and the inconsistent, contradictory reasoning behind them, show that *immoral conduct is irrational.*

To act irrationally is to act and to reason very badly. If Kant is right, then when we act immorally, we are reasoning poorly. But can this be right? Haven't we heard of lots of folks who act immorally while also being sharp, cunning, and strategic—in short, while being rational?

Well, in one sense, Kant allows that these wrongdoers are rational, because they are following what he called a **hypothetical imperative**. Specifically, these are imperatives—commands—of reason. They command us to do whatever is needed in order to get what we care about. Hypothetical imperatives tell us how to achieve our goals. They require us, on pain of irrationality, to do certain things, but only because such actions will get us what we want.

For instance, if my goal is to lose twenty pounds (as it often is), then reason requires me to forgo that pint of luscious coffee ice cream. If I want to get that Wall Street job, then reason requires that I line up a good summer internship. Reason demands that I look both ways at a busy intersection if I want to remain alive. These rational commands apply to me because of what I care about. I am irrational if I disregard them or act in a way that violates them.

But what if I don't care about acting morally? Then it seems that I can rationally ignore its requirements. But Kant would have none of that. He wanted to show that some rational requirements are, in his jargon, **categorical imperatives**. Like hypothetical imperatives, categorical imperatives are commands of reason. But unlike hypothetical imperatives, categorical imperatives are rational requirements that apply to a person regardless of what he or she cares about. They are requirements of reason that apply to everyone who possesses reason—in other words, everyone able to reflect on the wisdom of her actions, and able to use such reflections to guide her actions. Categorical imperatives command us to do things whether we want to or not, with the result that if we ignore or disobey them, we are acting contrary to reason (i.e., irrationally).

Kant thought that *all moral duties are categorical imperatives.* They apply to us just because we are rational beings. We must obey them even if we don't want to, and even if moral obedience gets us nothing that we care about.

One lesson Kant took from his thoughts about the Golden Rule is that the basic rules of morality do not depend on our desires. If they did, then moral rules would fail to apply to everyone, since our desires can differ from person to person. This would make morality too variable, and make it possible for people to escape from their moral duty just by changing what they want. Kant thought that he was defending common sense when he claimed that morality is, in this sense, universal—that everyone who can reason must obey its commands.

If moral duties really are categorical imperatives, then we act rationally when we act morally, and we act irrationally when we act immorally. Is that sort of view defensible? Can we really justify the claim that it is rational for everyone to act morally—even if we know that, for some people, moral conduct will only undermine their goals?

Kant thought he could do this. This is his line of reasoning:

The Argument for the Irrationality of Immorality

1. If you are rational, then you are consistent.
2. If you are consistent, then you obey the principle of universalizability.
3. If you obey the principle of universalizability, then you act morally.

4. Therefore, if you are rational, then you act morally.
5. Therefore, if you act immorally, then you are irrational.

It does seem that rationality requires consistency, as the first premise asserts. And, as we have discussed, the principle of universalizability is a demand of consistency. So, while more could certainly be said about these first two premises, let us take them for granted here and focus on the third. This is the claim that obedience to the principle of universalizability guarantees that our conduct is moral. Is this Kantian claim correct?

D. ASSESSING THE PRINCIPLE OF UNIVERSALIZABILITY

Unfortunately, the principle of universalizability fails as a general test for the morality of our actions. Look at premise 3 of Kant's Argument for the Irrationality of Immorality. It says that a maxim's universalizability is a guarantee of an action's rightness. That is false. We can act on universalizable maxims and still do wrong.

The principle of universalizability seems to be a very attractive way of pointing out how unfairness and inconsistency lead to immorality. So, for instance, when a thief robs a bank in order to gain riches, Kant can show why the robbery is immoral. If everyone acted on the thief's maxim, there would be no money in the bank to steal, and the thief's goal could not be achieved. But what if the criminal had robbed the bank in order to damage it and put it out of business? If everyone acted that way, then the thief's goal *could* be achieved. So the principle of universalizability fails to condemn the robbery. And yet such an act is surely wrong.

Recall the case of the fanatic that came up when we were discussing the *what if everyone did that?* test. The goals of fanatics are ones that can often be met in a world in which everyone shares their aims. Fanatics need not make exceptions of themselves. The murderous aims of any number of groups could easily be achieved in a world in which everyone supported them. Thus fanatics can be consistent in the relevant sense: their guiding principles could be fulfilled if everyone else were to adopt them.

I think this shows that the principle of universalizability fails to give us an adequate test of fairness, for we can follow its advice while still singling out individuals or groups for discriminatory treatment. There can be consistent Nazis, after all. It doesn't follow that their policies are fair or morally acceptable.

E. KANT ON ABSOLUTE MORAL DUTIES

Kant thought that certain sorts of actions are never permitted. Lying is one of them. In a much-discussed case, that of the inquiring murderer, Kant has us imagine a man bent on killing. This man knocks at your door and asks if you know the location of his intended victim. You do. Should you reveal it? If you do, your information is almost certainly going to lead to murder.

Kant thought you had two decent choices. Ideally, you'd just say nothing. That wouldn't help the murderer, and it wouldn't involve lying. But what if you have to say something? In that case, you have to tell the truth—because you must never lie, under any circumstances.

I think that this is the wrong answer, and the interesting thing is that Kant's own theory does not require him to give it. Kant was so convinced that lying was wrong that he misapplied his own theory.

Kant never provided an argument for the claim that the moral rules that prohibit such things as lying and killing are **absolute** (i.e., never permissibly broken). The closest he came to supplying such an argument was in his belief that moral considerations are more important than anything else. In any conflict between moral duty and other demands—say, those of the law, self-interest, or tradition—morality wins.

Still, it doesn't follow that moral duties are absolute, for even if they always outweigh other kinds of considerations, moral duties might conflict *with other moral duties*. And if they do, they can't all be absolute. Some of them must give way to others.

And can't moral duties conflict with one another? It seems, for instance, that there is a duty to avoid hurting people's feelings, a duty not to start a panic, and a duty to protect innocent people from dangerous attackers. It also seems that fulfilling each of these duties will sometimes require us to lie, and that there is a moral duty not to do so. Perhaps none of these is really a moral duty. Or perhaps, implausibly, we'd never need to lie in order to respect these duties. But it's much more likely that these are real duties, and that they really can conflict with one another. And if that is so, then these duties cannot all be absolute.

This does not spell disaster for Kant. He does not need to defend the existence of absolute moral duties. His philosophy can, for instance, justify lying to the inquiring murderer. Kant's hatred of lying made him overlook a crucial element of his own view—namely, that the morality of action depends on one's maxim. He just assumed that anyone who lied would be operating with a maxim like this: tell a lie so as to gain some benefit. That maxim is not universalizable. In a world in which everyone did this, no one could trust the words of others, and people would be unable to obtain any of the goals they were trying to achieve through lying.

But Kant's maxim is not the only one you could have in such a situation. A maxim is a principle that you give yourself. No one forces it on you. When confronted with a potential killer, I might adopt this maxim: *say whatever I need to say in order to prevent the murder of an innocent person*. That maxim is universalizable. The goal I am aiming for—to save an innocent person's life—could be achieved if everyone acted this way.

For Kant, we can't determine whether an act is right or wrong until we know its maxim. And for any given action, there are countless maxims that might support it. After all, we make up our own maxims, and mine may be very different from yours. It follows that there is only one way for Kant to absolutely ban a type of action. And that is to be sure in advance that, of all the hundreds or thousands of maxims that might support an action, *none* of them is universalizable. It is hard to see how we could ever know that.

As a result, it is much harder than Kant thought to defend the existence of absolute moral duties. And in this particular case, that is all to the good, since it opens up the possibility that it is sometimes acceptable to lie—for instance, to the inquiring murderer. Of course, if Kant is right, then we would have to have a universalizable maxim that permits this. But nothing Kant ever said should make us think that this is impossible. Contrary to Kant's personal view, we don't have to regard all (or perhaps any) moral duties as absolute.

F. THE PRINCIPLE OF HUMANITY

In the course of his work, Kant identified a number of different candidates for the role of ultimate moral principle. Although the principle of universalizability clearly emphasizes the moral importance of fairness, another of Kant's formulations directs our attention to the respect and dignity that serve as the basis of morality. This formulation is widely known as the **principle of humanity**:

> Always treat a human being (yourself included) as an end, and never as a mere means.

To understand this principle, we need to get clear about three things: humanity, ends, and means.

When Kant spoke of *humanity*, he wasn't thinking necessarily of *Homo sapiens*. Rather, he was referring to all rational and autonomous beings, no matter their species. Perhaps there are aliens, or some nonhuman animals, who are rational and autonomous. If so, then they count as human beings for purposes of Kant's principle.

Treating someone *as an end* is treating her with the respect she deserves. Treating someone *as a means* is dealing with her so that she helps you achieve one of your goals. This may be perfectly okay. I do this, for instance, when I hire a plumber to fix a broken water pipe in my kitchen. In an innocent sense, I am using him—he is needed to get me what I want (a functioning sink, in this case). Yet if I greet him at the door, give him any help he asks for, and then pay him as he leaves, I am also treating him with respect, and so, in Kantian terms, I am also treating him as an end.

But what if, while the plumber is checking the leak, I remove a wrench from his tool kit and whack him over the head with it? He's out cold—excellent. I then snugly fit his head into the space where the pipe has corroded, thus plugging the leak. While he's unconscious, I rush off to the hardware store and buy a cheap bit of PVC pipe. The plumber wakes up just as I am returning from the store. I scold him for falling asleep on the job and usher him out the door with a curt good riddance. Then I proceed to fix the leak myself, saving a hefty fee.

What has happened in this ridiculous scenario is that I've used the plumber literally as a thing, as a piece of pipe. He might as well have been an inanimate object. I failed to treat him in a way that recognized any of his distinctively human features. That's why I have treated him as a *mere means*.

Although it often happens that people do treat one another both as an end and as a means, one can't treat people both as an end and as a *mere* means. Treating someone as an end implies a degree of respect that is absent when treating someone as a mere means.

Most of us think that there is something about humanity that lends us dignity and makes us worthy of respect. Most of us also think that human beings are worthy of greater respect than anything else in creation. Humans are more important than monkeys or sharks or daffodils or amoebas. Is this a defensible position, or is it just a self-interested prejudice?

Kant had an answer. He claimed that we are each rational and autonomous, and that these traits are what justify our special moral status. These two powers make us worthy of respect. Being rational involves using our reason to tell us how to achieve our goals and to determine whether we can pursue them in a morally acceptable way. It takes a lot of brainpower to be able to formulate your goals, to imagine a world where everyone pursues them as you do, and then to ask about the consistency of your actions. Humans are the only beings on earth who can engage in such complex reasoning.

Being autonomous literally means being a self-legislator. Autonomous people are those who decide for themselves which principles are going to govern their life. You are an autonomous person. You possess the ultimate responsibility for the choices you make, the goals you aim for, and the manner in which you pursue them. You are not a slave to your passions; you can resist temptation, check your animal urges, and decide for yourself whether to indulge them. You are not forced to act as you do, but are free to choose your own path.

Kant thought that our rationality and autonomy made each of us literally priceless. Despite the work of actuaries, and juries in wrongful death suits, you can't really put a dollar figure on a human life. The assumption that we are infinitely valuable explains the agony we feel at the death of a loved one. If we had to choose between the destruction of the most beautiful art object in the world and the killing of a human being, we should choose the former. No matter how valuable the object, the value of a human life exceeds it by an infinite amount.

Kant argues that rationality and autonomy support the dignity of each human being, and that everyone is owed a level of respect because of these traits. This makes excellent sense of a number of deeply held moral beliefs. Here are the most important of them.

1. It explains, in the first place, the immorality of a fanatic's actions. Such people don't regard human life as infinitely precious, but rather treat their despised opponents as mere obstacles to the achievement of their goals. The principle of humanity forbids such behavior, even when it is consistently undertaken, and thus allows us to address the most severe problem facing the principle of universalizability.

2. The importance of autonomy explains why slavery and rape are always immoral. Slavery treats the oppressed without regard for their own goals and hopes. Rape is treating another human being solely as a source of one's own gratification, as if the victim had no legitimate say in the matter. These are the most extreme examples of duress and coercion. They are immoral because of their complete denial of the victim's autonomy. As such, these crimes are perhaps the clearest cases of treating other people as mere means.

3. The principle of humanity easily explains our outrage at **paternalism**. To be paternalistic is to assume the rights and privileges of a parent—toward another adult. Paternalism has us limit the liberty of others, for their own good, against their will. It is treating autonomous individuals as children, as if we, and not they, were best suited to making the crucial decisions of their lives.

It is paternalistic, for instance, if a roommate sells your TV set because he is worried about your spending too much time watching *Archer* reruns and too little time on your homework. Or imagine a classmate who thinks that your boyfriend is bad for you, and so writes him a nasty note and forges your signature, hoping that he'll break off your relationship. Anyone who has experienced paternalistic treatment knows how infuriating it can be. And the reason is simple: we are autonomous and rational, and the ability to create our own life plan entitles us to do so. We ought to be free to make a life for ourselves, even if we sometimes make a mess of things.

4. Our autonomy is what justifies the attitude of never abandoning hope in people. The chance that a very hard-hearted man will change his ways may be very small, but the probability never reduces to zero. No matter how badly he was raised, or how badly he has lived his life, he is still autonomous, and so can always choose to better himself. It is usually naïve to expect such a transformation. Changing your character and habits is hardly easy. But the possibility of redemption is always there, and that is only because we are free to set our own course in life.

5. Many people believe in universal human rights. These are moral rights that protect human beings from certain kinds of treatment and entitle each of us to a minimum of respect, just because we are human. Kant can explain why we have such rights. We have them because of our rationality and autonomy. These two traits are the basis for living a meaningful life. If you doubt this, just imagine a life without them. It is a life fit for an insect, or a plant. What endows our life with preciousness is our ability to reason and choose for ourselves how we are going to live it. Every person is rational and autonomous to some degree, and every person needs these powers protected in order to have the sorts of experiences, engage in the kinds of activities, and support the sorts of relationships that make life worth living. Human rights protect these powers at a very fundamental level.

6. Our autonomy is what explains our practices of holding one another accountable for our deeds and misdeeds. Because we are not robots, but rather free and rational human beings, we are morally responsible for our choices and actions. We are fit for praise and blame, and that is because our conduct is up to us. We don't blame sharks or falcons for killing their prey; neither do we condemn a wilted orchid or a nasty-smelling ginkgo tree. Plants and animals deserve neither

moral credit nor blame, and this is because their lives are not autonomous ones.

Despite its many attractions, the principle of humanity, with its emphasis on rationality and autonomy, is not trouble-free. In particular, the notion of treating someone as an end is vague, and so the principle is difficult to apply. Unlike the three-step process used to apply the principle of universalizability, there is no straightforward test that tells us how to apply the principle of humanity. It tells us to treat humanity as an end—in other words, with the respect that people deserve. It's sometimes crystal clear whether the principle is being honored. No one doubts, for instance, that the principle is violated by treating a plumber as a piece of pipe or by enslaving someone. But the vagueness of the notion of treating someone as an end often makes it difficult to know whether our actions are morally acceptable. Do we respect celebrities by telling the truth about their private lives—even when this is damaging to their reputations? Is it disrespectful to enemy soldiers to set landmines at our borders? Are we failing to give due respect to famine victims if we spend money on a new computer rather than donating it to an aid agency?

We can't know the answer to these questions without a better understanding of what it is to treat someone as an end. Without a more precise test of when we are respecting others and treating them as they deserve (i.e., as their rationality and autonomy demand), the principle of humanity fails to give us the guidance that we expect from an ultimate moral principle.

G. CONCLUSION

Kant's ethical views are rich and suggestive. They are extremely important in their own right, but it can also be quite helpful to contrast them with the consequentialist outlook that is so popular in political and economic circles these days. Whereas utilitarians think of benevolence as the central moral virtue, Kant thought that fairness occupied that role. Kant regarded many of the basic moral rules as absolute, and so insisted that it was never acceptable to break them—even if breaking them led to better results. He also rejected the exclusive emphasis on the future and an action's results in determining what is right and wrong, and instead asked us to focus on a person's maxim, since rational consistency, rather than the utilitarian's emphasis on maximizing happiness, is the test of morality.

Many of the shortcomings of consequentialism are nicely handled by the Kantian theory. But consequentialists are pleased to return the favor: the Kantian theory isn't without its own problems, and many of those are neatly addressed by consequentialism. Let's now have a look at another important contender, the social contract theory, whose defenders hope to secure many of the benefits of these two ethical outlooks, while escaping the problems that confront them.

ESSENTIAL CONCEPTS

Absolute: moral rules are absolute if and only if it is never permitted to break them.

Categorical imperative: a command of reason that requires us to act in a certain way regardless of whether doing so will get us anything we care about.

Golden Rule: the moral principle that requires you to treat others as you would like to be treated.

Hypothetical imperative: a command of reason that tells us to do whatever is needed in order to get what we care about.

Maxim: a principle of action you give yourself when you are about to do something.

Paternalism: the practice of assuming the rights and privileges of a parent toward another adult.

Principle of humanity: always treat a human being (yourself included) as an end, and never as a mere means.

Principle of universalizability: an act is morally acceptable if, and only if, its maxim is universalizable.

Universalizable: a maxim is universalizable if and only if the goal that it specifies can be achieved in a world in which everyone is acting on that maxim.

DISCUSSION QUESTIONS

1. Explain the difference between the Golden Rule and the *what if everyone did that?* test. What problems arise for each? Do you think that they can be remedied?

2. What is a maxim, and what does it mean for a maxim to be *universalizable*? Why does the principle of universalizability fail to be a good test of the morality of our actions?

3. According to Kant, it is always irrational to act immorally. What reasons does he give for thinking this? Do you agree with him?

4. What is the difference between hypothetical and categorical imperatives? Why did Kant think that morality consists of categorical imperatives?

5. Why does the existence of fanatics pose a challenge to Kant's moral theory? How do you think that the Kantian should respond to this challenge?

6. What is the relationship between Kant's principle of universalizability and the principle of humanity? Do the two ever give conflicting advice? If so, which do you think is a better guide to our moral obligations?

7. If rationality and autonomy explain why we are as important as we are, how (if at all) can we explain the moral importance of infants and nonhuman animals?

READING

The Good Will and the Categorical Imperative
Immanuel Kant

Immanuel Kant (1724–1804) was the greatest German philosopher who ever lived. In this excerpt from his *Groundwork of the Metaphysics of Morals*, Kant introduces two key elements of his moral philosophy. According to Kant, the first of these, the *good will*, is the only thing possessed of unconditional value: it is valuable in its own right, in every possible circumstance. The good will is the steady commitment to do our duty for its own sake. Our actions possess moral worth if, but only if, they are prompted by the good will.

The second important element is the *categorical imperative*, Kant's term for a requirement of reason that applies to us regardless of what we care about. Moral requirements are categorical imperatives—we must, for instance, sometimes give help to others in need, even if we don't want to, and even if such help gets us nothing that we care about. Kant believed that moral action is rational action. Each of us has a compelling reason to obey morality, even when doing so only frustrates our deepest desires.

Kant here sets out two tests for morally acceptable action. The first says that actions are morally acceptable only when the principles that inspire them can be acted on by everyone consistently. The second requires us to treat humanity always as an end in itself, and never as a mere means. Kant realizes that such formulations are somewhat abstract, and so here offers us a number of illustrations that are meant to help us understand and apply them.

THE GOOD WILL

It is impossible to think of anything at all in the world, or indeed even beyond it, that could be considered good without limitation except a good will. Understanding, wit, judgment and the like, whatever such *talents* of mind may be called, or courage, resolution, and perseverance in one's plans, as qualities of *temperament*, are undoubtedly good and desirable for many purposes, but they can also be extremely evil and harmful if the will which is to make use of these gifts of nature, and whose distinctive constitution is therefore called *character*, is not good. It is the same with *gifts of fortune*. Power, riches, honor, even health and that complete well-being and satisfaction with one's condition called *happiness*, produce boldness and thereby often arrogance as well unless a good will is present which corrects the influence of these on the mind and, in so doing, also corrects the whole principle of action and brings it into conformity with universal ends—not to mention that an impartial rational spectator can take no delight in seeing the uninterrupted prosperity of a being graced with no feature of a pure and good will, so that a good will seems to constitute the indispensable condition even of worthiness to be happy.

Some qualities are even conducive to this good will itself and can make its work much easier; despite this, however, they have no inner unconditional

From *Groundwork of the Metaphysics of Morals*, trans. Mary Gregor (New York: Cambridge University Press, 1998), pp. 7–11, 25–26, 30–32, 36–39.

worth but always presuppose a good will, which limits the esteem one otherwise rightly has for them and does not permit their being taken as absolutely good. Moderation in affects and passions, self-control, and calm reflection are not only good for all sorts of purposes but even seem to constitute a part of the *inner* worth of a person; but they lack much that would be required to declare them good without limitation (however unconditionally they were praised by the ancients); for, without the basic principles of a good will they can become extremely evil, and the coolness of a scoundrel makes him not only far more dangerous but also immediately more abominable in our eyes than we would have taken him to be without it.

A good will is not good because of what it effects or accomplishes, because of its fitness to attain some proposed end, but only because of its volition, that is, it is good in itself and, regarded for itself, is to be valued incomparably higher than all that could merely be brought about by it in favor of some inclination and indeed, if you will, of the sum of all inclinations. Even if, by a special disfavor of fortune or by the niggardly provision of a stepmotherly nature, this will should wholly lack the capacity to carry out its purpose—if with its greatest efforts it should yet achieve nothing and only the good will were left (not, of course, as a mere wish but as the summoning of all means insofar as they are in our control)—then, like a jewel, it would still shine by itself, as something that has its full worth in itself. Usefulness or fruitlessness can neither add anything to this worth nor take anything away from it. Its usefulness would be, as it were, only the setting to enable us to handle it more conveniently in ordinary commerce or to attract to it the attention of those who are not yet expert enough, but not to recommend it to experts or to determine its worth. . . .

We have, then, to explicate the concept of a will that is to be esteemed in itself and that is good apart from any further purpose, as it already dwells in natural sound understanding and needs not so much to be taught as only to be clarified—this concept that always takes first place in estimating the total worth of our actions and constitutes the condition of all the rest. In order to do so, we shall set before ourselves the concept of duty, which contains that of a good will though under certain subjective limitations and hindrances, which, however, far from concealing it and making it unrecognizable, rather bring it out by contrast and make it shine forth all the more brightly.

I here pass over all actions that are already recognized as contrary to duty, even though they may be useful for this or that purpose; for in their case the question whether they might have been done *from duty* never arises, since they even conflict with it. I also set aside actions that are really in conformity with duty but to which human beings have *no inclination* immediately and which they still perform because they are impelled to do so through another inclination. For in this case it is easy to distinguish whether an action in conformity with duty is done *from duty* or from a self-seeking purpose. It is much more difficult to note this distinction when an action conforms with duty and the subject has, besides, an *immediate* inclination to it. For example, it certainly conforms with duty that a shopkeeper not overcharge an inexperienced customer, and where there is a good deal of trade a prudent merchant does not overcharge but keeps a fixed general price for everyone, so that a child can buy from him as well as everyone else. People are thus served *honestly*; but this is not nearly enough for us to believe that the merchant acted in this way from duty and basic principles of honesty; his advantage required it; it cannot be assumed here that he had, besides, an immediate inclination toward his customers, so as from love, as it were, to give no one preference over another in the matter of price. Thus the action was done neither from duty nor from immediate inclination but merely for purposes of self-interest.

On the other hand, to preserve one's life is a duty, and besides everyone has an immediate inclination to do so. But on this account the often anxious care that most people take of it still has no inner worth and their maxim has no moral content. They look after their lives *in conformity with duty* but not *from duty*. On the other hand, if adversity and hopeless grief have quite taken away the taste for life; if an unfortunate man, strong of soul and more indignant about his fate than despondent or dejected, wishes for death and yet preserves his life without loving it, not from inclination or fear but from duty, then his maxim has moral content.

To be beneficent where one can is a duty, and besides there are many souls so sympathetically attuned that, without any other motive of vanity or self-interest they find an inner satisfaction in spreading joy around them and can take delight in the satisfaction of others so far as it is their own work. But I assert that in such a case an action of this kind, however it may conform with duty and however amiable it may be, has nevertheless no true moral worth but is on the same footing with other inclinations, for example, the inclination to honor, which, if it fortunately lights upon what is in fact in the common interest and in conformity with duty and hence honorable, deserves praise and encouragement but not esteem; for the maxim lacks moral content, namely that of doing such actions not from inclination but *from duty.* Suppose, then, that the mind of this philanthropist were overclouded by his own grief, which extinguished all sympathy with the fate of others, and that while he still had the means to benefit others in distress their troubles did not move him because he had enough to do with his own; and suppose that now, when no longer incited to it by any inclination, he nevertheless tears himself out of this deadly insensibility and does the action without any inclination, simply from duty; then the action first has its genuine moral worth. Still further: if nature had put little sympathy in the heart of this or that man; if (in other respects an honest man) he is by temperament cold and indifferent to the sufferings of others, perhaps because he himself is provided with the special gift of patience and endurance toward his own sufferings and presupposes the same in every other or even requires it; if nature had not properly fashioned such a man (who would in truth not be its worst product) for a philanthropist, would he not still find within himself a source from which to give himself a far higher worth than what a mere good-natured temperament might have? By all means! It is just then that the worth of character comes out, which is moral and incomparably the highest, namely that he is beneficent not from inclination but from duty. . . .

Thus the moral worth of an action does not lie in the effect expected from it and so too does not lie in any principle of action that needs to borrow its motive from this expected effect. For, all these effects (agreeableness of one's condition, indeed even promotion of others' happiness) could have been also brought about by other causes, so that there would have been no need, for this, of the will of a rational being, in which, however, the highest and unconditional good alone can be found. Hence nothing other than the *representation of the law* in itself, *which can of course occur only in a rational being,* insofar as it and not the hoped-for effect is the determining ground of the will, can constitute the preeminent good we call moral, which is already present in the person himself who acts in accordance with this representation and need not wait upon the effect of his action.

But what kind of law can that be, the representation of which must determine the will, even without regard for the effect expected from it, in order for the will to be called good absolutely and without limitation? Since I have deprived the will of every impulse that could arise for it from obeying some law, nothing is left but the conformity of actions as such with universal law, which alone is to serve the will as its principle, that is, *I ought never to act except in such a way that I could also will that my maxim should become a universal law.* Here mere conformity to law as such, without having as its basis some law determined for certain actions, is what serves the will as its principle, and must so serve it, if duty is not to be everywhere an empty delusion and a chimerical concept. Common human reason also agrees completely with this in its practical appraisals and always has this principle before its eyes. Let the question be, for example: may I, when hard pressed, make a promise with the intention not to keep it? Here I easily distinguish two significations the question can have: whether it is prudent or whether it is in conformity with duty to make a false promise. The first can undoubtedly often be the case. I see very well that it is not enough to get out of a present difficulty by means of this subterfuge but that I must reflect carefully whether this lie may later give rise to much greater inconvenience for me than that from which I now extricate myself;

and since, with all my supposed *cunning*, the results cannot be so easily foreseen but that once confidence in me is lost this could be far more prejudicial to me than all the troubles I now think to avoid, I must reflect whether the matter might be handled *more prudently* by proceeding on a general maxim and making it a habit to promise nothing except with the intention of keeping it. But it is soon clear to me that such a maxim will still be based only on results feared. To be truthful from duty, however, is something entirely different from being truthful from anxiety about detrimental results, since in the first case the concept of the action in itself already contains a law for me while in the second I must first look about elsewhere to see what effects on me might be combined with it. For, if I deviate from the principle of duty this is quite certainly evil; but if I am unfaithful to my maxim of prudence this can sometimes be very advantageous to me, although it is certainly safer to abide by it. However, to inform myself in the shortest and yet infallible way about the answer to this problem, whether a lying promise is in conformity with duty, I ask myself: would I indeed be content that my maxim (to get myself out of difficulties by a false promise) should hold as a universal law (for myself as well as for others)? and could I indeed say to myself that every one may make a false promise when he finds himself in a difficulty he can get out of in no other way? Then I soon become aware that I could indeed will the lie, but by no means a universal law to lie; for in accordance with such a law there would properly be no promises at all, since it would be futile to avow my will with regard to my future actions to others who would not believe this avowal or, if they rashly did so, would pay me back in like coin; and thus my maxim, as soon as it were made a universal law, would have to destroy itself.

I do not, therefore, need any penetrating acuteness to see what I have to do in order that my volition be morally good. Inexperienced in the course of the world, incapable of being prepared for whatever might come to pass in it, I ask myself only: can you also will that your maxim become a universal law? If not, then it is to be repudiated, and that not because of a disadvantage to you or even to others

forthcoming from it but because it cannot fit as a principle into a possible giving of universal law, for which lawgiving reason, however, forces from me immediate respect. Although I do not yet *see* what this respect is based upon (this the philosopher may investigate), I at least understand this much: that it is an estimation of a worth that far outweighs any worth of what is recommended by inclination, and that the necessity of my action from *pure* respect for the practical law is what constitutes duty, to which every other motive must give way because it is the condition of a will good *in itself*, the worth of which surpasses all else. . . .

THE CATEGORICAL IMPERATIVE

Now, all imperatives command either *hypothetically* or *categorically*. The former represent the practical necessity of a possible action as a means to achieving something else that one wills (or that it is at least possible for one to will). The categorical imperative would be that which represented an action as objectively necessary of itself, without reference to another end.

Since every practical law represents a possible action as good and thus as necessary for a subject practically determinable by reason, all imperatives are formulae for the determination of action that is necessary in accordance with the principle of a will which is good in some way. Now, if the action would be good merely as a means *to something else* the imperative is *hypothetical*; if the action is represented as *in itself* good, hence as necessary in a will in itself conforming to reason, as its principle, *then it is categorical*. . . .

There is one imperative that, without being based upon and having as its condition any other purpose to be attained by certain conduct, commands this conduct immediately. This imperative is categorical. It has to do not with the matter of the action and what is to result from it, but with the form and the principle from which the action itself follows; and the essential good in the action consists in the disposition, let the result be what it may. This imperative may be called the imperative of morality. . . .

When I think of a *hypothetical* imperative in general I do not know beforehand what it will contain;

I do not know this until I am given the condition. But when I think of a *categorical* imperative I know at once what it contains. For, since the imperative contains, beyond the law, only the necessity that the maxim[1] be in conformity with this law, while the law contains no condition to which it would be limited, nothing is left with which the maxim of action is to conform but the universality of a law as such; and this conformity alone is what the imperative properly represents as necessary.

There is, therefore, only a single categorical imperative and it is this: *act only in accordance with that maxim through which you can at the same time will that it become a universal law.*

Now, if all imperatives of duty can be derived from this single imperative as from their principle, then, even though we leave it undecided whether what is called duty is not as such an empty concept, we shall at least be able to show what we think by it and what the concept wants to say.

Since the universality of law in accordance with which effects take place constitutes what is properly called *nature* in the most general sense (as regards its form)—that is, the existence of things insofar as it is determined in accordance with universal laws—the universal imperative of duty can also go as follows: *act as if the maxim of your action were to become by your will a* universal law of nature.

We shall now enumerate a few duties in accordance with the usual division of them into duties to ourselves and to other human beings and into perfect and imperfect duties.[2]

(1) Someone feels sick of life because of a series of troubles that has grown to the point of despair, but is still so far in possession of his reason that he can ask himself whether it would not be contrary to his duty to himself to take his own life. Now he inquires whether the maxim of his action could indeed become a universal law of nature. His maxim, however, is: from self-love I make it my principle to shorten my life when its longer duration threatens more troubles than it promises agreeableness. The only further question is whether this principle of self-love could become a universal law of nature. It is then seen at once that a nature whose law it would be to destroy life itself by means of the same feeling whose destination is to impel toward the furtherance of life would contradict itself and would therefore not subsist as nature; thus that maxim could not possibly be a law of nature and, accordingly, altogether opposes the supreme principle of all duty.

(2) Another finds himself urged by need to borrow money. He well knows that he will not be able to repay it but sees also that nothing will be lent him unless he promises firmly to repay it within a determinate time. He would like to make such a promise, but he still has enough conscience to ask himself: is it not forbidden and contrary to duty to help oneself out of need in such a way? Supposing that he still decided to do so, his maxim of action would go as follows: when I believe myself to be in need of money I shall borrow money and promise to repay it, even though I know that this will never happen. Now this principle of self-love or personal advantage is perhaps quite consistent with my whole future welfare, but the question now is whether it is right. I therefore turn the demand of self-love into a universal law and put the question as follows: how would it be if my maxim became a universal law? I then see at once that it could never hold as a universal law of nature and be consistent with itself, but must necessarily contradict itself. For, the universality of a law that everyone, when he believes himself to be in need, could promise whatever he pleases with the intention of not keeping it would make the promise and the end one might have in it itself

---

1. A maxim is the subjective principle of acting, and must be distinguished from the objective principle, namely the practical law. The former contains the practical rule determined by reason conformably with the conditions of the subject (often his ignorance or also his inclinations), and is therefore the principle in accordance with which the subject acts; but the law is the objective principle valid for every rational being, and the principle in accordance with which he ought to act, i.e., an imperative.

2. I understand here by a perfect duty one that admits no exception in favor of inclination.

impossible, since no one would believe what was promised him but would laugh at all such expressions as vain pretenses.

(3) A third finds in himself a talent that by means of some cultivation could make him a human being useful for all sorts of purposes. However, he finds himself in comfortable circumstances and prefers to give himself up to pleasure than to trouble himself with enlarging and improving his fortunate natural predispositions. But he still asks himself whether his maxim of neglecting his natural gifts, besides being consistent with his propensity to amusement, is also consistent with what one calls duty. He now sees that a nature could indeed always subsist with such a universal law, although (as with the South Sea Islanders) the human being should let his talents rust and be concerned with devoting his life merely to idleness, amusement, procreation—in a word, to enjoyment; only he cannot possibly will that this become a universal law or be put in us as such by means of natural instinct. For, as a rational being he necessarily wills that all the capacities in him be developed, since they serve him and are given to him for all sorts of possible purposes.

(4) Yet a *fourth*, for whom things are going well while he sees that others (whom he could very well help) have to contend with great hardships, thinks: what is it to me? let each be as happy as heaven wills or as he can make himself; I shall take nothing from him nor even envy him; only I do not care to contribute anything to his welfare or to his assistance in need! Now, if such a way of thinking were to become a universal law the human race could admittedly very well subsist, no doubt even better than when everyone prates about sympathy and benevolence and even exerts himself to practice them occasionally, but on the other hand also cheats where he can, sells the right of human beings or otherwise infringes upon it. But although it is possible that a universal law of nature could very well subsist in accordance with such a maxim, it is still impossible to will that such a principle hold everywhere as a law of nature. For, a will that decided this would conflict with itself, since many cases could occur in which one would need the love and sympathy of others and in which, by such a law of nature arisen from his own will, he would rob himself of all hope of the assistance he wishes for himself. . . .

If we now attend to ourselves in any transgression of a duty, we find that we do not really will that our maxim should become a universal law, since that is impossible for us, but that the opposite of our maxim should instead remain a universal law, only we take the liberty of making an *exception* to it for ourselves (or just for this once) to the advantage of our inclination. Consequently, if we weighed all cases from one and the same point of view, namely that of reason, we would find a contradiction in our own will, namely that a certain principle be objectively necessary as a universal law and yet subjectively not hold universally but allow exceptions. . . .

Suppose there were something the *existence of which in itself* has an absolute worth, something which as *an end in itself* could be a ground of determinate laws; then in it, and in it alone, would lie the ground of a possible categorical imperative, that is, of a practical law.

Now I say that the human being and in general every rational being *exists* as an end in itself, *not merely as a means* to be used by this or that will at its discretion; instead he must in all his actions, whether directed to himself or also to other rational beings, always be regarded *at the same time as an end*. All objects of the inclinations have only a conditional worth; for, if there were not inclinations and the needs based on them, their object would be without worth. But the inclinations themselves, as sources of needs, are so far from having an absolute worth, so as to make one wish to have them, that it must instead be the universal wish of every rational being to be altogether free from them. Thus the worth of any object *to be acquired* by our action is always conditional. Beings the existence of which rests not on our will but on nature, if they are beings without reason, still have only a relative worth, as means, and are therefore called *things*, whereas rational beings are called *persons* because their nature already marks them out as an end in itself, that is, as something that may not be used merely as a means, and hence so far limits all choice (and is an object of respect). These, therefore, are not merely subjective ends, the existence of which as an effect of our action has a worth *for us*, but rather *objective ends*, that is, beings the existence of which is in itself an end, and indeed one such that no other end, to which they would serve *merely* as means, can be put in its place, since without it nothing of *absolute worth* would be found anywhere; but if all worth were conditional and therefore contingent, then no supreme practical principle for reason could be found anywhere.

If, then, there is to be a supreme practical principle and, with respect to the human will, a categorical imperative, it must be one such that, from the representation of what is necessarily an end for everyone because it is an *end in itself*, it constitutes an *objective* principle of the will and thus can serve as a universal practical law. The ground of this principle is: *rational nature exists as an end in itself.* The human being necessarily represents his own existence in this way; so far it is thus a *subjective* principle of human actions. But every other rational being also represents his existence in this way consequent on just the same rational ground that also holds for me; thus it is at the same time an *objective* principle from which, as a supreme practical ground, it must be possible to derive all laws of the will. The practical imperative will therefore be the following: *So act that you use humanity, whether in your own person or in the person of any other, always at the same time as an end, never merely as a means.* We shall see whether this can be carried out.

To keep to the preceding examples:

First, as regards the concept of necessary duty to oneself, someone who has suicide in mind will ask himself whether his action can be consistent with the idea of humanity *as an end in itself*. If he destroys himself in order to escape from a trying condition he makes use of a person *merely as a means* to maintain a tolerable condition up to the end of life. A human being, however, is not a thing and hence not something that can be used *merely* as a means, but must in all his actions always be regarded as an end in itself. I cannot, therefore, dispose of a human being in my own person by maiming, damaging or killing him. (I must here pass over a closer determination of this principle that would prevent any misinterpretation, e.g., as to having limbs amputated in order to preserve myself, or putting my life in danger in order to preserve my life, and so forth; that belongs to morals proper.)

Second, as regards necessary duty to others or duty owed them, he who has it in mind to make a false promise to others sees at once that he wants to make use of another human being *merely as a means*, without the other at the same time containing in himself the end. For, he whom I want to use for my purposes by such a promise cannot possibly agree to my way of behaving toward him, and so himself contain the end of this action. This conflict with the principle of other human beings is seen more distinctly if examples of assaults on the freedom and property of others are brought forward. For then it is obvious that he who transgresses the rights of human beings intends to make use of the person of others merely as means, without taking into consideration that, as rational beings, they are always to be valued at the same time as ends, that is, only as beings who must also be able to contain in themselves the end of the very same action.

Third, with respect to contingent (meritorious) duty to oneself, it is not enough that the action does not conflict with humanity in our person as an end in itself; it must also *harmonize with it*. Now there are in humanity predispositions to greater perfection, which belong to the end of nature with respect to humanity in our subject; to neglect these might admittedly be consistent with the *preservation* of humanity as an end in itself but not with the *furtherance* of this end.

Fourth, concerning meritorious duty to others, the natural end that all human beings have is their own happiness. Now, humanity might indeed subsist if no one contributed to the happiness of others but yet did not intentionally withdraw anything from it; but there is still only a negative and not a positive agreement with *humanity as an end in itself* unless everyone also tries, as far as he can, to further the ends of others. For, the ends of a subject who is an end in itself must as far as possible be also *my* ends, if that representation is to have its *full* effect in me. . . .

Immanuel Kant: The Good Will and the Categorical Imperative

1. Kant claims that a good will is the only thing that can be considered "good without limitation." What does he mean by this? Do you find this claim plausible?

2. Unlike hedonists, Kant believes that happiness is not always good. What reasons does he give for thinking this? Do you agree with him?

3. What is the difference between doing something "in conformity with duty" and doing something "from duty"? Is Kant correct in saying that only actions done *from duty* have moral worth?

4. Kant claims to have discovered a *categorical imperative*, a moral requirement that we have reason to follow regardless of what we happen to desire. Can people have reasons for action that are completely independent of their desires?

5. According to Kant, it is morally permissible to act on a particular principle (or "maxim") only if "you can at the same time will that it become a universal law." Do you think this is a good test of whether an action is morally permissible? Can you think of any immoral actions that would pass this test, or any morally permissible actions that would fail it?

6. Kant later gives another formulation of the categorical imperative: "So act that you use humanity, whether in your own person or in the person of any other, always at the same time as an end, never merely as a means." What does it mean to treat someone as an end? Are we always morally required to treat humans in this way?

CHAPTER 7

Social Contract Theory

The social contract theory, also known as contractarianism, originated as a political theory and only later developed into a theory of morality. It tells us that laws are just if, and only if, they reflect the terms of a social contract that free, equal, and rational people would accept as the basis of a cooperative life together. Its view of morality stems directly from that political ideal: *actions are morally right just because they are permitted by rules that free, equal, and rational people would agree to live by, on the condition that others obey these rules as well.*

A. THE BACKGROUND OF THE SOCIAL CONTRACT THEORY

The political origins of the social contract theory can be traced back to the ancient Greeks. Early in the *Republic*, Plato's brothers tell Socrates that they find the social contract view both appealing and troubling. They challenge Socrates to tell them what is wrong with it. His answer takes up almost the whole of the book, a testament to the power of contractarianism.

Here is the story that Socrates heard. We are all by nature largely, or entirely, self-interested. What we want is power over others, physical security, plenty of money, and sensual pleasure. Our deepest goal is to lord it over everyone else. Who among us wouldn't want the power of the president or the wealth of Bill Gates—or, ideally, both?

This points to an obvious problem. Everyone wants to be at the top of the heap, and only a few can make it there. Further, no one wants to be a patsy, the person who gets stepped on as others climb the ladder of success. We each want to be number one. But we know that the chances of making it are slim, and we want to avoid being trampled as others claw their way to the top. So what do we do?

If we are rational, we will each agree to curb our self-interest and cooperate with one another. We'll do this *conditionally*—that is, on the condition that others do so as well. A complete free-for-all is going to make everyone miserable. If we all stop trying to get the better of each other, and instead agree to seek a little less for ourselves, then we'll all be better off.

That is what reason and morality require of us, according to the social contract theory. Starting with the assumptions that we each are largely motivated by self-interest, and that it is rational to be that way, contractarianism tells us that we each do best for ourselves by agreeing to limit the direct pursuit of self-interest and accept a bargain that gets us a pretty decent life. That everyone gets such a life means that we give up the chance of an absolutely fabulous life. But we also protect ourselves from a really terrible one, a life in which we are in the thick of a cutthroat competition, vulnerable to the attacks of everyone around us. That is a deal worth making. Here's why.

B. THE PRISONER'S DILEMMA

Consider life's basic scenario: There is intense competition for scarce resources. We each want as much of those resources as we can get. Being rational, we each try to get as much as we can, knowing that more for us means less for someone else. Things are going to get very bad, very quickly.

This is what happened when baseball players, Tour de France cyclists, and Olympic weight lifters began to take increasingly dangerous anabolic steroids, in a bid to gain a competitive edge and lucrative championships. This is what happens when a politician starts a smear campaign and his opponent feels the need to ramp up the abuse in order to stand a fighting chance in the race. This is what always happens in turf battles over the spoils of an illegal drug trade.

These cases all share the same essential features. In each, there is mounting competition over a scarce resource, and many are trying their best to increase their share of it. That seems to be rational, and yet, if everyone stopped being so selfish, each person would be better off.

These sorts of situations, in which everyone would be better off by scaling back their pursuit of self-interest, are known as **prisoner's dilemmas**. The name comes from a scenario, introduced by economists, in which two thieves (call them Al and Bob) are caught and sent to separate detention cells. Being rational, Al and Bob previously made a deal with each other: if they get caught, they'll each keep silent, to thwart the police and protect themselves. Now that they have been captured, the police tell each one the same thing: "If you keep your promise to your partner by keeping quiet, and he rats you out, then he's off the hook, and you're looking at a six-year sentence. If *you* break your word and snitch on him, while he remains silent, you're home free, while he spends the next six years in jail. If you both keep quiet, you'll each get two years. But if you both confess, you'll each get four."

The following diagram will help you keep track of the options. Each number represents years in jail. The first number in each pair is Al's prison sentence; the second is Bob's.

Suppose that both criminals know about the various outcomes, and that both have only one concern at this point: to minimize their jail time. If they are both rational, what are they going to do?

You might think that it's impossible to know the answer, since you don't know enough about Al or Bob, their bond with each other, their trustworthiness, and so on, to make an informed guess. But really, there is no doubt that each is going to confess. They are going to break their promise to each other, landing themselves a four-year sentence apiece. That's a far cry from getting off scot-free, and double the two years they'd get if they each kept quiet.

The important point is that remaining silent is the cooperative strategy. Silence here means keeping one's word, honoring the terms of the deal. Confession is a betrayal, breaking one's promise, abandoning a partner.

Al and Bob are going to betray each other. That's certain. They'll do this because they know the odds, because they are self-interested, and because they are rational.

Why will they confess? Because *no matter what his accomplice does, each criminal will be better off by confessing.*

Consider Al's choices. Suppose that

Bob remains silent. Then if Al confesses, Al is home free. If Al keeps his mouth shut, Al gets two years. So if Bob remains silent, Al should confess. That will minimize his jail time. That is what he most wants. So, if Al is rational, he will confess.

Now suppose that

Bob confesses. Then if Al confesses, Al gets four years in jail. Silence gets him six. So if Bob confesses, Al should confess, too.

		Bob	
		Remains Silent (Cooperation)	Confesses (Betrayal)
Al	Remains Silent (Cooperation)	2, 2	6, 0
	Confesses (Betrayal)	0, 6	4, 4

Thus, either way, Al does best for himself by spilling the beans and breaking his promise to Bob. And of course Bob is reasoning in the same way. So they are both going to confess and end up with four years in jail.

The prisoner's dilemma isn't just some interesting thought experiment. It's real life. There are countless cases in which the rational pursuit of self-interest will lead people to refuse to cooperate with one another, even though this leaves everyone much worse off.

C. COOPERATION AND THE STATE OF NATURE

So why don't competitors cooperate? The answer is simple: because it is so risky. The criminals in the prisoner's dilemma could cooperate. But that would mean taking a chance at a six-year sentence and betting everything on your partner's good faith. Unilaterally keeping silent, refusing the use of steroids, forsaking negative campaigning or violence—these are strategies for suckers. Those who adopt them may be virtuous, but they are the ones who will be left behind, rotting in jail, economically struggling, off the Olympic podium, or the victim of an enemy's gunshot. If enough people are willing to do what it takes to ensure that they get ahead, then you've either got to join in the competition or be the sacrificial lamb.

Englishman Thomas Hobbes (1588–1679), the founder of modern contractarianism, was especially concerned with one sort of prisoner's dilemma. He invited the readers of his magnum opus, *Leviathan*, to imagine a situation in which there was no government, no central authority, no group with the exclusive power to enforce its will on others. He called this situation the **state of nature**. And he thought it was the worst place you could ever be.

In his words, the state of nature is a "war of all against all, in which the life of man is solitary, poor, nasty, brutish and short." People ruthlessly compete with one another for whatever goods are available. Cooperation is a sham, and trust is nonexistent. Hobbes himself lived through a state of nature—the English Civil War—and thus had first-hand knowledge of its miseries. If you've ever read *The Lord of the Flies*, you have an idea of what Hobbes is talking about. As I write this, I can turn on my television and see pictures of states of nature from around the world—in parts of Syria, Iraq, and Sudan. The scenes are terrible.

The Hobbesian state of nature is a prisoner's dilemma. By seeking to maximize self-interest, everyone is going to be worse off. In such dire circumstances, everyone is competing to gain as much as he can, at the expense of others. With so much at stake, an all-out competition is bound to be very bad for almost everyone. No one is so smart or strong or well-connected as to be free from danger.

There is an escape from the state of nature, and the exit strategy is the same for all prisoner's dilemmas. We need two things: beneficial rules that require cooperation and punish betrayal, and an enforcer who ensures that these rules are obeyed.

The rules are the terms of the social contract. They require us to give up the freedom to attack and to kill others, to cheat them and lie to them, to beat and threaten them and take from them whatever we can. In exchange for giving up these freedoms (and others), we gain the many advantages of cooperation. It is rational to give up some of your freedom, provided that you stand a good chance of getting something even better in return. The peace and stability of a well-ordered society is worth it. That is the promise of the social contract.

But you need more than good rules of cooperation to escape from a prisoner's dilemma. You also need a way to make sure the rules are kept.

The state of nature comes to an end when people agree with one another to give up their unlimited freedoms and to cooperate on terms that are beneficial to all. The problem with agreements, though, is that they can be broken.

And without a strong incentive to keep their promises, people in prisoner's dilemmas are going to break them. Just think of Al and Bob in our original example.

What's needed is a powerful person (or group) whose threats give everyone excellent reason to keep their word. The central power doesn't have to be a government—it could be a mob boss, who threatens Al and Bob with death if they were to break their silence. It could be the International Olympic Committee, with the power to suspend or disqualify athletes who test positive for illegal substances. But in the most general case, in which we are faced with anarchy and are trying to escape from utter lawlessness, what we need is a government to enforce basic rules of cooperation. Without a central government, the situation will spiral downhill into a battleground of competing factions and individuals, warlords and gang bosses, each vying for as much power and wealth as possible. A war of all against all won't be far behind.

D. THE ADVANTAGES OF CONTRACTARIANISM

Contractarianism has many advantages. One of these is that contractarianism explains and justifies the content of the basic moral rules. On the contractarian account, the moral rules are ones that are meant to govern social cooperation. When trying to figure out which standards are genuinely moral ones, contractarians ask us to imagine a group of free, equal, and rational people who are seeking terms of cooperation that each could reasonably accept. The rules they select to govern their lives together are the moral rules. These will closely match the central moral rules we have long taken for granted.

John Rawls (1921–2002), the most famous twentieth-century social contract theorist, had a specific test for determining the rules that the ideal social contractors would support. In his *Theory of Justice* (1971), by most accounts the most important work of political philosophy written in the last century, Rawls has us envision

contractors behind a **veil of ignorance**. This is an imaginary device that erases all knowledge of your distinctive traits. Those behind the veil know that they have certain basic human needs and wants, but they know nothing of their religious identity, their ethnicity, their social or economic status, their sex, or their moral character. The idea is to put everyone on an equal footing, so that the choices they make are completely fair.

When placed behind a veil of ignorance, or in some other condition of equality and freedom, what social rules will rational people select? These will almost certainly include prohibitions of killing, rape, battery, theft, and fraud, and rules that require keeping one's word, returning what one owes, and being respectful of others. Contractarianism thus easily accounts for why the central moral rules are what they are—rational, self-interested people, free of coercion, would agree to obey them, so long as others are willing to obey them, too.

The rules of cooperation must be designed to benefit everyone, not just a few. Otherwise, only a few would rationally endorse them, while the rest would rationally ignore them. This allows the contractarian to explain why slavery and racial and sexual discrimination are so deeply immoral. Biased policies undermine the primary point of morality—to create fair terms of cooperation that could earn the backing of everyone. Even if oppressed people identify with the interests of their oppressors, and staunchly defend the system of discrimination, that does not make it right. The correct moral rules are those that free people would endorse for their *mutual* benefit—not for the benefit of one group over another.

A second benefit of contractarianism is that it can explain the objectivity of morality. Moral rules, on this view, are objective. Anyone can be mistaken about what morality requires. Personal opinion isn't the final authority in ethics. Neither is the law or conventional wisdom—whole societies can be mistaken about what is right and wrong, because they may be mistaken about what free, equal, and rational people would include in their ideal social code.

Thus contractarians have an answer to a perennial challenge: if morality isn't a human creation, where did it come from? If contractarianism is correct, morality does not come from God. Nor does it come from human opinion. Rather, morality is the set of rules that would be agreed to by people who are very like us, only more rational and wholly free, and who are selecting terms of cooperation that will benefit each and every one of them.

Thus contractarians don't have to picture moral rules as eternally true. And they can deny that moral rules are just like the rules of logic or of natural science—other areas where we acknowledge the existence of objective truths. The moral rules are the outcomes of rational choice, tailored to the specifics of human nature and the typical situations that humans find themselves in. This removes the mystery of objective morality. Even if God doesn't exist, there can still be objective values, so long as there are mutually beneficial rules that people would agree to if they were positioned as equals, fully rational and free.

A third benefit of contractarianism is that it explains why it is sometimes acceptable to break the moral rules. Moral rules are designed for cooperative living. But when cooperation collapses, the entire point of morality disappears. When things become so bad that the state of nature approaches, or has been reached, then the ordinary moral rules lose their force.

One way to put this idea is to say that every moral rule has a built-in escape clause: do not kill, cheat, intimidate, and so on, *so long as others are obeying this rule as well*. When those around you are saying one thing and doing another, and cannot be counted on to limit the pursuit of their self-interest, then you are freed of your ordinary moral obligations to them.

The basis of morality is cooperation. And that requires trust. When that trust is gone, you

are effectively in a state of nature. The moral rules don't apply there, because the basic requirement of moral life—that each person be willing to cooperate on fair terms that benefit everyone—is not met.

This explains why you aren't bound to keep promises made at gunpoint, or to be the only taxpayer in a land of tax cheats. It explains why you don't have to wait patiently in line when many others are cutting in, or to obey a curfew or a handgun law if everyone else is violating it. When you can't rely on others, there is no point in making the sacrifices that cooperative living requires. There is no moral duty to play the sucker.

E. THE ROLE OF CONSENT

Most of us believe that we have a moral duty to honor our commitments. And a contract is a commitment—it is a promise given in exchange for some expected benefit. A social contract differs from other contracts only in the extent of the duties it imposes and the benefits it creates. Since we are morally required to keep our promises, we have a duty to honor the terms of the social contract.

But have we actually promised to live up to any social contract? The Pilgrims did, when they paused before the shores of Massachusetts and together signed the Mayflower Compact in 1620. In ancient Athens, free men were brought to the public forum and directly asked to promise obedience to their city—or leave, without penalty. Naturalized citizens in the United States have long been required to pledge allegiance to the nation's laws. But relatively few adults nowadays have done any such thing. It seems, therefore, that we are not really parties to any such contract, and so are not bound to obey its terms.

Contractarianism would be in deep trouble if it claimed that our moral and legal duties applied only to those who agreed to accept them. *But it makes no such claim.* The social contract that fixes our basic moral duties is not one that any of us has *actually* consented to; rather, it is one that we each *would* agree to were we all free and rational and seeking terms of mutually beneficial cooperation. So the fact that we have never signed a social contract or verbally announced our allegiance to one does not undermine the contractarian project.

Contractarianism does not require you to do whatever the existing laws and social customs tell you to do. Those standards are partly a product of ignorance, past deception and fraud, and imperfect political compromise. We are morally required to live up to the standards that free, rational people would accept as the terms of their cooperative living. It's safe to say that no existing set of laws perfectly lines up with those terms.

Thus contractarianism isn't a simple recipe to do whatever your society says. Rather, it provides a way to evaluate society's actual rules, by seeing how close (or how far) they are to the ideal social code that would be adopted if we were freer, more equal, and more rational than we are. If contractarianism is correct, this ideal social code is the moral law.

F. DISAGREEMENT AMONG THE CONTRACTORS

If the social contract theory is correct, then the moral rules are those that free, equal, and rational people would agree to live by. But what happens if such people disagree with one another? For instance, what if these idealized contractors can't reach a deal about the conditions under which a nation should go to war, or about the kind of aid we owe to the very poor? What happens then?

Rawls solved this problem by making every contractor a clone of every other. Behind the veil of ignorance, all of your distinguishing features go away. No one is any different from anyone else. And so there is no reason to expect any disagreement.

But Hobbes and other contractarians won't stand for this. They can't see why I should follow the rules of someone who is so completely unlike me—a person who is not only absolutely rational but also stripped of all knowledge of his social status, his friendships and family situation, his desires, interests, and hopes. Hobbes and his followers insist that the moral rules are those that we, *situated as we are*, would rationally agree to, provided of course that others would agree to live by them as well.

It's not easy to know how to solve this disagreement between contractarians. On the one hand, Rawls's view is likely to be fairer, since any information that could prejudice our choices is kept from us as we select rules to live by. But Hobbes also has a point, in that we want to make it rational, if we can, for everyone to live by the moral rules. Why should I live according to the rules set by some person who isn't at all like the real me? That's a pretty good question.

I'm sure that you've already figured out that I am not able to answer every good ethical question. This is another one I am going to leave for your consideration. Instead, let's return to our original problem: what should we say when the people choosing the social rules disagree with one another?

Perhaps Rawls is right, and there won't be any disagreement. But what if he's wrong? If contractors disagree, then the actions or policies they disagree about are morally neutral. They are neither required nor forbidden. That's because the moral rules are ones that *all* contractors would agree to. If there are some matters that they can't agree on, then these are not covered by the moral rules.

This could be pretty bad. Or it might be just fine. It all depends on where the disagreement arises (if it ever does). If there are only small pockets of disagreement, regarding relatively trivial matters, then this is hardly a problem. But what if contractors can't agree about war policy, about whether executions are just, about how to treat the poorest among us? Then this is really serious, since we do think that morality must weigh in on these issues.

So, how much disagreement will there be? There is no easy way to know. We can provide answers only after we know how to describe the contractors and their position of choice. Will they be clones of one another, situated behind the veil of ignorance? Or will they be aware of their different personalities and life situations? Will they be more or less equally situated, or are some going to have a lot more leverage than others? When we say that they are rational, do we have Kant's conception in mind? Or Hobbes's, according to which rationality amounts to reliably serving your self-interest? Or some other conception?

Answers to these questions will make a big difference in deciding on the specific moral rules that a social contract theory favors. These answers will also determine the amount of agreement we can expect from the contractors. There is no shortcut to discovering these answers. To get them, contractarians must defend their own specific version of the theory against competing versions. That is a major undertaking. Until it is done, we cannot know just what the moral rules are or how much contractual disagreement to expect.

G. CONCLUSION

Contractarianism starts with a very promising idea: morality is essentially a social matter, and it is made up of the rules that we would accept if we were free, equal, and fully rational. The heart of the theory is an ideal social code that serves as the true standard for what is right and wrong.

This theory has a lot going for it, as we've seen. It offers us a procedure for evaluating moral claims, and so offers the promise of being able to justify even our most basic moral views. It has an interesting explanation of the objectivity of morality. It can explain why we are sometimes allowed to break the moral rules. It does not require actual consent to the ideal social rules in order for them to genuinely apply to all people. In cases in which the contractors disagree with one another, the social contract theory ought to insist that actions are morally required only if all contractors agree. Whether this is a problem for the view is a matter left for your further reflection.

ESSENTIAL CONCEPTS

Prisoner's dilemma: a situation in which the pursuit of self-interest by all parties leads to a worse outcome than if each were to compromise.

State of nature: anarchy; a situation in which there was no government, no central authority, no group with the exclusive power to enforce its will on others.

Veil of ignorance: an imaginary device that erases all knowledge of your distinctive traits in preparation for selecting principles of justice or morality.

DISCUSSION QUESTIONS

1. What makes a situation a "prisoner's dilemma"? What is the rational thing to do in a prisoner's dilemma situation?

2. What is the state of nature, and why does Hobbes think that such a condition would be so bad? How does Hobbes think that people would be able to emerge from the state of nature?

3. How do contractarians justify moral rules against such things as slavery and torture? Do you find their justifications of such rules to be compelling?

4. Explain how a contractarian defends the objectivity of ethics. Do you find this defense plausible?

5. Suppose that the existing laws of a society require something that you regard as unjust. Does the social contract theory automatically support the morality of the existing law? Why or why not?

6. Would a group of free, equal, and rational people necessarily all agree on a set of rules to live by? If not, is this a problem for contractarianism?

READING

Leviathan
Thomas Hobbes

Thomas Hobbes (1588–1679) was the most brilliant of the modern social contract theorists. His theory, important in both ethics and political philosophy, views the basic moral rules of society as ones that rational people would adopt in order to protect their own interests. Without obedience to such rules, the situation deteriorates into a "war of all against all, in which the life of man is solitary, poor, nasty, brutish and short."

Hobbes was an ethical egoist—someone who thinks that our fundamental duty is to look after our own interests—as well as a social contract theorist. Many commentators have found a tension in this combination. See for yourself whether Hobbes succeeded in justifying the basic moral rules by reference to self-interest.

Among the many interesting features in this excerpt from Hobbes's classic *Leviathan* is his discussion of the fool. The fool is someone who allows that breaking one's promises is unjust, but who thinks that it may sometimes be rational to do so anyway. Hobbes resists this idea. He wants to show that it is always rational to do one's duty—to live by the laws of cooperation that would be accepted by free and rational people. His overall view is motivated by the thought that moral duties must provide each of us with excellent reasons to obey them, and that these reasons must ultimately stem from self-interest. As a result, Hobbes's discussion casts fascinating light on the perennial question of why we should be moral.

OF THE NATURAL CONDITION OF MANKIND AS CONCERNING THEIR FELICITY AND MISERY

Nature hath made men so equal in the faculties of body and mind as that, though there be found one man sometimes manifestly stronger in body or of quicker mind than another, yet when all is reckoned together the difference between man and man is not so considerable as that one man can thereupon claim to himself any benefit to which another may not pretend as well as he. For as to the strength of body, the weakest has strength enough to kill the strongest, either by secret machination or by confederacy with others that are in the same danger with himself.

And as to the faculties of the mind, setting aside the arts grounded upon words, and especially that skill of proceeding upon general and infallible rules, called science, which very few have and but in few things, as being not a native faculty born with us, nor attained, as prudence, while we look after somewhat else, I find yet a greater equality amongst men than that of strength. For prudence is but experience, which equal time equally bestows on all men in those things they equally apply themselves unto. That which may perhaps make such equality incredible is but a vain conceit of one's own wisdom, which almost all men think they have in a greater degree than the vulgar; that is, than all men but themselves, and a few others, whom by fame, or for concurring with themselves, they approve. For such is the nature of men that howsoever they may acknowledge many others to be more witty, or more eloquent or more learned, yet they will hardly believe there be many so wise as themselves; for they see their own wit at hand, and other men's at a distance. But this proveth rather that men are in that point equal, than unequal. For there is not ordinarily a greater sign of the equal distribution of anything than that every man is contented with his share.

From this equality of ability ariseth equality of hope in the attaining of our ends. And therefore if any two men desire the same thing, which nevertheless they cannot both enjoy, they become enemies; and in the way to their end (which is principally their own conservation, and sometimes their delectation only) endeavour to destroy or subdue one another. And from hence it comes to pass that where an invader hath no more to fear than another man's single power, if one plant, sow, build, or possess a convenient seat, others may probably be expected to come prepared with forces united to dispossess and deprive him, not only of the fruit of his labour, but also of his life or liberty. And the invader again is in the like danger of another.

And from this diffidence of one another, there is no way for any man to secure himself so reasonable as anticipation; that is, by force, or wiles, to master the persons of all men he can so long till he see no other power great enough to endanger him: and this is no more than his own conservation requireth, and is generally allowed. Also, because there be some that, taking pleasure in contemplating their own power in the acts of conquest, which they pursue farther than their security requires, if others, that otherwise would be glad to be at ease within modest bounds, should not by invasion increase their power, they would not be able, long time, by standing only on their defence, to subsist. And by consequence, such augmentation of dominion over men being necessary to a man's conservation, it ought to be allowed him.

Again, men have no pleasure (but on the contrary a great deal of grief) in keeping company where there is no power able to overawe them all. For every man looketh that his companion should value him at the same rate he sets upon himself, and upon all signs of contempt or undervaluing naturally endeavours, as far as he dares (which amongst them that have no common power to keep them in quiet is far enough to make them destroy each other), to extort a greater value from his contemners, by damage; and from others, by the example.

So that in the nature of man, we find three principal causes of quarrel. First, competition; secondly, diffidence; thirdly, glory.

The first maketh men invade for gain; the second, for safety; and the third, for reputation. The first use violence, to make themselves masters of other men's persons, wives, children, and cattle; the second, to defend them; the third, for trifles, as a word, a smile, a different opinion, and any other sign of undervalue, either direct in their persons or by reflection in their kindred, their friends, their nation, their profession, or their name.

Hereby it is manifest that during the time men live without a common power to keep them all in awe, they are in that condition which is called war; and such a war as is of every man against every man. For war consisteth not in battle only, or the act of fighting, but in a tract of time, wherein the will to contend by battle is sufficiently known: and therefore the notion of time is to be considered in the nature of war, as it is in the nature of weather. For as the nature of foul weather lieth not in a shower or two of rain, but in an inclination thereto of many days together: so the nature of war consisteth not in actual fighting, but in the known disposition thereto during all the time there is no assurance to the contrary. All other time is peace.

Whatsoever therefore is consequent to a time of war, where every man is enemy to every man, the same consequent to the time wherein men live without other security than what their own strength and their own invention shall furnish them withal. In such condition there is no place for industry, because the fruit thereof is uncertain: and consequently no culture of the earth; no navigation, nor use of the commodities that may be imported by sea; no commodious building; no instruments of moving and removing such things as require much force; no knowledge of the face of the earth; no account of time; no arts; no letters; no society; and which is worst of all, continual fear, and danger of violent death; and the life of man, solitary, poor, nasty, brutish, and short.

It may seem strange to some man that has not well weighed these things that Nature should thus dissociate and render men apt to invade and destroy one another: and he may therefore, not trusting to this inference, made from the passions, desire perhaps to have the same confirmed by experience. Let him therefore consider with himself: when taking a journey, he arms himself and seeks to go well accompanied; when going to sleep, he locks his doors; when even in his house he locks his chests; and this when he knows there be laws and public officers, armed, to revenge all injuries shall be done him; what opinion he has of his fellow subjects, when he rides armed; of his fellow citizens, when he locks his doors; and of his children, and servants, when he locks his chests. Does he not there as much accuse mankind by his actions as I do by my words? But neither of us accuse man's nature in it. The desires, and other passions of man, are in themselves no sin. No more are the actions that proceed from those passions till they know a law that forbids them; which till laws be made they cannot know, nor can any law be made till they have agreed upon the person that shall make it.

It may peradventure be thought there was never such a time nor condition of war as this; and I believe it was never generally so, over all the world: but there are many places where they live so now. For the savage people in many places of America, except the government of small families, the concord whereof dependeth on natural lust, have no government at all, and live at this day in that brutish manner, as I said before. Howsoever, it may be perceived what manner of life there would be, where there were no common power to fear, by the manner of life which men that have formerly lived under a peaceful government use to degenerate into a civil war.

But though there had never been any time wherein particular men were in a condition of war one against another, yet in all times kings and persons of sovereign authority, because of their independency, are in continual jealousies, and in the state and posture of gladiators, having their weapons pointing, and their eyes fixed on one another; that is, their forts, garrisons, and guns upon the frontiers of their kingdoms, and continual spies upon their neighbours, which is a posture of war. But because they uphold thereby the industry of their subjects, there does not follow from it that misery which accompanies the liberty of particular men.

To this war of every man against every man, this also is consequent; that nothing can be unjust. The notions of right and wrong, justice and injustice, have there no place. Where there is no common power, there is no law; where no law, no injustice. Force and fraud are in war the two cardinal virtues. Justice and injustice are none of the faculties neither of the body nor mind. If they were, they might be in a man that were alone in the world, as well as his senses and passions. They are qualities that relate to men in society, not in solitude. It is consequent also to the same condition that there be no propriety, no dominion, no mine and thine distinct; but only that to be every man's that he can get, and for so long as he can keep it. And thus much for the ill condition which man by mere nature is actually placed in; though with a possibility to come out of it, consisting partly in the passions, partly in his reason.

The passions that incline men to peace are: fear of death; desire of such things as are necessary to commodious living; and a hope by their industry to obtain them. And reason suggesteth convenient articles of peace upon which men may be drawn to agreement. These articles are they which otherwise are called the laws of nature, whereof I shall speak more particularly in the two following chapters.

OF THE FIRST AND SECOND NATURAL LAWS, AND OF CONTRACTS

The right of nature, which writers commonly call *jus naturale*, is the liberty each man hath to use his own power as he will himself for the preservation of his own nature; that is to say, of his own life; and consequently, of doing anything which, in his own judgement and reason, he shall conceive to be the aptest means thereunto.

By liberty is understood, according to the proper signification of the word, the absence of external impediments; which impediments may oft take away part of a man's power to do what he would, but cannot hinder him from using the power left him according as his judgement and reason shall dictate to him.

A law of nature, *lex naturalis*, is a precept, or general rule, found out by reason, by which a man is forbidden to do that which is destructive of his life, or taketh away the means of preserving the same, and to omit that by which he thinketh it may be best preserved.

And because the condition of man. . . is a condition of war of every one against every one, in which case every one is governed by his own reason, and there is nothing he can make use of that may not be a help unto him in preserving his life against his enemies; it followeth that in such a condition every man has a right to every thing, even to one another's body. And therefore, as long as this natural right of every man to every thing endureth, there can be no security to any man, how strong or wise soever he be, of living out the time which nature ordinarily alloweth men to live. And consequently it is a precept, or general rule of reason: that every man ought to endeavour peace, as far as he has hope of obtaining it; and when he cannot obtain it, that he may seek and use all helps and advantages of war. The first branch of which rule containeth the first and fundamental law of nature, which is: to seek peace and follow it. The second, the sum of the right of nature, which is: by all means we can to defend ourselves.

From this fundamental law of nature, by which men are commanded to endeavour peace, is derived this second law: that a man be willing, when others are so too, as far forth as for peace and defence of himself he shall think it necessary, to lay down this right to all things; and be contented with so much liberty against other men as he would allow other men against himself. For as long as every man holdeth this right, of doing anything he liketh; so long are all men in the condition of war. But if other men will not lay down their right, as well as he, then there is no reason for anyone to divest himself of his: for that were to expose himself to prey, which no man is bound to, rather than to dispose himself to peace. This is that law of the gospel: Whatsoever you require that others should do to you, that do ye to them.

Whensoever a man transferreth his right, or renounceth it, it is either in consideration of some right reciprocally transferred to himself, or for some other good he hopeth for thereby. For it is a voluntary act: and of the voluntary acts of every man, the object is some good to himself. And therefore there be some rights which no man can be understood by any words, or other signs, to have abandoned or transferred. As first a man cannot lay down the right of resisting them that assault him by force to take away his life, because he cannot be understood to aim thereby at any good to himself. The same may be said of wounds, and chains, and imprisonment, both because there is no benefit consequent to such patience, as there is to the patience of suffering another to be wounded or imprisoned, as also because a man cannot tell when he seeth men proceed against him by violence whether they intend his death or not. And lastly the motive and end for which this renouncing and transferring of right is introduced is nothing else but the security of a man's person, in his life, and in the means of so preserving life as not to be weary of it. And therefore if a man by words, or other signs, seem to despoil himself of the end for which those signs were intended, he is not to be understood as if he meant it, or that it was his will, but that he was ignorant of how such words and actions were to be interpreted.

The mutual transferring of right is that which men call contract. . . .

Signs of contract are either express or by inference. Express are words spoken with understanding of what they signify: and such words are either of the time present or past; as, I give, I grant, I have given, I have granted, I will that this be yours: or of the future; as, I will give, I will grant, which words of the future are called promise.

Signs by inference are sometimes the consequence of words; sometimes the consequence of silence; sometimes the consequence of actions; sometimes the consequence of forbearing an action: and generally a sign by inference, of any contract, is whatsoever sufficiently argues the will of the contractor.

Words alone, if they be of the time to come, and contain a bare promise, are an insufficient sign of a free gift and therefore not obligatory. For if they be of the time to come, as, tomorrow I will give, they are a sign I have not given yet, and consequently that my right is not transferred, but remaineth till I transfer it by some other act. . . .

If a covenant be made wherein neither of the parties perform presently, but trust one another, in the condition of mere nature (which is a condition of war of every man against every man) upon any reasonable suspicion, it is void: but if there be a common power set over them both, with right and force sufficient to compel performance, it is not void. For he that performeth first has no assurance the other will perform after, because the bonds of words are too weak to bridle men's ambition, avarice, anger, and other passions, without the fear of some coercive power; which in the condition of mere nature, where all men are equal, and judges of the justness of their own fears, cannot possibly be supposed. And therefore he which performeth first does but betray himself to his enemy, contrary to the right he can never abandon of defending his life and means of living.

But in a civil estate, where there is a power set up to constrain those that would otherwise violate their faith, that fear is no more reasonable; and for that cause, he which by the covenant is to perform first is obliged so to do.

OF OTHER LAWS OF NATURE

From that law of nature by which we are obliged to transfer to another such rights as, being retained, hinder the peace of mankind, there followeth a third; which is this: that men perform their covenants made; without which covenants are in vain, and but empty words; and the right of all men to all things remaining, we are still in the condition of war.

And in this law of nature consisteth the fountain and original of justice. For where no covenant hath preceded, there hath no right been transferred, and every man has right to everything and consequently, no action can be unjust. But when a covenant is made, then to break it is unjust and the definition of injustice is no other than the not performance of covenant. And whatsoever is not unjust is just.

But because covenants of mutual trust, where there is a fear of not performance on either part (as hath been said in the former chapter), are invalid, though the original of justice be the making of covenants, yet injustice actually there can be none till the cause of such fear be taken away; which, while men are in the natural condition of war, cannot be done. Therefore before the names of just and unjust

can have place, there must be some coercive power to compel men equally to the performance of their covenants, by the terror of some punishment greater than the benefit they expect by the breach of their covenant, and to make good that propriety which by mutual contract men acquire in recompense of the universal right they abandon: and such power there is none before the erection of a Commonwealth. And this is also to be gathered out of the ordinary definition of justice in the Schools, for they say that justice is the constant will of giving to every man his own. And therefore where there is no own, that is, no propriety, there is no injustice; and where there is no coercive power erected, that is, where there is no Commonwealth, there is no propriety, all men having right to all things: therefore where there is no Commonwealth, there nothing is unjust. So that the nature of justice consisteth in keeping of valid covenants, but the validity of covenants begins not but with the constitution of a civil power sufficient to compel men to keep them: and then it is also that propriety begins.

The fool hath said in his heart, there is no such thing as justice, and sometimes also with his tongue, seriously alleging that every man's conservation and contentment being committed to his own care, there could be no reason why every man might not do what he thought conduced thereunto: and therefore also to make, or not make; keep, or not keep, covenants was not against reason when it conduced to one's benefit. He does not therein deny that there be covenants; and that they are sometimes broken, sometimes kept; and that such breach of them may be called injustice, and the observance of them justice: but he questioneth whether injustice, taking away the fear of God (for the same fool hath said in his heart there is no God), may not sometimes stand with that reason which dictateth to every man his own good; and particularly then, when it conduceth to such a benefit as shall put a man in a condition to neglect not only the dispraise and revilings, but also the power of other men. The kingdom of God is gotten by violence: but what if it could be gotten by unjust violence? Were it against reason so to get it, when it is impossible to receive hurt by it? And if it be not against reason, it is not against justice: or else justice is not to be approved for good. From such reasoning as this, successful wickedness hath obtained the name of virtue: and some that in all other things have disallowed the violation of faith, yet have allowed it when it is for the getting of a kingdom. And the heathen that believed that Saturn was deposed by his son Jupiter believed nevertheless the same Jupiter to be the avenger of injustice, somewhat like to a piece of law in Coke's Commentaries on Littleton; where he says if the right heir of the crown be attainted of treason, yet the crown shall descend to him, and *eo instante* the attainder be void: from which instances a man will be very prone to infer that when the heir apparent of a kingdom shall kill him that is in possession, though his father, you may call it injustice, or by what other name you will; yet it can never be against reason, seeing all the voluntary actions of men tend to the benefit of themselves; and those actions are most reasonable that conduce most to their ends. This specious reasoning is nevertheless false.

For the question is not of promises mutual, where there is no security of performance on either side, as when there is no civil power erected over the parties promising; for such promises are no covenants: but either where one of the parties has performed already, or where there is a power to make him perform, there is the question whether it be against reason; that is, against the benefit of the other to perform, or not. And I say it is not against reason. For the manifestation whereof we are to consider; first, that when a man doth a thing, which notwithstanding anything can be foreseen and reckoned on tendeth to his own destruction, howsoever some accident, which he could not expect, arriving may turn it to his benefit; yet such events do not make it reasonably or wisely done. Secondly, that in a condition of war, wherein every man to every man, for want of a common power to keep them all in awe, is an enemy, there is no man can hope by his own strength, or wit, to defend himself from destruction without the help of confederates; where every one expects the same defence by the confederation that any one else does: and therefore he which declares he thinks it reason to deceive those that help him can in reason expect no other means of safety than what can be had from his own single power.

He, therefore, that breaketh his covenant, and consequently declareth that he thinks he may with reason do so, cannot be received into any society that unite themselves for peace and defence but by the error of them that receive him; nor when he is received be retained in it without seeing the danger of their error; which errors a man cannot reasonably reckon upon as the means of his security: and therefore if he be left, or cast out of society, he perisheth; and if he live in society, it is by the errors of other men, which he could not foresee nor reckon upon, and consequently against the reason of his preservation; and so, as all men that contribute not to his destruction forbear him only out of ignorance of what is good for themselves.

As for the instance of gaining the secure and perpetual felicity of heaven by any way, it is frivolous; there being but one way imaginable, and that is not breaking, but keeping of covenant.

And for the other instance of attaining sovereignty by rebellion; it is manifest that, though the event follow, yet because it cannot reasonably be expected, but rather the contrary, and because by gaining it so, others are taught to gain the same in like manner, the attempt thereof is against reason. Justice therefore, that is to say, keeping of covenant, is a rule of reason by which we are forbidden to do anything destructive to our life, and consequently a law of nature.

Thomas Hobbes: Leviathan

1. At the beginning of the selection, Hobbes argues that all humans are fundamentally equal. In what ways does Hobbes claim that we are equal? Do you agree with him?

2. Hobbes claims that without a government to enforce law and order, we would find ourselves in a "war . . . of every man against every man." What reasons does he give for believing this? Do you think he is right?

3. According to Hobbes, if there were no governments to establish laws, nothing would be just or unjust. Does this seem plausible? Would some actions be unjust, even if there were no authority around to punish those who committed them?

4. Hobbes says, "Of the voluntary acts of every man, the object is some good to himself." Is Hobbes correct in thinking that self-interest is what motivates every voluntary action?

5. Hobbes claims that it is always unjust to violate our covenants (or contracts), provided that there is a government with the power to enforce them. He also claims that any action that does not violate a covenant is just. Can you think of any counterexamples to either of these claims?

6. The "fool" claims that it is rational to unjustly break one's covenants in cases where doing so promotes one's self-interest. How does Hobbes respond to this claim? Do you find Hobbes's replies convincing?

CHAPTER 8

Natural Law

Perhaps the key to morality lies in understanding our place in the natural order of things. Many have thought so.

In trying to discover what makes for a good human life, we might take a cue from the rest of the animal kingdom and ask about why their lives go well, when they do. It seems that there is a common answer: animals live good lives when their nature is fulfilled, and bad lives when it isn't. A racehorse, by nature, is built for speed. Chameleons naturally blend in with their background. When fillies break a leg, or chameleons cannot camouflage themselves, their lives go poorly.

In each of these cases, nature is dictating the terms of appraisal. The things *in* nature *have* a nature. Such things are bad when they are unnatural, and good to the extent that they fulfill their nature. Perhaps we can say the same thing about human beings.

A. THE THEORY AND ITS ATTRACTIONS

That is the guiding thought of the **natural law theory**. By its lights, good human beings are those who fulfill their true nature; bad human beings are those who don't. The moral law is the natural law—the law that requires us to act in accordance with our nature. (As we'll see, this is a different kind of natural law from the one that physicists use to describe the workings of molecules or galaxies.) At its most basic, natural law theory tells us that *actions are right just because they are natural, and wrong just because they are unnatural. And people are good or bad to the extent that they fulfill their true nature—the more they fulfill their true nature, the better they are.*

The natural law theory promises to solve some very serious problems in ethics. Four of these are especially important.

1. *Natural law theory promises to explain how morality could possibly be objective, that is, how moral standards depend on something other than human opinion.*

According to this theory, human nature can serve as the objective standard of morality. We do right when our acts express human nature, and do wrong when they violate it. Since individuals and entire societies can be mistaken about what our true nature is, they can be badly off target about what morality asks of us.

Many natural law theorists are theists, who claim that our nature was given to us by God. Indeed, the most brilliant and influential exponent of natural law theory, St. Thomas Aquinas (1225–1275), melded Aristotelian and Christian views to argue that we are morally bound to fulfill our nature precisely because God endowed us with it. But that is not an essential element of the theory. What is crucial is that human nature is meant to serve as the ultimate moral standard, regardless of whether our nature has arisen from divine origins or in some other way. If this theory is correct, then so long as there is such a thing as human nature, there is an objective source of morality.

2. *Natural law theory easily explains why morality is specially suited for human beings, and not for anything else in the natural world.*

Almost everyone agrees that a distinctive human feature is our sophisticated reasoning abilities.

A few other animals may be able to reason in basic ways, but no species on earth can approach our ability to assess various ways of life, critically analyze the merits of actions and policies, and then govern our behavior on the basis of our reflections. This capacity for rational thought also seems to be the cornerstone of morality. **Moral agents**—those who bear responsibility for their actions, and who are fit for praise or blame—are those who can control their behavior through reasoning. That's why we don't hold animals (or trees or automobiles) morally responsible for the harms they sometimes cause. Only human beings have the sort of nature that enables them to be moral agents. Natural law theory can thus explain why moral duties apply only to human beings (or, if there are any, to other life forms who share our rational powers).

3. *Natural law theory has a clear account of the origins of morality.*

The theory tells us that morality is only as old as humanity itself, that morality dates to the earliest days of humankind. But that isn't because morality depends on human opinion, as so many people believe. Rather, it is because morality depends on human nature. No humans, no human nature. No human nature, no morality.

4. *Natural law theory may solve one of the hardest problems in ethics: how to gain moral knowledge.*

According to natural law theory, moral knowledge requires two things: we must know what our human nature is, and know whether various actions fulfill it. Knowledge of human nature may be quite difficult to get—that depends on how we conceive of human nature, which we will consider shortly. In principle, though, we should be able to investigate the matter and come up with some well-informed views. Equipped with this knowledge, we can then look carefully at individuals to see whether their actions line up with human nature.

Suppose, for instance, that we perform a vast study of human infants, across many different cultures, and discover that they are gentle and nonviolent. Many have thought that this sort of empirical evidence clinches the case for thinking that these traits are part of human nature. If we then see people acting aggressively and violently, we have all the evidence we need to convict them of immorality. That's because they would be acting in conflict with their true nature.

So, on the natural law view, gaining moral knowledge need not be mysterious. Armed solely with descriptions of a person's behavior, and knowledge of our human nature, we *can* determine whether actions are moral, by seeing whether they fulfill our nature.

B. THREE CONCEPTIONS OF HUMAN NATURE

We often approve of actions by declaring them to be perfectly natural, or we excuse someone's harmful conduct by saying that it was the natural thing to do under the circumstances. We also condemn certain actions as unnatural or say of an especially awful act that it was a crime against nature. This all makes excellent sense, on the assumption that natural law theory is true.

In order to apply the natural law theory to real moral problems, we need a sharp understanding of human nature, for it is human nature that, on this theory, will determine the standards of morality. Human nature is what makes us human. It is the set of features that is essential to being human, so that if we were to lose these features, we would also lose our humanity. Natural law theorists are committed to the idea that there is a human essence, a set of traits that define us as human beings.

What is the nature of human nature? Here are three familiar—and problematic—answers.

The first possibility is that we are animals by nature, and so to act according to our nature is just to behave as other animals do. Other animals need protection against predators and enough food to eat, and this explains why it is morally acceptable for us to defend ourselves against attackers and to grow food and feed ourselves. That certainly sounds plausible. But looking to other animals for moral guidance is actually quite a poor idea. After all, some animals kill their own young; others eat their own young; still others brutalize the weaker members of their own species. That doesn't make it right for us to do any of these things.

So the fact that we share many traits, needs, and interests with other animals is not going to unlock the puzzle of determining our human nature—at least if that nature is supposed to also provide moral standards that we must live by. We need to look elsewhere for an understanding of human nature that might be morally relevant.

The second possibility is that human nature is the set of traits that we have innately. **Innate** traits are ones we have from birth. They are natural in the sense of being inborn, natural as opposed to being learned, or acquired from parents and society. On this line of thinking, our true nature is the one we are born with; traits we acquire through socialization are artificial, and stain the purity of our earliest days. In principle, we can use scientific methods to discover what is innately human, and so solve the challenge of gaining moral knowledge.

If Jean-Jacques Rousseau (1712–1778) was right, we are innately angelic. Before society corrupts us, our noble nature shines through. We are by nature pleasant, cooperative, and considerate. If our nature holds the key to morality, then morality is largely as we think it is. It requires us to be kind, cooperative, and attentive to the needs of others.

That would be a comfort. But what if Thomas Hobbes (1588–1679) had it right? He thought that we are innately selfish, competitive, and distrustful. We are born that way and, for the most part, stay that way. If the natural is the innate, and if we are required to act on our true nature, then the Hobbesian view is going to force us to abandon many of our conventional ethical beliefs.

The view that the natural is what is innate is widely held. This explains why so many people think that studies focused on infants will unlock the key to human nature. The thought is that society is bound to change our natural state, and so we gain the deepest insight into human nature by discovering what we are like before society changes us in so many ways.

Yet if natural law theory is correct, and if the natural is the very same thing as the innate, then we need to resolve the nature/nurture debate before we can know what is right and wrong. And that seems mistaken. We are *very* confident that morality is not a counsel of selfishness, mistrust, and competition, even if we are uncertain about whether such traits are innate. We can be very sure that killing people because of their skin color is immoral, even if we aren't sure whether we have an innate tendency to harm people who don't look like us.

This raises a general point: *the ultimate origins of our impulses are irrelevant to the morality of our actions.* Rape and robbery are immoral, no matter whether the impulse to commit these crimes is innate or acquired. Cheerfully comforting the sick is a good thing, even if we weren't born with a desire to offer such help. Since the morality of our actions and our character traits does not depend on whether they are innate or acquired, natural law theorists must look elsewhere for an understanding of human nature.

A third conception of human nature says that our nature is whatever traits we all share. These universal human features would make up the essence of humanity. Such a view lets us scientifically determine our human nature. The data wouldn't always be easy to come by. But with a lot of effort, we could discover our human nature just by observing the features that all humans have in common.

There are two problems with such a view. First, there may be no universal human traits. And second, even if there are, they may not provide good moral guidance.

It may seem silly to deny that there are any universal human traits. Doesn't everyone want to have enough food and water to remain alive? Don't all adults have a sex drive? Aren't we all capable, to one degree or another, of complex thinking about our future? Yet some people want to die, not to live; others are indifferent to the attractions of sex; still others are so mentally impaired as to be unable to think at all about their future. For just about any trait (perhaps every trait) that is said to be part of human nature, we can find exceptions that undermine the rule.

Natural law theorists have a reply to this, which is best appreciated by considering an example. Return to the case of nonhuman animals and think about their nature. For instance, it is part of a buck's nature to be alert to predators, to have four legs, to grow antlers, and to be fawn-colored. Still, there are bucks with only three legs. A few fail to grow antlers; others are deaf to predators; still others are albinos. We might say of such specimens that they aren't really bucks, not fully bucks, or not all that a buck should be.

If that sounds right, then we might adopt the following strategy. Perhaps human nature, like that of nonhuman animals, is determined not by what *every* member of the species shares, but only by what *most* members share. Bucks can have a nature, even if some bucks fail to perfectly live up to it. The same goes for human beings.

This strategy won't work. There is the difficult problem of setting a threshold. Just how many humans need to have a trait before it qualifies as part of human nature? But leave that aside. The real problem is this: the fact that most humans have a certain trait is morally irrelevant.

Suppose, for instance, that most of us are selfish and mean. On this line of thinking, being selfish and mean would then be part of human nature. That would make such behavior morally right, on the natural law view. But that's awfully difficult to accept.

Even if everyone, or most of us, were cruel and malicious, that would not make cruelty and malice morally good. Even if people were usually or typically nasty and petty, these traits would still be vices, not virtues. The fact that many, most, or all people behave a certain way or have certain character traits is not enough to show that such behaviors and traits are morally good.

C. NATURAL PURPOSES

If human nature is not a matter of the (innate) traits that all or most of us have, then what is it? The answer given by most natural law theorists is this: human nature is what we are designed to be and to do. It is some function of ours, some purpose that we are meant to serve, some end that we were designed for.

It may seem that this conception of human nature places us squarely outside the realm of science and in the domain of religion. How could science tell us what our purpose is? Doesn't talk of our being designed for something imply the existence of an Intelligent Designer?

In fact many natural law theorists, following Thomas Aquinas's lead, have made just these assumptions and have developed their views within the context of one religious tradition or another. According to these views, God is our Intelligent Designer. When God created us, He assigned us a specific set of purposes. These are what make up our human nature. Since God is all-good, frustrating God's purpose is immoral. That's what we do when we act unnaturally. That's why it is wrong to act unnaturally.

There is a lot to say about such a view, but most of it has already been said in our earlier discussion (Chapter 1.E) of the divine command theory. On the present account, we must act naturally because that is the way we respect God's plans for us, which are at the heart of morality. Though this isn't quite the same thing as making God's *commands* the basis of morality, it is close enough to have inherited most of the strengths and weaknesses of the divine command theory. Rather than revisit that topic, let's consider a secular interpretation of natural purposes.

The challenge is to make sense of the idea that we have been designed to serve some purpose, without having to invoke an intelligent designer. Strictly speaking, of course, nature has no designs for us. Nature is not an intelligent being with intentions and plans. Still, it *can* make sense to speak of something's natural function or purpose. The mechanisms of evolution and natural selection, rather than God, can serve as the source of our natural purposes.

For instance, nature designed our brains to enable us to think, our liver to detoxify our blood, and our pancreas to regulate glucose levels. We can say what mitochondria are for, what the heart and kidneys are meant to do. In each case, there is a purpose that these organs serve, even if no one assigned them this purpose.

But that sort of talk doesn't easily translate to human lives. What is a human being *for*? Does the question even make sense?

To answer this question, we need to understand the idea of a natural purpose. Two basic secular accounts might offer some insight. Call the first account the *Efficiency Model*, and the second the *Fitness Model*.

Consider the Efficiency Model. Sticking with the example of a heart, we can say that pumping blood is its natural purpose, because nothing pumps blood as well as a heart. Hearts have a certain structure that enables them to pump blood more efficiently than anything else in the body. That is why the purpose of a heart is to pump blood.

Human beings can have a function or a purpose, then, if we are more efficient than anything else when it comes to certain tasks. Well, we are. But there are so many of them. For instance, we are better than anything else at designing puzzles and writing essays. But on this model, natural law theory cannot be correct, given its claim that unnatural action is immoral, for that would mean that we act immorally whenever we are bad at puzzle design or essay writing. We are also far better at building weapons than any other animal, and far more talented at using instruments of torture. But if acting naturally is always morally acceptable, then these actions, if they really are among our natural purposes, are beyond reproach. Something has gone wrong.

If the Efficiency Model is correct—if human nature is given by our natural purposes, and these purposes are whatever we are best able to accomplish—then natural law theory must fail.

There are too many such purposes, and many have nothing moral about them. Perhaps the Fitness Model will do better.

By this account, our organs have the purposes they do because it is extremely *adaptive* for them to serve these roles. The natural purpose of the heart, brain, liver, and lungs is to do what enhances **fitness**: roughly, our success at survival and reproduction. We are able to survive, and pass on our genes to our offspring, only because these organs function as well as they do. Nature has designed hearts and kidneys and brains (etc.) to improve our chances of survival. This is their natural purpose; it is ours, too. We are meant to survive and to transmit our genes to the next generation. That is what a human life is *for*.

Since our natural purposes are survival and procreation, we can see why so many natural law theorists have thought suicide immoral and have condemned birth control and homosexual activity. We also have a ready explanation of why courage, endurance, and fortitude are true virtues—those who possess them are (in the relevant sense) fitter than those who don't.

Suppose that the natural law theory is true. And suppose that we fulfill our human nature just when we fulfill our natural purposes. Two things follow:

1. Acting naturally—fulfilling our natural purposes—is always moral.
2. Acting unnaturally—frustrating our natural purposes—is always immoral.

But if the Fitness Model is correct, then both claims are false.

To see why claim 1 is false, recall that natural actions are those in which we use our mind and body to satisfy the purposes they were designed for. In the Fitness Model, these purposes are survival and reproduction. So natural actions are those that increase the chances of our survival and reproduction. But men can increase the chances of passing on their genes by raping as many women as they can. That is about as immoral as anything I can think of. And survival? Consider the words of Primo Levi, an Auschwitz prisoner: "the worst—that is, the fittest—survived. The best all died."[1] Sometimes those best schooled in violence and treachery are the ones likeliest to live another day. If we understand natural purposes as the Fitness Model advises, then claim 1 is false.

Claim 2 is also false. Not every act that frustrates a natural purpose is immoral. Nature has engineered our ears to be capable of hearing—the better to detect predators, to listen to the advice of our allies, to hear the threats posed by our attackers. But there is nothing immoral about wearing a set of headphones that block out noise. We have eyes so that we can see. But there is nothing wrong with crossing your eyes to make a joke, or closing them to shut out an unwanted sight.

It is worth noting that these examples can be successful even if it is God, and not nature alone, that has endowed us with these various purposes. Suppose that God made eyes to see, ears to hear. Still, isn't it morally acceptable to put on blindfolds, or wear headphones? Despite being "unnatural," these actions are perfectly acceptable.

What this shows is that the Fitness Model is as vulnerable as the Efficiency Model. Neither gives us a solid understanding of what human nature is that supports the natural law view that acting naturally is moral and that acting unnaturally is immoral. Until we are given a better method for determining our nature, the natural law theory is in trouble.

The weakness of the various understandings of human nature allows us to see why a classic moral argument fails. That argument goes like this:

The Natural Law Argument

1. If an act is unnatural, then it is immoral.
2. Suicide, contraception, and homosexual activity are unnatural.
3. Therefore suicide, contraception, and homosexual activity are immoral.

---

1. Primo Levi, *The Drowned and the Saved* (New York: Knopf, 1986), p. 82.

The first premise is false on all of the interpretations we have so far considered. Whether unnatural actions spring from acquired traits rather than innate ones; whether they are rare or unusual rather than typical or even universal; whether they frustrate nature's purposes rather than conform to them; still, such actions can be morally acceptable.

This does not prove that suicide, contraception, and homosexual activity are morally okay. What it shows, however, is that this popular argument is highly suspect, and it will certainly fail unless we have a better understanding of human nature to rely on.

D. THE DOCTRINE OF DOUBLE EFFECT

Natural law theories have always included supplemental principles to help guide our behavior. One of these—the **doctrine of double effect (DDE)**—has been extremely influential in moral philosophy. It is important in its own right, and also because of the role it plays in many contemporary discussions of ethical issues. The DDE refers to two relevant effects that actions can have: those that we intend to bring about, and those that we foresee but do not aim for. This principle says the following:

> Provided that your goal is worthwhile, you are sometimes permitted to act in ways that foreseeably cause certain types of harm, though you must never intend to cause such harms.

The DDE does not say that it is always wrong to intentionally harm others. It allows, for instance, that harmful punishment is sometimes acceptable. The DDE simply tells us that *some* harms may never be aimed for, even though those harms may be permitted as side effects of one's actions (i.e., as "collateral damage"). This list of such harms can differ from theorist to theorist, but there is at least one that they all agree on: one may never intentionally kill (or otherwise harm) an innocent human being.

There are times in life when, regrettably, we will harm someone no matter what we do.

Such situations can be extremely challenging, and just the moments when we look to moral philosophy for guidance. One such guide is the principle of utility (see Chapter 5), which tells us to minimize harm. In a wide variety of cases, this is exactly the right advice. But in others, it seems deeply problematic, and the DDE is often enlisted to explain why that's so.

We could minimize harm if we were secretly to abduct a small number of healthy people, anesthetize them, and cut them up to distribute their vital organs to those who would otherwise die from organ failure. We could minimize misery by "culling" the population of those whose lives are wretchedly unhappy, with little prospect of improvement—even if they didn't want to die. We could dramatically reduce terrorism if we adopted a policy of reliably executing a terrorist's child or spouse in response. But these ways of minimizing harm are deeply offensive.

The DDE can explain why such acts are wrong—in each case, they involve intending to harm an innocent person. Though the offending actions are each done in order to bring about some greater good—the reduction of misery—that does not seem to make those actions morally acceptable. The ends, no matter how good, do not always justify the means. Many believe that certain means are *never* to be utilized, even if employing them will help us minimize harm. The DDE makes this thought concrete by claiming that if the means—the actions one undertakes in the service of a larger goal—involve intending to harm an innocent person, then those actions are immoral. This enables the defender of the DDE to argue, for instance, that terrorist acts that target innocent civilians are always wrong. It delivers the same verdict when it comes to active euthanasia (see Chapter 15); since doctors in such cases are intending the death of their innocent patients, such killing is immoral, even though it is done at the request of the patient and undertaken with the aim of relieving the patient's suffering.

There is a difficulty with the DDE, and it must be solved before we can rely on it with confidence. The difficulty is that we lack a clear basis for distinguishing between intention and foresight. Without clarity on this point, the DDE will either fail to provide guidance about the morality of actions or will give us results that seem deeply mistaken.

Consider this challenge. Those who secretly abduct and carve up innocent people to distribute their organs could say that they intend only to save many innocent lives. They would be delighted if their innocent victims were (miraculously) to remain alive after the operation. Therefore, they *don't* intend to kill their victims. They merely foresee their death. Thus the DDE does not condemn their actions.

It is hard to imagine someone saying this with a straight face. But explaining precisely what is wrong with such a claim is not easy. It requires us to sharply define intention. Further, this definition must clearly distinguish intention from foresight, and also help us to see why intending harm is so much worse than foreseeing it. Can this be done? Have a look at these attempts:

(A) You intend to do X = You want X to occur as a result of your action.

But the surgeon carving up the kidnapped victims may not want them to die. He may want only to save the lives of the many patients who need these organs. So according to (A), the surgeon does not intend to kill the abducted patients. But he surely does, and that makes (A) implausible.

(B) You intend to do X = X is part of your plan of action.

Suppose there is a runaway trolley heading toward five innocent people. The only way to stop the train is by pushing a huge bystander (also innocent) onto the tracks at the last minute. His bulk will stop the train—though he will surely die as a result. Here we save five at the cost of one. But it seems a horrible thing to do. Yet if I were to push this guy, I could deny that his death was part of my plan of action. My plan was limited, let's say, to pushing this man and to stopping the train. I'd be pleased if the man were to escape with only bruises. According to (B), I didn't intend to kill the man. But I did. So (B) is problematic.

> (C) You intend to do X = You would regret it if X didn't occur as a result of your action.

Consider the last trolley case again. It seems clear that I intentionally killed the man I pushed to the tracks. But I would *not* regret it if he survived. Therefore, by (C), I did not intend his death. Again, something has gone wrong.

> (D) You intend to do X = X results from your actions in a nonaccidental way.

The problem here is that all merely foreseen results will now become results that we intend to produce. Consider another trolley case: the runaway trolley is speeding toward five innocents, but I can divert the trolley onto another track. Unfortunately, there is (you guessed it) one innocent person on the other track, and he won't be able to escape if the trolley heads his way. If I do divert the trolley, this man will die, and his death will be no accident. So, by (D), I have intended to kill him. But I haven't; I have foreseen that he will die, but I did not intend his death. So (D) is mistaken.

> (E) You intend to do X = You must cause X if you are to achieve your goals.

In the initial trolley case, it is false that the huge bystander's death must occur if I am to achieve my goals. All that *must* occur is that he stop the train with his body. And so, with (E), I do not intend his death. And so the DDE does not condemn my action. But I surely did intend his death, and my action is surely condemnable.

These aren't the only possibilities for defining what it is to intend to do something, but it's been a very difficult task for defenders of the DDE to provide a definition of intention that manages to track the moral distinctions that we feel so confident about. So if you are a fan of the DDE, here is your task: clarify the distinction between intended and merely foreseen results and do so in a way that shows why some intentional harms, just by virtue of being intended, are morally worse than harms that are foreseen. Perhaps it can be done. But it won't be easy.

E. CONCLUSION

The deep appeal of the natural law theory is its promise to base morality on something clear and unmysterious: nature and its workings. Moral laws, on this account, are just natural laws, though ones that regulate human beings rather than planets, molecules, or gravitational forces. Natural law theory promises many advantages. It promises to explain how morality could possibly be objective. It explains why morality is especially suited to human beings, rather than to other animate beings or inanimate objects. It has a clear account of the origins of morality. And it promises a blueprint for how to gain moral knowledge.

But as we have seen, it is difficult to try to glean recommendations for how we ought to act from descriptions of how nature actually operates. And that shouldn't be too surprising. Natural laws describe and predict how things will behave. They summarize the actual behavior of things, and, unless they are statistical laws (of the sort that assign a probability to outcomes, rather than a certainty), they cannot be broken.

Moral laws are different in every respect. They can be broken, and often are. They are not meant to describe how we actually behave, but rather to serve as ideals that we ought to aim for. Nor are they designed to predict our actions, since we so often fall short of meeting the standards they set.

Nature can define the limit of our possibilities. Our nature does not allow us to leap tall buildings in a single bound or to hold our breath for hours at a time. On the assumption that morality does not demand the impossible of us, nature can, in this way, set the outer bounds of what morality can require. But it can do no more. It cannot, in particular, tell us what we *are* required to do. Nor can it tell us what we are forbidden from trying to achieve. Nature has, at best, only a limited role to play in moral theory.

ESSENTIAL CONCEPTS

Doctrine of double effect: the principle that says that if your goal is worthwhile, you are sometimes permitted to act in ways that foreseeably cause certain types of harm, though you must never intend to cause such harms.

Fitness: a being's success at survival and reproduction.

Innate: traits that we have from birth.

Moral agents: those who bear responsibility for their actions, and who are fit for praise or blame, because they can control their behavior through reasoning.

Natural law theory: the view that actions are right just because they are natural and wrong just because they are unnatural. And people are good or bad to the extent that they fulfill their true nature—the more they fulfill their true nature, the better they are.

DISCUSSION QUESTIONS

1. Many people think of *human nature* as consisting of innate traits that all humans share. Is this conception of human nature a suitable basis for morality? Why or why not?

2. Suppose that most animals behaved in a certain way. Would that provide evidence that it is natural for us to follow their lead? If so, what implications would this have for natural law theory?

3. Do human lives have a purpose? Does knowing the purpose of human lives help us to determine what is morally required?

4. Is there a single correct definition of *human nature*? If not, is this a problem for the natural law theory?

5. How are moral laws different from the laws of physics or chemistry? Do these differences undermine the natural law theory?

READING

Natural Law

Thomas Aquinas

This is a short excerpt from St. Thomas Aquinas's magnum opus, *Summa Theologica*, which has served as a central basis of Roman Catholic theology since Aquinas wrote it over seven hundred years ago. Here Aquinas offers some of the essentials of his understanding of natural law. The text is difficult for contemporary readers but repays careful study. In it, Aquinas develops his conception of natural law by considering a series of objections to various aspects of it, then offering three sorts of reply: first, one that cites a biblical text in support of his position; second, a general reply that sets the objection in context; and third, a specific reply to each of the objections he considers.

In this selection Aquinas develops his views on natural law by first asking (and answering) the question of whether there is an unchanging, eternal law. He answers affirmatively, arguing that God (whose existence is presupposed throughout this selection) is himself unchanging and eternal, and that since God governs the entire universe by means of various principles (he calls these "dictates of practical reason"), these laws themselves are eternal and unchanging. The natural law is a subset of the eternal laws and is therefore itself eternal and in some respects unchanging. Aquinas divides the natural law into first principles—the fundamental ones that are taken as self-evident axioms and are entirely unchanging—and secondary ones, which might sometimes be difficult to discern and in rare cases admit of change.

Aquinas argues that everyone has God-given, innate knowledge of the basic principles of natural law, though our understanding may be clouded by various things. He then argues that virtuous acts are those prescribed by the natural law. He claims that we are naturally inclined to act in accordance with reason; acting in accordance with reason is always virtuous; and so acting naturally is always virtuous. And acting unnaturally—as, he claims, people do when having intercourse with others of the same sex—is invariably immoral. Aquinas then considers whether natural law might be different for those in different societies or for those of different temperaments. He argues that its general principles are universally binding on all human beings at all times, but allows that certain secondary principles might subtly differ depending on circumstances.

WHETHER THERE IS AN ETERNAL LAW?

Objection 1: It would seem that there is no eternal law. Because every law is imposed on someone. But there was not someone from eternity on whom a law could be imposed: since God alone was from eternity. Therefore no law is eternal.

Objection 2: Further, promulgation is essential to law. But promulgation could not be from eternity: because there was no one to whom it could be promulgated from eternity. Therefore no law can be eternal.

On the contrary, Augustine says (De Lib. Arb. i, 6): "That Law which is the Supreme Reason cannot be understood to be otherwise than unchangeable and eternal."

I answer that a law is nothing else but a dictate of practical reason emanating from the ruler who governs a perfect community. Now it is evident, granted that the world is ruled by Divine Providence . . . that the whole community of the universe is governed by Divine Reason. Wherefore the very Idea of the government of things in God the Ruler of the universe,

Summa Theologica, First Part of the Second Part, Question 91, Articles 1 and 2; Question 94, Articles 2–6. Benziger Brothers edition, 1947. Translated by Fathers of the English Dominican Province.

has the nature of a law. And since the Divine Reason's conception of things is not subject to time but is eternal, according to Prov. 8:23, therefore it is that this kind of law must be called eternal.

Reply to Objection 1: Those things that are not in themselves, exist with God, inasmuch as they are foreknown and preordained by Him, according to Rm. 4:17: "Who calls those things that are not, as those that are." Accordingly the eternal concept of the Divine law bears the character of an eternal law, in so far as it is ordained by God to the government of things foreknown by Him.

Reply to Objection 2: Promulgation is made by word of mouth or in writing; and in both ways the eternal law is promulgated: because both the Divine Word and the writing of the Book of Life are eternal. But the promulgation cannot be from eternity on the part of the creature that hears or reads.

WHETHER THERE IS IN US A NATURAL LAW?

Objection 1: It would seem that there is no natural law in us. Because man is governed sufficiently by the eternal law: for Augustine says (De Lib. Arb. i) that "the eternal law is that by which it is right that all things should be most orderly." But nature does not abound in superfluities as neither does she fail in necessaries. Therefore no law is natural to man.

Objection 2: Further, by the law man is directed, in his acts, to the end. But the directing of human acts to their end is not a function of nature, as is the case in irrational creatures, which act for an end solely by their natural appetite; whereas man acts for an end by his reason and will. Therefore no law is natural to man.

Objection 3: Further, the more a man is free, the less is he under the law. But man is freer than all the animals, on account of his free-will, with which he is endowed above all other animals. Since therefore other animals are not subject to a natural law, neither is man subject to a natural law.

On the contrary, A gloss on Rm. 2:14: "When the Gentiles, who have not the law, do by nature those things that are of the law," comments as follows: "Although they have no written law, yet they have the natural law, whereby each one knows, and is conscious of, what is good and what is evil."

I answer that law, being a rule and measure, can be in a person in two ways: in one way, as in him that rules and measures; in another way, as in that which is ruled and measured, since a thing is ruled and measured, in so far as it partakes of the rule or measure. Wherefore, since all things subject to Divine providence are ruled and measured by the eternal law; it is evident that all things partake somewhat of the eternal law, in so far as, namely, from its being imprinted on them, they derive their respective inclinations to their proper acts and ends. Now among all others, the rational creature is subject to Divine providence in the most excellent way, in so far as it partakes of a share of providence, by being provident both for itself and for others. Wherefore it has a share of the Eternal Reason, whereby it has a natural inclination to its proper act and end: and this participation of the eternal law in the rational creature is called the natural law. Hence the Psalmist: "The light of Thy countenance, O Lord, is signed upon us": thus implying that the light of natural reason, whereby we discern what is good and what is evil, which is the function of the natural law, is nothing else than an imprint on us of the Divine light. It is therefore evident that the natural law is nothing else than the rational creature's participation of the eternal law.

Reply to Objection 1: This argument would hold, if the natural law were something different from the eternal law: whereas it is nothing but a participation thereof.

Reply to Objection 2: Every act of reason and will in us is based on that which is according to nature: for every act of reasoning is based on principles that are known naturally, and every act of appetite in respect of the means is derived from the natural appetite in respect of the last end. Accordingly the first direction of our acts to their end must be in virtue of the natural law.

Reply to Objection 3: Even irrational animals partake in their own way of the Eternal Reason, just as the rational creature does. But because the rational creature partakes thereof in an intellectual and rational manner, therefore the participation of the eternal law in the rational creature is properly called a law, since a law is something pertaining to reason. Irrational creatures, however, do not partake thereof in a rational manner, wherefore there is no participation of the eternal law in them, except by way of similitude.

WHETHER THE NATURAL LAW CONTAINS SEVERAL PRECEPTS, OR ONLY ONE?

Objection 1: It would seem that the natural law contains, not several precepts, but one only. For law is a kind of precept. If therefore there were many precepts of the natural law, it would follow that there are also many natural laws.

Objection 2: Further, the natural law is consequent to human nature. But human nature, as a whole, is one; though, as to its parts, it is manifold. Therefore, either there is but one precept of the law of nature, on account of the unity of nature as a whole; or there are many, by reason of the number of parts of human nature. The result would be that even things relating to the inclination of the concupiscible faculty belong to the natural law.

Objection 3: Further, law is something pertaining to reason. Now reason is but one in man. Therefore there is only one precept of the natural law.

On the contrary, The precepts of the natural law in man stand in relation to practical matters, as the first principles to matters of demonstration. But there are several first indemonstrable principles.

Therefore there are also several precepts of the natural law.

I answer that the precepts of the natural law are to the practical reason, what the first principles of demonstrations are to the speculative reason; because both are self-evident principles. Now a thing is said to be self-evident in two ways: first, in itself; secondly, in relation to us. Any proposition is said to be self-evident in itself, if its predicate is contained in the notion of the subject: although, to one who knows not the definition of the subject, it happens that such a proposition is not self-evident. For instance, this proposition, "Man is a rational being," is, in its very nature, self-evident, since who says "man," says "a rational being": and yet to one who knows not what a man is, this proposition is not self-evident. Hence it is that, as Boethius says (De Hebdom.), certain axioms or propositions are universally self-evident to all; and such are those propositions whose terms are known to all, as, "Every whole is greater than its part," and, "Things equal to one and the same are equal to one another." But some propositions are self-evident only to the wise, who understand the meaning of the terms of such propositions: thus to one who understands that an angel is not a body, it is self-evident that an angel is not circumscriptively in a place: but this is not evident to the unlearned, for they cannot grasp it.

Now a certain order is to be found in those things that are apprehended universally. For that which, before aught else, falls under apprehension, is "being," the notion of which is included in all things whatsoever a man apprehends. Wherefore the first indemonstrable principle is that "the same thing cannot be affirmed and denied at the same time," which is based on the notion of "being" and "not-being": and on this principle all others are based. Now as "being" is the first thing that falls under the apprehension simply, so "good" is the first thing that falls under the apprehension of the practical reason, which is directed to action: since every agent acts for an end under the aspect of good. Consequently the first principle of practical reason is one founded on the notion of good, viz. that "good is that which all things seek after." Hence this is the first precept of law, that "good is to be done and pursued, and evil is to be avoided." All other precepts of the natural law are based upon this: so that whatever the practical reason naturally apprehends as man's good (or evil) belongs to the precepts of the natural law as something to be done or avoided.

Since, however, good has the nature of an end, and evil, the nature of a contrary, hence it is that all those things to which man has a natural inclination, are naturally apprehended by reason as being good, and consequently as objects of pursuit, and their contraries as evil, and objects of avoidance. Wherefore according to the order of natural inclinations, is the order of the precepts of the natural law. Because in man there is first of all an inclination to good in accordance with the nature which he has in common with all substances: inasmuch as every substance seeks the preservation of its own being, according to its nature: and by reason of this inclination, whatever is a means of preserving human life, and of warding off its obstacles, belongs to the natural law. Secondly, there is in man an inclination to things that pertain to him more specially, according to that nature which he has in common with other animals: and in virtue of this inclination, those things are said to belong to the natural law, "which nature has taught to all animals" [Pandect. Just. I, tit. i], such as sexual intercourse, education of offspring and so forth. Thirdly, there is in man an inclination to good, according to the nature of his reason, which nature is proper to him: thus man has a natural inclination to know the truth about God, and to live in society: and in this respect, whatever pertains to this inclination belongs to the natural law; for instance, to shun ignorance, to avoid offending those among whom one has to live, and other such things regarding the above inclination.

Reply to Objection 1: All these precepts of the law of nature have the character of one natural law, inasmuch as they flow from one first precept.

Reply to Objection 2: All the inclinations of any parts whatsoever of human nature, e.g. of the concupiscible and irascible parts, in so far as they are ruled by reason, belong to the natural law, and are reduced to one first precept, as stated above: so that the precepts of the natural law are many in themselves, but are based on one common foundation.

Reply to Objection 3: Although reason is one in itself, yet it directs all things regarding man; so that whatever can be ruled by reason, is contained under the law of reason.

WHETHER ALL ACTS OF VIRTUE ARE PRESCRIBED BY THE NATURAL LAW?

Objection 1: It would seem that not all acts of virtue are prescribed by the natural law. Because it is essential to a law that it be ordained to the common good. But some acts of virtue are ordained to the private good of the individual, as is evident especially in regards to acts of temperance. Therefore not all acts of virtue are the subject of natural law.

Objection 2: Further, every sin is opposed to some virtuous act. If therefore all acts of virtue are prescribed by the natural law, it seems to follow that all sins are against nature: whereas this applies [only] to certain special sins.

Objection 3: Further, those things which are according to nature are common to all. But acts of virtue are not common to all, since a thing is virtuous in one, and vicious in another. Therefore not all acts of virtue are prescribed by the natural law.

On the contrary, Damascene says (De Fide Orth. iii, 4) that "virtues are natural." Therefore virtuous acts also are a subject of the natural law.

I answer that, We may speak of virtuous acts in two ways: first, under the aspect of virtuous; secondly, as such and such acts considered in their proper species. If then we speak of acts of virtue, considered as virtuous, thus all virtuous acts belong to the natural law. For to the natural law belongs everything to which a man is inclined according to his nature. Now each thing is inclined naturally to an operation that is suitable to it according to its form: thus fire is inclined to give heat. Wherefore, since the rational soul is the proper form of man, there is in every man a natural inclination to act according to reason: and this is to act according to virtue. Consequently, considered thus, all acts of virtue are prescribed by the natural law: since each one's reason naturally dictates to him to act virtuously. But if we speak of virtuous acts, considered in themselves, i.e. in their proper species, then not all virtuous acts are prescribed by the natural law: for many things are done virtuously, to which nature does not incline at first; but which, through the inquiry of reason, have been found by men to be conducive to well-living.

Reply to Objection 1: Temperance is about the natural concupiscences of food, drink and sexual matters, which are indeed ordained to the natural common good, just as other matters of law are ordained to the moral common good.

Reply to Objection 2: By human nature we may mean either that which is proper to man—and in this sense all sins, as being against reason, are also against nature: or we may mean that nature which is common to man and other animals; and in this sense, certain special sins are said to be against nature; thus contrary to sexual intercourse, which is natural to all animals, is unisexual lust, which has received the special name of the unnatural crime.

Reply to Objection 3: This argument considers acts in themselves. For it is owing to the various conditions of men, that certain acts are virtuous for some, as being proportionate and becoming to them, while they are vicious for others, as being out of proportion to them.

WHETHER THE NATURAL LAW IS THE SAME IN ALL MEN?

Objection 1: It would seem that the natural law is not the same in all. For it is stated in the Decretals (Dist. i) that "the natural law is that which is contained in the Law and the Gospel." But this is not common to all men; because, as it is written (Rm. 10:16), "not all obey the gospel." Therefore the natural law is not the same in all men.

Objection 2: Further, "Things which are according to the law are said to be just," as stated in [Aristotle's] Ethic. v. But it is stated in the same book that nothing is so universally just as not to be subject to change in regard to some men. Therefore even the natural law is not the same in all men.

Objection 3: Further, to the natural law belongs everything to which a man is inclined according to his nature. Now different men are naturally inclined to different things; some to the desire of pleasures, others to the desire of honors, and other men to other things. Therefore there is not one natural law for all.

On the contrary, Isidore says (Etym. v, 4): "The natural law is common to all nations."

I answer that, to the natural law belongs those things to which a man is inclined naturally: and among these it is proper to man to be inclined to act according to reason. Now the process of reason is from the common to the proper, as stated in [Aristotle's] Phys. i. The speculative reason, however, is differently situated in this matter, from the practical reason. For, since the speculative reason is busied chiefly with the necessary things, which cannot be otherwise than they are, its proper conclusions, like the universal principles, contain the truth without fail. The practical reason, on the other hand, is busied with contingent matters, about which human actions are concerned: and consequently, although there is necessity in the general principles, the more we descend to matters of detail, the more frequently we encounter defects. Accordingly then in speculative matters truth is the same in all men, both as to principles and as to conclusions: although the truth is not known to all as regards the conclusions, but only as regards the principles which are called common notions. But in matters of action, truth or practical rectitude is not the same for all, as to matters of detail, but only as to the general principles: and where there is the same rectitude in matters of detail, it is not equally known to all.

It is therefore evident that, as regards the general principles whether of speculative or of practical reason, truth or rectitude is the same for all, and is equally known by all. As to the proper conclusions of the speculative reason, the truth is the same for all, but is not equally known to all: thus it is true for all that the three angles of a triangle are together equal to two right angles, although it is not known to all. But as to the proper conclusions of the practical reason, neither is the truth or rectitude the same for all, nor, where it is the same, is it equally known by all. Thus it is right and true for all to act according to reason: and from this principle it follows as a proper conclusion, that goods entrusted to another should be restored to their owner. Now this is true for the majority of cases: but it may happen in a particular case that it would be injurious, and therefore unreasonable, to restore goods held in trust; for instance, if they are claimed for the purpose of fighting against one's country. And this principle will be found to fail the more, according as we descend further into detail, e.g. if one were to say that goods held in trust should be restored with such and such a guarantee, or in such and such a way; because the greater the number of conditions added, the greater the number of ways in which the principle may fail, so that it be not right to restore or not to restore.

Consequently we must say that the natural law, as to general principles, is the same for all, both as to rectitude and as to knowledge. But as to certain matters of detail, which are conclusions, as it were, of those general principles, it is the same for all in the majority of cases, both as to rectitude and as to knowledge; and yet in some few cases it may fail, both as to rectitude, by reason of certain obstacles (just as natures subject to generation and corruption fail in some few cases on account of some obstacle), and as to knowledge, since in some the reason is perverted by passion, or evil habit, or an evil disposition of nature; thus formerly, theft, although it is expressly contrary to the natural law, was not considered wrong among the Germans, as Julius Caesar relates (De Bello Gall. vi).

Reply to Objection 1: The meaning of the sentence quoted is not that whatever is contained in the Law and the Gospel belongs to the natural law, since they contain many things that are above nature; but that whatever belongs to the natural law is fully contained in them. Wherefore Gratian, after saying that "the natural law is what is contained in the Law and the Gospel," adds at once, by way of example, "by which everyone is commanded to do to others as he would be done by."

Reply to Objection 2: The saying of the Philosopher [Aristotle] is to be understood of things that are naturally just, not as general principles, but as conclusions drawn from them, having rectitude in the majority of cases, but failing in a few.

Reply to Objection 3: As, in man, reason rules and commands the other powers, so all the natural inclinations belonging to the other powers must needs be directed according to reason. Wherefore it is universally right for all men, that all their inclinations should be directed according to reason.

WHETHER THE NATURAL LAW CAN BE CHANGED?

Objection 1: It would seem that the natural law can be changed. Because on Ecclus. 17:9, "He gave them instructions, and the law of life," the gloss says: "He wished the law of the letter to be written, in order to correct the law of nature." But that which is corrected is changed. Therefore the natural law can be changed.

Objection 2: Further, the slaying of the innocent, adultery, and theft are against the natural law. But we find these things changed by God: as when God commanded Abraham to slay his innocent son (Gen. 22:2); and when he ordered the Jews to borrow and purloin the vessels of the Egyptians (Ex. 12:35); and when He commanded Osee to take to himself "a wife of fornications" (Osee 1:2). Therefore the natural law can be changed.

Objection 3: Further, Isidore says (Etym. 5:4) that "the possession of all things in common, and universal freedom, are matters of natural law." But these things are seen to be changed by human laws. Therefore it seems that the natural law is subject to change.

On the contrary, It is said in the Decretals (Dist. v): "The natural law dates from the creation of the rational creature. It does not vary according to time, but remains unchangeable."

I answer that, A change in the natural law may be understood in two ways. First, by way of addition. In this sense nothing hinders the natural law from being changed: since many things for the benefit of human life have been added over and above the natural law, both by the Divine law and by human laws.

Secondly, a change in the natural law may be understood by way of subtraction, so that what previously was according to the natural law, ceases to be so. In this sense, the natural law is altogether unchangeable in its first principles: but in its secondary principles, which are certain detailed proximate conclusions drawn from the first principles, the natural law is not changed so that what it prescribes be not right in most cases. But it may be changed in some particular cases of rare occurrence, through some special causes hindering the observance of such precepts.

Reply to Objection 1: The written law is said to be given for the correction of the natural law, either because it supplies what was wanting to the natural law; or because the natural law was perverted in the hearts of some men, as to certain matters, so that they esteemed those things good which are naturally evil; which perversion stood in need of correction.

Reply to Objection 2: All men alike, both guilty and innocent, die the death of nature: which death of nature is inflicted by the power of God on account of original sin, according to 1 Kgs. 2:6: "The Lord killeth and maketh alive." Consequently, by the command of God, death can be inflicted on any man, guilty or innocent, without any injustice whatever. In like manner adultery is intercourse with another's wife; who is allotted to him by the law emanating from God. Consequently intercourse with any woman, by the command of God, is neither adultery nor fornication. The same applies to theft, which is the taking of another's property. For whatever is taken by the command of God, to Whom all things belong, is not taken against the will of its owner, whereas it is in this that theft consists. Nor is it only in human things, that whatever is commanded by God is right; but also in natural things, whatever is done by God, is, in some way, natural.

Reply to Objection 3: A thing is said to belong to the natural law in two ways. First, because nature inclines thereto: e.g. that one should not do harm to another. Secondly, because nature did not bring in the contrary: thus we might say that for man to be naked is of the natural law, because nature did not give him clothes, but art invented them. In this sense, "the possession of all things in common and universal freedom" are said to be of the natural law, because, to wit, the distinction of possessions and slavery were not brought in by nature, but devised by human reason for the benefit of human life. Accordingly the law of nature was not changed in this respect, except by addition.

WHETHER THE LAW OF NATURE CAN BE ABOLISHED FROM THE HEART OF MAN?

Objection 1: It would seem that the natural law can be abolished from the heart of man. Because on Rm. 2:14, "When the Gentiles who have not the law," etc. a gloss says that "the law of righteousness, which sin had blotted out, is graven on the heart of man when he is restored by grace." But the law of righteousness is the law of nature. Therefore the law of nature can be blotted out.

Objection 2: Further, the law of grace is more efficacious than the law of nature. But the law of grace is blotted out by sin. Much more therefore can the law of nature be blotted out.

Objection 3: Further, that which is established by law is made just. But many things are enacted by men, which are contrary to the law of nature. Therefore the law of nature can be abolished from the heart of man.

On the contrary, Augustine says (Confessions ii): "Thy law is written in the hearts of men, which iniquity itself effaces not." But the law which is written in men's hearts is the natural law. Therefore the natural law cannot be blotted out.

I answer that there belong to the natural law, first, certain most general precepts, that are known to all; and secondly, certain secondary and more detailed precepts, which are, as it were, conclusions following closely from first principles. As to those general principles, the natural law, in the abstract, can nowise be blotted out from men's hearts. But it is blotted out in the case of a particular action, in so far as reason is hindered from applying the general principle to a particular point of practice, on account of concupiscence or some other passion. But as to the other, i.e. the secondary precepts, the natural law can be blotted out from the human heart, either by evil persuasions, just as in speculative matters errors occur in respect of necessary conclusions; or by vicious customs and corrupt habits, as among some men, theft, and even unnatural vices, as the Apostle states (Rm. i), were not esteemed sinful.

Reply to Objection 1: Sin blots out the law of nature in particular cases, not universally, except perchance in regard to the secondary precepts of the natural law, in the way stated above.

Reply to Objection 2: Although grace is more efficacious than nature, yet nature is more essential to man, and therefore more enduring.

Reply to Objection 3: This argument is true of the secondary precepts of the natural law, against which some legislators have framed certain enactments which are unjust.

Thomas Aquinas: Natural Law

1. Aquinas believes that acting in accordance with one's natural inclinations is virtuous and that acting contrary to those inclinations is vicious (i.e., exemplifies a vice). What sense of 'natural' is required in order to make these claims as plausible as they can be?

2. Aquinas says that the natural law is a "dictate of practical reason." What do you think he means by this?

3. Aquinas's version of natural law clearly depends on its having been authored by God. Can you think of a way to defend a version of natural law theory that does not depend on divine authorship?

4. Aquinas believes that the general principles of the natural law apply to all human beings at all times. Do you find this view of the fundamental moral principles appealing? Why or why not?

5. What can be said on behalf of Aquinas's claim that the first principles of morality are known by everyone?

CHAPTER 9

The Ethic of Prima Facie Duties

Most moral theories are **absolutist**. To be absolutist is to insist that moral rules are absolute: never permissibly broken. If a moral rule is absolute, then it is always wrong to break it, no matter how much good is achieved or how much harm is prevented from doing so.

Most moral theories are also **monistic theories**. To be monistic is to insist that there is only one fundamental moral rule. Act utilitarianism, for instance, is a moral theory that is both absolutist and monistic. It is monistic, because it identifies just a single moral rule as the ultimate one: maximize the greatest balance of happiness over unhappiness. And it is absolutist because it says that breaking that rule is always wrong.

After reviewing different moral theories, you might have the following thought: each one seems to get something right, but its exclusive focus on one moral element is too restrictive. Perhaps we ought to abandon the monistic assumption and acknowledge that **ethical pluralism** might be right. Ethical pluralism is the view that there is more than one ultimate, fundamental moral principle.

A. ETHICAL PLURALISM AND PRIMA FACIE DUTIES

There are two basic ways to be an ethical pluralist. First, you might keep the absolutism and regard all fundamental moral rules as absolute. But there is a big potential problem with this: what if those rules ever conflict? If they do, then the theory yields contradiction, and so must be false. For if those rules are absolute, then it is always morally required to obey them. But if they conflict, they can't both be obeyed. Thus in any

case of conflict, you will respect one rule, and so do what is morally required, while violating another rule, and so do what is morally wrong. But no action can be morally right and wrong at the same time—that is a contradiction. It might be possible to construct a pluralistic moral theory such that all of its basic rules are guaranteed never, ever to conflict. But it won't be easy.

Here's another way to be an ethical pluralist: reject not only monism, but absolutism, too. Such theories are pluralistic; they endorse the existence of at least two fundamental moral rules. And each of these rules is nonabsolute; in some cases, it is morally acceptable to break them. The Oxford professor W. D. Ross (1877–1971) was the philosopher who first developed this version of pluralism. He had a special term for these nonabsolute rules. He called them principles of **prima facie duty**, and we will stick with that label in what follows.

A prima facie (Latin, "at first view") duty is an excellent, nonabsolute, permanent reason to do (or refrain from) something—to keep one's word, be grateful for kindnesses, avoid hurting others, and so on. As Ross saw it, each prima facie duty is of fundamental importance. None of these duties can be derived from one another, or from any more basic principle. Crucially, each prima facie duty may sometimes be overridden by other such duties. Though there is always good reason, say, to keep a promise or prevent harm to others, morality sometimes requires that we break a promise or do harm. Likewise for each of the other prima facie duties.

Ross was convinced that absolutism in all of its forms is implausible. As he saw it, those theories that endorse more than one absolute rule are bound to yield contradiction. Those that endorse only a single absolute moral rule are too narrow, failing to recognize that there are a number of independently important moral considerations. For instance, while Ross accepted the utilitarian emphasis on doing good and preventing harm to others, he also agreed with Kant that justice was morally important in its own right.

Ross identified seven prima facie duties, each of which is meant to represent a distinct basis of our moral requirements:

1. *Fidelity*: keeping our promises, being faithful to our word.
2. *Reparations*: repairing harm that we have done.
3. *Gratitude*: appropriately acknowledging benefits that others have given us.
4. *Justice*: ensuring that virtue is rewarded and vice punished.
5. *Beneficence*: enhancing the intelligence, virtue, or pleasure of others.
6. *Self-improvement*: making oneself more intelligent or virtuous.
7. *Nonmaleficence*: preventing harm to others.

Ross did not claim that this list was complete. He allowed that there might be other prima facie duties. But each of these seven duties, he thought, definitely did belong on the list.

The term *prima facie duty* can be misleading. That's because these things are not really duties, but rather permanent moral reasons that partly determine whether an action truly is, in the end, morally required. To say, for instance, that there is a prima facie duty of beneficence is to say the following:

1. There is *always* a strong reason to benefit others.
2. This reason may sometimes be outweighed by competing reasons.
3. If this reason is the only moral reason that applies in a given situation, then

benefiting others becomes our all-things-considered duty—in other words, what we are really, finally morally required to do in that situation.

Focus for a moment on the first item. It provides us with a way to test Ross's specific roster of prima facie duties. Suppose that there are situations in which there is *no reason at all* to benefit others. If that were so, there would be no prima facie duty of beneficence.

I will let you do the testing yourself, because I am most interested in the general theory of prima facie duties, rather than in any specific version of it. Even if Ross's group of seven rules includes too much, or too little, this would not undermine the ethic of prima facie duties. What it would show (and this would certainly be important) is that Ross's own list was off-base. But a better list might make the cut.

B. THE ADVANTAGES OF ROSS'S VIEW

The greatest attraction of the ethic of prima facie duties is its ability to accommodate our sense that there is, indeed, more than just a single fundamental moral consideration. To Ross, and to most of the rest of us, it does seem that the very fact of our having promised to do something generates *some* reason to follow through, even if keeping our promise fails to bring happiness, reward virtue, prevent misery, or do anything else. That we have given our word is reason enough to do what we have promised.

But no one believes that promising is the only thing like this. There does seem to be something immoral, for instance, when someone repays a kindness with ingratitude—even if, in unusual circumstances, being ungrateful is the right way to go.

Whether or not you agree with the whole of Ross's list, you may well sign on to the idea that fidelity and gratitude, at the very least, each possess moral importance in their own right. If you do, that is enough to force a shift away from monism.

Ross's position also easily explains the widespread belief that the moral rules may sometimes acceptably be broken. There is always something to be said in favor of keeping a promise—but I should break my promise to meet a student for coffee if my daughter has a medical emergency and needs to be taken to the hospital. We all accept that there are circumstances in which it is morally acceptable to break a promise, allow harm to others, pass up a chance at self-improvement, and so on. Ross's theory straightforwardly explains this.

The ethic of prima facie duties also appears to make good sense of our experience of moral conflict. Duties conflict when they can't all be fulfilled. On absolutist views, such conflict yields contradiction. But Ross's theory easily avoids this.

Consider the case of a poor single mother whose child is too sick to go to school. The mother has a duty to report to work. By taking the job, she has promised to reliably show up as scheduled. But suppose that she has just moved to town, has no friends or family there, and isn't allowed to bring her child to work. She also has a duty to care for her child, especially if no one else is available to do so. What should she do?

The Rossian can say of such a case that there is a conflict of prima facie duties. There is a strong case for showing up to work. There is a strong reason to care for one's child. Sometimes we can't do both. But no contradiction occurs, because we can distinguish between a standing reason (a prima facie duty) to do something and an all-things-considered, final duty to do it. When these final duties conflict—when we say, *in the end*, that you are absolutely required to show up at work and are also absolutely required to care for your child—then there is contradiction. Ross's view avoids this problem entirely.

I'm not intent on defending a specific verdict in this example. If Ross is correct, the key thing is that context will determine just how important a prima facie duty is. The consideration at the heart of such a duty (promise keeping,

preventing harm, righting one's wrongs, etc.) is always morally *important*. But it is not always morally *decisive*. That is precisely what distinguishes a prima facie duty from an absolute one.

Another benefit of Ross's theory is its view of moral regret. When moral claims conflict and we can't honor them all, we think that it is right to feel regret at having to give up something important. Regret is evidence that something of value has been sacrificed. When prima facie duties conflict and one takes priority over the other, the lesser duty doesn't just disappear. It still has some weight, even though in the circumstances it is not as morally powerful as the conflicting duty. Regret is our way of acknowledging this forsaken duty, our way of recognizing that something of value was lost in the conflict.

Indeed, this provides us with a reasonable test for knowing what our prima facie duties are. The test is simple: there is a prima facie duty to act in a certain way only if it would always be appropriate to regret our failure to act that way. If there were nothing valuable about gratitude, for instance, then missing a chance to express it would not be a cause for regret. But it is. And that shows that there is *something* important about gratitude, even if it isn't *all-important*. That's just what Ross believed.

C. A PROBLEM FOR ROSS'S VIEW

In Ross's view, preventing harm is always morally important. Sometimes it is the most important thing you can do. But not always. Seeing that the guilty get their just deserts is also, and always, very important. If Kant is right, it always takes priority over preventing harm. If utilitarians are right, it never takes priority. If Ross is right, it sometimes does, and sometimes doesn't.

This leads us naturally to what may be the hardest problem for Ross's view. Ross denies that there are any absolute moral rules. So each moral rule may sometimes be broken. *But when?*

The easiest way to answer that question would be to create a permanent ranking of the rules, by placing them in order from least to most morally important. Whenever a lower ranked rule conflicts with a higher ranked one, the higher rule wins out and determines our moral duty.

Ross rejects this strategy. He thinks that there is no fixed ranking of the various prima facie rules, no permanent ordering in terms of importance. And he is not alone in this. Though a ranking system is possible in principle, in practice no one has ever made it work. Sometimes it is morally more important to be grateful than to prevent harm. But not always. Sometimes it is more important to be honest with people than to spare them the hurt feelings that honesty may cause. And sometimes not. You get the picture.

The problem is that if we can't provide a fixed ranking of moral principles, then it isn't clear how we are to decide what to do when they conflict. That is because none of the prima facie duties has any kind of built-in moral weight. They are always important. But just how important? That depends on the specifics of the situation. Yet there are no guidelines that we can use from case to case to help us to know when a prima facie duty takes precedence over a competing duty. If a duty is sometimes, but not always, more important than another, then how do we know which one to obey when we cannot obey them both? This is an extremely hard question.

D. PRIMA FACIE DUTIES AND THE TESTING OF MORAL THEORIES

Ross thinks that his theory of prima facie duties is in deep harmony with common sense. And as he sees it, this is a great benefit of his theory. We should not overturn the biddings of common sense just because it conflicts with a pet theory.

Ross used the example of beauty to establish this point. Many of us feel sure that the *Mona Lisa* is a beautiful work. We should not abandon our belief in its beauty just because some theory of art declares that only Impressionist paintings or medieval altarpieces are really beautiful.

We should give up the theory before tossing aside our deepest, most secure beliefs.

What is true of our artistic judgments is also true of our moral ones. We can see how this plays out by considering Ross's rejection of consequentialism. Ross was quite clear-eyed about how tempting consequentialism can be. But he insisted that it was fatally flawed because it failed to appreciate the variety of fundamental moral concerns. Consequentialism imposes order, system, and a unifying principle onto our moral thinking. But he argued that we must resist such charms, because they conflict with our deepest beliefs about what is truly morally important. Our confidence in the independent value of promise keeping—or justice, or repairing our wrongs—should not be held hostage to a theory's demands.

If Ross is right, we use our deepest common-sense beliefs to test moral theories. These beliefs have a kind of priority in moral thinking. It isn't as if each moral belief we have is beyond scrutiny. Far from it. Some of our moral views, perhaps even our most cherished ones, may have to go, once we see that they conflict with beliefs that are even better justified. Still, the data of ethical thought, as Ross puts it, are those moral beliefs that have survived very careful reflection. Such beliefs are what moral theories must account for. These basic beliefs are to be given up only if we can show that they can't all be true.

To the extent that a moral theory cannot make room for such beliefs, it is the theory that must go. This was Ross's diagnosis of both consequentialism and Kantianism, for instance. They both understood morality too narrowly, as limited to a single fundamental moral rule. He thought that careful reflection would show us that there are at least seven such rules—none of them absolute.

Ross realized that his view offered little comfort to those who did not agree with his seven principles. But he was unapologetic. To someone who thought about justice, for instance, and failed to see its moral importance, Ross could do only one thing. He would invite that person to think more carefully about what justice really is. This can be done in many ways. We can offer the person examples to consider; draw analogies to cases that reveal the importance of justice; distinguish justice from other, possibly related, notions; ensure that particular beliefs opposing the importance of justice are not based on error. But suppose that the person remains unconvinced even after all of this further reflection. According to Ross, moral discussion now comes to an end, and the only verdict to render is that this person is mistaken. Nothing you can say will show him that he is wrong.

That may strike you as closed-minded, but two things can be said in Ross's defense. First, what are the alternatives? Why must it always be possible to offer something more in support of one's beliefs? If the process of offering justification for one's beliefs (whether ethical or nonethical) ever does stop somewhere, then once we have reached that stopping point, all that could possibly be done is to invite the doubters to reconsider.

Second, we should consider the possibility, in *nonmoral* contexts, of finding ourselves without any support for a claim that we rightly continue to believe. For instance, there may be nothing you can say that will convince a member of the Flat Earth Society of his mistake; no way to convince someone who believes in vampires that he is wrong; no clear path to showing a stubborn person that creating a square circle is impossible. You may be justified in your beliefs even if you can't always convince those who disagree with you. That holds for moral as well as for nonmoral beliefs.

E. KNOWING THE RIGHT THING TO DO

Even if our prima facie duties are obvious, we are still faced with the problem of knowing what to do when they conflict. And Ross has very little to say here, except that we can never

be certain that the balance we strike is the correct one. Ross acknowledged that our actual, all-things-considered moral duty on any given occasion is often anything but clear. We may feel very strongly about certain cases; indeed, most moral situations are easy and straightforward, ones we never give a second thought to. Still, there is no definite method for guiding us from an understanding of the prima facie duties to a correct moral verdict in any given case.

We must start our moral thinking about specific situations by understanding the kinds of things that can be morally important. This is a matter of clearly grasping the prima facie duties. These tell us what to look out for. Has a promise been made? A wrong been done? Is there an opportunity for self-improvement here? And so on. But once you answer such questions, you're on your own. You must bring your experience and insight to bear on the details of a given case. The bad news is that there is no fixed or mechanical procedure that tells us how to do this.

This can be very dissatisfying. There are several aims of moral theory, and one of them, surely, is to offer advice on deciding how to live. Ross denies that there is any general rule to follow in order to provide answers here. What a letdown.

But again, there are a few things we might say in order to make this a bit easier to swallow. First, the idea of a comprehensive moral decision procedure, one that can be consulted to provide definite answers to all moral questions, may not be so plausible. When faced with puzzling ethical questions, we may *want* a concrete set of guidelines to help us along. But do we really believe that there is such a thing? Each of the familiar options (e.g., the principle of utility, the Golden Rule, the *what if everyone did that?* test) has its problems. Perhaps the best explanation of this is that we are looking for something that does not exist.

Second, the absence of a decision procedure for arriving at conclusions is actually the *default* situation across all areas of thinking (except mathematics and its associated disciplines). For instance, scientists faced with a conflict between their data and some favored theory have no uniform method for determining whether to modify the theory or rethink their data. Further, even when the data are uncontroversial, selecting the best theory to account for it is anything but a rote, mechanical undertaking. Scientists must rely on good sense, too, since choosing which theory to believe is a matter of balancing the virtues of the competing theories. There is no precise rule to tell a scientist how to do this.

There are many theoretical virtues: parsimony (employing fewer assumptions than competing theories); conservatism (preserving as much as possible of what we already believe); generality (explaining the broadest range of things); testability (being open to experimental challenge and confirmation); and others. Suppose that one theory is more parsimonious and also more conservative, but another theory is more general and more testable. Or suppose that one theory is far more conservative than any competitor, but is also somewhat less general, and a fair bit less parsimonious. Science does not offer us a definite procedure for identifying the better theory. Sometimes it is just obvious that one theory is better or worse than another. But in close cases, scientists have no alternative but to use their judgment.

And that is precisely our situation when it comes to morality. There are many easy cases where the moral verdict is just obvious. These rarely get our attention, since they don't call for any hard thinking. It's the difficult cases—where different options each respect some prima facie duties but violate others—that require judgment. We can never be sure that we've exercised good judgment. We may be unable to convince ourselves, much less our opponents, that we have landed on the right answer to a hard ethical question. The lack of guidance we get from Ross's view of ethics can leave us feeling insecure and unsettled. That is regrettable. But it may also be inescapable.

F. CONCLUSION

The ethic of prima facie duties has a lot of things going for it. It is pluralistic, and so rejects the idea that the whole of morality can ultimately be explained by a single moral rule. It rejects absolutism, and so explains why it is sometimes permissible to break legitimate moral rules. It easily handles moral conflict without falling into contradictions. It offers an interesting role for regret in thinking about what is morally important.

Yet like all of the moral theories we have discussed, Ross's view is not without its problems. Perhaps the hardest of these concerns the question of how we can know what to do in particular situations. Since there is no permanent ranking of the prima facie rules, and no precise method for knowing how to strike a balance when the prima facie rules conflict, this leaves us with very little guidance for discovering what morality actually requires of us.

ESSENTIAL CONCEPTS

Absolutist theories: those theories that endorse the idea that there are absolute moral rules (those that are never permissibly broken).
Ethical pluralism: the view that there is more than one ultimate, fundamental moral principle.
Monistic theories: those theories that endorse the idea that there is just a single ultimate moral rule.
Prima facie duty: an excellent, nonabsolute, permanent reason to do (or refrain from) something.

DISCUSSION QUESTIONS

1. What exactly is a prima facie duty? How does an ethic of prima facie duties differ from monistic and absolutist ethical theories?
2. Do you think that Ross's list of prima facie duties is accurate and complete? If not, either explain why some of those on the list do not qualify as prima facie duties or provide examples of other prima facie duties that should have been included in his list.

3. Does the phenomenon of regret lend any support to Ross's theory? Why or why not?

4. To what extent does Ross's theory provide us with a method for deciding what the right thing to do is in particular situations? Is this a strength or a weakness of the theory?

5. Do you think that there is a formula for determining in every case what our moral duty is? If so, what is it?

6. How does Ross suggest that we test the plausibility of moral theories? Do you find his suggestion plausible? Why or why not?

READING

What Makes Right Acts Right?
W. D. Ross

W. D. Ross (1877–1971) developed a truly novel moral theory in his book *The Right and the Good* (1930), from which this selection is taken. He found something attractive about both utilitarianism and Kantianism, the major theoretical competitors of his day, but found that each had a major flaw. Ross applauded utilitarianism's emphasis on benevolence, but he rejected its idea that maximizing goodness is our sole moral duty. Kantianism preserved the attractive idea that justice is independently important but erred in claiming that the moral rules that specify such duties are absolute (never to be broken).

Ross created a kind of compromise theory, in which he identified a number of distinct grounds for moral duty (benevolence, fidelity to promises, truth-telling, avoiding harm, gratitude, justice, reparation). Each of these is a basis for a *prima facie duty*—an always-important reason that generates an "all-things-considered" duty, provided that no other reason or set of reasons is weightier in the situation. In other words, it is sometimes acceptable to violate a prima facie duty.

But when? We cannot offer a permanent ranking of these prima facie duties. Sometimes, for instance, it is right to promote the general happiness even if we have to commit an injustice to do so. But at other times, the balance should be struck in the opposite way.

Ross insisted that these prima facie duties are self-evident. Here he offers some very influential (and controversial) remarks on how we can gain moral knowledge, both of the moral principles themselves and of the correct verdicts to reach in particular cases.

The point at issue is that to which we now pass, viz. whether there is any general character which makes right acts right, and if so, what it is. Among the main historical attempts to state a single characteristic of all right actions which is the foundation of their rightness are those made by egoism and utilitarianism. But I do not propose to discuss

From W. D. Ross, *The Right and the Good* (1930), pp. 16–32. By permission of Oxford University Press.

these, not because the subject is unimportant, but because it has been dealt with so often and so well already, and because there has come to be so much agreement among moral philosophers that neither of these theories is satisfactory. A much more attractive theory has been put forward by Professor Moore: that what makes actions right is that they are productive of more *good* than could have been produced by any other action open to the agent.

This theory is in fact the culmination of all the attempts to base rightness on productivity of some sort of result. The first form this attempt takes is the attempt to base rightness on conduciveness to the advantage or pleasure of the agent. This theory comes to grief over the fact, which stares us in the face, that a great part of duty consists in an observance of the rights and a furtherance of the interests of others, whatever the cost to ourselves may be. Plato and others may be right in holding that a regard for the rights of others never in the long run involves a loss of happiness for the agent, that 'the just life profits a man.' But this, even if true, is irrelevant to the rightness of the act. As soon as a man does an action *because* he thinks he will promote his own interests thereby, he is acting not from a sense of its rightness but from self-interest.

To the egoistic theory hedonistic utilitarianism supplies a much-needed amendment. It points out correctly that the fact that a certain pleasure will be enjoyed by the agent is no reason why he ought to bring it into being rather than an equal or greater pleasure to be enjoyed by another, though, human nature being what it is, it makes it not unlikely that he will try to bring it into being. But hedonistic utilitarianism in its turn needs a correction. On reflection it seems clear that pleasure is not the only thing in life that we think good in itself, that for instance we think the possession of a good character, or an intelligent understanding of the world, as good or better. A great advance is made by the substitution of 'productive of the greatest good' for 'productive of the greatest pleasure.'

Not only is this theory more attractive than hedonistic utilitarianism, but its logical relation to that theory is such that the latter could not be true unless it were true, while it might be true though hedonistic utilitarianism were not. It is in fact one of the logical bases of hedonistic utilitarianism.

For the view that what produces the maximum pleasure is right has for its bases the views (1) that what produces the maximum good is right, and (2) that pleasure is the only thing good in itself. If, therefore, it can be shown that productivity of the maximum good is not what makes all right actions right, we shall *a fortiori* have refuted hedonistic utilitarianism.

When a plain man fulfils a promise because he thinks he ought to do so, it seems clear that he does so with no thought of its total consequences, still less with any opinion that these are likely to be the best possible. He thinks in fact much more of the past than of the future. What makes him think it right to act in a certain way is the fact that he has promised to do so—that and, usually, nothing more. That his act will produce the best possible consequences is not his reason for calling it right. What lends colour to the theory we are examining, then, is not the actions (which form probably a great majority of our actions) in which some such reflection as 'I have promised' is the only reason we give ourselves for thinking a certain action right, but the exceptional cases in which the consequences of fulfilling a promise (for instance) would be so disastrous to others that we judge it right not to do so. It must of course be admitted that such cases exist. If I have promised to meet a friend at a particular time for some trivial purpose, I should certainly think myself justified in breaking my engagement if by doing so I could prevent a serious accident or bring relief to the victims of one. And the supporters of the view we are examining hold that my thinking so is due to my thinking that I shall bring more good into existence by the one action than by the other. A different account may, however, be given of the matter, an account which will, I believe, show itself to be the true one. It may be said that besides the duty of fulfilling promises I have and recognize a duty of relieving distress, and that when I think it right to do the latter at the cost of not doing the former, it is not because I think I shall produce more good thereby but because I think it the duty which is in the circumstances more of a duty. This account surely corresponds much more closely with what we really think in such a situation. If, so far as I can see, I could bring equal amounts of good into being by fulfilling my promise and by helping some one to whom I had made no promise, I should not hesitate to regard the former as my duty. Yet on the view that what is right is right because it is productive of the most good I should not so regard it.

There are two theories, each in its way simple, that offer a solution of such cases of conscience. One is the view of Kant, that there are certain duties of perfect obligation, such as those of fulfilling promises, of paying debts, of telling the truth, which admit of no exception whatever in favor of duties of imperfect obligation, such as that of relieving distress. The other is the view of, for instance, Professor Moore and Dr. Rashdall, that there is only the duty of producing good, and that all 'conflicts of duties' should be resolved by asking 'by which action will most good be produced?' But it is more important that our theory fit the facts than that it be simple, and the account we have given above corresponds (it seems to me) better than either of the simpler theories with what we really think, viz. that normally promise-keeping, for example, should come before benevolence, but that when and only when the good to be produced by the benevolent act is very great and the promise comparatively trivial, the act of benevolence becomes our duty.

In fact the theory of 'ideal utilitarianism,' if I may for brevity refer so to the theory of Professor Moore, seems to simplify unduly our relations to our fellows. It says, in effect, that the only morally significant relation in which my neighbours stand to me is that of being possible beneficiaries by my action. They do stand in this relation to me, and this relation is morally significant. But they may also stand to me in the relation of promisee to promiser, of creditor to debtor, of wife to husband, of child to parent, of friend to friend, of fellow countryman to fellow countryman, and the like; and each of these relations is the foundation of a *prima facie* duty, which is more or less incumbent on me according to the circumstances of the case. When I am in a situation, as perhaps I always am, in which more than one of these *prima facie* duties is incumbent on me, what I have to do is to study the situation as fully as I can until I form the considered opinion (it is never more) that in the circumstances one of them is more incumbent than any other; then I am bound to think that to do this *prima facie* duty is my duty *sans phrase* in the situation.

I suggest '*prima facie* duty' or 'conditional duty' as a brief way of referring to the characteristic (quite distinct from that of being a duty proper) which an act has, in virtue of being of a certain kind (e.g. the keeping of a promise), of being an act which would be a duty proper if it were not at the same time of another kind which is morally significant. Whether an act is a duty proper or actual duty depends on *all* the morally significant kinds it is an instance of.

The phrase '*prima facie* duty' must be apologized for, since (1) it suggests that what we are speaking of is a certain kind of duty, whereas it is in fact not a duty, but something related in a special way to duty. Strictly speaking, we want not a phrase in which duty is qualified by an adjective, but a separate noun. (2) '*Prima' facie* suggests that one is speaking only of an appearance which a moral situation presents at first sight, and which may turn out to be illusory; whereas what I am speaking of is an objective fact involved in the nature of the situation, or more strictly in an element of its nature, though not, as duty proper does, arising from its whole nature.

There is nothing arbitrary about these *prima facie* duties. Each rests on a definite circumstance which cannot seriously be held to be without moral significance. Of *prima facie* duties I suggest, without claiming completeness or finality for it, the following division.

1. Some duties rest on previous acts of my own. These duties seem to include two kinds.

    A. Those resting on a promise or what may fairly be called an implicit promise, such as the implicit undertaking not to tell lies which seems to be implied in the act of entering into conversation (at any rate by civilized men), or of writing books that purport to be history and not fiction. These may be called the duties of fidelity.
    B. Those resting on a previous wrongful act. These may be called the duties of reparation.
2. Some rest on previous acts of other men, i.e. services done by them to me. These may be loosely described as the duties of gratitude.

3. Some rest on the fact or possibility of a distribution of pleasure or happiness (or of the means thereto) which is not in accordance with the merit of the persons concerned; in such cases there arises a duty to upset or prevent such a distribution. These are the duties of justice.

4. Some rest on the mere fact that there are beings in the world whose condition we can make better in respect of virtue, or of intelligence, or of pleasure. These are the duties of beneficence.

5. Some rest on the fact that we can improve our own condition in respect of virtue or of intelligence. These are the duties of self-improvement.

6. I think that we should distinguish from (4) the duties that may be summed up under the title of 'not injuring others.' No doubt to injure others is incidentally to fail to do them good; but it seems to me clear that non-maleficence is apprehended as a duty distinct from that of beneficence, and as a duty of a more stringent character.

The essential defect of the 'ideal utilitarian' theory is that it ignores, or at least does not do full justice to, the highly personal character of duty. If the only duty is to produce the maximum of good, the question who is to have the good—whether it is myself, or my benefactor, or a person to whom I have made a promise to confer that good on him, or a mere fellow man to whom I stand in no such special relation—should make no difference to my having a duty to produce that good. But we are all in fact sure that it makes a vast difference.

If the objection be made, that this catalogue of the main types of duty is an unsystematic one resting on no logical principle, it may be replied, first, that it makes no claim to being ultimate. It is a *prima facie* classification of the duties which reflection on our moral convictions seems actually to reveal. And if these convictions are, as I would claim that they are, of the nature of knowledge, and if I have not misstated them, the list will be a list of authentic conditional duties, correct as far as it goes though not necessarily complete. The list of *goods* put forward

by the rival theory is reached by exactly the same method—the only sound one in the circumstances—viz. that of direct reflection on what we really think. Loyalty to the facts is worth more than a symmetrical architectonic or a hastily reached simplicity. If further reflection discovers a perfect logical basis for this or for a better classification, so much the better.

It may, again, be objected that our theory that there are these various and often conflicting types of *prima facie* duty leaves us with no principle upon which to discern what is our actual duty in particular circumstances. But this objection is not one which the rival theory is in a position to bring forward. For when we have to choose between the production of two heterogeneous goods, say knowledge and pleasure, the 'ideal utilitarian' theory can only fall back on an opinion, for which no logical basis can be offered, that one of the goods is the greater; and this is no better than a similar opinion that one of two duties is the more urgent. And again, when we consider the infinite variety of the effects of our actions in the way of pleasure, it must surely be admitted that the claim which *hedonism* sometimes makes, that it offers a readily applicable criterion of right conduct, is quite illusory.

I am unwilling, however, to content myself with an *argumentum ad hominem*, and I would contend that in principle there is no reason to anticipate that every act that is our duty is so for one and the same reason. Why should two sets of circumstances, or one set of circumstances, not possess different characteristics, any one of which makes a certain act our *prima facie* duty? When I ask what it is that makes me in certain cases sure that I have a *prima facie* duty to do so and so, I find that it lies in the fact that I have made a promise; when I ask the same question in another case, I find the answer lies in the fact that I have done a wrong. And if on reflection I find (as I think I do) that neither of these reasons is reducible to the other, I must not on any a priori ground assume that such a reduction is possible.

It is necessary to say something by way of clearing up the relation between *prima facie* duties and the actual or absolute duty to do one particular act in particular circumstances. If, as almost all moralists except Kant are agreed, and as most plain men think, it is sometimes right to tell a lie or to break a promise, it must be maintained that there is a difference between *prima facie* duty and actual or absolute duty. When we think ourselves justified in breaking, and indeed morally obliged to break, a promise in order to relieve some one's distress, we do not for a moment cease to recognize a *prima facie* duty to keep our promise, and this leads us to feel, not indeed shame or repentance, but certainly compunction, for behaving as we do; we recognize, further, that it is our duty to make up somehow to the promisee for the breaking of the promise. We have to distinguish from the characteristic of being our duty that of tending to be our duty. Any act that we do contains various elements in virtue of which it falls under various categories. In virtue of being the breaking of a promise, for instance, it tends to be wrong; in virtue of being an instance of relieving distress it tends to be right.

Something should be said of the relation between our apprehension of the *prima facie* rightness of certain types of act and our mental attitude towards particular acts. It is proper to use the word 'apprehension' in the former case and not in the latter. That an act, *qua* fulfilling a promise, or *qua* effecting a just distribution of good, or *qua* returning services rendered, or *qua* promoting the good of others, or *qua* promoting the virtue or insight of the agent, is *prima facie* right, is self-evident; not in the sense that it is evident from the beginning of our lives, or as soon as we attend to the proposition for the first time, but in the sense that when we have reached sufficient mental maturity and have given sufficient attention to the proposition it is evident without any need of proof, or of evidence beyond itself. It is self-evident just as a mathematical axiom, or the validity of a form of inference, is evident. The moral order expressed in these propositions is just as much part of the fundamental nature of the universe (and, we may add, of any possible universe in which there were moral agents at all) as is the spatial or numerical structure expressed in the axioms of geometry or arithmetic. In our confidence that these propositions are true there is involved the same trust in our reason that is involved in our confidence in mathematics; and we should have no justification for trusting it in

the latter sphere and distrusting it in the former. In both cases we are dealing with propositions that cannot be proved, but that just as certainly need no proof.

Our judgements about our actual duty in concrete situations have none of the certainty that attaches to our recognition of the general principles of duty. A statement is certain, i.e. is an expression of knowledge, only in one or other of two cases: when it is either self-evident, or a valid conclusion from self-evident premises. And our judgements about our particular duties have neither of these characters. (1) They are not self-evident. Where a possible act is seen to have two characteristics, in virtue of one of which it is *prima facie* right, and in virtue of the other *prima facie* wrong, we are (I think) well aware that we are not certain whether we ought or ought not to do it; that whether we do it or not, we are taking a moral risk. We come in the long run, after consideration, to think one duty more pressing than the other, but we do not feel certain that it is so. And though we do not always recognize that a possible act has two such characteristics, and though there may be cases in which it has not, we are never certain that any particular possible act has not, and therefore never certain that it is right, nor certain that it is wrong. For, to go no further in the analysis, it is enough to point out that any particular act will in all probability in the course of time contribute to the bringing about of good or of evil for many human beings, and thus have a *prima facie* rightness or wrongness of which we know nothing. (2) Again, our judgements about our particular duties are not logical conclusions from self-evident premisses. The only possible premisses would be the general principles stating their *prima facie* rightness or wrongness *qua* having the different characteristics they do have; and even if we could (as we cannot) apprehend the extent to which an act will tend on the one hand, for example, to bring about advantages for our benefactors, and on the other hand to bring about disadvantages for fellow men who are not our benefactors, there is no principle by which we can draw the conclusion that it is on the whole right or on the whole wrong. In this respect the judgement as to the rightness of a particular act is just like the judgement as to the beauty of a particular natural object or work of art. A poem is, for instance, in respect of certain qualities beautiful and in respect of certain others not beautiful; and our judgement as to the degree of beauty it possesses on the whole is never reached by logical reasoning from the apprehension of its particular beauties or particular defects. Both in this and in the moral case we have more or less probable opinions which are not logically justified conclusions from the general principles that are recognized as self-evident.

There is therefore much truth in the description of the right act as a fortunate act. If we cannot be certain that it is right, it is our good fortune if the act we do is the right act. This consideration does not, however, make the doing of our duty a mere matter of chance. There is a parallel here between the doing of duty and the doing of what will be to our personal advantage. We never *know* what act will in the long run be to our advantage. Yet it is certain that we are more likely in general to secure our advantage if we estimate to the best of our ability the probable tendencies of our actions in this respect, than if we act on caprice. And similarly we are more likely to do our duty if we reflect to the best of our ability on the *prima facie* rightness or wrongness of various possible acts in virtue of the characteristics we perceive them to have, than if we act without reflection. With this greater likelihood we must be content.

The general principles of duty are obviously not self-evident from the beginning of our lives. How do they come to be so? The answer is, that they come to be self-evident to us just as mathematical axioms do. We find by experience that this couple of matches and that couple make four matches, that this couple of balls on a wire and that couple make four balls: and by reflection on these and similar discoveries we come to see that it is of the nature of two and two to make four. In a precisely similar way, we see the *prima facie* rightness of an act which would be the fulfilment of a particular promise, and of another which would be the fulfilment of another promise, and when we have reached sufficient maturity to think in general terms, we apprehend *prima facie* rightness to belong to the nature of any fulfilment of promise. What comes first in time is the apprehension of the self-evident *prima facie*

rightness of an individual act of a particular type. From this we come by reflection to apprehend the self-evident general principle of *prima facie* duty. From this, too, perhaps along with the apprehension of the self-evident *prima facie* rightness of the same act in virtue of its having another characteristic as well, and perhaps in spite of the apprehension of its *prima facie* wrongness in virtue of its having some third characteristic, we come to believe something not self-evident at all, but an object of probable opinion, viz. that this particular act is (not *prima facie* but) actually right.

In what has preceded, a good deal of use has been made of 'what we really think' about moral questions; a certain theory has been rejected because it does not agree with what we really think. It might be said that this is in principle wrong; that we should not be content to expound what our present moral consciousness tells us but should aim at a criticism of our existing moral consciousness in the light of theory. Now I do not doubt that the moral consciousness of men has in detail undergone a good deal of modification as regards the things we think right, at the hands of moral theory. But if we are told, for instance, that we should give up our view that there is a special obligatoriness attaching to the keeping of promises because it is self-evident that the only duty is to produce as much good as possible, we have to ask ourselves whether we really, when we reflect, are convinced that this is self-evident, and whether we really can get rid of our view that promise-keeping has a bindingness independent of productiveness of maximum good. In my own experience I find that I cannot, in spite of a very genuine attempt to do so; and I venture to think that most people will find the same.

I would maintain, in fact, that what we are apt to describe as 'what we think' about moral questions contains a considerable amount that we do not think but know, and that this forms the standard by reference to which the truth of any moral theory has to be tested, instead of having itself to be tested by reference to any theory. I hope that I have in what precedes indicated what in my view these elements of knowledge are that are involved in our ordinary moral consciousness.

It would be a mistake to found a natural science on 'what we really think,' i.e. on what reasonably thoughtful and well-educated people think about the subjects of the science before they have studied them scientifically. For such opinions are interpretations, and often misinterpretations, of sense-experience; and the man of science must appeal from these to sense-experience itself, which furnishes his real data. In ethics no such appeal is possible. We have no more direct way of access to the facts about rightness and goodness and about what things are right or good, than by thinking about them; the moral convictions of thoughtful and well-educated people are the data of ethics just as sense-perceptions are the data of a natural science. Just as some of the latter have to be rejected as illusory, so have some of the former; but as the latter are rejected only when they are in conflict with other more accurate sense-perceptions, the former are rejected only when they are in conflict with other convictions which stand better the test of reflection. The existing body of moral convictions of the best people is the cumulative product of the moral reflection of many generations, which has developed an extremely delicate power of appreciation of moral distinctions; and this the theorist cannot afford to treat with anything other than the greatest respect. The verdicts of the moral consciousness of the best people are the foundation on which he must build; though he must first compare them with one another and eliminate any contradictions they may contain.

W. D. Ross: What Makes Right Acts Right?

1. Ross begins by considering the view that the right action is the one that is "productive of more *good* than could have been produced by any other action open to the agent." What objections does he offer to this view? Do you think they are good ones?

2. Ross also considers Kant's view, according to which there are certain moral rules that must be followed without exception. What does Ross think is wrong with this theory? Do you agree with his criticism?

3. What does Ross mean by "*prima facie* duties," and how do these differ from "duty proper"? How does he think we should use our knowledge of prima facie duties to determine what our duty is in a particular situation?

4. How does Ross think we come to know prima facie duties? Do you find his view plausible?

5. What reasons does Ross give for his claim that we can never be certain about what the right thing to do is in a particular situation? Do you agree with him about this?

6. Ross claims that "the moral convictions of thoughtful and well-educated people are the data of ethics just as sense-perceptions are the data of a natural science." Is beginning with our own moral convictions the best way of doing ethics, or do you think there is a better way?

CHAPTER 10

Virtue Ethics

All of the moral theories we have reviewed thus far share a common assumption: that the moral philosopher's primary task is to define the nature of our moral duty. On this view, *What should I do?* is the crucial moral question. Once we have an answer to that, I can know what sort of person I should be—namely, the sort who will do my duty as reliably as possible.

But what if we approached ethics from a different starting point? What if we began by considering what makes for a desirable human life, examining the conditions and the character traits needed to flourish? Rather than begin with a theory of moral duty, we would start with a picture of the good life and the good person, and define our duty by reference to these ideals. That is precisely what virtue ethics recommends.[1]

Virtue ethics is not a single theory, but rather a family of theories that can trace its history (in the West) to the philosophy of the ancient Greeks. Aristotle's *Nicomachean Ethics*, written about 2,400 years ago, has had the greatest influence in this tradition and remains a primary inspiration for most who work in it. Aristotle's book develops most of the major themes that even today define the virtue ethical approach to the moral life. Let's consider some of the most important of these themes.

---

1. Actually, there is a strand of virtue ethics that abandons talk of moral duties and moral requirements altogether and instead suggests that we restrict our assessments to what is good and bad, virtuous and vicious. I invite you to reflect on whether it would be a gain or loss to give up on the concepts of moral duty and requirement, but for the remainder of the chapter, I will assume that virtue ethicists will allow a place for these notions.

A. THE STANDARD OF RIGHT ACTION

Virtue ethics insists that we understand right action by reference to what a virtuous person would characteristically do. To put it a bit more formally,

> (VE) An act is morally right just because it is one that a virtuous person, acting in character, would do in that situation.

According to virtue ethicists, actions aren't right because of their results, or because they follow from some hard-and-fast rule. Rather, they are right because they would be done by someone of true virtue. This person is a **moral exemplar**—someone who sets a fine example and serves as a role model for the rest of us. The ideal of the wholly virtuous person provides the goal that we ought to aim for, even if, in reality, each of us will fall short of it in one way or another.

Virtue ethics is actually a form of **ethical pluralism**. Though there is a single ultimate standard—do what the virtuous person would do—there are many cases where this advice is too general to be of use. At such times we need a set of more specific moral rules. Virtue ethics can provide these, too. For each virtue, there is a rule that tells us to act accordingly; for each vice, a rule that tells us to avoid it. So we will have a large set of moral rules—do what is honest; act loyally; display courage; deal justly with others; show wisdom; be temperate; avoid gluttony; refrain from infidelity; don't be timid, lazy, stingy, or careless; free yourself of prejudice; and so on.

When these rules conflict, how do we know what to do? We should follow the lead of the virtuous person. True, there will inevitably be disagreement about who counts as virtuous, and about the actions such a person would pursue. But this needn't hinder us. There is lots of room for critical discussion about who is virtuous and why. In the end, we may have to agree to disagree, since there may be no way to convince someone whose moral outlook is fundamentally opposed to our own. Those who have been raised to idolize Hitler or Stalin are going to have a skewed moral vision, and there may be no way to convince them of their error. Virtue ethicists deny that this undermines the existence of correct moral standards. It just shows that some people may always be blind to them.

B. MORAL COMPLEXITY

Many moral philosophers have hoped to identify a simple rule, or a precise method, that could tell us exactly what our moral duty is in each situation. What's more, this rule or method could be reliably used by anyone, so long as he or she is minimally intelligent. A classic example of this is the Golden Rule. Even a five-year-old can apply this test.

Virtue ethicists reject the idea that there is any simple formula for determining how to act. At the beginning of the *Nicomachean Ethics*, Aristotle cautions that we must not expect the same degree of precision in all areas of study, and implies that morality lacks rules and methods of thinking that are as precise as those, say, in mathematics. When it comes to morality, we must be content with general principles that allow for exceptions.

Virtue ethicists have followed Aristotle in this thought. To them, ethics is a complex, messy area of decision making, one that requires emotional maturity and sound judgment. One of the *problems* of the Golden Rule, for instance, is that even a child can use it with authority. Aristotle thought it obvious that even the most perceptive children are far short of true moral wisdom.

Virtue ethicists sometimes invite us to appreciate the complexity of morality by having us imagine a moral rule book. The book would contain all the true rules of ethics and all of the precise methods for applying them. It would state when exceptions were called for and when they were forbidden. It could be applied in a mechanical way, without any need of judgment.

Is this a real possibility? Not likely, according to virtue ethicists. Morality is not like geometry or civil engineering. We have moral rules of thumb that can help us in most situations. But strict obedience to such rules is bound to lead us into error. And the rules, of course, will sometimes conflict. What we need in all cases is a kind of sensitivity. It is something very different from a rote application of preset rules.

C. MORAL UNDERSTANDING

As virtue ethicists see things, moral understanding is not just a matter of knowing a bunch of moral facts. If it were, then a child prodigy might be one of the morally wisest among us. As we have seen, virtue ethicists deny this possibility. Imagine turning to such a child for advice about dealing with difficult coworkers, or helping a drug-addicted friend through recovery, or determining the best way to break off a relationship.

Moral understanding is a species of practical wisdom. Think of some familiar kinds of practical wisdom—knowing how to fix a car engine, how to skillfully play an instrument, or how to inspire teammates to come together behind an important project. Such knowledge does require an understanding of certain facts, but it is much more than that. We all know people with plenty of book smarts and very little in the way of good sense. Moral wisdom is a kind of know-how that requires a lot of training and experience. What it doesn't require is a superior IQ or a vast reading list.

Moral wisdom is an extremely complicated kind of skill. It does require knowledge of the way the world works, but it demands more than that. We must have a great deal of emotional intelligence as well. The moral virtues, which all require moral wisdom, therefore also require a combination of intellectual and emotional maturity. A person with only a crude appreciation for life's complexities, or a blank emotional life, is bound to be morally blind. Virtue ethics perfectly explains why that is so.

D. THE NATURE OF VIRTUE

The ultimate goal of a moral education is to make ourselves better people. A better person is a more virtuous person—someone who is more courageous, just, temperate, and wise (among other things).

A **virtue** is an admirable character trait. It's not a mere habit, or a tendency to act in certain ways. Habits don't define a person; character traits do. Some people are habitually loyal or generous. Yet they may lack virtue, because they don't really understand why it is appropriate to act this way. Virtues require wisdom about what is important, and why. While habits are defined as certain patterns of behavior, virtues require much more. In addition to routinely acting well, the virtuous person also has a distinctive set of perceptions, thoughts, and motives.

Let's make this concrete. Consider first the virtue of generosity. A generous person will often have different *perceptions* from a stingy person. Generous people will see the homeless person on the street, will take note of the shy child in the classroom, will realize that an injured person is having trouble with the door. Stingy people tend to look the other way.

A generous person has different *thoughts* from those of an ungenerous person. A generous person will think about how to be helpful, will not think only of his own needs, will value being of service, and will believe in the goodness of caring for the less fortunate.

A generous person's *motives* will differ from those of a stingy person. Generous people are not begrudging of their time, they are moved by the distress of others, and they take pleasure in freely giving what they can to those in need.

We can offer similar accounts of all of the other virtues. Courage, for instance, requires that we correctly perceive various threats or dangers, control our fear in a reasonable way, be moved by a noble end, and act accordingly. Though Aristotle considered courage primarily in the context of the battlefield, this virtue, like all virtues, has its place in any number of more ordinary situations. The new kid in school displays courage when taking an unpopular stand among those whose approval and companionship he hopes for. Gandhi displayed courage in peacefully resisting the nightsticks and attack dogs of the British colonial police. A whistleblower is courageous in revealing the corruption of her employers, knowing that she may be fired or sued for telling the truth.

Virtuous people are therefore defined not just by their deeds, but also by their inner life. They see, believe, and feel things differently from vicious people. They see what's important, know what is right and why it is right, and want to do things because they are right.

People are virtuous only when their understanding and their emotions are well integrated. A virtuous person who understands the right thing to do will also be strongly motivated to do it, without regret or reluctance, for all the right reasons. In Aristotle's view, and in the virtue ethical tradition, this is what distinguishes the truly virtuous from the merely **continent**—those who can keep it together, manage to do the right thing, but with little or no pleasure, and only by suppressing very strong contrary desires. As Aristotle insists, "Virtuous conduct gives pleasure to the lover of virtue."[2] This is one way to distinguish the truly virtuous from the merely continent.

E. DOES VIRTUE ETHICS OFFER ADEQUATE MORAL GUIDANCE?

The virtue ethical approach to life has a number of attractive features. I've tried to sketch some of the more important of them here. But given

---

2. *Nicomachean Ethics* 1099a12.

its unorthodox approach to morality, it is hardly surprising that virtue ethics has come in for its share of criticisms.

Moral philosophers sometimes accuse virtue ethics of failing to provide enough help in solving moral puzzles. When we are trying to figure out how to behave, we'd like to have something more than this advice: do what a virtuous person would do.

But virtue ethics *can* provide more advice. It will tell us to act according to a large number of moral rules, each based on doing what is virtuous or avoiding what is vicious: do what is temperate, loyal, modest, generous, compassionate, courageous, and so on. Avoid acting in a manner that is greedy, deceitful, malicious, unfair, short-tempered, and so on. The list of virtues and vices is a long one, and this may really be of some help in figuring out what to do.

Still, the virtue ethicist has to face the familiar problem of moral conflict. What happens when these virtue rules conflict with one another? Suppose, for instance, that you are on vacation and happen to see your best friend's husband intimately cozying up to another woman. Would a virtuous person reveal what she has seen? Well, there is a virtue of honesty, and that points to telling your friend. But being a busybody and rushing to judgment are vices; it's their marriage, not yours, and poking your nose into other people's business isn't a morally attractive thing to do.

That's all well and good. But you must do something. How to resolve this conflict (and countless others)? There *is* a right answer here, because there is something that a virtuous person would do. But virtue ethicists have offered very little instruction for deciding what that is. Once you appreciate which virtues and vices are involved in the situation, it is up to you to sort out how to balance them against one another.

This, of course, will be deeply unsatisfying to many people. They want their ethical theory to provide a clear rule that can tell them exactly what is required for each new situation. With

expectations set this high, virtue ethics is bound to disappoint.

Unsurprisingly, however, virtue ethicists think that such expectations are implausible and far too demanding. They deny that ethics is meant to provide us with a precise rule or mechanical decision procedure that can crank out the right answer for each morally complex case. There is no uniform moral guidebook, no formula or master rule that can tell us how to behave. We must figure it out for ourselves, through reflection, discussion, and experience.

Virtue ethicists can also argue that their theoretical competitors face similar problems. Most ethical theories incorporate a rule requiring promise keeping. But isn't it sometimes okay to break this rule? If so, is there any *other* rule that could tell us precisely when we may break our promises? Try it out. "You are allowed to break a promise if and only if _____." I don't know how to fill in that blank. That, of course, doesn't show that it can't be done. But anyone who can do it will also be able to know, in difficult situations, how to balance the virtue of fidelity against other considerations.

The bottom line is that almost every moral theory will require us to exercise good judgment in applying its rules. Virtue ethics requires more of us in this regard than some other theories, but that is a drawback only if morality can be made more precise than virtue ethicists believe. Whether that is so remains to be seen.

F. WHO ARE THE MORAL ROLE MODELS?

If virtue ethics is correct, then we can solve moral puzzles only by knowing how a virtuous person would act in our situation. Yet who are the moral exemplars? How do we decide who our role models should be, especially if different people endorse different candidates?

This is a very hard problem. After all, we pick our role models in large part by seeing how well they live up to our preexisting beliefs about what is right and wrong. Some people exalt suicide bombers as role models; others get sick just knowing that's so.

People can be truly virtuous even if we don't realize that they are. When we fail to choose the right role models, this is often explained by our own failure of virtue. Winston Churchill, for instance, though possessed of a great many virtues himself, was nevertheless so committed to maintaining British rule over India that he never saw past his racist attitudes toward Indians. Churchill once announced, "I hate Indians. They are a beastly people with a beastly religion." His racism prevented him from seeing Gandhi as a moral exemplar; indeed, Churchill was fully prepared to let Gandhi die in one of his hunger strikes. Churchill declared that Gandhi "ought to be lain bound hand and foot at the gates of Delhi and then trampled on by an enormous elephant with the new Viceroy [the British ruler of India] seated on its back."[3] Churchill's failure of virtue clouded his judgment so badly that he regarded Gandhi as deserving to die because of his threat to British imperial ambitions.

We become more insightful in selecting moral exemplars only by becoming morally wiser in general. And as we have seen, there is no fixed recipe for doing this. Moral education is a lifelong affair, and we are never fully wise. So we may indeed be off target in selecting our role models.

This isn't the whole story, of course. The whole story would involve a much more detailed account of how we gain moral knowledge, including knowledge of how to correctly identify our role models and how to resolve disputes about this matter. But in this respect, the virtue ethicist is in the same boat as everyone else. *Every* moral theorist has to answer hard

problems about how to gain moral wisdom, and how to resolve disagreements about fundamental moral issues.

G. CONFLICT AND CONTRADICTION

Contradictions are a fatal flaw in any theory. A **contradiction** occurs when one and the same claim is said to be both true and false. For instance, if an action is said to be both right and wrong at the same time, then it is true that it is right and false that it is right. That is a contradiction. Virtue ethics may be saddled with contradictions, and if that is so, then it is sunk.

The problem is simple. If there are many virtuous people, then what happens if they disagree about what to do in a given situation? If, in my shoes, some good people would act one way, and others would behave differently, then it seems that the same action would be both right (because some role models would do it) and not right (because others would not do it). This is a contradiction.

The very wise people I have known do not all think alike. They don't see every case in the same light. They temper justice with mercy to varying degrees. They disagree about the role and form that discipline should take in good parenting. Some are more optimistic than others; some are more willing to demand more personal sacrifice than others. It thus seems possible that virtuous role models, acting in character, would do different things in the same situation. And that would yield contradiction.

There are a few ways out of this problem. The first is to insist that there is really only a single truly virtuous person, and so the differences that cause the contradictions would disappear. The second is to insist that every virtuous person, acting in character, would do exactly the same thing in every situation. I don't find either of these replies very plausible, but perhaps there is more to be said for them than I am imagining.

The better option, I think, is to slightly modify the virtue ethical view of right action, given earlier in this chapter by the thesis labeled

3. These quotes appear in Johann Hari, "The Two Churchills," *New York Times Book Review* (August 15, 2010), p. 11. Hari was reviewing Richard Toye's book *Churchill's Empire* (New York: Henry Holt, 2010).

(VE). Assuming that virtuous people, acting in character, will sometimes do different things in the same situation, we should say the following:

1. An act in a given situation is morally required just because *all* virtuous people, acting in character, would perform it.
2. An act in a given situation is morally permitted just because *some but not all* virtuous people, acting in character, would perform it.
3. An act in a given situation is morally forbidden just because *no* virtuous person would perform it.

This really will solve the contradiction problem. If different virtuous people would act differently in the same situation, then we are no longer forced to say that an act is both right and wrong. Rather, we say that it is simply permitted, neither required nor forbidden. If different virtuous people would act differently were they in our shoes, then we are permitted to act as any one of them does. In that case, the theory will not tell us which role model to follow—it will be, morally speaking, up to us.

H. THE PRIORITY PROBLEM

How do we get a handle on the nature of virtue? Here is the standard way. We first get clear about our duty, and then define a virtue as a character trait that reliably moves us to do our duty for the right reasons. So, for instance, to understand the virtue of generosity, we first note that we are duty-bound to help the needy, and then define generosity as the character trait of giving to others in need, for the right reasons.

Virtue ethicists reject this strategy, because they deny that we can know our duty before knowing how virtuous people characteristically behave. For them, virtue has a kind of priority over duty—we must know what virtue is, and how the virtuous would behave, before knowing what we must do.

The issue is about which concept is morally fundamental—virtue, or right action. To help see the stakes here, consider this question: are people virtuous because they perform right actions, or are actions right because virtuous people perform them? Other moral theories go with the first option. Virtue ethics takes the second. And this raises a number of concerns.

Consider the evil of rape. The virtue ethicist explains its wrongness by claiming that virtuous people would never rape other people. But that seems backward. It is true, of course, that virtuous people are not rapists. But their rejection of rape is not what explains its wrongness. Rape is wrong because it expresses contempt for the victim, sends a false message of the rapist's superiority, violates the victim's rights, and imposes terrible harm without consent. We explain why virtuous people don't rape others by showing why rape is wrong. We don't explain why rape is wrong by showing that good people will not rape others.

The same goes for right actions. A bystander who sees a toddler about to walk into traffic should rush over to prevent the accident. Why? Not because a virtuous person would do such a thing (though of course she would). The real reason is to save a child's life, or at least to prevent her from being seriously injured. It's not that intervention is right because virtuous people would do it; rather, they would do it because it is right.

We can still look to virtuous role models for reliable guidance on how to act. But their choices do not turn otherwise neutral actions into ones that are right (or wrong). They are not so powerful as that. Virtuous people have keen insight into the reasons that make actions moral or immoral. They feel the compelling force of these reasons and act accordingly. That is what makes them virtuous.

If this line of thinking is on target, then we need to explain virtue in terms of duty, and not the other way around. But if that is so, then virtue ethics is in trouble, since one of its fundamental points is that rightness is defined in terms of the choices of the virtuous.

I. CONCLUSION

Virtue ethics represents an exciting continuation of an ancient tradition. It has a variety of attractions, not least of which is its emphasis on the importance of moral character. It represents a pluralistic approach to morality, and has interesting things to say about ethical complexity, moral education, and the importance of moral wisdom. Many of the criticisms that have been leveled at it can be met once we dig a bit deeper or introduce small changes to the theory.

But no ethical theory, at least in its present state, is immune to all real difficulties, and virtue ethics, too, has its vulnerable points. The greatest of these takes aim at one of its central claims: that right action must be understood by reference to virtue, rather than the other way around. Perhaps virtue can really enjoy this sort of priority. But it will take a great deal of further work to show it so.

ESSENTIAL CONCEPTS

Continent: those who manage to do the right thing, but with little or no pleasure, and only by suppressing very strong contrary desires.

Contradiction: when one and the same claim is said to be both true and false.

Ethical pluralism: the view that there is more than one ultimate, fundamental moral principle.

Moral exemplar: a moral role model; someone who exhibits the moral virtues to a great degree.

Virtue: an admirable character trait that helps to define a person.

DISCUSSION QUESTIONS

1. How might a person do the right thing but still fail to be morally admirable? How does virtue ethics account for this?
2. How do we come to know what the right thing to do is in a particular situation, according to virtue ethics?
3. Does virtue ethics demand too much of us? Why or why not?
4. Virtuous people sometimes disagree with one another about which actions are right. Is this a problem for virtue ethics? Why or why not?
5. What is the priority problem for virtue ethics? Do you think the virtue ethicist has an adequate reply to this problem?

READING

Nicomachean Ethics

Aristotle

Aristotle (384–322 BCE) was perhaps the greatest philosopher who ever lived. He worked in a variety of philosophical areas (logic, metaphysics, philosophy of mind, epistemology, ethics, rhetoric) and in each field produced work that exerted an influence across many centuries.

His seminal work in moral philosophy is *Nicomachean Ethics*, believed to be a set of carefully recorded lecture notes taken down by Aristotle's students. In this excerpt, from book 2 of the *Nicomachean Ethics*, Aristotle discusses the nature of virtue, its role in a good human life, and its relation to happiness and to "the golden mean." Aristotle's thoughts on the virtues have served as the basis of almost every version of virtue ethics developed in Western philosophy over the past two millennia.

MORAL VIRTUE

Moral Virtue, How Produced, in What Medium and in What Manner Exhibited

Moral virtue, like the arts, is acquired by repetition of the corresponding acts

VIRTUE, . . . being of two kinds, intellectual and moral, intellectual virtue in the main owes both its birth and its growth to teaching (for which reason it requires experience and time), while moral virtue comes about as a result of habit, whence also its name (ἠθική) is one that is formed by a slight variation from the word ἔθος (habit). From this it is also plain that none of the moral virtues arises in us by nature; for nothing that exists by nature can form a habit contrary to its nature. For instance the stone which by nature moves downwards cannot be habituated to move upwards, not even if one tries to train it by throwing it up ten thousand times; nor can fire be habituated to move downwards, nor can anything else that by nature behaves in one way be trained to behave in another. Neither by nature, then, nor contrary to nature do the virtues arise in us; rather we are adapted by nature to receive them, and are made perfect by habit.

Again, of all the things that come to us by nature we first acquire the potentiality and later exhibit the activity (this is plain in the case of the senses; for it was not by often seeing or often hearing that we got these senses, but on the contrary we had them before we used them, and did not come to have them by using them); but the virtues we get by first

exercising them, as also happens in the case of the arts as well. For the things we have to learn before we can do them, we learn by doing them, e.g. men become builders by building and lyre-players by playing the lyre; so too we become just by doing just acts, temperate by doing temperate acts, brave by doing brave acts.

These acts cannot be prescribed exactly, but must avoid excess and defect

Since, then, the present inquiry does not aim at theoretical knowledge like the others (for we are inquiring not in order to know what virtue is, but in order to become good, since otherwise our inquiry would have been of no use), we must examine the nature of actions, namely how we ought to do them; for these determine also the nature of the states of character that are produced, as we have said. Now, that we must act according to the right rule is a common principle and must be assumed—it will be discussed later, i.e. both what the right rule is, and how it is related to the other virtues. But this must be agreed upon beforehand, that the whole account of matters of conduct must be given in outline and not precisely, . . . that the accounts we demand must be in accordance with the subject-matter; matters concerned with conduct and questions of what is good for us have no fixity, any more than matters of health. The general account being of this nature, the account of particular cases is yet more lacking in exactness; for they do not fall under any art or precept, but the agents themselves must in each case consider what is appropriate to the occasion, as happens also in the art of medicine or of navigation.

But though our present account is of this nature we must give what help we can. First, then, let us consider this, that it is the nature of such things to be destroyed by defect and excess, as we see in the

Aristotle, from *Nicomachean Ethics*, trans. W. D. Ross, rev. by J. O. Urmson and J. L. Ackrill (New York: Oxford University Press, 1998), pp. 28–47. By permission of Oxford University Press.

case of strength and of health (for to gain light on things imperceptible we must use the evidence of sensible things); exercise either excessive or defective destroys the strength, and similarly drink or food which is above or below a certain amount destroys the health, while that which is proportionate both produces and increases and preserves it. So too is it, then, in the case of temperance and courage and the other virtues. For the man who flies from and fears everything and does not stand his ground against anything becomes a coward, and the man who fears nothing at all but goes to meet every danger becomes rash; and similarly the man who indulges in every pleasure and abstains from none becomes self-indulgent, while the man who shuns every pleasure, as boors do, becomes in a way insensible; temperance and courage, then, are destroyed by excess and defect, and preserved by the mean.

But not only are the sources and causes of their origination and growth the same as those of their destruction, but also the sphere of their actualization will be the same; for this is also true of the things which are more evident to sense, e.g. of strength; it is produced by taking much food and undergoing much exertion, and it is the strong man that will be most able to do these things. So too is it with the virtues; by abstaining from pleasures we become temperate, and it is when we have become so that we are most able to abstain from them; and similarly too in the case of courage; for by being habituated to despise things that are fearful and to stand our ground against them we become brave, and it is when we have become so that we shall be most able to stand our ground against them.

Pleasure in doing virtuous acts is a sign that the virtuous disposition has been acquired: a variety of considerations show the essential connexion of moral virtue with pleasure and pain

We must take as a sign of states of character the pleasure or pain that supervenes upon acts; for the man who abstains from bodily pleasures and delights in this very fact is temperate, while the man who is annoyed at it is self-indulgent, and he who stands his ground against things that are terrible and delights in this or at least is not pained is brave,

while the man who is pained is a coward. For moral excellence is concerned with pleasures and pains; it is on account of the pleasure that we do bad things, and on account of the pain that we abstain from noble ones. Hence we ought to have been brought up in a particular way from our very youth, as Plato says, so as both to delight in and to be pained by the things that we ought; this is the right education.

We assume, then, that this kind of excellence tends to do what is best with regard to pleasures and pains, and vice does the contrary.

That virtue, then, is concerned with pleasures and pains, and that by the acts from which it arises it is both increased and, if they are done differently, destroyed, and that the acts from which it arose are those in which it actualizes itself—let this be taken as said.

The actions that produce moral virtue are not good in the same sense as those that flow from it: the latter must fulfil certain conditions not necessary in the case of the arts

The question might be asked, what we mean by saying that we must become just by doing just acts, and temperate by doing temperate acts; for if men do just and temperate acts, they are already just and temperate, exactly as, if they do what is in accordance with the laws of grammar and of music, they are grammarians and musicians.

Or is this not true even of the arts? It is possible to do something that is in accordance with the laws of grammar, either by chance or under the guidance of another. A man will be a grammarian, then, only when he has both said something grammatical and said it grammatically; and this means doing it in accordance with the grammatical knowledge in himself.

Again, the case of the arts and that of the virtues are not similar; for the products of the arts have their goodness in themselves, so that it is enough that they should have a certain character, but if the acts that are in accordance with the virtues have themselves a certain character it does not follow that they are done justly or temperately. The agent also must be in a certain condition when he does them; in the first place he must have knowledge, secondly he must choose the acts, and choose them for their own sakes, and thirdly his action must proceed from a firm and unchangeable character. These are not reckoned in as conditions of the possession of the arts except the bare knowledge; but as a condition of the possession of the virtues knowledge has little or no weight, while the other conditions count not for a little but for everything, i.e. the very conditions which result from often doing just and temperate acts.

Actions, then, are called just and temperate when they are such as the just or the temperate man would do; but it is not the man who does these that is just and temperate, but the man who also does them *as* just and temperate men do them. It is well said, then, that it is by doing just acts that the just man is produced, and by doing temperate acts the temperate man; without doing these no one would have even a prospect of becoming good.

Definition of Moral Virtue

The genus of moral virtue: it is a state of character, not a passion, nor a faculty

Next we must consider what virtue is. Since things that are found in the soul are of three kinds—passions, faculties, states of character—virtue must be one of these. By passions I mean appetite, anger, fear, confidence, envy, joy, friendly feeling, hatred, longing, emulation, pity, and in general the feelings that are accompanied by pleasure or pain; by faculties the things in virtue of which we are said to be capable of feeling these, e.g. of becoming angry or being pained or feeling pity; by states of character the things in virtue of which we stand well or badly with reference to the passions, e.g. with reference to anger we stand badly if we feel it violently or too weakly, and well if we feel it moderately; and similarly with reference to the other passions.

Now neither the virtues nor the vices are *passions*, because we are not called good or bad on the ground of our passions, but are so called on the ground of our virtues and our vices, and because we are neither praised nor blamed for our passions (for the man who feels fear or anger is not praised, nor is the man who simply feels anger blamed, but the man who feels it in a certain way),

but for our virtues and our vices we *are* praised or blamed.

Again, we feel anger and fear without choice, but the virtues are modes of choice or involve choice. Further, in respect of the passions we are said to be moved, but in respect of the virtues and the vices we are said not to be moved but to be disposed in a particular way.

For these reasons also they are not *faculties*; for we are neither called good or bad, nor praised or blamed, for the simple capacity of feeling the passions; again, we have the faculties by nature, but we are not made good or bad by nature; we have spoken of this before.

If, then, the virtues are neither passions nor faculties, all that remains is that they should be *states of character*.

Thus we have stated what virtue is in respect of its genus.

The differentia of moral virtue: it is a disposition to choose the mean

We must, however, not only describe virtue as a state of character, but also say what sort of state it is. We may remark, then, that every virtue or excellence both brings into good condition the thing of which it is the excellence and makes the work of that thing be done well; e.g. the excellence of the eye makes both the eye and its work good; for it is by the excellence of the eye that we see well. Similarly the excellence of the horse makes a horse both good in itself and good at running and at carrying its rider and at awaiting the attack of the enemy. Therefore, if this is true in every case, the virtue of man also will be the state of character which makes a man good and which makes him do his own work well.

How this is to happen we have stated already, but it will be made plain also by the following consideration of the specific nature of virtue. In everything that is continuous and divisible it is possible to take more, less, or an equal amount, and that either in terms of the thing itself or relatively to us; and the equal is an intermediate between excess and defect. By the intermediate in the object I mean that which is equidistant from each of the extremes, which is one and the same for all men; by the intermediate relatively to us that which is neither too much nor too little—and this is not one, nor the same for all. For instance, if ten is many and two is few, six is the intermediate, taken in terms of the object; for it exceeds and is exceeded by an equal amount; this is intermediate according to arithmetical proportion. But the intermediate relatively to us is not to be taken so; if ten pounds are too much for a particular person to eat and two too little, it does not follow that the trainer will order six pounds; for this also is perhaps too much for the person who is to take it, or too little—too little for Milo, too much for the beginner in athletic exercises. The same is true of running and wrestling. Thus a master of any art avoids excess and defect, but seeks the intermediate and chooses this—the intermediate not in the object but relatively to us.

If it is thus, then, that every art does its work well—by looking to the intermediate and judging its works by this standard (so that we often say of good works of art that it is not possible either to take away or to add anything, implying that excess and defect destroy the goodness of works of art, while the mean preserves it; and good artists, as we say, look to this in their work), and if, further, virtue is more exact and better than any art, as nature also is, then virtue must have the quality of aiming at the intermediate. I mean moral virtue; for it is this that is concerned with passions and actions, and in these there is excess, defect, and the intermediate. For instance, both fear and confidence and appetite and anger and pity and in general pleasure and pain may be felt both too much and too little, and in both cases not well; but to feel them at the right times, with reference to the right objects, towards the right people, with the right motive, and in the right way, is what is both intermediate and best, and this is characteristic of virtue. Similarly with regard to actions also there is excess, defect, and the intermediate. Now virtue is concerned with passions and actions, in which excess is a form of failure, and so is defect, while the intermediate is praised and is a form of success; and being praised and being successful are both characteristics of virtue. Therefore virtue is a kind of mean, since, as we have seen, it aims at what is intermediate.

Again, it is possible to fail in many ways (for evil belongs to the class of the unlimited, as the Pythagoreans conjectured, and good to that of the limited), while to succeed is possible only in one way (for which reason also one is easy and the other difficult—to miss the mark easy, to hit it difficult); for these reasons also, then, excess and defect are characteristic of vice, and the mean of virtue; for men are good in but one way, but bad in many.

Virtue, then, is a state of character concerned with choice, lying in a mean, i.e. the mean relative to us, this being determined by a rational principle, and by that principle by which the man of practical wisdom would determine it. Now it is a mean between two vices, that which depends on excess and that which depends on defect; and again it is a mean because the vices respectively fall short of or exceed what is right in both passions and actions, while virtue both finds and chooses that which is intermediate. Hence in respect of what it is, i.e. the definition which states its essence, virtue is a mean, with regard to what is best and right an extreme.

But not every action nor every passion admits of a mean; for some have names that already imply badness, e.g. spite, shamelessness, envy, and in the case of actions adultery, theft, murder; for all of these and suchlike things imply by their names that they are themselves bad, and not the excesses or deficiencies of them. It is not possible, then, ever to be right with regard to them; one must always be wrong. Nor does goodness or badness with regard to such things depend on committing adultery with the right woman, at the right time, and in the right way, but simply to do any of them is to go wrong. It would be equally absurd, then, to expect that in unjust, cowardly, and voluptuous action there should be a mean, an excess, and a deficiency; for at that rate there would be a mean of excess and of deficiency, an excess of excess, and a deficiency of deficiency. But as there is no excess and deficiency of temperance and courage because what is intermediate is in a sense an extreme, so too of the actions we have mentioned there is no mean nor any excess and deficiency, but however they are done they are wrong; for in general there is neither a mean of excess and deficiency, nor excess and deficiency of a mean.

The above proposition illustrated by reference to particular virtues

We must, however, not only make this general statement, but also apply it to the individual facts. For among statements about conduct those which are general apply more widely, but those which are particular are more true, since conduct has to do with individual cases, and our statements must harmonize with the facts in these cases. We may take these cases from our table. With regard to feelings of fear and confidence courage is the mean; of the people who exceed, he who exceeds in fearlessness has no name (many of the states have no name), while the man who exceeds in confidence is rash, and he who exceeds in fear and falls short in confidence is a coward. With regard to pleasures and pains—not all of them, and not so much with regard to the pains—the mean is temperance, the excess self-indulgence. Persons deficient with regard to the pleasures are not often found; hence such persons also have received no name. But let us call them 'insensible.'

With regard to giving and taking of money the mean is liberality, the excess and the defect prodigality and meanness. In these actions people exceed and fall short in contrary ways; the prodigal exceeds in spending and falls short in taking, while the mean man exceeds in taking and falls short in spending. (At present we are giving a mere outline or summary, and are satisfied with this; later these states will be more exactly determined.) With regard to money there are also other dispositions—a mean, magnificence (for the magnificent man differs from the liberal man; the former deals with large sums, the latter with small ones), an excess, tastelessness and vulgarity, and a deficiency, niggardliness; these differ from the states opposed to liberality, and the mode of their difference will be stated later.

With regard to honour and dishonour the mean is proper pride, the excess is known as a sort of 'empty vanity,' and the deficiency is undue humility; and as we said liberality was related to magnificence, differing from it by dealing with small sums, so there is a state similarly related to proper pride, being concerned with small honours while that is concerned with great. For it is possible to desire honour as one ought, and more than one ought, and less, and the man who exceeds in his desires is called ambitious, the man who falls short unambitious, while the intermediate person has no name. The dispositions also are nameless, except that that of the ambitious man is called ambition. Hence the people who are at the extremes lay claim to the middle place; and we ourselves sometimes call the intermediate person ambitious and sometimes unambitious, and sometimes praise the ambitious man and sometimes the unambitious. The reason of our doing this will be stated in what follows; but now let us speak of the remaining states according to the method which has been indicated.

With regard to anger also there is an excess, a deficiency, and a mean. Although they can scarcely be said to have names, yet since we call the intermediate person good-tempered let us call the mean good temper; of the persons at the extremes let the one who exceeds be called irascible, and his vice irascibility, and the man who falls short an unirascible sort of person, and the deficiency unirascibility.

Characteristics of the Extreme and Mean States: Practical Corollaries

The extremes are opposed to each other and to the mean

There are three kinds of disposition, then, two of them vices, involving excess and deficiency respectively, and one a virtue, viz. the mean, and all are in a sense opposed to all; for the extreme states are contrary both to the intermediate state and to each other, and the intermediate to the extremes; as the equal is greater relatively to the less, less relatively to the greater, so the middle states are excessive relatively to the deficiencies, deficient relatively to the excesses, both in passions and in actions. For the brave man appears rash relatively to the coward, and cowardly relatively to the rash man; and similarly the temperate man appears self-indulgent relatively to the insensible man, insensible relatively to the self-indulgent, and the liberal man prodigal relatively to the mean man, mean relatively to the prodigal. Hence also the people at the extremes push the intermediate man each over to the other, and the brave man is called rash by the coward, cowardly by the rash man, and correspondingly in the other cases.

These states being thus opposed to one another, the greatest contrariety is that of the extremes to each other, rather than to the intermediate; for these are further from each other than from the intermediate, as the great is further from the small and the small from the great than both are from the equal. Again, to the intermediate some extremes show a certain likeness, as that of rashness to courage and that of prodigality to liberality; but the extremes show the greatest unlikeness to each other; now contraries are defined as the things that are furthest from each other, so that things that are further apart are more contrary.

To the mean in some cases the deficiency, in some the excess, is more opposed; e.g. it is not rashness, which is an excess, but cowardice, which is a deficiency, that is more opposed to courage, and not insensibility, which is a deficiency, but self-indulgence, which is an excess, that is more opposed to temperance. This happens from two reasons, one being drawn from the thing itself; for because one extreme is nearer and liker to the intermediate, we oppose not this but rather its contrary to the intermediate. E.g., since rashness is thought liker and nearer to courage, and cowardice more unlike, we oppose rather the latter to courage; for things that are further from the intermediate are thought more contrary to it. This, then, is one cause, drawn from the thing itself; another is drawn from ourselves; for the things to which we ourselves more naturally tend seem more contrary to the intermediate. For instance, we ourselves tend more naturally to pleasures, and hence are more easily carried away towards self-indulgence than towards propriety. We describe as contrary to the mean, then, rather the directions in which we more often go to great lengths; and therefore self-indulgence, which is an excess, is the more contrary to temperance.

The mean is hard to attain, and is grasped by perception, not by reasoning

That moral virtue is a mean, then, and in what sense it is so, and that it is a mean between two vices, the one involving excess, the other deficiency, and that it is such because its character is to aim at what is intermediate in passions and in actions, has been

sufficiently stated. Hence also it is no easy task to be good. For in everything it is no easy task to find the middle, e.g. to find the middle of a circle is not for everyone but for him who knows; so, too, anyone can get angry—that is easy—or give or spend money; but to do this to the right person, to the right extent, at the right time, with the right motive, and in the right way, *that* is not for everyone, nor is it easy; wherefore goodness is both rare and laudable and noble.

Hence he who aims at the intermediate must first depart from what is the more contrary to it, as Calypso advises—

Hold the ship out beyond that surf and spray.

For of the extremes one is more erroneous, one less so; therefore, since to hit the mean is hard in the extreme, we must as a second best, as people say, take the least of the evils; and this will be done best in the way we describe.

But we must consider the things towards which we ourselves also are easily carried away; for some of us tend to one thing, some to another; and this will be recognizable from the pleasure and the pain we feel. We must drag ourselves away to the contrary extreme; for we shall get into the intermediate state by drawing well away from error, as people do in straightening sticks that are bent.

Now in everything the pleasant or pleasure is most to be guarded against; for we do not judge it impartially. We ought, then, to feel towards pleasure as the elders of the people felt towards Helen, and in all circumstances repeat their saying; for if we dismiss pleasure thus we are less likely to go astray. It is by doing this, then, (to sum the matter up) that we shall best be able to hit the mean.

But this is no doubt difficult, and especially in individual cases; for it is not easy to determine both how and with whom and on what provocation and how long one should be angry; for we too sometimes praise those who fall short and call them good-tempered, but sometimes we praise those who get angry and call them manly. The man, however, who deviates little from goodness is not blamed, whether he do so in the direction of the more or of the less, but only the man who deviates more widely; for *he* does not fail to be noticed. But up to what point and to what extent a man must deviate before he becomes blameworthy it is not easy to determine by reasoning, any more than anything else that is perceived by the senses; such things depend on particular facts, and the decision rests with perception. So much, then, is plain, that the intermediate state is in all things to be praised, but that we must incline sometimes towards the excess, sometimes towards the deficiency; for so shall we most easily hit the mean and what is right.

Aristotle: Nicomachean Ethics

1. Some philosophers have maintained that people are naturally morally good, while others have held that people are naturally wicked. Aristotle takes a middle ground, saying, "Neither by nature, then, nor contrary to nature do the virtues arise in us." Which view do you think is correct, and why?

2. What do you think Aristotle means when he says that "matters concerned with conduct and questions of what is good for us have no fixity"? Do you agree with this statement?

3. What is the difference, according to Aristotle, between performing virtuous actions and being a virtuous person? Do you agree with him that the latter is more valuable?

4. Aristotle says that virtue is a "mean" between extremes. For instance, the virtue of courage consists of the disposition to feel neither too much nor too little fear, but rather some appropriate amount in between. Is this consistent with his claim that some actions (such as stealing or adultery) are always wrong in all circumstances?

5. What advice does Aristotle give regarding how we should go about seeking the mean between extremes? Do you think this is good advice?

CHAPTER 11

Feminist Ethics and the Ethics of Care

The most prominent authors and supporters of the ethical theories that we have considered so far have one thing in common. They are all men. Most of them lived in societies that systematically discriminated against women. Since even the most high-minded thinkers are bound to reflect some of the common assumptions of their times, it should come as no surprise that many important philosophers held views about women that nowadays make us cringe.

Aristotle said that "the male is by nature superior, and the female inferior; the one rules, and the other is ruled."[1] Aquinas claimed, "As regards her individual nature, each woman is defective and misbegotten."[2] Kant wrote that "laborious learning or painful pondering, even if a woman should greatly succeed in it, destroy the merits that are proper to her sex ... [and] they will weaken the charms with which she exercises her great power over the other sex. ... Her philosophy is not to reason, but to sense."[3] Rousseau said, "Women do wrong to complain of the inequality of man-made laws; this inequality is not of man's making, or at any rate it is not the result of mere prejudice, but of reason. ... [Women] must be trained to bear the yoke from the first, so that they may not feel

it, to master their own caprices and to submit themselves to the will of others."[4]

We might be tempted to downplay these slights by claiming that they did not influence the main lines of argument of these thinkers. And there is a sense in which this is correct—almost none of the major male philosophers of past centuries wrote very much about women. But there is also a sense in which it is incorrect, for there are two ways in which philosophers have shortchanged the lives of women. The first is to make false and damaging claims about them. The second is to ignore female experiences and perspectives. Both have been the norm in ethical thinking for centuries. **Feminist ethics** seeks to remedy both of these flaws.

A. THE ELEMENTS OF FEMINIST ETHICS

Feminist ethics is not a single theory, but rather a general approach to ethics that is defined by four central claims:

1. Women are the moral equals of men; views that justify the subordination of women or downplay their interests are thus mistaken on that account.

2. The experiences of women deserve our respect and are vital to a full and accurate understanding of morality. To the extent that philosophers ignore such experiences, their theories are bound to be

---

1. Aristotle, *Politics* 1254 b13.

2. Thomas Aquinas, *Summa Theologica*, Question 92, First article.

3. Immanuel Kant, *Observations on the Feeling of the Beautiful and the Sublime*, section 3.

4. Jean-Jacques Rousseau, *Emile: On Education.*

incomplete, and likely to be biased and inaccurate.

3. Traits that have traditionally been associated with women—empathy, sympathy, caring, altruism, mercy, compassion—are at least as morally important as traditionally masculine traits, such as competitiveness, independence, demanding one's fair share, a readiness to resort to violence, and the insistence on personal honor.

4. Traditionally feminine ways of moral reasoning, ones that emphasize cooperation, flexibility, openness to competing ideas, and a connectedness to family and friends, are often superior to traditionally masculine ways of reasoning that emphasize impartiality, abstraction, and strict adherence to rules.

Two cautionary notes. First, no one believes that every woman is compassionate and caring, or that every man is aggressive and competitive. These are generalizations that hold only to some extent, and allow for many exceptions. Second, when I speak of *traditionally* masculine and feminine traits, I mean just that. These are features that our cultures have long associated with men and with women, respectively. But there is no claim that such traits are innate. Many characteristics we associate with certain groups are a by-product of social influences. Stereotypes often fail to have any basis in fact. But even when they do, these facts are often a result of difficult circumstances and limited opportunities, rather than the expression of some inborn character.

The major moral theories we have discussed thus far are not designed with home and family life in mind. But since so many of our most important moments are spent with those we love, and since so many moral choices are made within the context of close relationships, why not imagine what an ethic would look like that took these as its starting points? Where standard ethical theories see morality as primarily about doing justice (Kantianism), seeking mutual benefit (contractarianism), or impartial benevolence (utilitarianism), many feminists point to care—especially a mother's care—as the model of moral relations and the basis of ethics. This maternal model has generated what feminist philosophers now call an *ethic of care*.

B. THE ETHICS OF CARE

We can better understand an **ethics of care** by first seeing what it is not. Unlike ethical egoism, care ethics does not insist that we always look out for number one. Mothers often rightly sacrifice their own interests in order to advance those of their children. Unlike Kantianism, an ethics of care does not place supreme importance on justice. Matters of justice are not entirely absent from parent–child relations, but they are certainly not the primary focus here. It is important that a parent not try to swindle her children, and that children show respect for their parents. But standing on one's rights, insisting on a fair share, and ensuring that the guilty are given their just deserts are not at the heart of loving relationships.

Contractarian theories see the authors of the moral law as indifferent to the needs of others, willing to make sacrifices for them only if there is a reasonable chance of being compensated in return. Good parents don't see things that way. A mother's care is not conditional on her child's obedience to a set of mutually beneficial rules. The rational pursuit of self-interest is not the ultimate goal; if the only way to help your child is to take a serious hit yourself, a good parent will often do just that.

And contrary to utilitarian demands for impartial benevolence, loving parents are much more concerned about their own children than about other people's kids. There is no thought of being impartial here; a good mother will demonstrate **partiality** toward her children, will give them more care and attention than she does anyone else's children. Love and care cannot be parceled out to everyone equally.

In addition to these specific differences, the ethics of care incorporates the following features. Most of these represent a point of departure from most traditional ethical theories, though as we'll see, there are some points of similarity between the ethics of care and both virtue ethics and Ross's ethical pluralism.

C. THE IMPORTANCE OF EMOTIONS

Care is an emotion, or a network of reinforcing emotions that involve some combination of sympathy, empathy, sensitivity, and love. Like all emotions, care has elements that involve thinking and feeling. The relevant thoughts are focused on the wants and needs of the one being cared for. The feelings are positive, friendly, helpful, nurturing, and often loving. Care helps us know what others need—parents often understand what their own child needs much better than anyone else. And care helps to motivate us to tend to those needs, even when we are exhausted, grudging, or angry. How many mothers and fathers have roused themselves from a sound sleep to soothe their crying infant? Care helps ease those parents out from under the covers.

Utilitarians don't place much importance on the emotions in knowing what's right and wrong. Calculating amounts of happiness and misery isn't an emotional task. Kant was quite dismissive of the emotions, claiming that reason alone could both tell us where our duty lay and get us to do it. Kant was surely right in thinking that our emotions cannot go unchecked—we need an ethic of care, and not just care itself. But feminist philosophers argue that care and its associated emotions are central to moral motivation and moral discovery, even if they are not the whole story.

Those who defend an ethics of care sometimes see themselves as working within a virtue ethics tradition. And this makes sense, given the emphasis not only on what we do, but on how we do it. The manner in which we do things is often as important as what we do.

Suppose, for instance, that my mother calls me up and asks that I spend the afternoon helping my aged father with some household chores. I do as she asks, but only grudgingly, and make it clear with my body language and my brusqueness that I resent being there. I've done the right thing, but in the wrong manner. I am not acting virtuously and am not displaying an appropriate level of care.

D. AGAINST UNIFICATION

Most of the traditional ethical theories offer us one **supreme moral rule**—one that is both absolute and fundamental—that determines the morality of all actions. Along with the ethic of prima facie duties and virtue ethics, care ethics rejects this picture. On this view, there is no sure-fire test for knowing what morality demands of us. Morality is complicated and messy. The drive to try to unify all of morality under a single supreme rule is an understandable one. Such a rule would lend clarity and structure to ethics. But care ethicists argue that this is a pipe dream.

We can see this as it plays out in the lives of many women (and men) faced with conflicting demands from children, work, spouses, and other sources. Suppose your parents call you up and proceed to criticize your boyfriend. He later asks you what you and your parents talked about. Do you tell him what they've said, knowing that he'll be hurt and that this is going to make a good relationship between him and your parents even harder to achieve? Or suppose your husband believes in disciplining children with a very firm hand. You disagree. He spanks his son—your son—after some minor misbehavior. Then he does it again. What do you do?

These aren't life-or-death cases. Rather, these are ordinary situations that arise in homes all the time. Feminist philosophers say of such examples that while there is often a right thing to do, we can't read off a recommendation from some simple rule. Rather, we have to appreciate the different sources of our moral duties. These stem primarily from relationships we have with other people. And they can conflict with one another. When they do, it can be very hard to know what to do. At such times, we may wish for some easy formula that could give us instant advice about how to behave. But if feminist philosophers are right, there is no such thing. Part of gaining moral maturity is recognizing this, facing life's difficult choices, and not pretending that overly simple answers will solve our problems.

E. PARTIALITY AND CONCRETENESS

There are many reasons why philosophers have been so attracted to the idea of a supreme moral rule. Here is one of them. The more general and abstract the rule, the less likely it is to include bias. A rule that applies only to certain people or to certain situations may reflect only a limited perspective. Philosophers have long sought an outlook that is free of prejudice and distortion, one that takes into account all people at all times.

But why is this so important? The traditional answer is that it gives us a way to ensure impartiality. We must think of everyone as moral equals, and that means giving each person equal weight when we determine what is right and wrong. But as we have seen, feminists reject the idea that we must proceed in this way. It is right that we give priority to those we care about. It is good to be partial to our loved ones.

Feminist ethicists resist the push to abstraction that we see so strongly in philosophy. Moral reasoning should not be centered on a single, very general rule, but rather should be guided by a more complicated understanding of the specifics of situations.

F. DOWNPLAYING RIGHTS

Feminists often argue that moral theories have placed too much emphasis on justice. Demanding our rights, insisting that others honor our claims, and making sure we get what we are entitled to—these are ways of asserting our independence from one another, rather than

our connectedness. Talk of rights can divide us more quickly. This is a common complaint about the abortion debates, for instance. Once we start speaking of the rights of a fetus and of a woman, the debate becomes bogged down, making it very difficult to find common ground with those on the other side of the fence.

Imagine that we instead emphasized our responsibilities to one another, based on the model of a caring parent toward her children. Society would be seen not as a venue for the pursuit of rational self-interest, but rather as a stage for cooperation where we took responsibility for one another, and especially for the most vulnerable among us. In the area of social policy, for instance, this would lead to placing much greater importance on education, on support for poor families, and on making sure that everyone had access to excellent medical care.

The emphasis on rights has often meant giving priority to our being free from coercion and unwanted interference. Rights protect autonomy and independence. And so we have rights, for instance, to say and to read what we want, or to do what we like within the privacy of our own homes.

But many (though not all) feminists have launched pointed criticisms of such priorities. They argue that rights tend to place us in opposition to others, creating a barrier beyond which no one may pass without permission. Individual rights often allow people to pursue their own paths at the expense of the community. Rights emphasize the ways in which we are separate from one another, rather than the ways in which we might be brought together.

After all, loving parents do not stand on their rights when their child needs them. They do not want to assert their independence from their son or daughter. Feminists argue that rather than finding ways to insulate ourselves from others, we should be looking to create more opportunities for people to help one another. We should emphasize our responsibilities to others, rather than our rights against them. To the extent that rights stand in the way of building community and forging close ties with others, most feminists regard them with suspicion.

G. CHALLENGES FOR FEMINIST ETHICS

Feminist ethics is an approach to morality, rather than a single unified theory with specific claims that all feminists endorse. As a result, a presentation of this family of views must settle for highlighting general lines of thought, rather than particular arguments and views that all feminists will accept.

Feminist ethicists currently deal with several challenges. And this is unsurprising, given that extensive work in the area is only a generation old. Here are some of the most important of these challenges.

1. *The feminist ethics of care threatens to restrict the scope of the moral community too greatly.* Indeed, early care ethicists argued that we have moral duties only to those we care about. This view is no longer argued for, as it leaves us without any moral duties to strangers or to those we thoroughly dislike. But if we are to model our moral behavior on the mother–child relation, then we need extensive advice about how this is supposed to work in the case of those we don't know or care about. After all, one way in which we seem to have made moral progress is by extending the scope of the moral community beyond those who are near and dear to us.

2. *The role of the emotions in helping us to know the right thing to do, and in moving us to do it, needs further exploration.* Moral clarity sometimes requires that we overcome our indifference and become more emotionally invested in an issue. But in other cases, emotions can cloud our judgment. We need a view of which emotions are appropriate, and when they are appropriate, since the very same emotion can sometimes be enlightening and at other times anything but. An emotion such as anger often blinds us to the truth and prevents us from doing right. And so it needs to be regulated. But anger can also correctly alert us to serious immorality and will sometimes move us to overcome our fear and to do the right thing. We need a much fuller story about the role of the emotions in the moral life.

3. *Downgrading impartiality has its costs.* There is a great deal to be said for the importance of impartiality. It is a definite virtue of judges and others who hold positions of civic responsibility. It is an important corrective for prejudice and bias. It is one of the best reasons for taking the interests of women as seriously as those of men. Impartiality may not always be the right way to go, but it is, at least sometimes and perhaps usually, the best perspective from which to make important moral decisions.

4. *Rejecting any supreme moral rule leaves it hard to know how to solve moral conflicts.* A virtue of the principle of universalizability, or the principle of utility, is that we have a definite standard to appeal to in trying to decide how to act in puzzling cases. Without such a standard, we may be left largely in the dark about what morality allows or requires of us.

5. *While cooperation is often an excellent thing, we also need to have strategies for dealing with uncooperative people or governments.* The world would be a much better place if we were all able to get along and put our differences behind us. But as we all know, good faith and flexibility are sometimes met with a sneer and an iron fist, and we need to plan for such occasions. Caring for our enemies will sometimes mean that they kill us or those we are entrusted to protect. Further, competition is sometimes a good thing. It can enhance efficiency in business. It can make

for inspiring athletic events. It can spur us to personal excellence. So we shouldn't give up on competition entirely. And that means developing a sophisticated view of when it is and isn't appropriate to prefer cooperation over competition.

6. *While justice and rights are not the whole of morality, they are nonetheless a very important part of it.* We can explain what is so immoral about the oppression of women by citing the rights that are violated by sexist actions and policies. Women have rights to be free of physical abuse; they have a moral right to be paid the same amount of money for doing the same work; it is a gross injustice to forcibly circumcise a teenage girl (or a grown woman, for that matter). Rights are a form of moral protection, and women are often the ones in need of the strongest protections. A plausible feminist ethic must therefore make room for the importance of moral rights and the demands of justice that they support.

H. CONCLUSION

Feminists have often been described as those who think that women ought to be treated exactly as we treat men. But this is a mistake. Feminists argue not for equal *treatment*—after all, many of the ways that men typically get treated are morally questionable. Rather, feminists argue for *equal consideration*. The interests of women are to be given the same importance as those of men. When setting social policies, when evaluating traditions, or when trying to settle conflicts between men and women, it is immoral to downgrade the interests of women just because they are women. Women are the moral equals of men. This simple idea, if taken seriously, would lead to radical change in most areas of the world.

Many of us, men as well as women, are more vulnerable and dependent than traditional moral theory allows. In the real world, there are severe inequalities of wealth and power, and it

pays to be sensitive to such things when deciding on our moral ideals. Making care the centerpiece of our moral life, and allowing emotions and our loving relations a larger role in moral thinking, can make a substantial difference in our ethical outlooks.

Feminist ethics is not just for women. Its recommendations are intended for men and women alike. The importance of care, and emotions generally; the emphasis on cooperation; the attractions of flexibility and compromise; the need for more than justice—each of these is as morally important for men as it is for women.

Feminist ethics is best seen as a general approach to morality, rather than as a well-developed theory that can at this point compete directly with the traditional moral theories. But this is not necessarily a weakness. Rather, it is evidence of the wide variety of views that can be developed by those who take the interests of women just as seriously as we have long taken those of men.

ESSENTIAL CONCEPTS

Ethics of care: a moral perspective that emphasizes the centrality of care as the model of admirable moral relations.

Feminist ethics: a family of moral theories committed to four central claims: (1) women are the moral equals of men; (2) the experiences of women deserve our respect and are vital to a full and accurate understanding of morality; (3) traits that have traditionally been associated with women are at least as morally important as traditionally masculine traits; (4) traditionally feminine ways of moral reasoning are often superior to traditionally masculine ways of reasoning.

Partiality: showing greater concern for, or assigning greater importance to, some beings rather than others.

Supreme moral rule: a moral rule that is both absolute and fundamental.

DISCUSSION QUESTIONS

1. What distinctively "female" experiences do feminists claim are neglected by

traditional ethical theories? Do you agree that moral philosophy should be more attentive to these experiences? If so, how should our ethical theories incorporate them?

2. Most ethical theories stress that impartiality is important to acting ethically. Why do care ethicists deny this? Do you think they are correct to do so?

3. Like Ross's pluralism, feminist ethics rejects the notion of a single supreme principle of morality. What are the advantages of this approach? What are the disadvantages?

4. How plausible do you think it is to model the moral relations between people on that of a caring mother to her child?

5. How is feminist ethics similar to virtue ethics? How do the two approaches differ?

6. Given that feminism is often associated with the idea of women's rights, it might seem strange that feminist ethics downplays the importance of rights. What are the reasons feminist ethicists give for doing so? Do you find this an attractive feature of the feminist approach to ethics?

READING

What Is Feminist Ethics?
Hilde Lindemann

Hilde Lindemann offers us a brief overview of feminist ethics in this selection. She first discusses the nature of feminism and identifies some of the various ways that people have defined it. Lindemann argues against thinking of feminism as focused primarily on equality, women, or the differences between the sexes. She instead invites us to think of feminism as based on considerations of gender—specifically, considerations to do with the lesser degree of power that women have, largely the world over, as compared with men.

Lindemann proceeds to discuss the sex/gender distinction and to identify the central tasks of feminist ethics: to understand, criticize, and correct the inaccurate gender assumptions that underlie our moral thinking and behavior. An important approach of most feminists is a kind of skepticism about the ability to distinguish political commitments from intellectual ones. Lindemann concludes by discussing this skepticism and its implications for feminist thought.

A few years ago, a dentist in Ohio was convicted of having sex with his female patients while they were

From Hilde Lindemann, "What Is a Feminist Ethics?" from *An Invitation to Feminist Ethics* (New York: McGraw-Hill, 2006), pp. 2–3, 6–16.

under anesthesia. I haven't been able to discover whether he had to pay a fine or do jail time, but I do remember that the judge ordered him to take a course in ethics. And I recall thinking how odd that order was. Let's suppose, as the judge apparently did, that the dentist really and truly didn't know it was wrong to have sex with anesthetized patients (this will tax your imagination, but try to suppose it anyway). Can we expect—again, as the judge apparently did—that on completing the ethics course, the dentist would be a better, finer man?

Hardly. If studying ethics could make you good, then the people who have advanced academic degrees in the subject would be paragons of moral uprightness. I can't speak for all of them, of course, but though the ones I know are nice enough, they're no more moral than anyone else. Ethics doesn't improve your character. Its *subject* is morality, but its relationship to morality is that of a scholarly study to the thing being studied. In that respect, the relationship is a little like the relationship between grammar and language.

Let's explore that analogy. People who speak fluent English don't have to stop and think about the correctness of the sentence "He gave it to *her*." But here's a harder one. Should you say, "He gave it to *her* who must be obeyed?" or "He gave it to *she* who must be obeyed?" To sort this out, it helps to know a little grammar—the systematic, scholarly description of the structure of the language and the rules for speaking and writing in it. According to those rules, the object of the preposition "to" is the entire clause that comes after it, and the subject of that clause is "she." So, even though it sounds peculiar, the correct answer is "He gave it to she who must be obeyed."

In a roughly similar vein, morally competent adults don't have to stop and think about whether it's wrong to have sex with one's anesthetized patients. But if you want to understand whether it's wrong to have large signs in bars telling pregnant women not to drink, or to sort out the conditions under which it's all right to tell a lie, it helps to know a little ethics. The analogy between grammar and ethics isn't exact, of course. For one thing, there's considerably more agreement about what language is than about what morality is. For another, grammarians are concerned only with the structure of language, not with the meaning or usage of particular words. In both cases, however, the same point can be made: You already have to know quite a lot about how to behave—linguistically or morally—before there's much point in studying either grammar or ethics. . . .

WHAT IS FEMINISM?

What, then, is feminism? As a social and political movement with a long, intermittent history, feminism has repeatedly come into public awareness, generated change, and then disappeared again. As an eclectic body of theory, feminism entered colleges and universities in the early 1970s as a part of the women's studies movement, contributing to scholarship in every academic discipline, though probably most heavily in the arts, social sciences, literature, and the humanities in general. Feminist ethics is a part of the body of theory that is being developed primarily in colleges and universities.

Many people in the United States think of feminism as a movement that aims to make women the social equals of men, and this impression has been reinforced by references to feminism and feminists in the newspapers, on television, and in the movies. But bell hooks has pointed out in *Feminist Theory from Margin to Center* (1984, 18–19) that this way of defining feminism raises some serious problems. Which men do women want to be equal to? Women who are socially well off wouldn't get much advantage from being the equals of the men who are poor and lower class, particularly if they aren't white. hooks's point is that there are no women and men in the abstract. They are poor, black, young, Latino/a, old, gay, able-bodied, upper class, down on their luck, Native American, straight, and all the rest of it. When a woman doesn't think about this, it's probably because she doesn't have to. And that's usually a sign that her own social position is privileged. In fact, privilege often means that there's something uncomfortable going on that others have to pay attention to but you don't. So, when hooks asks which men women want to be equal to, she's reminding us that there's an unconscious presumption of privilege built right in to this sort of demand for equality.

There's a second problem with the equality definition. Even if we could figure out which men are the ones to whom women should be equal, that way of putting it suggests that the point of feminism is somehow to get women to measure up to what (at least some) men already are. Men remain the point of reference; theirs are the lives that women would naturally want. If the first problem with the equality definition is "Equal to *which* men?" the second problem could be put as "Why equal to *any* men?" Reforming a system in which men are the point of reference by allowing women to perform as their equals "forces women to focus on men and address men's conceptions of women rather than creating and developing women's values about themselves," as Sarah Lucia Hoagland puts it in *Lesbian Ethics* (1988, 57). For that reason, Hoagland and some other feminists believe that feminism is first and foremost about women.

But characterizing feminism as about women has its problems too. What, after all, is a woman? In her 1949 book, *The Second Sex*, the French feminist philosopher Simone de Beauvoir famously observed, "One is not born, but becomes a woman. No biological, psychological, or economic fate determines the figure that the human female presents in society: it is civilization as a whole that produces this creature, intermediate between male and eunuch, which is described as feminine" (Beauvoir 1949, 301). Her point is that while plenty of human beings are born female, 'woman' is not a natural fact about them—it's a social invention. According to that invention, which is widespread in "civilization as a whole," man represents the positive, typical human being, while woman represents only the negative, the not-man. She is the Other against whom man defines himself—he is all the things that she is not. And she exists only in relation to him. In a later essay called "One Is Not Born a Woman," the lesbian author and theorist Monique Wittig (1981, 49) adds that because women belong to men sexually as well as in every other way, women are necessarily heterosexual. For that reason, she argued, lesbians aren't women.

But, you are probably thinking, everybody knows what a woman is, and lesbians certainly *are* women. And you're right. These French feminists aren't denying that there's a perfectly ordinary use of the word *woman* by which it means exactly what you think it means. But they're explaining what this comes down to, if you look at it from a particular point of view. Their answer to the question "What is a woman?" is that women are different from men. But they don't mean this as a trite observation. They're saying that 'woman' refers to *nothing but* difference from men, so that apart from men, women aren't anything. 'Man' is the positive term, 'woman' is the negative one, just like 'light' is the positive term and 'dark' is nothing but the absence of light.

A later generation of feminists have agreed with Beauvoir and Wittig that women are different from men, but rather than seeing that difference as simply negative, they put it in positive terms, affirming feminine qualities as a source of personal strength and pride. For example, the philosopher Virginia Held thinks that women's moral experience as mothers, attentively nurturing their children, may serve as a better model for social relations than the contract model that the free market provides. The poet Adrienne Rich celebrated women's passionate nature (as opposed, in stereotype, to the rational nature of men), regarding the emotions as morally valuable rather than as signs of weakness.

But defining feminism as about the positive differences between men and women creates yet another set of problems. In her 1987 *Feminism Unmodified*, the feminist legal theorist Catharine A. MacKinnon points out that this kind of difference, as such, is a symmetrical relationship: If I am different from you, then you are different from me in exactly the same respects and to exactly the same degree. "Men's differences from women are equal to women's differences from men," she writes. "There is an *equality* there. Yet the sexes are not socially equal" (MacKinnon 1987, 37). No amount of attention to the differences between men and women explains why men, as a group, are more socially powerful, valued, advantaged, or free than women. For that, you have to see differences as counting in certain ways, and certain differences being created precisely because they give men *power* over women.

Although feminists disagree about this, my own view is that feminism isn't—at least not directly—about equality, and it isn't about women, and it isn't about difference. It's about power. Specifically, it's about the social pattern, widespread across cultures and history, that distributes power asymmetrically to favor men over women. This asymmetry has been given many names, including the subjugation of women, sexism, male dominance, patriarchy, systemic misogyny, phallocracy, and the oppression of women. A number of feminist theorists simply call it gender, and throughout this book, I will too.

WHAT IS GENDER?

Most people think their gender is a natural fact about them, like their hair and eye color: "Jones is 5 foot 8, has red hair, and is a man." But gender is a *norm*, not a fact. It's a prescription for how people are supposed to act; what they must or must not wear; how they're supposed to sit, walk, or stand; what kind of person they're supposed to marry; what sorts of things they're supposed to be interested in or good at; and what they're entitled to. And because it's an *effective* norm, it creates the differences between men and women in these areas.

Gender doesn't just tell women to behave one way and men another, though. It's a *power* relation, so it tells men that they're entitled to things that women aren't supposed to have, and it tells women that they are supposed to defer to men and serve them. It says, for example, that men are supposed to occupy positions of religious authority and women are supposed to run the church suppers. It says that mothers are supposed to take care of their children but fathers have more important things to do. And it says that the things associated with femininity are supposed to take a back seat to the things that are coded masculine. Think of the many tax dollars allocated to the military as compared with the few tax dollars allocated to the arts. Think about how kindergarten teachers are paid as compared to how stockbrokers are paid. And think about how many presidents of the United States have been women. Gender operates through social institutions (like marriage and the law) and practices (like education and medicine) by disproportionately conferring entitlements and the control of resources on men, while disproportionately assigning women to subordinate positions in the service of men's interests.

To make this power relation seem perfectly natural—like the fact that plants grow up instead of down, or that human beings grow old and die—gender constructs its norms for behavior around what is supposed to be the natural biological distinction between the sexes. According to this distinction, people who have penises and testicles, XY chromosomes, and beards as adults belong to the male sex, while people who have clitorises and ovaries, XX chromosomes, and breasts as adults belong to the female sex, and those are the only sexes there are. Gender, then, is the complicated set of cultural meanings that are constructed around the two sexes. Your sex is either male or female, and your gender—either masculine, or feminine—corresponds socially to your sex.

As a matter of fact, though, sex isn't quite so simple. Some people with XY chromosomes don't have penises and never develop beards, because they don't have the receptors that allow them to make use of the male hormones that their testicles produce. Are they male or female? Other people have ambiguous genitals or internal reproductive structures that don't correspond in the usual manner to their external genitalia. How should we classify them? People with Turner's syndrome have XO chromosomes instead of XX. People with Klinefelter's syndrome have three sex chromosomes: XXY. Nature is a good bit looser in its categories than the simple male/female distinction acknowledges. Most human beings can certainly be classified as one sex or the other, but a considerable number of them fall somewhere in between.

The powerful norm of gender doesn't acknowledge the existence of the in-betweens, though. When, for example, have you ever filled out an application for a job or a driver's license or a passport that gave you a choice other than M or F? Instead, by basing its distinction between masculine and feminine on the existence of two and only two sexes, gender makes the inequality of power between men and women appear natural and therefore legitimate.

Gender, then, is about power. But it's not about the power of just one group over another. Gender always interacts with other social markers—such as race, class, level of education, sexual orientation, age, religion, physical and mental health, and ethnicity—to distribute power unevenly among women positioned differently in the various social orders, and it does the same to men. A man's social status, for example, can have a great deal to do with the extent to which he's even perceived as a man. There's a wonderful passage in the English travel writer Frances Trollope's *Domestic Manners of the Americans* (1831), in which she describes the exaggerated delicacy of middle-class young ladies she met in Kentucky and Ohio. They wouldn't dream of sitting in a chair that was still warm from contact with a gentleman's bottom, but thought nothing of getting laced into their corsets in front of a male house slave. The slave, it's clear, didn't count as a man—not in the relevant sense, anyway. Gender is the force that makes it matter whether you are male or female, but it always works hand in glove with all the other things about you that matter at the same time. It's one power relation intertwined with others in a complex social system that distinguishes your betters from your inferiors in all kinds of ways and for all kinds of purposes.

POWER AND MORALITY

If feminism is about gender, and gender is the name for a social system that distributes power unequally between men and women, then you'd expect feminist ethicists to try to *understand, criticize*, and *correct* how gender operates within our moral beliefs and practices. And they do just that. In the first place, they challenge, on moral grounds, the powers men have over women, and they claim for women, again on moral grounds, the powers that gender denies them. As the moral reasons for opposing gender are similar to the moral reasons for opposing power systems based on social markers other than gender, feminist ethicists also offer moral arguments against systems based on class, race, physical or mental ability, sexuality, and age. And because all these systems, including gender, are powerful enough to *conceal* many of the forces that keep them in place, it's often necessary to make the forces visible by explicitly identifying—and condemning—the various ugly ways they allow some people to treat others. This is a central task for feminist ethics.

Feminist ethicists also produce theory about the moral meaning of various kinds of *legitimate* relations of unequal power, including relationships of dependency and vulnerability, relationships of trust, and relationships based on something other than choice. Parent–child relationships, for example, are necessarily unequal and for the most part unchosen. Parents can't help having power over their children, and while they may have chosen to have children, most don't choose to have the particular children they do, nor do children choose their parents. This raises questions about the responsible use of parental power and the nature of involuntary obligations, and these are topics for feminist ethics. Similarly, when you trust someone, that person has power over you. Whom should you trust, for what purposes, and when is trust not warranted? What's involved in being trustworthy, and what must be done to repair breaches of trust? These too are questions for feminist ethics.

Third, feminist ethicists look at the various forms of power that are required for morality to operate properly at all. How do we learn right from wrong in the first place? We usually learn it from our parents, whose power to permit and forbid, praise and punish, is essential to our moral training. For whom or what are we ethically responsible? Often this depends on the kind of power we have over the person or thing in question. If, for instance, someone is particularly vulnerable to harm because of something I've done, I might well have special duties toward that person. Powerful social institutions—medicine, religion, government, and the market, to take just a few examples—typically dictate what is morally required of us and to whom we are morally answerable. Relations of power set the terms for who must answer to whom, who has authority over whom, and who gets excused from certain kinds of accountability to whom. But because so many of these power relations are illegitimate, in that they're instances of gender, racism, or other kinds of bigotry, figuring out which ones are morally justified is a task for feminist ethics.

DESCRIPTION AND PRESCRIPTION

So far it sounds as if feminist ethics devotes considerable attention to *description*—as if feminist ethicists were like poets or painters who want to show you something about reality that you might otherwise have missed. And indeed, many feminist ethicists emphasize the importance of understanding how social power actually works, rather than concentrating solely on how it ought to work. But why, you might ask, should ethicists worry about how power operates within societies? Isn't it up to sociologists and political scientists to describe how things *are*, while ethicists concentrate on how things *ought* to be?

As the philosopher Margaret Urban Walker has pointed out in *Moral Contexts*, there is a tradition in Western philosophy, going all the way back to Plato, to the effect that morality is something ideal and that ethics, being the study of morality, properly examines only that ideal. According to this tradition, notions of right and wrong as they are found in the world are unreliable and shadowy manifestations of something lying outside of human experience— something to which we ought to aspire but can't hope to reach. Plato's Idea of the Good, in fact, is precisely not of this earth, and only the gods could truly know it. Christian ethics incorporates Platonism into its insistence that earthly existence is fraught with sin and error and that heaven is our real home. Kant, too, insists that moral judgments transcend the histories and circumstances of people's actual lives, and most moral philosophers of the twentieth century have likewise shown little interest in how people really live and what it's like for them to live that way. "They think," remarks Walker (2001), "that there is little to be learned from what is about what ought to be" (3).

In Chapter Four [omitted here—ed.] we'll take a closer look at what goes wrong when ethics is done that way, but let me just point out here that if you don't know how things are, your prescriptions for how things ought to be won't have much practical effect. Imagine trying to sail a ship without knowing anything about the tides or where the hidden rocks and shoals lie. You might have a very fine idea of where you are trying to go, but if you don't know the waters, at best you are likely to go off course, and at worst you'll end up going down with all your shipmates. If, as many feminists have noted, a crucial fact about human selves is that they are always embedded in a vast web of relationships, then the forces at play within those relationships must be understood. It's knowing how people are situated with respect to these forces, what they are going through as they are subjected to them, and what life is like in the face of them, that lets us decide which of the forces are morally justified. Careful description of

how things are is a crucial part of feminist methodology, because the power that puts certain groups of people at risk of physical harm, denies them full access to the good things their society has to offer, or treats them as if they were useful only for other people's purposes is often hidden and hard to see. If this power isn't seen, it's likely to remain in place, doing untold amounts of damage to great numbers of people.

All the same, feminist ethics is *normative* as well as descriptive. It's fundamentally about how things ought to be, while description plays the crucial but secondary role of helping us to figure that out. Normative language is the language of "ought" instead of "is," the language of "worth" and "value," "right" and "wrong," "good" and "bad." Feminist ethicists differ on a number of normative issues, but as the philosopher Alison Jaggar (1991) has famously put it, they all share two moral commitments: "that the subordination of women is morally wrong and that the moral experience of women is worthy of respect" (95). The first commitment—that women's interests ought not systematically to be set in the service of men's—can be understood as a moral challenge to power under the guise of gender. The second commitment—that women's experience must be taken seriously—can be understood as a call to acknowledge how that power operates. These twin commitments are the two normative legs on which any feminist ethics stands. . . .

MORALITY AND POLITICS

If the idealization of morality goes back over two thousand years in Western thought, a newer tradition, only a couple of centuries old, has split off morality from politics. According to this tradition, which can be traced to Kant and some other Enlightenment philosophers, morality concerns the relations between persons, whereas politics concerns the relations among nation-states, or between a state and its citizens. So, as Iris Marion Young (1990) puts it, ethicists have tended to focus on intentional actions by individual persons, conceiving of moral life as "conscious, deliberate, a rational weighing of alternatives," whereas political philosophers have focused on impersonal governmental systems, studying "laws, policies, the large-scale distribution of social goods, countable quantities like votes and taxes" (149).

For feminists, though, the line between ethics and political theory isn't quite so bright as this tradition makes out. It's not always easy to tell where feminist ethics leaves off and feminist political theory begins. There are two reasons for this. In the first place, while ethics certainly concerns personal behavior, there is a long-standing insistence on the part of feminists that the personal *is* political. In a 1970 essay called "The Personal Is Political," the political activist Carol Hanisch observed that "personal problems are political problems. There are no personal solutions at this time" (204–205). What Hanisch meant is that even the most private areas of everyday life, including such intensely personal areas as sex, can function to maintain abusive power systems like gender. If a heterosexual woman believes, for example, that contraception is primarily her responsibility because she'll have to take care of the baby if she gets pregnant, she is propping up a system that lets men evade responsibility not only for pregnancy, but for their own offspring as well. Conversely, while unjust social arrangements such as gender and race invade every aspect of people's personal lives, "there are no personal solutions," either when Hanisch wrote those words or now, because to shift dominant understandings of how certain groups may be treated, and what other groups are entitled to expect of them, requires concerted political action, not just personal good intentions.

The second reason why it's hard to separate feminist ethics from feminist politics is that feminists typically subject the ethical theory they produce to critical political scrutiny, not only to keep untoward political biases out, but also to make sure that the work accurately reflects their feminist politics. Many nonfeminist ethicists, on the other hand, don't acknowledge that their work reflects their politics, because they don't think it should. Their aim, by and large, has been to develop ideal moral theory that applies to all people, regardless of their social position or experience of life, and to do that objectively, without favoritism, requires them to leave their own personal politics behind. The trouble, though, is that they aren't really leaving their own personal politics behind. They're merely refusing to notice that their

politics is inevitably built right in to their theories. (This is an instance of Lindemann's ad hoc rule Number 22: Just because you think you are doing something doesn't mean you're actually doing it.) Feminists, by contrast, are generally skeptical of the idealism nonfeminists favor, and they're equally doubtful that objectivity can be achieved by stripping away what's distinctive about people's experiences or commitments. Believing that it's no wiser to shed one's political allegiances in the service of ethics than it would be to shed one's moral allegiances, feminists prefer to be transparent about their politics as a way of keeping their ethics intellectually honest. . . .

FOR FURTHER READING

Baier, Annette. 1994. *Moral Prejudices: Essays on Ethics.* Cambridge, MA: Harvard University Press.

Beauvoir, Simone de. 1949 [1974]. *The Second Sex.* Trans. and ed. H. M. Parshley. New York: Modern Library.

Hanisch, Carol. 1970. "The Personal Is Political." In *Notes from the Second Year.* New York: Radical Feminism.

Hoagland, Sarah Lucia. 1988. *Lesbian Ethics: Toward New Value.* Palo Alto, CA: Institute of Lesbian Studies.

hooks, bell. 1984. *Feminist Theory from Margin to Center.* Boston: South End Press.

Jaggar, Alison. 1991. "Feminist Ethics: Projects, Problems, Prospects." In *Feminist Ethics,* ed. Claudia Card. Lawrence, KS: University Press of Kansas.

MacKinnon, Catharine A. 1987. *Feminism Unmodified.* Cambridge, MA: Harvard University Press.

Plumwood, Val. 2002. *Environmental Culture: The Ecological Crisis of Reason.* London: Routledge.

Walker, Margaret Urban. 2001. "Seeing Power in Morality: A Proposal for Feminist Naturalism in Ethics." In *Feminists Doing Ethics,* ed. Peggy DesAutels and Joanne Waugh. Lanham, MD: Rowman & Littlefield.

———. 2003. *Moral Contexts.* Lanham, MD: Rowman & Littlefield.

Wittig, Monique. 1981. "One Is Not Born a Woman." *Feminist Issues* 1, no. 2.

Young, Iris Marion. 1990. *Justice and the Politics of Difference.* Princeton, NJ: Princeton University Press.

Hilde Lindemann: What Is Feminist Ethics?

1. Near the beginning of her piece, Lindemann claims that studying ethics "doesn't improve your character." Do you think she is right about this? If so, what is the point of studying ethics?

2. What problems does Lindemann raise for the view that feminism is fundamentally about equality between men and women? Can these problems be overcome, or must we admit that feminism is concerned with equality?

3. What is the difference between sex and gender? Why does Lindemann think that gender is essentially about power? Do you think she is right about this?

4. Lindemann claims that feminist ethics is "*normative* as well as descriptive." What does she mean by this? In what ways is feminist ethics more descriptive than other approaches to ethics? Do you see this as a strength or a weakness?

5. What is meant by the slogan "The personal is political"? Do you agree with the slogan?

6. Lindemann claims that one should not set aside one's political views when thinking about ethical issues. What reasons does she give for thinking this? Do you agree with her?

2

Moral Problems

CHAPTER 12

Abortion

JUST THE FACTS

An **abortion** is the deliberate termination of a pregnancy. Depending on the point at which an abortion is performed, this procedure will result in the death of a **zygote**, **embryo**, or **fetus**.

At **conception**, a sperm enters and fertilizes an egg; together, they form a zygote, which (in humans) consists of a single cell with twenty-three chromosomes from the mother and twenty-three from the father. The zygote rapidly divides, from one to two cells, from two to four, and so on. After just a few days, and under normal conditions, it will lodge itself in the woman's uterus, where, at around a week and a half, it will be known as an embryo. The embryonic stage of development lasts for seven more weeks, at the end of which time the growing organism is known as a fetus.

Zygotes are invisible to the naked eye, as are embryos during the earliest stages of their development. At about a month an embryo is a bit smaller than a grain of rice; at two months (the beginning of the fetal stage), the fetus is about an inch in length and weighs about one-thirtieth of an ounce. At this point it has begun to develop bones and limbs and has a heartbeat. By the conclusion of the first **trimester** (a stage of three months), all of a healthy fetus's organs are present. The fetus is now about four inches long and weighs about an ounce.

Viability is the point at which a fetus can survive outside of the mother's womb. Medical consensus is that twenty weeks after conception marks the earliest point at which a fetus can do this—and even then, most fetuses born this early will die, and most who survive will do so with severe impairments.

There is also broad medical and scientific consensus that fetuses are incapable of experiencing pain until twenty-four or twenty-five weeks after conception. The studies that bear on this question are not decisive—after all, the fetus cannot tell us whether it is in pain or not. So scientists have had to make inferences based on other things they know, such as which elements of the brain and nervous system are responsible for the experience of pain in infants and young children. These elements are not sufficiently developed in a human fetus until the start of the third trimester, give or take a week.

Abortions can be performed either surgically or medically. The most common form is a surgical abortion, which involves inserting a thin, plastic tube into a woman's uterus and suctioning the embryo or fetus out of the uterine lining with a vacuum pump. Medical (i.e., non-surgical) abortions occur when a woman takes a prescribed drug or mix of drugs that operate to expel the embryo or fetus from the uterus.

Both forms of abortion are extremely safe. The vast majority of abortions require only outpatient visits to a medical facility and involve either no anesthesia or only local anesthetics. The risk of dying from a medically supervised abortion in the United States is less than 1 in 100,000; the odds of a woman dying from giving birth are 14 times greater (i.e., about 1 in 7,000). Studies have shown no general long-term medical or psychological harms from having had an abortion. Those who oppose abortion often point to cases of women who have come to regret their decision. There is no denying that such cases exist. But, on the other side, there are many millions of women who have experienced no regret from having had an abortion. Studies do not show a higher incidence of lasting psychological (or physical) harm on the part of women who have had abortions as compared with those who have not.

In 2012, about 700,000 abortions were performed in the United States. (This figure, taken from the Centers for Disease Control, excludes data from three states, so the exact number must be somewhat higher). Ninety-two percent of those abortions occurred during the first trimester; a bit more than 7 percent occurred during the second trimester; fewer than 1 percent took place during the third. The number of abortions in the United States has decreased steadily over the past three decades. There are many factors cited to explain this decrease, but there is broad consensus that better education about and access to birth control has had a substantial impact in reducing the number of unwanted pregnancies.

Before discussing some of the moral arguments that surround abortion, we must take note of the legal situation. Prior to 1973, each state was able to decide for itself whether to permit abortions and, if so, under what conditions. Many states simply outlawed it; others were more permissive. That all changed in 1973, when the US Supreme Court ruled in *Roe v. Wade* that a woman had a largely unlimited constitutional right to have an abortion during the first two trimesters of her pregnancy. The justices regarded viability as the crucial point at which the state may intervene to enact restrictions on abortion access, and saw the end of the second trimester as roughly the point at which a fetus might survive outside the womb.

Abortion is never mentioned in the US Constitution, but seven justices (with two dissenting) offered a two-step argument for the conclusion that women have a constitutional right to secure an abortion. The first step argued that the Constitution includes a right to privacy. This right is also unmentioned in the document itself, but Supreme Court justices had, in a series of prior cases, reasoned that many of the protections explicitly offered in the Constitution made sense only by assuming that there was an implied right to privacy. For instance, in 1965 the Court ruled (in *Griswold v. Connecticut*) that a state law prohibiting the sale of contraceptives was unconstitutional, because it violated the right of married couples to determine for themselves the intimate details of their private life together. The word *contraceptive* never appears in the Constitution, but this was not decisive in the eyes of the justices. Indeed, there are a great many rights that Supreme Court justices have located in the Constitution—rights, for example, to use a textbook of one's choosing when educating one's children, to marry a person of a different race, to be notified of one's rights when taken into custody—even though the Constitution never explicitly says anything about these legal protections.

The second step claimed that the right to privacy extended to a woman's choice of whether to terminate her pregnancy—at least until the fetus becomes viable. The Court was influenced by a case it had decided just a year earlier, when it ruled that unmarried couples also had a constitutional right to privacy that entitled them to the use of contraception. In that ruling, Justice William Brennan wrote that "[i]f the right to privacy means anything, it is the right of the individual, married or single, to be free from unwarranted government intrusion into matters so fundamentally affecting a person as the decision whether to bear or beget a child."[1] This set the stage for the *Roe* decision in 1973, which extended the quoted principle to include a right to an abortion.

Since federal law always takes priority over state law, and Supreme Court rulings are the final word on what counts as federal law, the abortion rights extended in *Roe v. Wade* became the law of the land. Any state that had previously had more restrictive abortion policies was

---

1. Eisenstadt v. Baird, 405 U.S. 438 (1972).

required to permit abortions during the first two trimesters. *Roe* allowed states to regulate abortion during the third trimester, but this has had little practical impact on the number of abortions performed in any given year. That's because less than 1 percent of all abortions occur during the last trimester; further, states allow abortions when the life of the mother or fetus is threatened by a continued pregnancy, and a great many of these late abortions fall into this class.

ARGUMENT ANALYSIS

Much of the debate about the morality of abortion has focused on whether a fetus is a human being. (From now on, I'll follow philosophical custom and use the term *fetus* to refer also to a zygote and embryo.) The thought seems to be that if we could just settle the status of the fetus, then the moral verdict about abortion will follow directly. Here is perhaps the classic anti-abortion attempt to capture the idea:

The Argument from Humanity

1. If the fetus is an innocent human being, then abortion is always (or perhaps almost always) immoral.
2. The fetus is an innocent human being.

Therefore,

3. Abortion is always (or perhaps almost always) immoral.

In support of premise 2, one might simply say that the fetus is a *human* fetus—after all, we are not talking about unborn dogs or monkeys. Further, the human fetus is a living, growing organism—although it is implanted in the mother's womb, connected via an umbilical cord, the fetus is its own individual, with its own genetic makeup. So, it seems, the fetus is a human being. Further, it is innocent of any wrongdoing. Because the fetus is not a **moral agent**—a being capable of understanding right and wrong, and then acting on the basis of that

understanding—a fetus cannot act immorally, even if it can, in some cases, cause harm. (If this sounds odd, compare: cars and lions and trees can sometimes cause harm, but they cannot act immorally. The explanation is that such things are not moral agents.)

Premise 1 can be supported by a very plausible general moral principle: it is wrong to deliberately kill innocent human beings. Now, there *might* be some rare exceptions to this principle—I leave it to you to decide this matter. Still, those rare cases aside, targeting innocent human beings for death certainly seems to be the height of immorality. If, as premise 2 says, a fetus is indeed an innocent human being, then it follows that abortion is always, or perhaps almost always, immoral.

This is probably the most popular line of argument against abortion. But it is not without its problems. These stem from the fact that the term *human being* is **ambiguous**—it has more than one meaning. There are at least two senses of the term used in these debates, and members of each camp tend to use their preferred meaning. The result is that a lot of the discussions about the morality of abortion end up going nowhere.

For our purposes, the important question is whether a fetus is an innocent human being. And that depends on how we define humanity. On a *biological* account, a human being is any member of the species *Homo sapiens*. If being human is a biological concept, then premise 2 is clearly true, since fetuses of our species are certainly innocent of any wrongdoing.

But if we give a purely biological definition of humanity, then premise 1 begs the question against pro-choice opponents. In other words, premise 1 assumes the truth of the conclusion it is meant to support. It does not provide an independent reason for rejecting the pro-choice position. Those who advance premise 1 without any supporting argument for it are preaching to the choir, since only those who already oppose abortion will accept this first premise. If humanity is defined in purely biological terms, then the first premise needs a lot of defense—indeed, as much defense as the argument's conclusion.

To see this, imagine pro-choice advocates who admit that, on a biological reading of *human being*, premise 2 is true. Yes, they'd say, the fetus is a member of our species and hasn't done anything wrong. So it's an innocent human being. But in that case, premise 1 is problematic. Pro-choicers could say that the moral rule against killing innocents is not directed at all members of our species. Rather, that moral rule is intended to protect **persons**: beings who are (at a minimum) rational, self-aware, possessed of emotions, able to reflect on the value of their experiences, and capable of communicating in original, sophisticated ways with one another. Science fiction tales aside, all the persons we know are in fact biological human beings. So it's easy to slide from a moral rule against killing persons to a moral rule against killing humans. Still, according to this pro-choice critic of the Argument from Humanity, all that means is that it is easy to make moral mistakes!

Pro-choicers might go on to say that what makes us special is not the fact that we are a member of a certain species, or the fact that we have a certain set of chromosomes in our cells, but rather the features that make us persons. We can't even *see* a zygote or an early embryo with the naked eye. More than 90 percent of abortions are performed on fetuses that are less than an inch long, that can't think, can't communicate, and have no emotions. A woman's interests in determining how her life is going to be lived are *very* important. Given the significance of these interests, and given that a human fetus is not a person, there is nothing immoral about abortion.

The point here isn't to assess this pro-choice reply—we'll do that soon enough. The point is rather to show how the Argument from Humanity involves an ambiguity about what is means to be a human being, and how that ambiguity makes real trouble for the argument. If we go with a biological understanding of humanity, then premise 2 is secure—but premise 1 needs a lot of further support, especially in light of the criticisms just aired by pro-choicers.

Alternatively, we might think of humanity not as a biological category, but rather as a *psychological* one. On such a view, being human is the same thing as being a person. We often use "human" and "person" interchangeably, so this is totally fine. But remember that in this context, "person" is a technical term—it denotes a being who can think rationally, feel emotions, communicate in sophisticated ways, and so on. On this reading, premise 1 of the Argument from Humanity is very plausible—it is (almost) always wrong to kill innocent persons. But premise 2 is false—fetuses are not persons in the sense currently under discussion. They possess none of the laundry list of features that make someone a person. So, if "human" = "person," the Argument from Humanity is unsound, since its second premise is false.

So the term *humanity* is ambiguous. This isn't any kind of problem, so long as we are very clear about which meaning we are relying on. But once we *are* clear about its different meanings, and make sure that the same meaning is being used in both premises, we can see that the Argument from Humanity is bound to land in trouble.

Now this hardly signals the downfall of the anti-abortion position. After all, those who oppose abortion have offered other arguments to support their views. Another familiar one is

The Argument from Potential

1. If the fetus has the potential to be a person, then it has the same moral status as a person.
2. Most fetuses have the potential to be a person.

Therefore,

3. Most fetuses have the same moral status as a person.
4. A person's moral status includes having a broad set of fundamental rights—including the **right to life** (the right not to be killed).

Therefore,

5. Most fetuses have a broad set of fundamental rights—including the right to life.
6. If a fetus has a right to life, then aborting it is immoral.

Therefore,

7. In most cases, abortion is immoral.

This argument has just four premises: 1, 2, 4, and 6. Premise 2 is uncontroversial: though some fetuses are lost due to miscarriage, most fetuses will grow to be healthy infants, who in turn will become persons like you and me. So most fetuses have the potential to become persons, which is what premise 2 says. Premise 4 is also highly plausible—though there are a lot of controversial details about how precisely to specify the moral status that you and I enjoy, it is widely accepted that we have a set of basic moral rights that protect our interests and choices. These rights include the right to life.

So the argument really hinges on premise 1 and premise 6. Now premise 6 may also seem obviously true: if the fetus has a right to life, then abortion is wrong, since a right to life is a protection against being killed, and abortion involves killing the fetus. As we'll soon see, things are a little trickier than they may seem. But before we investigate the trickiness, let us consider premise 1: the claim that if the fetus has the potential to be a person, then it has the same moral status as a person.

The best defense of this premise seems to be this general principle:

(P) If X has the potential to be Y, then X has the same moral status as Y.

But this principle is false. Just before the election in November 2016, Hillary Clinton had as much potential to become the president as a normal fetus does to become a person. Still, that potential did not entitle her to the moral status of the president—after all, she did not emerge victorious.

There are lots of other counterexamples to (P). A talented young actor may have the potential to become a star—that doesn't by itself give him celebrity status. A promising law student has the potential to become a judge—but she isn't yet qualified to send people to jail. I might buy up 80 percent of the lottery tickets this month, and so have great potential to win, but that does not yet entitle me to the jackpot. For a very close parallel to the abortion case, think, for example, of a dog embryo. It has just as much potential to become a dog as a human embryo has to become a person. But a dog embryo lacks the moral status of a puppy or a dog—we have various moral duties to dogs that we do not have to their embryos.

Now this doesn't show that premise 1 is false. But it does show that what is probably its best support, principle (P), is mistaken. So unless some other, better support for premise 1 can be found, we should not regard the Argument from Potential as sound.

Here is another familiar argument against abortion:

The Argument from Ensoulment

1. It is immoral to kill any innocent being who has a soul.
2. All human fetuses are both innocent and have a soul.

Therefore,

3. It is always immoral to kill a human fetus.

To assess the premises of this argument, we need to know what it is to have a soul. On most views, a soul is what makes you you—it is what makes you the unique individual you are. Most views also share the idea that the soul is immaterial—you can't touch it or see it; you can't pinpoint its exact location in space. I think that these are the two essential elements of being a soul.

Now one can have either a religious or a nonreligious view of the soul. On a nonreligious view, it seems to me that the soul is the equivalent of a personality. My personality is what makes me *me*. Further, you can't touch my personality or locate it at any particular point in space. But on this view, premise 2 is false, since fetuses, perhaps through an entire pregnancy, but certainly for the first couple of trimesters, lack personalities. They aren't funny or demanding or fastidious or moody or . . . anything, really.

If one holds to a religious view, and denies that a soul is a personality but rather something given by God to each zygote at conception, then lots of questions arise. If the soul is something other than a personality, what is it? How is it related to the cells of a zygote or embryo or fetus? Why think that God has, in fact, endowed each of us with a soul (or that God exists in the first place)? If God has given each human zygote a soul, does every other living thing have a God-given soul? If not, why not? Even if God endows all human zygotes with a soul, why think that God prohibits abortion, rather than giving priority to the important interests of a woman who wants to end her pregnancy? (After all, neither the Hebrew nor the Christian scriptures ever mention abortion.) It's true that some religious traditions believe that God has forbidden abortion—but many others reject this view. What evidence can be used to settle such a dispute?

Lots of questions here—and there are many others we could ask. But since this is not a book of theology, we will move on, noting only that if one hopes to utilize the Argument from Ensoulment, one needs answers to these (and other) questions.

Another argument opposing abortion is what we might call

The Infanticide Argument

1. If infanticide is immoral, so too is abortion.
2. Infanticide is immoral.

Therefore,

3. Abortion is immoral.

Some people might resist premise 2—many cultures have thought it perfectly fine to kill newborns. But most of us recoil at such a thought, and let us suppose that we are right to do so. (If we are wrong, then the argument collapses, because its second premise would be false.) So let's take premise 2 for granted.

But what is the thinking behind premise 1? It is a form of **sorites** reasoning. *Sorites* is the ancient Greek word for "heap," and it has given rise to a puzzle about how to draw a principled line between two things that exist along a spectrum. I know that sounds pretty vague, so let's make it concrete. In the ancient riddle, one starts with a grain of sand. Is this a heap? No. Now consider this principle: if X grains of sand is not a heap, then X + 1 grains is not a heap. That seems perfectly plausible—one grain of sand cannot make the difference between a heap and something that is not a heap. But note that if you start with a single grain of sand, and add one at a time, then, by this reasoning, you will *never* get a heap of sand—even if you took the time, say, to add 50 trillion grains of sand to the original one! So something has gone wrong. But it's puzzling, right? There are only two premises to a sorites argument: the status premise (one grain isn't a heap), and the arithmetic premise (adding a grain doesn't change something from a nonheap to a heap). And they both seem totally plausible.

Now what does this have to do with abortion? Well, consider this: suppose infanticide is wrong—it's wrong to deliberately kill infants. It seems that an hour should not make a difference in the moral status of a being. If it's wrong to kill a newborn, then, it seems, it would have been wrong to kill the fetus one hour prior to birth. After all, the fetus at that point has all of the same features as the newborn—except for its location. And one's location doesn't seem to be a morally important feature. But if it's wrong to kill a fetus one hour prior to birth, it's wrong to kill a fetus two hours prior to birth. And if it's wrong to kill a fetus two hours before birth, then it's wrong to kill it three hours before birth. You see where this is going. By continually applying the arithmetic premise that says that an hour cannot make a difference in the moral status of a human being, we will eventually be forced to say that if it is wrong to kill a newborn, then it is wrong to kill a fetus, embryo, or zygote. This is the support for premise 1.

It's very hard to know where this line of reasoning goes wrong, since its initial assumption (that infanticide is immoral) and its arithmetic premise both seem very appealing. Still, this argument for premise 1 does go wrong somewhere, as we can see from its original version. There is a difference between a grain of sand and a heap of sand, even if we can't point to a precise moment when adding a single grain turns a small collection of sand into a heap. There is a difference between an acorn and an oak, between day and night, between a dog zygote and a puppy, even if we are unable to identify a precise moment when one transforms into the other.

As a result, we don't yet have good reason to accept premise 1 of the Argument from Infanticide. The best argument we've considered for it depends on sorites reasoning, which, as we've just seen, generates lots of false conclusions (e.g., that a pile of 50 trillion grains of sand is not a heap). Ironically, though, some opponents of abortion have sought support for premise 1 by considering the implications of a standard *pro-choice* argument:

The Argument from Personhood

1. If a being is not a person, then it lacks any moral rights.
2. Fetuses aren't persons.

Therefore,

3. Fetuses lack moral rights.
4. If a being lacks moral rights, then it is morally acceptable to treat it in any way we like—including killing it.

Therefore,

5. It is morally acceptable to kill fetuses.

We'll assess the premises of this argument in a moment. But before we do, you might have picked up on a problem, one that is directly related to the Infanticide Argument. The problem is simple: infants aren't persons, either. They aren't rational; they aren't self-aware; they can't evaluate the attractions of various options. So if the Argument from Personhood is sound, and abortion is morally OK, then so too is infanticide. (Exercise: just replace "fetuses" with "infants" in the argument and see what happens.) That is just what premise 1 of the Infanticide Argument says.[2] And premise 2 of that argument is true, as we've seen. This puts the pro-choicer in a nice pickle—if she accepts the Argument from Personhood, which permits abortion, then it seems she must accept the Infanticide Argument, which forbids it! That is a contradiction.

The best route to take here is to reject the Argument from Personhood. As we have seen, its second premise is true: persons are individuals who have a set of pretty sophisticated cognitive abilities, which fetuses (and infants) lack. But there is an issue with premises 1 and 4. It is not easy to know whether premise 1 is true—that depends on some hard questions about the nature of moral rights and the conditions under which we possess them. We can't undertake that analysis here, so let's consider our options.

Perhaps premise 1 is false. In that case, this argument fails. Now suppose premise 1 is true. Then, because premise 2 is true, premise 3 would have to be true as well: fetuses lack moral rights. But that's not enough to show that abortion is

---

2. Actually, this is the contrapositive of premise 1 of the Infanticide Argument. Here is a reminder from the logic lesson in Chapter 2. A conditional is an "if P, then Q" claim. Its contrapositive is: "If Q is false, then P is false." A conditional and its contrapositive are logically equivalent. That means that if one is true, the other must be true; if one is false, then the other must be false as well. If the Personhood Argument is sound, then the following conditional is true: "if abortion is morally OK, then so too is infanticide." Its contrapositive is: "If infanticide is immoral, then so too is abortion." And that is premise 1 of the Infanticide Argument. So, if the Personhood Argument is sound, then premise 1 of the Infanticide Argument is true.

morally OK: the argument also requires premise 4 to be true. But premise 4 is not plausible. Dogs aren't persons; neither are monkeys, apes, or elephants. On this line of reasoning, premise 4 would tell us that we are morally allowed to treat them in any way we like—for example, starving them for the sadistic pleasure it affords us or torturing them just for sport. That's grossly immoral, which reflects the larger truth that there *are* moral limits to what we can do to nonpersons. It's not always easy to determine what those limits are—see Chapter 13 for in-depth discussion—but so long as there are limits, premise 4 is false. And so the Argument from Personhood is unsound.

The good news for pro-choicers is that once they abandon this argument, they are no longer forced to accept premise 1 of the Infanticide Argument. The bad news for pro-choicers is that they are now in need of a better argument that can justify their position. A famous possibility comes from Judith Jarvis Thomson, whose article on abortion, first published in 1971 and reprinted here, nearly single-handedly sparked widespread interest in the philosophical questions surrounding the morality of abortion.

Thomson did what few pro-choicers have been willing to do—namely, to grant, for purposes of argument, that fetuses have a moral right to life. You might think that once that's in place, it's game over for the pro-choicer. Look back at premise 6 of the Argument from Potential—it says that if a fetus has a right to life, then abortion is immoral. Isn't that just obviously true?

In Thomson's remarkable article, she directly challenged that view with an argument from analogy. She invited us to imagine a talented violinist in need of a life-saving blood transfusion—and only you have the right blood type. The Society of Music Lovers kidnaps you while you're asleep and hooks you up to a machine that will help transfuse him, with the result that if you were to unplug, you'd kill him. Luckily, say the kidnappers, the transfusion takes only nine months, at the end of which time he'll be completely cured. The violinist is obviously a person.

Further, he's innocent of any wrongdoing—he didn't put the Society members up to this task. So he has a right to life. And that means it would be wrong to kill him. If you unplug, you kill him. So you are morally forbidden to unplug.

Thomson thinks that this verdict is obviously mistaken: while it would be very nice of you to remain plugged to the violinist, it is not morally required. You are morally permitted to unplug if you want. In this situation, you are morally permitted to kill an innocent person with a right to life.

Now this is clearly a made-up tale, but Thomson offers it in the service of

Thomson's Argument from Analogy

1. If it is morally permitted to unplug from the violinist, then it is morally permitted to "unplug" from one's fetus, that is, to terminate one's pregnancy.
2. It is morally permitted to unplug from the violinist.

Therefore,

3. It is morally permitted to terminate one's pregnancy.

Thomson doesn't do much to argue for premise 2—it seems to her obviously correct. In my experience (having taught this paper many times), I've found that most readers agree with her.

But there is usually a lot of pushback regarding premise 1. The clearest parallel with the violinist case is one in which a woman becomes pregnant from having been raped. Just as you did not consent to be attached to the violinist, a rape victim did not consent to the actions that led to a fetus being dependent on her for its life. The principle that explains why you are free to unplug, or a rape victim is free to seek an abortion, seems to be this:

(R) If you bear no moral responsibility for putting others in a life-threatening situation, then you are not morally required to undertake a significant sacrifice in order to keep them alive.

In the violinist case, like a case of pregnancy from rape, sustaining another's life would be **supererogatory**: praiseworthy action that is above and beyond the call of duty.

The worry for Thomson's argument is that the parallel between the violinist case and pregnancy appears to diminish once we are talking about pregnancy that arises from consensual sex. In all such cases, principle (R) no longer seems to apply; even if a woman has used a reliable form of birth control, it has seemed to many that she bears at least some moral responsibility for becoming pregnant, because she knew, or should have known, that no form of birth control is guaranteed to work. Thomson rejects this reasoning—she claims that a person is not required to take *every possible* precaution to avoid creating a situation that makes someone else vulnerable to harm. She is only required to take all *reasonable* precautions. It's not reasonable to ask a woman who does not want children to remain celibate for her entire life—that is asking too much. If that is right, then if a woman uses a reliable form of contraception, she has done all that is reasonable to do in order to prevent a pregnancy. In that case, says Thomson, she is not morally responsible for her pregnancy, and so, by principle (R), not morally required to carry her pregnancy to term.

This line of reasoning has attracted a lot of critical attention; you be the judge of whether her argument works. But whatever the verdict, it cannot justify permitting abortion in cases where a woman *does* bear some moral responsibility for her pregnancy—as, for instance, where she engages in consensual sex without birth control. For those who want to justify abortions in those cases, they will need another argument.

Perhaps the best option takes inspiration from the Argument from Personhood, while trying to correct its problems. It is wrong to suppose that we are morally permitted to treat nonpersons in just any way we like. Still, it *is* sometimes morally acceptable to give the interests of persons priority over those of nonpersons. More strongly, there do seem to be cases where I am allowed to kill nonpersons for my own benefit. For example, if I am walking in a forest and am attacked by a bear—it's him or me—then I may kill it. If I live in an inhospitable area and have to choose between starving or fishing for my food, then I may kill some of the local salmon in order to survive.

Reflecting on these cases, it seems that we might be able to locate a different basis for the pro-choice position:

The Protection of Interests Argument

1. If the only way to protect a person's very important, morally legitimate interests is by killing a nonperson, then it is permissible to do so.
2. In almost all cases of unwanted pregnancies, the only way to protect a woman's very important, morally legitimate interests is by killing a nonperson—the fetus.

Therefore,

3. In almost all cases of unwanted pregnancies, it is permissible to kill the fetus.

Consider premise 2. A woman's interest in living a life as she chooses and plans, according to her own conception of what is valuable and significant, is both very important and morally legitimate. For women who want to terminate their pregnancies prior to viability—in other words, 99 percent of the women in the United States who do seek an abortion—the only way to protect this interest is to allow them the abortion they seek. So, if fetuses are not yet persons, then premise 2 is true.

Note that things are different once a fetus is viable. If a fetus can remain alive outside the womb, then a woman whose interests require her pregnancy to be terminated can undergo a **Cesarean section** (an operation that involves a surgical incision through the abdomen and uterus to remove the fetus from the womb, while seeking to preserve its life). The Protection of Interests Argument does not license a woman to abort her fetus once it is viable, so long as killing the fetus is not necessary to protecting the woman's interests.

That leaves premise 1 of the argument to consider. The earlier examples of defending oneself in the face of a bear attack, or avoiding starvation by fishing, help to support that premise. But all it takes to falsify a moral claim is one counterexample. Premise 1 is false if there is even a single case in which the only way to protect a person's very important, morally legitimate interests is to kill a nonperson, but doing so would be immoral anyway. Can you think of any such cases?

CONCLUSION

Abortion remains a politically contentious issue, but public discussions rarely reflect an appreciation of the complexities of the moral arguments on offer. Opponents of abortion are often content to cite the fetus's humanity as grounds for restricting abortion, failing to acknowledge the ambiguity of the notion of "humanity" and the difficulties that beset the Argument from Humanity. Citing a fetus's potential to develop into a person is also a precarious basis for defending opposition to abortion. In a selection reproduced in this chapter, Don Marquis offers a critique of abortion that, he claims, is different from an appeal to potential. Have a look and see whether you agree. Opponents of abortion have also sometimes relied on a line-drawing argument that cites the difficulties of identifying a point that distinguishes the newborn, who is assumed to enjoy a right to life, from a fetus at increasingly earlier staging of development. It's difficult to pinpoint exactly what goes wrong with this argument, but since it is structurally identical to other sorites arguments that are unsound, there is reason to think that this one is, too.

On the other side, those who defend a pro-choice position have often assumed that the fetus is a nonperson and so is eligible for any treatment we care to give it. As we have seen, this would give us too much license to treat nonpersons in immoral ways. The work of Judith Thomson has cast into doubt the idea that the morality of abortion hinges on whether the fetus possesses a right to life, but as we have seen, her argument is strongest only where defending the permissibility of abortion in cases of rape. The Protection of Interests argument seems to have the best chance of justifying a broader range of morally permitted abortion, but its success depends on whether persons, in order to defend their very important and morally legitimate interests, are allowed to kill nonpersons.

ESSENTIAL CONCEPTS

Abortion: the deliberate termination of a pregnancy.

Ambiguous: having more than one meaning.

Cesarean section: an operation that involves a surgical incision through the abdomen and uterus to remove the fetus from the womb, while seeking to preserve its life.

Conception: the point at which a sperm fertilizes an egg and a zygote is formed.

Embryo: the growing offspring that was once a zygote; the embryonic period of gestation lasts from roughly two weeks to eight weeks after conception.

Fetus: the growing offspring that was once an embryo; the fetal period begins at about the eighth week and lasts for the duration of the pregnancy.

Moral agent: a being capable of understanding right and wrong, and then conforming its behavior to that understanding.

Persons: beings who are rational, can think, feel emotions, feel pain and pleasure, reflect on the value of their experiences, and communicate in original, sophisticated ways with one another.

Right to life: the right not to be killed.

Sorites: a form of argument that relies on the difficulty of drawing a principled line between two things that exist along a spectrum.

Supererogatory: praiseworthy action that is above and beyond the call of duty.

Trimester: one of three three-month stages of a full-term pregnancy.

Viability: the point at which a fetus can survive outside of the mother's womb.

Zygote: the fertilized egg that marks conception and begins pregnancy.

STAT SHOT

1. In 2011, nearly half (45 percent) of all pregnancies among US women were unintended. That same year, about 40 percent of unintended pregnancies in the United States were terminated by abortion.[1]

2. From 2004 to 2013, the number of reported abortions in the United States decreased by 20 percent (Figure 12.1).

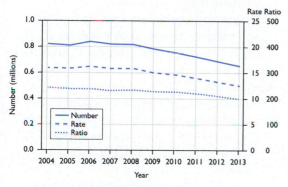

* Number of abortions per 1,000 women aged 15–44 years.
† Number of abortions per 1,000 live births.

‡ Data are for 47 reporting areas: excludes California, Louisiana, Maryland, New Hampshire, and West Virginia.

Figure 12.1. Number, rate,* and ratio† of abortions performed, by year—selected reporting areas,†† United States, 2004–2013.

Source: https://www.cdc.gov/reproductivehealth/data_stats/abortion.htm

3. In 2000, the FDA first approved a drug (RU-486, also known as mifepristone) for nonsurgical abortion. Nowadays this is used in combination with the drug misoprostol.

4. In 2013, 22 percent of all US abortions were medical (i.e., nonsurgical).[2]

5. Eighty-seven percent of all US counties have no abortion clinic.[3]

6. Estimates of the number of illegal abortions in the United States during the 1950s and 1960s range from 200,000 to 1.2 million per year. Prior to *Roe v. Wade*, as many as 5,000 American women died annually as a direct result of illegal abortions.[4]

7. Approximately 47,000 women die around the world from complications of unsafe abortion each year. Deaths due to illegal abortion constitute nearly 13 percent of all maternal deaths.[5]

1. https://www.guttmacher.org/fact-sheet/induced-abortion-united-states

2. https://www.cdc.gov/reproductivehealth/data_stats/abortion.htm

3. *Perspectives on Sexual and Reproductive Health* 43, no. 1 (2011), pp. 41–50, doi:10.1363/4304111

4. http://www.ourbodiesourselves.org/health-info/impact-of-illegal-abortion

5. https://www.guttmacher.org/fact-sheet/induced-abortion-worldwide

Cases for Critical Thinking

Sex-Selection Abortions

Ever since the late 1950s, medical professionals have used ultrasound technology to provide an image of the fetus within the womb. If conditions are favorable, it is possible by the middle of the second trimester to determine the sex of the fetus. Recently, however, a highly reliable blood test has been developed that can enable doctors to determine the sex of the fetus as early as week seven.[1]

These tests have been developed to provide vital information to parents about the well-being of their fetuses. But the tests have also been used by millions of potential parents to select fetuses for abortion just because they are one sex or the other. These are known as sex-selection abortions. In principle, male fetuses can be subject to sex-selection abortion, and doubtless some of them are. But in practice, female fetuses are overwhelmingly the ones selected on the basis of their sex to be aborted.

According to the Population Research Institute, 24 million sex-selection abortions have occurred since 2000.[2] Almost all have targeted female fetuses. There are often cultural and economic pressures that explain this. In India, for instance, parents of young women are expected to provide a dowry, which is an expensive proposition that many cannot afford. In China, a prolonged one-child policy, combined with elements of sexism within the predominant culture, provided incentive for many parents to terminate pregnancies when they discovered that it was to be a girl.

In areas where maternal health is generally good, the natural ratio of boys to girls at birth is 105:100—for every 100 girls born, there will be 105 boys. India's ratio is 112:100. China's is 116:100. In several regions of China, the ratio is 130:100.[3] This differential adds up quickly in the world's most populous countries. In China, for instance, there are 33 million more men than women in the population.[4]

This has serious implications for a society. On average, men are far more likely than women to perpetrate violent crimes. The entrenched sexism in many of the societies where sex-selection abortions are widespread is likely to become harder to combat with the numbers tilting as they are. With many more men than women in society, the marital hopes of many men are bound to be frustrated.

1. Stephanie A. Devaney, Glenn E. Palomaki, Joan A. Scott, "Noninvasive Fetal Sex Determination Using Cell-Free Fetal DNAA Systematic Review and Meta-analysis." *Journal of the American Medical Association* 306, no. 6 (2011): 627–636. doi:10.1001/jama.2011.1114

2. https://www.pop.org/project/stop-sex-selective-abortion/

3. Tania Branigan, "China's Great Gender Crisis." *The Guardian*, November 2, 2011.

4. http://www.rfa.org/english/news/china/gender-01222015125826.html.

Questions

1. Are there any circumstances in which a sex-selection abortion is morally justified? If so, what are they?

2. Various laws have been enacted to oppose sex-selection abortions. Is it feasible or otherwise good policy to criminalize abortions on the basis of the parents' motivations?

3. Many pro-choice feminists have been conflicted about the moral and legal status of sex-selection abortions. On the one hand, they support a right to choose. On the other, such abortions reinforce the status of girls and women as second-class citizens. How should pro-choice feminists think about sex-selection abortion?

4. In addition to those mentioned earlier, what sorts of harmful results can you anticipate from the practice of allowing sex-selection abortions? Are these sufficiently bad to justify outlawing the practice?

Abortion and Rape

In 2012, Todd Aiken, a Missouri Republican, was involved in a close race for a seat in the US Senate. During his campaign, he gave a televised interview during which he stated that pregnancy after rape "is really rare. If it's a legitimate [sic] rape, the female body has ways to try and shut that whole thing down."[1] James Leon Holmes, a federal judge in Arkansas, has written that "concern for rape victims is a red herring because conceptions from rape occur with approximately the same frequency as snowfall in Miami."[2]

It is unclear how widespread such views are, but there is no medical support for them and much medical evidence against them. A widely cited study[3] reports that there is a 5 percent chance that a rape victim will become pregnant as a result of having been raped. The study also reported that over 32,000 women in the United States each year become pregnant as a result of rape.

Some opponents of abortion argue that no abortions are morally permissible. They support their view by claiming that the fetus is possessed of a right to life from the moment of conception, and that the way in which a woman becomes pregnant has no bearing on the moral status of a fetus. As they see it, whatever endows us with a right to life is possessed by the zygote at conception, and this is sufficient to show that abortion is immoral. However, even many who are otherwise opposed to abortion are willing to allow for exceptions not only in cases of rape but also of incest.

1. http://usatoday30.usatoday.com/news/washington/story/2012-08-19/todd-akin-rape/57146944/1.

2. http://www.nytimes.com/2003/04/11/us/attack-on-judicial-nominee-leads-panel-to-delay-vote.html.

3. https://www.ncbi.nlm.nih.gov/pubmed/8765248.

Questions

1. Though most cases of incest are also cases of rape, some are not. For those cases of consensual incest, what basis would there be for opponents of abortion to grant an exception to their position?

2. Judith Jarvis Thomson argues that even if the fetus has a right to life, abortion may be permissible, especially in cases of pregnancies arising from rape. Do you find her line of reasoning plausible? Why or why not?

3. Other standard exceptions to prohibitions on abortion include allowing abortions in order to save a woman's life or to prevent the birth of a child whose medical status is bound to yield a terrible quality of life. Is either of these exceptions plausible? For those who oppose abortion, are there any legitimate exceptions to a general prohibition on abortion? If so, what are they, and what justifies these exceptions?

Defunding Planned Parenthood

Planned Parenthood is a nonprofit organization designed to aid women and men in making informed choices about becoming parents. It is the largest provider of prenatal and preventative women's health care in the country. According to its 2014–2015 annual report, Planned Parenthood and its affiliates provided over 4 million tests for sexually transmitted diseases, nearly 3 million contraception services, over 680,000 cancer screenings and prevention services, and over a million pregnancy tests.[1]

Planned Parenthood is also the largest abortion provider in the United States, performing about 327,000 abortions in a twelve-month period across 2013–2014. This has led to repeated calls from some legislators to withdraw all federal funding from the organization. It has long been the case that federal funds have been forbidden from being used for abortions, except in cases of rape, incest, or those in which a woman's life or health is endangered by carrying her pregnancy to term. Planned Parenthood receives about $500 million per year from the federal government—not as a direct grant, but rather indirectly, via Medicaid and Title X reimbursements for services provided to lower income patients. These funds are used to provide basic health care, contraceptives, and prenatal care for those who cannot otherwise afford it.

In the period between 2011 and 2016, at least 162 abortion clinics closed their doors across the country.[2] Many (though far from all) of these closures resulted from so-called TRAP (Targeted Regulation of Abortion Providers) laws, which are designed to effectively shut down abortion clinics under the guise of ensuring women's health. These laws require clinics to secure and maintain a level of staff or equipment that is so expensive as to make it impossible, practically speaking, for many to keep their doors open. The American Medical Association and the American College of Obstetricians and Gynecologists, among other medical organizations, have judged these requirements to be unnecessary to protect women's or fetal health. Though some of the most extreme TRAP measures were struck down by the US Supreme Court in 2016, twenty-five states still have such laws.[3]

Clinics that provide abortions rarely do only that—as noted earlier, Planned Parenthood clinics also provide an important variety of other services. If laws are enacted to prevent Medicaid and Title X reimbursement to Planned Parenthood for its services, this will certainly result in the closing of many of its clinics. This will surely result in fewer legal abortions being performed in the United States. But it will also mean that fewer girls and women will have access to basic medical and contraceptive services across the country, leading to an overall decrease in the quality of medical care for women and girls and an increase in the number of unwanted pregnancies.

1. Planned Parenthood Federation of America Annual 2014–15 Report: https://www.plannedparenthood.org/files/2114/5089/0863/2014-2015_PPFA_Annual_Report_.pdf.

2. https://www.bloomberg.com/news/articles/2016-02-24/abortion-clinics-are-closing-at-a -record-pace.

3. Details of the TRAP regulations can be found at https://www.guttmacher.org/state-policy/explore/targeted-regulation-abortion-providers.

Questions

1. How would a consequentialist (see Chapter 5) assess the question of whether to defund Planned Parenthood?

2. Because Planned Parenthood provides so many contraceptive services, it does a great deal to prevent unwanted pregnancies, and so reduce the demand for abortions in the first place. Might a law to prevent federal reimbursements for all Planned Parenthood services therefore increase the number of unwanted pregnancies, and so the demand for abortion?

3. If abortion is, in most cases, morally acceptable, then defunding Planned Parenthood would be a very bad thing. But suppose that abortion is immoral in most cases. On this assumption, Planned Parenthood is engaged in a lot of wrongful conduct. But it is also engaged in a lot of good conduct, by providing essential medical and contraceptive services. How should the government treat organizations that do a lot of good if those organizations also (per the assumption here) do a lot of harm?

READINGS

An Almost Absolute Value in History

John Noonan

John Noonan presents a variety of now-classic arguments against the moral permissibility of abortion. One of these is an argument from potential: since the fetus has the potential to be a mature human being, then it has the same moral status as you or I. Another is an argument from humanity: it is always wrong to kill an innocent human being, except perhaps in self-defense; a fetus is an innocent human being; therefore, it is wrong to kill a fetus except, perhaps, in self-defense. Yet another argument is a line-drawing one: there is no moment prior to birth where one can identify the point at which the fetus acquires a right to life; since newborns have a right to life, so too do embryos.

Noonan devotes some time to critiquing alternative points that might mark the division between fetuses that do, and those that do not, have a right to life. Viability is one such point; having sense experiences (sentience) is another; being the object of emotional attachment is yet another; being socially recognized one more. Noonan criticizes each of these criteria of independent moral importance; the result, he says, is that there is no point, other than conception, that marks the acquisition of such importance.

The most fundamental question involved in the long history of thought on abortion is: How do you determine the humanity of a being? To phrase the question that way is to put in comprehensive humanistic terms what the theologians either dealt with as an explicitly theological question under the heading of "ensoulment" or dealt with implicitly in their treatment of abortion. The Christian position as it originated did not depend on a narrow theological or philosophical concept. It had no relation to theories of infant baptism. It appealed to no special theory of instantaneous ensoulment. It took the world's view on ensoulment as that view changed from Aristotle to Zacchia. There was, indeed, theological influence affecting the theory of ensoulment finally adopted, and, of course, ensoulment itself was a theological concept, so that the position was always explained in theological terms. But the theological notion of ensoulment could easily be translated into humanistic language by substituting "human" for "rational soul"; the problem of knowing when a man is a man is common to theology and humanism.

If one steps outside the specific categories used by the theologians, the answer they gave can be analyzed as a refusal to discriminate among human beings on the basis of their varying potentialities. Once conceived, the being was recognized as man because he had man's potential. The criterion for humanity, thus, was simple and all-embracing:

From *The Morality of Abortion: Legal and Historical Perspectives*, edited by John T. Noonan, Jr. (Cambridge, MA: Harvard University Press). Copyright © 1970 by the President and Fellows of Harvard College.

if you are conceived by human parents, you are human.

The strength of this position may be tested by a review of some of the other distinctions offered in the contemporary controversy over legalizing abortion. Perhaps the most popular distinction is in terms of viability. Before an age of so many months, the fetus is not viable, that is, it cannot be removed from the mother's womb and live apart from her. To that extent, the life of the fetus is absolutely dependent on the life of the mother. This dependence is made the basis of denying recognition to its humanity.

There are difficulties with this distinction. One is that the perfection of artificial incubation may make the fetus viable at any time: it may be removed and artificially sustained. Experiments with animals already show that such a procedure is possible. This hypothetical extreme case relates to an actual difficulty: there is considerable elasticity to the idea of viability. Mere length of life is not an exact measure. The viability of the fetus depends on the extent of its anatomical and functional development. The weight and length of the fetus are better guides to the state of its development than age, but weight and length vary. Moreover, different racial groups have different ages at which their fetuses are viable. Some evidence, for example, suggests that Negro fetuses mature more quickly than white fetuses. If viability is the norm, the standard would vary with race and with many individual circumstances.

The most important objection to this approach is that dependence is not ended by viability. The fetus is still absolutely dependent on someone's care in order to continue existence; indeed a child of one or three or even five years of age is absolutely dependent on another's care for existence; uncared for, the older fetus or the younger child will die as surely as the early fetus detached from the mother. The unsubstantial lessening in dependence at viability does not seem to signify any special acquisition of humanity.

A second distinction has been attempted in terms of experience. A being who has had experience, has lived and suffered, who possesses memories, is more human than one who has not. Humanity depends on formation by experience. The fetus is thus "unformed" in the most basic human sense.

This distinction is not serviceable for the embryo which is already experiencing and reacting. The embryo is responsive to touch after eight weeks and at least at that point is experiencing. At an earlier stage the zygote is certainly alive and responding to its environment. The distinction may also be challenged by the rare case where aphasia has erased adult memory: has it erased humanity? More fundamentally, this distinction leaves even the older fetus or the younger child to be treated as an unformed inhuman thing. Finally, it is not clear why experience as such confers humanity. It could be argued that certain central experiences such as loving or learning are necessary to make a man human. But then human beings who have failed to love or to learn might be excluded from the class called man.

A third distinction is made by appeal to the sentiments of adults. If a fetus dies, the grief of the parents is not the grief they would have for a living child. The fetus is an unnamed "it" till birth, and is not perceived as personality until at least the fourth month of existence when movements in the womb manifest a vigorous presence demanding joyful recognition by the parents.

Yet feeling is notoriously an unsure guide to the humanity of others. Many groups of humans have had difficulty in feeling that persons of another tongue, color, religion, sex, are as human as they. Apart from reactions to alien groups, we mourn the loss of a ten-year-old boy more than the loss of his one-day-old brother or his 90-year-old grandfather. The difference felt and the grief expressed vary with the potentialities extinguished, or the experience wiped out; they do not seem to point to any substantial difference in the humanity of baby, boy, or grandfather.

Distinctions are also made in terms of sensation by the parents. The embryo is felt within the womb only after about the fourth month. The embryo is seen only at birth. What can be neither seen nor felt is different from what is tangible. If the fetus cannot be seen or touched at all, it cannot be perceived as man.

Yet experience shows that sight is even more untrustworthy than feeling in determining humanity. By sight, color became an appropriate index for saying who was a man, and the evil of racial discrimination was given foundation. Nor can touch provide the test; a being confined by sickness, "out of touch" with others, does not thereby seem to lose his humanity. To the extent that touch still has appeal as a criterion, it appears to be a survival of the old English idea of "quickening"—a possible mistranslation of the Latin *animatus* used in the canon law. To that extent touch as a criterion seems to be dependent on the Aristotelian notion of ensoulment, and to fall when this notion is discarded.

Finally, a distinction is sought in social visibility. The fetus is not socially perceived as human. It cannot communicate with others. Thus, both subjectively and objectively, it is not a member of society. As moral rules are rules for the behavior of members of society to each other, they cannot be made for behavior toward what is not yet a member. Excluded from the society of men, the fetus is excluded from the humanity of men.

By force of the argument from the consequences, this distinction is to be rejected. It is more subtle than that founded on an appeal to physical sensation, but it is equally dangerous in its implications. If humanity depends on social recognition, individuals or whole groups may be dehumanized by being denied any status in their society. Such a fate is fictionally portrayed in *1984* and has actually been the lot of many men in many societies. In the Roman empire, for example, condemnation to slavery meant the practical denial of most human rights; in the Chinese Communist world, landlords have been classified as enemies of the people and so treated as nonpersons by the state. Humanity does not depend on social recognition, though often the failure of society to recognize the prisoner, the alien, the heterodox as human has led to the destruction of human beings. Anyone conceived by a man and a woman is human. Recognition of this condition by society follows a real event in the objective order, however imperfect and halting the recognition. Any attempt to limit humanity to exclude some group runs the risk of furnishing authority and precedent for excluding other groups in the name of the consciousness or perception of the controlling group in the society.

A philosopher may reject the appeal to the humanity of the fetus because he views humanity as a secular view of the soul and because he doubts the existence of anything real and objective which can be identified as humanity. One answer to such a philosopher is to ask how he reasons about moral questions without supposing that there is a sense in which he and the others of whom he speaks are human. Whatever group is taken as the society which determines who may be killed is thereby taken as human. A second answer is to ask if he does not believe that there is a right and wrong way of deciding moral questions. If there is such a difference, experience may be appealed to: to decide who is human on the basis of the sentiment of a given society has led to consequences which rational men would characterize as monstrous.

The rejection of the attempted distinctions based on viability and visibility, experience and feeling, may be buttressed by the following considerations: Moral judgments often rest on distinctions, but if the distinctions are not to appear arbitrary *fiat*, they should relate to some real difference in probabilities. There is a kind of continuity in all life, but the earlier stages of the elements of human life possess tiny probabilities of development. Consider, for example, the spermatozoa in any normal ejaculate: There are about 200,000,000 in any single ejaculate, of which one has a chance of developing into a zygote. Consider the oocytes which may become ova: there are 100,000 to 1,000,000 oocytes in a female infant, of which a maximum of 390 are ovulated. But once spermatozoon and ovum meet and the conceptus is formed, such studies as have been made show that roughly in only 20 percent of the cases will spontaneous abortion occur. In other words, the chances are about 4 out of 5 that this new being will develop. At this stage in the life of the being there is a sharp shift in probabilities, an immense jump in potentialities. To make a distinction between the rights of spermatozoa and the rights of the fertilized ovum is to respond to an enormous shift in possibilities. For about twenty days after conception the egg may split to form twins or combine with another egg to form a chimera, but the probability of either event happening is very small.

It may be asked, What does a change in biological probabilities have to do with establishing humanity? The argument from probabilities is not aimed at establishing humanity but at establishing an objective discontinuity which may be taken into account in moral discourse. As life itself is a matter of probabilities, as most moral reasoning is an estimate of probabilities, so it seems in accord with the structure of reality and the nature of moral thought to found a moral judgment on the change in probabilities at conception. The appeal to probabilities is the most commonsensical of arguments; to a greater or smaller degree all of us base our actions on probabilities, and in morals, as in law, prudence and negligence are often measured by the account one has taken of the probabilities. If the chance is 200,000,000 to 1 that the movement in the bushes into which you shoot is a man's, I doubt if many persons would hold you careless in shooting; but if the chances are 4 out of 5 that the movement is a human being's, few would acquit you of blame. Would the argument be different if only one out of ten children conceived came to term? Of course this argument would be different. This argument is an appeal to probabilities that actually exist, not to any and all states of affairs which may be imagined.

The probabilities as they do exist do not show the humanity of the embryo in the sense of a demonstration in logic any more than the probabilities of the movement in the bush being a man demonstrate beyond all doubt that the being is a man. The appeal is a "buttressing" consideration, showing the plausibility of the standard adopted. The argument focuses on the decisional factor in any moral judgment and assumes that part of the business of a moralist is drawing lines. One evidence of the nonarbitrary character of the line drawn is the difference of probabilities on either side of it. If a spermatozoon is destroyed, one destroys a being which had a chance of far less than 1 in 200 million of developing into a reasoning being, possessed of the genetic code, a heart and other organs, and capable of pain. If a fetus is destroyed, one destroys a being already possessed of the genetic code, organs, and sensitivity to pain, and one which had an 80 percent chance of developing further into a baby outside the womb who, in time, would reason.

The positive argument for conception as the decisive moment of humanization is that at conception the new being receives the genetic code. It is this genetic information which determines his characteristics, which is the biological carrier of the possibility of human wisdom, which makes him a self-evolving being. A being with a human genetic code is man.

This review of current controversy over the humanity of the fetus emphasizes what a fundamental question the theologians resolved in asserting the inviolability of the fetus. To regard the fetus as possessed of equal rights with other humans was not, however, to decide every case where abortion might be employed. It did decide the case where the argument was that the fetus should be aborted for its own good. To say a being was human was to say it had a destiny to decide for itself which could not be taken from it by another man's decision. But human beings with equal rights often come in conflict with each other, and some decision must be made as to whose claims are to prevail. Cases of conflict involving the fetus are different only in two respects: the total inability of the fetus to speak for itself and the fact that the right of the fetus regularly at stake is the right to life itself.

The approach taken by the theologians to these conflicts was articulated in terms of "direct" and "indirect." Again, to look at what they were doing from outside their categories, they may be said to have been drawing lines or "balancing values." "Direct" and "indirect" are spatial metaphors; "line-drawing" is another. "To weigh" or "to balance" values is a metaphor of a more complicated mathematical sort hinting at the process which goes on in moral judgments. All the metaphors suggest

that, in the moral judgments made, comparisons were necessary, that no value completely controlled. The principle of double effect was no doctrine fallen from heaven, but a method of analysis appropriate where two relative values were being compared. In Catholic moral theology, as it developed, life even of the innocent was not taken as an absolute. Judgments on acts affecting life issued from a process of weighing. In the weighing, the fetus was always given a value greater than zero, always a value separate and independent from its parents. This valuation was crucial and fundamental in all Christian thought on the subject and marked it off from any approach which considered that only the parents' interests needed to be considered.

Even with the fetus weighed as human, one interest could be weighed as equal or superior: that of the mother in her own life. The casuists between 1450 and 1895 were willing to weigh this interest as superior. Since 1895, that interest was given decisive weight only in the two special cases of the cancerous uterus and the ectopic pregnancy. In both of these cases the fetus itself had little chance of survival even if the abortion were not performed. As the balance was once struck in favor of the mother whenever her life was endangered, it could be so struck again. The balance reached between 1895 and 1930 attempted prudentially and pastorally to forestall a multitude of exceptions for interests less than life.

The perception of the humanity of the fetus and the weighing of fetal rights against other human rights constituted the work of the moral analysts. But what spirit animated their abstract judgments? For the Christian community it was the injunction of Scripture to love your neighbor as yourself. The fetus as human was a neighbor; his life had parity with one's own. The commandment gave life to what otherwise would have been only rational calculation.

The commandment could be put in humanistic as well as theological terms: Do not injure your fellow man without reason. In these terms, once the humanity of the fetus is perceived, abortion is never right except in self-defense. When life must be taken to save life, reason alone cannot say that a mother must prefer a child's life to her own. With this exception, now of great rarity, abortion violates the rational humanist tenet of the equality of human lives.

For Christians the commandment to love had received a special imprint in that the exemplar proposed of love was the love of the Lord for his disciples. In the light given by this example, self-sacrifice carried to the point of death seemed in the extreme situations not without meaning. In the less extreme cases, preference for one's own interests to the life of another seemed to express cruelty or selfishness irreconcilable with the demands of love.

John Noonan: An Almost Absolute Value in History

1. Noonan claims that if we can't point to a precise moment during gestation when the fetus acquires a right to life, then the fetus has that right from conception. How plausible is this claim?

2. Conception is the point at which a fetus acquires its genetic makeup. Is Noonan right to think that this supports his claim that conception is the point at which a fetus acquires a right to life?

3. How important is the *potential* of a fetus to acquire the traits of a mature human being? In answering this question, consider how important potential is in other contexts besides abortion.

4. How does Noonan define what it is to be a human being? Is his definition plausible for the purposes he uses it for?

5. Noonan rejects the idea that sentience (the ability to have sense experiences and to feel pleasure or pain) marks the point that separates a fetus who lacks moral rights from a fetus that possesses them. Is his rejection plausible? Why or why not?

A Defense of Abortion

Judith Jarvis Thomson

In this article, Judith Thomson does what very few pro-choice advocates have been willing to do—namely, to grant, for the purposes of argument, that the fetus is as much a moral person as you or I. Still, she argues, being a person does not, by itself, entitle you to use someone else's resources, even if those resources are needed in order to preserve your life. Thus even if we grant that the fetus is a person, that is not enough to show that the fetus is entitled to the continued use of the mother's "resources" (her body). A pregnant woman has a right to bodily autonomy, and that right, in many cases, morally prevails over any rights possessed by a fetus.

Thomson uses a number of thought experiments to defend this claim. The most famous of these involves a world-class violinist. Suppose that you wake up one morning and find yourself connected to a transfusion machine that is providing life support for this musician. He surely has a right to life. But Thomson says that you would be within your rights to remove yourself from the apparatus—even knowing that, by doing this, he will die. The violinist, of course, is meant to be a stand-in for the fetus. According to Thomson, although it would be awfully nice of pregnant women to continue carrying their fetuses to term, they are not usually morally required to do so.

Thomson anticipates a variety of objections to this example, and provides further examples to support her view that women usually have a moral right to seek and obtain an abortion.

Most opposition to abortion relies on the premise that the fetus is a human being, a person, from the moment of conception. The premise is argued for, but, as I think, not well. Take, for example, the most common argument. We are asked to notice that the development of a human being from conception through birth into childhood is continuous; then it is said that to draw a line, to choose a point in this development and say "before this point the thing is not a person, after this point it is a person" is to make an arbitrary choice, a choice for which in the nature of things no good reason can be given. It is concluded that the fetus is, or anyway that we had better say it is, a person from the moment of conception. But this conclusion does not follow. Similar things might be said about the development of an acorn into an oak tree, and it does not follow that acorns are oak trees, or that we had better say they are. Arguments of this form are sometimes called "slippery slope arguments"—the phrase is perhaps self-explanatory—and it is dismaying that opponents of abortion rely on them so heavily and uncritically.

I am inclined to agree, however, that the prospects for "drawing a line" in the development of the fetus look dim. I am inclined to think also that we shall probably have to agree that the fetus has already become a human person well before birth. Indeed, it comes as a surprise when one first learns how early in its life it begins to acquire human characteristics. By the tenth week, for example, it already has a face, arms and legs, fingers and toes; it has internal organs, and brain activity is detectable. On the other hand, I think that the premise is false, that the fetus is not a person from the moment of conception. A newly fertilized ovum, a newly implanted clump of cells, is no more a person than an acorn is an oak tree. But I shall not discuss any of this. For it seems to me to be of great interest to ask what happens if, for the sake of argument, we allow the premise. How, precisely, are we supposed to get from there to the conclusion that abortion is morally impermissible? Opponents of abortion

From Judith Jarvis Thomson, "A Defense of Abortion," *Philosophy & Public Affairs* 1 (1971), pp. 47–53, 55–60, 65–66.

commonly spend most of their time establishing that the fetus is a person, and hardly any time explaining the step from there to the impermissibility of abortion. Perhaps they think the step too simple and obvious to require much comment. Or perhaps instead they are simply being economical in argument. Many of those who defend abortion rely on the premise that the fetus is not a person, but only a bit of tissue that will become a person at birth; and why pay out more arguments than you have to? Whatever the explanation, I suggest that the step they take is neither easy nor obvious, that it calls for closer examination than it is commonly given, and that when we do give it this closer examination we shall feel inclined to reject it.

I propose, then, that we grant that the fetus is a person from the moment of conception. How does the argument go from here? Something like this, I take it. Every person has a right to life. So the fetus has a right to life. No doubt the mother has a right to decide what shall happen in and to her body; everyone would grant that. But surely a person's right to life is stronger and more stringent than the mother's right to decide what happens in and to her body, and so outweighs it. So the fetus may not be killed; an abortion may not be performed.

It sounds plausible. But now let me ask you to imagine this. You wake up in the morning and find yourself back to back in bed with an unconscious violinist. A famous unconscious violinist. He has been found to have a fatal kidney ailment, and the Society of Music Lovers has canvassed all the available medical records and found that you alone have the right blood type to help. They have therefore kidnapped you, and last night the violinist's circulatory system was plugged into yours, so that your kidneys can be used to extract poisons from his blood as well as your own. The director of the hospital now tells you, "Look, we're sorry the Society of Music Lovers did this to you—we would never have permitted it if we had known. But still, they did it, and the violinist now is plugged into you. To unplug you would be to kill him. But never mind, it's only for nine months. By then he will have recovered from his ailment, and can safely be unplugged from you." Is it morally incumbent on you to accede to this situation? No doubt it would be very nice of you if you did, a great kindness. But do you *have* to accede to it? What if it were not nine months, but nine years? Or longer still? What if the director of the hospital says, "Tough luck, I agree, but you've now got to stay in bed, with the violinist plugged into you, for the rest of your life. Because remember this. All persons have a right to life, and violinists are persons. Granted you have a right to decide what happens in and to your body, but a person's right to life outweighs your right to decide what happens in and to your body. So you cannot ever be unplugged from him." I imagine you would regard this as outrageous, which suggests that something really is wrong with that plausible-sounding argument I mentioned a moment ago.

In this case, of course, you were kidnapped; you didn't volunteer for the operation that plugged the violinist into your kidneys. Can those who oppose abortion on the ground I mentioned make an exception for a pregnancy due to rape? Certainly. They can say that persons have a right to life only if they didn't come into existence because of rape; or they can say that all persons have a right to life, but that some have less of a right to life than others, in particular, that those who came into existence because of rape have less. But these statements have a rather unpleasant sound. Surely the question of whether you have a right to life at all, or how much of it you have, shouldn't turn on the question of whether or not you are the product of a rape. And in fact the people who oppose abortion on the ground I mentioned do not make this distinction, and hence do not make an exception in case of rape.

Nor do they make an exception for a case in which the mother has to spend the nine months of her pregnancy in bed. They would agree that would be a great pity, and hard on the mother; but all the same, all persons have a right to life, the fetus is a person, and so on. I suspect, in fact, that they would not make an exception for a case in which, miraculously enough, the pregnancy went on for nine years, or even the rest of the mother's life.

Some won't even make an exception for a case in which continuation of the pregnancy is likely to shorten the mother's life; they regard abortion as impermissible even to save the mother's life. Such cases are nowadays very rare, and many opponents of abortion do not accept this extreme view. All the same, it is a good place to begin: a number of points of interest come out in respect to it.

1. Let us call the view that abortion is impermissible even to save the mother's life "the extreme view." I want to suggest first that it does not issue from the argument I mentioned earlier without the addition of some fairly powerful premises. Suppose a woman has become pregnant, and now learns that she has a cardiac condition such that she will die if she carries the baby to term. What may be done for her? The fetus, being a person, has a right to life, but as the mother is a person too, so has she a right to life. Presumably they have an equal right to life. How is it supposed to come out that an abortion may not be performed? If mother and child have an equal right to life, shouldn't we perhaps flip a coin? Or should we add to the mother's right to life her right to decide what happens in and to her body, which everybody seems to be ready to grant—the sum of her rights now outweighing the fetus' right to life?

The most familiar argument here is the following. We are told that performing the abortion would be directly killing[1] the child, whereas doing nothing would not be killing the mother, but only letting her die. Moreover, in killing the child, one would be killing an innocent person, for the child has committed no crime, and is not aiming at his mother's death. And then there are a variety of ways in which this might be continued. (1) But as directly killing an innocent person is always and absolutely impermissible, an abortion may not be performed. Or, (2) as directly killing an innocent person is murder, and murder is always and absolutely impermissible, an abortion may not be performed. Or, (3) as one's duty to refrain from directly killing an innocent person is more stringent than one's duty to keep a person from dying, an abortion may not be performed. Or, (4) if one's only options are directly killing an innocent person or letting a person die, one must prefer letting the person die, and thus an abortion may not be performed.

Some people seem to have thought that these are not further premises which must be added if the conclusion is to be reached, but that they follow from the very fact that an innocent person has a right to life. But this seems to me to be a mistake, and perhaps the simplest way to show this is to bring out that while we must certainly grant that innocent persons have a right to life, the theses in (1) through (4) are all false. Take (2), for example. If directly killing an innocent person is murder, and thus is impermissible, then the mother's directly killing the innocent person inside her is murder, and thus is impermissible. But it cannot seriously be thought to be murder if the mother performs an abortion on herself to save her life. It cannot seriously be said that she *must* refrain, that she *must* sit passively by and wait for her death. Let us look again at the case of you and the violinist. There you are, in bed with the violinist, and the director of the hospital says to you, "It's all most distressing, and I deeply sympathize, but you see this is putting an additional strain on your kidneys, and you'll be dead within the month. But you *have* to stay where you are all the same. Because unplugging you would be directly killing an innocent violinist, and that's murder, and that's impermissible." If anything in the world is true, it is that you do not commit murder, you do not do what is impermissible, if you reach around to your back and unplug yourself from that violinist to save your life.

The main focus of attention in writings on abortion has been on what a third party may or may not do in answer to a request from a woman for an abortion. This is in a way understandable. Things being as they are, there isn't much a woman can safely do to abort herself. So the question asked is what a third party may do, and what the mother may do, if it is mentioned at all, is deduced, almost as an afterthought, from what it is concluded that third parties may do. But it seems to me that to treat the matter in this way is to refuse to grant to the mother that very status of person which is so firmly insisted on for the fetus. For we cannot simply read off what a person may do from what a third party

may do. Suppose you find yourself trapped in a tiny house with a growing child. I mean a very tiny house, and a rapidly growing child—you are already up against the wall of the house and in a few minutes you'll be crushed to death. The child on the other hand won't be crushed to death; if nothing is done to stop him from growing he'll be hurt, but in the end he'll simply burst open the house and walk out a free man. Now I could well understand it if a bystander were to say, "There's nothing we can do for you. We cannot choose between your life and his, we cannot be the ones to decide who is to live, we cannot intervene." But it cannot be concluded that you too can do nothing, that you cannot attack it to save your life. However innocent the child may be, you do not have to wait passively while it crushes you to death. Perhaps a pregnant woman is vaguely felt to have the status of house, to which we don't allow the right of self-defense. But if the woman houses the child, it should be remembered that she is a person who houses it.

I should perhaps stop to say explicitly that I am not claiming that people have a right to do anything whatever to save their lives. I think, rather, that there are drastic limits to the right of self-defense. If someone threatens you with death unless you torture someone else to death, I think you have not the right, even to save your life, to do so. But the case under consideration here is very different. In our case there are only two people involved, one whose life is threatened, and one who threatens it. Both are innocent: the one who is threatened is not threatened because of any fault, the one who threatens does not threaten because of any fault. For this reason we may feel that we bystanders cannot intervene. But the person threatened can.

In sum, a woman surely can defend her life against the threat to it posed by the unborn child, even if doing so involves its death. And this shows not merely that the theses in (1) through (4) are false; it shows also that the extreme view of abortion is false, and so we need not canvass any other possible ways of arriving at it from the argument I mentioned at the outset.

2. The extreme view could of course be weakened to say that while abortion is permissible to save the mother's life, it may not be performed by a third party, but only by the mother herself. But this cannot be right either. For what we have to keep in mind is that the mother and the unborn child are not like two tenants in a small house which has, by an unfortunate mistake, been rented to both: the mother *owns* the house. The fact that she does adds to the offensiveness of deducing that the mother can do nothing from the supposition that third parties can do nothing. But it does more than this: it casts a bright light on the supposition that third parties can do nothing. Certainly it lets us see that a third party who says "I cannot choose between you" is fooling himself if he thinks this is impartiality. If Jones has found and fastened on a certain coat, which he needs to keep him from freezing, but which Smith also needs to keep him from freezing, then it is not impartiality that says "I cannot choose between you" when Smith owns the coat. Women have said again and again "This body is *my* body!" and they have reason to feel angry, reason to feel that it has been like shouting into the wind. . . .

3. Where the mother's life is not at stake, the argument I mentioned at the outset seems to have a much stronger pull. "Everyone has a right to life, so the unborn person has a right to life." And isn't the child's right to life weightier than anything other than the mother's own right to life, which she might put forward as ground for an abortion?

This argument treats the right to life as if it were unproblematic. It is not, and this seems to me to be precisely the source of the mistake.

For we should now, at long last, ask what it comes to, to have a right to life. In some views having a right to life includes having a right to be given at least the bare minimum one needs for continued life. But suppose that what in fact *is* the bare minimum a man needs for continued life is something he has no right at all to be given? If I am sick unto death, and the only thing that will save my life is the touch of Henry Fonda's cool hand on my fevered brow, then all the same, I have no right to be given the touch of Henry Fonda's cool hand on my fevered brow. It would be frightfully nice of him to fly in from the West Coast to provide it. It would be less nice, though no doubt well meant, if my friends flew out to the West Coast and carried Henry Fonda back with them. But I have no right at all against anybody that he should do this for me. Or again, to return to the story I told earlier, the fact that for continued life that violinist needs the continued use of your kidneys does not establish that he has a right to be given the continued use of your kidneys. He certainly has no right against you that *you* should give him continued use of your kidneys. For nobody has any right to use your kidneys unless you give him such a right; and nobody has the right against you that you shall give him this right—if you do allow him to go on using your kidneys, this is a kindness on your part, and not something he can claim from you as his due. Nor has he any right against anybody else that *they* should give him continued use of your kidneys. Certainly he had no right against the Society of Music Lovers that they should plug him into you in the first place. And if you now start to unplug yourself, having learned that you will otherwise have to spend nine years in bed with him, there is nobody in the world who must try to prevent you, in order to see to it that he is given something he has a right to be given.

Some people are rather stricter about the right to life. In their view, it does not include the right to be given anything, but amounts to, and only to, the right not to be killed by anybody. But here a related difficulty arises. If everybody is to refrain from killing that violinist, then everybody must refrain from doing a great many different sorts of things. Everybody must refrain from slitting his throat, everybody must refrain from shooting him—and everybody must refrain from unplugging you from him. But does he have a right against everybody that they shall refrain from unplugging you from him? To refrain from doing this is to allow him to continue to use your kidneys. It could be argued that he has a right against us that *we* should allow him to continue to use your kidneys. That is, while he had no right against us that we should give him the use of your kidneys, it might be argued that he anyway has a right against us that we shall not now intervene and deprive him of the use of your kidneys. I shall come back to third-party interventions later. But certainly the violinist has no right against you that *you* shall allow him to continue to use your kidneys. As I said, if you do allow him to use them, it is a kindness on your part, and not something you owe him.

The difficulty I point to here is not peculiar to the right to life. It reappears in connection with all the other natural rights; and it is something which an adequate account of rights must deal with. For present purposes it is enough just to draw attention to it. But I would stress that I am not arguing that people do not have a right to life—quite to the contrary, it seems to me that the primary control we must place on the acceptability of an account of rights is that it should turn out in that account to be a truth that all persons have a right to life. I am arguing only that having a right to life does not guarantee having either a right to be given the use of or a right to be allowed continued use of another person's body—even if one needs it for life itself. So the right to life will not serve the opponents of abortion in the very simple and clear way in which they seem to have thought it would.

4. There is another way to bring out the difficulty. In the most ordinary sort of case, to deprive someone of what he has a right to is to treat him unjustly. Suppose a boy and his small brother are jointly given a box of chocolates for Christmas. If the older boy takes the box and refuses to give his brother any of the chocolates, he is unjust to him, for the brother has been given a right to half of them. But suppose that, having learned that otherwise it means nine years in bed with that violinist, you unplug yourself from him. You surely are not being unjust to him, for you gave him no right to use your kidneys, and no one else can have given him any such right. But we have to notice that in unplugging yourself, you are killing him; and violinists, like everybody else, have a right to life, and thus in the view we were considering just now, the right not

to be killed. So here you do what he supposedly has a right you shall not do, but you do not act unjustly to him in doing it.

The emendation which may be made at this point is this: the right to life consists not in the right not to be killed, but rather in the right not to be killed unjustly. This runs a risk of circularity, but never mind: it would enable us to square the fact that the violinist has a right to life with the fact that you do not act unjustly toward him in unplugging yourself, thereby killing him. For if you do not kill him unjustly, you do not violate his right to life, and so it is no wonder you do him no injustice.

But if this emendation is accepted, the gap in the argument against abortion stares us plainly in the face: it is by no means enough to show that the fetus is a person, and to remind us that all persons have a right to life—we need to be shown also that killing the fetus violates its right to life, i.e., that abortion is unjust killing. And is it?

I suppose we may take it as a datum that in a case of pregnancy due to rape the mother has not given the unborn person a right to the use of her body for food and shelter. Indeed, in what pregnancy could it be supposed that the mother has given the unborn person such a right? It is not as if there were unborn persons drifting about the world, to whom a woman who wants a child says "I invite you in."

But it might be argued that there are other ways one can have acquired a right to the use of another person's body than by having been invited to use it by that person. Suppose a woman voluntarily indulges in intercourse, knowing of the chance it will issue in pregnancy, and then she does become pregnant; is she not in part responsible for the presence, in fact the very existence, of the unborn person inside her? No doubt she did not invite it in. But doesn't her partial responsibility for its being there itself give it a right to the use of her body? If so, then her aborting it would be more like the boy's taking away the chocolates, and less like your unplugging yourself from the violinist—doing so would be depriving it of what it does have a right to, and thus would be doing it an injustice.

And then, too, it might be asked whether or not she can kill it even to save her own life: If she voluntarily called it into existence, how can she now kill it, even in self-defense?

The first thing to be said about this is that it is something new. Opponents of abortion have been so concerned to make out the independence of the fetus, in order to establish that it has a right to life, just as its mother does, that they have tended to overlook the possible support they might gain from making out that the fetus is *dependent* on the mother, in order to establish that she has a special kind of responsibility for it, a responsibility that gives it rights against her which are not possessed by any independent person—such as an ailing violinist who is a stranger to her.

On the other hand, this argument would give the unborn person a right to its mother's body only if her pregnancy resulted from a voluntary act, undertaken in full knowledge of the chance a pregnancy might result from it. It would leave out entirely the unborn person whose existence is due to rape. Pending the availability of some further argument, then, we would be left with the conclusion that unborn persons whose existence is due to rape have no right to the use of their mothers' bodies, and thus that aborting them is not depriving them of anything they have a right to and hence is not unjust killing.

And we should also notice that it is not at all plain that this argument really does go even as far as it purports to. For there are cases and cases, and the details make a difference. If the room is stuffy, and I therefore open a window to air it, and a burglar climbs in, it would be absurd to say, "Ah, now he can stay, she's given him a right to the use of her house—for she is partially responsible for his presence there, having voluntarily done what enabled him to get in, in full knowledge that there are such things as burglars, and that burglars burgle." It would be still more absurd to say this if I had had bars installed outside my windows, precisely to prevent burglars from getting in, and a burglar got in only because of a defect in the bars. It remains equally absurd

if we imagine it is not a burglar who climbs in, but an innocent person who blunders or falls in. Again, suppose it were like this: people-seeds drift about in the air like pollen, and if you open your windows, one may drift in and take root in your carpets or upholstery. You don't want children, so you fix up your windows with fine mesh screens, the very best you can buy. As can happen, however, and on very, very rare occasions does happen, one of the screens is defective; and a seed drifts in and takes root. Does the person-plant who now develops have a right to the use of your house? Surely not—despite the fact that you voluntarily opened your windows, you knowingly kept carpets and upholstered furniture, and you knew that screens were sometimes defective. Someone may argue that you are responsible for its rooting, that it does have a right to your house, because after all you *could* have lived out your life with bare floors and furniture, or with sealed windows and doors. But this won't do—for by the same token anyone can avoid a pregnancy due to rape by having a hysterectomy, or anyway by never leaving home without a (reliable!) army.

It seems to me that the argument we are looking at can establish at most that there are *some* cases in which the unborn person has a right to the use of its mother's body, and therefore *some* cases in which abortion is unjust killing. There is room for much discussion and argument as to precisely which, if any. But I think we should sidestep this issue and leave it open, for at any rate the argument certainly does not establish that all abortion is unjust killing.

5. There is room for yet another argument here, however. We surely must all grant that there may be cases in which it would be morally indecent to detach a person from your body at the cost of his life. Suppose you learn that what the violinist needs is not nine years of your life, but only one hour: all you need do to save his life is to spend one hour in that bed with him. Suppose also that letting him use your kidneys for that one hour would not affect your health in the slightest. Admittedly you were kidnapped. Admittedly you did not give anyone permission to plug him into you. Nevertheless it seems to me plain you *ought* to allow him to use your kidneys for that hour—it would be indecent to refuse.

Again, suppose pregnancy lasted only an hour, and constituted no threat to life or health. And suppose that a woman becomes pregnant as a result of rape. Admittedly she did not voluntarily do anything to bring about the existence of a child. Admittedly she did nothing at all which would give the unborn person a right to the use of her body. All the same it might well be said, as in the newly emended violinist story, that she *ought* to allow it to remain for that hour—that it would be indecent in her to refuse. . . .

6. My argument will be found unsatisfactory on two counts by many of those who want to regard abortion as morally permissible. First, while I do argue that abortion is not impermissible, I do not argue that it is always permissible. There may well be cases in which carrying the child to term requires only Minimally Decent Samaritanism[2] of the mother, and this is a standard we must not fall below. I am inclined to think it a merit of my account precisely that it does *not* give a general yes or a general no. It allows for and supports our sense that, for example, a sick and desperately frightened fourteen-year-old schoolgirl, pregnant due to rape, may *of course* choose abortion, and that any law which rules this out is an insane law. And it also allows for and supports our sense that in other cases resort to abortion is even positively indecent. It would be indecent in the woman to request an abortion, and indecent in a doctor to perform it, if she is in her seventh month, and wants the abortion just to avoid the nuisance of postponing a trip abroad. The very fact that the arguments I have been drawing attention to treat all cases of abortion, or even all cases of abortion in which the mother's life is not at stake, as morally on a par ought to have made them suspect at the outset.

Secondly, while I am arguing for the permissibility of abortion in some cases, I am not arguing for the right to secure the death of the unborn child. It is easy to confuse these two

things in that up to a certain point in the life of the fetus it is not able to survive outside the mother's body; hence removing it from her body guarantees its death. But they are importantly different. I have argued that you are not morally required to spend nine months in bed, sustaining the life of that violinist; but to say this is by no means to say that if, when you unplug yourself, there is a miracle and he survives, you then have a right to turn round and slit his throat. You may detach yourself even if this costs him his life; you have no right to be guaranteed his death, by some other means, if unplugging yourself does not kill him. There are some people who will feel dissatisfied by this feature of my argument. A woman may be utterly devastated by the thought of a child, a bit of herself, put out for adoption and never seen or heard of again. She may therefore want not merely that the child be detached from her, but more, that it die. Some opponents of abortion are inclined to regard this as beneath contempt—thereby showing insensitivity to what is surely a powerful source of despair. All the same, I agree that the desire for the child's death is not one which anybody may gratify, should it turn out to be possible to detach the child alive.

At this place, however, it should be remembered that we have only been pretending throughout that the fetus is a human being from the moment of conception. A very early abortion is surely not the killing of a person, and so is not dealt with by anything I have said here.

NOTES
1. The term "direct" in the arguments I refer to is a technical one. Roughly, what is meant by "direct killing" is either killing as an end in itself, or killing as a means to some end, for example, the end of saving someone else's life.
2. Meeting a standard of minimally decent treatment towards those in need.—Ed.

Judith Jarvis Thomson: A Defense of Abortion

1. Thomson's first thought experiment is the case of the violinist. Do you agree that it would be permissible to unplug yourself from the violinist? What conclusions about abortion should we draw from this thought experiment?

2. What is the "extreme view"? What are Thomson's objections to the view? Do you find her objections compelling?

3. Thomson claims that the notion of a "right to life" cannot be interpreted as a right to "the bare minimum one needs for continued life."

Why does she claim this? What, according to Thomson, does having a right to life amount to? Do you agree with her about this?

4. Why doesn't Thomson think that abortion always involves unjust killing? What does the justice of abortion depend on, according to Thomson?

5. Under what conditions (if any) do you think a woman grants a fetus the right to use her body?

On the Moral and Legal Status of Abortion
Mary Anne Warren

Mary Anne Warren argues for a pro-choice position according to which abortion is always morally permissible. The following argument presents the core of her view: persons have rights; fetuses are not persons, but only potential persons; the rights of persons always morally outweigh the rights of merely potential persons; so the rights of a woman always outweigh those of a fetus. Since one of the most important rights we have is to bodily autonomy or self-determination, it follows that a pregnant woman who wants to exercise that right is morally permitted to do so, even if it means the death of her fetus.

Warren begins by critiquing both Judith Thomson's and John Noonan's views on abortion. In the process, she introduces a crucial distinction between two conceptions of a human being—one of these is biological, according to which humans are members of the species *Homo sapiens*, and the other is moral, according to which humans are *persons*: beings possessed of full moral rights and independent moral importance. You and I are persons. Warren believes, however, that fetuses are not. She defends this position by identifying five criteria of personhood: consciousness, the ability to reason, self-motivated activity, the capacity to communicate, and self-awareness. She claims that a being who lacks all five of these traits cannot qualify as a person, and that fetuses lack all five. She concludes that fetuses are not persons.

We will be concerned with both the moral status of abortion, which for our purposes we may define as the act which a woman performs in voluntarily terminating, or allowing another person to terminate, her pregnancy, and the legal status which is appropriate for this act. I will argue that, while it is

From Mary Anne Warren, "On the Moral and Legal Status of Abortion," *The Monist* 57, no. 1 (1973), pp. 43–61.

not possible to produce a satisfactory defense of a woman's right to obtain an abortion without showing that a fetus is not a human being, in the morally relevant sense of that term, we ought not to conclude that the difficulties involved in determining whether or not a fetus is human make it impossible to produce any satisfactory solution to the problem of the moral status of abortion. For it is possible to show that, on the basis of intuitions which we may expect even the opponents of abortion to share, a fetus is not a person, and hence not the sort of entity to which it is proper to ascribe full moral rights.

Of course, while some philosophers would deny the possibility of any such proof, others will deny that there is any need for it, since the moral permissibility of abortion appears to them to be too obvious to require proof. But the inadequacy of this attitude should be evident from the fact that both the friends and the foes of abortion consider their position to be morally self-evident. Because proabortionists have never adequately come to grips with the conceptual issues surrounding abortion, most if not all, of the arguments which they advance in opposition to laws restricting access to abortion fail to refute or even weaken the traditional antiabortion argument, i.e., that a fetus is a human being, and therefore abortion is murder.

These arguments are typically of one of two sorts. Either they point to the terrible side effects of the restrictive laws, e.g., the deaths due to illegal abortions, and the fact that it is poor women who suffer the most as a result of these laws, or else they state that to deny a woman access to abortion is to deprive her of her right to control her own body. Unfortunately, however, the fact that restricting access to abortion has tragic side effects does not, in itself, show that the restrictions are unjustified, since murder is wrong regardless of the consequences of prohibiting it; and the appeal to the right to control one's body, which is generally construed as a property right, is at best a rather feeble argument for the permissibility of abortion. Mere ownership does not give me the right to kill innocent people whom I find on my property, and indeed I am apt to be held responsible if such people injure themselves while on my property. It is equally unclear that I have any moral right to expel an innocent person from my property when I know that doing so will result in his death.

Furthermore, it is probably inappropriate to describe a woman's body as her property, since it seems natural to hold that a person is something distinct from her property, but not from her body. Even those who would object to the identification of a person with his body, or with the conjunction of his body and his mind, must admit that it would be very odd to describe, say, breaking a leg, as damaging one's property, and much more appropriate to describe it as injuring one*self*. Thus it is probably a mistake to argue that the right to obtain an abortion is in any way derived from the right to own and regulate property.

But however we wish to construe the right to abortion, we cannot hope to convince those who consider abortion a form of murder of the existence of any such right unless we are able to produce a clear and convincing refutation of the traditional antiabortion argument, and this has not, to my knowledge, been done. With respect to the two most vital issues which that argument involves, i.e., the humanity of the fetus and its implication for the moral status of abortion, confusion has prevailed on both sides of the dispute. . . .

Our own inquiry will have two stages. In Section I, we will consider whether or not it is possible to establish that abortion is morally permissible even on the assumption that a fetus is an entity with a full-fledged right to life. I will argue that in fact this cannot be established, at least not with the conclusiveness which is essential to our hopes of convincing those who are skeptical about the morality of abortion, and that we therefore cannot avoid dealing with the question of whether or not a fetus really does have the same right to life as a (more fully developed) human being.

In Section II, I will propose an answer to this question, namely, that a fetus cannot be considered a member of the moral community, the set of beings with full and equal moral rights, for the simple reason that it is not a person, and that it is personhood, and not genetic humanity, i.e., humanity as defined by Noonan, which is the basis for membership in this community. I will argue that a fetus, whatever its stage of development, satisfies none of the basic criteria of personhood, and is not even enough *like* a person to be accorded even some of the same rights on the basis of this resemblance. Nor, as we will see, is a fetus's *potential* personhood a threat to the morality of abortion, since, whatever the rights of potential people may be, they are invariably overridden in any conflict with the moral rights of actual people.

I.

We turn now to Professor [Judith] Thomson's case[1] for the claim that even if a fetus has full moral rights, abortion is still morally permissible, at least sometimes, and for some reasons other than to save the woman's life. Her argument is based upon a clever, but I think faulty, analogy. She asks us to picture ourselves waking up one day, in bed with a famous violinist. Imagine that you have been kidnapped, and your bloodstream hooked up to that of the violinist, who happens to have an ailment which will certainly kill him unless he is permitted to share your kidneys for a period of nine months. No one else can save him, since you alone have the right type of blood. He will be unconscious all that time, and you will have to stay in bed with him, but after the nine months are over he may be unplugged, completely cured, that is provided that you have cooperated.

Now then, she continues, what are your obligations in this situation? The antiabortionist, if he is consistent, will have to say that you are obligated to stay in bed with the violinist: for all people have a right to life, and violinists are people, and therefore it would be murder for you to disconnect yourself from him and let him die (p. 49). But this is outrageous, and so there must be something wrong with the same argument when it is applied to abortion. It would certainly be commendable of you to agree to save the violinist, but it is absurd to suggest that your refusal to do so would be murder. His right to life does not obligate you to do whatever is required to keep him alive; nor does it justify anyone else in forcing you to do so. A law which required you to stay in bed with the violinist would clearly be an unjust law, since it is no proper function of the law to force unwilling people to make huge sacrifices for the sake of other people toward whom they have no such prior obligation.

Thomson concludes that, if this analogy is an apt one, then we can grant the antiabortionist his claim that a fetus is a human being, and still hold that it is at least sometimes the case that a pregnant woman has the right to refuse to be a Good Samaritan towards the fetus, i.e., to obtain an abortion. For there is a great gap between the claim that x has a right to life, and the claim that y is obligated to do whatever is necessary to keep x alive, let alone that he ought to be forced to do so. It is y's duty to keep x alive only if he has somehow contracted a *special* obligation to

do so; and a woman who is unwillingly pregnant, e.g., who was raped, has done nothing which obligates her to make the enormous sacrifice which is necessary to preserve the conceptus.

This argument is initially quite plausible, and in the extreme case of pregnancy due to rape it is probably conclusive. Difficulties arise, however, when we try to specify more exactly the range of cases in which abortion is clearly justifiable even on the assumption that the fetus is human. Professor Thomson considers it a virtue of her argument that it does not enable us to conclude that abortion is *always* permissible. It would, she says, be "indecent" for a woman in her seventh month to obtain an abortion just to avoid having to postpone a trip to Europe. On the other hand, her argument enables us to see that "a sick and desperately frightened schoolgirl pregnant due to rape may *of course* choose abortion, and that any law which rules this out is an insane law" (p. 65). So far, so good; but what are we to say about the woman who becomes pregnant not through rape but as a result of her own carelessness, or because of contraceptive failure, or who gets pregnant intentionally and then changes her mind about wanting a child? With respect to such cases, the violinist analogy is of much less use to the defender of the woman's right to obtain an abortion.

Indeed, the choice of a pregnancy due to rape, as an example of a case in which abortion is permissible even if a fetus is considered a human being, is extremely significant; for it is only in the case of pregnancy due to rape that the woman's situation is adequately analogous to the violinist case for our intuitions about the latter to transfer convincingly. The crucial difference between a pregnancy due to rape and the *normal* case of an unwanted pregnancy is that in the normal case we cannot claim that the woman is in no way responsible for her predicament; she could have remained chaste, or taken her pills more faithfully, or abstained on dangerous days, and so on. If, on the other hand, you are kidnapped by strangers, and hooked up to a strange violinist, then you are free of any shred of responsibility for the situation, on the basis of which it could be argued that you are obligated to keep the violinist alive. Only when her pregnancy is due to rape is a woman clearly just as nonresponsible.

Consequently, there is room for the antiabortionist to argue that in the normal case of unwanted pregnancy a woman has, by her own actions, assumed responsibility for the fetus. For if x behaves in a way which he could have avoided, and which he knows involves, let us say, a 1 percent chance of bringing into existence a human being, with a right to life, and does so knowing that if this should happen then that human being will perish unless x does certain things to keep him alive, then it is by no means clear that when it does happen x is free of any obligation to what he knew in advance would be required to keep that human being alive.

The plausibility of such an argument is enough to show that the Thomson analogy can provide a clear and persuasive defense of a woman's right to obtain an abortion only with respect to those cases in which the woman is in no way responsible for her pregnancy, e.g., where it is due to rape. In all other cases, we would almost certainly conclude that it was necessary to look carefully at the particular circumstances in order to determine the extent of the woman's responsibility, and hence the extent of her obligation. This is an extremely unsatisfactory outcome, from the viewpoint of the opponents of restrictive abortion laws, most of whom are convinced that a woman has a right to obtain an abortion regardless of how and why she got pregnant.

Of course a supporter of the violinist analogy might point out that it is absurd to suggest that forgetting her pill one day might be sufficient to obligate a woman to complete an unwanted pregnancy. And indeed it *is* absurd to suggest this. As we will see, the moral right to obtain an abortion is not in the least dependent upon the extent to which the woman is responsible for her pregnancy. But unfortunately, once we allow the assumption that a fetus has full moral rights, we cannot avoid taking this absurd suggestion seriously. Perhaps we can make this point more clear by altering the violinist story just enough to make it more analogous to a normal unwanted pregnancy and less to a pregnancy due to rape, and then seeing whether it is still obvious that you are not obligated to stay in bed with the fellow.

Suppose, then, that violinists are peculiarly prone to the sort of illness the only cure for which is the use of someone else's bloodstream for nine months, and that because of this there has been formed a society of music lovers who agree that whenever a violinist is stricken they will draw lots and the loser will, by some means, be made the one and only person capable of saving him. Now then, would you be obligated to cooperate in curing the violinist if you had voluntarily joined this society, knowing the possible consequences, and then your name had been drawn and you had been kidnapped? Admittedly, you did not promise ahead of time that you would, but you did deliberately place yourself in a position in which it might happen that a human life would be lost if you did not. Surely this is at least a prima facie reason for supposing that you have an obligation to stay in bed with the violinist. Suppose that you had gotten your name drawn deliberately; surely *that* would be quite a strong reason for thinking that you had such an obligation.

It might be suggested that there is one important disanalogy between the modified violinist case and the case of an unwanted pregnancy, which makes the woman's responsibility significantly less, namely, the fact that the fetus *comes into existence* as the result of the result of the woman's actions. This fact might give her a right to refuse to keep it alive, whereas she would not have had this right had it existed previously, independently, and then as a result of her actions become dependent upon her for its survival.

My own intuition, however, is that x has no more right to bring into existence, either deliberately or as a foreseeable result of actions he could have avoided, a being with full moral rights (y), and then refuse to do what he knew beforehand would be required to keep that being alive, than he has to enter into an agreement with an existing person, whereby he may be called upon to save that person's life, and then refuse to do so when so called upon. Thus, x's responsibility for y's existence does not seem to lessen his obligation to keep y alive, if he is also responsible for y's being in a situation in which only he can save him.

Whether or not this intuition is entirely correct, it brings us back once again to the conclusion that once we allow the assumption that a fetus has full moral rights it becomes an extremely complex and difficult question whether and when abortion is justifiable. Thus the Thomson analogy cannot help us produce a clear and persuasive proof of the moral permissibility of abortion. Nor will the opponents of the restrictive laws thank us for anything less; for their conviction (for the most part) is that abortion is obviously *not* a morally serious and extremely unfortunate, even though sometimes justified act, comparable to killing in self-defense or to letting the violinist die, but rather is closer to being a morally neutral act, like cutting one's hair.

The basis of this conviction, I believe, is the realization that a fetus is not a person, and thus does not have a full-fledged right to life. Perhaps the reason why this claim has been so inadequately defended is that it seems self-evident to those who accept it. And so it is, insofar as it follows from what I take to be perfectly obvious claims about the nature of personhood, and about the proper grounds for ascribing moral rights, claims which ought, indeed, to be obvious to both the friends and foes of abortion. Nevertheless, it is worth examining these claims, and showing how they demonstrate the moral innocuousness of abortion, since this apparently has not been adequately done before.

II.

The question which we must answer in order to produce a satisfactory solution to the problem of the moral status of abortion is this: How are we to define the moral community, the set of beings with full and equal moral rights, such that we can decide whether a human fetus is a member of this community or not? What sort of entity, exactly, has the inalienable rights to life, liberty, and the pursuit of happiness? Jefferson attributed these rights to all *men*, and it may or may not be fair to suggest that he intended to attribute them *only* to men. Perhaps he ought to have attributed them to all human beings. If so, then we arrive, first, at Noonan's problem of defining what makes a being human, and, second, at the equally vital question which Noonan does not consider, namely, What reason is there for identifying the moral community with the set of all human beings, in whatever way we have chosen to define that term?

1. On the Definition of 'Human'

One reason why this vital second question is so frequently overlooked in the debate over the moral status of abortion is that the term 'human' has two distinct, but not often distinguished, senses. This fact results in a slide of meaning, which serves to conceal the fallaciousness of the traditional argument that since (1) it is wrong to kill innocent human beings, and (2) fetuses are innocent human beings, then (3) it is wrong to kill fetuses. For if 'human' is used in the same sense in both (1) and (2) then, whichever of the two senses is meant, one of these premises is question-begging. And if it is used in two different senses then of course the conclusion doesn't follow.

Thus (1) is a self-evident moral truth,[2] and avoids begging the question about abortion, only if 'human being' is used to mean something like "a full-fledged member of the moral community." (It may or may not also be meant to refer exclusively to members of the species *Homo sapiens*.) We may call this the *moral* sense of 'human'. It is not to be confused with what we will call the *genetic* sense, i.e., the sense in which *any* member of the species is a human being, and no member of any other species could be. If (1) is acceptable only if the moral sense is intended, (2) is non-question-begging only if what is intended is the genetic sense.

In "Deciding Who is Human,"[3] Noonan argues for the classification of fetuses with human beings by pointing to the presence of the full genetic code, and the potential capacity for rational thought (p. 135). It is clear that what he needs to show, for his version of the traditional argument to be valid, is that fetuses are human in the moral sense, the sense in which it is analytically true that all human beings have full moral rights. But, in the absence of any argument showing that whatever is genetically human is also morally human, and he gives none, nothing more than genetic humanity can be demonstrated by the presence of the human genetic code. And, as we will see, the *potential* capacity for rational thought can at most show that an entity has the potential for *becoming* human in the moral sense.

2. Defining the Moral Community

Can it be established that genetic humanity is sufficient for moral humanity? I think that there are very good reasons for not defining the moral community in this way. I would like to suggest an alternative way of defining the moral community, which I will argue for only to the extent of explaining why it is, or should be, self-evident. The suggestion is simply that the moral community consists of all and only *people*, rather than all and only human beings;[4] and probably the best way of demonstrating its self-evidence is by considering the concept of personhood, to see what sorts of entity are and are not persons, and what the decision that a being is or is not a person implies about its moral rights.

What characteristics entitle an entity to be considered a person? This is obviously not the place to attempt a complete analysis of the concept of personhood, but we do not need such a fully adequate analysis just to determine whether and why a fetus is or isn't a person. All we need is a rough and approximate list of the most basic criteria of personhood, and some idea of which, or how many, of these an entity must satisfy in order to properly be considered a person.

In searching for such criteria, it is useful to look beyond the set of people with whom we are acquainted, and ask how we would decide whether a totally alien being was a person or not. (For we have no right to assume that genetic humanity is necessary for personhood.) Imagine a space traveler who lands on an unknown planet and encounters a race of beings utterly unlike any he has ever seen or heard of. If he wants to be sure of behaving morally toward these beings, he has to somehow decide whether they are people, and hence have full moral rights, or whether they are the sort of thing which he need not feel guilty about treating as, for example, a source of food.

How should he go about making this decision? If he has some anthropological background, he might look for such things as religion, art, and the manufacturing of tools, weapons, or shelters, since these factors have been used to distinguish our human from our prehuman ancestors, in what seems to be closer to the moral than the genetic sense of 'human'. And no doubt he would be right to consider the presence of such factors as good evidence that the alien beings were people, and morally human. It would, however, be overly anthropocentric of him to take the absence of these things as adequate evidence that they were not, since we can imagine people who have progressed beyond, or evolved without ever developing, these cultural characteristics.

I suggest that the traits which are most central to the concept of personhood, or humanity in the moral sense, are, very roughly, the following:

1. consciousness (of objects and events external and/or internal to the being), and in particular the capacity to feel pain;
2. reasoning (the *developed* capacity to solve new and relatively complex problems);
3. self-motivated activity (activity which is relatively independent of either genetic or direct external control);
4. the capacity to communicate, by whatever means, messages of an indefinite variety of types, that is, not just with an indefinite number of possible contents, but on indefinitely many possible topics;
5. the presence of self-concepts, and self-awareness, either individual or racial, or both.

Admittedly, there are apt to be a great many problems involved in formulating precise definitions of these criteria, let alone in developing universally valid behavioral criteria for deciding when they apply. But I will assume that both we and our explorer know approximately what (1)–(5) mean, and that he is also able to determine whether or not they apply. How, then, should he use his findings to decide whether or not the alien beings are people? We needn't suppose that an entity must have *all* of these attributes to be properly considered a person; (1) and (2) alone may well be sufficient for personhood, and quite probably (1)–(3) are sufficient. Neither do we need to insist that any one of these criteria is *necessary* for personhood, although once again (1) and (2) look like fairly good candidates for necessary conditions, as does (3), if activity is construed so as to include the activity of reasoning.

All we need to claim, to demonstrate that a fetus is not a person, is that any being which satisfies *none* of (1)–(5) is certainly not a person. I consider this claim to be so obvious that I think anyone who denied it, and claimed that a being which satisfied none of (1)–(5) was a person all the same, would thereby demonstrate that he had no notion at all of what a person is—perhaps because he had confused the concept of a person with that of genetic humanity. If the opponents of abortion were to deny the appropriateness of these five criteria, I do not know what further arguments would convince them. We would probably have to admit that our conceptual schemes were indeed irreconcilably different, and that our dispute could not be settled objectively.

I do not expect this to happen, however, since I think that the concept of a person is one which is very nearly universal (to people), and that it is common to both proabortionists and antiabortionists, even though neither group has fully realized the relevance of this concept to the resolution of their dispute. Furthermore, I think that on reflection even the antiabortionists ought to agree not only that (1)–(5) are central to the concept of personhood, but also that it is a part of this concept that all and only people have full moral rights. The concept of a person is in part a moral concept; once we have admitted that x is a person we have recognized, even if we have not agreed to respect, x's right to be treated as a member of the moral community. It is true that the claim that x is a *human being* is more commonly voiced as part of an appeal to treat x decently than is the claim that x is a person, but this is either because 'human being' is here used in the sense which implies personhood, or because the genetic and moral senses of 'human' have been confused.

Now if (1)–(5) are indeed the primary criteria of personhood, then it is clear that genetic humanity is neither necessary nor sufficient for establishing that an entity is a person. Some human beings are not people, and there may well be people who are not human beings. A man or woman whose consciousness has been permanently obliterated but who remains alive is a human being which is no longer a person; defective human beings, with no appreciable mental capacity, are not and presumably never will be people; and a fetus is a human being which is not yet a person, and which therefore cannot coherently be said to have full moral rights. Citizens of the next century should be prepared to recognize highly advanced, self-aware robots or computers, should such be developed, and intelligent inhabitants of other worlds, should such be found, as people in the fullest sense, and to respect their moral rights. But to ascribe full moral rights to an entity which is not a person is as absurd as to ascribe moral obligations and responsibilities to such an entity.

3. Fetal Development and the Right to Life

Two problems arise in the application of these suggestions for the definition of the moral community to the determination of the precise moral status of a human fetus. Given that the paradigm example of a person is a normal adult human being, then (1) How like this paradigm, in particular how far advanced since conception, does a human being need to be before it begins to have a right to life by virtue, not of being fully a person as of yet, but of being *like* a person? and (2) To what extent, if any, does the fact that a fetus has the *potential* for becoming a person endow it with some of the same rights? Each of these questions requires some comment.

In answering the first question, we need not attempt a detailed consideration of the moral rights of organisms which are not developed enough, aware enough, intelligent enough, etc., to be considered people, but which resemble people in some respects. It does seem reasonable to suggest that the more like a person, in the relevant respects, a being is, the stronger is the case for regarding it as having a right to life, and indeed the stronger its right to life is. Thus we ought to take seriously the suggestion that, insofar as "the human individual develops biologically in a continuous fashion the rights of a human person might develop in the same way." But we must keep in mind that the attributes which are relevant in determining whether or not an entity is enough like a person to be regarded as having some of the same moral rights are no different from those which are relevant to determining whether or not it is fully a person—i.e., are no different from (1)–(5)—and that being genetically human, or having recognizably human facial and other physical features, or detectable brain activity, or the capacity to survive outside the uterus, are simply not among these relevant attributes.

Thus it is clear that even though a seven-or eight-month fetus has features which make it apt to arouse in us almost the same powerful protective instinct as is commonly aroused by a small infant, nevertheless it is not significantly more personlike than is a very small embryo. It is *somewhat* more personlike; it can apparently feel and respond to pain, and it may even have a rudimentary form of consciousness, insofar as its brain is quite active. Nevertheless, it seems safe to say that it is not fully conscious, in the way that an infant of a few months is, and that it cannot reason, or communicate messages of indefinitely many sorts, does not engage in self-motivated activity, and has no self-awareness. Thus, in the *relevant* respects, a fetus, even a fully developed one, is considerably less personlike than is the average mature mammal, indeed the average fish. And I think that a rational person must conclude that if the right to life of a fetus is to be based upon its resemblance to a person, then it cannot be said to have any more right to life than, let us say, a newborn guppy (which also seems to be capable of feeling pain), and that a right of that magnitude could never override a woman's right to obtain an abortion, at any stage of her pregnancy.

There may, of course, be other arguments in favor of placing legal limits upon the stage of pregnancy in which an abortion may be performed. Given the relative safety of the new techniques of artifically inducing labor during the third trimester, the danger to the woman's life or health is no longer such an argument. Neither is the fact that people tend to respond to the thought of abortion in the later stages of pregnancy with emotional repulsion, since mere emotional responses cannot take the place of moral reasoning in determining what ought to be permitted. Nor, finally, is the frequently heard argument that legalizing abortion, especially late in the pregnancy, may erode the level of respect for human life, leading, perhaps, to an increase in unjustified euthanasia and other crimes. For this threat, if it is a threat, can be better met by educating people to the kinds of moral distinctions which we are making here than by limiting access to abortion (which limitation may, in its disregard for the rights of women, be just as damaging to the level of respect for human rights).

Thus, since the fact that even a fully developed fetus is not personlike enough to have any significant right to life on the basis of its personlikeness shows that no legal restrictions upon the stage of pregnancy in which an abortion may be performed can be justified on the grounds that we should protect the rights of the older fetus; and since there is no other apparent justification for such restrictions, we may conclude that they are entirely unjustified. Whether or not it would be *indecent* (whatever that means) for a woman in her seventh month to obtain an abortion just to avoid having to postpone a trip to Europe, it would not, in itself, be *immoral*, and therefore it ought to be permitted.

4. Potential Personhood and the Right to Life

We have seen that a fetus does not resemble a person in any way which can support the claim that it has even some of the same rights. But what about its *potential*, the fact that if nurtured and allowed to develop naturally it will very probably become a person? Doesn't that alone give it at least some right to life? It is hard to deny that the fact that an entity is a potential person is a strong prima facie reason for not destroying it; but we need not conclude from this that a potential person has a right to life, by virtue of that potential. It may be that our feeling that it is better, other things being equal, not to destroy a potential person is better explained by the fact that potential people are still (felt to be) an invaluable resource, not to be lightly squandered. Surely, if every speck of dust were a potential person, we would be much less apt to conclude that every potential person has a right to become actual.

Still, we do not need to insist that a potential person has no right to life whatever. There may well be something immoral, and not just imprudent, about wantonly destroying potential people, when doing so isn't necessary to protect anyone's rights. But even if a potential person does have some prima facie right to life, such a right could not possibly outweigh the right of a woman to obtain an abortion, since the rights of any actual person invariably outweigh those of any potential person, whenever the two conflict. Since this may not be immediately obvious in the case of a human fetus, let us look at another case.

Suppose that our space explorer falls into the hands of an alien culture, whose scientists decide to create a few hundred thousand or more human beings, by breaking his body into its component cells, and using these to create fully developed human beings, with, of course, his genetic code. We may imagine that each of these newly created men will have all of the original man's abilities, skills, knowledge, and so on, and also have an individual self-concept, in short that each of them will be a bona fide (though hardly unique) person. Imagine that the whole project will take only seconds, and that its chances of success are extremely high, and that our explorer knows all of this, and also knows that these people will be treated fairly. I maintain that in such a situation he would have every right to escape if he could, and thus to deprive all of these potential people of their potential lives; for his right to life outweighs all of theirs together, in spite of the fact that they are all genetically human, all innocent, and all have a very high probability of becoming people very soon, if only he refrains from acting.

Indeed, I think he would have a right to escape even if it were not his life which the alien scientists planned to take, but only a year of his freedom, or, indeed, only a day. Nor would he be obligated to stay if he had gotten captured (thus bringing all these people-potentials into existence) because of his own carelessness, or even if he had done so deliberately, knowing the consequences. Regardless of how he got captured, he is not morally obligated to remain in captivity for *any* period of time for the sake of permitting any number of potential people to come into actuality, so great is the margin by which one actual person's right to liberty outweighs whatever right to life even a hundred thousand potential people have. And it seems reasonable to conclude that the rights of a woman will outweigh by a similar margin whatever right to life a fetus may have by virtue of its potential personhood.

Thus, neither a fetus's resemblance to a person, nor its potential for becoming a person provides any basis whatever for the claim that it has any significant right to life. Consequently, a woman's right to protect her health, happiness, freedom, and even her life by terminating an unwanted pregnancy, will always override whatever right to life it may be appropriate to ascribe to a fetus, even a fully developed one. And thus, in the absence of any overwhelming social need for every possible child, the laws which restrict the right to obtain an abortion, or limit the period of pregnancy during which an abortion may be performed, are a wholly unjustified violation of a woman's most basic moral and constitutional rights.

NOTES

1. Judith Thomson, "A Defense of Abortion," *Philosophy and Public Affairs* 1 (1971), pp. 47–66.
2. Of course, the principle that it is (always) wrong to kill innocent human beings is in need of many other modifications, e.g., that it may be permissible to do so to save a greater number of other innocent human beings, but we may safely ignore these complications here.
3. John Noonan, "Deciding Who Is Human," *Natural Law Review* 13 (1968), p. 134.
4. From here on, we will use 'human' to mean genetically human, since the moral sense seems closely connected to, and perhaps derived from, the assumption that genetic humanity is sufficient for membership in the moral community.

Mary Anne Warren: On the Moral and Legal Status of Abortion

1. Warren claims that if we allow that the fetus is a person, then the pro-choice case collapses. Do you agree with her assessment? Why or why not?
2. Warren identifies five criteria of personhood. Do you think the fetus lacks each of these traits? If so, might there be a sixth criterion of personhood that the fetus does fulfill?
3. If even third-trimester fetuses are not persons—because they fail to fulfill any of the five criteria Warren associates with personhood—then newborn infants also fail to be persons. Is this correct? If so, would Warren's position also morally permit infanticide?
4. Warren argues that the rights of persons always outweigh the potential rights of potential persons by means of her astronaut example. Does this example establish what she thinks it does? Why or why not?
5. How important is a being's potential in determining its moral status?

Why Abortion Is Immoral
Don Marquis

In this article, Don Marquis argues, from entirely secular premises, to the conclusion that abortion is, in most circumstances, a form of murder. He does this by first trying to explain why it is immoral to kill people like you and me. After canvassing a few popular but mistaken options, he arrives at his answer. Such killing is immoral because it deprives us of a future of value.

Human fetuses—most of them, at least—also share this feature. And therefore it is ordinarily wrong to kill human fetuses. And so abortion is usually immoral. Marquis considers a variety of objections to his view and concludes his article by trying to show how each of them can be met.

The view that abortion is, with rare exceptions, seriously immoral has received little support in the recent philosophical literature. No doubt most philosophers affiliated with secular institutions of higher education believe that the anti-abortion position is either a symptom of irrational religious dogma or a conclusion generated by seriously confused philosophical argument. The purpose of this essay is to undermine this general belief. This essay sets out an argument that purports to show, as well as any argument in ethics can show, that abortion is, except possibly in rare cases, seriously immoral, that it is in the same moral category as killing an innocent adult human being. . . .

I.

A sketch of standard anti-abortion and pro-choice arguments exhibits how those arguments possess certain symmetries that explain why partisans of those positions are so convinced of the correctness of their own positions, why they are not successful in convincing their opponents, and why, to others, this issue seems to be unresolvable. An analysis of the nature of this standoff suggests a strategy for surmounting it.

Consider the way a typical anti-abortionist argues. She will argue or assert that life is present from the moment of conception or that fetuses look like babies

From Don Marquis, "Why Abortion Is Immoral," *Journal of Philosophy* 86 (1989), pp. 183–185, 189–192, 194, 198–199, 201.

or that fetuses possess a characteristic such as a genetic code that is both necessary and sufficient for being human. Anti-abortionists seem to believe that (1) the truth of all of these claims is quite obvious, and (2) establishing any of these claims is sufficient to show that abortion is morally akin to murder.

A standard pro-choice strategy exhibits similarities. The pro-choicer will argue or assert that fetuses are not persons or that fetuses are not rational agents or that fetuses are not social beings. Pro-choicers seem to believe that (1) the truth of any of these claims is quite obvious, and (2) establishing any of these claims is sufficient to show that an abortion is not a wrongful killing.

In fact, both the pro-choice and the anti-abortion claims do seem to be true, although the "it looks like a baby" claim is more difficult to establish the earlier the pregnancy. We seem to have a standoff. How can it be resolved?

As everyone who has taken a bit of logic knows, if any of these arguments concerning abortion is a good argument, it requires not only some claim characterizing fetuses, but also some general moral principle that ties a characteristic of fetuses to having or not having the right to life or to some other moral characteristic that will generate the obligation or the lack of obligation not to end the life of a fetus. Accordingly, the arguments of the anti-abortionist and the pro-choicer need a bit of filling in to be regarded as adequate.

Note what each partisan will say. The anti-abortionist will claim that her position is supported by such generally accepted moral principles as "It is always prima facie seriously wrong to take a human life" or "It is always prima facie seriously wrong to end the life of a baby." Since these are generally accepted moral principles, her position is certainly not obviously wrong. The pro-choicer will claim that her position is supported by such plausible moral principles as "Being a person is what gives an individual intrinsic moral worth" or "It is only seriously prima facie wrong to take the life of a member of the human community." Since these are generally accepted moral principles, the pro-choice position is certainly not obviously wrong. Unfortunately, we have again arrived at a standoff.

Now, how might one deal with this standoff? The standard approach is to try to show how the moral principles of one's opponent lose their plausibility under analysis. It is easy to see how this is possible. On the one hand, the anti-abortionist will defend a moral principle concerning the wrongness of killing which tends to be broad in scope in order that even fetuses at an early stage of pregnancy will fall under it. The problem with broad principles is that they often embrace too much. In this particular instance, the principle "It is always prima facie wrong to take a human life" seems to entail that it is wrong to end the existence of a living human cancer-cell culture, on the grounds that the culture is both living and human. Therefore, it seems that the anti-abortionist's favored principle is too broad.

On the other hand, the pro-choicer wants to find a moral principle concerning the wrongness of killing which tends to be narrow in scope in order that fetuses will *not* fall under it. The problem with narrow principles is that they often do *not* embrace enough. Hence, the needed principles such as "It is prima facie seriously wrong to kill only persons" or "It is prima facie wrong to kill only rational agents" do not explain why it is wrong to kill infants or young children or the severely retarded or even perhaps the severely mentally ill. Therefore, we seem again to have a standoff. The anti-abortionist charges, not unreasonably, that pro-choice principles concerning killing are too narrow to be acceptable; the pro-choicer charges, not unreasonably,

that anti-abortionist principles concerning killing are too broad to be acceptable. . . .

All this suggests that a necessary condition of resolving the abortion controversy is a more theoretical account of the wrongness of killing. After all, if we merely believe, but do not understand, why killing adult human beings such as ourselves is wrong, how could we conceivably show that abortion is either immoral or permissible?

II.

In order to develop such an account, we can start from the following unproblematic assumption concerning our own case: it is wrong to kill *us*. Why is it wrong? Some answers can be easily eliminated. It might be said that what makes killing us wrong is that a killing brutalizes the one who kills. But the brutalization consists of being inured to the performance of an act that is hideously immoral; hence, the brutalization does not explain the immorality. It might be said that what makes killing us wrong is the great loss others would experience due to our absence. Although such hubris is understandable, such an explanation does not account for the wrongness of killing hermits, or those whose lives are relatively independent and whose friends find it easy to make new friends.

A more obvious answer is better. What primarily makes killing wrong is neither its effect on the murderer nor its effect on the victim's friends and relatives, but its effect on the victim. The loss of one's life is one of the greatest losses one can suffer. The loss of one's life deprives one of all the experiences, activities, projects, and enjoyments that would otherwise have constituted one's future. Therefore, killing someone is wrong, primarily because the killing inflicts (one of) the greatest possible losses on the victim. To describe this as the loss of life can be misleading, however. The change in my biological state does not by itself make killing me wrong. The effect of the loss of my biological life is the loss to me of all those activities, projects, experiences, and enjoyments which would otherwise have constituted my future personal life. These activities, projects, experiences, and enjoyments are either valuable for their own sakes or are means to something else that is valuable for its own sake. Some parts of my future are not valued by me now, but will come to be valued by me as I grow older and as my values and capacities change. When I am killed, I am deprived both of what I now value which would have been part of my future personal life, but also what I would come to value. Therefore, when I die, I am deprived of all of the value of my future. Inflicting this loss on me is ultimately what makes killing me wrong. This being the case, it would seem that what makes killing *any* adult human being prima facie seriously wrong is the loss of his or her future.[1]

How should this rudimentary theory of the wrongness of killing be evaluated? It cannot be faulted for deriving an 'ought' from an 'is,' for it does not. The analysis assumes that killing me (or you, reader) is prima facie seriously wrong. The point of the analysis is to establish which natural property ultimately explains the wrongness of the killing, given that it is wrong. A natural property will ultimately explain the wrongness of killing, only if (1) the explanation fits with our intuitions about the matter and (2) there is no other natural property that provides the basis for a better explanation of the wrongness of killing. This analysis rests on the intuition that what makes killing a particular human or animal wrong is what it does to that particular human or animal. What makes killing wrong is some natural effect or other of the killing. Some would deny this. For instance, a divine-command theorist in ethics would deny it. Surely this denial is, however, one of those features of divine-command theory which renders it so implausible.

The claim that what makes killing wrong is the loss of the victim's future is directly supported by two considerations. In the first place, this theory explains why we regard killing as one of the worst of crimes. Killing is especially wrong, because it deprives the victim of more than perhaps any other crime. In the second place, people with AIDS or cancer who know they are dying believe, of course, that dying is a very bad thing for them. They believe that the loss of a future to them that they would otherwise have experienced is what makes their premature death a very bad thing for them. A better theory of the wrongness of killing would require a different natural property associated with killing

which better fits with the attitudes of the dying. What could it be?

The view that what makes killing wrong is the loss to the victim of the value of the victim's future gains additional support when some of its implications are examined. In the first place, it is incompatible with the view that it is wrong to kill only beings who are biologically human. It is possible that there exists a different species from another planet whose members have a future like ours. Since having a future like that is what makes killing someone wrong, this theory entails that it would be wrong to kill members of such a species. Hence, this theory is opposed to the claim that only life that is biologically human has great moral worth, a claim which many anti-abortionists have seemed to adopt. This opposition, which this theory has in common with personhood theories, seems to be a merit of the theory.

In the second place, the claim that the loss of one's future is the wrong-making feature of one's being killed entails the possibility that the futures of some actual nonhuman mammals on our own planet are sufficiently like ours that it is seriously wrong to kill them also. Whether some animals do have the same right to life as human beings depends on adding to the account of the wrongness of killing some additional account of just what it is about my future or the futures of other adult human beings which makes it wrong to kill us. No such additional account will be offered in this essay. Undoubtedly, the provision of such an account would be a very difficult matter. Undoubtedly, any such account would be quite controversial. Hence, it surely should not reflect badly on this sketch of an elementary theory of the wrongness of killing that it is indeterminate with respect to some very difficult issues regarding animal rights.

In the third place, the claim that the loss of one's future is the wrong-making feature of one's being killed does not entail, as sanctity of human life theories do, that active euthanasia is wrong. Persons who are severely and incurably ill, who face a future of pain and despair, and who wish to die will not have suffered a loss if they are killed. It is, strictly speaking, the value of a human's future which makes killing wrong in this theory. This being so, killing does not necessarily wrong some persons who are sick and dying. Of course, there may be other reasons for a prohibition of active euthanasia, but that is another matter. Sanctity-of-human-life theories seem to hold that active euthanasia is seriously wrong even in an individual case where there seems to be good reason for it independently of public policy considerations. This consequence is most implausible, and it is a plus for the claim that the loss of a future of value is what makes killing wrong that it does not share this consequence.

In the fourth place, the account of the wrongness of killing defended in this essay does straightforwardly entail that it is prima facie seriously wrong to kill children and infants, for we do presume that they have futures of value. Since we do believe that it is wrong to kill defenseless little babies, it is important that a theory of the wrongness of killing easily account for this. Personhood theories of the wrongness of killing, on the other hand, cannot straightforwardly account for the wrongness of killing infants and young children. Hence, such theories must add special ad hoc accounts of the wrongness of killing the young. The plausibility of such ad hoc theories seems to be a function of how desperately one wants such theories to work. The claim that the primary wrong-making feature of a killing is the loss to the victim of the value of its future accounts for the wrongness of killing young children and infants directly; it makes the wrongness of such acts as obvious as we actually think it is. This is a further merit of this theory. Accordingly, it seems that this value of a future-like-ours theory of the wrongness of killing shares strengths of both sanctity-of-life and personhood accounts while avoiding weaknesses of both. In addition, it meshes with a central intuition concerning what makes killing wrong.

The claim that the primary wrong-making feature of a killing is the loss to the victim of the value of its future has obvious consequences for the ethics of abortion. The future of a standard fetus includes a set of experiences, projects, activities, and such which are identical with the futures of adult human beings and are identical with the futures of young children. Since the reason that is sufficient to explain why it is wrong to kill human beings after the time of birth is a reason that also applies to fetuses, it follows that abortion is prima facie seriously morally wrong.

This argument does not rely on the invalid inference that, since it is wrong to kill persons, it is wrong to kill potential persons also. The category that is morally central to this analysis is the category of having a valuable future like ours; it is not the category of personhood. The argument to the conclusion that abortion is prima facie seriously morally wrong proceeded independently of the notion of person or potential person or any equivalent. Someone may wish to start with this analysis in terms of the value of a human future, conclude that abortion is, except perhaps in rare circumstances, seriously morally wrong, infer that fetuses have the right to life, and then call fetuses "persons" as a result of their having the right to life. Clearly, in this case, the category of person is being used to state the *conclusion* of the analysis rather than to generate the *argument* of the analysis. . . .

Of course, this value of a future-like-ours argument, if sound, shows only that abortion is prima facie wrong, not that it is wrong in any and all circumstances. Since the loss of the future to a standard fetus, if killed, is, however, at least as great a loss as the loss of the future to a standard adult human being who is killed, abortion, like ordinary killing, could be justified only by the most compelling reasons. The loss of one's life is almost the greatest misfortune that can happen to one. Presumably abortion could be justified in some circumstances, only if the loss consequent on failing to abort would be at least as great. Accordingly, morally permissible abortions will be rare indeed unless, perhaps, they occur so early in pregnancy that a fetus is not yet definitely an individual. Hence, this argument should be taken as showing that abortion is presumptively very seriously wrong, where the presumption is very strong—as strong as the presumption that killing another adult human being is wrong.

III.

How complete an account of the wrongness of killing does the value of a future-like-ours account have to be in order that the wrongness of abortion is a consequence? This account does not have to be an account of the necessary conditions for the wrongness of killing. Some persons in nursing homes may lack valuable human futures, yet it may be wrong to kill them for other reasons. Furthermore, this account does not obviously have to be the sole reason killing is wrong where the victim did have a valuable future. This analysis claims only that, for any killing where the victim did have a valuable future like ours, having that future by itself is sufficient to create the strong presumption that the killing is seriously wrong.

One way to overturn the value of a future-like-ours argument would be to find some account of the wrongness of killing which is at least as intelligible and which has different implications for the ethics of abortion....

One move of this sort is based upon the claim that a necessary condition of one's future being valuable is that one values it. Value implies a valuer. Given this one might argue that, since fetuses cannot value their futures, their futures are not valuable to them. Hence, it does not seriously wrong them deliberately to end their lives.

This move fails, however, because of some ambiguities. Let us assume that something cannot be of value unless it is valued by someone. This does not entail that my life is of no value unless it is valued by me. I may think, in a period of despair, that my future is of no worth whatsoever, but I may be wrong because others rightly see value—even great value—in it. Furthermore, my future can be valuable to me even if I do not value it. This is the case when a young person attempts suicide, but is rescued and goes on to significant human achievements. Such young people's futures are ultimately valuable to them, even though such futures do not seem to be valuable to them at the moment of attempted suicide. A fetus's future can be valuable to it in the same way. Accordingly, this attempt to limit the anti-abortion argument fails.

Another similar attempt to reject the anti-abortion position is based on Tooley's claim that an entity cannot possess the right to life unless it has the capacity to desire its continued existence. It follows that, since fetuses lack the conceptual capacity to desire to continue to live, they lack the right to life. Accordingly, Tooley concludes that abortion cannot be seriously prima facie wrong.[2]...

One might attempt to defend Tooley's basic claim on the grounds that, because a fetus cannot apprehend continued life as a benefit, its continued life cannot be a benefit or cannot be something it has a right to or cannot be something that is in its interest. This might be defended in terms of the general proposition that, if an individual is literally incapable of caring about or taking an interest in some X, then one does not have a right to X or X is not a benefit or X is not something that is in one's interest.

Each member of this family of claims seems to be open to objections. As John C. Stevens[3] has pointed out, one may have a right to be treated with a certain medical procedure (because of a health insurance policy one has purchased), even though one cannot conceive of the nature of the procedure. And, as Tooley himself has pointed out, persons who have been indoctrinated, or drugged, or rendered temporarily unconscious may be literally incapable of caring about or taking an interest in something that is in their interest or is something to which they have a right, or is something that benefits them. Hence, the Tooley claim that would restrict the scope of the value of a future-like-ours argument is undermined by counterexamples....[4]

IV.

In this essay, it has been argued that the correct ethic of the wrongness of killing can be extended to fetal life and used to show that there is a strong presumption that any abortion is morally impermissible. If the ethic of killing adopted here entails, however, that contraception is also seriously immoral, then there would appear to be a difficulty with the analysis of this essay.

But this analysis does not entail that contraception is wrong. Of course, contraception prevents the actualization of a possible future of value. Hence, it follows from the claim that futures of value should be maximized that contraception is prima facie immoral. This obligation to maximize does not exist, however; furthermore, nothing in the ethics of killing in this paper entails that it does. The ethics of killing in this essay would entail that contraception is wrong only if something were denied a human future of value by contraception. Nothing at all is denied such a future by contraception, however.

Candidates for a subject of harm by contraception fall into four categories: (1) some sperm or other, (2) some ovum or other, (3) a sperm and an ovum separately, and (4) a sperm and an ovum together. Assigning the harm to some sperm is utterly arbitrary, for no reason can be given for making a sperm the subject of harm rather than an ovum. Assigning the harm to some ovum is utterly arbitrary, for no reason can be given for making an ovum the subject of harm rather than a sperm. One might attempt to avoid these problems by insisting that contraception deprives both the sperm and the ovum separately of a valuable future like ours. On this alternative, too many futures are lost. Contraception was supposed to be wrong, because it deprived us of one future of value, not two. One might attempt to avoid this problem by holding that contraception deprives the combination of sperm and ovum of a valuable future like ours. But here the definite article misleads. At the time of contraception, there are hundreds of millions of sperm, one (released) ovum and millions of possible combinations of all of these. There is no actual combination at all. Is the subject of the loss to be a merely possible combination? Which one? This alternative does not yield an actual subject of harm either. Accordingly, the immorality of contraception is not entailed by the loss of a future-like-ours argument simply because there is no nonarbitrarily identifiable subject of the loss in the case of contraception.

NOTES

1. I have been most influenced on this matter by Jonathan Glover, *Causing Death and Saving Lives* (New York: Penguin, 1977), ch. 3; and Robert Young, "What Is So Wrong with Killing People?" *Philosophy*, LIV, 210 (1979): 515–528.

2. Michael Tooley, *Abortion and Infanticide* (New York: Oxford University Press, 1984), pp. 46–47.

3. "Must the Bearer of a Right Have the Concept of That to Which He Has a Right?" *Ethics*, xcv, 1 (1984): 68–74.

4. See Tooley again in *Abortion and Infanticide*, pp. 47–49.

Don Marquis: Why Abortion Is Immoral

1. Marquis begins by criticizing some common arguments on both sides of the abortion issue. Do his criticisms succeed in refuting the common arguments? Why or why not?

2. What, according to Marquis, is wrong with killing adult humans? Is his theory the best account of what is wrong with such killing?

3. Marquis claims that abortion is wrong for the same reason that killing adult humans is wrong. Are there any differences between the two that would justify abortion?

4. One might object to Marquis's claim that fetuses have a valuable future by pointing out that fetuses do not have the cognitive capacities to value anything. How does Marquis respond to this objection? Do you find his response convincing?

5. Marquis admits that his theory would be problematic if it led to the view that contraception is seriously morally wrong. How does he argue that his theory does not do this? Do you think he succeeds?

CHAPTER 13

Animals

JUST THE FACTS

If you slam a rock against a tree, or throw a rock in a fire, or put it in a freezer, it feels nothing. If you do the same to a person, he or she will feel it. That's because human beings possess **sentience**—we are able to have sense experiences and, as a result, can feel pleasure and pain. What about nonhuman animals ("animals," from now on): are they like rocks or like us? There's little doubt that almost all animals are sentient like us. There might be exceptions (maybe clams or corals, for instance), but we won't be concerned with them here. Though no animal has ever rated its pain on a scale of 1 to 10 for an experimenter, we have excellent reason to believe that animals experience pleasures and pains as we do. First, animals frequently exhibit the same sort of behavior that humans do when they receive the kind of treatment that would ordinarily cause humans to experience pain (e.g., being cut, struck, or subjected to extreme temperatures). Under these circumstances, animals kick, moan, squirm, squeal, and so on, just like we do. While it's possible that animals are merely exhibiting the behaviors we associate with being in pain without having the corresponding **subjective experiences**, this seems highly unlikely when you consider that many animals have complex brains and nervous systems very similar to our own. And we know that, for humans, the brain and the nervous system—that network of nerves and cells that carries messages to and from the brain—is the crucial biological structure that allows us to experience pleasure and pain. It would be quite surprising, then, if the brain and nervous system that serves as the biological basis for our subjective experiences played no role whatsoever in generating conscious experiences for animals. So, though we must admit that we are not (and likely never will be) *certain* that animals are sentient, we can be very confident that they are.

Humans use animals in a variety of ways. The first, and perhaps most obvious, is as a food source. Across the globe, humans eat enormous amounts of beef, chicken, pork, lamb, turkey, duck, fish, and many other kinds of meat. In 2015, 9.2 billion animals were slaughtered for food in the United States alone.[1] US citizens eat, on average, about 200 pounds of meat per person per year.[2] With a population of 320 million, that comes out to an annual overall consumption of about 64 billion pounds of meat.

Most animals used for food in the United States are raised on an intensive animal farm, or **factory farm**. These are industrial complexes where large numbers of animals are raised in a relatively small and tightly controlled space so that farmers can maximize meat production while minimizing their costs. Animals often find life in these conditions very uncomfortable.

For example, many chickens used for meat and egg production are put in **battery cages**, wire cages roughly the size of a piece of computer paper. In these cages, chickens are unable to fully spread their wings and can barely move. Due to the stress of these conditions, chickens (especially

---

1. http://www.humanesociety.org/news/resources/research/stats_slaughter_totals.html?referrer=https://www.google.com/
2. https://www.forbes.com/sites/niallmccarthy/2015/08/05/which-countries-eat-the-most-meat-each-year-infographic/#6988e5fb4f95

egg-laying hens) have a tendency to peck at one another, sometimes to death. To prevent this, farmers often cut off the tips of their beaks with a hot blade, a process called debeaking. This is quite painful for the birds, but farmers argue that it's better than the alternative, which is to leave their beaks unclipped, resulting in their mutilating or killing one another. Publicity surrounding these practices has led some large corporations to pledge to abandon these practices.[3]

Pigs don't have it much better. The natural life of a domestic pig is somewhere between ten and fifteen years. Pigs raised to be slaughtered for meat live for anywhere between six months to two years. Breeding pigs spend most of their lives in a cycle of pregnancy, birth, nursing, and pregnancy again until they're eventually slaughtered for food. During most of their life, they are confined to **gestation crates**, small cages only slightly larger than the pigs themselves. The tight space makes it impossible for the pigs to turn around and nearly impossible for them to sleep comfortably on the ground. The crates contain only slats and no solid floor, so as to make it easier to dispose of the waste. These crates have been banned in Canada and in nine US states, though many pork producers argue that such crates are needed to prevent sows from harming one another in more open, common spaces. As for nonbreeding pigs, they nurse for several weeks after birth. They're then separated from their mothers, castrated (if male), and placed in a pen with many other pigs where they live the majority of their lives. As soon as they are large enough, they're packed tightly into a truck and taken off to be slaughtered. In the summer, many pigs die on the way to the slaughterhouse, due to the intense heat inside the packed truck. In the winter, many freeze to death. Around a million pigs die each year en route to the slaughterhouse.[4]

In response to what many regard as cruel practices by the meat industry, millions of people across the world have chosen to adopt a **vegetarian** or **vegan** lifestyle. A vegetarian is someone who refrains from eating any meat products, while a vegan is someone who refrains from using any animal products at all (e.g., milk, cheese, eggs, leather belts, fur coats, animal skin shoes). In 2018, 5 percent of US citizens claimed to follow a strictly vegetarian diet—about 15 million people.[5]

Another way that humans use animals is by experimenting on them for research purposes. Though precise figures are hard to come by, the best estimates indicate that more than 100 million animals—for example, mice, guinea pigs, frogs, dogs, cats, rabbits, monkeys, fish, and birds—are killed annually in research labs.[6] The majority of those are rodents (e.g., mice, rats, hamsters). Pharmaceutical companies and medical researchers test vaccines, medications, and surgery techniques on animals before using them on humans. Similarly, many companies that sell cosmetics and want to be sure that their products are safe for human consumption begin by testing their products on animals. Some animals are forced to inhale toxic fumes; others are restrained while they have harmful chemicals dripped in their eyes; some have their skin repeatedly burned so that it never grows back. Anesthesia is used very rarely. As a result of these practices, the United Kingdom banned such experiments in 1998; the European Union did so in 2007. Though such experimentation is legal in the United States, greater knowledge of these experimental conditions has led some cosmetic companies to abandon such practices and to tout the "cruelty-free" origins of their products.

While animal experimentation can cause tremendous suffering for animals, it can also

3. http://www.humanesociety.org/issues/confinement_farm/facts/battery_cages.html?credit=web_id96878129
4. https://www.peta.org/issues/animals-used-for-food/factory-farming/pigs/pig-transport-slaughter/

5. https://news.gallup.com/poll/267074/percentage-americans-vegetarian.aspx.
6. http://lushprize.org/many-animals-used-experiments-around-world/

result in great benefits. For example, in 1921, an Ontario doctor experimented on dozens of dogs by severing the connection between their pancreas and digestive systems in an effort to understand diabetes. These experiments allowed him to isolate insulin, which eventually made it possible for millions of people with diabetes to be treated. More recently, Parkinson's disease was deliberately introduced to macaque monkeys in order to study ways to reduce the tremors that beset humans with the disease. Electrodes were implanted into the monkey's brains that managed to control the tremors; this procedure is now commonly used to help human victims of Parkinson's. Indeed, virtually any risky medical procedure now in use has been tested extensively on animals before it is ever attempted on humans. For example, the techniques for organ transplants and major organ surgeries (e.g., heart, brain, liver, kidney surgery) were developed by first attempting these procedures on animals. Vaccines are tested repeatedly on animals before they're introduced to humans on a large scale.

Advocates of animal testing point out that animals benefit from animal testing, too. Without animal research, millions of dogs, cats, birds, and farm animals would be dead (and continue to die) from more than two hundred diseases, including anthrax, rabies, distemper, feline leukemia, and canine parvo virus. Today, these diseases are largely preventable due to vaccines and treatments developed in animal research.

In the United States, there are laws in place to protect animals used for research purposes. The Animal Welfare Act (AWA) of 1966 requires all federally funded research facilities that conduct animal research to have an Institutional Animal Care and Use Committee (IACUC). These committees review research proposals from scientists who intend to use animals for research purposes. IACUCs try to ensure that no unnecessary harm is done to the animals, and they allow research on animals to proceed only if, in their judgment, there are no alternatives to animal testing. This doesn't mean, however, that IACUCs never permit harm to animals. On the contrary, often the only way to achieve the desired scientific result is to subject animals to intense suffering. If the expected benefits are great enough, an IACUC may still permit the research. The AWA does not apply to animals involved in meat production.

ARGUMENT ANALYSIS

If faced with the choice of having to toss a human or an animal overboard in order to keep a lifeboat afloat, few of us would send the human to a watery death. (Let's assume the human isn't a moral monster, but an everyday person like you or me.) This is a pretty plausible prediction. But most people also take it as wise moral advice—if we can't save them both, then we *ought* to spare the human, because humans are morally more important than animals. Is such a thought defensible, or is it perhaps just a prejudice that reflects our preference for those of our own kind?

Arguments designed to justify meat-eating and animal experimentation almost always proceed from the assumption that humans are morally more important than nonhuman animals. Almost no one would allow human beings to treat one another as we treat animals. But if you think that it is morally OK to kill animals for sport or for food, or to perform painful experiments on them, while also thinking that it isn't OK to do such things to your fellow humans, then you need some way to justify this differential treatment.

Such justifications are easy to find. Here is a popular one:

The Animals Kill Other Animals Argument

1. If animals kill other animals, then it is morally OK for humans to kill animals.
2. Animals do kill other animals.

Therefore,

3. It is morally OK for humans to kill animals.

There are several problems with premise 1. First, animals that eat other animals have no choice in the matter. We do. Second, a carnivore's survival depends on its eating other animals. Ours does not. With rare exceptions, human beings can survive perfectly well without eating animal flesh. Third, it is implausible to look to animals for moral guidance. Animals are not moral agents—they can't control their behavior through moral reasoning. That explains why they have no moral duties, and why they are immune from moral criticism. But we, obviously, are moral agents, and we can guide our behavior by the moral decisions we make. There is also a crucial problem for premise 2: none of the animals we routinely eat (chickens, cows, pigs, sheep, ducks, rabbits) are carnivores. They *don't* kill other animals. So if their behavior is supposed to guide our own, then we should eat only plants.

Rather than looking to animals as the models for our own moral behavior, some have suggested that we look to our power over animals as the basis for justifying their second-class status. Consider, then,

The Power Argument

1. If we are powerful enough to control an animal's behavior and the conditions under which it lives, then we are morally allowed to exercise that control.
2. We are powerful enough to control an animal's behavior and the conditions under which it lives.

Therefore,

3. We are morally allowed to control an animal's behavior and the conditions under which it lives.

Premise 2 of this argument is true for almost all animals. But premise 1 is deeply troubling. Might does not make right. That we are able to bend an animal to our will does not give us moral license to do so, any more than a slave-owner's power to control the life of his slaves gives him moral authority to treat them that way. Our coercive power is one thing; the morality of exercising it is another.

Consider, instead, the claim that since animals are dependent on farmers or lab researchers, those animals are rightly at the mercy of the humans who care for them. This dependence is of two sorts. Sometimes it is true that, were a farmer not in the business of breeding animals, certain animals would never have been born, and so they owe their lives to the farmers. In other cases, though farmers or lab researchers don't play a crucial role in seeing their animals into the world, these humans nevertheless maintain the animals under their care; the animals are in this sense dependent on humans for being able to remain alive. This gives rise to

The Dependency Argument

1. If animals depend for their existence or their sustenance on humans, then humans have a right to treat those animals in any way that best suits human interests.
2. Farm and lab animals depend for their existence or their sustenance on humans.

Therefore,

3. Humans have a right to treat farm and lab animals in any way that best suits human interests.

Though premise 2 is true in most cases, premise 1 is problematic. Regardless of which way the dependence relation is understood, dependence alone does not provide grounds for justifying anything like current farm or lab practices. Suppose a baby is dependent on her mother for her life. This certainly doesn't entitle the mother to kill or experiment upon the baby. Nor would an adoptive parent—one who exemplifies the second sort of dependence relation—be justified in treating a human baby this way. Dependence does not give free rein to the provider; we do not get license to kill or experiment on animals just because they owe their lives or sustenance to their keepers.

Here is another popular argument, not really in defense of the status quo with respect to our treatment of animals, but rather a critique of those who question it. It takes the form of

The Hypocrisy Argument

1. People who act in morally inconsistent ways are hypocrites, and so have flawed characters.
2. **Ethical vegetarians** and vegans act in morally inconsistent ways.

Therefore,

3. Ethical vegetarians and vegans are hypocrites.

Premise 1 is true, though it is important to note that hypocrisy is not the gravest moral flaw. (After all, some people are highly principled and act with perfect integrity—and yet their principles are terrible.) Consider one of literature's great hypocrites—the fictional character Huck Finn, as depicted in Mark Twain's 1884 novel *The Adventures of Huckleberry Finn*. Huck, like most whites of the day, has deeply racist attitudes. But his behavior doesn't always match up with his principles. For example, Huck shelters his runaway slave friend Jim, rather than turning him over to the slave catchers. Huck's compassion led him to hypocrisy, which in his case is to be applauded, rather than condemned—we think Huck's character is better than that of someone who would never sacrifice his racist principles to compassion.

Premise 2 refers to ethical vegetarians (those who are prompted by a concern for the rights or welfare of animals to refrain from eating them) and vegans (those who refuse to purchase or use any animal products). The thought behind the premise is simple: ethical vegetarians and vegans refuse to eat meat because of their moral objections to the ways in which animals are treated prior to and during slaughter. But these same people fail to protest other, more important injustices that target human beings. Their actions are thus inconsistent with their avowed opposition to cruelty and injustice.

There are three difficulties with this line of reasoning. First, there is simply no good evidence that most ethical vegetarians and vegans are as indifferent as this charge makes them out to be. Second, one cannot fight every injustice, and there is nothing wrong with selecting one's own particular area of concern for displaying extra effort. Failing to protest against every injustice does not amount to hypocrisy—or, if it does, then we are all hypocrites, in which case this criticism has no special force against ethical vegetarians and vegans. Third, this argument is, at its strongest, an ad hominem attack against ethical vegetarians and vegans. It says that they, as people, exhibit some sort of moral failing; they aren't active enough in protesting against human suffering. But even if this were true—and once again, there is no evidence to support this charge—it would do nothing to undermine the moral principles behind ethical vegetarianism or veganism. The charge of hypocrisy does not tell you which moral principles are correct. It just tells you that some people are not living up to the principles they endorse. You may know folks who talk a good game about the importance of giving generously to charity, while giving almost nothing. So they are hypocrites. That doesn't show that the principle of giving generously is mistaken. Likewise, even if ethical vegetarians and vegans did fail to live up to their principles, that doesn't show that those principles are mistaken.

Another familiar argument invites us to reflect on our emotional attachments to our fellow human beings and to compare them to those we have to other animals. Our bonds with our fellow humans are typically much stronger than those we have toward nonhuman animals. We love our pets, for sure, but we love our parents and our siblings and our friends even more. This greater emotional investment in members of our own species may give rise to

The Emotional Attachment Argument

1. If we feel greater emotional attachment to fellow human beings than to nonhuman

animals, then we are morally allowed to harm animals in order to promote human interests.

2. We do feel greater emotional attachment to fellow human beings than to nonhuman animals.

Therefore,

3. We are morally allowed to harm animals in order to promote human interests.

Premise 2 is true in most cases. That said, there are some misanthropes (those who dislike or hate their fellow humans) who prefer the company of their pets to that of other humans. The billionaire Leona Helmsley, a notorious misanthrope who earned the nicknamed "The Queen of Mean," left $12 million in her will to her dog while disinheriting two grandchildren.

As this example shows, it may not be a good idea (as premise 1 suggests) to make our moral relations with others depend on how much we happen to care about them. After all, white supremacists care more about whites than blacks; this doesn't license their treating blacks as inferiors. Many wealthy citizens feel distaste for the poor; this doesn't morally permit the rich to harm the poor. Similarly, though most of us care more about our fellow human beings than about animals, this greater emotional investment does not by itself allow us to harm animals.

Some justify eating and experimenting on animals by claiming that animals lack moral rights. Humans have such rights; animals don't; therefore we are allowed to confine, kill, and experiment upon animals, even if we are forbidden from treating our fellow human beings in these ways. These considerations combine to form

The Rights Argument

1. Humans have moral rights.
2. Animals lack moral rights.
3. Those with moral rights are morally permitted to treat beings without moral rights in whatever way the rights-holder thinks is best.

Therefore,

4. We humans are morally permitted to treat animals in any way we think best.

Premise 1 is true. But why think that premise 2 is true? Some argue that moral rights require an ability to (1) enter into reciprocal agreements, or (2) stand up for oneself, or (3) think about one's future in complex ways, or (4) conform one's behavior to principles one freely and rationally endorses. Animals lack all of these abilities.

Now it is a very difficult matter to determine whether any of these four abilities really is a necessary condition of having moral rights. But suppose they are, and premise 2 is true because of that. This raises a problem, though, since many human beings—newborn babies, young children, some adults who are severely mentally impaired—also lack these abilities. And that would mean that these humans also lack moral rights.

Now you might think—fine, not all human beings do have moral rights, after all. But now look at premise 3. If that premise is true, then the Rights Argument would morally allow us to treat babies, infants, toddlers, and the severely mentally incapacitated in any way we thought best. If we decided it was best to kill them, or keep them alive only to harvest their organs for our benefit, then it would be OK to do so. But (I am assuming) it's obviously wrong to do such things!

If you want to avoid this unhappy result, you have three choices. First, you could reject premise 2 and argue that animals do have moral rights after all. Second, you could reject premise 3 and argue that there are limits to the treatment we extend to those who lack rights. Or, third, you could accept all premises of the Rights Argument but challenge the assumption I've been using in my analysis of the argument. That assumption is that possessing moral rights depends on satisfying one of the conditions (1)–(4). The idea here is that there is a fifth source of moral rights, one that even human babies or late-stage Alzheimer's patients possess, but that animals lack. The project in that case is to identify it.

Let's consider this third strategy in more detail. You might believe that there is something special about humans—any human, no matter his or her abilities, talents, intelligence, or virtue. You might think that every human being is morally more important than any nonhuman animal. If you believe this—and most people seem to—the challenge is to defend it in the face of

The Argument from Marginal Cases

1. If it is immoral to kill and eat "marginal" human beings, and to painfully experiment on them, then it is immoral to treat nonhuman animals this way.
2. It is (almost) always immoral to kill and eat "marginal" human beings, and to painfully experiment on them.

Therefore,

3. It is (almost) always immoral to kill and eat animals, and to painfully experiment on them.

I dislike the name of this argument, because I think it distasteful to refer to any human being as "marginal." But its name is so familiar in philosophical circles that we will stick with it here.

"Marginal" human beings are those whose mental lives are no more developed than those of the nonhuman animals we routinely eat and experiment on. There are many causes of such developmental limitations: severe brain trauma, extreme intellectual disability, and so on. The basic idea behind the Argument from Marginal Cases is that such human beings are no more morally important than the animals we harm in our labs or factory farms. Since they are of equal importance, we must treat them equally. If we are not prepared to eat or experiment upon such human beings, then we shouldn't be willing to treat animals that way, either.

Almost no one rejects premise 2 of the Argument from Marginal Cases. You've got to be awfully hard-hearted to be willing to subject marginal human beings to the sort of treatment we apply to animals in our labs and farms. True, there *might* be rare exceptions where such treatment is acceptable—that's the point of saying that it is *almost* always wrong to do such things to human beings. But these would have to be extremely unusual cases.

So the real action occurs in premise 1. Its defenders support it in this way. They say that marginal human beings, and farm and lab animals, are moral equals. They are moral equals because they have the same capacity to experience pain or pleasure, and they also possess the same kind and degree of mental powers. Of course, different marginal human beings have diverse mental lives. But so, too, do animals—pigs are extremely smart, as are many of the primates that are kept caged in university and pharmaceutical labs, while other animals, such as chickens and turkeys, are far less intelligent. The idea behind premise 1, though, is that when an animal and a human being exhibit the same capacity for pleasure or pain and possess the same mental powers, then they are moral equals, and so morally ought to be given equal respect. Equal respect in this case cannot mean nurturing and caring for the "marginal" human being while killing, eating, or experimenting on the nonhuman animal.

The obvious place to attack this reasoning is with the claim that animals and marginal humans are moral equals. If you don't like that claim, then it is up to you to find a better test for moral importance than reference to mental powers and a capacity for experiencing pleasure and pain.

Here are some familiar alternatives: the ability (1) to communicate, (2) to have emotions, (3) to be self-aware, (4) to be self-governing, (5) to assert claims on one's behalf, (6) to plan for one's future, or (7) to figure out how to get what one wants.

The problem is that marginal human beings and many animals fare equally well on each of these tests. Many animals possess these abilities to the same degree as marginal human beings. In some cases, animals will pass these tests more readily than their human counterparts.

In my experience, most people at this point try to argue in one of three ways. First, some say that every human is more important than any animal, because God created each of us as an exalted being whose life has more value than that of any animal. That's a possibility, but defending it is a task for theologians, as the defense will ultimately rest on claims about God's existence and His purposes and intentions. So we are going to leave this aside.

Second, people often say that marginal human beings, *just because they are human*, are more important than animals. On this view, the test of whether you are morally important is whether you are human. No matter how "marginal" someone is, he or she is still a human being, and so more important than any animal.

But this is a bad argument. It clearly begs the question against the Argument from Marginal Cases. What we need to know is *why* all human beings are morally more important than all nonhuman animals. We don't answer that question by asserting that they are.

Third, some say that every human is especially morally important because human beings, *as a species*, are the most intelligent and powerful beings on the planet. Even though "marginal" human beings themselves are no different from many animals in terms of their mental powers and their capacity for pleasure and pain, still, marginal human beings belong to a group that, on the whole, exhibits greater mental powers than any other group of animals.

This is a popular line of argument, but it, too, is problematic. Suppose all members of your family—except you!—are criminals. It's wrong to treat you as a criminal, just because you are a member of a group whose typical members, or most of whose members, are criminals. We should treat you in a way that responds to your own individual traits. The same thing is true when it comes to benefitting others. Suppose a teacher decides to give a student a better grade than she deserves because all of her older siblings were academic overachievers. It would be wrong to give her a benefit just on the basis of her group membership (i.e., her family). The teacher should give her the grade she deserves, which depends on her specific effort, aptitude, and performance, rather than the achievements that are typical of her family members as a whole.

One of our authors, Peter Singer, popularized the term **speciesism** to refer to the view that humans, just by virtue of their species membership, are morally more important than nonhuman animals. He likened speciesism to racism and sexism, in that, as he sees it, all three give moral priority to one group over another on the basis of a morally irrelevant trait. Skin color doesn't make you morally superior to someone else; neither does your sex. Neither, according to Singer, does your species membership.

For those who disagree, let us ask why species membership is supposed to be the all-important test of moral status. Your genetic code, or the species of your parents, doesn't seem to be what establishes your moral importance. To see this, imagine a time, perhaps not so far in the future, in which we encounter (or create) beings who are like us in every way—except that they are made of silicon. They think like us. They feel emotions as we do. They are self-aware. They feel pain. They look exactly like us. The *only* difference between them and us is which species we belong to.

I don't know how to argue for this, and perhaps you disagree, but it seems to me that this difference doesn't justify treating these beings as second-class citizens. In fact, it seems that they are just as morally important as we are—after all, without cutting them open, we couldn't tell them apart from a human being, because they are identical to us in every way except the internal circuitry.

If you share my view about this case, then you should reject the idea that species membership is, in itself, a morally important trait. And if that is so, then we can't resist the Argument from Marginal Cases by claiming that marginal human beings, just by virtue of their humanity, are more important than animals.

Thus if you do think that every "marginal" human being is more important than every nonhuman animal, then you have to identify a litmus test of moral importance that is better than the one that makes it depend on a capacity for pleasure and pain and on one's mental powers. This test has to be defensible in its own right, and also give humans an edge, no matter how mentally developed they happen to be. It won't be easy to do this. Exercise: see for yourself.

CONCLUSION

There is a widespread feeling that humans, no matter their abilities, are morally more important than any nonhuman animal. Our current factory farming practices, and those in a great many research labs, reflect this outlook, insofar as they treat animals in ways that we would not allow any of our fellow human beings to be treated.

But perhaps these practices reflect a prejudice, rather than a defensible moral position. A number of the most popular arguments for assigning all humans moral priority over all other animals are quite weak, as we have seen. And the Argument from Marginal Cases poses a strong challenge to those who would invariably favor the interests of humans over those of nonhumans.

Suppose that the Argument from Marginal Cases is sound. What follows? It is important to see that we could still assign greater importance to the lives of *most* human beings over those of animals. The Argument requires that we give equal moral respect to those who are moral equals. It does not say that every animal is the moral equal of every human being—indeed, for all it says, most humans, who possess far greater mental powers than any nonhuman animal, may have a more exalted moral status as a result of these greater powers (of imagination, empathy, intelligence, comprehension, etc.). So the Argument does not force us to the conclusion that we must regard every human and every animal as morally on a par. Still, it does force us to think hard about why beings—humans and nonhumans alike—are morally important in the first place.

ESSENTIAL CONCEPTS

Battery cages: small wire cages housing chickens that can be lined up and stacked in a barn so that thousands of chickens can be stored in a very small space.

Ethical vegetarians: those who refrain from eating animals out of a moral concern for the rights or welfare of animals.

Factory farm: a large industrial complex where large volumes of animals are packed into a small space to make raising and slaughtering them (or collecting their eggs) maximally efficient.

Gestation crates: strong metal cages, barely larger than a pig, used to house breeding pigs.

Sentience: the capacity to have sense experiences (e.g., feelings of pleasure or pain).

Speciesism: the view that humans, just by virtue of their species membership, are morally more important than nonhuman animals.

Subjective experience: the sort of experience one has when one is conscious and occupying a perspective on the world.

Vegans: those who refrain from the purchase and consumption of all animal products.

Vegetarian: a person who refrains from eating meat.

STAT SHOT

1. In 2013,[1] the meat and poultry industry processed:
   - 8.6 billion chickens
   - 33.2 million cattle
   - 239.4 million turkeys
   - 2.3 million sheep and lambs
   - 112 million hogs
2. Among the top meat-consuming countries are developed countries and developing countries in South America (Figure 13.1).

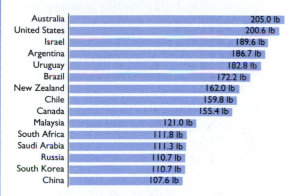

Figure 13.1. Annual meat consumption per capita worldwide in 2013.

Source: https://www.forbes.com/sites/niallmccarthy/2015/08/05/which-countries-eat-the-most-meat-each-year-infographic/#4d7331064f95

3. The size and number of pigs slaughtered in the United States have risen steadily since the early 1990s. The increase in average live weight is due, in part, to a steady dose of antibiotics, which allow pigs to devote energy to growing, rather than fighting disease.

4. Nine percent of US adults claim to be strictly or mostly vegetarian or vegan.[2]

5. In 2014, a slight majority of US adults (who didn't answer "don't know") opposed the use of animals in research (Figure 13.3). A significant majority of men favored research on animals, while a significant majority of women opposed it.

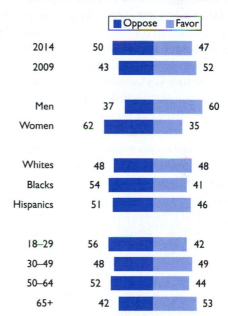

Figure 13.3. Percentage of US adults surveyed in 2014 saying they favor/oppose the use of animals in scientific research.

Source: http://www.pewinternet.org/2015/07/01/americans-politics-and-science-issues/pi_2015-07-01_science-and-politics_7-01/

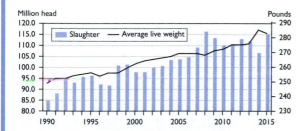

Figure 13.2. Commercial hog slaughter, number of head, and average live weight—United States.

Source: http://usda.mannlib.cornell.edu/usda/current/SlauOverview/SlauOverview-10-27-2016.pdf

1. https://www.meatinstitute.org/index.php?ht=d/sp/i/47465/pid/47465

2. http://www.pewinternet.org/2016/12/01/the-new-food-fights/ps_2016-12-01_food-science_1-07/

Cases for Critical Thinking

Exposé Videos

With the rise of YouTube and high-quality video cameras on cell phones, factory farm exposé videos have become increasingly numerous. These are videos taken by people, often animal rights activists, who go undercover to record farm workers abusing animals. These videos have been enormously successful tools at mobilizing large numbers of people to oppose the practices of the meat industry. In order to get the desired footage, though, activists must interview with, and be hired as employees by, factory farm managers. Once they've been hired and gain access to the farm, the videos they capture are deeply disturbing—even for supporters of factory farming. The worst of these show extreme abuses that are already illegal. In other cases, though, the films depict practices that are legally permitted but very unsettling to witness. Videos depicting illegal abuse have led to criminal prosecution in some cases, though they have been barred (because they were obtained through deception) in others.

Questions

1. To gain entrance to the factory farms, activists must deceive their employers by acting as though they're sincerely interested in working for the farm. Do you think it's morally permissible to deceive farm managers in this way? Why or why not? Suppose a condition of employment on the farm is that you sign a document promising never to take undercover video. Would it be morally permissible for an activist to sign that document and take undercover video anyway? Why or why not?

2. Usually, those who shoot exposé footage gain employment at a farm, take their video, and then immediately quit the job. But suppose an animal rights activist reasoned as follows: "Look, if I quit this job, the company will hire someone else to take my place and that person will likely not care about animal welfare. They might even be terribly cruel. If I continue working for this farm, however, I know that I will be kind to the animals. Now, to keep my job, I'll have to get my hands dirty by leading thousands of animals to their death. They won't keep me employed if I don't do the job they hired me for. So I'll certainly have to act in a way that I very much despise. But keeping this job is better for the animals than having someone else take the job. So, I'm going to keep working for this farm." Do you find this line of reasoning morally objectionable in any way, or does it sound like a pretty good idea? Why do you think that?

3. Imagine you work for a factory farm where employees are cruel to animals on a regular basis. The management is aware of the abuse, but they don't care. In fact, being compassionate to animals makes the work slower, so the management encourages the cruelty. Assuming you're certain you won't be caught, would it be permissible for you to set many of the animals free by opening up their cages so they can get away? If not, do you think it's ever permissible to take illegal means to alleviate the suffering of animals? Why or why not?

Experimenting on Chimpanzees

In the United States, many millions of people suffer from anxiety or depression.[1] Anxiety and depression can cause substance abuse, suicide, and other problems, especially in people who are not helped by today's medications and therapies. So, in 2014, researchers at the University of Wisconsin[2] interested in the neurobiology of anxiety and depression proposed the following experiment. They would take twenty rhesus macaque monkeys from their mothers in infancy. Periodically, they would expose the monkeys to stimuli intended to cause fear, stress, and anxiety. For example, they would put a strange monkey in the test monkey's cage, or put a strange human just outside of their cage, or expose the monkeys to a large snake. Shortly after, they would euthanize the monkeys and study their brains. Researchers hoped that, by conducting these experiments, they would be able to come up with new medication and psychotherapy strategies. Many on UW's campus opposed the study, claiming that the payoff didn't justify terrorizing the monkeys in the way the researchers proposed.

1. https://adaa.org/understanding-anxiety/facts-statistics

2. http://wisconsinwatch.org/2014/07/university-of-wisconsin-to-reprise-controversial-monkey-studies/

Questions

1. What do you think: Was this study morally justified? Why or why not?

2. Researchers would never dream of doing this kind of experiment to an infant human being. Are we justified in treating non-human subjects differently than human subjects who are, cognitively speaking, relevantly similar? Why or why not?

3. The UW study on monkeys was controversial, and even the researchers, though they ultimately supported the study, could see that there were powerful moral reasons to oppose it. But few researchers would think twice about doing painful research on rabbits, or frogs, or mice. Are we justified in treating some nonhuman subjects, such as primates, differently from others, such as mice? Why or why not?

Uplift: Cognitive Enhancement for Animals

In 2013, researchers at the University of Rochester and UCLA announced that they had made rodents smarter by injecting human brain cells into the forebrains of newborn mice. Scientists have also succeeded in dramatically improving the memories of rats and rhesus monkeys by using electronic brain implants.[1] These are the early stages of what many scientists believe is in our future: cognitive enhancement for animals, or, as science fiction novelists have called it for decades, "uplift." The benefits of uplift for animals could be tremendous. As one researcher said, uplifted animals could benefit by "find[ing] food more easily, being able to create a comfortable and secure environment, being able to avoid danger, and enjoying social interaction."[2] Though we are in the early stages, it can be instructive to think about the ethical implications of the fully developed animal uplift technology. Suppose, for example, that we were able to give animals a relatively cheap and easy treatment that would boost their intelligence to the level of a typical human adult.

1. https://www.bostonglobe.com/ideas/2013/03/30/should-make-animals-smarter/zbW4LTWkP8TZgB93Mqw7QJ/story.html

2. https://www.bostonglobe.com/ideas/2013/03/30/should-make-animals-smarter/zbW4LTWkP8TZgB93Mqw7QJ/story.html

Questions

1. Would this kind of cognitive enhancement be a benefit for animals? Why or why not?

2. Supposing that cognitively enhancing animals would be a benefit to them, would it be morally *permissible* to give this treatment to an animal? Why or why not? Would it be morally *required* that we give (at least some of) them the treatment? Why or why not?

3. If we get to the point that we can cognitively enhance animals to a significant degree, it will almost certainly be thanks to insights learned from extensive experimentation on animals. Assuming that cognitively enhancing animals would be to their benefit, would we have an obligation to enhance at least some animals as a way of compensating them for our extensive experimentation on them? Why or why not?

READINGS

All Animals Are Equal

Peter Singer

Peter Singer argues for a radical kind of equality among all animals—human and non-human alike. He knows that this is highly controversial, and seeks to protect against misunderstanding by distinguishing between a moral principle that requires equal treatment of all and a principle that requires equal consideration of interests. It is morally acceptable to treat different beings differently on many occasions. What we must not do, according to Singer, is to give the interests of humans greater importance than the same interests of nonhuman animals. His principle of equal consideration requires that identical interests be given identical moral weight, no matter whose interests they are. In many cases we share interests with nonhuman animals—interests, for instance, in avoiding hunger, staying warm, and avoiding pain. In cases where we have common interests, those interests are equally morally important, whether they belong to a human or to a nonhuman animal.

Singer believes that his equal consideration principle explains what is wrong with racism and sexism. It also explains what is immoral about *speciesism*—the view that one's species membership gives one greater moral importance than members of other species. For Singer, what confers moral importance on humans and nonhumans alike is the ability to experience pleasure and pain. He regards all other criteria—rationality, intelligence, or linguistic ability, for example—as arbitrary.

Singer presents the so-called Argument from Marginal Cases in defense of his claim that animal and human interests must be given equal weight. He argues that if it is wrong to kill or experiment on a "marginal" human—one whose mental life is no more developed than an animal's—then it is equally wrong to kill or experiment on an animal. After all, if their mental life is basically the same, then what else could morally distinguish them? They belong to different species, but Singer denies that species membership has any independent moral importance. They look different—but appearance is not itself morally important, either. We may care more about the human than the animal, but the emotional attachment of others is not a reliable basis for determining moral importance. Singer argues that animal experimentation may sometimes be morally justified, if it promises to yield great benefits. But then experimentation on "marginal" humans is also sometimes justified. Indeed, in some cases, we ought to experiment on humans *rather than* on animals, since human experimentation will be more reliable than animal experimentation.

In recent years a number of oppressed groups have campaigned vigorously for equality. The classic

From Peter Singer, "All Animals Are Equal," in Tom Regan and Peter Singer, eds., *Animal Rights and Human Obligations* (Prentice-Hall, 1989), pp. 148–162.

instance is the Black Liberation movement, which demands an end to the prejudice and discrimination that has made blacks second-class citizens. The immediate appeal of the black liberation movement and its initial, if limited, success made it a model for other oppressed groups to follow. We became familiar with liberation movements for Spanish-Americans, gay people, and a variety of other minorities. When a majority group—women—began their campaign, some thought we had come to the end of the road. Discrimination on the basis of sex, it has been said, is the last universally accepted form of discrimination, practiced without secrecy or pretense even in those liberal circles that have long prided themselves on their freedom from prejudice against racial minorities.

One should always be wary of talking of "the last remaining form of discrimination." If we have learnt anything from the liberation movements, we should have learnt how difficult it is to be aware of latent prejudice in our attitudes to particular groups until this prejudice is forcefully pointed out.

A liberation movement demands an expansion of our moral horizons and an extension or reinterpretation of the basic moral principle of equality. Practices that were previously regarded as natural and inevitable come to be seen as the result of an unjustifiable prejudice. Who can say with confidence that all his or her attitudes and practices are beyond criticism? If we wish to avoid being numbered amongst the oppressors, we must be prepared to re-think even our most fundamental attitudes. We need to consider them from the point of view of those most disadvantaged by our attitudes, and the practices that follow from these attitudes. If we can make this unaccustomed mental switch we may discover a pattern in our attitudes and practices that consistently operates so as to benefit one group—usually the one to which we ourselves belong—at the expense of another. In this way we may come to see that there is a case for a new liberation movement. My aim is to advocate that we make this mental switch in respect of our attitudes and practices towards a very large group of beings: members of species other than our own—or, as we popularly though misleadingly call them, animals. In other words, I am urging that we extend to other species the basic principle of equality that most of us recognize should be extended to all members of our own species.

All this may sound a little far-fetched, more like a parody of other liberation movements than a serious objective. In fact, in the past the idea of

"The Rights of Animals" really has been used to parody the case for women's rights. When Mary Wollstonecraft, a forerunner of later feminists, published her *Vindication of the Rights of Women* in 1792, her ideas were widely regarded as absurd, and they were satirized in an anonymous publication entitled *A Vindication of the Rights of Brutes*. The author of this satire (actually Thomas Taylor, a distinguished Cambridge philosopher) tried to refute Wollstonecraft's reasonings by showing that they could be carried one stage further. If sound when applied to women, why should the arguments not be applied to dogs, cats, and horses? They seemed to hold equally well for these "brutes"; yet to hold that brutes had rights was manifestly absurd; therefore the reasoning by which this conclusion had been reached must be unsound, and if unsound when applied to brutes, it must also be unsound when applied to women, since the very same arguments had been used in each case.

One way in which we might reply to this argument is by saying that the case for equality between men and women cannot validly be extended to nonhuman animals. Women have a right to vote, for instance, because they are just as capable of making rational decisions as men are; dogs, on the other hand, are incapable of understanding the significance of voting, so they cannot have the right to vote. There are many other obvious ways in which men and women resemble each other closely, while humans and other animals differ greatly. So, it might be said, men and women are similar beings and should have equal rights, while humans and nonhumans are different and should not have equal rights.

The thought behind this reply to Taylor's analogy is correct up to a point, but it does not go far enough. There are important differences between humans and other animals, and these differences must give rise to some differences in the rights that each have. Recognizing this obvious fact, however, is no barrier to the case for extending the basic principle of equality to nonhuman animals. The differences that exist between men and women are equally undeniable, and the supporters of Women's Liberation are aware that these differences may give rise to different rights. Many feminists hold that women have the right to an abortion on request. It does not follow that since these same people are campaigning for equality between men and women they must support the right of men to have abortions too. Since a man cannot have an abortion, it is meaningless to talk of his right to have one. Since a pig can't vote, it is meaningless to talk of its right to vote. There is no reason why either Women's Liberation or Animal Liberation should get involved in such nonsense. The extension of the basic principle of equality from one group to another does not imply that we must treat both groups in exactly the same way, or grant exactly the same rights to both groups. Whether we should do so will depend on the nature of the members of the two groups. The basic principle of equality, I shall argue, is equality of consideration; and equal consideration for different beings may lead to different treatment and different rights.

So there is a different way of replying to Taylor's attempt to parody Wollstonecraft's arguments, a way which does not deny the differences between humans and nonhumans, but goes more deeply into the question of equality and concludes by finding nothing absurd in the idea that the basic principle of equality applies to so-called "brutes." I believe that we reach this conclusion if we examine the basis on which our opposition to discrimination on grounds of race or sex ultimately rests. We will then see that we would be on shaky ground if we were to demand equality for blacks, women, and other groups of oppressed humans while denying equal consideration to nonhumans.

When we say that all human beings, whatever their race, creed, or sex, are equal, what is it that we are asserting? Those who wish to defend a hierarchical, inegalitarian society have often pointed out that by whatever test we choose, it simply is not true that all humans are equal. Like it or not, we must face the fact that humans come in different shapes and sizes; they come with differing moral capacities, differing intellectual abilities, differing amounts of benevolent feeling and sensitivity to the needs of others, differing abilities to communicate effectively, and differing capacities to experience pleasure and pain. In short, if the demand for equality were based on the actual equality of all human beings, we would have to stop demanding equality. It would be an unjustifiable demand.

Still, one might cling to the view that the demand for equality among human beings is based on the actual equality of the different races and sexes. Although humans differ as individuals in various ways, there are no differences between the races and sexes as such. From the mere fact that a person is black, or a woman, we cannot infer anything else about that person. This, it may be said, is what is wrong with racism and sexism. The white racist claims that whites are superior to blacks, but this is false—although there are differences between individuals, some blacks are superior to some whites in all of the capacities and abilities that could conceivably be relevant. The opponent of sexism would say the same: a person's sex is no guide to his or her abilities, and this is why it is unjustifiable to discriminate on the basis of sex.

This is a possible line of objection to racial and sexual discrimination. It is not, however, the way that someone really concerned about equality would choose, because taking this line could, in some circumstances, force one to accept a most inegalitarian society. The fact that humans differ as individuals, rather than as races or sexes, is a valid reply to someone who defends a hierarchical society like, say, South Africa, in which all whites are superior in status to all blacks. The existence of individual variations that cut across the lines of race or sex, however, provides us with no defense at all against a more sophisticated opponent of equality, one who proposes that, say, the interests of those with I.Q. ratings above 100 be preferred to the interests of those with I.Q.s below 100. Would a hierarchical society of this sort really be so much better than one based on race or sex? I think not. But if we tie the moral principle of equality to the factual equality of the different races or sexes, taken as a whole, our opposition to racism and sexism does not provide us with any basis for objecting to this kind of inegalitarianism.

There is a second important reason why we ought not to base our opposition to racism and sexism on any kind of factual equality, even the limited kind which asserts that variations in capacities and abilities are spread evenly between the different races and sexes: we can have no absolute guarantee that these abilities and capacities really are distributed evenly, without regard to race or sex, among human beings. So far as actual abilities are concerned, there do seem to be certain measurable differences between both races and sexes. These differences do not, of course, appear in each case, but only when averages are taken. More important still, we do not yet know how much of these differences is really due to the different genetic endowments of the various races and sexes, and how much is due to environmental differences that are the result of past and continuing discrimination. Perhaps all of the important differences will eventually prove to be environmental rather than genetic. Anyone opposed to racism and sexism will certainly hope that this will be so, for it will make the task of ending discrimination a lot easier; nevertheless it would be dangerous to rest the case against racism and sexism on the belief that all significant differences are environmental in origin. The opponent of, say, racism who takes this line will be unable to avoid conceding that if differences in ability did after all prove to have some genetic connection with race, racism would in some way be defensible.

It would be folly for the opponent of racism to stake his whole case on a dogmatic commitment to one particular outcome of a difficult scientific issue which is still a long way from being settled. While attempts to prove that differences in certain selected abilities between races and sexes are primarily genetic in origin have certainly not been conclusive, the same must be said of attempts to prove that these differences are largely the result of environment. At this stage of the investigation we cannot be certain which view is correct, however much we may hope it is the latter.

Fortunately, there is no need to pin the case for equality to one particular outcome of this scientific investigation. The appropriate response to those who claim to have found evidence of genetically-based differences in ability between the races or sexes is not to stick to the belief that the genetic explanation must be wrong, whatever evidence to the contrary may turn up: instead we should make it quite clear that the claim to equality does not depend on intelligence, moral capacity, physical strength, or similar matters of fact. Equality is a moral ideal, not a simple assertion of fact. There is no logically compelling reason for assuming that a factual difference in ability between two people justifies any difference in the amount of consideration we give to satisfying their needs and interests. The principle of the equality of human beings is not a description of an alleged actual equality among humans: it is a prescription of how we should treat humans.

Jeremy Bentham incorporated the essential basis of moral equality into his utilitarian system of ethics in the formula: "Each to count for one and none for more than one." In other words, the interests of every being affected by an action are to be taken into account and given the same weight as the like interests of any other being. A later utilitarian, Henry Sidgwick, put the point in this way: "The good of any one individual is of no more importance, from the point of view (if I may say so) of the Universe, than the good of any other."[1] More recently, the leading figures in contemporary moral philosophy have shown a great deal of agreement in specifying as a fundamental presupposition of their moral theories some similar requirement which operates so as to give everyone's interests equal consideration—although they cannot agree on how this requirement is best formulated.[2]

It is an implication of this principle of equality that our concern for others ought not to depend on what they are like, or what abilities they possess—although precisely what this concern requires us to do may vary according to the characteristics of those affected by what we do. It is on this basis that the case against racism and the case against sexism must both ultimately rest; and it is in accordance with this principle that speciesism is also to be condemned. If possessing a higher degree of intelligence does not entitle one human to use another for his own ends, how can it entitle humans to exploit nonhumans?

Many philosophers have proposed the principle of equal consideration of interests, in some form or other, as a basic moral principle; but, as we shall see in more detail shortly, not many of them have recognized that this principle applies to members of other species as well as to our own. Bentham was one of the few who did realize this. In a forward-looking passage, written at a time when black slaves in the British dominions were still being treated much as we now treat nonhuman animals, Bentham wrote:

> The day may come when the rest of the animal creation may acquire those rights which never could have been witholden from them but by the hand of tyranny. The French have already discovered that the blackness of the skin is no reason why a human being should be abandoned without redress to the caprice of a tormentor. It may one day come to be recognized that the number of the legs, the villosity of the skin, or the termination of the os sacrum, are reasons equally insufficient for abandoning a sensitive being to the same fate. What else is it that should trace the insuperable line? Is it the faculty of reason, or perhaps the faculty of discourse? But a full-grown horse or dog is beyond comparison a more rational, as well as a more conversable animal, than an infant of a day, or a week, or even a month, old. But suppose they were otherwise, what would it avail? The question is not, Can they *reason*? nor, Can they *talk*? but, Can they *suffer*?[3]

In this passage Bentham points to the capacity for suffering as the vital characteristic that gives a being the right to equal consideration. The capacity for suffering—or more strictly, for suffering and/or enjoyment or happiness—is not just another characteristic like the capacity for language, or for higher mathematics. Bentham is not saying that those who try to mark "the insuperable line" that determines whether the interests of a being should be considered happen to have selected the wrong characteristic. The capacity for suffering and enjoying things is a prerequisite for having interests at all, a condition that must be satisfied before we can speak of interests in any meaningful way. It would be nonsense to say that it was not in the interests of a stone to be kicked along the road by a schoolboy. A stone does not have interests because it cannot suffer. Nothing that we can do to it could possibly make any difference to its welfare. A mouse, on the other hand, does have an interest in not being tormented, because it will suffer if it is.

If a being suffers, there can be no moral justification for refusing to take that suffering into consideration. No matter what the nature of the being, the principle of equality requires that its suffering be counted equally with the like suffering—in so far as rough comparisons can be made—of any other being. If a being is not capable of suffering, or of experiencing enjoyment or happiness, there is nothing to be taken into account. This is why the limit of sentience (using the term as a convenient, if not strictly accurate, shorthand for the capacity to suffer or experience enjoyment or happiness) is the only defensible boundary of concern for the interests of others. To mark this boundary by some characteristic like intelligence or rationality would be to mark it in an arbitrary way. Why not choose some other characteristic, like skin color?

The racist violates the principle of equality by giving greater weight to the interests of members of his own race, when there is a clash between their interests and the interests of those of another race. Similarly the speciesist allows the interests of his own species to override the greater interests of members of other species.[4] The pattern is the same in each case. Most human beings are speciesists. I shall now very briefly describe some of the practices that show this.

For the great majority of human beings, especially in urban, industrialized societies, the most direct form of contact with members of other species is at mealtimes: we eat them. In doing so we treat them purely as means to our ends. We regard their life and well-being as subordinate to our taste for a particular kind of dish. I say "taste" deliberately—this is purely a matter of pleasing our palate. There can be no defense of eating flesh in terms of satisfying nutritional needs, since it has been established beyond doubt that we could satisfy our need for protein and other essential nutrients far more efficiently with a diet that replaced animal flesh by soy beans, or products derived from soy beans, and other high-protein vegetable products.[5]

It is not merely the act of killing that indicates what we are ready to do to other species in order to gratify our tastes. The suffering we inflict on the animals while they are alive is perhaps an even clearer indication of our speciesism than the fact that we are prepared to kill them.[6] In order to have meat on the table at a price that people can afford, our society tolerates methods of meat production that confine sentient animals in cramped, unsuitable conditions for the entire durations of their lives. Animals are treated like machines that convert fodder into flesh, and any innovation that results in a higher "conversion ratio" is liable to be adopted. As one authority on the subject has said, "cruelty is acknowledged only when profitability ceases."[7]...

Since, as I have said, none of these practices cater for anything more than our pleasures of taste, our practice of rearing and killing other animals in order to eat them is a clear instance of the sacrifice of the most important interests of other beings in order to satisfy trivial interests of our own. To avoid speciesism we must stop this practice, and each of us has a moral obligation to cease supporting the practice. Our custom is all the support that the meat-industry needs. The decision to cease giving it that support may be difficult, but it is no more difficult than it would have been for a white Southerner to go against the traditions of his society and free his slaves: if we do not change our dietary habits, how can we censure those slaveholders who would not change their own way of living?

The same form of discrimination may be observed in the widespread practice of experimenting on other species in order to see if certain substances are safe for human beings, or to test some psychological theory about the effect of severe punishment on learning, or to try out various new compounds just in case something turns up...

In the past, argument about vivisection has often missed the point, because it has been put in absolutist terms: Would the abolitionist be prepared to let thousands die if they could be saved by experimenting on a single animal? The way to reply to this purely hypothetical question is to pose another: Would the experimenter be prepared to perform his experiment on an orphaned human infant, if that were the only way to save many lives? (I say "orphan" to avoid the complication of parental feelings, although in doing so I am being overfair to the experimenter, since the nonhuman subjects of experiments are not orphans.) If the experimenter is not prepared to use an orphaned human infant, then his readiness to use nonhumans is simple discrimination, since adult apes, cats, mice, and other mammals are more aware of what is happening to them, more self-directing and, so far as we can tell, at least as sensitive to pain, as any human infant. There seems to be no relevant characteristic

that human infants possess that adult mammals do not have to the same or a higher degree. (Someone might try to argue that what makes it wrong to experiment on a human infant is that the infant will, in time and if left alone, develop into more than the nonhuman, but one would then, to be consistent, have to oppose abortion, since the fetus has the same potential as the infant—indeed, even contraception and abstinence might be wrong on this ground, since the egg and sperm, considered jointly, also have the same potential. In any case, this argument still gives us no reason for selecting a nonhuman, rather than a human with severe and irreversible brain damage, as the subject for our experiments.)

The experimenter, then, shows a bias in favor of his own species whenever he carries out an experiment on a nonhuman for a purpose that he would not think justified him in using a human being at an equal or lower level of sentience, awareness, ability to be self-directing, etc. No one familiar with the kind of results yielded by most experiments on animals can have the slightest doubt that if this bias were eliminated the number of experiments performed would be a minute fraction of the number performed today.

Experimenting on animals, and eating their flesh, are perhaps the two major forms of speciesism in our society. By comparison, the third and last form of speciesism is so minor as to be insignificant, but it is perhaps of some special interest to those for whom this article was written. I am referring to speciesism in contemporary philosophy.

Philosophy ought to question the basic assumptions of the age. Thinking through, critically and carefully, what most people take for granted is, I believe, the chief task of philosophy, and it is this task that makes philosophy a worthwhile activity. Regrettably, philosophy does not always live up to its historic role. Philosophers are human beings, and they are subject to all the preconceptions of the society to which they belong. Sometimes they succeed in breaking free of the prevailing ideology: more often they become its most sophisticated defenders. So, in this case, philosophy as practiced in the universities today does not challenge anyone's preconceptions about our relations with other species. By their writings, those philosophers who tackle problems that touch upon the issue reveal that they make the same unquestioned assumptions as most other humans, and what they say tends to confirm the reader in his or her comfortable speciesist habits.

I could illustrate this claim by referring to the writings of philosophers in various fields—for instance, the attempts that have been made by those interested in rights to draw the boundary of the sphere of rights so that it runs parallel to the biological boundaries of the species homo sapiens, including infants and even mental defectives, but excluding those other beings of equal or greater capacity who are so useful to us at mealtimes and in our laboratories. I think it would be a more appropriate conclusion to this article, however, if I concentrated on the problem with which we have been centrally concerned, the problem of equality.

It is significant that the problem of equality, in moral and political philosophy, is invariably formulated in terms of human equality. The effect of this is that the question of the equality of other animals does not confront the philosopher, or student, as an issue itself—and this is already an indication of the failure of philosophy to challenge accepted beliefs. Still, philosophers have found it difficult to discuss the issue of human equality without raising, in a paragraph or two, the question of the status of other animals. The reason for this, which should be apparent from what I have said already, is that if humans are to be regarded as equal to one another, we need some sense of "equal" that does not require any actual, descriptive equality of capacities, talents or other qualities. If equality is to be related to any actual characteristics of humans, these characteristics must be some lowest common denominator, pitched so low that no human lacks them—but then the philosopher comes up against the catch that any such set of characteristics which covers all humans will not be possessed only by humans. In other words, it turns out that in the only sense in which we can truly say, as an assertion of fact, that all humans are equal, at least some members of other species are also equal—equal, that is, to each other and to humans. If, on the other hand, we regard the statement "All humans are equal" in some non-factual way, perhaps as a prescription, then, as I have already argued, it is even more difficult to exclude non-humans from the sphere of equality.

This result is not what the egalitarian philosopher originally intended to assert. Instead of accepting the radical outcome to which their own reasonings naturally point, however, most philosophers try to reconcile their beliefs in human equality and animal inequality by arguments that can only be described as devious.

As a first example, I take William Frankena's well-known article "The Concept of Social Justice." Frankena opposes the idea of basing justice on merit, because he sees that this could lead to highly inegalitarian results. Instead he proposes the principle that

> all men are to be treated as equals, not because they are equal, in any respect, but simply because they are human. They are human because they have emotions and desires, and are able to think, and hence are capable of enjoying a good life in a sense in which other animals are not.[8]

But what is this capacity to enjoy the good life which all humans have, but no other animals? Other animals have emotions and desires and appear to be capable of enjoying a good life. We may doubt that they can think—although the behavior of some apes, dolphins, and even dogs suggests that some of them can—but what is the relevance of thinking? Frankena goes on to admit that by "the good life" he means "not so much the morally good life as the happy or satisfactory life," so thought would appear to be unnecessary for enjoying the good life; in fact to emphasize the need for thought would make difficulties for the egalitarian since only some people are capable of leading intellectually satisfying lives, or morally good lives. This makes it difficult to see what Frankena's principle of equality has to do with simply being human. Surely every sentient being is capable of leading a life that is happier or less miserable than some alternative life, and hence has a claim to be taken into account. In this respect the distinction between humans and nonhumans is not a sharp division, but rather a continuum along which we move gradually, and with overlaps between the species, from simple capacities for enjoyment and satisfaction, or pain and suffering, to more complex ones.

Faced with a situation in which they see a need for some basis for the moral gulf that is commonly thought to separate humans and animals, but can find no concrete difference that will do the job without undermining the equality of humans, philosophers tend to waffle. They resort to high-sounding phrases like "the intrinsic dignity of the human individual";[9] they talk of the "intrinsic worth of all men" as if men (humans?) had some worth that other beings did not,[10] or they say that humans, and only humans, are "ends in themselves," while "everything other than a person can only have value for a person."[11]

This idea of a distinctive human dignity and worth has a long history; it can be traced back directly to the Renaissance humanists, for instance to Pico della Mirandola's *Oration on the Dignity of Man*. Pico and other humanists based their estimate of human dignity on the idea that man possessed the central, pivotal position in the "Great Chain of Being" that led from the lowliest forms of matter to God himself; this view of the universe, in turn, goes back to both classical and Judeo-Christian doctrines. Contemporary philosophers have cast off these metaphysical and religious shackles and freely invoke the dignity of mankind without needing to justify the idea at all. Why should we not attribute "intrinsic dignity" or "intrinsic worth" to ourselves? Fellow-humans are unlikely to reject the accolades we so generously bestow on them, and those to whom we deny the honor are unable to object. Indeed, when one thinks only of humans, it can be very liberal, very progressive, to talk of the dignity of all human beings. In so doing, we implicitly condemn slavery, racism, and other violations of human rights. We admit that we ourselves are in some fundamental sense on a par with the poorest, most ignorant members of our own species. It is only when we think of humans as no more than a small sub-group of all the beings that inhabit our planet that we may realize that in elevating our own species we are at the same time lowering the relative status of all other species.

The truth is that the appeal to the intrinsic dignity of human beings appears to solve the egalitarian's problems only as long as it goes unchallenged. Once we ask why it should be that all humans—including infants, mental defectives, psychopaths, Hitler, Stalin, and the rest—have some kind of dignity or worth that no elephant, pig, or chimpanzee can ever achieve, we see that this question is as difficult

to answer as our original request for some relevant fact that justifies the inequality of humans and other animals. In fact, these two questions are really one: talk of intrinsic dignity or moral worth only takes the problem back one step, because any satisfactory defence of the claim that all and only humans have intrinsic dignity would need to refer to some relevant capacities or characteristics that all and only humans possess. Philosophers frequently introduce ideas of dignity, respect, and worth at the point at which other reasons appear to be lacking, but this is hardly good enough. Fine phrases are the last resource of those who have run out of arguments.

In case there are those who still think it may be possible to find some relevant characteristic that distinguishes all humans from all members of other species, I shall refer again, before I conclude, to the existence of some humans who quite clearly are below the level of awareness, self-consciousness, intelligence, and sentience, of many non-humans. I am thinking of humans with severe and irreparable brain damage, and also of infant humans. To avoid the complication of the relevance of a being's potential, however, I shall henceforth concentrate on permanently retarded humans.

Philosophers who set out to find a characteristic that will distinguish humans from other animals rarely take the course of abandoning these groups of humans by lumping them in with the other animals. It is easy to see why they do not. To take this line without re-thinking our attitudes to other animals would entail that we have the right to perform painful experiments on retarded humans for trivial reasons; similarly it would follow that we had the right to rear and kill these humans for food. To most philosophers these consequences are as unacceptable as the view that we should stop treating nonhumans in this way.

Of course, when discussing the problem of equality it is possible to ignore the problem of mental defectives, or brush it aside as if somehow insignificant.[12] This is the easiest way out. What else remains? My final example of speciesism in contemporary philosophy has been selected to show what happens when a writer is prepared to face the question of human equality and animal inequality without ignoring the existence of mental defectives, and without resorting to obscurantist mumbo jumbo.

Stanley Benn's clear and honest article "Egalitarianism and Equal Consideration of Interests"[13] fits this description.

Benn, after noting the usual "evident human inequalities" argues, correctly I think, for equality of consideration as the only possible basis for egalitarianism. Yet Benn, like other writers, is thinking only of "equal consideration of human interests." Benn is quite open in his defence of this restriction of equal consideration:

> . . . not to possess human shape is a disqualifying condition. However faithful or intelligent a dog may be, it would be a monstrous sentimentality to attribute to him interests that could be weighed in an equal balance with those of human beings . . . if, for instance, one had to decide between feeding a hungry baby or a hungry dog, anyone who chose the dog would generally be reckoned morally defective, unable to recognize a fundamental inequality of claims.
>
> This is what distinguishes our attitude to animals from our attitude to imbeciles. It would be odd to say that we ought to respect equally the dignity or personality of the imbecile and of the rational man . . . but there is nothing odd about saying that we should respect their interests equally, that is, that we should give to the interests of each the same serious consideration as claims to considerations necessary for some standard of well-being that we can recognize and endorse.

Benn's statement of the basis of the consideration we should have for imbeciles seems to me correct, but why should there be any fundamental inequality of claims between a dog and a human imbecile? Benn sees that if equal consideration depended on rationality, no reason could be given against using imbeciles for research purposes, as we now use dogs and guinea pigs. This will not do: "But of course we do distinguish imbeciles from animals in this regard," he says. That the common distinction is justifiable is something Benn does not question; his problem is how it is to be justified. The answer he gives is this:

> . . . we respect the interests of men and give them priority over dogs not *insofar* as they are rational, but because rationality is the human norm. We say it is *unfair* to exploit the deficiencies of the imbecile who falls short of the norm, just as it would be

unfair, and not just ordinarily dishonest, to steal from a blind man. If we do not think in this way about dogs, it is because we do not see the irrationality of the dog as a deficiency or a handicap, but as normal for the species. The characteristics, therefore, that distinguish the normal man from the normal dog make it intelligible for us to talk of other men having interests and capacities, and therefore claims, of precisely the same kind as we make on our own behalf. But although these characteristics may provide the point of the distinction between men and other species, they are not in fact the qualifying conditions for membership, to the distinguishing criteria of the class of morally considerable persons; and this is precisely because a man does not become a member of a different species, with its own standards of normality, by reason of not possessing these characteristics.

The final sentence of this passage gives the argument away. An imbecile, Benn concedes, may have no characteristics superior to those of a dog; nevertheless this does not make the imbecile a member of "a different species" as the dog is. Therefore it would be "unfair" to use the imbecile for medical research as we use the dog. But why? That the imbecile is not rational is just the way things have worked out, and the same is true of the dog—neither is any more responsible for their mental level. If it is unfair to take advantage of an isolated defect, why is it fair to take advantage of a more general limitation? I find it hard to see anything in this argument except a defense of preferring the interests of members of our own species because they are members of our own species. To those who think there might be more to it, I suggest the following mental exercise. Assume that it has been proven that there is a difference in the average, or normal, intelligence quotient for two different races, say whites and blacks. Then substitute the term "white" for every occurrence of "men" and "black" for every occurrence of "dog" in the passage quoted; and substitute "high I.Q." for "rationality" and when Benn talks of "imbeciles" replace this term by "dumb whites"—that is, whites who fall well below the normal white I.Q. score. Finally, change "species" to "race." Now retread the passage. It has become a defense of a rigid, no-exceptions division between whites and blacks, based on I.Q. scores, notwithstanding an admitted overlap between whites and blacks in this respect. The revised passage is, of course, outrageous, and this is not only because we have made fictitious assumptions in our substitutions. The point is that in the original passage Benn was defending a rigid division in the amount of consideration due to members of different species, despite admitted cases of overlap. If the original did not, at first reading strike us as being as outrageous as the revised version does, this is largely because although we are not racists ourselves, most of us are speciesists. Like the other articles, Benn's stands as a warning of the ease with which the best minds can fall victim to a prevailing ideology.

NOTES

1. *The Methods of Ethics* (7th Ed.), p. 382.
2. For example, R. M. Hare, *Freedom and Reason* (Oxford, 1963) and J. Rawls, *A Theory of Justice* (Harvard, 1972); for a brief account of the essential agreement on this issue between these and other positions, see R. M. Hare, "Rules of War and Moral Reasoning," *Philosophy and Public Affairs*, vol. 1, no. 2 (1972).
3. *Introduction to the Principles of Morals and Legislation*, ch. XVII.
4. I owe the term speciesism to Richard Ryder.
5. In order to produce 1 lb. of protein in the form of beef or veal, we must feed 21 lbs. of protein to the animal. Other forms of livestock are slightly less inefficient, but the average ratio in the United States is still 1:8. It has been estimated that the amount of protein lost to humans in this way is equivalent to 90 percent of the annual world protein deficit. For a brief account, see Frances Moore Lappe, *Diet for a Small Planet* (Friends of The Earth/Ballantine, New York 1971), pp. 4–11.
6. Although one might think that killing a being is obviously the ultimate wrong one can do to it, I think that the infliction of suffering is a clearer indication of speciesism because it might be argued that at least part of what is wrong with killing a human is that most humans are conscious of their existence over time and have desires and purposes that extend into the future—see, for instance, M. Tooley, "Abortion and Infanticide," *Philosophy and Public Affairs*, vol. 2, no. I (1972). Of course, if one took this view one would have to hold—as Tooley does—that killing a human infant or mental defective is not in itself wrong and is less serious than killing certain higher mammals that probably do have a sense of their own existence over time.
7. Ruth Harrison, *Animal Machines* (Stuart, London, 1964). For an account of farming conditions, see my *Animal Liberation* (New York Review Company, 1975).
8. In R. Brandt (ed.), *Social Justice* (Prentice Hall, Englewood Cliffs, 1962), p. 19.
9. Frankena, op. cit. p. 23.
10. H. A. Bedau, "Egalitarianism and the Idea of Equality," in *Nomos IX: Equality*, ed. J. R. Pennock and J. W. Chapman, New York, 1967.
11. C. Vlastos, "Justice and Equality," in Brandt, *Social Justice*, p. 48.
12. For example, Bernard Williams, "The Idea of Equality," in *Philosophy, Politics, and Society* (second series), ed. P. Laslett and W. Rundman (Blackwell, Oxford, 1962), p. 118; J. Rawls, *A Theory of Justice*, pp. 509–10.
13. *Nomos IX: Equality*; the passages quoted are on p. 62ff.

Peter Singer: All Animals Are Equal

1. Singer claims that speciesism commits the same sort of moral error as racism and sexism. Do you agree? Why or why not?
2. If you believe that animal experimentation is morally justified even when experimenting on mentally similar "marginal" human beings is not, what explains why such differential treatment is morally acceptable?
3. Singer claims that rationality or intelligence is as arbitrary a basis for determining moral importance as skin color. Do you find his claim plausible? Why or why not?
4. Does sentience really serve as the basis for independent moral importance? If so, why? If not, what other basis would you propose?
5. Does Singer's view allow for any circumstances in which it is morally acceptable to eat meat? If so, which circumstances are these, and why? If not, why not?

Virtue Ethics and the Treatment of Animals
Rosalind Hursthouse

In this essay, Rosalind Hursthouse gives a rich overview of virtue ethics and its implications for our treatment of nonhuman animals. As its name suggests, virtue ethics gives pride of place to the virtues and vices in determining the morality of our actions. A virtue is an excellent character trait—one that is morally good, admirable, or praiseworthy. A vice is a defective character trait—one that is morally bad, despicable, or regrettable. On Hursthouse's version of virtue ethics, morality tells us that we should act in ways that exemplify the virtues and avoid the vices.

After discussing the nature of the virtues, Hursthouse turns her attention to the moral status of eating animals. While vegetarianism is not itself a virtue—one can refrain from eating animals for all sorts of reasons, not just morally good ones—it is nevertheless correct, according to Hursthouse, that virtuous people, acting in character, would in most circumstances not eat meat. That's because most of today's animal farming practices are cruel and cause needless suffering. Virtuous people will not want to be party to such cruelty and suffering, and so will refrain from eating meat. There are exceptions—if you must eat meat to remain alive, for instance, then you needn't exhibit any vicious tendencies by sitting down to a steak dinner. But most of us are not in such exceptional circumstances, and so, for most of us, eating meat would be immoral, as it would reflect a defect in our character—an indifference to the suffering of others.

Hursthouse next turns to issues surrounding animal experimentation. She believes that matters here are more complicated, and that rendering a moral verdict is often more difficult than in the case of vegetarianism. In many cases, though, it is easy: much animal experimentation is indeed cruel and can be straightforwardly condemned. That said, even in such cases, individuals who are not lab researchers are rarely in a position to do anything directly to stop such experimentation, which takes place in labs funded by powerful organizations such as large corporations and universities. Unless you are in a special position of power, you just aren't in a position to meaningfully refrain from conducting such experiments, in the way that you are able to meaningfully refrain from eating meat. Hursthouse concludes by offering guidance on what ordinary folks who aspire to virtue can do in such situations.

WHAT IS VIRTUE ETHICS?

If we are going to think about the rights and wrongs of our treatment of nonhuman animals in terms of the virtues and vices, we have to be clear about these moral notions. Although some readers have

Rosalind Hursthouse, "Virtue Ethics and the Treatment of Animals," in *The Oxford Handbook of Animal Ethics*, ed. Tom Beauchamp and R. G. Frey (Oxford University Press, 2011), pp. 125–127, 129–133, 135–138.

an intuitive grasp of compassion and respect as virtues, and of cruelty, irresponsibility, selfishness, and dishonesty as vices, understanding of these and other concepts in modern virtue ethics merits careful discussion. So we must spend some time on the details.

Virtue and vice words can be used to assess both people and actions, and although the words "virtue" and "vice" are no longer common in ordinary conversation, we still employ a large and rich vocabulary of virtue and vice words. For example, we praise and admire people for being benevolent or altruistic, unselfish, fair, responsible, respectful, caring, courageous, honest, just, honorable, and the like. Similarly, we condemn, despise, or criticize people for being malevolent, selfish, callous, unfair, irresponsible, uncaring, cowardly reckless, cruel, unjust, dishonorable, and the like. Neither list is even close to complete, and some people will not agree with every example, but it gives the general idea of the language of virtue and vice. Applying these words to actions is often a fairly straightforward business. Applying them, especially the virtue words, to people in exactly the way virtue ethics does—as ascribing a virtue to them—calls for a bit of philosophical expertise.

In moral philosophy, we think of a virtue as a morally good, admirable, or praiseworthy character trait, the sort of thing that is cited in a character reference. Conversely, a vice or defect is a morally bad, despicable, or regrettable character trait, the sort of thing we condemn, despise, or deplore people for having. Another way to think of the virtues is as the ways we aspire to be or hope we are if we want to be a morally good person, or as what we try to instill in our children when we are giving them a moral education.

One can see immediately that few, if any, of the virtue words always operate as virtue terms in ordinary language. That is, they do not always function as terms that refer to morally good character traits. This is one of the main reasons why the intuitive grasp of virtue terms needs to be sharpened. Possession of the virtues is what makes an agent a morally good person, or someone who reliably and consistently does what is right; they enable their possessor to act well. However, many of the virtue words just listed can be used in ordinary language to pick out a character trait that actually enables or prompts its possessor to act wrongly.

Suppose I am the boss of a protection racket, looking to replace my right-hand man. I certainly do not want someone who is compassionate, caring, or honest. Nevertheless, I might well say that I do need someone who is responsible rather than irresponsible, industrious rather than lazy, and, most especially, courageous rather than cowardly or timid or reckless. This example might lead one to

think twice before admitting "responsible" and "industrious" as virtue words, but it seems beyond dispute that "courage" is one, and equally indisputable that a character trait that enables someone to face danger without giving in to fear will be what enables a member of a protection racket to act wrongly. So when, engaged in moral philosophy, we explicitly use "courage" as a virtue term, we need to restrict its application to facing danger *for a worthwhile end.* We may then say that those involved in protection rackets and other desperados may be daring, but do not possess the virtue of courage. Alternatively, we could say, as some philosophers do, that they do not have "virtuous courage."

However, this is not the only sort of case in which the ordinary use of virtue words does not pick out virtues. It is natural to say, for example, that some people who possess compassion could too easily be prevented by it from doing what they should. Might they not, for instance, find themselves unable to kill the bird their cat has mauled? Or might not their kindness prompt them to allow their dog too many treats, making him unhealthily fat? They are, we might say, "too compassionate, too kind, too virtuous."

We seem to have got into a muddle. Do we think that compassion can sometimes be a virtue and sometimes a fault, so that someone can be a compassionate person but thereby not be a morally good, admirable person? Or do we think that, if they are compassionate, of course they must be morally good, but that morally good people may be prompted by what makes them morally good to act wrongly?

We can get clear of this muddle by recalling that "virtue" is but one translation of the ancient Greek word *arête.* The other, more accurate, translation is "excellence," and the virtues are not just morally good character traits but *excellent* character traits. Here is how the "excellence" translation makes a difference: something that is excellent is as good of its kind as it could be reasonably expected to be, and we do not say that anything is "too excellent." However, someone whom we initially describe as "too compassionate or kind, too virtuous" is not as good as anyone could be. He would be better if he were the sort of person who could quickly wring the bird's neck or put his dog on a diet when he ought to. That is, he would be better if he had the *excellences* of compassion and kindness. Though he is, it seems, well on the way to being excellent in these ways, with his heart in the right place, we can readily imagine people who are compassionate without being squeamish or kind without being over-indulgent, and he is not as good as they are. So we should think of a virtue as an excellent moral character trait and, rather than describing someone as too compassionate, honest, or the like, find longer but more accurate descriptions. We now turn to considering what is involved in a virtue being a character trait.

An excellent character trait is a strongly entrenched dispositional state of a person or a certain sort of way they are all the way down, and the disposition is of a complex sort. It is, for a start, a disposition to act in certain ways, that is, in accordance with the virtue in question. As we noted above, the virtue terms are used to assess not only people but also actions, and people who can rightly be described as benevolent, honest, just, and so on consistently and reliably perform actions that can also rightly be described by those words. The benevolent consistently do what is benevolent, the honest consistently do what is honest, the just consistently do what is just, and so on. In general terms, someone with a particular virtue, V, consistently and reliably does what is V.

In looking to virtue ethics for action guidance, we can often simply employ the v-rules. What it is right to do is what a virtuous agent would do in the circumstances, and the virtuous agent typically does what falls under a virtue-rule and abstains from doing what falls under a vice-rule. Nevertheless, the connection between being virtuous and doing an action that can be correctly described by a virtue word is not entirely straightforward, because life presents us with moral dilemmas, that is, forced choices between actions such that no virtuous agent would willingly do either.

This "conflict problem" is one that all normative ethical theories, barring the simplest forms of act utilitarianism, face. All the theories employ basically the same strategy to deal with moral dilemmas, namely give an account of how they can be resolved correctly. A discriminating understanding of the virtues or moral principles in question, possessed only by those with practical wisdom or

provided by moral philosophers, will perceive that there is at least one feature of the situation that justifies doing one thing rather than the other. (If there are any irresolvable dilemmas, proponents of any normative approach may point out reasonably that it could only be a mistake to offer a resolution of what is, ex hypothesi, irresolvable.) So, having resolved a dilemma correctly, a virtuous agent may well do something that in different circumstances would fall under the prohibition of a vice-rule, or that, in the very circumstances in which she does it, may appear to the naive to do so, as a child may be shocked by my apparent callousness when I wring the wounded bird's neck.

Returning to the straightforward cases, people with the virtues or excellences of character not only typically do the V things, or act in virtuous ways, but also do so for the right reasons. They do not do what is compassionate merely on emotional impulse, nor do they do what is benevolent or honest for ulterior reasons. Thereby, they contrast with Kant's famous tradesman who does what is honest because it's to his advantage. Virtuous people do what is honest or benevolent because, in some sense, they think that the action is right, or worth doing for its own sake.

VEGETARIANISM

People sometimes suppose that virtue ethicists would say that vegetarianism is a virtue. Of course it isn't, because virtues are character traits and vegetarianism is not a character trait. It is a practice. So would they, perhaps, say that it is a virtuous practice? If we take that as meaning that those who practice it manifest virtue, then obviously not. One can be a vegetarian for a variety of reasons, not necessarily moral ones. However, if we take it as meaning that it is a practice that the virtuous, as such, tend to go in for, then the answer is yes.

Anyone who is reading this book knows, as I do, that in regularly eating commercially farmed meat we are being party to a huge amount of animal suffering, and it would be dishonest and hypocritical to pretend otherwise. Some people may not know this fact, but unless they are very young or mentally incapacitated, this is culpable ignorance; it is irresponsible not to think about how your dinner got onto your plate. Knowing that, we know that shrugging off such suffering as something that doesn't matter is callous. Knowing that our use of animals for food is not only unnecessary but positively wasteful, can we deny that our commercial farming practices are cruel? No, we cannot. So we should not be party to them.

Note that this apparently simple move, from "the practices are cruel and cause unnecessary suffering" to "we should not be party to them"—is not one that the act, or "direct," utilitarianism [Peter] Singer espoused in the first edition of *Practical Ethics* allows him to make, though he made it. It needs the rule, or "indirect," utilitarianism he added in the second edition.[1] However, within virtue ethics, given that a virtue is a disposition of a very complex sort that is expressed in a variety of sorts of actions, it is a simple move. The compassionate are not willingly party to cruelty any more than the just are willingly party to injustice or the honest to chicanery.

I want now to introduce a virtue the ancient Greeks made much of, *sophrosyne*, for which the usual translation is, unfortunately, "temperance." It is unfortunate because someone who possesses this virtue and thereby characteristically does what is temperate is unlikely to abstain totally from alcohol. Nor, though "moderation" is another possible translation, is it quite right to say that the temperate pursue the pleasures of food, drink, and sex "in moderation." Some people might do so solely because they thought it was healthy and would enable them to live longer, but still behave selfishly. Rather, the temperate characteristically pursue these physical pleasures in accordance with reason, which in this context entails not only in such a way as to maintain their health, but also in ways that are consistent with all the other virtues.

If the virtue is fully developed, the temperate characteristically abstain from such pleasure when they have reason to with no inner conflict, having brought their desires for food, drink, and sex into harmony with their reason. In this respect, temperance is the paradigm illustration of the Aristotelian point that our desires, even our most "animal" desires, are shaped and informed by our reason, for good or ill. Many people who convert to vegetarianism as adults are familiar with this phenomenon. Some find it remarkably easy, but for others, at first,

it is really hard; one's mouth waters at the thought of bacon or a juicy hamburger, and one eats one's tofu without enthusiasm. Gradually, however, the desires come into line.

Part of what goes into bringing such desires into line is coming to see them and their satisfaction in a different light. Midgley says, strikingly, "To himself, the meat-eater seems to be eating life. To the vegetarian, he seems to be eating death."[2] I have not yet managed to get myself that far, but I can at least now see my desires for meat as simply greedy and self-indulgent. "Self-indulgence" is a fortunate translation of the ancient Greek word for the vice opposed to temperance. Indulgence of one's own desires to the exclusion of regard for others' suffering is certainly a form of selfishness. Nonetheless, regard for others' suffering, though often the most relevant reason for restraining one's desires for certain foods, is not the only reason. We know that bottom trawling for fish is hugely destructive; we know that trawling in general is hugely wasteful because so much of the catch is thrown away. Should we not regard satisfying our desire for affordable fresh fish as self-indulgent when we have such good reason to boycott those practices, regardless of whether fish can feel pain?

Do the preceding paragraphs imply that, from the perspective of virtue ethics, one should never eat meat or fish? Consult your own grasp of the virtue and vice terms and you will surely find that the answer is no. After all, what would you think of someone who, accidentally stranded in the Australian outback without food, killed a rabbit and ate it rather than sitting down and waiting to die of starvation? Would you take it that they must be deficient in compassion? Callous? Self-indulgent? No. Of course, they might have all those vices, but their action, in *those* circumstances, gives us no reason to suppose that they have. When we try to imagine what a virtuous person, even an ideally virtuous person, would do in those circumstances, we do not usually imagine that she just resigns herself to death.

Nothing in our concepts of the individual virtues rules out our taking on board the idea that there may well be circumstances in which an ideally virtuous agent *would* lay down her life for a nonhuman animal. The concept of courage is just waiting for us to recognize the saving of a nonhuman animal as, sometimes, a worthwhile end, and that will enable us to say that that is what the ideally virtuous agent would do. As it is, there are some circumstances in which people at least *risk* their lives to save animal lives or rescue them from suffering, and we think they are compassionate and courageous to do so, not just cranks. As I write, those who are running interference on the Japanese whalers in the southern ocean are doing just that.

Comparing oneself unfavorably with the ideally virtuous agent is one thing; comparing others is quite different. In this connection, I should mention what Lisa Tessman has identified as one form of "moral trouble spawned by oppressive conditions," namely the form in which agents are "morally damaged [and] prevented from . . . exercising some of the virtues."[3] For millions of people, the business of getting hold of enough food to feed themselves and their children is a continual struggle. Whether they are getting it by killing for "bushmeat," scavenging in the rubbish of the wealthy, buying the cheapest of the limited range on offer, or surviving on the handouts of NGOs, they are in no position to pick and choose what they eat or give to their children and in no position to do much in the way of exercising compassion.

The above collection of examples is intended to illustrate the point that an action such as eating meat, which is exactly what a virtuous agent characteristically refrains from doing in many circumstances, may nevertheless be something that, in other circumstances, a virtuous agent does do. Hence, virtue ethics shares much of act utilitarianism's flexibility when applied to particular practical issues. However, "circumstances" are not just the same as "consequences." Whether my eating meat is compassionate or cruel or neither, temperate or self-indulgent or neither, is bound to depend on the circumstances in which I do it, and often (though not always) on my reasons, but only sometimes on its consequences.

SOME OTHER EXAMPLES

I now turn to considering some less familiar examples of actions that involve nonhuman animals to illustrate how virtue ethics engages with them. I begin by introducing a further virtue, namely love.

The virtue of compassion is a particular form or aspect of the virtue of love (which also gets called "benevolence" or "charity") because that virtue concerns itself with the good or well-being of others, and freedom from suffering, the concern of compassion, is part of the well-being of any sentient creature. As such it is, the virtue called forth by [a] utilitarian approach supports the usual objections to commercial farming. But we should note Kant's sapient observation that the virtue of love needs to be tempered with the virtue of respect.

In the Kantian context, limited to our relations with our fellow autonomous agents, love thus tempered—respectful love—is mindful of others' right to make their own choices, to live or die the way they want to, even if, in our view, they thereby jeopardize their own well-being. It is thus a corrective to the arrogance of paternalism, an undue even if well-intentioned assumption of authority or knowledge. Contrary to Kant, we may say that love, or benevolence, as a virtue is not limited in its concern to our fellow human beings, autonomous or otherwise. We may think of it, for example, as also governing our treatment of pets and other animals, such as horses, that we personally love. There is no doubt that many people love their cats, dogs, and horses, delighting in their company, mourning their deaths, and willingly, on occasion, going to considerable trouble on their behalf. However, following Kant, we may also say that, as a virtue, love has to be respectful love; our love for our pets should be shaped and informed by our recognition of the ways in which their needs and their lives are their *own*, peculiar to the sorts of animals they are.

Conscientious veterinarians frequently lament the fact that many pet-lovers have a view of their animal's good which, far from being informed and shaped by reason in this way, is largely informed by anthropomorphism or, worse, their own desires. It leads them, for example, to expend their resources on expensive food or treatment that their pet would be better off without, and even if their ignorance is not the result of arrogance or selfishness, it is culpable ignorance nonetheless. It is a form of folly, stupidity, or thoughtlessness, which leads them, unwittingly, to perform actions that are cruel, inconsiderate, and disrespectful.

Veterinarians also lament, rightly, the inbreeding of cats and dogs that produces animals which win "best in breed" at shows but have been bred to have traits that give them congenital health problems. No one with the virtue of respectful love or benevolence would be party to such a practice; buying such animals is vain and self-glorifying.

From the perspective of the major non-anthropocentric environmentalists, such as Aldo Leopold and Arne Naess, respectful love is something that should extend well beyond the limits of our fellow autonomous agents and sentient others to any living thing, because they all have a good of their own. In this context, respectful love loses any connection with rights, though it is still the corrective to our arrogant assumption not only of authority but also of superiority. Arrogance is not only displayed by riding roughshod over others' rights. We are not *the* beauty of the world, nor the paragon of animals. Our sublime rationality should enable us, especially now that we know as much as we do, to recognize that the living world contains a myriad of wonders that should make us humble as well as be a source of delight.

This anti-anthropocentric, "biocentric" claim, that *any* living thing is an appropriate object of respectful love, is more familiar in Eastern than in Western philosophy and one that we may find very hard to take on board. I do, but I can certainly find much that is true in it. One obvious point the claim is making is that "being alive" is a standing reason for not killing the thing in question that has to be overridden by another reason, and that the killing should never be done triumphantly or with glee or pride. This rules out all killing for sport as well as idly swatting flies or mindlessly slashing at plants as you walk through the countryside. Like the appeal to compassion, this claim supports the usual objections to commercial farming. Less obviously, with the emphasis on the "respectful," it correctly identifies what is wrong with the idea that we might, ingeniously, produce genetically engineered versions of the familiar farm animals that were non-sentient, thereby allowing ourselves to have our compassionate cake and eat it too. Or, to take, alas, a real-life example, it correctly identifies what is wrong with the creation, as a work of art, of a transgenic rabbit that glows green in the dark.[4]

Creating non-sentient animals for no better reason than to give ourselves guilt-free meat is, at the very least, arrogant and self-indulgent, as is the creation of the transgenic rabbit, though in neither of these cases could it be said that any animal's right has been violated. (No normal rabbit has had its putative right to enjoy a good rabbit life violated by the production of a non-sentient or glowing green rabbit.)

The virtue of respectful love may also help us on at least one issue concerning wild animals, namely what, if anything, we should do about the suffering that carnivores inflict in the wild. This is rarely discussed in the animal ethics literature. When it is, some theory-driven philosophers argue that we should interfere with the lives of wild animals to prevent the pain they inflict on other animals. This is sometimes given as a justification for keeping wild animals in zoos, sometimes proposed as part of a very-long-term project: "[T]he gradual supplanting of the natural by the just."[5] However, from the perspective of environmental ethics, the latter is yet another manifestation of anthropocentric arrogance. Respectful love of wild animals wishes them the good that really is their *own*, just as respectful love of our pets does. The difference is that the lives of most wild animals are red in tooth and claw, unlike those of our pets, but respect still entails leaving them to live their own form of life, not one that we, playing God, create for them.

EXPERIMENTATION

Much experimentation on nonhuman animals can be straightforwardly condemned as cruel. Some authors in animal ethics take the strange view that the act of inflicting unnecessary suffering on the sentient is cruel only if the agent enjoys or is indifferent to the animal's suffering. Perhaps these authors have been misled by the ambiguity of the phrase "an act of cruelty." It can indeed mean an act from the character trait of cruelty, or a characteristic act of a cruel person, and a cruel person is indeed someone who takes pleasure in or is indifferent to inflicting suffering on others. However, it can also mean "a cruel act," and a cruel act is nothing but the infliction of unnecessary suffering.

"Unnecessary" means "not necessary to secure some good which is worth the cost of, or suitably proportionate to, the suffering or evil involved," and hence much experimentation fails on at least one of four different counts. The first three of these are familiar in the animal ethics literature. The first is that what the suffering secures is not a good at all. The painful testing of new cosmetics on animals is the obvious example; new cosmetics are not a good, something worth pursuing or having. The old ones with new packaging will do just as well. The second is that it has little or no chance of securing the good which is supposed to justify it. Closely related to this is the third—that we can, or are more likely to, secure the good in other, better ways, such as avoiding duplication of the same experiments in different institutions and pooling any knowledge gained, or by using computer modeling of human organs. The fourth count is that the good in question, even when all other criteria are satisfied, is not suitably proportionate to the suffering or evil involved.

Much experimentation on animals is cruel and thereby, in virtue ethics terms, wrong, to be condemned, and not to be done. Thinking in virtue ethics terms makes us notice something about how the issues of animal experimentation and vegetarianism differ. Concluding that eating meat is, in many circumstances, not what a virtuous agent would do because she is not willingly party to cruelty, does not do what is self-indulgent, and so on, gives one clear guidance. However, the same is not true when we conclude that most animal experimentation is cruel. The question of abstaining from experimentation does not arise for most of us, and what counts as not being a party to this often cruel practice is somewhat obscure. It rules out buying cosmetics that have been tested on animals, and it could indicate that one should refuse to save or prolong one's life by accepting an organ transplant from a nonhuman animal as one should refuse to accept a kidney commercially obtained from someone in a developing country. But this is not an issue that commonly arises. Short of refraining from any of the benefits modern medicine offers, there does not seem to be anything that most of us could do that would count as "refraining from being party to the practice."

The lack of action guidance in this case is not peculiar to virtue ethics; proponents of the other approaches, having concluded that at least much of the experimentation on animals is wrong, leave it at that. But this is unsatisfactory, because normative ethics is supposed to provide action guidance; its point is to be practical.

So we should think about the question, what would a virtuous person do when he has recognized that most animal experimentation is cruel and therefore wrong? Given that he is conscientious and responsible, he thinks about what he could do to prevent it, but he immediately encounters a problem. Animal experimentation is a practice entrenched in powerful, well-established institutions, including medical schools, medical research centers, corporate research centers and laboratories aiming for profit, and universities training students to work in such institutions. The existence of this set of interlocked institutions is something that no one person has the power to change, not even heads of state.

Does the virtuous agent therefore give up in despair? Not if she has fortitude, or even just the commonsense that is part of practical wisdom. We know that people have been similarly situated, living in a society engaged in a wrong practice that they are quite powerless, individually, to change, and we know that the good ones haven't just given up in despair. They have looked around to see what individually insignificant but collectively influential contribution they could make to bring about change. One may be so situated that there is very little one can do as an individual, as was the case for many white people in the 1960s who deplored racism. Still, good people opposed to institutionalized racism did what they could, unremarkable as it was; they signed petitions, joined pressure groups, voted for politicians who spoke against racism, and any of us can do at least the first two to combat cruel animal experimentation.

Some people are in a position to do more. A growing number of science students refuse to experiment on or dissect animals, and in some universities, the system has been changed so that they are no longer required to do so. Many universities and corporations now have ethics committees that regulate the use of animals in research, and a significant number of experiments that are done in institutions that do not have such committees are no longer done in those that do. So some of us can join an ethics committee. However, there is no point in doing so determined to argue against every proposed experiment that uses animals; we will just be thrown off it and achieve nothing. Might it be said that that is what a truly virtuous agent would do? If you let some of the experiments through without protest, wouldn't this be hypocritical and lacking in integrity? No. Consult, again, your own understanding of the virtue and vice terms and think of Schindler, who consorted with the Nazis and "allowed" many Jews to go to the death camps without protest while he schemed to get some into the protection of his factory.[6] Far from condemning him for being hypocritical or lacking integrity, we regard him as admirable and his actions as exceptionally virtuous. Situated as he was, what could possibly count as acting better than he did? How could he have shown more virtue? By not saving anyone and getting himself killed?

More to the point, we can reflect on the career of Henry Spira,[7] one of the most effective animal rights activists of the twentieth century. His effectiveness is an excellent example of the practical wisdom that, according to Aristotle, is inseparable from the possession of any virtue in its perfected form. People with practical wisdom get things right in action, not only because they are virtuous and hence try to do what is right, but also because they are excellent at practical reasoning, at finding really good means to their virtuous ends. "Really good" means are really *effective* means, the ones that secure one's end in the most efficient (but non-vicious) way.

Full possession of practical wisdom, and hence perfected virtue and always getting things right in action, is no doubt an unrealizable ideal. Nevertheless, as an ideal it is the standard we rely on when, having failed to get things right and do what we intended to do, we say "I wish I had realized or known that or thought of so and so; then I wouldn't have done what I did." We say this—or should—not only when our error was the result of culpable ignorance, but even when it was not and we are not blameworthy, for our concern should be not the mere avoidance of wrongdoing, or being blameless, but being effective in good action.

We admire practical wisdom in people such as Spira in particular realms of action, without having to suppose they are perfect in every way. The general end he devoted himself to from his forties until his death was not the abolition of commercial farming and experimentation on animals as totally wrong, but reducing the amount of animal suffering caused. He always looked for really effective means to that end. Among the means he rejected as useless was the "self-righteous . . . hollering 'Abolition! All or nothing.'"[8] Among those he rejected as comparatively ineffective were the adversarial vilifications of animal-user industries in contrast to working with them in a friendly and cooperative way. This cooperative approach has been astonishingly effective.

It is not quite so astonishing when one looks at his unique campaigning methods and how he reasoned about securing his general end, the details of which are described in Singer's book on him. One striking detail is that for each campaign, he set a specific and in some ways modest end that he thought was achievable. For example, in his perhaps most famous campaign, he did not set out to stop all testing of cosmetics on animals, but just the Draize test; not to stop all companies using it, but largely Revlon; and, indeed, not to stop Revlon from using it entirely, but to get them to take the step of putting money into seeking alternatives. This final restriction on his target exemplifies another striking detail—his non-adversarial approach. Having dealt Revlon a hefty blow with a full page *New York Times* advertisement showing a rabbit with black patches over its eyes, he gave them the let out. He met with the vice president of Revlon who had been assigned the task of coping with the fallout from the advertisement and its follow-ups, and convinced him that he was someone who, in the vice president's own words, "would listen to us and be prepared to work something out that we could live with too."[9] Taking the step that was Spira's target was, it turned out, something Revlon could live with—unsurprisingly, because he had carefully selected it to be just that.

Spira's targets were, I think, modest in two ways: in being so limited in comparison with the enormous amount of animal suffering to be combated and also in being the targets of a modest man. When I read the details of what he did, I am struck not only by how dynamic and energetic he was—a real force to be reckoned with—but also by how modest and how lacking in self-centeredness he was. He was not interested in telling people about his moral views or in proving that they were right, or in what other people thought of his integrity, except insofar as that would have a bearing on the effectiveness of his campaigns. He was utterly lacking in the vanity that makes people think they can achieve great things that obviously no one can achieve: For over twenty years, he was focused on getting just *something* done about animal suffering, content to, in his own words, "move things on a little."[10]

At this point, I return to the topic of moral status, because I think Spira is an object lesson to moral philosophers who write on animal ethics and insist on making moral status the central issue. As I noted above, the fourth count on which experimentation on animals may be deemed unnecessary and hence cruel is that the good secured by the experiments is disproportionate to the suffering or evil involved. With respect to clinical research specifically directed toward the good of saving and improving the lives of human beings, the question of moral status is assumed to be crucial. If the animals used in medical experiments have the same moral status as human beings, then either we should be using brain-damaged orphans instead or we should stop it entirely, as it is all wrong.

However, insisting on making this claim, or insisting that rational argument shows that it must be accepted to avoid the speciesism that is just like racism, alienates many people who might otherwise be willing to contribute to campaigns against particular sorts of experiments. I have found, when teaching animal ethics, that many students who are reluctantly beginning to feel uncomfortable about our treatment of animals and drawn toward vegetarianism, seize on this claim when they come to it, finding in it an excuse to toss out everything that has gone before. Now they can see that it is all just silly and they need not worry about it. So, having lost all the ground I had gained, I then have to try to show them that the initial points stand independently of any claims about moral status, that much

medical experimentation is wrong, and that they should be thinking about what they can do about it. It is uphill work. I claimed previously that the concept of moral status drastically underestimated the range of features relevant to good decision making about what to do and that we did not need to use it. In the context of medical experimentation, I would claim further that the use of moral status as an evaluative concept is actually pernicious. It is the equivalent of hollering "Abolition! All or nothing," which is guaranteed to impede progress rather than to further it.

NOTES

1. Compare Singer, *Practical Ethics* (Cambridge: Cambridge University Press, 1979), p. 12, and *Practical Ethics*, 2nd edition (Cambridge: Cambridge University Press, 1993), pp. 13–14.
2. Midgley, *Animals and Why They Matter*, p. 27.
3. Lisa Tessman, *Burdened Virtues* (New York: Oxford University Press, 2005), p. 4.
4. http://www.genomenewsnetwork.org/articles/03_02/bunny_art.shtml.
5. Martha Nussbaum, *Frontiers of Justice* (Cambridge, MA: Harvard University Press, 2006), pp. 399-400.
6. See Thomas Keneally, *Schindler's Ark* (London: Hodder and Stoughton, 1982).
7. Peter Singer, *Ethics in Action: Henry Spira and the Animal Rights Movement* (Lanham, MD: Rowman and Littlefield, 1998).
8. Singer, *Ethics in Action: Henry Spira*, p. 53.
9. Singer, *Ethics in Action: Henry Spira*, p. 102.
10. Singer, *Ethics in Action: Henry Spira*, p. 198.

Rosalind Hursthouse: Virtue Ethics and the Treatment of Animals

1. How does Hursthouse define a virtue, and how does she believe the virtues to be related to morally right actions? Do you find her account plausible? Why or why not?
2. How does Hursthouse address the concern that virtue isn't that morally important, because it's possible to exhibit a virtue (such

as bravery) in the service of morally terrible goals? Why do you find her discussion persuasive (or unpersuasive)?

3. Hursthouse argues that virtuous people wouldn't be party to cruel practices, and so (unusual cases aside) such people would not eat meat. What does "being party to" mean? What if an ordinary consumer's meat eating has no impact on how animals on factory farms are treated—the same number of animals is killed on a given farm regardless of a single consumer's

purchasing or eating habits? Would that make a difference to Hursthouse's argument?

4. Hursthouse writes that "I can at least now see my desires for meat as simply greedy and self-indulgent." What are her grounds for this claim? Do they hold up to scrutiny?

5. Many animal experiments will definitely cause animal suffering, while it is far from certain that that they will help solve a real medical problem. Does virtue ethics condemn all such experiments? Why or why not?

Experimenting with Animals
Lori Gruen

Lori Gruen invites us to think about the morality of animal experimentation by focusing on two of the major positions in debates about its moral standing. The first of these is utilitarianism—the view that actions are morally acceptable if and only if they do, or are reasonably expected to, create the greatest balance of benefit over harm in the long run. The utilitarian also believes that species membership is by itself of no importance—the same interests (say, to avoid pain) are to be given equal weight in our moral calculations, no matter whether those interests are had by humans or by rats, cats, or primates. Utilitarians criticize a great many animal experiments, but allow that some can be morally justified—it all depends on whether the benefits are great enough to outweigh the inevitable suffering experienced by lab animals.

Gruen identifies two difficulties for utilitarianism. The first—known as the *incommensurability problem*—says that there is no principled way to strike a balance between one person's pleasures and the pain experienced by another person or animal. If this is right, then there just is no way at all to determine the moral status of an experiment that promises to relieve the pain of (say) 8,000 humans, at the cost of the pain and killing of 80,000 lab animals. The second problem—known as the *epistemic objection*—is that it is very difficult, and in many cases impossible, to know whether a given experiment really is likely to yield greater benefits than harms.

Gruen then considers the abolitionist position, which argues that all animal experimentation, no matter its potential benefits, is immoral. She presents three interrelated considerations in support of this view. First, animals are important in their own right and should not be treated as mere means—as mere tools or instruments, lacking any independent interests—for the benefits of others. Second, deliberately imposing harm for the benefit of others can be justified, but only with the consent of the victims.

Animals never give such consent. Third, it is wrong to impose suffering—especially extreme suffering and death—on some, solely in order to benefit others. Yet that is just what animal experimentation involves.

Gruen concludes that the difficulties with the utilitarian position, in tandem with the strength of the abolitionist arguments, makes it reasonable to believe that all animal experimentation is immoral and ought to be abolished.

Since animal experimentation began, the public has asked whether the practice is justifiable. Some people, who do not believe that useful information can be gained from experimenting on animals, answer the question with a resounding "NO!" Yet, there is good evidence to suggest that we have learned, and will continue to learn, from such experiments. While there are undoubtedly tens of thousands of animals who have suffered and died in laboratories in useless experiments, it is also true that some animal experiments have led to knowledge that has been central in the development of vaccines, pharmaceuticals, therapeutic procedures, and other protocols that directly improve the well-being of humans and other animals. But is the fact that some benefits have emerged from animal experiments enough to justify doing them?

When those who believe that experimenting on animals has led to some benefits attempt to justify the use of animals, they tend to appeal, knowingly or not, to a utilitarian or related consequentialist framework, one that tries to weigh the beneficial consequences of experimentation with the costs associated with it. On this account, animal experiments are justified ethically when the well-being of humans, and perhaps other animals, is enhanced by experiments that were done with the fewest number of animals possible experiencing the least amount of pain and suffering. Given that human disease causes so much suffering, if that suffering can be minimized by causing less suffering in medical experiments, then a utilitarian would probably find those experiments justified.

A controversy about the adequacy of the utilitarian approach to animal experimentation erupted

not long ago in Britain's popular press. At issue was a supportive comment utilitarian philosopher Peter Singer made in a British documentary about the research of Tipu Aziz, a scientist who performs primate neurological experimentation at Oxford University.[1] Aziz creates brain damage in monkeys in order to mimic the symptoms of Parkinson's disease. In his experiments, Aziz confines monkeys in primate-restraining chairs, drills into their skulls, implants electrodes, performs other electrical and surgical manipulations, and then observes their behavior for a period of time before killing them to remove and study their brains. According to the *Guardian*, Aziz claims that 40,000 people around the globe have benefited from the techniques he has developed, and only 100 monkeys have been sacrificed. For a utilitarian like Singer, if there were no other way to obtain this benefit, including the possibility of experimenting with fewer humans at a similar cognitive level to monkeys, then he would agree that it was a justifiable experiment.

I call Singer's test for when an experiment on a non-human animal is justified the "non-speciesist utilitarian test" or NSUT. According to NSUT, an experiment X would be justified if and only if:

1. Of all the options open, X generates more pleasure or benefit than pain or cost on balance; and
2. The justification for experiment X does not depend on irrelevant species prejudice, that is, equal interests are considered equally no matter who has them.

This framework has often been lauded for its simplicity and its practical usefulness. It apparently allows one to make a relatively clear determination about whether an experiment might be justified. In order to reach a conclusion about any particular

From Lori Gruen, *Ethics and Animals: An Introduction* (Cambridge University Press, 2011), pp. 118–129.

experiment, one has to measure and compare pleasures and pains across species to know that this was the only way to achieve a balance of pleasure over pain and to establish that the use of animals was not based on speciesist reasoning.

There are familiar objections to part 1 of NSUT, which is a straightforward utilitarian position, and there have long been utilitarian responses to the objections. There are also problems that emerge in the interpretation of part 2. Let's consider two familiar objections to part 1—the incommensurability objection and the epistemic objection or the cluelessness objection—in the context of stem cell research, in order to see the kinds of problems one particular case can raise for NSUT. Then we can turn to examining worries about part 2.

Since initially formulated, consequentialist theories that rely on being able to make interpersonal utility comparisons—that is, to compare the well-being of one person with the well-being of another and make judgments about the weight of a good for some versus the weight of a harm for others—have been scrutinized. It is often claimed that values are incommensurate, and thus meaningful comparisons cannot be made. It is hard enough to compare our own pleasure playing pushpin to our delight reading poetry; the exuberance of watching the Colts win the Super Bowl with the passion in seeing Venus Williams win at Wimbledon. How then are we supposed to compare the benefits a human gets from reading about Victorian gender relations with the benefits a dog gets catching a Frisbee? Since utilitarian theory relies on making just these sorts of comparisons, critics contend that utilitarian theories cannot guide our action.

In response, consequentialists have pointed out that, whether or not we are any good at it, we make these kinds of comparisons all the time in our daily lives. John Harsanyi suggests that the basic intellectual operation in making such comparisons is "imaginative empathy." When we are deciding between actions that will affect two different people, we try to put ourselves into both those individuals' positions, with their sets of interests and desires, to figure out the effect the action in question will have by their lights. Once we have done that, we can determine which course of action will lead to the most benefit (or, perhaps, least harm) and take that action. The more we develop our empathetic skills, and the more we learn about those around us who we are likely to affect more of the time, and about people generally, the better we will be at making these interpersonal utility comparisons.

This seems to be true when deciding which of one's children should get the bigger piece of pie, or which friend should get the theater tickets you are unable to use. But what about those cases in which the ethical stakes are quite high and the deliberation impersonal, as is often the case when thinking about such issues as animal experimentation? Consider one type of stem cell research designed to reverse the damage from spinal cord injuries (SCIs). The goal is to develop stem cell therapies that could eventually be used to replace destroyed nerves, to create supportive tissue environments to allow for axon regeneration, and to replace the myelin-forming cells that allow signaling along surviving axons. Such therapies, in principle, could help some reasonably large percentage of the roughly 8,000 people in the US, alone, who have suffered spinal cord injuries. Approximately 55 percent of these injuries are classified as incomplete injuries, signifying that these individuals experience varying degrees of constant pain in addition to the loss of mobility and function.[2] Most people are unaware of the fact that so many people with spinal cord injuries, even those who are paralyzed "from the neck down," experience pain, often excruciating neuropathic pain that most of us have never felt. Accurate empathy, in this case, requires fairly extensive study of spinal cord injuries and getting to know people who have experienced them. People involved in rehabilitation and care for those living with SCIs are in the best position to engage in this sort of imaginative empathy and can inform the rest of us. Those people doing research, particularly basic research on stem cells, often are not directly in contact with those suffering from spinal cord injuries, so their claims as to the extent of the potential benefits will generally not be as accurate as those who have more extensive knowledge of the particular suffering SCI survivors experience. Because SCIs vary so widely, determining the full nature and severity of the harms the injuries have caused to each individual and their families, friends, and support networks is also a challenge. Yet, despite the difficulties of trying to get a handle on the shape and intensity of the suffering in order to make interpersonal utility comparisons, it is not hard to conclude that eliminating or minimizing the suffering caused by SCIs would be a very good thing to do.

But, in order to do that very good thing, a vast amount of pain and suffering has to be inflicted deliberately on animals, the majority of which are rodents. (However, dogs, cats, and primates are also used in SCI research.) Animals used as models in SCI research generally have weights dropped onto their spines to cause precise types of injuries in particular locations. There is no way to obtain a reasonable estimate of the number of animals involved, but a conservative estimate, useful for illustrative purposes, would be that, at the very least, 80,000 animals annually will have to be experimented on and killed in the development of stem cell therapies for SCI. Animals have been, and will continue to be, used in the development of SCI models; in developing and refining various transplantation protocols; in generating neural stem cell progenitors and other cell types for transplantation; and in the stem cell transplantation protocols themselves. Training, modifications in procedures, and duplication of results will also involve the use of animals. And, of course, this does not include the animals that were used in the early basic research that led to increased understanding of both spinal cord function and mammalian developmental processes, as well as of the pluripotency of embryonic and fetal stem cells in the first place. If we suppose that, in ten years time, this use of animals will lead to a stem cell therapy for those humans suffering SCIs; that the human therapies will improve once human clinical trials and treatments are in place; and (quite unrealistically) that animal experiments for SCI treatments at that time will stop, we can—again, for illustrative purposes—say that, if this research is successful, the use of approximately 800,000 animals will lead to improvement in quality of life for people suffering spinal cord injuries into the future.

Can we compare the suffering and death of the animals used in the development of stem cell therapies for spinal cord injuries with the suffering of those individuals who suffer from SCIs and that of their families and friends? If we assume that 8,000 individuals suffer and survive SCIs per year and that the animal suffering is equivalent to human suffering, it would take 100 years to benefit 800,000 SCI sufferers. But, clearly, that isn't the right equation. The animals used may suffer horribly in the experiments, but their suffering comes to an end when they are killed. The benefit accrued to humans, whose suffering will presumably end with the successful development of stem cell therapies, is the avoidance of an average of twenty or so more years of pain and suffering. And there are other factors that make such comparisons troublesome. Humans suffering from SCIs don't just experience pain, but also depression, frustration, anger, grief, humiliation, and other taxing emotions as a result of being incapacitated, to varying degrees, by their injuries. They are also dependent on others who will suffer emotionally, and those dependent upon individuals who suffer SCIs will also suffer. Importantly, individuals who suffer SCIs can currently treat most of their pain and many, if not most, people suffering SCIs can achieve significant forms of independence allowing them to lead meaningful lives. Animals in spinal cord research generally do not have their pain relieved adequately, and there is no goal, such as independent living, for them to reach toward, and no pleasure in their short lives.

Comparing the benefits to humans who have suffered spinal cord injuries to the harms of those animals used in research, as part 1 of NSUT would have us do, is not straightforward, even when making specific (though unrealistic) assumptions about success and about numbers, as I have done here. Spinal cord injuries are complex, and, as one specialist recently acknowledged:

> [while] stem cell transplantation in mice and rats with partial spinal cord injuries has demonstrated improvement in locomotor functions, investigators have recognized that they must overcome biochemical inhibitors, provide appropriate growth factors at the correct time, while directing structural growth. The human central nervous system—the brain and the spinal cord—is 10 times

the length of a rodent's. To allow for healing you must cover ten times the distance that is present in rats and mice. Making the jump from the animal model to the human model is a fairly large leap.[3]

And herein lies another problem with part 1 of NSUT for practical deliberation—how do we know when we are justified in saying that, of all the options open, conducting these spinal cord injury experiments with animals will lead to the development of stem cell therapies that will benefit individuals with SCIs?

This "epistemic objection" has long plagued utilitarians—how can one know, in advance, what the consequences of one's actions will actually be? In most animal experimentation the goal is to gain information about basic biological processes, not to lead to any particular therapeutic consequence that will immediately or obviously change the world for the better. The suffering that is caused to animals may not even be expected to lead to any benefits down the road; as experimenters like to say, scientific research is not linear. Often unexpected knowledge is gained from experiments. Part 1 of NSUT suggests that, because we can't know what benefits might result from basic research, but we do know about the negative consequences in terms of animal suffering and deaths that are directly caused by the research, we would never be justified in supporting any basic research and that even comparative judgments between different types of basic research cannot be made. Consider a decision to use twenty sheep in a basic research experiment designed to get some ideas about whether there is a part of the brain that contributes to homosexual behavior, or to use sixty mice to try to figure out the mechanisms of diabetes. In neither case is there a clear or immediate therapeutic goal; experimenters are just trying to learn more about biological processes. NSUT would thus say neither is justified. However, it does seem that in the case of the homosexual sheep experiment, the question itself doesn't warrant either the use of scarce financial resources or the use of animals, whereas the case of diabetes might. Even in the context of basic research with animals, we can make distinctions between projects, but NSUT doesn't provide us with guidance in

making those distinctions, because no benefits are being promised.

Since it is not just hard, but in many cases impossible, to answer the question, "is performing experiment X the only action that will lead to greater benefit than the harms it causes?" it appears that part 1 of NSUT does not provide the kind of practical guidance in particular cases that we would expect from a theory that is meant to be practical and action-guiding. This difficulty becomes accentuated when we turn to the second part of the test. Even in those rare cases when we have an affirmative answer to part 1, in order to consider an experiment ethically justified, part 2 of NSUT must also be satisfied. Engaging in non-speciesist reasoning to determine the right animal model for a particular experiment involves considering the use of human animals as well as non-human animals. There is great scientific value to using humans as bio-models for human disease and injury, as the problem of extrapolating from one species to another would be avoided. Currently, clinical trials serve this function, as they are experiments on humans that occur after particular treatments have been tested on non-human animals but before the drug or therapy is released for use to the general public. Part 2 of NSUT suggests that human animals be considered earlier in the experimentation process.

Part 2 of NSUT would have us determine whether the decision to use mice, dogs, cats, and non-human primates was made without species prejudice.

To understand fully what this would mean, let's return to the stem cell research example for spinal cord injuries and again assume, for the sake of argument, that current research will lead to therapies in a decade or so that will allow people who suffer SCIs to recover both function, including mobility, and normal sensation. This would mean injuring the spinal cords of human experimental subjects who are at a similar "mental level" or "quality of life" to the non-human subjects, thus creating extraordinary pain in cases of purposely generated incomplete injuries. Pain relief will be withheld some of the time as it would interfere with the experimental protocol, and, for some of the induced SCIs, adequate pain-relieving pharmaceuticals have yet to be developed. It will also involve the introduction of neural progenitor embryonic stem cells into the spinal column. Initially, these cells may grow in inappropriate places or form tumors, leading to additional spinal cord damage and additional unrelievable pain. At some point, these human subjects would be killed and their spinal cords studied, as would be the case with the non-human animal subjects. As per our assumption above, after a decade or so, the technique would succeed and stem cell therapies would become available to people suffering from SCIs from that point forward. People, who would otherwise spend their lives confined to wheelchairs and in pain, would be able to walk, and their pain would be minimized if not eliminated. If we assume that fewer human experimental subjects would be needed than non-human subjects—let's say only 8,000 over the ten-year period, or 800 a year, which would be one hundred times less than the number of non-human animals proposed— would we be prepared to engage in the research?

This proposal should give us pause. There are two ways to evaluate this sort of proposal. One is to accept that experiments on animals and on humans are ethically justified. The other is to recognize that, insofar as we are unprepared to use human beings in spinal cord or any other painful experimentation, we should reject the idea that the research can ethically be performed on animals. As Singer has said, if a researcher using non-human animals is not prepared to use, for example, humans born with irreversible brain damage, then they are engaged in speciesist reasoning, and their experiments would not pass part 2 of NSUT.

So while, in the abstract, many would endorse the utilitarian justificatory scheme when it comes to animal experimentation, it looks as though the theory does not justify, and perhaps cannot justify, most of the current uses of animals in medical experiments.

ABOLITION OF ANIMAL EXPERIMENTATION

There are some people who object, in principle, to the utilitarian approach that would allow the possibility, however remote, that experimenting on animals is ethically justifiable. Like the utilitarians, the abolitionists hold that animals have lives that can go better or worse for them, that they should not suffer unnecessarily, and that they deserve to have their interests taken into consideration. Unlike utilitarians, however, abolitionists never think it is appropriate to use another individual as a means to one's own ends. Even if it is clear that the experiment would end more suffering than it would cause, it still would not be justifiable. There are three interrelated arguments that support the abolitionist position.

When we use others as means, we reduce them to instruments, and their value is based on how they serve in that role. Opponents of using animals in experimentation reject the notion that animals can or should serve as "model organisms" for human disease. Animals have their own lives to live and distinct ways of living those lives, all of which is denied them when they are seen as tools for research. Some have argued that the best way to see what is wrong with a view that reduces sensitive beings or subjects-of-a-life to tools or instruments is to consider cases in which individual humans were so reduced. The Nazi hypothermia experiments are often raised in this context. During the Second World War, Nazi soldiers faced hostile thermal environments, and there was very little information available about what the human body could withstand. Soldiers were being shot down over the North Sea, and the military needed information about how long they might survive in the cold water and how to warm them if they were rescued. Similar problems were faced by soldiers in damaged U-boats. In order successfully to rescue and ensure the well-being of the troops, the German government endorsed hypothermia experiments on human prisoners in Dachau. Even if they led to useful medical knowledge, the Nazi experiments were widely condemned as an affront to humanity. Nazis failed to appropriately value the lives of human beings. Those opposed to animal experimentation argue that the intrinsic value of animal lives is not being recognized in an analogous way. It's a mistake of ethical perception, a type of "blindness," that undermines our moral agency and our own animality.

However, under certain circumstances, we do allow experiments on human beings, and, when we do, we don't necessarily devalue the human subjects. This is because the only experiments with human subjects that are ethically acceptable are those done with the subject's full and informed consent. This wasn't always so. Between 1932 and 1972, in Tuskegee, Alabama, poor African Americans with "bad blood," actually syphilis, were used in experiments to track the progression of the disease for the US Public Health Service. Early in the study, in the 1940s, penicillin became the standard treatment for syphilis, but experimenters not only failed to provide penicillin and information about its curative affect to the men in the study, but they also prevented them from getting treatment anywhere. A quarter of the men in the study died of syphilis; many of their wives contracted the disease; and some of their children were born with congenital syphilis, which is life-threatening for infants. The subjects in the study were not informed about the nature of the study, and, in fact, they were being harmed by it. In the 1960s, another egregious set of experiments was performed, this time with a group of mentally retarded children living at the Willowbrook State Hospital in New York. The children were deliberately infected with hepatitis A and then treated in various ways. The facility would not admit new patients unless the parents consented to the experiments.

When these studies came to light, Congressional hearings were held, and, ultimately, laws were established to provide protection for human subjects, emphasizing the importance of respecting persons by requiring informed consent, minimizing risks to subjects, avoiding coercion and conflicts of interest, and requiring heightened scrutiny for any research on vulnerable populations. Those seeking to end experimentation with animals argue that because an animal can never give consent and because they have been historically oppressed and undervalued, they are a particularly vulnerable population and thus should not be used for research purposes, and that there should be strict regulations in place to protect them.

It is interesting, in thinking about the argument for informed consent, to consider that laws protecting human embryos from use in experimentation in the US currently are far more stringent than any regulations governing the use of animals. Animals cannot give verbal consent, nor can embryos. But we might think that existing animals would object, if they could, to being used in experiments. They would object to being held in cages, often in isolation; being subjected to invasive procedures; being denied the opportunity to exercise the capacities that are constitutive of their well-being. It makes little sense to think that embryos in Petri dishes, qua embryos, could similarly object, yet they have greater legal protection. Part of that protection is due to human exceptionalism that elevates the value of human life, even in vitro, over the value of other animals' lives; part comes from the institutional desire for people, in this case embryo donors, to have full knowledge of what sort of research they are consenting to. In the US, using federal funds for experimentation that involves creating embryos for research is prohibited. Federal money can only be used for research on human embryonic stem cell lines that were created from "excess" embryos created for reproductive purposes as long as the embryo donors provide full and informed consent to have the embryo destroyed in order to be used for research. There are few, if any, restrictions on funding for animal research.

The third type of argument that those seeking to abolish animal experimentation make is based on a view about the limits and stringency of ethical demands. There is a general moral presumption by those who do not hold utilitarian views that one should never be morally required to suffer for another, particularly if that suffering involves extreme sacrifice. Even utilitarians tend to limit ethical sacrifice to things of "comparable moral worth." Although it may be laudable for an individual to give up all her worldly goods for the sake of animal protection or to feed the hungry, it is not ethically required. It is a commendable choice one may make, but it is supererogatory, it goes beyond what any reasonable ethical theory can require. Since the animals who are used in experimentation do not benefit from it, indeed they are usually killed, this sort of sacrifice runs counter to the presumption against incurring the suffering of one individual to benefit another. Insofar as we think it is wrong to require someone to give up an organ for another in need, or to require transferring all of one's disposable income to provide education for every child, abolitionists believe it is wrong to force animals to endure experiments that will not directly benefit them.

When we take these three arguments together and when we look at the practical difficulties with the utilitarian position, it does indeed seem that the moral weight is heaviest on the side of ending research with animals. This has already happened with chimpanzee experiments that are now outlawed in every country in the world, except the US. In 1986, the British government banned the use of chimpanzees in research on ethical grounds, arguing that given how close chimpanzees are to humans, to treat them as expendable is immoral. The last research facility using chimpanzees in Europe stopped in 2004, when biomedical research with chimpanzees became illegal in the Netherlands. Japan ended biomedical experimentation on chimpanzees in 2006. Apparently, many countries have recognized that some research is beyond what a decent society can endorse. When we consider the vast and expensive infrastructure of animal experimentation, the vested interests of those engaged in animal use becomes rather clear. Virtually every scientific article ends by claiming "that more research is needed." This is how research scientists make their livings. There is little motivation for seeking alternatives, much as in the energy industry that has relied so heavily on fossil fuels. As long as animal interests are not taken into account and experimenters are unmotivated to change, it seems ethically reasonable to oppose animal experimentation.

NOTES

1. *Animal Testing—Monkeys, Rats and Me.* 2006.
2. According to the 2000 SCI database, the most frequent neurological category at discharge is incomplete quadriplegia (34.1 percent), followed by complete paraplegia (23.0 percent), complete quadriplegia (18.3 percent), and incomplete paraplegia (18.5 percent).
3. American Academy of Physical Medicine and Rehabilitation 2006.

Lori Gruen: Experimenting with Animals

1. One of Gruen's concerns about utilitarianism is that it requires us to be able to make interpersonal comparisons of utility—but that these are difficult or impossible to make. Do you think this is a genuine problem? If not, why not? If so, is it a merely practical problem—namely, that it is hard in practice to acquire all of the relevant information? Or it is a principled problem—namely, that there is no way, even armed with all information about who is receiving pleasure and who is receiving pain, to render such comparisons?

2. Another of Gruen's concerns with utilitarianism is what she calls the epistemic objection—that we cannot know or even reasonably believe in a great many cases what the outcomes of animal experiments will be, and so we are in no position to assess their morality before they are undertaken. How compelling do you find this criticism?

3. If utilitarianism is correct, then humans and lab animals who have equal mental capacities, or who enjoy equal quality of life, should be equally eligible for being experimented upon. Do you agree with this assessment? Why or why not?

4. One principle that the abolitionist relies on is that no one should be required to make large sacrifices for others. How does this principle apply to medical experimentation? Do you find this principle plausible? State your reasons.

5. Abolitionists also rely on the principle that no one should be made to suffer without giving their consent; since animals don't (and can't) give their consent to being experimented on, we should not make them suffer by experimenting on them. What do you think of the consent principle, and this argument? Does the consent principle have any exceptions? Are animal experiments among them? Defend your answers.

Puppies, Pigs, and People: Eating Meat and Marginal Cases

Alastair Norcross

Alastair Norcross opens his provocative piece with a fictional scenario that is both outrageous and meant to make a very serious philosophical point. As he sees it, current practices of factory farming are deeply immoral. One might think that meat-eaters are exempt from blame, though, since for the most part they are not the ones who are actually perpetrating the harms to animals on the factory farms that process the great majority of animal products. Norcross rejects this thought. As he sees it, meat-eaters—at least those who know of the cruelty of the treatment of factory-farmed animals—are fully blameworthy for their indulgence. The good they get from eating meat—primarily the gustatory pleasure they get from eating meat—is far outweighed by the awful suffering of the animals when confined and killed on factory farms.

Norcross considers a wide variety of replies to his charge. These include the claim that individual meat-eaters are off the moral hook because their purchases are so insignificant that they cannot affect the practices on factory farms. Another reply is that meat-eaters do not intend to harm animals, but only foresee animal harm as a result of contemporary farming practices. Norcross extensively criticizes both replies.

He then introduces a very popular argument in the literature on animal welfare: the argument from marginal cases. This argument says that we must treat animals and so-called marginal human beings as equals, since such humans have mental lives that are no more developed than those of the animals that are killed and eaten for food. He considers several replies to this argument and finds fault with each of them. If we are unwilling to cruelly confine, prematurely kill, and eat "marginal" human beings, then we should be equally reluctant to do such things to animals.

Norcross concludes with a discussion of the difference between being a moral agent (i.e., someone who can respond to moral reasons and control her behavior by means of such reasons) and a moral patient (i.e., a being to whom we owe duties, even if that being lacks rights or lacks the cognitive powers needed to be a moral agent). Norcross argues that animals qualify as moral patients, even if, because of their diminished or non-existent rationality, they cannot qualify as moral agents. We therefore owe them duties of respect, which protect them against the current practices involved in factory farming.

I. FRED'S BASEMENT

Consider the story of Fred, who receives a visit from the police one day. They have been summoned by Fred's neighbors, who have been disturbed by strange sounds emanating from Fred's basement. When they enter the basement they are confronted by the following scene: Twenty-six small wire cages, each containing a puppy, some whining, some whimpering, some howling. The puppies range in age from newborn to about six months. Many of them show signs of mutilation. Urine and feces cover the bottoms of the cages and the basement

From Alastair Norcross, "Puppies, Pigs and People: Eating Meat and Marginal Cases," *Philosophical Perspectives* 18 (2004), pp. 229–234, 239–244.

floor. Fred explains that he keeps the puppies for twenty-six weeks, and then butchers them while holding them upside-down. During their lives he performs a series of mutilations on them, such as slicing off their noses and their paws with a hot knife, all without any form of anesthesia. Except for the mutilations, the puppies are never allowed out of the cages, which are barely big enough to hold them at twenty-six weeks. The police are horrified, and promptly charge Fred with animal abuse. As details of the case are publicized, the public is outraged. Newspapers are flooded with letters demanding that Fred be severely punished. There are calls for more severe penalties for animal abuse. Fred is denounced as a vile sadist.

Finally, at his trial, Fred explains his behavior, and argues that he is blameless and therefore deserves no punishment. He is, he explains, a great lover of chocolate. A couple of years ago, he was involved in a car accident, which resulted in some head trauma. Upon his release from hospital, having apparently suffered no lasting ill effects, he visited his favorite restaurant and ordered their famous rich dark chocolate mousse. Imagine his dismay when he discovered that his experience of the mousse was a pale shadow of its former self. The mousse tasted bland, slightly pleasant, but with none of the intense chocolaty flavor he remembered so well. The waiter assured him that the recipe was unchanged from the last time he had tasted it, just the day before his accident. In some consternation, Fred rushed out to buy a bar of his favorite Belgian chocolate. Again, he was dismayed to discover that his experience of the chocolate was barely even pleasurable. Extensive investigation revealed that his experience of other foods remained unaffected, but chocolate, in all its forms, now tasted bland and insipid. Desperate for a solution to his problem, Fred visited a renowned gustatory neurologist, Dr. T. Bud. Extensive tests revealed that the accident had irreparably damaged the godiva gland, which secretes cocoamone, the hormone responsible for the experience of chocolate. Fred urgently requested hormone replacement therapy. Dr. Bud informed him that, until recently, there had been no known source of cocoamone, other than the human godiva gland, and that it was impossible to collect

cocoamone from one person to be used by another. However, a chance discovery had altered the situation. A forensic veterinary surgeon, performing an autopsy on a severely abused puppy, had discovered high concentrations of cocoamone in the puppy's brain. It turned out that puppies, who don't normally produce cocoamone, could be stimulated to do so by extended periods of severe stress and suffering. The research, which led to this discovery, while gaining tenure for its authors, had not been widely publicized, for fear of antagonizing animal welfare groups. Although this research clearly gave Fred the hope of tasting chocolate again, there were no commercially available sources of puppy-derived cocoamone. Lack of demand, combined with fear of bad publicity, had deterred drug companies from getting into the puppy torturing business. Fred appeals to the court to imagine his anguish, on discovering that a solution to his severe deprivation was possible, but not readily available. But he wasn't inclined to sit around bemoaning his cruel fate. He did what any chocolate lover would do. He read the research, and set up his own cocoamone collection lab in his basement. Six months of intense puppy suffering, followed by a brutal death, produced enough cocoamone to last him a week, hence the twenty-six cages. He isn't a sadist or an animal abuser, he explains. If there were a method of collecting cocoamone without torturing puppies, he would gladly employ it. He derives no pleasure from the suffering of the puppies itself. He sympathizes with those who are horrified by the pain and misery of the animals, but the court must realize that human pleasure is at stake. The puppies, while undeniably cute, are mere animals. He admits that he would be just as healthy without chocolate, if not more so. But this isn't a matter of survival or health. His life would be unacceptably impoverished without the experience of chocolate.

End of story. Clearly, we are horrified by Fred's behavior, and unconvinced by his attempted justification. It is, of course, unfortunate for Fred that he can no longer enjoy the taste of chocolate, but that in no way excuses the imposition of severe suffering on the puppies. I expect near universal agreement with this claim (the exceptions being those who are either inhumanly callous or thinking ahead, and wish to avoid the following conclusion, to which such agreement commits them). No decent person would even contemplate torturing puppies merely to enhance a gustatory experience. However, billions of animals endure intense suffering every year for precisely this end. Most of the chicken, veal, beef, and pork consumed in the US comes from intensive confinement facilities, in which the animals live cramped, stress-filled lives and endure unanaesthetized mutilations. The vast majority of people would suffer no ill health from the elimination of meat from their diets. Quite the reverse. The supposed benefits from this system of factory farming, apart from the profits accruing to agribusiness, are increased levels of gustatory pleasure for those who claim that they couldn't enjoy a meat-free diet as much as their current meat-filled diets. If we are prepared to condemn Fred for torturing puppies merely to enhance his gustatory experiences, shouldn't we similarly condemn the millions who purchase and consume factory-raised meat? Are there any morally significant differences between Fred's behavior and their behavior?

2. FRED'S BEHAVIOR COMPARED WITH OUR BEHAVIOR

The first difference that might seem to be relevant is that Fred tortures the puppies himself, whereas most Americans consume meat that comes from animals that have been tortured by others. But is this really relevant? What if Fred had been squeamish and had employed someone else to torture the puppies and extract the cocoamone? Would we have thought any better of Fred? Of course not.

Another difference between Fred and many consumers of factory-raised meat is that many, perhaps most, such consumers are unaware of the treatment of the animals, before they appear in neatly wrapped packages on supermarket shelves. Perhaps I should moderate my challenge, then. If we are prepared to condemn Fred for torturing puppies merely to enhance his gustatory experiences, shouldn't we similarly condemn those who purchase and consume factory-raised meat, in full, or even partial, awareness of the suffering endured by the animals? While many consumers are still blissfully ignorant of the appalling treatment meted out to meat, that number

is rapidly dwindling, thanks to vigorous publicity campaigns waged by animal welfare groups. Furthermore, any meat-eating readers of this article are now deprived of the excuse of ignorance.

Perhaps a consumer of factory-raised animals could argue as follows: While I agree that Fred's behavior is abominable, mine is crucially different. If Fred did not consume his chocolate, he would not raise and torture puppies (or pay someone else to do so). Therefore Fred could prevent the suffering of the puppies. However, if I did not buy and consume factory-raised meat, no animals would be spared lives of misery. Agribusiness is much too large to respond to the behavior of one consumer. Therefore I cannot prevent the suffering of any animals. I may well regret the suffering inflicted on animals for the sake of human enjoyment. I may even agree that the human enjoyment doesn't justify the suffering. However, since the animals will suffer no matter what I do, I may as well enjoy the taste of their flesh.

There are at least two lines of response to this attempted defense. First, consider an analogous case. You visit a friend in an exotic location, say Alabama. Your friend takes you out to eat at the finest restaurant in Tuscaloosa. For dessert you select the house specialty, "Chocolate Mousse à la Bama," served with a small cup of coffee, which you are instructed to drink before eating the mousse. The mousse is quite simply the most delicious dessert you have ever tasted. Never before has chocolate tasted so rich and satisfying. Tempted to order a second, you ask your friend what makes this mousse so delicious. He informs you that the mousse itself is ordinary, but the coffee contains a concentrated dose of cocoamone, the newly discovered chocolate-enhancing hormone. Researchers at Auburn University have perfected a technique for extracting cocoamone from the brains of freshly slaughtered puppies, who have been subjected to lives of pain and frustration. Each puppy's brain yields four doses, each of which is effective for about fifteen minutes, just long enough to enjoy one serving of mousse. You are, naturally, horrified and disgusted. You will certainly not order another serving, you tell your friend. In fact, you are shocked that your friend, who had always seemed to be a morally decent person, could have both recommended the dessert to you and eaten one himself, in full awareness of the loathsome process necessary for the experience. He agrees that the suffering of the puppies is outrageous, and that the gain in human pleasure in no way justifies the appalling treatment they have to endure. However, neither he nor you can save any puppies by refraining from consuming cocoamone. Cocoamone production is now Alabama's leading industry, so it is much too large to respond to the behavior of one or two consumers. Since the puppies will suffer no matter what either of you does, you may as well enjoy the mousse.

If it is as obvious as it seems that a morally decent person, who is aware of the details of cocoamone production, couldn't order Chocolate Mousse à la Bama, it should be equally obvious that a morally decent person, who is aware of the details of factory farming, can't purchase and consume factory-raised meat. If the attempted excuse of causal impotence is compelling in the latter case, it should be compelling in the former case. But it isn't.

The second response to the claim of causal impotence is to deny it. Consider the case of chickens, the most cruelly treated of all animals raised for human consumption, with the possible exception of veal calves. In 1998, almost 8 billion chickens were slaughtered in the US, almost all of them raised on factory farms. Suppose that there are 250 million chicken eaters in the US, and that each one consumes, on average, 25 chickens per year (this leaves a fair number of chickens slaughtered for nonhuman consumption, or for export). Clearly, if only one of those chicken eaters gave up eating chicken, the industry would not respond. Equally clearly, if they all gave up eating chicken, billions of chickens (approximately 6.25 billion per year) would not be bred, tortured, and killed. But there must also be some number of consumers, far short of 250 million, whose renunciation of chicken would cause the industry to reduce the number of chickens bred in factory farms. The industry may not be able to respond to each individual's behavior, but it must respond to the behavior of fairly large numbers. Suppose that the industry is sensitive to a reduction in demand for chicken equivalent to 10,000 people becoming vegetarians. (This seems like a reasonable guess, but I have no idea what the actual numbers

are, nor is it important.) For each group of 10,000 who give up chicken, a quarter of a million fewer chickens are bred per year. It appears, then, that if you give up eating chicken, you have only a one in ten thousand chance of making any difference to the lives of chickens, unless it is certain that fewer than 10,000 people will ever give up eating chicken, in which case you have no chance. Isn't a one in ten thousand chance small enough to render your continued consumption of chicken blameless? Not at all. . . . A one in ten thousand chance of saving 250,000 chickens per year from excruciating lives is morally and mathematically equivalent to the certainty of saving 25 chickens per year. We commonly accept that even small risks of great harms are unacceptable. That is why we disapprove of parents who fail to secure their children in car seats or with seat belts, who leave their small children unattended at home, or who drink or smoke heavily during pregnancy. Or consider commercial aircraft safety measures. The chances that the oxygen masks, the lifejackets, or the emergency exits on any given plane will be called on to save any lives in a given week are far smaller than one in ten thousand. And yet we would be outraged to discover that an airline had knowingly allowed a plane to fly for a week with non-functioning emergency exits, oxygen masks, and lifejackets. So, even if it is true that your giving up factory-raised chicken has only a tiny chance of preventing suffering, given that the amount of suffering that would be prevented is in inverse proportion to your chance of preventing it, your continued consumption is not thereby excused.

But perhaps it is not even true that your giving up chicken has only a tiny chance of making any difference. Suppose again that the poultry industry only reduces production when a threshold of 10,000 fresh vegetarians is reached. Suppose also, as is almost certainly true, that vegetarianism is growing in popularity in the US (and elsewhere). Then, even if you are not the one, newly converted vegetarian, to reach the next threshold of 10,000, your conversion will reduce the time required before the next threshold is reached. The sooner the threshold is reached, the sooner production, and therefore animal suffering, is reduced. Your behavior, therefore, does make a difference. Furthermore, many people who become vegetarians influence others to become vegetarian, who in turn influence others, and so on. It appears, then, that the claim of causal impotence is mere wishful thinking, on the part of those meat lovers who are morally sensitive enough to realize that human gustatory pleasure does not justify inflicting extreme suffering on animals.

Perhaps there is a further difference between the treatment of Fred's puppies and the treatment of animals on factory farms. The suffering of the puppies is a necessary means to the production of gustatory pleasure, whereas the suffering of animals on factory farms is simply a by-product of the conditions dictated by economic considerations. Therefore, it might be argued, the suffering of the puppies is *intended as a means* to Fred's pleasure, whereas the suffering of factory-raised animals is merely *foreseen* as a side-effect of a system that is a means to the gustatory pleasures of millions. The distinction between what is intended, either as a means or as an end in itself, and what is 'merely' foreseen is central to the Doctrine of Double Effect. Supporters of this doctrine claim that it is sometimes permissible to bring about an effect that is merely foreseen, even though the very same effect could not permissibly be brought about if intended. (Other conditions have to be met in order for the Doctrine of Double Effect to judge an action permissible, most notably that there be an outweighing good effect.) Fred acts impermissibly, according to this line of argument, because he intends the suffering of the puppies as a means to his pleasure. Most meat-eaters, on the other hand, even if aware of the suffering of the animals, do not intend the suffering.

In response to this line of argument, I could remind the reader that Samuel Johnson said, or should have said, that the Doctrine of Double Effect is the last refuge of a scoundrel. I won't do that, however, since neither the doctrine itself, nor the alleged moral distinction between intending and foreseeing can justify the consumption of factory-raised meat. The Doctrine of Double Effect requires not merely that a bad effect be foreseen and not intended, but also that there be an outweighing good effect. In the case of the suffering of factory-raised animals, whatever good could plausibly be claimed to come out of the system clearly doesn't outweigh the bad.

Furthermore, it would be easy to modify the story of Fred to render the puppies' suffering 'merely' foreseen. For example, suppose that the cocoamone is produced by a chemical reaction that can only occur when large quantities of drain-cleaner are forced down the throat of a conscious, unanaesthetized puppy. The consequent appalling suffering, while not itself a means to the production of cocoamone, is nonetheless an unavoidable side-effect of the means. In this variation of the story, Fred's behavior is no less abominable than in the original.

One last difference between the behavior of Fred and the behavior of the consumers of factory-raised meat is worth discussing, if only because it is so frequently cited in response to the arguments of this paper. Fred's behavior is abominable, according to this line of thinking, because it involves the suffering of *puppies*. The behavior of meat-eaters, on the other hand, 'merely' involves the suffering of chickens, pigs, cows, calves, sheep, and the like. Puppies (and probably dogs and cats in general) are morally different from the other animals. Puppies *count* (morally, that is), whereas the other animals don't, or at least not nearly as much.

So, what gives puppies a higher moral status than the animals we eat? Presumably there is some morally relevant property or properties possessed by puppies but not by farm animals. Perhaps puppies have a greater degree of rationality than farm animals, or a more finely developed moral sense, or at least a sense of loyalty and devotion. The problems with this kind of approach are obvious. It's highly unlikely that any property that has even an outside chance of being ethically relevant is both possessed by puppies and not possessed by any farm animals. For example, it's probably true that most puppies have a greater degree of rationality (whatever that means) than most chickens, but the comparison with pigs is far more dubious. Besides, if Fred were to inform the jury that he had taken pains to acquire particularly stupid, morally obtuse, disloyal and undevoted puppies, would they (or we) have declared his behavior to be morally acceptable? Clearly not.

I have been unable to discover any morally relevant differences between the behavior of Fred, the puppy torturer, and the behavior of the millions of people who purchase and consume factory-raised meat, at least those who do so in the knowledge that the animals live lives of suffering and deprivation. If morality demands that we not torture puppies merely to enhance our own eating pleasure, morality also demands that we not support factory farming by purchasing factory-raised meat. . . .

3. HUMANS' VERSUS ANIMALS' ETHICAL STATUS—THE RATIONALITY GAMBIT

For the purposes of this discussion, to claim that humans have a superior ethical status to animals is to claim that it is morally right to give the interests of humans greater weight than those of animals in deciding how to behave. Such claims will often be couched in terms of rights, such as the rights to life, liberty or respect, but nothing turns on this terminological matter. One may claim that it is generally wrong to kill humans, but not animals, because humans are rational, and animals are not. Or one may claim that the suffering of animals counts less than the suffering of humans (if at all), because humans are rational, and animals are not. . . .

What could ground the claim of superior moral status for humans? Just as the defender of a higher moral status for puppies than for farm animals needs to find some property or properties possessed by puppies but not by farm animals, so the defender of a higher moral status for humans needs to find some property or properties possessed by humans but not by other animals. The traditional view, dating back at least to Aristotle, is that rationality is what separates humans, both morally and metaphysically, from other animals.

One of the most serious challenges to the traditional view involves a consideration of what philosophers refer to as 'marginal cases.' Whatever kind and level of rationality is selected as justifying the attribution of superior moral status to humans will either be lacking in some humans or present in some animals. To take one of the most commonly-suggested features, many humans are incapable of engaging in moral reflection. For some, this incapacity is temporary, as is the case with infants, or the temporarily cognitively disabled. Others who once had the capacity may have permanently lost it, as is the case with

the severely senile or the irreversibly comatose. Still others never had and never will have the capacity, as is the case with the severely mentally disabled. If we base our claims for the moral superiority of humans over animals on the attribution of such capacities, won't we have to exclude many humans? Won't we then be forced to the claim that there is at least as much moral reason to use cognitively deficient humans in experiments and for food as to use animals? Perhaps we could exclude the only temporarily disabled, on the grounds of potentiality, though that move has its own problems. Nonetheless, the other two categories would be vulnerable to this objection.

I will consider two lines of response to the argument from marginal cases. The first denies that we have to attribute different moral status to marginal humans, but maintains that we are, nonetheless, justified in attributing different moral status to animals who are just as cognitively sophisticated as marginal humans, if not more so. The second admits that, strictly speaking, marginal humans are morally inferior to other humans, but proceeds to claim pragmatic reasons for treating them, at least usually, *as if* they had equal status.

As representatives of the first line of defense, I will consider arguments from three philosophers, Carl Cohen, Alan White, and David Schmidtz. First, Cohen:

> [the argument from marginal cases] fails; it mistakenly treats an essential feature of humanity as though it were a screen for sorting humans. The capacity for moral judgment that distinguishes humans from animals is not a test to be administered to human beings one by one. Persons who are unable, because of some disability, to perform the full moral functions natural to human beings are certainly not for that reason ejected from the moral community. The issue is one of kind. . . . What humans retain when disabled, animals have never had.[1]

Alan White argues that animals don't have rights, on the grounds that they cannot intelligibly be spoken of in the full language of a right. By this he means that they cannot, for example, claim, demand, assert, insist on, secure, waive, or surrender a right. This is what he has to say in response to the argument from marginal cases:

Nor does this, as some contend, exclude infants, children, the feeble-minded, the comatose, the dead, or generations yet unborn. Any of these may be for various reasons empirically unable to fulfill the full role of right-holder. But . . . they are logically possible subjects of rights to whom the full language of rights can significantly, however falsely, be used. It is a misfortune, not a tautology, that these persons cannot exercise or enjoy, claim, or waive, their rights or do their duty or fulfil their obligations.[2]

David Schmidtz defends the appeal to typical characteristics of species, such as mice, chimpanzees, and humans, in making decisions on the use of different species in experiments. He also considers the argument from marginal cases:

Of course, some chimpanzees lack the characteristic features in virtue of which chimpanzees command respect as a species, just as some humans lack the characteristic features in virtue of which humans command respect as a species. It is equally obvious that some chimpanzees have cognitive capacities (for example) that are superior to the cognitive capacities of some humans. But whether every human being is superior to every chimpanzee is beside the point. The point is that we can, we do, and we should make decisions on the basis of our recognition that mice, chimpanzees, and humans are relevantly different *types*. We can have it both ways after all. Or so a speciesist could argue.[3]

There is something deeply troublesome about the line of argument that runs through all three of these responses to the argument from marginal cases. A particular feature or set of features is claimed to have so much moral significance that its presence or lack can make the difference to whether a piece of behavior is morally justified or morally outrageous. But then it is claimed that the presence or lack of the feature in any *particular* case is not important. The relevant question is whether the presence or lack of the feature is *normal*. Such an argument would seem perfectly preposterous in most other cases. Suppose, for example, that ten famous people are on trial in the afterlife for crimes against humanity. On the basis of conclusive evidence, five are found

guilty and five are found not guilty. Four of the guilty are sentenced to an eternity of torment, and one is granted an eternity of bliss. Four of the innocent are granted an eternity of bliss, and one is sentenced to an eternity of torment. The one innocent who is sentenced to torment asks why he, and not the fifth guilty person, must go to hell. Saint Peter replies, "Isn't it obvious Mr. Gandhi? You are male. The other four men—Adolph Hitler, Joseph Stalin, George W. Bush, and Richard Nixon—are all guilty. Therefore the normal condition for a male defendant in this trial is guilt. The fact that you happen to be innocent is irrelevant. Likewise, of the five female defendants in this trial, only one was guilty. Therefore the normal condition for female defendants in this trial is innocence. That is why Margaret Thatcher gets to go to heaven instead of you."

As I said, such an argument is preposterous. Is the reply to the argument from marginal cases any better? Perhaps it will be claimed that a biological category such as a species is more 'natural,' whatever that means, than a category like 'all the male (or female) defendants in this trial.' Even setting aside the not inconsiderable worries about the conventionality of biological categories, it is not at all clear why this distinction should be morally relevant. What if it turned out that there were statistically relevant differences in the mental abilities of men and women? Suppose that men were, on average, more skilled at manipulating numbers than women, and that women were, on average, more empathetic than men. Would such differences in what was 'normal' for men and women justify us in preferring an innumerate man to a female math genius for a job as an accountant, or an insensitive woman to an ultra-sympathetic man for a job as a counselor? I take it that the biological distinction between male and female is just as real as that between human and chimpanzee.

A second response to the argument from marginal cases is to concede that cognitively deficient humans really do have an inferior moral status to normal humans. Can we, then, use such humans as we do animals? I know of no-one who takes the further step of advocating the use of marginal humans for food. . . . How can we advocate this second response while blocking the further step? Mary Anne

Warren suggests that "there are powerful practical and emotional reasons for protecting non-rational human beings, reasons which are absent in the case of most non-human animals."[4] It would clearly outrage common human sensibilities, if we were to raise retarded children for food or medical experiments. Here is Steinbock in a similar vein:

> I doubt that anyone will be able to come up with a concrete and morally relevant difference that would justify, say, using a chimpanzee in an experiment rather than a human being with less capacity for reasoning, moral responsibility, etc. Should we then experiment on the severely retarded? Utilitarian considerations aside, we feel a special obligation to care for the handicapped members of our own species, who cannot survive in this world without such care.... In addition, when we consider the severely retarded, we think, 'That could be me.' It makes sense to think that one might have been born retarded, but not to think that one might have been born a monkey.... Here we are getting away from such things as 'morally relevant differences' and are talking about something much more difficult to articulate, namely, the role of feeling and sentiment in moral thinking.[5]

This line of response clearly won't satisfy those who think that marginal humans really do deserve equal moral consideration with other humans. It is also a very shaky basis on which to justify our current practices. What outrages human sensibilities is a very fragile thing. Human history is littered with examples of widespread acceptance of the systematic mistreatment of some groups who didn't generate any sympathetic response from others. That we do feel a kind of sympathy for retarded humans that we don't feel for dogs is, if true, a contingent matter. To see just how shaky a basis this is for protecting retarded humans, imagine that a new kind of birth defect (perhaps associated with beef from cows treated with bovine growth hormone) produces severe mental retardation, green skin, and a complete lack of emotional bond between parents and child. Furthermore, suppose that the mental retardation is of the same kind and severity as that caused by other birth defects that don't have the other two effects. It seems likely that denying

moral status to such defective humans would not run the same risks of outraging human sensibilities as would the denial of moral status to other, less easily distinguished and more loved defective humans. Would these contingent empirical differences between our reactions to different sources of mental retardation justify us in ascribing different direct moral status to their subjects? The only difference between them is skin color and whether they are loved by others. Any theory that could ascribe moral relevance to differences such as these doesn't deserve to be taken seriously.

Finally, perhaps we could claim that the practice of giving greater weight to the interests of all humans than of animals is justified on evolutionary grounds. Perhaps such differential concern has survival value for the species. Something like this may well be true, but it is hard to see the moral relevance. We can hardly justify the privileging of human interests over animal interests on the grounds that such privileging serves human interests!

6. AGENT AND PATIENT—THE SPECIESIST'S CENTRAL CONFUSION

Although the argument from marginal cases certainly poses a formidable challenge to any proposed criterion of full moral standing that excludes animals, it doesn't, in my view, constitute the most serious flaw in such attempts to justify the status quo. The proposed criteria are all variations on the Aristotelian criterion of rationality. But what is the moral relevance of rationality? Why should we think that the possession of a certain level or kind of rationality renders the possessor's interests of greater moral significance than those of a merely sentient being? In Bentham's famous words "The question is not, Can they reason? nor Can they talk? But, Can they suffer?"[6]

What do defenders of the alleged superiority of human interests say in response to Bentham's challenge? Some, such as Carl Cohen, simply reiterate the differences between humans and animals that they claim to carry moral significance. Animals are not members of moral communities, they don't engage in moral reflection, they can't be moved by moral reasons, *therefore* (?) their interests don't count as much as ours. Others, such as Steinbock and Warren, attempt to go further. Here is Warren on the subject:

> Why is rationality morally relevant? It does not make us "better" than other animals or more "perfect." . . . But it is morally relevant insofar as it provides greater possibilities for cooperation and for the nonviolent resolution of problems.[7]

Warren is certainly correct in claiming that a certain level and kind of rationality is morally relevant. Where she, and others who give similar arguments, go wrong is in specifying what the moral relevance amounts to. If a being is incapable of moral reasoning, at even the most basic level, if it is incapable of being moved by moral reasons, claims, or arguments, then it cannot be a moral agent. It cannot be subject to moral obligations, to moral praise or blame. Punishing a dog for doing something "wrong" is no more than an attempt to alter its future behavior.

All this is well and good, but what is the significance for the question of what weight to give to animal interests? That animals can't be moral *agents* doesn't seem to be relevant to their status as moral *patients*. Many, perhaps most, humans are both moral agents and patients. Most, perhaps all, animals are only moral patients. Why would the lack of moral agency give them diminished status as moral patients? Full status as a moral patient is not some kind of reward for moral agency. I have heard students complain in this regard that it is *unfair* that humans bear the burdens of moral responsibility, and don't get enhanced consideration of their interests in return. This is a very strange claim. Humans are subject to moral obligations, because they are the kind of creatures who *can* be. What grounds moral agency is simply different from what grounds moral standing as a patient. It is no more unfair that humans and not animals are moral agents, than it is unfair that real animals and not stuffed toys are moral patients.

. . . It seems that any attempt to justify the claim that humans have a higher moral status than other animals by appealing to some version of rationality as the morally relevant difference between humans and animals will fail on at least two counts. It will fail to give an adequate answer to the argument from marginal cases, and, more importantly, it will

fail to make the case that such a difference is morally relevant to the status of animals as moral patients as opposed to their status as moral agents.

I conclude that our intuitions that Fred's behavior is morally impermissible are accurate. Furthermore, given that the behavior of those who knowingly support factory farming is morally indistinguishable, it follows that their behavior is also morally impermissible.

NOTES

1. Carl Cohen, "The Case for the Use of Animals in Biomedical Research," *The New England Journal of Medicine,* vol. 315, 1986.
2. Alan White, *Rights,* (OUP 1984). Reprinted in *Animal Rights and Human Obligations,* 2nd edition, Tom Regan and Peter Singer (eds.) (Prentice Hall, 1989), 120.
3. David Schmidtz, "Are All Species Equal?," *Journal of Applied Philosophy*, Vol. 15, no. 1 (1998), 61, my emphasis.
4. Warren, op. cit. 483. Mary Anne Warren, "Difficulties with the Strong Animal Rights Position," *Between the Species* 2, no. 4, 1987. Reprinted in *Contemporary Moral Problems,* 5th edition, James E. White (ed.) (West, 1997), 482.
5. Steinbock, op. cit. 469–470. Bonnie Steinbock, "Speciesism and the Idea of Equality," *Philosophy* 53, no. 204 (April 1978). Reprinted in *Contemporary Moral Problems,* 5th edition, James E. White (ed.) (West, 1997) 467–468.
6. Jeremy Bentham, *Introduction to the Principles of Morals and Legislation,* (Various) chapter 17.
7. Warren, op. cit. 482.

Alastair Norcross: Puppies, Pigs, and People: Eating Meat and Marginal Cases

1. Do you agree that Fred acts immorally in the case that Norcross describes? If so, what exactly is it about Fred's behavior that is morally objectionable? If not, why not?
2. Some might claim that eating meat from factory farms is relevantly different from Fred's behavior because individual consumers are powerless to change the factory-farming system, whereas Fred is fully in control of the puppies. How does Norcross respond to this claim?

3. Another disanalogy between Fred's behavior and that of most meat-eaters is that Fred *intends* to make the puppies suffer, while most consumers of meat don't intend to make any animals suffer. Does this disanalogy undermine Norcross's argument? Why or why not?

4. What is the "argument from marginal cases" and what is it supposed to show? What do you think is the strongest objection to the argument?

5. What is the difference between being a moral agent and being a moral patient? Why does Norcross think that nonhuman animals are moral patients? Do you agree with him?

Against the Moral Standing of Animals

Peter Carruthers

Peter Carruthers argues that nonhuman animals lack moral standing. This is one way of saying that animals have no moral importance in their own right. While this may seem morally offensive, Carruthers takes pains to argue that his position does not usually allow us to treat animals in whatever way we like. On the contrary, he is intent on showing that acts that display, say, cruelty or indifference to animal suffering are as morally wrong as we intuitively take them to be.

Carruthers develops his views within a *contractualist* (i.e., a contractarian) moral framework. He discusses the two most prominent versions of contractualism, those of philosophers John Rawls and Thomas Scanlon. On either theory, the moral rules that rational contractors would agree to would include ones that extend protection to all human beings, regardless of whether they are themselves rational. So, for instance, infants and the extremely mentally incompetent would have independent moral importance, despite the fact that they lack the sort of rationality that Carruthers thinks is so important.

By contrast, Carruthers believes that rational contractors would have no reason to include animals among those who are protected by the social rules that are meant to govern us. And so animals lack moral standing. They have no moral rights, and we have no duties directly to them. Nevertheless, Carruthers does argue that we have duties not to treat them in ways that display moral vices. So, for instance, we should not treat animals cruelly, because cruelty is a moral vice. This duty arises not because animals are morally important, but rather because rational contractors would endorse principles that required us to display moral virtues and avoid moral vices.

Peter Carruthers, "Against the Moral Standing of Animals," in C. Morris (ed.), *Questions of Life and Death: Readings in Practical Ethics* (Oxford University Press, 2011), 274–284.

I shall argue in this essay that the lives and sufferings of non-human animals (hereafter "animals") make no direct moral claims on us. At the same time I shall argue that the lives and sufferings of human infants and senile old people *do* make such claims on us. In short: I shall argue that no animals possess *moral standing*, while arguing that all human beings possess such standing. I shall allow, however, that some of the things that one might do (or fail to do) to an animal might attract justified moral criticism. But this will be criticism of an indirect (and perhaps culturally local) sort, not deriving from any violations of the rights that the animal might possess. On the contrary, because animals lack standing, they have no rights.

I. ASSUMPTIONS

In this section I shall lay out two sets of assumptions that form the background to my argument. One is about the mental lives and cognitive capacities of animals; the other is about the correct framework for moral theory. While I shall make no attempt to defend these assumptions here, they are quite widely shared, and each is, I believe, fully defensible.

1.1. Animal Minds

I shall assume that most animals have minds much like our own. They have beliefs and desires, and engage in practical reasoning in the light of their beliefs and desires. (This is true even of some invertebrates, including bees and jumping spiders, I believe.) Many animals feel pain and fear, and (in some cases) an emotion much like grief. In short: most animals can *suffer*. Stronger still, I shall assume for these purposes that most animals undergo experiences and feelings that are *conscious*, having the same kind of rich phenomenology and inner "feel" as do our own conscious mental states.

I shall also assume, however, that animals don't count as *rational agents* in the following (quite demanding) sense: a rational agent is a creature that is capable of governing its behavior in accordance with universal rules (such as "Don't tell lies"), and that is capable of thinking about the costs and benefits of the general adoption of a given rule, to be obeyed by most members of a community that includes other rational agents. This assumption is quite obviously true in connection with most animals. I believe that it is also true (although this is slightly more controversial) in connection with members of other species of great ape, such as chimpanzees and gorillas. (If it should turn out that the members of some species of animal *do* count as rational agents in the above sense, then those creatures will be accorded full moral standing, on the approach taken here.) Why the absence of rational agency should matter will emerge in the sections that follow.

1.2. Moral Theory

I shall assume that some or other version of contractualist moral theory is correct. (The problems with utilitarian theories are notorious, and well known. Forms of virtue theory are best pursued and accounted for within the framework of contractualism, I believe.) All contractualists agree that moral truths are, in a certain sense, human constructions, emerging out of some or other variety of hypothetical rational agreement concerning the basic rules to govern our behavior.

In one version of contractualism, moral rules are those that would be agreed upon by rational agents choosing, on broadly self-interested grounds, from behind a "veil of ignorance" (Rawls, 1972). On this account, we are to picture rational agents as attempting to agree on a set of rules to govern their conduct for their mutual benefit in full knowledge of all facts of human psychology, sociology, economics, and so forth, but in ignorance of any particulars about themselves—their own strengths, weaknesses, tastes, life plans, or position in society. All they are allowed to assume as goals when making their choice are the things that they will want *whatever* particular desires and plans they happen to have—namely, wealth, happiness, power, and self-respect. Moral rules are then the rules that would be agreed upon in this situation, provided that the agreement is made on rational grounds. The governing intuition behind this approach is that justice is fairness: since the situation behind the veil of ignorance is fair (all rational agents are equivalently placed), the resulting agreement must also be fair.

In another version of contractualism, moral rules are those that no rational agent could reasonably reject who shared (as their highest priority) the aim of reaching free and unforced general agreement on the rules that are to govern their behavior (Scanlon, 1982, 1998). On this account, we start from agents who are allowed full knowledge of their particular qualities and circumstances (as well as of general truths of psychology and so forth). But we imagine that they are guided, above all, by the goal of reaching free and unforced agreement on the set of rules that are to govern everyone's behavior. Here each individual agent can be thought of as having a veto over the proposed rules. But it is a veto that will only be exercised if it doesn't derail the agreement process, making it impossible to find any set of rules that no one can reasonably reject.

It should be stressed that within a contractualist approach, as I shall understand it, rational agents aren't allowed to appeal to any moral beliefs as part of the idealized contract process. Since moral truths are to be the output of the contract process, they cannot be appealed to at the start. Put differently: since morality is to be constructed through the agreement of rational agents, it cannot be supposed to exist in advance of that agreement. It is also worth pointing out that on each of the above approaches, some moral rules will be mere local conventions. This will happen whenever the contract process entails that there should be *some* moral rule governing a behavior or set of circumstances, but where there are no compelling grounds for selecting one candidate rule over the others.[1]

In what follows I shall often consider arguments from the perspective of *both* of the above forms of contractualism. In that way we can increase our confidence that the conclusions are entailed by contractualist approaches as such, rather than by the specifics of some or other particular variety.

2. ALL HUMANS HAVE STANDING

In the present section I shall argue that all human beings have moral standing, irrespective of their status as rational agents. I shall argue first that all rational agents have standing, and will then show that the same basic sort of standing should be accorded to human infants and senile (or otherwise mentally defective) adult humans.[2] Since these arguments don't extend to animals (as we will see in Section 3), they constitute a reply to [Peter] Singer's (1979) challenge. For Singer claims that contractualism can't consistently deny moral standing to animals without *also* withholding it from infants and mentally defective humans. This section and the one following will demonstrate that he is mistaken.

2.1. The Basic Case: Rational Agents Have Standing

The contractualist framework plainly entails that all rational agents should have the same moral standing. For moral rules are here conceived to be constructed *by* rational agents *for* rational agents. It is obvious that rational agents behind a veil of ignorance would opt to accord the same basic rights, duties, and protections to themselves (that is to say: to all rational agents, since they are choosing in ignorance of their particular identities). And likewise within Scanlon's framework: it is obvious that any proposed rule that would withhold moral standing from some sub-set of rational agents could reasonably be rejected by the members of that sub-set.

It should be stressed that contractualism accords the same basic moral standing to all rational agents as such, and not merely to the members of some actual group or society. On Rawls' approach, contracting agents don't even know which group or society they will turn out to be members of once the veil is drawn aside. And on Scanlon's account, although we are to picture rational agents seeking to agree on a framework of rules in full knowledge of who they are and the groups to which they belong, those rules can be vetoed by *any* rational agent, irrespective of group membership. It follows that if Mars should turn out to be populated by a species of rational agent, then contractualism will accord the members of that species full moral standing.

2.2. Non-Rational Humans: The Argument from Social Stability

It seems that rational contractors wouldn't automatically cede moral standing to those human beings who are *not* rational agents (e.g. infants and senile old people), in the way that they must cede standing to each other. But there are considerations that should induce them to do so, nevertheless. The main one is this.[3] Notice that the basic goal of the contract process is to achieve a set of moral rules that will provide social stability and preserve the peace. This means that moral rules will have to be *psychologically supportable*, in the following sense: they have to be such that rational agents can, in general, bring themselves to abide by them without brainwashing. (Arguably, no rational agent would consent to the loss of autonomy involved in any form of the latter practice.) But now the contractors just have to reflect that, if anything counts as part of "human nature" (and certainly much does; see Pinker, 2002), then people's deep attachment to their infants and aged relatives surely belongs within it. In general, people care as deeply about their immediate relatives as they care about anything (morality included), irrespective of their relatives' status as rational agents. In which case contracting agents should accord moral standing to all human beings, and not just to those human beings who happen to be rational agents.

Consider what a society would be like that denied moral standing to infants and/or senile old people. The members of these groups would, at most, be given the same type of protection that gets accorded to items of private property,

deriving from the legitimate concerns of the rational agents who care about them. But that would leave the state or its agents free to destroy or cause suffering to the members of these groups whenever it might be in the public interest to do so, provided that their relatives receive financial compensation. (For example, senile old people might be killed so that their organs can be harvested, or it might be particularly beneficial to use human infants in certain painful medical experiments.) We can see in advance that these arrangements would be highly unstable. Those whose loved ones were at risk would surely resist with violence, and would band together with others to so resist. Foreseeing this, contracting rational agents should agree that all human beings be accorded moral standing.[4]

2.3. A Reply from Anthropology

It might be replied against this argument that there have been many communities in the world where infanticide and the killing of the old have been sanctioned, without any of the predicted dire consequences for the stability of those societies. Thus in many traditional societies the smaller of a pair of twins, or any infant born deformed, might be abandoned by its mother to die (Hrdy, 1999). And some Inuit tribes are said to have had the practice of forsaking their old people to die in the snow when the latter became too infirm to travel.

One point to be made in response to this objection is that all of the communities in question were sustained and stabilized by systems of traditional belief (often religious belief: "The gods require it", might be the justification given). This is no longer possible for us in conditions of modernity, where it is acceptable for any belief, no matter how revered and long-standing, to be subjected to critical scrutiny. And plainly, the contract process envisaged by contractualism can't make appeal to such traditional beliefs, either.

Another point to be made in response to the objection is that all of the communities in question were teetering on the edge of survival for their members; or at the very least the costs to individuals for acting differently would have been *very* high. In which case it is far from obvious that the practices we are considering involve the denial of moral standing to infants and/or the old, anyway. For notice that in these communities death occurs from failure to support, or from the withdrawal of aid, rather than by active killing. And we, too, accept that it can be permissible to withdraw support, allowing someone to die, when the costs to oneself become too great. Think, for example, of someone in the process of rescuing another person from drowning, who has to give up their effort when they realize that the current is too strong, and that they themselves are in danger of drowning.

2.4. Conclusion: All Humans Have Standing

We can conclude the following. If, as I claim, contractualism is the correct framework for moral theorizing, then it follows that all human beings—whether infant, child, adult, old, or senile—should be accorded the same basic structure of rights and protections. In Section 3 I shall show, in contrast, that contractualism leaves all animals beyond the moral pale, withholding moral standing from them.

Before completing this section it is worth noting that infants and senile old people aren't by any means accorded "second class moral citizenship" by contractualism. Although it is only rational agents who get to grant moral standing through the contract process, and although the considerations that should lead them to grant moral standing to humans who aren't rational agents are indirect ones (not emerging directly out of the structure of the contract process, as does the moral standing of rational agents themselves), this has no impact on the product. Although the considerations that demonstrate the moral standing of rational agents and of non-rational humans may differ from one another, the result is the same: both groups have moral standing, and both should have similar basic rights and protections.

3. NO ANIMALS HAVE STANDING

In this section I shall maintain, first, that the argument just given for according moral standing to all human beings doesn't extend to animals. Then, second, I shall consider two further attempts to secure moral standing for animals within contractualism, showing that they fail. The upshot can be captured in the slogan: "Humans in, animals out."

3.1. Social Stability Revisited

The argument of Section 2.3 was that non-rational humans should be accorded moral standing in order to preserve social stability, since people's attachments to their infants and aged relatives are generally about as deep as it is possible to go. Someone might try presenting a similar argument to show that animals, too, should be accorded moral standing, citing the violence that has *actually* occurred in Western societies when groups of people (like members of the Animal Liberation Front) have acted in defense of the interests of animals. Such an argument fails, however, because members of these groups are acting, not out of attachments that are a normal product of human emotional mechanisms, but out of (what they take to be justified) moral beliefs.

Recall that rational agents engaging in the contract process are forbidden from appealing to any antecedent moral beliefs—whether their own or other people's. (This is because moral truth is to be the outcome of the contract, and shouldn't be presupposed at the outset.) So contracting rational agents should *not* reason that animals ought to be accorded moral standing on the grounds that some people have a moral belief in such standing, and may be prepared to kill or engage in other forms of violence in pursuit of their principles. The proper response is that such people aren't entitled to their belief in the moral standing of animals unless they can show that rational agents in the appropriate sort of contract situation would agree to it.

Many people come to care quite a bit about their pets, of course, and this is something that rational contractors might be expected to know. Could this give rise to a social-stability argument for moral standing? The answer is "No", for at least two distinct reasons.[5] One is that it is far from clear that the phenomenon of pet-keeping and attachment to pets is a human universal (in contrast with attachment to infants and aged relatives). It may rather a product of local cultural forces operating in some societies but not others. And if the latter is the case, then such attachments aren't a "fixed point" of human nature that should constrain rational contractors in their deliberations. They might appropriately decide, instead, that society should be arranged in such a way that people don't develop attachments that are apt to interfere with correct moral decision making.

A second problem with the suggestion is that attachment to pets is rarely so deep as attachments to relatives, in any case. Hence people should have little difficulty in coming to accept that pets can only be accorded the sorts of protections granted to other items of private property. Most of us would think that it would be foolish (indeed, reprehensible) to continue to keep a pet that threatens the life of a child (e.g., through severe allergic reactions). And when the state declares that the public interest requires that someone's dog be put down (e.g., because it is dangerous), it would surely be unreasonable to take up arms to defend the life of the animal, just as it would be unreasonable to kill to preserve a house that had been condemned for demolition.

3.2. Representing the Interests of Animals

While the argument from social stability doesn't show that animals should be accorded moral standing, other arguments could still be successful. One suggestion would be that some rational agents behind the veil of ignorance should be assigned to represent the interests of animals, much as a lawyer might be assigned to represent the interests of a pet in a court of law in a case involving a disputed will. If it was the job of those representatives to look out for the interests of animals in the formulation of

the basic moral contract, then they might be expected to insist upon animals being granted moral standing.

This suggestion, however, is plainly at odds with the guiding idea of contractualism. For what possible motive could there be for assigning some agents to represent the interests of animals in the contract process, unless it were believed that animals *deserve* to have their interests protected? But that would be to assume a moral truth at the outset: the belief, namely, that animals deserve to be protected. We noted above, in contrast, that contractualism assumes that the contracting parties should come to the contract situation either without any moral beliefs at all, or setting aside (taking care not to rely upon) such moral beliefs as they do have.

The point is even easier to see in Scanlon's version of contractualism. Real individual agents with knowledge of their own particulars, but who either lack moral beliefs or have set aside their moral beliefs while trying to agree to rules that no one could reasonably reject, could have no reason to assign some of their number to represent the interests of animals. For to do so would be tantamount to insisting at the outset that animals should be accorded moral standing, preempting and usurping the constructive contract process.

3.3. Ignorance of Species

Another suggestion is that people behind the veil of ignorance should be selecting moral rules in ignorance of their species, just as they are ignorant of their life-plans, age, strength, intelligence, gender, race, position in society, and so on (Regan, 1984). Then, just as rational agents might be expected to agree on rules to protect the weak, since for all they know they might end up to *be* weak, so, too, rational agents might be expected to agree on a system of fundamental rights for animals, since for all they know they might end up *being* an animal.

One problem with this suggestion is that Rawls' veil of ignorance is designed to rule out reliance upon factors that are widely agreed to be morally irrelevant. Amongst the intuitions that a good moral theory should preserve is the belief that someone's moral standing shouldn't depend upon such factors as their age, or gender, or race. In contrast we don't (or don't all) think that species is morally irrelevant. On the contrary, this is highly disputed, with (I would guess) a clear majority believing that differences of species (e.g., between human and dog) *can* be used to ground differential moral treatment.

The veil of ignorance is a theoretical device designed to ensure that deeply held moral beliefs about what is, or isn't, morally relevant should be preserved in the resulting theory. So although the contracting agents aren't allowed to appeal to any moral beliefs in the contract process, in effect the moral theorist has relied upon his prior moral beliefs in designing the surrounding constraints. Scanlon's version of contractualism, in contrast, digs deeper. It has the capacity to *explain why* the properties mentioned in the veil of ignorance are morally irrelevant. This is because one should be able to see in advance as one approaches the contract situation that if one proposes a rule favoring men, then this will be vetoed by those rational agents who are women, and vice versa; and so on for differences of age, intelligence, strength, race, and so on. So if we are motivated by the goal of reaching free and unforced general agreement among rational agents, we should abjure proposals that might favor one group over another. For we can foresee that these would be vetoed, and that others could equally well suggest proposals favoring other groups, in any case, which *we* would need to veto. But in contrast there is no reason for us to abjure rules that favor humans over animals.

The idea of choosing rules in ignorance of one's species isn't even coherent within the framework of Scanlon's form of contractualism, in which agents are supposed to have full knowledge of their own particular qualities and circumstances, as well as of general truths of psychology, economics, and so forth. So there is no way to argue for the moral significance of animals from such a standpoint. Indeed, one should be able to see in advance that a proposed rule that would accord moral standing to animals would be vetoed by some, because of the costs and burdens that it would place on us.

3.4. Conclusion: No Animals Have Standing

I conclude that while the moral standing of all humans (including infants and senile old people) is entailed by contractualism, by the same token such standing should be denied to animals. Even if this position is theoretically impeccable, however, it faces a serious challenge. This is that most people believe very strongly indeed that it is possible to act wrongly in one's dealings with animals. And most people believe, too, that it is something about what is happening *to the animal* that warrants the moral criticism. These are intuitions that need to be explained, or explained away. This will form the topic of Sections 4 and 5.

4. FORMS OF INDIRECT MORAL SIGNIFICANCE FOR ANIMALS

Imagine that while walking in a city one evening you turn a corner to confront a group of teenagers who have caught a cat, doused it in kerosene, and are about to set it alight. Of course you would be horrified. You would think that the teenagers were doing something very wrong; and the vast majority of people would agree with you. It would be a serious black mark against contractualist moral theories in general, and against the line that I am pursuing in this essay in particular, if this intuition couldn't be accommodated.

4.1. Offence to Animal-Lovers

One suggestion would be that we have *indirect* duties towards animals. These fail to have any corresponding rights on the part of the animal, but rather derive from a direct duty not to cause unnecessary offence to the feelings of animal-lovers or animal owners. Compare the above scenario with this one: while walking through a city you come across a pair of young people, stark naked, making love on a park bench in broad daylight. Here, too, you would be horrified, and you would think that what they were doing was wrong. But the wrongness isn't, as it were, intrinsic to the activity. It is rather that the love-making is being conducted in a way that might be disturbing or distressing to other people: namely, in public. Likewise, it might be said, in the case of the teenagers setting light to the cat: what they are doing is wrong because it is likely to be disturbing or distressing to other people.

On the face of it this proposal isn't very promising. For while it can explain why the teenagers are wrong to set light to a cat in the street (since there is a danger that they might be observed), it can't so easily explain our intuition that it would be wrong of them to set light to the cat in the privacy of their own garage. Admittedly, there is some wiggle room here if one wanted to defend the proposal. For animals, having minds of their own, are apt to render public a suffering that was intended to remain private. The burning cat might escape from the garage, for example, or might emit such ear-piercing screams that the neighbors feel called upon to investigate. But we can demonstrate the inadequacy of this whole approach through an example where such factors are decisively controlled for. This is the example of Astrid the astronaut.

You are to imagine that Astrid is an extremely rich woman who has become tired of life on Earth, and who purchases a space rocket for herself so that she can escape that life permanently. She blasts off on a trajectory that will eventually take her out of the solar system, and she doesn't even carry with her a radio or other means of communication. We can therefore know that she will never again have any contact with another human being. Now suppose that Astrid has taken with her a cat for company, but that at a certain point in the journey, out of boredom, she starts to use the cat for a dart-board, or does something else that would cause the cat unspeakable pain. Don't we think that what Astrid does

is very wrong? But of course the ground of its wrongness can't be the danger that animal-lovers will discover what she has done and be upset. For we know from the description of the case that there is no such danger.

4.2. Judging Acts by Character

Another approach, which I shall spend most of the remainder of this essay developing and defending, would be to claim that the action of torturing a cat is wrong because of what it shows about the moral character of the actor, not because it infringes any rights or is likely to cause distress to other people. Specifically, what the teenagers do in the street and what Astrid does on her space-rocket show them to be *cruel*. And this would be our ground for saying that the actions themselves are wrong. In order for this account to work, however, it needs to be shown more generally that we sometimes judge actions by the qualities of moral character that they evince, irrespective of any morally significant harm that they cause, or of any rights that they infringe. I shall argue as much here, before briefly providing a contractualist rationale in Section 5.

Return to the example of Astrid the astronaut. But now suppose that, in addition to a cat, she has taken with her another person. In one version of the story, this might be her beloved grandfather. In another version of the story (to avoid contaminating our intuitions with beliefs about family duties) it might be an employee whom she hires to work for her as a lifetime servant. Now at a certain point in the journey this other person dies. Astrid's response is to cut up the corpse into small pieces, thereafter storing them in the refrigerator and feeding them one by one to the cat.

Surely what Astrid does is wrong. But why? It causes no direct harm of a morally relevant sort. (Her companion, after all, is dead, and can't know or be upset.) And nor can any harm be caused indirectly to others. For in the nature of the case, no one else can ever know and be offended. Nor are any rights infringed. For even if one thinks that the dead have rights (which is doubtful), Astrid might know that her companion was an atheist who took not the slightest interest in ceremonies for the dead. Indeed, he might once have said to her, "Once I am dead I don't care what happens to my corpse; you can do what you like with it," thus waiving any rights that he might have in the matter. But still what Astrid does is very wrong.

Why is what Astrid does wrong? Surely this is because of what it shows about *her*. Just as her treatment of her cat shows her to be cruel, so her treatment of her dead companion displays a kind of disrespectful, inhuman, attitude towards humanity in general, and her companion in particular. (Note that practices for honoring the dead, and for treating corpses with respect, are a human universal. They are common to all cultures across all times.) And in each case we judge the action to be wrong because of the flaw that it evinces (both manifesting and further encouraging and developing) in her moral character.

Consider a different sort of example. Suppose that Lazy Jane is a doctor who is attending a conference of other medical professionals at a large hotel. She is relaxing in the bar during the evening, sitting alone with her drink in a cubicle. The bar is so arranged that there are many separate cubicles surrounding it, from each of which the bar itself is plainly visible, but the insides of which are invisible to each other. Jane is idly watching someone walk alone towards the bar when he collapses to the floor with all the signs of having undergone a serious heart-attack. Jane feels no impulse to assist him, and continues calmly sipping her martini.

Plainly what Jane does (or in this case, doesn't do) is wrong. But why? For we can suppose that no harm is caused. Since the man collapses in plain view of dozens of medical personnel, expert help is swift in arriving; and she had every reason to believe that this would be so in the circumstances. And no rights are infringed. For even if there is

such a thing as a general right to medical assistance when sick (which is doubtful), the man had no claim on *her* help in particular. If he had still been able to speak, he could have said, and (perhaps) said truly, "Someone should help me." But he certainly wouldn't have been correct if he had said, "Jane, in particular, should help me." Since our belief in the wrongness of Jane's inactivity survives these points, the explanation must be the one that we offered in connection with Astrid above: it is wrong because of what it reveals about *her*. Specifically, it shows her to be callous and indifferent to the suffering of other people; or at least it shows that she lacks the sort of spontaneous, emotional, non-calculative, concern for others that we think a good person should have.

My suggestion, then, is that our duties towards animals are indirect in the following way. They derive from the good or bad qualities of moral character that the actions in question would display and encourage; where those qualities *are* good or bad in virtue of the role that they play in the agent's interactions with other human beings. On this account, the most basic kind of wrong-doing towards animals is *cruelty*. A cruel action is wrong because it evinces a cruel character. But what makes a cruel character bad is that it is likely to express itself in cruelty towards *people*, which would involve direct violations of the rights of those who are caused to suffer.[6] Our intuition that the teenagers and Astrid all act wrongly is thereby explained, but explained in a way that is consistent with the claim that animals lack moral standing.

5. CONTRACTUALISM, VIRTUE ETHICS, AND ANIMALS

How, in general, do qualities of character acquire their significance within a contractualist moral framework? This question needs to be answered before the position sketched above can be considered acceptable. And we need to investigate, too, in what ways cruelty to animals and cruelty to humans are linked to one another.

5.1. Contractualism and Character

Contracting rational agents should know in advance that human beings aren't calculating machines. We have limited time, limited memory, limited attention, and limited intellectual powers. In consequence, in everyday life we frequently have to rely on a suite of "quick and dirty" heuristics for decision making, rather than reasoning our way slowly and laboriously to the optimal solution (Gigerenzer et al., 1999). Contracting rational agents should realize, too, the vital role that motivational states and emotional reactions play in human decision making (Damasio, 1994). Hence they should do far more than agree on a framework of rules to govern their behavior. They should also agree to foster certain long-term dispositions of motivation and emotion that will make right action much more likely (especially when action is spontaneous, or undertaken under severe time constraints). That is to say: contracting agents should agree on a duty to foster certain qualities of character, or *virtues*.

For example, contracting agents should agree on a duty to develop the virtue of *beneficence*. This is because they should foresee that more than merely rules of justice (which are for the most part negative in form: "don't steal, don't kidnap, don't kill, etc.") are necessary for human beings to flourish. People also need to develop positive attachments to the welfare of others, fostering a disposition and willingness to help others when they can do so at no important cost to themselves. For there are many ways in which people will inevitably, at some point in their lives, need the assistance of others if they are to succeed with their plans and projects, ranging from needing the kindness of a neighbor to jump-start one's car on a frosty morning, to needing someone on the river bank to throw one a life-buoy or a rope when one is drowning.[7]

Rational contractors should also agree that people's actions can be judged (that is, praised or blamed) for the qualities of character they evince, independently of the harm caused, and independently of violations of right. This is because people *should possess*, or should develop, the required good qualities. Although these good qualities *are* good, in general, because of their effects on the welfare and rights of other people, their display on a given occasion can be independent of such effects. Hence we can, and should, evaluate the action in light of the qualities of character that it displays, independently of other considerations.

5.2. Cruelty to Animals and Cruelty to Humans

If the account given above of the reasons why it is wrong for the teenagers to set light to a cat is to be successful, then cruelty to animals must be psychologically and behaviorally linked to cruelty to humans. To a first approximation, it must be the case that there is a single virtue of kindness, and a single vice of cruelty, that can be displayed towards either group. How plausible is this?

Certainly it would appear that attitudes towards the sufferings of animals and of humans are quite deeply linked in Western culture. For many of us have pets whom we treat as honorary family members, towards whom we feel filial obligations. And our practices of child-rearing make central use of animal subjects in moral education. Indeed, a child's first introduction to moral principles will frequently involve ones that are focused upon animals. A parent says, "Don't be cruel—you mustn't pull the whiskers out of the cat," "You must make sure that your pet gerbil has plenty of water," and so on and so forth. It would not be surprising, then, if attitudes towards the sufferings and welfare of animals and humans should thereafter be pretty tightly linked. This will warrant us in saying that the teenagers who are setting light to a cat are doing something wrong, not because the cat has moral standing, but because they are evincing attitudes that are likely to manifest themselves in their dealings with human beings (who do have moral standing, of course).

It seems possible, however, that the linkages that exist between attitudes to animal and to human suffering depend upon local cultural factors. For it seems implausible that these linkages should reflect properties of a universal human nature. In cultures where pets aren't kept, where people's interactions with animals are entirely pragmatic (e.g., through farming), and where animals aren't used as exemplars in moral education, it is possible that these attitudes are pretty cleanly separable. In which case, someone in such a culture who hangs a dog in a noose, strangling it slowly to death (perhaps because this is believed to make the meat taste better), won't be displaying cruelty, although someone in our culture who behaved likewise would be.

It may therefore be that our Western moral attitudes towards animals form part of the *conventional* content of our morality. If there is nothing in our human nature that links cruelty to animals with cruelty to humans, then contracting rational agents would have no reason to insist upon a rule forbidding cruelty to animals, or a rule mandating a virtue of kindness that extends to animals. But contracting agents have to settle upon some or other way of bringing up their children, and cultural practices (such as pet-keeping) may be adopted for reasons having nothing to do with the moral contract itself, but which nevertheless have an impact upon morals. Given such facts, we can become obliged not to be cruel to animals.

5.3. Acting for the Sake of the Animal

Notice that in our culture, someone with the right sort of kindly character who acts to prevent suffering to an animal will do so *for the sake of the animal*. For this is what having the right sort of sympathetic attitude consists in. It involves a spontaneous upwelling of sympathy at the sight or sound of suffering. Likewise it is something about the animal itself (its pain) that forms the immediate object of the emotion, and of the subsequent response. Certainly someone acting to ease the suffering of an animal won't be doing it to try to make himself into a better person! Nevertheless, the reason why this attitude is a virtue at all can be because of the way in which

it is likely to manifest itself in the person's dealings with other human beings.

We can therefore *explain away* the common-sense intuition that when we are morally required to act to prevent the suffering of an animal, we are required to do so *for the sake of the animal*, where this is understood to mean that the animal itself has moral standing. As a theoretical claim about what grounds our duties towards animals this is false, since animals lack standing. But as a psychological claim about the state of mind and motivations of the actor, who has acquired the right sort of kindly attitude, it is true. While agents should act as they do for the animal's sake (with the animal's interests in mind), the reason why they are required to do so doesn't advert to facts about the animal (which would require animals to have standing), but rather to wider effects on human beings.

6. CONCLUSION

I have argued in this essay that moral standing is possessed by all and only human beings (together with other rational agents, if there are any), who thus make direct moral claims upon us. Animals, in contrast, lack standing and make no direct claims upon us. Nevertheless, I have shown how there can be justified moral criticism for things that we do, or don't do, to an animal. This derives from the good or bad qualities of character that our actions evince. But these criticisms may have a conventional and culturally local quality, deriving from contingent facts about contemporary Western cultures. They aren't criticisms that are warranted by rules that no rational agents could reasonably reject (whatever their culture) when guided by facts about human nature.

NOTES

1. By way of analogy, think of the rule requiring us (in the United States) to drive on the right. Obviously there should be a rule requiring people to drive on one side of the road or the other, or chaos will ensue. But it doesn't much matter which side is chosen.

2. It is an interesting question what this and related arguments show about the moral status of abortion. I believe (although I shall not argue here) that they would show early (e.g., first trimester) abortions to be permissible, while ruling out most later forms of abortion.

3. For other arguments for the same conclusion, see Carruthers (1992), chapter 5.

4. This doesn't mean that all humans are accorded the same rights, however. While normal human adults might be given a right to autonomy, for example, it will make little sense to accord such a right to a human who isn't an autonomous agent.

5. A third problem is that moral standing would only be accorded, in any case, to those animals that are often kept as pets, such as dogs and cats. Animal species to whose members it is difficult to become emotionally attached would be left beyond the pale.

6. The UK's Royal Society for the Prevention of Cruelty to Animals claims on its website to have amassed voluminous evidence that people who are cruel to animals are also likely to engage in cruelty that involves human beings, and that the Society's prosecutions for cruelty to animals are almost always built upon this premise. The ASPCA in the United States makes similar claims on its "information for professionals" website, citing a number of empirical studies.

7. Notice that this does *not* mean that actions undertaken out of generosity are really self-interested ones. (On the contrary, generous people are people who feel an impulse to help another simply because they can see that the other person needs it.) It only means that self-interest enters into the explanation of why generosity is a virtue. This is because self-interested rational agents attempting to agree on a framework of rules that no one could reasonably reject would agree on a duty to become a generous sort of person.

REFERENCES

Carruthers, P. (1992). *The Animals Issue*. Cambridge University Press.

Damasio, A. (1994). *Descartes' Error*. Papermac.

Gigerenzer, G., Todd, P., and the ABC Research Group. (1999). *Simple Heuristics That Make Us Smart*. Oxford University Press.

Hrdy, S. (1999). *Mother Nature*. Pantheon Press.

Pinker, S. (2002). *The Blank Slate*. Viking Press.

Rawls, J. (1972). *A Theory of Justice*. Oxford University Press.

Regan, T. (1984). *The Case for Animal Rights*. Routledge.

Scanlon, T. (1982). Contractualism and Utilitarianism. In A. Sen and B. Williams (eds.), *Utilitarianism and Beyond*, Cambridge University Press.

Scanlon, T. (1998). *What We Owe to Each Other*. Harvard University Press.

Singer, P. (1979). *Practical Ethics*. Cambridge University Press.

Peter Carruthers: Against the Moral Standing of Animals

1. How plausible do you find the contractualist framework that Carruthers utilizes in his essay?

2. Carruthers thinks that both Rawls's and Scanlon's versions of contractarianism would yield identical verdicts regarding the moral standing of animals. Do you agree? If so, explain why. If not, explain why not.

3. Carruthers thinks that actions that cause no harm and violate no rights can still be immoral. Why does he think this? Do you find that claim plausible? Why or why not?

4. Suppose that an action displays a moral vice. Carruthers thinks that is not just evidence that the action is wrong; it is what *makes* the action wrong. Why does he think this? Are his reasons compelling? Why or why not?

5. Do you think that animals have moral standing? If so, what accounts for their having such standing? If not, why not?

CHAPTER 14

The Environment

JUST THE FACTS

There are plenty of reasons to worry about the current and future state of the environment. We can't consider them all in detail, so we'll focus on what many regard as the two most serious environmental problems facing humanity: **climate change** and **deforestation**.

"Climate change" refers to the change in weather patterns across the globe over an extended period of time (e.g., thousands of years). Climate change certainly includes **global warming** (the Earth's rising average atmospheric temperatures), but it also includes the meteorological consequences of global warming, namely, an increase in the frequency and severity of precipitation (leading to increased flooding), more frequent drought, and more frequent heat waves. These changes are expected to bring about a number of unwelcome consequences. For example, rising global temperatures are causing the melting of large parts of the polar ice caps. This has led to a rise in global sea levels, which, if left unchecked, will likely cause widespread coastal flooding, displacing millions from their homes. So far, sea levels have risen about eight inches since statistics were first kept in 1880. They're expected to rise between one and four feet by the end of this century.[1] More frequent droughts and flooding will cause a greater proportion of crops to fail, leading to widespread food shortages and a significant increase in world hunger. The social consequences are harder to predict, but history has shown that food shortages and land disputes often lead to very serious social harms.

Most climate scientists agree that the main cause of the current global warming trend is human expansion of the **greenhouse effect**—warming that results when greenhouse gases (e.g., carbon dioxide, methane, water vapor, nitrous oxide, and ozone) in the atmosphere trap heat radiating from the Earth's surface toward outer space. Ordinarily, the greenhouse effect is beneficial. Without it, Earth's average temperature would be near 0°F, instead of its current average (58.4°F). The trouble is that having too much greenhouse gas in the atmosphere leads to the problems described earlier.

As of 2017, carbon dioxide (CO_2) levels in the atmosphere are higher than they've been at any time in the past 400,000 years. During past ice ages, CO_2 levels were around 200 parts per million (ppm). During the warmer interglacial periods, they hovered around 280 ppm. In 2013, however, CO_2 levels surpassed 400 ppm for the first time in recorded history.[2]

The two greatest contributors to these unprecedented CO_2 levels are the burning of fossil fuels for manufacturing, meat production, and other industrial purposes, and changes in land use, especially deforestation (which we'll discuss shortly). When industrial plants burn coal, oil, and other fossil fuels, they release enormous amounts of carbon into the atmosphere, exacerbating the greenhouse effect. The animals on factory farms produce a huge amount of waste that generates an amount of greenhouse gas that exceeds that of the global transportation

---

1. http://nca2014.globalchange.gov/report/our-changing-climate/sea-level-rise

2. https://climate.nasa.gov/climate_resources/24/

industry.[3] China, still a developing country with the largest population on Earth (about 19 percent of the world population), is far and away the biggest contributor of greenhouse gases—releasing 23 percent of all greenhouse gases in the world. The United States is next, dwarfing the contribution of most countries, with about 15 percent—though the United States is only 4 percent of the world's population. Next are India, Russia, Brazil, and Japan, each contributing somewhere between 4 percent and 5 percent. All other countries contribute 2 percent or less.[4]

One of the biggest obstacles to slowing the progress of global warming has been convincing people that it is actually occurring and that humans are the primary cause. For instance, from 2011 to June 2017, US President Donald Trump tweeted 115 different times expressing his doubts about **anthropogenic** climate change (i.e., climate change that is caused by human beings).[5] That skepticism seems to be shared by a significant number of Americans, but not a majority. According to a 2017 Gallup poll, 68 percent of US citizens believe that climate change is caused by human activities; 32 percent do not.[6]

The other major environmental challenge we face is deforestation—the large-scale destruction of forests. Today, forests cover 31 percent of the land area on our planet, but each year an area roughly the size of Greece is destroyed—about forty-eight football fields every minute. Over the last century, about half of the Earth's forest cover was lost.[7] Forests produce vital

oxygen and provide homes for people, plants, and wildlife—somewhere between 70 percent and 90 percent of the world's biodiversity. Forests also play a crucial role in mitigating climate change because they act as a **carbon sink**, soaking up enormous amounts of carbon dioxide that would otherwise float free in the atmosphere. If deforestation continues at its current rate, the world's rainforests will vanish within one hundred years, thereby eliminating the majority of plant and animal species on Earth.[8]

When most people think of the causes of deforestation, they usually think of commercial logging—cutting down trees for sale as timber or pulp. While logging accounts for a significant amount of deforestation across the globe, its impact is dwarfed by deforestation due to agriculture (e.g., planting crops, grazing cattle). Poor farmers, especially in South America, often chop down small areas (usually just a few acres) and burn the tree trunks—a process called **slash and burn agriculture**. They use this land just to get by, growing food to support themselves and their families. Industrial agriculture occurs on a much larger scale, sometimes deforesting several square miles at a time. These larger areas of land are cleared for beef cattle to graze upon. The cattle are then slaughtered and much of the meat is sold to countries where demand is especially high (e.g., the United States, Canada). Cattle ranching is the number-one cause of deforestation in South America, accounting for 80 percent of it on the continent. Thus, environmentalists have long argued that one of the best ways that individuals can help slow deforestation and climate change is by avoiding meat, adopting a plant-based diet, and encouraging others to do so as well.

ARGUMENT ANALYSIS

Though environmental ethics covers a huge range of issues, perhaps the most fundamental one concerns moral standing. The issue is which parts of the environment have independent moral

3. https://www.ecowatch.com/how-factory-farming-contributes-to-global-warming-1881690535.html

4. http://www.ucsusa.org/global_warming/science_and_impacts/science/each-countrys-share-of-co2.html#.WclDS9Frw2w

5. https://www.vox.com/policy-and-politics/2017/6/1/15726472/trump-tweets-global-warming-paris-climate-agreement

6. http://www.gallup.com/poll/206030/global-warming-concern-three-decade-high.aspx

7. https://www.worldwildlife.org/threats/deforestation

8. https://www.conserve-energy-future.com/various-deforestation-facts.php

importance—importance in their own right, apart from any benefits that treating them well might bring about. Relying on a distinction we've seen in other discussions, the question, really, is which elements of the environment are **intrinsically valuable**—good and important in and of themselves—and which elements are merely **instrumentally valuable**—good because of the other good things they make possible. You are intrinsically valuable. A hammer or screwdriver, by contrast, can be only instrumentally valuable. Their goodness resides in their usefulness—if they were defective, for instance, and only frustrated our efforts to build or repair things, then they wouldn't be good at all. But people are valuable regardless of how useful they are.

The question we need to address is which nonhuman elements of the environment are intrinsically valuable. We can put the question in terms of membership in the moral community: members of the moral community are those possessed of independent moral importance, those who are valuable in and of themselves, regardless of how useful they are to others. Since we discussed nonhuman animals in Chapter 13, where various positions about their moral standing are assessed, our question here is actually a bit narrower: are there any elements of the nonanimal environment that are members of the moral community?

The answer standardly given by Western philosophers is no. On this view, even the most magnificent elements of the natural environment—the Grand Canyon, say, or the massive stands of sequoias and redwoods in northern California—are valuable only because of the enjoyment they provide us, or the resources (minerals, wood) that we can utilize by exploiting them. Kantians defend this view by means of

The Kantian Argument about Moral Standing

1. You are a member of the moral community if, and only if, you are rational and autonomous.
2. Only humans are rational and autonomous.

Therefore,

3. Only humans are members of the moral community; only humans are morally important in their own right.

Kant, as you may recall from Chapter 6, had very high standards for being rational and autonomous. You had to be able to freely choose a plan of life, to contemplate and weigh the value of different alternatives, to imagine what the world would be like were everyone to act on your principles, and to have your behavior conform to your decisions. Given these rigorous standards for rationality and autonomy, premise 2 is true. But premise 1 is problematic—it forces us to say that human infants, very young children, the severely mentally impaired, and all nonhuman animals have no value in their own right. They lack independent moral importance. That is very difficult to accept.

Social contract theorists have a similarly restrictive view of who is and isn't a member of the moral community. They defend their view by means of

The Contractarian Argument about Moral Standing

1. You are a member of the moral community if, and only if, you are able to enter into reciprocal agreements that promise to benefit those who have benefitted you, and to harm those who have harmed you.
2. Only humans are able to enter into such reciprocal agreements.

Therefore,

3. Only humans are members of the moral community.

As indicated in Chapter 7, there is a lot to like about the social contract theory. Still, its tough entry standards for membership in the moral community exclude the most vulnerable among us, just as Kantian views do.

Utilitarians have a broader conception of membership in the moral community. They allow that most nonhuman animals are valuable in their own right. They defend this by means of

The Utilitarian Argument about Moral Standing

1. A being is a member of the moral community if, and only if, it can experience pleasure or pain.
2. Almost every human being and most nonhuman animals can experience pleasure or pain.
3. Nothing else can experience pleasure or pain.

Therefore,

4. Almost every human being and most nonhuman animals are members of the moral community; nothing else is.

Utilitarians let many more beings into the moral community than Kantians and contractarians do. Unlike those positions, utilitarianism allows infants, young children, the severely mentally impaired, and most nonhuman animals to be members. But like those views, utilitarianism bars entry to all other elements of the environment. Majestic mountain ranges, diverse ecosystems, remarkable coral reefs—none of these are valuable in themselves. Their value lies solely in what they can do for us, and for other animals. Nature can nourish us, and we can take pleasure in its contemplation. But in and of itself, the natural environment—animals (including us) aside—has no value.

Some environmentalists accept these conclusions but argue that we must nevertheless do much more than we currently do in order to protect the natural environment. Their reasoning is straightforward. Although nonanimal elements of the natural environment have no intrinsic value, it is vital that we preserve them against exploitation, because doing so is essential to securing our long-term interests. When we treat the environment as if we were its rulers rather than its stewards, we are harming ourselves and future generations. In a word, we are acting shortsightedly.

This is a strategic argument for greater environmental protections, and it is often a compelling one. A great many of our current practices—especially, but not exclusively, in the United States—are undertaken with only short-term profits in mind. Of course, compelling arguments often fall on deaf ears, and the ignorance or self-interest of individuals, corporations, and politicians often conspires to stand in the way of sensible policies that are much more beneficial in the long run. Still, some environmentalists are dissatisfied with arguments that appeal only to the interests of humans and other animals. These environmentalists argue that other elements of nature are intrinsically valuable.

But which ones? Is a pebble or a blade of grass independently morally important? Or (for instance) only mountain ranges, or species, or entire ecosystems? Kantians and contractarians and utilitarians have sometimes been accused of chauvinism—of assigning intrinsic value on the basis of traits that we humans have, but that the rest of nature doesn't. Still, their criteria for membership in the moral community do seem to pick out morally important features, even if, as their critics argue, those features are not *all*-important. A stand of redwoods isn't rational, it can't enter agreements, and it doesn't feel pleasure or pain. So what feature (if any) qualifies it for independent moral importance?

One idea, championed by philosopher Paul Taylor, is that *being alive* is the crucial feature. His central thought can be cast in terms of

The Biocentrism Argument

1. Something has independent moral importance if, and only if, it is alive.
2. Plants and animals are alive.

Therefore,

3. Plants and animals have independent moral importance.

Biocentrism is the view that all living things are important in their own right, and that all living things are equally intrinsically valuable. A human is just as alive as a tree—as a result, in and of themselves, humans and trees are equally valuable. Of course we may be allowed to give priority to humans over trees in many cases, just as we are allowed to take actions that benefit some humans at the expense of others. But the trees will sometimes win out, too—in some cases, we must protect them even at the expense of the interests of humans who would wish to use or destroy them.

There is no arguing with premise 2; premise 1 is where the action is. Why is it that being alive, no matter the quality of one's experiences or abilities, is so important? It's difficult to answer that question, but then again, it is difficult to answer it for *any* candidate feature that is supposed to be the ultimate basis for moral importance. Why is *suffering* morally important? Why is *rationality* morally important? It's very hard to know how to answer these questions.

The typical line of argument on behalf of premise 1 says that being alive is the central basis for intrinsic value because so long as a being is alive, things can go better or worse for it, and that is a nonarbitrary basis for assigning it importance. Biocentrists also claim that any *other* basis is arbitrary. Rationality or reciprocity or suffering very conveniently gives *us* intrinsic importance. The biocentrist argues there is no good basis for restricting the moral community in these ways.

But we might wonder whether being able to be better or worse off is really the key to moral importance. It's true that a sapling can fare well or poorly—just fail to give it water and see. But it's also true that things can go well or poorly with my ten-year-old Toyota. Just fail to give it oil and watch it deteriorate. Paint the exterior of a windowsill and you will make it better off by protecting it against the elements. But no one thinks that Toyotas or windows are intrinsically valuable. So it's not clear why the ability to improve or worsen is so morally important.

We might also question the biocentrist's commitment to the equal intrinsic importance of all living things. Suppose that being alive is, in itself, morally important. But why think that this feature is the *only* thing that confers intrinsic value? Why isn't rationality or the capacity to suffer also important in its own right? Think of a region where mosquitoes are transmitting malaria. About 655,000 people die each year from this disease. Suppose you are located in such an area, and you see a mosquito land on a child's arm. For all you know, its bite may result in the child's death. It seems obvious that killing the mosquito is morally better than letting it alone. Part of the reason it's obvious is because the child possesses so many more valuable traits than the mosquito. The mosquito is alive. But the mosquito can't reflect on its life, can't make plans for the future, can't deliberate about what's right and wrong, can't forge and maintain loving relations, and can't forsake its own interests in the name of a higher cause. These abilities do seem to be valuable in their own right. If they are, then some living things are, in themselves, more important than others, because some beings have many more of these abilities than other living things.

The Biocentric Argument is expansive in one way and restrictive in another. Compared to the traditional moral theories, it broadens the moral community significantly by providing membership for all animals and plants. But some environmentalists want more. They believe that some things that are not themselves living beings (e.g., species, ecosystems, mountain ranges, or the atmosphere) are intrinsically valuable. These environmentalists argue, for instance, that strip-mining a mountaintop can be immoral—not (just) because of the pollutants that so often end up in local riverbeds and harm local communities, and not (just) because humans will no longer be able to take pleasure in viewing the landscape or in hiking the mountain trails. Rather, there is something valuable about the mountain itself, something that extends beyond the use to which it can be put for our benefit. The mountain, though, is not alive. Nor is the atmosphere. Nor are species or ecosystems themselves (though of course these last two include many living things). On this view, then, biocentrism is too narrow—it excludes certain elements of nature that possess moral importance in their own right, even though these elements are not alive.

The most common way to defend this idea is by invoking the importance of the natural. The thought is that there is something important, in itself, about being natural—so important, in fact, that preservation of the natural environment is sometimes more important than the benefits to be gained by altering it.

One difficulty we face when assessing this proposal is that the term *natural* has so many different meanings and can be applied to so many different things. We consider most of the morally relevant meanings in Chapter 22, so here we can be brief. In the context of environmentalism, what is **natural** is usually contrasted with what is **artificial**: artificial things are those that have been created or modified by human activity; natural things are not.

No one argues that everything that is natural is good in itself. Salmonella bacteria (which cause infections that lead to over 200,000 human deaths worldwide each year) are natural. It's hard to think of why an individual Salmonella bacterium should be considered intrinsically valuable. The same holds for a small pebble on a distant, uninhabited planet, or a dried-out splinter of wood in a remote desert. So being natural is not a sufficient condition of being intrinsically valuable. Still, many environmentalists believe that some nonliving elements of the natural environment are intrinsically valuable, just because they are natural, rather than artificial.

It's not easy to identify a principle that sorts the natural things that are thought to be intrinsically valuable (mountain ranges, ecosystems, species) from natural things that lack such value (stray pebbles, individual bacteria). You might think that things in the former category are valuable because we value them, whereas things in the latter category lack value because we are indifferent to their existence. But this is not the story these environmentalists want to tell. Instead, they believe that parts of nature have value in themselves. If we appreciate them, that's because we are recognizing a value that they have independently of the value we place on them.

If a mountain range can't think or feel, and isn't alive, then why think that it possesses any value in itself? A famous reply was given by philosopher Richard Routley, who invited his readers to reflect on what we think of the options available to the last person on Earth.[9] Suppose that person knows that he's the end of the line; once he dies, there's nothing left of humanity. Now suppose he has a choice. He can just die peacefully, or he can set out beforehand to do as much environmental damage as he can—exterminating whole species, polluting entire ecosystems, dynamiting mountain ranges, destroying the atmosphere. If we think (and we do, don't we?) that he'd be very wrong to take the second path, then this seems to show that we are committed to thinking of these elements of the natural environment as important in their own right. By hypothesis, no human will be around to value such things. If their importance depended on our valuing them, then in the absence of humans, they'd have no value. But if they were valueless, then it wouldn't be wrong to destroy them. We can formulate this line of thinking in

The Last Person Argument

1. If the natural environment lacked intrinsic value, then it would be morally OK for the last person on earth to destroy it.
2. That wouldn't be morally OK.

Therefore,

3. The natural environment possesses intrinsic value.

A parallel line of thought, inspired by the great English philosopher G. E. Moore, yields the same conclusion. Imagine two worlds with no humans or animals in them. One world is lush and beautiful—picture your scene of paradise and insert it here. The second world is completely barren—no life, permanently baked by a

---

9. This first appeared in Richard Routley, "Is There a Need for a New, an Environmental, Ethic?" *Proceedings of the XVth World Congress of Philosophy* 1 (1973): 205–210.

fiery sun, with a flat, featureless surface. Is one world more valuable than another? To test your answer, imagine that you were forced by someone to push a button that would destroy just one of these two worlds. I'd preserve the first world. (Wouldn't you?) I think it's more valuable than the second. But the value isn't instrumental—after all, nothing in the first world is useful to anyone. So the value is intrinsic.

Even if you find these two arguments persuasive, however, two more questions arise. First: *why* do only some elements of the natural environment, but not others, possess intrinsic value? And, second: how can we balance the value of the natural environment against human interests? We need to alter the natural environment in order to remain alive—we need food, water, and shelter. Meeting those needs requires us to change the natural environment. It follows that unless we are all morally required to die immediately, so as to no longer have any impact on the natural environment, we are morally permitted to modify the natural environment to some extent. But in what ways, and how much?

Suppose that you are convinced that some elements of the natural environment require protection, either for instrumental reasons (e.g., to ensure that we have enough food to eat) or because you assign some intrinsic value to nature. Still, the scope of our moral duties is unclear. Protecting the natural environment is a communal enterprise—the actions of a single individual don't seem to make much difference. Indeed, there seems little that you, as an individual, can do to prevent climate change, for instance. So even if we can settle the issues of the value of nature, we still may be puzzled about what we are morally required to do about it.

Some philosophers argue that we are obligated to do very little—perhaps nothing at all. They support their view by means of

The No Difference Argument

1. You are morally required to change your behavior or refrain from doing something only if that would improve the situation.

2. Changing or refraining from your ordinary consumer practices would not improve the environmental situation.

Therefore,

3. You are not morally required to change or refrain from your ordinary consumer practices in order to improve the environmental situation.

The idea behind premise 1 is that if your actions make no difference to a bad outcome, then you are not morally required to refrain from them. That sounds pretty sensible. If something bad is going to happen no matter what you do, and if you aren't going to make a bad situation even worse, then you are free to do what you want. In general, we are morally allowed to do as we please, at least so long as we are not worsening things. Premise 1 makes perfect sense of these thoughts.

Here are two cases designed to put pressure on this principle. See what you think. First, imagine someone with a fascination for Nazi artifacts. He discovers a lampshade for sale, one that was made from the flesh of concentration camp victims. He wants to buy the lampshade and keep it in a private viewing area in his home. Purchasing it is not going to support Nazi policies. So it doesn't look like the purchase of this piece is going to lead to anyone being worse off. If there is nevertheless something wrong with what this person is doing, then this casts doubt on premise 1.

The second case is one in which I cast a vote for a political candidate who runs on a platform that is popular with many but that is deeply immoral. Suppose that the other candidate is a reasonable, experienced person who stands for policies that are morally good. Still, the first politician wins by a large margin. Since he would have won easily even without my vote, it seems that my vote did not change the outcome. And if it didn't change the outcome, then it didn't make things worse. Still, you might think that my voting as I did was immoral. If so, you cannot accept premise 1.

Suppose, though, that neither of these examples fazed you, and you are committed to premise

1. Still, you might wonder about whether premise 2 is true. On the one hand, your environmental impact does seem negligible, a drop in the bucket. Suppose you gave up your car and biked everywhere, drastically reduced your energy consumption at home, and purchased only locally grown food. Now try to think of all of the harms that will ensue over the next decades as a result of climate change. Changing your habits will make no difference to the existence or intensity of these harms. Of course, it's a different matter entirely if you are the CEO of a large utility company or major corporation and have the power to effect change on a large scale. But for the rest of us individuals, a change in our daily practices doesn't seem to make any difference at all.

And yet the practices of millions of individuals *do* add up to something quite serious, just as the votes of millions of individuals, when taken together, signify something very important. If there is a major harm being done collectively, then the harm has to come from somewhere. One suggestion is that it comes from each of us; our individual contributions, even if they are very small, are still something. On this view, each of us *is* harming the environment when we drive, when we purchase foods transported from a different continent, when we throw things in the trash. Each harm is minuscule. But very tiny harms can add up to very large ones. If it's true that our ordinary habits are making the environment (perhaps imperceptibly) worse off, then premise 2 is mistaken.

CONCLUSION

As we have seen from discussions of abortion and animals, it is not easy to locate the precise basis of membership in the moral community. Beings are valuable in their own right if, only if, and because _____. Filling in that blank is a challenge, to put it mildly.

Kantians, contractarians, and utilitarians have given it a shot. Some environmentalists embrace one or the other of these theories. In doing so, they thereby deny the intrinsic value of the natural environment, and argue that we must extend our protection of it on instrumental grounds: such protection is useful to us, or perhaps to other animals or to future generations.

Other environmentalists, though, want to defend the claim that at least some nonhuman and nonanimal elements of nature are important in their own right. Biocentrism is one such effort. If true, it would extend independent moral importance to all living things, no matter how useful (or harmful) to us they happen to be. Biocentrism doesn't go far enough for some, however, as it fails to explain why (for instance) mountain ranges are important in themselves. The challenge for such views is to explain why some nonliving elements of the natural environment are intrinsically valuable, while others are not.

There is also the matter of the scope of our moral duties to protect the natural environment. Our individual actions seem to make either no difference at all, or, at most, only the tiniest difference to whether environmental harms occur. Given this, are we free to do as we please? Or is there some basis for arguing that we are duty-bound to change our individual practices?

ESSENTIAL CONCEPTS

Anthropogenic: originated by human beings.
Artificial: created or modified by human activity.
Biocentric: focused on all living things and their interests and denying the greater intrinsic importance of human beings vis-à-vis other life forms.
Carbon sink: a large system (e.g., an ocean, a forest) that absorbs and stores carbon dioxide from the atmosphere.
Climate change: a change in weather patterns that lasts for a long time (e.g., thousands or millions of years).
Deforestation: the destruction of a forest to make land available for other uses (e.g., agriculture).
Global warming: a rise in average atmospheric temperatures across the world.
Greenhouse effect: warming that results when greenhouse gases in the atmosphere (e.g., carbon dioxide, methane) trap heat radiating from the Earth's surface toward outer space.

STAT SHOT

1. Atmospheric CO_2 levels are higher than they've been in the last 400,000 years. They've risen dramatically since the Industrial Revolution (Figure 14.1).

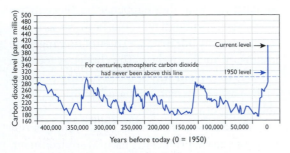

Figure 14.1.

Source: https://climate.nasa.gov/climate_resources/24/

2. Average global temperature has been trending upward since at least 1870 (Figure 14.2).

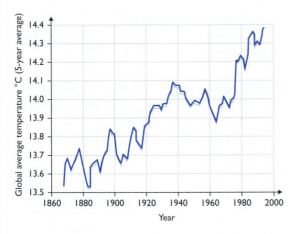

Figure 14.2.

Source: http://www.bbc.co.uk/schools/gcsebitesize/science/aqa_pre_2011/rocks/fuelsrev6.shtml

3. China emits more CO_2 than the next two biggest contributors combined. The United States still contributes far more

CO_2 per capita (since the US population is a quarter of China's) (Figure 14.3).

Rank	Country	Share of Global CO_2 Emissions
1	China	23.43%
2	United States	14.69%
3	India	5.70%
4	Russian Federation	4.87%
5	Brazil	4.17%
6	Japan	3.61%
7	Indonesia	2.31%
8	Germany	2.23%
9	Korea	1.75%
10	Canada	1.57%
11	Iran	1.57%

Figure 14.3.

Source: http://www.worldatlas.com/articles/biggestcontributors-to-global-warming-in-the-world.html

4. Sixty-eight percent of US citizens believe that climate change is caused by human activities; 32 percent do not (Figure 14.4).

	2001–2014 (average)	2015	2016	2017
Say most scientists believe global warming is occurring	60%	62%	65%	71%
Believe global warming is caused by human activities	57%	55%	65%	68%
Believe effects of global warming have already begun	54%	55%	59%	62%
Worry a great deal about global warming	32%	32%	37%	45%
Think global warming will pose a serious threat in their lifetime	35%	37%	41%	42%

Figure 14.4. Summary of Americans' views on global warming.

Source: http://www.gallup.com/poll/206030/global-warming-concern-three-decade-high.aspx

Instrumentally valuable: something good because of the other good things it makes possible.

Intrinsically valuable: something good and important in and of itself.

Natural: neither created nor altered by humans.

Slash and burn agriculture: a process in which a subsistence farmer cuts down the trees on a small parcel of land, then burns their stumps, so as to create an area suitable for agriculture.

Cases for Critical Thinking

Destroying Ancient Rock Formations

In 2014, two Boy Scout leaders, David Hall and Glenn Taylor, were leading a group of scouts on a hike in Utah's Goblin Valley State Park.[1] They came across a hoodoo, an ancient rock formation. The one they saw dates back to the Jurassic Period—145 to 170 million years ago. Hoodoos are often shaped like long slender pillars of rock, but the one these men encountered looked like a giant round boulder joined to the earth by a very thin piece of rock. With a great deal of effort, and the video camera on Hall's cell phone recording, Taylor proceeded to push the rock from its perch. The rock fell five or six feet to the ground and landed with a thud while the men danced and giggled. They claimed that they were just preventing the rock from falling on an unsuspecting passerby. They posted the video on social media and it went viral—garnering 5.5 million views as of 2017.[2] Most who saw the video were not amused. When the leadership of the Boy Scouts saw the video, they immediately kicked both men out of the organization, forbidding them from ever leading another troop. Emery County law enforcement in Utah charged Taylor with criminal mischief for pushing the rock and charged Hall with assisting criminal mischief for capturing the video. Both

are felonies. There were no signs posted prohibiting the men's behavior.

1. http://www.npr.org/sections/thetwo-way/2014/02/01/269926160/men-filmed-toppling-ancient-rock-formation-are-charged-in-utah

2. https://www.youtube.com/watch?v=AYFD18BwmJ4

Questions

1. Did Hall and Taylor do something morally wrong here? Why or why not?

2. Most people who saw the video were outraged at the men's behavior. But suppose that people reacted to the video the way the men themselves did—by laughing in amusement. And suppose that the Emery County police decided not to press any charges. Would that change your view about the moral permissibility of their actions? Why or why not?

3. The same year the video went viral, Goblin Valley State Park saw a 25 percent increase in attendance. The spike began almost immediately after the video was posted. Nearly every month since Hall and Taylor's stunt, the park has seen a new record in attendance. The following spring, nearly 60,000 people visited the park, doubling the 30,081 who visited the entire year of 2006. Thus, the controversial video has resulted in tens of thousands more people enjoying the park and learning about its ancient rock formations. Park employees have been able to educate thousands more people, not only about rock formations, but about how to treat them properly. There have even been proposals for the park to expand from its current 3,500 acres to 132,000 acres—an enormous increase in size.[3] The park and its visitors seem to have benefited a great deal from this episode. Imagine that you could go back to that day in 2014—the day the men destroyed the hoodoo—knowing what

you know now. Do you think you should try to stop the men, or should you let things proceed precisely as they actually did? Why?

3. http://www.deseretnews.com/article/865626278/A-tale-of-2-cameras.html

Taxing Meat

The meat industry is one of the biggest contributors to global warming—about 25 percent of all greenhouse emissions. Animals' digestive systems, as well as the production and shipment of their feed, produce lots of greenhouse gas. If, however, people around the world decided to eat much less meat, the meat industry would reduce their production of it. This would reduce both deforestation and greenhouse emissions, which would do wonders for the environment. But it's highly unlikely that enough people would give up eating meat so that it would make an appreciable difference to the environment. One way to achieve this desired reduction in the demand for meat, however, might be to tax it. If governments, especially the United States and Chinese governments, imposed high taxes on the purchase of meat, people would probably be less inclined to buy it. Researchers at Oxford University recently found that, in order to compensate for the damage done to the environment by meat production, governments should impose a 40 percent tax on beef, 15 percent on lamb, 8.5 percent on chicken, 7 percent on pork, and 5 percent on eggs.[1] On their proposal, the money received in tax revenue could then be used to fight climate change. Citing both the health and environmental advantages of such a tax policy, the lead researcher on the Oxford study commented, "Either we have climate change and more heart disease, diabetes and obesity, or we do something about the food system."[2]

1. https://www.theguardian.com/environment/2016/nov/07/tax-meat-and-dairy-to-cut-emissions-and-save-lives-study-urges

2. https://www.theguardian.com/environment/2016/nov/07/tax-meat-and-dairy-to-cut-emissions-and-save-lives-study-urges

Questions

1. What do you find attractive about the idea of a tax on meat? What do you find unattractive about it?

2. All things considered, do you think we ought to endorse a policy of taxing meat? Or do you think that such taxes ought to be opposed? Why? If you object to a meat tax, is it because you object to the tax rates for various meats mentioned earlier, or is it because you object, in principle, to a tax on meat?

3. There don't seem to be many overwhelmingly attractive options for achieving a significant reduction in worldwide greenhouse gas emissions. Do you think there are any better, or even equally good, alternatives to a meat tax?

Kenyan Deforestation

In 2009, the Kenyan government began enacting a plan to evict 8,000 Kenyans from their homes without compensating them.[1] These Kenyans had, years before, settled illegally in the Mau forest, one of Kenya's national forests, and the Kenyan government turned a blind eye. Drought elsewhere in Kenya was causing many farmers' crops to fail and their grazing land to become barren. These Kenyan "squatters" (as the government called them) entered the Mau looking for a way to support their families. They began clearing away parts of the forest so they could plant crops and give their cattle a place to graze. After clearing roughly 1,500 square miles of land—an area a third the size of Rhode Island—the Kenyan government decided that enough was enough. In their judgment, the rapid deforestation was threatening the Mau, and they very much wished to preserve it. The government began removing squatters from their homes and erecting electrified fences around the area to keep them out.[2]

1. https://www.theguardian.com/world/2009/nov/18/kenya-forest-squatters-evicted

2. https://www.theguardian.com/world/2009/may/10/kenya-climate-change-mau-park

Questions

1. Was the Kenyan government justified in preventing its citizens from settling in the Mau to make a living?

2. Whether or not the Kenyan law prohibiting deforestation was justified, it was (and is) the law. But do you think it's morally permissible for the so-called squatters, who depend on the Mau to provide for their families, to disobey the law by continuing to farm?

3. The turmoil in Kenya is, in part, the product of droughts caused by global warming. Do you think that countries who have contributed significantly to global warming (e.g., the United States, China, members of the European Union) ought to compensate Kenya for the damage global warming has done? Why or why not?

READINGS

The Ethics of Respect for the Environment
Paul Taylor

Paul Taylor argues against the anthropocentric view that human interests, and the human perspective generally, are morally superior to all others. Instead, Taylor encourages us to take what he calls "an attitude of respect for nature," in which we regard all elements of nature as possessed of as much inherent worth as all others. He develops a "life-centered ethic" that assigns importance to the well-being of every living thing, regardless of whether it is rational, able to suffer, or even conscious. That something is alive, or is (like the biosphere or specific ecosystems) composed of living things, is enough to grant it moral importance.

Taylor proceeds to identify the four essential claims that make up a *biocentric* (i.e., life-centered) outlook on nature: (1) humans are members of the Earth's community of life; (2) the Earth's natural ecosystems are a complex web of interconnected environments; (3) each individual living thing has a good of its own; (4) the assertion of greater human merit or inherent worth is nothing but irrational bias. The remainder of the article is devoted to a discussion of each of these four elements. The last claim, (4), receives the most attention.

Human beings have long thought of themselves as more important than members of any other species. But what could justify this attitude? We have rationality and autonomy—they don't. But cheetahs have speed that we lack; birds can fly; eagles can see things we can't. Why think of our special traits as more important than theirs? Taylor says that there is no good answer to this question. From our perspective, we are likely to give more value to the features that we alone possess. But there is no neutral reason to assign our perspective any more importance than any other—to argue otherwise is already to assume the superiority of humanity. Taylor concludes by sketching some of the significant implications of taking up the life-centered ethic.

HUMAN-CENTERED AND LIFE-CENTERED SYSTEMS OF ENVIRONMENTAL ETHICS

In this paper I show how the taking of a certain ultimate moral attitude toward nature, which I call "respect for nature," has a central place in the foundations of a life-centered system of environmental ethics. I hold that a set of moral norms (both standards of character and rules of conduct) governing human treatment of the natural world is a rationally grounded set if and only if, first, commitment to those norms is a practical entailment of adopting the attitude of respect for nature as an ultimate moral attitude, and second, the adopting of that attitude on the part of all rational agents can itself be justified. . . .

In designating the theory to be set forth as life-centered, I intend to contrast it with all anthropocentric views. According to the latter, human actions affecting the natural environment and its nonhuman inhabitants are right (or wrong) by either of two criteria: they have consequences which are favorable (or unfavorable) to human well-being, or they are consistent (or inconsistent) with the system of norms that protects and implements human rights. From this human-centered standpoint it is to humans and only to humans that all duties are ultimately owed. We may have responsibilities *with regard to* the natural ecosystems and biotic communities of our planet, but these responsibilities are in every case based on the contingent fact that our treatment of those ecosystems and communities of life can further the realization of human values and/or human rights. We have no obligation to promote or protect the good of nonhuman living things, independently of this contingent fact.

From Paul Taylor, "The Ethics of Respect for the Environment," *Environmental Ethics* 3 (1981): pp. 197–201, 211–218.

A life-centered system of environmental ethics is opposed to human-centered ones precisely on this point. From the perspective of a life-centered theory, we have prima facie moral obligations that are owed to wild plants and animals themselves as members of the Earth's biotic community. We are morally bound (other things being equal) to protect or promote their good for *their* sake. . . .

THE GOOD OF A BEING AND THE CONCEPT OF INHERENT WORTH

What would justify acceptance of a life-centered system of ethical principles? In order to answer this it is first necessary to make clear the fundamental moral attitude that underlies and makes intelligible the commitment to live by such a system. It is then necessary to examine the considerations that would justify any rational agent's adopting that moral attitude.

Two concepts are essential to the taking of a moral attitude of the sort in question. . . . These concepts are, first, that of the good (well-being, welfare) of a living thing, and second, the idea of an entity possessing inherent worth. I examine each concept in turn.

(1) Every organism, species population, and community of life has a good of its own which moral agents can intentionally further or damage by their actions. To say that an entity has a good of its own is simply to say that, without reference to any *other* entity, it can be benefited or harmed. . . . We can think of the good of an individual nonhuman organism as consisting in the full development of its biological powers. Its good is realized to the extent that it is strong and healthy. . . .

The idea of a being having a good of its own, as I understand it, does not entail that the being must have interests or take an interest in what affects its life for better or for worse. We can act in a being's interest or contrary to its interest without its being interested in what we are doing to it in the sense of wanting or not wanting us to do it. It may, indeed, be wholly unaware that favorable and unfavorable events are taking place in its life. I take it that trees, for example, have no knowledge or desires or feelings. Yet it is undoubtedly the case that trees can be harmed or benefited by our actions. . . .

(2) The second concept essential to the moral attitude of respect for nature is the idea of inherent worth. We take that attitude toward wild living things (individuals, species populations, or whole biotic communities) when and only when we regard them as entities possessing inherent worth. Indeed, it is only because they are conceived in this way that moral agents can think of themselves as having validly binding duties, obligations, and responsibilities that are *owed* to them as their *due*. I am not at this juncture arguing why they *should* be so regarded; I consider it at length below. But so regarding them is a presupposition of our taking the attitude of respect toward them and accordingly understanding ourselves as bearing certain moral relations to them. This can be shown as follows:

What does it mean to regard an entity that has a good of its own as possessing inherent worth? Two general principles are involved: the principle of moral consideration and the principle of intrinsic value.

According to the principle of moral consideration, wild living things are deserving of the concern and consideration of all moral agents simply in virtue of their being members of the Earth's community of life. From the moral point of view their good must be taken into account whenever it is affected for better or worse by the conduct of rational agents. This holds no matter what species the creature belongs to. The good of each is to be accorded some value and so acknowledged as having some weight in the deliberations of all rational agents. Of course, it may be necessary for such agents to act in ways contrary to the good of this or that particular organism or group of organisms in order to further the good of others, including the good of humans. But the principle of moral consideration prescribes that, with respect to each being an entity having its own good, every individual is deserving of consideration.

The principle of intrinsic value states that, regardless of what kind of entity it is in other respects, if it is a member of the Earth's community of life, the realization of its good is something *intrinsically* valuable. This means that its good is prima facie worthy of being preserved or promoted as an end in itself and for the sake of the entity whose good it is. Insofar as we regard any organism, species population, or life community as an entity having inherent worth, we believe that it must never be treated as if it were a mere object or thing whose entire value lies in being instrumental to the good of some other entity. The well-being of each is judged to have value in and of itself.

Combining these two principles, we can now define what it means for a living thing or group of living things to possess inherent worth. To say that it possesses inherent worth is to say that its good is deserving of the concern and consideration of all moral agents, and that the realization of its good has intrinsic value, to be pursued as an end in itself and for the sake of the entity whose good it is.

The duties owed to wild organisms, species populations, and communities of life in the Earth's natural ecosystems are grounded on their inherent worth. When rational, autonomous agents regard such entities as possessing inherent worth, they place intrinsic value on the realization of their good and so hold themselves responsible for performing actions that will have this effect and for refraining from actions having the contrary effect. . . .

THE BIOCENTRIC OUTLOOK ON NATURE

The biocentric outlook on nature has four main components. (1) Humans are thought of as members of the Earth's community of life, holding that membership on the same terms as apply to all the nonhuman members. (2) The Earth's natural ecosystems as a totality are seen as a complex web of interconnected elements, with the sound biological functioning of each being dependent on the sound biological functioning of the others. (This is the component referred to above as the great lesson that the science of ecology has taught us.) (3) Each individual organism is conceived of as a teleological center of life, pursuing its own good in its own way. (4) Whether we are concerned with standards of merit or with the concept of inherent worth, the claim that humans by their very nature are superior to other species is a groundless claim and, in the light of elements (1), (2), and (3) above, must be rejected as nothing more than an irrational bias in our own favor. . . .

THE DENIAL OF HUMAN SUPERIORITY

This fourth component of the biocentric outlook on nature is the single most important idea in establishing the justifiability of the attitude of respect for nature. Its central role is due to the special relationship it bears to the first three components of the outlook. This relationship will be brought out after the concept of human superiority is examined and analyzed.

In what sense are humans alleged to be superior to other animals? We are different from them in having certain capacities that they lack. But why should these capacities be a mark of superiority? From what point of view are they judged to be signs of superiority and what sense of superiority is meant? After all, various nonhuman species have capacities that humans lack. There is the speed of a cheetah, the vision of an eagle, the agility of a monkey. Why should not these be taken as signs of *their* superiority over humans?

One answer that comes immediately to mind is that these capacities are not as *valuable* as the human capacities that are claimed to make us superior. Such uniquely human characteristics as rational thought, aesthetic creativity, autonomy and self-determination, and moral freedom, it might be held, have a higher value than the capacities found in other species. Yet we must ask: valuable to whom, and on what grounds?

The human characteristics mentioned are all valuable to humans. They are essential to the preservation and enrichment of our civilization and culture. Clearly it is from the human standpoint that they are being judged to be desirable and good. It is not difficult here to recognize a begging of the question. Humans are claiming human superiority from a strictly human point of view, that is, from a point of view in which the good of humans is taken as the standard of judgment. All we need to do is

to look at the capacities of nonhuman animals (or plants, for that matter) from the standpoint of *their* good to find a contrary judgment of superiority. The speed of the cheetah, for example, is a sign of its superiority to humans when considered from the standpoint of the good of its species. If it were as slow a runner as a human, it would not be able to survive. And so for all the other abilities of nonhumans which further their good but which are lacking in humans. In each case the claim to human superiority would be rejected from a nonhuman standpoint.

When superiority assertions are interpreted in this way, they are based on judgments of *merit*. To judge the merits of a person or an organism one must apply grading or ranking standards to it. (As I show below, this distinguishes judgments of merit from judgments of inherent worth.) Empirical investigation then determines whether it has the "good-making properties" (merits) in virtue of which it fulfills the standards being applied. In the case of humans, merits may be either moral or nonmoral. We can judge one person to be better than (superior to) another from the moral point of view by applying certain standards to their character and conduct. Similarly, we can appeal to nonmoral criteria in judging someone to be an excellent piano player, a fair cook, a poor tennis player, and so on. Different social purposes and roles are implicit in the making of such judgments, providing the frame of reference for the choice of standards by which the nonmoral merits of people are determined. Ultimately such purposes and roles stem from a society's way of life as a whole. Now a society's way of life may be thought of as the cultural form given to the realization of human values. Whether moral or nonmoral standards are being applied, then, all judgments of people's merits finally depend on human values. All are made from an exclusively human standpoint.

The question that naturally arises at this juncture is: why should standards that are based on human values be assumed to be the only valid criteria of merit and hence the only true signs of superiority? This question is especially pressing when humans are being judged superior in merit to nonhumans. It is true that a human being may be a better mathematician than a monkey, but the monkey may be a better tree climber than a human being. If we humans value mathematics more than tree climbing, that is because our conception of civilized life makes the development of mathematical ability more desirable than the ability to climb trees. But is it not unreasonable to judge nonhumans by the values of human civilization, rather than by values connected with what it is for a member of *that* species to live a good life? If all living things have a good of their own, it at least makes sense to judge the merits of nonhumans by standards derived from *their* good. To use only standards based on human values is already to commit oneself to holding that humans are superior to nonhumans, which is the point in question.

A further logical flaw arises in connection with the widely held conviction that humans are *morally* superior beings because they possess, while others lack, the capacities of a moral agent (free will, accountability, deliberation, judgment, practical reason). This view rests on a conceptual confusion. As far as moral standards are concerned, only beings that have the capacities of a moral agent can properly be judged to be *either* moral (morally good) *or* immoral (morally deficient). Moral standards are simply not applicable to beings that lack such capacities. Animals and plants cannot therefore be said to be morally inferior in merit to humans. Since the only beings that can have moral merits *or be deficient in such merits* are moral agents, it is conceptually incoherent to judge humans as superior to nonhumans on the ground that humans have moral capacities while nonhumans don't.

Up to this point I have been interpreting the claim that humans are superior to other living things as a grading or ranking judgment regarding their comparative merits. There is, however, another way of understanding the idea of human superiority. According to this interpretation, humans are superior to nonhumans not as regards their merits but as regards their inherent worth. Thus the claim of human superiority is to be understood as asserting that all humans, simply in virtue of their humanity, have *a greater inherent worth* than other living things.

The inherent worth of an entity does not depend on its merits.[1] To consider something as possessing inherent worth, we have seen, is to place intrinsic value on the realization of its good. This is done regardless of whatever particular merits it might have or might lack, as judged by a set of grading or ranking standards. In human affairs, we are all familiar with the principle that one's worth as a person does not vary with one's merits or lack of merits. The same can hold true of animals and plants. To regard such entities as possessing inherent worth entails disregarding their merits and deficiencies, whether they are being judged from a human standpoint or from the standpoint of their own species.

The idea of one entity having more merit than another, and so being superior to it in merit, makes perfectly good sense. Merit is a grading or ranking concept, and judgments of comparative merit are based on the different degrees to which things satisfy a given standard. But what can it mean to talk about one thing being superior to another in inherent worth?. . .

The vast majority of people in modern democracies . . . do not maintain an egalitarian outlook when it comes to comparing human beings with other living things. Most people consider our own species to be superior to all other species and this superiority is understood to be a matter of inherent worth, not merit. There may exist thoroughly vicious and depraved humans who lack all merit. Yet because they are human they are thought to belong to a higher class of entities than any plant or animal. That one is born into the species *Homo sapiens* entitles one to have lordship over those who are one's inferiors, namely, those born into other species. The parallel with hereditary social classes is very close. Implicit in this view is a hierarchical conception of nature according to which an organism has a position of superiority or inferiority in the Earth's community of life simply on the basis of its genetic background. The "lower" orders of life are looked down upon and it is considered perfectly proper that they serve the interests of those belonging to the highest order, namely humans. The intrinsic value we place on the well-being of our fellow humans reflects our recognition of their rightful position as our equals. No such intrinsic value is to be placed on the good of other animals, unless we choose to do so out of fondness or affection for them. But their well-being imposes no moral requirement on us. In this respect there is an absolute difference in moral status between ourselves and them.

This is the structure of concepts and beliefs that people are committed to insofar as they regard humans to be superior in inherent worth to all other species. I now wish to argue that this structure of concepts and beliefs is completely groundless. If we accept the first three components of the biocentric outlook and from that perspective look at the major philosophical traditions which have supported that structure, we find it to be at bottom nothing more than the expression of an irrational bias in our own favor. The philosophical traditions themselves rest on very questionable assumptions or else simply beg the question. I briefly consider three of the main traditions to substantiate the point. These are classical Greek humanism, Cartesian dualism, and the Judeo-Christian concept of the Great Chain of Being.

The inherent superiority of humans over other species was implicit in the Greek definition of man as a rational animal. Our animal nature was identified with "brute" desires that need the order and restraint of reason to rule them (just as reason is the special virtue of those who rule in the ideal state). Rationality was then seen to be the key to our superiority over animals. It enables us to live on a higher plane and endows us with a nobility and worth that other creatures lack. This familiar way of comparing humans with other species is deeply ingrained in our Western philosophical outlook. The point to consider here is that this view does not actually provide an argument *for* human superiority but rather makes explicit the framework of thought that is implicitly used by those who think of humans as inherently superior to nonhumans. The Greeks who held that humans, in virtue of their rational capacities, have a kind of worth greater than that of any nonrational being, never looked at rationality as but one capacity of living things among many others. But when we consider rationality from the standpoint of the first three elements of the ecological outlook, we see that its value lies in its importance for *human* life. Other creatures achieve their species-specific good without the need of rationality, although they often make use of capacities that humans lack. So the humanistic outlook of classical Greek thought does not give us a neutral (nonquestion-begging) ground on which to construct a scale of degrees of inherent worth possessed by different species of living things.

The second tradition, centering on the Cartesian dualism of soul and body, also fails to justify the claim to human superiority. That superiority is supposed to derive from the fact that we have souls while animals do not. Animals are mere automata and lack the divine element that makes us spiritual beings. I won't go into the now familiar criticisms of this two-substance view. I only add the point that, even if humans are composed of an immaterial, unextended soul and a material, extended body, this in itself is not a reason to deem them of greater worth than entities that are only bodies. Why is a soul substance a thing that adds value to its possessor? Unless some theological reasoning is offered here (which many, including myself, would find unacceptable on epistemological grounds), no logical connection is evident. An immaterial something which thinks is better than a material something which does not think only if thinking itself has value, either intrinsically or instrumentally. Now it is intrinsically valuable to humans alone, who value it as an end in itself, and it is instrumentally valuable to those who benefit from it, namely humans.

For animals that neither enjoy thinking for its own sake nor need it for living the kind of life for which they are best adapted, it has no value. Even if "thinking" is broadened to include all forms of consciousness, there are still many living things that can do without it and yet live what is for their species a good life. The anthropocentricity underlying the claim to human superiority runs throughout Cartesian dualism.

A third major source of the idea of human superiority is the Judeo-Christian concept of the Great Chain of Being. Humans are superior to animals and plants because their Creator has given them a higher place on the chain. It begins with God at the top, and then moves to the angels, who are lower than God but higher than humans, then to humans, positioned between the angels and the beasts (partaking of the nature of both), and then on down to the lower levels occupied by nonhuman animals, plants, and finally inanimate objects. Humans, being "made in God's image," are inherently superior to animals and plants by virtue of their being closer (in their essential nature) to God.

The metaphysical and epistemological difficulties with this conception of a hierarchy of entities are, in my mind, insuperable. Without entering into this matter here, I only point out that if we are unwilling to accept the metaphysics of traditional Judaism and Christianity, we are again left without good reasons for holding to the claim of inherent human superiority.

The foregoing considerations (and others like them) leave us with but one ground for the assertion that a human being, regardless of merit, is a higher kind of entity than any other living thing. This is the mere fact of the genetic makeup of the species *Homo sapiens*. But this is surely irrational and arbitrary. Why should the arrangement of genes of a certain type be a mark of superior value, especially when this fact about an organism is taken by itself, unrelated to any other aspect of its life? We might just as well refer to any other genetic makeup as a ground of superior value. Clearly we are confronted here with a wholly arbitrary claim that can only be explained as an irrational bias in our own favor.

That the claim is nothing more than a deep-seated prejudice is brought home to us when we look at our relation to other species in the light of the first three elements of the biocentric outlook. Those elements taken conjointly give us a certain overall view of the natural world and of the place of humans in it. When we take this view we come to understand other living things, their environmental conditions, and their ecological relationships in such a way as to awake in us a deep sense of our kinship with them as fellow members of the Earth's community of life. Humans and nonhumans alike are viewed together as integral parts of one unified whole in which all living things are functionally interrelated. Finally, when our awareness focuses on the individual lives of plants and animals, each is seen to share with us the characteristic of being a teleological center of life striving to realize its own good in its own unique way.

As this entire belief system becomes part of the conceptual framework through which we understand and perceive the world, we come to see ourselves as bearing a certain moral relation to nonhuman forms of life. Our ethical role in nature takes on a new significance. We begin to look at other species as we look at ourselves, seeing them as beings which have a good they are striving to realize just as we have a good we are striving to realize. We accordingly develop the disposition to view the world from the standpoint of their good as well as from the standpoint of our own good. Now if the groundlessness of the claim that humans are inherently superior to other species were brought clearly before our minds, we would not remain intellectually neutral toward that claim but would reject it as being fundamentally at variance with our total world outlook. In the absence of any good reasons for holding it, the assertion of human superiority would then appear simply as the expression of an irrational and self-serving prejudice that favors one particular species over several million others.

Rejecting the notion of human superiority entails its positive counterpart: the doctrine of species impartiality. One who accepts that doctrine regards all living things as possessing inherent worth—the *same* inherent worth, since no one species has been shown to be either "higher" or "lower" than any other. Now we saw earlier that, insofar as one thinks of a living thing as possessing inherent worth, one considers it to be the appropriate object of the attitude of respect and believes that attitude to be the only fitting or suitable one for all moral agents to take toward it.

Here, then, is the key to understanding how the attitude of respect is rooted in the biocentric outlook of nature. The basic connection is made through the denial of human superiority. Once we reject the claim that humans are superior either in merit or in worth to other living things, we are ready to adopt the attitude of respect. The denial of human superiority is itself the result of taking the perspective on nature built into the first three elements of the biocentric outlook.

Now the first three elements of the biocentric outlook, it seems clear, would be found acceptable to any rational and scientifically informed thinker who is fully "open" to the reality of the lives of nonhuman organisms. Without denying our distinctively human characteristics, such a thinker can acknowledge the fundamental respects in which we are members of the Earth's community of life and in which the biological conditions necessary for the realization of our human values are inextricably linked with the whole system of nature. In addition, the conception of individual living things as teleological centers of life simply articulates how a scientifically informed thinker comes to understand them as the result of increasingly careful and detailed observations. Thus, the biocentric outlook recommends itself as an acceptable system of concepts and beliefs to anyone who is clear-minded, unbiased, and factually enlightened, and who has a developed capacity of reality awareness with regard to the lives of individual organisms. This, I submit, is as good a reason for making the moral commitment involved in adopting the attitude of respect for nature as any theory of environmental ethics could possibly have.

MORAL RIGHTS AND THE MATTER OF COMPETING CLAIMS

I have not asserted anywhere in the foregoing account that animals or plants have moral rights. This omission was deliberate. I do not think that the reference class of the concept, bearer of moral rights, should be extended to include nonhuman living things. My reasons for taking this position, however, go beyond the scope of this paper. I believe I have been able to accomplish many of the same ends which those who ascribe rights to animals or plants wish to accomplish. There is no reason, moreover, why plants and animals, including whole species populations and life communities, cannot be accorded *legal* rights under my theory. To grant them legal protection could be interpreted as giving them legal entitlement to be protected, and this, in fact, would be a means by which a society that subscribed to the ethics of respect for nature could give public recognition to their inherent worth.

There remains the problem of competing claims, even when wild plants and animals are not thought of as bearers of moral rights. If we accept the biocentric outlook and accordingly adopt the attitude of respect for nature as our ultimate moral attitude,

how do we resolve conflicts that arise from our respect for persons in the domain of human ethics and our respect for nature in the domain of environmental ethics? This is a question that cannot adequately be dealt with here. My main purpose in this paper has been to try to establish a base point from which we can start working toward a solution to the problem. I have shown why we cannot just begin with an initial presumption in favor of the interests of our own species. It is after all within our power as moral beings to place limits on human population and technology with the deliberate intention of sharing the Earth's bounty with other species. That such sharing is an ideal difficult to realize even in an approximate way does not take away its claim to our deepest moral commitment.

NOTE

1. For this way of distinguishing between merit and inherent worth, I am indebted to Gregory Vlastos, "Justice and Equality," in R. Brandt, ed., *Social Justice* (Englewood Cliffs, N.J.: Prentice-Hall, 1962), pp. 31–72.

Paul Taylor: The Ethics of Respect for the Environment

1. In what sense is Taylor's view "life-centered"? How does his view differ from anthropocentric views?

2. What does it mean to say that an entity has "a good of its own"? Which entities does Taylor think have goods of their own? Do you agree with him on this?

3. What is the difference, according to Taylor, between merit and worth? Which does he think is important to determining whether an entity is morally considerable? Do you agree with him?

4. One reason people have given for thinking that humans are morally considerable while animals are not is that only humans are *rational*. How does Taylor respond to this line of argument? Do you find his response persuasive?

5. Taylor claims that the view that humans are morally superior to animals is "an irrational bias in our own favor." How does he argue for this claim? Is his argument a good one?

Ideals of Human Excellence and Preserving Natural Environments

Thomas Hill, Jr.

According to Thomas Hill, Jr., the standard moral theories have difficulty explaining what is wrong with the destruction of the environment. Utilitarianism runs into trouble, because it is possible that overall happiness is maximized when cutting down a virgin forest or bulldozing a field to make way for suburban homes. Kantian and rights-based moral theories have just as much trouble here, because it is very difficult to defend the idea that plants or ecosystems—incapable of reasoning, asserting claims, or even feeling anything—are possessed of rights. Contractarian theories are just as vulnerable on this score. If our basic duties are owed only to our fellow members of the social contract, then plants and ecosystems will again be left out in the cold.

These concerns lead Hill to consider an alternative way of understanding our ethical relations with the environment. Rather than focusing on the question of whether we have any duties directly toward the environment, Hill invites us to consider a virtue ethical approach, which places primary emphasis on the sort of person we should try to become. He argues that those who fail to treat the environment with respect are almost certainly going to be less than fully virtuous. They will fail to be admirable in a number of ways and will exemplify a variety of vices. In particular, those who are indifferent to the value of nature will almost certainly be ignorant and self-important. They will lack proper humility, and will either fail to have a well-developed sense of beauty or will be insufficiently grateful for the good things in life. Thus even if we can't defend the claim that nature has rights, or that we owe nature anything, there is still excellent reason to respect and preserve natural environments. For if we don't, we will fall short of plausible ideals of human excellence.

I.

A wealthy eccentric bought a house in a neighborhood I know. The house was surrounded by a beautiful display of grass, plants, and flowers, and it was shaded by a huge old avocado tree. But the grass required cutting, the flowers needed tending, and the man wanted more sun. So he cut the whole lot down and covered the yard with asphalt. After all it was his property and he was not fond of plants.

It was a small operation, but it reminded me of the strip mining of large sections of the Appalachians. In both cases, of course, there were reasons

From Thomas Hill, Jr., "Ideals of Human Excellence and Preserving Natural Environments," *Environmental Ethics* 5 (1983), pp. 211–214.

for the destruction, and property rights could be cited as justification. But I could not help but wonder, "What sort of person would do a thing like that?"

Many Californians had a similar reaction when a recent governor defended the leveling of ancient redwood groves, reportedly saying, "If you have seen one redwood, you have seen them all."

Incidents like these arouse the indignation of ardent environmentalists and leave even apolitical observers with some degree of moral discomfort. The reasons for these reactions are mostly obvious. Uprooting the natural environment robs both present and future generations of much potential use and enjoyment. Animals too depend on the environment; and even if one does not value animals for their own sakes, their potential utility for us is incalculable. Plants are needed, of course, to replenish the atmosphere quite aside from their aesthetic value. These reasons for hesitating to destroy forests and gardens are not only the most obvious ones, but also the most persuasive for practical purposes. But, one wonders, is there nothing more behind our discomfort? Are we concerned solely about the potential use and enjoyment of the forests, etc., for ourselves, later generations, and perhaps animals? Is there not something else which disturbs us when we witness the destruction or even listen to those who would defend it in terms of cost/benefit analysis?

Imagine that in each of our examples those who would destroy the environment argue elaborately that, even considering future generations of human beings and animals, there are benefits in "replacing" the natural environment which outweigh the negative utilities which environmentalists cite. No doubt we could press the argument on the facts, trying to show that the destruction is shortsighted and that its defenders have underestimated its potential harm or ignored some pertinent rights or interests. But is this all we could say? Suppose we grant, for a moment, that the utility of destroying the redwoods, forests, and gardens is equal to their potential for use and enjoyment by nature lovers and animals. Suppose, further, that we even grant that the pertinent human rights and animal rights, if any, are evenly divided for and against destruction. Imagine that we also concede, for argument's sake, that the forests contain no potentially useful endangered species of animals and plants. Must we then conclude that there is no further cause for moral concern? Should we then feel morally indifferent when we see the natural environment uprooted?

II.

Suppose we feel that the answer to these questions should be negative. Suppose, in other words, we feel that our moral discomfort when we confront the destroyers of nature is not fully explained by our belief that they have miscalculated the best use of natural resources or violated rights in exploiting them. Suppose, in particular, we sense that part of the problem is that the natural environment is being viewed exclusively as a natural resource. What could be the ground of such a feeling? That is, what is there in our system of normative principles and values that could account for our remaining moral dissatisfaction?

Some may be tempted to seek an explanation by appeal to the interests, or even the rights, of plants. After all, they may argue, we only gradually came to acknowledge the moral importance of all human beings, and it is even more recently that consciences have been aroused to give full weight to the welfare (and rights?) of animals. The next logical step, it may be argued, is to acknowledge a moral requirement to take into account the interests (and rights?) of plants. The problem with the strip miners, redwood cutters, and the like, on this view, is not just that they ignore the welfare and rights of people and animals: they also fail to give due weight to the survival and health of the plants themselves.

The temptation to make such a reply is understandable if one assumes that all moral questions are exclusively concerned with whether *acts* are right or wrong, and that this, in turn, is determined entirely by how the acts impinge on the rights and interests of those directly affected. On this assumption, if there is cause for moral concern, some right or interest has been neglected; and if the rights and interests of human beings and animals have already been taken into account, then there must be some other pertinent interests, for example, those of plants. A little reflection will show that the assumption is mistaken; but, in any case, the conclusion that plants have rights or morally relevant interests is surely untenable. We do speak of what is "good for" plants, and they can "thrive" and also be "killed." But this does not imply that they have "interests" in any morally relevant sense. Some people apparently believe that plants grow better if we talk to them, but the idea that the plants suffer and enjoy, desire and dislike, etc., is clearly outside the range of both common sense and scientific belief. The notion that the forests should be preserved to avoid *hurting* the trees or because they have a *right* to life is not part of a widely shared moral consciousness, and for good reason.

Another way of trying to explain our moral discomfort is to appeal to certain religious beliefs. If one believes that all living things were created by a God who cares for them and entrusted us with the use of plants and animals only for limited purposes, then one has a reason to avoid careless destruction of the forests, etc., quite aside from their future utility. Again, if one believes that a divine force is immanent in all nature, then too one might have reason to care for more than sentient things. But such arguments require strong and controversial premises, and, I suspect, they will always have a restricted audience.

Early in this century, due largely to the influence of G. E. Moore, another point of view developed which some may find promising.[1] Moore introduced, or at least made popular, the idea that certain states of affairs are intrinsically valuable— not just valued, but valuable, and not necessarily because of their effects on sentient beings. . . . The intrinsic goodness of something, he thought, was an objective, nonrelational property of the thing, like its texture or color, but not a property perceivable by sense perception or detectable by scientific instruments. In theory at least, a single tree thriving alone in a universe without sentient beings, and even without God, could be intrinsically valuable. . . . The survival of a forest might have worth beyond its worth *to* sentient beings.

Even if we try to . . . think in Moore's terms, it is far from obvious that everyone would agree that the existence of forests, etc., is intrinsically valuable. The test, says Moore, is what we would say when we imagine a universe with just the thing in question, without any effects or accompaniments, and then we ask, "Would its existence be better than its nonexistence?" Be careful, Moore would remind us, not to construe this question as, "Would you *prefer* the existence of that universe to its nonexistence?" The question is, "Would its existence have the objective, nonrelational property, intrinsic goodness?"

Now even among those who have no worries about whether this really makes sense, we might well get a diversity of answers. Those prone to destroy natural environments will doubtless give one answer, and nature lovers will likely give another. When an issue is as controversial as the one at hand, intuition is a poor arbiter.

The problem, then, is this. We want to understand what underlies our moral uneasiness at the destruction of the redwoods, forests, etc., even apart from the loss of these as resources for human beings and animals. But I find no adequate answer by pursuing the questions, "Are rights or interests of plants neglected?" "What is God's will on the matter?" and "What is the intrinsic value of the existence of a tree or forest?" My suggestion, which is in fact the main point of this paper, is that we look at the problem from a different perspective. That is, let us turn for a while from the effort to find reasons why certain *acts* destructive of natural environments are morally wrong to the ancient task of articulating our ideals of human excellence. Rather than argue directly with destroyers of the environment who say, "Show me why what I am doing is *immoral*," I want to ask, "What sort of person would want to do what they propose?" The point is not to skirt the issue with an *ad hominem*, but to raise a different moral question, for even if there is no convincing way to show that the destructive acts are wrong (independently of human and animal use and enjoyment), we may find that the willingness to indulge in them reflects the absence of human traits that we admire and regard as morally important.

This strategy of shifting questions may seem more promising if one reflects on certain analogous situations. Consider, for example, the Nazi who asks, in all seriousness, "Why is it wrong for me to make lampshades out of human skin— provided, of course, I did not myself kill the victims to get the skins?" We would react more with shock and disgust than with indignation, I suspect, because it is even more evident that the question reveals a defect in the questioner than that the proposed act is itself immoral. Sometimes we may not regard an act wrong at all though we see it as reflecting something objectionable about the person who does it. Imagine, for example, one who laughs spontaneously to himself when he reads a newspaper account of a plane crash that kills hundreds. Or, again, consider an obsequious grandson who, having waited for his grandmother's inheritance with mock devotion, then secretly spits on her grave when at last she dies. Spitting on the grave may have no adverse consequences and perhaps it violates no rights. The moral uneasiness which it arouses is explained more by our view of the agent than by any conviction that what he did was immoral. Had he hesitated and asked, "Why shouldn't I spit on her grave?" it seems more fitting to ask him to reflect on the sort of person he is than to try to offer reasons why he should refrain from spitting.

III.

What sort of person, then, would cover his garden with asphalt, strip mine a wooded mountain, or level an irreplaceable redwood grove? Two sorts of answers, though initially appealing, must be ruled out. The first is that persons who would destroy the environment in these ways are either shortsighted, underestimating the harm they do, or else are too little concerned for the well-being of other people. Perhaps too they have insufficient regard for animal life. But these considerations have been set aside in order to refine the controversy. Another tempting response might be that we count it a moral virtue, or at least a human ideal, to love nature. Those who value the environment only for its utility must not really love nature and so in this way fall short of an ideal. But such an answer is hardly satisfying in the present context, for what is at issue is *why* we feel moral discomfort at the activities of those who admittedly value nature only for its utility. That it is ideal to care for nonsentient nature beyond its possible use is really just another way of expressing the general point which is under controversy.

What is needed is some way of showing that this ideal is connected with other virtues, or human excellences, not in question. To do so is difficult and my suggestions, accordingly, will be tentative and subject to qualification. The main idea is that, though indifference to nonsentient nature does not *necessarily* reflect the absence of virtues, it often signals the absence of certain traits which we want to encourage because they are, in most cases, a natural basis for the development of certain virtues. It is often thought, for example, that those who would destroy the natural environment must lack a proper appreciation of their place in the natural order, and so must either be ignorant or have too little humility. Though I would argue that this is not necessarily so, I suggest that, given certain plausible empirical assumptions, their attitude may well be rooted in ignorance, a narrow perspective, inability to see

things as important apart from themselves and the limited groups they associate with, or reluctance to accept themselves as natural beings. Overcoming these deficiencies will not guarantee a proper moral humility, but for most of us it is probably an important psychological preliminary. Later I suggest, more briefly, that indifference to nonsentient nature typically reveals absence of either aesthetic sensibility or a disposition to cherish what has enriched one's life and that these, though not themselves moral virtues, are a natural basis for appreciation of the good in others and gratitude.

Consider first the suggestion that destroyers of the environment lack an appreciation of their place in the universe. Their attention, it seems, must be focused on parochial matters, on what is, relatively speaking, close in space and time. They seem not to understand that we are a speck on the cosmic scene, a brief stage in the evolutionary process, only one among millions of species on Earth, and an episode in the course of human history. Of course, they know that there are stars, fossils, insects, and ancient ruins; but do they have any idea of the complexity of the processes that led to the natural world as we find it? Are they aware how much the forces at work within their own bodies are like those which govern all living things and even how much they have in common with inanimate bodies? Admittedly scientific knowledge is limited and no one can master it all; but could one who had a broad and deep understanding of his place in nature really be indifferent to the destruction of the natural environment?

This first suggestion, however, may well provoke a protest from a sophisticated anti-environmentalist. "Perhaps *some* may be indifferent to nature from ignorance," the critic may object, "but I have studied astronomy, geology, biology, and biochemistry, and I still unashamedly regard the nonsentient environment as simply a resource for our use. It should not be wasted, of course, but what should be preserved is decidable by weighing long-term costs and benefits." "Besides," our critic may continue, "as philosophers you should know the old Humean formula, 'You cannot derive an *ought* from an *is*.' All the facts of biology, biochemistry, etc., do not entail that I ought to love nature or want to preserve it. What one understands is one thing; what one values is something else. Just as nature lovers are not necessarily scientists, those indifferent to nature are not necessarily ignorant."

Although the environmentalist may concede the critic's logical point, he may well argue that, as a matter of fact, increased understanding of nature tends to heighten people's concern for its preservation. If so, despite the objection, the suspicion that the destroyers of the environment lack deep understanding of nature is not, in most cases, unwarranted, but the argument need not rest here.

The environmentalist might amplify his original idea as follows: "When I said that the destroyers of nature do not appreciate their place in the universe, I was not speaking of intellectual understanding alone, for, after all, a person can *know* a catalog of facts without ever putting them together and seeing vividly the whole picture which they form. To see oneself as just one part of nature is to look at oneself and the world from a certain perspective which is quite different from being able to recite detailed information from the natural sciences. What the destroyers of nature lack is this perspective, not particular information."

Again our critic may object, though only after making some concessions: "All right," he may say, "*some* who are indifferent to nature may lack the cosmic perspective of which you speak, but again there is no *necessary* connection between this failing, if it is one, and any particular evaluative attitude toward nature. In fact, different people respond quite differently when they move to a wider perspective. When I try to picture myself vividly as a brief, transitory episode in the course of nature, I simply get depressed. Far from inspiring me with a love of nature, the exercise makes me sad and hostile. . . . " In sum, the critic may object, "Even if one should try to see oneself as one small transitory part of nature, doing so does not dictate any particular normative attitude. Some may come to love nature, but others are moved to live for the moment; some sink into sad resignation; others get depressed or angry. So indifference to nature is not necessarily a sign that a person fails to look at himself from the larger perspective."

The environmentalist might respond to this objection in several ways. He might, for example, argue that even though some people who see themselves as part of the natural order remain indifferent to nonsentient nature, this is not a common reaction. Typically, it may be argued, as we become more and more aware that we are parts of the larger whole we come to value the whole independently of its effect on ourselves. Thus, despite the possibilities the critic raises, indifference to nonsentient nature is still in most cases a sign that a person fails to see himself as part of the natural order.

If someone challenges the empirical assumption here, the environmentalist might develop the argument along a quite different line. The initial idea, he may remind us, was that those who would destroy the natural environment fail to *appreciate* their place in the natural order. "Appreciating one's place" is not simply an intellectual appreciation. It is also an attitude, reflecting what one values as well as what one knows. When we say, for example, that both the servile and the arrogant person fail to *appreciate* their place in a society of equals, we do not mean simply that they are ignorant of certain empirical facts, but rather that they have certain objectionable attitudes about their importance relative to other people. Similarly, to fail to appreciate one's place in nature is not merely to lack knowledge or breadth of perspective, but to take a certain attitude about what matters. A person who *understands* his place in nature but still views nonsentient nature merely as a resource takes the attitude that nothing is *important* but human beings and animals. Despite first appearances, he is not so much like the pre-Copernican astronomers who made the intellectual error of treating the Earth as the "center of the universe" when they made their calculations. He is more like the racist who, though well aware of other races, treats all races but his own as insignificant.

So construed, the argument appeals to the common idea that awareness of nature typically has, and should have, a humbling effect. The Alps, a storm at sea, the Grand Canyon, towering redwoods, and "the starry heavens above" move many a person to remark on the comparative insignificance of our daily concerns and even of our species, and this is generally taken to be a quite fitting response. What seems to be missing, then, in those who understand nature but remain unmoved is a proper humility.[2] Absence of proper humility is not the same as selfishness or egoism, for one can be devoted to self-interest while still viewing one's own pleasures and projects as trivial and unimportant. And one can have an exaggerated view of one's own importance while grandly sacrificing for those one views as inferior. Nor is the lack of humility identical with belief that one has power and influence, for a person can be quite puffed up about himself while believing that the foolish world will never acknowledge him. The humility we miss seems not so much a belief about one's relative effectiveness and recognition as an attitude which measures the importance of things independently of their relation to oneself or to some narrow group with which one identifies. A paradigm of a person who lacks humility is the self-important emperor who grants status to his family because it is *his*, to his subordinates because *he* appointed them, and to his country because *he* chooses to glorify it. Less extreme but still lacking proper humility is the elitist who counts events significant solely in proportion to how they affect his class. The suspicion about those who would destroy the environment, then, is that what they count important is too narrowly confined insofar as it encompasses only what affects beings who, like us, are capable of feeling.

This idea that proper humility requires recognition of the importance of nonsentient nature is similar to the thought of those who charge meat eaters with "species-ism." In both cases it is felt that people too narrowly confine their concerns to the sorts of beings that are most like them. But, however intuitively appealing, the idea will surely arouse objections from our nonenvironmentalist critic. "Why," he will ask, "do you suppose that the sort of humility I *should* have requires me to acknowledge the importance of nonsentient nature aside from its utility? You cannot, by your own admission, argue that nonsentient nature *is* important, appealing to religious or intuitionist grounds. And simply to assert, without further argument, that an ideal humility requires us to view nonsentient nature as important for its own sake begs the question at issue. If proper humility is acknowledging the relative importance of things as one should, then to show that I must lack this you must first establish that one *should* acknowledge the importance of nonsentient nature."

Though some may wish to accept this challenge, there are other ways to pursue the connection between humility and response to nonsentient nature. For example, suppose we grant that proper humility requires only acknowledging a due status to sentient beings. We must admit, then, that it is logically possible for a person to be properly humble even though he viewed all nonsentient nature simply as a resource. But this logical possibility may be a psychological rarity. It may be that, given the sort of beings we are, we would never learn humility before persons without developing the general capacity to cherish, and regard important, many things for their own sakes. The major obstacle to humility before persons is self-importance, a tendency to measure the significance of everything by its relation to oneself and those with whom one identifies. The processes by which we overcome self-importance are doubtless many and complex, but it seems unlikely that they are exclusively concerned with how we relate to other people and animals. Learning humility requires learning to feel that something matters besides what will affect oneself and one's circle of associates. What leads a child to care about what happens to a lost hamster or a stray dog he will not see again is likely also to generate concern for a lost toy or a favorite tree where he used to live. Learning to value things for their own sake, and to count what affects them important aside from their utility, . . . is necessary to the development of humility and it seems likely to take place in experiences with nonsentient nature as well as with people and animals. If a person views all nonsentient nature merely as a resource, then it seems unlikely that he has developed the capacity needed to overcome self-importance.

IV.

This last argument, unfortunately, has its limits. It presupposes an empirical connection between experiencing nature and overcoming self-importance, and this may be challenged. Even if experiencing nature promotes humility before others, there may be other ways people can develop such humility in a world of concrete, glass, and plastic. If not, perhaps all that is needed is limited experience of nature in one's early, developing years; mature adults, having overcome youthful self-importance, may live well enough in artificial surroundings. More importantly, the argument does not fully capture the spirit of the intuition that an ideal person stands humbly before nature. That idea is not simply that experiencing nature tends to foster proper humility before other people; it is, in part, that natural surroundings encourage and are appropriate to an ideal sense of oneself as part of the natural world. Standing alone in the forest, after months in the city, is not merely good as a means of curbing one's arrogance before others; it reinforces and fittingly expresses one's acceptance of oneself as a natural being.

Previously we considered only one aspect of proper humility, namely, a sense of one's relative importance with respect to other human beings. Another aspect, I think, is a kind of *self-acceptance*. This involves acknowledging, in more than a merely intellectual way, that we are the sort of creatures that we are. Whether one is self-accepting is not so much a matter of how one attributes *importance* comparatively to oneself, other people, animals, plants, and other things as it is a matter of understanding, facing squarely, and responding appropriately to who and what one is, e.g., one's powers and limits, one's affinities with other beings and differences from them, one's unalterable nature and one's freedom to change. Self-acceptance is not merely intellectual awareness, for one can be intellectually aware that one is growing old and will eventually die while nevertheless behaving in a thousand foolish ways that reflect a refusal to acknowledge these facts. On the other hand, self-acceptance is not passive resignation, for refusal to pursue what one truly wants within one's limits is a failure to accept the freedom and power one has. Particular behaviors, like dying one's gray hair and dressing like those twenty years younger, do not *necessarily* imply lack of self-acceptance, for there could be reasons for acting in these ways other than the wish to hide from oneself what one really is. One fails to accept oneself when the patterns of behavior and emotion are rooted in a desire to disown and deny features of oneself, to pretend to oneself that they are not there. This is not to say that a self-accepting person makes no value judgments about himself, that he likes all facts about himself, wants equally to develop and display them; he can, and should feel remorse for

his past misdeeds and strive to change his current vices. The point is that he does not disown them, pretend that they do not exist or are facts about something other than himself. Such pretense is incompatible with proper humility because it is seeing oneself as better than one is.

Self-acceptance of this sort has long been considered a human excellence, under various names, but what has it to do with preserving nature? There is, I think, the following connection. As human beings we are part of nature, living, growing, declining, and dying by natural laws similar to those governing other living beings; despite our awesomely distinctive human powers, we share many of the needs, limits, and liabilities of animals and plants. These facts are neither good nor bad in themselves, aside from personal preference and varying conventional values. To say this is to utter a truism which few will deny, but to accept these facts, as facts about oneself, is not so easy—or so common. Much of what naturalists deplore about our increasingly artificial world reflects, and encourages, a denial of these facts, an unwillingness to avow them with equanimity. . . .

My suggestion is not merely that experiencing nature causally promotes such self-acceptance, but also that those who fully accept themselves as part of the natural world lack the common drive to disassociate themselves from nature by replacing natural environments with artificial ones. A storm in the wilds helps us to appreciate our animal vulnerability, but, equally important, the reluctance to experience it may *reflect* an unwillingness to accept this aspect of ourselves. The person who is too ready to destroy the ancient redwoods may lack humility, not so much in the sense that he exaggerates his importance relative to others, but rather in the sense that he tries to avoid seeing himself as one among many natural creatures.

V.

My suggestion so far has been that, though indifference to nonsentient nature is not itself a moral vice, it is likely to reflect either ignorance, a self-importance, or a lack of self-acceptance which we must overcome to have proper humility. A similar idea might be developed connecting attitudes toward nonsentient nature with other human excellences. For example, one might argue that indifference to nature reveals a lack of either an aesthetic sense or some of the natural roots of gratitude.

When we see a hillside that has been gutted by strip miners or the garden replaced by asphalt, our first reaction is probably, "How ugly!" The scenes assault our aesthetic sensibilities. We suspect that no one with a keen sense of beauty could have left such a sight. Admittedly not everything in nature strikes us as beautiful, or even aesthetically interesting, and sometimes a natural scene is replaced with a more impressive architectural masterpiece. But this is not usually the situation in the problem cases which environmentalists are most concerned about. More often beauty is replaced with ugliness.

At this point our critic may well object that, even if he does lack a sense of beauty, this is no moral vice. His cost/benefit calculations take into account the pleasure others may derive from seeing the forests, etc., and so why should he be faulted?

Some might reply that, despite contrary philosophical traditions, aesthetics and morality are not so distinct as commonly supposed. Appreciation of beauty, they may argue, is a human excellence which morally ideal persons should try to develop. But, setting aside this controversial position, there still may be cause for moral concern about those who have no aesthetic response to nature. Even if aesthetic sensibility is not itself a moral virtue, many of the capacities of mind and heart which it presupposes may be ones which are also needed for an appreciation of other people. Consider, for example, curiosity, a mind open to novelty, the ability to look at things from unfamiliar perspectives, empathetic imagination, interest in details, variety, and order, and emotional freedom from the immediate and the practical. All these, and more, seem necessary to aesthetic sensibility, but they are also traits which a person needs to be fully sensitive to people of all sorts. The point is not that a moral person must be able to distinguish beautiful from ugly people; the point is rather that unresponsiveness to what is beautiful, awesome, dainty, dumpy, and otherwise aesthetically interesting in nature probably reflects a lack of the openness of mind and spirit necessary to appreciate the best in human beings.

The anti-environmentalist, however, may refuse to accept the charge that he lacks aesthetic sensibility. If he claims to appreciate seventeenth-century miniature portraits, but to abhor natural wildernesses, he will hardly be convincing. Tastes vary, but aesthetic sense is not *that* selective. He may, instead, insist that he *does* appreciate natural beauty. He spends his vacations, let us suppose, hiking in the Sierras, photographing wildflowers, and so on. He might press his argument as follows: "I enjoy natural beauty as much as anyone, but I fail to see what this has to do with preserving the environment independently of human enjoyment and use. Nonsentient nature is a resource, but one of its best uses is to give us pleasure. I take this into account when I calculate the costs and benefits of preserving a park, planting a garden, and so on. But the problem you raised explicitly set aside the desire to preserve nature as a means to enjoyment. I say, let us enjoy nature fully while we can, but if all sentient beings were to die tomorrow, we might as well blow up all plant life as well. A redwood grove that no one can use or enjoy is utterly worthless."

The attitude expressed here, I suspect, is not a common one, but it represents a philosophical challenge. The beginnings of a reply may be found in the following. When a person takes joy in something, it is a common (and perhaps natural) response to come to cherish it. To cherish something is not simply to be happy with it at the moment, but to care for it for its own sake. This is not to say that one necessarily sees it as having feelings and so wants it to feel good; nor does it imply that one judges the thing to have Moore's intrinsic value. One simply wants the thing to survive and (when appropriate) to thrive, and not simply for its utility. We see this attitude repeatedly regarding mementos. They are not simply valued as a means to remind us of happy occasions; they come to be valued for their own sake. Thus, if someone really took joy in the natural environment, but was prepared to blow it up as soon as sentient life ended, he would lack this common human tendency to cherish what enriches our lives. While this response is not itself a moral virtue, it may be a natural basis of the virtue we call "gratitude." People who have no tendency to cherish things that give them pleasure may be poorly disposed to respond gratefully to persons who are good to them. Again the connection is not one of logical necessity, but it may nevertheless be important. A nonreligious person unable to "thank" anyone for the beauties of nature may nevertheless feel "grateful" in a sense; and I suspect that the person who feels no such "gratitude" toward nature is unlikely to show proper gratitude toward people.

Suppose these conjectures prove to be true. One may wonder what is the point of considering them. Is it to disparage all those who view nature merely as a resource? To do so, it seems, would be unfair, for, even if this attitude typically stems from deficiencies which affect one's attitudes toward sentient beings, there may be exceptions and we have not shown that their view of nonsentient nature is itself blameworthy. But when we set aside questions of blame and inquire what sorts of human traits we want to encourage, our reflections become relevant in a more positive way. The point is not to insinuate that all anti-environmentalists are defective, but to see that those who value such traits as humility, gratitude, and sensitivity to others have reason to promote the love of nature.

NOTES

1. G. E. Moore, *Principia Ethica* (Cambridge: Cambridge University Press, 1903); *Ethics* (London: H. Holt, 1912).
2. By "*proper* humility" I mean that sort and degree of humility that is a morally admirable character trait. How precisely to define this is, of course,

a controversial matter; but the point for present purposes is just to set aside obsequiousness, false modesty, underestimation of one's abilities, and the like.

Thomas Hill, Jr.: Ideals of Human Excellence and Preserving Natural Environments

1. Why does Hill think it is sometimes difficult to explain what is wrong with destroying the environment in terms of rights and welfare? What alternative framework does he propose for looking at the issue?
2. Hill presents several examples of acts which may not necessarily be immoral, but which would clearly reveal a defect in any person who performed them. Do you find his examples convincing? Is harming the environment relevantly similar to these actions?
3. Hill suggests that many environmentally destructive actions might be performed as a result of ignorance. How does he argue for this claim, and how might an "anti-environmentalist" respond?
4. What exactly is *humility*, and why does Hill claim that those who are unmoved by nature lack it? Do you agree with him?
5. What connection, if any, is there between self-acceptance and preserving nature? Can a person fully accept himself or herself while at the same time destroying natural environments?

The Public and Private Morality of Climate Change
John Broome

John Broome begins his essay by introducing two important distinctions. The first is between public morality, which directs government actions, and private morality, which directs those of individuals. The second is between duties of justice, which focus on what we owe to particular people, and duties of goodness, which are duties to make the world better.

Broome argues that when it comes to private morality and what we, as individuals, must do to address climate change, we have only duties of justice. For a variety of reasons, the good we can do to prevent climate change harms is relatively small, and our resources would be better spent in trying to yield greater benefits in non-climate-related areas. Governments, though, *do* have climate-based duties of goodness; given their much greater resources, they can address severe problems, such as medical crises, while also taking steps to reduce damage to the climate.

Both individuals and governments have duties of justice to redress the harms imposed by our emissions. Broome reviews seven different features of the harms that come from our emissions, in support of the claim that such harmful behavior, both on the part of individuals and governments, amounts to an injustice. When it comes to individuals, his verdict is succinct: "Your carbon footprint ought to be zero unless you make restitution." That said, Broome does not in fact advise individuals to compensate everyone who is harmed by our carbon emissions. That would be too unwieldy. Rather, he proposes that we reduce our emissions where we can, and *offset* the rest. This amounts to taking steps to remove or prevent emissions in proportion to causing them.

Broome then turns his attention to a government's duty of goodness to improve climate conditions. He argues that, as a practical matter, governments can discharge their duties of goodness to future generations without asking current citizens to make any net sacrifice. How is such a thing possible? By reducing greenhouse emissions (a sacrifice), but compensating current citizens by allowing them to use up more non-emissions-generating resources. Future generations would therefore be left with fewer of these other resources, but a cleaner environment.

We as individuals are subject to various moral duties. We have a duty to be kind to strangers, to keep our promises, to look after our parents when they are old, and so on. Collective entities, including our governments, are also subject to moral duties, or so I assume. I assume that a government should not imprison innocent people, it should protect refugees, it should support the destitute, and so on, and that these are moral duties.

The moral duties of governments—whatever they are—I call "public morality." They generate derivative moral duties for citizens: we should do what is appropriate to get our government to act rightly, and support it when it does. These duties I call "civic morality." By "private morality," I mean the morality of our private lives; private morality does not include our civic duties.

Climate change creates duties within both public and private morality. I shall describe some of them.

DUTIES OF JUSTICE AND DUTIES OF GOODNESS

Moral duties fall into two broad classes: duties of justice and duties of goodness or beneficence. There may be other sorts of moral duties, too, but I shall be concerned only with these two. I start by making the distinction between them.

The duty of goodness is to make the world better. Some libertarians deny that people as individuals have this duty. I disagree with those libertarians, but I have no need to argue with them here. My conclusions about private morality will not call on this duty of goodness. However, I shall assume that governments have a duty of goodness; I assume they have a duty to make the world better

John Broome, "The Public and Private Morality of Climate Change," from the Tanner Lectures, vol. 32, 2013, pp. 5–20.

for their own citizens at least. For instance, they should create their country's economic infrastructure and design their banking regulations with that aim in mind.

Improving the world is not our only moral duty. When an action of yours would improve the world, you are not necessarily morally required to do it, and sometimes you are not even morally permitted to do it. A famous example is the case of a surgeon who has five patients, each needing an organ in order to survive: one needs a heart, another a liver, a third a kidney, and so on. Suppose the surgeon kills an innocent visitor to the hospital and distributes her organs to the five patients, thereby saving five lives at the expense of one. That leads to a net benefit; it improves the world. Yet this surgeon's act is not morally permissible.

So there must be some other source of moral duties that can oppose the duty of goodness. There is evidently some sort of a moral duty not to harm people, even for the sake of the greater overall good. . . . The duty not to harm is not unlimited; there are occasions when it is morally permissible to harm someone. For instance, you may do harm in self-defense, and you may harm a person when you are inflicting a deserved punishment on her. I am sorry to say I cannot accurately delineate the boundaries of the duty not to harm, but I hope soon to identify one instance of it convincingly.

I take this duty not to harm to be a duty of justice. Other philosophers may classify it differently, and nothing will turn on the classification. It does have at least one feature that is characteristic of justice. It is a duty *owed* to a particular person, or to particular people. If you breach a duty of justice, you are doing an injustice, and there is always someone to whom you do it. To express this fact, we often say that the person has a *right* to your performing the duty. Rights go along with justice. When you have a duty of justice to do something, someone has a right to your doing it.

By contrast, duties of goodness are not owed to particular people. The difference is nicely illustrated by the views of the eighteenth-century philosopher William Godwin. Godwin thought that the duty to promote good is indeed owed to the people whose

good you should promote.[1] He explicitly classified it as a duty of justice. For instance, he thought that if someone else can make better use of your horse than you can, she has a right to it. He thought you do her an injustice if you do not let her have it. Few of us agree with Godwin about that. Most of us think we have a duty to promote goodness, but we think the duty is not owed to particular people, and we therefore do not take it to be a duty of justice.

JUSTICE AND GOODNESS IN PUBLIC AND PRIVATE MORALITY

I am now going to apply this distinction among sorts of duty to the moral duties that arise from climate change. My first point is that the relative importance of justice and goodness differs between private morality and public morality. Justice is relatively more important for private morality, goodness relatively more important for public morality. Indeed, I shall argue that the private morality of climate change is governed entirely by the duty of justice, whereas public morality is also aimed at goodness.

Why do I say this? For two main reasons. The first is known as the "nonidentity problem." It was made prominent by the philosopher Derek Parfit.[2] Remember that a duty of justice is owed to particular people, who have a right to its performance. Take a particular person who is alive 150 years from now—call her "Sarah." Suppose Sarah's life is not very good because we, the current generation, allow climate change to go unchecked. Could she claim we do her an injustice by our profligacy? Could she say she has a right to a better life, which we deny her by emitting so much greenhouse gas? She could not, for a reason I shall now explain.

Suppose we were instead to take the trouble to reduce our emissions. By "we" I am referring to the present generation either in the whole world or within a particular nation. We would live lives of a different sort. The richer among us would travel less by car and plane and buy fewer consumer goods. The poorer would find farming easier and find less need to migrate to the cities; they would also find less need to move to higher ground to escape from the rising sea. There would be many other differences. Indeed, everyone's life would be different. Consequently, many people would have babies with different partners. Even those who would have the same partner as they actually do have would conceive their babies at different times.

The identity of a person depends on the sperm and egg she originates from. No one could have come from a different egg or a different sperm from the one she actually does come from. To put it differently: anyone who originated from a different sperm or a different egg would be a different person. Consequently, even the slightest variation in the timing of conception makes a different person. A slight change in a couple's lives means that they conceive different people. Were we to significantly reduce our emissions of greenhouse gas, it would change the lives of nearly everyone in the world. Within a couple of generations, the entire population of the world would consist of different people. Call this the "nonidentity effect."

Our Sarah would therefore not exist at all, were we to take the trouble to reduce our emissions. If she would not even exist were we to reduce our emissions, she cannot plausibly claim she had a right to a better life, which we violate by not doing so. We could not give Sarah a better life by emitting less gas, so we do not violate a right of hers by emitting profligately. Suppose we did owe a duty to Sarah to reduce emissions. Were we to carry out this duty, there would be no Sarah and therefore no duty. It would be a duty that cannot be satisfied. That makes no sense. We can conclude that our emissions do no injustice to Sarah. The same goes for nearly everyone in her generation.

In a way, the nonidentity effect excuses us as a generation from a charge of injustice toward future generations. Please do not think it excuses us from every moral duty to reduce emissions. Our continued emissions make the lives of future generations much less good than they could be. So they constitute a serious violation of our duty of goodness. This is not in any way a minor violation of morality; making the world less good is a serious moral fault. But it is not a violation of justice.

The nonidentity effect of a generation's or a country's emissions will obviously be much bigger than the nonidentity effect of a single person's emissions.

If you reduce your own emissions of greenhouse gas, that will affect the identity of some people in the next few generations, but probably not very many. So the nonidentity effect provides individuals with little excuse against a charge of injustice to future generations. That is the first reason justice is relatively more important for individuals than it is for nations and their governments.

THE HARM DONE BY AN INDIVIDUAL

The second reason justice is relatively more important in the private morality of climate change is that the duty of goodness demands very little of an individual. It requires you to reduce your greenhouse gas emissions only insofar as you can do so at a very small cost. Probably it requires you to turn off the light when you leave a room—that sort of thing. The reason is quantitative, and to explain it I need to start by giving you some idea of the quantity of harm a person's emissions do.

I shall use a calculation shown to me by David Frame, now of Victoria University in New Zealand.[3] I must emphasize that Frame means it to be very rough. The figures are intended only to show you the order of magnitude of the harm you do, nothing more. Frame calculates that an average person from a rich country, if she was born in 1950, will emit during the course of her whole life about 800 tonnes of carbon dioxide. This will warm the atmosphere by about half a billionth of a degree. A major part of the harm climate change will do is the killing of people. The World Health Organization has published predictions of the number who will be killed, and on that basis we can estimate that this 800 tonnes will shorten people's lives in total by some months. Each year of a rich person's emissions shortens lives by one or two days. We will not shorten any single person's life that much, but each of us shortens lives in total by that amount.

This is a serious harm. None of us would want to be responsible for shortening people's lives to that extent. This figure shows you, read conversely, how much good you could do by reducing your emissions. Some people despair in the face of climate change. They think the problem is so huge that nothing they can do as individuals will do any good. But they are wrong. By reducing your emissions, you can do significant good through extending people's lives. If you stop your emissions, each year you will extend lives by a day or two.

But the main point I want to make is that the good you can do by reducing your emissions, though significant, is small compared with other opportunities you have. Suppose you reduce your annual emissions to zero in the cheapest possible way (which is by offsetting them, as I shall explain later). It will cost you a few hundred dollars per year. For that you will extend people's lives by one or two days each year. But for a few hundred dollars, a charity that treats tuberculosis can cure a person's infection, and thereby extend her life for many years or decades. Of course, reducing emissions will do good in other ways as well as by saving lives, but they are not enough to close this very large gap in benefits. So if you aim to use your resources to improve the world, reducing emissions of greenhouse gas is not the way to do it. To improve the world, you should carry on emitting, and send the money you save by doing so to a tuberculosis charity. This is why I say that the duty of goodness does not require you to reduce your emissions significantly.

Why does the same argument not apply to governments? It's because governments—at least the governments of large countries—control more resources. Like individuals, they have more effective ways of using resources to do good, by treating tuberculosis, controlling malaria and polio, providing clean drinking water around the world, and so on. But even if they were to do all those things, they could *still* improve the world further by using their power to reduce greenhouse gas emissions. A government's duty of goodness requires it to treat tuberculosis, control malaria, provide clean water, and so on, *and* control climate change. That is not so for an individual. If you were to devote all your resources to improving the world, even when they were completely exhausted, the need for tuberculosis treatment would still be more pressing than the need to reduce greenhouse gas emissions.

THE INJUSTICE OF EMISSIONS

The private morality of climate change therefore does not arise from the duty of goodness. It arises instead from the duty of justice. What justice does the duty of justice require of individuals?

I am concerned with the particular duty of justice not to harm. I have already said that each person's emissions of greenhouse gas do harm. I have even given a rough estimate of the amount of one particular harm they do: the harm of shortening lives. Earlier I pointed out that not all harms are necessarily unjust, but next I shall argue that the harm done by emissions is indeed an injustice. I cannot do this conclusively, because I am not able to identify exactly where the boundary lies between harms that are unjust and those that are not. But I shall mention seven different characteristics of the harm done by our emissions, and by the time I have reached the end of the list, I think it will be clear that this harm lies on the side of injustice. Several points beside the seven are so obvious that I do not include them in the list: the harm caused by emissions is not a merited punishment, it is done without the consent of the person harmed, and so on. Here is the list.

First, the harm done by our emissions is the result of something we *do*. Many of us make a distinction between doing harm and failing to prevent harm. If you fail to donate to a charity that relieves poverty, you fail to prevent the harm of poverty, but many of us do not think this failure is an injustice. Emitting greenhouse gas is different. In living our lives, we *act* in ways that cause greenhouse gases to be emitted. We *cause* carbon dioxide to spew from our chimneys and the exhaust pipes of our cars. These are consequences of things we do, rather than of things we omit to do.

Second, the harm we do by our emissions is serious. It may be permissible to do a trivial amount of harm, but this harm is far from trivial. I have given an idea of its size.

Third, the harm we do is not accidental. Indeed, we do it knowingly, though not deliberately. Few people in the developed world are ignorant of the greenhouse effect. Accidental harms are not an injustice, but emissions are not in that category.

Fourth, we do not compensate the victims of our harm. An injustice can sometimes be canceled by compensation, but our emissions are not canceled in this way.

Fifth, most of us make our emissions for our own benefit. That is not true of all of us. Some people are exceptionally altruistic and act for the sake of others. They may use the money they save by not cutting their emissions to benefit mankind. I am addressing not them, but the less altruistic majority. I said that justice normally prohibits you from harming other people even in order to make the world better. It more strongly prohibits you from harming other people in order to benefit yourself.

Sixth, the harms done by the emissions of the rich are not fully reciprocated. Some environmental harms are reciprocal. Traffic congestion is an example. If you drive to work, the presence of your car on the roads impedes other people on their way to work. They equally impede you. Each of you is significantly harming others by delaying them, but because the harm is reciprocal, we do not think that each of you is doing an injustice to others. Climate change is different. It is mostly a one-way transaction in which the present rich harm the present poor and future generations and are not much harmed in return. When I say that greenhouse gas emissions are an injustice, I am referring to the emissions of the present rich.

A seventh characteristic of greenhouse gas emissions is that we could easily reduce them. I shall soon explain that this is easier than you may think. You might be excused for causing harms that it would be very hard to avoid causing, but emitting greenhouse gas is not in that category.

I conclude from all these considerations that our emissions of greenhouse gas are an injustice.

THE INDIVIDUAL DUTY NOT TO CAUSE EMISSIONS

It follows that each of us is under a duty of justice not to cause the emission of greenhouse gas, at least without compensating the people who are harmed as a result. Your carbon footprint ought to be zero unless you make restitution. This is strong advice, but I find I cannot avoid drawing this conclusion. It puts me in an unusual position for a moral philosopher. Normally, moral philosophers talk in generalities. We avoid preaching to people about particular moral demands. But here I am doing that. Fortunately, you will see in a moment that this duty turns out to be less onerous than it may at first appear.

By what means should you perform this duty of justice? You might try to do it by compensating the people you harm. Doing so would be remarkably cheap. Most of the harm you cause will not happen till far in the future. This means that if you put aside money now to compensate the victims of your harm, you can exploit the power of compound interest before you have to pay it over. William Nordhaus calculates that if you are lucky enough to be able to invest your money at 5.5 percent per year, $7.40 is enough to compensate for the harm done by a tonne of carbon dioxide.[4] Since you emit perhaps twenty or thirty tonnes in a year, a couple of hundred dollars a year will suffice.

However, I do not recommend this means of trying to achieve justice, because it will fail. Remember that duties of justice are owed to particular people. Your emissions of greenhouse gas are an injustice done to a large fraction of the world's population over a long period of time. You will not be able to compensate each of them individually.

You might try to make restitution through a collective international scheme of some sort. That way, you will not compensate all the individuals you harm, but you might manage some sort of surrogate compensation, by compensating large populations rather than individuals. Possibly you might satisfy justice by other means. But there remains another problem. You do not know how much compensation you actually owe. None of us knows how much harm we cause by our emissions. We may be able to compute how much gas we emit, but the harm that gas does is very uncertain. Predictions of the effects of climate change are recognized to be very uncertain indeed. I have mentioned Nordhaus's figure, but I do not think he would claim it is particularly reliable.

You would do much better not to make the emissions in the first place; no compensation will then be required. This is possible. We all know some steps we might take: do not live wastefully, be frugal with energy in particular, switch off lights, do not waste water, eat less meat, eat local food, and so on. Many of these are steps you can take at little or no cost to yourself, and you should take those ones. However, you could not live in a way that does not cause the emission of any greenhouse gas at all. Virtually anything you buy has been produced using energy from fossil fuels. You can certainly reduce your emissions. But your most effective way of re-ducing your emissions to zero is to cancel or *offset* the emissions that you will still be causing after you have taken the obvious steps. Offsetting is a good way to fulfill your duty of justice. I shall explain how it works in a moment.

I am not telling you that offsetting is a way to solve the problem of climate change. I have already said that reducing your individual emissions of greenhouse gas—by offsetting or in other ways—is not the most effective way for you to improve the world. Your duty to have a zero carbon footprint does not derive from your duty of goodness. You must do it to avoid committing an injustice to other people—simply that. So far as solving the problem of climate change is concerned, your best route is through political action to induce your government to do what it should.

OFFSETTING

Offsetting your emissions means ensuring that for every unit of greenhouse gas you cause to be added to the atmosphere, you also cause a unit to be subtracted from it. If you offset, on balance you add nothing. Offsetting does not remove the very molecules that you emit, but the climate does not care which particular molecules are warming it. If you offset all your emissions, you make sure that your presence in the world causes no addition to the greenhouse gas in the atmosphere. You do not contribute to warming the atmosphere, so you do no harm through climate change. It is not that you do harm, which you then compensate for; offsetting is not a sort of compensation. It is a way to avoid harming in the first place.

It will not be easy to calculate the offset you need. You must make sure you offset not just the gas that is directly emitted by your own actions, but also the gas that supplied the energy used in making everything you consume. The average emissions in your own country will not be a good guide, because much of what you consume will have been manu-factured abroad. It would be safest to overestimate. But in any case, this calculation is much less per-vaded by uncertainty than trying to calculate how much harm your emissions do, with the aim of compensating people for them. This adds to the reasons for preferring offsetting to compensating.

How do you offset in practice? You may be able to subtract gas from the atmosphere yourself. One way of doing so is to grow trees. As they grow, trees remove carbon from the air to build their bodies: they take in carbon dioxide molecules, keep the carbon, and release the oxygen. But you would need to make sure that your trees' carbon is perma-nently kept out of the air, and that would be hard to achieve. Eventually, your trees will die and de-compose, and their carbon will return to the air. Somehow you will have to ensure your forest will be replanted again and again perpetually even after your death. For that reason, effective do-it-yourself offsetting is difficult.

More easily practicable means of offsetting are "preventive," as I call them. Instead of taking carbon dioxide out of the atmosphere, they prevent it from getting into the atmosphere in the first place.

Plenty of commercial organizations offer to prevent carbon emissions on your behalf. You pay them a fee per tonne of offsetting you ask them to do. They use your money to finance projects that diminish emissions somewhere in the world. Most projects create sources of renewable energy. For instance, they build hydroelectric power stations or wind farms. Others promote the efficient use of energy. One installs efficient cooking stoves in people's homes in Africa and Asia. Cooking with firewood is an important cause of carbon emis-sions, and efficient stoves reduce the quantity that is emitted.

Preventive offsetting is cheap. Responsible com-panies will offset a tonne of emissions for around ten dollars. This means you can offset all your emis-sions for a few hundred dollars. That is why I said you can easily avoid harming people through your emissions.

Many environmentalists are strongly opposed to offsetting. Greenpeace is opposed, for example. One of its arguments is: "The truth is, once you've put a tonne of CO_2 into the atmosphere, there's nothing off-setting can do to stop it changing our climate."[5] I do not think this is true. If at the same time you put a tonne of carbon dioxide into the atmosphere, you subtract another tonne, your actions together do not change the climate. So, since the climate does not change, the tonne you emit does not change it. Certainly, *you* do not change the climate, which is what matters.

Still, I recognize there are significant moral and practical problems connected with offsetting. One of them is that it is difficult to be sure that the reduction in emissions you pay for really happens. But I prefer to leave these for our discussion, because I want to get on to public morality.

GOVERNMENTS' DUTIES OF GOODNESS

Governments, like individuals, bear duties of justice. However, in responding to climate change, they also have duties of goodness. I am going to concentrate on those because I have already talked about justice. I want to survey a different part of the morality of climate change.

When governments try to promote goodness, they must generally do some complex calculations. Their actions, especially over climate change, benefit many people and also impose costs on many people. Different benefits have to be aggregated together somehow, and so do different costs. Then benefits have to be weighed against costs. Cost-benefit analysis of some sort is inevitable. Climate change is a problem on a vast scale, affecting the whole world for centuries, and the quantitative methods of economics are necessary for coping with it.

Cost-benefit analysis also calls for ethical analysis, because the valuing and weighing of benefits and costs raise moral questions of many sorts. How should benefits to the rich be weighed against benefits to the poor? How should we value the loss of a person's life against the mundane good things that life contains? How should we take account of the huge uncertainty that surrounds climate change, including the small chance of total catastrophe? How should we weigh distant future benefits against present costs? How should we take into account the changes in the world's population that climate change will undoubtedly cause, including the small chance that our population will collapse to small numbers or even to extinction?

EFFICIENCY

All of those questions are fertile sources of disagreement and argument. But I have decided to leave them aside and take up one subject that does not involve weighing and aggregating. Instead, it involves what economists call efficiency. Having spent most of this lecture talking about private duties of justice that particularly do not aim to solve the problem of climate change, I am going to spend the rest of it on something that perhaps might solve it. It is a point that I have come to think is extremely important for the practical politics of climate change.

Oddly enough, it is a point of simple economics. When a person engages in some activity that emits greenhouse gas, the gas spreads around the globe and delivers small harms everywhere. These harms are among the costs of what the person does, but the person who causes the gas to be emitted does not bear this cost. It is borne by all people who suffer the harm. In economists' terminology, it is an "external cost" of the activity. Emissions of greenhouse gas constitute an "externality," as economists put it.

Externalities cause *inefficiency*. From the point of view of economics, this is what principally makes climate change a problem. Inefficiency here is what is sometimes called more specifically "Pareto inefficiency." It is defined as a situation in which it would be technically possible to make some people better off without making anyone worse off; a change of this sort is called a "Pareto improvement." Because emissions are an externality, they cause inefficiency in this sense, so a Pareto improvement is possible. I can go further. It would be technically possible to go so far as to remove the externality through a Pareto improvement.

This is a consequence of very elementary economic theory, though I admit I had to be reminded of its implications for climate change by my one-time teacher Duncan Foley.[6] The elementary economics needs to be modified to take account of the nonidentity effect, but it is nevertheless true that no one needs to make any sacrifice to solve the problem caused by the externality of greenhouse gas emissions.

I can describe in broad terms how the externality could be solved without any sacrifices. Although we are bequeathing to our successors a dirty atmosphere, we are doing quite a lot of good things for them in other ways. We are leaving them a lot of resources: cities, economic infrastructure, cultivated land, knowledge, and also those natural resources that we do not use up. Suppose we reduce our emissions of greenhouse gas. Other things being equal, that would require a sacrifice on our part. But we could fully compensate ourselves for the sacrifice by consuming more of other resources and leaving less to future generations in other ways. We could compensate ourselves to the extent that we are no worse off on balance. In macroeconomic terms, we could keep our own consumption constant and redirect our investment toward reducing greenhouse gas emissions. Future generations would receive from us fewer resources of other sorts, but they would have a cleaner atmosphere, and they would end up better off on balance.

Here is a slightly more concrete example of how this could be done. We could impose a carbon tax equal to the external damage done by emissions. Then we could compensate each person in some way for the carbon tax she pays. For example, we could reduce her income tax to the extent that she is just as well off as she was before. The carbon tax itself would finance some of the compensation, but it will not be enough to finance full compensation for everybody. The balance could be financed by a loan that will be repaid by future generations.

The externality of climate change could be removed without anyone's making a sacrifice. This raises a puzzle. When delegates come each year to meetings of the United Nations Framework Convention on Climate Change, at Copenhagen or Durban or somewhere else, they take themselves to be negotiating about how to distribute among the nations the burden of reducing climate change. No government will agree to accept a burden—to impose a sacrifice on its people—so the meetings regularly fail to achieve the reductions in emissions that are required. Yet I am saying that eliminating the problem of climate change requires no sacrifices at all. What is going on?

EFFICIENCY VERSUS OPTIMIZATION

I am telling the truth. It would indeed be possible in principle to eliminate the externality without any sacrifices. Doing so would be an improvement on the present situation, since some people would be better off and no one would be worse off. But it does not follow that this is the best thing that can be done about climate change. Most of the economists who work on climate change have chosen to look for this best thing, and their thinking has influenced the political process. These economists approach the problem as one of *optimization*. They look for the *best* way of managing our resources: the way that will do the most good. They work out how the international community can best meet its duty of goodness. This involves weighing benefits and costs in the way I have described. It turns out that, if their calculations are correct and founded on correct ethical principles, it would be best if the present generation did make some sacrifices for the future. . . .

Compare these three options:

Business as usual. ("BAU")

Reduce emissions and fully compensate ourselves for doing so, so there is no sacrifice. ("Compensation")

Reduce emissions and do not fully compensate ourselves for doing so, so there is sacrifice. ("Optimum")

. . .

Compensation is unattractive. Not only is it worse than Optimum, but it also incorporates injustice. BAU is an unjust situation: the present rich harm the present poor by our emissions of greenhouse gas, and that is unjust. If we move from there to Compensation, the rich are paid for reducing their emissions by those who suffer from them. This is an improvement for those who suffer, but it nevertheless perpetuates the injustice. If someone unjustly hurts you every day, you may be able to improve your situation by paying her to stop it, but that does not remove the injustice.

So I understand why the political process aims toward Optimum rather than Compensation. But the constant failure of the political process has made me cynical. National leaders will not commit their presently living people—in most cases their electorate—to the sacrifices they must make to achieve Optimum. I no longer think Optimum can be reached through negotiation, and I now favor aiming instead at Compensation. The issue at stake would then be how to distribute the *benefits* of controlling climate change—not the burdens—among the nations. Putting the question in this optimistic form might break the political logjam.

The difference between Compensation and Optimum is a matter of the distribution of resources between people: between the rich and the poor and between present and future generations. This distribution is not primarily determined by climate change, and dealing with climate change need not involve putting it right. If you aim for the very best outcome, you are aiming to correct all the present ills of the world. For example, suppose you think that the correct rate for discounting future commodities is below the interest rate in the market. By implication, you think the market does not pass as many resources to the future as it should; present people are consuming too much and not leaving enough for our successors. If, in dealing with climate change, you choose policies that are optimal according to your lower discount rate, you will find yourself making up for this general failure, as well as for the particular problem of climate change. Now that I have become cynical, I think we should concentrate on solving the particular problem and temporarily leave aside the general one.

PUBLIC MORALITY

Should we understand this as a moral duty of goodness, resting on governments and the international community? It could be argued that promoting efficiency is not even a moral duty at all. It is in everyone's interests. We could think of this task of government as merely one of coordinating people's activities in pursuing their own interests. We might even think a government in this domain acts not as an agent in its own right, but as a mere mechanism through which individual people coordinate their activities by mutual agreement. Many economists claim that ethics has nothing to do with economics, and many of those same economists claim that economics is concerned with efficiency only. I think this idea may be the basis of their thinking.

But governments have too many of the characteristics of agency for this to be plausible. For example, governments clearly have intentions. After two centuries, the Monroe Doctrine still expresses one of the US government's intentions, even though the personnel who constitute the government have changed many times. True, it remains a topic for

philosophical research how a collective entity can have intentions, but it is a fact. As agents, governments are potentially bearers of moral duties, and improving the world is one duty they actually bear. Moreover, they cannot be merely a forum where agents coordinate their interests, since many of the relevant interests belong to people who are not yet born. Governments have a moral responsibility toward those people.

If governments cannot achieve the best outcome, Optimum, their duty of goodness requires them at least to aim for Compensation.

This sets a task for the economics profession. The theory tells us that Compensation, where no one makes a sacrifice, is possible. But to make it possible in practice requires some work. We are to reduce our emissions, financing the cost of doing so by loans that will be repaid by future people. But we know well that there is a limit to the amount that governments can borrow, and several governments seem to have already reached their limit. We therefore need new economic institutions that are robust enough to support enough borrowing to achieve Compensation. Economists must design these institutions.

I hope institutions can be created that will make Compensation possible. If so, I hope it will allow progress to be made on climate change. But remember that Compensation is not a good solution. If Compensation can be achieved, Optimum still remains a possibility. Getting from Compensation to Optimum is a matter of the distribution of resources between generations. It could be achieved by canceling the debt that builds up under Compensation. I hope that by making Compensation a real possibility, we might achieve something more like Optimum in the end. In taking the cynical position, I have not abandoned the aim of doing the best.

NOTES

1. William Godwin, *Enquiry Concerning Political Justice*, 3rd ed. (1798; reprint, Harmondsworth: Penguin Press, 1976).
2. Derek Parfit, *Reasons and Persons* (Oxford: Oxford University Press, 1984), chap. 16.
3. David Frame, "Personal and Intergenerational Carbon Footprints" (forthcoming).
4. William Nordhaus, *A Question of Balance* (New Haven, CT: Yale University Press, 2008), 15, 178.

5. Statement by Charlie Kronick of Greenpeace, January 17, 2007.

6. See Duncan Foley, "The Economic Fundamentals of Global Warming," in *Twenty-First Century Microeconomics: Responding to the Climate Challenge*, edited by Jonathan M. Harris and Neva R. Goodwin (Cheltenham, UK: Edward Elgar, 2009), 115–26.

John Broome: The Public and Private Morality of Climate Change

1. Explain the non-identity effect. Does it have the implications for duties to address climate change that Broome thinks?

2. Broome believes that individuals have no duties of justice to redress climate change harms they cause. Why does he say this? Do you agree with his reasons? Why or why not?

3. What is the difference between efficiency and optimization? Do you agree with the use Broome makes of this distinction?

4. What is offsetting, and is this a plausible way for individuals to fulfill their duties of goodness regarding climate change?

5. Broome emphasizes the possibility of governments addressing their duties of goodness to future generations without asking their citizens to undertake any sacrifices. What are his reasons for this emphasis, and do you find them attractive? Why or why not?

It's Not My Fault: Global Warming and Individual Moral Obligations

Walter Sinnott-Armstrong

Global warming, and climate change more generally, is causing huge problems. Sinnott-Armstrong believes that governments have moral duties to address these problems. These duties fall especially to the wealthier countries, which are responsible for the vast majority of the harms that arise from global warming. But the case is far less clear when it comes to individuals, since individuals are far less able to reduce or prevent these harms and are far less responsible for causing them in the first place. To bring out the challenge, Sinnott-Armstrong invites us to consider a case of wasteful driving. Suppose I take a pleasure drive in a gas-guzzling car. Have I violated any moral obligation in doing so?

Sinnott-Armstrong admits that he has the intuition that I have indeed done wrong in taking such a drive. But he offers many reasons to be suspicious of moral intuitions, and so he argues that if we are to be rightly confident of a verdict here, then we must enlist some general moral principle to show that my pleasure ride is immoral. Sinnott-Armstrong considers a wide variety of such principles: that we oughtn't to do harm or worsen harms that are already occurring, the Kantian principle of universalizability and principle of humanity, the doctrine of double effect, and several others. He then argues that none of these principles implies that I have done wrong in taking such a pleasure drive. According to Sinnott-Armstrong, my moral obligation is to prompt my government to take action to combat the harms of global warming—only in that way will my actions make a real contribution to solving the problem.

From W. Sinnott-Armstrong, "It's Not *My* Fault: Global Warming and Individual Moral Obligations," in W. Sinnott-Armstrong and Richard Howarth, eds., *Perspectives on Climate Change* (Elsevier, 2006), pp. 295–315. Notes have been edited.

. . . . Even if scientists establish that global warming is occurring, even if economists confirm that its costs will be staggering, and even if political theorists agree that governments must do something about it, it is still not clear what moral obligations regarding global warming devolve upon individuals like you and me. That is the question to be addressed in this essay.

I. ASSUMPTIONS

To make the issue stark, let us begin with a few assumptions. I believe that these assumptions are probably roughly accurate, but none is certain, and I will not try to justify them here. Instead, I will simply take them for granted for the sake of argument.

First, global warming has begun and is likely to increase over the next century. We cannot be sure exactly how much or how fast, but hot times are coming.

Second, a significant amount of global warming is due to human activities. The main culprit is fossil fuels.

Third, global warming will create serious problems for many people over the long term by causing climate changes, including violent storms, floods from sea level rises, droughts, heat waves, and so on. Millions of people will probably be displaced or die.

Fourth, the poor will be hurt most of all. The rich countries are causing most of the global warming, but they will be able to adapt to climate changes more easily. Poor countries that are close to sea level might be devastated.

Fifth, governments, especially the biggest and richest ones, are able to mitigate global warming. They can impose limits on emissions. They can require or give incentives for increased energy efficiency. They can stop deforestation and fund reforestation. They can develop ways to sequester carbon dioxide in oceans or underground. These steps will help, but the only long-run solution lies in alternatives to fossil fuels. These alternatives can be found soon if governments start massive research projects now.

Sixth, it is too late to stop global warming. Because there is so much carbon dioxide in the atmosphere already, because carbon dioxide remains in the atmosphere for so long, and because we will remain dependent on fossil fuels in the near future, governments can slow down global warming or reduce its severity, but they cannot prevent it. Hence, governments need to adapt. They need to build seawalls. They need to reinforce houses that cannot withstand storms. They need to move populations from low-lying areas.

Seventh, these steps will be costly. Increased energy efficiency can reduce expenses, adaptation will create some jobs, and money will be made in the research and production of alternatives to fossil fuels. Still, any steps that mitigate or adapt to global warming will slow down our economies, at least in the short run. That will hurt many people, especially many poor people.

Eighth, despite these costs, the major governments throughout the world still morally ought to take some of these steps. The clearest moral obligation falls on the United States. The United States caused and continues to cause more of the problem than any other country. The United States can spend more resources on a solution without sacrificing basic necessities. This country has the scientific expertise to solve technical problems. Other countries follow its lead (sometimes!). So the United States has a special moral obligation to help mitigate and adapt to global warming.

2. THE PROBLEM

Even assuming all of this, it is still not clear what I as an individual morally ought to do about global warming. That issue is not as simple as many people assume. I want to bring out some of its complications.

It should be clear from the start that *individual* moral obligations do not always follow directly from *collective* moral obligations. The fact that your government morally ought to do something does not prove that *you* ought to do it, even if your government fails. Suppose that a bridge is dangerous because so much traffic has gone over it and continues to go over it. The government has a moral obligation to make the bridge safe. If the government fails to do its duty, it does not follow that I personally have a moral obligation to fix the bridge. It does not even follow that I have a moral obligation to fill in one crack in the bridge, even if the bridge would be fixed if everyone filled in one crack, even if I drove over the bridge many times, and even if I still drive over it every day. Fixing the bridge is the government's job, not mine. While I ought to encourage the government to fulfill its obligations, I do not have to take on those obligations myself.

All that this shows is that government obligations do not *always* imply parallel individual obligations. Still, maybe *sometimes* they do. My government has a moral obligation to teach arithmetic to the children in my town, including my own children. If the government fails in this obligation, then I do take on a moral obligation to teach arithmetic to my children. Thus, when the government fails in its obligations, sometimes I have to fill in, and sometimes I do not.

What about global warming? If the government fails to do anything about global warming, what am I supposed to do about it? There are lots of ways for me as an individual to fight global warming. I can protest against bad government policies and vote for candidates who will make the government fulfill its moral obligations. I can support private organizations that fight global warming, such as the Pew Foundation, or boycott companies that contribute too much to global warming, such as most oil companies. Each of these cases is interesting, but they all differ. To simplify our discussion, we need to pick one act as our focus.

My example will be wasteful driving. Some people drive to their jobs or to the store because they have no other reasonable way to work and eat. I want to avoid issues about whether these goals justify driving, so I will focus on a case where nothing so important is gained. I will consider driving for fun on a beautiful Sunday afternoon. My drive is not necessary to cure depression or calm aggressive impulses. All that is gained is pleasure: Ah, the feel of wind in your hair! The views! How spectacular! Of course, you could drive a fuel-efficient hybrid car. But fuel-efficient cars have less "get up and go." So let us consider a gas-guzzling sport utility vehicle. Ah, the feeling of power! The excitement! Maybe you do not like to go for drives in sport utility vehicles on sunny Sunday afternoons, but many people do.

Do we have a moral obligation not to drive in such circumstances? This question concerns driving, not *buying* cars. To make this clear, let us assume that I borrow the gas-guzzler from a friend. This question is also not about *legal* obligations. So let us assume that it is perfectly legal to go for such drives. Perhaps it ought to be illegal, but it is not. Note also that my question is not about what would be *best*. Maybe it would be better, even morally better, for me not to drive a gas-guzzler just for fun. But that is not the issue I want to address here. My question is whether I have a *moral* obligation not to drive a gas-guzzler just for fun on this particular sunny Sunday afternoon.

One final complication must be removed. I am interested in global warming, but there might be other moral reasons not to drive unnecessarily. I risk causing an accident, since I am not a perfect driver. I also will likely spew exhaust into the breathing space of pedestrians, bicyclists, or animals on the side of the road as I drive by. Perhaps these harms and risks give me a moral obligation not to go for my joyride. That is not clear. After all, these reasons also apply if I drive the most efficient car available, and even if I am driving to work with no other way to keep my job. Indeed, I might scare or injure bystanders even if my car gave off no greenhouse gases or pollution. In any case, I want to focus on global warming. So my real question is whether the facts about global warming give me any moral obligation not to drive a gas-guzzler just for fun on this sunny Sunday afternoon.

I admit that I am *inclined* to answer, *Yes*. To me, global warming does *seem* to make such wasteful driving morally wrong.

Still, I do not feel confident in this judgment. I know that other people disagree (even though they are also concerned about the environment). I would probably have different moral intuitions about this case if I had been raised differently or if I now lived in a different culture. My moral intuition might be distorted by overgeneralization from the other cases where I think that other entities (large governments) do have moral obligations to fight global warming. I also worry that my moral intuition might be distorted by my desire to avoid conflicts with my environmentalist friends. The issue of global warming generates strong emotions because of its political implications and because of how scary its effects are. It is also a peculiarly modern case, especially because it operates on a much grander scale than my moral intuitions evolved to handle long ago when acts did not have such long-term effects on future generations (or at least people were not aware of such effects). In such circumstances, I doubt that we are justified in trusting our moral intuitions alone. We need some kind of confirmation.

One way to confirm the truth of my moral intuitions would be to derive them from a general moral principle. A principle could tell us why wasteful driving is morally wrong, so we would not have to depend on bare assertion. And a principle might be supported by more trustworthy moral beliefs. The problem is *which* principle?

3. ACTUAL ACT PRINCIPLES

One plausible principle refers to causing harm. If one person had to inhale all of the exhaust from my car, this would harm him and give me a moral obligation not to drive my car just for fun. Such cases suggest:

> *The harm principle*: We have a moral obligation not to perform an act that causes harm to others.

This principle implies that I have a moral obligation not to drive my gas-guzzler just for fun *if* such driving causes harm.

The problem is that such driving does *not* cause harm in normal cases. If one person were in a position to inhale all of my exhaust, then he would get sick if I did drive, and he would not get sick if I did not drive (under normal circumstances). In contrast, global warming will still occur even if I do not drive just for fun. Moreover, even if I do drive a gas-guzzler just for fun for a long time, global warming will not occur unless lots of other people also expel greenhouse gases. So my individual act is neither necessary nor sufficient for global warming. . . .

Another argument leads to the same conclusion: the harms of global warming result from the massive quantities of greenhouse gases in the atmosphere. Greenhouse gases (such as carbon dioxide and water vapor) are perfectly fine in small quantities. They help plants grow. The problem emerges only when there is too much of them. But my joyride by itself does not cause the massive quantities that are harmful.

Contrast someone who pours cyanide poison into a river. Later someone drinking from the river downstream ingests some molecules of the poison. Those molecules cause the person to get ill and die. This is very different from the causal chain in global warming, because no particular molecules from my car cause global warming in the direct way that particular molecules of the poison do cause the drinker's death. Global warming is more like a river that is going to flood downstream because of torrential rains. I pour a quart of water into the river upstream (maybe just because I do not want to carry it). My act of pouring the quart into the river is not a cause of the flood. Analogously, my act of driving for fun is not a cause of global warming.

Contrast also another large-scale moral problem: famine relief. Some people say that I have no moral obligation to contribute to famine relief because the famine will continue and people will die whether or not I donate my money to a relief agency. However, I could help a certain individual if I gave my donation directly to that individual. In contrast, if I refrain from driving for fun on this one Sunday, there is no individual who will be helped in the least. I cannot help anyone by depriving myself of this joyride.

The point becomes clearer if we distinguish global warming from climate change. You might think that my driving on Sunday raises the temperature of the globe by an infinitesimal amount. I doubt that, but, even if it does, my exhaust on that Sunday does not cause any climate change at all. No storms or floods or droughts or heat waves can be traced to my individual act of driving. It is these climate changes that cause harms to people. Global warming by itself causes no harm without climate change. Hence, since my individual act of driving on that one Sunday does not cause any climate change, it causes no harm to anyone.

The point is not that harms do not occur from global warming. I have already admitted that they do. The point is also not that my exhaust is overkill, like poisoning someone who is already dying from poison. My exhaust is not sufficient for the harms of global warming, and I do not intend those harms. Nor is it the point that the harms from global warming occur much later in time, if I place a time bomb in a building, I can cause harm many years later. And the point is not that the harm I cause is imperceptible. I admit that some harms can be imperceptible because they are too small or for other reasons. Instead, the point is simply that my individual joyride does not cause global warming, climate change, or any of their resulting harms, at least directly. . . .

Of course, even if I do not cause climate change, I still might seem to contribute to climate change in the sense that I make it worse. If so, another principle applies:

> The contribution principle: We have a moral obligation not to make problems worse.

This principle applies if climate change will be worse if I drive than it will be if I do not drive.

The problem with this argument is that my act of driving does not even make climate change worse. Climate change would be just as bad if I did not drive. The reason is that climate change becomes worse only if more people (and animals) are hurt or if they are hurt worse. There is nothing bad about global warming or climate change in itself if no people (or animals) are harmed. But there is no individual person or animal who will be worse off if I drive than if I do not drive my gas-guzzler just for fun. Global warming and climate change occur on such a massive scale that my individual driving makes no difference to the welfare of anyone.

Some might complain that this is not what they mean by "contribute." All it takes for me to contribute to global warming in their view is for me to expel greenhouse gases into the atmosphere. I do *that* when I drive, so we can apply:

> The gas principle: We have a moral obligation not to expel greenhouse gases into the atmosphere.

If this principle were true, it would explain why I have a moral obligation not to drive my gas-guzzler just for fun.

Unfortunately, it is hard to see any reason to accept this principle. There is nothing immoral about greenhouse gases in themselves when they cause no harm. Greenhouse gases include carbon dioxide and water vapor, which occur naturally and help plants grow. The problem of global warming occurs because of the high quantities of greenhouse gases, not because of anything bad about smaller quantities of the same gases. So it is hard to see why I would have a moral obligation not to expel harmless quantities of greenhouse gases. And that is all I do by myself.

Furthermore, if the gas principle were true, it would be unbelievably restrictive. It implies that I have a moral obligation not to boil water (since water vapor is a greenhouse gas) or to exercise (since I expel carbon dioxide when I breathe heavily). When you think it through, an amazing array of seemingly morally acceptable activities would be ruled out by the gas principle. These implications suggest that we had better look elsewhere for a reason why I have a moral obligation not to drive a gas-guzzler just for fun.

Maybe the reason is risk. It is sometimes morally wrong to create a risk of a harm even if that harm does not occur. I grant that drunk driving is immoral, because it risks harm to others, even if the drunk driver gets home safely without hurting anyone. Thus, we get another principle:

> The risk principle: We have a moral obligation not to increase the risk of harms to other people.

The problem here is that global warming is not like drunk driving. When drunk driving causes harm, it is easy to identify the victim of this particular drunk driver. There is no way to identify any particular victim of my wasteful driving in normal circumstances.

In addition, my earlier point applies here again. If the risk principle were true, it would be unbelievably restrictive. Exercising and boiling water also expel greenhouse gases, so they also increase the risk of global warming if my driving does. This principle implies that almost everything we do violates a moral obligation.

Defenders of such principles sometimes respond by distinguishing significant from insignificant risks or increases in risks. That distinction is problematic, at least here. A risk is called significant when it is "too" much. But then we need to ask what makes this risk too much when other risks are not too much. The reasons for counting a risk as significant are then the real reasons for thinking that there is a moral obligation not to drive wastefully. So we need to specify those reasons directly instead of hiding them under a waffle-term like "significant"

4. INTERNAL PRINCIPLES

None of the principles discussed so far is both defensible and strong enough to yield a moral obligation not to drive a gas-guzzler just for fun. Maybe we can do better by looking inward.

Kantians claim that the moral status of acts depends on their agents' maxims or "subjective principles of volition"[1]—roughly what we would call motives or intentions or plans. This internal focus is evident in Kant's first formulation of the categorical imperative:

> *The universalizability principle*: We have a moral obligation not to act on any maxim that we cannot will to be a universal law.

The idea is not that universally acting on that maxim would have bad consequences. (We will consider that kind of principle below.) Instead, the claim is that some maxims "cannot even be thought as a universal law of nature without contradiction."[2] However, my maxim when I drive a gas-guzzler just for fun on this sunny Sunday afternoon is simply to have harmless fun. There is no way to derive a contradiction from a universal law that people do or may have harmless fun. Kantians might respond that my maxim is, instead, to expel greenhouse gases. I still see no way to derive a literal contradiction from a universal law that people do or may expel greenhouse gases. There would be bad consequences, but that is not a contradiction, as Kant requires. In any case, my maxim (or intention or motive) is not to expel greenhouse gases. My goals would be reached completely if I went for my drive and had my fun

without expelling any greenhouse gases. This leaves no ground for claiming that my driving violates Kant's first formula of the categorical imperative.

Kant does supply a second formulation, which is really a different principle:

> *The means principle*: We have a moral obligation not to treat any other person as a means only.[3]

It is not clear exactly how to understand this formulation, but the most natural interpretation is that for me to treat someone as a means implies my using harm to that person as part of my plan to achieve my goals. Driving for fun does not do that. I would have just as much fun if nobody were ever harmed by global warming. Harm to others is no part of my plans. So Kant's principle cannot explain why I have a moral obligation not to drive just for fun on this sunny Sunday afternoon.

A similar point applies to a traditional principle that focuses on intention:

> *The doctrine of double effect*: We have a moral obligation not to harm anyone intentionally (either as an end or as a means).

This principle fails to apply to my Sunday driving both because my driving does not cause harm to anyone and because I do not intend harm to anyone. I would succeed in doing everything I intended to do if I enjoyed my drive but magically my car gave off no greenhouse gases and no global warming occurred. . . .

5. COLLECTIVE PRINCIPLES

Maybe our mistake is to focus on individual persons. We could, instead, focus on institutions. One institution is the legal system, so we might adopt.

> *The ideal law principle*: We have a moral obligation not to perform an action if it ought to be illegal.

I already said that the government ought to fight global warming. One way to do so is to make it illegal to drive wastefully or to buy (or sell) inefficient gas-guzzlers. If the government ought to pass such laws, then, even before such laws are passed, I have a moral obligation not to drive a gas-guzzler just for fun, according to the ideal law principle.

The first weakness in this argument lies in its assumption that wasteful driving or gas-guzzlers ought to be illegal. That is dubious. The enforcement costs of a law against joyrides would be enormous. A law against gas-guzzlers would be easier to enforce, but inducements to efficiency (such as higher taxes on gas and gas-guzzlers, or tax breaks for buying fuel-efficient cars) might accomplish the same goals with less loss of individual freedom. Governments ought to accomplish their goals with less loss of freedom, if they can. Note the "if." I do not claim that these other laws would work as well as an outright prohibition of gas-guzzlers. I do not know. Still, the point is that such alternative laws would not make it illegal (only expensive) to drive a gas-guzzler for fun. If those alternative laws are better than outright prohibitions (because they allow more freedom), then the ideal law principle cannot yield a moral obligation not to drive a gas-guzzler now.

Moreover, the connection between law and morality cannot be so simple. Suppose that the government morally ought to raise taxes on fossil fuels in order to reduce usage and to help pay for adaptation to global warming. It still seems morally permissible for me and for you not to pay that tax now. We do not have any moral obligation to send a check to the government for the amount that we would have to pay if taxes were raised to the ideal level. One reason is that our checks would not help to solve the problem, since others would continue to conduct business as usual. What would help to solve the problem is for the taxes to be increased. Maybe we all have moral obligations to try to get the taxes increased. Still, until they are increased, we as individuals have no moral obligations to abide by the ideal tax law instead of the actual tax law.

Analogously, it is actually legal to buy and drive gas-guzzlers. Maybe these vehicles should be illegal. I am not sure. If gas-guzzlers morally ought to be illegal, then maybe we morally ought to work to get them outlawed. But that still would not show that now, while they are legal, we have a moral obligation not to drive them just for fun on a sunny Sunday afternoon.

Which laws are best depends on side effects of formal institutions, such as enforcement costs and loss of freedom (resulting from the coercion of laws). Maybe we can do better by looking at informal groups.

Different groups involve different relations between members. Orchestras and political parties, for example, plan to do what they do and adjust their actions to other members of the group in order to achieve a common goal. Such groups can be held responsible for their joint acts, even when no individual alone performs those acts. However, gas-guzzler drivers do not form this kind of group. Gas-guzzler drivers do not share goals, do not make plans together, and do not adjust their acts to each other (at least usually).

There is an abstract set of gas-guzzler drivers, but membership in a set is too arbitrary to create moral responsibility. I am also in a set of all terrorists plus me, but my membership in that abstract set does not make me responsible for the harms that terrorists cause.

The only feature that holds together the group of people who drive gas-guzzlers is simply that they all perform the same kind of act. The fact that so many people carry out acts of that kind does create or worsen global warming. That collective bad effect is supposed to make it morally wrong to perform any act of that kind, according to the following:

> *The group principle*: We have a moral obligation not to perform an action if this action makes us a member of a group whose actions together cause harm.

Why? It begs the question here merely to assume that, if it is bad for everyone in a group to perform acts of a kind, then it is morally wrong for an individual to perform an act of that kind. Besides, this principle is implausible or at least questionable in many cases. Suppose that everyone in an airport is talking loudly. If only a few people were talking, there would be no problem. But the collective effect of so many people talking makes it hard to hear announcements, so some people miss their flights. Suppose, in these circumstances, I say loudly (but not too loudly), "I wish everyone would be quiet." My speech does not seem immoral, since it alone does not harm anyone. Maybe there should be a rule (or law) against such loud speech in this setting (as in a library), but if there is not (as I am assuming), then it does not seem immoral to do what others do, as long as they are going to do it anyway, so the harm is going to occur anyway.

Again, suppose that the president sends everyone (or at least most taxpayers) a check for $600. If all recipients cash their checks, the government deficit will grow, government programs will have to be slashed, and severe economic and social problems will result. You know that enough other people will cash their checks to make these results to a great degree inevitable. You also know that it is perfectly legal to cash your check, although you think it should be illegal, because the checks should not have been issued in the first place. In these circumstances, is it morally wrong for you to cash your check? I doubt it. Your act of cashing your check causes no harm by itself, and you have no intention to cause harm. Your act of cashing your check does make you a member of a group that collectively causes harm, but that still does not seem to give you a moral obligation not to join the group by cashing your check, since you cannot change what the group does. It might be morally good or ideal to protest by tearing up your check, but it does not seem morally obligatory.

Thus, the group principle fails. Perhaps it might be saved by adding some kind of qualification, but I do not see how.

6. COUNTERFACTUAL PRINCIPLES

Maybe our mistake is to focus on actual circumstances. So let us try some counterfactuals about what would happen in possible worlds that are not actual. Different counterfactuals are used by different versions of rule-consequentialism.

One counterfactual is built into the common question, "What would happen if everybody did that?" This question suggests a principle:

> *The general action principle*: I have a moral obligation not to perform an act when it would be worse for everyone to perform an act of the same kind.

It does seem likely that, if everyone in the world drove a gas-guzzler often enough, global warming would increase intolerably. We would also quickly run out of fossil fuels. The general action principle is, thus, supposed to explain why it is morally wrong to drive a gas-guzzler.

Unfortunately, that popular principle is indefensible. It would be disastrous if every human had no children. But that does not make it morally wrong for a particular individual to choose to have no children. There is no moral obligation to have at least one child.

The reason is that so few people *want* to remain childless. Most people would not go without children even if they were allowed to. This suggests a different principle:

> *The general permission principle*: I have a moral obligation not to perform an act whenever it would be worse for everyone to be permitted to perform an act of that kind.

This principle seems better because it would not be disastrous for everyone to be permitted to remain childless. This principle is supposed to be able to explain why it is morally wrong to steal (or lie, cheat, rape, or murder), because it would be disastrous for everyone to be permitted to steal (or lie, cheat, rape, or murder) whenever (if ever) they wanted to.

Not quite. An agent is permitted or allowed in the relevant sense when she will not be liable to punishment, condemnation (by others), or feelings of guilt for carrying out the act. It is possible for someone to be permitted in this sense without knowing that she is permitted and, indeed, without anyone knowing that she is permitted. But it would not be disastrous for everyone to be permitted to steal if nobody knew that they were permitted to steal, since then they would still be deterred by fear of punishment, condemnation, or guilt. Similarly for lying, rape, and so on. So the general permission principle cannot quite explain why such acts are morally wrong. . . .

7. WHAT IS LEFT?

We are left with no defensible principle to support the claim that I have a moral obligation not to drive a gas-guzzler just for fun. Does this result show that this claim is false? Not necessarily.

Some audiences have suggested that my journey through various principles teaches us that we should not look for general moral principles to back up our moral intuitions. They see my arguments as a *reductio ad absurdum* of principlism, which is the view that moral obligations (or our beliefs in them) depend on principles. Principles are unavailable, so we should focus instead on particular cases, according to the opposing view called particularism.

However, the fact that we cannot find any principle does not show that we do not need one. I already gave my reasons why we need a moral principle to back up our intuitions in this case. This case is controversial, emotional, peculiarly modern, and likely to be distorted by overgeneralization and partiality. These factors suggest that we need confirmation for our moral intuitions at least in this case, even if we do not need any confirmation in other cases.

For such reasons, we seem to need a moral principle, but we have none. This fact still does not show that such wasteful driving is not morally wrong. It only shows that we do not *know* whether it is morally wrong. Our ignorance might be temporary. If someone comes up with a defensible principle that does rule out wasteful driving, then I will be happy to listen and happy if it works. However, until some such principle is found, we cannot claim to know that it is morally wrong to drive a gas-guzzler just for fun.

The demand for a principle in this case does not lead to general moral skepticism. We still might know that acts and omissions that cause harm are morally wrong because of the harm principle. Still, since that principle and others do not apply to my wasteful driving, and since moral intuitions are unreliable in cases like this, we cannot know that my wasteful driving is morally wrong.

This conclusion will still upset many environmentalists. They think that they know that wasteful driving is immoral. They want to be able to condemn those who drive gas-guzzlers just for fun on sunny Sunday afternoons.

My conclusion should not be so disappointing. Even if individuals have no such moral obligations, it is still morally better or morally ideal for individuals not to waste gas. We can and should praise those who save fuel. We can express our personal dislike for wasting gas and for people who do it. We might even be justified in publicly condemning wasteful driving and drivers who waste a lot, in circumstances where such public rebuke is appropriate. Perhaps people who drive wastefully should feel guilty for their acts and ashamed of themselves, at least if they perform such acts regularly; and we should bring up our children so that they will feel these emotions. All of these reactions are available even if we cannot truthfully say that such driving violates a moral *obligation*. And these approaches might be more constructive in the long run than accusing someone of violating a moral obligation.

Moreover, even if individuals have no moral obligations not to waste gas by taking unnecessary Sunday drives just for fun, governments still have moral obligations to fight global warming, because they can make a difference. My fundamental point has been that global warming is such a large problem that it is not individuals who cause it or who need to fix it. Instead, governments need to fix it, and quickly. Finding and implementing a real solution is the task of governments. Environmentalists should focus their efforts on those who are not doing their job rather than on those who take Sunday afternoon drives just for fun.

This focus will also avoid a common mistake. Some environmentalists keep their hands clean by withdrawing into a simple life where they use very little fossil fuels. That is great. I encourage it. But some of these escapees then think that they have done their duty, so they rarely come down out of the hills to work for political candidates who could and would change government policies. This attitude helps nobody. We should not think that we can do enough simply by buying fuel-efficient cars, insulating our houses, and setting up a windmill to make our own electricity. That is all wonderful, but it neither does little or nothing to stop global warming, nor does this focus fulfill our real moral obligations, which are to get governments to do their job to prevent the disaster of excessive global warming. It is better to enjoy your Sunday driving while working to change the law so as to make it illegal for you to enjoy your Sunday driving.

NOTES

1. Immanuel Kant (1959), *Foundations of the Metaphysics of Morals* (L. W. Beck, trans.). Indianapolis, IN: Bobbs-Merrill. (Original work published in 1785.)
2. *ibid*, 429.
3. *ibid*, 429.

Walter Sinnott-Armstrong: It's Not *My* Fault: Global Warming and Individual Moral Obligations

1. Sinnott-Armstrong claims that individual actions, such as taking a pleasure drive, do not cause any global warming at all. Do you agree?

2. If *everyone* took such drives, then global warming would increase. Does that have any impact on the issue of whether each individual has a moral duty to refrain from such driving? Why or why not?

3. Sinnott-Armstrong thinks that individuals have moral obligations to help end global warming, but that these obligations are restricted to influencing governments to change their climate policies. Are people like you and I powerful enough to do that? If so, then why aren't we powerful enough to partially prevent global warming? Alternatively, if, as individuals, we cannot cause global warming, can we, as individuals, cause governments to change their climate policies?

4. The ideal law principle says that we have a moral obligation not to perform an action if that action ought to be illegal. Why does Sinnott-Armstrong think that this principle fails to generate a moral obligation for individuals to refrain from pleasure drives? Is his argument successful? Why or why not?

5. What is a counterfactual principle? Is there any such principle that is both a plausible test for moral requirements and yields a moral obligation to refrain from taking a pleasure drive?

CHAPTER 15

Euthanasia

JUST THE FACTS

Euthanasia is the practice of assisting in a patient's death, where such assistance is motivated by the hope of benefitting the patient. This beneficial motivation distinguishes euthanasia from most other behavior that results in an innocent person's death. Whether this difference is enough to make a moral difference is a matter of great debate, as we shall see.

All types of euthanasia have this in common: they are meant to benefit the patient, whose death is the end result. While this has an air of paradox—how can someone be better off dead than alive?—the cases we are concerned with are all ones in which a patient is looking at a very dire forecast that involves a drastic reduction in quality of life. Typically, this is a matter either of great physical pain or of substantial cognitive impairment. When faced with such a choice, a patient may, after careful reflection, decide to end things on her own terms, rather than suffer through such a radical deterioration.

Not all patients are in a position to make such a choice. To see this, consider a distinction among three types of euthanasia: voluntary, nonvoluntary, and involuntary. **Involuntary euthanasia** occurs when a person makes a voluntary choice to remain alive, but someone else overrides that choice and seeks to end the person's life, for his own good. Now this may be incoherent—it may be impossible actually to benefit a person by killing him, if he prefers to remain alive. Or it may be coherent. But if it is, it's certainly immoral! So let's consider the other two forms of euthanasia, to see whether either of them might do better, morally speaking.

Nonvoluntary euthanasia occurs when patients are incapable of making voluntary choices. These are some of the most publicized cases of euthanasia—ones, typically, where a patient has suffered extreme brain damage as a result of an overdose or an accident. This patient isn't ever going to wake up; her cerebral cortex is so damaged that there is no chance of regaining consciousness. She doesn't feel anything; she doesn't think any thoughts. Her body is functioning at a minimal level, sometimes with the aid of life-sustaining treatment. These cases raise some very difficult issues. Are such people even alive? Their bodies are, to be sure. But are people identical to their bodies? Who gets to decide for such patients? Parents? Spouses? Children? What if there is disagreement among the nearest and dearest of the unfortunate patient? Even if we can settle this issue, on what basis should the decision makers make their decision? Most medical ethicists agree that we should defer to the expressed wishes of the patient while she was *compos mentis* (i.e., of sound mind). But what if the patient never made her desires known, either verbally or in writing? What if she did, but had conflicting opinions, or was undecided about which choice she would want her guardian to make?

I raise these issues only to set them to one side—not because they are in any way unimportant, but because the readings in this chapter, and the vast majority of ethical thinking about euthanasia, have instead focused on issues surrounding **voluntary euthanasia**. This occurs when patients voluntarily consent to end their lives and seek the assistance of others to do so. A patient might request in person that her doctor administer lethal drugs. Alternatively, the request might come in the form of an **advance directive**. This is a document the patient has written in advance instructing her doctor about the kind of care she would like to receive if she can no longer communicate or is no longer competent to make decisions about her own care. It's uncommon, but some advance directives specify conditions under which the patient would like to be euthanized. From now on, I'll be talking just about voluntary euthanasia, and so will leave the "voluntary" qualifier implicit.

Another dimension along which we could distinguish acts of euthanasia is with respect to the doctor's level of involvement in the act. **Passive euthanasia** occurs when a doctor omits doing something, such as providing life-sustaining care, so that the suffering patient may die relatively painlessly. For example, a doctor may give a patient powerful analgesics (painkillers) and refrain from giving her food and water while she dies of starvation or dehydration. **Active euthanasia**, by contrast, is the intentional termination of a patient's life that involves taking means to hasten her death. For example, a doctor might inject a patient with lethal drugs or expose the patient to a lethal amount of carbon monoxide. In these cases, the doctor doesn't merely allow the patient to die, as in the case of withholding nutrition; rather, the doctor actively brings about the patient's death.

With the voluntary/nonvoluntary and the active/passive distinctions in hand (having set involuntary euthanasia aside), we can identify four kinds of euthanasia:

1. Active voluntary (e.g., lethal injection by a doctor at the patient's request)
2. Active nonvoluntary (e.g., lethal injection for a terminally ill infant whose parents consent to the procedure)
3. Passive voluntary (e.g., withholding life-extending antibiotics, with the patient's consent, leaving her underlying condition to kill her while she's sedated)
4. Passive nonvoluntary (e.g., withholding nutrition from a permanently unconscious patient and allowing her to die of dehydration with her family's consent)

One further act in the vicinity of, but distinct from, euthanasia is worth mentioning. Sometimes patients want to end their suffering themselves—not to have a doctor do it for them. Since most people don't have lethal drugs in their medicine cabinet, they need help from a doctor. In such cases, a patient may ask a doctor to prescribe a lethal dose of drugs that the patient can then administer to herself, thereby ending her suffering. When a doctor helps a person commit suicide in this way, it's called **physician-assisted suicide**.

Doctors have at their disposal several methods for peacefully ending a patient's life. The most common method of passive euthanasia is called "terminal sedation." This occurs when a doctor gives a terminally ill patient a powerful sedative over an extended period of time. The patient is rendered unconscious, and during that time, food and water are withheld until the patient dies of dehydration or starvation. If all goes as intended, the patient experiences very little discomfort after being sedated.

Lethal injection is the most common method of active euthanasia. This consists of three different drugs injected successively into a patient's veins. The first drug is a powerful sedative, the second is a powerful muscle relaxant, and the third stops the heart from beating—roughly the same procedure as the one used for death row inmates executed by lethal injection.

The most common method of physician-assisted suicide is orally taking a lethal dose of secobarbital—a sedative commonly used as anesthesia for minor surgeries. About an hour before taking the lethal drug, patients take an antiemetic (a drug that prevents vomiting). They then mix the lethal dose with a sweet substance to mask the bitter taste. Once the drugs are ingested, the patient loses consciousness and dies within a matter of minutes.

Active voluntary euthanasia is legal in only four countries in the world: the Netherlands (since 2002), Belgium (2002), Luxembourg (2009), and Colombia (2015). Active nonvoluntary euthanasia is illegal in every country, but is decriminalized (i.e., not prosecuted by the government) in the Netherlands when parents of terminally ill infants enduring "unbearable suffering" consent to euthanasia for their child. Passive nonvoluntary euthanasia is legal almost everywhere. And passive voluntary euthanasia is legal in most European Union countries, Canada, and the United States.

Physician-assisted suicide is legal in Switzerland, Germany, Japan, Canada, and the US states of California, Colorado, Montana, Oregon, Vermont, Washington, and Washington, DC. In the United States, candidates for physician-assisted suicide must have a terminal illness and a prognosis of six months or fewer to live. To legally obtain lethal drugs in Washington, DC, a patient is required to make two oral requests, separated by at least fifteen days, to an attending physician. The patient must then submit a written request to the attending physician before the patient makes her second oral request and must wait at least forty-eight hours before an insurance-covered medication may be prescribed. Other states have very similar regulations to ensure that the patient is fully informed about, and committed to, her decision to end her life.

Oregon began permitting physician-assisted suicide in 1997. Since that time, 1,127 patients have died by a self-administered lethal dose of a prescription medication—52 percent male, 48 percent female. Seventy percent of those people were over the age of sixty-five, and about 80 percent had metastatic cancer.

The majority of Americans favor legalizing active voluntary euthanasia. According to a 2018 Gallup poll, 72 percent of US citizens say that a doctor should be allowed to end a patient's life by painless means if the patient requests it. That has been the majority view in the United States since about 1970.[1]

ARGUMENT ANALYSIS

Some critics of euthanasia argue that patients can never choose to end their lives voluntarily. Whether such critics are correct depends in part on the nature of voluntary choice. Unsurprisingly, this question has vexed philosophers for a very long time. Aristotle argued that there are two essential elements to such choice: adequate information, and the absence of coercion or compulsion. When we know enough about our options, and no one is twisting our arm, then our choice is voluntary. While philosophers have added nuance to Aristotle's conception, his two elements remain central to contemporary notions of voluntary choice.

Now the question: *can* anyone voluntarily choose to seek aid in ending one's life? One argument answers no:

The Impossibility of Voluntary Euthanasia Argument

1. Euthanasia is morally permissible only if patients voluntarily choose it.
2. Patients cannot voluntarily choose to be euthanized.

Therefore,

3. Euthanasia is not morally permissible.

Depending on the verdicts we reach about nonvoluntary euthanasia, premise 1 may be mistaken. After careful reflection, we might determine that some instances of nonvoluntary euthanasia are morally acceptable. But assume for now that premise 1 is true. Why think that premise 2 is true?

Those who support premise 2 argue that anyone who would be eligible for euthanasia cannot be choosing voluntarily, because the

---

1. https://news.gallup.com/poll/235145/americans-strong-support-euthanasia-persists.aspx

person would have to be in such agony or fear that he cannot think clearly. He would be unable to process all of the relevant information about his situation, or his condition would effectively be coercing him into any such choice.

This reasoning is problematic, for two reasons. First, it assumes without argument that the only patients who might be eligible for euthanasia are those who are in intense agony, or the depths of fear, or so heavily medicated that they are unable to coherently think through their options. There is no doubt that end-of-life circumstances sometimes include these factors. But they needn't. Some patients at the end of life can take in the relevant information about their diagnosis and their prognosis. They can balance the choices they face. One might say that they can never rationally choose to end their life before their condition does, but it's unclear why we should think this. Some have undergone numerous surgeries and invasive or debilitating treatments and have decided they'd rather seek assistance in dying than try to fight the disease that is killing them. There doesn't seem to be anything necessarily irrational about such a choice. Some have said that anyone choosing to end his own life must be deeply depressed, and so irrational, and so not choosing voluntarily. But this, too, seems like unfounded speculation. Not all who elect euthanasia are depressed. And for many who are depressed, that may be a perfectly rational response to a situation that presents only terrible choices. Depression need not be clinical depression, of the sort whose presence in a life could undercut one's rational capacity to make life-and-death decisions.

Let's assume for now that it is possible for people to sometimes voluntarily choose to seek assistance to end their life, for their own good. Still, many questions remain. Because everyone believes that passive euthanasia is often morally acceptable—it has been common practice for centuries, in diverse societies across the world—we will restrict our focus from now on to active euthanasia, which has long been illegal in most

countries and, in the United States, has been opposed by the American Medical Association since its inception.

There are at least two angles one might take: legal and moral. Many discussions fail to carefully distinguish between these, and the explanation here is simple: if you think that active euthanasia is immoral, you think that it is a form of unjustified killing, and it's then clear that it should be illegal as well. But things are more complicated if you think that active euthanasia is at least sometimes morally acceptable. Many people who think this also think that it should be illegal. This is an unusual combination—in almost every case, we criminalize behavior only if we regard it as immoral, since punishment has an element of moral condemnation that would not make sense if the convict had done nothing immoral. Still, some people do hold this interesting combination of views, because they are convinced by

The Slippery Slope Argument

1. If legalizing active euthanasia would eventually lead to widespread terrible abuse, then active euthanasia should be illegal.
2. Legalizing active euthanasia would eventually lead to widespread terrible abuse.

Therefore,

3. Active euthanasia should be illegal.

A **slippery slope argument** is designed to criticize certain social innovations on the grounds that allowing them will lead to terrible results in the long run. The metaphor works like this: imagine that we are securely positioned at the top of a very steep hill. At the bottom of the hill lies disaster. Once we take even a tiny step from our safe perch, we are destined to tumble all the way down—the slope is slippery precisely because we can't stop ourselves from the inevitable crash.

Premise 1 seems pretty plausible, so let us grant it in order to consider premise 2. Its supporters often argue as follows: if we allow this practice, then we will be authorizing doctors and nurses to sometimes kill their patients.

And once medical professionals are making decisions about whose life is worth living and whose life is not, then, over time—not next week, next year, or even five years from now, but perhaps in a generation or two—our commitment to protecting innocent life will inevitably weaken. Down the road, we will become so morally corrupted that we won't even recognize it as corruption. Medical professionals will be killing elderly patients who want to live, but whose care is extremely expensive. They will be killing infants born with various illnesses and deformities. Perhaps, in a move reminiscent of the Nazi "euthanasia" programs (which were simply disguised campaigns to murder patients in mental hospitals), we will allow the killing of the mentally incapacitated, justifying such practices with the claim that we are really doing these people a favor.

Such an outcome rightly strikes us as horrific. And we might think that there is no way that allowing a merciful end to patients' lives will land us in such a morally compromised position. But proponents of this slippery slope argument claim that once we take the fateful step of letting doctors kill their patients, then centuries of moral inhibitions will begin to be erased.

It is sometimes easy to determine when a prediction of disaster is unreasonable. Many people crafted slippery slope arguments to defend segregationist policies, or those that denied women the right to vote. These arguments were based on unwarranted fears, long-standing prejudice, and deep-seated ignorance. But sometimes it's quite difficult to know whether a prediction at the heart of a slippery slope argument is plausible. This is often the case with truly radical social reforms, ones that have rarely (if ever) been tested. Only a very small number of places have allowed active euthanasia, for instance, and even where it is permitted, it has been legal only for a relatively short time. Without a substantial track record to rely on, it might be unclear whether allowing it will have the disastrous results that opponents predict. In that case, we need further arguments to tell us how to respond to such uncertainty.

Opponents of voluntary active euthanasia may argue that we should allow it only if we have clear evidence that it won't lead to disaster. Since we lack such evidence, we should continue to forbid it. Supporters will argue that such a rule would prevent all sorts of morally important social innovations; after all, we can't prove that they will be beneficial if we are never permitted to test them in the first place. Those who favor allowing active euthanasia will further argue that the status quo results in needless suffering, that it undermines a patient's right to self-determination, and that a doctor's primary moral duty is to benefit her patients—and that, in unusual cases, assisting in a patient's death is the best way to benefit him.

Let's consider some of these reasons by building up arguments that incorporate them. The first of these is

The Compassion Argument

1. If an act is compassionate and prevents needless suffering, then it is morally acceptable.
2. Active euthanasia is compassionate and prevents needless suffering.

Therefore,

3. Active euthanasia is morally acceptable.

Premise 2 is ordinarily true. Those of you who have been pet owners: consider the situation when you have had to "put your pet down," that is, actively euthanize it. Why did you do such a thing, ending the animal's life hours or days before the fatal condition killed your beloved pet? The answer is simple: compassion. You wanted to spare it the needless suffering it would have experienced had you let nature take its course. You judged that it was better for the animal to be painlessly killed than to deteriorate any further.

If we extend this kindness to animals, why shouldn't we do so to our fellow human beings who have asked for similar treatment? That is the rhetorical way of asking about the merits of premise 1. Critics of this argument need to show that some compassionate actions are nevertheless immoral, and that those cases are relevantly similar to the case of active euthanasia. In particular, we need examples in which a person voluntarily requests to be relieved of her suffering, though granting that request would be immoral. There *may* be such cases. For instance, if some very bad people deserve to suffer and ask to be let off the hook, it may be wrong to grant that request. But this isn't relevantly similar, since, we are assuming, those who request to be euthanized do not deserve the suffering they are facing. If a child asks to be spared a minor difficulty, it is immoral to say yes every time—you will harm the child in the long run by preventing the development of strength of character needed to weather the inevitable difficulties faced in later years. But here, too, it seems that the case is relevantly different, since patients at the end of their life already have a well-formed character, and should not be asked to endure possibly excruciating suffering on the chance that it might fortify their character.

Another argument for active euthanasia claims that there is no morally relevant difference between killing people and letting them die. In both cases, the result is the same, and the specific means—*doing* something (killing) that ends in someone's death, versus *allowing* something that has the same outcome—makes no moral difference. So they are morally equivalent. Since passive euthanasia is morally OK, so too is active euthanasia. We can summarize this line of thought in

The Equivalence Argument

1. If there is no morally relevant difference between killing someone and letting him die, then there is no morally relevant difference between active and passive euthanasia.
2. There is no morally relevant difference between killing someone and letting him die.

Therefore,

3. There is no morally relevant difference between active and passive euthanasia.

Philosopher James Rachels proposed this argument in a very influential article written several decades ago.[2] He argued for premise 2 as follows. Think of a case that is identical in every way except one: in the first case, someone kills. In the second, someone lets another person die. Then see whether there is any moral difference. He claims that you won't find any.

Here is Rachels's example. Imagine that Smith stands to gain a large inheritance from the death of his six-year-old cousin. When his cousin is taking a bath, Smith proceeds to drown him, solely out of desire for the inheritance money. Now imagine Jones, who is in exactly the same situation, with exactly the same motives and intentions. Just as he is about to drown *his* cousin, the child slips under the water and drowns. Jones watches the entire thing and is prepared to push the child's head back under water if he has to. But he doesn't have to—the child dies without Jones having done anything. Rachels predicts that when we reflect on the case, we will come to believe that Smith's action is no worse than Jones's inaction, and so, in itself, killing someone is no worse than letting that person die.

Of course, there are lots of cases where killing someone *is* morally worse than letting him die. For instance, one might set out intentionally to betray and murder a friend, which is much worse, we think, than what happens when we fail to write a check to a famine relief agency, thereby letting a stranger halfway around the world die from hunger or preventable disease. But in such cases, there is some *other* difference, besides the fact that the first death involves a killing and the second death involves allowing someone to die, that explains why one is morally worse than the other.

It's true that the case Rachels uses is *not* a case of euthanasia, but rather a case of straight-up murder. Smith and Jones are not trying to promote the best interests of their cousin; rather,

---

2. James Rachels, "Active and Passive Euthanasia," *New England Journal of Medicine* 292 (1975): 78–80.

they are selfishly acting from greedy motives. But Rachels asks us not to get distracted by this point. He is presenting a controlled experiment, in which all variables are identical except one: the means of securing the death of their cousin. As with the best controlled experiments, we isolate just a single difference to see whether it makes a difference. Rachels claims that once you think hard about the Smith-Jones case, you will see that when the intentions, motivations, circumstances, and the results are the same, then whether those results were obtained by killing or letting die does not matter, morally speaking. Do you agree?

Another argument in favor of active euthanasia invites us to reflect on the importance of autonomy—the capacity to determine for ourselves how we are going to live our life. Autonomy is crucially important to living a decent life, as we can see when we contemplate its violation. The basic problem with slavery, exploitation, manipulation, and coercion is that these are all violations of autonomy. These immoral practices fail to treat a person with the respect she deserves, instead regarding her simply as a means to fulfilling someone else's desires.

While autonomy is very important, we cannot, of course, let people do just whatever they want—our autonomy does not extend so far as to allow me to violate your rights. For instance, I have a right to life. So even if someone wanted very much to kill me, he can't justify his action by claiming that he chose to do so autonomously!

With this limitation on autonomous action in place, we are now in a position to develop an argument that focuses explicitly on whether the law ought to permit active euthanasia:

The Autonomy Argument

1. If an action is autonomous and violates no one else's rights, then the law ought to allow it.
2. Many requests for active euthanasia are both autonomous and such that granting that request will violate no one's rights.

Therefore,

3. Many instances of active euthanasia should be legally permitted.

The core idea is this: it's my life, and I can do with it as I please. No one else should be in a position to tell me how to live my life, or, for that matter, tell me how to end it—unless, in doing so, I threaten to violate someone else's rights.

In some cases, choosing to die might indeed threaten someone else's rights. If a single parent who was terminally ill requested euthanasia without having taken steps to ensure that her children were well cared for after her death, then she would at least arguably be violating their rights. But this is a pretty unusual case. One might, of course, cause loved ones to suffer by requesting to be euthanized, but they don't have a right to be spared emotional pain of this sort. We don't violate the rights of others every time we cause them to suffer. (Suppose, for instance, that in becoming engaged to John, you cause intense suffering to Ted, who was hoping to marry you. You are not thereby violating Ted's rights.)

So premise 2 seems pretty plausible. What about premise 1? Many people find this attractive. But others have their concerns. The two major sources of worry come from those who endorse **legal moralism** and **legal paternalism**. Legal moralism says that we can legally prohibit behavior that violates no one's rights, so long as that behavior is immoral. Legal paternalism says that we can legally prohibit a person's behavior for her own good, even if that behavior is autonomous and violates no one's rights. To give you a sense of these views, those who favor legal moralism have tried to ban "indecent" books, to criminalize homosexual sex, to outlaw gambling, and to forbid the sale of liquor on Sundays, despite the fact that adults could autonomously choose to engage in these activities without violating anyone's rights in doing so. Legal paternalism has been used to require the use of seat belts in cars and helmets for motorcycle riders, even though people can autonomously choose to take the risks of going without them and, in doing so, needn't violate anyone's rights.

We could write a book about each of these two doctrines, and many have done so. Rather than engage them, though, let me make two brief points. First, both doctrines may be mistaken. If so, they give us no grounds for rejecting premise 1 of the Autonomy Argument. But, second, even if they are correct, legal moralism threatens premise 1 only if active euthanasia is immoral. We will shortly consider various arguments for that conclusion, so stay tuned. As far as legal paternalism is concerned, it gives us grounds for rejecting premise 1 only if a ban on euthanasia will protect the well-being of patients. But that is quite controversial. After all, such a ban would prevent some patients who have considered the matter carefully from doing what they most want to do. It will cause some to experience more suffering than they want to endure. It substitutes the judgment of lawmakers for the judgment of the patients themselves. Perhaps all of these measures are appropriate, but much further argument would be needed to show it so.

Let's turn now to arguments that oppose active euthanasia. The first one appeals to a doctor's special duties of care.

Doctors Must Not Kill

1. Active euthanasia is the intentional killing of an innocent person.
2. It is never morally permissible for doctors to intentionally kill their patients.

Therefore,

3. It is never morally permissible for doctors to perform active euthanasia.

Before we analyze the premises, a word about the conclusion. Even if it is true, this would not represent a complete argument against the morality of active euthanasia. That's because active euthanasia need not be performed by doctors. It might be performed by other medical professionals, such as nurses, or even a loved one with no medical expertise but in possession of medical advice, say, about how many pain pills will make for a lethal dose. So this argument, even if sound, does not show that all active euthanasia is morally forbidden.

With that qualification, let's consider the argument's premises. Premise 1 is true by definition. We might challenge premise 2, though, in the following way. A doctor's Hippocratic Oath, her professional pledge of allegiance to ethical principles, states that the first duty of a doctor is to *do no harm*. In ordinary cases, intentionally killing an innocent person is certainly doing him harm. But we are not speaking of ordinary cases. If a patient makes a repeated voluntary request for euthanasia, then intentionally terminating his life may be benefitting him, rather than harming him, because doing so respects his autonomy and reduces the overall amount of suffering that he has to experience. Premise 2 might instead be supported by a slippery slope argument: once we permit doctors to perform active euthanasia, then centuries of prohibitions against doctors killing their patients will slowly erode, leading eventually to murderous abuse. (See the earlier discussion of slippery slope arguments for an appraisal.)

Opponents of premise 2 might also argue that a doctor's primary moral duty is to benefit her patients, which requires deferring to their deepest autonomous wishes. If that conception of a doctor's role is correct, then so long as patients can indeed elect euthanasia in an autonomous way, then assisting in that procedure may not only be morally permitted but, in fact, a doctor's moral responsibility.

Another argument against active euthanasia enlists a ban against intentionally killing innocent people:

The Absolutist Argument

1. Active euthanasia is the intentional killing of an innocent person.
2. It is never morally acceptable to intentionally kill an innocent person.

Therefore,

3. Active euthanasia is never morally acceptable.

Premise 1 should look familiar (see the previous argument), and is true by definition. Premise 2 is an example of an absolute rule—one that is always wrong to break. There is a huge debate in moral philosophy about whether there are any absolute rules. We can't solve that here, so let's focus on just a couple of points.

First, the reason that it is ordinarily wrong to kill an innocent person is because the victim doesn't want to die. But that reason is absent in the sort of case we are discussing. Second, if a rule is absolute, then there are *no* circumstances in which breaking the rule is morally OK. We must obey the rule no matter how horrible the results of doing so may be. So, for instance, if you were faced with a choice in which you had to kill one innocent person in order to save *a million* other innocent people (put that creativity of yours to work and think up such a case), premise 2 would forbid you from doing that. You'd have to let those million people die. Most people have found that very difficult to stomach, not because they'd find anything pleasant in the prospect of killing someone, but rather because they'd find it hard to identify the rationale behind being forced to let a million innocents die when they could have been saved. The natural rationale seems to be this: Innocent human life is morally very important. That's why you shouldn't deliberately end it. But if it is so important, why not protect a million lives at the expense of one? That's a very hard question. Until we have an excellent answer to it, there is some reason to doubt whether premise 2 is true. Perhaps, after all, there are exceptions to the general moral rule against killing innocents. If so, then active euthanasia *might* be one of them.

Another argument focuses on the chance of medical error in offering a diagnosis or prognosis of a patient's condition. This is an argument not against the moral permissibility of active euthanasia, but rather against the advisability of legalizing it. The thought is that if we allow active euthanasia, then some patients may elect it on the basis of mistaken medical information, and so end their lives prematurely. Hence

The Medical Error Argument

1. We should outlaw practices that will mistakenly result in the loss of innocent life.
2. Active euthanasia will sometimes mistakenly result in the loss of innocent life.

Therefore,

3. We should outlaw active euthanasia.

Premise 2 seems very plausible. Doctors are only human; despite their best intentions, they will sometimes make mistakes when it comes to diagnosing a terminal condition or predicting its outcome. But premise 1 is suspect. We rightly allow people to take walks along country roads, bike for pleasure, or drive to work, even though we know in advance that many innocent people will die each year as a result of such behavior. Further, and perhaps ironically, allowing *passive* euthanasia, which every state and country does, also violates premise 1. Patients may decide not to undergo surgery, may forgo a round of chemotherapy, or may otherwise alter their medications or treatment, owing to medical errors of diagnosis and prognosis. When patients opt for passive euthanasia, they typically cease any further treatments or medical interventions. But these steps can also lead to premature death. If we allow passive euthanasia despite such risks, it's not clear why those risks justify outlawing active euthanasia.

The last argument against active euthanasia that we'll consider is

The Playing God Argument

1. Playing God is immoral.
2. Committing active euthanasia is playing God.

Therefore,

3. Active euthanasia is immoral.

What is it to play God? The most straightforward understanding is: to make life-or-death decisions about someone else's life. On that understanding, premise 2 is true. But premise 1 is false. Emergency room doctors do this all the time, and rightly so. So do military commanders in battle zones. So do parents of young children who seek to vaccinate them against deadly diseases. These counterexamples show that we need a different understanding if premise 1 is to be plausible. The best alternative is to say that playing God is making life-or-death decisions about someone else's life *when one lacks the moral authority to do so.* That handles these problem cases. On this understanding, premise 1 seems to be true. But now premise 2 becomes problematic.

It's not clear why patients lack the moral authority to request euthanasia. It might be that they lack such authority because active euthanasia is immoral, but we can't assume that here, since that is what this argument is meant to show! Perhaps they lack the authority because only God has the right to decide when a person is going to end her life. This gets us into lots of tricky matters, but for now, consider just three points. First, defenders of this view need to justify their claim that God exists. (Don't worry, we're not going there.) Second, they must justify their claim that they know what God wants of us. Third, they also need to defend the claim that God forbids us from seeking to end our lives. But this will be quite complicated, and it is noteworthy that a number of thinkers from different religious traditions have rejected such a view. They have argued that God created human beings as autonomous individuals, and so intended us to exercise our autonomy not just over small issues but over the very largest ones as well. They also believe that God is benevolent and compassionate, and that such a deity would not want to see His creatures suffer needlessly. While it is true that suffering can sometimes be essential for improving one's character, it is also the case that in many instances, especially of the sort we are concerned with in this chapter, the suffering at issue is so intense as to break a patient, rather than facilitate her character development. When things are this bad, it isn't clear why an all-loving God would require a person to experience such agony. There may be a good answer to that question, but that takes us into the realm of religious speculation, which we must leave to others.

CONCLUSION

Euthanasia presents an especially difficult set of moral issues for at least two reasons. First, there are distinct issues about the morality and the legality of euthanasia, and these are sometimes run together. Interestingly and unusually, some people allow that the most controversial form of euthanasia, active euthanasia, is morally acceptable, while also arguing that we should outlaw the practice. Second, euthanasia involves taking steps that are known, and in some cases intended, to result in the death of innocent people, which in almost every other context is clearly wrong. On the one hand, then, euthanasia—really, voluntary active euthanasia—starts off with a significant strike against it. On the other hand, though, we might think that such a practice is, by default, morally legitimate, since it can honor a patient's right to self-determination and can be the option that minimizes suffering for an innocent person.

ESSENTIAL CONCEPTS

Active euthanasia: euthanasia that occurs as the intentional termination of a patient's life that involves taking means to hasten her death.
Advance directive: a document detailing a person's wishes about medical treatment in the event that that person can no longer communicate those wishes to a doctor.
Euthanasia: the practice of assisting in a patient's death, where such assistance is motivated by the hope of benefitting the patient.
Involuntary euthanasia: euthanasia that occurs when a person makes a voluntary choice to remain alive, but someone else overrides that choice and seeks to end the person's life, for his own good.
Legal moralism: the doctrine that we can legally prohibit behavior that violates no one's rights, so long as that behavior is immoral.
Legal paternalism: the doctrine that we can legally prohibit a person's behavior for her own

good, even if that behavior is autonomous and violates no one's rights.

Nonvoluntary euthanasia: euthanasia that occurs when patients are incapable of making voluntary choices.

Passive euthanasia: euthanasia that occurs when we "let nature take its course," allowing someone's terminal condition to worsen with the awareness that she will die as a result, all the while intending to make her as comfortable as possible.

Physician-assisted suicide: a suicide performed with the help of a medical professional whose role is usually to prescribe and to oversee the administration of (but not to administer) lethal drugs.

Slippery slope argument: an argument designed to criticize certain social innovations on the grounds that allowing them will lead to terrible results in the long run.

Voluntary euthanasia: euthanasia that occurs when patients voluntarily consent to end their lives and seek the assistance of others to do so.

STAT SHOT

1. In the Netherlands, there were 5,516 reported cases of assisted dying in 2015. In 208 of those cases the patient self-administered the lethal drugs. In 5,277 cases, the doctor administered the drugs.[1]

2. In Oregon, 1,749 prescriptions have been written for lethal drugs for physician-assisted suicide since 1997. As of February 2017, 1,127 patients have died from ingesting those drugs. The others refrained from taking them.[2]

3. In 2017, 73 percent of US citizens said that a doctor should be *legally* permitted to end a patient's life by painless means if the patient requests it. That has been the majority view in the United States since about 1970 (Figure 15.1).

4. In 2017, 57 percent of Americans said that physician-assisted suicide is *morally acceptable*; 37 percent said it is *morally wrong* (Figure 15.2).

Regardless of whether or not you think [this issue] should be legal, for each one, please tell me whether you personally believe that in general it is morally acceptable or morally wrong. How about doctor-assisted suicide?

Figure 15.2.

Source: http://news.gallup.com/poll/211928/majorityamericans-remain-supportive-euthanasia.aspx

1. http://www.dyingforchoice.com/resources/fact-files/netherlands-2015-euthanasia-report-card

2. http://www.cnn.com/2014/11/26/us/physician-assisted-suicide-fast-facts/index.html

When a person has a disease that cannot be cured, do you think doctors should be allowed by law to end the patient's life by some painless means if the patient and his or her family request it?

Figure 15.1.

Source: http://news.gallup.com/poll/211928/majorityamericans-remain-supportive-euthanasia.aspx

Cases for Critical Thinking

Dax Cowart

In the summer of 1973, twenty-five-year-old Donald "Dax" Cowart and his father were working on a broken-down automobile when an explosion, caused by a leaking gas line, erupted, killing Cowart's father. Cowart began running, his body engulfed in flames. He made it about a half mile, with severe burns over 65 percent of his body and his eyes badly damaged, before he collapsed. A local farmer found Cowart shortly after. Cowart asked the farmer to run, get a gun, and bring it back so he could shoot himself. The farmer refused and called an ambulance instead. Cowart spent the next 232 days in the hospital receiving daily baths in a chlorine bleach solution to clean his wounds and having his bandages painfully peeled off and replaced.[1] He would later compare this treatment to being "skinned alive" each day.[2] He lost both eyes and all of his fingers. Every day, he was in constant, excruciating pain, and every day he asked his doctors to help him die. The doctors refused. He was also refused a significant amount of pain medicine, since the risks of such medication were poorly understood at the time. Once he was released from the hospital, Cowart made several unsuccessful attempts to end his life. Eventually, however, he completed a law degree and got married. He successfully sued the gas company whose leaky line caused his horrific injury, and he's now financially secure for life. When asked to describe his life, Cowart says, "Today I'm happy; in fact I even feel that I'm happier than most people."[3] And yet Cowart has never wavered from his insistence that he ought to have been allowed to die. He now speaks often at medical ethics conferences arguing for the importance of patient autonomy about end-of-life decisions.

1. https://www.youtube.com/watch?v=WAQHuaua4W0

2. http://digitalcommons.law.yale.edu/cgi/viewcontent.cgi?article=1702&context=fss_papers

3. http://digitalcommons.law.yale.edu/cgi/viewcontent.cgi?article=1702&context=fss_papers

Questions

1. Assuming that the farmer was in no danger of legal prosecution, would it have been morally *permissible* for him to provide Dax with a gun to kill himself? Would it have been morally *required*? Why or why not?

2. Do you think that the severity of Dax's pain rendered him incapable of making an informed and rational decision about his medical treatment? Why or why not?

3. Dax didn't have a terminal illness or injury. He survived and later thrived. Yet Dax has always said that the doctors ought to have respected his wishes and allowed him to die—either by active euthanasia or by physician-assisted suicide. Do you agree with Dax that he should have been allowed to die, or do you think the doctors did the right thing in continuing to treat him? Why?

4. Is it ever morally permissible to perform euthanasia (either passive or active) on a person without a terminal illness or injury? Why or why not?

Dementia and Advance Directives

In the Netherlands, active nonvoluntary euthanasia is decriminalized. This means that, under certain circumstances, medical professionals will not be prosecuted if they euthanize a person who is not competent to make decisions about her own medical care. For example, if a patient has severe dementia, but has an advance directive specifying that she is to be euthanized if she reaches a state of severe dementia, then doctors will not be prosecuted if they euthanize that patient (given that the patient *now* has severe dementia). This led to the following unfortunate scenario.[1]

In February 2017, an elderly Dutch woman with dementia was held down by her family as she resisted her doctor's attempts to inject her with lethal drugs. After being diagnosed with dementia, but before the disease had rendered her incompetent to make medical decisions, the patient told doctors that she would like to be euthanized "when the time was right." When doctors judged that the time was right, they slipped a sleep-inducing drug into her coffee. She fell asleep, but woke unexpectedly when they began the process of injecting the lethal drugs. The patient resisted, apparently not wishing to have the procedure done to her. Nevertheless, the doctors and the patient's family successfully restrained her and were able to administer the lethal drugs. She died soon after. The doctor who gave the order to proceed with the procedure was under investigation for a time, but officials determined that the doctor acted "in good faith" and was cleared of any wrongdoing.

1. http://www.independent.co.uk/news/world/europe/doctor-netherlands-lethal-injection-dementia-euthanasia-a7564061.html

Questions

1. Was it morally *permissible* for the doctor to euthanize this patient? Why or why not? Was it morally *required*, given that the patient clearly specified in her advance directive that she wanted to be euthanized? Why or why not?

2. Suppose the doctors explained to the patient that they were going to euthanize her and that she understood what they were saying (though the doctors still judged that she was not competent to make decisions about her own care). And suppose that the patient said that she didn't *ever* want to be euthanized, no matter what she said years earlier when she wrote her advance directive. Should the doctors respect the patient's current wishes or her wishes as they were when she wrote her advance directive? Why?

3. Can people without dementia make accurate judgments about what life with dementia is like? Why or why not? What does your answer suggest about the morality of

advance directives instructing doctors to perform euthanasia on a future version of oneself with dementia?

Children and Euthanasia

In 1963, a woman at The Johns Hopkins Hospital gave birth to a premature baby boy. Soon after, the child was diagnosed with duodenal atresia (an intestinal blockage) and Down syndrome. The blockage could be corrected with a very low-risk operation. Without the operation, food could not make its way to the intestines to be absorbed and the child would starve to death. The parents opted not to have the operation to correct the blockage. They thought that taking care of a child with Down syndrome would be enormously time consuming and didn't want to take too much time away from their two other children. The physicians decided to respect the parents' decision. They withheld food and water from the child, and, over the course of several days, he slowly died of dehydration.[1]

1. https://muse.jhu.edu/article/405764/pdf

2. http://www.independent.co.uk/news/world/europe/doctor-netherlands-lethal-injection-dementia-euthanasia-a7564061.html

Questions

1. Was it permissible for the parents to refuse to consent to the surgery that would have saved their child's life? Why or why not? If you think not, would it have been permissible for the doctors to save the child against the parents' wishes? If you think it was permissible to allow the child to die, would it have been permissible for doctors to actively euthanize the child painlessly? Why or why not?

2. Is there any disability a child might have that would justify euthanizing that child (either passively or actively)?

3. In the Netherlands, children between twelve and sixteen can be euthanized if they request it (and meet other conditions, such as being terminally ill), but they need consent

from their parents. From ages sixteen to eighteen, minors can be euthanized without parental consent if they request it—even in the face of parental opposition.[2] Is it ever morally justified to euthanize a sixteen-year-old minor against her parent's wishes? If so, under what conditions? If not, why not?

READINGS

The Morality of Euthanasia

James Rachels

James Rachels (1941–2003) argues that active euthanasia is sometimes morally permissible. Active euthanasia occurs when someone (typically a medical professional) takes action to deliberately end a patient's life, at the patient's request, for the patient's own good. Rachels argues that considerations of mercy play a vital role in justifying active euthanasia in many cases.

He first considers a utilitarian argument on behalf of active euthanasia, but finds problems with utilitarianism that are weighty enough to undermine this argument. However, Rachels believes that a different version can succeed. In this one, Rachels claims that any action that promotes the best interests of all concerned, and that violates no rights, is morally acceptable. Since, he claims, active euthanasia sometimes satisfies this description, it is sometimes morally acceptable.

The single most powerful argument in support of euthanasia is the argument from mercy. It is also an exceptionally simple argument, at least in its main idea, which makes one uncomplicated point. Terminally ill patients sometimes suffer pain so horrible that it is beyond the comprehension of those who have not actually experienced it. Their suffering can be so terrible that we do not like even to read about it or think about it; we recoil even from the descriptions of such agony. The argument from mercy says euthanasia is justified because it provides an end to *that*.

From James Rachels, "Euthanasia," in Tom Regan, ed., *Matters of Life and Death*, second edition (New York: McGraw Hill, 1986), pp. 49–52.

The great Irish satirist Jonathan Swift took eight years to die, while, in the words of Joseph Fletcher, "His mind crumbled to pieces." At times the pain in his blinded eyes was so intense he had to be restrained from tearing them out with his own hands. Knives and other potential instruments of suicide had to be kept from him. For the last three years of his life, he could do nothing but sit and drool: and when he finally died it was only after convulsions that lasted thirty-six hours.

Swift died in 1745. Since then, doctors have learned how to eliminate much of the pain that accompanies terminal illness, but the victory has been far from complete. So, here is a more modern example.

Stewart Alsop was a respected journalist who died in 1975 of a rare form of cancer. Before he died, he wrote movingly of his experiences as a terminal patient. Although he had not thought much about euthanasia before, he came to approve of it after rooming briefly with someone he called Jack:

> The third night that I roomed with Jack in our tiny double room in the solid-tumor ward of the cancer clinic of the National Institutes of Health in Bethesda, Md., a terrible thought occurred to me.
>
> Jack had a melanoma in his belly, a malignant solid tumor that the doctors guessed was about the size of a softball. The cancer had started a few months before with a small tumor in his left shoulder, and there had been several operations since. The doctors planned to remove the softball-sized tumor, but they knew Jack would soon die. The cancer had metastasized—it had spread beyond control.
>
> Jack was good-looking, about 28, and brave. He was in constant pain, and his doctor had prescribed an intravenous shot of a synthetic opiate—a pain-killer, or analgesic—every four hours. His wife spent many of the daylight hours with him, and she would sit or lie on his bed and pat him all over, as one pats a child, only more methodically, and this seemed to help control the pain. But at night, when his pretty wife had left (wives cannot stay overnight at the NIH clinic) and darkness fell, the pain would attack without pity.
>
> At the prescribed hour, a nurse would give Jack a shot of the synthetic analgesic, and this would control the pain for perhaps two hours or a bit more. Then he would begin to moan, or whimper, very low, as though he didn't want to wake me. Then he would begin to howl, like a dog.
>
> When this happened, either he or I would ring for a nurse, and ask for a pain-killer. She would give him some codeine or the like by mouth, but it never did any real good—it affected him no more than half an aspirin might affect a man who had just broken his arm. Always the nurse would explain as encouragingly as she could that there was not long to go before the next intravenous shot—"Only about 50 minutes now." And always poor Jack's whimpers and howls would become more loud and frequent until at last the blessed relief came.
>
> The third night of this routine the terrible thought occurred to me. "If Jack were a dog," I thought, "what would be done with him?" The answer was obvious: the pound, and chloroform. No human being with a spark of pity could let a living thing suffer so, to no good end.
>
> The NIH clinic is, of course, one of the most modern and best-equipped hospitals we have. Jack's suffering was not the result of poor treatment in some backward rural facility; it was the inevitable product of his disease, which medical science was powerless to prevent.

I have quoted Alsop at length not for the sake of indulging in gory details but to give a clear idea of the kind of suffering we are talking about. We should not gloss over these facts with euphemistic language or squeamishly avert our eyes from them. For only by keeping them firmly and vividly in mind can we appreciate the full force of the argument from mercy: If a person prefers—and even begs for—death as the only alternative to lingering on *in this kind of torment*, only to die anyway after a while, then surely it is not immoral to help this person die sooner. As Alsop put it, "No human being with a spark of pity could let a living thing suffer so, to no good end."

THE UTILITARIAN VERSION OF THE ARGUMENT

In connection with this argument, the utilitarians deserve special mention. They argued that actions and social policies should be judged right or wrong *exclusively* according to whether they cause happiness or misery; and they argued that when judged by this standard, euthanasia turns out to be morally acceptable. The utilitarian argument may be elaborated as follows:

(1) Any action or social policy is morally right if it serves to increase the amount of happiness in the world or to decrease the amount of misery. Conversely, an action or social policy is morally wrong if it serves to decrease happiness or to increase misery.

(2) The policy of killing, at their own request, hopelessly ill patients who are suffering great pain would decrease the amount of misery in the world. (An example could be Alsop's friend Jack.)

(3) Therefore, such a policy would be morally right.

The first premise of this argument, (1), states the Principle of Utility, which is the basic utilitarian assumption. Today most philosophers think that this principle is wrong, because they think that the promotion of happiness and the avoidance of misery are not the *only* morally important things. Happiness, they say, is only one among many values that should be promoted: freedom, justice, and a respect for people's rights are also important. To take one example: people *might* be happier if there were no freedom of religion, for if everyone adhered to the same religious beliefs, there would be greater harmony among people. There would be no unhappiness caused within families by Jewish girls marrying Catholic boys, and so forth. Moreover, if people were brainwashed well enough, no one would mind not having freedom of choice. Thus happiness would be increased. But, the argument continues, even if happiness *could* be increased this way, it would not be right to deny people freedom of religion, because people have a right to make their own choices. Therefore, the first premise of the utilitarian argument is unacceptable.

There is a related difficulty for utilitarianism, which connects more directly with the topic of euthanasia. Suppose a person is leading a miserable life—full of more unhappiness than happiness—but does *not* want to die. This person thinks that a miserable life is better than none at all. Now I assume that we would all agree that the person should not be killed; that would be plain, unjustifiable murder. Yet it *would* decrease the amount of misery in the world if we killed this person—it would lead to an increase in the balance of happiness over unhappiness—and so it is hard to see how, on strictly utilitarian grounds, it could be wrong. Again, the Principle of Utility seems to be an inadequate guide for determining right and wrong. So we are on shaky ground if we rely on *this* version of the argument from mercy for a defense of euthanasia.

DOING WHAT IS IN EVERYONE'S BEST INTERESTS

Although the foregoing utilitarian argument is faulty, it is nevertheless based on a sound idea. For even if the promotion of happiness and avoidance of misery are not the *only* morally important things, they are still very important. So, when an action or a social policy would decrease misery, that is *a* very strong reason in its favor. In the cases of voluntary euthanasia we are now considering, great suffering is eliminated, and since the patient requests it, there is no question of violating individual rights. That is why, regardless of the difficulties of the Principle of Utility, the utilitarian version of the argument still retains considerable force.

I want now to present a somewhat different version of the argument from mercy, which is inspired by utilitarianism but which avoids the difficulties of the foregoing version by not making the Principle of Utility a premise of the argument. I believe that the following argument is sound and proves that active euthanasia *can* be justified:

1. If an action promotes the best interests of *everyone* concerned and violates *no one's* rights, then that action is morally acceptable.
2. In at least some cases, active euthanasia promotes the best interests of everyone concerned and violates no one's rights.
3. Therefore, in at least some cases, active euthanasia is morally acceptable.

It would have been in everyone's best interests if active euthanasia had been employed in the case of Stewart Alsop's friend Jack. First, and most important, it would have been in Jack's own interests, since it would have provided him with an easier, better death, without pain. (Who among us would choose Jack's death, if we had a choice, rather than a quick painless death?) Second, it would have been in the best interests of Jack's wife. Her misery, helplessly watching him suffer, must have been almost unbearable. Third, the hospital staff's best interests would have been served, since if Jack's dying had not been prolonged, they could have turned their attention to other patients whom they could have helped. Fourth, other patients would have benefited, since medical resources would no longer have been used in the sad, pointless maintenance of Jack's physical existence. Finally, if Jack himself requested to be killed, the act would not have violated his rights. Considering all this, how can active euthanasia in this case be wrong? How can it be wrong to do an action that is merciful, that benefits everyone concerned, and that violates no one's rights?

James Rachels: The Morality of Euthanasia

1. Would someone in circumstances like Jack's be better off dead? That is, would dying quickly and painlessly be in his best interest?
2. What are Rachels's objections to the principle of utility? Do you find them convincing?
3. How does Rachels's second argument differ from the utilitarian argument? Do you agree with Rachels that it is a stronger argument?

4. Rachels claims that euthanasia cannot be said to violate anyone's rights, given that the patient requests it. Do you find this claim plausible? Is it possible to do something that violates someone's rights even if he or she consents to it?
5. Rachels claims that (in some cases) active euthanasia promotes the interests of everyone concerned. If our society were to allow active euthanasia, would this be harmful to anyone's interests? Why or why not?

Why Doctors Must Not Kill
Leon R. Kass

Leon Kass argues that doctors must never be allowed to kill their patients, even if they request to be euthanized. As a general matter, Kass believes that permitting active euthanasia will lead to the deterioration of the doctor–patient relationship at all levels, thereby undercutting doctors' abilities to care for their patients' well-being.

Kass insists that patients who are deeply suffering are unlikely to be in a good position to offer informed consent to end their life. If euthanasia is an option, they may also feel pressure to exit life more quickly. And doctors may tire of certain patients and so end their life without gaining consent. Once people become aware of these dynamics, they are sure to lose trust in their doctors, thus eroding the doctor–patient relationship. Furthermore, once the absolute ban on medical killing is weakened, doctors will invariably end up taking the lives of patients even without their consent. Indeed, Kass claims, physicians in the Netherlands, where euthanasia is legal, have already reached that point.

Kass believes that there are three absolute limits on what a doctor is morally permitted to do. Each of these limits is enshrined in the Hippocratic Oath. A physician must not breach patient confidentiality; must not sleep with patients; and must not kill them. Within these outer limits there is much discretion and no fixed rules. But these limits are absolute, says Kass, precisely because they protect against a physician's deepest temptations.

Do you want your doctor licensed to kill? Should he or she be permitted or encouraged to inject or prescribe poison? Shall the mantle of privacy that protects the doctor-patient relationship, in the service of life and wholeness, now also cloak decisions for death? Do you want *your* doctor deciding, on the basis of his own private views, when you still deserve to live and when you now deserve to die? And what about the other fellow's doctor—that shallow

From Leon R. Kass, "Why Doctors Must Not Kill," *Commonweal* 14 Supp. (August 9, 1991), pp. 472–475.

technician, that insensitive boor who neither asks nor listens, that unprincipled money-grubber, that doctor you used to go to until you got up the nerve to switch: do you want *him* licensed to kill? Speaking generally, shall the healing profession become also the euthanizing profession?

Common sense has always answered, "No." For more than two millennia, the reigning medical ethic, mindful that the power to cure is also the power to kill, has held as an inviolable rule, "Doctors must not kill." Yet this venerable taboo is now under attack. Proponents of euthanasia and physician-assisted suicide would have us believe that it is but an irrational vestige of religious prejudice, alien to a true ethic of medicine, which stands in the way of a rational and humane approach to suffering at the end of life. Nothing could be further from the truth. The taboo against doctors killing patients (even on request) is the very embodiment of reason and wisdom. Without it, medicine will have trouble doing its proper work; without it, medicine will have lost its claim to be an ethical and trustworthy profession; without it, all of us will suffer—yes, more than we now suffer because some of us are not soon enough released from life.

Consider first the damaging consequences for the doctor-patient relationship. The patient's trust in the doctor's whole-hearted devotion to the patient's best interests will be hard to sustain once doctors are licensed to kill. Imagine the scene: you are old, poor, in failing health, and alone in the world; you are brought to the city hospital with fractured ribs and pneumonia. The nurse or intern enters late at night with a syringe full of yellow stuff for your intravenous drip. How soundly will you sleep? It will not matter that your doctor has never yet put anyone to death; that he is legally entitled to do so will make a world of difference.

And it will make a world of psychic difference too for conscientious physicians. How easily will they be able to care whole-heartedly for patients when it is always possible to think of killing them as a "therapeutic option"? Shall it be penicillin and a respirator one more time, or, perhaps, this time just an overdose of morphine? Physicians get tired of treating patients who are hard to cure, who resist their best efforts, who are on their way

down—"gorks," "gomers," and "vegetables" are only some of the less than affectionate names they receive from the house officers. Won't it be tempting to think that death is the best "treatment" for the little old lady "dumped" again on the emergency room by the nearby nursing home?

It is naive and foolish to take comfort from the fact that the currently proposed change in the law provides "aid-in-dying" only to those who request it. For we know from long experience how difficult it is to discover what we truly want when we are suffering. Verbal "requests" made under duress rarely reveal the whole story. Often a demand for euthanasia is, in fact, an angry or anxious plea for help, born of fear of rejection or abandonment, or made in ignorance of available alternatives that could alleviate pain and suffering. Everyone knows how easy it is for those who control the information to engineer requests and to manipulate choices, especially in the vulnerable. Paint vividly a horrible prognosis, and contrast it with that "gentle, quick release": which will the depressed or frightened patient choose, especially in the face of a spiraling hospital bill or children who visit grudgingly? Yale Kamisar asks the right questions: "Is this the kind of choice, assuming that it can be made in a fixed and rational manner, that we want to offer a gravely ill person? Will we not sweep up, in the process, some who are not really tired of life, but think others are tired of them; some who do not really want to die, but who feel that they should not live on, because to do so when there looms the legal alternative of euthanasia is to do a selfish or cowardly act? Will not some feel an obligation to have themselves 'eliminated' in order that funds allocated for their terminal care might be better used by their families or, financial worries aside, in order to relieve their families of the emotional strain involved?"

Euthanasia, once legalized, will not remain confined to those who freely and knowingly elect it—and the most energetic backers of euthanasia do not really want it thus restricted. Why? Because the vast majority of candidates who merit mercy-killing cannot request it for themselves: adults with persistent vegetative state or severe depression or senility or aphasia or mental illness or Alzheimer's disease; infants who are deformed; and children who are retarded or dying. All incapable of requesting death, they will thus be denied our new humane "assistance-in-dying." But not to worry. The lawyers and the doctors (and the cost-containers) will soon rectify this injustice. The enactment of a law legalizing mercy killing (or assisted suicide) on voluntary request will certainly be challenged in the courts under the equal-protection clause of the Fourteenth Amendment. Why, it will be argued, should the comatose or the demented be denied the right to such a "dignified death" or such a "treatment" just because they cannot claim it for themselves? With the aid of court-appointed proxy consenters, we will quickly erase the distinction between the right to choose one's own death and the right to request someone else's—as we have already done in the termination-of-treatment cases.

Clever doctors and relatives will not need to wait for such changes in the law. Who will be around to notice when the elderly, poor, crippled, weak, powerless, retarded, uneducated, demented, or gullible are mercifully released from the lives their doctors, nurses, and next of kin deem no longer worth living? In Holland, for example, a recent survey of 300 physicians (conducted by an author who supports euthanasia) disclosed that over 40 percent had performed euthanasia *without the patient's request*, and over 10 percent had done so in more than five cases. Is there any reason to believe that the average American physician is, in his private heart, more committed than his Dutch counterpart to the equal worth and dignity of every life under his care? Do we really want to find out what he is like, once the taboo is broken?

Even the most humane and conscientious physician psychologically needs protection against himself and his weaknesses, if he is to care fully for those who entrust themselves to him. A physician-friend who worked many years in a hospice caring for dying patients explained it to me most convincingly: "Only because I knew that I could not and would not kill my patients was I able to enter most fully and intimately into caring for them as they lay dying." The psychological burden of the license to kill (not to speak of the brutalization of the physician-killers) could very well be an intolerably high price to pay for the physician-assisted euthanasia.

The point, however, is not merely psychological: it is also moral and essential. My friend's horror at the thought that he might be tempted to kill his patients, were he not enjoined from doing so, embodies a deep understanding of the medical ethic and its intrinsic limits. We move from assessing consequences to looking at medicine itself.

The beginning of ethics regarding the use of power generally lies in nay-saying. The wise setting of limits on the use of power is based on discerning the excesses to which the power, unrestrained, is prone. Applied to the professions, this principle would establish strict outer boundaries—indeed, inviolable taboos—against those "occupational hazards" to which each profession is especially prone. *Within* these outer limits, no fixed rules of conduct apply; instead, prudence—the wise judgment of the man-on-the-spot—finds and adopts the best course of action in the light of the circumstances. But the outer limits themselves are fixed, firm, and non-negotiable.

What are those limits for medicine? At least three are set forth in the venerable Hippocratic Oath: no breach of confidentiality; no sexual relations with patients; no dispensing of deadly drugs. These unqualified, self-imposed restrictions are readily understood in terms of the temptations to which the physician is most vulnerable, temptations in each case regarding an area of vulnerability and exposure that the practice of medicine requires of patients. Patients necessarily divulge and reveal private and intimate details of their personal lives; patients necessarily expose their naked bodies to the physician's objectifying gaze and investigating hands; patients necessarily expose and entrust the care of their very lives to the physician's skill, technique, and judgment. The exposure is, in all cases, one-sided and asymmetric: the doctor does not reveal his intimacies, display his nakedness, offer up his embodied life to the patient. Mindful of the meaning of such nonmutual exposure, the physician voluntarily sets limits on his own conduct, pledging not to take advantage of or to violate the patient's intimacies, naked sexuality, or life itself.

The prohibition against killing patients, the first negative promise of self-restraint sworn to in the Hippocratic Oath, stands as medicine's first and most abiding taboo: "I will neither give a deadly drug to anybody if asked for it, nor will I make a suggestion to this effect. . . . In purity and holiness I will guard my life and my art." In forswearing the giving of poison, the physician recognizes and restrains a god-like power he wields over patients, mindful that his drugs can both cure and kill. But in forswearing the giving of poison, *when asked for it*, the Hippocratic physician rejects the view that the patient's choice for death can make killing him—or assisting his suicide—right. For the physician, at least, human life in living bodies commands respect and reverence—*by its very nature*. As its respectability does not depend upon human agreement or patient consent, revocation of one's consent to live does not deprive one's living body of respectability. The deepest ethical principle restraining the physician's power is not the autonomy or freedom of the patient; neither is it his own compassion or good intention. Rather, it is the dignity and mysterious power of human life itself, and, therefore, also what the oath calls the purity and holiness of the life and art to which he has sworn devotion. A person can choose to be a physician, but he cannot simply choose what physicianship means.

The central meaning of physicianship derives not from medicine's powers but from its goal, not from its means but from its end: to benefit the sick by the activity of healing. The physician as physician serves only the sick. He does not serve the relatives or the hospital or the national debt inflated due to Medicare costs. Thus he will never sacrifice the well-being of the sick to the convenience or pocketbook or feelings of the relatives or society. Moreover, the physician serves the sick not because they have rights or wants or claims, but because they are sick. The healer works with and for those who need to be healed, in order to help make them whole. Despite enormous changes in medical technique and institutional practice, despite enormous changes in nosology and therapeutics, the center of medicine has not changed: it is as true today as it was in the days of Hippocrates that the ill desire to be whole; that wholeness means a certain well-working of the enlivened body and its unimpaired powers to sense, think, feel, desire, move, and maintain itself;

and that the relationship between the healer and the ill is constituted, essentially even if only tacitly, around the desire of both to promote the wholeness of the one who is ailing.

Can wholeness and healing ever be compatible with intentionally killing the patient? Can one benefit the patient as a whole by making him dead? There is, of course, a logical difficulty: how can any good exist for a being that is not? But the error is more than logical: to intend and to act for someone's good requires his continued existence to receive the benefit.

To be sure, certain attempts to benefit may in fact turn out, unintentionally, to be lethal. Giving adequate morphine to control pain might induce respiratory depression leading to death. But the intent to relieve the pain of the living presupposes that the living still live to be relieved. This must be the starting point in discussing all medical benefits: no benefit without a beneficiary.

Against this view, someone will surely bring forth the hard cases: patients so ill-served by their bodies that they can no longer bear to live, bodies riddled with cancer and racked with pain, against which their "owners" protest in horror and from which they insist on being released. Cannot the person "in the body" speak up against the rest, and request death for "personal" reasons?

However sympathetically we listen to such requests, we must see them as incoherent. Such person-body dualism cannot be sustained. "Personhood" is manifest on earth only in living bodies; our highest mental functions are held up by, and are inseparable from, lowly metabolism, respiration, circulation, excretion. There may be blood without consciousness, but there is never consciousness without blood. Thus one who calls for death in the service of personhood is like a tree seeking to cut its roots for the sake of growing its highest fruit. No physician, devoted to the benefit of the sick, can serve the patient as person by denying and thwarting his personal embodiment.

To say it plainly, to bring nothingness is incompatible with serving wholeness: one cannot heal—or comfort—by making nil. The healer cannot annihilate if he is truly to heal. The physician-euthanizer is a deadly self-contradiction.

But we must acknowledge a difficulty. The central goal of medicine—health—is, in each case, a perishable good: inevitably, patients get irreversibly sick, patients degenerate, patients die. Healing the sick is *in principle* a project that must at some point fail. And here is where all the trouble begins: How does one deal with "medical failure"? What does one seek when restoration of wholeness—or "much" wholeness—is by and large out of the question?

Contrary to the propaganda of the euthanasia movement, there is, in fact, much that can be done. Indeed, by recognizing finitude yet knowing that we will not kill, we are empowered to focus on easing and enhancing the *lives* of those who are dying. First of all, medicine can follow the lead of the hospice movement and—abandoning decades of shameful mismanagement—provide truly adequate (and now technically feasible) relief of pain and discomfort. Second, physicians (and patients and families) can continue to learn how to withhold or withdraw those technical interventions that are, in truth, merely burdensome or degrading medical additions to the unhappy end of a life—including, frequently, hospitalization itself. Ceasing treatment and allowing death to occur when (and if) it will seem to be quite compatible with the respect life itself commands for itself. Doctors may and must allow to die, even if they must not intentionally kill.

Ceasing medical intervention, allowing nature to take its course, differs fundamentally from mercy killing. For one thing, death does not necessarily follow the discontinuance of treatment; Karen Ann Quinlan lived more than ten years after the court allowed the "life-sustaining" respirator to be removed. Not the physician, but the underlying fatal illness becomes the true cause of death. More important morally, in ceasing treatment the physician need not *intend* the death of the patient, even when the death follows as a result of his omission. His intention should be to avoid useless and degrading medical *additions* to the already sad end of a life. In contrast, in active, direct mercy killing the physician must, necessarily and indubitably, intend *primarily* that the patient be made dead. And he must knowingly and indubitably cast himself in the role of the agent of death. This remains true even if he is merely an assistant in suicide. A physician who provides the pills or lets the patient plunge the syringe after he leaves the room is *morally* no different from one who does the deed himself. "I will neither give a deadly drug to anybody if asked for it, nor will I make a suggestion to this effect."

Once we refuse the technical fix, physicians and the rest of us can also rise to the occasion: we can learn to act humanly in the presence of finitude. Far more than adequate morphine and the removal of burdensome machinery, the dying need our presence and our encouragement. Dying people are all too easily reduced ahead of time to "thinghood" by those who cannot bear to deal with the suffering or disability of those they love. Withdrawal of contact, affection, and care is the greatest single cause of the dehumanization of dying. Not the alleged humaneness of an elixir of death, but the humanness of connected living-while-dying is what medicine—and the rest of us—most owe the dying. The treatment of choice is company and care.

The euthanasia movement would have us believe that the physician's refusal to assist in suicide or perform euthanasia constitutes an affront to human dignity. Yet one of their favorite arguments seems to me rather to prove the reverse. Why, it is argued, do we put animals out of their misery but insist on compelling fellow human beings to suffer to the bitter end? Why, if it is not a contradiction for the veterinarian, does the medical ethic absolutely rule out mercy killing? Is this not simply inhumane?

Perhaps *inhumane*, but not thereby *inhuman*. On the contrary, it is precisely because animals are not human that we must treat them (merely) humanely. We put dumb animals to sleep because they do not know that they are dying, because they can make nothing of their misery or mortality, and, therefore, because they cannot live deliberately—i.e., humanly—in the face of their own suffering and dying. They cannot live out a fitting end. Compassion for their weakness and dumbness is our only appropriate emotion, and given our responsibility for their care and well-being, we do the only humane thing we can. But when a conscious human being asks us for death, by that very action he displays the presence of something that precludes our regarding him as a dumb animal. Humanity is owed humanity, not humaneness. Humanity is owed the bolstering of the human, even or especially in its dying moments, in resistance to the temptation to ignore its presence in the sight of suffering.

What humanity needs most in the face of evils is courage, the ability to stand against fear and pain and thoughts of nothingness. The deaths we most admire are those of people who, knowing that they are dying, face the fact frontally and act accordingly: they set their affairs in order, they arrange what could be final meetings with their loved ones, and yet, with strength of soul and a small reservoir of hope, they continue to live and work and love as much as they can for as long as they can. Because such conclusions of life require courage, they call for our encouragement—and for the many small speeches and deeds that shore up the human spirit against despair and defeat.

Many doctors are in fact rather poor at this sort of encouragement. They tend to regard every dying or incurable patient as a failure, as if an earlier diagnosis or a more vigorous intervention might have avoided what is, in truth, an inevitable collapse. The enormous successes of medicine these past fifty years have made both doctors and laymen less prepared than ever to accept the fact of finitude. Doctors behave, not without some reason, as if they have godlike powers to revive the moribund; laymen expect an endless string of medical miracles. Physicians today are not likely to be agents of encouragement once their technique begins to fail.

It is, of course, partly for these reasons that doctors will be pressed to kill—and many of them will, alas, be willing. Having adopted a largely technical approach to healing, having medicalized so much of the end of life, doctors are being asked—often with thinly veiled anger—to provide a final technical solution for the evil of human finitude and for their own technical failure: If you cannot cure me, kill me. The last gasp of autonomy or cry for dignity is asserted against a medicalization and institutionalization of the end of life that robs the old and the incurable of most of their autonomy and dignity: intubated and electrified, with bizarre mechanical companions, once proud and independent people find themselves cast in the roles of passive, obedient, highly disciplined children. People who

care for autonomy and dignity should try to reverse this dehumanization of the last stages of life, instead of giving dehumanization its final triumph by welcoming the desperate goodbye-to-all-that contained in one final plea for poison.

The present crisis that leads some to press for active euthanasia is really an opportunity to learn the limits of the medicalization of life and death and to recover an appreciation of living with and against mortality. It is an opportunity for physicians to recover an understanding that there remains a residual human wholeness—however precarious—that can be cared for even in the face of incurable and terminal illness. Should doctors cave in, should doctors become technical dispensers of death, they will not only be abandoning their posts, their patients, and their duty to care; they will set the worst sort of example for the community at large—teaching technicism and so-called humaneness where encouragement and humanity are both required and sorely lacking. On the other hand, should physicians hold fast, should doctors learn that finitude is no disgrace and that human wholeness can be cared for to the very end, medicine may serve not only the good of its patients, but also, by example, the failing moral health of modern times.

Leon R. Kass: Why Doctors Must Not Kill

1. Kass claims that "[t]he physician-euthanizer is a deadly self-contradiction." What does Kass mean by this? Is his claim plausible?

2. Kass argues that respect for human life, which requires that it never be deliberately taken, is an ethical principle that is deeper than respecting patient autonomy and being compassionate. What argument does he give for this view? Is it plausible?

3. Kass believes that doctors must allow their patients to die, though doctors may never kill. Is this a morally defensible position?

4. Kass claims that intending to kill a patient is always wrong, but that taking steps that are known to lead to a patient's death is not. Does this difference make a moral difference?

5. Kass offers a slippery slope argument against active euthanasia. How plausible is that argument?

The Survival Lottery

John Harris

In this paper, John Harris invites us to consider the merits of a special sort of organ transplant scheme, which he calls the survival lottery. Each year, many thousands of people die because of organ failure and the lack of a suitable donor organ. Harris proposes that we remedy this situation by instituting a lottery among (almost) all citizens. Whenever two or more people are in need of a vital organ, we pick a citizen at random to be vivisected (dissected while alive—though presumably under anesthesia!), so that his or her organs can be distributed to those who need them to survive.

We don't do this with any sort of punitive intent, but rather in order to minimize the number of people who die, through no fault of their own, because of organ failure. True, the organ donor being killed is wholly innocent. But then so are those who are dying for lack of a donor organ.

Harris is well aware that the lottery sounds like outright murder, and he devotes the bulk of the article to presenting, and then countering, a great many objections to it. He acknowledges that there may be problems with making such a system feasible in practice. If these problems could be ironed out, however, Harris thinks that rational and morally enlightened people would endorse this proposal for their own society.

Let us suppose that organ transplant procedures have been perfected; in such circumstances if two dying patients could be saved by organ transplants then, if surgeons have the requisite organs in stock and no other needy patients, but nevertheless allow their patients to die, we would be inclined to say, and be justified in saying, that the patients died because the doctors refused to save them. But if there are no spare organs in stock and none otherwise available, the doctors have no choice, they cannot save their patients and so must let them die. In this case we would be disinclined to say that the doctors are in any sense the cause of their patients' deaths. But let us further suppose that the two dying patients, Y and Z, are not happy about being left to die. They might argue that it is not strictly true that there are no organs which could be used to save them. Y needs a new heart and Z new lungs. They point out that if just one healthy person were to be killed his organs could be removed and both of them be saved. We and the doctors would probably be alike in thinking that such a step, while technically possible, would be out of the question. We would not say that the doctors were killing their patients if they refused to prey upon the healthy to save the sick. And because this sort of surgical Robin Hoodery is out of the question we can tell Y and Z that they cannot be saved, and that when they die they will have died of natural causes and not of the neglect of their doctors. Y and Z do not however agree; they insist that if the doctors fail to kill a healthy man and use his organs to save them, then the doctors will be responsible for their deaths.

Many philosophers have for various reasons believed that we must not kill even if by doing so we could save life. They believe that there is a moral difference between killing and letting die. On this view, to kill A so that Y and Z might live is ruled out because we have a strict obligation not to kill but a duty of some lesser kind to save life. A. H. Clough's dictum "Thou shalt not kill but need'st not strive officiously to keep alive" expresses bluntly this

John Harris, "The Survival Lottery" from *Philosophy* 50 (1975), pp. 81–87. Reprinted with the permission of Cambridge University Press.

point of view. The dying Y and Z may be excused for not being much impressed by Clough's dictum. They agree that it is wrong to kill the innocent and are prepared to agree to an absolute prohibition against so doing. They do not agree, however, that A is more innocent than they are. Y and Z might go on to point out that the currently acknowledged right of the innocent not to be killed, even where their deaths might give life to others, is just a decision to prefer the lives of the fortunate to those of the unfortunate. A is innocent in the sense that he has done nothing to deserve death, but Y and Z are also innocent in this sense. Why should they be the ones to die simply because they are so unlucky as to have diseased organs? Why, they might argue, should their living or dying be left to chance when in so many other areas of human life we believe that we have an obligation to ensure the survival of the maximum number of lives possible?

Y and Z argue that if a doctor refuses to treat a patient, with the result that the patient dies, he has killed that patient as sure as shooting, and that, in exactly the same way, if the doctors refuse Y and Z the transplants that they need, then their refusal will kill Y and Z, again as sure as shooting. The doctors, and indeed the society which supports their inaction, cannot defend themselves by arguing that they are neither expected, nor required by law or convention, to kill so that lives may be saved (indeed, quite the reverse) since this is just an appeal to custom or authority. A man who does his own moral thinking must decide whether, in these circumstances, he ought to save two lives at the cost of one, or one life at the cost of two. The fact that so called "third parties" have never before been brought into such calculations, have never before been thought of as being involved, is not an argument against their now becoming so. There are, of course, good arguments against allowing doctors simply to haul passers-by off the streets whenever they have a couple of patients in need of new organs. And the harmful side-effects of such a practice in terms of terror and distress to the victims, the witnesses and society generally, would give us further reasons for dismissing the idea. Y and Z realize this and have a proposal, which they will shortly produce, which would largely meet objections to

placing such power in the hands of doctors and eliminate at least some of the harmful side-effects.

In the unlikely event of their feeling obliged to reply to the reproaches of Y and Z, the doctors might offer the following argument: they might maintain that a man is only responsible for the death of someone whose life he might have saved, if, in all the circumstances of the case, he ought to have saved the man by the means available. This is why a doctor might be a murderer if he simply refused or neglected to treat a patient who would die without treatment, but not if he could only save the patient by doing something he ought in no circumstances to do—kill the innocent. Y and Z readily agree that a man ought not to do what he ought not to do, but they point out that if the doctors, and for that matter society at large, ought on balance to kill one man if two can thereby be saved, then failure to do so will involve responsibility for the consequent deaths. The fact that Y's and Z's proposal involves killing the innocent cannot be a reason for refusing to consider their proposal, for this would just be a refusal to face the question at issue and so avoid having to make a decision as to what ought to be done in circumstances like these. It is Y's and Z's claim that failure to adopt their plan will also involve killing the innocent, rather more of the innocent than the proposed alternative.

To back up this last point, to remove the arbitrariness of permitting doctors to select their donors from among the chance passers-by outside hospitals, and the tremendous power this would place in doctors' hands, to mitigate worries about side-effects and lastly to appease those who wonder why poor old A should be singled out for sacrifice, Y and Z put forward the following scheme: they propose that everyone be given a sort of lottery number. Whenever doctors have two or more dying patients who could be saved by transplants, and no suitable organs have come to hand through "natural" deaths, they can ask a central computer to supply a suitable donor. The computer will then pick the number of a suitable donor at random and he will be killed so that the lives of two or more others may be saved. No doubt if the scheme were ever to be implemented a suitable euphemism for "killed" would be employed. Perhaps we would begin to talk about citizens being called upon to "give life" to others. With the refinement of transplant procedures such a scheme could offer the chance of saving large numbers of lives that are now lost. Indeed, even taking into account the loss of the lives of donors, the numbers of untimely deaths each year might be dramatically reduced, so much so that everyone's chance of living to a ripe old age might be increased. If this were to be the consequence of the adoption of such a scheme, and it might well be, it could not be dismissed lightly. It might of course be objected that it is likely that more old people will need transplants to prolong their lives than will the young, and so the scheme would inevitably lead to a society dominated by the old. But if such a society is thought objectionable, there is no reason to suppose that a program could not be designed for the computer that would ensure the maintenance of whatever is considered to be an optimum age distribution throughout the population.

Suppose that inter-planetary travel revealed a world of people like ourselves, but who organized their society according to this scheme. No one was considered to have an absolute right to life or freedom from interference, but everything was always done to ensure that as many people as possible would enjoy long and happy lives. In such a world a man who attempted to escape when his number was up or who resisted on the grounds that no one had a right to take his life, might well be regarded as a murderer. We might or might not prefer to live in such a world, but the morality of its inhabitants would surely be one that we could respect. It would not be obviously more barbaric or cruel or immoral than our own.

Y and Z are willing to concede one exception to the universal application of their scheme. They realize that it would be unfair to allow people who have brought their misfortune on themselves to benefit from the lottery. There would clearly be something unjust about killing the abstemious B so that W (whose heavy smoking has given him lung cancer) and X (whose drinking has destroyed his liver) should be preserved to overindulge again.

What objections could be made to the lottery scheme? A first straw to clutch at would be the desire for security. Under such a scheme we would never know when we would hear *them* knocking at the door. Every post might bring a sentence of death, every sound in the night might be the sound of boots on the stairs. But, as we have seen, the chances of actually being called upon to make the ultimate sacrifice might be slimmer than is the present risk of being killed on the roads, and most of us do not lie trembling a-bed, appalled at the prospect of being dispatched on the morrow. The truth is that lives might well be more secure under such a scheme.

If we respect individuality and see every human being as unique in his own way, we might want to reject a society in which it appeared that individuals were seen merely as interchangeable units in a structure, the value of which lies in its having as many healthy units as possible. But of course Y and Z would want to know why A's individuality was more worthy of respect than theirs.

Another plausible objection is the natural reluctance to play God with men's lives, the feeling that it is wrong to make any attempt to re-allot the life opportunities that fate has determined, that the deaths of Y and Z would be "natural," whereas the death of anyone killed to save them would have been perpetrated by men. But if we are able to change things, then to elect not to do so is also to determine what will happen in the world.

Neither does the alleged moral differences between killing and letting die afford a respectable way of rejecting the claims of Y and Z. For if we really want to counter proponents of the lottery, if we really want to answer Y and Z and not just put them off, we cannot do so by saying that the lottery involves killing and object to it for that reason, because to do so would, as we have seen, just beg the question as to whether the failure to save as many people as possible might not also amount to killing.

To opt for the society which Y and Z propose would be then to adopt a society in which saintliness would be mandatory. Each of us would have to recognize a binding obligation to give up his own life for others when called upon to do so. In such a society anyone who reneged upon this duty would be a murderer. The most promising objection to such a society, and indeed to any principle which required us to kill A in order to save Y and Z, is, I suspect, that we are committed to the right of self-defence. If I can kill A to save Y and Z then he can kill me to save P and Q, and it is only if I am prepared to agree to this that I will opt for the lottery or be prepared to agree to a man's being killed if doing so would save the lives of more than one other man. Of course there is something paradoxical about basing objections to the lottery scheme on the right of self-defence since, *ex hypothesi*, each person would have a better chance of living to a ripe old age if the lottery scheme were to be implemented. None the less, the feeling that no man should be required to lay down his life for others makes many people shy away from such a scheme, even though it might be rational to accept it on prudential grounds, and perhaps even mandatory on utilitarian grounds. Again, Y and Z would reply that the right of self-defence must extend to them as much as to anyone else; and while it is true that they can only live if another man is killed, they would claim that it is also true that if they are left to die, then someone who lives on does so over their dead bodies.

It might be argued that the institution of the survival lottery has not gone far to mitigate the harmful side-effects in terms of terror and distress to victims, witnesses and society generally, that would be occasioned by doctors simply snatching passers-by off the streets and disorganizing them for the benefit of the unfortunate. Donors would after all still have to be procured, and this process, however it was carried out, would still be likely to prove distressing to all concerned. The lottery scheme would eliminate the arbitrariness of leaving the life and death decisions to the doctors, and remove the possibility of such terrible power falling into the hands of any individuals, but the terror and distress would remain. The effect of having to apprehend presumably unwilling victims would give us pause. Perhaps only a long period of education or propaganda could remove our abhorrence. What this abhorrence reveals about the rights and wrongs of the situation is however more difficult to assess. We might be inclined to say that only monsters could ignore the promptings of conscience so far as to operate the lottery scheme. But the promptings

of conscience are not necessarily the most reliable guide. In the present case Y and Z would argue that such promptings are mere squeamishness, an over-nice self-indulgence that costs lives. Death, Y and Z would remind us, is a distressing experience whenever and to whomever it occurs, so the less it occurs the better. Fewer victims and witnesses will be distressed as part of the side-effects of the lottery scheme than would suffer as part of the side-effects of not instituting it.

Lastly, a more limited objection might be made, not to the idea of killing to save lives, but to the involvement of "third parties." Why, so the objection goes, should we not give X's heart to Y or Y's lungs to X, the same number of lives being thereby preserved and no one else's life set at risk? Y's and Z's reply to this objection differs from their previous line of argument. To amend their plan so that the involvement of so called "third parties" is ruled out would, Y and Z claim, violate their right to equal concern and respect with the rest of society. They argue that such a proposal would amount to treating the unfortunate who need new organs as a class within society whose lives are considered to be of less value than those of its more fortunate members. What possible justification could there be for singling out one group of people whom we would be justified in using as donors but not another? The idea in the mind of those who would propose such a step must be something like the following: since Y and Z cannot survive, since they are going to die in any event, there is no harm in putting their names into the lottery, for the chances of their dying cannot thereby be increased and will in fact almost certainly be reduced. But this is just to ignore everything that Y and Z have been saying. For if their lottery scheme is adopted they are not going to die anyway—their chances of dying are no greater and no less than those of any other participant in the lottery whose number may come up. This ground for confining selection of donors to the unfortunate therefore disappears. Any other ground must discriminate against Y and Z as members of a class whose lives are less worthy of respect than those of the rest of society.

It might more plausibly be argued that the dying who cannot themselves be saved by transplants, or by any other means at all, should be the priority selection group for the computer programme. But how far off must death be for a man to be classified as "dying"? Those so classified might argue that their last few days or weeks of life are as valuable to them (if not more valuable) than the possibly longer span remaining to others. The problem of narrowing down the class of possible donors without discriminating unfairly against some sub-class of society is, I suspect, insoluble.

Such is the case for the survival lottery. Utilitarians ought to be in favour of it, and absolutists cannot object to it on the ground that it involves killing the innocent, for it is Y's and Z's case that any alternative must also involve killing the innocent. If the absolutist wishes to maintain his objection, he must point to some morally relevant difference between positive and negative killing. This challenge opens the door to a large topic with a whole library of literature, but Y and Z are dying and do not have time to explore it exhaustively. In their own case the most likely candidate for some feature which might make this moral difference is the malevolent intent of Y and Z themselves. An absolutist might well argue that while no one intends the deaths of Y and Z, no one necessarily wishes them dead, or aims at their demise for any reason, they do mean to kill A (or have him killed). But Y and Z can reply that the death of A is no part of their plan, they merely wish to use a couple of his organs, and if he cannot live without them . . . *tant pis!* None would be more delighted than Y and Z if artificial organs would do as well, and so render the lottery scheme otiose.

One form of absolutist argument perhaps remains. This involves taking an Orwellian stand on some principle of common decency. The argument would then be that even to enter into the sort of "macabre" calculations that Y and Z propose displays a blunted sensibility, a corrupted and vitiated mind. Forms of this argument have recently been advanced by Noam Chomsky (*American Power and the New Mandarins*) and Stuart Hampshire (*Morality and Pessimism*). The indefatigable Y and Z would of course deny that their calculations are in any sense "macabre," and would present them as the most humane course available in the circumstances. Moreover they would claim that the Orwellian stand on decency is the product of a closed mind, and not susceptible to rational argument. Any reasoned defence of such a principle must appeal to notions like respect for human life, as Hampshire's argument in fact does, and these Y and Z could make conformable to their own position.

Can Y and Z be answered? Perhaps only by relying on moral intuition, on the insistence that we do feel there is something wrong with the survival lottery and our confidence that this feeling is prompted by some morally relevant difference between our bringing about the death of A and our bringing about the deaths of Y and Z. Whether we could retain this confidence in our intuitions if we were to be confronted by a society in which the survival lottery operated, was accepted by all, and was seen to save many lives that would otherwise have been lost, it would be interesting to know.

There would of course be great practical difficulties in the way of implementing the lottery. In so many cases it would be agonizingly difficult to decide whether or not a person had brought his misfortune on himself. There are numerous ways in which a person may contribute to his predicament, and the task of deciding how far, or how decisively, a person is himself responsible for his fate would be formidable. And in those cases where we can be confident that a person is innocent of responsibility for his predicament, can we acquire this confidence in time to save him? The lottery scheme would be a powerful weapon in the hands of someone willing and able to misuse it. Could we ever feel certain the lottery was safe from unscrupulous computer programmers? Perhaps we should be thankful that such practical difficulties make the survival lottery an unlikely consequence of the perfection of transplants. Or perhaps we should be appalled.

It may be that we would want to tell Y and Z that the difficulties and dangers of their scheme would be too great a price to pay for its benefits. It is as well to be clear, however, that there is also a high, perhaps an even higher, price to be paid for the rejection of the scheme. That price is the lives of Y and Z and many like them, and we delude ourselves if we suppose that the reason why we reject their plan is that we accept the sixth commandment.

John Harris: The Survival Lottery

1. What exactly is a survival lottery, and how would it work? Do you think it would be morally permissible to institute one?

2. Some people might object to Harris's proposal by claiming that it is never morally permissible to kill innocent people. Why doesn't Harris think this is a good objection? Do you find his criticisms of this objection convincing?

3. Another objection to the survival lottery claims that any such policy would cause widespread terror, since anyone could be selected to have his or her organs harvested. Is this a good objection? How does Harris respond?

4. Harris allows one exception to the universal application of the survival lottery. What is the exception? Do you agree that these individuals should be excluded from the lottery?

5. Some might think that instituting a survival lottery amounts to "playing God." What does it mean to "play God"? Is it always wrong to do so?

6. What "practical difficulties" does Harris think we would face if we tried to institute a survival lottery? Could these difficulties be overcome?

CHAPTER 16

Economic Justice
and Economic Inequality

JUST THE FACTS

Economic inequality refers to the difference in economic well-being between different groups or between individuals within a group. There are various measures of economic well-being, such as income, consumption, and wealth. There are therefore a variety of ways to measure economic inequality. For the most part, however, we'll focus on **wealth inequality**—the unequal distribution of wealth among groups or individuals within a group. Many discussions of economic inequality have focused on wealth and wealth inequality because being more wealthy tends to afford one many advantages over the less wealthy. To the extent that one is wealthy, one can achieve both short- and long-term financial security, gain social prestige and political power, and create still more wealth.

There are many ways to measure a person's wealth, but perhaps the most common way is to measure that person's **net worth**—her assets minus her liabilities. People's assets include the value of their banking and savings accounts, residences, cars, boats, real estate holdings, retirement accounts, investments, and so on. Their liabilities include their debts, such as their mortgage, credit card debt, student loans, car loans, and unpaid medical bills. Thus, one can be very wealthy while having very low income (or no income at all), as in the case of a retired person living on the interest from a large retirement account. Conversely, one can have a very high income but very low (even negative) wealth, as in the case, say, of a professional athlete with a large salary but a negative net worth due to enormous credit card and mortgage debt.

Most people have probably heard that there is significant wealth inequality both between people within the same country and between people across countries. Few, however, are aware of the severity of the inequality. Indeed, a 2011 study found that US citizens dramatically underestimate the degree of wealth inequality in the United States and would prefer a far more equal distribution of it.[1] It's therefore worth taking a long look at the actual numbers to better appreciate the current state of things.

We'll begin with global wealth inequality. According to a recent study,[2] the combined wealth of the richest 1 percent of people in the world (about 75 million people) exceeded the combined wealth of the other 99 percent (about 7.4 billion people). The twenty-six richest people on the planet own roughly the same amount of wealth as the poorest 50 percent (about 3.75 billion people) combined.[3] Bill Gates, founder of Microsoft, has more wealth than the gross domestic product (GDP) of more than one hundred different countries (individually, not combined), including Myanmar, Ethiopia, Luxembourg, Croatia, Belarus, Tunisia, and Lithuania. The

---

1. http://www.people.hbs.edu/mnorton/norton%20ariely%20in%20press.pdf
2. https://www.bbc.com/news/business-35339475
3. https://www.theguardian.com/business/2019/jan/21/world-26-richest-people-own-as-much-as-poorest-50-per-cent-oxfam-report

1,810 billionaires on the 2016 Forbes list of billionaires own as much wealth as the poorest 70 percent of humanity (5.25 billion people). According to UNICEF, 80 percent of the world's population (6 billion) lives on $10 or less a day—less than $3,650 per year.[4] All the while, 22,000 children die each day due to poverty.[5]

The difference in wealth between the rich and the poor in the United States is also enormous and continues to grow. Indeed, the wealth gap in the United States is wider than that of any other major developed nation. For example, the wealthiest 1 percent of Americans (3.2 million people) own roughly 40 percent of the nation's wealth, while the poorest 80 percent (256 million people) own just 7 percent. In 2011, the 400 wealthiest Americans had more wealth than the poorest 50 percent of Americans (160 million people) combined.[6]

Inequality along racial lines is large and growing in the United States, too. In 1983, the median household wealth of white families was 8 times that of black families. By 2013, that gap had grown; at that point, median white families owned 12 times the wealth ($134,230) of median black families ($11,030). There is still significant inequality among white and Hispanic families, but Hispanic families have managed to close the gap a small bit. In 1983, median white families had 11 times the wealth of median Hispanic families; thirty years later, median white families had 10 times the wealth ($134,230) of median Hispanic families ($13,730).[7] In 2013, white families had over $100,000 more (about 7 to 11 times more) in average retirement savings than African American and Hispanic families—a gap that is becoming more important as 401(k)s and similar retirement plans replace more traditional pension plans. The billionaires who make up the Forbes 400 list of richest Americans—the vast majority of whom are white—now have as much wealth as all African American households, plus one-third of America's Hispanic population, combined. In other words, 400 extremely wealthy individuals have as much wealth as 21 million African American and Hispanic households in America. As of 2018, there were more than 7.5 million vacation homes in the United States,[8] while more than half a million people were homeless.[9]

As with any economic phenomenon, the causes of wealth inequality are complex. There are, however, a few factors that most agree contribute to wealth inequality—even if none of these factors is by itself sufficient to explain the phenomenon. Those factors are income inequality, educational inequality, advancement in technology, and globalization. Obviously, income inequality—the disparity in wages earned between people—will make a difference in wealth inequality, because money earned in wages can be invested, or saved, or used to acquire further assets, thereby contributing to one's wealth. Differences in income are often due to differences in education. In general, the more education a person has, the more employers are willing to pay for the knowledge and skills acquired as a result of that education. Thus, better educated people tend to have higher-paying jobs and better job security. As for technology, computers and robots now perform many highly repetitious jobs formerly carried out by humans. As new technology can perform those tasks more efficiently, those jobs are eliminated. And those jobs have tended to be filled by low-skilled,

4. https://www.unicef.org/publications/files/UNICEF_SOWC_2016.pdf

5. https://www.unicef.org/media/media_56045.html

6. http://www.politifact.com/wisconsin/statements/2011/mar/10/michael-moore/michael-moore-says-400-americans-have-more-wealth-/

7. https://www.pewresearch.org/fact-tank/2017/11/01/how-wealth-inequality-has-changed-in-the-u-s-since-the-great-recession-by-race-ethnicity-and-income/

8. https://eyeonhousing.org/2020/10/nations-stock-of-second-homes-2/

9. https://www.hudexchange.info/resource/5948/2019-ahar-part-1-pit-estimates-of-homelessness-in-the-us/

and therefore low-paid, laborers. Thus, poorer people tend to be hurt most by advances in technology—in the short term, at least. Finally, globalization—the business practice of operating on an international scale—means that businesses in America can find laborers outside the American labor market. Laborers in poorer countries are often willing to work for lower wages than American workers. Thus, businesses stand to make higher profits if they hire laborers in those other countries and lay off, or refrain from hiring, American laborers.

Americans and Canadians tend to be less concerned about wealth inequality than members of other developed and developing countries. According to a 2013 Pew Research study, 47 percent of Americans and 45 percent of Canadians said that the gap between the rich and poor was a "very big problem."[10] That differs significantly from other developed economies such as Greece, Italy, and Spain, where the numbers were 84 percent, 75 percent, and 75 percent, respectively. Concern about inequality is highest among developing countries, where a median of 74 percent say that the gap between the rich and poor is a "very big problem." This includes 86 percent of Lebanese, 85 percent of Pakistanis, and 82 percent of Tunisians. Japan and Australia were especially noteworthy for their lack of concern with inequality, as only 34 percent of Japanese and 33 percent of Australians said that inequality was a "very big problem."[11]

ARGUMENT ANALYSIS

Statistics like the ones mentioned earlier point to great wealth and income gaps in the United States. Is the wide gulf between rich and poor cause for moral concern? Or is this extreme sort of economic inequality morally acceptable?

To help us answer this question, recall a distinction made in several other chapters:

10. http://www.pewglobal.org/2013/05/23/chapter-3-inequality-and-economic-mobility/
11. Ibid.

that between instrumental and intrinsic value. Things are instrumentally valuable when they cause good things to occur or prevent bad things from happening. Things are intrinsically valuable when they are good in and of themselves, considered entirely apart from any results they may bring about. Many people think that closing the wealth and income gaps would be of great *instrumental* value. For instance, reducing inequality might enable those who are relatively poor to have access to better health care, educational opportunities, legal defense, and improved career options. Lessening the wealth and income gaps might help many at the lower end of the economic spectrum to feel more allegiance to society. And less poverty might lead to less crime.

But many also think that there is something good, in and of itself, with a situation of equality among people. This is reflected in the idea that each person is of equal fundamental importance—every person has a basic dignity, a core set of moral rights, an intrinsic value that is the same as that of every other person. Suppose we grant that people are in these ways fundamentally equal. Does that also mean that economic equality is intrinsically valuable?

Many people say no and insist that economic equality is, at best, of only instrumental value. One line of reasoning in support of this position is

The Leveling-Down Argument

1. If equality is intrinsically valuable, then it is morally good to **level down**, even if doing so fails to benefit the worse-off.
2. It wouldn't be morally good to level down in such circumstances.

Therefore,

3. Equality is not intrinsically valuable.

To level down is to decrease the resources or benefits of the better-off. One way to do this—we might call it the Robin Hood way—is to take from the rich and give to the poor. This would level down the wealthy and level up the poor, yielding a more egalitarian outcome. But we could also increase equality by simply taking from the rich and destroying that wealth, without redistributing it at all. This would make the rich much closer in economic status to the poor, and so increase equality. But this sort of leveling down seems objectionable, as premise 2 asserts. Why act so as to harm some people if you won't thereby benefit anyone else?

Attention to the plight of the poor often motivates people to endorse some form of **economic egalitarianism**—the view that it is morally important to distribute wealth and income equally. But as the previous paragraph revealed, it is possible to construct an egalitarian system that only harms the better-off and fails to benefit any of the worse-off.

Those who advocate for egalitarianism are often motivated by a concern to improve the condition of the poor. But on some plausible (though contested) assumptions, we can in fact best improve the economic status of the worst-off by allowing for inequalities. The idea is that the poor are better off living in a society with such things as life-saving drugs, cell phones, and safe cars. These innovations are possible (the thought goes) only because we promise innovators a chance at becoming wealthy from the investment of their time and energy. If everyone earned the same income, regardless of how hard they worked or how innovative they were, then this would drastically reduce the incentive to develop so many life-enhancing and life-saving products. So economic inequality may be the price we have to pay in order to live in a society that offers such benefits.

Note that even if this line of reasoning is sound, it does not support anything like the level of inequality we see in the United States. Innovations have flourished in our own country, and others, when the upper income tax rates were much higher than they are today. There are also means of redistributing wealth other than through income taxes. We could, for instance,

prevent the concentration of wealth across generations by imposing higher **estate taxes** (those paid by the estate of a person who has died) or **inheritance taxes** (paid by those who have inherited the wealth of the deceased). Doing such things wouldn't have much impact on incentives to innovate for the greater good.

Objections to economic equality can come both from those who are **conservative** (in its original and strict meaning: those who want to preserve the status quo), who argue for protecting the wealthy from increased taxation, as well as from those who want to see greater redistribution of wealth from the rich to the poor. As an example of a conservative argument, consider

The Legal Argument

1. If one obeys the law (including paying all legally required taxes), then one is morally entitled to all of one's remaining wealth and income.
2. A great many of the rich fully obey the law.

Therefore,

3. A great many of the rich are morally entitled to their riches.

Premise 2 is true. But premise 1 not very plausible. For it assumes that whatever the tax code allows or requires is morally legitimate. As a general matter, it is false that we are morally entitled to do whatever the law allows us. After all, the law has allowed people to enslave one another. It has sometimes allowed powerful elites to rape or kill their servants with impunity. We are always able to step back from the law and ask about its moral legitimacy. The same holds for tax law. Even if a given law allows the rich to keep most of their wealth, that does not automatically mean that the rich are *morally* entitled to it. We cannot just assume that existing tax codes are morally correct. Some may err too heavily in favor of the wealthy; others, of course, may err in the opposite direction.

Conservatives might instead opt for a more nuanced attempt to preserve the economic status quo. It takes the form of

The Liberty Argument

1. The government can ensure economic equality only by constantly interfering with its citizens to adjust for any inequality, even when it arises from free exchanges.
2. It is wrong for the government to interfere in this way.

Therefore,

3. It is wrong for the government to ensure economic equality.

The idea behind this argument is simple. We are morally at liberty to do whatever we want, so long as we don't violate the rights of others. A legitimate government will respect that liberty. But if it is called on to ensure economic equality, the government will have to continuously monitor our economic situation and intrude on our privacy. Further, this sort of radical redistribution of wealth will violate the property rights of the better-off, when they have achieved their economic gains through free exchanges.

Suppose you tell me of a great idea for a new company you want to start. You're honest with me, describing the risks and the potential rewards. I tell you I'll invest $25,000 in exchange for 90 percent of the profits in your company—if it ever does make a profit, which most start-ups don't. The company is a great success and I become rich—for a short while. Now that I am much wealthier than you, and indeed than most people, the government steps in and takes most of those profits away, in the form of an equality tax. This seems to be a violation of my rights, since our deal was made freely, and in making my newfound wealth, I broke no laws and violated no one's rights.

But this is too quick. After all, most of us, when earning our pay, break no laws and violate no rights. And yet we are all subject to income taxes, and rightly so. Unless you are an **anarchist**—someone who rejects the legitimacy of all governments and thinks that government ought to be abolished—you should believe that some taxes are morally legitimate, since governments require tax revenue in order to provide their services. The question, then, is not *whether* we are morally required to return a portion of our income to the government, but how much. People frequently complain about how high their taxes are. But how much is too much?

Others argue against an egalitarian ideal not because they seek to protect the interests of the wealthy but because, perhaps surprisingly, they believe that economic equality fails to do enough for the worst-off enough among us. Call this

The Insufficiency Argument

1. Distributing equal resources to citizens will still leave many of the worst-off with little chance of a decent life.
2. Governments should not adopt policies that yield this sort of result; governments should instead adopt policies that maximize the chance that every citizen has an equal opportunity to live a sufficiently good life.

Therefore,

3. The government should not distribute resources equally to its citizens.

The core thought behind this argument is that a substantial number of people are very badly off and need an unusually large number of resources to bring them to a level of well-being that is even close to what the average person enjoys. Imagine poor citizens who require medicines, nursing care, hospitalizations, rehabilitative therapies or surgeries that cost hundreds of thousands of dollars. Guaranteeing economic equality would fall far short of giving such people what they need in order to live a decent life.

According to proponents of the Insufficiency Argument, **distributive justice**—justice in the social distribution of resources and opportunities—requires that we do what we can to ensure that everyone has an equal chance at living a sufficiently good life. That can require giving some people much more than the average, and much more than an equal monetary distribution would require. So economic egalitarianism is mistaken—not because it takes too much from the wealthy, but rather because it fails to give enough to many of the poor.

One potential criticism of this argument is that many societies lack the resources to meet the demands it sets. *Perhaps* the richest countries could tax their wealthier citizens enough so as to ensure that even the neediest are able to live a decent life. But other countries may simply be too poor to provide all of their citizens a chance at a decent life.

As you might also have suspected, another problem with this argument is that it requires the government to take a stand on what qualifies as a sufficiently good life and to be committed to enabling each of its citizens to live such a life. Some argue that there is too much controversy over what counts as a good life for this demand to have any force. Others argue that the government should not be in the business of trying to define the nature of a good life—this is something that each citizen should decide for herself. Finally, even if we could agree on what did and didn't qualify as a sufficiently good life, many claim that it's not the government's business to ensure that we are able to live it.

Addressing these points would require that we investigate the proper purpose of government and the limits of its legitimate reach. Some believe that government is best when it interferes the least; it must maintain a hands-off policy so long as we are respecting the rights of others. Others envision a more proactive role for government, arguing that it is uniquely well positioned to bring about important social benefits that make nearly everyone's life better off. On this view, the government may tax us at a greater rate and constrain us in various ways (e.g., by requiring that we wear seat belts or helmets while driving), even when we are not threatening to violate the rights of others. While properly analyzing these fascinating debates is unfortunately beyond the scope of our present discussion, we can consider some related arguments that have an indirect bearing on the merits of these two visions of the role and limits of good government.

One such argument keeps the focus on the poor and claims once again that an economic egalitarian policy fails to do enough for them. The argument comes from John Rawls (1921–2002), who was perhaps the greatest political philosopher of the twentieth century. He defended what he called the **difference principle**: when distributing resources and opportunities, societies are required to give the greatest priority to the interests of the worst-off among us. Priority is not the same as equality—when you give one group priority over another, you are treating these groups unequally. Rawls's argument for the difference principle has several steps and involves some jargon, but it is not really that complicated.

To appreciate Rawls's view, we need to get two technical terms under our belt. The first is one that Rawls coined: the **original position**. Rawls defended a social contract theory of justice (see Chapter 7), according to which the fundamental principles of social justice are the outcome of contractual negotiations among free, equal, and rational people. The negotiation takes place in the original position, which for Rawls has a very distinctive feature. The negotiators in the original position are not real people. He does not believe that the principles of justice emerge from any actual negotiation. Rather, we are to imagine a group of fictitious people who know almost nothing about themselves. They do know the basic facts about human psychology. They care about what happens to them post-negotiation and know that they have some set of values. But they don't know which values they embrace. Nor do they know their age, economic status, religion, sex, gender, personality type, or social position. For Rawls, the extent of this ignorance ensures the fairness of the principles these contractors agree to. Since no one knows the features that distinguish him or her from anyone else, everyone will be negotiating from an impartial perspective.

Their task: come to agreement on which principles they are going to be governed by. They have no idea of where they're going to land once these principles are enforced. Rawls claims that if we face such an uncertain future, and if we are comfortable accepting a sufficiently good outcome, then we must use the **maximin principle** of rational choice. This tells us to survey all of the options, determine what the worst-case scenario is in each of them, and pick the option that yields the best of the worst-case scenarios. In effect, you are maximizing the minimum—hence, maximin. The basic idea is that when you are really unsure about your choices, then do your best to protect against disaster by picking the option that will guarantee you the best of the worst outcomes. According to Rawls, the difference principle does just that:

The Rawlsian Argument for the Difference Principle

1. The correct principles of social justice are those that would be chosen in the original position.
2. Those principles should be selected by utilizing the maximin principle.
3. The maximin principle, as applied in the original position, tells us to choose the difference principle to distribute social resources and opportunities.

Therefore,

4. The difference principle is one of the correct principles of social justice.

The reasoning behind premise 3 is interesting. Rawls thinks that there are going to be better and worse-off citizens in every country—no matter how hard a government tried to ensure economic equality, some people are going to end up better off than others, through harder work or good fortune. Still, we have to strive to identify the fairest distribution of social resources and opportunities. Rawls thinks that utilitarianism is the view of social justice that *appears* to be the fairest, because it assigns each person's interests equal importance. Rawls asks us to imagine

what the worst-case scenario would be like in a society governed by utilitarian principles. And the answer is: terrible. You might be the sacrificial lamb, the one whose interests get crushed if doing so improves the interests of enough others. (Recall the discussion of the problem of justice in Chapter 5.C.) But under the difference principle, the worst-off citizens get top priority. That doesn't guarantee that they will become as well-off as the rich, but it does guarantee that society will focus its attention and its resources to bettering their plight. Since the occupants of the original position are rational, they'd use the maximin principle to select principles of justice. The difference principle makes the condition of the worst-off the best it can be, since the difference principle requires society to give them greatest priority. Because, as Rawls sees it, principles selected in the original position are fair, and specify what justice requires, it follows that a fair and just society would adopt the difference principle.

Critics of Rawls, and of the general idea that we must give priority to the worst-off, often argue as follows. Whether we should give priority to some citizens over others depends not on the condition they find themselves in, but how they got there. For instance, if those at the bottom rung of the social and economic ladder are there because they don't like to work, or because they opted out of educational opportunities that would have enabled their economic advancement, then society need not do anything to give them a helping hand. The thought is that if a person is responsible for his poverty, then the government owes him nothing by way of offering greater resources or opportunities. This can be summed up in

The Effort Argument

1. If economic equality is a worthy moral ideal, then we should do our best to ensure that everyone receives the same economic resources.
2. We shouldn't do that; those who work much harder than others should receive greater economic reward; those who

expend less effort when working should receive less economic reward.

Therefore,

3. Economic equality is not a worthy moral ideal.

Premise 1 is quite plausible. And there is certainly something appealing about premise 2. Compare a hard-working, industrious person with a lazy, entitled one—why create economic policies designed to give them both the same resources? And yet—many have argued that we bear (at best) only partial responsibility for our work habits. Those who lack initiative, or who are averse to hard work, may be born with traits that make them so, or may be raised by parents who bear a lot of responsibility for reinforcing these characteristics. Here we enter deep territory—how responsible are we for our personality and character traits? Many of our practices assume that people are genuinely responsible for their motivations and actions. But once we see that so much of who we are depends on factors outside of our control—our genetic endowment, our parents, the influences of those we grew up with, the messages being sent by acquaintances, teachers, the media, community members—the scope of our responsibility seems to dwindle.

Suppose we are indeed responsible for how much effort we put into our work. In that case, premise 2 would have some very interesting implications. There is no reason to think that most millionaires work any harder than the average plumber or school teacher. If the Effort Argument is sound, then most CEOs should earn no more than most construction workers. Indeed, those millionaires who have inherited their wealth and never worked at all should, by this argument, be very heavily taxed. It's also the case that many of the poor live in areas where it is very difficult to find work at all, much less well-paying work. What if people are willing to work quite hard, but unable to find such employment? Because the unemployed are not expending any effort at a job,

the Effort Argument offers no basis for providing such people with any economic resources at all.

Those who like this result are committed to rejecting the existence of a social safety net for some of the most vulnerable members of society. This rejection is sometimes motivated by the following consideration. People have many needs. But the fact that someone else has unmet needs does not, by itself, impose a duty on me to meet those needs. Suppose I have a lot of money. You, a complete stranger, have been unable to afford health insurance and have broken your knee in a fall. The surgery and hospitalization will cost $20,000, which you don't have. You've heard of my wealth and ask me to give you the funds for the surgery. It would be really nice of me to do that—I am so wealthy that the money is a drop in the bucket. But it doesn't seem that you have a right to the money, or that I have a duty to give it to you.

The lesson many draw from this is that needs do not entail rights; just because I need something does not mean that I am entitled to it. This thought gives rise to the last argument we'll consider here:

The Needs Argument

1. The government's moral obligations are limited to respecting its citizens' entitlements.
2. Citizens need many things to which they are not entitled.

Therefore,

3. The government is not morally obligated to meet all of the needs of its citizens.

Premise 2 is very plausible. I may need to be loved, for instance, but that doesn't entitle me to anyone's affection. Premise 1, though, is highly controversial. Many people think, for instance, that even if a person does not have a right to affordable health insurance, the government is required to provide it so as to protect its vulnerable citizens against catastrophic loss. On this view, a government's proper role is much more expansive than premise 1 allows. As indicated earlier, we can't resolve debates about the limits of government here, but we can note the following. When it comes time to defend specific policy proposals, those who endorse the Needs Argument must make further arguments about what citizens are and are not entitled to. For instance, you might love this argument, but also believe that citizens *are* entitled to decent health care. In that case, you'll argue that the government ought to provide it to all citizens. Others, who favor a more limited government, will allow that everyone needs good health care, but then argue that this is one of those needs that does not generate an entitlement. To make progress on this debate, we'd need to answer the following question: Why are citizens entitled to the fulfilment of some needs—to be safe from attack, to have an efficient police force and a fair judicial system—while other needs fail to generate an entitlement?

CONCLUSION

It turns out that there are surprisingly few arguments for the conclusion that economic equality is intrinsically valuable. And concerns about leveling down have convinced most people that economic egalitarianism is not what we should be striving for. Rather, the animating spirit of economic egalitarianism seems to be better captured by the view that society in some way must give priority to the needs and interests of the poor, even if, in the end, there is still an unequal distribution of wealth and income. On this front, perhaps the most philosophically influential argument has been Rawls's argument for the difference principle. But many have sought to defend something closer to the status quo, thereby preserving the very large wealth and income gaps between rich and poor, by arguing that a substantial redistribution of wealth would infringe the rights of the better-off, wrongly reward those who make little effort at work, and mistakenly treat needs as entitlements. As we have seen, resolving these debates will in many cases require a more extensive investigation into the proper role and limits of government.

ESSENTIAL CONCEPTS

Anarchist: someone who rejects the legitimacy of all governments and thinks that government ought to be abolished.

Conservative: someone who wants to preserve the status quo and endorses policies designed to do so.

Difference principle: the principle that says that when distributing resources and opportunities, societies are required to give the greatest priority to the interests of the worst-off among us.

Distributive justice: justice in the social distribution of resources and opportunities.

Economic egalitarianism: the view that it is morally important to distribute wealth and income equally.

Economic inequality: the difference in economic well-being between different groups or between individuals within a group.

Estate tax: a tax paid by the estate of a person who has died.

Inheritance tax: a tax paid by the recipients who have inherited the wealth of the deceased.

Level down: to decrease the resources or benefits of the better-off.

Maximin principle: a principle of rational choice that tells us to survey all of the options, determine the worst-case scenario in each of them, and pick the option that has the best of the worst-case scenarios.

Net worth: a measure of wealth calculated by subtracting liabilities (i.e., debts or financial obligations) from assets (i.e., holdings regarded as having economic value).

Original position: John Rawls's term for the situation in which imaginary negotiators, stripped of all knowledge of the features that distinguish them from one another, come together to decide on social principles that will govern them.

Wealth inequality: a difference in wealth between groups or individuals within a group.

STAT SHOT

1. Since 2015, the combined wealth of the richest 1 percent of people in the world (about 75 million people) exceeded the combined wealth of the other 99 percent (about 7.4 billion people).[1]

2. High-income populations are scarce outside of North America and Western Europe (Figure 16.1).

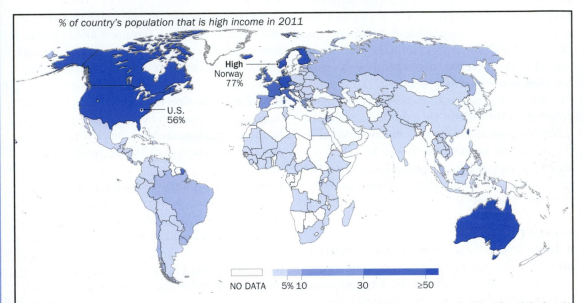

% of country's population that is high income in 2011

High
Norway
77%

U.S.
56%

NO DATA   5% 10   30   ≥50

Note: This map shows the proportion of people within a country that were high income in 2011. It is one of five maps showing the shares of population in each county that live at different income levels. The income groups are as follows: the poor who live on $2 or less daily, low income on $2.01–10, middle income on $10.01–20, upper-middle income on $20.01–50, and high income on more than $50; figures expressed in 2011 purchasing power parities in 2011 prices.

Figure 16.1.
Source: Pew Research Center analysis of data from the World Bank Povcal/Net database (Center for Global Development version available on the Harvard Dataverse Network) and the Luxembourg Income Study Center. http://www.pewglobal.org/2015/07/08/ mapping-the-global-population-how-many-live-on-how-much-and-where/

3. In 2015, the poorest 71 percent of people in the world owned just 3 percent of the wealth. The richest 0.7 percent owned 45.2 percent of the wealth (Figure 16.2).

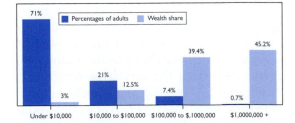

Figure 16.2. Global adult population and share of total wealth by wealth group, 2015.
Source: Credit Suisse Research Institute, Global Wealth Report 2015. https://inequality.org/facts/global-inequality/

NOTE

1. https://www.oxfam.org/sites/www.oxfam.org/ files/file_attachments/bp-economy-for-99-percent-160117-en.pdf

continued

continued

4. In 2013, the top 10 percent of wealthiest Americans owned the overwhelming majority of wealth in the United States. The 51st to 90th percentiles owned about 15 percent. The bottom 50 percent owned somewhere in the vicinity of 1 percent of the wealth (Figure 16.3).

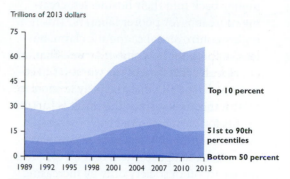

Trillions of 2013 dollars

Figure 16.3.
Source: https://www.cbo.gov/publication/51846

Cases for Critical Thinking

Economic Inequality and Taxes

People often complain that the richest people in America get too many tax breaks from the government. But the richest Americans often point out that they pay significantly more taxes than anyone else.[1] For example, according to this graphic (Figure 16.4) from the Pew Research Center,[2] the richest 2.7 percent of Americans pay nearly 52 percent of all income tax. Americans making less than $100,000 per year in income (84 percent of Americans) pay only 20.5 percent of the income tax collected by the US government. The poorest 24.3 percent of Americans pay only 0.1 percent of the nationally collected

Individual income tax statistics, by income group

Adjusted Gross Income	% of Returns Filed	% of Income Tax Paid
Less than $15,000	24.3	0.1
$15,000 to $29,999	20.4	1.4
$30,000 to $49,999	17.6	4.1
$50,000 to $99,999	21.7	14.9
$100,000 to $199,999	11.8	21.9
$200,000 to $249,999	1.5	5.9
$250,000 and above	2.7	51.6

Figure 16.4.
Source: http://www.pewresearch.org/fact-tank/2016/04/13/
high-income-americans-pay-most-income-taxes-but-enough-to-be-fair/

income taxes. These poorest Americans are the same ones that receive a host of benefits from the government in the form of welfare payments, disability payments, Medicaid, SNAP (also known as "food stamps"), and so on. The result is that, for the poorest Americans, the monetary value of the benefits they receive from the government far exceeds the amount of money that they pay to the government. Some people think that it's unfair that poorer Americans receive more from the government than they pay in while richer Americans receive less from the government than they pay in.

[1] http://www.nationalreview.com/article/433887/
tax-fairness-high-income-moral-fiscal

[2] http://www.pewresearch.org/fact-tank/2016/04/13/
high-income-americans-pay-most-income-taxes-but-enough-to-be-fair/

Questions

1. Do you think that the richest Americans should pay still more in income taxes, less, or is the income tax structure basically correct? What reasons can you offer in support of your view?

2. Economic conservatives often argue that giving big tax cuts to the rich helps the poor and the worst-off in society, because this

allows business owners to invest even more money back into their businesses, creating more jobs for poorer laborers. This is a highly controversial economic claim, but let's suppose for now that it's true—that tax cuts for the rich benefit the worst-off in society. Still, such a policy is likely to increase wealth inequality, since the result is further profits for businesses and their owners, only a fraction of which will be passed on to workers. Suppose, then, that we can help the worst-off in society only by increasing economic inequality. Should we do it? Or should we refrain from helping the worst-off so as to reduce economic inequality?

3. "Taxation is theft" is a slogan endorsed by some economic conservatives. The idea is that people who earn money in an honest way by making voluntary exchanges with other consenting adults ought to be able to use their earnings as they see fit. If, for example, I tried to take your hard-earned money by force in order to give it to a poorer person, that would be theft. I would have stolen from you. The same, some say, is true of the government. When it redistributes money from rich to poor via taxation, the government has committed theft. Is this line of reasoning correct? Why or why not? If not, what justifies the state in redistributing wealth from some citizens to others?

Global Versus Domestic Economic Inequality

In 2016, Vermont senator Bernie Sanders ran for the Democratic nomination for president, receiving 43 percent of votes in the primaries. One of the issues he was most passionate about was wealth inequality in America. He proposed thirteen strategies for combating such inequality. Here was his fourth strategy: "Reversing trade policies like [the free-trade agreements] NAFTA, CAFTA, and PNTR with China that

have driven down wages and caused the loss of millions of jobs. If corporate America wants us to buy their products, they need to manufacture those products in this country, not in China or other low-wage countries."[1] In short, he proposed to constrain trade between nations to preserve American jobs.

Also in 2016, Republican presidential nominee Donald Trump proposed taking drastic measures—for example, building a wall between the United States and Mexico—to stop the flow of immigrants from Latin America. One of the stated justifications for this plan was that it would preserve American jobs from immigrants who wished to find employment in the United States.

Both candidates favored creating or preserving jobs for poorer Americans rather than for poorer people from other countries. The likely result is that wealth inequality in the United States would be, to some extent, lessened while global inequality would be increased (since even many of the poorest Americans are vastly richer than the poorest people elsewhere).

Questions

1. To the extent that governments ought to try to reduce economic inequality, should they be more concerned about economic inequality *in their own country* or should they be more concerned with *global* economic inequality? Why?

2. Do owners of large businesses (e.g., Nike, Dell, Apple) have a moral obligation not to outsource jobs to other countries—or, at least to limit outsourcing—to preserve jobs for poorer citizens in their own country? Why or why not?

3. Every now and then, when a major company announces that it will eliminate several hundred local jobs and outsource them

1. https://berniesanders.com/issues/income-and-wealth-inequality

to workers in another country (e.g., India, Mexico), consumers respond by trying to organize boycotts against those businesses. Do you, as a consumer, have an obligation to refrain from buying from businesses that eliminate local jobs to the benefit of workers in other countries? Why or why not?

Walmart

Walmart is the world's largest company by revenue and the largest private employer in the world. The company employs 1.4 million people in the United States alone—about 1 percent of the American workforce. The company also has a reputation for being a less-than-ideal place to work. The average pay for nonmanagement positions, as of 2017, is $9.41 per hour. That's well below the $13 per hour national average for other retail positions.[1] In 2005, a Walmart memo, sent by its board of directors, advised store managers to begin eliminating full-time positions in favor of hiring part-time employees because part-time employees were ineligible for the more expensive health insurance.[2] In 2010, the wealth of the Walton family (the family that owns Walmart) was valued at $89.5 billion—equal, at the time, to the combined wealth of the poorest 41.5 percent of families in America. In response to Walmart's

treatment of its employees, many have called on the government to force Walmart to pay higher wages and provide better health insurance programs for its employees. Others have called for consumers to boycott the company.

Questions

1. Would the government be justified in forcing Walmart, and similar companies, to pay its employees higher wages or to provide health insurance for its uninsured or underinsured employees? Why or why not?

2. Many defenders of Walmart argue that its employees agree to the wages and benefits that they receive. Walmart doesn't force anyone to accept a job at their company; nor does Walmart prevent their employees from quitting if they so desire. If associates agree to work for the wages and benefits that Walmart provides, should we conclude that those wages and benefits are fair? Why or why not?

3. Walmart can provide a wide range of products at exceptionally low prices, in part because they pay their employees such low wages and provide such poor benefits. The result is that there are a wide range of low-price goods available for poor people to purchase—products that are significantly more expensive at stores like Whole Foods that pay their employees much higher wages. Given these facts, should we be glad that Walmart exists? Why or why not?

1. https://www.glassdoor.com/Salary/Walmart-Salaries-E715.htm
2. http://www.nytimes.com/2005/10/26/business/walmart-memo-suggests-ways-to-cut-employee-benefit-costs.html

READINGS

A Theory of Justice

John Rawls

In this selection, John Rawls sets out some of the basic elements of his famous theory of justice. Rawls, the most influential English-speaking political philosopher of the twentieth century, sought to identify the method for selecting principles of domestic justice. He tells us that we ought to choose principles that are fair, both in content and in their method of selection.

Rawls develops a social contract theory of justice, according to which principles of justice are those that would be selected by people who know nothing of the features that distinguish them from one another. Such people are rational, know the basic facts of human psychology, know that they have some conception of what is valuable, but don't know what that specific conception is. Nor do they know their economic or social status, their religion, their sex, their family history, or their skin color. This sort of widespread ignorance protects against bias and partiality in the selection of principles of justice.

When it comes to determining the principles that are to govern the basic economic structure of society, Rawls defends what he calls the *difference principle*. This principle recommends laws that give priority in the distribution of opportunities and resources to the worst-off members of society. He argues that the social contractors described earlier would select this principle because it is rational to do so. That claim, in turn, is defended by invoking the *maximin rule*—a principle about how to make decisions when you are uncertain of the chances or the value of the possible outcomes of your choice. The maximin rule tells us to maximize the minimum: we are to survey our options, identify the worst-case scenario associated with each option, and then select the one that yields the best of these worst-case scenarios. Rawls argues that since those who are selecting principles of justice don't know where they will end up in the social hierarchy, and since the difference principle gives priority to the worst-off in society, then rational contractors will select the difference principle. As a result, domestic economic policies are just only if they distribute greater resources and opportunities to the worst-off among us.

The Main Idea of the Theory of Justice

My aim is to present a conception of justice which generalizes and carries to a higher level of abstraction

the familiar theory of the social contract as found, say, in Locke, Rousseau, and Kant. In order to do this we are not to think of the original contract as one to enter a particular society or to set up a particular form of government. Rather, the guiding idea is that the principles of justice for the basic structure of society are the object of the original agreement. They are the principles that free and rational persons concerned to further their own interests would accept in an initial position of equality as defining the fundamental terms of their association. These principles are to regulate all further agreements: they specify the kinds of social cooperation that can be entered into and the forms of government that can be established. This way of regarding the principles of justice I shall call justice as fairness.

Thus we are to imagine that those who engage in social cooperation choose together, in one joint act, the principles which are to assign basic rights and duties and to determine the division of social benefits. Men are to decide in advance how they are to regulate their claims against one another and what is to be the foundation charter of their society. Just as each person must decide by rational reflection what constitutes his good, that is, the system of ends which it is rational for him to pursue, so a group of persons must decide once and for all what is to count among them as just and unjust. The choice which rational men would make in this hypothetical situation of equal liberty, assuming for the present that this choice problem has a solution, determines the principles of justice.

In justice as fairness the original position of equality corresponds to the state of nature in the traditional theory of the social contract. This original position is not, of course, thought of as an actual historical state of affairs, much less as a primitive condition of culture. It is understood as a purely hypothetical situation characterized so as to lead to a certain conception of justice. Among the essential features of this situation is that no one knows his place in society, his class position or social status, nor does any one know his fortune in the distribution of natural assets and abilities, his intelligence, strength, and the like. I shall even assume that the parties do not know their conceptions of the good or their special psychological propensities. The principles of justice are chosen behind a veil of ignorance. This ensures that no one is advantaged or disadvantaged in the choice of principles by the outcome of natural chance or the contingency of social circumstances. Since all are similarly situated and no one is able to design principles to favor his particular condition, the principles of justice are the result of a fair agreement or bargain. For given the circumstances of the original position, the symmetry of everyone's relations to each other, this initial situation is fair between individuals as moral persons, that is, as rational beings with their own ends and capable, I shall assume, of a sense of justice. The original position is, one might say, the appropriate initial status quo, and thus the fundamental agreements reached in it are fair. This explains the propriety of the name "justice as fairness": it conveys the idea that the principles of justice are agreed to in an initial situation that is fair. The name does not mean that the concepts of justice and fairness are the same, any more than the phrase "poetry as metaphor" means that the concepts of poetry and metaphor are the same.

Justice as fairness begins, as I have said, with one of the most general of all choices which persons might make together, namely, with the choice of the first principles of a conception of justice which is to regulate all subsequent criticism and reform of institutions. Then, having chosen a conception of justice, we can suppose that they are to choose a constitution and a legislature to enact laws, and so on, all in accordance with the principles of justice initially agreed upon. Our social situation is just if it is such that by this sequence of hypothetical agreements we would have contracted into the general system of rules which defines it. Moreover, assuming that the original position does determine a set of principles (that is, that a particular conception of justice would be chosen), it will then be true that whenever social institutions satisfy these principles those engaged in them can say to one another that they are cooperating on terms to which they would agree if they were free and equal persons whose relations with respect to one another were fair. They could all view their arrangements as meeting the stipulations which they would acknowledge in an initial situation that embodies widely accepted and reasonable constraints on the choice of principles. The general recognition of this fact would provide the basis for a public acceptance of the corresponding principles of justice. No society can, of course, be a scheme of cooperation which men enter voluntarily in a literal sense; each person finds himself placed at birth in some particular position in some particular society, and the nature of this position materially affects his life prospects. Yet a society satisfying the principles of justice as fairness comes as close as a society can to being a voluntary scheme, for it meets the principles which free and equal persons would assent to under circumstances that are fair. In this sense its members are autonomous and the obligations they recognize self-imposed.

One feature of justice as fairness is to think of the parties in the initial situation as rational and mutually disinterested. This does not mean that the parties are egoists, that is, individuals with only certain kinds of interests, say in wealth, prestige, and domination. But they are conceived as not taking an interest in one another's interests. They are to presume that even their spiritual aims may be opposed, in the way that the aims of those of different religions may be opposed. Moreover, the concept of rationality must be interpreted as far as possible in the narrow sense, standard in economic theory, of taking the most effective means to given ends. I shall modify this concept to some extent, as explained later, but one must try to avoid introducing into it any controversial ethical elements. The initial situation must be characterized by stipulations that are widely accepted.

In working out the conception of justice as fairness one main task clearly is to determine which principles of justice would be chosen in the original position. To do this we must describe this situation in some detail and formulate with care the problem of choice which it presents. These matters I shall take up in the immediately succeeding chapters. It may be observed, however, that once the principles of justice are thought of

as arising from an original agreement in a situation of equality, it is an open question whether the principle of utility would be acknowledged. Offhand it hardly seems likely that persons who view themselves as equals, entitled to press their claims upon one another, would agree to a principle which may require lesser life prospects for some simply for the sake of a greater sum of advantages enjoyed by others. Since each desires to protect his interests, his capacity to advance his conception of the good, no one has a reason to acquiesce in an enduring loss for himself in order to bring about a greater net balance of satisfaction. In the absence of strong and lasting benevolent impulses, a rational man would not accept a basic structure merely because it maximized the algebraic sum of advantages irrespective of its permanent effects on his own basic rights and interests. Thus it seems that the principle of utility is incompatible with the conception of social cooperation among equals for mutual advantage. It appears to be inconsistent with the idea of reciprocity implicit in the notion of a well-ordered society. Or, at any rate, so I shall argue.

I shall maintain instead that the persons in the initial situation would choose two rather different principles: the first requires equality in the assignment of basic rights and duties, while the second holds that social and economic inequalities, for example inequalities of wealth and authority, are just only if they result in compensating benefits for everyone, and in particular for the least advantaged members of society. These principles rule out justifying institutions on the grounds that the hardships of some are offset by a greater good in the aggregate. It may be expedient but it is not just that some should have less in order that others may prosper. But there is no injustice in the greater benefits earned by a few provided that the situation of persons not so fortunate is thereby improved. The intuitive idea is that since everyone's well-being depends upon a scheme of cooperation without which no one could have a satisfactory life, the division of advantages should be such as to draw forth the willing cooperation of everyone taking part in it, including those less well situated. Yet this can be expected only if reasonable terms are proposed. The two principles mentioned seem to be a fair agreement on the basis of which those better endowed, or more fortunate in their social position, neither of which we can be said to deserve, could expect the willing cooperation of others when some workable scheme is a necessary condition of the welfare of all. Once we decide to look for a conception of justice that nullifies the accidents of natural endowment and the contingencies of social circumstance as counters in quest for political and economic advantage, we are led to these principles. They express the result of leaving aside those aspects of the social world that seem arbitrary from a moral point of view. . . .

Justice as fairness is an example of what I have called a contract theory. The merit of the contract terminology is that it conveys the idea that principles of justice may be conceived as principles that would be chosen by rational persons, and that in this way conceptions of justice may be explained and justified. The theory of justice is a part, perhaps the most significant part, of the theory of rational choice. Furthermore, principles of justice deal with conflicting claims upon the advantages won by social cooperation; they apply to the relations among several persons or groups. The word "contract" suggests this plurality as well as the condition that the appropriate division of advantages must be in accordance with principles acceptable to all parties. The condition of publicity for principles of justice is also connoted by the contract phraseology. Thus, if these principles are the outcome of an agreement, citizens have a knowledge of the principles that others follow. It is characteristic of contract theories to stress the public nature of political principles. . . .

The Veil of Ignorance

The idea of the original position is to set up a fair procedure so that any principles agreed to will be just. The aim is to use the notion of pure procedural justice as a basis of theory. Somehow we must nullify the effects of specific contingencies which put men at odds and tempt them to exploit social and natural circumstances to their own advantage. Now in order to do this I assume that the parties are situated behind a veil of ignorance. They do not know how the various alternatives will affect their own particular case and they are obliged to evaluate principles solely on the basis of general considerations.

It is assumed, then, that the parties do not know certain kinds of particular facts. First of all, no one knows his place in society, his class position or social status; nor does he know his fortune in the distribution of natural assets and abilities, his intelligence and strength, and the like. Nor, again, does anyone know his conception of the good, the particulars of his rational plan of life, or even the special features of his psychology such as his aversion to risk or liability to optimism or pessimism. More than this, I assume that the parties do not know the particular circumstances of their own society. That is, they do not know its economic or political situation, or the level of civilization and culture it has been able to achieve. The persons in the original position have no information as to which generation they belong. These broader restrictions on knowledge are appropriate in part because questions of social justice arise between generations as well as within them, for example, the question of the appropriate rate of capital saving and of the conservation of natural resources and the environment of nature. There is also, theoretically anyway, the question of a reasonable genetic policy. In these cases too, in order to carry through the idea of the original position, the parties must not know the contingencies that set them in opposition. They must choose principles the consequences of which they are prepared to live with whatever generation they turn out to belong to.

As far as possible, then, the only particular facts which the parties know are that their society is subject to the circumstances of justice and whatever this implies. It is taken for granted, however, that they know the general facts about human society. They understand political affairs and the principles of economic theory; they know the basis of social organization and the laws of human psychology. Indeed, the parties are presumed to know whatever general facts affect the choice of the principles of justice. There are no limitations on general information, that is, on general laws and theories, since conceptions of justice must be adjusted to the characteristics of the systems of social cooperation which they are to regulate, and there is no reason to rule out these facts. It is, for example, a consideration against a conception of justice that in view of the laws of moral psychology, men would not acquire a desire to act upon it even when the institutions of their society satisfied it. For in this case there would be difficulty in securing the stability of social operation. It is an important feature of a conception of justice that it should generate its own support. That is, its principles should be such that when they are embodied in the basic structure of society men tend to acquire the corresponding sense of justice. Given the principles of moral learning, men develop a desire to act in accordance with its principles. In this case a conception of justice is stable. This kind of general information is admissible in the original position. . . .

Thus there follows the very important consequence that the parties have no basis for bargaining in the usual sense. No one knows his situation in society nor his natural assets, and therefore no one is in a position to tailor principles to his advantage. We might imagine that one of the contractees threatens to hold out unless the others agree to principles favorable to him. But how does he know which principles are especially in his interests? The same holds for the formation of coalitions: if a group were to decide to band together to the disadvantage of the others, they would not know how to favor themselves in the choice of principles. Even if they could get everyone to agree to their proposal, they would have no assurance that it was to their advantage, since they cannot identify themselves either by name or description. . . .

The Rationality of the Parties

I have assumed throughout that the persons in the original position are rational. In choosing between principles each tries as best he can to advance his interests. But I have also assumed that the parties do not know their conception of the good. This means that while they know that they have some rational plan of life, they do not know the details of this plan, the particular ends and interests which it is calculated to promote. How, then, can they decide which conceptions of justice are most to their advantage? Or must we suppose that they are reduced to mere guessing? To meet this difficulty, I postulate . . . that they would prefer more primary social goods rather than less [i.e., rights and liberties, powers and opportunities, income and wealth and self-respect]. . . . Of course, it may turn out once the veil of ignorance is removed, that some of them for religious or other reasons may not, in fact, want more of these goods. But from the standpoint of the original position, it is rational for the parties to suppose that they do want a larger share, since in any case they are not compelled to accept more if they do not wish to nor does a person suffer from a greater liberty. Thus even though the parties are deprived of information about their particular ends, they have enough knowledge to rank the alternatives. They know that in general they must try to protect their liberties, widen their opportunities, and enlarge their means for promoting their aims whatever these are. Guided by the theory of the good and the general facts of moral psychology, their deliberations are no longer guesswork. They can make a rational decision in the ordinary sense. . . .

The assumption of mutually disinterested rationality, then, comes to this: the persons in the original position try to acknowledge principles which advance their system of ends as far as possible. They do this by attempting to win for themselves the highest index of primary social goods, since this enables them to promote their conception of the good most effectively whatever it turns out to be. The parties do not seek to confer benefits or to impose injuries on one another; they are not moved by affection or rancor. Nor do they try to gain relative to each other; they are not envious or vain. Put in terms of a game, we might say: they strive for as high an absolute score as possible. They do not wish a high or a low score for their opponents, nor do they seek to maximize or minimize the difference between their successes and those of others. The idea of a game does not really apply, since the parties are not concerned to win but to get as many points as possible judged by their own system of ends. . . .

Once we consider the idea of a contract theory it is tempting to think that it will not yield the principles we want unless the parties are to some degree at least moved by benevolence, or an interest in one another's interests. . . . Now the combination of mutual disinterest and the veil of ignorance achieves the same purpose as benevolence. For this combination of conditions forces each person in the original position to take the good of others into account. In justice as fairness, then, the effects of good will are brought about by several conditions working jointly. The feeling that this conception of justice is egoistic is an illusion fostered by looking at but one of the elements of the original position. . . .

THE PRINCIPLES OF JUSTICE

Two Principles of Justice

I shall now state in a provisional form the two principles of justice that I believe would be chosen in the original position. In this section I wish to make only the most general comments, and therefore the first formulation of these principles is tentative. As we go on I shall run through several formulations and approximate step by step the final statement to be given much later. I believe that doing this allows the exposition to proceed in a natural way.

The first statement of the two principles reads as follows.

> First: each person is to have an equal right to the most extensive basic liberty compatible with a similar liberty for others.
>
> Second: social and economic inequalities are to be arranged so that they are both (a) reasonably expected to be to everyone's advantage, and (b) attached to positions and offices open to all.

There are two ambiguous phrases in the second principle, namely "everyone's advantage" and "equally open to all." Determining their sense more exactly will lead to a second formulation of the principle. . . .

By way of general comment, these principles primarily apply, as I have said, to the basic structure of society. They are to govern the assignment of rights and duties and to regulate the distribution of social and economic advantages. As their formulation suggests, these principles presuppose that the social structure can be divided into two more or less distinct parts, the first principle applying to the one, the second to the other. They distinguish between those aspects of the social system that define and secure the equal liberties of citizenship and those that specify and establish social and economic inequalities. The basic liberties of citizens are, roughly speaking, political liberty (the right to vote and to be eligible for public office) together with freedom of speech and assembly; liberty of conscience and freedom of thought; freedom of the person along with the right to hold (personal) property; and freedom from arbitrary arrest and seizure as defined by the concept of the rule of law. These liberties are all required to be equal by the first principle, since citizens of a just society are to have the same basic rights.

The second principle applies, in the first approximation, to the distribution of income and wealth and to the design of organizations that make use of differences in authority and responsibility, or chains of command. While the distribution of wealth and income need not be equal, it must be to everyone's advantage, and at the same time, positions of authority and offices of command must be accessible to all. One applies the second principle by holding positions open, and then, subject to this constraint, arranges social and economic inequalities so that everyone benefits.

These principles are to be arranged in a serial order with the first principle prior to the second. This ordering means that a departure from the institutions of equal liberty required by the first principle cannot be justified by, or compensated for, by greater social and economic advantages. The distribution of wealth and income, and the hierarchies of authority, must be consistent with both the liberties of equal citizenship and equality of opportunity.

It is clear that these principles are rather specific in their content, and their acceptance rests on certain assumptions that I must eventually try to explain and justify. A theory of justice depends upon a theory of society in ways that will become evident as we proceed. For the present, it should be observed that the two principles (and this holds for all formulations) are a special case of a more general conception of justice that can be expressed as follows.

All social values—liberty and opportunity, income and wealth, and the bases of self-respect—are to be distributed equally unless an unequal distribution of any, or all, of these values is to everyone's advantage.

Injustice, then, is simply inequalities that are not to the benefit of all. Of course, this conception is extremely vague and requires interpretation.

As a first step, suppose that the basic structure of society distributes certain primary goods, that is, things that every rational man is presumed to want. These goods normally have a use whatever a person's rational plan of life. For simplicity, assume that the chief primary goods at the disposition of society are rights and liberties, powers and opportunities,

income and wealth. These are the social primary goods. Other primary goods such as health and vigor, intelligence and imagination, are natural goods; although their possession is influenced by the basic structure, they are not so directly under its control. Imagine, then, a hypothetical initial arrangement in which all the social primary goods are equally distributed: everyone has similar rights and duties, and income and wealth are evenly shared. This state of affairs provides a benchmark for judging improvements. If certain inequalities of wealth and organizational powers would make everyone better off than in this hypothetical starting situation, then they accord with the general conception. . . .

Now the second principle insists that each person benefit from permissible inequalities in the basic structure. This means that it must be reasonable for each relevant representative man defined by this structure, when he views it as a going concern, to prefer his prospects with the inequality to his prospects without it. One is not allowed to justify differences in income or organizational powers on the ground that the disadvantages of those in one position are outweighed by the greater advantages of those in another. Much less can infringements of liberty be counterbalanced in this way. Applied to the basic structure, the principle of utility would have us maximize the sum of expectations of representative men (weighted by the number of persons they represent, on the classical view); and this would permit us to compensate for the losses of some by the gains of others. Instead, the two principles require that everyone benefit from economic and social inequalities. It is obvious, however, that there are indefinitely many ways in which all may be advantaged when the initial arrangement of equality is taken as a benchmark. How then are we to choose among these possibilities? . . .

Democratic Equality and the Difference Principle

The democratic interpretation [of the second principle] is arrived at by combining the principle of fair equality of opportunity with the difference principle. This principle singles out a particular position from which the social and economic inequalities of the basic structure are to be judged. Assuming the framework of institutions required by equal liberty and fair equality of opportunity, the higher expectations of those better situated are just if and only if they work as part of a scheme which improves the expectations of the least advantaged members of society. The intuitive idea is that the social order is not to establish and secure the more attractive prospects of those better off unless doing so is to the advantage of those less fortunate. . . .

To illustrate the difference principle, consider the distribution of income among social classes. Let us suppose that the various income groups correlate with representative individuals by reference to whose expectations we can judge the distribution. Now those starting out as members of the entrepreneurial class in a property-owning democracy, say, have a better prospect than those who begin in the class of unskilled laborers. It seems likely that this will be true even when the social injustices which now exist are removed. What, then, can possibly justify this kind of initial inequality in life prospects? According to the difference principle, it is justifiable only if the difference in expectation is to the advantage of the representative man who is worse off, in this case the representative unskilled worker. The inequality in expectation is permissible only if lowering it would make the working class even more worse off. Supposedly, given the rider in the second principle concerning open positions, and the principle of liberty generally, the greater expectations allowed to entrepreneurs encourages them to do things which raise the long-term prospects of the laboring class. Their better prospects act as incentives so that the economic process is more efficient, innovation proceeds at a faster pace, and so on. Eventually the resulting material benefits spread throughout the system and to the least advantaged. I shall not consider how far these things are true. The point is that something of this kind must be argued if these inequalities are to be just by the difference principle. . . .

. . . And therefore, as the outcome of the last several sections, the second principle is to read as follows.

> Social and economic inequalities are to be arranged so that they are both (a) to the greatest benefit of the least advantaged and (b) attached to offices and positions open to all under conditions of fair equality of opportunity.

THE REASONING LEADING TO THE TWO PRINCIPLES

. . . It is useful as a heuristic device to think of the two principles as the maximin solution to the problem of social justice. There is an analogy between the two principles and the maximin rule for choice under uncertainly. This is evident from the fact that the two principles are those a person would choose for the design of a society in which his enemy is to assign him his place. The maximin rule tells us to rank alternatives by their worst possible outcomes: we are to adopt the alternative the worst outcome of which is superior to the worst outcomes of the others. The persons in the original position do not, of course, assume that their initial place in society is decided by a malevolent opponent. As I note below, they should not reason from false premises. The veil of ignorance does not violate this idea, since an absence of information is not misinformation. But that the two principles of justice would be chosen if the parties were forced to protect themselves against such a contingency explains the sense in which this conception is the maximin solution. And this analogy suggests that if the original position has been described so that it is rational for the parties to adopt the conservative attitude expressed by this rule, a conclusive argument can indeed be constructed for these principles. Clearly the maximin rule is not, in general, a suitable guide for choices under uncertainty. But it is attractive in situations marked by certain special features. My aim, then, is to show that a good case can be made for the two principles based on the fact that the original position manifests these features to the fullest possible degree, carrying them to the limit, so to speak.

Consider the gain-and-loss table below. It represents the gains and losses for a situation which is not a game of strategy. There is no one playing against the person making the decision; instead he is faced with several possible circumstances which may or may not obtain. Which circumstances happen to exist does not depend upon what the person choosing decides or whether he announces his moves in advance. The numbers in the table are monetary values (in hundreds of dollars) in comparison with some initial situation. The gain (g) depends upon the individual's decision (d) and the circumstances (c). Thus $g = f(d, c)$. Assuming that there are three possible decisions and three possible circumstances, we might have this gain-and-loss table.

Decisions	Circumstances		
	C_1	C_2	C_3
d_1	−7	8	12
d_2	−8	7	14
d_3	5	6	8

The maximin rule requires that we make the third decision. For in this case the worst that can happen is that one gains five hundred dollars, which is better than the worst for the other actions. If we adopt one of these we may lose either eight or seven hundred dollars. Thus, the choice of d_3 maximizes $f(d, c)$ for that value of c, which for a given d, minimizes f. The term "maximin" means the *maximum minimorum*; and the rule directs our attention to the worst that can happen under any proposed course of action, and to decide in the light of that.

Now there appear to be three chief features of situations that give plausibility to this unusual rule. First, since the rule takes no account of the likelihoods of the possible circumstances, there must be some reason for sharply discounting estimates of these probabilities. Offhand, the most natural rule of choice would seem to be to compute the expectation of monetary gain for each decision and then to adopt the course of action with the highest prospect. . . . Thus it must be, for example, that the

situation is one in which a knowledge of likelihoods is impossible, or at best extremely insecure. . . .

The second feature that suggests the maximin rule is the following: the person choosing has a conception of the good such that he cares very little, if anything, for what he might gain above the minimum stipend that he can, in fact, be sure of by following the maximin rule. It is not worthwhile for him to take a chance for the sake of a further advantage, especially when it may turn out that he loses much that is important to him. This last provision brings in the third feature, namely, that the rejected alternatives have outcomes that one can hardly accept. The situation involves grave risks. Of course these features work most effectively in combination. The paradigm situation for following the maximin rule is when all three features are realized to the highest degree. This rule does not, then, generally apply, nor of course is it self-evident. Rather, it is a maxim, a rule of thumb, that comes into its own in special circumstances. Its application depends upon the qualitative structure of the possible gains and losses in relation to one's conception of the good, all this against a background in which it is reasonable to discount conjectural estimates of likelihoods. . . .

Some Main Grounds for the Two Principles of Justice

. . . The first confirming ground for the two principles can be explained in terms of what I earlier referred to as the strains of commitment. I said that the parties have a capacity for justice in the sense that they can be assured that their undertaking is not in vain. Assuming that they have taken everything into account, including the general facts of moral psychology, they can rely on one another to adhere to the principles adopted. Thus they consider the strains of commitment. They cannot enter into agreements that may have consequences they cannot accept. They will avoid those that they can adhere to only with great difficulty. Since the original agreement is final and made in perpetuity, there is no second chance. In view of the serious nature of the possible consequences, the question of the burden of commitment is especially acute. A person is choosing once and for all the standards which are to govern his life prospects. Moreover, when we enter an agreement we must be able to honor it even should the worst possibilities prove to be the case. Otherwise we have not acted in good faith. Thus the parties must weigh with care whether they will be able to stick by their commitment in all circumstances. Of course, in answering this question they have only a general knowledge of human psychology to go on. But this information is enough to tell which conception of justice involves the greater stress.

In this respect the two principles of justice have a definite advantage. Not only do the parties protect their basic lights but they insure themselves against the worst eventualities. They run no chance of having to acquiesce in a loss of freedom over the course of their like for the sake of a greater good enjoyed by others, an undertaking that in actual circumstances they might not be able to keep. Indeed, we might wonder whether such an agreement can be made in good faith at all.

. . . A second consideration invokes the condition of publicity as well as that of the constraints on agreements. . . . When the basic structure of society is publicly known to satisfy its principles for an extended period of time, those subject to these arrangements tend to develop a desire to act in accordance with these principles and to do their part in institutions which exemplify them. A conception of justice is stable when the public recognition of its realization by the social system tends to bring about the corresponding sense of justice. Now whether this happens depends, of course, on the laws of moral psychology and the availability of human motives. I shall discuss these matters later on. At the moment we may observe that the principle of utility seems to require a greater identification with the interests of others than the two principles of justice. Thus the latter will be a more stable conception to the extent that this identification is difficult to achieve. . . . Looking at the question from the stand-point of the original position, the parties recognize that it would be highly unwise if not irrational to choose principles which may have consequences so extreme that they could not accept them in practice. They would reject the principle of utility and adopt the more realistic idea of designing the social order on a principle of reciprocal advantage. We need not suppose, of course, that persons never make substantial sacrifices for one another, since moved by affection and ties of sentiment they often do. But such actions are not demanded as a matter of justice by the basic structure of society.

Furthermore, the public recognition of the two principles gives greater support to men's self-respect and this in turn increases the effectiveness of social cooperation. Both effects are reasons for choosing these principles. . . .

John Rawls: A Theory of Justice

1. Do you think that principles of justice ought to be selected by those who are ignorant of their distinguishing features? Why or why not?

2. Is the maximin rule well suited for helping to select principles of justice? If so, why? If not, what alternative principle would you suggest and why?

3. Does the maximin rule yield the result that Rawls thinks it does, or is there an alternative principle of justice that this rule would recommend?

4. Rawls thinks that principles of justice are fair only if they would earn the allegiance of all of those who have to live under them. Do you think that the difference principle meets this condition? Why or why not?

5. Utilitarians argue that giving equal consideration to everyone's interests is fair, and that economic resources and opportunities are therefore fairly distributed when they maximize overall happiness. Rawls disagrees. Who has the better of this disagreement, and why?

Why Does Inequality Matter?

T. M. Scanlon

Among political philosophers and economists, there is a large debate about the moral importance of inequality. Some think that it is intrinsically bad—a bad thing in itself, regardless of how it came about or what harms it may cause down the line. Others think that there is nothing intrinsically bad about inequality, and indeed think that our focus on it is misplaced. These thinkers, known as *prioritarians*, believe that our focus should be on improving the lives of the poor, even if doing so requires that we also improve the lives of the wealthy and perhaps even increase inequality along the way.

T. M. Scanlon wants to walk a line between these two positions. He does not believe that inequality is bad in itself. But he does think that it is often quite bad, and that it calls for responses that range beyond improving the lives of the poor. He calls his position *pluralism*, because he thinks that there are a number of different reasons for finding inequality objectionable, when it is.

One sort of problem arises when a society is obligated to equally distribute some good, such as police protection or childhood education, but instead, without adequate justification, treats a favored group better than a disfavored group. This leads to one sort of wrongful inequality. A second sort arises when inequality is a source of shame or social deprivation on the part of the poorest within a society. A third problem occurs when the wealthiest are able to exert an undue influence on the lives of the less wealthy. A fourth scenario is one in which inequality undermines equality of opportunity.

These four kinds of objection to inequality point to ways in which inequality can have bad results. Inequality can also be morally objectionable when and because the institutions that produce it are themselves morally unjustified. This occurs, for instance, when tax laws unfairly favor the wealthy or are unduly punitive toward the poor.

Why does inequality matter? That is to say, what reason do we have for being concerned with the *difference* between what some have and what others have, as opposed to just trying to make the poor better off? My idea in asking this question is not that inequality is more important than poverty. Often it is not. The fact that millions have been lifted out of extreme poverty in recent decades matters more than the increased inequality among people in rich countries. I am interested in inequality not because it is more important than poverty but because it is more puzzling. People have obvious reasons for wanting to be better off, and particularly strong reasons for wanting to escape from poverty. But it is less clear what reason they have to be concerned with the difference between what they have and what others have. Why isn't this just envy, as critics of egalitarianism often claim?

Some philosophers, called *prioritarians*, think we should be concerned only with improving the welfare of the poor.[1] In their view, the fact that there are some who have more than the poor is relevant only for the reason that the bank robber Willy Sutton is said to have given when asked why he robbed banks: "That's where the money is." Other

From T. M. Scanlon, "Why Does Inequality Matter? Presented at the conference "Combating Inequality: Rethinking Policies to Reduce Inequality in Advanced Economies," October 17, 2019, at the Peterson Institute for International Economics.

philosophers think that inequality is bad in itself, unless it results simply from the free choices of those who have less.[2]

I disagree with both. I think that there are a number of different reasons for objecting to inequality, which arise either from its effects or from the unjustifiability of the institutions that produce it. The plurality of these objections matters, since different objections to inequality call for different policies to combat it. In this paper I will summarize this pluralist view.[3]

Inequality is not always objectionable. The fact that people Scandinavia live longer than people in the United States indicates that we could do better in this regard. But the inequality involved is not what is troubling. The fact that women live longer than men is also not a troubling inequality. But if men in the U.S. lived longer than women this would be worrying, because it seems likely to be due to male babies getting better nourishment, or men getting better medical care.

This illustrates one way in which inequality can be objectionable because of the institutions that produce it. An inequality is objectionable if it results from the fact that an individual or institution that has the same obligation to provide a certain benefit to each member of a group provides this benefit at a higher level for some than for others, without special justification (Scanlon 2018, Chapter 2). It is objectionable in this way, for example, if a municipality (without justification) provides better street paving, sanitation, or other conditions of public health to some residents than to others. This objection depends on the existence of a specific obligation to provide the benefit to those people. It is not a case of objectionable inequality if I give more to one charity than to some other that is equally worthy. I have no general account of when such obligations exist. My point is only that this particular objection to inequality depends on there being an obligation of this kind.

To illustrate some different objections to inequality, imagine two societies, in each of which 99% of the residents have the same quite tolerable level of income. In society A, 1% of the people are much poorer than this, and in society B 1% are much richer, by the same amount. Since these societies are mirror images of one another, they may have the same Gini coefficient [a statistical measure of wealth or income inequality]. But there are different objections to the inequality that they involve.

One thing that comes to mind about society A is what would it be like to be one of the poor people in this society—not just what it would be like to have so little money, but what it would be like to be so much poorer than almost everyone else. As Adam Smith observed (Smith 1910, 351–352), it is a serious objection to a society that it forces some to live and dress in such a way that they cannot go out in public without shame. Whether having so little money is an occasion for shame depends, of course, on the prevailing attitudes of the society: on whether being poor involves being regarded as inferior, less desirable as a friend or neighbor, and unsuitable for positions of authority (Ci 2014). Where such attitudes exist, poverty is an objectionable form of status inequality, like race and gender (Scanlon 2018, Chapter 3).

This particular objection would not apply to the inequality in society B, since it is unlikely that members of the 99% in that society have reason to feel ashamed for not living in the way that the rich do. If the rich are just a few entertainers and athletes with no political power, this inequality might not matter very much. But things are different if the rich own the factories where everyone else has to work, or can dominate the political process. Economic inequality is objectionable it if gives some an unacceptable degree of control over the lives of others or if it undermines the fairness of a society's political institutions. The inequality in society A may be objectionable in these ways as well, if the 99% control the political process and the opportunities available to the poor.

Inequality is also objectionable when it interferes with equality of opportunity (Scanlon 2018, Chapters 4, 5). Equality of opportunity involves two requirements. Procedural fairness requires that individuals should be selected for positions of advantage on the basis of relevant criteria. Substantive opportunity requires that all individuals should have the opportunity to develop the capabilities required to be successful candidates, and to decide whether to do so. Economic inequality can interfere with both of these requirements. In the case of university admissions, for example, procedural fairness is violated if the rich bribe admissions officers to give preference to their children or if the need to raise money leads universities to give preference to children from rich families. Substantive opportunity is violated if children from rich families have much better opportunities to develop the abilities that make them good candidates for admission.

It is important to note that equality of opportunity is not actually achieved in the contemporary U.S., and that even if it were achieved it would not, in itself, justify the unequal outcomes that it leads to. Rather, equality of opportunity is merely a necessary condition for the justice of these unequal outcomes, which presupposes some other justification for the unequal positions involved. The "relevant" criteria for selection that define procedural fairness depend on this justification: they are just the properties that those who are selected for positions of advantage need to have in order for those positions to serve the purposes that are supposed to justify them.

Inequality in income and wealth can be objectionable not only because of its consequences but also because of the unjustifiability of the institutional mechanisms that produce it. Discussion of reducing inequality often focuses on "redistribution" as the main means for doing this. But in considering inequality of income and wealth we should look first at what produces inequality in pretax income in the first place, treating redistributive taxation as a secondary matter. Many institutional mechanisms that generate inequality, such as intellectual property laws, and laws governing limited liability corporations and various forms of financial instruments, and laws making it difficult to form unions and engage in collective bargaining, could be changed without infringement of anyone's liberty. So, in the case of the two societies I mentioned, we should ask where the money of the rich in society A comes from, and what keeps the poor in society B down?

The basic egalitarian idea here is that institutional mechanisms that generate large scale economic inequality in either of these ways need to be justified. They cannot merely be arbitrary. Commonly heard objections to "the one percent" may be based in part on the consequences of this inequality for equality of opportunity and political fairness. But I believe that these objections also reflect the sense that these large holdings are unjustifiable.

How, then, might the institutional mechanisms that produce such differences be justified? I argue that they cannot be justified by appeal to property rights or to ideas of desert. Property rights are important, but they are the creatures of economic institutions, which need to be justified in some other way (Scanlon 2018, Chapter 7). And the only forms of desert that are relevant to economic distribution are, again, dependent on institutions (Scanlon 2018, Chapter 8).

Transactions that generate inequality can sometimes be justified on the ground that restricting them would involve unacceptable interference with individual liberty. For example, we could not prevent Wilt Chamberlain from becoming rich, in the way Robert Nozick (Nozick 1974) imagined him doing, by telling people that they could not spend their money on basketball tickets if they wish to do so. But this covers only a few cases. Today, even the large incomes of sports figures depend on institutional mechanisms such as television licensing and anti-trust law rather than on individual fans putting an extra dollar into a box for the pleasure of watching Wilt play, as Nozick imagined they might do.

Mechanisms that generate inequality cannot be justified simply on the ground that they lead to increases in GDP, independent of how these increases are distributed. How, then, can such institutions be justified? I suggest that it is only by the fact that they are to the benefit even of those who receive smaller shares, and therefore could not be eliminated in a way that would leave those in this position better off.

We thus arrive at Rawls's Difference Principle (Rawls 1971), by means of a direct moral argument rather than by appeal to the idea of rational choice behind a veil of ignorance. (Although the basic elements of this argument are ones that Rawls mentions.)

I have so far been considering inequality in pretax income. Taxation can be justified in a number of different ways, including, among others: as a fair way to fund benefits owed to all, including the provision of education and other conditions that are required by Substantive Opportunity; as a way of reducing inequality in order to ward off its ill effects; and as a way of restraining the growth of inequality by reducing the reasons individuals have to demand higher incomes.

Summary: I have identified six reasons for objecting to inequality. Some of these objections are based on its consequences: inequality of status, unacceptable control of some by others, interference with equality of opportunity and with the fairness of political institutions. Other objections arise from the way the inequality is produced, though the unequal provision of benefits owed to all or by institutions that generate unequal incomes without adequate justification.

Some implications of this pluralist view:

1. There is no specific degree of inequality that should obtain in complex society (no "pattern" or Gini coefficient that must be maintained.) A degree of inequality is acceptable if it is not open to objection of these kinds (or perhaps others.)

2. Since there are many reasons for taxation, the appropriate rate of taxation depends on many different factors.

3. There is no single answer to the question "equality of what?" The kind of inequality that is objectionable varies, depending on the objection to inequality that is in question.

NOTES

1. Parfit 2000. For discussion, see O'Neill 2008.
2. Cohen 1989. For critical discussion, see Anderson 1999 and Scheffler 2003.
3. For a fuller statement see Scanlon 2018.

WORKS CITED

Anderson, Elizabeth, 1999, "What Is the Point of Equality?" *Ethics* 109, 287–337.

Ci, Jiwei, 2014, "Agency and Other Stakes of Poverty," *Journal of Political Philosophy* 21, 125–150.

Cohen, G. A., 1989, "On the Currency of Egalitarian Justice," *Ethics* 99, 906–944.

Nozick, Robert, 1974, *Anarchy, State, and Utopia* (New York: Basic Books).

O'Neill, Martin, 2008, "What Should Egalitarians Believe?" *Philosophy and Public Affairs* 36, 119–156.

Parfit, Derek, 2000, "Equality or Priority?" in Michael Clayton and Andrew Williams, eds., *The Idea of Equality* (New York: Palgrave Macmillan), 81–125.

Rawls, John, 1971, *A Theory of Justice* (Cambridge, MA: Harvard University Press).

Scanlon, T. M., 2018, *Why Does Inequality Matter?* (Oxford: Oxford University Press).

Scheffler, Samuel, 2003, "What Is Egalitarianism?" *Philosophy and Public Affairs* 31, 5–39.

Smith, Adam, 1910, *The Wealth of Nations* (London: J.M. Dent).

T. M. Scanlon: Why Does Inequality Matter?

1. Is inequality bad in itself, or only when it is an indication of something else (such as a history of unfair treatment) that is morally important?

2. Suppose that in a given situation one could either improve the needs of the poor or reduce inequality, but not both. Which would you recommend, and why?

3. Is there anything especially problematic about inequality of wealth, as compared to inequality of income?

4. Scanlon discusses four ways in which inequality can be morally objectionable because of its problematic consequences. Do you find each of the four kinds of case as worrisome as Scanlon does? Is there a fifth kind of case that he has failed to mention?

5. Scanlon's discussion focuses on inequality of wealth. Do you think that his claims extend to other sorts of inequality? If so, which sorts of inequality? If not, why not?

A Bleeding Heart Libertarian View of Inequality

Andrew J. Cohen

Bleeding heart libertarianism combines two views. The libertarian element reflects a commitment to the substantial value of so-called negative liberty—freedom to do whatever you want, so long as you do not violate the rights of others. On a libertarian view, the state ought to ensure a free market and limit its activities to both protecting the negative liberties of its citizens and ensuring that injustices are remedied. The bleeding heart element comes from an emphasis on the plight of the poor. Bleeding heart libertarians claim that securing the negative liberties of all is the best route to elevating the status of the poor.

Andrew Jason Cohen believes that a free market economy, where people are allowed to exchange with anyone they want, on mutually acceptable terms, will inevitably create inequalities of wealth. But he denies that such inequality is bad in itself, and thinks that having a free market is in fact likely to do more to benefit the poor than an economy that is riddled with government regulations. He offers a series of thought experiments to get his readers to question whether there is anything morally problematic with wealth inequality per se. If Cohen is right, free markets not only allow the poor to improve their economic status but also expose everyone to more people, thereby increasing the chance that we'll find new friends or partners, introducing us to a greater diversity of ideas, and giving us more opportunities to try out different ways of life.

Cohen is not blind to the real injustices that have contributed to inequality and poverty. But he believes that the best way to remedy them is by creating more liberty for individuals, rather than more regulations. Cohen is well aware that real markets are not ideal. But that's true of governments, too. He doubts that more government regulation is going to fix the problems that have so frequently allowed the poor to be treated unjustly. He is especially concerned with what he calls "legal plunder"—the manipulation by powerful, wealthy individuals to shape the law so as to benefit themselves, at the expense of the less fortunate. "What we want," writes Cohen, "is a system wherein people live by mutual cooperation, a system wherein no one systematically and/or wrongfully hurts others." Cohen believes that bleeding heart libertarianism fits the bill.

We live in a market system and witness much economic inequality. Although such inequality may not be an essential characteristic of market systems, it seems historically inevitable. How we should evaluate this inequality, on the other hand, is contentious. I propose that bleeding heart libertarians provide the best diagnosis and prescription.

Jason Cohen, "A Bleeding Heart Libertarian View of Inequality," in *Ethics in Practice*, 5th ed., ed. Hugh LaFollette (Wiley, 2020), pp. 624–631.

In the first section, I explain "bleeding heart libertarianism" (hereafter, "BHL"). In section II, I indicate why, as a matter of theory, a market generally includes economic inequality. In the third section, I discuss the inequality in contemporary market systems. Here, I step away from theory to comment on the real-world situation—and indicate the real moral problems often associated with inequality. In section IV, I extend my discussion to global inequality. Then, in the fifth section, I explain that although inequality that arises in a libertarian market is morally acceptable, the inequality of our market system is morally questionable. While some claim that inequality requires government intervention, I suggest that the key difference between our market system and a libertarian market system is precisely the government intervention we have—I argue, that is, that there is too much unjustified interference in contemporary markets.

I. BLEEDING HEART LIBERTARIANISM

To start with the obvious, BHL is a form of libertarianism. If anything distinguishes it from other versions of libertarianism, it is that bleeding heart libertarians (BHLs) are explicitly bleeding hearts—concern for the plight of the less fortunate is central to our project. In short, BHL is a family of libertarian (and hence liberal) views that take suffering to be a moral problem; like all libertarians, however, we recognize that not all moral problems require state action—and, indeed, that state action sometimes causes the problem.

The BHL concern for the plight of the less fortunate does not mean we endorse socialism or increased redistributive welfare policies. It means we think the world should be set up in a way such that the least well-off (whomever they are) are as well-off as possible, consistent with ensuring liberty for all. . . .

Perhaps it is worth noting that BHLs endorse the free market but are eager to consider what empirical economic science—as well as economic theory—has to teach us. The emphasis on empirical evidence is significant. Many BHLs will thus look at the effects of particular government policies before announcing their views of those policies. We likely all oppose redistributive policies in principle, but may endorse some policies, in specific circumstances, that actually help the poorest individuals in our society. We all oppose policies that redistribute resources from poorer people to richer people or that otherwise place unfair burdens on poorer people. . . .

While law is meant to protect, Frédéric Bastiat noted that it is often "perverted through the influence of two very different causes—naked greed and misconceived philanthropy."[1] The naked greed

by those with power encourages them to use the law to take from the poor and others; this is "legal plunder." Misconceived philanthropy may start in a seemingly better intention of wanting to help, but requires imposing a view about what is good for people (a view they may not share) and encourages ill-feeling between citizens, as well as other problems. By contrast, "When law and force keep a man within the bounds of justice, they impose nothing upon him but a mere negation. They only oblige him to abstain from doing harm."[2] This simply means that individuals should be free to trade with one another as they wish, with no interference. No individual ought to be forced to trade with anyone else. Markets where such freedom is present require no force except that needed to prevent or rectify harm—where harm is not merely being hurt, but suffering a hurt because of the wrongful action of another. Force used even to help the poor (which often has perverse effects) where no harm is present or, perhaps worse, to help the wealthy at the expense of the poor, is impermissible on this view.

BHL is a family of views that take some form of negative liberty (freedom from interference) to be a normatively primary (and guiding) value in the organization of a just state, insisting it must be present for all (some call this "classical liberalism"), but that also share a deep concern to prevent suffering (and perhaps promote at least minimal individual well-being). Some in this camp may approve of limited government interventions to end suffering; all agree that allowing individuals extensive (negative) liberty is likely to create the least suffering possible. Some may favor pretty strong, if not absolute, property rights. . . . Put simply, we believe that ensuring negative freedom as a matter of law will also allow people the most de facto positive freedom (freedom to do as one wants)—and we value that positive freedom. By contrast, socialists seek to ensure positive freedom as a matter of law, believing that will allow most people extensive de facto negative freedom. Rawlsians and other left-leaning liberals who favor some redistributive welfare scheme, by contrast, seek to ensure some of both positive and negative liberty as a matter of law. . . .

---

1. Frédéric Bastiat, *The Law* (Auburn, AL: Ludwig von Mises Institute, 2007), 5.

2. Ibid., 19.

II. MARKETS BRING INEQUALITY BUT . . .

It may be hard for those of us in the developed world in the 21st century to believe, but the history of the world is a history almost entirely of subsistence. It's not until the 19th century and the Industrial Revolution that we see substantial accumulation of wealth. In what some call "the Great Divergence," Europe and the US saw a growth in wealth completely anomalous with all of preceding history (and, at that time, the rest of the world—from which Europe and the US diverged). In the 20th century, such growth continued throughout the world. To take just one simple example, as late as 1981, 90% of the people in China lived in poverty; in 2018, under 7% do. This is a truly phenomenal change that means the number of people that would be in the group that is the least well-off has been dramatically reduced. This is a clear gain for humankind that should not be understated. According to the World Bank, the world "cut the 1990 poverty rate in half by 2015" while "Nearly 1.1 billion people have moved out of extreme poverty."[3] While there are still too many living with poverty, the numbers are good—and not only has poverty been reduced, but the rest of us have gotten wealthier.

Historically speaking, subsistence poverty was the norm; wealth, the anomaly. Though there are many factors that contributed to the tremendous growth in wealth in the last 200 years—while the previous 2000 years human kind languished—freer and more extensive trade is clearly the single biggest factor. The accumulation of capital and the tremendous reduction of poverty that we continue to see is a direct result of the market system and property rights that make such a system possible. This, more than anything else, likely explains why BHLs take trade so seriously. Indeed, it may be that the single clearest difference between BHLs and other libertarians is that while other libertarians start with economic freedom as a value and thus support

markets, BHLs are concerned with human welfare, see that markets improve human welfare, and thus support economic freedom and the markets it enables.

Trade is good because it brings wealth and wealth means improved human welfare. Wealth should not be conceived of as mere money. Wealth is the means that one has to do as one wishes. As a form of wealth, money allows one to buy the goods and services one needs or wishes to use. Increasing wealth (as money or otherwise), means increasing one's ability to live as one wishes. It means improving one's life. Of course, increased wealth does not mean all lives are equally improved. The "Great Divergence" was, after all, a period in which the lives of some—primarily those in Europe and the US—were improved at a vastly quicker rate than those elsewhere. Within Europe and the US, we also see differential gains, with some doing exponentially better than others. There is, no doubt, economic inequality in developed markets. Let us step back from this simple and acknowledged fact for a moment to consider where the inequality comes from.

According to Adam Smith, "there is a natural propensity in human nature . . . to truck, barter, and exchange one thing for another."[4] If this is not inherent in human nature, it is certainly widespread. Say I have four sticks and two stones and prefer a third stone to two of the four sticks; meanwhile, you have two sticks and five stones and prefer more sticks. We trade and are both happier for doing so. Say I prefer to spend my days reading moral and political philosophy, economics, and political science; you prefer to spend your days raising cattle or apples. You might not want to trade your meat or fruit for my reading (or my explaining what I read), but I can find buyers for my teaching services, accepting some relatively stable currency (through the intermediary of the University) and then trade some of that currency for your meat or fruit.

Importantly, you might not be a great farmer. It may be, in fact, that I would be a better farmer than you if I decided to dedicate my days to it. I might, that is, have an absolute advantage over you with

---

3. See http://www.worldbank.org/en/topic/poverty/overview. Some raise concerns with the numbers (see, e.g., https://www.aljazeera.com/indepth/opinion/2014/08/exposing-great-poverty-reductio-201481211590729809.html), but the overall prognosis is clearly positive.

---

4. *An Inquiry into the Nature and Causes of the Wealth of Nations*, Book I, Chapter II, Paragraph 1.

regard to farming. Why don't I spend my days farming? In part, this is simply my own preference, but it's also related to the fact that while I might be able to more efficiently produce food than you, doing so would not be the most efficient use of my time because I can produce teaching more efficiently than I can produce food. My opportunity cost of producing food is higher than yours (assume you have no other talents, or no other talents that result in marketable goods or services). You have a comparative advantage in food production. Though I could produce food more efficiently than you, doing so would leave me less well-off than producing teaching and trading with you for the food. This is the principle of comparative advantage.

The principle of comparative advantage shows that even someone with an absolute advantage in producing a good may be better off trading for that good from someone else. Having trading partners with comparative advantages producing most of the goods and services we value benefits us. Having more trading partners—indeed, having more trading partners with more diverse skills—improves our ability to trade for goods and services we value. So long as we also produce goods or services valued by others, we do better than trying to produce all we value ourselves.

Given the propensity to trade, natural or not, and the principle of comparative advantage, we do better to divide labor into more and more segments. The division of labor, as Smith notes, results in increased productivity and wealth due to the increased dexterity (itself due to increased simplicity of tasks), the time we save from not having to switch tasks, and the increased use of machinery for those tasks. It's unlikely that the increased productivity and wealth would be spread equally amongst all participants. The fact is that some will be more generally skilled and talented; they will thus have absolute advantages over others in a greater array of tasks, and thus be able to choose from that greater array in a way that they benefit more than others. They will be able to earn a greater income and accumulate more wealth.

Economic inequality is to be expected in markets where people freely sell their labor or the goods and services they produce. On the other hand, we

should realize that there are economic gains to all. In all but the rarest cases, even those with relatively few absolute advantages will find themselves with a comparative advantage in something. This may be some form of menial labor, but that labor will still be productive and valuable to the overall system and those who participate in it.

We should not fail to note that the advantage to market systems is not merely the economic wealth it produces. Given the need to trade with a wide array of people with a wide array of skill sets, markets open the door for each of us to meet many more people than we would if we continued to live the subsistence lives our ancestors lived. We have more contact with others—some similar to us but many different—and thus more opportunity to find compatible friends and even spouses than we would otherwise. We have more chances to choose a different way to live—including with different people, in different jobs, different churches, and so on.

To summarize, markets bring more wealth for all and also more contact with others, some who become friends and family. They also likely bring inequality. This inequality is a factor of all doing better, though some more than others. This is not necessarily something to bemoan. At least part of the reason China was able to reduce poverty from 90% to 7% in less than 40 years, after all, is simply that when people are allowed to trade freely, they are more likely to take responsibility for production. When they are not free to trade—when they can only receive as much as someone else declares is sufficient—they have no incentive to take such responsibility. Without legal ownership (i.e., property), that is, no one will—to use the colloquialism—take ownership (i.e., take responsibility for production, regardless of who legally owns what). With a legal system of property, by contrast, people take ownership and invest themselves in their work to create more for all as a means of promoting their own welfare. In the process, all do better.

III. THE INEQUALITY IN OUR MARKET SYSTEM AND THE REAL PROBLEMS

What we have seen thus far is that property rights and the market systems they make possible provide great benefits for all—especially increased wealth and more social ties—but do so unequally. Inequality on its own, though, is not a problem. To see this, imagine there is a society with rising income and rising inequality such that:

At Time 1, 90% of the population has income of $10,000/year and 10% have income of $50,000/year.

At later Time 2, 90% of the population has income of $50,000/year and 10% have income of $500,000/year.

At the earlier time, each member of the smaller and richer tenth of the population brings in five times the amount of those in the larger and poorer nine-tenths. At the later time, they bring in ten times their poorer compatriots. Income inequality has increased. Why we should be concerned about this is less clear. Of course, if the wealthy became wealthy by exploiting (or stealing from or . . .) the others, we should be concerned—but the concern would be with the exploitation (or theft or . . .) rather than the inequality itself.

To make the point starker, consider a later date:

At Time 3, 95% of the population has income of $100,000/year and 5% have income of $5 million/year.

Now the richer twentieth brings in 50 times what their poorer compatriots bring in. More drastic inequality, but at this later date, it is unreasonable to think anyone is poor. (Holding the value of dollars constant.) That fact—that no one is poor—is significant. As Harry Frankfurt says, "From the point of view of morality, it is not important that everyone should have the same. What is morally important is that each should have enough."[5] "Enough" is "what is needed for the kind of life a person would most sensibly and appropriately seek for himself."[6]

Frankfurt's view captures an important intuition very well: what we care about is suffering. We find suffering morally bad without need for argument (which is not to say no argument can be made) and we tend to think that where there is inequality, those with the least will suffer. Historically, this may have been the case. Given the general subsistence level of wealth throughout the world, being on the lower end of income or wealth meant always

being close to death. But that is a contingent fact. As shown earlier, inequality can easily exist even where no one is poor or suffering. (I am not saying that is our situation.) We can be morally unconcerned with inequality and exceedingly concerned with poverty and suffering. That is the BHL stance.

To be clear, there are two contingent but real moral problems associated with inequality. One is poverty or other suffering on the low end of the spectrum of economic inequality, as just discussed. The other is the abuse (exploitation, etc.) those on the high end can engage in. Specifically, those on the high end can use their wealth to influence government in ways that improve their lot at the expense of everyone else (what economists call "rent-seeking" behavior). This is the legal plunder I discussed earlier. . . .

Examples that are worth considering in this light include the entire institution of slavery (which benefited wealthy white landowners) and, more recently, in the US, overcriminalization and overincarceration (which benefit the entrenched elite in various law enforcement agencies and the businesses that serve them at the expense of poor people, especially those of color).

In her book *The New Jim Crow*,[7] while discussing the "drug war" in the US, Michelle Alexander notes that "Between 1980 and 1984, FBI antidrug funding increased from $8 million to $95 million. Department of Defense antidrug allocations increased from $33 million in 1981 to $1,042 million in 1991. During that same period, DEA antidrug spending grew from $86 to $1,026 million, and FBI antidrug allocations grew from $38 to $181 million."[8] It is hard to read about these increases and not think rent-seeking on behalf of these agencies greatly influenced policy. Indeed, when Alexander discusses the rise of civil asset forfeiture, she notes that "local police departments, as well as state and federal law enforcement agencies . . . have a direct pecuniary interest in the profitability and longevity of the drug war."[9] She goes on to show how the

---

5. *On Inequality* (Princeton: Princeton University Press, 2015), 7.
6. Ibid., 11.

7. New York: The New Press, 2010.
8. Ibid., 49.
9. Ibid., 83.

drug war disproportionately affects minorities—in extremely serious ways. Indeed, these examples of rent-seeking . . . involve widespread massive violations of individual rights, resulting in harms to millions of people.

What we have seen here is that the sort of inequality that exists in the contemporary western world is morally problematic, not because people earn different amounts or have unequal wealth, but because some suffer and some use their wealth to warp government policy in their favor while causing damage to others. Obviously, this is not a new problem. The attempt "to enrich all classes at the expense of each other" that Bastiat found so rightly concerning, is always seductive.

IV. GLOBAL AND DOMESTIC INEQUALITY

Many who express concern about domestic inequality seem unclear about why they are concerned. In the US, demonstrators claiming they are in the 99% indicate opposition to the vast amount of wealth owned or controlled by the 1%. They do not seem bothered by the fact that they themselves are in the top 1% if we are talking about world population rather than US population.

CNBC reports that "To reach the threshold of the top 1 percent of income earners in the US, you need to make $389,436 a year or more, a 2013 Economic Policy Institute report finds."[10] "But the threshold required to make it in to" the top 1 percent of income earners in the world is "just $34,000 per person."[11] The global median income is just $1,225 a year, meaning most of the demonstrators in the US are amongst the wealthiest in the world, something they seem largely oblivious to. Most do not think they are taking advantage of poorer people elsewhere. (Some do—and protest against that as well.)

Whether global inequality is a problem is a question separate from whether domestic inequality is a

problem. We cannot, in any case, just look at average national incomes to determine if they are unequal in real value. If living expenses in a country are 10% of what they are in the US, we should not be bothered if people there earn 10% of what people in the US earn. That said, there is no doubt that Americans and Europeans are richer than people elsewhere on any reasonable metric. It's not merely that we have higher nominal earnings, but that those earnings provide us far more real wealth than can be had elsewhere.

For BHLs, global inequality, like domestic inequality, is only contingently problematic. If some suffer, it should give us pause. If that suffering is the result of harmful actions by others—especially harmful actions taken to elevate some at the expense of those who suffer—interference is pro tanto [i.e., presumptively] permissible. Such actions are likely the result of wealthier individuals wielding influence on government bodies in ways that allow them to capture rents at the expense of those with less (as already discussed). This is true globally as well as domestically.

Domestically, municipal governments in the US normally grant monopoly rights to cable companies, thereby limiting competition. Some have rent control or zoning laws that make housing more expensive, hurting those needing less expensive housing. Governments frequently require professional licenses for those working in industries as diverse as medicine, law, plumbing, and hair dressing, thereby limiting the competition. In these ways, governments provide assistance to some—typically those already in the field—at the expense of others—those who might wish to provide the service at a reduced cost and those who might wish to buy the service at the lower cost. The same is true globally.

Import tariffs imposed by the US Federal Government on dishwashers, for example, is meant to help US manufacturers sell more of their product. The imported machines are more expensive with the taxes than they would be without, so fewer people buy them. The tariffs amount to a gift to US manufacturers that sets back the interests of foreign producers and those in the US who wish to buy those products or to have more (often less expensive) options to choose from.

10. https://www.cnbc.com/2017/11/06/how-much-you-need-to-earn-to-be-in-the-top-1-percent-at-every-age.html.

11. http://www.dailymail.co.uk/news/article-2082385/We-1--You-need-34k-income-global-elite--half-worlds-richest-live-U-S.html.

To the BHL, the domestic and global issues are on par. With domestic interventions, domestic players are helped and domestic players are hurt. With global interventions, domestic players are helped and both domestic and international players are hurt. To the BHL, anyone's being hurt should give us pause. . . .

[I]t remains unclear why we should be concerned about social inequality only within our own polities. As already indicated, there may be no reason to worry about different wage levels in different places, but this does not mean we should be unconcerned with suffering in different places—especially when such suffering is the result of wrongful impositions caused by those with wealth and power.

When wealthy business and political leaders in one country agree to buy a natural resource—diamonds or oil, perhaps—from the hereditary political leaders of a small county though they know the latter will use the finances they receive to suppress dissent or worse, all of those involved contribute to maintaining the power structure that causes people to suffer. To use only one recent example, when the US continues to encourage firms to do business with Saudi Arabia, it is not difficult to see how the latter gets the economic and military power to bomb Houthi rebels in Yemen, causing great suffering.

While I am here primarily concerned with economic inequality, it is worth considering how it impacts other areas. (E.g., the overcriminalization and overincarceration problem in the US and continued warfare in the Middle East already discussed.) We should recognize that economic inequality matters when, as a contingent matter, some people abuse the political (and economic) system for their own gain and, in the process, cause others to suffer. We should recognize that this matters internationally as well as domestically. The fact is, the economic system we live in is international. This does not mean all people across the globe should be political equals. On the other hand, we must not refuse to recognize that individuals matter morally no matter where they are. This is part of the BHL stance.

V. GOVERNMENT INTERVENTION IS THE CAUSE, NOT THE ANSWER

Inequality matters, but the way it matters has naught to do with national borders. It matters when it includes suffering by those who are not well-off and it matters when those who are well-off use their positions to inflict their desires on others. What we want is a system wherein people live by mutual co-operation, a system wherein no one systematically and/or wrongfully hurts others. To be clear, what matters is not inequality per se, but two possible phenomena that are often (but not necessarily) correlated with inequality. As we saw in section III, even substantial inequality might be completely unproblematic if all are doing well.

Some might object that I seem to believe that real-world markets work in ways that are required in economic theory without realizing that the latter idealizes in its models. I do not think this is right; I am not blind to the fact that real markets are not ideal markets. Importantly, though, we should also not be blind to the fact that real governments are not ideal governments. We should not think we can replace the very flawed real markets we live in with ideal government programs. The question we ought to be concerned with here is "why do markets go awry?"

From the perspective of BHL, the main cause of markets misfiring is the perversion of law, as discussed in section I. . . . The problem comes when some—those with the ability to convince government about how such laws should work—use that power to enrich themselves at the expense of others without enriching those others or receiving their agreement. Yet this is pervasive—and perverse. Regulatory capture—where those being regulated essentially do the regulating—is also pervasive. And perverse. The idea that some professional services should be licensed so as to protect consumers will likely meet with widespread approval (unfortunately). The problem comes when some use licensing laws to their advantage without enriching others. When licensing laws primarily enrich those who are licensed but add little to no value to consumers, or, worse, remove value by making it impossible to purchase the service at a lower cost—which is also pervasive—law is again perverse.

When law is perverted, some—usually those already well-off—use it to enrich themselves at the expense of others—often the less well-off—without their agreement. This is the opposite of what BHLs, as well as all other libertarians, want. We want a free market wherein, as already discussed, no one is coerced to trade with anyone else. A genuinely free market system is one wherein each is free to do as they wish, trading with whomever would freely trade with him or her on terms they both find mutually beneficial. When this is what happens, we have a system wherein people flourish by providing value for others. This is obviously morally permissible. It would be a mistake to consider it either selfless or altruistic, but it is a system wherein people do better by doing well for others.

When government interferes, some manage to do well for themselves by seeking and receiving rents from government action. They might receive higher pay because they have few competitors due to licensing requirements. They may receive their pay even if their investments failed in predictable ways. That pay comes from others, forced to pay taxes to support bad bets of those who can get the government to cover their risks. They might be able to charge more for their goods because they convinced the government to impose tariffs on competition from elsewhere. And so on. When this is the case, we have immorality built into a hybrid market system. While some trades may be freely entered into and mutually beneficial, others are forced (either literally, or by the artificial limiting of options by government power, or via other factors that make various trades such that genuine informed consent is impossible).

The point here is simple: when government interferes, it renders mutual benefit through consent impossible. When it does that, there is immorality in the system. The inequality that results is immoral and likely to be more extreme than otherwise. To make this vivid, imagine you want to marry Donna. Donna does not want to marry you. You are hurt by her rejection, but nothing immoral has occurred; she married me and you went on and found someone else (we hope). Imagine, though, that the reason Donna married me is that I convinced the government to require a "Donna marrying license" law that allowed only one license per decade and I, knowing it was being instituted, got to the licensing board first. Or imagine she married me because I managed to get the government to make your travel to Donna's home town illegal. Or to make your profession illegal. Or to subsidize mine (making me wealthier and so more attractive). In such situations,

you would rightly be aggrieved. You failed to marry who you wanted but only (let us assume) because of unjust interference by the government on my behalf. Now imagine this example multiplied by a million—that is, with government determining the outcome in millions of cases, leaving it impossible for millions to do what they wish.

Recognizing that every market transaction has winners and losers, one should worry about having an agency that operates in ways that determine the winners and losers. If I win Donna because of my superior charm, humor, intellect, looks, or what have you, it is one thing. If I win her because of undue interference on my behalf, it is another. If Microsoft, Apple, Google, or whoever sells the most software because it makes the best (most desirable) software, it is one thing. If it sells the most software because of undue interference, it is another. If medical doctors earn more money than professors because they work harder, longer, or are simply deemed to provide a more valuable service by most people, it is one thing. If they earn more money because of undue limits to their competition, it is another.

Import tariffs, immigration restrictions, agricultural and industrial subsidies, licensing requirements, government grants of monopolies of any sort, real estate zoning laws, and so on, are all ways that the government aids some at the expense of others. These are all ways that markets are made less free and less fair. Importantly, it's worse than this discussion thus far may make it seem—simply because we are not likely to have government determining the winner of a single transaction in isolation from all other transactions. More likely, if the government sets things so that I win and you lose in one transaction, it will set things so that I win in a lot of transactions (and perhaps that you lose in a lot of transactions) since the winner of a transaction will seek to persuade government to continue setting things in his favor and, by virtue of a "win," will have the resources to do so, offering compensation to government officials that help them.

The objection raised earlier might now be restated: I remain blind to the problems of markets unimpeded by government interference. Of course, government does interfere and (most) BHLs want government to interfere—at least to protect property rights and the consensual actions of market participants. The claim might be that this always occurs and I've provided little reason to think interfering to ensure market transactions that are consensual is anything more than aiding a group of market participants at the expense of others. Those protected, after all, will be benefited at the cost of those they are protected against (as well as those who pay taxes to support the system). The response here can be made straightforwardly, even if its defense would need to be more extensive. Protecting those who consensually trade with others is protecting them from harm by those who would unjustly seek to set back their interests. It is justified by the injustice. By contrast, interfering on behalf of some who are not the subjects of unjust attempts to set back their interests is interference not justified by injustice. It is itself an unjust use of force.

Andrew Jason Cohen: A Bleeding Heart Libertarian View of Inequality

1. Both bleeding heart libertarianism and John Rawls's difference principle assign importance to addressing the needs of the poor. As a general matter, how do these two approaches differ? Can you think of a concrete example in which the advice of one of these approaches would conflict with that of the other?

2. Many think that the best way to stop legal plunder is to enact regulations designed to prevent it. What does Cohen think of such a proposal? Do you find his ideas plausible? Why or why not?

3. What are the advantages of a free market, according to Cohen? He spends little time discussing its disadvantages. What (if any) do you think these are? Do the advantages outweigh the disadvantages?

4. Are you convinced by Cohen's thought experiments designed to show that there is nothing, in itself, morally problematic with economic inequality?

5. Cohen argues against import tariffs, which are designed to protect domestic manufacturers from foreign competition. Do you think that such tariffs are morally acceptable? Why or why not?

How Not to Complain about Taxes
Elizabeth Anderson

In this selection, Elizabeth Anderson considers two common complaints people have about taxation. The first complaint is that, in taxing private citizens, the government takes what is rightfully a citizen's private property. This complaint is often inspired by John Locke's famous defense of the institution of private property in his *Second Treatise of Civil Government*. Anderson argues that Locke himself didn't oppose certain forms of taxation—even extensive taxation. For instance, Locke held that every person has duties of charity that the government can legitimately enforce. Thus, Anderson argues, appeals to Locke's work to oppose the kind of taxation now common in welfare states is unsuccessful.

From Elizabeth Anderson, "How Not to Complain about Taxes," Left2Right blog, January 6 and January 26, 2005. http://left2right.typepad.com/main/2005/01/how_not_to_comp.html

The second complaint is that, in a capitalist society like the United States, earned income is deserved income. The idea is that the income a person makes by trading with others in the free market is owed to the one who earned it—not the government. If so, this would count strongly against taxation for redistributive purposes. Anderson argues that this thought is mistaken because it's implausible to think that the market distributes income and goods in proportion to a person's virtue or moral worth. She makes the case by considering the work of another famous defender of capitalism: Friedrich Hayek. Hayek argued that prices function to send signals to producers and consumers about the relative abundance or scarcity of goods in the market. If so, then, Anderson argues, there is virtually no connection between a person's moral excellence and the amount of money that person earns by selling his goods or labor in the free market.

Anderson proceeds to argue that, since capitalist economies are by their very nature volatile, having good insurance is necessary. Thus, there is good reason for the government to help protect its citizens from this predictable volatility. And providing this protection would require some taxation for redistributive purposes.

I.

Governments cannot be supported without great charge, and it is fit every one who enjoys his share of the protection, should pay out of his estate his proportion for the maintenance of it.

That's John Locke, the great defender of private property, writing (*Second Treatise of Government*, ch. XI, par. 140). It pays for defenders of private property to listen to Locke, so as to avoid silly complaints about taxation. Here's one common one I hear: that government, in taxing my property, is taking away what is really mine. This complaint is often conjoined with the accusation that liberals, in order to justify taxation, must believe that the government owns all property to begin with and by rights could confiscate it all. Two points should put these fallacies to rest.

First, a technical point: the fact that some property is mine does not entail that other people do not have rightful claims to some portion of it. I am entitled to my salary; it's mine. But my children have a rightful claim to support from my income. In some states, such as California, I have a legal obligation to support my parents out of my income, if they cannot support themselves. I have to pay my bills out of my income. If I negligently injure someone, I am liable to pay them damages

from my income. The fact that this income is mine does not settle anything about who else might have legitimate claims to some portion of it, and on what grounds. Note also that I did not have to give my personal consent for some of these others to have a claim on it.

So far, I've just been talking about property as a legal institution. But perhaps the complaint I am criticizing is talking about supposed "natural" property rights, following theorists such as Locke. So here's my second point: unless one is a bomb-throwing anarchist, an advocate of natural property rights must concede the legitimacy and indeed necessity of a state, at least as an institution for collective protection and impartial adjudication of claims—the so-called "minimal state." And such a state will have a legitimate claim on every member's property, to the extent necessary for everyone to pay their fair share for its maintenance, as Locke rightly insisted. Even in a minimal state, the fact that my income is mine does not constitute an argument against the taxation necessary to support the state.

In fact, Locke himself went much further than this minimal claim. In the Lockean mythology loved by libertarians, it is supposed that individuals, upon joining a minimal state, retain full claim to all of their natural property rights, except to the small extent needed to support a minimal state. The fallacy here is to suppose that, when people join together to form a state for the protection of their property, they are concerned only to protect their property from the encroachment of others. According to Locke, however, individuals form a state not just for protection against violations of their negative liberties but for the *preservation* of their lives (which are part of their property):

> the first and fundamental natural law, which is to govern even the legislature itself, is the preservation of society, and (as far as will consist with the public good) of every person in it. (Locke, *Second Treatise*, ch. 11, par. 134)

Unless one could show, contrary to fact, that death rates under publicly funded health care systems are higher than under systems that leave people to pay for their health care with whatever resources are at their disposal, some kind of publicly funded health insurance entitlements are compatible with, and may even be required by, Locke's theory of natural property rights. Moreover, Locke insists on our obligation to provide for the poor:

> God hath not left one man so to the mercy of another, that he may starve him if he please: God the Lord and Father of all, has given no one of his children such a property in his peculiar portion of the things of this world, but that he has given his needy brother a *right* to the surplusage of his goods; so that it cannot justly be denied him, when his pressing wants call for it. . . . As justice gives every man a title to the product of his honest industry, and the fair acquisitions of his ancestors descended to him; so charity gives every man a *title* to so much out of another's plenty, as will keep him from extreme want, where he has no means to subsist otherwise: and a man can no more justly make use of another's necessity to force him to become his vassal, by with-holding that relief God requires him to afford to the wants of his brother, than he that has more strength can seize upon a weaker, master him to his obedience, and with a dagger at his throat, offer his death or slavery. (*First Treatise*, ch. 4, par. 42, emphasis mine)

Locke's point is not just that some kind of *entitlement*-based welfare system is required by

morality and built into the structure of natural property rights (the poor have a *title* to what they need). It's also that, *to prevent a free property system from degenerating into feudalism, constraints on freedom of contract are required*. Just as contracts into slavery are invalid, contracts into vassalage are. People are not entitled to use their superior bargaining power to drive others to the wall, or into subjection.

So, you can't get an argument against a welfare state from Locke's theory of natural property rights. I won't pretend that Locke was as generous as modern welfare states; his preferred system of provision for the poor was in fact very harsh. And, given the primitive state of medicine in his day, no one at the time imagined it would have done much good to universalize access to it. But nothing in his system prevents a more generous welfare state. . . .

Does it follow that Locke, in accepting the legitimacy of taxation to promote the general welfare, including the establishment of welfare entitlements, really believes that the government owns everything and so could by rights dispose of all property arbitrarily? Of course not. He lays out the following constraints on legitimate taxation in ch. 11 of the *Second Treatise*:

1. It must be consistent with some system of private property or other (par. 138).

2. It cannot confiscate people's private property arbitrarily, but only in accordance with duly passed laws (par. 135–8).

3. The people must consent to these laws, *not* in the sense that they must obtain the personal consent of each individual, but in the sense that they have the consent of the majority of representatives in the legislature (taxation "must be with his own consent, i.e. the consent of the majority, giving it either by themselves, or their representatives chosen by them") (par. 140).

4. The laws must be for the common good of society, and in particular, promote the preservation of each member in it (par. 134–5).

5. The level of taxation cannot be so great as to reduce anyone to poverty or subjection ("It [the legislative power] . . . can never have a right to destroy, enslave, or designedly to impoverish the subjects" par. 135).

Although I'm no Lockean, I'm happy with these constraints, as I think all liberals are. (Personally, I would add another constraint, that requires the distribution of tax burdens to be fair. Locke may also implicitly be insisting on fairness in the quote that opens this post.)

So please, stop the silly rhetoric that liberals suppose that the government owns everything already. Stop the silly rhetoric that supposes that the fact that some property is mine offers any argument whatsoever against the legitimacy of taxing it.

I hasten to add that this still leaves plenty of room for reasonable dispute about proper levels of taxation. For all I've said so far, it's fine to argue that current levels of government spending are excessive, so that the levels of taxation required to support those levels are unjustified. It's fine to argue that the tax system we have unfairly distributes its burdens on the rich. It's fine to argue that our tax system stupidly rigs incentives in unproductive ways. . . . This post is simply a plea to focus on real arguments about taxation, not silly rhetoric.

II.

The claim "I deserve my income," as applied to an individual's pretax income in free market economies, has considerable intuitive force. If true, it suggests a powerful moral claim against taxation for redistributive purposes, on the intuitively plausible supposition that a just economic order ought to ensure that people get what they morally deserve.

But, however intuitive these claims may be, they are unjustified. In two of his important works of political economy, *The Constitution of Liberty* (see esp. ch. 6), and *Law, Legislation, and Liberty* (vol. 2), Hayek explained why free market prices cannot, *and should not*, track claims of individual moral desert.

1. Let's consider first Hayek's claim that prices in free market capitalism do not give people what they morally deserve. Hayek's deepest economic insight was that the basic function of free market prices is informational. Free market prices send signals to producers as to where their products are most in demand (and to consumers as to the opportunity costs of their options). They reflect

the sum total of the inherently dispersed information about the supply and demand of millions of distinct individuals for each product. Free market prices give us our *only* access to this information, and then only in aggregate form. This is why centralized economic planning is doomed to failure: there is no way to collect individualized supply and demand information in a single mind or planning agency, to use as a basis for setting prices. Free markets alone can effectively respond to this information.

It's a short step from this core insight about prices to their failure to track any coherent notion of moral desert. Claims of desert are essentially backward-looking. They aim to reward people for virtuous conduct that they undertook in the past. Free market prices are essentially forward-looking. Current prices send signals to producers as to where the demand is *now*, not where the demand was when individual producers decided on their production plans. Capitalism is an inherently dynamic economic system. It responds rapidly to changes in tastes, to new sources of supply, to new substitutes for old products. This is one of capitalism's great virtues. But this responsiveness leads to volatile prices. Consequently, capitalism is constantly pulling the rug out from underneath even the most thoughtful, foresightful, and prudent production plans of individual agents. However virtuous they were, by whatever standard of virtue one can name, individuals cannot count on their virtue being rewarded in the free market. For the function of the market isn't to reward people for past good behavior. It's to direct them toward producing for *current* demand, regardless of what they did in the past.

This isn't to say that virtue makes no difference to what returns one may expect for one's productive contributions. The exercise of prudence and foresight in laying out one's production and investment plans, and diligence in carrying them out, generally improves one's odds. But sheer dumb luck is also, ineradicably, a prominent factor determining free market returns. And nobody deserves what comes to them by sheer luck.

2. If free market prices don't give people what they morally deserve, should we try to regulate factor prices so that they *do* track producers' moral deserts? Hayek offered two compelling arguments against this proposal. First, if you fix prices on a backward-looking standard, they will no longer be able to perform their informational function. Producers will produce for what was demanded last quarter, even if it isn't demanded today. This creates enormous waste and generates huge opportunity costs. We'd be *much* poorer in an economy that worked like this.

One could imagine a way around this problem. Let prices move according to the free market. But set up a government agency to compensate people for their undeserved bad luck, from taxes raised on that part of people's property that they receive on account of their undeserved good luck. This way, prices would retain their informational function. This idea, which I have dubbed "luck egalitarianism," now dominates contemporary egalitarian thinking. I have argued in print that it's a very bad idea ("What is the Point of Equality?," *Ethics* 109 (1999): 287–337), for numerous reasons. One is that there is no coherent way to determine how much of what people get is due to luck, and how much is truly their responsibility. Hayek focused on a more fundamental reason: any attempt to regulate people's rewards according to judgments of how much they morally deserve would destroy liberty. It would involve the state in making detailed, intrusive judgments of how well people used their liberty, and penalize them for not exercising their liberty in the way the state thinks best. This is no way to run a free society.

Hayek was right. It might *sound* like a compelling idea, to make sure that people receive the income they morally deserve. But orienting the economy around this goal, assuming it is achievable at all (and there are principled doubts about that), would doom us to poverty and serfdom. It would abolish capitalism, along with its chief virtues. It isn't worth the draconian costs.

3. Several implications follow from Hayek's insights into the nature of capitalism.

(a) The claim "I deserve my pretax income" is not generally true. Nor should the basic organization of property rules be based on considerations of moral desert. Hence, claims about desert have no standing in deciding whether taxation for the purpose of funding social insurance is just.

(b) The claim that people rocked by the vicissitudes of the market, or poor people generally, are getting what they deserve is also not generally true. To moralize people's misfortunes in this way is both ignorant and mean. Capitalism continuously and randomly pulls the rug out from under even the most prudent and diligent people. It is *in principle* impossible for even the most prudent to forsee all the market turns that could undo them. (If it were possible, then efficient socialist planning would be possible, too. But it isn't.)

(c) Capitalist markets are highly dynamic and volatile. This means that at any one time, lots of people are going under. Often, the consequences of this would be catastrophic, absent concerted intervention to avert the outcomes generated by markets. For example, the economist Amartya Sen has documented that sudden shifts in people's incomes (which are often due to market volatility), and not absolute food shortages, are a principal cause of famine.

(d) The volatility of capitalist markets creates a profound and urgent need for insurance, over and above the insurance needs people would have under more stable (but stagnant) economic systems. This need is increased also by the fact that capitalism inspires a love of personal independence, and hence brings about the smaller ("nuclear") family forms that alone are compatible with it. We no longer belong to vast tribes and clans. This sharply reduces the ability of individuals under capitalism to pool risks within families, and limits the claims they can effectively make on non-household (extended) family members for assistance. To avoid or at least ameliorate disaster and disruption, people need to pool the risks of capitalism.

This fact does not yet clinch the case for *social insurance*—that is, universal, compulsory, government-provided, tax-funded insurance. For all I've said so far, maybe private insurance would do a better job meeting people's needs for insurance in the event of unemployment, disability, loss of a household earner, sickness, and old age. That depends on the relative performance of social and private insurance with respect to each of these events. Or perhaps some kind of mixed system, combining social and private insurance, would be optimal (I'm inclined to this position).

I do think, however, that the arguments I have provided so far go a considerable way towards justifying the view that, whether the insurance provider is public or private, not all individuals can reasonably be expected to pay for their insurance premiums out of their pretax incomes. For the reasons just discussed, pretax incomes provide a morally arbitrary baseline for determining the means within which people may reasonably be expected to live. Equilibrium factor prices may well be below subsistence or a decent life for millions. (This doesn't mean we should seek to institute a morally deserved baseline. My goal is not to ensure that people get what they morally deserve. It's to avoid gratuitous suffering, and to ensure that everyone has effective access, over their whole lifespan, to the means needed for a decent life.) And so far, no argument that people have a moral claim to their pretax incomes, sufficient to preclude taxing it for insurance purposes, has survived critical scrutiny. Certainly, "I deserve it" doesn't.

Elizabeth Anderson: How Not to Complain about Taxes

1. Which of the complaints against taxation that Anderson considers do you find most compelling (even if, in the end, you don't find it persuasive)?

2. Anderson distinguishes between legal property rights and natural property rights. What is the difference? Can you think of a legal property right that is not also a natural property right?

3. Anderson cites Locke, who thinks that we have moral duties to aid the poor. Do you agree that we have such duties? If so, is the government justified in ensuring, by means of taxation, that we live up to those duties?

4. Why doesn't Anderson think that we necessarily deserve the income we make by trading our goods or labor in the free market? Do you agree with her? Why or why not?

5. Anderson argues that capitalist societies are more volatile than more socialistic societies. Why does she think this? Does the government have a duty to protect its citizens from such volatility?

CHAPTER 17

Globalization and Immigration

JUST THE FACTS

There are about 7.5 billion people on the planet. Most of them are quite poor—much poorer than a typical poor person in a developed country. Developed countries provide many more, and better, jobs for low-skilled laborers and much more in the way of social welfare programs. Developed countries thus tend to provide a kind of economic prosperity and stability that is still quite uncommon in our world.

One way to improve the lot of the desperately poor who do not enjoy this kind of prosperity is to allow them to immigrate to developed countries where they could earn much higher wages. There are, however, at least two factors that make such immigration difficult. The first is that immigration often costs a nontrivial amount of money—precisely what the desperately poor lack. The second is that developed countries have immigration laws. Each year, these countries block tens of thousands of immigrants from entering, thereby denying them the opportunity to find work in their stronger economies. The result is that many of the world's desperately poor occupy an economic status that might be much improved were they allowed to work in a more affluent country.

When one is desperately poor, it's difficult to secure food, clean water, medical care, shelter, education, employment, and protection from theft and violence. Almost 3 billion people lack access to toilets and almost 1 billion lack access to clean drinking water; 179 million infants in the least developed countries fail to be protected from diseases by routine immunization; 3.2 million children under the age of fifteen currently live with HIV. And according to World Health Organization estimates, there were 212 million cases of malaria and 429,000 deaths from that disease in 2015 alone.[1] Virtually all these deaths were preventable with the allocation of resources that those in developed countries take for granted.

One of the best ways to pull oneself out of crushing poverty is to get an education, but 161 million children in the developing world do not attend primary school, either because they cannot afford it, their community doesn't provide it, or they're forced to work to help their families survive.[2] Without an education, upward economic mobility is practically impossible.

The good news is that those of us in the developed world have the power to make a difference in the lives of the desperately poor. In 2008, the United Nations estimated that it would take about $30 billion per year to end world hunger.[3] This sounds like an enormous figure, but it's dwarfed by the $737 billion the United States Congress spends each year on defense and the $223 billion Americans spend each year on alcohol.[4] In 2000, the United Nations estimated that the cost of supplying clean water to everyone on the planet was $10 billion per year. [5] Even if that figure has doubled since then, Americans could pay for more than three years of clean water for

---

1. http://www.who.int/mediacentre/factsheets/fs094/en/

2. https://borgenproject.org/global-poverty/

3. http://www.nytimes.com/2008/06/04/news/04iht-04food.13446176.html

4. https://www.statista.com/statistics/207936/us-total-alcoholic-beverages-sales-since-1990/

5. http://www.nytimes.com/2000/11/23/world/price-of-safe-water-for-all-10-billion-and-the-will-to-provide-it.html

everyone on the planet with the money they spend on lottery tickets each year—$76 billion.[6]

Technology has made it easier than ever to give aid, too. Anyone can donate to traditional aid organizations like Oxfam or UNICEF in a matter of minutes by paying online. Smartphones have made donating easier still. Through an organization called GiveDirectly, one can, in a matter of seconds with a smartphone app, make a cash transfer from a personal bank account to a person in extreme poverty in East Africa. One can also (again, via smartphone) provide an interest-free loan to a poor entrepreneur via an organization called Kiva. The beauty of these advances in technology is that transaction costs are so low—much lower than traditional organizations with large bureaucracies. A much greater percentage of one's donations thereby go to one's intended recipients, rather than to pay for administrative costs.

While aid from people in developed countries can help the global poor, so too can the opportunity to immigrate. Some of the benefits of immigration are noneconomic—the opportunity, for instance, to live in a stable, well-ordered, relatively nonviolent society. In particular, immigration provides an opportunity for people to escape the horrors of war. While refugees often find it difficult (at least initially) to thrive in a new land, there is little doubt that they are much better off immigrating than remaining in their war-torn countries. Since the Syrian civil war began in 2011, more than 6.6 million Syrians have become refugees.[7] Nearly 1 million refugees applied for asylum in the European Union (EU) in 2015; less than a third were successful in their application. This led many unsuccessful asylum seekers to apply elsewhere or to try to enter EU countries illegally. In 2016, an estimated 1 million unauthorized immigrants entered EU countries.[8]

Other benefits of immigration are economic. For example, according to 2015 UN estimates, about 12 million people living in the United States were born in Mexico. About half of them were undocumented.[9] The majority of these immigrants come to find work in the United States, and many of them send a portion of their earnings back to Mexico to help support their families. The same is true of Indians immigrating to the United Arab Emirates (UAE). Annual migration of Indians to the UAE, which stood at 4,600 in 1975, rose to over 125,000 by 1985, nearly 200,000 in 1999, and now stands at 2.6 million. The increase is the result of the thriving UAE oil economy, and the beneficiaries are both native UAE citizens (who get a relatively cheap labor force) and the millions of Indian immigrants who are now much better able to support themselves and their families than they were in their home country.[10]

ARGUMENT ANALYSIS

In most ways, the world we live in now is more globally connected than ever. We can have cost-free conversations with people halfway around the world in real time. Information about the most distant events is available at the touch of a key or the click of a mouse. National markets are increasingly interconnected with one another. The number of international travelers continues to rise. The life we live is more than ever influenced by events occurring outside our own borders.

These facts naturally raise questions about our duties to those who are not our compatriots.

6. https://moneywise.com/managing-money/debt/lendedu-lottery-spending-report-2020

7. https://www.worldvision.org/refugees-news-stories/syrian-refugee-crisis-facts

8. https://www.washingtonpost.com/news/wonk/wp/2016/07/01/europes-immigration-crisis-is-just-beginning/?utm_term=.c1ce9325cfdd

9. http://www.pewresearch.org/fact-tank/2016/05/18/5-facts-about-the-u-s-rank-in-worldwide-migration/

10. http://www.pewresearch.org/fact-tank/2016/05/18/5-facts-about-the-u-s-rank-in-worldwide-migration/

While our moral thinking is often focused quite close to home—on our relations to friends and family, our workmates, or fellow citizens—we take a broader perspective in this chapter and ask about our moral duties to distant strangers. While there is a host of issues that arise in this context, we will restrict ourselves to two: the desperate poverty suffered by tens of millions of the distant poor, and the immigration policies of the wealthier nations that are often designed to keep those people from coming to our shores.

Aid to Distant Strangers

The primary argument for offering aid to distant strangers is very simple: we are in a position to help, at relatively little cost to ourselves. So we should do so. All humans are of fundamentally equal moral importance. So it doesn't matter whether those needing help are my neighbors or distant strangers—if I can prevent their suffering, without causing myself to suffer much, then I should offer my help. This line of reasoning can be summarized in

The Reduction of Suffering Argument

1. If we can reduce the suffering of others without incurring significant sacrifice on our part, then we are morally obligated to do so.
2. We can reduce the suffering of the world's poor without incurring significant sacrifice on our part.

Therefore,

3. We are morally obligated to reduce the suffering of the world's poor—as much as we can, just shy of making a significant sacrifice.

Premise 2 is true of me, and perhaps of you, too. Of course, there are some citizens of the wealthier nations who are themselves desperately poor, such that any aid they were to offer others *would* amount to a significant sacrifice. This argument doesn't apply to such people—for them, the argument is unsound, because its second

premise is false. But the rest of us cannot get off so easily. According to a recent study, it costs about $50 to feed a school-aged girl for an entire year in many developing countries.[11] That's about $4 per month. Though the boundaries for what qualifies as a *significant* sacrifice are unspecified, this amount easily qualifies as insignificant for me, and for most of you who are reading this book. Think of what you can buy at your local store for $4. Now think of having to forgo that purchase. Not a significant loss, most likely.

Premise 1 also seems sensible, and can be supported by a famous example offered by one of our authors, Peter Singer.[12] Imagine you are taking a walk and see a child drowning nearby in a shallow pond. You don't spot anyone near him. Though it would cost you something—wet shoes, a couple of minutes of your time—you are nevertheless morally required to save the child, even though (we are assuming) he's a complete stranger to you. Morally speaking, it would be wrong just to walk away. Nor would it suffice to call 9-1-1, since (let's assume) you can tell that the child would drown well before any emergency assistance would arrive on the scene. What explains your moral duty in this case? Premise 1 seems to do a very nice job.

Some say, however, that premise 1 is too demanding—we needn't do everything we can, shy of significant sacrifice, to help others in need. Instead, we must only do our *fair share*. The idea remains that the needs of others, including strangers, impose some duty of assistance on us. But to determine the extent of our duty, we first need to understand what it would take to fully meet the need, and then figure out how many people are in a position to help. Then we do a calculation. To make things far simpler than they are in practice, suppose we could prevent starvation and malnutrition around the world at

---

11. "Hunger Price Tags." *www.wfp.org*. World Food Programme, May 18, 2012.

12. The example appears in Singer's "Famine, Affluence and Morality," *Philosophy and Public Affairs* 2 (1972).

a cost of $50 billion a year. (We can't; just suppose, though, that money alone could solve these problems and that $50 billion is the required amount.) Next, suppose that there are a billion people in so-called first-world countries, people who are significantly more affluent than those who are in danger of starvation. Now divide $50 billion by a billion, and you've arrived at each person's fair share—$50. On this line of thinking, even if you're quite rich and could easily make a $1,000 contribution to an aid agency without incurring any significant sacrifice, you are morally required to give only $50.

Defenders of the Reduction of Suffering Argument have a standard reply: giving only one's fair share will leave many, many people to die preventable deaths. After all, very few of us do give our fair share to aid distant strangers. To modify Singer's example, suppose that I live in a community whose members take turns on a neighborhood patrol watch. We each have to do a shift once per month, walking the streets and offering help where needed. I did my service last Monday. But today I'm the one who happens upon the drowning child. The fact that I've already done my fair share does not let me off the hook, morally speaking. I need to do more than my fair share, precisely because someone else desperately needs my help right now.

A different kind of argument takes no stand on whether the needs of others, all by themselves, impose duties of aid. Instead, the motivating idea here is that people are morally bound to right the wrongs they have committed. Injustice requires **reparations**—repairing the harm done to those who have suffered from our injustice. The United States and other major economic powers in the world have become as rich as they are in part because of some quite terrible behavior that includes colonizing other countries and exploiting their resources without adequate compensation (or, in many cases, any compensation at all). This checkered history naturally gives rise to

The International Reparations Argument

1. If Country A has perpetrated extensive injustices against Country B, then A has a duty to B to repair the harms caused by those injustices.
2. Most of the wealthiest countries of the West have perpetrated extensive injustices against poorer countries.

Therefore,

3. Most of the wealthiest countries in the West have a duty to repair the harms caused by those injustices.[13]

Premise 2 is true. This is not the place to record the many unsavory examples of the more powerful countries exploiting weaker ones—one can consult any number of sources to confirm its truth. I'm not saying that that all or even most of a wealthy country's riches are a result of such exploitation—that is a more complex and controversial matter that we can't, and don't need to, enter here. But so long as wealthier countries have indeed exploited weaker ones, then, if premise 1 is also true, the wealthier nations have a duty to repair those wrongs.

Premise 1 is a direct application, to countries, of the basic principle of reparation—that wrongdoers must repair the damage they've done to their victims. It is hard to argue with this principle. It's true that the principle, and the argument's conclusion, do not specify the precise ways in which reparations are to be made. So, for all this argument says, reparations could take the form of direct monetary aid, providing infrastructure support, sending needed medical supplies, or other methods.

There are critics, of course, of giving aid to distant strangers. One common objection to such aid is that it is often extremely wasteful and sometimes counterproductive. This criticism is

---

13. Reparations also figure importantly in Chapter 18; for instructive comparison, have a look at the Reparations Argument in that chapter.

correct. In many cases, donations to aid agencies go primarily to administrative costs, rather than to help the intended recipients. In other cases, aid agencies spend millions of dollars on projects that are doomed to fail, owing to a lack of understanding of the local culture and the conditions that have caused the problems in the first place.

While this objection is legitimate, it ultimately fails to undermine the moral case for giving aid. For example, there are now reliable websites that help potential donors track the efficiency of aid organizations, so that one can have a much more informed take on the benefits that different agencies actually bring to the desperate poor.[14]

Interestingly, the ethical outlook behind the Reduction of Suffering Argument—a utilitarian one, concerned primarily to minimize long-term suffering—can be used as a basis for a skeptical argument about the merits of providing famine relief and other forms of aid to distant strangers. The idea, articulated in an influential article by the population biologist Garrett Hardin,[15] is that saving the lives of famine victims will bring great short-term good, but at the cost of far greater long-term harm. We can present the details after laying out the basics of

The Utilitarian Argument

1. We are morally required to do something only if it will improve long-term happiness or reduce overall long-term suffering.
2. Providing famine relief will fail to do either—in fact, it will only increase long-term suffering.

Therefore,

3. We are not morally required to provide famine relief.

Hardin doesn't argue for the first premise—he just assumes the truth of utilitarianism, which is a very controversial doctrine among moral philosophers. We can't revisit those controversies here; for the many benefits of utilitarianism, as well as some of its drawbacks, see Chapter 5. Let's suppose, though, that utilitarianism is true. Why think that premise 2 is also true?

Hardin answered that question by introducing the notion of a **ratchet effect**. This refers to an exponential increase in a population over time, occurring in poor communities with scarce resources. Hardin believes that if we spare the lives of famine victims by delivering life-sustaining aid, then they will procreate at an exponential rate. If, for instance, we save a million famine victims now, then a generation from now we can expect the population of that famine-stricken area to have increased to (say) 3 million. Now suppose that the area is once again hit by famine, and we once again come to the rescue of the local population. Then, two generations from now, we are likely to encounter a population of about 9 million people. This cycle will lead eventually to a population so large that no one will be able to provide enough resources to sustain it. At that point—many years down the road, but an inevitable consequence of the ratchet effect, and the fact that we cannot increase resources exponentially—the next famine or natural disaster will lead to the deaths of *many* millions of people. But the lives of those who live in the future are no less valuable than our own. If we have to choose between letting a million people die now, or letting many millions die in the future—and this is indeed our choice, says Hardin—then, with regret, we must let the million die now.

There is much evidence to support Hardin's predictions about population growth. In the

---

14. These include GiveWell (https://www.givewell.org/), The Life You Can Save (https://www.thelifeyoucansave.org/), and Giving What We Can (https://www.givingwhatwecan.org/).

15. "Lifeboat Ethics: The Case Against Helping the Poor," *Psychology Today* (September 1974), 800–814.

decades since the publication of his article (in 1974), the population of hard-hit countries such as Bangladesh or Somalia has increased dramatically. In 1974, Bangladesh had a population of 70 million. In 2016 it had more than doubled, to 163 million.[16] Somalia had a population of 3.6 million in 1974; in 2016, the number had increased by about 400 percent, to 14.3 million.[17] The question, though, is whether the ratchet effect can be avoided, and whether we are able to increase resources in ways that meet the greater demands caused by population growth. Optimists will answer both questions with yes; pessimists, such as Hardin, will say no. The correct answers are matters well beyond a philosopher's expertise—political economists, geographers, biologists, environmental scientists, and food experts are the ones whose research will provide these answers.

Immigration

People opposed to immigration often rely on ugly stereotypes and appeals to fear in order to gain political support for their cause. This is as true nowadays as it was a century ago, when loud cries could be heard in support of closing the borders against the grandparents of many of today's fiercest critics of immigration. We will leave the ugliness aside—after all, one might entirely avoid crude caricatures of immigrants, and sympathize with their plight, but still believe that a nation has a right to restrict entry to its own territory. After considering some of the better arguments for immigration restriction, we'll then turn to some of the arguments for open borders.

One reason to oppose immigration stems from the desire to protect the economic interests of a country's citizens. This can be expressed in terms of

16. https://www.google.com/search?q=1970+bangladesh+population+statistics&ie=utf-8&oe=utf-8

17. https://www.google.com/search?q=1970+somalia+population+statistics&ie=utf-8&oe=utf-8

The Economics Argument

1. Nations have a right to protect their economic interests.
2. Restricting immigration will protect the interests of wealthier countries.

Therefore,

3. Wealthier countries have a right to restrict immigration.

Premise 1 is highly plausible. There are limits to this right, of course—nations are not allowed to promote their economic interests by violating treaties, exploiting weaker nations, or fraudulently manipulating markets. But such cases aside, nations are morally entitled to protect their own economic interests. So let's focus on premise 2. On its behalf, we should note that the poorest workers are usually those threatened the most by immigrants, since immigrants are usually willing to work for lower wages. Sometimes this displaces local workers; at others times, though it doesn't do that, it nevertheless drives down their pay. It's also the case that providing social benefits—medical care, housing subsidies, free education to immigrant children—can be quite costly, especially for smaller nations or communities that are asked to take in substantial numbers of immigrants.

But that is not the entire story. Frequently, a lower paid workforce increases profits for businesses—their owners and shareholders. It also enables businesses to lower the price of goods and services, thereby benefitting consumers as well. Immigrants are often needed to cover domestic worker shortages or to do work that locals are unwilling to do. So there are economic benefits as well as harms associated with immigration. Further, the government could offset the harms to displaced workers by offering them unemployment compensation and vocational retraining. It's also the case that many immigrants are highly skilled workers—doctors, professors, engineers, and so on—and that the presence of these new citizens usually has substantial economic benefits to society at large, in addition to the immigrants themselves. And policies could be designed so that various social benefits are conferred only after an immigrant has paid into the system for a specified amount of time, helping to defray the costs associated with these benefits. So, while immigration certainly has its economic costs, it also has its benefits, and it's far from clear that the former always outweigh the latter.

Another concern about permissive immigration policies is that they open the door to foreign terrorists. This worry gives rise to

The Security Argument

1. States have a moral duty to protect their citizens against dangerous attack.
2. Restricting immigration is required to offer that protection.

Therefore,

3. States have a moral duty to restrict immigration.

Premise 1 is true. A government's legitimacy depends on its effectively protecting its citizens from preventable threats of substantial harm. Premise 2, though, is more controversial.

It is true that if a state entirely excluded foreigners from its shores, then it would thereby prevent all attacks by foreigners. But the relevance of this observation for premise 2 is unclear. Very few foreign terrorists would be deterred by anti-immigration laws. If they are intent on risking their lives to kill the citizens of another country, then they will (try to) enter the country illegally or will enter legally as a visitor, rather than by application as an immigrant. So it's unclear just how effective a wholesale immigration ban would be in preventing terrorism.

Of course, a country has the right to deny entry to those it reasonably suspects of being dangerous. But it is not reasonable to suppose that a person is a likely terrorist just because he or she is a citizen of a certain country. President Donald Trump sought in 2017 to ban entry to the United States of all citizens of Iran, Iraq, Libya, Somalia, Sudan, Syria, and Yemen. Between 1975 and 2015, six Iranians, six Sudanese, two Somalis, two Iraqis, and one Yemeni were convicted of perpetrating acts of terrorism on US soil. (No Syrians or Libyans have been convicted of such crimes during that time.) In those four decades, the United States allowed entry to 3.25 million refugees; twenty of them have been convicted of attempting or committing a terrorist act on US soil.[18] I am not trying to minimize the horror of terrorist actions. But these figures challenge the view that one's passport is good evidence of terrorist intentions.

Another argument for restricting immigration comes from a basic moral and political principle: we have the right to determine how our lives are going to go, at least so long as we do not violate the rights of others along the way. The thought is that nations, as well as individuals, have this right. This is the basis of

The National Self-Determination Argument

1. Nations have a right to political self-determination.
2. The right to self-determination includes a right to refuse to associate with others.
3. A nation's right to refuse to associate with others includes the right to close its borders to potential immigrants and others.

Therefore,

4. Nations have a right to close their borders to potential immigrants and others.

Premise 1 is highly plausible, at least when it comes to morally legitimate states. One thing it means for a state to be a sovereign nation is that it gets to decide for itself how to run its affairs. Premise 2 is also plausible. Think about the individual case—if you have a right to self-determination, then others can't force you to be

---

18. https://www.theatlantic.com/international/archive/2017/01/trump-immigration-ban-terrorism/514361/

their friend or lover. The right includes a right to say no to the company of those you prefer to distance yourself from. Premise 3 looks like a direct application of premise 2—just as a nation's right to self-determination allows it to refuse to enter into economic or military alliances with other nations, it also entitles it to refuse to associate with individuals who are not citizens of the country. And that may amount to a closing of its borders.

   The right to self-determination, like most and perhaps all other rights, has its limits. Two are most relevant here. First, the needs of others may sometimes limit our right to self-determination. Think of the case of the drowning child. I have a right to determine how I'm going to live my life. But if I am the only one who can save the drowning child, then it seems that his needs create a moral duty on my part to save him, whether I want to do so or not. If this is correct, then perhaps the need for refugees to gain life-saving entry to our shores creates a moral duty to take a great many of them in. Second, the need to offer reparations limits one's right to self-determination. Wealthy people cannot refuse to right their wrongs by claiming that their right to self-determination entitles them to ignore the harm they've done. So, too, with countries: if a wealthy nation has exploited a weaker one and caused some of the harms that are now prompting its citizens to emigrate, then the wealthy nation may morally have to accept those immigrants as a way of discharging its duty to repair the wrongs it has committed.

   Let's now consider some arguments in favor of permissive immigration policies. Supporters of such policies often cite a different fundamental freedom as the basis for their view. This is the freedom of movement, which morally allows us to go where we like, without impediment. The core idea can be put simply:

The Freedom of Movement Argument

1. Freedom of movement is a human right, and so had by all humans.

2. Freedom of movement entails going where you like.

Therefore,

3. Every human has a right to go wherever he or she likes.

Therefore,

4. Nations are morally required to open their borders to anyone who wants to gain entry.

Premise 1 is plausible. And so is premise 2—to the extent that we have freedom of movement, we are allowed to go where we like. Together, premises 1 and 2 provide strong support for 3. But the move from 3 to 4 is invalid. That's because the right to go where you like is not absolute or unlimited. I may really want to attend a celebrity's wedding, or a closed business meeting, but am not entitled to do so without an invitation. I may very much want to enter your home, but my freedom of movement doesn't entitle me to do so if you don't permit it. If, in these personal contexts, we are allowed to bar our homes and businesses from unwanted outsiders, it's not clear why a state should be forbidden from doing so as well.

   Now if you do not legitimately occupy a house—if, for instance, you are squatting there—then you don't have a right to exclude others from that property. So, too, if a government is morally illegitimate, as many governments are, then it lacks a right to exclude others from its territory. In that case, an emigrant's freedom of movement may well entitle her to entry to a given land. But when a nation's government is morally legitimate, it has a right to control who may and may not enter its territory.

   Another argument in favor of open borders begins by reflecting on the very different opportunities for a good life had by people in different parts of the world. If you were lucky enough to have been born into a stable, democratic, and prosperous country, then you have a far better chance of living a good life than if you were born in Syria or Somalia. And this disparity seems not only deeply unfortunate but also, in a way, unfair, since those who live in such desperate conditions have done nothing to deserve their poor life chances. We can put this thought to work in

The Anti-Luck Argument

1. Nations are morally required to give everyone an equal chance at a good life if their poor prospects are due to bad luck (i.e., circumstances beyond their control).
2. Wealthy nations are able to give everyone such an equal chance only if they allow open borders.

Therefore,

3. Wealthy nations are morally required to allow open borders.

The thought behind premise 1 is that nations are morally required to be just; justice requires giving people what they deserve; giving people what they deserve requires correcting for cases in which people suffer undeservedly; some emigrants from unstable and poverty-stricken countries are suffering undeservedly; so justice requires that such suffering be eased, if it can be.

Critics of this argument may well agree to the line of reasoning sketched in the previous paragraph. However, they may claim that the duties of a government are limited to addressing the undeserved suffering of its own citizens and the suffering of foreigners that it has wrongly caused. But if a nation is not responsible for the undeserved suffering of a potential immigrant, then it has no duty to try to ease that suffering. It would, of course, be nice were a nation to undertake to do this. But doing so is not morally required.

Defenders of the Anti-Luck Argument point to cases in which nations are morally required to intervene in other countries solely for humanitarian purposes. If any such intervention really is morally required, then the moral duties of nations are not limited to meeting the needs of its own citizens and redressing the wrongs it has done to the citizens of other countries.

Suppose for now that we accept premise 1. Still, critics of the Anti-Luck Argument might take issue with premise 2 and claim that there are other ways to ease the undeserved suffering of foreigners. A wealthy nation could, for instance, offer various forms of support designed to strengthen the institutions and economy of the impoverished country. So long as this is a genuine possibility, it's not clear why wealthy nations are also required to open their borders in order to improve lives of foreigners who have been born in dire, undeserved circumstances.

The final argument that we'll consider on behalf of open borders is the most popular. It is very like the Reduction of Suffering Argument we considered earlier, only in this case as applied specifically to immigration, rather than to the general unmet needs of the distant poor:

The Humanitarian Aid Argument

1. If we are able to drastically improve someone's life at relatively little cost to ourselves, then we are morally obligated to do so.
2. Opening our borders to immigrants would drastically improve their lives at relatively little cost to ourselves.

Therefore,

3. We are morally obligated to open our borders to immigrants.

We needn't say much about this argument, as it relies on various claims that we have already discussed. We could enlist the drowning child example in support of premise 1. On the other side, most people deny that I am required to feed you, pay for your surgery, or let you sleep the night in my home just because you need me to do one of these things.

Regarding premise 2, there is no doubt that opening our borders to many immigrants would indeed drastically improve their lives. The question is whether that benefit comes at an acceptable cost. There will certainly be economic costs. But as we've seen earlier with the Economic Argument for closing borders, there are often substantial economic benefits to opening one's borders as well. That said, there may be other, noneconomic costs associated with a liberal immigration policy—for instance, the possible erosion of a national culture.

It's true that mass immigration may change a culture in various ways. But, first, that change may sometimes be for the better— many aspects of many cultures are morally problematic. Second, it's unclear how important the preservation of culture is when weighed against meeting the basic needs of desperate people. Third, the culture of many immigrants will be significantly similar to that of a host country, so this worry isn't that serious in those cases. Finally, even in harder cases—for instance, where immigrants bring with them a deeply sexist and religiously intolerant outlook—their entry can be tied to an education program that provides history and context about the host culture, its value, and the importance of partial assimilation to the core values of a country that has extended itself in opening its borders.

CONCLUSION

We live in a globally interconnected world. We are aware of events happening in real time across the world in a way that was hardly possible until very recently. This greater awareness raises questions about the scope of our moral duty to aid distant strangers in need.

The needs can be very acute, and we can meet many of those needs at relatively little cost. Many think that this decides the matter, morally: we are under obligation to meet those needs and to offer such aid. Those who disagree argue that the needs of others do not impose duties on us unless we have either agreed to fulfill those needs or have acted wrongly in ways that require us to repair the damage we've done. When neither condition is met, they say, then we are under no moral duty to offer any assistance.

In many cases, the most good we can do for such people is to allow them to immigrate to our country (so long as our country is stable, democratic, and prosperous). The worries about opening our borders—incurring economic costs, endangering our citizenry, violating our right to national self-determination, threatening the preservation of our culture—are countered by those who cite the human right to freedom of movement, the need to correct for undeserved suffering, and the moral importance of preventing humanitarian crises. I think it safe to say that we have yet to see a decisive argument for closing our borders against all would-be immigrants, but neither has there been a decisive argument for opening our borders to all who would like to come.

ESSENTIAL CONCEPTS

Ratchet effect: an exponential increase of a population over time, occurring in poor communities confronted with scarce resources.
Reparations: repairing the harm one has done to the victims of one's unjust conduct.

STAT SHOT

1. Worldwide, 3 billion people lack access to toilets and almost 1 billion lack access to clean drinking water.[1]

2. The percentage of people living in extreme poverty (defined in 2011 as earning less than $1.90 per day) has been steadily decreasing since 1990 (Figure 17.1).

significantly from 1970, when it was just 4.7 percent (Figure 17.2).

4. As of 2015, there were 44.7 million foreign-born people in the United States. About 1 in every 4 was an unauthorized immigrant (Figure 17.3).

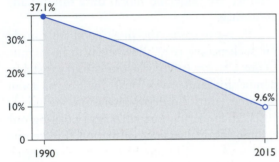

Share of population below $1.90 a day (2011 PPP)

Figure 17.1.

Source: The World Bank and https://www.weforum.org/agenda/2016/01/has-the-world-overlooked-a-major-achievement/

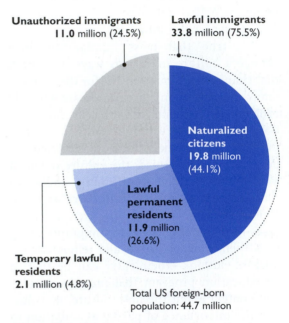

Unauthorized immigrants
11.0 million (24.5%)

Lawful immigrants
33.8 million (75.5%)

**Naturalized citizens
19.8** million (44.1%)

**Lawful permanent residents
11.9** million (26.6%)

**Temporary lawful residents
2.1** million (4.8%)

Total US foreign-born population: 44.7 million

Figure 17.3. Foreign-born population estimates, 2015. All numbers are rounded independently and are not adjusted to sum to US total or other totals.

Source: Pew Research Center estimates for 2015 based on augmented American Community Survey (IPUMS). https://www.pewresearch.org/ph_16-06-02_foreign-bornbreakdown/

1. https://borgenproject.org/global-poverty/

3. *As of 2015, 13.4 percent of the United States population was foreign-born. That's up*

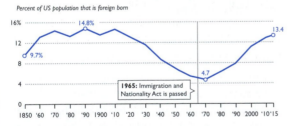

Percent of US population that is foreign born

1965: Immigration and Nationality Act is passed

Figure 17.2.

Source: US Census Bureau, "Historical Census Statistics on the Foreign-Born Population of the United States: 1850-2000" and Pew Research Center tabulations of 2010 and 2015 American Community Survey (IPUMS). https://www.pewresearch.org/ft_17-04-10_immigrant_share/

Cases for Critical Thinking

GiveDirectly

GiveDirectly is a nonprofit organization operating in East Africa—specifically Kenya, Uganda, and Rwanda. They help families living in extreme poverty by facilitating unconditional cash transfers to them from donors via mobile phone. Every year since 2012, GiveDirectly has been a top-rated charity according to Give Well—a nonprofit organization that grades charities according to their cost-effectiveness. GiveDirectly's website allows donors to quickly make a direct transfer to an extremely poor person with almost no transaction costs. If you're reading this text, then you're likely the kind of person who has enough disposable income to make a big difference in the life of a very poor person. For example, a transfer of $50—what many spend on a pair of blue jeans—would be more than what many GiveDirectly recipients make in a month.[1]

1. https://www.givedirectly.org/

Questions

1. Do you have a moral obligation to give at least something to GiveDirectly or a similar organization? Why or why not?
2. If you think that you do have an obligation to give, at what point would you no longer be obligated to give?
3. If you think that you don't have an obligation to give, why not? Does anyone have such an obligation (e.g., the very rich)? Why or why not?
4. Some people think that you have an obligation to give to the global poor for the following reason: You're relatively rich only because you were born into a relatively rich country. And the only reason that the desperately poor are poor is that they were born into a desperately poor country. But neither of you had a say about where you were born. The only difference between you and the desperately poor is luck—good luck for you, bad luck for them. And no one should have to suffer while others live in comfort if the only difference between them is luck. Is this line of reasoning correct? Why or why not?

Citizenship for Children Born to Undocumented Immigrants

The Fourteenth Amendment to the US Constitution states that "All persons born or naturalized in the United States, and subject to the jurisdiction thereof, are citizens of the United States and of the State wherein they reside." Thus, children born in the United States (besides children of foreign diplomats) are US citizens, regardless of their parents' nationality. This amendment was originally intended to make the children of slaves into US citizens, even if their parents weren't born in the United States. But the law also made it possible for undocumented immigrants to enter the country illegally, give birth on US soil, and claim US citizenship for their newborn children. These children would then have the legal rights to public education and public assistance for health care, retirement, and so on. US citizenship for a child can also make it easier for the undocumented parents to gain citizenship through family reunification programs. Thus, millions of people who have not paid into the United States tax system could wind up benefiting from programs paid for by US taxpayers.

Opponents of the citizenship-by-birth provisions in the Constitution argue that these measures encourage undocumented immigration because it creates an easier alternative to the standard, and much more difficult, immigration procedures. Further, these protections create an incentive for already present undocumented immigrants to expand their families, thereby exacerbating the problem of paying for welfare programs for people who have paid nothing, or very little, into those programs. These opponents argue that such rights and privileges should not be given to families whose members have already violated law.

Proponents of the citizenship-by-birth protections, however, argue that punishing children for illegal acts committed by their parents is unjust. Children have no say about where they are born, and returning them to their parents' home country may be highly traumatic for them once they've been integrated into a community in the United States. And to deprive these children of education, health care, and the other benefits of citizenship in what to them has always been their home threatens to create a population of second-class people. Due to deportation or other circumstances, children of illegal immigrants are somewhat more likely to grow up without a stable family or become orphaned. Removing citizenship provisions would jeopardize these children's protection from social services organizations. If children of illegal immigrants born in the United States were not granted citizenship, the US government would be in the awkward position of keeping and protecting young noncitizens within its borders or deporting them to a country that has never had anything to do with them. Neither option holds out much hope for a child's future.

Questions

1. Is it unjust to taxpaying citizens to make it easy for undocumented immigrants and their children to gain access to social welfare benefits when they haven't paid much or anything into those programs? Why or why not?

2. Is it unjust to children born in the United States to undocumented immigrants to deport them, when they haven't themselves broken any laws and have lived most of their lives in the United States? Why or why not?

3. Should children born in the United States to undocumented immigrants be granted citizenship? Why or why not?

4. What is the point of laws restricting who can and cannot enter, or reside in, a country? How does your answer to this question bear on your answer to Question 3?

Asylum for Refugees

In early 2011, over 30,000 Tunisian refugees arrived on the island of Lampedusa, Italy's southernmost point. Following the outbreak of the Libyan Civil War a few weeks later, thousands more Libyan refugees escaped to Italy. The number of refugees continued to swell as refugees from Somalia, Ethiopia, Egypt, and Eritrea joined other African refugees making their way to Italy. European Union law requires the country where refugees first arrive to carry out the asylum process. Italy, overwhelmed by refugees and its own high unemployment rate, asked for help from the other twenty-six EU countries, particularly in resettling refugees who have family members in other EU countries. The other EU member states responded that Italy had the resources and the responsibility to deal with the crisis on its own.[1]

Italy responded to the European Union's refusal to accept the refugees by issuing six-month temporary residency papers and travel permits, granting 25,000 Tunisian refugees the right to travel to other EU countries. Many of the French-speaking Tunisians set their sights on France. French riot police met scores of Tunisian refugees at the French-Italian border and turned them back, preventing ten trains from crossing the border and closing ancient footpaths between France and Italy. French officials insisted that they were not trying to undermine the agreement between EU countries to allow freedom of movement between member countries but were instead responding to threats to public order.

1. http://www.nytimes.com/2011/03/31/world/europe/31italy.html

Questions

1. Did Italy have a responsibility to receive and offer asylum to the refugees, as the leaders of the other EU countries claimed? Why?

2. Would it have been justified for Italy or France to accept some refugees that they deemed useful to them (e.g., doctors, metalworkers) while turning the rest away? Or should they have accepted refugees without reference to judgments about who would best serve their country's interests?

3. Once Italy did offer asylum to the refugees, did the other EU countries have a duty to aid Italy in accommodating them? Why or why not?

4. The United States allowed six hundred Tunisian refugees to settle in its territory. It was, at the time, more prepared than most EU countries to absorb an influx of refugees. Did the United States, and similarly prepared countries (such as Canada), have a duty to assist Italy by taking in refugees, or was this above and beyond the call of their moral duty? Why?

READINGS

The Singer Solution to World Poverty

Peter Singer

Peter Singer argues that our ordinary patterns of spending money on ourselves are immoral. Such spending involves the purchase of many things that are not essential to preserving our lives or health. The money we spend on fancy dinners, new clothes, or vacations could instead be sent to relief agencies that save people's lives. We don't know our potential beneficiaries, but that is morally irrelevant. Our decision not to spend money to save their lives is morally inexcusable.

Singer offers us a series of fascinating examples in which people have the opportunity to prevent an innocent person's death but fail to do so. We regard the person in each example as having done something extremely immoral. Singer argues that we who spend money on inessential personal pleasures are no better.

But what if most of the people we know are also failing to give anything to famine relief or aid agencies? That doesn't let us off the hook—it just means that they are also behaving in a deeply immoral way.

Perhaps the money sent overseas will not do as much good as advertised? Singer mentions some very reliable aid agencies (and provides contact information) that will not squander your money. For a couple hundred dollars, you can save a child's life, or purchase a few new additions to your wardrobe. If Singer is right, then choosing to spend that money on yourself means knowingly allowing an innocent person to die. Given the relatively small sacrifice you would be making if you sent that money overseas, and given the great benefit you would be providing if you did, morality gives you no choice. World poverty could largely be solved if we in the wealthier nations did our moral duty and gave much more than we currently do to those in greatest need.

In the Brazilian film *Central Station*, Dora is a retired schoolteacher who makes ends meet by sitting at the station writing letters for illiterate people. Suddenly she has an opportunity to pocket $1,000. All she has to do is persuade a homeless 9-year-old boy to follow her to an address she has been given. (She is told he will be adopted by wealthy foreigners.) She delivers the boy, gets the money, spends some of it on a television set, and settles down to enjoy her new acquisition. Her neighbor spoils the fun, however, by telling her that the boy was too old to be adopted—he will be killed and his organs sold for transplantation. Perhaps Dora knew this all along, but after her neighbor's plain speaking, she spends a troubled night. In the morning Dora resolves to take the boy back.

Suppose Dora had told her neighbor that it is a tough world, other people have nice new TVs too, and if selling the kid is the only way she can get one, well, he was only a street kid. She would then have become, in the eyes of the audience, a monster. She redeems herself only by being prepared to bear considerable risks to save the boy.

At the end of the movie, in cinemas in the affluent nations of the world, people who would have been quick to condemn Dora if she had not rescued the boy go home to places far more comfortable than her apartment. In fact, the average family in the United States spends almost one-third of its income on things that are no more necessary to them than Dora's new TV was to her. Going out to nice restaurants, buying new clothes because the old ones are no longer stylish, vacationing at beach

resorts—so much of our income is spent on things not essential to the preservation of our lives and health. Donated to one of a number of charitable agencies, that money could mean the difference between life and death for children in need.

All of which raises a question: In the end, what is the ethical distinction between a Brazilian who sells a homeless child to organ peddlers and an American who already has a TV and upgrades to a better one—knowing that the money could be donated to an organization that would use it to save the lives of kids in need?

Of course, there are several differences between the two situations that could support different moral judgments about them. For one thing, to be able to consign a child to death when he is standing right in front of you takes a chilling kind of heartlessness; it is much easier to ignore an appeal for money to help children you will never meet. Yet for a utilitarian philosopher like myself—that is, one who judges whether acts are right or wrong by their consequences—if the upshot of the American's failure to donate the money is that one more kid dies on the streets of a Brazilian city, then it is, in some sense, just as bad as selling the kid to the organ peddlers. But one doesn't need to embrace my utilitarian ethic to see that, at the very least, there is a troubling incongruity in being so quick to condemn Dora for taking the child to the organ peddlers while, at the same time, not regarding the American consumer's behavior as raising a serious moral issue.

In his 1996 book, *Living High and Letting Die*, the New York University philosopher Peter Unger presented an ingenious series of imaginary examples designed to probe our intuitions about whether it is wrong to live well without giving substantial

---

From Peter Singer, "The Singer Solution to World Poverty," *New York Times Magazine*, September 5 (1999), pp. 60–63.

amounts of money to help people who are hungry, malnourished or dying from easily treatable illnesses like diarrhea. Here's my paraphrase of one of these examples:

Bob is close to retirement. He has invested most of his savings in a very rare and valuable old car, a Bugatti, which he has not been able to insure. The Bugatti is his pride and joy. In addition to the pleasure he gets from driving and caring for his car, Bob knows that its rising market value means that he will always be able to sell it and live comfortably after retirement. One day when Bob is out for a drive, he parks the Bugatti near the end of a railway siding and goes for a walk up the track. As he does so, he sees that a runaway train, with no one aboard, is running down the railway track. Looking farther down the track, he sees the small figure of a child very likely to be killed by the runaway train. He can't stop the train and the child is too far away to warn of the danger, but he can throw a switch that will divert the train down the siding where his Bugatti is parked. Then nobody will be killed—but the train will destroy his Bugatti. Thinking of his joy in owning the car and the financial security it represents, Bob decides not to throw the switch. The child is killed. For many years to come, Bob enjoys owning his Bugatti and the financial security it represents.

Bob's conduct, most of us will immediately respond, was gravely wrong. Unger agrees. But then he reminds us that we, too, have opportunities to save the lives of children. We can give to organizations like UNICEF or Oxfam America. How much would we have to give one of these organizations to have a high probability of saving the life of a child threatened by easily preventable diseases? (I do not believe that children are more worth saving than adults, but since no one can argue that children have brought their poverty on themselves, focusing on them simplifies the issues.) Unger called up some experts and used the information they provided to offer some plausible estimates that include the cost of raising money, administrative expenses and the cost of delivering aid where it is most needed. By his calculation, $200 in donations would help a sickly 2-year-old transform into a healthy 6-year-old—offering safe passage through childhood's most dangerous years. To show how practical philosophical argument can be, Unger even tells his readers that they can easily donate funds by using their credit card and calling one of these toll-free numbers: (800) 367-5437 for UNICEF; (800) 693-2687 for Oxfam America. [http://supportunicef.org/forms/whichcountry2.html for UNICEF and http://www.oxfam.org/eng/donate.htm for Oxfam—PS.]

Now you, too, have the information you need to save a child's life. How should you judge yourself if you don't do it? Think again about Bob and his Bugatti. Unlike Dora, Bob did not have to look into the eyes of the child he was sacrificing for his own material comfort. The child was a complete stranger to him and too far away to relate to in an intimate, personal way. Unlike Dora, too, he did not mislead the child or initiate the chain of events imperiling him. In all these respects, Bob's situation resembles that of people able but unwilling to donate to overseas aid and differs from Dora's situation.

If you still think that it was very wrong of Bob not to throw the switch that would have diverted the train and saved the child's life, then it is hard to see how you could deny that it is also very wrong not to send money to one of the organizations listed above. Unless, that is, there is some morally important difference between the two situations that I have overlooked.

Is it the practical uncertainties about whether aid will really reach the people who need it? Nobody who knows the world of overseas aid can doubt that such uncertainties exist. But Unger's figure of $200 to save a child's life was reached after he had made conservative assumptions about the proportion of the money donated that will actually reach its target.

One genuine difference between Bob and those who can afford to donate to overseas aid organizations but don't is that only Bob can save the child on the tracks, whereas there are hundreds of millions of people who can give $200 to overseas aid organizations. The problem is that most of them aren't doing it. Does this mean that it is all right for you not to do it?

Suppose that there were more owners of priceless vintage cars—Carol, Dave, Emma, Fred, and so on, down to Ziggy—all in exactly the same situation as

Bob, with their own siding and their own switch, all sacrificing the child in order to preserve their own cherished car. Would that make it all right for Bob to do the same? To answer this question affirmatively is to endorse follow-the-crowd ethics—the kind of ethics that led many Germans to look away when the Nazi atrocities were being committed. We do not excuse them because others were behaving no better.

We seem to lack a sound basis for drawing a clear moral line between Bob's situation and that of any reader of this article with $200 to spare who does not donate it to an overseas aid agency. These readers seem to be acting at least as badly as Bob was acting when he chose to let the runaway train hurtle toward the unsuspecting child. In the light of this conclusion, I trust that many readers will reach for the phone and donate that $200. Perhaps you should do it before reading further.

Now that you have distinguished yourself morally from people who put their vintage cars ahead of a child's life, how about treating yourself and your partner to dinner at your favorite restaurant? But wait. The money you will spend at the restaurant could also help save the lives of children overseas! True, you weren't planning to blow $200 tonight, but if you were to give up dining out just for one month, you would easily save that amount. And what is one month's dining out, compared to a child's life? There's the rub. Since there are a lot of desperately needy children in the world, there will always be another child whose life you could save for another $200. Are you therefore obliged to keep giving until you have nothing left? At what point can you stop?

Hypothetical examples can easily become farcical. Consider Bob. How far past losing the Bugatti should he go? Imagine that Bob had got his foot stuck in the track of the siding, and if he diverted the train, then before it rammed the car it would also amputate his big toe. Should he still throw the switch? What if it would amputate his foot? His entire leg?

As absurd as the Bugatti scenario gets when pushed to extremes, the point it raises is a serious one: only when the sacrifices become very significant indeed would most people be prepared to say that Bob does nothing wrong when he decides not to throw the switch. Of course, most people could be wrong; we can't decide moral issues by taking opinion polls. But consider for yourself the level of sacrifice that you would demand of Bob, and then think about how much money you would have to give away in order to make a sacrifice that is roughly equal to that. It's almost certainly much, much more than $200. For most middle-class Americans, it could easily be more like $200,000.

Isn't it counterproductive to ask people to do so much? Don't we run the risk that many will shrug their shoulders and say that morality, so conceived, is fine for saints but not for them? I accept that we are unlikely to see, in the near or even medium-term future, a world in which it is normal for wealthy Americans to give the bulk of their wealth to strangers. When it comes to praising or blaming people for what they do, we tend to use a standard that is relative to some conception of normal behavior. Comfortably off Americans who give, say, 10 percent of their income to overseas aid organizations are so far ahead of most of their equally comfortable fellow citizens that I wouldn't go out of my way to chastise them for not doing more. Nevertheless, they should be doing much more, and they are in no position to criticize Bob for failing to make the much greater sacrifice of his Bugatti.

At this point various objections may crop up. Someone may say: "If every citizen living in the affluent nations contributed his or her share I wouldn't have to make such a drastic sacrifice, because long before such levels were reached, the resources would have been there to save the lives of all those children dying from lack of food or medical care. So why should I give more than my fair share?" Another, related, objection is that the Government ought to increase its overseas aid allocations, since that would spread the burden more equitably across all taxpayers.

Yet the question of how much we ought to give is a matter to be decided in the real world—and that, sadly, is a world in which we know that most people do not, and in the immediate future will not, give substantial amounts to overseas aid agencies. We know, too, that at least in the next year, the United

States Government is not going to meet even the very modest United Nations–recommended target of 0.7 percent of gross national product; at the moment it lags far below that, at 0.09 percent, not even half of Japan's 0.22 percent or a tenth of Denmark's 0.97 percent. Thus, we know that the money we can give beyond that theoretical "fair share" is still going to save lives that would otherwise be lost. While the idea that no one need do more than his or her fair share is a powerful one, should it prevail if we know that others are not doing their fair share and that children will die preventable deaths unless we do more than our fair share? That would be taking fairness too far.

Thus, this ground for limiting how much we ought to give also fails. In the world as it is now, I can see no escape from the conclusion that each one of us with wealth surplus to his or her essential needs should be giving most of it to help people suffering from poverty so dire as to be life-threatening. That's right: I'm saying that you shouldn't buy that new car, take that cruise, redecorate the house or get that pricey new suit. After all, a $1,000 suit could save five children's lives.

So how does my philosophy break down in dollars and cents? An American household with an income of $50,000 spends around $30,000 annually on necessities, according to the Conference Board, a nonprofit economic research organization. Therefore, for a household bringing in $50,000 a year, donations to help the world's poor should be as close as possible to $20,000. The $30,000 required for necessities holds for higher incomes as well. So a household making $100,000 could cut a yearly check for $70,000. Again, the formula is simple: whatever money you're spending on luxuries, not necessities, should be given away.

Now, evolutionary psychologists tell us that human nature just isn't sufficiently altruistic to make it plausible that many people will sacrifice so much for strangers. On the facts of human nature, they might be right, but they would be wrong to draw a moral conclusion from those facts. If it is the case that we ought to do things that, predictably, most of us won't do, then let's face that fact head-on. Then, if we value the life of a child more than going to fancy restaurants, the next time we dine out we will know that we could have done something better with our money. If that makes living a morally decent life extremely arduous, well, then that is the way things are. If we don't do it, then we should at least know that we are failing to live a morally decent life—not because it is good to wallow in guilt but because knowing where we should be going is the first step toward heading in that direction.

When Bob first grasped the dilemma that faced him as he stood by that railway switch, he must have thought how extraordinarily unlucky he was to be placed in a situation in which he must choose between the life of an innocent child and the sacrifice of most of his savings. But he was not unlucky at all. We are all in that situation.

Peter Singer: The Singer Solution to World Poverty

1. Was it morally wrong of Bob to refrain from throwing the switch, thus allowing the child to die? Is there any moral difference between Bob's decision and the decision of well-off people to spend money on luxuries rather than the alleviation of poverty?

2. One difference between the case of Bob and the case of someone not giving to charity is that Bob is the only person in a position to prevent the child's death, while many people are in a position to give to charity. Why doesn't Singer think that this is a morally relevant difference? Do you agree with him?

3. How much of our income does Singer think we are morally required to give away? Do you find his standard reasonable?

4. How does Singer respond to the objection that his theory is too demanding, and that people will never make the sacrifices he suggests? Do you find his response convincing?

5. One might respond to Singer's proposals by claiming that instead of individuals contributing money to alleviate world poverty, governments should be responsible for handling such efforts. Why doesn't Singer think that this undermines his view that middle-class people should give large percentages of their income to charity?

A Kantian Approach to Famine Relief
Onora O'Neill

Onora O'Neill opens this selection by providing a very helpful summary of the central ideas of Kant's principle of humanity, which calls on us to treat human beings as ends, and never as mere means. These dual notions require interpretation, as O'Neill (one of the preeminent scholars of Kantian ethics in the last several decades) well recognizes. To treat someone as a means is innocent enough—it is simply to rely on her to help you to achieve one of your goals. But to treat someone as a *mere* means is to treat her in a way that she cannot in principle consent to. Treating someone as an end is to show her the respect that she is due, owing to her rationality and autonomy. This amounts to treating her in ways that she *can* consent to.

The question here is whether, in spending money on our own pleasures rather than on giving to aid agencies that will save the lives of famine victims, we are thereby violating our moral obligations. O'Neill applies the rudiments of the Kantian ethic to provide an answer. Our moral obligations to aid others are discretionary—we must do some good, but we are allowed to choose the times and the ways in which we offer such help. Of course, we must treat no such victims as mere means—we must not coerce or deceive them, for instance. But how much (if anything) must we do for them?

In addressing this question, O'Neill contrasts the Kantian view with a utilitarian one, which requires that we give such aid until the point at which, were we to give any more, we would become as badly off as our intended beneficiaries. The Kantian view is less demanding. As O'Neill indicates, the Kantian can offer no precise formula for specifying the amount and kind of aid that one must give to victims of famine relief. Still, because of its emphasis on the importance of developing one's capacities for autonomous choice, and because of the severe ways in which famine threatens those capacities, Kantian ethics places a high priority on providing such aid.

THE FORMULA OF THE END IN ITSELF

Kant states the Formula of the End in Itself as follows:

> Act in such a way that you always treat humanity, whether in your own person or in the person of any other, never simply as a means but always at the same time as an end.

To understand this we need to know what it is to treat a person as a means or as an end. According to Kant, each of our acts reflects one or more *maxims*. The maxim of the act is the principle on which one sees oneself as acting. A maxim expresses a person's policy, or if he or she has no settled policy, the principle underlying the particular intention or decision on which he or she acts. Thus, a person who decides "This year I'll give 10 percent of my income to famine relief" has as a maxim the principle of tithing his or her income for famine relief.

Whenever we act intentionally, we have at least one maxim and can, if we reflect, state what it is. When we want to work out whether an act we propose to do is right or wrong, according to Kant, we should look at our maxims. We just have to check that the act we have in mind will not use anyone as a mere means, and, if possible, that it will treat other persons as ends in themselves.

From Onora O'Neill, "A Kantian Approach to Famine Relief," in Tom Regan, ed., *Matters of Life and Death,* second edition (New York: Random House, 1986), pp. 322–329.

USING PERSONS AS MERE MEANS

To use someone as a *mere means* is to involve them in a scheme of action *to which they could not in principle consent.* Kant does not say that there is anything wrong about using someone as a means. Evidently we have to do so in any cooperative scheme of action. If I cash a check I use the teller as a means, without whom I could not lay my hands on the cash; the teller in turn uses me as a means to earn his or her living. But in this case, each party consents to her or his part in the transaction. Kant would say that though they use one another as means, they do not use one another as *mere* means. Each person assumes that the other has maxims of his or her own and is not just a thing or a prop to be manipulated.

But there are other situations where one person uses another in a way to which the other could not in principle consent. For example, one person may make a promise to another with every intention of breaking it. If the promise is accepted, then the person to whom it was given must be ignorant of what the promisor's intention (maxim) really is. Successful false promising depends on deceiving the person to whom the promise is made about what one's real maxim is. And since the person who is deceived doesn't know that real maxim, he or she can't in principle consent to his or her part in the proposed scheme of action. The person who is deceived is, as it were, a prop or a tool—a mere means—in the false promisor's scheme. In Kant's view, it is this that makes false promising wrong.

In Kant's view, acts that are done on maxims that require deception or coercion of others, and so cannot have the consent of those others, are wrong. When we act on such maxims, we treat others as mere means, as things rather than as ends in themselves. If we act on such maxims, our acts are not only wrong but unjust: such acts wrong the particular others who are deceived or coerced.

TREATING PERSONS AS ENDS IN THEMSELVES

To treat someone as an end in him or herself requires in the first place that one not use him or her as mere means, that one respect each as a rational person with his or her own maxims. But beyond that, one may also seek to foster others' plans and maxims by sharing some of their ends. To act beneficently is to seek others' happiness, therefore to intend to achieve some of the things that those others aim at with their maxims. Beneficent acts try to achieve what others want. However, we cannot seek everything that others want; their wants are too numerous and diverse, and, of course, sometimes incompatible. It follows that beneficence has to be selective.

There is a sharp distinction between the requirements of justice and of beneficence in Kantian ethics. Justice requires that we act on *no* maxims that use others as mere means. Beneficence requires that we act on *some* maxims that foster others' ends, though it is a matter for judgment and discretion which of their ends we foster. Kantians will claim that they have done nothing wrong if none of their acts is unjust, and that their duty is complete if in addition their life plans have been reasonably beneficent.

KANTIAN DELIBERATIONS ON FAMINE PROBLEMS

The theory I have just sketched may seem to have little to say about famine problems. For it is a theory that forbids us to use others as mere means but does not require us to direct our benevolence first to those who suffer most. A conscientious Kantian, it seems, has only to avoid being unjust to those who suffer famine and can then be beneficent to those nearer home. He or she would not be obliged to help the starving, even if no others were equally distressed.

Kant's moral theory does make less massive demands on moral agents than utilitarian moral theory. On the other hand, it is somewhat clearer just what the more stringent demands are, and they are not negligible. We have here a contrast between a theory that makes massive but often indeterminate demands and a theory that makes fewer but less unambiguous demands and leaves other questions, in particular the allocation of beneficence, unresolved.

KANTIAN DUTIES OF JUSTICE IN TIMES OF FAMINE

In famine situations, Kantian moral theory requires unambiguously that we do no injustice. We should not act on any maxim that uses another as mere means, so we should neither deceive nor coerce others. Such a requirement can become quite exacting when the means of life are scarce, when persons can more easily be coerced, and when the advantage of gaining more than what is justly due to one is great.

First, where there is a rationing scheme, one ought not to cheat and seek to get more than one's share—any scheme of cheating will use someone as mere means. Nor may one take advantage of others' desperation to profiteer or divert goods onto the black market or to accumulate a fortune out of others' misfortunes. Transactions that are outwardly sales and purchases can be coercive when one party is desperate. All the forms of corruption that deceive or put pressure on others are also wrong: hoarding unallocated food, diverting relief supplies for private use, corruptly using one's influence to others' disadvantage. Such requirements are far from trivial and frequently violated in hard times. In severe famines, refraining from coercing and deceiving may risk one's own life and require the greatest courage.

Second, justice requires that in famine situations one still try to fulfill one's duties to particular others. For example, even in times of famine, a person has duties to try to provide for dependents. These duties may, tragically, be unfulfillable. If they are, Kantian ethical theory would not judge wrong the acts of a person who had done her or his best. A conscientious attempt to meet the particular obligations one has undertaken may also require of one many further maxims of self-restraint and of endeavor—for example, it may require a conscientious attempt to avoid having (further) children; it may require contributing one's time and effort to programs of economic development. Where there is no other means to fulfill particular obligations, Kantian principles may require a generation of sacrifice.

The obligations of those who live with or near famine are undoubtedly stringent and exacting; for those who live further off it is harder to see what a Kantian moral theory demands. Might it not, for example, be permissible to do nothing at all about those suffering famine? Might one not ensure that one does nothing unjust to the victims of famine by adopting no maxims whatsoever that mention them? To do so would, at the least, require one to refrain from certain deceptive and coercive practices frequently employed during the European exploration and economic penetration of the now underdeveloped world and still not unknown. For example, it would be unjust to "purchase" valuable lands and resources from persons who don't understand commercial transactions or exclusive property rights or mineral rights, and so do not understand that their acceptance of trinkets destroys their traditional economic pattern and way of life. The old adage "trade follows the flag" reminds us to how great an extent the economic penetration of the less-developed countries involved elements of coercion and deception, so was on Kantian principles unjust (regardless of whether or not the net effect has benefited the citizens of those countries).

Few persons in the developed world today find themselves faced with the possibility of adopting on a grand scale maxims of deceiving or coercing persons living in poverty. But at least some people find that their jobs require them to make decisions about investment and aid policies that enormously affect the lives of those nearest to famine. What does a commitment to Kantian moral theory demand of such persons?

It has become common in writings in ethics and social policy to distinguish between one's *personal responsibilities* and one's *role responsibilities*. So a person may say, "As an individual I sympathize, but in my official capacity I can do nothing"; or we may excuse persons' acts of coercion because they are acting in some particular capacity—e.g., as a soldier or a jailer. On the other hand, this distinction isn't made or accepted by everyone. At the Nuremberg trials of war criminals, the defense "I was only doing my job" was disallowed, at least for those whose command position meant that they had some discretion in what they did. Kantians generally would play down any distinction between a person's own responsibilities and his or her role responsibilities. They would not deny that in any capacity one is accountable for certain things for which as a private person one is not accountable. For example, the treasurer of an organization is accountable to the board and has to present periodic reports and to keep specified records. But if she fails to do one of these things for which she is held accountable she will be held responsible for that failure—it will be imputable to her as an individual. When we take on positions, we *add* to our responsibilities those that the job requires; but we do not lose those that are already required of us. Our social role or job gives us, on Kant's view, no license to use others as mere means.

If persons are responsible for all their acts, it follows that it would be unjust for aid officials to coerce persons into accepting sterilization, wrong for them to use coercive power to achieve political advantages (such as military bases) or commercial advantages (such as trade agreements that will harm the other country). Where a less-developed country is pushed to exempt a multinational corporation from tax laws, or to construct out of its meager tax revenues the infrastructure of roads, harbors, or airports (not to mention executive mansions) that the corporation—but perhaps not the country—needs, then one suspects that some coercion has been involved.

The problem with such judgments—and it is an immense problem—is that it is hard to identify coercion and deception in complicated institutional settings. It is not hard to understand what is coercive about one person threatening another with serious injury if he won't comply with the first person's suggestion. But it is not at all easy to tell where the outward forms of political and commercial negotiation—which often involve an element of threat—have become coercive.

KANTIAN DUTIES OF BENEFICENCE IN TIMES OF FAMINE

The grounds of duties of beneficence are that such acts develop or promote others' ends and, in particular, foster others' capacities to pursue ends, to be autonomous beings.

Clearly there are many opportunities for beneficence. But one area in which the *primary* task of developing others' capacity to pursue their own ends is particularly needed is in the parts of the world where extreme poverty and hunger leave people unable to pursue *any* of their other ends. Beneficence directed at putting people in a position to pursue whatever ends they may have has, for Kant, a stronger claim on us than beneficence directed at sharing ends with those who are already in a position to pursue varieties of ends. It would be nice if I bought a tennis racquet to play with my friend who is tennis mad and never has enough partners; but it is more important to make people able to plan their own lives to a minimal extent. It is nice to walk a second mile with someone who requests one's company; better to share a cloak with someone who may otherwise be too cold to make any journey. Though these suggestions are not a detailed set of instructions for the allocation of beneficence by Kantians, they show that relief of famine must stand very high among duties of beneficence.

THE LIMITS OF KANTIAN ETHICS: INTENTIONS AND RESULTS

Kantian ethics differs from utilitarian ethics both in its scope and in the precision with which it guides action. Every action, whether of a person or of an agency, can be assessed by utilitarian methods, provided only that information is available about all the consequences of the act. The theory has unlimited scope, but, owing to lack of data, often lacks precision. Kantian ethics has a more restricted scope. Since it assesses actions by looking at the maxims of agents, it can only assess intentional acts. This means that it is most at home in assessing individuals' acts; but it can be extended to assess acts of agencies that (like corporations and governments and student unions) have decision-making procedures.

It may seem a great limitation of Kantian ethics that it concentrates on intentions to the neglect of results. It might seem that all conscientious Kantians have to do is to make sure that they never intend to use others as mere means, and that they sometimes intend to foster others' ends. And, as we all know, good intentions sometimes lead to bad results, and correspondingly, bad intentions sometimes do no harm, or even produce good. If Hardin is right, the good intentions of those who feed the starving lead to dreadful results in the long run.

If some traditional arguments in favor of capitalism are right, the greed and selfishness of the profit motive have produced unparalleled prosperity for many.

But such discrepancies between intentions and results are the exception and not the rule. For we cannot just *claim* that our intentions are good and do what we will. Our intentions reflect what we expect the immediate results of our action to be. Nobody credits the "intentions" of a couple who practice neither celibacy nor contraception but still insist "we never meant to have (more) children." Conception is likely (and known to be likely) in such cases. Where people's expressed intentions ignore the normal and predictable results of what they do, we infer that (if they are not amazingly ignorant) their words do not express their true intentions. The Formula of the End in Itself applies to the intentions on which one acts—not to some prettified version that one may avow. Provided this intention—the agent's real intention—uses no other as mere means, he or she does nothing unjust. If some of his or her intentions foster others' ends, then he or she is sometimes beneficent. It is therefore possible for people to test their proposals by Kantian arguments even when they lack the comprehensive causal knowledge that utilitarianism requires. Conscientious Kantians can work out whether they will be doing wrong by some act even though they know that their foresight is limited and that they may cause some harm or fail to cause some benefit.

UTILITARIANISM AND RESPECT FOR LIFE

Utilitarians value happiness and the absence or reduction of misery. As a utilitarian one ought (if conscientious) to devote one's life to achieving the best possible balance of happiness over misery. If one's life plan remains in doubt, this will be because the means to this end are often unclear. But whenever the causal tendency of acts is clear, utilitarians will be able to discern the acts they should successively do in order to improve the world's balance of happiness over unhappiness.

This task is not one for the faint-hearted. First, it is dauntingly long, indeed interminable. Second,

it may at times require the sacrifice of happiness, and even of lives, for the sake of a greater happiness. As our control over the means of ending and preserving human life has increased, analogous dilemmas have arisen in many areas for utilitarians. Should life be preserved at the cost of pain when modern medicine makes this possible? Should life be preserved without hope of consciousness? Should triage policies, because they may maximize the number of survivors, be used to determine who should be left to starve? All these questions can be fitted into utilitarian frameworks and answered *if* we have the relevant information. And sometimes the answer will be that human happiness demands the sacrifice of unwilling lives. Further, for most utilitarians, it makes no difference if the unwilling sacrifices involve acts of injustice to those whose lives are to be lost. Utilitarians do not deny these possibilities, though the imprecision of our knowledge of consequences often blurs the implications of the theory. If we peer through the blur, we see that the utilitarian view is that lives may indeed be sacrificed for the sake of a greater good even when the persons are not willing. There is nothing wrong with using another as a mere means provided that the end for which the person is so used is a happier result than could have been achieved any other way, taking into account the misery the means have caused. In utilitarian thought, persons are not ends in themselves. Their special moral status derives from their being means to the production of happiness. Human life has therefore a high though derivative value, and one life may be taken for the sake of greater happiness in other lives, or for ending of misery in that life. Nor is there any deep difference between ending a life for the sake of others' happiness by not helping (e.g., by triaging) and doing so by harming.

Utilitarian moral theory has then a rather paradoxical view of the value of human life. Living, conscious humans are (along with other sentient beings) necessary for the existence of everything utilitarians value. But it is not their being alive but the state of their consciousness that is of value. Hence, the best results may require certain lives to be lost—by whatever means—for the sake of the total happiness and absence of misery that can be produced.

KANT AND RESPECT FOR PERSONS

Kantians reach different conclusions about human life. Human life is valuable because humans (and conceivably other beings, e.g., angels or apes) are the bearers of rational life. Humans are able to choose and to plan. This capacity and its exercise are of such value that they ought not to be sacrificed, for anything of lesser value. Therefore, no one rational or autonomous creature should be treated as mere means for the enjoyment or even the happiness of another. We may in Kant's view justifiably—even nobly—risk or sacrifice our lives for others. For in doing so we follow our own maxim and nobody uses us as mere means. But no others may use either our lives or our bodies for a scheme that they have either coerced or deceived us into joining. For in doing so they would fail to treat us as rational beings; they would use us as mere means and not as ends in ourselves.

Onora O'Neill: A Kantian Approach to Famine Relief

1. O'Neill contrasts the Kantian and utilitarian views about the nature and extent of our moral obligations to famine victims. Which elements of these views do you find especially attractive or objectionable?
2. The Kantian offers people a lot of discretion about how to fulfill their general obligation to benefitting others. How appealing do you find such discretion?
3. Contrast the Kantian and utilitarian views about respect for life. Which do you find more attractive and why?
4. O'Neill does not discuss the Kantian principle of universalizability (see Chapter 6). What are the implications of this principle for our duties to give to famine relief?
5. How does the importance of autonomy and rationality figure into the Kantian picture of our obligations to famine victims?

Human Rights and Global Wrongs
Thomas Pogge

Thomas Pogge opens this brief selection by recounting many sobering details of the extent of global poverty, the growing inequality among rich and poor, and the relatively small contributions made by developing countries to improve the situation. As Pogge makes clear, the world's wealthier countries have fallen short even relative to their stated commitments to relieving the suffering of the world's poor—and these commitments, he finds, are themselves woefully inadequate.

Many people in richer countries argue that their obligation to relieve poverty is restricted to so-called negative duties—duties not to harm or interfere with the rights of others. On this view, we fulfill our duties so long as we keep a hands-off policy and refrain from making a bad situation any worse. One might reject this restriction and argue instead that human rights include, for instance, the right not to starve or the right to receive inexpensive life-saving medical treatment. On such a view, we have positive duties to the poor—duties to improve their lives by giving help where it is most needed.

Pogge argues that even if we reject the existence of such positive duties, those in wealthy countries are not off the hook. If we look at all carefully at how the wealth of these countries was acquired, we see a long track record of exploitation and injustice. Rich countries owe a great deal of their wealth to a terrible history that has involved massive violations of human rights—violations that have included theft, fraud, wars of aggression, colonialism, enslavement, and genocide. True, very few of our contemporaries are involved in such behavior; they are not responsible for these injustices. But neither, says Pogge, are they entitled to benefit by them. We who are comparatively wealthy enjoy our status because of past injustices; as a result, we are morally obligated to relieve the suffering of those whose poverty results from that injustice.

Half of humankind is poor, living on less than 3 percent of global household income, as against 69 percent captured by the top tenth. Even on the narrowest conception of ("extreme") poverty, the number of poor is somewhere around the 1.02 billion counted as chronically undernourished (2009)[1] or the 1.377 billion counted in 2005 as living below the World Bank's international poverty line of $1.25 per person per day at 2005 PPPs (Purchasing Power Parities).[2] About one third of all human deaths—eighteen million per annum—are due to poverty-related causes, mostly diseases that cause little or no damage in more affluent populations.[3]

Surprisingly, the world poverty problem—so unimaginably large in human terms—is also tiny in economic terms. The World Bank quantifies the collective shortfall in 2005 of all those living in extreme poverty at 0.33 percent (at PPPs) of the sum of all gross domestic products.[4] At currency exchange rates this shortfall is merely $76 billion or one-sixth of one percent of world income or about one-ninth of current U.S. military spending.[5] And even the collective shortfall of the 3.085 billion whom the World Bank counts as living on less than twice its poverty line have a collective shortfall from this line ($2.50 per person per day at 2005 PPPs) of only $506 billion or 1.13 percent of world income or about two-thirds of U.S. military spending.[6]

Though modest institutional reforms, affecting just over 1 percent of the global income distribution, could overcome severe poverty, existing institutional arrangements drive this distribution in the opposite direction: they induce greater inequality.

From Thomas Pogge, "Human Rights and Global Wrongs," *Reflections* (Yale Divinity School, Fall 2010), pp. 44–46.

The nearby table shows how humanity's top few percentiles are growing their share of global household income while the remainder, and especially the bottom quarter, are losing ground.[7]

This pattern manifests itself in the evolution of hunger. The number of chronically undernourished people has not declined from the 800-million level reported in the mid-1990s. In fact, a spike in global food prices (2006–08) and the recent global financial crisis have caused this number to break above the one-billion mark for the first time in human history[8]—even while the ranks of the hungry are continuously thinned by millions of deaths each year from poverty-related causes.

The rich countries' response to world poverty is mainly rhetorical. Though official development assistance (ODA) has in the aftermath of 9/11 reversed its long-term decline, it is still only $120 billion annually or 0.3 percent of Gross National Income (2008) as compared to the 0.7 percent target promised over thirty years ago.[9] More importantly, only $15 billion of annual ODA is earmarked for basic social services.[10]

And even the rhetoric is appalling. At the 1996 World Food Summit in Rome, the world's governments pledged themselves "to reducing the number of undernourished people to half their present level no later than 2015,"[11] implicitly accepting 25,000 daily poverty deaths in 2015 and some 250 million such deaths in the interim. In the 2000 *UN Millennium Declaration*, they substituted a diluted promise "to halve, by the year 2015, the proportion of the world's people" living in extreme poverty.[12] Because of 2000–15 population growth, this promise requires only a 40 percent reduction in the number of poor. The poverty promise was diluted

Segment of World Population	% Share World of Global Household Income 1988	% Share of Global Household Income 2005	Absolute % Change in Income Share	Relative % Change in Income Share
Richest 5%	42.87%	46.36%	+3.49%	+8.1%
Next 20%	46.63	43.98	−2.65	−5.7%
Second Quarter	6.97	6.74	−0.23	−3.3%
Third Quarter	2.37	2.14	−0.23	−9.8%
Poorest Quarter	1.15	0.77	−0.38	−32.9%

again in the final formulation of the first Millennium Development Goal (MDG-1), which defines poverty as a "proportion of people in the developing world"[13] and thus takes advantage of even faster population growth in the reference group (denominator of the proportion). MDG-1 also backdates the baseline to 1990. It thereby counts China's poverty reduction in the 1990s toward the goal and, by lengthening the plan period, doubles population growth in the reference group. The 50-percent reduction in the number of extremely poor people promised in Rome for the 1996–2015 period has thus been twisted into a 20-percent reduction of this number; and 496 million were thereby added to the number of those whose extreme poverty in 2015 will be deemed consistent with having kept the grand poverty promise. Half a billion additional extremely poor people mean about six million additional deaths from poverty-related causes in 2015 and each subsequent year.[14]

HELPING AND HURTING THE POOR

Confronted with such facts, citizens of the rich countries may concede that we affluent should do more to help the poor. But they see this as a demand of humanity or charity—not as a demand of justice and certainly not as a moral duty imposed on us by the human rights of the poor. As the U.S. government declared after the World Food Summit: "the attainment of any 'right to adequate food' or 'fundamental right to be free from hunger' is a goal or aspiration to be realized progressively that does not give rise to any international obligations."[15]

The presumption behind this denial is that, internationally at least, human rights entail only negative duties: they require that one not deprive foreigners of secure access to the objects of their human rights. They do not require that one help them attain such secure access by protecting them against other threats. This presumption can be attacked by arguing that human rights do impose positive duties toward foreigners. But, even if the presumption is accepted, it shields the rich from human-rights-based obligations only insofar as they bear no responsibility for the existing ever-more-radically unequal global economic distribution. And this claim to innocence is highly dubious at best.

For one thing, the existing radical inequality is deeply tainted by how it accumulated through one historical process that was deeply pervaded by enslavement, colonialism, even genocide. The affluent are quick to point out that they cannot inherit their ancestor's sins. Indeed. But how can they then be entitled to the fruits of these sins: to their huge inherited advantage in power and wealth over the rest of the world? If we are not so entitled, then we are, by actively excluding the global poor from our lands and possessions, contributing to their deprivations.

RULES OF THE GAME

Moreover, even the causes of the current persistence of severe poverty are by no means exclusively domestic to the countries in which it occurs. The asymmetries inherent in the current global economic (World Trade Organization) regime are well documented: it allows the rich countries to favor their own companies through tariffs, quotas, antidumping duties, export credits and huge subsidies. The United Nations Conference on Trade and Development estimates that the latter market distortions cost the developing countries $700 billion annually in lost export revenue—a huge amount relative to the needs of their poor.[16] And the constrained trading opportunities the rich countries afford the poor do not come for free. To obtain them, poor countries must spend large amounts on enforcing the intellectual property rights of the rich, thereby depriving their own populations of access to cheap generic versions of patented life-saving medicines, seeds, and clean green technologies.

To be sure, many developing countries are run by corrupt and incompetent leaders, unwilling or unable to make serious poverty-eradication efforts. But their ability to rule, often against the will and interests of the population, crucially depends on outside factors. It depends, for instance, on their being recognized by the rich countries as entitled to borrow in their country's name, to confer legal title to its natural resources, and with the proceeds to buy the weapons they need to stay in power. By assigning these privileges to such rulers, on the basis of their effective power alone, the rich countries support their banks and secure their resource imports. But they also greatly strengthen the staying power of oppressive rulers and the incentives toward coup attempts and civil wars, especially in the resource-rich countries.

More generally, bad leadership, civil wars, and widespread corruption in the developing countries are not wholly homegrown, but strongly encouraged by the existing international rules and extreme inequalities. The rulers and officials of these countries have vastly more to gain from catering to the interests of wealthy foreign governments, corporations, and tourists than from meeting the basic needs of their impoverished compatriots.

Are the rich countries violating human rights when they, in collaboration with Southern elites, impose a global institutional order under which, foreseeably and avoidably, hundreds of millions cannot attain "a standard of living adequate for the health and well-being of himself and of his family, including food, clothing, housing and medical care" (*Universal Declaration of Human Rights,* §25)? The *Declaration* itself makes quite clear that they do when it proclaims that "everyone is entitled to a social and international order in which the rights and freedoms set forth in this Declaration can be fully realized" (ibid., §28).

The existing international institutional order fails this test. It aggravates extreme poverty through protectionism and aggressive enforcement of intellectual property rights in seeds and essential medicines. And it fosters corrupt and oppressive government in the poorer countries by recognizing any person or group holding effective power—regardless of how they acquired or exercise it—as entitled to sell the country's natural resources and to dispose of the proceeds of such sales, to borrow in the country's name and thereby to impose debt service obligations upon it, to sign treaties on the country's behalf and thus to bind its present and future population, and to use state revenues to buy the means of internal repression.

Some parts of international law contain inspiring affirmations of human rights. Other parts contribute massively to the underfulfillment of these same rights. These contributions are foreseeable and avoidable. To avoid them, human rights must be mainstreamed to constrain the design of all global institutional arrangements.

NOTES

1. FAO (Food and Agriculture Organization of the United Nations). "1.02 Billion People Hungry." News Release. June 19, 2009. www.fao.org/news/story/en/item/20568/icode/(accessed July 31, 2010).
2. Shaohua Chen and Martin Ravallion. "The Developing World Is Poorer than We Thought, But No Less Successful in the Fight against Poverty," World Bank Policy Research Working Paper WPS 4703 (Washington DC, 2008), http://econ.world-bank.org/docsearch. The World Bank counts as poor only those living on less, per person per day, than what $1.25 could buy in the US in 2005. The UN follows this definition.
3. WHO (World Health Organization). *The Global Burden of Disease: 2004 Update* (WHO Publications, 2008), table A$_1$, pp. 54–9.
4. Chen and Ravallion (n.2), p. 27.
5. Thomas Pogge. *Politics as Usual: What Lies Behind the Pro-Poor Rhetoric* (Polity, 2010), pp. 69–70.
6. Ibid.
7. Data kindly supplied by Branko Milanovic of the World Bank in a personal e-mail of April 25, 2010.
8. FAO (Food and Agriculture Organization of the United Nations). "1.02 Billion People Hungry."

News Release. June 19, 2009. www.fao.org/news/story/en/item/20568/icode/(accessed July 31, 2010).

9. See http://mdgs.un.org/unsd/mdg/SeriesDetail.aspx?srid=569&crid= (accessed August 1, 2010) for ODA allocations. The corresponding CNIs can be found in World Bank, *World Development Report* 2010 (The World Bank, 2010), pp. 378-9.

10. See http://mdgs.un.org/unsd/mdg/SeriesDetail.aspx?srid=592&crid= (accessed Aug. 1, 2010).

11. *Rome Declaration on World Food Security.* November 1996. www.fao.org/wfs.

12. UN General Assembly. *United Nations Millennium Declaration.* A/res/55/2, Sept. 8, 2000. www.un.org/millennium/declaration/ares552e.htm. Article 19.

13. United Nations. *The Millennium Development Goals Report 2008* (UN Department of Economic and Social Affairs, 2008), p. 6.

14. Pogge, pp. 58–62.

15. Rome Declaration (n.11), Annex II to the *Final Report of the World Food Summit.*

16. UNCTAD, *Trade and Development Report: Fragile Recovery and Risks* (UN Publications 1999), p. IX. Available at www.unctad.org/en/docs/tdr1999_en.pdf.

Thomas Pogge: Human Rights and Global Wrongs

1. What are human rights, and how might the existence of such rights be justified?

2. Do human rights include any positive rights? If so, which ones? If not, why not?

3. Historically, wealthy countries have become wealthy in substantial part by having exploited poorer countries. Does this impose obligations on the wealthier countries to improve the conditions of the poorer ones?

4. Pogge claims that many *current* practices supported by wealthy countries work to enforce and increase poverty in poorer ones. He believes that this imposes a duty of the wealthy countries to relieve the poverty that they are now causing. Do you agree with his claim? Why or why not?

5. One argument for giving aid is that many people desperately need it to survive, and the wealthy can provide it at relatively little cost to themselves. Is this a good argument? Why or why not?

International Aid: Not the Cure You Were Hoping For

Jason Brennan

Jason Brennan focuses on two questions in this piece. First: Why are some countries rich and others poor? Second: Does international aid actually succeed in lifting people out of poverty? The answers he offers may be surprising.

Brennan thinks that many people, and most philosophers, mistake their way when thinking about these questions because they fail to appreciate the relevant economic facts about how nations become wealthy and about how ineffective international aid really is. In this selection he emphasizes the importance of relying on claims that have achieved consensus among economists.

Many people think that some countries are rich, and others poor, because rich countries either have much greater natural resources than poor ones, or have gained their riches by exploiting poor countries. Brennan claims instead that wealthy countries got that way, and stay that way (when they do), because they have excellent institutions. A poor country can transform its wealth if it reorganizes itself to reduce corruption, increase the freedoms of its citizens, and free its markets of needless government control.

In answer to the second question, Brennan claims that international aid does very little good. It can, he concedes, save some lives in emergency situations. But the chances that it leads to long-term benefits for poor populations are slim to none. It's a common assumption, but mistaken nonetheless, that we can easily end world poverty if rich countries simply gave some portion of their wealth to the poor. The problem with this thinking, according to Brennan, is that it fails to appreciate how crucial the existence of good institutions is to sustaining the health and well-being of a nation's population. Giving money or food aid directly to impoverished countries rarely improves their institutions and so does little, in the end, to improve the lives of the needy.

Many people are too poor to meet their basic needs. The good news is that extreme poverty (defined as living on less than $1.90 per capita per day) is disappearing before our eyes. In 1820, about 95 percent of people lived in extreme poverty. By 1960, that had only dropped to about 66 percent. Now, less than 10 percent of the world lives in extreme poverty. Perhaps most remarkably, these numbers are proportions. There are many more people around, and they're living better than ever before.[1] This is a miracle, but hardly anyone notices it.

Nevertheless, many remain mired in poverty. Surely, most of us think, something must be done. Immediately, a facile solution comes to mind: Some countries—Germany or the United States—have more than enough. (Even a person at the "poverty line" the US is, despite the high cost of US living, among the top 14 percent of income earners worldwide.) So, it seems, curing world poverty is easy: The rich countries could just donate a bunch of money to the poor countries. Voila!

I wish it were that simple. This is a topic where normative reasoning and moral philosophy, in isolation, tend to lead us astray. If we genuinely care about solving world poverty, we need the tools of economics to help us answer two questions:

1. Why are some countries rich and others poor?
2. Does international aid, whether through private charities, government-to-government aid, or government-to-charity aid, actually succeed in lifting people out of poverty?

Philosophy might uncover what our obligations are *in light of the facts*, but it does not help us discover what the facts are. Unfortunately, philosophers of global justice are uninterested in or even hostile to learning the facts. Philosophers tend to advocate the policies economists know don't work, and tend to reject the institutions economists know work.

The overwhelming consensus in economics is that rich countries are rich because they have good institutions, while poor countries are poor because they have bad institutions. Further, the consensus is that aid generally doesn't work. Under special conditions, certain targeted forms of aid can prevent death during an immediate crisis, but that's about it. I'll explain both of these points below.

FALSE STARTS

Many people believe that global justice requires wealth redistribution from rich to poor countries. Most who find redistributive views appealing do so

---

Jason Brennan, "International Aid: Not the Cure You Were Hoping for," in *Ethics, Left and Right: The Moral Issues that Divide Us*, ed. Robert Fischer (Oxford University Press, 2019), pp. 160–168.

because they also hold mistaken beliefs about empirical matters. They usually accept one or more the following claims:

1. The reason some countries are rich and others are poor is that natural resources are unevenly distributed around the globe. The rich are rich because they have or had access to more or better resources than the poor countries did.

2. The reason some countries are rich and others are poor is that the rich countries (through conquest, colonialism, and empire) *extracted* resources from the poor countries.

3. We can easily end world poverty if rich countries simply gave some portion of their wealth to the poor.

These are *economic* claims. But they play an important role in many people's normative reasoning. People who accept these claims regard world poverty as a simple problem of misallocation: too much here, too little there. The obvious next step is to argue for redistribution in order to fix the misallocation. But the problem here is that each of these three claims is *false*.

The first two claims hold that differences in wealth result from a zero-sum process. I'll take a closer look below. But here, let's pause to note that wealth has been made, not simply moved around. We've seen an explosion of wealth and income over the past two hundred years. In 1990 US dollars, GDP/capita in 1 AD was about $457, rising to $712 by 1820. But look what's happened since:

When the history of economic growth is drawn on a chart, as in Fig. 1, it looks like a hockey stick. In the past 200 years, *real* (that is, inflation and cost-of-living adjusted) per capita world product has increased by a factor of at least 30. The United States' economy this year will produce *more*, in real terms, than the entire world did in 1950.

When the Great Enrichment began, Western Europe and the Western European offshoots grew faster than the rest of the world. As a result, the gap between Europe's standard of living and the rest of the world also grew. But even the poorest regions enjoyed *some* growth. It's not that Western Europe and the European offshoots grew rich

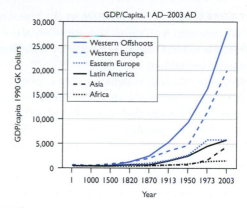

Fig. 1.[2]

while the other countries became even poorer. It's not as though Western Europe grew rich at the rate others grew poor, which would suggest a zero-sum reallocation of a fixed stock of wealth. Rather, all countries started off as poor; some got *slightly* richer over time, while the European countries and their offshoots got *much* richer over time.

Why?

Wrong Answer One: Natural Resources

Philosopher Thomas Pogge claims the world's rich have excluded the poor from their fair share of the world's natural resources. Pogge thinks this unjust. He claims people worldwide have a right to "a proportional resource share."[3]

Philosophers often assume differential natural resources explain why some countries are rich and others poor. But, as economist David Weil summarizes the empirical literature in his widely-used textbook *Economic Growth*, "the effect of natural resources on income is weak at best."[4] For instance, China after the 1950s was and remains poorer (in per capita income and other standard measures) than Singapore or Hong Kong, though the latter have almost *no* natural resources to speak of. The USSR was much poorer than the USA, though the USSR had far better natural resources. In Adam Smith's time, the Netherlands and England were richer than France, though France had far better natural resources. And so on.

Indeed, while natural resources can sometimes spur growth, they more frequently *inhibit* growth.

Economists refer to this problem as the "resource curse": countries with a high concentration of easily extractable natural resources frequently suffer from economic stagnation.

Just why this is so is debated. One explanation may be that countries with abundant natural resources "do not develop the cultural attributes necessary for economic success," in part because necessity is the mother of invention.[5] Another theory is that countries that enjoy resource booms tend to consume the sudden influx income in an unsustainable way. They don't develop capital, but eat away the extra income until it's gone. (See, e.g., Venezuela.) Perhaps the most popular theory (or, more precisely, the theory thought to identify the most significant set of causes) is that when a country enjoys abundant resources, this encourages governments to act in destructive ways. Regardless, the idea that resources explain wealth is widely accepted by laypeople, but widely rejected by economists.

Wrong Answer Two: Imperialism

A second popular view holds that that rich countries are rich because they (or their predecessors) through policies of colonialism, imperialism, and resource extraction, stole from the so-called third world. . . . As Pogge says,

> [E]xisting radical inequality is deeply tainted by how it accumulated through one historical process that was deeply pervaded by enslavement, colonialism, even genocide. The rich are quick to point out that they cannot inherit their ancestor's sins. Indeed. But how can they then be entitled to the fruits of these sins: to their huge inherited advantage in power and wealth over the rest of the world?[6]

On this view, imperialist extraction explains (or helps to explain) why developed countries became wealthy and why undeveloped countries are poor. Our wealth is inherited stolen wealth.

European countries indeed conquered Africans, Asians, and Native Americans, murdered and enslaved them, and stole their resources for use back home. Does such theft explain why European countries and some of their offshoots are rich? If you've never taken an economics class, you'll probably presume, as Pogge does, that the answer is yes.

But economists think the answer is no. Indeed, Adam Smith's 1776 *Wealth of Nations*—the book that founded modern economics—is fundamentally an economic critique of imperialism. Smith carefully survey the economic value of the goods Britain and other countries had extracted from the Americas and elsewhere, and then compared that to the costs these countries incurred to create and maintain those empires. Smith concluded:

> The rulers of Great Britain have, for more than a century past, amused the people with the imagination that they possessed a great empire on the west side of the Atlantic. This empire, however, [is] . . . not a gold mine, but the project of a gold mine; a project which has cost, which continues to cost, and which, if pursued in the same way as it has been hitherto, is likely to cost, immense expense, without being likely to bring any profit; for the effects of the monopoly of the colony trade, it has been shown, are, to the great body of the people, mere loss instead of profit.[7]

Smith found that a minority of politically well-connected people benefitted from the empire, but the majority of British subjects *lost* money. The losers lost more than the winners won. The costs of creating and maintaining the empire greatly *exceeded* the value of the raw materials obtained. (To illustrate: Imagine you paid $50K to buy a gun to rob people, but you only got $25K in earnings from all your muggings. You thereby *lost* money on your robberies.) Further, Smith showed, imperialism distorted the economy (by encouraging inefficient production methods) and so further hurt Britain and other imperial powers. Britain was getting richer despite its empire, not because of it.

The thrust of Smith's views is widely accepted. The general view among economists—who have better data today than Smith did back then—is that empires do not pay for themselves, even if we focus narrowly on the economic interests of imperial powers and ignore the harm they did to those they conquered.

However, while imperialism does not explain why some countries are rich, it may partly explain why some now remain poor. When imperialist powers established colonies, they replaced existing institutions with new institutions. As economists Daron Acemoglu, Simon Johnson, and James Robinson show, the kinds of institutions imperial powers set up depended on whether Europeans could settle in the colonies. In places such as North America, where European settlers faced low mortality rates (because there were low risks of disease), imperial powers exported well-functioning, growth-creating institutions.[8] In places such as the Congo, where Europeans faced high mortality rates (because of disease), imperial powers established growth-inhibiting extractive institutions. When the European powers abandoned or lost their colonies, these bad institutions remained behind, and generally morphed into current dysfunctional institutions those countries have today.

You might think this concession justifies redistribution: "Aha! Belgium should redistribute some of its wealth to the Congo. After all, even if the Belgians lost money in their rape, murder, and robbery of the Congo, it's still their fault that the Congo is doing badly today." In the same way, this argument goes, suppose I spent $500 to buy a gun, and then rob you, but only get $250 from doing so. Even though I lost money when I robbed you, I still owe you compensation.

But this argument treats countries as if they were people, and it obscures morally important facts. It's not that the Belgian or British people choose, as a group, to steal from Africans or Native Americans. Rather, what really happened was that, years ago, in what were non-democratic countries, the kings and queens, plus some political insiders, taxed the Belgian and British subjects to buy guns, soldiers, and warships, and then used those to steal from the Africans and Native

Americans. The Belgian and British subjects were *also* victims of imperialism—their leaders exploited them (through taxes and conscription) to then exploit others (through conquest and theft). So, demanding the Belgians pay restitution to the Congo is demanding the descendants of some victims pay restitution to the descendants of other victims. Imagine Queen Isabella robs my grandpa to buy a gun, which she then uses to kill your grandpa. It's bizarre to hold that this would require me to compensate you.

INSTITUTIONS ARE THE ANSWER, UNFORTUNATELY

The dominant view in mainstream development economics is that sustained economic growth results mainly from having good economic and political institutions. Institutions "are the rules of the game in a society or, more formally, are the humanly devised constraints that shape human interaction."[9] As economist Dani Rodrik summarizes, when it comes to explaining economic growth and why some countries are rich and others poor, "the quality of institutions trumps everything else."[10]

Which institutions produce growth? Countries with (a) robust systems of private property and (b) open markets, (c) protected by the rule of law enforced by (d) stable and inclusive governments, offer much better prospects for significant and sustained development than those that lack such institutions. The countries with institutions a–d, such as Switzerland, Canada, Singapore, or Hong Kong, are nearly always rich; the countries that lack a–d are nearly always poor. The reasons why are well understood, though I can only summarize them here.

As Acemoglu and Robinson argue in *Why Nations Fail*, the main difference between good and bad institutions concerns the degree to which they foster extractive activity or instead encourage cooperation and productivity. The main difference concerns whom the institutions empower, and thus whom the institutions benefit. What they call *inclusive* institutions, such as open markets and strong protections for private property, empower people across society, and thus tend to benefit all. They give people a stake in and ability to invest long term and engage in mutually beneficial capital accumulation. By contrast, *extractive* institutions—such as dictatorships where the government owns the natural resources, or overly regulated economies where rent seekers rig the rules—empower only some, and thus tend to benefit only small groups of people at others' expense.

It's "unfortunate" that the institutional theory of wealth is correct. The reason it's unfortunate is that while we know which institutions create growth and which impede it, we don't know how to induce social change. We don't know how to get countries with bad institutions to switch to good institutions. Part of the reason institutional change is so difficult is that the leaders of countries with bad institutions nearly always have a stake in those bad institutions—they make their living by exploiting their subjects or selling favors.

THE AID ILLUSION

Though developed countries didn't get rich at the expense of poor countries, you might still hope we could solve world poverty by giving away money. It's a simple idea. We're rich. They're poor. We give them some cash. They stop being poor.

As Nobel Laureate economist Angus Deaton (himself an aid skeptic) notes, if that argument were sound, then curing world poverty would require barely anything from us:

> One of the stunning facts about global poverty is how little it would take to fix it, at least if we could magically transfer money into the bank accounts of the world's poor. In 2008, there were about 800 million people in the world living on less than $1.00 a day. On average, each of these people is "short" about $0.28 a day. . . . We could make up that shortfall with less than a quarter billion dollars a day. . . Taking . . . into account [differences in purchasing power in poor countries], . . . world poverty could be eliminated if every American adult donated $0.30 a day; or, if we could build a coalition of the willing from all the adults of Britain, France, Germany, and Japan, each would need to give only $0.15 a day.[11]

People may be selfish, but surely no one would balk at 15 cents a day to end extreme world poverty. It seems so easy!

But it's not easy, as Deaton then explains. In the past 50 years, hundreds of billions of dollars have been spent on government-to-government and other forms of international aid. Just between 2000 and 2010, governments provided $128 billion in foreign aid.[12] Has it done any good?

Looking at Africa over the past 50 years, Deaton finds an inverse relationship between growth and aid. He summarizes the empirics:

> Growth *decreased* steadily while aid *increased* steadily. When aid fell off, after the end of the Cold War, growth picked up; the end of the Cold War took away one of the main rationales for aid to Africa, and African growth rebounded . . . [A] more accurate punchline would be "the Cold War is over, and Africa won," because the West reduced aid.[13]

Economists Left and Right generally agree. (Philosophers of global justice generally ignore such economics or cherry-pick the minority dissenting studies.) In a comprehensive review of the existing empirical literature, Hristos Doucouliagos and Martin Paldam conclude that, overall, "after 40 years of years of development aid, the evidence indicates that aid has not been effective."[14] Overall, the research generally finds that aid is more likely to hurt than help. In general, economists find that aid helps a bit in countries that have pretty good institutions, but tends to hurt in countries with bad institutions.[15]

Why would it *hurt*? Acemoglu and Robinson write,

> The idea that rich Western countries should provide large amounts of "development aid" in order to solve the problem of [world] poverty . . . is based on an incorrect understanding of what causes poverty. Countries such as Afghanistan are poor because of their extractive institutions—which result in a lack of property rights, law and order, or well-functioning legal systems and the stifling domination of national and, more often, local elites over political and economic life. The same institutional problems mean that foreign aid will be ineffective,

as it will be plundered and is unlikely to be delivered where it is supposed to go. In the worst-case scenario, it will prop up the regimes that are the very root of the problems of those societies.[16]

The problem is that poor countries suffer negative feedback loops. They are governed by abusive elites, people who make a living (and stay in power) by extracting resources from their countries and people. In such conditions, to pour more money into a country usually means lining the pockets of the abusers, not feeding the hungry.

When rulers make a living by extracting resources from their societies, sending more money means increasing the rewards of being in power. Foreign aid tends to make bad governments thrive without the support of their citizens, encourage factions within those countries (different agencies, bureaucracies, strongmen) to compete for power in order to gain control of the incoming aid, and tends to subsidize corruption. It escalates conflicts, civil wars, and human rights violations. Rather than inducing development and growth, aid often prolongs and worsens the conditions that produce poverty and need in the first place.

No one denies that aid *can* do good sometimes. Christopher Coyne, himself another major critic of foreign aid, finds that aid seems to be most effective in increasing pre-determined outputs in response to clear-cut crises. If there's a sudden famine, buying and distributing food stops starvation. (Though, as Coyne documents, if can also fail at that, and sometimes even makes things worse.[17])

But there is distinction between *aid* and *development*. Development happens when a society begins to grow economically, and the conditions that cause people's poverty start to disappear. There is simply no track record of aid helping to spur economic development. The reasons why are clear: To get rich, countries need good institutions, but you can't export good institutions the way you can send a sack of rice.

AN OBLIGATION TO HELP IS AN OBLIGATION TO HELP

Philosophers of global justice spend their time debating which normative principles would ground duties of international aid. To induce their readers to have moral intuitions which favor redistribution, they often rely on thought experiments like these:

1. If grandma gave 20 of her grandchildren 80 percent of the pie, and the other 166 grandkids only 20 percent, should the rich 20 give the poor 166 more pie?

2. Suppose my grandpa stole your grandpa's watch, which I then inherit. Should I give it "back" to you?

3. If I see a kid drowning in a puddle, shouldn't I save him, even if saving him ruins my expensive shoes?

Philosophers think the actual world is analogous to thought experiments like these. This makes foreign aid seem morally mandatory.

But economics, surprisingly, tells us that philosophers are bad at philosophy. The problem is that these three thought experiments, and all the variations on them, are *irrelevant*. The gap between rich and poor did not result from an unfair initial distribution of resources or from theft. And saving the world's poor from poverty looks almost nothing like pulling a drowning kid from a pond.

In 1799, US President George Washington got a bad sore throat. His family called in doctors, who then killed him. Yes, killed him. His doctors (the best available in his day) subscribed to false and counterproductive beliefs about medicine. They bled him multiple times, extracting at least forty-eight ounces of blood. They also blistered his skin, induced vomiting, and administered an enema. The dehydrated president then died. When Martha Washington sent for the doctors, despite her best intentions, she was ordering a death sentence.

An obligation to help the poor is an obligation to actually help them. Good intentions don't matter. Too often, developed countries play the part of Washington's doctors, killing instead of helping, administering a medicine worse than the disease. Philosophers of global justice today play the role of Martha Washington. They mean well, but they're calling in the bad doctors.

I'm not saying we should do nothing. I'm instead claiming we should do what works. "We" (the people in the developed world) helped Taiwan,

Hong Kong, South Korea, and Japan—countries that were poor in the 1950s but are rich today—become rich not by giving them aid, but by buying their products as they liberalized their economies. If we want to help, we will open borders to immigrants and we'll increase international trade. We'll confine foreign aid to its rightful place and stop pretending it's the solution.

NOTES

1. Max Roser and Esteban Ortiz-Ospina, "Global Extreme Poverty," in *Our World in Data,* accessed February 2, 2018, https://ourworldindata.org/extreme-poverty/.

2. Chart made using data from Angus Maddison, *Contours of the World Economy, 1–2030 AD: Essays in Macro-Economic History* (New York: Oxford University Press 2007), 70.

3. Thomas Pogge, "Eradicating Systemic Poverty: Brief for a Global Resources Dividend," *Journal of Human Development* 2 (2001): 59–77, p. 65.

4. David Weil, *Economic Growth*, 3rd Edition (New York: Pearson, 2013), 453.

5. Weil, *Economic Growth*, 450.

6. Thomas Pogge, "Poverty and Human Rights," accessed Feb. 2, 2018, http://www2.ohchr.org/english/issues/poverty/expert/docs/Thomas_Pogge_Summary.pdf

7. Adam Smith, *The Wealth of Nations,* V.3.92.

8. Or better, ended up being forced to set up inclusive institutions. See Daron Acemoglu, Simon Johnson, and James Robinson, "The Colonial Origins of Comparative Development: An Empirical Investigation," *American Economic Review* 91 (2001): 1369–1401; Daron Acemoglu and James Robinson, *Why Nations Fail* (New York: Crown Business, 2013).

9. North, *Institutions, Institutional Change, and Economic Performance*, 3.

10. Dani Rodrik, Arvind Subramanian, and Francisco Trebbi, "Institutions Rule: The Primacy of Institutions over Geography and Integration in Economic Development," *Journal of Economic Growth* 9 (2004): 131–165.

11. Angus Deaton, *The Great Escape* (Princeton: Princeton University Press, 2013), 268–269.

12. Christopher Coyne, *Doing Bad by Doing Good: Why Humanitarian Aid Fails* (Stanford: Stanford University Press, 2013), 47.

13. Deaton, *Great Escape*, 285.

14. Hristos Doucouliagos and Martin Paldam, "Aid Effectiveness on Accumulation. A Meta Study," *Kyklos* 59 (2006): 227–254.

15. Here, I draw from Coyne, *Doing Bad by Doing Good*, 51.

16. Acemoglu and Robinson, *Why Nations Fail*, 452–453.

17. Coyne, *Doing Bad by Doing Good.*

Jason Brennan: International Aid: Not the Cure You Were Hoping For

1. If Brennan is right, the solution to world poverty requires massive change to the institutions of poorer countries. Assuming that is correct, what, if anything, are the obligations of richer countries to help with such institutional change?

2. Brennan allows that many rich nations have a history of exploiting ones that are now poor, but denies that this generates any duty of compensation or reparation. Do you agree with his reasoning? Why or why not?

3. Does the dire need of others ever, by itself, impose a moral duty to assist them? If not, why not? If so, does this justify some duty to provide aid to distant strangers?

4. Would it be morally acceptable for wealthier countries to provide aid to poorer ones, but only on the condition that the poorer nations improved their institutions?

5. Brennan says that, when it comes to foreign aid, "good intentions don't matter." Results do. If an aid program fails to help the needy, then it is unjustified, no matter how well-meaning the donors. Do you agree? Why or why not?

Refugees and the Right to Control Immigration

Christopher Heath Wellman

Christopher Heath Wellman's article is an extended defense of the moral rights of legitimate states to exclude outsiders, including those who hope to immigrate to such states. The right to exclude is not, he thinks, absolute. But while there may be some exceptions, the right is more robust and extensive than many assume. It is so strong that legitimate states typically have a moral right to exclude even refugees from their borders, should they choose to do so.

Wellman's core argument is built upon three assumptions. First, legitimate states are morally entitled to self-determination. Second, freedom of association is a very important element of self-determination. And, third, freedom of association entitles one to refuse to associate with others. Together, these support the view that legitimate states are morally entitled to refuse to "associate" with non-citizens, which means, in practical terms, that such states may deny outsiders entry to the state's territory or an offer of citizenship.

Wellman uses an argument from analogy to support his views. A person has a right to self-determination, which entitles her to freedom of association, which gives her a right to refuse to associate with others at her discretion. This right explains why it would be wrong to force a person to get married against her will, or to take someone into her home when she wants to bar the door against him. Legitimate states possess these rights as well, and they entitle such states to refuse, at their discretion, to extend citizenship or residence to outsiders.

Wellman realizes that many wealthier countries have a history of exploiting the countries whose citizens are seeking to emigrate. But he believes that there are usually ways, other than by allowing immigration, by which those wealthier states can fulfill their duties of justice to those they have wronged.

I believe that legitimate states have a right to political self-determination which entitles them to design and enforce their own immigration policies.[1] This right is admittedly not absolute, but I do not think it is outweighed as easily or as often as most presume. To support these claims, I shall defend a legitimate state's right to exclude outsiders and then argue that this right is typically not outweighed by the competing claims of refugees.

THE RIGHT TO EXCLUDE

My argument for a legitimate state's right to exclude outsiders is built on three foundational premises: (1) legitimate states are entitled to self-determination, (2) freedom of association is an integral component of self-determination, and (3) freedom of association entitles one to refuse to associate with others as one sees fit. Based on this reasoning, I conclude that, just as an individual's right to

This essay was commissioned for the fifth edition of *The Ethical Life* (New York: Oxford University Press, 2021).

1. This paper utilizes excerpts from my book (co-authored with Phillip Cole), *Debating the Ethics of Immigration: Is There a Right to Exclude?* (New York: Oxford University Press, 2011), in which these ideas and arguments are developed and defended at greater length.

self-determination explains why she may choose whether or not to marry any given suitor, the citizens of a legitimate state are free collectively to offer or refuse membership in their political community to any given prospective immigrant.

It is not difficult to establish the truth of the second and third premises. To see that freedom of association is integral to self-determination and that enjoying freedom of association requires that one be free to refuse to associate with others, we need only imagine a setting in which one's father, say, has sole discretion to choose who his children will marry. Whatever one might think of this type of arrangement, it clearly does not respect rights to self-determination. Freedom of association involves more than merely the right to get married; it includes the right to reject any and all suitors one prefers not to marry. And this explains why those of us who value individual autonomy take such offense at the thought of institutions which bestow upon parents the authority to force spouses on their children.

But while few deny that individuals have a right to freedom of association in the marital realm, some may question whether corporate political entities are the types of things that could have such a right. To see that states are entitled to an analogous sphere of political self-determination, think of a country like Norway and its relations with Sweden and the European Union. Norway is currently an associate member of the EU, and it enjoys close relations with Sweden, the country from which it seceded in 1905. But now imagine that Sweden (inspired, perhaps by the reunification of Germany) wanted to reunite with Norway or that the EU wanted Norway to become a full member. Would Sweden or the EU have the right to unilaterally annex Norway, or would it be impermissible for them to do so without Norway's consent? It seems clear that neither Sweden nor the EU is morally entitled to forcibly annex Norway. If either wants to merge with Norway, it may invite Norway to join forces, but Norway is free to either accept or decline such an invitation. Indeed, even if it is clear to all that the Norwegians would be better off after the merger, it remains Norway's decision to make, and no other country or international organization may

permissibly force itself onto Norway without its consent.

And notice that one cannot insist upon Norway's right to remain independent of Sweden without implicitly affirming its right to self-determination, because the best explanation for the impermissibility of Sweden's unilateral annexation of Norway is that it violates Norway's sovereign right to independence. But if Norway's right to self-determination entitles it to refuse to associate with other corporate political entities like Sweden or the EU, then why is it not similarly within its rights to refuse to associate with any given Swedish or European citizen? It seems to me, then, that just as an individual has a right to determine whom (if anyone) he or she would like to marry, a group of fellow-citizens has a right to determine whom (if anyone) it would like to invite into its political community. And just as an individual's freedom of association entitles one to remain single, a legitimate state's freedom of association entitles it to exclude all foreigners from its political community.

Here two potential objections present themselves. First, it may strike some as misleading to compare having discretion over one's partner in marriage to the selection of potential immigrants, because having control over one's associates is plainly paramount in marital relations but seems of little consequence within the relatively impersonal context of political life. Second, even if we concede that a legitimate state's right to freedom of association applies in its relations to other countries or international institutions, this seems quite different from alleging that large political regimes enjoy freedom of association with respect to individual foreigners.

In response to the first worry, I admit that freedom of association is considerably more important in intimate relations. Acknowledging this is unproblematic, however, since it amounts to conceding only that rights to freedom of association are more valuable in intimate contexts, not that they do not exist elsewhere. At most, then, this objection merely highlights that it may require more to defeat the presumptive right in intimate contexts. Notice, however, that there are many non-intimate associations where we rightly value freedom of association very highly. Religious associations in which people attend to matters of conscience and political groups through which members express themselves can often be large and impersonal, and yet we are extremely reluctant to restrict their associative rights.

Despite the admitted lack of intimacy, freedom of association is also clearly important for political states. To appreciate this, notice that even members of relatively insignificant associations like golf clubs are often (understandably) concerned about their control over potential members. These members typically care about their club's membership rules for at least two sets of reasons. First and most obviously, the size of the club affects one's experience as a member. In the case of a private golf club, for instance, some may want to expand membership, so that each individual will be required to pay less in dues, while others might well be against adding new members for fear that the increased number of golfers will result in limited access to, and more wear and tear on, the golf course. In short, whereas some might be motivated to cut costs, others will be happy to pay higher fees for a more exclusive golfing experience. Second and perhaps less obviously, members will care about the rules of membership because all new members will subsequently have a say in how the club is organized. In other words, caring about one's experience as a club member gives one reason to care about the rules for admitting new members, because, once admitted, new members will typically have a say in determining the future course of the club.

And if the reasons to concern oneself with the membership rules of one's golf club are straightforward, there is nothing curious about people caring so much about the rules governing who may enter their political communities, even though a citizen will typically never meet, let alone have anything approaching intimate relations with, the vast majority of her compatriots. Indeed, there are a number of obvious reasons why citizens would care deeply about how many and which type of immigrants can enter their country. Even if we put to one side all concerns about the state's culture, economy, and political functioning, for instance, people's lives are obviously affected by substantial changes in population density, so it seems only natural that

citizens who like higher population density would welcome huge numbers of immigrants, while those with contrary tastes would prefer a more exclusive policy. And in the real world, of course, a substantial influx of foreigners will also almost invariably affect the host state's cultural make-up, the way its economy functions, and/or how its political system operates. And let me be clear: I am not assuming that all of these changes will necessarily be for the worse. More modestly, I am emphasizing only that citizens will often care deeply about their country's culture, economy and political arrangements, and thus, depending upon their particular preferences, may well seek more or fewer immigrants, or perhaps more or fewer immigrants of a given linguistic, cultural, economic and/or political profile.

In the case of Mexican immigrants into the United States, for instance, it is not the least bit surprising that some favor a more open policy, while others lobby for the government to heighten its efforts to stem what they regard as a "flood" of unwelcome newcomers. Without taking a stand on this particular controversy, here I wish to stress only the obvious point that, even with large anonymous groups like contemporary bureaucratic states, the number and types of constituents have an obvious and direct effect upon what it is like to be a member of these groups. Thus, unless one questions why anyone would care about their experience as citizens, there is no reason to doubt that we should be so concerned about our country's immigration policy. What is more, as in the case of golf clubs, the crucial point is that—whether one interacts personally with them or not—one's fellow citizens play roles in charting the course that one's country takes. And since a country's immigration policy determines who has the opportunity to join the current citizens in shaping the country's future, this policy will matter enormously to any citizen who cares what course her political community will take.

This connection between a group's membership and its future direction underscores why freedom of association is such an integral component of self-determination. No collective can be fully self-determining without enjoying freedom of association because, when the members of a group can change, an essential part of group self-determination is exercising control over what the "self" is. To appreciate this point, consider again the controversy over Mexican immigration into the United States. It is not merely that large numbers of these immigrants would almost certainly change the culture of those areas where they tend to relocate *en masse*; it is also that (if legally admitted and given the standard voting rights of citizenship) these new members will help determine future laws in the United States, including its immigration policy toward other potential immigrants from Mexico (and elsewhere). Thus, if I am right that legitimate political states are entitled to political self-determination, there appears to be every reason to conclude that this privileged position of sovereignty includes a weighty presumptive right to freedom of association, a right which entitles these states to include or exclude foreigners as they see fit.

Consider now the worry that, while legitimate states are indeed entitled to freedom of association, this right applies only against other corporate entities, such as foreign countries or international institutions; it does not hold against individual persons who would like to enter a given political community. An objector of this stripe shies away from a blanket denial of political freedom of association in recognition of the unpalatable implications such a position would allow. Think again of contemporary Norway, for instance. If one denied Norway's right to freedom of association, then there seems to be no principled way to explain why Sweden or the European Union would act impermissibly if either were to forcibly annex it. Presumably neither Sweden nor the EU may unilaterally merge with Norway; rather, Norway has the right to either accept or refuse these unions. But affirming Norway's right to reject these mergers is just to say that Norway enjoys a right to freedom of association which holds against foreign countries like Sweden and international organizations like the EU. It does not necessarily follow, this objection continues, that Norway therefore has the right to deny admittance to any given Swede or citizen of an EU country who would like to enter Norway. Indeed, in terms of self-determination, the contrast between merging with Sweden and admitting an individual Swede is striking, in that only the former would appear to seriously impact Norway's

control over its internal affairs. Thus, insofar as freedom of association is defended as an important component of self-determination, perhaps sovereign states enjoy freedom of association only with respect to macro institutions and not in their micro dealings with individual persons.

An individual immigrant would admittedly not have anything like the impact on Norway's political self-determination that a forced merger with Sweden or the EU would. Nonetheless, I am unmoved by this objection for at least two basic reasons. First, we routinely (and rightly, I think) ascribe rights of freedom of association against individuals to large, nonpolitical institutions. Second, political states would lose a crucial portion of their self-determination if they were unable to refuse to associate with individuals. Consider these points in turn.

Let us begin by considering two garden-variety large institutions like Microsoft Corporation and Harvard University. Presumably each of these institutions enjoys freedom of association, and thus Microsoft could choose to either accept or reject an offer to merge with Cisco Systems and Harvard would have the discretion as to whether or not to accept an offer to form a cooperative alliance with, say, Stanford University. But notice that we do not restrict their freedom of association exclusively to their dealings with other corporate entitles; Microsoft's and Harvard's rights to self-determination also give them discretion over their relations with individuals. No matter how qualified I may be, I may not simply assign myself a paying job at Microsoft, for instance, nor may I unilaterally decide to enroll in Harvard as a student or assume a position on their faculty. And if large bureaucratic organizations like Microsoft and Harvard are perfectly within their rights to refuse to associate with various individuals, why should we think that freedom of association would operate any differently for political states? At the very least, it seems as though anyone who wanted to press this second objection would owe us an explanation as to why the logic of freedom of association does not apply to political states as it plainly does in other contexts.

The best way to make this case would presumably be to point out that, because political states are so enormous, an individual's immigration will have no discernible impact upon any given country's capacity for self-determination. I acknowledge that one person's immigration is typically insignificant, but this fact strikes me as insufficient to vindicate the objection. Notice, for instance, that one unilaterally appointed student at Harvard or a single employee at Microsoft would not make much of a difference at either institution, but we would never conclude from this that Harvard and Microsoft lack discretion over their respective admissions and hiring processes. What is more, as the example of Mexican immigrants into the U.S. illustrates, even if a solitary immigrant would be unlikely to have much of an impact on any given state, a sufficient number of immigrants certainly could make an enormous difference. And unless a state is able to exercise authority over the individuals who might immigrate, it is in no position to control its future self-determination. Thus, the very same principle of political self-determination which entitles Norway to either join or reject an association with other countries like those in the EU also entitles Norway to set its own immigration policy for potential individual immigrants.

To summarize our discussion of these two potential objections: Even though (1) the association among compatriots may be far less important than the intimate relations among family members, and (2) a single immigrant is likely to have no discernible influence upon a political community's capacity to be self-determining, legitimate political states have weighty presumptive rights to freedom of association which entitle them to either accept or reject individual applicants for immigration as they see fit. In short, the principle of political self-determination explains why countries have a right to design and enforce their own immigration policies. Whether any given (legitimate) state wants to have entirely open borders, exclude all outsiders, or enact some intermediate policy, it has a presumptive right to do so.

As mentioned earlier, though, this right is merely presumptive and thus remains liable to being overridden in any given set of circumstances. Below I will consider whether this presumptive right is necessarily outweighed by the competing claims of refugees. First, though, I want to emphasize that I am arguing on behalf of a *deontological* right to limit immigration rather than a *consequential* recommendation as to how any given state should act.

There is a big difference between defending an agent's right to X and recommending that this agent actually do X. One can defend Norway's right to remain independent of Sweden or the EU, for instance, without taking a stand on the separate question of whether Norway would be wise to join. This combination of positions may at first seem contradictory, but it is not. What Norway ought to do and who is entitled to decide what Norway does are two separate issues. Thus, it is important to bear in mind that, in defending a legitimate state's right to exclude potential immigrants, I am offering no opinion on the separate question as to how countries might best exercise this right.

There are several reasons I am not comfortable making any recommendations as to how jealously states should guard their borders. First and most obviously, determining what immigration policy would be best for a country's citizens and/or humanity as a whole requires knowledge of a great deal of detailed empirical information that I simply lack. Just as importantly, though, it seems to me that there is unlikely to be any "one size fits all" prescription which would be appropriate for every country in the world. On the contrary, there is no reason why a certain number and type of immigrants could not be beneficial in one country and yet quite harmful in another; it all depends on the particular social, cultural, economic and political circumstances of the host country. Consider, for instance, the economic impact of immigration. While some writers warn that opening a country's markets to outsiders will have potentially disastrous effects, others counter that the impact of open borders will (in the long run, at least) invariably be beneficial, since removing any artificial boundary will allow the market to operate more efficiently. I would guess, however, that the truth lies somewhere between these two polar positions. Even if we restrict our focus exclusively to the economic impact upon those who were initially in the host state (as these debates often implicitly presume we should), how helpful any given influx of newcomers would be seems to me to depend upon a number of factors, such as this country's antecedent level of unemployment and the types of skills and work ethic these immigrants have. In addition to determining what the overall effect of the immigrants would be, it is important to consider how the various costs and benefits are distributed. In many cases the influx of relatively unskilled workers may disproportionately help relatively wealthy business owners (who benefit from the increased supply of labor) and hurt working-class people (who now face greater competition for jobs whose wages have been decreased). Thus, if one believes that we should be especially concerned about our worst-off compatriots, then this might provide a reason of justice to limit immigration even in circumstances in which the overall net economic impact of more porous borders would be positive.

In light of these observations, I am reluctant to recommend a specific immigration policy as the ideal solution for any given (let alone every) state to follow. If forced to show my hand, however, I must confess that I would generally favor more open borders than the status quo. I appreciate that countries have a variety of good reasons to refrain from completely opening their borders, but I suspect that many of the world's current policies are more the result of unprincipled politicians' exploiting the xenophobia of their constituents for short-term political gain than of well-reasoned assessments of what will be to the long-term advantage. In saying this, however, I am in no way retreating from my contention that legitimate regimes may set their own immigration policy. In my view, there are deontological reasons to respect a legitimate state's rights of political self-determination, and so those countries which qualify have a deontologically based moral right to freedom of association. Thus, whether they exercise this right rationally or not, it is their call to make. Just as my friends and family may not forcibly interfere with my imprudent decisions to get married or divorced, for instance, external parties must respect a legitimate state's dominion over its borders, even if the resulting policy seems plainly irrational.

To recapitulate the highlights of what has been a relatively long discussion: One cannot adequately capture why it is in principle wrong for an external body such as Sweden or the EU to forcibly annex a country like Norway without invoking a state's right to political self-determination. But if legitimate political regimes enjoy a sphere of self-determination which allows them to refuse relations with foreign countries and international organizations, it seems only natural to conclude that they are similarly entitled to reject associating with individual foreigners. Thus, any regime which satisfactorily protects and respects human rights is entitled to unilaterally design and enforce its own immigration policy. In sum, just as an individual has the right to determine whom (if anyone) she would like to marry, a group of fellow-citizens has a right to determine whom (if anyone) it would like to invite into its political community. And just as an individual's freedom of association entitles her to remain single, a corporate political entity's freedom of association entitles it to exclude all foreigners.

As striking as this conclusion may sound, it is not ultimately all that controversial once one recalls that the right in question is not absolute, but merely presumptive. Many who insist that morality requires (more) open borders might happily concede all of the conclusions for which I have argued to this point, for instance, because they are confident that whatever presumptive rights legitimate states have to exclude foreigners are often (if not always) overridden by more weighty moral concerns. Space limitations do not allow me to attend to the many powerful arguments that have been offered in defense of open borders, but I will argue below that even refugees do not necessarily have as strong of a claim to immigrate as one might initially suspect. This will not establish that legitimate states may exclude all prospective immigrants, of course, but hopefully it will lend credence to my claim that a state's presumptive right to exclude outsiders holds up quite well against the competing claims of outsiders.

REFUGEES

Following the 1951 Convention Relating to the Status of Refugees, international law defines a refugee as someone who "owing to a well-founded fear of being persecuted for reasons of race, religion, nationality, membership of a particular social group, or political opinion, is outside the country of his nationality, and is unable to or, owing to such fear, is unwilling to avail himself of the protection of that country."[2] Critics have protested that this definition is too narrow in at least three important ways.[3] First, why focus exclusively on victims of group-based persecution? And even if we do think in terms of groups, why restrict ourselves to these particular groups? What if someone is persecuted *qua* woman or *qua* homosexual, for instance? Second, given the variety of threats to living a minimally decent human life, why insist that only those vulnerable to persecution can qualify as refugees? What about so-called economic refugees or those who are fleeing a civil war, for instance? Third, why think that someone must already be "outside the country of his nationality" in order to qualify? What if an individual is being detained at the border or is too frail or impoverished to migrate without assistance, for example?

I share these worries about this restricted definition of refugees. If human rights are best understood as the protections humans need against the standard threats to living a minimally decent life, then it strikes me that anyone whose human rights are in jeopardy should qualify as a refugee. Defined thusly, a refugee would be anyone who has a particularly urgent claim to help because her current state is either unable or unwilling to protect her human rights. I will not press this issue here, however, because our interest in refugees is a potential exception to my claim that legitimate states have the right to exclude outsiders. Retaining the traditional, narrow definition seems appropriate, then, since this provides the toughest challenge to my account.

It is not difficult to see why refugees are thought to be an especially compelling counterexample to anyone who seeks to defend a state's discretion over immigration. First, unlike someone who merely wants to migrate to improve an already good life (such as an artist who wants to live in New York, for example), the refugee is unable to live a minimally decent human life in her home country. More importantly, insofar as this person specifically needs protection from her state, she cannot be helped from abroad. Unlike a poor Chadian to whom Norwegians might ship resources, for instance, an Iraqi Kurd persecuted by Saddam Hussein's Baathist regime apparently could not be helped in any other way than by being given refuge in a foreign country. Finally, given that the refugee has fled her home country and is requesting asylum from the new state, the latter is now involved in the situation. As regrettable as it might be for Norway to refuse to send funds to starving Chadians, for instance, Norway is not thought to be implicated in their starvation in the same way it would be if it forcibly returned a Kurdish asylum seeker to Iraq, where she was subsequently tortured. Combining these points, a refugee's plight appears morally tantamount to that of a baby who has been left on one's doorstep in the dead of winter. Only a moral monster would deny the duty to bring this infant into her home, and no theorist who endorses human rights could deny that states must admit refugees.

I agree that the citizens of wealthy states are obligated to help refugees, but I am not convinced that this assistance must come in the form of more open admissions. Just as we might send food and other resources to the world's poor, we can try to help persecuted foreigners in their home state. Imagine that Iraqi Kurds request asylum in Norway, for instance. Assuming that these Kurds are in fact being persecuted, it is natural to conclude that Norway has no choice but to allow them to immigrate. But this conclusion is too hasty. While there would presumably be nothing wrong with welcoming these Iraqis into the Norwegian political community, there are other options if the Norwegians would prefer not to expand their citizenship. If Norway were able to protect these Kurds in their homeland, creating a safe haven with a no-fly zone in Northern Iraq, for instance, then there would be nothing wrong with Norway's assisting them in this fashion. (Indeed, in many ways, helping in this manner seems preferable.) The core point, of course, is that

---

2. Convention, art. 1A(2).

3. For an excellent discussion of these matters, see Andrew E. Shacknove, "Who Is a Refugee?" *Ethics* 95 (January 1985): 274–284.

if these persecuted Kurds have a right against Norwegians, it is a general right to protection from their persecutors, not the more specific right to refuge *in Norway*. If Norway provides these Kurds refuge in Iraq, then the Kurds cease to qualify as refugees and thus no longer have any special claim to migrate to Norway.

Some will resist my proposal on the grounds that Norway should not meddle in Iraq's domestic affairs, but this objection wrongly presumes an orientation in which every *de facto* state occupies a privileged position of moral dominion over all matters on its territory. On my view, only *legitimate* states are entitled to political self-determination, where legitimacy is understood in terms of satisfactorily protecting the rights of one's constituents and respecting the rights of all others. And any state that persecutes its own citizens (as the Baathist regime did when it targeted Kurds) clearly does not adequately secure the human rights of its citizens and thus is manifestly not entitled to the normal sovereign rights which typically make humanitarian intervention in principle wrong. And note: I am not saying that it will always be easy or advisable to intervene and fix a refugee's problem at its source. (On the contrary, I would think that countries would more often prefer to admit refugees than to forcibly intervene on their behalf.) I allege only there is nothing in principle which necessarily prohibits foreign states like Norway from providing refuge to persecuted groups like Iraqi Kurds in their native countries.

At this point, one might protest that Norway must admit these Kurdish refugees at least until it has adequately secured a safe haven in Northern Iraq. This may be right: No matter how jealously the Norwegians might guard their political membership, the Kurds must not be returned until their protection against persecution can be guaranteed. It is important to notice, however, that Norwegians need not extend the benefits of political membership to these temporary visitors any more than it must give citizenship to other guests, like tourists, who are in the country for only a short time. What is more, if I am right that there is nothing wrong with Norway's intervening in Iraq once the Kurdish refugees have already arrived on Norway's doorstep, then presumably it would equally be permissible for Norway to intervene preemptively, so as to avert the mass migration. After all, Norway's intervention is justified by the initial acts of Iraqi persecution, not by the subsequent migration of masses of refugees.

Before closing, I would like to return to the analogy of the baby on the doorstep, not to insist that it is inapt, but because I think reflecting upon this domestic case actually confirms my analysis of refugees. Suppose, then, that I open my front door in the dead of winter and find a newborn baby wrapped in blankets. Clearly, I must bring the infant in from the cold, but it does not follow that I must then adopt the child and raise her as my own. Perhaps it would be permissible to do so, but it seems clear that I would not be required to incorporate this child into my family if I would prefer not to. This child has a right to a decent future, and its arrival on my doorstep may well obligate me to attend to her needs until I can find her a satisfactory home, but the infant's valid claim not to be left out in the cold does not entail the entirely distinct right to permanent inclusion in my family. I thus conclude that the analogy between a refugee and a baby left on one's doorstep is both apt and instructive. In both cases, one can non-voluntarily incur a stringent duty to help the imperiled individual. But just as one can satisfactorily discharge one's duty to the vulnerable child without permanently adopting it, a state can entirely fulfill its responsibility to persecuted refugees without allowing them to immigrate into its political community.

In the end, then, I respond to the challenge posed by the plight of refugees by conceding a stringent duty to help but insisting that this obligation is disjunctive. Just as wealthy states may permissibly respond to global poverty either by opening their borders or by helping to eliminate this poverty at its source, countries that receive refugees on their political doorstep are well within their rights either to invite these refugees into their political communities or to intervene in the refugees' home state to ensure that they are effectively protected from persecution there. I thus conclude that, as tragic as the cases of many refugees no doubt are, they do not necessarily constitute an exception to my thesis that legitimate states are entitled to exclude all outsiders, even those who desperately seek to gain admission.

Christopher Heath Wellman: Refugees and the Right to Control Immigration

1. Reconstruct Wellman's central argument for allowing legitimate states to refuse entry or citizenship to outsiders. Which premise do you think most vulnerable, and why?

2. How plausible is Wellman's analogy between, on the one hand, an individual's right to refuse to marry a suitor or refuse to let someone into her home, and, on the other, a state's right to refuse entry or citizenship to outsiders?

3. Here is another analogy: you are lost in the woods, starving, and see a cabin. It's locked, but through a window you see that there is food inside. You can either remain outside and die of exposure or starvation, or break into the cabin and save yourself. Many would say that you are morally permitted to save yourself, and—here's the analogy—refugees are in exactly the same position with regard to wealthy countries. What are the implications of Wellman's view for this case? Do you find those implications plausible or implausible?

4. Many states have become wealthy through a long history of exploiting other countries, some of whose citizens are now seeking to emigrate. Does this history impose any duties on wealthy states to open their borders? Why or why not?

5. Some argue that an open borders policy is morally problematic because it creates "brain drain"—a situation in which a significant proportion of the most educated and talented within a struggling nation decide to emigrate, leaving the struggling country in even worse shape. Does this constitute a good reason for restricting immigration?

Open Borders

Javier Hidalgo

Imagine that you wake up one morning and see a wall of barbed wire surrounding your neighborhood. When you try to cross, in order to look for work, go to church, or visit a relative, a guard forbids you from doing so. In anything but a very unusual, emergency situation, enforcing this barrier violates your freedom of movement and your freedom of association. And that, in turn, threatens your freedom to seek an occupation, practice your religion, and sustain family relations.

Javier Hidalgo introduces this thought experiment to draw a clear parallel with immigration policies that place barriers against migrant entry. He allows that there may be exceptional cases where, all things considered, it is justified to block a migrant from entering a country, but those special cases aside, every country (including our own)

This essay was commissioned expressly for *Living Ethics*, second edition. © Javier Hidalgo, 2021.

should have open borders. Failing to do so, he argues, violates rights to freedom of movement, association, occupational choice, and religious freedom.

Hidalgo then confronts various criticisms of an open borders policy. Some claim that while it would be generous to open borders to noncitizens, we have no moral duty to do so. Hidalgo replies that we owe everyone, citizen and noncitizen alike, a wide variety of duties that require us not to interfere with their rights (including the right to move about freely). Others argue that immigration ends up costing citizens more, in order to pay for various social benefits of the new entrants. But Hidalgo points to data that indicate that more immigration tends to make societies wealthier and better off. Some claim that crime rates rise with immigration; Hidalgo denies that this is so. He then argues that closing borders would be immoral even if immigration had unavoidably negative overall social costs for existing citizens, as there are strict limits on what governments may do to help their citizens. Hidalgo once more argues by analogy: "If it's wrong for me to coerce and assault strangers in order to benefit my children, then it is hard to see why it would be fine for the government to coerce and assault foreigners for the benefit of citizens. But that's just what immigration restrictions do." Another argument is that the preservation of culture allows us to close our borders if we choose. Hidalgo replies that many immigrants assimilate to the prevailing culture, that many countries, such as the United States, are already highly multicultural, and that we are not allowed to preserve a culture if doing so requires denying the important rights of others. Finally, he considers the objection that countries are like private clubs and, therefore, are allowed to forbid others from becoming members. Hidalgo argues that this analogy is flawed; while private clubs may restrict what people wear, what they say, and the religion they practice, governments are forbidden from doing these things. This shows, says Hidalgo, that the analogy between governments and private associations is misleading.

INTRODUCTION

Gabriel Hernández Cortez is a Mexican citizen from Guanajuato in central Mexico. In Guanajuato, Gabriel worked in construction and earned a few dollars daily. Gabriel's son, Carlos, became ill and was hospitalized. The cost of Carlos' medical care was ruinous for his family's finances. His wife and two children had to move in with her parents. Meanwhile, Gabriel set out for the United States to earn more money. Gabriel says: "I prefer to stay home. But the only way to make it is to come north . . . I just want a very tiny slice of pie. I just want to work for a little bit of money."

But Gabriel couldn't reach the United States. Gabriel tried crossing the border four times. Each time American immigrant agents caught him and turned him back. In one case, border agents caught Gabriel as he was climbing a barbed-wire fence. An agent grabbed Gabriel by his hair and the barbed wire cut his leg. He says: "I don't blame la migra. They're just doing their jobs, enforcing the laws that come down from above." Gabriel remained in Naco, Sonora and slept out in a central plaza in the city, pondering how to cross the border. I don't know what happened to him.[1]

Here's another case. Gloria lived in Phoenix with her four children where she worked as a

This chapter draws heavily on my past work, particularly: Javier Hidalgo, "The Libertarian Case for Open Borders," in *The Routledge Handbook of Libertarianism*, ed. Jason Brennan, Bas Van der Vossen, and David Schmidtz (New York, NY: Routledge, 2017), 377–389; Javier Hidalgo, *Unjust Borders: Individuals and the Ethics of Immigration* (New York, NY: Routledge, 2018), chapter 1.

housekeeper. She was a single mom and she was also undocumented. One day she was arrested. Her employer had been operating drop houses where unauthorized migrants would stay after crossing the border. Gloria says that she had nothing to do with it, but she was charged as an accomplice. After serving time in prison, she was deported to Mexico and lost custody of her children. The children were separated and put into foster care. Gloria now lives in Nogales, Mexico. She works in a factory for $15 per day and lives in a plywood shed. Gloria rarely sees her children. Gloria says: "when I was young and my kids were little, I thought that I could never live without them. I never thought that one day they'd grow up and I'd be far away from them. But you have to learn how to live like this." Her children visit her at the border where they can talk through a mesh fence, but these visits are infrequent. Gloria's son says: "I just sometimes feel like I'm a stranger to her. And sometimes she's a stranger to me."[2]

The laws and policies that forbid migrants like Gabriel from crossing borders and that deport migrants like Gloria are immigration restrictions. Immigration restrictions stop foreigners from crossing borders and permanently residing in another state's territory. There's nothing special about the United States, of course. Every state enforces immigration restrictions.

Are immigration restrictions justified? My answer: generally speaking, no. My overall argument goes like this. Immigration restrictions interfere with valuable freedoms, such as freedom of association and occupational choice. So there's a presumption against immigration restrictions. Other moral considerations can in principle defeat this presumption. But they usually don't. We thus have reason to conclude that actual immigration restrictions are unjust.

I. FREEDOM OF MOVEMENT IS VALUABLE

Let's start with the claim that immigration restrictions interfere with valuable freedoms. To motivate this claim, let's consider a thought experiment.

Imagine that tomorrow you wake up in the morning and you start getting ready for work, just like every other day. As you're pulling out of your driveway, you notice something strange. You see walls topped with barbed wire encircling your neighborhood. You also notice police officers patrolling the area around the walls, and pulling down people who try to scale them.

You angrily ask the police officers why they're doing this. They respond: "The local government has determined that the members of your community are taking jobs from other citizens and using too many welfare benefits. Besides, your community is culturally distinct from the broader community and we can't have your community changing our culture in bad ways. Finally, doesn't the rest of the community have a right to self-determination? We can decide who we want to associate with and we've decided that we don't want to associate with you!"

Needless to say, you don't accept these arguments and you're eager to escape your neighborhood. You need to get to work, for one thing. But you also want to visit friends and family members in other parts of the city, attend concerts and classes, eventually move to a new apartment across the city, and so on. But state officials stop you from leaving. You might be injured if you evade these officials and scale the walls. Maybe you'll cut yourself on barbed wire. If you are undeterred and try to leave anyway, these officers will overpower and imprison you. Moreover, state officials will probably track you down and return you to your neighborhood even if you do manage to escape. Finally, let's suppose that public officials make it illegal for people outside of your neighborhood to interact with you by employing or sheltering you. Let's call this case: *Neighborhood*.

At first glance, the actions of state officials in Neighborhood seem seriously wrong. Why's that? Well, we have strong moral reasons to refrain from coercing and harming other people. Almost everyone thinks that assault and violent threats are usually wrong. The reasons against coercion and violence speak against the actions of the state employees. After all, state officials threaten you with physical force in Neighborhood and deploy this force against you if you disobey their commands.

The deeper story is that state employees infringe on valuable liberties when they prohibit you from leaving your neighborhood. If you're unable to leave your neighborhood, you can't search for work, you can't associate with your friends and family, you can't attend your church, and you can't explore cultural opportunities outside of your neighborhood. So state employees seem to violate your rights to freedom of association, occupational choice, religious freedom, and so on. Your personal liberties in Neighborhood are curtailed by restrictions on freedom of movement.

Reflection on Neighborhood suggests that freedom of movement is intimately connected with core freedoms. To exercise occupational freedom or religious liberty, we must have the freedom to move around. Your religious freedom is impaired if the state forbids you from traveling to the church of your choice. You lack occupational freedom if other people stop you from searching for a job or traveling to employers who are willing to hire you. The state should respect basic liberal freedoms like freedom of conscience, freedom of association, freedom of speech, and occupational freedom. And, if the state should respect these basic liberties and freedom of movement is necessary for people to exercise their basic liberties, then the state should allow freedom of movement. So we can conclude that the state should allow freedom of movement.

You might concede that it's wrong for state officials to restrict your freedom of movement in Neighborhood. But you might argue that this is an extreme case. Sure, it's wrong for governments to put you in prison without justification. It hardly follows from this that states are obligated to respect your freedom of movement in general. Instead, maybe states are only obligated to ensure that you have an adequate range of options. The government avoids violating your rights if it restricts your freedom of movement *and* you already have an adequate range of options to live a decent life. So this objection says that it's wrong to restrict your freedom of movement if you lack enough options to live a decent life. Otherwise, though, it can be permissible to restrict your freedom of movement.

The problem with this line of argument is that we have strong reasons to avoid restricting freedom of movement even when people already have adequate or decent options. Let's consider a new variation on Neighborhood. Imagine that you live in a major city—say, Los Angeles. You have plenty of good options in this city. You can access a range of jobs, associate with a wide variety of people, and access many different cultural opportunities. After all, there are more people in Los Angeles County than there are in many countries, such as Denmark or New Zealand. So you can have a decent life if you stay in Los Angeles. But imagine that state officials decide to stop you from leaving the city or that all other towns and cities in the United States deny you admission. If you try to get to San Francisco, the police will track you down and force you to come back to Los Angeles. Let's call this case: *City*.

It's less bad for officials to stop you from leaving Los Angeles than it is for someone to prevent you from leaving your neighborhood. It's still wrong, though. This indicates that, even if you have decent options where you live, states should still respect your freedom to move. To drive this point home, let's compare freedom of movement to other freedoms, such as freedom of occupational choice. Suppose that you already have a good job and you can easily satisfy your basic needs. You are a tenured college professor, say. But you want to pursue a new career in a different industry because you are bored with your work and you want a career that you'll find more meaningful. Let's imagine that the government forbids you from changing jobs. Government officials explain: "you already have a job, plenty of decent options, and you already have enough options to live a good life. So it's permissible for us to prohibit you from quitting your tenured professorship."

This is a bad argument. It's wrong to stop you from exercising your occupational freedom even if you can already satisfy your basic needs or have decent options. The same point again applies to other valuable liberties. Take freedom of religion. It's unjust for the government to forbid me from practicing the Jedi religion, despite the fact that I have plenty of other religious options. We can apply this point to freedom of movement too. States should still respect your freedom of movement regardless of whether you are already well-off or not.

With these clarifications on the table, let's now turn to immigration restrictions.

2. AGAINST IMMIGRATION RESTRICTIONS

Immigration restrictions infringe on freedom of movement. Immigration restrictions coercively stop many millions of people from moving to other countries, and they in effect forbid citizens of states that restrict immigration from associating with foreigners.

Let's return to the case that I discussed in the beginning of this chapter: the case of Gabriel Hernández Cortez. To recap: Gabriel is a Mexican citizen who lives in poverty and who wants to immigrate to the United States. He tried to cross the border, but border agents used physical force to stop him, imprison him, and deport him back to Mexico. Most people would judge that the conduct of state officials in Neighborhood and City is wrong. But many people also endorse immigration restrictions that prevent people like Gabriel from crossing borders.

Why, though? If it's wrong to restrict your freedom of movement in Neighborhood and City, then why is it permissible for American officials to prevent people like Gabriel from immigrating to the United States? Here's my view: the same reasons bear on each of these cases. Public officials have strong moral reasons to refrain from restricting your freedom of movement in Neighborhood and City and, if public officials have these reasons, then the United States government has strong moral reasons to refrain from restricting Gabriel's freedom of movement, too.

Let's consider some different ways of blocking this conclusion. An objector might argue that governments lack obligations to maximize the freedoms of foreigners. This critic might reason as follows: "It would be *nice* if the United States allowed Gabriel to immigrate. But the United States only has obligations to expand and protect the freedom of Americans, not the freedoms of foreigners. So it's permissible for the United States to refuse to allow Gabriel to immigrate. In contrast, state officials have duties to respect the liberties of their citizens. These duties explain why it's wrong for state employees to forbid you from leaving your neighborhood or city."

It's false, though, that governments only have obligations to respect the freedom of their own citizens. They are obligated to respect the liberty of foreigners too. This is so because we have "negative" duties to other people. Negative duties are duties to refrain from harming or coercing people. Negative duties are universal. They apply to all other people

simply in virtue of their humanity. The reason I ought to refrain from beating other people up is simply that they're people, rather than because they're my compatriots.

Here are some other examples to illustrate the point that our reasons to avoid coercing and harming people don't depend on whether they're foreigners or not:

(A) Imagine that a Mexican police officer, Fernando, decides to assault and imprison an American tourist, Tracy, while she is visiting Mexico.

(B) An American public official, Roy, goes on a vacation to Mexico and he assaults Mexican citizens without provocation.

(C) American public officials decide to forcibly round up foreign tourists in the United States and place them in a prison camp.

(D) The president of the United States orders a military strike on a Mexican city, killing hundreds of non-combatants. This strike is unprovoked.

The actions (A–D) seem wrong. But why? The answer again is that we have negative duties to refrain from interfering with other people, even if they're foreigners. We might say that the negative duty to refrain from harmful interference is a "general" duty, a duty that we *prima facie* owe to all other people. So we can't coerce, assault, or imprison foreigners without a good justification.

What about Gabriel's case, though? It looks like state officials in this example are violating negative duties here, too—in particular, their negative duties to refrain from coercing Gabriel. Maybe this duty is overridden by other considerations. But at first glance officials do have these duties. After all, if the people in (A–D) have duties to respect the rights and liberties of foreigners, then it stands to reason that immigration agents have these duties, too. The point generalizes. The United States government has obligations to respect the freedom of Gabriel and others who want to immigrate. These obligations are moral reasons to oppose immigration restrictions.

You might object to my argument by pointing out that rights to immigrate involve more than just the permission to enter a territory. When someone immigrates, they also become entitled to public services, such as police protection and access to the courts, and eventually other resources, like welfare benefits. These benefits can be costly. Citizens might need to foot the bill for public benefits in the form, say, of higher taxes. So the decision about whether to admit Gabriel into the United States is not just about the decision to refrain from forcibly stopping him from immigrating. It's also about whether citizens are obligated to bear the costs of allowing Gabriel to immigrate. For this reason, you might reasonably doubt whether we can ground the right to immigrate solely in the negative duty to refrain from coercing foreigners.

Maybe allowing Gabriel to immigrate would impose costs on citizens. Yet this fails to break the analogy between immigration and Neighborhood and City. If the police allow you to leave your neighborhood or city, then your movement might impose costs on other people. Suppose that, if the government lets you leave your neighborhood or city, then you will move to a nearby city. And, once you live in this town, you'll become entitled to public services there. You will be entitled to police protection, access to the courts, and so on. This may impose costs on the other residents of the town where you now live. Yet the actions of state officials in Neighborhood are unjust nevertheless. Gabriel's immigration seems no different. It looks like it's wrong to deny a person freedom of movement just because this person *might* impose costs on others.

Suppose that you agree with me that it seems unjust for the United States to exclude people like Gabriel. But you could deny that this judgment generalizes to immigration restrictions more broadly. You could argue that it's wrong to exclude Gabriel, because Gabriel is unable to satisfy his basic needs or the basic needs of his child where he is currently situated. Maybe Gabriel lacks adequate options to live a decent life. He's unable to find a decent job and source of income. However, you might claim that it's permissible to restrict the immigration of someone who is already well off. Thus, Gabriel's case fails to ground a *general* objection to immigration restrictions. So, on this line of argument, it's wrong to deny admission to foreigners if this imperils their ability to satisfy their basic needs, but it may be permissible to restrict their entry otherwise.

Yet it seems wrong to restrict the immigration even of people who are already well off. Let's return to my thought experiment City. To recap, you live in Los Angeles, you are already well off, and you have plenty of options for living a decent life. Nonetheless, it seems unjust for government officials to trap you in Los Angeles. Thus, despite the fact that you have decent options where you live, the government should still respect your freedom to move. The same goes for foreigners. Even if Gabriel were well off, there would still be strong reasons to allow him to immigrate to the United States. Like other liberties such as occupational freedom, states have good reasons to respect your freedom of movement regardless of whether you already have plenty of options.

That said, it *is* morally worse for the United States to stop Gabriel from immigrating than it is for United States to prevent the immigration of someone who is already well-off. Everything else being equal, it's worse to coercively stop a person from moving from one place to another if this person's interest in doing so is stronger. Gabriel has a strong interest in moving to the United States. If Gabriel had the chance to immigrate to the United States, this would make him much better off. Thus, the United States has an especially strong reason to admit him. And it turns out the same point applies for millions and millions of foreigners. Migrants like Gabriel are desperate and destitute. These cases are not exceptional. States prohibit many destitute and desperate foreigners from immigrating. So actual immigration restrictions set back the urgent interests of many people.

To get a sense of how harmful immigration restrictions are, let's consider how much people would benefit from immigrating. The economist Branko Milanovic finds that location of birth is the biggest predictor of a person's lifetime income.[3] Your prospects in life are probably determined less by your class or sex than by the place where you were born. If location determines your prospects in life, then this suggests that moving your location could improve your prospects. And this is what economists find. Estimates indicate that low-skilled immigrants from Mexico raise their wages by over 400 percent after they migrate to the United States. Unskilled Salvadorians increase their annual incomes from about $1,200 to $18,000 by moving to the United States.[4] In general, low-skilled workers in poor countries can more than triple their real earnings by moving to the United States or a similar country.

Why do migrants benefit from immigrating? Here're a few reasons. Richer states tend to have better institutions. They do a *relatively* good job of protecting property rights, implementing the rule of law, and avoiding inefficient regulations. Rich states also tend to have more human capital, better technology, and superior infrastructure. These attributes help people to become more productive when they move to rich countries. Productivity is the main determinant of income. So we should expect that moving people from a poor to a rich country would significantly increase their incomes. In fact, migration from, say, Nigeria or Chad to an affluent country massively boosts people's standard of living. To take another example, computer programmers earn dramatically more in the United States than they do in India, even though they're performing similar tasks.[5] Thus, to the extent that immigration restrictions prevent these people from moving, these restrictions deny foreigners large benefits.

There is more to life than money, of course. People want to immigrate for non-economic reasons, too. People move in order to escape authoritarian governments, political instability, and violence. Authoritarian regimes rule a large fraction of the human race. The residents of these countries often want to immigrate to states that protect civil and political liberties. Many people also live in societies with high rates of violence. For example, many Latin American countries experience high rates of drug-related violence. This violence has caused hundreds of thousands of people to immigrate to other countries, such as the United States. Civil wars in the Middle East have recently generated millions of refugees who desperately want to find safety abroad.

So it appears that a large number of people would benefit a great deal if they could immigrate, but they cannot do so. But you may still harbor doubts that borders should be left relatively open even if immigration is such a good deal for the global poor. One common concern is that, if states allowed more immigration, then skilled workers from poor countries would immigrate. If skilled workers left, this would deprive poor countries of human capital. The most talented entrepreneurs and the most educated citizens would seek their fortunes in rich countries. Poor countries would thus lose their most skilled citizens. Wouldn't this make the global poor worse off?

Economists actually disagree about the effects of skilled migration. While some economists think that the emigration of skilled workers has negative effects on poor countries, others believe that this emigration has neutral or even positive impacts.[6] Skilled workers may benefit the compatriots that they leave behind by forming technological and trade networks between their new and old countries. They also spread valuable ideas and send home remittances. Also, migration is often circular. Skilled people might work in, say, Britain for a few years and return home with more education and skills. Anyway, the current order makes it much easier for skilled workers to immigrate to rich countries. Rich countries are eager to recruit doctors and computer programmers from poor countries while they shun construction workers and taxi drivers. Even if skilled migration creates more overall harm than benefit for the global poor, people in poor countries would benefit if more *unskilled* workers had the legal opportunity to immigrate to rich countries.

To sum up, immigration has large benefits for migrants and immigration restrictions deny these benefits to many millions of people. This information is relevant because it tells us something about the magnitude of the harms that immigration restrictions inflict. Immigration restrictions curtail valuable freedoms and this fact grounds a powerful objection to these restrictions. I think that immigration restrictions are unjust even if they avoid trapping people in poverty or oppression. But it's morally worse to coercively stop people from immigrating if their interest in doing so is stronger. People have weighty interests in substantially improving their standard of living, escaping authoritarian governments, and living in conditions free from violence. Actual immigration restrictions trample on these interests.

3. OBJECTIONS AND RESPONSES

Commentators in public debate often defend immigration restrictions by pointing out that immigration can harm our fellow citizens. Immigrants compete with citizens for jobs and this competition drives down wages, which creates more poverty. Immigrants end up using welfare and other public benefits and this strains government budgets. And maybe immigrants cause other problems too, such as crime and terrorism. Many people say that governments should restrict immigration to prevent these bad things from happening. Let's call this *the bad consequences objection* to open borders.

The bad consequences objection says that immigrants harm the societies that admit them. Yet people frequently exaggerate the costs of immigration. Consider the effects of immigration on wages. Most economists who study the labor market effects of immigration conclude that immigration has small effects on the wages of citizens.[7] Foreigners often don't compete with citizens for jobs. Instead, foreigners have different skills and attributes than many citizens and this leads them to complement the labor of citizens. Consequently, immigration can actually raise the wages of citizens. Or take the fiscal effects of immigration. Many people worry that immigrants will end up using a lot of public services and welfare benefits, thereby imposing costs on the rest of us. But, in reality, researchers find that the effects of immigration on public finances are small and hard to detect.[8] Most immigrants find work and pay taxes; immigrants usually pay their own way.

Think about it this way. Imagine that half of the population of the country where you lived disappeared right now. Would you be better off economically? Probably not. That's because all those other people add something to the economy. They buy stuff, which creates demand for your labor. And their talents and knowledge on the whole make your country more productive, which increases your wages in the long-run, too. Immigrants are people, too. It stands to reason that they also add something to a society's prosperity. And this is what economists find. More immigration tends to make societies wealthier and better-off.[9]

What about the threat that immigration poses to our physical security? Popular opinion is also wrong about the relationship between immigration and crime. Most studies on the relationship between immigration and crime conclude that immigration does not increase crime and may in fact reduce it.[10] Or consider terrorism. The number of immigrants who are terrorists is infinitesimal. The United States admitted 3.25 million refugees over the past four decades and only twenty of them have been convicted of attempting or committing terrorism on U.S. territory. The chance of an American being killed by a foreign terrorist is about 1 in about 3,600,000.[11] Falling furniture is much more likely to kill you than an immigrant terrorist, to say nothing of car accidents, ordinary homicides, or heart disease. The lesson is that, when you review the evidence and compare this evidence to popular perceptions about immigration, you'll find that people tend to overestimate the costs of immigration and underestimate its benefits.

Let's suppose though that immigration does have serious costs for citizens. We still need to ask ourselves: is it necessary to restrict immigration in order to prevent bad outcomes or is there another alternative? For example, let's assume that immigrants end up consuming a lot of welfare benefits and straining the government's budget. It doesn't follow that we should restrict immigration. Here's another option: states can deny immigrants access to public services and welfare benefits. You might object: "that's unfair!" But surely it's better than excluding immigrants outright. If so, we can address the problem without restricting immigration. And the same goes for most other potential costs of immigration.

Let's assume, though, that immigration does harm some citizens and that we can't find a feasible way to avoid these costs. Even then, immigration restrictions would be unjustified. Notice that the bad consequences objection assumes that, if immigration imposes costs on citizens, then that's a good reason to restrict immigration. Yet there's a problem with this assumption: it ignores immigrants. The rights and interests of immigrants matter, too. As I argued earlier, we have obligations to refrain from harming and coercing other people, including foreigners. And these obligations can trump our obligations to our fellow citizens.

Here's an analogy. I think that I owe more to my children than I owe to random strangers. I should show more concern for my children than I should show for other people's children. Nonetheless, it would be wrong for me to coerce, kidnap, or assault strangers in order to benefit my children. Suppose that, if I mugged strangers on the street, I could afford to buy my children presents that they really wanted. Obviously though, that wouldn't be okay. The economist Bryan Caplan observes that "almost everyone knows that 'it would help my son' is not a good reason for even petty offenses—like judging a Tae Kwon Do tournament unfairly because your son's a contestant."[12]

The same point applies to governments. Many of us think that governments owe more to their citizens than they owe to foreigners. Governments have stronger obligations to benefit their own citizens. But there are strict limits on what governments can do to help their citizens. If it's wrong for me to coerce and assault strangers in order to benefit my children, then it is hard to see why it would be fine for the government to coerce and assault foreigners for the benefit of citizens. But that's just what immigration restrictions do: immigration restrictions involve coercion and violence. So even if immigration restrictions are necessary to benefit citizens, we should still doubt whether it's morally okay to enforce them.

Here's another common objection to open borders: some people argue that states should restrict immigration in order to preserve a society's national culture. Foreigners have different values and cultural practices. If they immigrate, then this will change a society's culture and identity. But we have good reasons to preserve our culture. So we should restrict immigration. Let's call this: *the cultural objection* to open borders.

One response to the cultural objection is to point out that most immigrants assimilate and adopt the cultural practices of recipient societies. [13] Another response to the cultural objection is to ask: so what if immigration causes cultural change? The exercise of many individual rights can change a society's culture and identity. Consider rights to free speech. Free speech can change a society's culture by encouraging people to adopt new values and practices. Suppose that Mormons are successful at persuading many Americans to convert. This could change a society's culture—let's assume that Mormons have somewhat different values and practices than the dominant culture. But it would clearly be wrong to forbid Mormons from proselytizing.

Or consider rights to reproductive freedom. Imagine that Muslims are a minority in a society, but Muslims have more children than the rest of the population and most of these children adopt the practices and values of their parents. As a result, Muslims' exercise of reproductive freedom generates cultural change. We should clearly condemn any restrictions on Muslim's reproductive freedom that aim to stop this change. Individual rights trump the goal of cultural preservation. Foreigners' rights to immigrate should override this goal as well. Thus, the cultural objection to open borders is unsound.

Let's consider one final objection to open borders. Some people think of states like private clubs or property. We can rightfully exclude people from our private associations and property. Suppose that you and your friends form a chess club. It seems okay for you to refuse to allow strangers to join your club. Or assume that you own your house. You are within your rights to prevent homeless people from sleeping in your home. Maybe we can defend immigration restrictions on similar grounds. States might be analogous to private clubs or perhaps states have property rights in their national territories. If that's true, then we can exclude immigrants just as we can exclude people from our clubs and houses. Let's call this the *rights-based objection* to open borders.

But here's the problem with the rights-based objection. If states have rights to freedom of association or property rights over their territories, then states can permissibly do more than just restrict immigration. They can restrict all individual rights. To illustrate, consider that private associations, such as clubs, churches, or businesses, can permissibly exclude non-members. For example, the Catholic Church can permissibly refuse to baptize Satanists. In this sense, the Catholic Church has the right to exclude people. But private associations can also regulate the behavior of their members in illiberal ways. This is why the Catholic Church can forbid its members from using birth control, having sex out of wedlock, worshipping Satan, and so on.

Now, suppose you think that states are like private associations in that both can permissibly exclude non-members. Well, if states really are like private associations, then states should also be able to regulate the behavior of their members in the same way that private associations do. States should also have the right to forbid citizens from using birth control, having sex out of wedlock, or worshipping Satan. Thus, the same logic that justifies immigration restrictions also implies that states can restrict any liberty, such as freedom of speech or sexual freedom. If states are like clubs, they might exercise their rights by excluding outsiders. Or states may exercise their rights to freedom of association by curtailing the individual liberties of their members.

Suppose, alternatively, you think that citizens collectively own their territories or institutions and that these property rights permit the exclusion of outsiders. On this view, countries are like big private estates. And aren't private estates well within their rights to exclude trespassers? The problem is, once again, that this justifies too much. Consider a private establishment, like a restaurant. A restaurant may have a dress code that forbids customers from taking off their shirt, wearing clothes with profanity on them, or wearing baggy pants, and that requires workers to wear a uniform. They can also forbid people from such activities as staging a political protest in their restaurant. Why is it permissible for a restaurant to do this? Ownership rights. Private property rights give people the right to control what happens on their property, within some limits. If countries are essentially private property, then they should be able to forbid residents from wearing baggy pants, uttering profanity, holding political protests, and so on.

I submit that these are not policies that we should accept. It would be unjust for states to behave in these ways. But, to reject the implications that countries can act in illiberal ways, we must also reject the view that countries are analogous to private property or private clubs. And, if countries are not like private property or clubs, then we can't appeal to these analogies to justify immigration restrictions. For this reason, the rights-based objection to open borders fails.

4. CONCLUSION

Advocates of open borders aren't crazy. They acknowledge that immigration can cause problems and that, in rare cases, there are good arguments for immigration restrictions. If allowing immigration would cause disaster, then that's a solid reason for restricting it. But open borders advocates just happen to believe that a careful evaluation of the evidence reveals that immigration has far fewer downsides and many more upsides than most people think. Once you work through the evidence, you find that most people's fears about immigration are exaggerated or even baseless.

So what would a world with open borders look like? You're already familiar with it. You know how you can just move around your country freely? Tomorrow you can wake up and decide to move to another city or town. I live in Richmond, Virginia. If I wanted to, I could get up right now, buy a plane ticket to Alaska, and move there. Advocates of open borders say that the whole world should be like that.

Sometimes when I lecture about immigration, I show the audience pictures of what open and closed borders look like. Here's a picture of an open border:[14]

This is the border between Germany and Switzerland. Germany on the left side of the street and Switzerland is on the right side. Here's another picture:[15]

This is the border between Spain and Portugal. Spain and Portugal are members of the European Union, which has open borders between member states. What do we observe in these two pictures? Not much. Just countryside and open roads. It's peaceful. No walls, guns, or border guards.

Now, contrast these pictures with this one:[16]

This is the border between Hungary and Serbia, which is not an open border. Notice the high fences

topped with razor wires and the police officer ready to stop migrants from crossing. Or consider this picture:[17]

This is the border between Texas, United States, and the Mexican state of Chihuahua. Also not an open border.

Think about what kind of world you want to live in. Do we want to live in a world where borders look like the first two pictures? Or do want to live in a world where borders look like the third and fourth pictures? I hope to have given you some reason to prefer the first two.

NOTES

1. This story is reported in Margaret Regan, *The Death of Josseline: Immigration Stories from the Arizona Borderlands* (Boston, Mass.: Beacon Press, 2010), pp. 16–20.

2. This story is from: This American Life, *The Walls*, March 18, 2018, accessed June 1, 2018, https://www.thisamericanlife.org/641/the-walls.

3. Branko Milanovic, "Global Inequality of Opportunity: How Much of Our Income Is Determined by Where We Live?," *Review of Economics and Statistics*, 2014.

4. Lant Pritchett, *Let Their People Come: Breaking the Gridlock on Global Labor Mobility* (Washington, D.C.: Center for Global Development, 2006), p. 22.

5. Michael A Clemens, "Why Do Programmers Earn More in Houston than Hyderabad? Evidence from Randomized Processing of US Visas," *American Economic Review* 103, no. 3 (2013): 198–202.

6. For contrasting perspectives on skilled immigration, see: Devesh Kapur and John McHale, *Give Us Your Best and Brightest: The Global Hunt for Talent and Its Impact on the Developing World* (Baltimore, MD: Brooking Institution Press, 2005); Michael Clemens, "Losing Our Minds? New Research Directions on Skilled Emigration and Development," *International Journal of Manpower* 37, no. 7 (2016): 1227–1248.

7. Giovanni Peri, "Do Immigrant Workers Depress the Wages of Native Workers?" *IZA World of Labor* 42 (2014): 1–10.

8. The National Academy of Sciences, ed., *The Economic and Fiscal Consequences of Immigration* (National Academies Press, 2017).

9. Amandine Aubry, Michał Burzyński, and Frédéric Docquier, "The Welfare Impact of Global Migration in OECD Countries," *Journal of International Economics* 101 (July 2016): 1–21.

10. Graham C. Ousey and Charis E. Kubrin, "Immigration and Crime: Assessing a Contentious Issue," *Annual Review of Criminology* 1, no. 1 (2018): 63–84.

11. Alex Nowrasteh and 2016, "Terrorism and Immigration: A Risk Analysis" (Washington, D.C.: CATO Institute, 2016), https://www.cato.org/publications/policy-analysis/terrorism-immigration-risk-analysis.

12. Bryan Caplan, "Patria, Parenti, Amici," *Econlog* (blog), December 25, 2011, http://econlog.econlib.org/archives/2011/12/patria_parenti.html.

13. Jack Citrin et al., "Testing Huntington: Is Hispanic Immigration a Threat to American Identity?," *Perspectives on Politics* 5, no. 1 (2007): 31–48.

14. Hansueli Krapf, "Canton of Schaffhausen, Swiss/German Border in Dörflingen," *Wikipe<RSL: I checked and the URL that follows works fine>dia Commons*, April 22, 2012, https://commons.wikimedia.org/wiki/File:2012-04-22_19-33-46_Switzerland_Kanton_Schaffhausen_D%C3%B6rflingen,_Hinterdorf.JPG (accessed July 3, 2020).

15. M. Peinado, "España-Portugal," *Wikipedia Commons*, May 3, 2013, https://commons.wikimedia.org/wiki/File:007422_-_Espa%C3%B1a-Portugal_(8735025539).jpg (accessed July 3, 2020).

16. Bőr Benedek, "Police Car Near Hungary-Serbia Border Barrier," *Wikipedia Commons*, September 14, 2015, https://commons.wikimedia.org/wiki/File:Police_car_at_Hungary-Serbia_border_barrier.jpg (accessed July 3, 2020).

17. Dicklyon, "Border Wall between Sunland Park, New Mexico United States and Anapra, Chihuaha, Mexico" *Wikipedia Commons*, January 26, 2019, https://commons.wikimedia.org/wiki/File:Border_wall_at_Anapra.jpg (accessed July 3, 2020).

Javier Hidalgo: Open Borders

1. Hidalgo opens his piece with the thought experiment he calls *Neighborhood*. Do you think that Neighborhood is a good analogy for closed borders? Can we justifiably draw lessons for immigration policy from this thought experiment? Why or why not?

2. Hidalgo argues that freedom of association supports open borders. Others have argued that freedom of association supports immigration limits. Their thinking goes like this: Freedom of association protects your right to refuse marriage or friendship with a suitor, so it likewise protects a country's right to decline to be associated with migrants who seek entry. Do you find this analogy plausible? Does freedom of association better support open borders or immigration restrictions (or neither)?

3. Many fear that open borders will result in the destruction of a nation's culture. How important is it to protect such culture? What, if any, are the permissible limits a nation can take in order to preserve its culture? Do immigration limits fall within those limits?

4. Hidalgo writes that "if it's wrong for me to coerce and assault strangers in order to benefit my children, then it is hard to see why it would be fine for the government to coerce and assault foreigners for the benefit of citizens. But that's just what immigration restrictions do." What do you think of this claim? If you agree with this claim, offer your reasons in support of it; if you disagree, offer the reasons that lead you to reject it.

5. There's an old saying: a picture's worth a thousand words. Consider the photos at the end of Hidalgo's article. Are these legitimate philosophical devices for trying to persuade readers? Why or why not?

CHAPTER 18

The Legacy of Racism

JUST THE FACTS

It's no secret that the United States has a long history of **racism** (the view that members of a given race are inferior by virtue of their racial identity). We couldn't possibly tell that full history here. The best we can do is make a start. We'll focus on the racial discrimination endured by minorities at the hands of the US government, passing over, almost entirely, the horrific treatment endured by minorities at the hands of private citizens.

Slave traders began bringing kidnapped Africans to the Americas as early as 1619, around the time the first British colonists settled in Jamestown, Virginia. The practice continued for the next 246 years, until it was abolished in 1865 with the passing of the Thirteenth Amendment. In total, close to 400,000 Africans were forcibly taken from their homes and thrown into dark, cramped transport ships.[1] They were given little food and water, and they had little idea what would happen to them. Many died in transit. Once in North America, they were sold to white colonists (American citizens, after 1776) as slaves. Many were sold separately from their family members, never to be reunited again. The products of their labor were taken by their owners and sold for profits that slaves would never see. Slaves enjoyed virtually no legal protections. If they attempted to escape, they were hunted down and their punishment was left to the discretion of their owners. For perceived bad behavior or lack of productivity, slaves were,

among many other things, beaten, whipped, isolated, starved, and burned.

The abolition of slavery in 1865 made it illegal to buy, sell, or own slaves, but it would still be a long time before African Americans would be granted anything approaching legal equality. In the 1880s, state and local governments began passing **Jim Crow laws** mandating racial segregation in public facilities such as schools, restaurants, and restrooms in the states of the former Confederacy. These laws were judged not to violate the Fourteenth Amendment requiring equal protection under the law for all citizens, on the grounds that blacks and whites were entitled to "separate but equal" services. So long as the facilities provided to each race were equally available and of roughly equal quality, state and local governments could require that public facilities be segregated by race. Of course, in practice, things were anything but equal. Black schools and public facilities were clearly underfunded and understaffed relative to their white counterparts, but little was done about it. Legally, the downfall of Jim Crow laws came only in 1954, when the US Supreme Court ruled (in the landmark case *Brown v. Board of Education*) that state laws mandating segregation in public schools were unconstitutional.

Though school segregation was legally prohibited in 1954, government-sanctioned racism did not immediately disappear. In 1934, the US government created the Federal Housing Administration (FHA) to assist people in becoming homeowners by insuring their loans. The FHA, however, explicitly refused to back loans to black people or people who lived near black people until 1964—a practice called

---

1. http://www.pbs.org/wnet/african-americans-many-rivers-to-cross/history/how-many-slaves-landed-in- the-us/

redlining. The result was that many black people were unable to buy homes, and any attempt to improve their neighborhoods with even small-scale business ventures was obstructed by lenders refusing to underwrite loans to potential investors. Those ventures were judged to be too risky; the lack of businesses led to the reduction of property values in black neighborhoods, and declining property values discouraged new businesses from entering the neighborhood—a vicious cycle that has yet to right itself in many minority communities.

In the 1980s and 1990s, crack cocaine became a cheaper alternative to the powder cocaine that was popular in the 1970s. In 1986, Congress passed the Anti-Drug Abuse Act as part of the War on Drugs. The new law mandated a minimum sentence of five years in prison without parole for possession of five grams of crack cocaine, which was more likely to be used by African Americans. For powder cocaine, more frequently used by wealthier white Americans, it took possession of five hundred grams for a minimum sentence of five years. The stated justification for this enormous disparity was that crack had a much higher association with violent crime than powder cocaine. The result, however, was predictable: African Americans were incarcerated for crack-related crimes at a much higher rate than whites were for cocaine-related crimes. Black Americans also received much harsher sentences for comparable drug offenses. In 2010, nearly twenty-five years after the Anti-Drug Abuse Act's passage, President Barack Obama signed the Fair Sentencing Act into law, thereby reducing the disparity between the amount of crack cocaine and powder cocaine needed to trigger federal criminal penalties. He also eliminated the mandatory five-year minimum sentence for simple crack possession.

In the mid-1990s, psychologists began performing experiments to test subjects' implicit attitudes—those they aren't consciously aware of—toward all kinds of things, such as foods, brands, clothes, and political views. Psychologists also began to conduct experiments about attitudes taken toward racial and ethnic minorities. The most common way to measure such implicit attitudes is to use the Implicit Association Test (IAT). In a standard IAT, subjects attempt to sort words or pictures into categories as fast as possible without making any errors. An IAT score is computed by comparing speed and error rates on the "blocks" (or trials) in which the pairing of concepts is consistent with common stereotypes (e.g., "black" and "bad," "white" and "good") to the blocks in which the pairing of the concepts is inconsistent with common stereotypes. A review in 2007 that tested over 700,000 subjects on the race-evaluation IAT found that over 70 percent of white subjects associated black faces with negative words (e.g., war, bad) and white faces with positive words (e.g., peace, good).

Researchers are worried that **such implicit bias** will translate into discrimination against minorities, and there's some reason to think that this worry is well founded. In 2003, researchers mailed thousands of résumés to employers with job openings and measured which ones were selected for callbacks for interviews.[2] Before sending them, however, researchers randomly used stereotypically African American names (e.g., "Jamal") on some and stereotypically white names (e.g., "Connor") on others. The same résumé was roughly 50 percent more likely to result in a callback for an interview if it had a stereotypically white name. In another study, white state legislators (both Republican and Democrat) were found to be less likely to respond to calls or emails by constituents with stereotypically African American names.[3] And in yet another study, emails sent to faculty members at universities, asking to talk about research

---

2. https://www.aeaweb.org/articles?id=10.1257/0002828042002561

3. http://onlinelibrary.wiley.com/doi/10.1111/j.1540-5907.2011.00515.x/full

opportunities, were more likely to get a reply if a stereotypically white name was used.[4]

To be free from many of the consequences of these implicit biases and to be part of a racial group that does not have a history of crushing oppression can be quite an advantage. Peggy McIntosh has given a name to this kind of advantage: **white privilege**.[5] Here are a few of her examples of such privilege. White people can turn on the television or open to the front page of the paper and see white people widely represented. When white people are told about their national heritage or about "civilization," they are shown people of their own color. White people do not have to educate their children to be aware of systemic racism for their own daily physical protection. They can swear, or dress in second-hand clothes, or not answer letters, without having people attribute these choices to the bad morals, or the poverty, or the illiteracy of their race. If a traffic cop pulls a white person over or if the IRS audits his tax return, he can be sure he hasn't been singled out because of his race. The striking thing about these advantages is that white people are often completely unaware that they enjoy them.

African Americans are just one of many groups that have been the victims of implicit and explicit discrimination in the United States. In addition to having their population decimated by disease and war, Native Americans have repeatedly had their land forcibly taken from them. For example, in 1830, the federal Indian Removal Act called for the removal of the "Five Civilized Tribes"—the Cherokee, Chickasaw, Choctaw, Creek, and Seminole—from their homelands in the southern United States. Between 1830 and 1838, government officials, working on behalf of white cotton growers, forced nearly 100,000 Native Americans to so-called Indian Territory in Oklahoma. Along the way, some 4,000 Cherokee people died of cold, hunger, and disease—an event now known as the "Trail of Tears."[6]

After the Japanese attacks on Pearl Harbor, Hawaii, in December 1941, many Americans were suspicious about the loyalty of Japanese residents and citizens of the United States. There were rumors that many Japanese Americans knew of the attacks before they happened but remained silent. The FBI knew that these rumors were false but did nothing to rebut them. In 1942, emboldened by these suspicions common among the public, the US government began forcing Japanese and Japanese Americans citizens into **internment camps**—crowded and uncomfortable barracks surrounded by barbed wire, located in remote areas far from their homes. In total, 110,000 Japanese and Japanese Americans living on the West Coast were forced into camps for two and half years—from 1942 to 1944.[7]

The sort of explicit and implicit discrimination we've been discussing is race based. Recently, though, work by philosophers and biologists on the concept of race has cast some doubt on whether races really exist. The skepticism about the biological reality of race is motivated by the realization that it is extraordinarily difficult to characterize the essence of, or the necessary and sufficient conditions for, membership in a particular race. For example, what biological feature is shared by Spaniards and Russians that makes them both white, but is not shared by Russians and Mongolians, making the former white and the latter Asian? There have been many attempts to answer this (and similar) kinds of questions, but there have been few satisfying answers.

---

4. https://papers.ssrn.com/sol3/papers.cfm?abstract_id=2063742

5. McIntosh, "White Privilege: Unpacking the Invisible Knapsack," *Independent School* (Winter 1990).

6. http://www.cherokee.org/About-The-Nation/History/Trail-of-Tears/A-Brief-History-of-the-Trail-of-Tears

7. https://www.pbs.org/childofcamp/history/

ARGUMENT ANALYSIS

Racism is immoral. As a result, we are not going to follow the usual procedure and offer arguments for and against the main topic of the chapter. There are no good arguments for racist attitudes and practices.

While the immorality of racism is clear, the best way to respond to racism is anything but. Here we enter into difficult and controversial territory. As usual, there are many more topics and arguments than can be canvassed, so we have to be selective. Here we will focus on just two large topics: **affirmative action** and the wisdom of **reparations**.

Affirmative Action

Affirmative action is a social policy that increases a qualified applicant's chances in hiring or admissions on the basis of his or her status as a member of a group that has suffered extensive discrimination. Affirmative action is often applied to women and to the disabled, as well as to racial and ethnic minorities, but we will focus here just on affirmative action as it applies to the latter groups.

Many people object to affirmative action because they regard it as essentially unfair. At its most extreme, the charge is that affirmative action is a form of racism in reverse. Since racism is wrong, and since two wrongs don't make a right, affirmative action is immoral. This line of reasoning can be put in the form of

The Racism Argument

1. Racism is immoral.
2. Affirmative action is a form of racism.

Therefore,

3. Affirmative action is immoral.

Premise 1 is true. But premise 2 is false. Affirmative action policies are not motivated by, and do not convey, the view that whites are inferior in any way to minorities. Affirmative action policies do not stigmatize whites, do not express any form of hatred or condemnation toward white people, and do not claim any kind of moral, emotional, or spiritual superiority for minorities. Affirmative action gives preference in hiring and admissions to members of minority groups, but does not stereotype white citizens thereby and does not contribute to the reinforcement of **oppression**. Racism is a form of oppression: a system of unjust and unequal social forces that systematically limit opportunities and impose other harms on members of a given population. Whites as a group are not oppressed—there is no systemic limitation of their opportunities just because they are white. Of course many white people suffer great disadvantages of one kind or another. But the color of their skin in almost all contexts affords them privilege, rather than a thoroughgoing disadvantage.

Another criticism of affirmative action policies is that they violate the **principle of merit**: positions should be awarded on the basis of qualifications. A qualification is a trait that makes you well-suited to promoting a legitimate goal of the organization you are applying to or are already serving. If one person is better qualified than another for a job, then the better qualified candidate should get the position. If one student has better grades and a higher SAT score than a second student, and if there's not room for both in a college's entering class, then the first student should gain admission and the second shouldn't. But affirmative action policies give those who are somewhat less qualified priority over the more qualified. That is unfair:

The Qualifications Argument

1. Fairness requires that positions should be awarded solely on the basis of merit, that is, of who is best qualified for the position.
2. Affirmative action does not award positions solely on the basis of an applicant's qualifications, but instead partly on the basis of racial or ethnic identity.

Therefore,

3. Affirmative action is unfair.

Let's start with premise 2. Recall that affirmative action is not designed to give unqualified applicants a leg up. Affirmative action is restricted to qualified applicants who, by the ordinary measures of merit, are somewhat less qualified than whites who are competing for the same spots. I think premise 2 is usually true. Your skin color or ethnic background is not usually something that makes you better at a given job. But there are exceptions; racial or ethnic identity can *sometimes* be a further qualification of a position. Given the long history of police violence within minority neighborhoods, an African American community liaison officer will be more likely than a white officer to be effective in such a neighborhood. An African American actress is better qualified than a white one to portray Rosa Parks in a new bio-pic. But these are exceptions to the rule. Being white only rarely makes applicants better qualified for a job—it doesn't make them likely to be better farmers, cashiers, or insurance agents. The same goes for members of minority groups.

Premise 1 is very plausible. Suppose a less qualified white person gets a job over a much better qualified black person, owing to the prejudices of an employer. That is unfair. It is unfair because the black person deserved the job. She deserved it by virtue of her superior qualifications. This seems to make perfect sense. If it does, then it lends strong support to premise 1.

Suppose premise 1 is true, and suppose, too, that premise 2 is true for most cases. Then it is also true that affirmative action is ordinarily unfair. But, perhaps surprisingly, that does not settle the issue of whether affirmative action is morally acceptable. That is because we are sometimes morally allowed to sacrifice fairness in order to achieve other valuable goals.

Consider a couple of examples, each designed to illustrate the general point that fairness is not the supreme moral value. Here's the first. Suppose I need my house repaired and I receive bids from several contractors to do the work. One of these stands out as the best. But just before I hire this person, I hear that one of the contractors who submitted a competing bid—a good one, just not the best—needs this job in order to avoid bankruptcy. So I hire him instead. He's certainly qualified, but not the best qualified. I thereby violated the principle of merit. But my decision is still morally permitted—the job was mine to bestow, and in denying the job to the most qualified person, I did not disqualify him on immoral grounds (for instance, sexism, racism, or anti-Semitism).

Here is a second example. The United States gives veterans preferential treatment in employment and college admissions and financial aid decisions. These policies allow institutions to hire or admit veterans who are qualified, but less qualified than some other applicants. This policy thus violates the principle of merit. But the policy might be justified by pointing to the important social goals it achieves—rewarding veterans for their service to the country and providing incentive to others to enlist.

What these examples show is that it is permissible to violate the principle of merit in a range of cases, including those where valuable goals (such as helping others stay on their feet or honoring our veterans) are achieved by doing so. Affirmative action, too, is designed to achieve a laudable goal—the reduction of oppression and the increase of equal opportunity for those who are members of historically disadvantaged groups. So even if affirmative action is unfair, that unfairness might be outweighed by the good it can do.

Many defenders of affirmative action make this claim. They argue that in the face of lots of evidence (some of it provided earlier) that employers are either overtly racist or, perhaps more commonly nowadays, subject to implicit bias (prejudice that we do not realize we have), we need affirmative action in order to improve the likelihood that minority applicants will stand an equal chance of success in the job market and in college. This is the basis for

The Equal Opportunity Argument

1. A society is morally required to provide its citizens with equal opportunity to gain valuable resources and positions.
2. If a policy helps society to meet its moral requirements, then the policy is morally legitimate.
3. Affirmative action helps to achieve such equal opportunity.

Therefore,

4. Affirmative action is morally legitimate.

Look at the conclusion. It does not say that affirmative action is itself morally required, just that it is legitimate. Its defenders hope that one day there will be no need for affirmative action, because minorities, women, and other oppressed groups will in fact stand an equal chance of fulfilling their potential. Should such a day ever come, affirmative action will no longer be morally legitimate. But in the meantime, its defenders claim that it can move us closer to the point at which the historically disadvantaged are as likely to enjoy the same opportunities for education, health care, and wealth as their fellow citizens.

Premises 1 and 2 are quite plausible. One critique of premise 3 comes from the thought that affirmative action is not needed for helping us gain conditions of equal opportunity, because *we already live in a society of equal opportunity*. The thought here is that equal opportunity exists so long as laws are not discriminatory. Federal and state laws no longer allow racial discrimination, and in many contexts explicitly forbid it. So, the thought goes, we live in a land of equal opportunity. But this overlooks a distinction, taken from the law, between **de jure equality** and **de facto equality**. De jure equality is equality in the content of the law. In the United States, there is now de jure equality among all citizens. De facto equality refers to the situation on the ground,

the real, lived experience of citizens. It is deeply implausible to suppose that the United States, or nearly any other country, offers de facto equality of opportunity to its citizens.

To appreciate the point here, imagine someone saying the following: everyone has an equal opportunity to buy a yacht. No person, and no law, is preventing you from doing so. True, you only have a few hundred dollars in your bank account, and Bill Gates has billions. But you and he have the same opportunity to buy a yacht.

In one sense this is true. There is de jure equality of opportunity here. If I were to plunk down the millions needed to buy the boat, and do so before Bill Gates managed to do the deal, then I would own that ship. But in another sense there is no such equality, since I lack the funds to buy the yacht. The real chance that he and I would make the purchase isn't equal; I have no chance at all, no real opportunity. Now given the disparities of wealth and education between whites, on the one hand, and blacks and Native Americans, on the other, we are far from a situation of de facto equality of opportunity. Affirmative action is designed to help remedy that.

Another criticism of premise 3—probably the one most often heard—comes from the worries about unfairness that were the focus of the Qualifications Argument. The thought is that if you give someone other than the most qualified person a job, then that violates equal opportunity. That thought might seem appealing. But things are actually more complicated than they at first appear.

That's because the status quo is not itself a level playing field. Think of college admissions. These are based partly on SAT or ACT results, scores in Advanced Placement courses, and extracurricular activities. Students from better educated and wealthier families have a huge advantage with respect to these criteria. Wealthy parents can afford tutors to prep their children for these standardized tests. AP classes are rarely offered in poor communities. If your after-school and summer jobs are essential to keeping your family financially afloat, you won't be able to afford the sorts of costly summer activities—volunteer work in a distant country, intensive language school, unpaid internships at the local hospital or the big law firm run by a relative or family friend—that make the applications of so many affluent students so strong. These students have a huge leg up in the competition for social advantages. Their wealth means that they are very likely to be white. Of course there are affluent members of minority groups, and millions of very poor whites. But white households, on average, have 20 times the wealth of African American households. On average, schools in African American, Native American, and Hispanic neighborhoods pay teachers less and are far less well equipped than schools in predominantly white neighborhoods. (More information about the vast inequalities in the United States between whites and blacks is available in Chapter 16.)

This isn't at all to place blame on affluent white families for being wealthy or for providing their children with excellent opportunities. The Equal Opportunity Argument says nothing about enacting affirmative action as a means to harm whites or to punish them for wrongdoing. Rather, it is designed to help to equalize a playing field that is very uneven. It's not that whites need to be "put in their place," but rather that minorities ought to have an equal chance at the valuable things in life. No one believes that affirmative action alone will secure this. But the claim is that without affirmative action, there's even less reason to suppose that the current state of deep inequality will correct itself.

The Equal Opportunity Argument is consequentialist: it seeks to justify affirmative action by claiming that it will help bring about a great good down the road—a society of true equality of opportunity. Other defenders, though, think that affirmative action is justified not necessarily because of the good results it might have, but instead because of what has happened in the past. Specifically, they see affirmative action as one element in a package of reparations for past injustices.

Reparations

Reparations are a special form of **compensation**. Compensation involves improving the condition of a victim of harm. Ordinary compensation does not require a wrongdoer, and need not be paid by the perpetrator of the harm. For example, compensation could be provided by an insurance company for property damage suffered by flood victims. Reparations, though, are triggered by someone having acted immorally; the justification of reparations is to *repair* the relationship between victims and perpetrators. This in turn requires an acknowledgment by the blameworthy parties that they have done wrong, and demands that the wrongdoers, rather than some innocent third party such as an insurance company, provide their victims with the needed repair.

As applied to the legacy of racism, the core idea is that the US government has committed terrible and extensive injustices in its dealings with certain communities—most notably (though not exclusively) Native Americans and African Americans. As a result, it must seek to repair these wrongs, and so offer reparations to victims in these communities. One possible means of doing so is to enact affirmative action policies that give preference in hiring and admissions. But this is just one option. It could be combined with, or replaced by, other possible policies, such as a substantial financial payment over several years, accompanied by official expressions of apology. This serves as the basis of

The Reparations Argument

1. If one party has imposed systemic harms on members of a targeted group, then the wrongdoer is morally required to provide reparations to the victims.
2. The US government has imposed systemic harms on members of at least two

targeted groups: Native Americans and African Americans.

Therefore,

3. The US government owes reparations to Native Americans and African Americans.

Though this argument (like our broader discussion) is couched in terms of the United States, its central point applies to any other country that has targeted segments of its population for discriminatory treatment. (See Chapter 17 for further discussion of international reparations claims.)

Premise 2 is true. This is not the place to engage in a history lesson, but a quick glance (if needed) at the Just the Facts section should suffice to establish its plausibility.

Premise 1 is also very plausible. You must right your wrongs; you are not permitted to ignore your harmful conduct and pretend that it never happened. Nor are you allowed merely to pay someone else to aid your victim—that might provide compensation, but not reparation. And you must discharge your duty to your victim, specifically—you are not off the hook if you ignore your victim but offer the money you would have given him to a charity instead. Premise 1 does a fine job of explaining why claims like these are true.

Still, opponents of the Reparations Argument will rightly point out that premise 1, as it stands, is incomplete. To see this, note that there can be genuine repair of a relationship between perpetrator and victim only if both parties are alive. It's an obvious point, but one that critics have seized on in order to resist this argument.

One might object that those who perpetrated the evils of slavery and the forced resettlement of native tribes are long dead. And the administrations that allowed and perpetrated such harms are different from the current administration. These points are correct. Still,

governments do inherit the obligations of their predecessors. The United States cannot simply cancel its foreign debt, for instance, whenever a new administration is voted into office. So if past governments acted wrongly and did not repair those wrongs—and there can be little doubt that the US government has in fact failed to repair the horrific damage it did in allowing and enforcing slavery and in violently resettling native tribes—then there is a case to be made that today's government inherits those duties of repair.

Rather than argue that reparations are unjustified because the wrongdoers are no longer around to repair their harms, one can argue instead that the *victims* of these injustices are long dead. As a result, the relations between them and the government cannot be repaired. Hence there is no call for reparations.

There is something clearly right about this criticism. Chattel slavery in the United States, for instance, was outlawed over 150 years ago. The Choctaw nation was forcibly removed from its lands in 1830; the Cherokee nation was resettled at gunpoint in 1838, when several thousand tribal members lost their lives on the Trail of Tears. The United States can do nothing for these victims.

But there are two points of complication here. The first is that it might make sense to speak of today's members of the African American and Native American communities as victims of these past injustices. Although today's African Americans are not enslaved, and Native Americans are under no threat of being forcibly removed from their reservations, there is a sense in which the poor life prospects of so many members of these communities are due to the legacy of racism that their communities have suffered for generations.

That said, the claim of victimhood weakens as generations pass. Consider: if I kill some guy, it makes sense to regard his children as victims, too. Even though I didn't kill them, they have been victimized by my immoral action. *Perhaps* the victim's grandchildren are also victims of my crime. But things get very shaky when we trace this down to the fourth, fifth, or sixth generation. Both slaves and the Native Americans whose land was taken from them were clearly victimized, and it's sensible to speak of their children as victims, too. But we are now several generations away from these events, so it is less plausible to speak of today's African American and Native American citizens as victims of these historic injustices. If that is so, then the government does not owe them reparations for those injustices.

The second complication is that the injustices done to these communities did not end in the mid-nineteenth century. For instance, many older members of the African American community alive today suffered the injustices of Jim Crow laws, of federally mandated housing discrimination, and of federal "urban redevelopment" projects that destroyed middle-class black communities. Neither the federal government nor the state governments responsible for such policies have done much (and in some cases, have done nothing) to repair these wrongs.

In other words, claims to reparations need not be based on wrongs done before anyone today was alive. Racism has persisted in the decades since slavery was abolished and native communities were forced at gunpoint from their tribal lands. So perhaps reparations are owed after all—not in order to repair wrongs done over a century ago, but rather more recent wrongs.

Even if this were so, however, there is the extremely difficult question of what is required in order to repair the wrongs done. Many defenders of reparations argue that reparation should take the form of compensation for harms suffered. To know how much compensation is required, you ask a question: how well off would the victim be had the harm not occurred? This is what is called a **counterfactual question**. It asks about an outcome that would have occurred if, *contrary to fact*, some other event did not take place. In this case, the thought is that

governments are morally required to restore the victims of government-sponsored and government-tolerated racism to the level of well-being they would have enjoyed if, contrary to fact, they had not been the victims of racist policies and practices.

The problem with this approach is obvious. Racism has been a pervasive feature of US society for centuries. It is simply impossible to tell how well off African Americans and Native Americans would be today in the absence of the long history of racism. A quick and glib reply is: much better! But if we erase racism from the history of the United States, most of today's African Americans would never have been born, since their enslaved ancestors would never have met one another. So for all of these people, there is no way to answer the question: how well off would you be if slavery had never existed? And there are hundreds of different scenarios, each equally plausible, that might have arisen had US government policies toward native tribes been respectful rather than racist. As a result, there is no fact of the matter about what our world would look like if racism were removed from history. We know that racism has done a huge amount of harm. What we don't, and can't, know is how the world would be if all that harm never happened. But that is what we need to know in order to make sense of a claim to compensation. As a result, there is no measure, really, for determining the nature and extent of reparations that governments might owe to citizens who have suffered from racist oppression.

If these reflections are correct, then focusing on past injustices, and so on reparation, may not be a good guide to determining a government's responsibilities to correct for racism. This does not mean that the government is off the hook. As we indicated earlier, the government has a responsibility for creating conditions of equal opportunity. This responsibility may impose substantial obligations to change policies and practices so as to level the playing field and ensure that African American and Native Americans—and other members of historically disadvantaged groups—have an equal chance at living a good life.

CONCLUSION

Racism has been a deep moral stain on a country built on a premise of equal freedom. Nor is racism of only historical interest; racism persists, despite de jure equality. The difficulty of eradicating racism naturally invites us to reflect on how best to respond to it.

Some argue that policies of affirmative action are one element of a legitimate response. Against this, some critics mistakenly claim that affirmative action policies are racist; others take a subtler approach, and level their criticisms on the basis of the unfairness that comes from violating the principle of merit. But as we have seen, this principle, though important, is not absolute—there can be justified exceptions to it, cases in which we are morally allowed to assign positions of advantage to people even if they are not the best qualified for those positions. The strongest cases are ones in which a very important goal is gained by violating the principle of merit. Many would argue that advancing de facto equality of opportunity qualifies as such a goal.

Others defend affirmative action as a form of reparations that the government owes to the citizens of groups that have been targeted for discriminatory treatment. Reparations are justified, when they are, as a way of righting wrongs, of correcting for past injustices. There are complicated questions to do with the identities of the perpetrators and the victims, but even if we set them aside, the hardest question is how to determine what might be owed by way of reparations. The difficulty stems from our having to answer a question that seems to admit of no answer, namely: how well off would African American and Native American citizens be today if there were no legacy of racism? Perhaps there are ways around this difficulty. But even if there are not, appeals to equal opportunity may be able to justify the distribution of greater advantages to members of these historically disadvantaged groups.

ESSENTIAL CONCEPTS

Affirmative action: a social policy that increases the chances of hiring or admissions on the basis of an applicant's status as a member of a group that has suffered extensive discrimination.

Compensation: the means of restoring those who have been harmed to the condition they were in prior to the harm having occurred. Compensation does not require a wrongdoer, and it need not be paid by the perpetrator of the harm.

Counterfactual question: a question that asks what would have occurred if, contrary to fact, something else had not taken place.

De facto equality: equality in real, lived experience.

De jure equality: equality in the content of the law.

Implicit bias: prejudice that we do not realize we have.

Internment camps: barbed-wire-enclosed living quarters where thousands of Japanese and Japanese American people were forced to live for two and half years during World War II.

Jim Crow laws: state and local laws passed in the 1880s, in the southern United States, enforcing segregation between white and black people in public places such as schools, restrooms, and restaurants.

Oppression: a system of unjust and unequal social forces that systematically limit opportunities and impose other harms on members of a given population.

Principle of merit: positions should be awarded on the basis of qualifications.

Racism: the belief that members of a given race are inferior by virtue of their racial identity.

STAT SHOT

1. An estimated 10 million Native Americans were living in the territory that is the present-day United States when European settlers first arrived. Fewer than 300,000 were living in 1900. In the 2010 census, 5.2 million claimed to be Native American or Alaska Native.[1]

2. White people in America are significantly less likely than black people to believe that blacks are treated less fairly than whites (Figure 18.1).

% Saying blacks are treated less fairly than whites in the country

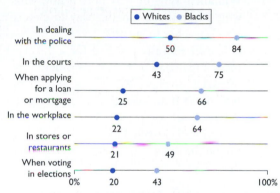

Note: Whites and blacks include only non-Hispanics.

Figure 18.1.
Source: http://www.pewsocialtrends.org/2016/06/27/on-views-of-race-and-inequality-blacks-and-whites-are-worlds-apart/st_2016-06-27_race-inequality-overview-02/

3. White people are more likely to use drugs, but black people are more likely to be arrested and sentenced for a drug offense (Figure 18.2).

4. Only 36 percent of white Americans said that racial discrimination was a major reason that blacks in the United States may have a harder time getting ahead than whites (Figure 18.3).

1. http://endgenocide.org/learn/past-genocides/native-americans/

Prisoners under state jurisdiction sentenced for drug offenses by race, December 31, 2011

White 29%
Black 40%

Percent who have ever used these drugs, by race, 2011   ■ White ■ Black

	White	Black
Cocaine	17.1%	9.9%
Crack	3.4%	5%
Hallucinogens	17.2%	6.7%
Inhalants	9.6%	3.2%
Marijuana	46.3%	40.4%
Unprescribed painkillers	15.2%	10.6%

Figure 18.2.
Source: National Survey on Drug Use and Health, Bureau of Justice Statistics, and The Huffington Post, http://www.huffingtonpost.com/2014/07/02/civil-rights-act-anniversary-racism-charts_n_5521104.html

% saying each of these is a major reason that blacks in the U.S. may have a harder time getting ahead than whites

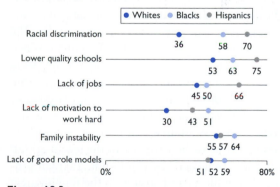

Figure 18.3.
Source: http://www.pewsocialtrends.org/2016/06/27/on-views-of-race-and-inequality-blacks-and-whites-are-worlds-apart/st_2016-06-27_race-inequality-overview-06/

Redlining: the practice of denying services to residents of certain areas based on their racial or ethnic identities.

Reparations: repairing a wrong one has done to a victim. This requires acknowledgment that one has done wrong, and it requires that the wrongdoer provide the victim with the needed repair.

White privilege: the set of social, political, and economic advantages enjoyed by white people in Western countries that are not enjoyed by other racial or ethnic groups in those countries.

Cases for Critical Thinking

Piscataway School Board v. Taxman

Deborah Williams, a black woman, and Sharon Taxman, a white woman, were business teachers at Piscataway High School in New Jersey in the 1980s. Their school district was forced to make budget cuts, and the board decided to lay off one of the business teachers. In ordinary circumstances, the board's policy is to lay off the teacher with the least seniority. In this case, however, Williams and Taxman had the same seniority—both were hired on the same day. The board eventually chose to lay off Taxman. When Taxman inquired into the reason for her being laid off rather than Williams, she found that she was not laid off for being less qualified, or for inferior job performance, or the like. It was rather that Williams, being black, would help preserve the racial diversity of the teaching staff in a way that Taxman would not. Taxman proceeded to file a complaint with the Employment Opportunity Commission. Her case eventually came before the US District Court in Newark in 1993. She won her case and was awarded $144,000. The school board appealed the decision, but lost again. The US Court of Appeals, in its opinion following the case, argued that the school board had violated the Civil Rights Act of 1964 outlawing discrimination on the basis of race, color, religion, sex, or national origin. Diversity alone, they argued, could never justify hiring and firing on the basis of race. The US Supreme Court agreed to hear the case, but Taxman and the Piscataway School Board settled the suit. Taxman received $433,500 in back pay, legal fees, and damages.[1]

1. http://www.nytimes.com/1997/11/22/nyregion/affirmative-action-settlement-overview-settlement-ends-high-court-case.html

Questions
1. What value, if any, is there in having a racially diverse faculty at a high school?
2. Did the school board make the right decision to lay off Taxman rather than Williams? Why or why not? If not, what would have been a better way to choose which teacher to lay off?
3. Is it ever morally justified for a government organization to use considerations of racial diversity for hiring and firing purposes? If so, when? If not, why not? What about for private businesses: is it ever morally justified for them to hire and fire on the basis of considerations of racial diversity?

The Georgetown 272

In the fall of 1838, Georgetown College (later Georgetown University) was deep in debt and in danger of closing its doors. To prevent this, the college sold 272 slaves for the equivalent of $3.3 million in today's dollars. Georgetown was thus able to pay all its debts and keep its doors open.

The slaves were shipped to the port of New Orleans. Until recently, almost nothing was known about what had become of them. Thanks to generous private funding, however, a team of genealogists has been able to trace more than two hundred of the slaves from Maryland to Louisiana. They believe that there may be thousands of the slaves' living descendants in Louisiana today—many of them in the town of Maringouin, Louisiana.

In 2016, Georgetown students organized protests and sit-ins, using the hashtag #GU272 on Twitter to put pressure on the university to acknowledge its connection to slavery and to make amends in some way. In November 2016, the university issued a formal apology and agreed to remove the names of the Rev. Thomas F. Mulledy and the Rev. William McSherry, the college presidents involved in the sale, from two campus buildings. It was also announced that descendants of the Georgetown 272 would be granted the legacy status—a kind of preferential, but not guaranteed, admission—that relatives of the school's faculty, staff, and alumni enjoy.[1,2]

1. https://www.nytimes.com/2016/04/17/us/georgetown-university-search-for-slave-descendants.html.

2. http://www.theadvocate.com/baton_rouge/news/communities/westside/article_b221befe-0f26-11e7-8783-330932e2f352.html

Questions

1. Was Georgetown University morally required to do something to acknowledge and make amends for an event that happened 178 years ago in the university's history—a time when no one who is now associated with the university or the Georgetown 272 was alive? Why or why not?

2. Did Georgetown University do *enough* to respond to this event in their past? Why or why not? If you think they should have done more, what else should they have done?

3. Once news of the Georgetown 272 came to light, the Georgetown University administration responded relatively quickly. Many attribute this quick response to the hundreds of Georgetown student activists who called for Georgetown to respond appropriately. Do college students and faculty who know of grave injustices perpetrated by their universities have a duty to hold their universities accountable for responding

appropriately, or is such activism above and beyond the call of moral duty? Why or why not?

Statues of Historically Significant Racists

A statue of Andrew Jackson, the president who ordered the forcible resettlement of thousands of Native Americans on the Trail of Tears, leading many to their deaths, stands prominently in Jackson Square in New Orleans, Louisiana. In 1960, the square was declared a National Historic Landmark. In 2012, the American Planning Association named Jackson Square one of America's "Great Public Spaces." In the Tennessee state capitol building in Nashville, there is a large statue of Nathan Bedford Forrest, commander in the Confederate army and former Grand Wizard of the Ku Klux Klan. Eight statues of Confederate leaders currently reside in the National Statuary Hall Collection on Capitol Hill in Washington, DC. Among them are Confederate president Jefferson Davis, vice president Alexander Stephens, and general Robert E. Lee. In Monroe, Michigan, there stands a statue honoring George Armstrong Custer, who oversaw the killing of thousands of Native Americans as a commander in the US Army.

Many are convinced that statues and monuments to known racists, such as the ones described here, have no place in America. It would obviously be wrong for there to be statues of historically significant Nazi leaders displayed all over present-day Germany. It is equally out of place, many say, for there to be standing monuments to men like Jackson, Forrest, and Lee in present-day America.

Others think that, for better or worse, such monuments represent America's history. As such, they ought to be left alone. On behalf of this proposal, some claim that none of us would look very good if we were judged by the standards of people hundreds of years in the future. Further, if we had to topple the statue of every person guilty of something terrible, there would be very few statues standing at all. No one is un-ambiguously good, and that includes the notable people of the past.

Questions

1. What do you say: Should monuments to such people be taken down? Why or why not?
2. In your estimation, what is the best argument, or strongest consideration, against your position? What do you say in response?
3. What is the purpose of displaying statues in public places such as parks and government buildings? To remind us of our history? To honor the people represented in the statue? Something else? How does your answer to this question support your answer to Question 1?

READINGS

Letter from Birmingham City Jail

Martin Luther King, Jr.

In this now-classic piece, written while in jail for having violated a court injunction against participating in a demonstration, Martin Luther King, Jr., replies to criticisms from his fellow clergymen. These criticisms target the actions undertaken by King and other civil rights activists in the 1950s and 1960s. The criticisms are largely variations of a single theme: King advocated that laws be broken in order to pursue his goals, and his fellow clergymen disapprove of the means he is taking to try to achieve them.

King has several replies. One of them emphasizes that law-breaking should be used only as a last-resort response to grave injustice. But he and his fellow protesters had exhausted all efforts to engage in good-faith negotiations with the civic leaders who were committed to maintaining segregation within their communities. A second reply highlights two features of the civil disobedience practiced by King and his followers: first, that it was nonviolent, and second, that those who engaged in protest were doing so openly, and thereby willing to accept the punishments that they received. These features enable King to offer a third reply, namely, that such open and nonviolent protest actually expresses a respect for law, rather than a disregard for its authority. Finally, he also invokes St. Augustine's claim that "an unjust law is no law at all." Since the segregationist laws were deeply unjust, it would follow that they are no law at all, and so do not need to be followed.

King's remarks are punctuated by his disappointment with his fellow clergymen and by a steady commitment to a moderate response to injustice. At one extreme are those who have accommodated themselves to the status quo. At the other extreme are those who are so upset by failure to change it that they support violence to change the system. King advocates for a middle path—that of nonviolent, persistent protest—as the most principled and effective way to further the cause of justice.

16 April 1963

My Dear Fellow Clergymen:

While confined here in the Birmingham city jail, I came across your recent statement calling my present activities "unwise and untimely." Seldom do I pause to answer criticism of my work and ideas. If I sought to answer all the criticisms that cross my desk, my secretaries would have little time for anything other than such correspondence in the course of the day, and I would have no time for constructive work. But since I feel that you are men of genuine good will and that your criticisms are sincerely set forth, I want to try to answer your statement in what I hope will be patient and reasonable terms.

I think I should indicate why I am here in Birmingham, since you have been influenced by the view which argues against "outsiders coming in." I have the honor of serving as president of the Southern Christian Leadership Conference, an organization operating in every southern state, with headquarters in Atlanta, Georgia. We have some eighty-five affiliated organizations across the South, and one of them is the Alabama Christian Movement for Human Rights. Frequently we share staff, educational and financial resources with our affiliates. Several months ago the affiliate here in Birmingham asked us to be on call to engage in a nonviolent direct action program if such were deemed necessary. We readily consented, and when the hour came we lived up to our promise. So I, along with several members of my staff, am here because I was invited here. I am here because I have organizational ties here.

But more basically, I am in Birmingham because injustice is here. Just as the prophets of the eighth century B.C. left their villages and carried their "thus saith the Lord" far beyond the boundaries of their home towns, and just as the Apostle Paul left his village of Tarsus and carried the gospel of Jesus Christ to the far corners of the Greco Roman world, so am I compelled to carry the gospel of freedom beyond my own home town. Like Paul, I must constantly respond to the Macedonian call for aid.

Moreover, I am cognizant of the interrelatedness of all communities and states. I cannot sit idly by in Atlanta and not be concerned about what happens in Birmingham. Injustice anywhere is a threat to justice everywhere. We are caught in an inescapable network of mutuality, tied in a single garment of destiny. Whatever affects one directly, affects all indirectly. Never again can we afford to live with the narrow, provincial "outside agitator" idea. Anyone who lives inside the United States can never be considered an outsider anywhere within its bounds.

You deplore the demonstrations taking place in Birmingham. But your statement, I am sorry to say, fails to express a similar concern for the conditions that brought about the demonstrations. I am sure that none of you would want to rest content with the superficial kind of social analysis that deals merely with effects and does not grapple with underlying causes. It is unfortunate that demonstrations are taking place in Birmingham, but it is even more unfortunate that the city's white power structure left the Negro community with no alternative.

In any nonviolent campaign there are four basic steps: collection of the facts to determine whether injustices exist; negotiation; self-purification; and direct action. We have gone through all these steps in Birmingham. There can be no gainsaying the fact that racial injustice engulfs this community. Birmingham is probably the most thoroughly segregated city in the United States. Its ugly record of brutality is widely known. Negroes have experienced grossly unjust treatment in the courts. There have been more unsolved bombings of Negro homes and churches in Birmingham than in any other city in the nation. These are the hard, brutal facts of the case. On the basis of these conditions, Negro leaders sought to negotiate with the city fathers. But the latter consistently refused to engage in good faith negotiation. . . .

You may well ask: "Why direct action? Why sit ins, marches and so forth? Isn't negotiation a better path?" You are quite right in calling for negotiation. Indeed, this is the very purpose of direct action. Nonviolent direct action seeks to create such a crisis and foster such a tension that a community which has constantly refused to negotiate is forced to confront the issue. It seeks so to dramatize the issue that it can no longer be ignored. My citing the creation of tension as part of the work of the nonviolent resister may sound rather shocking. But I must confess that I am not afraid of the word "tension." I have earnestly opposed violent tension, but there is a type of constructive, nonviolent tension which is necessary for growth. Just as Socrates felt that it was necessary to create a tension in the mind so that individuals could rise from the bondage of myths and half-truths to the unfettered realm of creative analysis and objective appraisal, so must we see the need for nonviolent gadflies to create the kind of tension in society that will help men rise from the dark depths of prejudice and racism to the majestic heights of understanding and brotherhood. The purpose of our direct action program is to create a situation so crisis packed that it will inevitably open the door to negotiation. I therefore concur with you in your call for negotiation. Too long has our beloved Southland been bogged down in a tragic effort to live in monologue rather than dialogue.

One of the basic points in your statement is that the action that I and my associates have taken in Birmingham is untimely. Some have asked: "Why didn't you give the new city administration time to act?" The only answer that I can give to this query is that the new Birmingham administration must be prodded about as much as the outgoing one, before it will act. We are sadly mistaken if we feel that the election of Albert Boutwell as mayor will bring the millennium to Birmingham. While Mr. Boutwell is a much more gentle person than Mr. Connor, they are both segregationists, dedicated to maintenance of the status quo. I have hope that Mr. Boutwell will be reasonable enough to see the futility of massive resistance to desegregation. But he will not see this without pressure from devotees of civil rights. My friends, I must say to you that we have not made a single gain in civil rights without determined legal and nonviolent pressure. Lamentably, it is an historical fact that privileged groups seldom give up their privileges voluntarily. Individuals may see the moral light and voluntarily give up their unjust posture; but, as Reinhold Niebuhr has reminded us, groups tend to be more immoral than individuals.

We know through painful experience that freedom is never voluntarily given by the oppressor; it must be demanded by the oppressed. Frankly, I have yet to engage in a direct action campaign that was "well timed" in the view of those who have not suffered unduly from the disease of segregation. For years now I have heard the word "Wait!" It rings in the ear of every Negro with piercing familiarity. This "Wait" has almost always meant "Never." We must come to see, with one of our distinguished jurists, that "justice too long delayed is justice denied."

We have waited for more than 340 years for our constitutional and God given rights. The nations of Asia and Africa are moving with jetlike speed toward gaining political independence, but we still creep at horse and buggy pace toward gaining a cup of coffee at a lunch counter. Perhaps it is easy for those who have never felt the stinging darts of segregation to say, "Wait." But when you have seen vicious mobs lynch your mothers and fathers at will and drown your sisters and brothers at whim; when you have seen hate filled policemen curse, kick and even kill your black brothers and sisters; when you see the vast majority of your twenty million Negro brothers smothering in an airtight cage of poverty in the midst of an affluent society; when you suddenly find your tongue twisted and your speech stammering as you seek to explain to your six year old daughter why she can't go to the public amusement park that has just been advertised on television, and see tears welling up in her eyes when she is told that Funtown is closed to colored children, and see ominous clouds of inferiority beginning to form in her little mental sky, and see her beginning to distort her personality by developing an unconscious bitterness toward white people; when you have to concoct an answer for a five year old son who is asking: "Daddy, why do white people treat colored people so mean?"; when you take a cross country drive and find it necessary to sleep night after night in the uncomfortable corners of your automobile because no motel will accept you; when you are humiliated day in and day out by nagging signs reading "white" and "colored"; when your first name becomes "nigger," your middle name becomes "boy" (however old you are) and your last name becomes "John," and your wife and mother are never given the respected title "Mrs."; when you are harried by day and haunted by night by the fact that you are a Negro, living constantly at tiptoe stance, never quite knowing what to expect next, and are plagued with inner fears and outer resentments; when you are forever fighting a degenerating sense of "nobodiness"—then you will understand why we find it difficult to wait. There comes a time when the cup of endurance runs over, and men are no longer willing to be plunged into the abyss of despair. I hope, sirs, you can understand our legitimate and unavoidable impatience. You express a great deal of anxiety over our willingness to break laws. This is certainly a legitimate concern. Since we so diligently urge people to obey the Supreme Court's decision of 1954 outlawing segregation in the public schools, at first glance it may seem rather paradoxical for us consciously to break laws. One may well ask: "How can you advocate breaking some laws and obeying others?" The answer lies in the fact that there are two types of laws: just and unjust. I would be the first to advocate obeying just laws. One has not only a legal but a moral responsibility to obey just laws. Conversely, one has a moral responsibility to disobey unjust laws. I would agree with St. Augustine that "an unjust law is no law at all."

Now, what is the difference between the two? How does one determine whether a law is just or unjust? A just law is a man-made code that squares with the moral law or the law of God. An unjust law is a code that is out of harmony with the moral law. To put it in the terms of St. Thomas Aquinas: An unjust law is a human law that is not rooted in eternal law and natural law. Any law that uplifts human personality is just. Any law that degrades human personality is unjust. All segregation statutes are unjust because segregation distorts the soul and damages the personality. It gives the segregator a false sense of superiority and the segregated a false sense of inferiority. Segregation, to use the terminology of the Jewish philosopher Martin Buber, substitutes an "I-it" relationship for an "I-thou" relationship and ends up relegating persons to the status of things. Hence segregation is not only politically, economically and sociologically unsound, it is morally wrong and sinful. Paul Tillich has said that sin is separation. Is not segregation an existential expression of man's tragic separation, his awful estrangement, his terrible sinfulness? Thus it is that I can urge men to obey the 1954 decision of the Supreme Court, for it is morally right; and I can urge them to disobey segregation ordinances, for they are morally wrong.

Let us consider a more concrete example of just and unjust laws. An unjust law is a code that a numerical or power majority group compels a minority group to obey but does not make binding on itself. This is difference made legal. By the same token, a just law is a code that a majority compels a minority to follow and that it is willing to follow itself. This is sameness made legal. Let me give another explanation. A law is unjust if it is inflicted on a minority that, as a result of being denied the right to vote, had no part in enacting or devising the law. Who can say that the legislature of Alabama which set up that state's segregation laws was democratically elected? Throughout Alabama all sorts of devious methods are used to prevent Negroes from becoming registered voters, and there are some counties in which, even though Negroes constitute a majority of the population, not a single Negro is registered. Can any law enacted under such circumstances be considered democratically structured?

Sometimes a law is just on its face and unjust in its application. For instance, I have been arrested on a charge of parading without a permit. Now, there is nothing wrong in having an ordinance which requires a permit for a parade. But such an ordinance becomes unjust when it is used to maintain segregation and to deny citizens the First-Amendment privilege of peaceful assembly and protest.

I hope you are able to see the distinction I am trying to point out. In no sense do I advocate evading or defying the law, as would the rabid segregationist. That would lead to anarchy. One who breaks an unjust law must do so openly, lovingly, and with a willingness to accept the penalty. I submit that an individual who breaks a law that conscience tells him is unjust, and who willingly accepts the penalty of imprisonment in order to arouse the conscience of the community over its injustice, is in reality expressing the highest respect for law. . . .

We should never forget that everything Adolf Hitler did in Germany was "legal" and everything the Hungarian freedom fighters did in Hungary was "illegal." It was "illegal" to aid and comfort a Jew in Hitler's Germany. Even so, I am sure that, had I lived in Germany at the time, I would have aided and comforted my Jewish brothers. If today I lived in a Communist country where certain principles dear to the Christian faith are suppressed, I would openly advocate disobeying that country's antireligious laws.

I must make two honest confessions to you, my Christian and Jewish brothers. First, I must confess that over the past few years I have been gravely disappointed with the white moderate. I have almost reached the regrettable conclusion that the Negro's great stumbling block in his stride toward freedom is not the White Citizen's Counciler or the Ku Klux Klanner, but the white moderate, who is more devoted to "order" than to justice; who prefers a negative peace which is the absence of tension to a positive peace which is the presence of justice; who constantly says: "I agree with you in the goal you seek, but I cannot agree with your methods of direct action"; who paternalistically believes he can set the timetable for another man's freedom; who lives by a mythical concept of time and who constantly advises the Negro to wait for a "more convenient season." Shallow understanding from people of good will is more frustrating than absolute misunderstanding from people of ill will. Lukewarm acceptance is much more bewildering than outright rejection. . . .

In your statement you assert that our actions, even though peaceful, must be condemned because they precipitate violence. But is this a logical assertion? Isn't this like condemning a robbed man because his possession of money precipitated the evil act of robbery? Isn't this like condemning Socrates because his unswerving commitment to truth and his philosophical inquiries precipitated the act by the misguided populace in which they made him drink hemlock? Isn't this like condemning Jesus because his unique God consciousness and never ceasing devotion to God's will precipitated the evil act of crucifixion? We must come to see that, as the federal courts have consistently affirmed, it is wrong to urge an individual to cease his efforts to gain his basic constitutional rights because the quest may precipitate violence. Society must protect the robbed and punish the robber.

I had also hoped that the white moderate would reject the myth concerning time in relation to the struggle for freedom. I have just received a letter from a white brother in Texas. He writes:

"All Christians know that the colored people will receive equal rights eventually, but it is possible that you are in too great a religious hurry. It has taken Christianity almost two thousand years to accomplish what it has. The teachings of Christ take time to come to earth." Such an attitude stems from a tragic misconception of time, from the strangely irrational notion that there is something in the very flow of time that will inevitably cure all ills. Actually, time itself is neutral; it can be used either destructively or constructively. More and more I feel that the people of ill will have used time much more effectively than have the people of good will. We will have to repent in this generation not merely for the hateful words and actions of the bad people but for the appalling silence of the good people. Human progress never rolls in on wheels of inevitability; it comes through the tireless efforts of men willing to be co-workers with God, and without this hard work, time itself becomes an ally of the forces of social stagnation. . . .

Oppressed people cannot remain oppressed forever. . . . The Negro has many pent up resentments and latent frustrations, and he must release them. So let him march; let him make prayer pilgrimages to the city hall; let him go on freedom rides—and try to understand why he must do so. If his repressed emotions are not released in nonviolent ways, they will seek expression through violence; this is not a threat but a fact of history. So I have not said to my people: "Get rid of your discontent." Rather, I have tried to say that this normal and healthy discontent can be channeled into the creative outlet of nonviolent direct action. And now this approach is being termed extremist.

But though I was initially disappointed at being categorized as an extremist, as I continued to think about the matter I gradually gained a measure of satisfaction from the label. Was not Jesus an extremist for love: "Love your enemies, bless them that curse you, do good to them that hate you, and pray for them which despitefully use you, and persecute you." Was not Amos an extremist for justice: "Let justice roll down like waters and righteousness like an ever flowing stream." Was not Paul an extremist for the Christian gospel: "I bear in my body the marks of the Lord Jesus." Was not Martin

Luther an extremist: "Here I stand; I cannot do otherwise, so help me God." And John Bunyan: "I will stay in jail to the end of my days before I make a butchery of my conscience." And Abraham Lincoln: "This nation cannot survive half slave and half free." And Thomas Jefferson: "We hold these truths to be self-evident, that all men are created equal . . ." So the question is not whether we will be extremists, but what kind of extremists we will be. Will we be extremists for hate or for love? Will we be extremists for the preservation of injustice or for the extension of justice? In that dramatic scene on Calvary's hill three men were crucified. We must never forget that all three were crucified for the same crime—the crime of extremism. Two were extremists for immorality, and thus fell below their environment. The other, Jesus Christ, was an extremist for love, truth and goodness, and thereby rose above his environment. Perhaps the South, the nation and the world are in dire need of creative extremists.

I had hoped that the white moderate would see this need. Perhaps I was too optimistic; perhaps I expected too much. I suppose I should have realized that few members of the oppressor race can understand the deep groans and passionate yearnings of the oppressed race, and still fewer have the vision to see that injustice must be rooted out by strong, persistent and determined action. I am thankful, however, that some of our white brothers in the South have grasped the meaning of this social revolution and committed themselves to it. . . . Unlike so many of their moderate brothers and sisters, they have recognized the urgency of the moment and sensed the need for powerful "action" antidotes to combat the disease of segregation. . . .

Perhaps I have once again been too optimistic. Is organized religion too inextricably bound to the status quo to save our nation and the world? Perhaps I must turn my faith to the inner spiritual church, the church within the church, as the true ekklesia and the hope of the world. But again I am thankful to God that some noble souls from the ranks of organized religion have broken loose from the paralyzing chains of conformity and joined us as active partners in the struggle for freedom. They have left their secure congregations and walked the streets of Albany, Georgia, with us. They have gone down the highways of the South on tortuous rides for freedom. Yes, they have gone to jail with us. Some have been dismissed from their churches, have lost the support of their bishops and fellow ministers. But they have acted in the faith that right defeated is stronger than evil triumphant. Their witness has been the spiritual salt that has preserved the true meaning of the gospel in these troubled times. They have carved a tunnel of hope through the dark mountain of disappointment.

I hope the church as a whole will meet the challenge of this decisive hour. But even if the church does not come to the aid of justice, I have no despair about the future. I have no fear about the outcome of our struggle in Birmingham, even if our motives are at present misunderstood. We will reach the goal of freedom in Birmingham and all over the nation, because the goal of America is freedom. Abused and scorned though we may be, our destiny is tied up with America's destiny. Before the pilgrims landed at Plymouth, we were here. Before the pen of Jefferson etched the majestic words of the Declaration of Independence across the pages of history, we were here. For more than two centuries our forebears labored in this country without wages; they made cotton king; they built the homes of their masters while suffering gross injustice and shameful humiliation—and yet out of a bottomless vitality they continued to thrive and develop. If the inexpressible cruelties of slavery could not stop us, the opposition we now face will surely fail. We will win our freedom because the sacred heritage of our nation and the eternal will of God are embodied in our echoing demands.

Before closing I feel impelled to mention one other point in your statement that has troubled me profoundly. You warmly commended the Birmingham police force for keeping "order" and "preventing violence." I doubt that you would have so warmly commended the police force if you had seen its dogs sinking their teeth into unarmed, nonviolent Negroes. I doubt that you would so quickly commend the policemen if you were to observe their ugly and inhumane treatment of Negroes here in the city jail; if you were to watch them push and curse old Negro women and young

Negro girls; if you were to see them slap and kick old Negro men and young boys; if you were to observe them, as they did on two occasions, refuse to give us food because we wanted to sing our grace together. I cannot join you in your praise of the Birmingham police department. . . .

I wish you had commended the Negro sit inners and demonstrators of Birmingham for their sublime courage, their willingness to suffer and their amazing discipline in the midst of great provocation. One day the South will recognize its real heroes. They will be the James Merediths, with the noble sense of purpose that enables them to face jeering and hostile mobs, and with the agonizing loneliness that characterizes the life of the pioneer. They will be old, oppressed, battered Negro women, symbolized in a seventy-two-year-old woman in Montgomery, Alabama, who rose up with a sense of dignity and with her people decided not to ride segregated buses, and who responded with ungrammatical profundity to one who inquired about her weariness: "My feets is tired, but my soul is at rest." They will be the young high school and college students, the young ministers of the gospel and a host of their elders, courageously and nonviolently sitting in at lunch counters and willingly going to jail for conscience' sake. One day the South will know that when these disinherited children of God sat down at lunch counters, they were in reality standing up for what is best in the American dream and for the most sacred values in our Judaeo Christian heritage, thereby bringing our nation back to those great wells of democracy which were dug deep by the founding fathers in their formulation of the Constitution and the Declaration of Independence.

Never before have I written so long a letter. I'm afraid it is much too long to take your precious time. I can assure you that it would have been much shorter if I had been writing from a comfortable desk, but what else can one do when he is alone in a narrow jail cell, other than write long letters, think long thoughts and pray long prayers?

If I have said anything in this letter that overstates the truth and indicates an unreasonable impatience, I beg you to forgive me. If I have said anything that understates the truth and indicates my having a patience that allows me to settle for anything less than brotherhood, I beg God to forgive me.

I hope this letter finds you strong in the faith. I also hope that circumstances will soon make it possible for me to meet each of you, not as an integrationist or a civil-rights leader but as a fellow clergyman and a Christian brother. Let us all hope that the dark clouds of racial prejudice will soon pass away and the deep fog of misunderstanding will be lifted from our fear drenched communities, and in some not too distant tomorrow the radiant stars of love and brotherhood will shine over our great nation with all their scintillating beauty.

Yours for the cause of Peace and Brotherhood,
Martin Luther King, Jr.

Martin Luther King, Jr.: Letter from Birmingham City Jail

1. King endorses St. Augustine's view that "an unjust law is no law at all." Do you agree? Why or why not?

2. King supports a policy of nonviolent resistance to injustice. Do you think that violent resistance is ever morally justifiable? If not, why not? If so, under what conditions?

3. King also endorses the need of his followers to openly break the law. Why does he say this, and are his reasons plausible ones?

4. Can you express respect for the rule of law while also openly breaking the law? Why or why not?

5. King says that "there is a type of constructive, nonviolent tension which is necessary for growth." What does he mean by this, and is his thought plausible?

Time for a New Black Radicalism

Chris Lebron

Chris Lebron argues that the persistence of racism in the United States calls for the development of a new black radicalism. Such a political movement requires, in his words, "the explicit intention to use strong, nonconventional and unsanctioned means to effect systemic change by either disrupting the status quo or reinstating a preferred previous status quo." Lebron is not advocating a return to earlier, better times—he thinks that African Americans have never enjoyed anything remotely like social equality in the United States. In order to stand a better chance of enjoying a social status at least much closer to one that whites have long enjoyed, Lebron argues that a new version of black radicalism is required.

After criticizing three popular reasons for believing that radical social movements are morally problematic, Lebron explains a psychological dynamic that has long characterized the black community, that of shifting between rage and despair and trying to locate a rational basis for hope in the prospects of racial equality. Lebron argues that such a basis can be provided only through a form of unified political activism guided by a central leadership. Further, he questions whether the passive, nonviolent resistance that characterized Martin Luther King, Jr.'s campaign of social activism is appropriate for our times. Lebron does not seek to answer this question but to raise the possibility that King's program, effective as it was for his era, may no longer be an effective tool in the search for real racial justice in the United States.

Here are two statements:

1. *The Negro must love the white man, because the white man needs his love to remove his tensions, insecurities and fears.*
2. *You do too much singing. Today it is time to stop singing, and start swinging.*

Which of the above is emblematic of black radicalism? The answer is not as clear-cut as many of us might think.

The first statement was made by Martin Luther King Jr. in support of his much lauded and widely known strategy of nonviolent resistance.

King's call comes from his 1958 account of the Montgomery, Ala., bus boycott, "Stride Toward Freedom." In it, he articulated what he saw as an essential form of communal love that had its roots in New Testament Christianity but one that King felt was best described by the ancient Greek word "agape," a redeeming love that "springs from the need of the other person." Certainly, the families of the murdered congregationalists of Emanuel African Methodist Episcopal Church, in Charleston, S.C., were practicing that sort of love last week when they publicly forgave Dylann Roof, the young white supremacist who committed those murders.

The second statement was made in a characteristically biting tone by Malcolm X some six years after King's, in a 1964 speech in Detroit, known as "The Ballot or the Bullet," urging a more active resistance in the face of the government's repeated failure to protect black people's rights and lives. It was clearly directed at those who still affirmed King's program of nonviolent resistance, and raised the possibility that the continuation of that government failure might require blacks to take up arms.

Today, as we face a seemingly endless number of black lives being unjustifiably threatened, damaged and lost, and the resulting emotional cycle among black Americans of rage-despair-hope, it seems urgent that we ask again whether now is the time to make black radicalism central to black politics and activism. And if so, what should it demand of American citizens?

By radicalism I mean the explicit intention to use strong, nonconventional and unsanctioned means to effect systemic change by either disrupting the status quo or reinstating a preferred previous status quo. If the convention in a capitalist society is for the tech industry to charge for all services and you offer yours for free on the principle that "knowledge wants to be free," you are a radical; if you're a state legislator who cuts against the separation of church and state by lobbying to make the Bible the official book of the state, you are a radical.

It would be a disservice to the diverse tradition of black thought and activism to present the black radicalism monolithically, but we can identify a central motivation across its various iterations: to secure for blacks, against the history of white supremacy and the persistent racial oppression it has spawned, a degree of respect and dignity by means that directly confront and reconfigure both the discourse of and policies around racial justice. This is typically done with an eye toward not merely rationally persuading white Americans, but to intentionally unsettle and dislodge them from the comforts of white privilege.

We don't typically assign the term "radical" to people like the computer programmer or the legislator described above, for a number of reasons. First, radicalism, especially in the political sphere, is thought to necessarily entail violence. Second, radicalism is often used as a substitute for "fundamentalism." Lastly, radicalism is thought to represent (some form of) insurgency as a way of life or lifestyle. This last reason when combined with the first is what makes the idea of radicalism, especially black radicalism, alarming to many Americans. Yet it turns out that all of these reasons for treating radicalism as a dangerous doctrine are wrong.

It is important to begin by challenging the claim that radicalism and fundamentalism are interchangeable. Fundamentalism is an ideology and all ideologies share one critical flaw. They begin with a basic proposition (for example, the lives of all nonbelievers in religion X are expendable) and assert that proposition as a true statement about the world and then proceed to interpret all evidence in the light of that purported truth; thus ideology short-circuits effective means of assessing the reality of social, economic and political situations. Radicalism, in contrast, is significantly (but not entirely) post hoc—it is inherently pragmatic and arises in response to real threats, actual slights, suffered deprivations and obvious oppression.

When we take radicalism to be the same kind of thing as fundamentalism, it is a short step to the third charge—that radicalism is a way of life. This is clearly mistaken. Radicalism responds to real conditions of oppression that bring it into being, thus, seeks to eliminate the very conditions that make its existence necessary.

If one accepts these two clarifications, it also becomes clear that it is a mistake to think that radicalism is necessarily bound up with violence. Yes, it can be. America's founding fathers brought two nations into open warfare in the name of freedom—to disrupt the status quo imposed from without by Britain. This is a form of radicalism represented by Malcolm X. When he exhorted black Americans to stop singing and start swinging, he openly affirmed the legitimacy of violent self-defense against white supremacy and its murderous practitioners. Malcolm certainly sought to disrupt the status quo of white supremacy by unsanctioned means. But what of King teaching that blacks must love whites in order to ease their insecurities and fears? You should accept this as black radicalism as well.

The more obvious radical aspect of King's teaching has to do with the use of nonviolence as a doctrine of insurgent political action. While today political marches in the name of racial justice are common, in the middle of the 20th century large scale protests cut directly against the prevailing sentiment that blacks had no right to express themselves politically and publicly. King's challenge to various police forces to exact violence on a passive gathering sought to effectively and strongly disrupt a white supremacist status quo.

But here is another aspect: King's teachings also sought to disrupt the status quo *within the black community*, where despair risked deactivating the will to political action and rage compelled increasing numbers of black youth to begin considering taking up arms. King always held that passive resistance was the strategy of the truly strong person at a time when the black status quo had reason to view white Americans only as enemies, as undeserving of blacks' love.

In a manner unsettlingly resonant with the heart of the civil rights era, blacks today continue to find themselves moving between rage and despair. Rage at the abuses that should have ended when the slaves were freed, despair because the claim that black lives matter was dismissed up to and beyond the signing of the Civil Rights Act. This leaves hope, a disposition taken up when one thinks the expression of rage and despair might have compelled one's oppressors to finally act with a sense of justice. Have the many decades of expressing rage and despair done its work making space for hope?

As things stand, there is no rational space for *mere* hope—recent events in the light of the facts of history discourage naïveté. A truly intelligent hope leaves little to chance and encourages conviction and action to better secure a preferred future—in our case, a racially just America. It seems to me the way to hope today lies in the promise of a resurgent black radical politics.

Systemic racial inequality is a daily fact of American life. There is no shortage of news of vigilantes and police literally getting away with murdering blacks; white supremacist ideologies still thrive, and at times produce awful consequences, as we saw in the Charleston massacre. And that is just the overtly grim news. When we add to that the persistent racial inequalities in income, housing, education, medical care and employment, there is no denying that the withholding from black Americans of resources, opportunity and basic sympathy is the status quo in America. It is an unjust status quo, thus it must be disturbed, disrupted. The hope here, then, would focus on a future wherein blacks' needs, aspirations, and basic humanity are not only beyond question, but recognized as having equal importance and worth as whites'.

However, maybe you are more concerned with this question: *Which* flavor of black radicalism should be embraced—Malcolm's or Martin's? In a society in which blacks must insist and remind their fellow citizens that black lives matter, that really is the question, isn't it? Maybe we should turn to history as our guide.

Blacks have tried for more than 150 years, since the Emancipation Proclamation was signed, to reasonably engage American institutions and whites with a very uneven, and in important respects, failed record of adequate responsiveness. It can be difficult to imagine what else one can say to get what one is owed after so long. But we should accept at least two propositions. First, that any resurgent black radical politics must also be a unified politics, one that values central leadership coupled with an explicit program of action. The protests and movements in response to the past year's abuse of black citizens have shown that local and spontaneous protests can be effective, but also limited in scope—they have not led to adequate action at the level of national politics. Even when local protests have persisted in places like Ferguson, Mo., they tend to quickly fall from the American public's view, and thus their conscience.

Second, some 50 years after King, maybe blacks should not desire his second coming. Though he is consistently invoked by leaders at every political level, it seems to me that the days of sitting at the lunch counter and enduring inhumane abuses must be left to history. Rather, black Americans have tragically earned the right to ask a question more appropriately radical for our present moment: Where is the love *for us*?

It is time that blacks not be expected nor expect of themselves to set the standard for goodness and upstanding character in a society that regularly treats them cruelly. When I ask, *where is the love*, I am really asking you to tell me in return, to speak by your actions and take responsibility for the kind of radicalism it is now appropriate for blacks to take up: Should we heed Martin's counsel and open our arms in embrace or should we be wary of yet another painful and bloody era of speaking and acting in bad faith, and as Malcolm advised, close our fists?

Chris Lebron: Time for a New Black Radicalism

1. How does Lebron characterize radicalism? Does his characterization tally with your understanding of what radicalism is?

2. Must radicalism be violent? If radicalism is a plausible response to oppression, is violence ever a justified element of a radical response? If so, when? If not, why not?

3. Lebron claims that black radical activism "is typically done with an eye toward not merely rationally persuading white Americans, but to intentionally unsettle and dislodge them from the comforts of white privilege." Why does he think such actions are warranted? Do you agree or disagree with his assessment?

4. Lebron enumerates and rejects three popular reasons for thinking radicalism a dangerous doctrine. Present these reasons and assess his critique of them.

5. Lebron claims that "the way to hope today lies in the promise of a resurgent black radical politics." Explain what he means by this and assess the merits of his claim.

6. Lebron writes that "some 50 years after King, maybe blacks should not desire his second coming." Explain what Lebron means by this and assess the merits of his claim.

The New Jim Crow

Michelle Alexander

In this selection Michelle Alexander summarizes some of the central lines of thinking from her important 2010 book of the same title. The work is not philosophical in its orientation, but advances a series of claims that provide crucial historical and sociological background for philosophical inquiry into the continuing legacy of racism in the United States.

Alexander opens her account by recalling her former belief in a familiar narrative of steady improvement in race relations in the United States. The narrative goes something like this: While far from perfect, today's situation for African Americans is in kind and degree hugely better than it was fifty or one hundred years ago. The continual progress has culminated in the election of Barack Obama, whose presidency ushered in a "postracial" society where the color of one's skin is now largely irrelevant for one's life prospects and the ways one is treated on a daily basis.

Alexander's main thesis is that the fundamental facts of life for African Americans have changed very little over the past century. Although laws are no longer couched explicitly in racist terms, the *practice* of the law—especially the criminal law—has effects that are deeply discriminatory. The harms caused by the rise of mass incarceration since the 1970s have fallen disproportionately on members of the African American community. Nor is this any accident, according to Alexander—many of those who developed and sustained the harmful policies did so in order to ensure the preservation of a racial caste system in the United States. While the laws on the books may look color-blind, the story on the ground is anything but, leading Alexander to call the regime of mass incarceration the *new* Jim Crow.

The subject that I intend to explore today is one that most Americans seem content to ignore. Conversations and debates about race—much less racial caste—are frequently dismissed as yesterday's news, not relevant to the current era. Media pundits and more than a few politicians insist that we, as a nation, have finally "moved beyond race." We have entered into the era of "post-racialism," it is said, the promised land of colorblindness. Not just in America, but around the world, President Obama's election has been touted as the final nail in the coffin of Jim Crow, the bookend placed on the history of racial caste in America.

This triumphant notion of post-racialism is, in my view, nothing more than fiction—a type of Orwellian doublespeak made no less sinister by virtue of the fact that the people saying it may actually believe it. Racial caste is not dead; it is alive and well in America. The mass incarceration of poor people of color in the United States amounts to a new caste system—one specifically tailored to the political, economic, and social challenges of our time. It is the moral equivalent of Jim Crow.

I am well aware that this kind of claim may be hard for many people to swallow. Particularly if you, yourself, have never spent time in prison or been labeled a felon, the claim may seem downright absurd. I, myself, rejected the notion that something akin to a racial caste system could be functioning in the United States more than a decade ago—something that I now deeply regret.

I first encountered the idea of a new racial caste system in the mid-1990s when I was rushing to catch the bus in Oakland, California, and a bright orange poster caught my eye. It screamed in large bold print: THE DRUG WAR IS THE NEW JIM CROW. I recall pausing for a moment and skimming the text of the flyer. A radical group was holding a community meeting about police brutality, the new three-strikes law in California, the drug war, and the expansion of America's prison system. The meeting was being held at a small community church a few blocks away; it had seating capacity for

Michelle Alexander, "The New Jim Crow," *The Ohio State Journal of Criminal Law* 9 (2011), pp. 7–26.

no more than fifty people. I sighed and muttered to myself something like, "Yeah, the criminal justice system is racist in many ways, but it really doesn't help to make such absurd comparisons. People will just think you're crazy." I then crossed the street and hopped on the bus. I was headed to my new job, director of the Racial Justice Project for the ACLU in Northern California.

When I began my work at the ACLU, I assumed the criminal justice system had problems of racial bias, much in the same way that all major institutions in our society are plagued to some degree with problems associated with conscious and unconscious bias. As a civil rights lawyer, I had litigated numerous class-action employment discrimination cases, and I understood well the many ways in which racial stereotyping can permeate subjective decision-making processes at all levels of an organization with devastating consequences. While at the ACLU, I shifted my focus from employment discrimination to criminal justice reform, and dedicated myself to the task of working with others to identify and eliminate racial bias whenever and wherever it reared its ugly head.

By the time I left the ACLU, I had come to suspect that I was wrong about the criminal justice system. It was not just another institution infected with racial bias, but rather a different beast entirely. The activists who posted the sign on the telephone phone were not crazy; nor were the smattering of lawyers and advocates around the country who were beginning to connect the dots between our current system of mass incarceration and earlier forms of social control. Quite belatedly, I came to see that mass incarceration in the United States had, in fact, emerged as a stunningly comprehensive and well-disguised system of racialized social control that functions in a manner strikingly similar to Jim Crow.

I state my basic thesis in the introduction to my book, *The New Jim Crow:*

What has changed since the collapse of Jim Crow has less to do with the basic structure of our society than the language we use to justify it. In the era of colorblindness, it is no longer socially permissible to use race, explicitly, as a justification for discrimination, exclusion, and social contempt. So we don't. Rather than rely on race, we use our criminal justice system to label people of color "criminals" and then engage in all the practices we supposedly left behind. Today it is perfectly legal to discriminate against criminals in nearly all the ways it was once legal to discriminate against African Americans. Once you're labeled a felon, the old forms of discrimination—employment discrimination, housing discrimination, denial of the right to vote, and exclusion from jury service—are suddenly legal. As a criminal, you have scarcely more rights, and arguably less respect, than a black man living in Alabama at the height of Jim Crow. We have not ended racial caste in America; we have merely redesigned it.[1]

I reached this conclusion reluctantly. Like many civil rights lawyers, I was inspired to attend law school by the civil rights victories of the 1950s and 1960s. Even in the face of growing social and political opposition to remedial policies such as affirmative action, I clung to the notion that the evils of Jim Crow are behind us and that, while we have a long way to go to fulfill the dream of an egalitarian, multiracial democracy, we have made real progress. I understood the problems plaguing poor communities of color, including problems associated with crime and rising incarceration rates, to be a function of poverty and lack of access to quality education—the continuing legacy of slavery and Jim Crow. I strenuously resisted the idea that a new caste system was operating in this country; I was nearly offended by the notion. But after years of working on issues of racial profiling, police brutality, drug law enforcement in poor communities of color, and attempting to assist people released from prison "re-enter" into a society that never seemed to have much use for them in the first place, I had a series of experiences that began what I call my "awakening." I began to awaken to a racial reality that is so obvious to me now that what seems odd in retrospect is that I was blind to it for so long.

Here are some facts I uncovered in the course of my work and research that you probably have not heard on the evening news:

* More African American adults are under correctional control today—in prison or jail, on probation or parole—than were enslaved in 1850, a decade before the Civil War began.
* In 2007 more black men were disenfranchised than in 1870, the year the Fifteenth Amendment was ratified prohibiting laws that explicitly deny the right to vote on the basis of race. During the Jim Crow era, African Americans continued to be denied access to the ballot through poll taxes and literacy tests. Those laws have been struck down, but today felon disenfranchisement laws accomplish what poll taxes and literacy tests ultimately could not.
* In many large urban areas in the United States, the majority of working-age African American men have criminal records. In fact, it was reported in 2002 that, in the Chicago area, if you take into account prisoners, the figure is nearly 80%.

Those bearing criminal records and cycling in and out of our prisons today are part of a growing under-caste—not class, caste—a group of people, defined largely by race, who are relegated to a permanent second-class status by law. They can be denied the right to vote, automatically excluded from juries, and legally discriminated against in employment, housing, access to education, and public benefits, much as their grandparents and great-grandparents were during the Jim Crow era.

I find that when I tell people that mass incarceration amounts to a New Jim Crow, I am frequently met with shocked disbelief. The standard reply is: "How can you say that a racial caste system exists? Just look at Barack Obama! Just look at Oprah Winfrey! Just look at the black middle class!"

The reaction is understandable. But we ought to question our emotional reflexes. The mere fact that some African Americans have experienced

---

1. Michelle Alexander, *The New Jim Crow: Mass Incarceration in the Age of Colorblindness*, 2 (2010).

great success in recent years does not mean that something akin to a caste system no longer exists. No caste system in the United States has ever governed all black people. There have always been "free blacks" and black success stories, even during slavery and Jim Crow. During slavery, there were some black slave owners—not many, but some. And during Jim Crow, there were some black lawyers and doctors—not many, but some. The unprecedented nature of black achievement in formerly white domains today certainly suggests that the old Jim Crow is dead, but it does not necessarily mean the end of racial caste. If history is any guide, it may have simply taken a different form.

Any honest observer of American racial history must acknowledge that racism is highly adaptable. The rules and reasons the legal system employs to enforce status relations of any kind evolve and change as they are challenged. Since our nation's founding, African Americans have been repeatedly controlled through institutions, such as slavery and Jim Crow, which appear to die, but then are reborn in new form—tailored to the needs and constraints of the time.

For example, following the collapse of slavery, the system of convict leasing was instituted—a system many historians believe was worse than slavery. After the Civil War, black men were arrested by the thousands for minor crimes, such as loitering and vagrancy, and sent to prison. They were then leased to plantations. It was our nation's first prison boom. The idea was that prisoners leased to plantations were supposed to earn their freedom. But the catch was they could never earn enough to pay back the plantation owner the cost of their food, clothing and shelter to the owner's satisfaction, and thus they were effectively re-enslaved, sometimes for the rest of their lives. It was a system more brutal in many respects than slavery, because plantation owners had no economic incentive to keep convicts healthy or even alive. They could always get another one?

Today, I believe the criminal justice system has been used once again in a manner that effectively re-creates caste in America. Our criminal justice system functions more like a caste system than a system of crime control.

For those who find that claim difficult to swallow, consider the facts. Our prison system has quintupled for reasons that have stunningly little do with crime. In less than 30 years, the U.S. penal population exploded from around 300,000 to more than 2 million.[2] The United States now has the highest rate of incarceration in the world, dwarfing the rates of nearly every developed country, including highly repressive regimes like China and Iran.[3]

In fact, if our nation were to return to the incarceration rates of the 1970s—a time, by the way, when civil rights activists thought that imprisonment rates were egregiously high—we would have to release four out of five people who are in prison today. More than a million people employed by the criminal justice system could lose their jobs. That is how enormous and deeply entrenched the new system has become in a very short period of time.

As staggering as those figures are, they actually obscure the severity of the crisis in poor communities of color. Professor Loïc Wacquant has argued that the term "mass incarceration" itself is a misnomer, since it implies that nearly everyone has been subject to the new system of control.[4] But, of course that is not the case. The overwhelming majority of the increase in imprisonment has been poor people of color, with the most astonishing rates of incarceration found among black men. It was estimated several years ago that, in Washington, D.C.—our nation's capital—three out of four young black men (and nearly all those in the poorest neighborhoods) could expect to serve time in prison. Rates of incarceration nearly as shocking can be found in other communities of color across America.

So what accounts for this vast new system of control? Crime rates? That is the common answer. But no, crime rates have remarkably little to do

---

2. *Key Facts at a Glance: Correctional Populations*, Bureau of Justice Statistics (updated Dec. 16, 2010), available at http://bjs.ojp.usdoj.gov/content/glance/tables/corr2tab.cfm:

3. Pew Ctr. On the States, One in 100: Behind Bars in America 2008, at 5 (Feb. 2008), http://www.pewcenteronthestates.org/uploadedFiles/One%20in%20100.pdf.

4. See Loïc Wacquant, "Class, Race & Hyperincarceration in Revanchist America," *Daedalus*, Summer 2010, at 74.

with skyrocketing incarceration rates. Crime rates have fluctuated over the past thirty years, and are currently at historical lows, but incarceration rates have consistently soared. Most criminologists and sociologists today acknowledge that crime rates and incarceration rates have, for the most part, moved independently of one another. Rates of imprisonment—especially black imprisonment—have soared regardless of whether crime has been rising or falling in any given community or the nation as a whole.

So what does explain this vast new system of control, if not crime rates? Ironically, the activists who posted the sign on that telephone pole were right: The War on Drugs. The War on Drugs and the "get tough" movement explain the explosion in incarceration in the United States and the emergence of a vast, new racial undercaste. In fact, drug convictions alone accounted for about two-thirds of the increase in the federal system, and more than half of the increase in the state prison population between 1985 and 2000. Drug convictions have increased more than 1000% since the drug war began, an increase that bears no relationship to patterns of drug use or sales.[5]

People of all races use and sell drugs at remarkably similar rates, but the enemy in this war has been racially defined.[6] The drug war has been waged almost exclusively in poor communities of color, despite the fact that studies consistently indicate that people of all races use and sell drugs at remarkably similar rates. This evidence defies our basic stereotype of a drug dealer, as a black kid standing on a street corner, with his pants hanging down. Drug dealing happens in the ghetto, to be sure, but it happens everywhere else in America as well. Illegal drag markets, it turns out—like American society generally—are relatively segregated by race. Blacks tend to sell to blacks, whites to whites, Latinos sell to each other. University students sell to each other. People of all races use and sell drugs. A kid in rural Kansas does not drive to the 'hood to get his pot, or meth, or cocaine, he buys it from somebody down the road. In fact, the research suggests that where significant differences by race can be found, white youth are more likely to commit drug crimes than youth of color.[7]

But that is not what you would guess when entering our nation's prisons and jails, overflowing as they are with black and brown drug offenders. In the United States, those who do time for drug crime are overwhelmingly black and brown.[8] In some states, African Americans constitute 80 to 90% of all drug offenders sent to prison.[9]

I find that many people are willing to concede these racial disparities once they see the data. Even so, they tend to insist that the drug war is motivated by concern over violent crime. They say: just look at our prisons. Nearly half of the people behind bars are violent offenders. Typically this is where the discussion ends.

The problem with this abbreviated analysis is that violent crime is not responsible for the prison boom. To get a sense of how large a contribution the drug war has made to mass incarceration, consider this: there are more people in prison today just for drug offenses than were incarcerated in 1980 for all

---

5. Marc Mauer & Ryan S. King, "A 25-Year Quagmire: The War on Drugs and Its Impact on American Society," pp. 2, 4 (Sept. 2007), available at https://www.sentencingproject.org/publications/a-25-year-quagmire-the-war-on-drugs-and-its-impact-on-american-society/.

6. The overwhelming majority of those arrested and incarcerated for drug crimes during the past few decades have been black and brown. When the War on Drugs gained full steam in the mid-1980s, prison admissions for African Americans "skyrocketed, nearly quadrupling in three years, then increasing steadily until it reached in 2000 a level more than twenty-six times the level in 1983." Jeremy Travis, *But They All Come Back: Facing the Challenges of Prison Reentry*, 28 (2002).

7. The National Household Survey on Drug Abuse reported in 2000 that white youth aged 12–17 were more likely to have used and sold illegal drugs than African American youth. Neelum Arya & Ian Augarten, *Campaign for Youth Justice, Critical Condition: African-American Youth in The Justice System* (2003), at table 5, p. 16 and p. 19.

8. Although the majority of illegal drug users and dealers nationwide are white, roughly three-fourths of all people imprisoned for drug offenses since the War on Drugs began have been African American or Latino. Marc Mauer & Ryan S. King, *The Sentencing Project, Schools and Prisons: Fifty Years After Brown v. Board of Education*, 3 (Apr. 2004).

9. Human Rights Watch, "Punishment and Prejudice: Racial Disparities in the War on Drugs," Vol. 12, No. 2, at 19 (May 2000).

reasons.[10] The reality is that the overwhelming majority of people who are swept into this system are non-violent offenders.

In this regard, it is important to keep in mind that most people who are under correctional control are not in prison or jail. As of 2008, there were approximately 2.3 million people in prisons and jails, and a staggering 5.1 million people under "community correctional supervision"—i.e., on probation or parole. Millions more have felony records and spend their lives cycling in and out of prison, unable to find work or shelter, unable to vote or to serve on juries. This system depends on the prison label, not prison time. It does not matter whether you have actually spent time in prison; your second-class citizenship begins the moment you are branded a felon. It is this badge of inferiority—the criminal record—that ushers you into a parallel social universe in which discrimination is, once again, perfectly legal.

How did this extraordinary system of control, unprecedented in world history, come to pass? Most people insist upon a benign motive. They seem to believe that the War on Drugs was launched in response to rising drug crime and the emergence of crack cocaine in inner city communities. For a long time, I believed that too. But that is not the case. Drug crime was actually declining, not rising, when President Ronald Reagan officially declared the drug war in 1982. President Richard Nixon was the first to coin the term a "war on drugs," but President Reagan turned the rhetorical war into a literal one. From the outset, the war had little to do with drug crime and much to do with racial politics.

The drug war was part of a grand and highly successful Republican Party strategy—often known as the Southern Strategy—of using racially coded political appeals on issues of crime and welfare to attract poor and working class white voters who were resentful of, and threatened by, desegregation, busing, and affirmative action. Poor and working class whites had their world rocked by the Civil Rights Movement. White elites could send their kids to private schools and give them all of the advantages wealth has to offer. But poor and working class whites were faced with a social demotion. It was their kids who might be bused across town, and forced to compete for the first time with a new group of people they had long believed to be inferior for decent jobs and educational opportunities. Affirmative action, busing, and desegregation created an understandable feeling of vulnerability, fear, and anxiety among a group already struggling for survival.

Republican party strategists found that thinly veiled promises to "get tough" on "them"—the racially defined others—could be highly successful in persuading poor and working class whites to defect from the Democratic New Deal Coalition and join the Republican Party. H.R. Haldeman, President Richard Nixon's former Chief of Staff, reportedly summed up the strategy: "[T]he whole problem is really the blacks. The key is to devise a system that recognizes this while not appearing to."[11]

A couple years after the drag war was announced, crack cocaine hit the streets of inner-city communities. The Reagan administration seized on this development with glee, hiring staff who were responsible for publicizing inner-city crack babies, crack mothers, the so-called "crack whores," and drug-related violence. The goal was to make inner-city crack abuse and violence a media sensation that, it was hoped, would bolster public support for the drag war and would lead Congress to devote millions of dollars in additional funding to it.

The plan worked like a charm. For more than a decade, black drug dealers and users became regulars in newspaper stories and saturated the evening TV r news—forever changing our conception of who the drug users and dealers are. Once the enemy in the war was racially defined, a wave of punitiveness took over. Congress and state legislatures nationwide devoted billions of dollars to the drug war and passed harsh mandatory minimum sentences for drug crimes—sentences longer than murderers receive in many countries. Many black politicians

---

10. "Unfairness in Federal Cocaine Sentencing: Is it Time to Crack the 100 to 1 Disparity?" Hearing on H.R. 1459, H.R. 1466, H.R. 265, H.R. 2178 and H.R. 18 Before the H. Subcomm. On Crime, Terrorism, and Homeland Security of the H. Comm. On the Judiciary, 111th Cong. 2 (2009) (testimony of Marc Mauer, Executive Director, Sentencing Project).

11. Willard M. Oliver, *The Law & Order Presidency*, 126–127 (2003).

joined the "get tough" bandwagon, apparently oblivious to their complicity with the emergence of a system of social control that would, in less than two decades, become unprecedented in world history.

Almost immediately, Democrats began competing with Republicans to prove that they could be even tougher on "them." In President Bill Clinton's boastful words, "I can be nicked on a lot, but no one can say I'm soft on crime."[12] The facts bear him out. Clinton's "tough on crime" policies resulted in the largest increases in federal and state prison inmates of any president in American history. But Clinton was not satisfied with exploding prison populations. In an effort to appeal to the "white swing voters," he and the so-called new Democrats championed legislation banning drug felons from public housing (no matter how minor the offense) and denying them basic public benefits, including food stamps, for life. Discrimination in virtually every aspect of political, economic, and social life is now perfectly legal, once you're labeled a felon.

All of this has been justified on the grounds that getting brutally tough on "them" is the only way to root out violent offenders or drug kingpins. The media images of violence in ghetto communities—particularly when crack first hit the street— led many to believe that the drug war was focused on the most serious offenders. Yet nothing could be further from the truth. Federal funding has flowed to those state and local law enforcement agencies that increase dramatically the volume of drug arrests, not the agencies most successful in bringing down the bosses. What has been rewarded in this war is sheer numbers—the sheer volume of drug arrests. To make matters worse, federal drug forfeiture laws allow state and local law enforcement agencies to keep for their own use 80% of the cash, cars, and homes seized from drug suspects, thus granting law enforcement a direct monetary interest in the profitability of the drug market itself.[13]

The results are predictable. People of color have been rounded up en masse for relatively minor, nonviolent drug offenses. In 2005, for example, four out of five drug arrests were for possession, only one out of five for sales.[14] Most people in state prison for drug offenses have no history of violence or even of significant selling activity.[15] In fact, during the 1990s—the period of the most dramatic expansion of the drug war—nearly 80% of the increase in drug arrests was for marijuana possession, a drug generally considered less harmful than alcohol or tobacco and at least as prevalent in middle-class white communities as in the inner city.

In this way, a new racial undercaste has been created in an astonishingly short period of time. Millions of people of color are now saddled with criminal records and legally denied the very rights that were supposedly won in the Civil Rights Movement.

The U.S. Supreme Court, for its part, has mostly turned a blind eye to race discrimination in the criminal justice system. The Court has closed the courthouse doors to claims of racial bias at every stage of the criminal justice process from stops and searches to plea bargaining and sentencing. Law enforcement officials are largely free to discriminate on the basis of race today, so long as no one admits it. That's the key. In *McCleskey v. Kemp* and *United States v. Armstrong,* the Supreme Court made clear that only evidence of conscious, intentional racial bias—the sort of bias that is nearly impossible to prove these days in the absence of an admission— is deemed sufficient.[16] No matter how impressive the statistical evidence, no matter how severe the racial disparities and racial impacts might be, the Supreme Court is not interested. The Court has, as a practical matter, closed the door to claims of racial bias in the criminal justice system. It has immunized the new caste system from judicial scrutiny for racial bias, much as it once rallied to legitimate and protect slavery and Jim Crow.

---

12. Michael Kramer, "The Political Interest Frying Them Isn't the Answer," *Time,* Mar. 14, 1994, at 32.

13. See Eric Blumenson & Eva Nilsen, *Policing for Profit: The Drug War's Hidden Economic Agenda,* 65 U. Chi. L. Rev. 35, 44–45, 51 (1998).

14. Mauer & King, *supra* note 20, at 3.

15. *Id.* at 2.

16. See *United States v. Armstrong,* 517 U.S. 456 (1996); *McCleskey v. Kemp,* 481 U.S. 279 (1987).

In my experience, those who have been incarcerated have little difficulty recognizing the parallels between mass incarceration and Jim Crow. Many former prisoners have told me, "It's slavery on the inside; Jim Crow when you get out." Prisoners are often forced to work for little or no pay. Once released, they are denied basic civil and human rights until they die. They are treated as though they possess an incurable defect, a shameful trait that can never be fully eradicated or redeemed. In the words of one woman who is currently incarcerated:

> When I leave here it will be very difficult for me in the sense that I'm a felon. That I will always be a felon . . . it will affect my job, it will affect my education . . . custody [of my children], it can affect child support, it can affect everywhere—family, friends, housing. . . . People that are convicted of drug crimes can't even get housing anymore. . . . Yes, I did my prison time. How long are you going to punish me as a result of it?[17]

Willie Johnson, a forty-three year old African American man recently released from prison in Ohio, explained it this way:

> My felony conviction has been like a mental punishment, because of all the obstacles. . . . Every time I go to put in a [job] application—I have had three companies hire me and tell me to come to work the next day. But then the day before they will call me and tell me don't come in— because you have a felony. And that is what is devastating because you think you are about to go to work and they call you and say because of your felony we can't hire [you]. I have run into this at least a dozen times. Two times I got very depressed and sad because I couldn't take care of myself as a man. It was like I wanted to give up—because in society nobody wants to give us a helping hand.[18]

Not surprisingly, for many trapped in the undercaste, the hurt and depression gives way to anger. A black minister in Waterloo, Mississippi put it this way:

> "Felony" is the new N-word. They don't have to call you a nigger anymore. They just say you're a felon. In every ghetto you see alarming numbers of young men with felony convictions. Once you have that felony stamp, your hope of employment, for any kind of integration into society, it begins to fade out. Today's lynching is a felony charge. Today's lynching is incarceration. Today's lynch mobs are professionals. They have a badge; they have a law degree. A felony is a modern way of saying, "I'm going to hang you up and bum you." Once you get that *F*, you're on fire.[19]

What is painfully obvious to many trapped within the system, remains largely invisible to those of us who have decent jobs and zoom around on freeways, passing by the virtual and literal prisons in which members of the undercaste live.

None of this is to say, of course, that mass incarceration and Jim Crow are the "same." There are significant differences between mass incarceration and earlier forms of racial control, to be sure—many of which are described in some detail in my book. Just as there were vast differences between slavery and Jim Crow, there are important differences between Jim Crow and mass incarceration. Yet all three (slavery, Jim Crow, and mass incarceration) have operated as tightly networked systems of laws, policies, customs, and institutions that operate collectively to ensure the subordinate status of a group defined largely by race. When we step back and view the system of mass incarceration as a whole, there is a profound sense of déjà vu. There is a familiar stigma and shame. There is an elaborate system of control, complete with political disenfranchisement and legalized discrimination in every major realm of economic and social life.

---

17. Jeff Manza & Christopher Uggen, *Locked Out: Felon Disenfranchisement and American Democracy*, 152 (2006).

18. Interview by Guylando A. M. Moreno with Willie Thompson, in Cincinnati, Ohio (Mar. 2005). See also Alexander, supra note 2, at 158–159.

19. Sasha Abramsky, *Conned: How Millions Went to Prison, Lost the Vote, and Helped Send George W. Bush to the White House*, 140 (2006).

And there is the production of racial meaning and racial boundaries. Just consider a few of the rules, laws, and policies that apply to people branded felons today and ask yourself if they remind you of a bygone era:

*   Denial of the right to vote. Forty-eight states and the District of Columbia deny prisoners the right to vote. That, of course, is just the tip of the iceberg. Even after the term of punishment expires, states are free to deny people who have been labeled felons the right to vote for a period of years or their entire lives. In a few states, one in four black men have been permanently disenfranchised.[20] Nationwide, nearly one in seven black men are either temporarily or permanently disenfranchised as a result of felon disenfranchisement laws.[21]

*   Exclusion from jury service. One hallmark of Jim Crow was the systematic exclusion of blacks from juries. Today, those labeled felons are automatically excluded from juries, and to make matters worse, people are routinely excluded from juries if they "have had negative experiences with law enforcement." Good luck finding a person of color in a ghetto community today who has not yet had a negative experience with law enforcement. The all-white jury is no longer a thing of the past in many regions of the country, in part, because so many African Americans have been labeled felons and excluded from juries.

*   Employment discrimination. Employment discrimination against felons is deemed legal and absolutely routine. Regardless of whether your felony occurred three months ago or thirty-five years ago, for the rest of your life you're required to check that box on employment applications asking the dreaded question: "Have you ever been convicted of a felony?" In one survey, about 70% of employers said they would not hire a drug felon convicted for sales or possession.[22] Most states also deny a wide range of professional licenses to people labeled felons. In some states, you can't even get license to be a barber if you're a felon.

*   Housing discrimination. Housing discrimination is perfectly legal. Public housing projects as well as private landlords are free to discriminate against criminals. In fact, those labeled felons may be barred from public housing for five years or more and legally discriminated against for the rest of their lives.[23]

*   Public benefits. Discrimination is legal against those who have been labeled felons in public benefits. In fact, federal law renders drug offenders ineligible for food stamps for the rest of their lives.[24] Fortunately, some states have opted out of the federal ban, but it remains the case that thousands of people, including pregnant women and people with HIV/AIDS, are denied even food stamps, simply because they were once caught with drugs.

*   Fees and fines. What do we expect people convicted of drug felonies to do? Even if they manage to escape jail time and get nothing more than probation, they will be discriminated against in employment, denied public housing, locked out of the private housing market, and possibly denied even food stamps. Apparently what we expect them to do is to pay hundreds or thousands of dollars

20. Jamie Fellner & Marc Mauer, *The Sentencing Project, Losing the Vote: The Impact of Felony Disenfranchisement Laws in the United States*, 1 (1998), available at https://www.sentencingproject.org/publications/losing-the-vote-the-impact-of-felony-disenfranchisement-laws-in-the-united-states/

21. *Id.* These figures may understate the impact of felony disenfranchisement, because they do not take into account the millions of formerly incarcerated people who cannot vote in states that require people convicted of felonies to pay fines or fees before their voting rights can be restored.

22. Employers Grp. Research Servs., *Employment of Ex-Offenders: A Survey of Employer's Policies and Practices*, 6 (2002).

23. See *Human Rights Watch, No Second Chance: People with Criminal Records Denied Access to Public Housing*, 33 (2004).

24. See Temporary Assistance for Needy Family Program (TANF), 21 U.S.C. § 862a(a)(2) (2006).

in fees, fines, court costs, and accumulated back child support—frequently as a condition of probation or parole.[25] And here's the kicker: Even if a former prisoner manages to get a job, up to 100% of their wages can be garnished to pay for the costs of their imprisonment, court processing fees, and back payments in child support.[26] Yes, 100% of their wages can be garnished.

What, realistically, do we expect these folks to do? What is this system designed to do? It seems designed to send them right back to prison, which is what in fact happens most of the time. About 70% of released prisoners are rearrested within three years, and the majority of those who return to prison do so within a matter of months, because the barriers to mere survival on the outside are so immense.

Remarkably, as bad as all the formal barriers to political and economic inclusion are, many formerly incarcerated people tell me that is not the worst of it. The worst is the stigma that follows you for the rest of your life. It is not just the denial of the job, but the look that crosses an employer's face when he sees the "box" has been checked. It is not just the denial of public housing, but the shame of being a grown man having to ask your grandma to sleep in her basement at night. The shame associated with criminality can be so intense that people routinely try to "pass."

During the Jim Crow era, light-skinned blacks often tried to pass as white in order to avoid the stigma, shame, and discrimination associated with their race. Today, people labeled criminals lie not only to employers and housing officials, but also to their friends, acquaintances and family members. Children of prisoners lie to friends and relatives saying, "I don't know where my daddy is." Grown men who have been released from prison for years still glance down and look away when asked who they will vote for on election day, ashamed to admit they can't vote. They try to "pass" to avoid the stigma and discrimination associated with the new caste system.

There are two major reasons, I believe, that so many of us are in denial about the existence of racial caste in America. The first is traceable to a profound misunderstanding regarding how racial oppression actually works. If someone were to visit the United States from another country (or another planet) and ask: "Is the U.S. criminal justice system some kind of tool of racial control?," most Americans would swiftly deny it. Numerous reasons would leap to mind why that could not possibly be the case. The visitor would be told that crime rates, black culture, or bad schools were to blame. "The system is not run by a bunch of racists," the apologist would explain. They would say, "It is run by people who are trying to fight crime." Because mass incarceration is officially colorblind, and because most people today do not think of themselves as racist, it seems inconceivable that the system could function much like a racial caste system.

But more than forty-five years ago, Martin Luther King Jr. warned of the danger of precisely this kind of thinking. He insisted that blindness and indifference to racial groups is actually more important than racial hostility to the creation and maintenance of systems of racial control. Those who supported slavery and Jim Crow, he argued, typically were not bad or evil people; they were just blind.[27] Many segregationists were kind to their black shoe shiners and maids and genuinely wished them well. Even the Justices who decided the infamous Dred Scott case, which ruled "that the Negro had no rights which the white man was bound to respect," were not wicked men, he said.[28] On the whole, they were decent and dedicated men. But, he hastened to add, "They were victims of spiritual and intellectual blindness. They knew not what they did. The whole system of slavery was largely perpetuated by sincere though spiritually ignorant persons."[29]

The same is true today. People of good will—and bad—have been unwilling to see black and brown men, in their humanness, as entitled to the same care, compassion, and concern that would be extended to one's friends, neighbors, or loved ones.

---

25. Rachel L. McLean & Michael D. Thompson, *Council of State Gov'ts Justice Ctr., Repaying Debts*, 7–8 (2007).

26. *Id.* at 22.

27. Martin Luther King, Jr., *Strength to Love*, 45 (Fortress Press 1981) (1963).

28. *Id.*

29. *Id.*

After all, who among us would want a loved one struggling with drug abuse to be put in a cage, labeled a felon, and then subjected to a lifetime of discrimination, scorn and social exclusion? Most Americans would not wish that fate on anyone they cared about. But whom do we care about? In America, the answer to that question is still linked to race. Dr. King recognized that it was this indifference to the plight of African Americans that supported the institutions of slavery and Jim Crow. And this callous racial indifference supports mass incarceration today.

Another reason that we remain in deep denial is that we, as a nation, have a false picture of our racial reality. Prisoners are literally erased from the nation's economic picture. Unemployment and poverty statistics do not include people behind bars. During the much heralded economic boom of the 1990s—the Clinton years—African American men were the only group to experience a steep increase in real joblessness, a development directly traceable to the increase in the penal population. During the 1990s—the best of times for the rest of America—the true jobless rates for non-college black men was a staggering 42%.

Affirmative action, though, has put a happy face on this racial reality. Seeing black people graduate from Harvard and Yale and become CEOs or corporate lawyers—not to mention President of the United States—causes us all to marvel at what a long way we have come. As recent data shows, though, much of black progress is a myth.[30] In many respects, if you take into account prisoners, African Americans as a group are doing no better than they were when King was assassinated and uprisings swept inner cities across America. And that is with affirmative action!

When we pull back the curtain and take a look at what our so-called colorblind society creates without affirmative action, we see a familiar social, political and economic structure—the structure of racial caste. And the entry into this new caste system can be found at the prison gate.

So where do we go from here? What can be done to dismantle this new system of control? What is clear, I think, is that those of us in the civil rights community have allowed a human rights nightmare to occur on our watch. While many of us have been fighting for affirmative action or clinging to the perceived gains of the Civil Rights Movement, millions of people have been rounded up en masse, locked in cages, and then released into a parallel social universe in which they can be discriminated against for the rest of their lives—denied the very rights our parents and grandparents fought for and some died for. The clock has been turned back on racial progress in America, yet scarcely anyone seems to notice.

What is needed, I believe, is a broad based social movement, one that rivals in size, scope, depth, and courage the movement that was begun in the 1960s and left unfinished. It must be a multi-racial, multi-ethnic movement that includes poor and working class whites—a group that has consistently been pit against poor people of color, triggering the rise of successive new systems of control.

The drug war was born with black folks in mind, but it is a hungry beast; it has caused incalculable suffering in communities of all colors. A white youth given a prison sentence rather than the drug treatment he desperately needs is suffering because of a drug war born of racial anxieties and resentments raging long before he was born. In California and throughout the Southwest, Latinos are a primary target of the drug war. And now that Wall Street executives have found they can profit from prisons, private prison companies have lobbied for punitive laws aimed at suspected illegal immigrants, in the hopes of building new immigration detention centers—the newest market for caging human beings.[31] The impulse to exploit racial fears and biases for political and economic gain is leading to a prison-building boom aimed at immigrants. If we are going to succeed in bringing this brutal system to an end, we must map the linkages between the suffering of

---

30. See The Eisenhower Foundation, *What We Can Do Together: A Forty Year Update of the National Advisory Commission on Civil Disorders: Preliminary Findings* (2008), available at http://www.eisenhowerfoundation.org/docs/Kerner%20 40%20Year%20Update,%20Executive%20Summary.pdf.

---

31. Laura Sullivan, *Prison Economics Help Drive Arizona Immigration Law*, National Public Radio (Oct. 28, 2010), http:// www.npr.org/templates/story/story.php?storyId=130833741.

African Americans in the drug war to the experiences of other oppressed and marginalized groups. We must connect the dots. This movement must be multi-racial and multi-ethnic, and it must have a keen sense of the racial history and racial dynamics that brought us to this moment in time.

But before this movement can even get underway, a great awakening is required. We must awaken from our colorblind slumber to the realities of race in America. And we must be willing to embrace those labeled criminals—not necessarily their behavior, but them—their humanness. For it has been the refusal and failure to fully acknowledge the humanity and dignity of *all* persons that has formed the sturdy foundation of all caste systems.

It is our task, I firmly believe, to end not just mass incarceration, but the history and cycle of caste in America.

Michelle Alexander: The New Jim Crow

1. "THE DRUG WAR IS THE NEW JIM CROW." Alexander was skeptical of this poster when she first saw it. Having read her piece, what do you think of it?

2. As Alexander notes, though many leaders who endorsed the tough-on-crime legislation were motivated by a desire to reinforce racism, there were exceptions. For instance, some leaders within the African American community also supported that legislation. Does this make any difference when assessing the morality of those laws?

3. According to Alexander, if we returned to incarceration rates from the 1970s, we would have to release four out of five convicts currently in prison, and at least a million people employed in our expanded prison system would lose their jobs. What ethical implications, if any, do you take away from these claims?

4. What steps do you think we can take in order to reduce the effects of racism in the criminal justice system?

5. Though Alexander does not focus on matters of racist police brutality, an increasing number of videos displaying such behavior have led to calls to reduce police forces or to defund entire police departments. What do you think of such appeals? What reasons support your view, and what are the best reasons against your view?

Affirmative Action: Bad Arguments and Some Good Ones

Daniel M. Hausman

In this paper, Daniel Hausman sets himself two goals. First, he wants to reveal the flaws of some popular arguments for and against policies of preferential hiring and admissions (PHA). Second, he offers an argument in favor of PHA that he believes is successful in showing that the practice can be justified.

Many people favor or oppose PHA on the basis of their view of its results. But, as Hausman notes, the actual results of PHA programs are difficult to determine and are highly disputed. Hausman does not take a stand, for instance, on whether PHA has actually improved or damaged the self-esteem of minorities, reduced or increased prejudice, and so on. The evidence, he thinks, is inconclusive. But we can still assess the merits of arguments for and against PHA even in the absence of such evidence.

One classic argument opposing PHA claims that it is "racism in reverse." Hausman rejects this line of reasoning, pointing out that PHA is not grounded in assumptions of racial inferiority or racial hatred, and that it is not designed to oppress, humiliate, and exclude. Hausman also rejects arguments against PHA that assume that it is morally wrong in hiring or admissions to take into account anything other than the applicant's qualifications.

On the other side, defenders of PHA often rely on arguments from rectification or reparation to make their case. Many defenders think that harms should be rectified (remedied); racist acts are harmful; so they must be rectified, and PHA will do a good job of that. Hausman agrees that harms should be remedied, but by those who have actually done the harm. The harms of slavery, for instance, can no longer be rectified by those who perpetrated them, so this is a poor basis on which to justify PHA.

Arguments from reparations fare no better. Reparations are compensation owed by the government for wrongs that it has done or permitted. Hausman agrees that the US and state governments were indeed responsible for many racist harms. But he offers a variety of reasons for thinking that PHA is not a good way of correcting for those harms.

Hausman concludes with an argument in favor of PHA. Ensuring equality of opportunity is a fundamental government responsibility. Hausman argues that PHA will help to advance this important goal. PHA won't by itself solve all of the problems that our long legacy of racism has created. But it will to some degree level a playing field that unjustly favors white males.

Affirmative action has many aspects. Some, such as requiring that job openings be advertised so that minorities can learn of them, are not controversial. Other aspects, such as preferential hiring and admissions (PHA), with which this essay is concerned, are hotly disputed. PHA takes minority status to increase an applicant's chance of getting a job or getting admitted to a university. Though the policy favors applicants with minority status, it does not imply that minority status should determine hiring or admission all by itself. (Nobody is proposing hiring blind bus drivers because they are minorities.) The idea is to favor otherwise qualified applicants who belong to disadvantaged groups. Because the pool of qualified minority applicants is often small, the direct benefits of PHA are also rather small. To limit the discussion, I shall focus in this essay largely on preferential hiring and admissions of African Americans, because they have a special history of slavery and oppression—even though the greatest beneficiaries of PHA have in fact been women.

There are many arguments defending preferential hiring and admissions and many criticizing it. Many of these arguments depend crucially on facts about the consequences. So, for example, critics have argued that PHA harms those it intends to benefit by undermining their self-confidence or by putting them in positions beyond their abilities in which they are bound to fail. Critics have also argued that those favored by PHA are often incompetent, and PHA thus undermines the credentials of beneficiaries, incites racism, and diminishes economic efficiency. Defenders argue that PHA has changed the American population's conception of what minorities and women can aspire to and that PHA has lessened racial disparities. These arguments would be powerful if their factual premises were true. But it is hard to know what the effects of PHA have been, and there is little evidence supporting any of these claims about the consequences of PHA. Heartwarming tales of successes of recipients of PHA and horror stories of harms and abuses are not serious evidence.[1]

The most prominent arguments do not rely on controversial factual premises. Critics argue that PHA is racism in reverse: discrimination is wrong, regardless of whether it is directed against or for African Americans. Defenders argue that PHA helps to rectify past injustices committed against African Americans. These are the arguments one most often hears. But they are not good arguments. Defenders and critics should stop making them.

"RACISM IN REVERSE"

If it was morally impermissible to exclude African Americans from universities and jobs on the basis of their race, how can it be morally permissible to exclude whites on the basis of their race? Lisa Newton, a philosopher at Fairfield University, enunciates this criticism as follows: "The quota system, as employed by the University of California's medical school at Davis or any similar institution, is unjust, for all the same reasons that the discrimination it attempts to reverse is unjust."[2].

Let us formulate this argument precisely. The word "discrimination" causes confusion, because it has both a neutral and a negative sense. In the neutral sense, discrimination is simply drawing distinctions, which may be a good or a bad thing to do. An admissions office does nothing wrong when it discriminates (in this sense) among candidates on the basis of factors such as test scores and high school grade averages. In the negative sense, discrimination consists in drawing distinctions unjustly. In the neutral sense, PHA obviously involves discriminating among candidates. Does it also discriminate in the negative sense—that is, unjustly? To avoid confusing the two meanings, it is best to avoid the word "discrimination" altogether, and ask instead whether the distinctions PHA draws among candidates are unjust.

Why might it be unjust to allow an applicant's race to influence hiring or admissions? Perhaps injustice lies simply in allowing race to influence choices. But it not always wrong to take race into account. A director making a movie of the life of Martin Luther King commits no injustice in refusing to consider white actors for the lead role. Refusing to hire a white short-order cook is, on the other hand, harder to justify. What's the difference? The answer seems to be that race is relevant to playing Martin Luther King, while it is not relevant to frying eggs.

One way to capture the racism in reverse argument is as follows:

1. It is wrong in hiring or admissions to take into account anything other than the applicant's qualifications.
2. PHA takes the applicant's race into account.
3. Race is almost always not a qualification.
4. Thus, PHA is almost always wrong.

I hope the reader agrees that this is a good way to formulate the racism in reverse argument, because I am trying to get at the truth rather than to win points in a political debate by misrepresenting the critic's position.

Crucial to this argument is the notion of a "qualification." A qualification is any fact about an applicant that is relevant to how successfully the applicant can promote the legitimate goals of the organization to which the applicant is applying. For example, high school class rank and ACT scores are qualifications, because they are correlated with academic performance in college. Running the 100-meter dash in under ten seconds is also a qualification for admission if the success of its athletic teams is among the legitimate goals of a university. For universities without sports teams, like those in Europe, it is not a qualification. The race of applicants would be relevant to a university devoted to white racial supremacy, but the promotion of racial supremacy is not a legitimate goal. Since, as the Martin Luther King movie example illustrates, race is sometimes a qualification, this argument does not conclude that PHA is always wrong, just that it is almost always wrong. On the view that this argument makes precise, what was wrong with the exclusion and special hurdles faced by African Americans during the Jim Crow era was that their prospects were not determined exclusively by their qualifications.

The argument formulated above is a valid argument. The conclusion follows logically from the premises. To assert all three of the premises and at the same time deny the conclusion is to contradict oneself. Constructing valid arguments can be very helpful. If those whom you are trying to persuade grant the premises, then, on pain of contradiction, they must accept the conclusion. Alternatively, if those you are attempting to persuade reject the conclusion, then they must reject at least one of the premises.

Let us examine whether the argument is also sound—that is, whether as well as being valid, all its premises are true. Premise 2 is obviously true: preferential hiring and admission of African Americans takes race into account. Premise 3 in contrast is debatable, because diversity among students and employees arguably serves legitimate goals of universities and some firms. Among the objectives of universities is to train business and political leaders who can interact with and understand people from many different backgrounds. Diversity within the student body serves this purpose.

More can be said about premise 3 and the importance of diversity, but let us focus on premise 1, which says that hiring and admissions should depend exclusively on qualifications. Premise 1 may seem plausible. It apparently explains why the racist exclusion of African Americans from schools, unions, and many professions was wrong: those exclusions were not based on qualifications. But premise 1 is false, and it does not correctly identify what was wrong with racist exclusions of African Americans. Consider three examples of hiring or admissions that depend on more than just qualifications:

- Case 1: Veterans are given preferences on civil service examinations and in college admissions.
- Case 2: An owner of a small grocery store hires his teenageasons that the discriminatiomore responsible teenager) to deliver groceries after school because he wants to keep an eye on her.
- Case 3: My father, who owned his own small company, often hired ex-convicts rather than applicants without criminal records because he thought that people who had served their time deserved a second chance. He did not hire ex-convicts because he had any illusions that they would be better workers.

Are the hiring or admissions policies in these three examples wrong?

Before answering, it is important to set aside unrelated reasons why the conduct may be wrong. Suppose, for example, that instead of owning his own company, my father was the personnel officer in a corporation, and he was instructed to hire the most qualified employees. If he then hired less qualified ex-cons because of his concern about their plight, he would be failing in his duties to the company that pays his salary. His actions would be wrong, because they violated company policy,

whether or not it is permissible to take factors other than qualifications into account. If instead he had instructions to give preferences to ex-cons and refused to follow them, he would be equally at fault. Second, if the grocery store owner were to put out a sign saying "Help wanted. I shall hire whoever is most qualified," and he then hired his daughter even though he knew there were more qualified applicants, he would be acting wrongly. The wrong consists in deceiving the applicants, not in taking into account his personal relationship to his daughter.

There is no defensible general principle that requires hiring and admissions to depend only on qualifications. It is not automatically wrong to take into account a veteran's past service to the nation when providing education or hiring, even when having patrolled the streets of Baghdad or losing a limb is not a qualification. I'm proud of my father's hiring, even though it was not based only on qualifications. If PHA is wrong, it is not because it takes into account factors other than qualifications.

If it is sometimes acceptable to take factors other than qualifications into account, does that mean that it was okay to exclude blacks from universities, from unions, from neighborhoods, swimming pools, even bathrooms? Of course not! Those policies were despicable, but what explains those wrongs is not that they took factors other than qualifications into account. Consider segregated bathrooms, which are of no economic importance and superficially appear to treat the races equally. (I was with my father almost sixty years ago, when he was thrown out of a "whites only" bathroom in Florida.) What's wrong with having separate bathrooms for different races? Is it only that the bathrooms for whites were nicer? If the bathrooms had been equally nice and the restrictions had been symmetrical, with whites not allowed into the "colored only" bathrooms as blacks were not allowed into the "whites only" bathroom, how could the policy be unjust or harmful to blacks?

Social context is crucial. In a racist black nation where there was a widespread view that contact with whites was defiling, segregated bathrooms would be a racist insult to whites. In the U.S., segregated bathrooms, hotels, train cars, and so forth were a humiliating insult to blacks, not to whites. In 1941, when Marian Anderson, the great African-American contralto, gave a concert at Lawrence University, she could not spend the night in Appleton, Wisconsin, where I used to live. In the 1940s, Appleton did not allow African Americans to reside within city limits. Fortunately, Anderson could stay in a hotel in a nearby town. The inconvenience was not enormous, but the insult was. Think about how it feels to be treated as if you were "unclean"—as if mere contact was defiling.

As these examples suggest, the mistreatment of African Americans that constituted Jim Crow consisted in their systematic denigration by white society, which resulted in their poverty, oppression, and exclusion. It relied on intimidation, beatings, humiliation, and murder. It was deeply wrong because of how it treated African Americans, not because it picked its victims by their race. If those mistreated were chosen not because of their skin color but via lottery and then marked as inferior, perhaps with a tattoo on their foreheads, the mistreatment would be no less repugnant and unjust.

In contrast, preferential hiring and admissions policies—whatever their virtues or vices—are not grounded in hatred of whites. PHA does not denigrate or oppress whites, or exclude them from the mainstream of American life. The admissions offices at universities are not full of white-hating racists out to keep whites from soiling their universities. Lisa Newton is wrong: PHA is not unjust "for all the same reasons that the discrimination it attempts to reverse is unjust." If PHA is unjust, it is not for any of the reasons that racial discrimination against blacks is unjust.

The failure of this common criticism of preferential hiring and admissions does not mean that PHA is fair or advisable. There may be other and better criticisms. But there is no moral prohibition on taking factors other than qualification into account in hiring and admissions, and in any case race is sometimes a qualification. PHA is not reverse racism.

RECTIFICATION, REPARATIONS, AND PHA

The main argument in defense of PHA fares no better. It maintains that PHA is a good way of rectifying past injustices perpetrated against African Americans. Rectification is a familiar idea. If my neighbor, Henry, were to steal my bicycle, justice would require that Henry give it back to me and compensate me for the inconvenience. When rights have been violated, justice requires that, as far as possible, the injustice be "rectified"—that the world be restored to how it would have been if there had been no injustice. African Americans have over the past centuries been the victims of incalculable injustices. They were enslaved, kidnapped, beaten, raped, tortured, and murdered and, after the Civil War brought slavery to an end, African Americans suffered more than a century of lynching, peonage, and relegation to the status of second-class citizens. Though racism persists, things are obviously better now. But these past injustices have not been rectified. Accordingly, many argue that PHA is justified as a form of rectification.

One might state the core of their argument as follows:

1. Those who commit injustices owe their victims damages.
2. Massive injustices have been perpetrated against African Americans.
3. Thus, those who committed these injustices owe damages to their African-American victims.

If intended to justify PHA, this argument has three problems. First, to rectify past injustice, one needs to identify the perpetrators of injustices and the victims of injustices and to determine the magnitude of the damages the perpetrators should pay to the victims. With respect to slavery, both perpetrators and victims are long dead. Descendants of victims of crimes may have claims to particular goods stolen from parents or grandparents, but their claims are limited. Children are not responsible for their parents' and grandparents' crimes, and members of a race are not responsible for injustices committed by other members of their race. How could PHA constitute the compensation that perpetrators of past injustices owe to their victims?

Second, rectification of an injustice is designed to restore people and their circumstances to that condition that would have obtained if no injustice had been done. Rectification in this sense for the wrongs of slavery is impossible. There is no way to know how the world would have been if there had been no slavery. Life in this country would have been utterly different. Few of our parents or more distant ancestors would have met, and consequently only a small portion of contemporary Americans would have existed in a hypothetical world without slavery. How can we possibly envision how things would have been under circumstances so different that they do not even contain the same people?

Third, identifying those who should pay compensation and those to whom compensation is owed would lead to a divisive inquiry into the virtues and vices of our ancestors, when they came to the United States, whether they conserved or squandered ill-gotten gains, and so forth. This is not a road that those who hope to improve race relations should want to follow.

Although widely misunderstood, invoking reparations rather than rectification solves the problem of identifying the responsible party. Reparations are a form of compensation provided by the government (and hence ultimately taxpayers) to acknowledge and partly to rectify past injustices perpetrated or permitted by the government. For example, the U.S. government provided $20,000 in reparations to Japanese-Americans who were interned during World War II, or to their immediate descendants. The funds were raised through taxation of all Americans, including Japanese-Americans. There was no distinction between those people who may have profited from the internment and the great majority who did not benefit from it, because reparations are a civic responsibility for a civic wrong, rather than a personal responsibility for personal wrongs. Because government at all levels perpetrated injustices toward African Americans and acquiesced in many other injustices that could and should have been prevented, it bears a great responsibility for past injustices toward African Americans.

Conceptualizing PHA as the paying of reparations rather than as rectifying individual injustices should thus in principle avoid divisive inquiries

into the vices of our ancestors. But public discussion tramples subtle distinctions, and, unfortunately, proponents and critics misunderstand reparations and turn discussion of the issue into acrimonious finger pointing concerning the intergenerational transmission of personal guilt. A few years ago David Horowitz placed advertisements criticizing reparations in a number of college newspapers. These advertisements led to violent protests by those concerned about the disadvantages that African Americans must deal with. Among Horowitz's ten reasons to oppose reparations were: (1) we cannot identify the descendants of the perpetrators of the crimes of slavery; (2) few Americans owned slaves, and (3) most Americans have no clear connection to slavery. Since reparations are a civic responsibility for the wrongs government caused or permitted, these claims are irrelevant, but neither Horowitz nor most of his readers appear to have understood that. Supporters of reparations are just as confused. For example, in an op-ed piece in the *New York Times* (April 23, 2010), Henry Louis Gates takes the most vexing problem of reparations to be "how to parcel out blame to those directly involved in the capture and sale of human beings for immense economic gain," and he believes that historical research now makes it possible "to publicly attribute responsibility and culpability where they truly belong, to white people and black people."

Even if reparations did not cause such confusions, other problems with rectification apply equally to reparations. How much should be paid? To whom should reparations be paid? Though there are powerful reasons to diminish the huge racial disparities that divide our nation, those policies should not be regarded as reparations. The risks of misunderstanding, the problems in identifying the recipients, and the problems in determining how much should be paid are reasons not to invoke reparations to justify policies that diminish racial disparities.

Furthermore, even if reparations could be ascertained without provoking confused racial animosity, preferential hiring and admissions policies are not a defensible way of paying reparations. PHA does not focus on those who have been most harmed by past injustices, and it does not distribute the costs of paying reparations in a justifiable way. It unfairly imposes the cost of reparations—a civic responsibility—entirely on non-minority college applicants and job seekers, who bear no more responsibility for past injustices than anyone else. These costs, like the benefits PHA provide, are generally small, but it is still unjust both to make one group in society pay all the costs and arbitrarily to benefit just one group. If PHA were only one of a set of programs whose costs were distributed throughout the population, this objection would not be cogent. But apart from PHA, public policy does little to address racial disparities.

I am not arguing that Americans should forget past injustices. Without understanding the past, how could we understand the present and know what to do about it? Moreover, the fact that the problems of the present arose through past injustices creates a special obligation to address them. But it is impossible to undo the past or rectify old and large-scale injustices. We have no idea what would constitute rectification, and could not carry it out if we did. Although we need to look to the past for understanding, our moral concern should focus on the future. How can we free it of racism and of the disparities that racism has caused?

PREFERENTIAL ADMISSIONS AND EQUAL OPPORTUNITY

The other major arguments that do not depend on factual knowledge of details of the consequences of PHA invoke the value of equal opportunity. Critics maintain that equal opportunity condemns PHA. Defenders maintain that PHA promotes equal opportunity. Obviously, both cannot be right.

Consider an analogy. Suppose that in the local elementary school there are two first-grade and two second-grade classes. One of the first-grade teachers is excellent, and one is terrible. One of the second-grade teachers is also excellent, and one is terrible. The socioeconomic status of the families in this community is uniform, and the children have had similar preschool experiences. The school board assigns students to first-grade teachers by lottery on the grounds that the fairest policy gives every student an equal chance at a good first-grade experience.

There is disagreement, however, about how to assign children to the second-grade teachers. Some school board members argue that every child should have one good and one bad teacher. Those children who had the good first-grade teacher should get the bad second-grade teacher and vice versa. These board members say, "If every child has both a good teacher and a bad teacher, then the children's schooling and overall future opportunities will be as close to equal as we can make them." Other school board members argue for a second lottery. They say, "Why should students be punished for having had a good teacher in first grade? Equal opportunity demands that every child should have an equal chance of having a good second-grade teacher."

This analogy is helpful in several regards. First, it explains why it can appear that PHA both promotes and impedes equal opportunity. If one is thinking narrowly about the chance of getting a good second-grade teacher, then a second lottery equalizes opportunity, just as (if there were no racism) the absence of PHA would equalize the chances of being hired or admitted of otherwise equally qualified applicants of different races. On the other hand, if one is concerned with opportunities over a lifetime, insuring that every child has one good teacher and one bad one promotes equality of opportunity, just as PHA does (on the assumption that the opportunities and resources available previously to black applicants have, on average, been worse than those available to white applicants). Those concerned with equal opportunity should be concerned with lifetime opportunities, not opportunities to acquire one or another immediate benefit or burden. Because of past inequalities and continued racism, PHA lessens inequalities in opportunity.

The school analogy also makes clear that PHA does not punish white applicants, just as assigning children who had the good first-grade teacher to the bad second-grade teacher does not punish them. These kids have done nothing wrong. Indeed, it may be that nobody has done anything wrong. The policy of making sure that each student has one good and one bad teacher is not a way of rectifying in second grade an injustice done in first grade, because no injustice has been done. The justification for the second-grade teacher assignments is to provide children with similar overall opportunities, not to restore children to where they would have been if they had not previously been treated unjustly. In the case of PHA, unlike the elementary school analogy, some of the past inequalities in opportunity have been the result of injustices, but the point is to diminish inequality rather than to rectify injustice.

It is important to distinguish between compensation as rectifying injustice and compensation as equalizing opportunity. The former does not justify PHA, because, as I argued earlier, it is unfair to impose the costs of reparations or rectification on white applicants, since reparations are a social responsibility, and rectification is the responsibility of individual wrongdoers. By contrast, equalizing opportunity can justify PHA, because it is not unjust to diminish the chances of applicants whose prospects have on average been inflated by previous inequalities. The relevant question for a rejected white applicant is not "With my qualifications, would I have been admitted or hired if there were no PHA policy?" Nor is it "With my qualifications, would I have been admitted or hired if I were black?" The relevant question is "If the qualifications of all the applicants (including me) had not been skewed by past inequalities in opportunity and if there were no continuing racism, would I have been admitted or hired?"

Given previous inequalities and continuing discrimination, PHA brings us on average closer to equal opportunity.[3] Like the children who had the good first-grade teacher, white applicants on average have had previous advantages. PHA diminishes these inequalities and counteracts some of the continued racist discrimination in hiring.

This argument assumes that the opportunities for black applicants have been in fact on average worse than the opportunities for white applicants. But there can be no serious doubt about its truth. According to the Pew Research Center, the median wealth of African Americans in 2009 was one-twentieth that of whites. There is no plausible explanation of inequalities in outcomes that are this enormous other than unequal opportunities, and such large inequalities in outcomes obviously translate into inequalities in opportunity. A far higher percentage of black children live in poverty and in single-parent homes. On average the parents of African-American children are likely to have had less education, and the schools African-American children attend typically have worse facilities, lower-paid teachers, and larger class sizes. Some black applicants are highly privileged and many white applicants have grown up in dire circumstances, but on average, black applicants have had to cope with greater poverty, more difficult environments, and worse schooling. Their opportunities have been on average considerably worse, and they face the additional burden of continued discrimination.[4] PHA does a little to lessen these inequalities in opportunity. Valuing equal opportunity (not equal results) is a reason to support it, not to oppose it.

CONCLUSIONS

This essay has focused on the most popular arguments concerning PHA. Their popularity does not reflect well on the subtlety of public discourse, because they are not good arguments. PHA is not racism in reverse. It is not racist. It does not aim to denigrate, exclude, oppress, or punish whites. The main argument in defense of PHA is just as weak. PHA is not justified as a form of rectification or of reparations. Reparations and rectification are impractical, racially divisive, and incapable of justifying a policy that imposes costs arbitrarily on only one segment of the population.

As we have seen, there are good arguments to be made in defense of PHA as promoting diversity and equal opportunity, but it could turn out that other consequences of PHA are so harmful that there is good reason to abandon the policies. If we knew the effects of PHA on racial animosity, on the self-conception and status of the minorities it aims to benefit, and on the extent to which they and others are successful, we would be in a better position to reach a definite conclusion concerning whether PHA is beneficial. But we do not know its effects well enough.

One other consideration should be mentioned. Preferential hiring and admissions policies are more or less the only social policies in the United States that acknowledge the special handicaps disadvantaged minorities face and, in a small way, concretely aim to lessen them. Disadvantaged minorities would inevitably see the abandonment of PHA, without putting something substantial in its place, as white

America turns its back on a disgracefully unjust situation. The deck is stacked, and white America gets to shuffle the cards. Will it do anything about the poor hands that minorities have been dealt?

NOTES

1. There have been serious investigations of the effects, which I cannot summarize here. In my view, the results have been inconclusive.

2. *National Forum* 58.1 (Winter 1978), pp. 22–23.

3. For example, in one study mailed applications with common African-American names were only half as likely to get callbacks as applications with names that are not associated with African Americans. See "Are Emily and Greg More Employable than Lakisha and Jamal? A Field Experiment on Labor Market Discrimination" by Marianne Bertrand and Sendhil Mullainathan (2004) (http://www.economics.harvard.edu/faculty/mullainathan/files/emilygreg.pdf).

4. This conclusion does not rest on the silly view that all differences in outcomes among members of different social groups result from differences in opportunities.

Daniel M. Hausman: Affirmative Action: Bad Arguments and Some Good Ones

1. Why isn't it racist for schools to offer preferential admissions to blacks and Hispanics? What's the difference between not admitting someone because they are black or Hispanic and not admitting someone because they are white?

2. If what was wrong with slavery and "Jim Crow" laws was not their racial basis, then what was wrong with them?

3. Suppose that the United States government were to pay reparations to the descendants of slaves. Why should people who are not descended from slave holders (such as recent immigrants) have to pay taxes to support paying these reparations?

4. What is the point of the parable of the two first-grade and two second-grade classes? Is it a good analogy to the circumstances in which preferential hiring or admissions might be called for?

5. What other arguments can you think of supporting or criticizing preferential hiring and admissions? Can you provide logically valid formulations of these arguments?

The Future of Racial Integration

Elizabeth Anderson

Elizabeth Anderson argues for the importance of racial integration as an ideal that should govern the development of our social and legal policies. She begins by identifying four stages of integration: (1) formal desegregation, which occurs when explicitly racist laws and social policies are abolished; (2) spatial integration, which occurs when members of all races are able to share public spaces on terms of equality; (3) formal social integration, which requires that members of different races fully cooperate with well-defined social roles that are not themselves racially identified; and (4) informal social integration, which occurs when members of different races engage with one another on the basis of trust, intimacy, familiarity, and ease. Anderson focuses her article on conditions in the United States, where only the first stage of integration has been largely achieved.

To make her case for racial integration, Anderson describes the many different kinds of harms that racial segregation imposes, mostly on members of minority groups. Failures of integration threaten the dignity of racial minorities, impose huge costs in terms of unequal social and economic opportunities, and undermine our democratic institutions, whose success is based on cooperative decision-making by equal citizens.

Anderson argues that these failures generate a moral obligation to foster racial integration in our society. Four reasons explain this moral obligation. First, citizens are entitled to social institutions that treat them with respect, rather than demean their dignity. Second, societies have a duty to ensure that a citizen's racial identity is not a pervasive liability when trying to make use of social and economic opportunities and public goods. Third, citizens are entitled to real, effective participation in democratic decision-making. Finally, public institutions in the United States bear a great deal of responsibility for past racial injustices and for many of the current racial disparities in opportunities, and so are morally required to remedy the harms they have done.

Anderson then critiques anti-integrationist arguments from both the political right and left. On the right, opponents of racial integration argue that current failures of integration are largely the result of voluntary self-segregation on the part of black citizens, rather than of racist attitudes and practices on the part of white citizens. On the left, Anderson distinguishes three strands of identity politics that deny the importance of racial integration. According to the first, proponents argue that racial self-segregation is required in order for black citizens to develop psychologically mature and healthy racial identities. The second asserts that such self-segregation fosters mutual aid and the building of a distinctive racial culture that implies no animosity toward white majority citizens. In a third model, self-segregated communities, such as those represented by all-black college houses, help to generate knowledge from racially distinctive perspectives, knowledge of just the sort needed to counter racism. Anderson allows that there are valid points to each of these arguments but denies that they are sufficient to justify anti-integrationist practices.

Racial integration was once the rallying cry of the civil rights movement. Today, a half-century after *Brown v. Board of Education* declared public school segregation unconstitutional, integration is barely mentioned as an issue in the major media or by politicians. Conservatives tend to argue that whites now welcome integration and that current patterns of segregation are due to the voluntary choices of minority groups to stay apart. As if to confirm this argument, many activists on the Left express disillusionment with integration and defend the virtues of self-segregation. It is time to put integration back on the public agenda, and to reorient policies from voting rights and housing to affirmative action toward integrationist goals.

From Elizabeth Anderson, "The Future of Racial Integration," in Laurence Thomas, ed., *Contemporary Debates in Social Philosophy* (Blackwell, 2008), pp. 229–240.

I. THE STATE OF INTEGRATION TODAY

Racial integration consists in the full inclusion and participation as equals of the members of all races in all aspects of social interaction, especially in the main institutions of society that define its opportunities for recognition, educational and economic advancement, access to public goods, and political influence. It takes place in four stages: (1) formal desegregation, (2) spatial integration, (3) formal social integration, and (4) informal social integration. Formal desegregation consists in the abolition of laws and policies enforcing separation of public facilities and accommodations on racial grounds. Spatial integration consists in the common use of facilities and public spaces on terms of equality by substantial numbers of all races. A spatially integrated neighborhood may still be socially segregated, in that neighbors of different races may not interact in neighborly ways—welcome them to the neighborhood, engage in small talk, do small favors for one another. Similarly, a school may be spatially but not socially integrated if students of different races attend different "tracked" classes, participate in different school clubs, sit apart at the lunch table, and, in residential schools, inhabit different halls or dormitories. As Glenn Loury has stressed (2002: 95–6), even when people observe anti-discrimination laws, and so avoid "discrimination in contract," they may still practice "discrimination in contact," which often amounts to the shunning of marginalized groups by avoiding neighborly, collegial, or friendly relationships with them.

Social integration requires genuine cooperation on terms of racial equality. It can be formal or informal. Formal social integration occurs when members of different races fully cooperate in accordance with institutionally defined social roles, and all races occupy all roles in enough numbers that roles are not racially identified. It happens when white privates obey orders issued to them by black lieutenants, with the same degree of alacrity as they would have had the orders been issued by white lieutenants. It happens when white students and Latino students cooperate as equal lab partners, or as members of the school football team. Informal social integration involves forms of cooperation, ease, welcome, trust, affiliation, and intimacy that go beyond the official requirements of organizationally defined roles. It happens when members of different races form friendships, date, marry, bear children, or adopt different race children. At school and at work, it happens when members of different races share conversations at the lunch table, hobnob over the coffee break, and play together at recess.

I call these "stages" of integration because they are ordered by degree of difficulty, and attaining the easier ones is typically a prerequisite to substantial attainment of the harder ones. Measured by these stages, how far have Americans gone up the ladder of integration? The first stage, formal desegregation, has largely been attained. This was the signal achievement of the civil rights movement. It immediately enabled spatial integration of public accommodations—the common use by all races of restaurants, buses, hotels, drinking fountains, restrooms, and other facilities generally open to the public.

But formal desegregation did not bring about spatial integration in neighborhoods, and only partially achieved it in public schools and workplaces. Even in the workplace, however, social integration is far from complete. Even when blacks have "made it" to managerial and professional positions, they still report high levels of discriminatory and disrespectful treatment.

Informal social integration lags far behind formal social integration. Only 1.9 percent of married couples and 4.3 percent of unmarried cohabiting couples are interracial. Asians have the highest rate of interracial coupling, at 19 percent, followed by Hispanics at 18 percent, and blacks at 5 percent (Fields and Casper 2001: 15). Racially mixed families, in which at least one parent is of a different race from at least one child, are more common: 17 percent of adoptees are of a different race from at least one of their parents. Here again, Asian children are most integrated with other-race households, black children by far the least (Kreider 2003: 13, 14). Informal social integration, especially of blacks, is a largely unfinished agenda.

2. THE HARMS OF SEGREGATION

Notwithstanding dramatic progress in integration since the Jim Crow era, substantial levels of segregation, especially of blacks, and especially at later stages, remain. Should we care? I think we must. Integration is needed to realize three types of goods: dignity, socioeconomic opportunity for marginalized racial groups, and democracy for us all. Each stage of integration has its own role to play in advancing these goods.

2.1 Dignity

Racial segregation by law or policy has a fundamental expressive point: to constitute the excluded group as an untouchable caste. Formal desegregation is therefore necessary to remove the dignitary harm entailed by official segregation. But it is not sufficient. Habits of racial aversion, conceits of racial superiority, and stigmatizing fears of disorder stemming from interracial contact persist for generations after their official props have been removed. If, as a result of entrenched residential, school, and workplace segregation, dominant groups have hardly any contact with marginalized ones, how are they to learn more respectful habits of interracial interaction? Habits cannot be taught like a creed. They can only be learned by practice. Spatial integration provides the opportunities needed for practicing the first stage of respectful interaction: extending the common courtesies of civil society to other races—observing queues, yielding the right of way, manifesting the demeanor and bearing of one who accepts the sharing of public facilities with other races as a matter of course. The demands of respect go beyond those of bare civility, however. They include a readiness to welcome others as eligible equal partners in cooperative projects. Formal social integration is needed to learn and express such respect.

It might be thought that the demands of respect fall short of informal social integration. Can't people get along respectfully without being more intimately involved? The answer depends on what is keeping them apart. If it is just a lack of personal chemistry, no disrespect is involved. But the causes of informal social segregation in the US are inextricable from racial stigma. About 12 percent of whites openly reject integration with blacks (Patterson 1997: 47). This factor should not be exaggerated, however. The main problem is not the small hard core of self-avowed racists, but the mismatch between whites' sincerely avowed beliefs and their habits of the heart. Conscious beliefs are the first, easiest, and most superficial thing to change, because they are most fully under our rational control, and most responsive to arguments and evidence. Such beliefs often have relatively weak connections to our feelings, unconscious habits, and somatic responses. To change the latter takes steady practice and a transformation of the conditions that trigger them.

Multiple independent lines of evidence point to a systematic mismatch between whites' conscious non-racist beliefs and their unconscious aversive attitudes toward blacks. Survey research has consistently found a dramatic gap between whites' support for antiracist principles and their opposition to doing anything that would put these principles into practice. Experiments show that people who avow antiracist beliefs nevertheless help blacks less than whites, especially when the blacks occupy higher-status social roles (Gaertner and Dovidio 1986). They also favor whites over blacks when their relative qualifications are ambiguous (Dovidio and Gaertner 2000). Psychological tests demonstrate pervasive unconscious associations of blacks with negative attributes, even on the part of people who explicitly reject racist beliefs and behavior. Such associations are correlated with negative social interactions with blacks (McConnell and Leibold 2001).

This evidence suggests that, while lack of social integration need not in principle express disrespect for others, the particular antipathy whites display toward social integration with blacks does express stigmatizing attitudes toward blacks. The social segregation of blacks therefore manifests a dignitary harm to blacks. Policies aimed at facilitating social integration in settings conducive to reducing prejudice would reduce this harm.

2.2 Socioeconomic Opportunity

Spatial segregation has profound material implications. Predominantly black neighborhoods are isolated from areas of job growth. This "spatial mismatch" of residence and jobs causes high unemployment in urban black neighborhoods, and high commuting costs for employed residents of poor and middle-class black neighborhoods. It also deprives black neighborhoods of commercial property and hence of a decent tax base. Residents of black neighborhoods therefore pay higher taxes for public services than their equal-income counterparts in predominantly white neighborhoods. Consulting firms advise banks, retailers, and chain restaurants to avoid black neighborhoods, even when their middle-class status indicates a high density of spending power per block. Thus, black neighborhoods enjoy relatively poor shopping, restaurants, and other commercial services (Cashin 2004: 117–23).

White flight tends to suppress demand for houses in neighborhoods with many blacks, leading to low housing appreciation. This deprives blacks of home investment opportunities, the chief source of middle-class wealth. Low housing values limit blacks' access to the credit they need to start businesses. Racial segregation also leads the black middle class to be far more integrated with lower classes than the white middle class. In fragmented metropolitan areas, the black middle class therefore carries a higher burden of taxation for local public services to the poor than the white middle class, leaving even less money to support the kinds of public services that the middle class demands— for example, decent parks, well-maintained streets, and good schools. The black middle class is also less able to escape crime, even when moving to the suburbs.

The black poor suffer additional disadvantages when they are spatially segregated and hence live in neighborhoods with concentrated poverty. Segregation multiplies and spreads the effects of unemployment by filling poor blacks' social networks with people who have been similarly shut out of job opportunities. Concentrated poverty depresses the prospects of local businesses. It also depresses children's school performance: poor children do better in middle-class schools than in schools where most of their peers are poor (Brooks-Gunn et al. 1993).

Social segregation produces disadvantages over and above spatial segregation. It isolates marginalized groups from the mostly white social networks that govern access to jobs. Moreover, access to opportunities for human development is a function not simply of where one lives but of who one knows, both formally and informally. Discrimination in contact generates "development bias" in disadvantaged communities segregated from the mainstream. If the people in one's community have suffered disadvantages in the acquisition of human capital, one will tend to inherit those same disadvantages (Borjas 1992; Loury 2002: 99–104).

Every organization works through informal as well as formal channels. Managers, for instance, typically have particularly trusted subordinates, whose advice they especially solicit and rely on. Such informal relationships provide critical opportunities for the development and demonstration of highly valued but objectively unmeasurable personal traits, such as loyalty, judgment, and leadership. Even when blacks assume the privileges and responsibilities of their formal titles, they are still often shut out from these informal relationships. Consequently, they tend to be confined to narrow, highly formalized paths to promotion, based on objective criteria such as degrees earned and years of experience, while whites enjoy additional access to informal paths to promotion based on mentoring and impressionistic criteria (Wilson et al. 1999).

Competence in interracial interaction is a two-way street. Disadvantaged racial groups suffer from others' lack of interracial skills. When white teachers and managers feel uncomfortable around blacks and Latinos, instinctively take the side of white students and employees in conflicts, and otherwise manifest unconscious racial aversion, they are rarely the ones to suffer. Whites can acquire interracial interpersonal skills only through practice, which requires that they be socially integrated with other racial groups.

Social integration of dominant and subordinate groups in institutionally supported cooperative settings works to reduce dominant group prejudice and incompetence in interracial interaction. This is known as the "contact hypothesis." It has been updated and confirmed in light of recent research on unconscious biases (Gaertner and Dovidio 2000; Dovidio et al. 2001; Wright et al. 1997). Thus, while social segregation is a major cause of continuing black disadvantage, social integration is a cure.

2.3 Democracy

Segregation harms us all, by undermining democracy. Democracy is a form of collective self-governance based on discussion among equal citizens. Democratic discussion involves reciprocal claim-making, in light of which citizens from all walks of life, through their representatives, work out the rules for living together and decide which collective projects to pursue. The legitimacy of decisions in a democracy depends on their responsiveness to the reasonable concerns of all. This discussion takes place in civil society as well as in the institutions of government. Segregation undermines democratic discussion in both domains.

Consider first civil society, the spaces in which citizens come together to communicate and thereby shape the contours of public opinion. For this process to work democratically, citizens from all walks of life need to share their experiences and concerns, to work out a sense of the problems they share that need a collective response, and what those responses might look like. Political opinions drawn up in ignorance of or indifference to the interests, needs, and concerns of others are defective from a democratic point of view. This is why the "capacity to regard oneself from the perspective of the other . . . is the foundation of the critical interaction necessary for active and effective citizenship" (Post 1998: 23). Segregation obstructs the development and exercise of this capacity. Racial segregation and stigmatization put people of different races in different walks of life: their life circumstances and prospects, the ways they and others view them, are different in politically significant ways. Yet spatial segregation prevents these citizens from different walks of life from communicating; social segregation makes them averse to and awkward in interaction.

The same difficulties arise for discussions among the representatives who occupy political offices. Spatial segregation, exacerbated by racial and partisan gerrymandering of legislative districts, produces a large group of overwhelmingly white districts, along with a handful of majority black, Latino, and integrated districts. Since the residents of the overwhelmingly white districts don't benefit from public spending in the other districts, the ordinary competition among districts for public goods acquires a racial cast. The same lack of benefit means that segregated blacks are less able to find coalition partners of other races (Massey and Denton 1993: 154–5). Even when politics is not overtly racially divisive, it is still likely to be racially negligent, in the sense that policies may be developed and advanced without significant responsiveness to the impact of those policies on racially segregated groups. A politician in an overwhelmingly white district is free to advance policies that have a grossly differential negative impact on disadvantaged racial groups, without being held to account for the costs imposed on other racial groups, and possibly without even knowing the costs.

3. THE IMPERATIVE OF INTEGRATION

We have seen that racial integration is needed to undo the dignitary, socioeconomic, and democratic harms of segregation. Promoting integration is not simply a good thing; it is an obligation. This is so for four reasons. First, citizens are entitled to the social bases of self-respect—that is, to social arrangements that recognize rather than demean their dignity. Second, citizens are entitled to a basic structure of society that satisfies at least the following weak principle of racial equality of opportunity: that their racial status not constitute a pervasive liability in gaining access to socioeconomic opportunity and publicly provided goods. Third, citizens are entitled to effective inclusion in democratic discussion, so that democratic processes are actually responsive to the reasonable articulated concerns and claims of people from all walks of life. Since segregation undermines all three entitlements, society has an obligation to undo it.

These reasons would provide a compelling case for the state and other central institutions to promote integration, even if segregation had been produced by purely private choices. A fourth reason for holding these institutions responsible for promoting integration is that they created segregation through systematic historical wrongdoing. Current patterns of residential and school segregation are largely the product of a century of concerted unconstitutional social engineering by all levels of government: state policies promoting racially exclusive zoning and racial covenants, underwriting mortgages only in all-white neighborhoods, redlining black and integrated neighborhoods to discourage banks from making loans there, locating public housing exclusively in dominantly black neighborhoods, destroying thriving black business districts in the name of urban renewal, deliberately driving highways between black and white neighborhoods to reinforce residential segregation, and locating public schools so as to encourage segregated settlement patterns (Massey and Denton 1993: 17–59). Wrongdoers are obligated not merely to cease engaging in such practices, but to remedy the continuing effects of their past wrongdoing. This is not a matter of compensating for past wrongs, but of dismantling a mechanism—segregation—put in place by past illegal state action that continues to perpetuate injustice.

Given the compelling interest in promoting integration, how is this interest to be advanced? Critics of integration imagine that it must proceed by interfering with freedom of association and destroying black institutions (MacDonald 2000: 212; Young 2000: 216, 226). This confuses means with ends. Of course, informal social integration cannot be forced; this would violate people's rights to freedom of association and be self-defeating besides. But integration can be facilitated, by creating more occasions for interracial cooperation in settings conducive to reducing prejudice.

The integrationist agenda proceeds on four fronts: political, residential, educational, and economic. Political integration aims to redraw political boundaries and powers so that different racial groups share public resources and services, and work together to solve their problems. They urge the formation of cross-border metropolitan regional authorities to deal cooperatively with issues such as public transportation, urban sprawl, and regional planning (Cashin 2004). Political integrationists also urge that state and federal legislative districts be drawn, where possible, to include substantial numbers of each racial group. The aim is to insure that politics proceeds on the basis of interracial engagement, and that politicians, even in majority white districts, have to compete for minority votes and so listen seriously to the concerns of members of disadvantaged racial groups.

On the residential front, the integrationist agenda includes, but looks beyond, vigorous enforcement of housing discrimination laws. For example, the zoning power currently enables municipalities to prohibit the construction of housing affordable to the poor and working class. Because this power is used most frequently by towns close to concentrations of poor blacks, the class-exclusionary zoning power functions as an effective proxy for racial exclusion. From an integrationist point of view, it is high time that the class-exclusionary zoning power be sharply limited, both for the sake of blacks and Latinos and for the sake of the poor of all races.

At selective schools and at work, affirmative action is a primary tool of racial integration. Because work settings enforce cooperation among their participants, they bring about significant formal social integration, which creates a bridge to informal social integration and interracial civic engagement. In selective schools, affirmative action aims to produce a racially integrated and hence democratically responsive and legitimate elite.

The integrationist rationale for affirmative action differs from the standard compensatory and diversity rationales in several ways. The compensatory rationale is backward-looking, and focuses on delivering benefits to the targets of affirmative action preferences, conceived as victims of past discrimination. Integrationist affirmative action is forward-looking: it aims to dismantle current obstacles to racial equality and democracy, and views the targets of affirmative action as agents of this mission rather than victims. While not neglecting the benefits that targets receive from affirmative action, the integrationist perspective stresses the benefits these agents bring to others: expanding the social networks, human capital, and access to employment and professional services of their less integrated same-race associates; stimulating awareness of racial disadvantage and enabling the development of competence in interracial interaction on the part of racially isolated whites doing their part to realize the promise of democracy, especially in constituting a competent, legitimate, representative elite. The integrationist perspective thereby avoids a standard objection to compensatory affirmative action: the mismatch between those targeted for preferences and those most victimized by discrimination.

The integrationist rationale shares with the diversity rationale a forward-looking focus on the ways affirmative action targets bring benefits to others. Unlike the diversity rationale, it does not confine its vision to the ways diversity advances the internal educational mission of schools, but looks to its effects in the wider world. It also resists the capture of affirmative action by identity politics operating under the guise of multiculturalism. It thereby avoids many standard objections to diversity-based affirmative action: that it amounts to a racial spoils system, conflates race with culture, places grossly excessive weight on race compared to other dimensions of diversity, and unjustifiably uses race as a proxy for the diversity features, such as political ideology, that really matter. When racial integration rather than diversity is the goal, the relevance of racial means to achieving it is evident; indeed, race-based selection is inherently the most narrowly tailored means to integration. Moreover, integration raises not merely differences in rationale but in the implementation of affirmative action. Where the diversity rationale tends to favor the preservation and celebration of racial group differences, integration favors conditions that bring people together across racial divides. As I shall discuss later, this means that integrationists look skeptically upon the voluntarily segregated college residential halls that were established by the partisans of identity politics.

4. THE ORDEAL OF INTEGRATION (I): CONSERVATIVE VIEWS

The dramatic costs to disadvantaged racial groups and to democracy of racial segregation make a compelling case for adopting racial integration as a major political imperative. Racial integration is an indispensable means to promoting the dignity of marginalized racial groups, advancing their access to the goods enjoyed in other neighborhoods, developing their social and human capital, enhancing everyone's competence in interracial interaction, reducing racial prejudice, and realizing democracy.

Despite the harms of segregation and the benefits of integration, a surprising confluence of opinion between conservatives and left-wing advocates of identity politics has arisen to rationalize segregation and resist active pro-integration policies. Their views highlight some problems with integration that must be addressed. Their recommendations, however, misunderstand the dynamics of racial segregation and integration, and neglect the material and social conditions for the realization of their own professed goals.

Consider first the conservative view, exemplified by Stephan and Abigail Thernstrom (1997). Their position reflects a pattern typical of white opinion in America: support in principle for racial integration, combined with resolute opposition to any active policies for achieving this end. It rests on two arguments: that segregation is due to voluntary black self-segregation, and that attempts to actively promote integration are self-defeating.

The idea that black segregation is voluntary grounds the Thernstroms' complacency about integration. They argue that most whites are willing to accept substantial numbers of blacks in their neighborhoods. If whites avoid neighborhoods with many blacks, this is because these neighborhoods have other undesirable qualities, such as high crime and low-income neighbors. Since this aversion is based on color-blind considerations, whites' avoidance of neighborhoods with many blacks does not reflect racial antipathy. The Thernstroms infer that any segregation that exists today is the result of voluntary black self-segregation (1997: 220–31). Indeed, few blacks are willing to be the first entrants into an all-white neighborhood, and most prefer a neighborhood that is evenly divided between blacks and whites, or one with a predominance of blacks.

The Thernstroms' interpretation of white preferences fails to grasp the changed character of white antipathy for blacks, from overt hatred to unconscious stigmatization. While most whites do not feel hatred for individual blacks, they still hold demeaning stereotypical views about settings in which blacks are numerous or visibly increasing (Ellen 2000). "There goes the neighborhood." This is not a color-blind attitude, nor is it innocent. Such racial profiling of neighborhoods helps create the very conditions—declining property values in "blackening" neighborhoods, with cascading negative consequences—that "justify" it.

Nevertheless, the Thernstroms are right to claim that black self-segregation is a factor in the perpetuation of spatial segregation. But *why* do blacks prefer self-segregation to being pioneers in nearly all-white communities? Is this due to racial solidarity, or fear of an unwelcome reception from whites? Many blacks express pride in controlling their own communities and feel more at home in black majority neighborhoods. The obverse of this is that they *don't* feel at home in majority white neighborhoods. Many blacks who work in majority white settings report "integration fatigue," a response to the constant stresses of exposure to the conscious and unconscious racial prejudice, aversion, and interracial incompetence of whites. To them, going back home to a majority black neighborhood, where they will be welcomed wholeheartedly, their dignity will not be affronted, and their right to be there will be taken for granted, is a blessed refuge from the strains and humiliations of integration. By contrast, commuting back home to an overwhelmingly white neighborhood, where their children may be shunned by some of the neighbors, or suspected as hoodlums by the local police, where a small but hard core of neighbors may actively express hostility to their presence, and most of the others may be cordial but distant, hardly provides the same comfort and affirmation.

Conservatives observe high levels of racial conflict (Rothman et al. 2003) and self-segregation on more racially integrated campuses, and infer from these facts that "socially engineered" integration doesn't work. Indeed, they argue that it is self-defeating, in that it arouses racial discord and resentment (Schuck 2003). Integrationists argue that racial conflict and self-segregation are symptoms of habits established in students' prior segregated lives. Given that most students come from segregated backgrounds, it is no wonder that their interactions at first are marred by stereotypes and prejudice, that they are relatively incompetent at respectful interracial interaction, and that they self-segregate at first, out of habit and comfort, when they enter an integrated setting. The question is whether experience with integration enables them to *learn* how to manage interracial interactions in more positive ways.

This can be tested. If the conservative argument is right, then racial conflict would drive out positive experiences of interracial interaction, and people's tendencies to self-segregate would be stable or increase over time. If the integrationist argument is right, then integration in settings of institutionalized support for cooperation increases opportunities for both negative *and positive* interracial interaction. Over time, people learn to better manage interracial relationships, and thereby lead more integrated lives. Studies consistently confirm the integrationist hypothesis. Students who attend more racially integrated schools lead more racially integrated lives after graduation: they have more racially diverse co-workers, neighbors, and friends than students who attend less diverse schools (Braddock et al. 1994; Gurin 1999: 133).

The facts of unconscious racial stigma and the dynamics of racial interaction highlight the unreality of conservative insistence on "color-blind" policies. On the Thernstroms' view, racial discord is caused by race consciousness (1997: 539). Any policy, such as affirmative action, that heightens race consciousness, is therefore self-defeating. Such a view could make sense only on the supposition that beliefs, habits, and attitudes don't exist if we aren't aware of them. Once we acknowledge that mental states reside at various levels of consciousness, the call for conscious color-blindness effectively amounts to a call to let unconscious racial biases operate unopposed by conscious policies that might change them.

5. THE ORDEAL OF INTEGRATION (II): IDENTITY POLITICS IN THE TWENTY-FIRST CENTURY

If conservatives have been complacent about integration, many on the Left actively promote racial self-segregation. In contrast with conservatives, they do so in recognition of the persistence of unjust racial inequality. The question is whether their prescriptions are up to the task of advancing racial justice. What's missing from their defenses of black and Latino self-segregation, I'll argue, is a clear understanding of the negative consequences of white segregation that this entails, as well as a gross undervaluation of the importance of forging *racially integrated* collective identities: forms of collective self-understanding, of who "we" are, that take for granted that "we" includes people of all races. Let's consider three models of self-segregation advanced by the Left. Call them the "identity development," "benign ethnocentrism," and "epistemological" models.

Beverly Tatum is a leading theorist of the identity development model of self-segregation. She argues that self-segregation is needed for individuals to develop psychologically healthy and mature racial identities. Black self-segregation emerges among children as a way to cope with racism and negative images of blacks. Blacks turn to one another for a sympathetic rather than a dismissive ear in discussing negative encounters with whites, to forge more positive black identities than those prevalent in mainstream culture, and to share their experiences of interpersonal racism and learn how to deal with it (Tatum 1997: 54–74).

Iris Young advances a different model of self-segregation, based on benign ethnocentrism, a kind of morally innocent in-group affinity. On this model, a social subgroup can legitimately prefer affiliating with "their own," without implying any antipathy toward outgroups. Residential "clustering" by race is morally permissible

> when its purpose is mutual aid and culture building among those who have affinity with one another, as long as the process of clustering does not exclude some people from access to benefits and opportunities. Such a clustering desire based on lifestyles or comfort is not wrong even when acted on by privileged or formerly privileged groups . . . if it can be distinguished from the involuntary exclusion of others and the preservation of privilege. (Young 2000: 217)

Integration, Young argues, focuses on the wrong issues. The mere fact that neighborhoods are racially identifiable is no cause for concern. What matters is the equal allocation of benefits to different areas, not the equal allocation of racial groups to different areas.

Aimee MacDonald (2000) defends an epistemological model of self-segregation in the course of defending racial program houses on college campuses. Racial self-segregation provides a locus for the generation of knowledge from racially distinctive perspectives, knowledge that is needed to counter racism. Because race defines people's social locations, their opportunities, and the ways people perceive and treat them, people experience the social world differently in virtue of the ways they are racially classified. Arriving at an understanding of how this is so requires people to come to grips with their racial identities, which in turn requires that people of the same race share their experiences and work together to interpret them as a basis for antiracist action.

Taken together, the arguments of Tatum, Young, and MacDonald offer a powerful account of the benefits of self-segregation. *I happily acknowledge that these benefits exist*, or, in Young's idealized case of benign ethnocentrism, which abstracts from the fact that ethnocentrism in today's world is inextricable from outgroup antipathy and responses to it, might exist. Yet none of their accounts is grounded in a realistic appraisal of the material and social conditions for advancing racial equality. To achieve racial equality, blacks need to change, whites need to change, and we need to change. All of these changes can happen only through racial integration. Let us recall why.

Young imagines a world in which racial equality can be achieved by moving resources to the people, rather than moving people to the resources. We could imagine this strategy working if disadvantaged racial groups lacked only material resources. But, as we have seen, people's access to advantages is mediated not simply by impersonal allocative rules, but through social, including personal, relationships. To some degree, affirmative action functions for blacks and Latinos as a formal substitute for the informal social connections that enable whites to get ahead. But it is a fantasy to suppose that the substitute is or ever could be perfect, especially at higher rungs of the occupational ladder, where people need to prove themselves through more intangible criteria, such as trust, that develop and become salient through personal relationships. Moreover, as Patterson and Loury stress, blacks need experience in integrated settings to acquire the skills needed to manage and lead racially integrated, majority white institutions. This is a matter of acquiring human capital, not of assimilation. Integration does not assume that the habits learned and deployed at work or in other integrated settings replace those that prevail in other settings. Racial equality therefore requires that blacks and Latinos change, in that they acquire forms of human and social capital that can be obtained only through social integration.

When blacks and Latinos self-segregate, whites are of necessity racially isolated. Tatum argues that all-white groups can work out positive antiracist white identities for themselves, without having to ask blacks and Latinos to take up the burden of helping them deal with their prejudices (Tatum 1997: 90–113). Yet whites have to be made aware of their own racial privilege for this to happen. Tatum and Young acknowledge that it is hard for whites to become aware of this if they are isolated from blacks and Latinos.

No doubt, among whites eager to have a non-racist identity, the opinions they express in an all-white group could be managed by a skilled psychologist of race relations, such as Tatum herself. The real difficulty lies deeper than people's conscious opinions. To focus on their beliefs about racial privilege or their quest for a non-racist self-understanding is to imagine that acquiring a politically correct consciousness is what whites need to be able to treat blacks and Latinos as equals. Yet we have seen that what most urgently needs to change are people's unconscious habits of interracial interaction and perception. And the fundamental way to change these is to practice respectful interaction in settings that promote interracial cooperation. Whites need this practice more than anyone else, since they have the least experience in integrated settings.

Racial equality cannot be achieved without interracial interaction. To achieve this, we need to generate practical knowledge of how to work together on terms of equality. Only by working and

thinking *together* can *we* work out mutually respectful and cooperative habits of interaction. To be sure, MacDonald is right to point out that blacks and Latinos at times need to talk among themselves to work out strategies for coping with the stresses of integration. But she is wrong to suppose that the possibilities for generating such knowledge would be under threat by closing down racial program housing. Self-segregation is the default position of black, white, and Latino Americans. Black and Latino students will find one another and work out racially defined identities and epistemological perspectives without needing to be housed together. The most scarce, important, and difficult community of meaning we need to construct is that of a racially integrated "us." And this community cannot be achieved if black and Latino students institutionalize their self-segregation.

MacDonald's epistemological argument can also be questioned on its own terms, to the extent that it focuses on the *preservation* of racially exclusive communities of meaning. There is no point in preserving the races, understood as social positions in a racialized social hierarchy. But there may be a point in preserving cultural meanings and practices that are independent of racism and the struggle against it. This is why MacDonald, like Young, shifts from a structural account of race to a cultural account. It is no doubt true that cultural meanings and practices that originated in black and Latino communities have immeasurably enriched American culture. But only a spurious association of culture with blood or ancestry can support the thought that racial self-segregation is needed to preserve or develop diverse cultural meanings and practices, even those that originated among segregated groups. Whites and Asians can, and do, play jazz. No group "owns" any particular cultural practice or has any particular entitlement to exclusive development rights to it. In a free and democratic society, culture is part of the commons and is no racial group's intellectual property. The demand to "preserve" particular cultural communities of meaning freezes culture in racialized cubicles, prevents its free appropriation by racial others and, most importantly, prevents its free development by an integrated "us."

The idea that institutionalized self-segregation is needed to preserve epistemic diversity is equally spurious. It makes sense only against a background assumption that integration is the same as assimilation and cultural homogenization, or that it presumes the fixity of mainstream culture. To the contrary, integration is a constant generator of new cultural diversities and epistemic perspectives, just as cross-pollination constantly generates novel combinations of genes in plants. And far from presuming that mainstream culture should remain static, integration aims to *change* it, especially to the extent that it embodies unconscious racial stereotypes and prejudices.

I conclude that the integrated "us," not the self-segregated racial group, is the critical agent of racial justice that most urgently awaits deeper and richer construction. This is consistent with affirming that "effective resistance to racial domination requires that the black victims of that domination organize and motivate themselves to collective action through the systematic practice of pro-black discrimination in contact" (Loury 2002: 97). My point is that neither justice nor democracy can be realized if the self-segregated racial group is celebrated as a more worthy site of identity and emotional investment than the integrated "us," as multiculturalists would have it. Identity politics, in the form of ethnoracial nationalism, was no doubt a necessary moment in the struggle for racial equality (Patterson 1997: 65–6). But it is time to strike a new balance between moments of self-segregation and of integration, decidedly in favor of the racially inclusive "us."

REFERENCES

Borjas, George J. (1992) "Ethnic Capital and Intergenerational Mobility," *Quarterly Journal of Economics* 107: 123–50.

Braddock, J. H., Dawkins, M. P., and Trent, W. (1994) "Why Desegregate? The Effect of School Desegregation on Adult Occupational Desegregation of African Americans, Whites, and Hispanics," *International Journal of Contemporary Sociology* 31: 273–83.

Brooks-Gunn, Jeanne, Duncan, Greg J., Klebanov, Pamela Kato, and Sealan, Naomi (1993) "Do Neighborhoods Influence Child and Adolescent Development?" *American Journal of Sociology* 99: 353–95.

Cashin, Sheryll (2004) *The Failures of Integration: How Race and Class Are Undermining the American Dream* (New York: Public Affairs).

Dovidio, John, and Gaertner, Samuel (2000) "Aversive Racism and Selection Decisions: 1989 and 1999," *Psychological Science* 11(4): 315–19.

Dovidio, John, Gaertner, Samuel, and Kawakami, Kerry (2001) "Intergroup Contact: The Past, Present, and the Future," *Group Processes & Intergroup Relations* 6(1): 5–20.

Ellen, Ingrid Gould (2000) *Sharing America's Neighborhoods: The Prospects for Stable Racial Integration* (Cambridge, MA: Harvard University Press).

Fields, Jason, and Casper, Lynne (2001) *America's Families and Living Arrangements: March 2000.* Current Population Reports, P20–537. Washington, DC: US Census Bureau: http://www.census.gov/prod/2001pubs/p20–537.pdf.

Gaertner, Samuel, and Dovidio, John (1986) "The Aversive Form of Racism," in John Dovidio and Samuel Gaertner, eds., *Prejudice, Discrimination, and Racism* (New York: Academic Press).

Gaertner, S. L., and Dovidio, John (2000) *Reducing Intergroup Bias: The Common Ingroup Identity Model* (Philadelphia: Psychology Press).

Gurin, Patricia (1999) Expert Report of Patricia Gurin. "The Compelling Need for Diversity in Higher Education." Gratz et al. v. Bollinger et al., No. 97–75321 (E. D. Mich.) Grutter et al. v. Bollinger, et al., No. 97–75928 (E. D. Mich.) (Ann Arbor MI: University of Michigan).

Kreider, Rose (2003) *Adopted Children and Stepchildren: 2000.* Census 2000 Special Reports, CENSR-5RV (Washington, DC: US Census Bureau): http://www.census.gov/prod/2003pubs/censr–6.pdf.

Loury, Glenn (2002) *The Anatomy of Racial Inequality* (Cambridge, MA: Harvard University Press).

MacDonald, Aimee (2000) "Racial Authenticity and White Separatism: The Future of Racial Program Housing on College Campuses," in Paula Moya, ed., *Reclaiming Identity: Realist Theory and the*

Predicament of Postmodernism (Berkeley and Los Angeles: University of California Press).

Massey, Douglas, and Denton, Nancy (1993) *American Apartheid* (Cambridge, MA: Harvard University Press).

McConnell, Allen, and Leibold, Jill (2001) "Relations Among the Implicit Association Test, Discriminatory Behavior, and Explicit Measures of Racial Attitudes," *Journal of Experimental Social Psychology* 37(5): 435–42.

Patterson, Orlando (1997) *The Ordeal of Integration: Progress and Resentment in America's "Racial" Crisis* (Washington, DC: Civitas/Counterpoint).

Post, Robert (1998) "Introduction: After Bakke," in Robert Post and Michael Rogin, eds., *Race and Representation: Affirmative Action* (New York: Zone Books).

Rothman, Stanley, Lipset, Seymour Martin, and Nevitte, Neil (2003) "Racial Diversity Reconsidered," *The Public Interest* (Spring).

Schuck, Peter (2003) *Diversity in America: Keeping Government at a Safe Distance* (Cambridge, MA: Belknap Press).

Tatum, Beverly (1997) *"Why Are All the Black Kids Sitting Together in the Cafeteria?" and Other Conversations About Race* (New York: Basic Books).

Thernstrom, Stephen, and Thernstrom, Abigail (1997) *America in Black and White: One Nation, Indivisible* (New York: Simon and Schuster).

Wilson, George, Sakura-Lemessy, Ian, and West, Jonathan P. (1999) "Reaching the Top: Racial Differences in Mobility Paths to Upper-Tier Occupations," *Work and Occupations* 26: 165–86.

Wright, Stephen C., Aron, Arthur, McLaughlin-Volpe, Tracy, and Ropp, Stacy A. (1997) "The Extended Contact Effect: Knowledge of Cross-Group Friendships and Prejudice," *Journal of Personality and Social Psychology* 73: 73–90.

Young, Iris Marion (2000) *Inclusion and Democracy* (Oxford: Oxford University Press).

Elizabeth Anderson: The Future of Racial Integration

1. Do you think that Anderson has accurately identified the stages of racial integration? If so, give your assessment of where your community stands with regard to her four stages.

2. Anderson offers a distinctive rationale for policies of affirmative action. What is it, and how plausible is it?

3. Anderson presents one politically conservative argument against racial integration. Reconstruct that argument and critically assess Anderson's replies to it.

4. Anderson presents three politically liberal arguments against racial integration. Reconstruct one of those arguments and then critically assess Anderson's reply to it.

5. Do you think that racial integration is valuable for its own sake, valuable only as a means to some further valuable situation, or neither? Defend your answer.

CHAPTER 19

Privacy

JUST THE FACTS

The amount of **privacy** a person has depends on the amount of control she has over the accessibility of information about herself. The more control a person has over such information, the more privacy she has.

One way a person's privacy can be reduced is by being put under constant **surveillance**, which amounts to any action that involves monitoring someone with the aim of collecting information about them. A recent event that highlighted the threat to privacy posed by **government surveillance** (i.e., that undertaken under orders by the state) was Edward Snowden's 2013 unveiling of highly classified information from the National Security Agency (NSA), a federal intelligence agency of the U.S. Department of Defense. This information revealed details about government surveillance programs of the nations comprising "Five Eyes"—the intelligence alliance between Australia, Canada, New Zealand, the United Kingdom, and the United States.[1] These programs had been kept secret from the general public, and raised worries among the citizens of these nations that their privacy was being violated on an unprecedented scale. One of the surveillance programs goes by the codename "PRISM," a U.S. operation that enables the NSA to collect private communications data—including emails and social media posts—of the users of at least nine major internet and technology companies, including Google, Yahoo, Microsoft, and Facebook. After going through certain protocols,[2] the NSA is allowed to collect data directly from the servers of these companies via PRISM as part of their efforts to surveil foreign targets,[3] provided that federal judges overseeing the use of the Foreign Intelligence Surveillance Act (FISA) determine that the data collection complies with FISA.[4]

Another surveillance program revealed by Snowden's leaked information goes by the codenames "XKeyscore." Like PRISM, XKeyscore is an NSA program that collects internet data. But XKeyscore's data collection abilities are apparently much greater than PRISM's. The *Guardian*'s initial report on Snowden's XKeyscore leaks notes that the NSA considers XKeyscore its "widest-reaching" data collection program.[5] XKeyscore is reportedly connected to the fiber-optic cables that make up the "backbone" of the world's communication network, and it can apparently track all of an individual user's internet activities. According to *The Intercept*'s 2015 analysis of documents on XKeyscore, the data collected by XKeyscore "not only include emails, chats and web-browsing traffic, but also pictures, documents, voice calls, webcam photos, web searches, advertising analytics traffic, social

1. https://www.dni.gov/index.php/who-we-are/organizations/enterprise-capacity/chco/chco-related-menus/chco-related-links/recruitment-and-outreach/217-about/organization/icig-pages/2660-icig-fiorc

2. https://www.washingtonpost.com/wp-srv/special/politics/prism-collection-documents/

3. https://www.theguardian.com/world/2013/jun/08/nsa-prism-server-collection-facebook-google

4. https://www.washingtonpost.com/wp-srv/special/politics/prism-collection-documents/

5. https://www.theguardian.com/world/2013/jul/31/nsa-top-secret-program-online-data

media traffic, botnet traffic, logged keystrokes, computer network exploitation (CNE) targeting, intercepted username and password pairs, file uploads to online services, Skype sessions and more."[6] As with PRISM, the NSA's use of XKeyscore is also regulated by FISA.

Under FISA, the NSA is legally forbidden from intentionally targeting US citizens for surveillance without individualized warrants.[7] However, FISA legally permits the NSA to collect data without a warrant if the data are incidentally obtained while carrying out surveillance that targets others.[8] This has happened, for instance, when the recorded phone call of a foreign target of surveillance was made to a US citizen. And some have expressed worry that the NSA might (or in fact does) exploit legal loopholes to effectively achieve targeted surveillance of US citizens while remaining in compliance with FISA's restrictions. The NSA's use of a provision of the Patriot Act to acquire access to all of Verizon's records of phone calls on their network[9] is one example that has been cited as evidence that the US government may be willing to adopt very permissive interpretations of laws, under which the NSA can constantly surveil everyone in the United States.[10]

In nations where privacy laws are less restrictive, government surveillance programs appear to be even more extensive than those of the Five Eyes nations. In addition to internet and telephone surveillance technologies, the Chinese government has been expanding its surveillance capabilities by building up a repertoire of other tools, including widely dispersed facial-recognition cameras, phone scanners and apps, and fingerprinting databases.[11] The Chinese government hopes to be capable of the sort of fine-grained surveillance needed for the success of their plans of implementing a "Social Credit System" (SCS) by the end of 2020. Persons will be assigned publicly accessible trustworthiness scores by the SCS based on things various things, including their compliance with contracts and their spending habits;[12] those who score poorly will face penalties, including travel restrictions and an inability to buy property or take out loans.[13] The hope is that sweeping surveillance will leave no actions unaccounted for by the SCS.

Various polls show that most Americans are distrustful of both states and private companies when it comes to collecting and handling data about them. A Pew Research Center study found that 79 percent of Americans are concerned about how companies use their collected data, and 64 percent are similarly concerned about the government.[14] Most also feel they have little or no control over the data that companies (81 percent) or the government (84 percent) collect, though some feel that they are more in control of some sorts of information rather than others (e.g., slightly more people feel they are least a little in control over data about their physical location than data about websites they visit).[15] The same study also suggests that Americans are much more accepting of

6. https://theintercept.com/2015/07/01/nsas-google-worlds-private-communications/

7. https://www.theguardian.com/world/2013/jul/31/nsa-top-secret-program-online-data

8. https://www.washingtonpost.com/news/wonk/wp/2013/06/12/heres-everything-we-know-about-prism-to-date/?arc404=true

9. https://www.theguardian.com/world/2013/jun/06/nsa-phone-records-verizon-court-order

10. https://www.washingtonpost.com/news/wonk/wp/2013/06/12/heres-everything-we-know-about-prism-to-date/?arc404=true

11. https://www.nytimes.com/2019/12/17/technology/china-surveillance.html

12. https://www.wired.co.uk/article/chinese-government-social-credit-score-privacy-invasion

13. https://www.wired.co.uk/article/china-social-credit-system-explained

14. https://www.pewresearch.org/internet/2019/11/15/americans-and-privacy-concerned-confused-and-feeling-lack-of-control-over-their-personal-information/

15. Ibid.

having their data collected for some purposes rather than others. For example, 49 percent of Americans find it acceptable for the government to collect data on all Americans to assess potential terrorist threats, but the same number also find it unacceptable for smartphone makers to share audio recordings with law enforcement to assist criminal investigations.

Another Pew Research Center study found that a majority of Americans (74 percent) say that it is more important that people be able to "keep things about themselves that might be potentially damaging from being searchable online" than that they be able to "discover potentially useful information about others,"[16] suggesting that they value the privacy of their own information over the ability to acquire information about others. The same study found that a majority of Americans believe there is a right to have certain information held by other people or organizations deleted, though there is more agreement that there is such a right when that information concerns certain content rather than others. For example, 87 percent of Americans agreed that there was such a right when it comes to potentially embarrassing photos or videos, but only 36 percent agreed that there was such a right when it comes to "data collected by law enforcement, like criminal records, mugshots." The study also found that across most information types, the proportion of older Americans who believe in such rights is greater than the proportion of younger Americans.

Despite their privacy concerns, Pew Research Center data suggest that most Americans do not read privacy policies and terms of service before agreeing to them. Only 38 percent of Americans sometimes read such policies, and the proportions that always (9 percent) or often (13 percent) read such policies are even smaller.[17] Moreover, the number of users of various social media

platforms continues to be at or near all-time highs. Statistical survey data suggest that as of the first quarter of 2020, there are over 2.6 billion monthly active Facebook users,[18] of which over 223 million are American.[19] And as of February 2019, there are over 330 million active users on Twitter,[20] of which over 68 million are American.[21]

ARGUMENT ANALYSIS

How much of our privacy should we be willing to give up? Is anyone ever morally obligated to *sacrifice* at least some of their privacy? Is anyone ever morally obligated to *maintain* privacy over at least some sorts of information? And when is it permissible for others to acquire information about us that we desire to keep private?

Before considering some arguments meant to address these questions, let's first distinguish **active surveillance** from **passive surveillance**. The first involves surveillance by another person. Here, there is no gap between the acquisition of information about a person and the processing of that information. Contrast that with passive surveillance, undertaken by devices that collect information about us without immediately making it known to other people. For example, facial recognition cameras can record our whereabouts even if no one person is actively monitoring the information being collected.

For consequentialists, engaging in either active or passive surveillance of others is not

16. https://www.pewresearch.org/fact-tank/2020/01/27/most-americans-support-right-to-have-some-personal-info-removed-from-online-searches/

17. https://www.pewresearch.org/internet/2019/11/15/americans-and-privacy-concerned-confused-and-feeling-lack-of-control-over-their-personal-information/

18. https://www.statista.com/statistics/264810/number-of-monthly-active-facebook-users-worldwide/

19. https://www.statista.com/statistics/408971/number-of-us-facebook-users/

20. https://www.statista.com/statistics/282087/number-of-monthly-active-twitter-users/

21. https://www.statista.com/statistics/274564/monthly-active-twitter-users-in-the-united-states/

just permissible but is in fact morally required whenever doing so would maximize good results. Their argument is pretty straightforward:

The Consequentialist Argument for Surveillance

1. Actions are morally required if and only if they would maximize good results.
2. Active and passive surveillance does sometimes maximize good results.

Therefore,

3. Both active and passive surveillance are sometimes morally required.
4. Any action that is morally required is morally permitted.

Therefore,

5. Both active and passive surveillance are sometimes morally permitted.

We won't pause to assess premise 1 (see Chapter 5 for discussion). And premise 4 is extremely plausible. So the action is with premise 2. There are surely cases in which revealing information that someone wishes to be keep private would lead to suboptimal consequences. In all such cases, consequentialists will judge such surveillance actions impermissible. Still, it's hard to deny the truth of premise 2. Both active and passive surveillance may yield optimal results, at least in some cases.

To help see this, consider some of the benefits that can come from allowing for state surveillance of its population. First, 2013 NSA documents on the XKeyscore program claim that the program provided intelligence that led to the capture of over three hundred terrorists.[22] Such claims might be cited as apparent evidence of the **public safety** benefits of surveillance programs that include both active and passive elements. Second, wide-reaching surveillance

might deter people from attempting to carry out criminal activities: if you know you're being watched, you're less likely to try to commit a crime in the first place. Third, government surveillance might provide evidence that would improve the reliability of legal verdicts, resulting in less wrongful convictions and less guilty persons escaping prosecution.

Many argue that states are not only right to surveil their citizens but are also required to sometimes keep their own secrets. This amounts to a kind of privacy that would attach to information that is held by government officials. Standardly, the arguments for keeping state secrets also take a consequentialist form:

The Consequentialist Argument for State Secrecy

1. Actions are morally required if and only if they would maximize good results.
2. Keeping state secrets will sometimes maximize good results.

Therefore,

3. The state is sometimes morally required to keep secrets from the public.
4. Any action that is morally required is also morally permitted.

Therefore,

5. The state is sometimes morally permitted to keep secrets from the public.

As before, we won't pause to consider premises 1 or 4. Premise 2 is quite plausible. Though we might sometimes, especially in the face of government abuse or corruption, wish for political leaders who are completely transparent, there do seem to be occasions where state secrecy is required to promote the best results. Think of cases in which governments need to conceal their bottom line when negotiating with other nations, or where a nation has invested huge resources to develop a valuable item whose

---

22. https://www.nytimes.com/2013/08/01/us/nsa-surveillance.html?pagewanted=2&_r=0

details, if leaked, would lead to the collapse of any advantage (financial, diplomatic, etc.) that it had hoped to gain from its investment. Or suppose, as some have argued, that the NSA's use of various surveillance programs can minimize harm only if the public is not informed about some of the relevant details of those programs—for instance, the fact that they can pinpoint someone's physical location from her internet activities regardless of whether she uses a virtual private network. If details such as these must be kept secret in order to yield the best results, then consequentialism both permits and requires that the NSA keep the public from knowing about them.

Even if surveillance programs and policies of government secrecy yield the benefits just discussed, they may also cause substantial harms. Indeed, some of the benefits may come only at the expense of certain harms. Consider, for instance, that the deterrence benefits in reducing crime require that the public knows of surveillance program in the first place. But such knowledge might lead to a huge amount of stress in people's lives. It might also inhibit the way they permissibly behave towards others when in public. And clandestine surveillance programs, hidden to the public, are more easily manipulated and subject to uncheckable abuses by those who staff them. It is an open question in each case whether the benefits outweigh the costs.

Nonconsequentialist approaches to privacy, surveillance, and secrecy will look to things other than the results of a surveillance or secrecy program in order to determine its morality. For nonconsequentialists, certain things are morally important independently of an action's results, and our judgments about intrusions of privacy and nondisclosures of information must appropriately account for the moral weightiness of these things. When it comes to judging the permissibility of privacy-affecting actions, then, what should we consider besides

the value that might be had by the consequences of such actions?

One possibility is the importance of protecting our **autonomy**, which is the power to guide our life through our own free choices. There are various ways that someone can lose her autonomy, but two standard ways are by being **coerced** (i.e., manipulated to make a choice among a set of options that have been wrongfully narrowed) or by being deprived of information needed to make an autonomous choice.

Some scholars have argued that certain infringements of privacy are immoral because they frustrate our ability to maintain our autonomy. The following supplies one basis for their view:

The Privacy Argument from Autonomy

1. If our interests in maintaining our autonomy are morally significant, then any limitation of our autonomy is morally suspect.
2. Our interests in maintaining our autonomy are morally significant.

Therefore,

3. Any limitation of our autonomy is morally suspect.
4. Infringements of privacy limit our autonomy.

Therefore,

5. Infringements of privacy are morally suspect.

Given that what saying that something is "morally significant" amounts to is saying that it is morally weighty and should be treated as such in our moral deliberations, premise 1 is a truism: if an interest of ours is morally weighty, then the fact that an action would frustrate our ability to satisfy that interest counts against the permissibility of that action. Note that an action can be morally suspect but still be, in the end, morally acceptable. We might find grounds to remove or outweigh the suspicion. When it comes to autonomy, though limiting it is always suspect, there are surely some good reasons for doing so in some cases. For instance, I might autonomously choose to do something deeply immoral or absolutely disastrous; in such a case, it may well be OK to limit my autonomy and prevent the serious immorality or disaster from occurring.

Premise 2 is highly plausible. If Kantians are right (see Chapter 6), our autonomy is the basis of human dignity. But even if they are off-base about that, there is still much to be said on behalf of premise 2. We want to be free to make our own choices, even if that freedom must have limits. Exercising autonomous choice is a pre-condition for living the life we want. It is the basis for our personal responsibility, and so the basis for thinking that we have earned praise or criticism for our actions. We are not robots or mindless devices, and should not be treated as if we had no will of our own.

Premise 4 is also plausible, at least for many cases. Our privacy might be infringed through coercive measures or by accessing personal information. Either sort of case may well result in limiting the options available to us. These two sorts of considerations aren't the only ones that bear on the plausibility of premise 4, but they are especially salient when privacy infringements involve active or passive surveillance.

As I've indicated, though, not every limitation of autonomy is, in the end, morally wrong. In particular, we might ask about the moral status of state surveillance, given that it will at least sometimes limit our autonomy. Being constantly monitored by such programs might compromise your autonomy; after all, those who are constantly monitored may end up being effectively coerced to (for example) conform to prevailing social norms, when they might otherwise be freer spirits. Whether wide-reaching surveillance programs do exert this sort of coercive pressure is something that requires psychological and sociological research to resolve. Perhaps people tend to eventually get accustomed to being constantly surveilled, such that they no longer feel any pressure to modify their behavior when they are "on camera." Another issue for further research is whether both active and passive versions of surveillance programs have the same coercive effects (if any). Perhaps active but not passive versions do have coercive effects that compromise autonomy, in which case the former but not the latter would be impermissible by the lights of the Argument from Autonomy.

State secrecy, rather than state surveillance, might also limit peoples' autonomy. It can do this by withholding information that we need to make certain choices. Think for a moment of a case that doesn't involve the state. A doctor's failure to inform a patient of relevant treatment options would compromise her ability to autonomously choose which sort of medical care is best for her. Perhaps state secrecy analogously compromises the autonomy of those it keeps in the dark. Of course, if such secrecy only prevented people from making immoral or disastrous choices, then that wouldn't be so problematic. But if such secrecy instead prevented us from knowing of attractive and viable options, then it would indeed work to infringe our autonomy.

Another important value that privacy may protect is our ability to form close relationships with others. Different sorts of relationships are associated with different standards of what personal information can be appropriately shared: the closer the relationship between two people, the more fitting it is that they share personal information. I share things with my wife that I wouldn't do with friends, much less strangers; my control over that information is part of what helps me to determine my relations with others. Generally, at least part of our ability to control the nature of our relationships involves being able to control how our personal information is shared, which in turn requires control over the privacy of that information. Thus any action that compromises our control over the privacy of such information is at least initially morally problematic and will be impermissible all-things-considered if there aren't sufficiently strong reasons in favor of that action. This line of reasoning can be summed up by

The Privacy Argument from Personal Relations

1. Any action that compromises our ability to sustain personal relationships is morally suspect.
2. Many infringements of privacy compromise our ability to sustain personal relationships.

Therefore,

3. Many infringements of privacy are morally suspect.

Premise 1 of this argument is quite plausible. There is something morally worrisome about actions that threaten our ability to maintain our relationships with others. As before, though, an action's being morally suspect does *not* mean that it is always immoral. It just means that there is ordinarily some moral strike against it. Still, many morally suspect actions might be, when everything is said and done, morally OK after all. Premise 2 is also plausible. If you're like most people, you're embarrassed or ashamed by some details of your life that you'd much rather keep to yourself. Maybe your life partner should know about them, but even here, it is an open question whether complete transparency is the ideal. Surely others, though, especially only casual acquaintances or work colleagues, needn't know everything about your personal life. The disclosure of most such information, against your will, would represent a violation of your privacy that might well threaten their ability to look you in the eye and your ability to sustain a working relationship with them. It follows

that in many cases, infringements of privacy are indeed morally suspect.

The Privacy Argument from Personal Relations suggests that some surveillance programs would be impermissible, insofar as the information collected from such programs was made publicly accessible and compromised the privacy of the owner of the information. But what about programs whose collected information was never made accessible to anyone you ever interact with? Whether the surveillance is active or passive, there doesn't seem to be any obvious way that such programs would compromise your control over the nature of your relationships. This points to a limitation of the argument we're currently considering, namely, that the real threat of state surveillance with respect to one's personal relationships is not in the surveillance itself, but in making public the information that it has collected.

A closely related argument appeals to our interest in having intimate relationships in particular, where a relationship is intimate insofar as it involves a significant degree of some combination of love, friendship, trust, and respect. This argument relies on the claim that a certain amount of privacy is a necessary condition for having intimate relationships at all. The thought is that at least part of what it is to be an intimate relationships is to be a relationship that involves a sort of **shared privacy** over personal information. Such privacy amounts to one person sharing private information only with some select second party, where that second party ensures that the information remains known only by the two parties. A common example is the secrets that loving couples share only between themselves. The importance of shared privacy supports

The Argument from Intimacy

1. Any action that compromises our ability to sustain intimate personal relationships is morally suspect.

2. Many infringements of privacy compromise our ability to sustain intimate personal relationships.

Therefore,

3. Many infringements of privacy are morally suspect.

Premise 1 is highly plausible. That's because the value of intimate relationships is pretty substantial. Our ability to enter and sustain intimate relationships is an essential part of our ability to define ourselves as persons. Intimate relationships can also contribute a great deal of happiness to one's life. And though this is controversial, some philosophers have argued that such relationships are intrinsically valuable—they are good in and of themselves, quite apart from the good they bring in their wake.

Premise 2 is also quite plausible. Infringing a person's privacy can indeed compromise her ability to sustain intimate relationships. After all, such relationships are built in part upon a fund of shared privacy, which is a kind of intimate exclusivity. The intimacy is defined by information that is effectively a secret held by the parties with access to the information. If someone videos your intimate conversations without your consent, or reads your love letters and then posts them on social media, then this infringement of privacy can be devastating for the relationship.

It follows that some infringements of privacy are morally suspect, because they threaten the intimate relationships of those whose shared privacy has been breached. But we should once more distinguish between a violation of privacy and the publication of the information that has been taken. Think again about a case in which others read your love letters without your consent, and perhaps even after you've explicitly forbidden them from doing so. Surely there is something morally suspect about this behavior. But suppose that those who have violated your shared privacy never reveal what they have read. Is such conduct damaging to your intimate relationship? If so, what does such damage consist in?

Even if it is difficult to pinpoint the harm here, that does not mean that such infringements of privacy are morally acceptable. After all, if the Argument from Intimacy is sound, then there is something morally suspect about privacy infringements. Whether they are morally acceptable in the end depends on whether there are strong enough moral reasons to outweigh the morally problematic features of privacy infringements. Suppose you secretly read someone's love letters just for kicks, or publish them for the pleasure of seeing the authors squirm. There are no good moral reasons, much less any strong ones, for engaging in such behavior. So in that case, the violation of privacy is not just morally suspect, but immoral, all things considered.

But suppose instead that government officials surveilled a couple whom they rightly suspected of espionage, and that the surveillance was credibly designed to gain information that could prove helpful in preventing a murderous attack. In such a case it might well be that privacy infringement, despite being itself morally suspect, was nevertheless the right thing to do, all things considered.

In some cases we want to control who has access to our personal information for reasons other than retaining control over our relationships (whether intimate or not). Rather, we seek to control our personal information precisely because it is *ours*, to do with as we please. If someone takes our information from us without our consent, then it's as if he has stolen something from us, and so has wronged us. Wronging others is immoral. Those who violate our privacy act immorally because they take what is not theirs to take.

There can be many reasons to want to retain control over personal information. In some cases, the information might be embarrassing if revealed. In others, it might bring to light a vulnerability whose publication would lead to harmful results. There are lots of other bad results that might follow from an unlicensed invasion of privacy. And there are good ones, too—as we've seen, these include the ability to determine one's relationships with others. In these respects, privacy has instrumental value—it enables us to prevent harms and achieve goods that we might otherwise be unable to acquire. In addition to playing these instrumental roles, privacy might simply be valued for its own sake. We may value control over our own information not just for the good it can do, but for itself alone. As well as being instrumentally beneficial, it might also be intrinsically valuable. Consider this parallel: we may want to protect our personal space in order to prevent various harms or gain various benefits, but we might also value our control over that space for its own sake. The same goes for the control we exercise over our privacy.

It's not easy to argue for something's intrinsic value. A standard way to do this is to invite reflection on what things would be like in the absence of something, holding everything else fixed, and then try to determine whether things would be worse. This is a way to argue, for instance, that happiness is intrinsically valuable. Imagine a world without happiness and compare it to the same world once you add happiness back into the picture. The second world strikes me as a much better one. If you share that view, then you have some reason to think that happiness, in itself, is valuable.

Now run the test with privacy, rather than happiness. Imagine a world as similar as possible to ours, except that no one had any privacy. Is that world less appealing than ours? Has something valuable gone missing? If so, then you have some reason for thinking that privacy is intrinsically valuable.

Another way we might try to establish the intrinsic value of privacy is to drill down and think about its nature. At bottom, it amounts

to control over personal information. Though it may sound a bit odd to put it this way, the information in question is information you *own*. It's yours. When someone else takes it without your consent, that is a kind of theft. And theft is ordinarily wrong. This thinking can be summarized in

The Control of Privacy Argument

1. If something is ours, then others may permissibly take it only if we offer our consent to do so.
2. Violations of privacy involve others taking our information without our consent.

Therefore,

3. Violations of privacy are impermissible.

Premise 1 is very plausible. Part of what it means to own something is to have a moral right to its exclusive use. Others may permissibly use what is ours, but only with our permission. To be sure, there may be exceptions, but these are rare and unusual. Think, for instance, of a case in which your home has been destroyed by a natural disaster and the only food available to you is what you can find in someone else's home. You knock and no one answers. If you are on the verge of starvation, it may be permissible for you to enter their home and take some of their food, even without their consent. Likewise, if a privacy violation is required in order to save lives, then it might be permitted to access your information even without your consent. These sorts of extreme cases aside, though, it is wrong to take what others own without their consent, just as premise 1 says.

Premise 2 is also plausible. Your privacy isn't *violated* if you've given someone permission to access the information he's taken. When consenting to someone else's use of your information, you have waived your right to exclusive use of that information, and you are not wronged when that person (or that state agency) accesses the information you've permitted them to see.

Underlying this argument is the thought that our personal information is ours—we own it. But this is something that needs to be argued for. Imagine, for instance, that a government official claims that all personal information is the property of the state, rather than its individual citizens. When a state surveils you, it does so in order to get what it's entitled to—information about you. The state may consent to give you a restricted amount of privacy, but then again it may not. And if it doesn't, then you cannot complain that the state is taking what it has no right to take, since it owns your information to begin with.

This sounds nightmarish—Big Brother on steroids. Though the line of reasoning in the previous paragraph may well be mistaken, it's important to note that revealing the error requires an argument about the proper limits of state control over those living in its territory. If the state gets its legitimacy from the consent of the governed, then the state owns our personal information only if we consent to give it that power. If, instead, the state gets its legitimacy in some other way, then there is more room for the possibility that the state owns our personal information. Settling this matter requires a lot of thinking about what gives the state its authority to govern. Since that discussion takes us far from matters of privacy, we're unfortunately going to have to leave the matter here.

CONCLUSION

Privacy is certainly instrumentally important—it can enhance our autonomy and help to sustain our relationships with others. It can protect us from embarrassing revelations and give us a competitive edge. It may also be important in its own right. But no one thinks that respecting privacy is required in every circumstance. The state may rightly engage in active or passive surveillance of a terrorist cell that is plotting an atrocity. In such cases, the state is also allowed to make use of the information it gathers, in order to prevent disaster—even if the conspirators don't give their consent. Other cases are more complicated; while it may be acceptable to surveil a person, it would be unacceptable to actually access or use that information. As usual, consequentialists will argue that the overall permissibility of privacy infringements depends on their results, while nonconsequentialists will point to certain values (say, autonomy, or private ownership) that we must respect even if, on a given occasion, it would be optimal to thwart them.

ESSENTIAL CONCEPTS

Active surveillance: any form of surveillance that is carried out by an actual person such that, when it is successful, the information collected on the target(s) of surveillance is immediately made known to the person conducting the surveillance.

Autonomy: the power to guide our life through our own free choices.

Government surveillance: surveillance carried out by the state or by orders of the state.

Passive surveillance: any form of surveillance that is not carried out by an actual person such that the information collected on the target(s) of surveillance is not immediately made known to anyone.

Privacy: the level of accessibility of one's personal information to others.

Public safety: the level of protection citizens and social institutions have against threats to their well-being.

Shared privacy: one person sharing private information only with some select second party, where that second party ensures that the information remains known only by the two parties.

Surveillance: any action that involves monitoring someone with the aim of collecting information about them.

STAT SHOT

Majority of Americans fees as if they have little control over data collected about them by companies and the government

% of U.S. adults who say

		Companies	The government
Lack of control	They have very little/no control over the data _____ collect(s)	**81%**	**84%**
Risks outweigh benefits	Potential risks of _____ collecting data about them outweigh the benefits	**81%**	**66%**
Concern over data use	They are very/somewhat concerned about how _____ use(s) the data collected	**79%**	**64%**
Lack of understanding about data use	They have very little/no understanding about what _____ do/does with the data collected	**59%**	**78%**

Note: Those who did not give an answer or who gave other responses are not shown.
Source: PEW Research Center, "Americans and Privacy: Concerned, Confused and Feeling Lack of Control Over Their Personal Information."

Figure 19.1.

Source: https://www.pewresearch.org/internet/2019/11/15/americans-and-privacy-concerned-confused-and-feeling-lack-of-control-over-their-personal-information/

Americans are more accepting of using personal data to help improve schools or assess potential terrorist threats, but are more wary of some other data uses

% of U.S. adults who say the following uses of data of personal information are . . .

	Not acceptable	Acceptable	Not sure
Poorly perfoming schools sharing student data with a nonprofit seeking to improve educational outcomes	27	49	24
The government collecting data about all Americans to assess potential terrorist threats	31	49	19
DNA testing companies sharing customers' genetic data with law enforcement to help solve crimes	33	48	18
Fitness tracking app makers sharing user data with medical researchers to better understand the link between exercise and heart disease	35	41	22
Social media companies monitoring users' posts for signs of depression to identify users at risk for self-harm and connect them to counselors	45	27	27
Smart speaker makers sharing users' audio recordings with law enforcement to help with criminal investigations	49	25	25

Note: Those who did not give an answer are not shown.
Source: PEW Research Center, "Americans and Privacy: Concerned, Confused and Feeling Lack of Control Over Their Personal Information."

Figure 19.2.

Source: https://www.pewresearch.org/internet/2019/11/15/americans-and-privacy-concerned-confused-and-feeling-lack-of-control-over-their-personal-information/

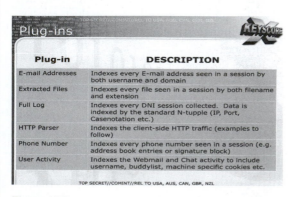

Figure 19.3.
Slide from leaked NSA presentation on XKeyscore.
Source: https://www.theguardian.com/world/interactive/2013/jul/31/nsa-xkeyscore-program-full-presentation

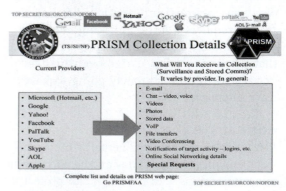

Figure 19.4.
Slide from leaked NSA presentation on PRISM.
Source: https://www.washingtonpost.com/wp-srv/special/politics/prism-collection-documents/

Cases for Critical Thinking

Surveillance by Civilians

British police encourage members of the public to report information to them that might aid investigations of potential terrorist attacks. Former Assistant Commissioner of the Metropolitan Police Service Mark Rowley was quoted saying that contributions from the public have been "extraordinary" in helping with such investigations.[23] One noteworthy case where public reporting reportedly helped lead to an arrest that thwarted a terrorist attack involved a student named Isa Ibrahim.[24] In 2008, Ibrahim was arrested after police were informed of his plans to set off explosives in a shopping center in Bristol. Ibrahim's is considered a landmark case because it was the first time public reporting from members of the Muslim community led to an arrest that prevented a major terrorist attack in the United Kingdom.

The BBC reported that most of the respondents of a survey of 2,198 British adults agreed that it was important for communities to work with police to prevent terrorism. That said, a quarter of respondents to that survey indicated that they might not report what they thought was suspicious activity because of fears that they'd be wasting police time, and two out of five indicated that they were unsure about what suspicious behavior might look like. Rowley suggested that members of the public should "trust [their] instinct" and should not "be cautious" when reporting things of concern. He said, "If it turns out to be a call where you made it with good intent but actually there was no problem at the end of it, that's fine. We'd rather have many calls like that, rather than miss out on the critical one that helps us stop an attack."[25]

Questions

1. Should states encourage civilians to assist in terrorism surveillance efforts? What potential drawbacks might be involved in such a policy?
2. Is there a morally relevant difference between reporting your suspicions about terrorist activity versus other sorts of criminal activity? If so, what are these differences? Do they have any implications for whether civilians are obligated to report potential terrorism risks?
3. If someone is falsely accused by civilian reporting of plotting to commit terrorism, are they owed any sort of compensation? If not, why not? If so, would people be owed similar compensation if it was the state that mistakenly accused them of plotting to commit terrorism?

SURVEILLANCE OF STATE OFFICIALS

On August 9, 1974, former U.S. president Richard Nixon resigned from office after it appeared that he would be impeached for the Watergate scandal. Nixon's administration had been involved in the break-in of the Democratic National Committee headquarters (located at the Watergate Office Building in Washington, DC) on June 17, 1972. His administration actively resisted investigation of the scandal, but the existence of audio recordings of conversations in the White House eventually came to light, and Nixon's refusal to hand over the recordings after receiving a congressional subpoena ultimately formed the basis for an article of impeachment.

The audio recordings that Nixon refused to hand over were produced by a sound-activated taping system. The recordings revealed

23. https://www.bbc.com/news/uk-39,176,110

24. http://news.bbc.co.uk/nol/ukfs_news/mobile/newsid_8150000/newsid_8155900/8155978.stm#sa-link_location=story-body&intlink_from_url=https%3A%2F%2Fwww.bbc.com%2Fnews%2Fuk-39,176,110&intlink_ts=1,598,066,112,237-sa

25. https://www.bbc.com/news/uk-39,176,110

conversations Nixon had with members of his administration, which clearly implicated his involvement in both the 1972 break-in of the Democratic National Committee headquarters and the subsequent attempts to cover it up. The existence of these tapes played a major role in the investigation that pressured Nixon to resign.

Questions

1. The investigation of the Watergate scandal might have turned out much differently without the tape recordings that revealed Nixon's involvement in the scandal. Given this, do you think records should be made of all state communications?

2. It's clear that Nixon did not want his role in the Watergate scandal to be disclosed. This seems to give us good grounds for believing that Nixon would not have ordered the break-in had he known that his involvement would be discovered. Given this, if there were a way to enable to the public to constantly monitor the activities of state officials, should it be implemented?

3. Are there any kinds of state activity that we have special reason to keep secret? If not, why not? If so, what are those activities, and what are the reasons to prevent the public from knowing of them?

SILENCING THE PRESS

The Guardian, a British newspaper, was one of the first outlets to publish articles on the documents leaked by NSA whistleblower Edward Snowden. After running several articles, *The Guardian* was pressured by the British government to either destroy or surrender its computer hard drives containing copies of Snowden's files.[26] Despite the fact that other copies of those files existed outside the country, British officials argued that the risk of the information being stolen by a foreign government was too great to allow the newspaper to retain its files.

In its defense, *The Guardian* argued that there was substantial public interest letting the public know about the extent of government surveillance. Its editors also sought to protect their source; they were worried that handing over the files would make Snowden vulnerable to having the information on those hard drives used against him in his prosecution.

Questions

1. If a civilian acquires state secrets, does she have a right to free speech that would make it permissible for her to spread that information to the public?

2. In general, are civilians obligated to help the state maintain its secrets? If not, why not? If so, what is the basis of this obligation?

3. If it's permissible for the state to keep a piece of information secret, does it follow that the state is always permitted to prevent a civilian from spreading that information to the public if she somehow acquires that information? Why or why not?

---

26. https://www.theguardian.com/world/2013/aug/20/nsa-snowden-files-drives-destroyed-london

Visible Man: Ethics in a World Without Secrets

Peter Singer

In this selection, Peter Singer investigates the ethical implications of new technologies that help governments keep tabs on their citizens and those that enable groups such as WikiLeaks to reveal state secrets on a wide scale. Nowadays, governments (and some large corporations, such as Facebook) have access to more personal data than any totalitarian government has ever had. Much of this is data that we freely share, via (say) social media postings. But other personal information is taken from us without our consent, especially by governments engaged in mass surveillance of their citizens. Singer asks, "Will this technology be a form of tyranny, or will it free us from tyranny? Will it upend democracy or strengthen it?"

 Singer considers answers to this question by focusing on what he calls "the inspection principle," which tells us that the greater the information revealed, the better the decisions are likely tocrnments to justify mass surveillance—after all, the thought goes, if the information gathered by such surveillance can stop another 9/11, then it may well seem worth it. But the very same principle can also be used to target governmental secrecy—after all, a well-informed citizenry, one that knows what government officials are really up to, will be better placed to call for action in the face of government corruption and mismanagement. The more our lives are subject to inspection, the less informational privacy we enjoy. Singer's piece invites the question: How much inspection is too much? Singer doesn't offer an answer. Instead, he invites readers to reflect for themselves on how best to strike the balance between individual privacy and social good.

 In 1787, the philosopher Jeremy Bentham proposed the construction of a "Panopticon," a circular building with cells along the outer walls and, at the center, a watchtower or "inspector's lodge" from which all the cells could be seen but no one would know, at any given moment, due to a system of blinds and partitions, whether he was actually being observed. Bentham thought this design would be particularly suited to prisons but suggested it could also be applied to factories, hospitals, mental asylums, and schools. Not only would prisoners, workers, the ill, the insane, and students be subject to observation, but also—if the person in charge of the facility visited the inspector's area—the warders, supervisors, caregivers, and teachers. The gradual adoption of this "inspection principle," would, Bentham predicted, create "a new scene of things," transforming the world into a place with "morals reformed, health preserved, industry invigorated, instruction diffused, public burdens lightened."

 The modern Panopticon is not a physical building, and it doesn't require the threat of an inspector's presence to be effective. Technological breakthroughs have made it easy to collect, store, and disseminate data on individuals, corporations, and even the government. With surveillance technology like closed-circuit television cameras and digital cameras now linked to the Internet, we have the means to implement Bentham's inspection principle on a much vaster scale. What's more, we have helped construct this new Panopticon, voluntarily

From Peter Singer, "Visible Man," *Harper's* (August 2011), pp. 31–36.

giving up troves of personal information. We blog, tweet, and post what we are doing, thinking, and feeling. We allow friends and contacts, and even strangers, to know where we are at any time. We sign away our privacy in exchange for the conveniences of modern living, giving corporations access to information about our financial circumstances and our spending habits, which will then be used to target us for ads or to analyze our consumer habits.

Then there is the information collected without our consent. Since 2001, the number of U.S. government organizations involved in spying on our own citizens, both at home and abroad, has grown rapidly. Every day, the National Security Agency intercepts 1.7 billion emails, phone calls, instant messages, bulletin-board postings, and other communications. This system houses information on thousands of U.S. citizens, many of them not accused of any wrongdoing. Not long ago, when traffic police stopped a driver they had to radio the station and wait while someone checked records. Now, handheld devices instantly call up a person's Social Security number and license status, records of outstanding warrants, and even mug shots. The FBI can also cross-check your fingerprints against its digital archive of 96 million sets.

Yet the guarded have also struck back, in a sense, against their guardians, using organizations like WikiLeaks, which, according to its founder Julian Assange, has released more classified documents than the rest of the world's media combined, to keep tabs on governments and corporations. When Assange gave the *Guardian* 250,000 confidential cables, he did so on a USB drive the size of your little finger. Efforts to close down the WikiLeaks website have proven futile, because the files are mirrored on hundreds of other sites. And in any case, WikiLeaks isn't the only site revealing private information. An array of groups are able to release information anonymously. Governments, corporations, and other organizations interested in protecting privacy will strive to increase security, but they will also have to reckon with the likelihood that such measures are sometimes going to fail.

New technology has made greater openness possible, but has this openness made us better off? For those who think privacy is an inalienable right, the modern surveillance culture is a means of controlling behavior and stifling dissent. But perhaps the inspection principle, universally applied, could also be the perfection of democracy, the device that allows us to know what our governments are really doing, that keeps tabs on corporate abuses, and that protects our individual freedoms just as it subjects our personal lives to public scrutiny. In other words, will this technology be a form of tyranny or will it free us from tyranny? Will it upend democracy or strengthen it?

The standards of what we want to keep private and what we want to make public are constantly evolving. Over the course of Western history, we've developed a desire for more privacy, quite possibly as a status symbol, since an impoverished peasant could not afford a house with separate rooms. Today's affluent Americans display their status not only by having a bedroom for each member of the family, plus one for guests, but also by having a bathroom for every bedroom, plus one for visitors so that they do not have to see the family's personal effects. It wasn't always this way. A seventeenth-century Japanese *shunga* depicts a man making love with his wife while their daughter kneels on the floor nearby, practicing calligraphy. The people of Tikopia, a Pacific island inhabited by Polynesians, "find it good to sleep side by side crowding each other, next to their children or their parents or their brothers and sisters, mixing sexes and generations," according to the anthropologist Dorothy Lee. "[A]nd if a widow finds herself alone in her one-room house, she may adopt a child or a brother to allay her intolerable privacy." The Gebusi people in New Guinea live in communal longhouses and are said to "shun privacy," even showing reluctance to look at photos in which they are on their own.

With some social standards, the more people do something, the less risky it becomes for each individual. The first women to wear dresses that did not reach their knees were no doubt looked upon with disapproval, and may have risked unwanted sexual attention; but once many women were revealing more of their legs, the risks dissipated. So too with privacy: when millions of people are prepared to post personal information, doing so becomes less risky for everyone. And those collective, large-scale forfeitures of personal privacy have other benefits as well, as tens of thousands of Egyptians showed when they openly became fans of the Facebook page

"We are all Khaled Said," named after a young man who was beaten to death by police in Alexandria. The page became the online hub for the protests that forced the ouster of President Hosni Mubarak.

Whether Facebook and similar sites are reflecting a change in social norms about privacy or are actually driving that change, that half a billion are now on Facebook suggests that people believe the benefits of connecting with others, sharing information, networking, self-promoting, flirting, and bragging outweigh breaches of privacy that accompany such behavior.

More difficult questions arise when the loss of privacy is not in any sense a choice. Bentham's Panopticon has become a symbol of totalitarian intrusion. Michel Foucault described it as "the perfection of power." We all know that the police can obtain phone records when seeking evidence of involvement in a crime, but most of us would be surprised by the frequency of such requests. Verizon alone receives 90,000 demands for information from law-enforcement agencies annually. Abuses have undoubtedly accompanied the recent increase in government surveillance. One glaring example is the case of Brandon Mayfield, an Oregon attorney and convert to Islam who was jailed on suspicion of involvement in the 2004 Madrid train bombings. After his arrest, Mayfield sued the government and persuaded a federal judge to declare the provision of the Patriot Act that the FBI used in investigating him unconstitutional. But as with most excesses of state power, the cause is not so much the investigative authority of the state as the state's erroneous interpretation of the information it uncovers and the unwarranted detentions that come about as a result. If those same powers were used to foil another 9/11, most Americans would likely applaud.

There is always a danger that the information collected will be misused—whether by regimes seeking to silence opposition or by corporations seeking to profit from more detailed knowledge of their potential customers. The scale and technological sophistication of this data-gathering enterprise allow the government to intercept and store far more information than was possible for secret police of even the most totalitarian states of an earlier era, and the large number of people who have access to sensitive information increases the potential for misuse.[1] As with any large-scale human activity, if enough people are involved eventually someone will do something corrupt or malicious. That's a drawback to having more data gathered, but one that may well be outweighed by the benefits. We don't really know how many terrorist plots have been foiled because of all this data-gathering.[2] We have even less idea how many innocent Americans were initially suspected of terrorism but *not* arrested because the enhanced data-gathering permitted under the Patriot Act convinced law-enforcement agents of their innocence.

The degree to which a government is repressive does not turn on the methods by which it acquires information about its citizens, or the amount of data it retains. When regimes want to harass their opponents or suppress opposition, they find ways to do it, with or without electronic data. Under President Nixon, the administration used tax audits to harass those on his "enemies list." That was mild compared with how "enemies" were handled during the dirty wars in Argentina, Guatemala, and Chile, and by the Stasi in East Germany. These repressive governments "disappeared" tens of thousands of dissidents, and they targeted their political enemies with what now seem impossibly cumbersome methods of collecting, storing, and sorting data. If such forms of abuse are rare in the United States, it is not because we have prevented the state from gathering electronic data about us. The crucial step in preventing a repressive government from misusing information is to have alert and well-informed citizens with a strong sense of right and *wrong* who work to keep the government democratic, open, just, and under the rule of law. The technological innovations used by governments and corporations to monitor citizens must be harnessed to monitor those very governments and corporations.

One of the first victories for citizen surveillance came in 1991, when George Holliday videotaped Los Angeles police officers beating Rodney King. Without that video, yet another LAPD assault on a black man would have passed unnoticed. Instead,

---

1. Including those involved in international operations relating to homeland security and intelligence, 854,000 people currently hold top-secret security clearances, according to the Washington Post.

2. In 2003, FBI director Robert Mueller claimed that the number of thwarted plots was more than one hundred.

racism and violence in police departments became a national issue, two officers went to prison, and King received $3.8 million in civil damages. Since then, videos and photographs, many of them taken on mobile phones, have captured innumerable crimes and injustices. Inverse surveillance—what Steve Mann, professor of computer engineering and proponent of wearing imaging devices, terms "sousveillance"—has become an effective way of informing the world of abuses of power.

We have seen the usefulness of sousveillance again this year in the Middle East, where the disclosure of thousands of diplomatic cables by WikiLeaks helped encourage the Tunisian and Egyptian revolutions, as well as the protest movements that spread to neighboring countries. Yet most government officials vehemently condemned the disclosure of state secrets. Secretary of State Hillary Clinton claimed that WikiLeaks' revelations "tear at the fabric of the proper function of responsible government." In February of this year, at George Washington University, she went further, saying that WikiLeaks had endangered human rights activists who had been in contact with U.S. diplomats, and rejecting the view that governments should conduct their work in full view of their citizens. As a counterexample, she pointed to U.S. efforts to secure nuclear material in the former Soviet states. Here, she claimed, confidentiality was necessary in order to avoid making it easier for terrorists or criminals to find the materials and steal them.

Clinton is right that it is not a good idea to make public the location of insecurely stored nuclear materials, but how much of diplomacy is like that? There may be some justifiable state secrets, but they certainly are few. For nearly all other dealings between nations, openness should be the norm. In any case, Clinton's claim that WikiLeaks releases documents "without regard for the consequences" is, if not deliberately misleading, woefully ignorant. Assange and his colleagues have consistently stated that they are motivated by a belief that a more transparent government will bring better consequences for all, and that leaking information has an inherent tendency toward greater justice, a view Assange laid out on his blog in December 2006, the month in which WikiLeaks published its first document:

The more secretive or unjust an organization is, the more leaks induce fear and paranoia in its leadership and planning coterie. . . . Since unjust systems, by their nature induce opponents, and in many places barely have the upper hand, leaking leaves them exquisitely vulnerable to those who seek to replace them with more open forms of governance.

Assange could now claim that WikiLeaks' disclosures have confirmed his theory. For instance, in 2007, months before a national election, WikiLeaks posted a report on corruption commissioned but not released by the Kenyan government. According to Assange, a Kenyan intelligence official found that the leaked report changed the minds of 10 percent of Kenyan voters, enough to shift the outcome of the election.

Two years later, in the aftermath of the global financial crisis, WikiLeaks released documents on dealings by Iceland's Kaupthing Bank, showing that the institution made multibillion-dollar loans, in some cases unsecured, to its major shareholders shortly before it collapsed. Kaupthing's successor, then known as New Kaupthing, obtained an injunction to prevent Iceland's national television network from reporting on the leaked documents but failed to prevent their dissemination. WikiLeaks' revelations stirred an uproar in the Icelandic parliament, which then voted unanimously to strengthen free speech and establish an international prize for freedom of expression. Senior officials of the bank are now facing criminal charges.

And of course, in April 2010, WikiLeaks released thirty-eight minutes of classified cockpit-video footage of two U.S. Army helicopters over a Baghdad suburb. The video showed the helicopter crews engaging in an attack on civilians that killed eighteen people, including two Reuters journalists, and wounded two children. Ever since the attack took place, in 2007, Reuters had unsuccessfully sought a U.S. military inquiry into the deaths of its two employees, as well as access to the cockpit video under the Freedom of Information Act. The United States had claimed that the two journalists were killed during a firefight. Although no action has been taken against the soldiers involved, if the military is ever going to exercise greater restraint when civilian lives are at risk, it will have been compelled to do so through the release of material like this.

Months before the Arab Spring began, Assange was asked whether he would release the trove of secret diplomatic cables that he was rumored to have obtained. Assange said he would, and gave this reason: "These sort of things reveal what the true state of, say, Arab governments are like, the true human rights abuses in those governments." As one young Tunisian wrote to the *Guardian*, his countrymen had known for many years that their leaders were corrupt, but that was not the same as reading the full details of particular incidents, rounded off with statements by American diplomats that corruption was keeping domestic investment low and unemployment high. The success of Tunisia's revolution undoubtedly influenced the rest of the Arab world, putting U.S. diplomats in an uncomfortable predicament. A mere three months after condemning WikiLeaks for releasing stolen documents "without regard to the consequences," Secretary Clinton found herself speaking warmly about one of those outcomes: the movement for reform in the Middle East.

WikiLeaks' revelations have had profound ramifications, but as with any event of this scale, it is not easy to judge whether those consequences are, on the whole, desirable. Assange himself admitted to the *Guardian* that as a result of the leaked corruption report in Kenya, and the violence that swept the country during its elections, 1,300 people were killed and 350,000 displaced; but, he added, 40,000 Kenyan children die every year from malaria, and these and many more are dying because of the role corruption plays in keeping Kenyans poor.[3] The Kenyan people, Assange believes, had a right to the information in the leaked report because "decision-making that is based upon lies or ignorance can't lead to a good conclusion."

In making that claim, Assange aligned himself with a widely held view in democratic theory, and a standard argument for freedom of speech: elections can express the will of the people only if the people are reasonably well informed about the issues on which they base their votes. That does not mean that decision-making based on the truth always leads to better outcomes than decision-making based on ignorance. There is no reason for Assange to be committed to that claim, any more than a supporter of democracy must be committed to the claim that democratic forms of government always reach better decisions than authoritarian regimes. Nor does a belief in the benefits of transparency imply that people must know the truth about everything; but it does suggest that more information is generally better, and so provides grounds for a presumption against withholding the truth.

What of Clinton's claims that the leaks have endangered human rights activists who gave information to American diplomats? When WikiLeaks released 70,000 documents about the war in Afghanistan, in July 2010, Admiral Mike Mullen, chairman of the Joint Chiefs of Staff, said that Assange had blood on his hands, yet no casualties resulting from the leaks have been reported—unless you count the ambassadors forced to step down due to embarrassing revelations. Four months after the documents were released, a senior NATO official told CNN that there had not been a single case of an Afghan needing protection because of the leaks. Of course, that may have been "just pure luck," as Daniel Domscheit-Berg, a WikiLeaks defector, told the *New York Times* in February. Assange himself has admitted that he cannot guarantee that the leaks will not cost lives, but in his view the likelihood that they will save lives justifies the risk.

WikiLeaks has never released the kind of information that Clinton pointed to in defending the need for secrecy. Still, there are other groups out there, such as the Russian anticorruption site Rospil.info, the European Union site Brussels-Leaks, the Czech PirateLeaks, Anonymous, and so on, that release leaked materials with less scrupulousness. It is entirely possible that there will be leaks that everyone will regret. Yet given that the leaked materials on the wars in Afghanistan and Iraq show tens of thousands of civilian lives lost due to the needless, reckless, and even callous

---

3. The United Nations claimed that as many as 600,000 Kenyans were displaced after the election.

actions of members of the U.S. military, it is impossible to listen to U.S. leaders blame WikiLeaks for endangering innocent lives without hearing the tinkle of shattering glass houses.

In the Panopticon, of course, transparency would not be limited to governments. Animal rights advocates have long said that if slaughterhouses had glass walls, more people would become vegetarian, and seeing the factory farms in which most of the meat, eggs, and milk we consume are produced would be more shocking even than the slaughterhouses. And why should restaurant customers have to rely on occasional visits by health inspectors? Webcams in food-preparation areas could provide additional opportunities for checking on the sanitary conditions of the food we are about to eat.

Bentham may have been right when he suggested that if we all knew that we were, at any time, liable to be observed, our morals would be reformed. Melissa Bateson and her colleagues at England's Newcastle University tested this theory when they put a poster with a pair of eyes above a canteen honesty box. People taking a hot drink put almost three times as much money in the box with the eyes present as they did when the eyes were replaced by a poster of flowers. The mere suggestion that someone was watching encouraged greater honesty. (Assuming that the eyes did not lead people to overpay, the study also implies a disturbing level of routine dishonesty.)

We might also become more altruistic. Dale Miller, a professor of organizational behavior at Stanford University, has pointed out that Americans assume a "norm of self-interest" that makes acting altruistically seem odd or even irrational. Yet Americans perform altruistic acts all the time, and bringing those acts to light might break down the norm that curtails our generosity. Consistent with that hypothesis, researchers at the University of Pennsylvania found that people are likely to give more to listener-sponsored radio stations when they are told that other callers are giving above-average donations. Similarly, when utility companies send customers a comparison of their energy use with the average in their neighborhood, customers with above-average use reduce their consumption.

The world before WikiLeaks and Facebook may have seemed a more secure place, but to say whether it was a better world is much more difficult. Will fewer children ultimately die from poverty in Kenya because WikiLeaks released the report on corruption? Will life in the Middle East improve as a result of the revolutions to which WikiLeaks and social media contributed? As the Chinese communist leader Zhou Enlai responded when asked his opinion of the French Revolution of 1789, it is too soon to say. The way we answer the question will depend on whether we share Assange's belief that decision-making leads to better outcomes when based on the truth than when based on lies and ignorance.

Peter Singer: Visible Man: Ethics in a World without Secrets

1. "New technology has made greater openness possible, but has this openness made us better off?" How do you respond to Singer's question? Support your answer.

2. Singer suggests at one point that a desire for greater privacy may be a desire for superior status and reflect a parochial Western perspective. What do you think of this suggestion?

3. Singer claims that "[t]he degree to which a government is repressive does not turn on the methods by which it acquires information about its citizens, or the amount of data it retains." How does he support this claim? Do you agree with his line of reasoning? Why or why not?

4. Singer argues that state secrets are only rarely justified; for the most part, government workings ought to be transparent. What principle could serve as the basis for justifying state secrecy on a given matter?

5. Singer points to studies that show that people behave more honestly when they believe that others are watching them. Suppose these studies are correct. When (if ever) would the benefits of increased honesty justify restrictions in privacy?

Why Privacy Is Important
James Rachels

James Rachels opens this selection with a nice series of scenarios that point clearly to the value of privacy. In these cases, privacy is important because it conceals from others things that might cause us embarrassment or shame, or cause us to be unfairly treated by those who gain access to some bit of personal information. But Rachels thinks that focusing on such cases is bound to distract us from what is really valuable about privacy. Even in cases where we are doing something perfectly ordinary, whose revelation will cause us no harm or disadvantage, we may rightly value having the power the decide for ourselves whether others can have access to our personal information. Certain things are *our business*; we may allow others to learn of these things, but then again, we may not. Our decisions should control whether others are allowed to know various things about us. Rachels's goal is to understand why that is.

On the account that Rachels prefers, privacy is important because it is required in order to maintain the sorts of relationships with others that we value. We behave differently depending on whether we are dealing with our siblings, parents, children, friends, work associates, or casual acquaintances. Some think that this reveals a kind of dishonesty; honest people will behave in just the same ways no matter who they happen to be with. Rachels thinks that this common view is mistaken, for it is often appropriate to reveal different parts of yourself to others depending on what relationship they bear to you. We don't want our dentist or the mail carrier to know our intimate secrets, though we may be fine sharing them with our partner or best friend. Our ability to control what we reveal about ourselves helps to determine which relationships we bear to other people, and those relationships, in turn, help to determine the quality of our lives. In this way, the ability to control who has what information about us plays a central role in determining how well our life is going.

Why, exactly, is privacy important to us? There is no one simple answer to this question, since people have a number of interests that may be harmed by invasions of their privacy.

(a) Privacy is sometimes necessary to protect people's interests in competitive situations. For example, it obviously would be a disadvantage to Bobby Fischer if he could not analyze the adjourned position in a chess game in private, without his opponent learning his results.

(b) In other cases someone may want to keep some aspect of his life or behavior private simply because it would be embarrassing for other people to know about it. There is a splendid example of this in John Barth's novel *End of the Road*. The narrator of the story, Jake Horner, is with Joe Morgan's wife, Rennie, and they are approaching the Morgan house where Joe is at home alone:

From James Rachels, "Why Privacy Is Important," *Philosophy and Public Affairs* 4, no. 4 (1975), pp. 323–331.

"Want to eavesdrop?" I whispered impulsively to Rennie. "Come on, it's great! See the animals in their natural habitat."

Rennie looked shocked. "What for?"

"You mean you never spy on people when they're alone? It's wonderful! Come on, be a sneak! It's the most unfair thing you can do to a person."

"You disgust me, Jake!" Rennie hissed. "He's just reading. You don't know Joe at all, do you?"

"What does that mean?"

"*Real* people aren't any different when they're alone. No masks. What you see of them is authentic."

. . . . Quite reluctantly, she came over to the window and peeped in beside me.

It is indeed the grossest of injustices to observe a person who believes himself to be alone. Joe Morgan, back from his Boy Scout meeting, had evidently intended to do some reading, for there were books lying open on the writing table and on the floor beside the bookcase. But Joe wasn't reading. He was standing in the exact center of the bare room, fully dressed, smartly executing military commands. About face! Right *dress*! 'Ten-*shun*! Parade *rest*! He saluted briskly, his cheeks blown out and his tongue extended, and then proceeded to cavort about the room–spinning, pirouetting, bowing, leaping, kicking. I watched entranced by his performance, for I cannot say that in my strangest moments (and a bachelor has strange ones) I have surpassed him. Rennie trembled from head to foot.[1]

The scene continues even more embarrassingly.

(c) There are several reasons why medical records should be kept private, having to do with the consequences to individuals of facts about them becoming public knowledge. "The average patient doesn't realize the importance of the confidentiality of medical records. Passing out information on venereal disease can wreck a marriage. Revealing a pattern of alcoholism or drug abuse can result in a man's losing his job or make it impossible for him to obtain insurance protection."[2]

(d) When people apply for credit (or for large amounts of insurance or for jobs of certain types) they are often investigated, and the result is a fat file of information about them. Now there is something to be said in favor of such investigations, for business people surely do have the right to know whether credit-applicants are financially reliable. The trouble is that all sorts of other information goes into such files, for example, information about the applicant's sex-life, his political views, and so forth. Clearly it is unfair for one's application for credit to be influenced by such irrelevant matters.

These examples illustrate the variety of interests that may be protected by guaranteeing people's privacy, and it would be easy to give further examples of the same general sort. However, I do not think that examining such cases will provide a complete understanding of the importance of privacy, for two reasons.

First, these cases all involve relatively unusual sorts of situations, in which someone has something to hide or in which information about a person might provide someone with a reason for mistreating him in some way. Thus, reflection on these cases gives us little help in understanding the value which privacy has in *normal* or *ordinary* situations. By this I mean situations in which there is nothing embarrassing or shameful or unpopular in what we are doing, and nothing ominous or threatening connected with its possible disclosure. For example, even married couples whose sex-lives are normal (whatever that is), and so who have nothing to be ashamed of, by even the most conventional standards, and certainly nothing to be blackmailed about, do not want their bedrooms bugged. We need an account of the value which privacy has for us, not only in the few special cases but in the many common and unremarkable cases as well.

---

1. John Barth, *End of the Road* (New York, 1960), pp. 57–58.

2. Dr. Malcolm Todd, President of the A.M.A., quoted in the *Miami Herald*, 6 October 1973, p. 18-A.

Second, even those invasions of privacy that *do* result in embarrassment or in some specific harm to our other interests are objectionable on other grounds. A woman may rightly be upset if her credit-rating is adversely affected by a report about her sexual behavior because the use of such information is unfair; however, she may also object to the report simply because she feels—as most of us do—that her sex-life is *nobody else's business*. This, I think, is an extremely important point. We have a "sense of privacy" which is violated in such affairs, and this sense of privacy cannot adequately be explained merely in terms of our fear of being embarrassed or disadvantaged in one of these obvious ways. An adequate account of privacy should help us to understand what makes something "someone's business" and why intrusions into things that are "none of your business" are, as such, offensive.

These considerations lead me to suspect that there is something important about privacy which we shall miss if we confine our attention to examples such as (a), (b), (c), and (d). In what follows I will try to bring out what this something is.

I want now to give an account of the value of privacy based on the idea that there is a close connection between our ability to control who has access to us and to information about us, and our ability to create and maintain different sorts of social relationships with different people. According to this account, privacy is necessary if we are to maintain the variety of social relationships with other people that we want to have, and that is why it is important to us. By a "social relationship" I do not mean anything especially unusual or technical; I mean the sort of thing which we usually have in mind when we say of two people that they are friends or that they are husband and wife or that one is the other's employer.

The first point I want to make about these relationships is that, often, there are fairly definite patterns of behavior associated with them. Our relationships with other people determine, in large part, how we act toward them and how they behave toward us. Moreover, there are *different* patterns of behavior associated with different relationships. Thus a man may be playful and affectionate with his children (although sometimes firm), businesslike with his employees, and respectful and polite with his mother-in-law. And to his close friends he may show a side of his personality that others never see—perhaps he is secretly a poet, and rather shy about it, and shows his verse only to his best friends.

It is sometimes suggested that there is something deceitful or hypocritical about such differences in behavior. It is suggested that underneath all the role-playing there is the "real" person, and that the various "masks" that we wear in dealing with some people are some sort of phony disguise that we use to conceal our "true" selves from them. I take it that this is what is behind Rennie's remark, in the passage from Barth, that, *"Real* people aren't any different when they're alone. No masks. What you see of them is authentic." According to this way of looking at things, the fact that we observe different standards of conduct with different people is merely a sign of dishonesty. Thus the cold-hearted businessman who reads poetry to his friends is "really" a gentle poetic soul whose businesslike demeanor in front of his employees is only a false front; and the man who curses and swears when talking to his friends, but who would never use such language around his mother-in-law, is just putting on an act for her.

This, I think, is quite wrong. Of course the man who does not swear in front of his mother-in-law may be just putting on an act so that, for example, she will not disinherit him, when otherwise he would curse freely in front of her without caring what she thinks. But it may be that his conception of how he ought to behave with his mother-in-law is very different from his conception of how he may behave with his friends. Or it may not be appropriate for him to swear around *her* because "she is not that sort of person." Similarly, the businessman may be putting up a false front for his employees, perhaps because he dislikes his work and has to make a continual, disagreeable effort to maintain the role. But on the other hand he may be, quite comfortably and naturally, a businessman with a certain conception of how it is appropriate for a businessman to behave; and this conception is compatible with his also being a husband, a father, and a friend, with different conceptions of how it is appropriate to behave with his wife, his children, and his friends. There need be nothing dishonest or hypocritical in any of this, and neither side of his personality need be the "real" him, any more than any of the others.

It is not merely accidental that we vary our behavior with different people according to the different social relationships that we have with them. Rather, the different patterns of behavior are (partly) what define the different relationships; they are an important part of what makes the different relationships what they are. The relation of friendship, for example, involves bonds of affection and special obligations, such as the duty of loyalty, which friends owe to one another; but it is also an important part of what it means to have a friend that we welcome his company, that we confide in him, that we tell him things about ourselves, and that we show him sides of our personalities which we would not tell or show to just anyone. Suppose I believe that someone is my close friend, and then I discover that he is worried about his job and is afraid of being fired. But, while he has discussed this situation with several other people, he has not mentioned it at all to me. And then I learn that he writes poetry, and that this is an important part of his life; but while he has shown his poems to many other people, he has not shown them to me. Moreover, I learn that he behaves with his other friends in a much more informal way than he behaves with me, that he makes a point of seeing them socially much more than he sees me, and so on. In the absence of some special explanation of his behavior, I would have to conclude that we are not as close as I had thought.

The same general point can be made about other sorts of human relationships: businessman to employee, minister to congregant, doctor to patient, husband to wife, parent to child, and so on. In each case, the sort of relationship that people have to one another involves a conception of how it is appropriate for them to behave with each other, and what is more, a conception of the kind and degree of knowledge concerning one another which it is appropriate

for them to have. (I will say more about this later.) I do not mean to imply that such relationships are, or ought to be, structured in exactly the same way for everyone. Some parents are casual and easy-going with their children, while others are more formal and reserved. Some doctors want to be friends with at least some of their patients; others are business-like with all. Moreover, the requirements of social roles may vary from community to community—for example, the role of wife may not require exactly the same sort of behavior in rural Alabama as it does in New York or New Guinea. And, the requirements of social roles may change: the women's liberation movement is making an attempt to redefine the husband-wife relationship. The examples that I have been giving are drawn, loosely speaking, from contemporary American society; but this is mainly a matter of convenience. The only point that I want to insist on is that *however* one conceives one's relations with other people, there is inseparable from that conception an idea of how it is appropriate to behave with and around them, and what information about oneself it is appropriate for them to have.

The point may be underscored by observing that new types of social institutions and practices sometimes make possible new sorts of human relationships, which in turn make it appropriate to behave around people, and to say things in their presence, that would have been inappropriate before. "Group therapy" is a case in point. Many psychological patients find the prospect of group therapy unsettling, because they will have to speak openly to the group about intimate matters. They sense that there is something inappropriate about this: one simply does not reveal one's deepest feelings to strangers. Our aspirations, our problems, our frustrations and disappointments are things that we may confide to our husbands and wives, our friends, and perhaps to some others—but it is out of the question to speak of such matters to people that we do not even know. Resistance to this aspect of group therapy is overcome when the patients begin to think of each other not as strangers but as *fellow members of the group*. The definition of a kind of relation between them makes possible frank and intimate conversation which would have been totally out of place when they were merely strangers.

All of this has to do with the way that a crucial part of our lives—our relations with other people—is organized, and as such its importance to us can hardly be exaggerated. Thus we have good reason to object to anything that interferes with these relationships and makes it difficult or impossible for us to maintain them in the way that we want to. Conversely, because our ability to control who has access to us, and who knows what about us, allows us to maintain the variety of relationships with other people that we want to have, it is, I think, one of the most important reasons why we value privacy.

First, consider what happens when two close friends are joined by a casual acquaintance. The character of the group changes; and one of the changes is that conversation about intimate matters is now out of order. Then suppose these friends could *never* be alone; suppose there were always third parties (let us say casual acquaintances or strangers) intruding. Then they could do either of two things. They could carry on as close friends do, sharing confidences, freely expressing their feelings about things, and so on. But this would mean violating their sense of how it is appropriate to behave around casual acquaintances or strangers. Or they could avoid doing or saying anything which they think inappropriate to do or say around a third party. But this would mean that they could no longer behave with one another in the way that friends do and further that, eventually, they would no longer *be* close friends.

Again, consider the differences between the way that a husband and wife behave when they are alone and the way they behave in the company of third parties. Alone, they may be affectionate, sexually intimate, have their fights and quarrels, and so on; but with others, a more "public" face is in order. If they could never be alone together, they would either have to abandon the relationship that they would otherwise have as husband and wife or else behave in front of others in ways they now deem inappropriate.

These considerations suggest that we need to separate our associations, at least to some extent, if we are to maintain a system of different relationships with different people. Separation allows us to behave with certain people in the way that is appropriate to the sort of relationship we have with them, without at the same time violating our sense of how it is appropriate to behave with, and in the presence of, others with whom we have a different kind of relationship. Thus, if we are to be able to control the relationships that we have with other people, we must have control over who has access to us.

We now have an explanation of the value of privacy in ordinary situations in which we have nothing to hide. The explanation is that, even in the most common and unremarkable circumstances, we regulate our behavior according to the kinds of relationships we have with the people around us. If we cannot control who has access to us, sometimes including and sometimes excluding various people, then we cannot control the patterns of behavior we need to adopt (this is one reason why privacy is an aspect of liberty) or the kinds of relations with other people that we will have. But what about our feeling that certain facts about us are "simply nobody else's business"? Here, too, I think the answer requires reference to our relationships with people. If someone is our doctor, then it literally is his business to keep track of our health; if someone is our employer, then it literally is his business to know what salary we are paid; our financial dealings literally are the business of the people who extend us credit; and so on. In general, a fact about ourselves is someone's business if there is a specific social relationship between us which entitles them to know. We are often free to choose whether or not to enter into such relationships, and those who want to maintain as much privacy as possible will enter them only reluctantly. What we cannot do is accept such a social role with respect to another person and then expect to retain the same degree of privacy relative to him that we had before. Thus, if we are asked how much money we have in the bank, we cannot say, "It's none of your business," to our banker, to prospective creditors, or to our spouses, because their relationships with us do entitle them to know. But, at the risk of being boorish, we could say that to others with whom we have no such relationship.

James Rachels: Why Privacy Is Important

1. Consider the examples Rachels uses at the outset of his paper. Does his preferred view of the value of privacy make sense of those examples? Why or why not?

2. Some believe that a person of integrity will behave in the same way no matter the social context she finds herself in. Why does Rachels disagree? Do you find his objection plausible?

3. Rachels discusses an example in which a person feels comfortable swearing with his friends but not with his mother-in-law. Why does he think that this example raises issues that help us understand the importance of privacy? Is he right about that?

4. Rachels never explicitly defines privacy in his article. Based on your reading, what definition of privacy do you think he is operating with?

5. Rachels writes, "If we are to be able to control the relationships that we have with other people, we must have control over who has access to us." Is this claim plausible? Why or why not?

What Must We Hide: The Ethics of Privacy and the Ethos of Disclosure

Anita L. Allen

Anita L. Allen opens her wide-ranging piece on the ethics of privacy with a sociological note. Given the widespread use of technology, we are nowadays losing a sense of privacy, our interest in it, and a willingness to respect the privacy of others. On the assumption that these observations are correct, we can ask this philosophical question: are these losses to be welcomed, or are they problematic?

Allen plausibly maintains that answering such questions requires first getting clear about the many values that support informational privacy—the control over access to, and disclosure of, personal information. The list of such values is lengthy. But so, too, is the list of those values that can be promoted by restricting our rights to privacy. Allen does not give a formula for how to balance these values. Instead, she focuses on some specific conflicts among them.

One of these is the value of free speech, which can sometimes be exercised by publicly revealing information about others that they want to keep private. In such cases it's easy to see the conflict, even if it's difficult to formulate a principle that can always tell you which value takes priority in a given case. Allen then considers cases in which a person voluntarily discloses what strikes us as information that ought to be kept private. But the idea raises an interesting question: if privacy involves control over your own information, what could be ethically problematic about voluntarily disclosing *your own* personal information?

Allen explores this question using fascinating examples that range from the private diaries of John Adams to the Christian scriptures. Unsurprisingly, she finds different rationales for an ethical demand to keep maintain personal privacy. Adams thought that personal concealment was sometimes required to protect against danger and dishonor; the Gospel of Matthew instructs us to conceal our good deeds, for fear that we might become motivated by the desire for good reputation, rather than a desire to do good for its own sake. Though she doesn't side with one of these authors over the other, she does affirm the idea that there are some personal disclosures that are indeed morally questionable.

I. INTRODUCTION

We live in an era of personal revelation. We are preoccupied by seeking, gathering, and disclosing information about others and ourselves. In the age of revelation, individuals and enterprises are fond of ferreting out what is buried away. We are fond of broadcasting what we know, think, do, and feel; and we are motivated by business and pleasure because we care about friendship, kinship, health, wealth, education, politics, justice, and culture. A lot of this has to do with technology, of course. We live at a historical moment characterized by the wide availability of multiple modes of communication and stored data, easily and frequently accessed. Our communications are capable of disclosing breadths and depths of personal, personally identifiable, and sensitive information to many people rapidly. In this era of revelation—dominated by portable electronics, internet social media, reality television, and traditional talk radio—many of us are losing our sense of privacy, our taste for privacy, and our willingness to respect privacy. Is this set of losses a bad thing? If it is a bad thing, what can be done about it?

My reflections on these questions begin with a series of diverse examples from the past several years. The first and second examples portray voluntary self-revelation for amusement and monetary gain; a third and fourth example depict revelations concerning others, motivated by a desire for amusement in one case and geopolitical justice in another.

Former Congressman Anthony Weiner was a Democratic member of the United States House of Representatives elected by the people of New York. Congressman Weiner sent sexually suggestive images of himself as attachments to Twitter

From Anita Allen, "What Must We Hide: The Ethics of Privacy and the Ethos of Disclosure," *St. Thomas Law Review* 25 (2013), pp. 1–17.

messages to young women, ages twenty-one and seventeen, he did not even know. When knowledge of his "sexting" conduct became public in 2011, he was forced to resign from office under pressure from fellow Democrats. There was no obvious, objectively urgent need for Congressman Weiner's messages. We have to assume he was simply amusing himself in an especially risky and presumptuous manner. He cared little for the privacy of his body and sexual urges, so little that he risked the grave consequences of their exposure to strangers whom he had no reason to trust.

When Joyce Maynard was only eighteen years old, she had an intimate affair with famed writer J. D. Salinger. He was fifty-three years old. For a short while, the mismatched lovers lived together in his New Hampshire hideaway where his fame and genius seduced her. In 2006, Maynard announced she would sell the fourteen unpublished love letters that the reclusive Salinger wrote to her between April 25, 1972, and August 17, 1973. Sotheby's auction house agreed to manage the sale. Maynard knew how greatly Salinger valued his privacy and that he would be offended by her decision; but, she said that the letters were her property and, moreover, that she needed money to send her children to college. Her own privacy no longer mattered to her since she had already published *At Home in the World,* a memoir of the fascinating, scandalous affair. Was it ethical for Maynard to exploit the law and further offend and embarrass a former lover for profit? It is not self-evident that ethics allow a person in Maynard's position this particular freedom.

My next example, like the Congressman Weiner example, involves contemporary communications technologies. In 2010, a talented young musician named Tyler Clementi was a freshman at Rutgers University, the state university of New Jersey. He asked his roommate, Dharun Ravi, to let him have their room for the night for a date. Ravi consented, but decided to pull a prank on Clementi. He switched on a webcam in their dormitory room, webcasting Clementi's same-sex intimacies all over the Internet. When Clementi learned what had been done to him, the distraught, gay youth bid farewell to his friends online and then committed suicide. On September 22, 2010, the teenager leapt to his death off of New York City's George Washington Bridge. In my view, the ethics of Congressman Weiner's and Joyce Maynard's revelations are somewhat debatable, but the ethics of Ravi's are not. Ravi's thoughtless advantage taking was unethical; and, as moral luck would have it, it also had a devastating outcome compounding the sense of its wrongfulness. Ravi was convicted of the New Jersey crimes of "bias intimidation" and criminal privacy invasion.

My final example is WikiLeaks. WikiLeaks describes itself as "a non-profit media organization dedicated to bringing important news and information to the public." It does this by providing a "secure and anonymous way for independent sources around the world to leak information to its journalists."[1] While a member of the United States armed forces on active duty, then twenty-two year old Private Bradley Manning provided WikiLeaks with sensitive United States Government documents without authority, including field reports from wars in Iraq and Afghanistan, classified State Department diplomatic cables, records concerning Guantanamo Bay detainees, and videos of United States military missions. Manning was arrested in 2010 and tried in 2011. The sensitive documents he handed over to Wikileaks were published by WikiLeaks and then republished by major mainstream media and social media alike. Many people were appalled that such a thing could occur. But strikingly, many were not appalled either because they failed to recognize any legitimate expectations of privacy, confidentiality or security, or because they believed the social good of disclosure far outweighed any embarrassment to diplomats and nations.

What is the social good at issue? According to WikiLeaks, it publishes "material of ethical, political and historical significance while keeping the identity of [its] sources anonymous, thus providing a universal way for the revealing of suppressed and censored injustices."[2] Julian Assange defends his group's approach to forced government accountability—"shining the light on the secret crimes of the powerful."[3] Some link the "Arab Spring" pro-democracy movements afoot in North Africa to distrust and disgust fueled by WikiLeaks.[4] Nonetheless, some professors of foreign relations initially said they would not incorporate information revealed by WikiLeaks into their university courses because it was acquired and published unethically.

In the age of revelation, sensitive information will come to light whether it ought to or not. Whether it is our love lives or political strategies, all will come to light. For better or worse, everything from furtive street crimes to genomes will come to light.

II. THE VALUE OF PRIVACY

The four examples with which I began raise concerns about the value of privacy. They show that some people especially do not value their own privacy, and some do not value the privacy of others. Philosophically, these examples say something about the positive ethics of informational privacy. By informational privacy, I mean conditions of limited access to and limited disclosure of personal data. In situations in which people actually want privacy protected, allowing individuals to control personal information about themselves has been an important way to achieve desired forms of limited access.

So what can be said in favor of privacy and its protection? Let me list the values, good, and ends that I, and other like-minded scholars, relate to privacy:

- *Self-expression:* Opportunities for privacy allow individuals to better express their true personalities and values.

---

2. *Id.*

3. Charlie Osborne & Zack Whittaker, *Assange: U.S. 'witch hunt' against Wikileaks must end*, ZDNET.COM (Aug. 19, 2021).

4. State Department Press Releases & Documents, *Internet Freedom; Promoting Human Rights in the Digital Age—A Panel Discussion*, FED. INFO. & NEWS DISPATCH, INC., May 3, 2011, *available at* 2011 WLNR 8610506.

---

1. Main, WIKILEAKS.FDN (last visited Oct. 9, 2012), http://wikileaks.fdn.fr.

- *Good Reputation:* Privacy helps preserve reputations.
- *Repose:* Privacy may enable tranquility and relaxation.
- *Intellectual Life:* Privacy may enhance creativity and reflection, which may be good for an individual's own sake, but which can lead to useful cultural products and inventions.
- *Intimacy and Formality:* Opportunities for privacy are thought to enable individuals to keep some people at a distance, so that they can enjoy intense intimate relationships with others.
- *Preferences and Traditions:* Privacy allows the individual or groups of like-minded individuals the ability to plan undertakings and live in accord with preferences and traditions.
- *Civility:* Privacy norms sustain civility by condemning behaviors that offend courtesy, honor, and appropriateness.
- *Human Dignity:* Philosophers have said that respect for privacy is, in many ways, respect for human dignity itself.
- *Limited Government:* Privacy rights against government demand that state power is limited and unobtrusive, as liberal democracy requires.
- *Toleration:* Privacy rights demand that government tolerate differences among individuals and groups.
- *Autonomy:* An aspect of liberty, privacy fosters the development and exercise of autonomy.
- *Individualism:* Privacy fosters individualism, and it is not fairly condemned as a purely individualistic value at odds with ideals of a cooperative, efficient democratic community.

Anyone who makes the case for privacy must contend with the case against it and against the rights protecting it. Indeed, not all philosophers emphasize the good of privacy. A few have emphasized values, good, and ends that properly limit personal privacy:

- *National Security:* Privacy interferes with national security measures.
- *Law Enforcement:* Privacy interferes with effective and efficient law enforcement.
- *Public Health:* Privacy hampers effective and efficient public health protection, e.g., it burdens the delivery of routine medical care and health research.
- *Public Right to Know:* Privacy rights chill free speech and a free press. Privacy keeps information the public has a right to know in private or government hands.
- *Administrative Costs:* Privacy rights enable individuals to bring trivial lawsuits involving little more than hurt feelings to court, thereby taking up time judges could devote to more serious personal injury cases.
- *Selfish Individualism:* Privacy is unduly individualistic.
- *Inefficiency:* Privacy protection practices are inefficient for business.
- *Excess of Protections:* The United States has too many privacy laws. Privacy rights can keep socially valuable information out of the hands of people who could use and learn from it.
- *Privacy Rights Should Be Limited:* The law should provide a remedy only against intrusions and publications that are "highly offensive." The law should protect only "reasonable expectations of privacy" and bar state interference only if it is wholly irrational or "unduly burdensome."

III. THE LURE OF FREE SPEECH

Why not reveal? Why not disclose? Why hide anything? Courts have been asked to support ideals of anonymous Internet speech that would allow bold, even cruel, speech to reign free and immunize speakers from exposure and even liability. In a high-profile federal district court case from the United States District Court for the District of Connecticut, *Doe I and Doe II v. Individuals, whose true names are unknown,*[5] the plaintiffs were two female students at Yale Law School. The two students were targets of defamatory, threatening, and

---

5. Doe I v. Individuals, 561 F. Supp. 2d 249 (D. Conn. 2008)

harassing statements posted on AutoAdmit.com from 2005 to 2007.

AutoAdmit is an Internet discussion board that, in the mid-2000s, drew between 800,000 and one million visitors per month. Participants posted and reviewed comments about universities and law schools. A photograph of one of the plaintiffs was published on AutoAdmit without her permission. An anonymous commentator encouraged others to "[r]ate this HUGE breasted cheerful big tit girl from YLS." In two months, nearly two hundred threads about the women were posted. One post stated that plaintiff fantasized about being raped by her father, that she enjoyed having sex while family members watched, that she encouraged others to punch her in the stomach while seven months pregnant, that she had a sexually transmitted disease, that she had abused heroin, and a poster said that she "hope[s] she gets raped and dies."[6]

After plaintiffs filed a lawsuit, many posts were published discussing the lawsuit. The Yale women brought federal copyright claims and state law claims for libel, invasion of privacy, and emotional distress against unknown individuals using thirty-nine different pseudonymous names. In the course of the suit, and here is where the free speech issues arise, the plaintiffs issued a subpoena to Internet service provider AT&T for information relating to the identity of the person assigned to the Internet Protocol ("IP") address from which an individual posted comments about one of the plaintiffs. AT&T sent a letter to the person whose Internet account corresponded with the IP address, and he filed a motion to quash disclosure of his identity and a motion to proceed anonymously in the suit.

The court held the plaintiffs were entitled to disclosure of the poster's identity. The court stated that the protection afforded anonymous speech by the First Amendment of the United States Constitution extends to speech on the Internet, as cyberlibertarians prefer to think, but that this right is not absolute and does not protect speech that otherwise would be unprotected. Libel is not protected speech. The plaintiffs established a prima facie case of libel against the poster through evidence tending to show that the poster's discussion of her alleged sexual behavior in a message that clearly identified her by name harmed her reputation.

As for the allegation that he should be able to proceed anonymously as "John Doe" out of regard for his free speech rights and reputation, the court also held against the poster. The rule of procedure requiring parties to a lawsuit to identify themselves protects the public's legitimate interest in knowing all of the facts involved, including the identities of the parties. The risk that an Internet user might be exposed to ridicule or lose employment upon disclosure of his identity was not grounds to allow him to proceed anonymously.

The lawsuit settled out of court. I believe the district court came to the right decision with respect to both issues—forcing AT&T to hand over the name of the person behind the IP address of the AutoAdmit poster and forcing the poster to litigate under his real name. Free speech ideals should not give persons *carte blanche* to defame others and invade their privacy. But in the age of revelation, we not only have to concern ourselves with free speech being used to justify disclosures about others, but we also need to concern ourselves with free speech seeming to give persons *carte blanche* to make disclosures about themselves.

IV. VOLUNTARY SELF-DISCLOSURE

One has to be especially intrigued by the voluntary self-disclosure that characterizes our era, which is why I began with the Congressman Weiner incident and the Maynard-Salinger affair. Congressman Weiner exposed himself. Maynard exposed Salinger, but after she had made an industry of exposing herself. We make disclosures about ourselves and do not imagine anyone having ethical grounds to object to our doing so. Fun, popular social media, like Facebook and Twitter, make personal disclosures easy and nearly irresistible. Is there an ethics problem with self-disclosure? Is there any reason to be reserved, private, secret, or contained offline?

Television programs are one semi-authentic personally revealing reality show after another. The World Wide Web is a site of exhibitionism and voyeurism. Videos of everything are posted on the Web—childbirth, breast cancer surgery,

---

6. *Individuals*, 561 F. Supp. 2d at 251.

professional events, and social events, like your granddad's seventieth birthday. Youtube is an amazing resource; but, some of its content are videos posted by people who think every forgettable moment of fun should be filmed, uploaded, and shared.

My teenagers have iPhones that keep them connected to the world and accountable to family and friends. They expect me always to have my smart phone close at hand, turned on, and fully charged. They expect me to answer their text messages immediately—"But I texted you, Mom" and "Why didn't you answer my text?!" They are baffled and disappointed if I do not go along. Today, a mom who does not text and video chat is worse than a mom who does not cook. So, I oblige.

But it is not just teenagers who have embraced the ethos of revelation. Earlier this year, I was visiting a museum with my brother. He is fifty years old and a lawyer. While we were in the museum, he took a minute to update his status on Facebook. He let hundreds of "friends" and acquaintances know where he was and what he was doing. Far from home, he used the popular social networking application, Foursquare, to figure out if anyone he knew might be in the museum too. If you think, "Well, of course he did," then you have embraced and normalized the ethos I am problematizing.

In the age of revelation many of us make disclosures about other people and feel ethically fine about it. In the age of revelation, there is an emerging bias towards "nothing-is-sacred" disclosure, toward knowing, and toward finding out. The WikiLeaks diplomatic cable disclosure was illustrative. WikiLeaks took the concept of "government watchdog" to a whole new level.

A case involving nursing students who posted images of themselves on Facebook raises an interesting set of questions about whether voluntary self-disclosures offend personal or professional ethics.[7] Doyle Byrnes was a nursing student at Johnson County Community College. In 2010, she was expelled from nursing school for what college administrators viewed as inappropriate conduct on

Facebook. Byrnes apologized for her conduct but felt expulsion was not called for. So, she sued to get back into school. The Kansas federal district court judge that heard her case sided with her. On January 19, 2011, Judge Eric Melgren issued a preliminary injunction ordering not only that Byrnes be reinstated, but also that she be allowed to make up missed assignments and exams.[8]

What had Byrnes done to get herself expelled in the first place? On November 10, 2010, she participated in a clinical course on obstetrics and gynecology at Olathe Medical Center in Olathe, Kansas. As part of the course she examined fresh placenta from recently delivered pregnancies. Byrnes and three other nursing students (witnesses Chrystie North, Jamie Vande Brake, and Danielle Thompson) wanted to photograph themselves examining the placenta to post on Facebook. They obtained permission from the course supervisor, Defendant Amber Delphia, to photograph themselves examining a placenta specimen derived from a recent birth. Permission was granted on the condition that no identifying marks be present in the photograph.

It was not until after class that Delphia asked the students what they intended to do with the photographs. One of the women responded that they were going to post them on Facebook, to which they said Delphia replied, "Oh, you girls." When it came to the attention of the college that photographs of the nursing students with placenta were posted on Facebook, the girls were expelled.

The judge enjoined Byrnes' expulsion for several reasons. First, he noted that the conduct in question may have been inappropriate or offensive to the nursing college, but it did not violate any clear policy or disciplinary rule. Second, since photographs are meant to be shared, granting permission to photograph was in effect granting permission to share— face to face, on Facebook, or anywhere presumably. Moreover, by only saying, "Oh, you girls," as was alleged, Delphia missed an opportunity to object on school policy, legal, or ethical grounds to posting images with placenta and instead gave the students the impression that it would be alright to post.

7. Byrnes v. Johnson Cnty Comm. Coll., Civ. Action No. 10-2690-EFM-DJW, 2011 WL 166715 (Dist. Kan. Jan, 19, 2011).

8. *Id.* at 5.

The judge did not buy the arguments that someone might be able to figure out the identity of the patient, from whom the placenta was donated, from information about the day and time of the picture. This is not a case of likely re-identification. So, the ethical failing is not so much a breach of patient confidentiality or invasion of patient privacy, but rather, it is a lack of professional dignity and respect for patients that is of concern.

We are curious, inquisitive, and accountable. It is perhaps because I have children about the same age as those involved in the Rutgers tragedy that I can so easily understand Dharun Ravi's point of view. At the time, Ravi did not think that he was doing anything seriously wrong when he activated a webcam to spy on his roommate Clementi. After all, it was Ravi's dorm room, too; webcams exist and everyone knows it; the camera only revealed what was true; he was really "making out" with another dude; and it is his own fault if he gets pranked.

Clearly, there has been a shift in ethos, invisible to youth who have known no other way to live and discernable to anyone who was already an adult in the 1980s. A shift in ethos is not necessarily a problem for ethics. But let us consider whether this one is a problem for ethics. One can readily comprehend the ethical concerns raised by WikiLeaks and cyber-bullying. However, the privacy-related ethical concerns raised by voluntary self-disclosure are not as readily comprehended. I believe there are reasons to think that you may be doing something unethical when you are just revealing facts about yourself to others. But I have to go back in time 200 years, or even 2000 years, to explain them.

V. WHY KEEP YOUR MOUTH SHUT

Consider the entry in John Adams' diary dated Monday, August 20, 1770. Adams was a patriot of the American Revolution and an eventual United States President. In Adams' view, privacies of concealment, secrecy, and reserve are both moral virtues and moral duties. Worldly wisdom dictates that we protect ourselves from "damage, danger, and confusion" by generally keeping "our sentiments, actions, desires, and resolutions" to ourselves. Revelations to enemies and indiscreet friends alike risk "loss, disgrace, or mortification." On occasion, though, virtue and duty run in the other direction: "the cause of religion, of government, of liberty, the interest of the present age and of posterity, render it a necessary duty for a man to make known his sentiments and intentions boldly and publicly."[9]

Adams' take is modern. Privacy aligns, not with raw preference, but with prudent self-interest. The good of privacy is contingent. Sometimes we ought to go public when we might prefer to hide; sometimes we ought to hide when we might prefer to go public. The important thing is that privacy, like information sharing, has a place in free society. Our moral interests include freedom from judgment, freedom to don masks, freedom to build and maintain reputations, and freedom to and from intimacy. What must we hide? Adams' diary points to a general answer: hide the things where disclosure would lead to danger, disgrace, and dishonor.

But a distinctly different rationale for self-concealment is suggested by the book of Matthew in the New Testament of the Christian Bible. We should hide the things where disclosure leads to approval and admiration. The righteousness of pious acts such as giving to the poor, praying, and fasting is undermined by intentionally seeking public notice. Through modesty and reserve we are taking God alone into confidence. Thus:

> So whenever you give alms, do not sound a trumpet before you, as the hypocrites do. . . . But when you give alms, do not let your left hand know what your right hand is doing, so that your alms may be done in secret; and your Father who sees in secret will reward you.[10]

> [A]nd whenever you pray, do not be like the hypocrites; for they love to stand and pray . . . at the street corners, so that they may be seen by others. . . . they have received their reward. But whenever you pray, go into your room and shut the door and pray to your Father who is in secret; and your Father who sees in secret will reward you.[11]

---

9. Diary Entry by John Adams (Aug. 20, 1770), *in* JOHN ADAMS DIARY, PAPER BOOK NO 15Vol. 3 (1961), *available at* http://www.masshist.org/digitaladams/aea/cfm/doc.cfm?id=D15.

10. *Matthew* 6:2–12 (New Revised Standard).

11. *Matthew* 6:1–6 (New Revised Standard).

And when you fast, do not look dismal, like the hypocrites. . . . But when you fast, anoint your head and wash your face, that your fasting may be seen not by men but by your Father who is in secret; and your Father who sees in secret will reward you.[12]

There is a ready secular rendering of the message in this passage. Keeping your goodness to yourself makes you really good. Virtue is its own reward. Do not be a show off. Ancient and early American texts offer a way of thinking about privacy that the buzz of continuous networking threatens to drown out. Status updating on Facebook and Twitter risks offending the ethics of Adams and the ethics of Matthew. The status update such as "I am giving a lecture in Paris" reads like a brag; and it is also an "all clear" message to house thieves and rivals in romance.

VI. PRIVACY LAW

Does anyone care about all data giveaways and data collection that have come to characterize daily life? Is there anything to be done about it? I believe there are moral duties of privacy—duties to ourselves and duties to others. I believe there are also moral rights of privacy.

The right to privacy means it is wrong to do what Rutgers freshman Ravi did to his roommate Clementi. The moral right to privacy may mean that Maynard should not have published Salinger's letters to her during his lifetime. As it happens, the law sided with Maynard, but not with Ravi.

Americans have a legal right to privacy. It is enshrined in the United States Constitution, our common law, and in acts of Congress. For the right to privacy, all Americans owe a debt of gratitude to United States Supreme Court Justice Louis D. Brandeis, who was a key architect of the American right to privacy.

In law school at Harvard, Justice Brandeis formed a friendship with classmate Samuel D. Warren. Together they founded a successful law partnership. They remained close even after Warren—a wealthy, upper crust Bostonian, married to a snobby anti-semitic senator's daughter—was called away from the bar to take over his family's business. Warren was annoyed by all the attention the popular tabloid press paid to his extravagant life. So he convinced the brilliant Justice Brandeis to write an article, to be published under both of their names, calling for the creation of a new legal right against so-called "yellow journalism." Their article, simply titled, "The Right to Privacy," was published in the Harvard Law Review in the winter of 1890.

The right to privacy that Warren and Justice Brandeis conceived would deter and redress publication in newspapers of gossip and photographs that "invaded the sacred precincts of private and domestic life" and thereby injured "inviolate personality." A rhetorical tour de force, the article inspired the bar and the judiciary. Today, you may very well be entitled to a lawsuit to recover for your hurt feelings and lost dignity if, in a highly offensive manner, someone intrudes into your seclusion, publishes embarrassing private facts, places you in a false light, or uses your name or photo without your consent. In this way, Ravi clearly violated Clementi's common law privacy rights to have his intimate sex life kept secret.

VII. PRIVACY ETHICS

The law can only do so much. An ethic of privacy is needed to complement (dare I say, counteract?) the ethos of revelation. Such an ethic would include the general rule that "felt immorality does not automatically warrant denying someone informational privacy."

Consider the facts of a recent lawsuit, *Yath v. Fairview Clinic.*[13] Candace Yath brought the suit against a medical facility and members of her family. A member of Yath's husband's extended family happened to work at a clinic where she was tested for sexually transmitted diseases, and saw Yath at the clinic. The curious relative accessed Yath's electronic medical record and then told another family member, resulting in someone setting up an insulting MySpace page. The offensive page depicted Yath as a dirty adulteress: "Rotten Candy." Was this a bald exercise of free speech? Yes. Was

---

12. *Matthew* 6:16–23 (New Revised Standard).

13. Yath v. Fairview Clinics, 767 N.W.2d 34, 38 (Minn. Ct. App. 2009)

this a bald invasion of privacy and breach of medical confidentiality? Yes, too.

In the era of revelation, we need an ethic that includes a general rule against needlessly sacrificing privacy in the name of protecting speech, and, by the way, property. A striking example of the latter is the webcam scandal that rocked the Philadelphia, Pennsylvania suburb of Lower Merion in 2009. On November 11, 2009, Lindy Matsko, an Assistant Principal at Hamton High School ("HHS"), approached fifteen-year-old Blake Robbins, then a sophomore, and informed him that school administrators believed that he was "engaged in improper behavior in his home."[14] Matsko cited as evidence an image taken from the webcam of Robbins' school-issued Macintosh laptop computer. Matsko believed the images captured implicated Robbins in illegal drug usage. Robbins, however, claimed at one television interview that the images showed him consuming Mike & Ike candy, which school administrators only mistook for drugs. Prior to this incident, neither Robbins' parents nor any other high school parent or student in the Lower Merion School District were aware of the School District's ability to capture screenshots and webcam images from the student's school-issued laptops using so-called "Theft Track" software. But the school could capture webcam shots "of anyone or anything appearing in front of the camera at the time of activation" taken from any location in which the [school-issued] computer was kept, including the student's home.[15]

In a statement to a newspaper after Robbins filed a lawsuit claiming privacy intrusions prohibited by state and federal law, a school district official, Connie DiMedio, confirmed that the School District did not disclose the Theft Track remote activation feature to teachers or students for obvious reasons, since "[i]t involved computer security, and that is all it was being used for."[16] On October 11,

2010, the Lower Merion School Board voted unanimously to settle Robbins' and another invasion of privacy lawsuit that resulted from its webcam spying for a total of $610,000. The school agreed never again to use tracking software on student-issued laptops without the consent of students and their parents.

How can a society enthralled by technology-aided revelatory communication give privacy its ethical due? The question is imperative as social media and social networking continue to take flight, as cloud computing becomes the norm for storing our documents and mementos, and as advances in genomics and neuroimaging create volumes of biomedical data which potentially reveal us to ourselves and others as never before.

To ask the questions I am raising is not to deny that there is value in freedom of speech, sociality, and community.

Privacy can be a "Machivellian," even antisocial, asset-enabling immorality. But it does not have to be. It can be a bit of sanctuary from judgment and for repose. Privacy can be of a piece with Adamsonian, Aristotelian, and Christian virtue: prudence, modesty, humility, and reserve.

VIII. INDIFFERENCE TO PRIVACY

Without a doubt, in the era of revelation, some of us are indifferent to our own privacy. We may be unwisely indifferent to our own privacy because we are young, or because we are busy, or because we are unfamiliar with the risks of data collection, sharing, and storage that come with the mysterious technology we enjoy. In March 2011, the European Union announced that it would seek measures to require social networking sites to take down and destroy pages. In the era of revelation, we are beginning to see that we can be harmed by the habit of self-disclosure. There must be a right to forget and be forgotten.

There are things we must hide. We must hide what is necessary to preserve our common dignity and separate virtues. We must hide what is necessary to keep ourselves safe from harm. We must hide what our roles and responsibilities and professions dictate that we hide as matters of efficacy, beneficence, or contract; and we must hide,

---

14. Class Action Complaint at 6, Robbins v. Lower Merion Sch. Dist., No. 10-cv-00665-JD (E.D. Pa. Feb. 16, 2010) [hereinafter Robbins Complaint].

15. Robbins Complaint, *supra* note 37, at 6, 7.

16. Dan Hardy & Bonnie Clark, *Student Claims School Spied on Him Via Computer Webcamm*, PHILA. INQUIRER, Feb. 19, 2010 at A01.

notwithstanding all of technology's attractions, what good relationships and reputations—now and in our distant and uncertain futures—renders it prudent to hide. Telling us exactly what and why we hide—this is the work of a comprehensive ethic of privacy in an era of revelation.

Anita L. Allen: What We Must Hide: The Ethics of Privacy and the Ethos of Disclosure

1. Those who sext are giving up some of their privacy. Are there any conditions where sexting is immoral? If not, why not? If so, what are those conditions?
2. Consider the case of Joyce Maynard that Allen describes early in her article. Was Maynard's disclosure of Salinger's letters ethical? Why or why not?
3. When WikiLeaks founder Julian Assange decided to reveal classified information about US military operations, he did so on the grounds that the public has a right to know about injustices that would otherwise be hidden. Do states have a right to privacy that protects their freedom to conceal injustices? If so, why? If not, are there any circumstances in which a nation could legitimately conceal the misbehavior of state workers? If you believe there are, describe those circumstances and explain why such concealment would be legitimate.
4. When does a right of free speech allow you to post information about others that they would want to keep private?
5. Allen believes that you can be doing something unethical simply by revealing facts about yourself. What reasons does she give? Do you find her line of reasoning plausible? Why or why not?

In Praise of Big Brother: Why We Should Stop Worrying and Learn to Love Big Government

James Stacey Taylor

James Stacey Taylor's thesis is that "the State should place all of its citizens under surveillance at all times and in all places, including their offices, classrooms, shops—and even their bedrooms." Taylor knows that, unless you are a fan of totalitarian dictatorships, your first reaction to this thesis is likely going to be shock and horror. His aim is to convince you that it's a much better option than it might appear to be.

The key to making his case is to introduce a crucial distinction between surveillance records and their use. While he believes that everyone's every action ought to be recorded, he also believes that the recordings should not be accessible to government officials unless there is excellent reason to allow them viewing rights. In other words, no one would be allowed to view most of those videotapes. Indeed, there should be important safeguards that protect individuals from having their records accessed, unless special circumstances arise.

Stacey argues that it is sometimes permissible for the state to secure information about past events—for instance, to determine who has committed a crime. Given this, the only question is about the best means to obtain that information. Stacey argues that surveillance recordings would be the most reliable source of such information, and so using them would be morally acceptable.

But state officials have no right to look at such recordings unless there is reasonable basis for thinking that doing so is crucial to securing some very important state interest, such as apprehending a criminal. While people have rights to privacy, Taylor believes that those rights are not violated if the state has reasonable grounds for investigating one's activities during a given time span. Given the value that surveillance recordings offer, both in terms of catching criminals and supporting the alibis of the innocent who might not otherwise have the evidence to back up their case, Taylor thinks that complete state surveillance of an entire population is justified.

In recent years surveillance technology has undergone a revolution. Spy satellites are now so accurate that they can be used to track the movements of individual people, and even read license plates on cars. It is now simple to intercept faxes, pager messages, and telephone messages, for rooms to be bugged, and for tracking devices to be installed on vehicles, goods, and even individual persons. Spyware software can now be covertly and remotely implanted onto Internet-linked computers to monitor the keystrokes that their users make and the websites that they visit. And in many areas of the developed world persons now live much of their public lives under the panoptic gaze of closed-circuit television monitors that record their every move.

This revolution in surveillance technology is often regarded with horror. Discussions of its ethical implications frequently draw analogies between it and Big Brother's sinister surveillance of the citizens of Oceania in George Orwell's 1984. Worse yet, as many of the participants in such discussions note, the surveillance capabilities that are now available to governments and corporations dwarf that which Big Brother had access to. In 1984, people could be sure that they could not be watched by Big Brother's telescreens if they were in a crowd. Face-recognition software now renders such a hope futile. In 1984 people could escape the omnipresence of Big Brother's telescreens by going out of the cities and into the country, where they only had to take care that their conversations were not monitored by hidden microphones. Such escape is now impossible, for spy satellites can be used to monitor people wherever they go.

With the dystopic vision of 1984 lurking in the background it is clear that one need not possess any pronounced Luddite tendencies to oppose the expanding use of surveillance technology. It will be argued in this paper, however, that rather than opposing such an expansion of surveillance technology, its use should be *encouraged*—and not only in the public realm. Indeed, the State should place all of its citizens under surveillance at all times and in all places, including their offices, classrooms, shops—and even their bedrooms.

AN OVERVIEW OF THE ARGUMENT

At first sight, the conclusion that the State should place all of its citizens under constant surveillance is undoubtedly alarming. Yet this alarm can be dispelled once it is realized that this conclusion flows naturally from the plausible and widely held view that, in certain circumstances, it is morally permissible for the State to secure information about past events. It is, for example, widely held that in certain circumstances it is morally permissible for the State to compel witnesses to testify about past events in criminal trials. The State, however, can only use hindsight to determine what information it is morally permitted to have access to, for it will only become clear in retrospect what information is relevant to (for example) solving a crime or judging mitigating circumstances. To ensure that it gleans all of the information that it is morally permitted to access, then, the State can gather information about all events that occur, provided it only accesses that which it is morally permitted. Given this, then, the State is in principle morally permitted to place its citizens under constant surveillance. The purpose of this paper is not, however, only to show that the State is morally permitted to place its citizens under constant surveillance. It is also to show that a situation in which the State used such surveillance

From James Stacey Taylor, "In Praise of Big Brother: Why We Should Stop Worrying and Learn to Love Big Government," *Public Affairs Quarterly* 19, no. 3 (2005), pp. 227–239.

would be morally *preferable* to one where it did not. To establish this it will be shown that under such a system of surveillance it is likely that crime will decrease, that justice will be better served, and that fewer costs will be imposed on witnesses. Finally, four objections to the use of such a system of State surveillance will be examined and rejected: that it would be open to abuse, that it is not morally permissible for the State to secure information about past events, and that such surveillance would violate citizens' privacy, or autonomy, or both.

Before moving to develop the above argument in favor of constant State surveillance an important initial clarification is in order. This argument is based on two claims: (i) that if it is ever morally permissible for the State to secure information about past events, then it is morally permissible for it to do so through the use of surveillance devices, and (ii) that in some cases it is permissible for the State to secure information about past events. As it stands, however, it is not clear whether (ii) is the claim that the State's acquisition of information respects a person's moral rights (e.g., to privacy or autonomy), or the claim that in some cases the consequences of securing such information justify the State's acquisition of it. That is, it is not clear whether this argument is one that would be acceptable to a rights theorist, or only to a consequentialist. This unclarity can be dispelled once it is recognized that the argument presented here is compatible with *both* a rights-based and a consequentialist approach to ethics. This argument is acceptable to a rights theorist because, as will be argued below, when the State is morally permitted to access information it will not violate anyone's rights in so doing. If the arguments below are sound, then, claim (ii) will be true if one accepts a rights-based approach to ethics. This argument is also acceptable to consequentialists, who could also accept claim (ii). For a consequentialist to accept (ii) it must be the case that there is at least *one* time at which it is clear that the consequences justify the State's acquisition of information about a certain past event. And, as will be argued below, such a situation is simple to envisage. As such, the argument of this paper is amenable to both rights theorists and consequentialists alike.

SURVEILLANCE AND TESTIMONY

Despite appearances, then, the conclusion that there is no principled reason why a State should not place all of it citizens under constant surveillance is by no means a radical one. It is merely an extrapolation of the widely accepted view that, under certain circumstances, it is morally permissible for agents of the State to secure information about past events. It is, for example, widely accepted that it is morally permissible for judges to subpoena witnesses to require them to disclose information. It is also widely accepted that it is morally permissible for judges to permit law enforcement agencies to install surveillance devices to monitor the activities of persons they suspect of criminal activity, provided that such agencies demonstrate that they have probable cause for their suspicions. The claim that it is morally permissible for agents of the State to secure information about past events is thus innocuous. Moreover, if it is morally permissible for agents of the State to secure information about past events through the subpoenaing of witnesses or the use of surveillance devices, then there should be no moral bar to their gaining such information through securing access to records of past events that might have been generated by preexisting surveillance devices. (Provided, of course, that in securing such information the agents of the State are subject to the same restrictions on their powers that are in place with respect to their subpoenaing of witnesses or the placing of suspects under surveillance.)

However, that it is morally permissible for agents of the State to secure access to information about past events that has been gathered through the use of surveillance devices does not show that it is morally permissible for the State to place its citizens under constant surveillance. To reach this further conclusion it must first be noted that it cannot (typically) be known in advance what information it would be morally permissible for the agents of the State to have access to. Instead, one can only use hindsight to determine what events it would be morally permissible for them to access information about. For example, it could not have been predicted that knowledge of the actions performed by Billy Nolan Lovelady, a worker at the

Texas School Book Depository in Dallas on 22 November 1963, would be relevant to assessing who assassinated the president of United States. However, the defenders of Lee Harvey Oswald (who was accused of this assassination) claimed that at the time of the shooting Oswald was standing unarmed in the doorway of the Texas School Book Depository and produced a photograph purporting to prove this. Once this had occurred, knowledge of Lovelady's actions became relevant in showing that the man in the photograph who was claimed to be Oswald was actually Lovelady. In this situation, then, it was morally permissible for agents of the State to take steps to secure information about Lovelady's whereabouts at the time in question to disprove Oswald's alibi—and this could not have been predicted beforehand.

As well as it being clear that one usually cannot know in advance what information the agents of the State are morally permitted to secure, it is also clear that once it becomes evident what information they are permitted to secure, gathering this is frequently difficult—as the continuing controversy over "who shot JFK" indicates. Putting these two facts together, then, it is evident that there should be no moral bar against the agents of the State installing surveillance devices to secure all the information that they might potentially be permitted to secure access to. (Provided that they only access the information thus gathered in circumstances where this access is morally permissible.) Thus, since it is *potentially* morally permissible for agents of the State to secure information about events no matter when or where they take place, it is morally permissible for the State to subject its citizens to surveillance at all times and in all places, provided that the information thus gathered was accessed only in the morally appropriate circumstances.

FURTHER CLARIFYING THE ARGUMENT

Yet, despite the above disclaimer that this argument is by no means as radical as it appears, the conclusion that it is morally permissible for the State to subject its citizens to constant surveillance might still seem chilling. To alleviate this concern the above pro-surveillance argument should be

clarified in two ways. First, it must be emphasized that although this argument leads to the conclusion that it is morally permissible for the State to place its citizens under constant surveillance, it does *not* lead to the conclusion that it is morally permissible for the State to have access to *all* of the information that its surveillance devices secure. Instead, this argument leads only to the conclusion that the State should have access to the information recorded by these devices that it is morally permissible for it to have access to. Of course, the question of the extent to which the State is morally permitted to secure information about the actions of its citizens, or the events that they are involved in, is a vexed one. It is, for example, debatable as to how far the privilege that is accorded to information divulged within certain professional relationships (such as those between clergy and penitents, doctors and patients, lawyers and clients, counselors and clients, or journalists and sources) should extend, and for what reasons (if any) such privilege should be trumped by other considerations. It is also debatable as to whether the increased powers accorded to law enforcement agencies by the Patriot Act to secure information about suspects or "persons of interest" are morally legitimate. However, it must be stressed that the question of *what* information the State that subjects its citizens to constant and universal surveillance should have access to is separate from the question of *whether it is morally permissible* to *place them under surveillance at all*—and it is the *latter* question that is at issue here.

The second way in which this pro-surveillance argument must be clarified is related to the first. In cases where agents of the State *are* morally permitted to access information about the actions of others, the information that they are morally permitted to secure is limited to the *minimum* that is needed for them to achieve the (legitimate) purposes for which they need it. Accordingly they are not morally permitted to have access to (for example) videotaped records of the actions of others if the information that they are morally permitted to secure could be gleaned from an automatic transcription of such videotape. Thus, although it might be morally permissible for an agent of the State to secure detailed information about a criminal defendant's past adultery if this is relevant to the State's case against him in a criminal trial, it does not follow that it is also morally permissible for this agent to watch a videotape of the defendant in the act. Similarly, the agents of the State would only be morally permitted to place citizens under surveillance in private areas such as their homes or offices if they could achieve this without accessing more information than they were morally permitted to access. It would thus not be morally permissible, for example, for the agents of the State to enter a person's house to install surveillance devices in it. This is because in doing so they would access more information than they were morally permitted to access (e.g., they would find out information about his domestic habits and the interior of his home during the installation process), for the installation of such devices would have to occur *before* there was reason to believe that the State was morally permitted to secure such information. Indeed, it is likely that, with respect to the interiors of the homes of most of the State's citizens, such reason will never be forthcoming.

This second clarification of the above pro-surveillance argument is important in three respects. First, it underscores the fact that this argument does not cede to the State any information-gathering powers that it does not already enjoy. Second, it emphasizes that the conclusion of this argument is a parsimonious one, insofar as it only supports the State's securing the *minimum* amount of information that it needs for its morally legitimate purposes. This argument will thus *not* support the use of any surveillance devices that enable the State to secure more information than is necessary for its morally legitimate purposes. Finally, and in a related vein, once it becomes possible for surveillance technology automatically to provide a written narrative of events, the use of any type of surveillance technology that provides *more* than this information (such as, for example, manned closed-circuit television monitors, and videotapes) will *cease* to be morally justified by the above pro-surveillance argument. Rather than justifying the *expansion* of the State's powers of surveillance, then, the above pro-surveillance argument will instead eventually justify their *curtailment*.

THE ADVANTAGES OF UNIVERSAL STATE SURVEILLANCE

The most obvious advantages to the State's installing such a surveillance system would result from the fact that witnesses would no longer be needed in either criminal or civil cases, for their testimony would be supplanted by information supplied by surveillance devices. Unlike witness testimony, this information would be accurate. It would, for example, be unaffected by any biases (whether conscious or unconscious) that human witnesses might be subject to and which could taint their testimony. It would also be free from distortions, whether deliberate (e.g., the witness is lying, or omitting parts of the truth), or accidental (e.g., the witness has a faulty memory). Moreover, the juries and judges to whom the information taken from surveillance devices would be presented in a court could take it at its face value, rather than having subjectively to assess its accuracy in the light of the perceived reliability of the witness from whom it was taken. Furthermore, that witnesses would no longer be needed under a system of constant and universal State surveillance would also benefit those who would otherwise have served in this capacity. Most obviously, they would no longer be burdened with the task of testifying, which might have required them to travel, or to take time off work. They would also be relieved from any threats that they might have faced from persons who would be adversely affected either by their testimony (e.g., the defendants or their associates), or by its lack (e.g., the prosecutors).

A system of constant State surveillance would have other advantages, too. Under the current criminal justice system a wealthy defendant who is innocent of the charges that she is faced with can use her wealth to hire private investigators to demonstrate her innocence, either by finding persons who witnessed the crime of which she is accused, or by finding persons who can provide her with a legitimate alibi. This option is not open to poorer defendants who are similarly innocent, but who cannot afford to hire private investigators. Since this is so, innocent, poor defendants are more likely than innocent, wealthy defendants to accept plea bargains, or to be convicted of crimes that they did not commit. If, however, a poor person were to be accused of a crime in a State that subjected its citizens to constant surveillance, the judge in her case would be morally justified (indeed, would be morally *required*) in enabling the defense to secure information that would prove her innocence, and that would have been gathered by the State's surveillance devices. A State's use of constant surveillance could thus reduce the number of persons who are wrongfully convicted. This would not only be good in itself, but it would also lead to a more equitable justice system, for the disparity in wrongful conviction rates between the wealthy (who could use their wealth to prove their innocence) and the poor could be eliminated.

In addition to these advantages constant State surveillance would also benefit the State's citizenry at large, by serving as a deterrent to crime. This would not be because the citizens who lived under State surveillance would never know when they were being watched, and so would refrain from committing crimes for fear of being caught in the act. As is clear from the second clarification of this pro-surveillance argument, above, this argument does not justify the State watching its citizens, for in doing so it would acquire more information about them than it is morally permitted to acquire. However, if the State were to subject its citizens to the degree of surveillance that would be justified on the above argument, its citizens would know that whenever a crime was committed its performance would be recorded, and so its perpetrator would be likely to be apprehended. This knowledge would deter many potential criminals from committing crimes. (It would also deter law enforcement officers from extending the limits of their authority.) To be sure, the knowledge that one's criminal act would be recorded would not deter all potential criminals from committing crimes. Some persons would still commit crimes of passion, and of anger: others would succumb to the temptation to commit an opportunistic theft, act under the influence of drugs or alcohol, or act on the belief that they would not be caught. But most persons would simply judge the commission of crime not to be worthwhile, once they realized that they were subject to constant State surveillance, and so such surveillance would serve as an effective deterrent to most criminal activity.

TWO INITIAL OBJECTIONS

Despite the advantages that would accrue to a system of constant State surveillance of the type that is defended above there are two immediate objections that its proponents must face. The first is that such a surveillance system would be open to abuse. The second denies the claim that it is morally permissible for agents of the State (e.g., judges) to compel witness testimony or authorize information-gathering surveillance.

The Objection from Potential Abuse

It must be admitted that, in practice, a system of constant State surveillance is likely to be abused to some extent. However, if one adopts a rights-based understanding of claim (ii) above (i.e., if one holds that such a system of State surveillance is permissible as long as it does not in itself violate persons' moral rights), this objection can be readily rebutted. On such an understanding of claim (ii) one could first note that this abuse-based objection gets its force from the view that such abuse would violate persons' moral rights. The proponent of a rights-based understanding of claim (ii) would certainly agree with this underlying view, and would join with its advocates in condemning such abuse. However, the rights theorist who was in favor of such a system of State surveillance would also note that the condemnation of the *abuse* of State surveillance is not to condemn State surveillance *itself*. To condemn the use of *x* for the purposes of *y*. where *y* violates persons' rights (e.g., to privacy or autonomy) is *not* also to condemn the use of *x* for the purposes of *z*, where *z* does *not* violate persons' rights. Thus, a rights theorist who was a proponent of State surveillance could argue, to offer the possibility of abuse as an objection to constant State surveillance is to confuse the moral status of different possible uses of such surveillance. For such proponents of State surveillance, then, this first objection can be readily dismissed.

If one adopts a consequentialist understanding of claim (ii), however, defending the use of constant

State surveillance against this objection is more difficult. This is because the likelihood of such abuse together with the likelihood of such abuse causing harm must be weighed against the benefits (as outlined above) that such a system is likely to provide. And, given that such a system has not yet been implemented, such a weighing and balancing of its relative costs and benefits will be difficult to assess with certainty. Despite this, however, there is good reason to believe that little harm will accrue from the abuse of such a system of surveillance. Thus, given the likelihood that such a system of State surveillance will bring important benefits to the citizens of the State in which it is installed, the possibility of its abuse should not deter consequentialists from endorsing the above pro-surveillance argument.

To show why there is good reason to believe that little harm would accrue from such a system of State surveillances consequentialist proponents should first distinguish between major abuses of such a system and minor abuses of it. A major abuse of such a system would be one in which the State used its power together with its improved surveillance capabilities to persecute or oppress its citizens, either individually or as a whole. A minor abuse of the system would be one in which some of the agents of the State secured access to the information gathered by its surveillance devices for their own nefarious purposes, such as voyeurism or the mockery of the persons whose recorded actions they are viewing. The consequentialist proponent of constant and universal State surveillance need not be unduly concerned about the possibility of major abuses of the State surveillance system. If the State were prone to abuse its citizens in this way prior to the installation of such a system, this would provide good consequentialist grounds for resisting its introduction. The consequentialist proponent of constant State surveillance is thus only concerned with defending the introduction of such a surveillance system in those cases where the State was *not* prone to abusing its citizens in this way. This is not to say, however, that a State (or the agents of a State) that was not prone to persecuting or oppressing its citizens might not occasionally persecute individual citizens. In response to this the consequentialist proponent of constant State surveillance should note that given its power, were the State (or its agents) to decide to persecute some of its citizens in this way it would not need a system of surveillance to do this effectively. Thus, although such a surveillance system might make it easier for the State (or its agents) to engage in the persecution that it had decided upon, this would not make things any worse for the person or persons thus persecuted. As such, then, the possibility of the major abuse of a system of constant and universal State surveillance by a State that was not prone to persecuting its citizens would not, for a consequentialist, be a significant objection to the introduction of such a system.

What, then, of the concern that such a system of constant State surveillance would be subject to minor abuses? The most obvious response to this concern is to argue that if such a system of surveillance is introduced then it must be accompanied by a series of safeguards that would reduce the possibility that the information that it gathers would be abused in this way. It might, for example, be that such a system should be accompanied by the requirement that only a very few persons have access to the information that it gathers, that such persons be screened carefully and supervised closely, and that they are subject to draconian penalties for any abuses that they might perpetrate. If they were severe enough such safeguards would be likely to reduce the possibility of the minor abuse of such a system of surveillance to a level whereby the harm that its abusers might cause would be outweighed by the advantages that it would provide to the State's citizens as a whole.

However, the consequentialist proponent of State surveillance also has a second—and more philosophically interesting—response to the concern that such surveillance would be subject to minor abuse: that such abuse would not be harmful, and so would not detract from the advantages outlined above. This response is based on observing that given the penalties for abuse by which such a system would be accompanied (as outlined above), any such abuse would be perpetrated covertly. As such, its victims (e.g., persons subjected to the voyeuristic gaze of some of the agents of the State) would not know that they were victims. Yet even though this is so, the proponents of this second response to the above abuse-based objection do not use this observation to argue that, since such persons did not know that they were being watched, this watching did not harm them. This is because, the mere fact that a person is ignorant of the frustration of her interests (e.g., her interest not to be the unwilling subject of voyeurism) does not mean that she has not thereby been harmed. Rather, this second consequentialist response to the above abuse-based objection conjoins this observation with the claim that for a person to be harmed her life must have been adversely affected in some way, whether she knew of this or not.

Given this, then, although the consequentialist proponent of constant State surveillance should not argue that if a person did not know that she was the object of voyeurism then she would not be harmed by this, he *should* argue that if such abuse of the State surveillance system did not affect this person's life then she would not be harmed by it. And it is plausible that such minor abuse would indeed fail to affect the lives of those subject to it. Given the draconian penalties that would be imposed upon those who engaged in such minor abuse of the system, it is unlikely that its victims would come to learn of their victimization, and so it is unlikely that they would come to be upset by it as a result of gaining such knowledge. The system of State surveillance that would be justified by the above pro-surveillance argument would not be one in which the State's citizens were constantly watched, but just one in which their actions were recorded. As such, the perpetrators of such minor abuses as voyeurism would have no direct contact with their victims. Thus, since such minor abuses of the State surveillance system as voyeurism would neither upset their unwitting victims, nor compromise their autonomy through subjecting them to deception, they would not harm them in any way.

Through instituting safeguards, then, one could ensure that the minor abuse of the type of State surveillance system that was argued for above could be reduced to a minimum—or, perhaps, even eliminated altogether. Yet even if such abuse did occur it would not necessarily harm its victims, for it would not necessarily adversely affect their lives. As such, then, even though the consequentialist proponents of such a system of constant State surveillance must take into account the possibility of the harm that its abuse might cause, they still have good reason to believe that, all things considered, the State should be morally permitted to subject its citizens to it.

Compelling Testimony Is Morally Impermissible

Both the rights theorists and the consequentialists who support the introduction of a system of constant State surveillance can thus meet the objection that such a system might be abused. What, then, of the second objection with which they are faced: that it is not morally permissible for the agents of the State (e.g., judges) to compel witness testimony or authorize information-gathering surveillance with probable cause? This second objection is less plausible than the first. As was noted in the initial clarificatory section of this essay, the above pro-surveillance argument is a conditional argument, such that if it is ever morally permissible for an agent of the State (e.g., a judge or a prosecutor) to secure information from a witness about past events, then it is morally permissible for her to use State surveillance devices to secure the same information. For the antecedent clause of this argument to be true all that needs to be true is that in at least one case it would be morally permissible for (e.g.) a judge to secure information from a witness. And this latter claim is very plausible indeed, for both rights theorists and consequentialists alike. To see this, assume that Lee Harvey Oswald really was innocent of the assassination of John F. Kennedy, and, to prove his innocence, needed to secure the photograph that was taken of him standing in the doorway to the Texas School Book Depository at the time of the shooting. Assume also that the owner of this photograph disliked Oswald, and wanted to see him wrongly convicted. Here, it would clearly be morally permissible for the judge in Oswald's case to require that the owner of the photograph produce it in evidence.

It is simple to construct examples in which the ill effects that result from a person's refusal to produce an item of information in evidence are vast, and where the costs to him of supplying this information are tiny. Imagine, for example, a case in which ten men will be executed for a crime that they did not commit unless a man who (for idiosyncratic reasons of his own) dislikes discussing what clothes he wore in the past discloses to their judge which clothes he wore on the day of the crime. (In this case the clothes that the uncooperative witness wore are, for some reason, crucial to establishing whether it is the accused, or another group of ten men, who committed the crime in question.) Clearly, in this case it would be counterintuitive to claim that the judge was not justified in requiring this man to reveal what clothes he wore on the day in question. And, once one accepts that for *any* case outlined in an example such as this, it would be morally permissible for a judge to secure the information in question, then one will have granted the truth of the antecedent claim on which this conditional argument in favor of surveillance rests. That is, once one grants that for any given case that it would be permissible for a judge to secure the withheld information, then one must also grant that it would be permissible to use State surveillance to secure the same information. And, since the State cannot tell where or when the actions or events that this information pertains to would occur, one would then also have to grant that the State would be justified in gathering information about *all* actions and events that occur. (With, of course, the proviso that it can only *access* that which it is morally permissible for it to access.)

SURVEILLANCE, PRIVACY, AND AUTONOMY

The two most obvious and immediate objections to the above pro-surveillance argument can thus be met. However, it still faces two more. The first of these is based on the claim that such a surveillance system would violate the privacy of those subjected to it. The second is based on the claim that it would illegitimately compromise their autonomy.

Neither of these objections is sound. The objection that constant State surveillance would violate the privacy of those subject to it rests on a failure to acknowledge the limits of the proposed surveillance. On the system of surveillance argued for above, the State would only be permitted to access the information that its surveillance devices gather *when it is morally permissible for it to do so.* As such,

the State's use of such a surveillance system would not enable it justly to access any more information than it is morally permitted to access already. This point is not reiterated to defend the system of State surveillance advocated above on the grounds that it would not violate the privacy of its citizens any more than this is violated already. Rather, it has been reiterated to provide the basis for a *stronger defense of this system of State surveillance: that it would not violate the citizens' privacy at all.*

To develop this strong defense of the system of State surveillance advocated above, it must be recognized that privacy is both a relative notion and a normative notion. A certain item of information is private *relative to* a certain person, if that person cannot *legitimately* (a normative concept) require that that item of information be disclosed to her. For example, my use of the checking account that I share with my wife is not private with respect to her, for she can legitimately require that I disclose my use of it to her. However, it is private with respect to my colleagues, who cannot legitimately require that I disclose my use of it to them. Similarly, the examination score of a student in my class is not private with respect to the student, since she can legitimately require its disclosure, but it is private with respect to my wife, who cannot. Given, then, that privacy is both a relative notion and a normative notion, and since, according to the pro-surveillance argument above, the agents of the State can only access those items of information that they are morally permitted to access, it is clear that the above pro-surveillance argument does not justify the violation of the privacy of the State's citizens. According to that argument, the only time at which the State could permissibly access information about actions or events would be when it was morally permitted to do so; that is, when it could *legitimately* require that this information be disclosed to it. This being so, under the system of State surveillance argued for above, the State could only access information that is *not* private relative to it. Thus, in accessing such information the State would not violate the privacy of its citizens.

Just as constant and universal State surveillance of the sort argued for above would not violate the privacy of the persons subject to it, neither would it compromise their autonomy—although it is easy to see why one might think that it would. In *1984* Oceania's citizens adjusted their behavior when they were in the presence of telescreens to conform to the way that they believed that Big Brother's Party wanted them to behave. Were they not to do this, and were they to be observed by agents of Big Brother during their refusal to conform, they risked severe punishment. To avoid the penalties that the Party would impose on them if they failed to conform to its expectations, then, Oceania's citizens ceded a degree of control over their actions to the Party. That is, when they acted out of fear that Party members were observing them, and so acted to conform to the Party's view of how they should behave, the citizens of Oceania satisfied their desires to "Perform the actions that the Party wants me to perform." To the extent that they thus ceded control to the Party, then, Big Brother's citizens suffered from compromised autonomy as a result of being subjected to (or, potentially subjected to) State surveillance.

Fortunately, however, the citizens of a State that utilized the type of constant surveillance that would be justified on the above pro-surveillance argument would not similarly suffer from compromised autonomy. As noted earlier such a surveillance system would not utilize the type of in-person surveillance that was used by Big Brother's Party in *1984*. Instead, it would merely record the actions of the citizens and the events that they participated in. Since this is so, most of the citizens subject to this form of State surveillance would not believe that they needed to alter their behavior to conform to the State's view of how they should act (were the State even to hold such a view), for they would recognize that the State would not actually be watching them. Moreover, if they were law-abiding, then they would also recognize that the chances of the State having just cause to access information about their actions would be very slim indeed. Free from the pressure to conform of the sort that was imposed upon the citizens of Oceania, then, most citizens whose State subjected them to constant and universal surveillance of the type outlined above would *not* cede control over their acts to the State. The citizens of such a State would thus retain their autonomy with

respect to it. Moreover, the claim that most citizens placed under constant State surveillance would not suffer from any diminution in their autonomy is not merely a speculative one. Persons subjected to surveillance are unlikely to alter their behavior once they become used to being "on tape" (unless they previously performed acts that they believed they should not have been performing) when they realize that there is little chance that the information that the surveillance devices record would ever be required, and so there is little chance of their actions ever being observed.

Of course, not all the citizens of a State that utilized the type of surveillance advocated above would retain full autonomy with respect to all of their actions. The exceptions would be those who are criminally inclined, and who, as a result of being placed under State surveillance, would alter their behavior by refraining from committing crimes. Such persons would suffer from compromised autonomy with respect to their deliberate omission of criminal activity, insofar as they alter their behavior solely to avoid incurring criminal penalties. Yet, given that the actions that these persons refrain from performing are criminal ones, the diminution in autonomy that these persons would experience as a result of being placed under State surveillance is one that it is morally legitimate to inflict upon them.

CONCLUSION

It is now time to take stock. Although it is often claimed that the recent proliferation of surveillance technology is turning the West into an "Orwellian nightmare" it was argued in this paper that, rather than condemning the prospect of constant State surveillance, we should instead welcome it. Such surveillance would not, however, involve any expansion of State power into the lives of its citizens. This is because if, under certain circumstances, it is morally permissible for judges to secure information relevant to their cases from witnesses, then, under the same circumstances, it should also be morally permissible for them to secure this information through the use of surveillance devices. Constant State surveillance is thus no different in principle from the current system of subpoenaing witnesses. Moreover, the State's use of such surveillance would be morally *preferable* to the subpoenaing of witnesses. It would, for example, avoid the need to impose costs on those who would otherwise be called as witnesses, and it would result in the provision of more accurate information. There are, of course, practical concerns that must be addressed before any such State surveillance system is put in place. But since, as has been argued in this paper, there is no *principled* reason to oppose such a system, but there is reason to endorse it, once worries about the possibility of such a system being abused are laid to rest the road would be clear for its introduction. Big Brother would then indeed be watching over us. But, unless one has criminal tendencies, this should be a cause for relief, rather than concern.

James Stacey Taylor: In Praise of Big Brother

1. Is there any way to protect against governmental abuse of a system of total surveillance? If so, how? If not, does that imply that such a system cannot be morally justified?

2. What do you think of the following slippery slope argument: if we allow complete surveillance of citizens, then over time we will lose respect for individual privacy rights. When we do, we won't even recognize the moral error we've fallen into. So we should not start up such a surveillance system in the first place.

3. What information do you think the government ought to be allowed to have about our activities? What information should we be allowed to hide from government officials? What principle explains your answers to these questions?

4. Do people have a moral right not to be under surveillance at all? If not, why not? If so, what is the basis for such a right?

5. Taylor claims that a system of state surveillance would neither compromise people's privacy nor violate their autonomy. How does he support this claim? Do you find his argument persuasive? Why or why not?

CHAPTER 20

The Death Penalty

JUST THE FACTS

Capital punishment, commonly known as the death penalty, is the government-authorized practice of executing people (i.e., putting them to death) as punishment for a crime.

Capital punishment is illegal, or legal but almost never practiced, in the majority of countries in the world. It remains legal, however, and is regularly practiced in the world's most populous countries (e.g., China, India, Indonesia, the United States). Thus, roughly 60 percent of the world's population lives in a country where capital punishment is both legal and practiced. According to Amnesty International (an organization that opposes the death penalty), in 2016, there were twenty-three countries (about an eighth of all countries) that were known to have executed a total of 1,032 convicted criminals. Most of those executions were carried out by Iran, Saudi Arabia, Iraq, and Pakistan (in that order). China is believed to have carried out more executions than any other country, but there are no good data on China's practices, since China refuses to divulge figures on their use of the death penalty. Thus, the 1,032 figure cited earlier does not count the executions authorized by the Chinese government. Among so-called first-world countries, executions are uncommon, but the United States is a notable exception. Capital punishment is outlawed in every country in the European Union.

In the United States, capital punishment is legal in thirty-one states and illegal in nineteen states (as well as the District of Columbia). Since 1976, the US government and individual states have executed 1,455 inmates—twenty of them in 2016. The number of inmates executed in the United States has dropped every year since 2009, when there were fifty-two executions, and executions have trended downward since 1999, when there were ninety-eight of them.

Prior to 1972, capital punishment was legally permitted by the US government. In the 1972 Supreme Court case *Furman v. Georgia*, however, the Court ruled (in a 5-to-4 decision) that the death penalty violated the Eighth Amendment of the US Constitution and was therefore **unconstitutional**. The Eighth Amendment says that "Excessive bail shall not be required, nor excessive fines imposed, *nor cruel and unusual punishments inflicted.*" The court's majority view was that sentences of capital punishment were applied in ways that were either **arbitrary** or **discriminatory** (or both)—at least, as things were practiced then in 1972. Thus, in the Court's view, the death penalty violated the "cruel and unusual punishment" clause. Capital punishment was therefore outlawed in the United States beginning in 1972. This prohibition, however, didn't last long. States reacted to *Furman* by providing juries with objective criteria for when (and when not) to sentence a convicted felon to death, in the hopes that this would address the Court's concerns that the death penalty was being arbitrarily applied. Once these policies were in place, the Supreme Court ruled, in the 1976 case *Woodson* v. *North Carolina*, that the death penalty was constitutional so long as the safeguards preventing the death penalty from being arbitrarily applied continued to be in place. The death penalty has been legal and practiced in the United States ever since.

There are two kinds of crimes for which a person is liable to be sentenced to death in the United States: murder (usually **aggravated murder**) and crimes against the state (e.g., treason, espionage, high-volume drug trafficking). No one has been executed for crimes against the state since 1976, so most of our discussion will concern the death penalty for supposed murderers. Murder consists in the **premeditated** killing of one person by another in an attempt to harm the victim (thus distinguishing murder from euthanasia—see Chapter 15). Aggravated murder consists in murder plus so-called **aggravating conditions**. Aggravating conditions are features of a crime that significantly increase the severity or the harmful consequences of that crime. What constitutes an aggravating condition differs from state to state, but a few conditions are common to most states. For instance, a murder preceded by rape or torture is an instance of aggravated murder, since these features make the crime significantly more heinous.

Methods of capital punishment currently in use across the world include beheading, electrocution, firing squad, hanging, lethal gas, and **lethal injection**. Lethal injection is by far the most common method used in the United States, though electrocution (by electric chair), hanging, firing squad, and lethal gas remain on the books in some states as a legal means of execution.

Lethal injection involves injecting three different drugs into a prisoner's veins in a very specific order. The first drug is sodium thiopental (or, in some states, midazolam), a fast-acting form of anesthesia that causes a person to lose consciousness within thirty to forty-five seconds. If all goes according to plan, prisoners will not feel anything that happens to them after they receive this injection. They'll be in a medically induced coma. The next drug, pancuronium bromide, is a powerful muscle relaxant. It paralyzes all of a person's muscles, including the diaphragm, which is necessary for breathing. The last drug, potassium chloride, disrupts electrical signals in the heart, causing it to fail and stop beating. Once the heart stops, the prisoner is dead and the execution is complete. The entire process usually lasts less than five minutes.

Executions in the United States are not evenly distributed along sex and racial lines. The overwhelming majority of **death row** inmates are male—less than 2 percent are female. And of the 1,455 inmates executed in the United States since 1976, only sixteen have been female—about 1 percent. With respect to race, 42 percent of all death row inmates in the United States are African American, 42 percent white, and 13 percent Hispanic. For reference, white people constitute roughly 64 percent of the US population, while African Americans constitute roughly 12 percent, and Hispanic people 16 percent. Thus African Americans are significantly overrepresented among the death row population and white people are significantly underrepresented. Not surprisingly, African Americans are also overrepresented among those who have been executed. Since 1976, 34.5 percent of all inmates executed were African American, while 55.7 percent were white. During that time, 307 inmates have been executed for committing an interracial murder, where a white person murders a black person or a black person murders a white person. In 287 of those executions (93 percent), a black person was executed for murdering a white person. In twenty of those executions (7 percent), a white person was executed for murdering a black person.

In general, US citizens favor the death penalty for convicted murderers. According to a recent Pew Research Center poll,[1] 49 percent of US citizens said that they favor the death penalty while 42 percent said they oppose it, with opinions differing along sex and racial lines. On the whole, both men and women in the United States favor the death penalty, but men favor it much more. The poll found that 45 percent of

---

1. http://www.pewresearch.org/fact-tank/2016/09/29/support-for-death-penalty-lowest-in-more-than-four-decades/

women favor the death penalty, while 43 percent oppose it. Fifty-five percent of men said they favor the death penalty; only 38 percent oppose it. There is a significant divergence of opinion among white people and minorities, too: whites generally favor the death penalty while minorities overwhelmingly oppose it. The poll found that 57 percent of white respondents favor the death penalty; only 35 percent oppose it. Among black people, 29 percent favored it, while 63 percent opposed. Hispanics, too, generally opposed the death penalty—36 percent favored, 50 percent opposed.

ARGUMENT ANALYSIS

There is something morally suspect about punishment—after all, when we punish, we deliberately try to make someone suffer, at a point where he is defenseless and within our control. In any other context, such behavior would certainly be immoral. So if punishment is ever morally acceptable, we need some excellent reason to remove our suspicions. There are three primary justifications of punishment, only two of which have any application when it comes to the death penalty.

The first justification is rehabilitation—the state punishes criminals in order to make them better people. The idea is that forcing wrongdoers to suffer will give them the needed incentive to reflect on their wrongdoing and then turn themselves around, so that they can eventually be successfully integrated into society. This justification obviously fails as a basis for supporting the death penalty—we aren't going to improve people's moral character by executing them.

By contrast, the other two justifications of punishment have often been used to defend capital punishment. The first of these is the **deterrence theory**, which has its roots in consequentialist moral theories. The basic idea here is that punishment is justified because of its good results; in particular, punishment is morally acceptable if, only if, and because it is likely to efficiently prevent crime. When it comes to the

death penalty, the view says that killing criminals is itself a bad thing, but this can sometimes be outweighed by the good we can secure by preventing the deaths of innocent people in the future. That prevention occurs through what is known as **special deterrence** (deterring the criminal himself) and **general deterrence** (deterring law-abiding people who might otherwise be tempted to commit serious crimes).

The remaining justification of punishment is known as **retributivism**, which has its roots in nonconsequentialist moral theories. On this view, punishment is morally justified if, only if, and because it gives criminals their **just deserts** (i.e., what they justly deserve). Retributivism tells us that when we want to determine whether a punishment is morally justified, we don't look into the future to see whether punishing a criminal will yield good results. Instead, we look to the past, assess how guilty a criminal is, and then set a punishment that is proportional to the crime. When it comes to the death penalty, the retributivist justification is that murderers deserve to die; we must give people what they deserve; and so we must execute murderers.

Of course, there are also opponents of the death penalty. Such critics, known as **abolitionists**, believe that capital punishment cannot be morally justified and so seek to abolish it where it exists. In addition to criticizing the arguments of deterrence theorists and retributivists who support the death penalty, abolitionists also offer some positive arguments of their own. Let's consider these, before assessing the merits of the arguments used to support capital punishment.

One popular critique of the death penalty asserts that there is a kind of incoherence at its heart. The state can't consistently prohibit murder while also approving of it, in the form of capital punishment. A common way to express this idea is by means of

The Incoherence Argument

1. Murder is immoral.
2. Capital punishment is murder.

Therefore,

3. Capital punishment is immoral.

This argument won't work. Though the first premise is true by definition, the second premise begs the question. In other words, it is assuming the truth of the conclusion it is meant to support. What premise 2 really says is: Capital punishment is immoral killing. Suppose you are wondering what to think about the morality of the death penalty. This argument isn't going to help—you need as much support for premise 2 as for the conclusion. If anyone presented this argument to you, you'd rightly say that you haven't yet been given any reason to believe the conclusion. Asserting premise 2 is just another way of stating that conclusion, rather than an independent reason to believe it.

Abolitionists might try another tack:

The Absolutist Argument

1. Killing people is absolutely wrong, that is, wrong always and everywhere.
2. Capital punishment kills people.

Therefore,

3. Capital punishment is absolutely wrong.

Premise 2 of this argument is true, no doubt about it. But premise 1 is very hard to defend. There seem to be justified exceptions, as when we kill in self-defense as a last resort. Or when we engage in a just war and kill an enemy combatant who is intent on genocide. If there are exceptions to premise 1, perhaps capital punishment is one of them.

True, there are some pacifists who oppose all killing, no matter the circumstances. But this form of pacifism is very difficult to defend. Until we have a satisfying defense of such rigorous pacifism, the jury is out on the merits of premise 1, and so of this argument.

But perhaps a more familiar argument will do the trick. It is well known that if you are a person of color in the United States, you stand

a much greater chance of being charged with a **capital offense** in the first place, then convicted, and eventually sentenced to death, than if you are a white person who has been suspected of committing murder. There is no denying that there is systemic discrimination that occurs in the administration of the death penalty, and that such discrimination is morally unjustified. This serves as the basis of

The Argument from Discrimination

1. If a punishment is applied in a systemically discriminatory way, then it is morally unjustified and ought to be abolished.
2. The death penalty is applied in a systemically discriminatory way.

Therefore,

3. The death penalty is morally unjustified and ought to be abolished.

Defenders of the death penalty have replied in three ways to this argument. First, some have conceded that the argument is sound, and that it represents an indictment of the way that the death penalty is actually administered. But, they say, this is a flaw that can be remedied—the death penalty is, *in principle*, morally justified, even if, as it is currently practiced, it is not. Whether this reply is satisfactory depends on whether you think that we can someday erase systemic discrimination from our society. I leave it to you to defend your optimism or pessimism on this matter.

A second reply denies premise 2, and argues that in fact there is no such systemic discrimination that occurs in today's legal system. Though settling this issue requires an in-depth consideration of the evidence, the evidence does seem very clearly to support this premise.

Since the argument is valid and premise 2 is (I am assuming) true, that leaves only premise 1 as the target for those who wish to reject the conclusion. But how can we deny that *systemic* discrimination—bias that is not the rare exception, but rather the normal circumstance—undermines the legitimacy of the death penalty? Perhaps it does. But death penalty defenders point out that such discrimination is not likely to be restricted only to capital cases. If it really is systemic, then discrimination affects all levels of the legal system. And if systemic discrimination really is sufficient to undermine the moral justification of punishment, then it is sufficient to undermine the morality *of the entire legal system*. Further, since this argument is designed to show that the death penalty should be abolished because it is morally unjustified, then its soundness would imply that we should abolish our entire criminal justice system, because it, too, is infected with systemic discrimination and so morally unjustified.

Some abolitionists will endorse this radical conclusion. But many others will resist. Every human institution is imperfect, they will say, and our legal system, while far from ideal in its workings, has enough merit to warrant our allegiance. If that is so, then perhaps the fact that the death penalty is administered in a discriminatory way is not enough to show that we ought to abolish it. Resolving this debate requires extensive knowledge of the facts about how our legal system actually works, including the extent of discrimination faced by people of color. But it also requires thinking deeply about how much injustice an institution can tolerate before it becomes morally unjustified on the whole.

I invite you to reflect further on these issues, but in the meantime, we should move to another abolitionist argument. This one points to the fact that the legal system is bound to be error-prone. It's folks like you and I who sit on juries, and we make mistakes. Even if we could correct for our biases, we are still fallible. Evidence is rarely complete. Some defense lawyers are much better than others. Some judges are more impartial and better versed in the law than others. As a result, even if we were all pure at heart, some innocent people would be wrongly convicted. This is bad enough. But when their conviction leads to their death, that, says abolitionists, is too much. This line of thinking can be expressed in

The Killing Innocents Argument

1. If we know that a social practice will result in killing innocents, then it is immoral and ought to be abolished.
2. We know that the death penalty will result in killing innocents.

Therefore,

3. The death penalty is immoral and ought to be abolished.

Some defenders of the death penalty reject premise 2. They claim that given the appeals available to those sentenced to death, we are bound to weed out erroneous convictions, with the result that the innocent are never sent to their deaths. But this is an extraordinarily optimistic assumption, and is cast into doubt by the best study we have.[2] True, studies on this matter are not themselves perfect, because it is sometimes so difficult to establish the truth about whether the defendant in a capital case is really guilty. But precisely because of this difficulty, it is impossible to be justly confident that innocents are never sent to their death.

Defenders of the death penalty might instead say that in at least some cases, we can be absolutely sure that the defendant is guilty—we have him on video, say, or we have his confession, or we have several eyewitnesses who testify to his guilt. There are two problems with such a reply. First, each of these sources of evidence is sometimes misleading. Many people have signed confessions to crimes they didn't commit. Eyewitness testimony has often proven to be unreliable. And videos have sometimes been tampered with. Still, imagine that in a given case you *can* be absolutely sure that the defendant committed the crime he's accused of. Now a second problem arises—how are you going to craft a law that ensures that only *these* defendants are

---

2. http://www.newsweek.com/one-25-executed-us-innocent-study-claims-248,889; http://phenomena.nationalgeographic.com/2014/04/28/how-many-people-are-wrongly-convicted-researchers-do-the-math/

convicted and sentenced to death? We rightly ask jurors and judges to follow the law, rather than use their own instincts, to determine whether a defendant is guilty. Suppose we wrote a law that restricted the death penalty just to cases in which all jurors were sure of the defendant's guilt. Given human fallibility, it seems that even *that* law would in some cases be misapplied, thereby sending some innocent people to their death.

A stronger reply to the Killing Innocents Argument criticizes premise 1. As it stands, that premise is implausible, since we rightly allow many other social practices that are known to impose substantial risks of killing innocents. Think of driving cars, building bridges, manufacturing prescription drugs. We know that each of these practices is going to result in the loss of innocent life, and yet we allow them anyway.

The abolitionist might reply that there is something especially awful when the state is taking innocent life. While there does seem something correct about that, this reply won't fix the problem here. Suppose that the state took over the health care system, and all doctors and pharmacists became state employees. (If you're opposed to such an idea, that's fine. I'm not arguing for the advisability of such a plan, but just asking you to imagine what might happen if it were implemented.) In that case, we'd know in advance that some state employees, acting in the name of the state, are going to inadvertently kill some innocent people. Yet that fact would not by itself show that we oughtn't to have state-run medical care.

Though there are difficulties with each of these abolitionist arguments, it may be that defenses of the death penalty do no better. Let's turn our attention now to some of those defenses. We'll consider the arguments from deterrence theorists first, and then shift the focus to retributivist arguments.

The basic deterrence argument for the death penalty is perfectly simple:

The Basic Deterrence Argument

1. If a punishment efficiently deters crime, then that punishment is morally justified.

2. The death penalty efficiently deters murder.

Therefore,

3. The death penalty is morally justified.

It's very important to note that qualification about a punishment *efficiently* deterring crime. Loads of punishments will have a deterrent effect that prevents a given crime. For instance, if I was the town mayor and wanted to stop people from littering, I could ask the town council to impose the death penalty on litterers. That would *definitely* be a good deterrent! Don't think we'd see too much litter around town after that. But it's absurd to think that death for litterers is a justified punishment. That's because the death penalty is not an efficient punishment—it imposes more harm than is needed to generate the good result of crime prevention. An efficient punishment is one that will hurt the criminal *no more than is necessary* in order to get the beneficial effect of crime prevention. Efficiency here means getting the greatest crime reduction for the least cost—where such cost is measured not just in dollars but also in the suffering of the criminals themselves.

So the Basic Deterrence Argument says, in effect, that in order to prevent murders, you have to threaten to execute murderers. No lesser punishment will do. That's what is conveyed by premise 2, which says that the death penalty is an efficient way to prevent murder.

There are two problems with the Basic Deterrence Argument. The first is that premise 1 may license some very bad behavior. Suppose we do a lot of scientific studies and it turns out that no amount of jail time will efficiently deter certain criminals. Nor will the prospect of a lethal injection. The only thing that will do the trick is to threaten to kill them in some horrible way, like slowly cutting them in half without anesthesia or throwing them off a very tall building. Premise 1 says that under these circumstances, such punishments are morally justified. It is hard to accept that.

But suppose you do. Still, premise 2 of this argument is also problematic, because there is no good evidence that it is true. Despite countless studies of the issue, the consensus among social scientists is that we lack strong reasons for thinking that the death penalty actually is an efficient deterrent of murder. That doesn't prove that premise 2 is false. But it does show that until better evidence comes along, we are not yet justified in thinking it true, and so not yet justified in thinking that the Basic Deterrence Argument is sound.

There are two further points to make about premise 2. First, one might insist that although the way the death penalty is currently administered fails to be an efficient deterrent, that just shows that we aren't doing it right. After all, we execute only about one in a thousand of those who are convicted of murder. If we performed a lot more executions, people would start to get the message, and the murder rate would drop accordingly. The problem with this reply, though, is that executing a lot more convicts increases the chance that we will end up killing more wrongly convicted innocent people.

Faced with the absence of hard evidence in support of premise 2, deterrence theorists have come up with an armchair reason to support it. The thought is simple: the greater one fears a punishment, the greater the deterrence it provides. People fear execution more than any other punishment. So the death penalty provides greater deterrence than any other punishment.

Yet this very plausible line of thinking is actually somewhat problematic. I fear being beheaded more than I do a lethal injection. So, according to the previous paragraph, beheading deters me more. But it doesn't. The prospect of a lethal injection is fearful enough to deter me from doing anything truly horrible. In other words, beheading is an inefficient punishment—it is harsher than punishment needs to be in order to deter me from murdering anyone.

Now the problem: execution, even if more fearful than life in prison, may be harsher than

what is needed to deter would-be murderers. Some criminals, of course, might not be deterrable at all, either because they are so intent on killing their victim or because they aren't thinking things through, and are acting, say, on impulse, or under the influence of drugs, or because they are so mentally ill that they are unable to calculate the risks. But for those criminals who can be deterred, a lesser punishment than execution—perhaps life imprisonment—may do. Defenders of the Basic Deterrence Argument have to show that murderers would abandon their plans if faced with the prospect of execution, but would carry out their plans if faced with life in prison. That has yet to be shown.

Turn now to retributivist efforts to justify capital punishment. Retributivists can entirely avoid having to answer questions about how likely it is that the death penalty will reduce crime. Their focus is instead on giving criminals their just deserts. This can be expressed in

The Argument from Just Deserts

1. If murderers deserve to die, then the state should execute them.
2. Murderers deserve to die.

Therefore,

3. The state should execute murderers.

The defense of premise 1 is straightforward. The state should be in the business of acting justly, and acting justly means giving people what they deserve. The defense of premise 2 is also straightforward: murderers have killed their victims. If you harm someone, then justice demands that you be harmed in the same way. So murderers deserve to die.

This argument is very popular. It is also deeply problematic.

Consider premise 1. You might think that it is obviously true, because it is based on two extremely plausible principles:

(D1) If a person deserves X, then justice demands that she get X.

(D2) The state should treat its citizens justly.

But there are three problems with premise 1, which, surprisingly, derive from doubts we might have about D2. I'm not sure that any of these problems is sufficient to undermine the premise, but taken together, they do put real pressure on its appeal.

First, most of us think that giving people the punishment they deserve sometimes has to take a back seat to other moral concerns. Our practice of allowing for parole, plea bargains, executive clemency, pardons, and suspended sentences attests to that. Each of these can be seen as an exercise in mercy—in treating people more kindly than they deserve. And mercy is a virtue. So perhaps it's not the case that just because murderers deserve to die—if they do—that we should be in the business of executing them.

Second, suppose that maintaining a system of capital punishment required so much money that we had to drastically sacrifice funds for schooling, for health programs, and for national defense. Studies show that a system of capital punishment is *much* more expensive than a system that has abolished it.[3] Each state with the death penalty spends hundreds of thousands of dollars more per death row inmate than for a convict who is sentenced to life in prison. Perhaps we should punish criminals a bit less than they deserve, so as to save resources to meet these other social needs.

Third, suppose that by instituting the death penalty, a state thereby *increased* the crime rate. I should stress that there is no conclusive evidence that this has occurred. There is a strong correlation between states that have the death penalty and states that have murder rates that are higher than average. But correlation is not the same thing as causation—studies have not shown that these higher murder rates are *caused by* the death penalty. Still, suppose that allowing capital punishment

had a brutalizing effect, making people less respectful of human life than they'd otherwise be, and so making people less inhibited about taking the lives of others. (Again, I am not saying that this is in fact the case, just inviting you to think about what would follow if it were.) If capital punishment actually increases, rather than decreases, the murder rate, then that would be an excellent reason to suspend the death penalty—even if it is true that this is what murderers deserve.

Giving people their just deserts is very important. But these considerations should make us wonder whether it is *all*-important. Premise 1 stands for the idea that justice must always be done, no matter its costs. But perhaps there are limits to when it is appropriate to give people what they deserve. Resolving this issue is very hard, and I am not claiming that these three points, taken together, are decisive refutations of premise 1. Indeed, let's suppose for now that premise 1 can survive these concerns. Still, premise 2 (the claim that murderers deserve to die) is actually very hard to defend.

Here's a radical critique of premise 2: no one deserves to suffer. There is a classic argument for this view. People deserve to suffer only if they freely choose to do wrong. But we have no free choice. So no one deserves to suffer.

We have no free choice? Really? I bet you don't believe that. I don't, either. But there's a powerful argument for this view. Our choices are determined by our beliefs and desires, which in turn are determined by how we were raised, by the society and the era in which we live, by the messages we take in through the media, our social networks, our parents, our clergy (if we are religious). We cannot control these influences. But that means that our choices are ultimately the product of factors beyond our control. If we don't control the ultimate causes of our choices, then we don't control our choices. And if we do not control our choices, then we lack free choice.

I said this was a radical idea, right? The basic line of thought is that we are justly punished only if we have freely chosen to do wrong. But

---

3. http://www.deathpenaltyinfo.org/costs-death-penalty

no one has freely chosen to do wrong, because no one has freely chosen to do *anything*. So no one can be justly punished. Note that this way of pushing back against the retributivist would show not only that the death penalty is immoral, but that *all* punishment is immoral. Most people are going to want to find a way to refute this argument. Have fun!

Let's assume we can answer this radical challenge, and so assume that some people are responsible for their poor choices and the terrible actions prompted by them. Still, why think that murderers who freely choose to kill are deserving of death? The classic retributivist response invokes the famous **lex talionis**. This principle (Latin for "law of retaliation") is the eye-for-an-eye, tooth-for-a-tooth, life-for-a-life guideline that says, more specifically, that a punishment is deserved if and only if it treats the criminal just as he treated his victim(s).

Punishment that is administered as lex talionis advises can be deeply satisfying. It can get criminals to see things from their victims' perspective, and so open their eyes to the true nature of the damage they have done. Further, punishment in line with lex talionis seems perfectly just, since the criminal can't rightly complain of being mistreated, given that he was willing to treat someone else in exactly the same way. Lastly, in the difficult matter of determining how to punish criminals, lex talionis often gives us concrete, practical advice. What to do with a murderer, for instance? Treat him as he has treated his victim.

These attractions account for lex talionis's broad appeal. Despite the widespread enthusiasm, however, lex talionis is fatally flawed. Three reasons explain its failure.

First, lex talionis cannot explain why criminals who intentionally hurt their victims should be punished more than those who accidentally cause the same harm. Lex talionis tells us to set the punishment by reference to the suffering of the victim. But victims can suffer the same harm, whether the perpetrator has carefully planned to cause it or has caused it by accident.

If I am recklessly practicing archery in my backyard and unintentionally skewer my neighbor, I deserve less punishment than a cold-blooded murderer. Or so we think. Lex talionis does not allow for that, since the victims in both cases have suffered the same harm.

We could say that what criminals deserve is determined not only by the harm they have done, but also by how blameworthy they are in bringing it about. So a hired killer should be punished more than a reckless archer, because the murderer displays a kind of moral corruption that the archer lacks. This does give us the right answer—the callous killer *should* be punished more. But it comes at the cost of abandoning lex talionis.

That's because we are no longer required to treat the criminal as he treated his victim. If an assassin deserves to be executed, then those who kill, but are less guilty than an assassin, should receive a lighter sentence than death. That undermines the letter and spirit of lex talionis, since these less guilty killers will not be harmed just as they have harmed their victims. And it also removes one of the great virtues of lex talionis—that of offering precise guidance on how much criminals should be punished.

A second problem with lex talionis is that it cannot tell us what many criminals deserve. This is most obvious in crimes that lack victims. Suppose an assassin attempts (but fails) to kill his victim, and the victim never discovers this. No harm, no foul? Suppose that someone leaves a bar well and truly drunk, and then manages to drive home without hurting anyone. Still, she deserves to be punished, but since there is no victim, lex talionis offers no basis for punishment.

Other crimes may have victims, and yet lex talionis offers no advice about their punishment. What to do with a hijacker or a counterfeiter? A kidnapper? Someone who transports stolen mattresses across state lines? The idea of treating these people just as they've treated their victims makes little sense.

Lastly, the guidance that lex talionis provides, when it does prescribe a punishment, is sometimes deeply immoral. It's a sad truth: any horror you can imagine people doing to one another has probably already been done. People have raped and tortured others, have burned whole families as they slept in their homes, have severed their limbs, tossed acid in their faces, and thrown handcuffed victims out of helicopters. Does morality really require that we do these things to the criminals who committed such deeds? We don't want official torturers, rapists, and arsonists on the state payroll. Legal punishment is the state's business, and we insist that the state meet certain minimum moral standards. A state that rapes its rapists is failing, miserably.

These three problems show that lex talionis cannot be the whole story about justice, because lex talionis sometimes fails to give advice when it is needed, and sometimes gives bad advice. This doesn't show that premise 2 is false. It may still be true that murderers deserve to die. But the classic defense of this claim is mistaken. If you believe in premise 2, your task is now to come up with a better defense than the one offered by lex talionis.

CONCLUSION

Abolitionists about capital punishment have offered several critiques that seek to undermine its moral legitimacy. The strongest of these are worries about systemic discrimination and the danger of killing innocents who have been wrongly convicted. Although these are very serious concerns, it isn't clear as yet that they can be fashioned into airtight arguments that threaten the morality of capital punishment. That said, the central arguments offered by deterrence theorists and retributivists are also vulnerable to criticisms. There is little evidence that the death penalty is an efficient deterrent, and the standard way to show that murderers deserve to die is deeply flawed. Given these

argumentative difficulties, how should we as a society respond? One principle says: maintain the status quo, until there is a compelling argument to shift from it. A different principle directs us to refrain from deliberately killing any of our citizens until we have a compelling argument that licenses such killing. Which of these do you find more plausible, and why?

ESSENTIAL CONCEPTS

Abolitionists: those who believe that the death penalty is not morally justified (and so seek to abolish it where it exists).

Aggravated murder: a murder that is made even more severe by especially violent or harmful circumstances in connection with the murder.

Aggravating conditions: features of a crime that increase its severity or harmful consequences.

Arbitrary: capricious, unprincipled, without a discernible rationale.

Capital offenses: those crimes that carry the death penalty as a possible punishment.

Capital punishment: the death penalty.

Death row: the part of a prison with cells for people sentenced to death.

Deterrence theory: the view that punishment is justified if, only if, and because it is an efficient way of preventing crime.

Discriminatory: marked by unjustified bias for or against a particular group.

General deterrence: using the threat of punishment to prevent crimes that might be committed by those other than the criminal himself.

Just deserts: what a person deserves.

Lethal injection: a method of executing a person by introducing deadly poison into his bloodstream.

Lex talionis: literally, the law of retaliation, which requires that one treat criminals in just the way they treated their victims.

Premeditated: planned or thought out in advance.

STAT SHOT

1. The United States has executed 1,455 prisoners since 1976 (Figure 20.1).

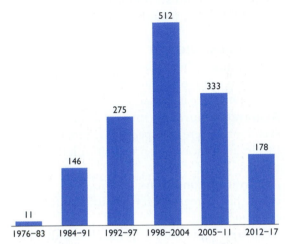

Figure 20.1.

Source: https://deathpenaltyinfo.org/documents/FactSheet.pdf

2. Five US states executed people in 2016. Georgia (nine executions) and Texas (seven executions) together were responsible for 80 percent of the twenty executions during the year.[1]

3. Since 1976, more than 155 people in twenty-seven states have been released from death row after courts reconsidered existing evidence or received new evidence of the prisoner's innocence.[2]

4. US citizens favor the death penalty more than they oppose it, but there are significant differences of opinion along gender, racial, and partisan lines (Figure 20.2).

1. https://www.amnesty.org/en/latest/news/2017/04/death-penalty-2016-facts-and-figures/

2. https://deathpenaltyinfo.org/documents/FactSheet.pdf

% who____ the death penalty for persons convicted of murder

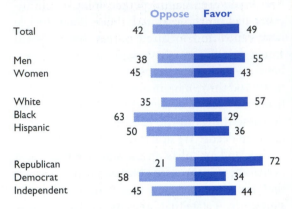

Note: Whites and blacks include only those who are not Hispanic; Hispanics are of any race. Don't know responses not shown.

Figure 20.2.

Source: http://www.pewresearch.org/fact-tank/2017/04/24/5-facts-about-the-death-penalty/

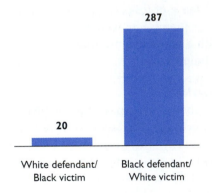

Figure 20.3

Source: https://deathpenaltyinfo.org/documents/FactSheet.pdf

5. Black people are executed for murdering white people much more often than white people are executed for murdering black people (Figure 20.3).

Retributivism: the view that punishment is justified if, only if, and because it gives a criminal his just deserts.

Special deterrence: using the threat of punishment to deter the criminal himself.

Unconstitutional: not permitted by, or in violation of, a country's political constitution.

Cases for Critical Thinking

The Pickax Murders

After binging on drugs for an entire weekend in June of 1983, Karla Faye Tucker and David Garrett broke into Jerry Dean's house and brutally murdered him by beating him over the head with a hammer and hacking him to death with a pickax. After Dean was dead, Tucker and Garrett noticed that another person, Deborah Thornton, was in the room and shivering under the bed covers. Tucker and Garrett proceeded to murder Thornton in the same way they murdered Dean. Far from showing remorse, Tucker bragged to her friends and would later testify in court that she experienced intense sexual satisfaction with each blow of the pickax. The case quickly became known worldwide for the events that followed.[1]

While awaiting her trial in jail, Tucker claimed to experience a powerful religious conversion. She was now a born-again Christian, she said. Though she originally pleaded not guilty to the murders, after her conversion, Tucker confessed and expressed deep sorrow and remorse for what she had done. She began counseling her fellow inmates and married the prison minister. Nevertheless, Tucker and Garrett were sentenced to death.

During the process of appealing her sentence, many people and organizations across the world asked the state of Texas to commute Tucker's sentence to life in prison. Among the supporters were Pope John Paul II, Jesse Jackson, televangelist Pat Robertson, the European

Parliament, and even Deborah Thornton's brother, Ronald Carlson. These appeals fell on deaf ears. Governor George W. Bush refused to block her execution and on February 3, 1998, Tucker was executed by lethal injection.

1. http://www.nytimes.com/1998/02/04/us/execution-texas-overview-divisive-case-killer-two-ends-texas-executes-tucker.html

Questions

1. Suppose Tucker's apparent change of heart was sincere and that she was enormously sorry for her past crimes. Suppose that she completely turned her life around and was, as she claimed during her trial, not a threat to society but rather a positive contributor. If so, should Tucker's sentence have been commuted to life in prison? More generally, should juries or legal officials consider whether an inmate is genuinely remorseful or rehabilitated when deliberating about whether to issue a death sentence? Why or why not?

2. Tucker and Garrett committed their crimes under the influence of powerful drugs. Does this fact affect what sort of sentence they ought to receive? Why or why not?

3. Many in the popular media were upset that the state of Texas would execute a woman. In the United States, women are executed much less often than men—only 16 of the 1,455 people executed since 1976 were women. Tucker was the first woman executed in the state of Texas since 1863. Do you think this disparity is indicative of a bias in favor of women when it comes to death sentences? Do you think this disparity should be corrected or is it appropriate? If you think the disparity should be corrected, how should it be done: by executing more women or by executing fewer men?

4. Tucker confessed to committing the murder. While false confessions do happen, Tucker's doesn't seem like a plausible candidate. Hers seems about as genuine as

they come. Should murderers be rewarded for confessing by being exempt from the death penalty? Or should those who confess be prime candidates for the death penalty since, one might think, we can be much more confident that those who confess are guilty?

Botched Executions

The people performing executions (in most countries, at least) try to make the process as painless as possible for the prisoner. But no human being is perfect and that includes the people who perform executions. Sometimes things go awry. These are called botched executions. A botched execution usually results in the death of the prisoner, but only after the prisoner experiences a prolonged period of pain and suffering. Other times, the execution fails entirely, so that the execution must be postponed for another day or canceled altogether.[1] In any case, when an execution is botched, things can get pretty gruesome.

For instance, Pedro Medina, who in 1997 was executed by electric chair in Florida, was subjected to two minutes of painful electrocution before he was killed. Witnesses reported that a "crown of foot-high flames shot from the headpiece during the execution, filling the execution chamber with a stench of thick smoke and gagging the two dozen official witnesses." Investigators later determined that the error was caused by "the improper application of a sponge" designed to conduct electricity to Medina's head.[2] Commenting on a different botched electrocution in Florida two years later, Florida Supreme Court Justice Leander Shaw commented that "The color photos of [the executed inmate] depict a man who—for all appearances—was brutally tortured to death by the citizens of Florida."[3]

Lethal injections can be botched, too. Usually it's because prison staff have difficulty finding a vein suitable for the catheter carrying the lethal drugs. This results in long periods, sometimes hours, of prison staff repeatedly sticking the inmate with a needle until they can locate a suitable vein. All the while the prisoner is left to contemplate his fate. Other times, the problem is that prison staff poke the needle all the way through the vein so that the lethal drugs are injected into soft tissue rather than the bloodstream. This is what happened to Angel Diaz in a 2006 execution in Florida. It took thirty-four minutes for the lethal drugs to finally stop Diaz's heart—plenty of time for the anesthesia to wear off and for Diaz to experience intense pain.[4]

1. http://www.cnn.com/2016/08/23/us/ohio-death-row-inmate-supreme-court/index.html

2. https://deathpenaltyinfo.org/some-examples-post-furman-botched-executions#_edn3

3. http://articles.chicagotribune.com/1999-10-27/news/9910270092_1_electric-chair-allen-lee-tiny-davis-thomas-provenzano

4. http://www.nbcnews.com/id/16241245/ns/us_news-crime_and_courts/t/botched-execution-likely-painful-doctors-say/

5. https://deathpenaltyinfo.org/some-examples-post-furman-botched-executions#_edn3

Questions

1. Does the treatment that Medina and Diaz received constitute cruel and unusual punishment? If not, what would it take for a punishment to qualify as cruel and unusual?

2. For each individual execution, the chances of botching it are small. But, over time, the chance that some execution or other will be botched and that a prisoner will endure extraordinary suffering is very high—a near certainty. There have been dozens of botched executions since 1979.[5] Does this fact affect how you think about the moral permissibility of the death penalty? Why or why not?

3. It's not a legal requirement for medical professionals to be present at an execution.

Nevertheless, states often have medical professionals on hand to help if anything goes wrong. Many in the medical profession think that doctors should refuse to participate in executions, since, in their view, helping to execute a prisoner violates a doctor's duty to heal, and not to harm, people under their care. Do you think doctors have a duty to refrain from participating in executions? Why or why not?

Jury Selection and Race

In 1986, Timothy Tyrone Foster, an eighteen-year-old African American man, brutally tortured and murdered Queen Madge White, an elderly white woman, in her home in Rome, Georgia. Her jaw was broken, she had gashes on the top of her head, and she had been sexually assaulted and strangled. Foster confessed to everything and was sentenced to death. Later, Foster challenged his sentence in a court of appeals, claiming that there was racial bias in the jury selection process for his sentencing. He claimed that prosecutors purposely struck all four black prospective jurors, leaving his sentencing to an all-white jury.[1]

1. https://www.nytimes.com/2016/05/24/us/supreme-court-black-jurors-death-penalty-georgia.html

Questions

1. It's well known that the United States has a history of racism and discrimination against African Americans. It's also well known that African Americans are significantly overrepresented in the death row population, while white people are significantly underrepresented. Given these facts, do you think it's fair for a black person to be sentenced to death by an all-white jury? If so, why? If not, why not? And what should be done to make the process fair?

2. The brutal nature of White's murder led many to speculate that Foster suffered from some sort of mental illness. Foster never received such a diagnosis. If, however, a doctor had diagnosed Foster with a mental illness that made him more likely to commit such a brutal murder, would that influence your view about what sort of punishment Foster ought to receive? Why or why not?

3. When Foster murdered White, he was eighteen years old. But suppose he had been a few months younger and was only seventeen. Would that influence your view about what punishment Foster ought to receive? More generally, should mature minors, or very young adults, be liable to receive the death penalty for brutal murders? Why or why not?

READINGS

On Deterrence and the Death Penalty
Ernst van den Haag

When deciding whether considerations of deterrence favor the death penalty, you might confront this argument from abolitionists:

1. The death penalty is morally justified only if there is substantial evidence that it is an effective deterrent.
2. We lack such evidence.

Therefore,

3. The death penalty is not morally justified.

Van den Haag rejects the first premise of this argument. He mentions, very briefly, that he is also attracted to a retributivist justification—he believes that the death penalty is justified because it gives murderers their just deserts. Perhaps more interesting, though, is that he accepts the second premise. He believes that, from a deterrence perspective, considerations of deterrence can justify imposing the death penalty even if we lack evidence that it does a good job at preventing crime.

He makes three points in defense of this view. The first is designed to prevent an error on the part of his critics, who sometimes claim that death's irrevocability means that we must have better evidence of its deterrent effects than we do for less severe penalties. Van den Haag replies that this is not so; all we need is reason to believe that the death penalty will yield more deterrence than a lesser penalty would. And, second, we do have such reason, in the form of this general principle: the more fearful a penalty is, the greater its deterrent effect. Most people fear death more than any other potential punishment, so we have reason to think that capital punishment is indeed a more effective deterrent than lesser punishments. Van den Haag's third point is that given our uncertainty about the deterrent effects of the death penalty, we are bound to be risking lives no matter whether we impose the death penalty or abolish it. Given that we are risking things either way, van den Haag believes that we should risk the life of a convicted murderer so as to spare the lives of potential innocent victims.

If rehabilitation and the protection of society from unrehabilitated offenders were the only purposes of legal punishment the death penalty could be abolished: it cannot attain the first end, and is not needed for the second. No case for the death penalty can be made unless "doing justice," or "deterring others," are among our penal aims. Each of these purposes can justify capital punishment by itself; opponents, therefore, must show that neither actually does, while proponents can rest their case on either.

Although the argument from justice is intellectually more interesting, and, in my view, decisive

From Ernst van den Haag, "On Deterrence and the Death Penalty," *The Journal of Criminal Law, Criminology, and Political Science* 60, no. 2 (1969), pp. 141–147. Reprinted by special permission of Northwestern University School of Law, *The Journal of Criminal Law and Criminology.* Notes have not been reprinted.

enough, utilitarian arguments have more appeal: the claim that capital punishment is useless because it does not deter others, is most persuasive. I shall, therefore, focus on this claim. . . .

For I doubt that the presence or absence of a deterrent effect of the death penalty is likely to be demonstrable by statistical means. . . .

It is on our uncertainty that the case for deterrence must rest. If we do not know whether the death penalty will deter others, we are confronted with two uncertainties. If we impose the death penalty, and achieve no deterrent effect thereby, the life of a convicted murderer has been expended in vain (from a deterrent viewpoint). There is a net loss. If we impose the death sentence and thereby deter some future murderers, we spared the lives of some future victims (the prospective murderers gain too; they are spared punishment because they were deterred). In this case, the death penalty has led to a net gain, unless the life of a convicted murderer is valued more highly than that of the unknown victim, or victims (and the non-imprisonment of the deterred non-murderer).

The calculation can be turned around, of course. The absence of the death penalty may harm no one and therefore produce a gain—the life of the convicted murderer. Or it may kill future victims of murderers who could have been deterred, and thus produce a loss—their life.

To be sure, we must risk something certain—the death (or life) of the convicted man, for something uncertain—the death (or life) of the victims of murderers who may be deterred. This is in the nature of uncertainty—when we invest, or gamble, we risk the money we have for an uncertain gain. Many human actions, most commitments—including marriage and crime—share this characteristic with the deterrent purpose of any penalization, and with its rehabilitative purpose (and even with the protective).

More proof is demanded for the deterrent effect of the death penalty than is demanded for the deterrent effect of other penalties. This is not justified by the absence of other utilitarian purposes such as protection and rehabilitation; they involve no less uncertainty than deterrence.

Irrevocability may support a demand for some reason to expect more deterrence than revocable penalties might produce, but not a demand for more proof of deterrence, as has been pointed out above. The reason for expecting more deterrence lies in the greater severity, the terrifying effect inherent in finality. Since it seems more important to spare victims than to spare murderers, the burden of proving that the greater severity inherent in irrevocability adds nothing to deterrence lies on those who oppose capital punishment. Proponents of the death penalty need show only that there is no more uncertainty about it than about greater severity in general.

The demand that the death penalty be proved more deterrent than alternatives cannot be satisfied any more than the demand that six years in prison be proved to be more deterrent than three. But the uncertainty which confronts us favors the death penalty as long as by imposing it we might save future victims of murder. This effect is as plausible as the general idea that penalties have deterrent effects which increase with their severity. Though we have no proof of the positive deterrence of the penalty, we also have no proof of zero, or negative effectiveness. I believe we have no right to risk additional future victims of murder for the sake of sparing convicted murderers; on the contrary, our moral obligation is to risk the possible ineffectiveness of executions. However rationalized, the opposite view appears to be motivated by the simple fact that executions are more subjected to social control than murder. However, this applies to all penalties and does not argue for the abolition of any.

Ernst van den Haag: On Deterrence and the Death Penalty

1. Van den Haag claims that we are not required to provide more proof of capital punishment's deterrent effect than of other punishments' deterrent effect. Can you think of a good reason to support this claim?
2. Is it true that the more fearful a punishment is, the more deterrence it will yield?
3. Explain the way (if any) in which the death penalty is uniquely irrevocable. Does this status impose any special argumentative burdens on defenders of the death penalty? If so, which ones?

4. Given that we are unsure of the deterrent effects of the death penalty, is it acceptable to take the life of a convict—a certain loss, according to van den Haag—for the chance that doing so will save innocent lives in the future? Why or why not?

5. Do you think it plausible to support the death penalty on deterrence grounds even if we are unsure of its deterrent effects? If your answer is yes, explain how your case agrees with or differs from van den Haag's. If your answer is no, defend your belief that such support is implausible.

Civilization, Safety, and Deterrence

Jeffrey H. Reiman

Jeffrey Reiman believes that murderers deserve to die. But he denies that the death penalty is morally justified. By sparing the life of a murderer, we communicate the great value of human life, the disvalue of pain, and the horror at allowing one person complete control over another. Reiman also believes that by sending this message, we will, over the long run, contribute to a society that is more civilized, more respectful of human life, and consequently less violent. In short, sparing the lives of convicted murderers may well have a deterrent effect.

Reiman devotes the bulk of this selection to critiquing Ernst van den Haag's claim that capital punishment is likely to be our most effective deterrent because it inspires more fear than any other punishment. Reiman identifies four grounds of suspicion.

First, a less fearful punishment may be fearful enough, and may deter all who can be deterred. Second, people assess risks in a very crude fashion, so even if people fear death more than other punishments, the prospect of facing death may not deter them from their criminal preparations. Third, while van den Haag claims that capital punishment deters by sending a message of the wrongness of murder, Reiman counters (as earlier) that refraining from executing murderers sends a civilizing message that stands an equal chance of preventing crime. Finally, Reiman alleges that van den Haag's argument proves too much. If it were sound, then we should torture people to death, since that is more feared than lethal injection; since we shouldn't torture people to death, it follows that van den Haag's argument is unsound.

. . . By placing execution alongside torture in the category of things we will not do to our fellow human beings even when they deserve them, we broadcast the message that totally subjugating a person to the power of others *and* confronting him with the advent of his own humanly administered demise is too horrible to be done by civilized human beings to their fellows even when they have earned it: too horrible to do, and too horrible to be capable of doing. And I contend that

From Jeffrey H. Reiman, "Civilization, Safety, and Deterrence," *Philosophy and Public Affairs* 14 (1985), pp. 142–147.

broadcasting this message loud and clear would in the long run contribute to the general detestation of murder and be, to the extent to which it worked itself into the hearts and minds of the populace, a deterrent. In short, refusing to execute murderers though they deserve it both reflects and continues the taming of the human species that we call civilization. Thus, I take it that the abolition of the death penalty, though it is a just punishment for murder, is part of the civilizing mission of modern states. . . .

. . . I said that judging a practice too horrible to do even to those who deserve it does not exclude the possibility that it could be justified if necessary to avoid even worse consequences. Thus, were the death penalty clearly proven a better deterrent to the murder of innocent people than life in prison, we might have to admit that we had not yet reached a level of civilization at which we could protect ourselves without imposing this horrible fate on murderers, and thus we might have to grant the necessity of instituting the death penalty. But this is far from proven. The available research by no means clearly indicates that the death penalty reduces the incidence of homicide more than life imprisonment does. . . .

Conceding that it has not been proven that the death penalty deters more murders than life imprisonment, van den Haag has argued that neither has it been proven that the death penalty does *not* deter more murders, and thus we must follow common sense which teaches that the higher the cost of something, the fewer people will choose it, and therefore at least some potential murderers who would not be deterred by life imprisonment will be deterred by the death penalty Van den Haag writes:

> . . . our experience shows that the greater the threatened penalty, the more it defers.
>
> . . . Life in prison is still life, however unpleasant. In contrast, the death penalty does not just threaten to make life unpleasant—it threatens to take life altogether. This difference is perceived by those affected. We find that when they have the choice between life in prison and execution, 99 percent of all prisoners under sentence of death prefer life in prison. . . .
>
> From this unquestioned fact a reasonable conclusion can be drawn in favor of the superior deterrent effect of the death penalty. Those who have the choice in practice . . . fear death more than they fear life in prison. . . . If they do, it follows that the threat of the death penalty, all other things equal, is likely to deter more than the threat of life in prison. One is most deterred by what one fears most. From which it follows that whatever statistics fail, or do not fail, to show, the death penalty is likely to be more deterrent than any other.[1]

Those of us who recognize how commonsensical it was, and still is, to believe that the sun moves around the earth, will be less willing than Professor van den Haag to follow common sense here, especially when it comes to doing something awful to our fellows. Moreover, there are good reasons for doubting common sense on this matter. Here are four:

1. From the fact that one penalty is more feared than another, it does not follow that the more feared penalty will deter more than the less feared, unless we know that the less feared penalty is not fearful enough to deter everyone who can be deterred—and this is just what we don't know with regard to the death penalty. Though I fear the death penalty more than life in prison, I can't think of any act that the death penalty would deter me from that an equal likelihood of spending my life in prison wouldn't deter me from as well. Since it seems to me that whoever would be deterred by a given likelihood of death would be deterred by an *equal* likelihood of life behind bars, I suspect that the commonsense argument only seems plausible because we evaluate it unconsciously assuming that potential criminals will face larger likelihoods of death sentences than of life sentences. If the likelihoods were equal, . . . where life imprisonment was improbable enough to make it too distant a possibility to worry much about, a similar low probability of

death would have the same effect. After all, we are undeterred by small likelihoods of death every time we walk the streets. And if life imprisonment were sufficiently probable to pose a real deterrent threat, it would pose as much of a deterrent threat as death. And this is just what most of the research we have on the comparative deterrent impact of execution versus life imprisonment suggests.

2. In light of the fact that roughly 500 to 700 suspected felons are killed by the police in the line of duty every year, and the fact that the number of privately owned guns in [the United States] is substantially larger than the number of households . . . , it must be granted that anyone contemplating committing a crime *already* faces a substantial risk of ending up dead. . . . It's hard to see why anyone *who is not already deterred by this* would be deterred by the addition of the more distant risk of death after apprehension, conviction, and appeal. Indeed, this suggests that people consider risks in a much cruder way than van den Haag's appeal to common sense suggests—which should be evident to anyone who contemplates how few people use seatbelts (14 percent of drivers, on some estimates), when it is widely known that wearing them can spell the difference between life (outside prison) and death.

3. Van den Haag has maintained that deterrence does not work only by means of cost-benefit calculations made by potential criminals. It works also by the lesson about the wrongfulness of murder that is slowly learned in a society that subjects murderers to the ultimate punishment.[2] But if I am correct in claiming that the refusal to execute even those who deserve it has a civilizing effect, then the refusal to execute also teaches a lesson about the wrongfulness of murder. My claim here is admittedly speculative, but no more so than van den Haag's to the contrary. [My] view has the added virtue of accounting for the failure of

research to show an increased deterrent effect from executions *without having to deny the plausibility of van den Haag's commonsense argument that at least some additional potential murders will be deterred by the prospect of the death penalty*. If there is a deterrent effect from *not executing*, then . . . while executions will deter some murderers, this effect will be balanced by the weakening of the deterrent effect of not executing, such that no net reduction in murders will result. And this . . . also disposes of van den Haag's argument that, in the absence of knowledge one way or the other on the deterrent effect of executions, we should execute murderers rather than risk the lives of innocent people whose murders might have been deterred. . . . If there is a deterrent effect of not executing, it follows that we risk innocent lives either way. And if this is so, it seems that the only reasonable course of action is to refrain from imposing what we know is a horrible fate.

4. Those who still think that van den Haag's commonsense argument for executing murderers is valid will find that the argument proves more than they bargained for. Van den Haag maintains that, in the absence of conclusive evidence on the relative deterrent impact of the death penalty versus life imprisonment, we must follow common sense and assume that if one punishment is more fearful than another, it will deter some potential criminals not deterred by the less fearful punishment. Since people sentenced to death will almost universally try to get their sentences changed to life in prison, it follows that death is more fearful than life imprisonment, and thus. . . will deter some additional murderers. Consequently, we should institute the death penalty to save the lives these additional murderers would have taken. But, since people sentenced to be tortured to death would surely try to get their sentences changed to simple execution, the same argument

proves that death-by-torture will deter still more potential murderers. Consequently, we should institute death-by-torture to save the lives these additional murderers would have taken. Anyone who accepts van den Haag's argument is then confronted with a dilemma: Until we have conclusive evidence that capital punishment is a greater deterrent to murder than life imprisonment, he must grant *either* that we should not follow common sense and not impose the death penalty; *or* we should follow common sense and torture murderers to death. In short, either we must abolish the electric chair or reinstitute the rack. Surely, this is the *reductio ad absurdum* of van den Haag's commonsense argument.

NOTES

1. Ernest van den Haag and John P. Conrad, *The Death Penalty: A Debate* (New York: Plenum Press, 1983), pp. 68–69.
2. Ibid., p. 63.

Jeffrey Reiman: Civilization, Safety, and Deterrence

1. Reiman claims that abolishing the death penalty advances the cause of civilization. Do you think he is right about that?
2. Do you think that abolishing the death penalty would have as much deterrent effect as retaining it? Why or why not?
3. Deterrence theorists argue that we should impose the least harmful punishment that can effectively deter crime. Does this thought help to answer Reiman's claim that van den Haag's argument proves too much?
4. There is plenty of evidence that people fail to assess risk in a rational way. How does Reiman use this evidence to argue against van den Haag? Are his critiques on this point sound?
5. Reiman claims that if the prospect of life imprisonment doesn't deter a would-be murderer, then the chance of the death penalty won't, either. Do you think Reiman is right about that? Why or why not?

Justifying Legal Punishment
Igor Primoratz

In this excerpt from his book *Justifying Legal Punishment* (1989), Igor Primoratz defends the retributivist idea that a punishment is justified only if it gives a criminal his just deserts. But what do criminals deserve? Primoratz argues for the following principle: criminals deserve to be deprived of the same value that they deprived their victims of. Primoratz regards all human beings as possessed of lives of equal moral worth, and also believes that nothing is as valuable as human life. So murderers deserve to die. Since justice is a matter of giving people what they deserve, it follows that justice demands that murderers be executed.

Primoratz considers the most popular arguments of the opposing camp and finds problems for each of them. Opponents claim that capital punishment violates a murderer's right to life; that killing murderers is contradictory; that capital punishment is disproportionally harsh; that the innocent are inevitably going to be executed; and that systematic discrimination undermines any chance at moral legitimacy.

Primoratz carefully considers each objection and offers his replies. In the end, he thinks that justice requires the death penalty, that justice is the supreme legal virtue, and that none of the objections is strong enough to undermine the case for capital punishment. Therefore the state ought to execute convicted murderers.

. . . According to the retributive theory, consequences of punishment, however important from the practical point of view, are irrelevant when it comes to its justification; *the* moral consideration is its justice. Punishment is morally justified insofar as it is meted out as retribution for the offense committed. When someone has committed an offense, he deserves to be punished: it is just, and consequently justified, that he be punished. The offense is the sole ground of the state's right and duty to punish. It is also the measure of legitimate punishment: the two ought to be proportionate. So the issue of capital punishment within the retributive approach comes down to the question, Is this punishment ever proportionate retribution for the offense committed, and thus deserved, just, and justified?

The classic representatives of retributivism believed that it was, and that it was the only proportionate and hence appropriate punishment, if the offense was *murder*—that is, criminal homicide perpetrated voluntarily and intentionally or in wanton disregard of human life. In other cases, the demand for proportionality between offense and punishment can be satisfied by fines or prison terms; the crime of murder, however, is an exception in this respect, and calls for the literal interpretation of the *lex talionis*. The uniqueness of this crime has to do with the uniqueness of the value which has been deliberately or recklessly destroyed. We come across this idea as early as the original formulation of the retributive view—the biblical teaching on punishment: "You shall accept no ransom for the life of a murderer who is guilty of death; but he shall be put to death."[1] The rationale of this command—one that clearly distinguishes the biblical conception of the criminal

From Igor Primoratz, *Justifying Legal Punishment* (Amherst, NY: Humanity Books, 1989), pp. 158–159, 161–166. Copyright © 1989 by Igor Primoratz. All rights reserved. Used with permission of the publisher; www.prometheusbooks.com.

law from contemporaneous criminal law systems in the Middle East—is that man was not only created *by* God, like every other creature, but also, alone among all the creatures, *in the image of God*:

> That man was made in the image of God . . . is expressive of the peculiar and supreme worth of man. Of all creatures, Genesis 1 relates, he alone possesses this attribute, bringing him into closer relation to God than all the rest and conferring upon him the highest value. . . . This view of the uniqueness and supremacy of human life . . . places life beyond the reach of other values. The idea that life may be measured in terms of money or other property . . . is excluded. Compensation of any kind is ruled out. The guilt of the murderer is infinite because the murdered life is invaluable; the kinsmen of the slain man are not competent to say when he has been paid for. An absolute wrong has been committed, a sin against God which is not subject to human discussion. . . . Because human life is invaluable, to take it entails the death penalty.[2]

This view that the value of human life is not commensurable with other values, and that consequently there is only one truly equivalent punishment for murder, namely death, does not necessarily presuppose a theistic outlook. It can be claimed that, simply because we have to be alive if we are to experience and realize any other value at all, there is nothing equivalent to the murderous destruction of a human life except the destruction of the life of the murderer. Any other retribution, no matter how severe, would still be less than what is proportionate, deserved, and just. As long as the murderer is alive, no matter how bad the conditions of his life may be, there are always at least *some* values he can experience and realize. This provides a plausible interpretation of what the classical representatives of retributivism as a philosophical theory of punishment, such as Kant and Hegel, had to say on the subject.[3]

It seems to me that this is essentially correct. With respect to the larger question of the justification of punishment in general, it is the retributive theory that gives the right answer. Accordingly, capital punishment ought to be retained where it obtains, and reintroduced in those jurisdictions that have abolished it, although we have no reason to believe that, as a means of deterrence, it is any better than a very long prison term. It ought to be retained, or reintroduced, for one simple reason: that justice be done in cases of murder, that murderers be punished according to their deserts.

There are a number of arguments that have been advanced against this rationale of capital punishment. . . .

[One] abolitionist argument . . . simply says that capital punishment is illegitimate because it violates the right to life, which is a fundamental, absolute, sacred right belonging to each and every human being, and therefore ought to be respected even in a murderer.

If any rights are fundamental, the right to life is certainly one of them; but to claim that it is absolute, inviolable under any circumstances and for any reason, is a different matter. If an abolitionist wants to argue his case by asserting an absolute right to life, she will also have to deny moral legitimacy to taking human life in war, revolution, and self-defense. This kind of pacifism is a consistent but farfetched and hence implausible position.

I do not believe that the right to life (nor, for that matter, any other right) is absolute. I have no general theory of rights to fall back upon here; instead, let me pose a question. Would we take seriously the claim to an absolute, sacred, inviolable right to life—coming from the mouth of a *confessed murderer*? I submit that we would not, for the obvious reason that it is being put forward by the person who confessedly denied another human being this very right. But if the murderer cannot plausibly claim such a right for himself, neither can *anyone else* do that in his behalf. This suggests that there is

an element of reciprocity in our general rights, such as the right to life or property. I can convincingly claim these rights only so long as I acknowledge and respect the same rights of others. If I violate the rights of others, I thereby lose the same rights. If I am a murderer, I have no *right* to live.

Some opponents of capital punishment claim that a criminal law system which includes this punishment is contradictory, in that it prohibits murder and at the same time provides for its perpetration: "It is one and the same legal regulation which prohibits the individual from murdering, while allowing the state to murder. . . . This is obviously a terrible irony, an abnormal and immoral logic, against which everything in us revolts."[4]

This seems to be one of the more popular arguments against the death penalty, but it is not a good one. If it were valid, it would prove too much. Exactly the same might be claimed of other kinds of punishment: of prison terms, that they are "contradictory" to the legal protection of liberty; of fines, that they are "contradictory" to the legal protection of property. Fortunately enough, it is not valid, for it begs the question at issue. In order to be able to talk of the state as "murdering" the person it executes, and to claim that there is "an abnormal and immoral logic" at work here, which thrives on a "contradiction," one has to use the word "murder" in the very same sense—that is, in the usual sense, which implies the idea of the *wrongful* taking the life of another—both when speaking of what the murderer has done to the victim and of what the state is doing to him by way of punishment. But this is precisely the question at issue: whether capital punishment *is* "murder," whether it is wrongful or morally justified and right.

The next two arguments attack the retributive rationale of capital punishment by questioning the claim that it is only this punishment that satisfies the demand for proportion between offense and punishment in the case of murder. The first points out that any two human lives are different in many important respects, such as age, health, physical and mental capability, so that it does not make much sense to consider them equally valuable. What if the murdered person was very old, practically at the very end of her natural life, while the murderer is young, with most of his life still ahead of him, for instance? Or if the victim was gravely and incurably ill, and thus doomed to live her life in suffering and hopelessness, without being able to experience almost anything that makes a human life worth living, while the murderer is in every respect capable of experiencing and enjoying things life has to offer? Or the other way round? Would not the death penalty in such cases amount either to taking a more valuable life as a punishment for destroying a less valuable one, or *vice versa*? Would it not be either too much, or too little, and in both cases disproportionate, and thus unjust and wrong, from the standpoint of the retributive theory itself?

Any plausibility this argument might appear to have is the result of a conflation of differences between, and value of, human lives. No doubt, any two human lives are *different* in innumerable ways, but this does not entail that they are not *equally valuable*. I have no worked-out general theory of equality to refer to here, but I do not think that one is necessary in order to do away with this argument. The modern humanistic and democratic tradition in ethical, social, and political thought is based on the idea that all human beings are equal. This finds its legal expression in the principle of equality of people under the law. If we are not willing to give up this principle, we have to stick to the assumption that, all differences notwithstanding, any two human lives, *qua* human lives, are equally valuable. If, on the other hand, we allow that, on the basis of such criteria as age, health, or mental or physical ability, it can be claimed that the life of one person is more or less valuable than the life of another, and we admit such claims in the sphere of law, including criminal law, we shall thereby give up the principle of equality of people under the law. In all consistency, we shall not be able to demand that property, physical and personal integrity, and all other rights and interests of individuals be given equal consideration in courts of law either—that is, we shall have to accept systematic discrimination between individuals on the basis of the same criteria across the whole field. I do not think anyone would seriously contemplate an overhaul of the whole legal system along these lines.

The second argument having to do with the issue of proportionality between murder and capital punishment draws our attention to the fact that the law normally provides for a certain period of time to elapse between the passing of a death sentence and its execution. It is a period of several weeks or months; in some cases it extends to years. This period is bound to be one of constant mental anguish for the condemned. And thus, all things considered, what is inflicted on him is disproportionately hard and hence unjust. It would be proportionate and just only in the case of "a criminal who had warned his victim of the date at which he would inflict a horrible death on him and who, from that moment onward, had confined him at his mercy for months."[5]

The first thing to note about this argument is that it does not support a full-fledged abolitionist stand; if it were valid, it would not show that capital punishment is *never* proportionate and just, but only that it is *very rarely* so. Consequently, the conclusion would not be that it ought to be abolished outright, but only that it ought to be restricted to those cases that would satisfy the condition cited above. Such cases do happen, although, to be sure, not very often; the murder of Aldo Moro, for instance, was of this kind. But this is not the main point. The main point is that the argument actually does not hit at capital punishment itself, although it is presented with that aim in view. It hits at something else: a particular way of carrying out this punishment, which is widely adopted in our time. Some hundred years ago and more, in the Wild West, they frequently hanged the man convicted to die almost immediately after pronouncing the sentence. I am not arguing here that we should follow this example today; I mention this piece of historical fact only in order to show that the interval between sentencing someone to death and carrying out the sentence is not a *part* of capital punishment itself. However unpalatable we might find those Wild West hangings, whatever objections we might want to voice against the speed with which they followed the sentencing, surely we shall not deny them the *description* of "executions." So the implication of the argument is not that we ought to do away with capital punishment altogether, nor that we ought to restrict it to those cases of murder where the murderer had warned the victim weeks or months in advance of what he was going to do to her, but that we ought to reexamine the procedure of carrying out this kind of punishment. We ought to weigh the reasons for having this interval between the sentencing and executing, against the moral and human significance of the repercussions such an interval inevitably carries with it.

These reasons, in part, have to do with the possibility of miscarriages of justice and the need to rectify them. Thus we come to the argument against capital punishment which, historically, has been the most effective of all: many advances of the abolitionist movement have been connected with discoveries of cases of judicial errors. Judges and jurors are only human, and consequently some of their beliefs and decisions are bound to be mistaken. Some of their mistakes can be corrected upon discovery; but precisely those with most disastrous repercussions—those which result in innocent people being executed—can never be rectified. In all other cases of mistaken sentencing we can revoke the punishment, either completely or in part, or at least extend compensation. In addition, by exonerating the accused we give moral satisfaction. None of this is possible after an innocent person has been executed; capital punishment is essentially different from all other penalties by being completely irrevocable and irreparable. Therefore, it ought to be abolished.

A part of my reply to this argument goes along the same lines as what I had to say on the previous one. It is not so far-reaching as abolitionists assume; for it would be quite implausible, even fanciful, to claim that there have *never* been cases of murder which left no room whatever for reasonable doubt as to the guilt and full responsibility of the accused. Such cases may not be more frequent than those others, but they do happen. Why not retain the death penalty at least for them?

Actually, this argument, just as the preceding one, does not speak out against capital punishment itself, but against the existing procedures for trying capital cases. Miscarriages of justice result in innocent people being sentenced to death and executed, even in the criminal-law systems in which greatest

care is taken to ensure that it never comes to that. But this does not stem from the intrinsic nature of the institution of capital punishment; it results from deficiencies, limitations, and imperfections of the criminal law procedures in which this punishment is meted out. Errors of justice do not demonstrate the need to do away with capital punishment; they simply make it incumbent on us to do everything possible to improve even further procedures of meting it out.

To be sure, this conclusion will not find favor with a diehard abolitionist. "I shall ask for the abolition of Capital Punishment until I have the infallibility of human judgement demonstrated to me," that is, as long as there is even the slightest possibility that innocent people may be executed because of judicial errors, Lafayette said in his day.[6] Many an opponent of this kind of punishment will say the same today. The demand to do away with capital punishment altogether, so as to eliminate even the smallest chance of that ever happening—the chance which, admittedly, would remain even after everything humanly possible has been done to perfect the procedure, although then it would be very slight indeed—is actually a demand to give a privileged position to murderers as against all other offenders, big and small. For if we acted on this demand, we would bring about a situation in which proportionate penalties would be meted out for all offenses, *except* for murder. Murderers would not be receiving the only punishment truly proportionate to their crimes, the punishment of death, but some other, lighter, and thus disproportionate penalty. All other offenders would be punished according to their deserts; only murderers would be receiving less than *they* deserve. In all other cases justice would be done in full; only in cases of the gravest of offenses, the crime of murder, justice would not be carried out in full measure. It is a great and tragic miscarriage of justice when an innocent person is mistakenly sentenced to death and executed, but systematically giving murderers advantage over all other offenders would also be a grave injustice. Is the fact that, as long as capital punishment is retained, there is a possibility that over a number of years, or even decades, an injustice of the first kind may be committed, unintentionally and unconsciously, reason enough to abolish it altogether, and thus end up with a system of punishments in which injustices of the second kind are perpetrated daily, consciously, and inevitably?

There is still another abolitionist argument that actually does not hit out against capital punishment itself, but against something else. Figures are sometimes quoted which show that this punishment is much more often meted out to the uneducated and poor than to the educated, rich, and influential people; in the United States, much more often to blacks than to whites. These figures are adduced as a proof of the inherent injustice of this kind of punishment. On account of them, it is claimed that capital punishment is not a way of doing justice by meting out deserved punishment to murderers, but rather a means of social discrimination and perpetuation of social injustice.

I shall not question these findings, which are quite convincing, and anyway, there is no need to do that in order to defend the institution of capital punishment. For there seems to be a certain amount of discrimination and injustice not only in sentencing people to death and executing them, but also in meting out other penalties. The social structure of the death rows in American prisons, for instance, does not seem to be basically different from the general social structure of American penitentiaries. If this argument were valid, it would call not only for abolition of the penalty of death, but for doing away with other penalties as well. But it is not valid; as Burton Leiser has pointed out,

> . . . this is not an argument, either against the death penalty or against any other form of punishment. It is an argument against the unjust and inequitable distribution of penalties. If the trials of wealthy men are less likely to result in convictions than those of poor men, then something must be done to reform the procedure in criminal courts. If those who have money and standing in the community are less likely to be charged with serious offenses than their less affluent fellow citizens, then there should be a major overhaul of the entire system of criminal justice. . . . But the

maldistribution of penalties is no argument against any particular form of penalty.[7]

NOTES

1. Numbers 35.31 (R.S.V.).
2. M. Greenberg, "Some Postulates of Biblical Criminal Law," in J. Goldin (ed.), *The Jewish Expression* (New York: Bantam, 1970), pp. 25–26. (Post-biblical Jewish law evolved toward the virtual abolition of the death penalty, but that is of no concern here.)
3. "There is no *parallel* between death and even the most miserable life, so that there is no equality of crime and retribution [in the case of murder] unless the perpetrator is judicially put to death" (I. Kant, "The Metaphysics of Morals," *Kant's Political Writings*, ed. H. Reiss, trans. H. B. Nisbet [Cambridge: Cambridge University Press, 1970], p. 156). "Since life is the full compass of a man's existence, the punishment [for murder] cannot simply consist in a 'value,' for none is great enough, but can consist only in taking away a second life" (G. W. F. Hegel, *Philosophy of Right*, trans. T. M. Knox [Oxford: Oxford University Press, 1965], p. 247).
4. S. V. Vulović, *Problem smrtne kazne* (Belgrade: Geca Kon, 1925), pp. 23–24.
5. A. Camus, "Reflections on the Guillotine," *Resistance, Rebellion and Death*, trans. J. O'Brien (London: Hamish Hamilton, 1961), p. 143.
6. Quoted in E. R. Calvert, *Capital Punishment in the Twentieth Century* (London: G. P. Putnam's Sons, 1927), p. 132.
7. B. M. Leiser, *Liberty, Justice and Morals: Contemporary Value Conflicts* (New York: Macmillan, 1973), p. 225.

Igor Primoratz: Justifying Legal Punishment

1. Retributivists such as Primoratz hold that the punishment of a crime ought to be proportional to the offense. Do you find such a view plausible? Are there any other morally relevant considerations when considering how someone should be punished?
2. Primoratz argues that the only punishment proportional to the offense of murder is the death penalty. What reasons does he give for thinking this? Do you think he is correct?

3. Some argue that capital punishment violates the right to life. Primoratz responds that the right to life is not "absolute." What does he mean by this, and how does he argue for it? Do you agree with him?

4. How does Primoratz respond to the objection that the death penalty is hypocritical because it involves killing people for the offense of killing other people? Do you find his response convincing?

5. Many people object to the death penalty on the grounds that it sometimes results in innocent people being executed, and is often applied in a discriminatory way. Why doesn't Primoratz think these concerns justify abolishing the death penalty? Do you agree?

An Eye for an Eye?

Stephen Nathanson

In this excerpt from his book *An Eye for an Eye?* (1987), Stephen Nathanson argues against the classic retributivist principle of punishment: lex talionis. This principle tells us to treat criminals just as they treated their victims—an eye for an eye, a tooth for a tooth. Nathanson finds two major problems for lex talionis. First, it advises us to commit highly immoral actions—raping a rapist, for instance, or torturing a torturer. Second, it is impossible to apply in many cases of deserved punishment—for instance, the principle offers no advice about what to do with drunk drivers, air polluters, embezzlers, or spies.

Retributivists might replace lex talionis with a principle of proportional punishment, according to which increasingly bad crimes must be met with increasingly harsher punishment. This proposal is plausible, says Nathanson, but it offers no justification for the death penalty. All it tells us is that the worst crimes ought to be met with the harshest punishments. But it says nothing about how harsh those punishments should be.

Nathanson concludes by discussing the symbolism of abolishing the death penalty, and claims that we express a respect for each person's inalienable rights by refraining from depriving a murderer of his life.

Suppose we . . . try to determine what people deserve from a strictly moral point of view. How shall we proceed?

The most usual suggestion is that we look at a person's actions because what someone deserves would appear to depend on what he or she does.

From Stephen Nathanson, *An Eye for an Eye?* (Totowa, NJ: Rowman and Littlefield, 1987), pp. 72–77, 138–140, 145.

A person's actions, it seems, provide not only a basis for a moral appraisal of the person but also a guide to how he should be treated. According to the *lex talionis* or principle of "an eye for an eye," we ought to treat people as they have treated others. What people deserve as recipients of rewards or punishments is determined by what they do as agents.

This is a powerful and attractive view, one that appears to be backed not only by moral common sense but also by tradition and philosophical thought. The most famous statement of philosophical support for this view comes from Immanuel Kant, who linked it directly with an argument for the death penalty. Discussing the problem of punishment, Kant writes,

> What kind and what degree of punishment does legal justice adopt as its principle and standard? None other than the principle of equality . . . the principle of not treating one side more favorably than the other. Accordingly, any undeserved evil that you inflict on someone else among the people is one that you do to yourself. If you vilify, you vilify yourself; if you steal from him, you steal from yourself; if you kill him, you kill yourself. Only the law of retribution (*jus talionis*) can determine exactly the kind and degree of punishment.[1]

Kant's view is attractive for a number of reasons. First, it accords with our belief that what a person deserves is related to what he does. Second, it appeals to a moral standard and does not seem to rely on any particular legal or political institutions. Third, it seems to provide a measure of appropriate punishment that can be used as a guide to creating laws and instituting punishments. It tells us that the punishment is to be identical with the crime. Whatever the criminal did to the victim is to be done in turn to the criminal.

In spite of the attractions of Kant's view, it is deeply flawed. When we see why, it will be clear that the whole "eye for an eye" perspective must be rejected.

PROBLEMS WITH THE EQUAL PUNISHMENT PRINCIPLE

. . . [Kant's view] does not provide an adequate criterion for determining appropriate levels of punishment.

. . . We can see this, first, by noting that for certain crimes, Kant's view recommends punishments that are not morally acceptable. Applied strictly, it would require that we rape rapists, torture torturers, and burn arsonists whose acts have led to deaths. In general, where a particular crime involves barbaric and inhuman treatment, Kant's principle tells us to act barbarically and inhumanly in return. So, in some cases, the principle generates unacceptable answers to the question of what constitutes appropriate punishment.

This is not its only defect. In many other cases, the principle tells us nothing at all about how to punish. While Kant thought it obvious how to apply his principle in the case of murder, his principle cannot serve as a general rule because it does not tell us how to punish many crimes. Using the Kantian version or the more common "eye for an eye" standard, what would we decide to do to embezzlers, spies, drunken drivers, airline hijackers, drug users, prostitutes, air polluters, or persons who practice medicine without a license? If one reflects on this question, it becomes clear that there is simply no answer to it. We could not in fact design a system of punishment simply on the basis of the "eye for an eye" principle.

In order to justify using the "eye for an eye" principle to answer our question about murder and the death penalty, we would first have to show that it worked for a whole range of cases, giving acceptable answers to questions about amounts of punishment. Then, having established it as a satisfactory general principle, we could apply it to the case of murder. It turns out, however, that when we try to apply the principle generally, we find that it either gives wrong answers or no answers at all. Indeed, I suspect that the principle of "an eye for an eye" is no longer even a principle. Instead, it is simply a metaphorical disguise for expressing belief in the death penalty. People who cite it do not take it seriously. They do not believe in a kidnapping for a kidnapping, a theft for a theft, and so on. Perhaps "an eye for an eye" once was a genuine principle, but now it is merely a slogan. Therefore, it gives us no guidance in deciding whether murderers deserve to die.

In reply to these objections, one might defend the principle by saying that it does not require that punishments be strictly identical with crimes. Rather, it requires only that a punishment produce an amount of suffering in the criminal which is equal to the amount suffered by the victim. Thus, we don't have to hijack airplanes belonging to airline hijackers, spy on spies, etc. We simply have to reproduce in them the harm done to others.

Unfortunately, this reply really does not solve the problem. It provides no answer to the first objection, since it would still require us to behave barbarically in our treatment of those who are guilty of barbaric crimes. Even if we do not reproduce their actions exactly, any action which caused equal suffering would itself be barbaric. Second, in trying to produce equal amounts of suffering, we run into many problems. Just how much suffering is produced by an airline hijacker or a spy? And how do we apply this principle to prostitutes or drug users, who may not produce any suffering at all? We have rough ideas about how serious various crimes are, but this may not correlate with any clear sense of just how much harm is done.

Furthermore, the same problem arises in determining how much suffering a particular punishment would produce for a particular criminal. People vary in their tolerance of pain and in the amount of unhappiness that a fine or a jail sentence would cause them. Recluses will be less disturbed by banishment than extroverts. Nature lovers will suffer more in prison than people who are indifferent to natural beauty. A literal application of the principle would require that we tailor punishments to individual sensitivities, yet this is at best impractical. To a large extent, the legal system must work with standardized and rather crude estimates of the negative impact that punishments have on people.

The move from calling for a punishment that is identical to the crime to favoring one that is equal in the harm done is no help to us or to the defense of the principle. "An eye for an eye" tells us neither what people deserve nor how we should treat them when they have done wrong.

PROPORTIONAL RETRIBUTIVISM

The view we have been considering can be called "equality retributivism," since it proposes that we repay criminals with punishments equal to their crimes. In the light of problems like those I have cited, some people have proposed a variation on this view, calling not for equal punishments but rather for punishments which are *proportional* to the crime. In defending such a view as a guide for setting criminal punishments, Andrew von Hirsch writes:

> If one asks how severely a wrongdoer deserves to be punished, a familiar principle comes to mind:

Severity of punishment should be commensurate with the seriousness of the wrong. Only grave wrongs merit severe penalties; minor misdeeds deserve lenient punishments. Disproportionate penalties are undeserved—severe sanctions for minor wrongs or vice versa. This principle has variously been called a principle of "proportionality" or "just deserts"; we prefer to call it commensurate deserts.[2]

Like Kant, von Hirsch makes the punishment which a person deserves depend on that person's actions, but he departs from Kant in substituting proportionality for equality as the criterion for setting the amount of punishment.

In implementing a punishment system based on the proportionality view, one would first make a list of crimes, ranking them in order of seriousness. At one end would be quite trivial offenses like parking meter violations, while very serious crimes such as murder would occupy the other. In between, other crimes would be ranked according to their relative gravity. Then a corresponding scale of punishments would be constructed, and the two would be correlated. Punishments would be proportionate to crimes so long as we could say that the more serious the crime was, the higher on the punishment scale was the punishment administered.

This system does not have the defects of equality retributivism. It does not require that we treat those guilty of barbaric crimes barbarically. This is because we can set the upper limit of the punishment scale so as to exclude truly barbaric punishments. Second, unlike the equality principle, the proportionality view is genuinely general, providing a way of handling all crimes. Finally, it does justice to our ordinary belief that certain punishments are unjust because they are too severe or too lenient for the crime committed.

The proportionality principle does, I think, play a legitimate role in our thinking about punishments. Nonetheless, it is no help to death penalty advocates, because it does not require that murderers be executed. All that it requires is that if murder is the most serious crime, then murder should be punished by the most severe punishment on the scale. The principle does not tell us what this punishment should be, however, and it is quite compatible with the view that the most severe punishment should be a long prison term.

This failure of the theory to provide a basis for supporting the death penalty reveals an important gap in proportional retributivism. It shows that while the theory is general in scope, it does not yield any *specific* recommendations regarding punishment. It tells us, for example, that armed robbery should be punished more severely than embezzling and less severely than murder, but it does not tell us how much to punish any of these. This weakness is, in effect, conceded by von Hirsch, who admits that if we want to implement the "commensurate deserts" principle, we must supplement it with information about what level of punishment is needed to deter crimes.[3] In a later discussion of how to "anchor" the punishment system, he deals with this problem in more depth, but the factors he cites as relevant to making specific judgments (such as available prison space) have nothing to do with what people deserve. He also seems to suggest that a range of punishments may be appropriate for a particular crime. This runs counter to the death penalty supporter's sense that death alone is appropriate for some murderers.[4]

Neither of these retributive views, then, provides support for the death penalty. The equality principle fails because it is not in general true that the appropriate punishment for a crime is to do to the criminal what he has done to others. In some cases this is immoral, while in others it is impossible. The proportionality principle may be correct, but by itself it cannot determine specific punishments for specific crimes. Because of its flexibility and open-endedness, it is compatible with a great range of different punishments for murder.[5] . . .

THE SYMBOLISM OF ABOLISHING THE DEATH PENALTY

What is the symbolic message that we would convey by deciding to renounce the death penalty and to abolish its use?

I think that there are two primary messages. The first is the most frequently emphasized and is usually expressed in terms of the sanctity of human life, although I think we could better express it in terms of respect for human dignity. One way we express our respect for the dignity of human beings is by abstaining from depriving them of their lives, even if they have done terrible deeds. In defense of human well-being, we may punish people for their crimes, but we ought not to deprive them of everything, which is what the death penalty does.

If we take the life of a criminal, we convey the idea that by his deeds he has made himself worthless and totally without human value. I do not believe that we are in a position to affirm that of anyone. We may hate such a person and feel the deepest anger against him, but when he no longer poses a threat to anyone, we ought not to take his life.

But, one might ask, hasn't the murderer forfeited whatever rights he might have had to our respect? Hasn't he, by his deeds, given up any rights that he had to decent treatment? Aren't we morally free to kill him if we wish?

These questions express important doubts about the obligation to accord any respect to those who have acted so deplorably, but I do not think that they prove that any such forfeiture has occurred. Certainly, when people murder or commit other crimes, they do forfeit some of the rights that are possessed by the law-abiding. They lose a certain right to be left alone. It becomes permissible to bring them to trial and, if they are convicted, to impose an appropriate—even a dreadful—punishment on them.

Nonetheless, they do not forfeit all their rights. It does not follow from the vileness of their actions that we can do anything whatsoever to them. This is part of the moral meaning of the constitutional ban on cruel and unusual punishments. No matter how terrible a person's deeds, we may not punish him in a cruel and unusual way. We may not torture him, for example. His right not to be tortured has not been forfeited. Why do these limits hold? Because this person remains a human being, and we think that there is something in him that we must continue to respect in spite of his terrible acts.

One way of seeing why those who murder still deserve some consideration and respect is by reflecting again on the idea of what it is to *deserve* something. In most contexts, we think that what people deserve depends on what they have done, intended, or tried to do. It depends on features that are qualities of individuals. The best person for the job deserves to be hired. The person who worked especially hard deserves our gratitude. We can call the concept that applies in these cases *personal desert*.

There is another kind of desert, however, that belongs to people by virtue of their humanity itself and does not depend on their individual efforts or achievements. I will call this impersonal kind of desert *human* desert. We appeal to this concept when we think that everyone deserves a certain level of treatment no matter what their individual qualities are. When the signers of the Declaration of Independence affirmed that people had inalienable rights to "life, liberty, and the pursuit of happiness," they were appealing to such an idea. These rights do not have to be earned by people. They are possessed "naturally," and everyone is bound to respect them.

According to the view that I am defending, people do not lose all of their rights when they commit terrible crimes. They still deserve some level of decent treatment simply because they remain living, functioning human beings. This level of moral desert need not be earned, and it cannot be forfeited. This view may sound controversial, but in fact everyone who believes that cruel and unusual punishment should be forbidden implicitly agrees with it. That is, they agree that even after someone has committed a terrible crime, we do not have the right to do anything whatsoever to him.

What I am suggesting is that by renouncing the use of death as a punishment, we express and reaffirm our belief in the inalienable, unforfeitable core of human dignity.

Why is this a worthwhile message to convey? It is worth conveying because this belief is both important and precarious. Throughout history, people have found innumerable reasons to degrade the humanity of one another. They have found qualities in others that they hated or feared, and even when they were not threatened by these people, they have sought to harm them, deprive them of their liberty, or take their lives from them. They have often felt that they had good reasons to do these things, and they have invoked divine commands, racial purity, and state security to support their deeds.

These actions and attitudes are not relics of the past. They remain an awful feature of the contemporary world. By renouncing the death penalty, we show our determination to accord at least minimal respect even to those whom we believe to be personally vile or morally vicious. This is, perhaps, why we speak of the *sanctity* of human life rather than its value or worth. That which is sacred remains, in some sense, untouchable, and its value is not dependent on its worth or usefulness to us. Kant expressed this ideal of respect in the famous second version of the Categorical Imperative: "So act as to treat humanity, whether in thine own person or in that of any other, in every case as an end withal, never as a means only." . . .

When the state has a murderer in its power and could execute him but does not, this conveys the idea that even though this person has done wrong and even though we may be angry, outraged, and indignant with him, we will nonetheless control ourselves in a way that he did not. We will not kill him, even though we could do so and even though we are angry and indignant. We will exercise restraint, sanctioning killing only when it serves a protective function.

Why should we do this? Partly out of a respect for human dignity. But also because we want the state to set an example of proper behavior. We do not want to encourage people to resort to violence to settle conflicts when there are other ways available. We want to avoid the cycle of violence that can come from retaliation and counter-retaliation. Violence is a contagion that arouses hatred and anger, and if unchecked, it simply leads to still more violence. The state can convey the message that the contagion must be stopped, and the most effective principle for stopping it is the idea that only defensive violence is justifiable. Since the death penalty is not an instance of defensive violence, it ought to be renounced.

We show our respect for life best by restraining ourselves and allowing murderers to live, rather than by following a policy of a life for a life. Respect for life and restraint of violence are aspects of the same ideal. The renunciation of the death penalty would symbolize our support of that ideal.

NOTES

1. Kant, *Metaphysical Elements of Justice*, translated by John Ladd (Indianapolis: Bobbs-Merrill, 1965), p. 101.

2. *Doing Justice* (New York: Hill & Wang, 1976), p. 66; reprinted in *Sentencing*, edited by H. Gross and A. von Hirsch (Oxford University Press, 1981), p. 243. For a more recent discussion and further defense by von Hirsch, see his *Past or Future Crimes* (New Brunswick, N.J.: Rutgers University Press, 1985).

3. Von Hirsch, *Doing Justice*, pp. 93–94. My criticisms of proportional retributivism are not novel. For helpful discussions of the view, see Hugo Bedau, "Concessions to Retribution in Punishment," in *Justice and Punishment*, edited by J. Cederblom and W. Blizek (Cambridge, Mass.: Ballinger, 1977), and M. Golding, *Philosophy of Law* (Englewood Cliffs, N.J.: Prentice Hall, 1975), pp. 98–99.

4. See von Hirsch, *Past or Future Crimes*, ch. 8.

5. For more positive assessments of these theories, see Jeffrey Reiman, "Justice, Civilization, and the Death Penalty," *Philosophy and Public Affairs* 14 (1985): 115–48; and Michael Davis, "How to Make the Punishment Fit the Crime," *Ethics* 93 (1983).

Stephen Nathanson: An Eye for an Eye?

1. Nathanson rejects the principle of lex talionis, according to which we ought to treat criminals as they have treated others. What reasons does he give for rejecting this principle? Do you find his reasons convincing?

2. Nathanson considers the following modification of the principle of lex talionis: "a punishment [should] produce an amount of suffering in the criminal which is equal to the amount suffered by the victim." Do you think this is a plausible principle? What objections does Nathanson offer to the principle?

3. What is the principle of proportional retributivism? Why doesn't Nathanson think that this principle supports the death penalty? Do you agree with him?

4. What symbolic message does Nathanson think that abolishing the death penalty would convey? Is this a good reason to abolish the death penalty?

5. Are there any reasons for supporting the death penalty that Nathanson does not consider? If so, are these reasons ever strong enough to justify sentencing someone to death?

CHAPTER 21

Drugs

JUST THE FACTS

Drugs are chemicals that, when introduced into the bloodstream (e.g., by drinking, smoking, snorting, injecting), predictably alter the way we feel. We'll focus specifically on recreational drugs—those used to have fun, rather than for medical purposes.

Recreational drugs fall into four broad categories: depressants, stimulants, opioids, and psychedelics. Depressants, colloquially known as "downers," produce a feeling of calmness and relaxation. These include substances such as alcohol, marijuana, Xanax, Valium, Ambien, and ketamine. Stimulants, by contrast, also known as "uppers," enhance users' concentration and give them a sense of energy and alertness. These include caffeine, nicotine, Adderall, MDMA (ecstasy), cocaine, and methamphetamine. Opioids, such as morphine, heroin, fentanyl, methadone, oxycodone, and hydrocodone, are a family of drugs that function as painkillers. With the exceptions of heroin, these drugs usually enter circulation by being prescribed by a doctor. Finally, psychedelics give users what's often described as a "trippy" experience, altering or heightening their visual and auditory experiences and giving them an enhanced sense of openness. Psychedelics include LSD, mescaline (peyote's active ingredient), DMT, and hallucinogenic mushrooms.

One of the major concerns people have about drugs is **drug addiction**—a chronic disease characterized by drug seeking and use that is compulsive, or difficult to control, despite harmful consequences.[1] Most recreational drugs work by affecting the brain's reward circuit, flooding it with the chemical messenger dopamine. This overstimulation of the reward circuit causes the intensely pleasurable "high" that leads users to take a drug again and again. Over time, the brain adjusts to the excess dopamine, thereby reducing the high that users feel compared to the high they felt when they first started taking the drug—an effect known as **tolerance**. Addicts eventually become physically dependent on their drug of choice. When they go for a while without it, they begin to exhibit symptoms of withdrawal—anxiety, fatigue, vomiting, depression, seizures, or hallucinations associated with denying the body a substance on which it depends. To avoid these symptoms, and to achieve their usual high, users take more of their drug of choice. Thus begins a vicious cycle of taking more drugs, building more tolerance, becoming more addicted, and taking still more drugs. Too often, the cycle ends in lethal **overdose**. Drug overdose is the leading cause of accidental death in the United States, with 52,404 lethal drug overdoses in 2015.[2]

Recently, the United States has seen a significant increase in drug overdoses due to opioids, especially prescription painkillers. The United States makes up 4 percent of the world's population but consumes 75 percent of the world's prescription drugs.[3] More than 15 million

---

1. https://www.drugabuse.gov/publications/drugfacts/understanding-drug-use-addiction

2. https://www.asam.org/docs/default-source/advocacy/opioid-addiction-disease-facts-figures.pdf

3. https://www.cnbc.com/2016/04/27/americans-consume-almost-all-of-the-global-opioid-supply.html

Americans abuse prescription drugs, and 52 million Americans over the age of twelve have used prescription drugs nonmedically in their lifetime.[4] The use of heroin, a cheaper alternative to prescription opioids, rose by 75 percent between 2007 and 2011. Four in five new heroin users started out misusing prescription painkillers. As a result, the number of men who lost their lives to opioid overdoses rose 250 percent between 1999 and 2010. For women, that number increased even more dramatically—rising 415 percent in the same period.

While opioid use is on the rise, by far the most used and abused drug across the world is alcohol. One in six US adults **binge drinks**—that is, drinks heavily in a short time to get severely intoxicated—about four times a month, consuming about eight drinks per binge.[5] According to a 2015 study, 26.9 percent of people aged eighteen or older reported that they engaged in binge drinking in the past month. Also, 15.1 million adults ages eighteen and older (6.2 percent of this age group) had alcohol use disorder (AUD)—9.8 million men and 5.3 million women. About 1.3 million of these adults received treatment for AUD at a specialized facility; this represents only 8.3 percent of adults who needed treatment.[6] An estimated 88,000 people die from alcohol-related causes annually, making alcohol the fourth leading preventable cause of death in the United States.

The abuse of alcohol has brought with it enormous costs. According to the Centers for Disease Control and Prevention, drinking too much, including binge drinking, cost the United States $249 billion in 2010. These costs resulted from losses in workplace productivity, health care expenditures, criminal justice costs, and other expenses. Binge drinking was responsible for 77 percent of these costs—about $191 billion.[7]

After alcohol, marijuana is the most commonly used drug in the United States In 2013, there were 19.8 million marijuana users in the United States—about 7.5 percent of people aged twelve or older.[8] The drug is now legal in nine states—Alaska, California, Colorado, Maine, Massachusetts, Nevada, Oregon, Vermont, and Washington—and the District of Columbia. As with many drugs in the United States, most of the supply of marijuana comes from Mexico. Mexican drug cartels are estimated to earn between $19 billion and $29 billion annually from the United States.[9] As a result, violence associated with the drug trade is a major problem in Mexico. For instance, since the beginning (in 2006) of Mexico's war on drugs, an estimated 200,000 people have been killed and 28,000 are missing. In the first ten months of 2016 alone, there were more than 17,000 reported homicides.[10]

A very large number of people in America are incarcerated for drug crimes. According to the Bureau of Prisons, 207,847 people were incarcerated in federal prisons in 2015. Roughly half (48.6 percent) were in for drug offenses.[11] The average prison sentence for federal drug offenders was more than eleven years. Almost all (99.5 percent) drug offenders in federal prison

4. http://www.drugfreeworld.org/drugfacts/prescription/abuse-international-statistics.html

5. https://www.cdc.gov/alcohol/fact-sheets/binge-drinking.htm

6. https://www.niaaa.nih.gov/alcohol-health/overview-alcohol-consumption/alcohol-facts-and-statistics

7. https://www.niaaa.nih.gov/alcohol-health/overview-alcohol-consumption/alcohol-facts-and-statistics

8. https://www.drugabuse.gov/publications/drugfacts/nationwide-trends

9. https://borgenproject.org/facts-about-mexican-drug-cartels/

10. https://borgenproject.org/facts-about-mexican-drug-cartels/

11. https://fivethirtyeight.com/features/releasing-drug-offenders-wont-end-mass-incarceration/

were serving sentences for drug trafficking—not simple possession or use.[12]

The punishment for drug crimes falls disproportionately on people of color. For instance, black people make up 50 percent of the state and local prisoners incarcerated for drug crimes. And black youth (under eighteen) are 10 times more likely to be arrested for drug crimes than white youths—even though white youths are more likely to abuse drugs.[13]

In 2013, the United States spent $25.6 billion on drug prevention and law enforcement; $15 billion of that went to law enforcement, interdiction, and international efforts.[14] The pro-reform Drug Policy Alliance estimates that when we combine state and local spending on everything from drug-related arrests to prison, the total cost adds up to at least $51 billion per year. Over four decades, the group says, enforcing drug laws has cost American taxpayers about $1 trillion.[15]

ARGUMENT ANALYSIS

When discussing the morality of drugs, it is essential to make at least two important distinctions. The first is between the *morality* and *legality* of drug use. The moral status of drug use is one thing; its legal status, another. We can ask whether drug use is itself immoral; we can also ask whether laws that prohibit such use are immoral. As we will see, many believe that there should be tight connections between our answers to these questions, though others disagree, and think that even if there is nothing immoral about drug use, laws that prohibit such use are morally acceptable.

12. https://www.bjs.gov/content/pub/pdf/dofp12.pdf

13. http://www.sentencingproject.org/publications/racial-disparities-in-youth-commitments-and-arrests/

14. http://www.huffingtonpost.com/2013/04/08/drug-war-mass-incarceration_n_3034310.html

15. http://www.huffingtonpost.com/2013/04/08/drug-war-mass-incarceration_n_3034310.html

The second distinction is between drug *use*, on the one hand, and a drug's *manufacture and sale*, on the other. As we will see, it is possible to have one set of views about the morality of drug use and the laws that regulate such use, while having a quite different set of opinions about the morality and legality of making and selling drugs. For instance, though there has been relatively little public discussion of this option, one might think that drug use is morally acceptable and should be decriminalized, while also arguing that its sale and manufacture are immoral and ought to be illegal.

In the discussion that follows, we'll focus primarily (but not exclusively) on this question: should drug use be criminalized? As we'll see, addressing this question requires us to consider the morality of drug use as well.

Let's begin with those who defend the idea that laws prohibiting drug use are morally justified. One reason that is often offered in support of criminalization is that drug use leads to a great deal of harm to others. People under the influence engage in all sorts of harmful behavior. And a desire or need for drugs among those who can't pay for their habit often leads to theft, robbery, battery, and assault. These concerns can be expressed in

The Harm to Others Argument

1. If an activity ordinarily imposes serious and wrongful harm on others, then it is rightly outlawed.
2. Drug use ordinarily imposes wrongful harm on others.

Therefore,

3. Drug use is rightly outlawed.

Premise 1 is plausible, but only because it includes its qualifications about the kind of harm that triggers criminalization. That an action *occasionally* harms someone else does not by itself justify legal prohibition—after all, driving a car occasionally leads to serious harm to others, but this doesn't justify a legal ban on driving. Indeed, that a kind of action *ordinarily* harms others is still not enough to justify criminalizing it—football players routinely harm one another, but since they have consented to the risks, this should be enough to protect them from going to jail for playing their sport. We need to show something more: namely, that that the harms occur with some frequency, and that those harms are also **wrongs**—violations of rights. Even this is not enough, however. If those wrongful harms are of only minor importance, then it's best not to get the law involved. But if the wrongful harms are serious ones, then it is appropriate to make them illegal.

Premise 2, though, isn't very plausible. It's true, of course, that drug users under the influence do sometimes wrongfully harm others. But they very often do not. Further, the wrongful harms do not consist of taking drugs—that in itself violates no one's rights. The wrongs occur when a user, under the influence, commits actions that are already criminalized. To see why this is important, consider that people under the influence of alcohol sometimes drive drunk, beat their spouses, or start fights at bars. Such behavior should be outlawed, whether it is fueled by alcohol or not. But having a glass of wine with a meal, or a bourbon after dinner, is not itself an action that wrongfully harms others. Drinking alcohol violates no one's rights. The same can be said about the use of other drugs.

That said, suppose that there was a drug that reliably caused its users to become violent or terribly reckless toward others. Even if the use of that drug did not itself violate anyone's rights, still, it would ordinarily lead to behavior that *did* wrongfully harm others. In that case, premise 2 would be true of such a drug; assuming the truth of premise 1, we would have a sound argument in support of some drug criminalization.

But most drugs do *not* routinely lead users to harm others. It's true that some addicts may, in desperation, rob or steal from others in order to support their habit. But that is not itself a strong reason to criminalize drug use. After all, this sort of desperate behavior is true of most kinds of addiction. Some sex addicts rob and steal in order to pay for their habit—we should not thereby criminalize sex. Once again, we should criminalize the behavior that itself wrongfully harms others—robbery and theft, for instance—but this does not yet provide any reason to criminalize most drug use, which is only occasionally linked with these wrongs.

Another reason offered in support of criminalizing drug use is that people often harm *themselves* when using drugs, and it is the state's job to protect people from such dangerous behavior. The list of such harms is substantial: one might die from an overdose, suffer cognitive damage, degrade one's personality, or ruin oneself financially. If the state can prevent its citizens from suffering such fates, shouldn't it do so?

That question reveals a commitment to the idea that **paternalism** is a legitimate goal of the criminal law. Paternalism has us limit the liberty of others, for their own good, against their will. In this case, advocates of drug criminalization argue that laws prohibiting drug use will spare thousands of users the terrible outcomes just mentioned. That thought underlies

The Paternalism Argument

1. Most drug users are subject to a significant chance of serious harm from their drug use.
2. The government should prohibit people from doing things that threaten a significant chance of serious harm to themselves.

Therefore,

3. The government should prohibit drug use.

Premise 1 is true of many drugs, though it is false of others. Let's focus on those drugs that do pose a serious threat (heroin and other opioids, for instance). On behalf of premise 2, many think of the government's proper role in consequentialist terms—the purpose of government is to do what it can to minimize harm to its citizens, and this includes self-harm, as well as harm to others. This is what permits the government to require that we wear seat belts, that motorcyclists use helmets, and that boat owners have life vests on board.

Despite the substantial good that has been achieved by these laws, they represent a contentious vision of the state's proper role. (For more discussion of this general issue, see Chapter 16.) Many critics of paternalism argue that it amounts to treating adults as children, as if they either didn't know what's good for them, or did not have the moral authority to engage in risky behavior. The state, they argue, should limit criminal sanctions to actions that threaten to violate the rights of others. We shouldn't send people to jail for consuming unhealthy foods, participating in dangerous sports or hobbies, marrying unwisely, or placing all of their money in extremely risky investments. And yet such activities pose substantial risk of harm to their participants.

The defender of the Paternalism Argument could agree with these verdicts but offer the following reply: Of course the state should not be in the business of protecting citizens from *every* sort of risk. Sometimes—as in the case in which people marry unwisely—the state should keep a hands-off policy, because state officials lack the knowledge it would take to prevent bad marriages, and the damage to privacy of enacting such a law would be very high. In short, the costs of such a marriage law would outweigh the benefits. But this isn't always the case with paternalistic laws. Think again about seat belt laws, for instance. Like all paternalistic laws, these are harmful to some extent, precisely because they limit our freedom. Those who don't want to wear a seat belt are forced to do something they don't want to do. Thinking in consequentialist terms, however, policies that impose some harms can be justified if they are the least costly way of minimizing overall harm. Seat belt laws prevent a huge amount of harm, at relatively little cost to personal freedom. Further, there doesn't seem to be any less costly way to save all the lives that seat belt laws do. So, if consequentialism is correct, seat belt laws are morally justified.

Can we say the same thing of drug laws? That depends on two things: (a) whether some form of consequentialism is correct, and (b) whether criminalizing drug use is the least costly way to prevent harms to drug users. Many of the pros and cons of consequentialism were discussed in Chapter 5, and we won't pause to rehearse them here. It is important to note, however, that some consequentialists *reject* the Paternalism Argument, because they are skeptical about (b): they doubt that criminalization really is the most effective way to reduce the harms associated with drug use. After all, criminalizing conduct is itself very costly, not only economically, but also in terms of the loss of a convict's liberty, and the harms suffered by any family members who depend on him or her for economic and emotional support. Given these costs, sending someone to jail should always be a last resort. Consequentialist doubts about whether this last resort is justified for drug use take the form of

The Efficiency Argument for Legalization

1. Criminal sanctions are morally justified only if they are the most efficient (i.e., least costly and most likely to succeed) means of reducing harm.
2. Criminal sanctions against drug use are not the most efficient means of reducing harm.

Therefore,

3. Criminal sanctions against drug use are not morally justified.

Premise 1 is a straightforward application of consequentialism. Supporters of premise 2 argue that spending the money we do on criminal prohibition (see Just the Facts for more detail) would yield much greater benefit if it were spent instead on educating citizens about the harmful effects of drug use, on drug rehabilitation programs, and on a variety of social programs that would increase the prospects of those who have resorted to drugs to numb them to life's miseries. *If* they are right—a question too complex to consider here—then consequentialists would be best advised to affirm this argument and so reject the Paternalistic Argument.

Another argument for the legalization of drug use comes not from a focus on results but rather on the nature of punishment. Punishment is a unique kind of harm, in response to a unique kind of offense—a violation of the criminal law. The state can hurt you in a lot of ways—by upping your tax rate, denying you citizenship, forcing you to fulfill the terms of a contract you breached, making you pay stiff licensing fees to register your car or business, or by requiring that you compensate your neighbor for damaging her property. But punishment is different. Not only does punishment hurt (sometimes literally), it, unlike all of these other state responses, is *intended* to hurt. Furthermore, it is designed to convey condemnation for the convict's wrongful conduct; the expression of the community's moral outrage is essential to punishment.

These thoughts provide the basis for the

Legal Punishment Requires Immorality Argument

1. Actions are justifiably criminalized only if they are immoral.
2. Drug use is not immoral.

Therefore,

3. Drug use is not justifiably criminalized.

Premise 1 is pretty plausible. Here is an argument for it:

(A) Actions are justifiably criminalized only if it is morally justified to condemn their performance.

This follows from the understanding of legal punishment given earlier, and is part of what distinguishes punishment from other harmful or costly legal responses, such as licensing fees. Further,

(B) It is morally justified to condemn the performance of an action only if it is immoral.

Suppose an action *isn't* immoral—then it wouldn't be right to morally condemn someone for performing it. (A) and (B) together entail premise 1. In other words, if (A) and (B) are true, then so is premise 1.

What of premise 2? We can assess its pros and cons by considering the three most prominent criticisms of it. One might think that drug use is immoral because (1) it is against the law, or (2) it wrongfully harms others, or (3) it harms drug users themselves. Let's review these in order.

The first option is not very plausible. We can't show that drug use is immoral just by showing that it is illegal. In the first case, there are some jurisdictions where drug use is *legal*. Even where drug use is illegal, though, the important point is that an action's illegality is not sufficient for its immorality. There are lots of counterproductive or morally bankrupt laws; violating such laws need not be immoral. Those who peacefully protested the segregationist Jim Crow laws in the 1950s and 1960s were violating the law but were not acting immorally. Perhaps drug laws are like these laws in being morally unjustified. I'm not saying they are. But neither can we just assume that drug laws are morally justified, since their moral status is precisely the matter under investigation!

The second option is also problematic. As we noted earlier, drug use itself does not wrongfully harm others, although in some cases it does lead to such harm, as when a user, under the influence, becomes violent or recklessly endangers the lives of others. These actions are indeed immoral, and are already rightly criminalized. But drug use, considered in itself, does not wrongfully harm others.

There is a wrinkle here, noted earlier. Some actions, though they do not wrongfully harm others, nevertheless very reliably lead to such harm. Think about conspiracy. This is just a bunch of folks talking to one another. Such talk doesn't harm anyone. Still, conspiring to commit harm is immoral, precisely because of its reliable connection to wrongfully harming others. I think there is a parallel here to certain drugs, such as crack cocaine. Their use doesn't by itself harm anyone else. But for certain users, there is a reliable connection between taking these drugs and harming others. If you take a drug that is known to reliably cause its users to harm others, then, at the very least, this reveals a kind of recklessness, an indifference to the well-being of others, and that *is* morally suspect. In most cases, though, drug use does not reliably lead most users to commit such harms. For those drugs, then, this second basis for thinking that drug use is immoral will not work.

According to the third option, harming *oneself* can be immoral. Drug use sometimes becomes drug abuse; when this happens, the harms to oneself are sometimes as grave as can be. Those who overdose or become addicts have certainly harmed themselves. Still, it's unclear whether these unfortunate people are also thereby acting immorally, by virtue of having harmed themselves. Of course, if one becomes the sort of addict who neglects one's children, or betrays one's friend or spouse, then we have grounds for condemnation—but once again, on the basis of these harms to others, rather than the drug use itself. If we focus on a case where drug abuse does not lead to harm to others but does lead to real self-harm—say, by contracting HIV from dirty needles or by becoming financially ruined—then it may be more apt to judge this person's behavior to be pitiable, unwise, or imprudent, rather than immoral.

Questions about whether self-harm is immoral are deep ones; I don't pretend to have resolved the matter here, but I invite you to reflect further on whether such harm can qualify as immoral. It's important to note that consequentialists (see Chapter 5) answer in the affirmative:

if, in harming yourself, you are failing to do the most good you can, then your action is immoral. Kantians (see Chapter 6) also think that self-harm can be immoral, if it is prompted by a maxim that cannot be universalized. Natural law theorists (see Chapter 8) claim that certain types of self-harm, such as suicide, are immoral, because they are contrary to our nature.

Abolitionists—those who seek to abolish laws, in this case, those that criminalize drug use—have another argument against criminalizing drug laws. This one relies on the idea that we have certain **moral rights**—moral entitlements or liberties that protect our interests and choices. According to the argument we are about to consider, one of these rights is the right to use drugs. It is wrong to punish people for exercising their rights. So it is wrong to punish people for using drugs:

The Rights Argument

1. If people have a moral right to do X, then punishing them for doing X is unjust.
2. In most cases, people have a moral right to take drugs.

Therefore,

3. In most cases, punishing people for taking drugs is unjust.

Premise 1 is plausible. If I am morally entitled to air my views, or peacefully assemble, or practice a given faith, then it would be wrong of the government to criminalize such conduct. As we have seen, the proper role of the government is contested. But nearly everyone agrees that legitimate governments are designed, at the very least, to *protect* the moral rights of their citizens. Governments become illegitimate—they are moral failures whose coercion of citizens is morally unjustified—when they fail to protect those rights or, even worse, actively violate them. So if people have a moral right to do something, then governments should not punish people for exercising those rights. That is what premise 1 says.

But what of premise 2—why think that people have a moral right to use drugs? Here is an answer, by way of an argument:

(A) If an action violates no one else's rights, then people have a moral right to perform that action.
(B) In most cases, drug use violates no one else's rights.

Therefore,

2. In most cases, people have a moral right to take drugs.

Premise (A) rests on the general idea that we are autonomous, sovereign beings who get to determine how we are to live our lives. Other people may advise us and seek to influence us, but we are morally at liberty to resist such advice and influence. This moral right to self-determination is not unlimited, of course. As the old adage goes, the liberty to swing my fist ends where your nose begins. Other people's rights limit one's own. But, as a general point, so long as I am respecting your rights, I am morally at liberty to do as I please.

Premise (B) is also plausible. There are some cases, discussed earlier, where taking a drug would reliably lead to violence or recklessness towards others. In such cases, drug use would violate the rights of others. But most cases of drug use are not like this. (A) and (B) together entail premise 2; if they are true, premise 2 is true.

A final argument for drug legalization is a familiar one. It begins by noting that alcohol and tobacco are also drugs. We do not criminalize their use, even though their consumption does *far* more damage than illegal drug use does. The idea is that we are being inconsistent if we forbid the use of some recreational drugs, like cigarettes and beer, while outlawing the use of others. We should either criminalize them all or legalize them all. Since we shouldn't criminalize alcohol and tobacco use, we should legalize all recreational drugs. We can summarize this line of reasoning in

The Tobacco-Alcohol Argument

1. If tobacco and alcohol use should be legal, then other recreational drug use should be legal.
2. Tobacco and alcohol use should be legal.

Therefore,

3. Other recreational drug use should be legal.

Nowadays very few people object to premise 2, for reasons given in the two preceding arguments. If adults know the dangers of using alcohol and tobacco but opt to drink or smoke, it's their decision to make—the government should not prevent us from engaging in risky behavior if we know what we're doing. And few people regard smoking or having a drink as immoral. There just doesn't seem to be a good reason to send millions of people to jail for using tobacco or having a beer.

Defenders of premise 1 rely on these points to support their analogy between alcohol, tobacco, and other recreational drugs. Tobacco is highly addictive and is a primary cause of millions of deaths around the world—over 480,000 per year in the United States alone.[16] This is nearly *ten times* the number of deaths from all other drugs (except alcohol) combined.[17] Abolitionists often point to figures such as these in the service of their cause. But we need to be careful with statistics here (as elsewhere), since the number of drug deaths and other harms from drug use would almost certainly increase if we were to legalize their use—more people would use drugs, and current users may well use more often, if the threat of legal punishment disappeared. That said, the harm caused by tobacco use is *huge*. Though we can expect a substantial increase in drug-related harms if we legalize their use,

16. https://www.cdc.gov/tobacco/data_statistics/fact_sheets/fast_facts/index.htm

17. https://www.drugabuse.gov/related-topics/trends-statistics/overdose-death-rates

we lack good evidence for thinking that those harms would come close to those caused by tobacco use. If such harm is not sufficient to justify criminalization, then it is not clear why the harms caused by other drugs should warrant their criminalization.

One reply is that harms from tobacco use (leaving second-hand smoke aside for now) are harms to the users themselves, which should not be punished. This abandons the paternalistic rationale for drug laws. But other drugs are mood altering and consciousness altering, making their users liable to cause harm to *others*. We have examined this form of argument already, but it's worth making a new point in the present context: alcohol use is also mood and consciousness altering, and also causes a huge amount of harm to others. Again, we have no way of reasonably predicting how much more harm would result from legalizing drugs that are currently prohibited. But the point made at the end of the last paragraph holds for alcohol as well: if we refrain from criminalizing alcohol use despite the massive harms it causes, then it's not clear why we should continue to send people to jail for using drugs that are no worse than alcohol in this regard.

An interesting hybrid view toward drug legalization has recently been developed. (See the reading by Peter de Marneffe later in this chapter.) The idea is that while drug *use* ought to be decriminalized, drug *manufacture* and *sale* ought to remain illegal. On this view, if you can get your hands on drugs, you should be free to use them. But those who make and distribute these drugs should go to jail for doing so. This can sound paradoxical, but the basic idea is pretty straightforward. People have a moral right to use drugs, for reasons given in the discussion of the Rights Argument. And if you have a moral right to do something, you shouldn't be punished for doing it. But drug use does lead to a great deal of harm, and this is something that a society should try to prevent if it can. The best way to do it, while respecting the rights of its citizens, is to criminalize the manufacture and sale of drugs. Hence

The Social Harm Argument

1. If a law greatly reduces social harm and does not violate anyone's rights, then the law is morally justified.
2. Laws criminalizing drug manufacture and distribution greatly reduce social harm and do not violate anyone's rights.

Therefore,

3. Laws criminalizing drug manufacture and distribution are morally justified.

Premise 1 is meant to combine the best of both worlds—the consequentialist emphasis on reducing harm, with the nonconsequentialist focus on protecting rights. Both considerations are of central moral importance, and this premise captures that point.

We can support premise 2 as follows. Prohibiting the manufacture and sale of drugs will greatly reduce their supply. If we greatly reduce the supply, then we'll greatly reduce drug use. And if we greatly reduce drug use, then we'll greatly reduce the harms that come from such use. Further, because we would not criminalize drug use itself, we violate no one's rights. Though people have a moral right to use drugs, they don't have a moral right to make them or sell them. So prohibiting the sale and manufacture of drugs respects people's rights while greatly reducing social harm. That's what premise 2 says.

There are three points that might be pressed by critics of this line of argument. First, while prohibition usually does reduce supply and use of the prohibited item, it also has side effects that are themselves very harmful. As is well known, forbidding the manufacture and sale of a much-desired item, such as alcohol during Prohibition (1920–1933) or cocaine or heroin today, can lead to the creation of a lucrative and violent black market. The vast wealth to be made from the sale of illegal drugs also leads to the corruption of political institutions, from the local police to federal judges and, in some cases, all the way to the presidential palace. Imagine instead that the manufacture and sale of drugs were legal and heavily taxed. The violence associated with the black market would be greatly reduced. The added tax would increase cost, thereby reducing demand, and so moderating use. These tax revenues could provide the resources to invest in far more extensive drug rehabilitation services and better education about the harms wrought by drug use.

Second, as noted earlier, criminalizing behavior is a very costly social response. The United States spends billions of dollars each year on its "war on drugs." Legalizing drugs would allow that money to be either returned to taxpayers or to be spent on social programs that might greatly reduce harm. So, while the consequences of prohibition are likely to be fewer harms from drug use, the consequences of legalization are likely to be far less drug-related violence and far more tax revenues that can be used for the social good. It's unclear at this point whether the outcomes of prohibiting the manufacture and sale of drugs are, on the whole, better than those we might see with legalization.

Third, it may be that, contrary to premise 2, people *do* have a moral right to manufacture and sell drugs. Recall another point made earlier, when discussing the Rights Argument: we have a moral right to do what we like, so long as this does not violate the rights of others. It doesn't seem that growing marijuana, for instance, or selling it to willing buyers or distributors, violates anyone's moral rights. The same holds for "harder" drugs, such as cocaine or heroin. Given that processing tobacco leaves into cigarettes or distilling gin from juniper berries doesn't violate anyone's moral rights, it is difficult to see why processing coca leaves into cocaine or poppies into heroin would do so. It's true that selling cigarettes, alcohol, or other drugs to minors could be understood as violating their rights, because they may suffer serious harm without being able to adequately understand the risks.

But it is not easy to see how selling any of these drugs violates the rights of adults who are capable of making informed decisions about whether to use them. If this line of reasoning is correct, then people have as much of a right to make and sell drugs as they do to use them. *If* that is correct, then criminalizing the manufacture and sale of drugs would, after all, violate people's rights, thereby undermining premise 2 of the Social Harms Argument.

CONCLUSION

Many tens of thousands of our fellow citizens are in jail or prison today because of drug possession charges. Is that morally legitimate?

Those who defend the status quo say yes. They argue that drug use often leads to serious harm—either to users themselves, to others who are harmed by users who are under the influence, or both. These defenders say that it is society's responsibility to reduce such harm, and that the most effective way to do so is by criminalizing drug use.

Those who argue for legalization claim that drug use is not immoral—indeed, that there is a moral right to use drugs if we wish—thereby casting doubt on the legitimacy of criminalizing drug use. These abolitionists allow, of course, that drug use sometimes leads people to perform actions that wrongfully harm others, but they insist that criminalization be reserved for those harms, rather than drug use itself. Legalizers also argue by analogy: if tobacco and alcohol users should not be sent to jail for their indulgence, neither should those who use "harder" drugs.

Perhaps a compromise can be struck, according to which drug use should be legal, though drug manufacture and sales should not. The basis for this compromise is the thought that adults have a right to self-determination that entitles them to do as they please, so long as they respect the rights of others. The success of this compromise position depends on whether the right to self-determination also entitles us to make and sell drugs.

STAT SHOT

Do you think the use of marijuana should be made legal, or not? (%)

All adults

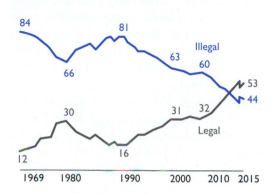

% saying 'legal' among generations

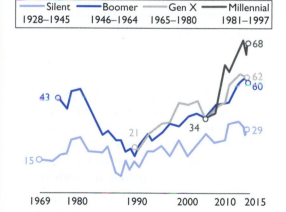

1. Abuse of tobacco, alcohol, and illicit drugs costs the United States more than $740 billion annually in costs related to crime, lost work productivity, and health care.[1]

2. In 2015, a slim majority of Americans supported legalizing marijuana. Younger Americans tended to support legalizing marijuana more than older Americans (Figure 21.1).

1. https://www.drugabuse.gov/related-topics/trends-statistics

Figure 21.1

Source: http://www.people-press.org/2015/04/14/in-debate-over-legalizing-marijuana-disagreement-over-drugs-dangers/#current-opinion-on-legalizing-marijuana

ESSENTIAL CONCEPTS

Abolitionists: those who seek to abolish laws (in this case, laws that criminalize drug use).

Binge drinks: consumes an excessive amount of alcohol in a short period of time to become severely intoxicated.

Drug addiction: a chronic disease characterized by drug seeking and use that is compulsive, or difficult to control, despite harmful consequences.

Drugs: chemicals that, when introduced into the bloodstream, predictably alter the way we feel.

Moral rights: moral entitlements or liberties that protect our interests and choices.

Overdose: a dangerously excessive and sometimes lethal amount of a drug.

Paternalism: the practice of limiting someone's liberty, against his will, for his own good.
Tolerance: the effect that occurs when the brain adjusts to a pattern of drug use, in which the high that users feel, compared to the high they felt when they first started taking a drug, is reduced.
Wrongs: violations of rights.

Cases for Critical Thinking

DanceSafe: Raving Mad?

A rave is an electronic music dance party that lasts all night. They're usually held in dark rooms, such as dance clubs or abandoned warehouses, filled with lasers and strobe lights. When raves began their rise to popularity in the late 1980s, many participants used the drug ecstasy to enhance the experience of pulsing music, bright lights, and wild dancing. Ecstasy is still popular, but rave-goers nowadays also use cocaine, methamphetamine, and hallucinogens.

Since these drugs are illegal in the United States, there is always the danger that they are "cut" with harmful substances. Illegal drugs often contain cutting agents (or bulking agents), such as sugar, baking soda, caffeine, laundry detergent, or pesticides.[1] Dealers include these cheap substances in their drugs to make it appear as if their drugs contain more of the active ingredient than they really do. This allows dealers to make more money from a given supply of drugs than if they did not cut them. Some cutting agents are harmless, but some are toxic—especially when combined with powerful drugs such as ecstasy, cocaine, and methamphetamine.

DanceSafe is an organization that attends rave parties and offers to test drugs for dangerous cutting agents.[2] The idea is that rave-goers are going to take drugs no matter what. It's best to make sure that the drugs they take are safe rather than potentially lethal. DanceSafe also sells drug testing kits that can be used at home when drug users are by themselves.

Some have applauded DanceSafe's potentially life-saving efforts. Others, however, worry that, when DanceSafe gives users assurance that their drugs are pure, it is causing significant harm by further encouraging people to use powerful and potentially deadly drugs. This, critics worry, pushes drug addicts further into addiction. Critics also worry that the service makes attending raves even more attractive. Though there aren't enough data to confirm or disconfirm this, many worry that raves are places with significantly increased rates of heatstroke (due to overheating while dancing on drugs), STI (sexually transmitted infection) transmission, sexual assault, and rape. If DanceSafe makes taking drugs safer, then, the thought goes, more people will attend raves and be harmed by these associated dangers.

1. http://www.cph.org.uk/wp-content/uploads/2012/08/cut-a-guide-to-the-adulterants-bulking-agents-and-other-contaminants-found-in-illicit-drugs.pdf

2. https://dancesafe.org/

Questions
1. Do DanceSafe and similar services encourage drug use? If so, is that a reason to think that they morally ought to stop providing their services? Why or why not?
2. Suppose data came in confirming the claim that raves are places with significantly increased rates of heatstroke, STI transmission, sexual assault, and rape. Would it be morally justified for DanceSafe to continue to provide their service at raves?
3. According to DanceSafe, the US government has never arrested a DanceSafe employee for providing drug testing services. Nor has anyone who has had his or her drugs tested by DanceSafe been arrested on that basis. Law enforcement lets DanceSafe provide their service without any interference. Is this the correct stance for law enforcement to take toward DanceSafe and similar services? Why or why not?

Drug Cartels

On August 25, 2010, the corpses of seventy-two migrants from South and Central America were discovered on a ranch in Tamaulipas, Mexico. These fifty-eight men and fourteen women were kidnapped by the Los Zetas cartel and killed for refusing to traffic drugs. In April 2011, several mass graves holding 177 bodies were discovered in the same area—almost certainly victims of the cartels, too. In July 2011, Edgar Jimenez Lugo, known as "El Ponchis" or "The Cloak," a four-teen-year-old American citizen with drug cartel ties, was found guilty of beheading at least four people. In September of that same year, a mur-dered man and woman were found hanging from a bridge in Nuevo Laredo, Mexico. Near their mu-tilated bodies was a sign saying they were killed for denouncing drug cartel activities on a social media site. The sign also threatened to kill others who post "funny things on the internet." And in March of 2017, a mass grave containing more than 250 human skulls—more victims of drug cartels—was uncovered in Veracruz, Mexico.[1]

Many Americans who buy illegal drugs are convinced that there is nothing morally prob-lematic about merely using recreational drugs. But most of the illegal drugs in the United States were either produced or trafficked through Mexico by the Mexican drug cartels. Thus, a large proportion of the money paid to buy illegal drugs in the United States is likely to find its way back to these violent organizations.

Questions

1. Is buying illegal marijuana morally permis-sible if there is a fairly high likelihood that the money used for such purchases will end up in the hands of exceedingly violent drug cartels? Why or why not?

2. Many argue that the drug cartels' biggest fear is that drugs will be legalized in the United States.[2] If this happened, they say, then US citizens could safely buy, sell, and produce cheap marijuana and other drugs on their own. This would significantly reduce the cartels' demand and significantly reduce their violent activities. Does this sound plausible? Why or why not? Suppose that it's correct. Would this justify legal-izing drugs, or at least marijuana, in the United States?

3. Many argue that the only reason that drug cartels are violent is that marijuana and other drugs are illegal in Mexico. After all, almost no one is killed in the alcohol trade in Mexico, since alcohol is legal there. According to proponents of this idea, cartels resort to violence only because they cannot safely settle their business disputes in the court system. Does this sound plausible? Why or why not? Suppose that it's correct—that violence would be significantly reduced if drugs were legalized in Mexico. Would this justify legalizing drugs in Mexico, or at least less powerful drugs such as marijuana? Why or why not?

The Ethics of Staged Interventions

It's often heartbreaking to watch a loved one deal with the consequences of drug addiction: loss of interest in things they once loved, depression, erratic behavior, theft, lying, significant health problems, and so on. To help a loved one escape the grip of addiction, friends and family some-times stage an intervention. This is a planned confrontation by an addict's loved ones for the addict's benefit. In an intervention, each loved one is given an opportunity to express love for the addicted family member or friend and is in-vited to describe the harmful effects drug addic-tion has had on their relationship. Then there is usually a request for the addict to agree to get professional help. The request often comes in

---

1. http://www.cnn.com/2013/09/02/world/americas/mexico-drug-war-fast-facts/index.html

2. http://www.npr.org/templates/transcript/transcript.php?storyId=280741858

the form of an ultimatum: go into rehabilitation immediately or risk losing contact, income, or other privileges from the loved ones who staged the intervention. The hope is that such a drastic measure will help addicts to see that their addiction needs to be addressed.

Questions

1. Interventions are often a desperate measure used by family members after years of difficult conversations that have failed. Loved ones often know that addicts would never willingly attend an intervention. Thus, they must often resort to deception and even lying to get an addict to walk into an intervention. Is it morally justified for people to lie to and deceive their addicted loved one in an effort to help them overcome addiction?

2. Sometimes parents with addicted adult sons or daughters living in their house threaten to kick them out if they don't agree to treatment. This would leave the addicted son or daughter homeless. But the hope is that facing such a desperate situation will influence the addict to get help. Is it morally justified for parents to refuse to house their addicted adult sons or daughters if they refuse treatment? Why or why not?

3. Sometimes family members destroy their addicted loved one's stash of drugs (or alcohol) by flushing them down the toilet or throwing them in the garbage. The hope is that this will make it more difficult to use the drugs that are doing such harm. But drugs and alcohol can be incredibly expensive or dangerous to obtain. Is it morally justified to destroy a stash of drugs or alcohol as a way of helping an addict? Why or why not?

4. Staged interventions work (when they do) because they put enormous social pressure on an addict to get help. Are such measures objectionably paternalistic, since addicts for whom an intervention is necessary would almost never willingly agree to get professional help for their addiction?

READINGS

Against the Legalization of Drugs

Peter de Marneffe

Peter de Marneffe argues for a moderate position on the sale and use of drugs. On the one hand, he believes that drug *use* ought to be decriminalized. According to de Marneffe, people have a moral right to self-sovereignty—a right to do as they please, so long as their actions do not harm or wrong others—that entitles them to put into their bodies anything they like, so long as this does not involve violating the rights of others. The right to self-sovereignty implies that people have a moral right to use drugs, so long as such use is not likely to lead to drug users violating the rights of others. And if they have a moral right to use drugs, then it is wrong of the government to criminalize such use.

On the other hand, the government does have the moral authority to criminalize the manufacture and sale of substantial amounts of drugs. And, according to de Marneffe, the government is fully justified in using that authority to criminalize such behavior. The argument against drug legalization is simple: if the sale and manufacture of drugs is legalized, then many more people will abuse drugs, or abuse them more often than they currently do. Such abuse has terrible consequences. Governments should do what they can to reduce the terrible consequences that beset their citizens. So governments should make the manufacture and sale of drugs illegal.

De Marneffe devotes the bulk of his article to presenting and then replying to a variety of objections to his proposal. These include the objection that such governmental prohibitions are ineffective; that they are objectionably paternalistic; that they violate the rights of drug users; that they have led to the many problems of the so-called War on Drugs; that they have immoral effects on imprisoned youth; that they lead to and reinforce racial discrimination; that they only increase the amount of violence in society; that they foster the corruption of government officials in the foreign countries where drugs are manufactured; that it is inconsistent to legally allow the sale and manufacture of cigarettes and alcohol while prohibiting the sale and manufacture of other drugs; that if drugs ought to be illegal then so too should the sale and manufacture of unhealthy foods; and, finally, that there is no scientific proof that drug abuse would increase with the legalization of drugs.

INTRODUCTION

By the *legalization of drugs* I mean the removal of criminal penalties for the manufacture, sale, and possession of large quantities of recreational drugs, such as marijuana, cocaine, heroin, and methamphetamine. In this chapter, I present an argument against drug legalization in this sense. But I do not argue against *drug decriminalization*, by which I mean the removal of criminal penalties for recreational drug use and the possession of small quantities of recreational drugs. Although I am against drug legalization, I am for drug decriminalization. So one of my goals here is to explain why this position makes sense as a matter of principle.

The argument against drug legalization is simple. If drugs are legalized, they will be less expensive and more available. If drugs are less expensive and more available, drug use will increase, and with it, proportionately, drug abuse. So if drugs are

From Andrew I. Cohen and Christopher Heath Wellman, eds., *Contemporary Debates in Applied Ethics*, second edition (Wiley, 2014), pp. 346–357.

legalized, there will be more drug abuse. By *drug abuse* I mean drug use that is likely to cause harm.

INEFFECTIVENESS OBJECTION

A common objection is that drug laws do not work. The imagined proof is that people still use drugs even though they are illegal. But this is a bad argument. People are still murdered even though murder is illegal, and we do not conclude that murder laws do not work or that they ought to be repealed. This is because we think these laws work well enough in reducing murder rates to justify the various costs of enforcing them. So even if drug laws do not eliminate drug abuse, they might likewise reduce it by enough to justify their costs.

Why should we think that drug laws reduce drug abuse? For one thing, our general knowledge of human psychology and economic behavior provides a good basis for predicting that drug use will increase if drugs are legalized. People use drugs because they enjoy them. If it is easier and less expensive to do something enjoyable, more people will do it and those who do it already will do it more often.

Laws against the manufacture and sale of drugs make drugs less available, because they prohibit their sale in convenient locations, such as the local drug or liquor or grocery store, and more expensive, because the retail price of illegal drugs reflects the risk to manufacturers and sellers of being arrested and having their goods confiscated. So if drugs are legalized, the price will fall and they will be easier to get. "Hey honey, feel like some heroin tonight?" "Sure, why not stop at Walgreens on the way home from picking up the kids?"

The claim that drug laws reduce drug abuse is also supported by the available empirical evidence. During Prohibition it was illegal to manufacture, sell, and transport "intoxicating liquors" (but not illegal to drink alcoholic beverages or to make them at home for one's own use). During this same period, deaths from cirrhosis of the liver and admissions to state hospitals for alcoholic psychosis declined dramatically compared to the previous decade (Warburton, 1932, pp. 86, 89). Because cirrhosis and alcoholic psychosis are highly correlated with heavy drinking, this is good evidence that Prohibition reduced heavy drinking substantially. Recent studies of alcohol consumption also conclude that heavy drinking declines with increases in price and decreases in availability (Edwards et al., 1994; Cook, 2007). Further evidence that drug use is correlated with availability is that the use of controlled psychoactive drugs is significantly higher among physicians and other health care professionals (who have much greater access to these drugs) than it is among the general population (Goode, 2012, pp. 454–455), and that veterans who reported using heroin in Vietnam, where it was legal, reported not using it on returning to the USA, where it was illegal (Robins et al., 1974).

For all these reasons it is a safe bet that drug abuse would increase if drugs were legalized, and it is hard to find an expert on drug policy who denies this. This alone, however, does not settle whether laws against drugs are a good policy because we do not know by how much drug abuse would increase if drugs were legalized and we do not know how much harm would result from this increase in drug abuse. It is important to recognize, too, that drug laws also cause harm by creating a black market, which fosters violence and government corruption, and by sending people to prison. It is possible that the harms created by drug laws outweigh their benefits in reducing drug abuse. I will say more about this possibility below, but first I address some philosophical objections to drug laws.

PATERNALISM OBJECTION

One objection is that drug laws are paternalistic: they limit people's liberty for their own good. A related objection is that drug laws are moralistic: they impose the view that drug use is wrong on everyone, including those who think it is good. It is true that drug use can be harmful, but most people who use drugs do not use them in a way that harms someone or that creates a significant risk of harm. This is true even of so-called "hard drugs" such as heroin and cocaine. Is it not wrong for the government to prohibit us from doing something we enjoy if it causes no harm?

To oppose drug legalization, however, is to oppose the removal of penalties for the *commercial manufacture* and *sale* and *possession of large quantities* of drugs; it is not to support criminal penalties for the use or possession of small quantities of drugs. To oppose drug legalization is therefore not to hold that anyone should be prohibited from doing something they enjoy for their own good, or that the government should impose the controversial view that drug use is wrong on everyone.

VIOLATION OF RIGHTS OBJECTION

A more fundamental objection to drug laws is that they violate our rights. I believe there is some truth to this. So I want to explain why it makes sense to oppose drug legalization even though some drug laws do violate our rights.

Each of us has a right of self-sovereignty: a moral right to control our own minds and bodies. Laws that prohibit people from using drugs or from possessing small quantities of them violate this right because the choice to use drugs involves an important form of control over our minds and bodies, and recreational drug use does not usually harm anyone or pose a serious risk of harm. The choice to use drugs involves an important form of control over our minds partly because recreational drug use is a form of mood control, which is an important aspect of controlling our minds. There are also perceptual experiences that we can have only as the result of using certain drugs, such as LSD, and certain kinds of euphoria that we can experience only as the result of using certain drugs, such as heroin. The choice to put a drug into one's body—to snort it, smoke it, inject it, or ingest it—is also an important form of control over one's body. Because we have a right to control our own minds and bodies, the government is justified in prohibiting us from using a drug only if the choice to use this drug is likely to harm someone, which is not true of most recreational drug use. Laws that prohibit us from using recreational drugs therefore violate our right of self-sovereignty and for this reason should be repealed.

The choice to manufacture or sell drugs, in contrast, does not involve an important form of control over one's own mind or body—no more than the choice to manufacture or sell any commercial product does. These are choices to engage in a commercial enterprise for profit, and may therefore be regulated or restricted for reasons of public welfare, just as any other commercial enterprise may be. One might think that there is something "hypocritical" or "inconsistent" about prohibiting the manufacture and sale of drugs and not prohibiting their possession and use, but this is confused. If one opposes drug legalization on the ground that the government should do whatever it can to reduce drug abuse, regardless of whether it violates anyone's rights, then it would be inconsistent to oppose drug criminalization. But it is not inconsistent to oppose drug criminalization if one opposes drug legalization on the ground that the government should do whatever it can to reduce drug abuse consistent with respect for individual rights. This is because it makes sense to hold that whereas drug criminalization violates the right of self-sovereignty, non-legalization does not (de Marneffe, 2013).

Some might argue that non-legalization violates the right of self-sovereignty too, because it is not possible to use drugs if no one is legally permitted to sell them. But this is obviously false because people still use drugs even though selling them is illegal. Although this fact is sometimes cited to demonstrate the futility of drug control, ironically it makes drug control easier to justify. If drug non-legalization really did make it impossible to use drugs, and so to have the unique experiences they provide, this policy would arguably violate the right of self-sovereignty on this ground. But drug control laws do not make drug use impossible; they only increase the price and reduce the availability of drugs. This is no more a violation of self-sovereignty than a decision by the local supermarket not to carry a certain food or to double its price.

HIGH COSTS OF THE DRUG WAR OBJECTION

Laws against the manufacture and sale of drugs might of course still be a bad policy even if they do not violate the right of self-sovereignty. This is because these laws have costs, and these costs might outweigh the benefits of these laws in reducing drug abuse. Laws against the manufacture and sale of drugs create a black market, which fosters violence, because when disputes arise in an illegal trade the disputants cannot go to the legal system for resolution. The black market also fosters government corruption, because those in an illegal trade must pay government officials for protection from arrest and confiscation. Drug laws also cost money to enforce, which might be better spent in other ways. Finally, drug laws result in some people being arrested and imprisoned and being left with criminal records. It is certainly possible that these costs outweigh the benefits of drug control in reducing drug abuse.

It is important to understand, though, that drug control policy need not be as costly as the so-called War on Drugs, which is current US policy. So even if the War on Drugs is too costly, as critics maintain, it does not follow that drugs should be legalized. The case against drug legalization rests on the assumption that the benefits of drug control in reducing drug abuse are sufficient to justify the costs of drug control *once these costs are reduced as much as possible consistent with effective drug control*. By *effective* drug control, I mean a policy that reduces drug abuse substantially compared to the amount of drug abuse that would exist if drugs were legalized. I do not mean a policy that eliminates drug abuse altogether. It is no more possible to eliminate drug abuse than it is to eliminate crime. But just as effective crime control is still possible, effective drug control is possible too. And if it is possible to have effective drug control without the high costs of the War on Drugs, then the benefits of prohibiting the manufacture and sale of drugs are more likely to justify the costs.

One compelling objection to the War on Drugs is to the sentencing rules for drug law violations, which require judges to impose long prison terms for drug trafficking offenses. Critics rightly argue that mandatory sentences and long prison terms for selling drugs are morally indefensible. These are not, however, necessary features of effective drug control policy. They are not features of European drug control policy, for example. So it makes sense to oppose harsh mandatory penalties while also opposing drug legalization.

Drug control works primarily by increasing price and reducing availability, which can be accomplished by reliably enforcing laws against the manufacture and sale of drugs with moderate penalties. Where it is illegal to manufacture and sell drugs, most business persons avoid the drug trade because they do not want to be arrested and have their goods confiscated. This reduces supply, which increases price. Where it is illegal to sell drugs, stores that aim to retain their licenses also do not sell them, which reduces availability. Heavy penalties no doubt drive the price up even higher and decrease availability even more by increasing the risks of drug trafficking—but the biggest increases in price and the biggest reductions in availability come simply from the illegality of the trade itself together with reliable enforcement of laws against manufacture and sale (Kleiman et al., 2011, pp. 48–50). If effective drug control does not require harsh mandatory penalties, then the fact that such penalties are unjustifiable is not a good argument for drug legalization.

EFFECT ON IMPRISONED YOUTHS OBJECTION

Another objection to US drug control policy is that it results in many young people being arrested, imprisoned, and left with criminal records, who would otherwise not suffer these misfortunes. Some might retort that if a person chooses to deal drugs illegally, he cannot legitimately complain about the foreseeable consequences of his choice. But this response is inadequate because by making drugs illegal the government creates a hazard that otherwise would not exist. By making the manufacture and sale of drugs illegal, the government creates a lucrative illegal market, and the money-making opportunities that this market creates are attractive, especially to young people who lack a college education or special training, because they can make much more money by dealing drugs than by doing anything else. When the government creates a system of penalties for manufacturing and selling drugs it therefore creates a hazard; it creates a tempting opportunity to make money and then imposes penalties for making money in this way.

In general, the government has an obligation to reduce the risk to individuals of being harmed by the hazards it creates. When the government tests weapons, for example, it must take care that people do not wander into the testing areas. Bright signs are not enough; it must also build fences and monitor against trespass. The government also has an obligation to help young people avoid the worst consequences of their willingness to take unwise risks. It has an obligation to require teenagers to wear helmets when they ride a motorcycle, for example. So when the government creates the hazard of imprisonment by making the manufacture and sale of drugs illegal, it must guard against the likelihood of imprisonment, and it must take special care to reduce this likelihood for young people who commonly lack a proper appreciation of the negative impact that conviction and imprisonment will have on their lives. For all these reasons, the government must structure drug laws so that young people have an adequate opportunity to avoid being imprisoned for drug offenses, and to avoid acquiring a criminal record. This means, among other things, that no one should be arrested for a drug offense prior to receiving an official warning; no penalty for a first conviction should involve prison time; initial jail or prison sentences should be short and subject to judicial discretion; and imprisonment for subsequent convictions should increase in length only gradually and also be subject to judicial discretion.

RACIAL DISCRIMINATION OBJECTION

A related objection to the War on Drugs is that those imprisoned for drug offenses in the USA are disproportionately black inner city males (Alexander, 2012). This objection would be addressed to some degree by the changes in sentencing policy just proposed, but one might predict that any effective drug control policy would result in the same sort of disproportionality, which some might see as an argument for drug legalization. However, it also is important to consider the potential negative impact of drug legalization on inner city communities. Drug legalization will result in a substantial increase in drug abuse. Drug abuse commonly leads parents to neglect their children, and to neglect their own health and jobs, which harms their children indirectly. Drug abuse also distracts teenagers from their schoolwork, interferes with the development of a sense of responsibility, and makes young people less likely to develop the skills necessary for acquiring good jobs as adults. If drugs are legalized, there will therefore be more child neglect as a result and more truancy by teenagers. This is likely to have an even more devastating impact on the life prospects of young people in non-affluent inner city communities than it has on the life prospects of young people in affluent suburbs. I suspect this is the primary reason why many inner city community leaders oppose drug legalization.

It is true that incarcerating large numbers of inner city youths for drug offenses also has a negative impact on inner city communities. A man who is in jail cannot be present as a parent or make money to support his children, and a person with a criminal record has a harder time finding a decent job. These consequences alone would warrant drug legalization if there were no downside. If we assume, however, that drug legalization would result in a substantial increase in child neglect and adolescent truancy, then legalization does not seem like a good way to improve the life prospects of inner city youth overall. It seems better to maintain laws against the manufacture and sale of drugs, and reduce the number of those who are convicted and imprisoned for drug offenses. This would be consistent with effective drug control because the number of dealers in prison could be reduced dramatically without making drugs noticeably cheaper or easier to get (Kleiman et al., 2011, p. 203).

INCREASE IN VIOLENCE OBJECTION

Another objection to US drug control policy is that it has increased violence in other countries, particularly Mexico. Americans enjoy using drugs and are willing to pay for them. Because it is illegal to manufacture and sell drugs in the USA, American drug control policy creates opportunities for people south of the border to get rich by making drugs and selling them wholesale to retailers north of the border. Because those in the drug trade use violence to control market share and to intimidate law enforcement, US drug laws result in violence. If drugs were legalized in the USA, the recreational drug market would presumably be taken over by large US drug, liquor, and food companies and it would not be possible for anyone in Mexico to get rich by selling illegal drugs to Americans, which would eliminate the associated violence there.

Drug legalization, however, is not the only way to reduce drug-related violence abroad. Here are some alternative strategies:

- The USA might legalize the private production of marijuana for personal use (the way it was legal during Prohibition to make alcoholic beverages at home). Because much of the Mexican drug trade is in marijuana, this would reduce its profitability, and so presumably the associated violence.
- The USA might also concentrate its drug enforcement efforts in Mexico on the most violent drug trafficking organizations, as opposed to concentrating on the biggest and most profitable organizations, which would create incentives for those in the Mexican drug trade to be less violent.
- The USA might also ease border control at entry points not on the US-Mexico border. The violence in Mexico is created partly by the fact that it is the primary conduit of cocaine from South and Central America to North America. If the USA were to loosen border control in Florida, fewer drugs would travel through Mexico. Because the USA

imports so many goods, it is not possible to stop drugs from coming into this country. Some would cite this as proof that drug control is futile, but this conclusion is unwarranted because border controls still raise the retail price of drugs substantially, which results in less drug abuse (Kleiman et al., 2011, pp. 162–163). The suggestion here is that a general policy of border control is consistent with US law enforcement experimenting with different border control policies with an eye to reducing violence abroad (Kleiman et al., 2011, p. 170).

None of these proposals would eliminate drug-related violence in Mexico, but it is unrealistic to think that criminal violence in Mexico would be eliminated by drug legalization in the USA. After all, what will career criminals in Mexico do once they cannot make money via the drug trade? Presumably they will turn to other criminal activities, such as kidnapping, extortion, and human trafficking, which also involve violence.

CORRUPTION OF FOREIGN GOVERNMENTS OBJECTION

Another objection to US drug control policy is that it fosters the corruption of foreign governments. Because those in the foreign drug trade need protection from arrest, prosecution, and confiscation of assets, because they are willing to pay government officials to look the other way, and because some government officials are willing to accept this payment, the drug trade increases government corruption. If drugs were legalized in the USA, this would destroy the illegal market abroad, which would remove an important contributing factor in government corruption.

It is naive, though, to think that US drug control policy is the primary cause of government corruption abroad. Although we associate police corruption with drug trafficking, the latter tends to flourish where government officials are already corrupt (Kleiman et al., 2011, p. 177). [A] foreign police force that is not fully professionalized will be susceptible to financial corruption regardless of whether the USA legalizes drugs.

THE INCONSISTENCY OBJECTION

Another argument against drug laws is that it is hypocritical or inconsistent for our government to prohibit the manufacture and sale of heroin, cocaine, and methamphetamine while permitting the manufacture and sale of alcohol and cigarettes. Drinking and smoking cause far more harm than other kinds of recreational drug use. This is partly because there is so much more drinking and smoking, which is partly because the manufacture and sale of alcohol and cigarettes are legal. But drinking and smoking are also inherently more harmful than other forms of drug use. Drinking alcohol is correlated much more highly with violence, property crime, and accidental injury than the use of heroin is, and a regular user of heroin who uses it safely—in moderate doses with clean equipment—does not face any significant health risk as a result, whereas cigarette smoking is known to cause heart and lung disease. So it can seem that if the government is justified in prohibiting the manufacture and sale of heroin, it must also be justified in prohibiting the manufacture and sale of alcohol and cigarettes.

This would be a good objection to drug laws if laws against the manufacture and sale of alcoholic beverages and cigarettes were wrong in principle, but it is hard to see why they would be. After all, drinking and smoking cause a lot of harm and neither policy would violate the right of self-sovereignty discussed above, because a law that prohibits only the manufacture and sale of a drug does not prohibit its possession or make its use impossible. Of course, the suggestion that alcohol prohibition might be justified is commonly dismissed with the incantation that Prohibition was a disastrous failure, but historians agree that Prohibition succeeded in substantially reducing heavy drinking, and it would have been even more effective had its enforcement been adequately funded and had it been administered from the outset by law enforcement professionals instead of by political appointees (Okrent, 2010, pp. 134–145, 254–261). Prohibition did fail politically, but so did Reconstruction and the Equal Rights Amendment. The fact that a policy is rejected or abandoned does not show that it was wrong in principle. Finally, it is worth noting that alcohol prohibition still exists in some parts of this country, on Indian reservations, for example, and that these policies make sense as part of an effort to reduce alcoholism and the harms associated with it.

It is not necessary, though, to advocate alcohol prohibition in order to defend other drug laws, because there are relevant differences between them. For one thing, the institution of alcohol prohibition now is likely not to reduce heavy drinking by as much as drug non-legalization reduces drug abuse. Drinking is widely accepted and a part of normal social rituals, in a way that heroin, cocaine, and methamphetamine use is not. This means that alcohol prohibition now would not work in tandem with a strong social stigma, which would presumably reduce its effectiveness in reducing alcohol abuse. It is possible, too, that in an environment of social acceptance, sharply increasing the excise taxes on alcoholic beverages would achieve almost as much as prohibition in reducing the harms caused by heavy drinking with none of the costs of prohibition (though it is worth noting here that liquor industry lobbying has been more effective in preventing excise tax increases than it was in preventing Prohibition). There are also important ways in which instituting alcohol prohibition now would be more burdensome than continuing with drug non-legalization. Many people have built their lives around the alcoholic beverage industry. If alcohol were now prohibited, many of these people would lose their jobs, and many companies, restaurants and bars would go out of business, which would be a serious hardship for owners and employees. In contrast, people who go into the drug trade do so knowing that it is illegal. So the burden on them of maintaining drug laws is not as great as the burden that alcohol prohibition would impose on those who have built their lives around the liquor trade on the assumption that the manufacture and sale of alcohol will remain legal. Ironically, it is drug *legalization* that would burden those in the illegal drug trade, in much the same way as Prohibition burdened those in the legal liquor trade: by depriving them of their livelihood.

There are also important differences between illicit drugs and cigarettes. Drug legalization, I assume, would result in a substantial increase in drug abuse, which, I assume, would also result in a substantial increase in child neglect and adolescent truancy, which would have a substantial negative impact on the life prospects of many young people. Cigarette smoking, in contrast, does not make someone a worse parent or a worse student or employee. Furthermore, because heavy smoking typically has a negative impact on a person's life only toward the end when he or she is older, smoking as a young person is less likely than adolescent drug abuse to have a negative impact on the *kind* of life a person has. Finally, although psychologically challenging, it is quite possible to quit smoking as an adult and so to reduce the long-term health consequences of starting to smoke as a teenager—much easier than it is to reverse the long-term negative consequences of having had inadequate parenting or having failed out of high school as the result of drug abuse. Given these differences between the consequences of smoking and drug abuse, one can consistently oppose the legalization of drugs for the reasons I have given here without advocating prohibiting the manufacture and sale of cigarettes.

In explaining above how one might consistently oppose the legalization of drugs without advocating alcohol prohibition, I observed that drinking is so widespread and socially accepted that alcohol prohibition is likely to reduce heavy drinking by less than drug abuse is reduced by laws against the manufacture and sale of illicit drugs. This same point might now be given as an argument for legalizing marijuana: marijuana use is so widespread and socially accepted that laws against the manufacture and sale of marijuana do not do very much to reduce it. It might also be argued that legalizing marijuana would not result in a dramatic increase in drug abuse because marijuana is less subject to abuse than other drugs (including alcohol). Finally, legalizing marijuana in the USA would dramatically reduce the drug trade in Mexico, which would result in a corresponding reduction in violence and government corruption there. Should not marijuana be legalized, then, even if other drugs should not be?

In this chapter I am arguing against the view that the manufacture and sale of *all* drugs should be legalized; I am not arguing that there is *no* drug that should be legalized. Suppose that marijuana legalization would not result in a substantial increase in drug abuse. Suppose that most of those who would use marijuana if it were legalized are already using it and using it almost as much as they want to. Or suppose that marijuana use itself is harmless and does not lead to the use of more harmful drugs. If either of these things is true, then marijuana should be legalized. It is also possible, though, that, as a result of legalization, many more young people would use marijuana than do now, and that a sizable fraction of them would use it in ways that interfere with their education or employment, and that a sizable fraction of them would go on to abuse more harmful drugs who would otherwise never have tried them. Because I am not sure that these things would not happen, I do not support legalizing marijuana. With more information, though, I might change my mind. So it is important to make clear that whether a drug should be legalized depends on the consequences of legalizing it, and not on whether any *other* drug should be legalized. Hence, even if marijuana should be legalized, it would not follow that heroin, cocaine, and methamphetamine should be legalized too.

UNHEALTHY FOODS OBJECTION

Another argument against drug laws is that if the government is justified in prohibiting us from putting a drug into our bodies for our own good, then it is also justified in prohibiting us from putting unhealthy foods into our bodies for our own good. The suggestion that the government is entitled to control what we eat strikes many of us as outrageous. Why is it not likewise outrageous for the government to prohibit us from using recreational drugs?

For the reasons given above, I think it is. Laws that prohibit us from using drugs—or drinking alcohol or smoking cigarettes—violate our right of self-sovereignty in the same way that laws that prohibit us from eating high fat or high sugar foods would. However, just as laws that prohibit the manufacture and sale of drugs do not violate our self-sovereignty, laws that regulate the sale of fatty or sugary foods do not either. So if the government

prohibits fast food restaurants from selling humongous hamburgers, or prohibits convenience stores from selling sugary soda in giant cups, or prohibits vending machines in schools from stocking items with high fat or sugar content, no one's right of self-sovereignty is violated. Whether these policies are a good idea is a separate question, but if they are a bad idea, it is not because they violate anyone's rights.

NO SCIENTIFIC PROOF OBJECTION

In arguing against drug legalization, I assume that drug abuse would increase substantially if drugs were legalized. Some might now object that there is no proof of this, and this is true, but there is also no proof that murder rates will rise if murder is decriminalized. That is, this assumption is not warranted by any set of controlled laboratory experiments or randomized field trials. Should murder therefore be decriminalized? Obviously not. Some might say that the freedom to murder is not a very important liberty, so the standard of proof need not be so high. But most of us also support on the basis of assumptions for which there is no scientific proof policies that do impinge on important liberties. For example, many of us support restrictions on campaign contributions on the assumption that unrestricted contributions would result in more political corruption. But there is no scientific proof of this, and restrictions on campaign contributions impinge on the important freedom of political speech. Many of us also support immigration laws on the assumption that unrestricted immigration would lower our quality of life. But there is also no scientific proof of this, and freedom of movement is also an important liberty. Should we withdraw our support for these policies just because we support them on the basis of scientifically unproven assumptions? I think not. In general we are justified in supporting a legal restriction for a reason if two conditions are met: (a) this reason would justify this restriction if it was based on true assumptions, and (b) we are warranted by the available evidence in believing that the relevant assumptions are true. So if we are warranted by the available evidence in believing that drug abuse will increase if drugs are legalized, then we are justified in making this assumption for the purpose of evaluating drug control policy. And we are warranted in making this assumption—by what we know about patterns of alcohol and drug consumption and more generally about human psychology and economic behavior.

CONCLUSION

If drug abuse would increase substantially if drugs were legalized, and laws that prohibit the manufacture and sale of drugs do not violate our right of self-sovereignty, and effective drug control requires only moderate penalties reliably and conscientiously enforced, then it makes sense to oppose drug legalization. This, in essence, is the argument I have made here. In evaluating drug policy, it is important, too, to consider how public policy would be shaped if drugs were legalized. Beer, liquor, and cigarette companies already do as much as they can to prevent the government from adopting policies that would reduce drinking and smoking and so their associated harms. They do as much as they can to prevent increases in excise taxes, which increase the price of alcohol and cigarettes, and so reduce their sales, and so smoking and drinking. They do as much as they can to prevent restrictions on the hours and locations of the sale of alcohol and cigarettes. They do as much as they can to prevent licensing and rationing policies, which would reduce the amount of alcohol consumed by problem drinkers. And they do as much as they can to make their products attractive through advertising, particularly to young people. We should expect that if drugs are legalized, drug companies will behave in the same way: that they will do everything they can to prevent the enactment of laws that restrict the marketing and sale of heroin, cocaine, and methamphetamine, and that they will do everything they can to market these drugs successfully, particularly to young people, who will be their most profitable market. Because drug use is currently stigmatized, drug companies are unlikely to be as successful as liquor companies in preventing sound public policy, at least initially. But if we envision a world in which legal drug companies are legally trying to persuade consumers to buy recreational drugs from legal vendors and legally trying to prevent any socially responsible legislation that reduces their legal sales, it is hard to envision a world that does not have much more drug abuse.

REFERENCES

Alexander, M. (2012) *The New Jim Crow: Mass Incarceration in the Age of Colorblindness*. New York: New Press.

Cook, P. J. (2007) *Paying the Tab: The Economics of Alcohol Policy*. Princeton, NJ: Princeton University Press.

de Marneffe, P. (2013) Vice laws and self-sovereignty. *Criminal Law and Philosophy* 7: 29–41.

Edwards, G., Anderson, P., Babor, T. F. et al. (1994) *Alcohol Policy and the Public Good*. New York: Oxford University Press.

Goode, E. (2012) *Drugs in American Society*, 8th ed. New York: McGraw-Hill.

Kleiman, M.A.R. et al. (2011) *Drugs and Drug Policy: What Everyone Needs to Know*. New York: Oxford University Press.

Okrent, D. (2010) *Last Call: The Rise and Fall of Prohibition*. New York: Scribner.

Robins, L. N. et al. (1974) Drug use by U.S. army in Vietnam: a follow-up on their return home. *American Journal of Epidemiology* 99: 235–249.

Warburton, C. (1932) *The Economic Results of Prohibition*. New York: Columbia University Press.

Peter de Marneffe: Against the Legalization of Drugs

1. Is it consistent to favor drug decriminalization while also urging that the sale and manufacture of drugs be illegal? Why or why not?

2. Reconstruct the argument from self-sovereignty in support of drug decriminalization. Is that argument sound?

3. Is there another objection to the criminalization of the sale and manufacture of drugs that de Marneffe has failed to consider and that you find compelling? If so, what is it?

4. De Marneffe has considered eleven objections to his argument. Are any of these objections stronger than he supposes? If so, which ones?

America's Unjust Drug War

Michael Huemer

Michael Huemer argues that the recreational use of drugs, including cocaine and heroin, ought to be legal, and that the long-standing US policy of criminalizing their possession and sale is morally unjustified. He presents, and then seeks to rebut, what he regards as the two most prominent arguments for their criminalization.

The first argument is that drugs are very harmful to those who use them, and the prevention of such harm justifies the state in criminalizing drug use. The second is that drug use reliably causes harm to third parties, and since the state's mission is to prevent such harm, the state is again justified in outlawing drug use. Huemer agrees that there are some cases in which drug use does threaten others (such as when one drives while under the influence), and agrees that such activity ought to be prohibited. But, he argues, this represents a small minority of cases—in all other situations, drug use ought to be legally permitted.

Huemer then turns from criticizing prohibitionist arguments, and offers a positive argument for decriminalization. This argument claims that we have a natural moral right—that is, one that exists independently of its recognition by society—to use our bodies as we please, so long as we do not violate the rights of others in doing so. Unusual exceptions aside, we do not violate another's rights when we use drugs. Therefore we have a moral right to use drugs. Huemer thinks that the government thus violates our moral rights when it prohibits most drug use.

Should the recreational use of drugs such as marijuana, cocaine, heroin, and LSD be prohibited by law? *Prohibitionists* answer yes. They usually argue that drug use is extremely harmful both to drug users and to society in general, and possibly even immoral, and they believe that these facts provide sufficient reasons for prohibition. *Legalizers* answer no. They usually give one or more of three arguments: First, some argue that drug use is not as harmful as prohibitionists believe, and even that it is sometimes beneficial. Second, some argue that drug prohibition "does not work," in other words, it is not very successful in preventing drug use and/or has a number of very bad consequences. Lastly, some argue that drug prohibition is unjust or violates rights.

From Michael Huemer, "America's Unjust Drug War," in Bill Masters, ed., *The New Prohibition* (Accurate Press, 2004), pp. 133–144. www.accuratepress.net

I won't attempt to discuss all these arguments here. Instead, I will focus on what seem to me the three most prominent arguments in the drug legalization debate: first, the argument that drugs should be outlawed because of the harm they cause to drug users; second, the argument that they should be outlawed because they harm people other than the user; and third, the argument that drugs should be legalized because drug prohibition violates rights. I shall focus on the moral/philosophical issues that these arguments raise, rather than medical or sociological issues. I shall show that the two arguments for prohibition fail, while the third argument, for legalization, succeeds.

I. DRUGS AND HARM TO USERS

The first major argument for prohibition holds that drugs should be prohibited because drug use is extremely harmful to the users themselves, and prohibition decreases the rate of drug abuse.

This argument assumes that the proper function of government includes preventing people from harming themselves. Thus, the argument is something like this:

1. Drug use is very harmful to users.
2. The government should prohibit people from doing things that harm themselves.
3. Therefore, the government should prohibit drug use.

Obviously, the second premise is essential to the argument; if I believed that drug use was very harmful, but I did *not* think that the government should prohibit people from harming themselves, then I would not take this as a reason for prohibiting drug use. But premise (2), if taken without qualification, is extremely implausible. Consider some examples of things people do that are harmful (or entail a risk of harm) to themselves: smoking tobacco, drinking alcohol, eating too much, riding motorcycles, having unprotected or promiscuous sex, maintaining relationships with inconsiderate or abusive boyfriends and girlfriends, maxing out their credit cards, working in dead-end jobs, dropping out of college, moving to New Jersey, and being rude to their bosses. Should the government prohibit all of these things?[1] Most of us would agree that the government should not prohibit *any* of these things, let alone all of them. And this is not merely for logistical or practical reasons; rather, we think that controlling those activities is not the business of government.

Perhaps the prohibitionist will argue, not that the government should prohibit *all* activities that are harmful to oneself, but that it should prohibit activities that harm oneself in a certain way, or to a certain degree, or that also have some other characteristic. It would then be up to the prohibitionist to explain how the self-inflicted harm of drug use differs from the self-inflicted harms of the other activities mentioned above. Let us consider three possibilities.

(1) One suggestion would be that drug use also harms people other than the user; we will discuss this harm to others in section II. If, as I will contend, neither the harm to drug users nor the harm to others justifies prohibition, then there will be little plausibility in the suggestion that the combination of harms justifies prohibition. Of course, one could hold that a certain threshold level of total harm must be reached before prohibition of an activity is justified, and that the combination of the harm of drugs to users and their harm to others passes that threshold even though neither kind of harm does so by itself. But if, as I will contend, the "harm to users" and "harm to others" arguments both fail because it is not the government's business to apply criminal sanctions to prevent the kinds of harms in question, *then* the combination of the two harms will not make a convincing case for prohibition.

(2) A second suggestion is that drug use is generally *more* harmful than the other activities listed above. But there seems to be no reason to believe this. As one (admittedly limited) measure of harmfulness, consider the mortality statistics. In the year 2000, illicit drug use directly or indirectly caused an estimated 17,000 deaths in the United States.[2] By contrast, tobacco caused an estimated 435,000 deaths.[3] Of course, more people use tobacco than use illegal drugs,[4] so let us divide by the number of users: tobacco kills 4.5 people per 1000 at-risk persons per year; illegal drugs kill 0.66 people per 1000 at-risk persons per year.[5] Yet almost no one favors outlawing tobacco and putting smokers in prison. On a similar note, obesity caused an estimated 112,000 deaths in the same year (due to increased incidence of heart disease, strokes, and so on), or 1.8 per 1000 at-risk persons.[6] Health professionals have warned about the pandemic of obesity, but no one has yet called for imprisoning obese people.

There are less tangible harms of drug use—harms to one's general quality of life. These are difficult to quantify. But compare the magnitude of the harm to one's quality of life that one can bring about by, say, dropping out of high school, working in a dead-end job for several years, or marrying a jerk—these things can cause extreme and lasting detriment to one's well-being. And yet no one proposes jailing those who drop out, work in bad jobs, or make poor marriage decisions. The idea of doing so would seem ridiculous, clearly beyond the state's prerogatives.

(3) Another suggestion is that drug use harms users *in a different way* than the other listed activities. What sorts of harms do drugs cause?

First, illicit drugs may worsen users' health and, in some cases, entail a risk of death. But many other activities—including the consumption of alcohol, tobacco, and fatty foods; sex; and (on a broad construal of "health") automobiles—entail health risks, and yet almost no one believes those activities should be criminalized.

Second, drugs may damage users' relationships with others—particularly family, friends, and lovers—and prevent one from developing more satisfying personal relationships.[7] Being rude to others can also have this effect, yet no one believes you should be put in jail for being rude. Moreover, it is very implausible to suppose that people should be subject to criminal sanctions for ruining their personal relationships. I have no general theory of what sort of things people should be punished for, but consider the following example: suppose that I decide to break up with my girlfriend, stop calling my family, and push away all my friends. I do this for no good reason—I just feel like it. This would damage my personal relationships as much as anything could. Should the police now arrest me and put me in jail? If not, then why should they arrest me for doing something that only has a *chance* of indirectly bringing about a similar result? The following seems like a reasonable political principle: If it would be wrong (because not part of the government's legitimate functions) to punish people for *directly bringing about* some result, then it would also be wrong to punish people for doing some other action on the grounds that the action has a *chance* of bringing about that result indirectly. If the state may not prohibit me from *directly cutting off* my relationships with others, then the fact that my drug use *might have the result* of damaging those relationships does not provide a good reason to prohibit me from using drugs.

Third, drugs may harm users' financial lives, costing them money, causing them to lose their jobs or not find jobs, and preventing them from getting promotions. The same principle applies here: if it would be an abuse of government power to prohibit me from directly bringing about those sorts of negative financial consequences, then surely the fact that drug use might indirectly bring them about is not a good reason to prohibit drug use. Suppose that I decide to quit my job and throw all my money out

the window, for no reason. Should the police arrest me and put me in prison?

Fourth and finally, drugs may damage users' moral character, as James Q. Wilson believes:

> [I]f we believe—as I do—that dependency on certain mind-altering drugs *is* a moral issue and that their illegality rests in part on their immorality, then legalizing them undercuts, if it does not eliminate altogether, the moral message. That message is at the root of the distinction between nicotine and cocaine. Both are highly addictive; both have harmful physical effects. But we treat the two drugs differently not simply because nicotine is so widely used as to be beyond the reach of effective prohibition, but because its use does not destroy the user's essential humanity. Tobacco shortens one's life, cocaine debases it. Nicotine alters one's habits, cocaine alters one's soul. The heavy use of crack, unlike the heavy use of tobacco, corrodes those natural sentiments of sympathy and duty that constitute our human nature and make possible our social life.[8]

In this passage, Wilson claims that the use of cocaine (a) is immoral, (b) destroys one's humanity, (c) alters one's soul, and (d) corrodes one's sense of sympathy and duty. One problem with Wilson's argument is the lack of evidence supporting claims (a)–(d). Before we put people in prison for corrupting their souls, we should require some objective evidence that their souls are in fact being corrupted. Before we put people in prison for being immoral, we should require some argument showing that their actions are in fact immoral. Perhaps Wilson's charges of immorality and corruption all come down to the charge that drug users lose their sense of sympathy and duty—that is, claims (a)–(c) all rest upon claim (d). It is plausible that *heavy* drug users experience a decreased sense of sympathy with others and a decreased sense of duty and responsibility. Does this provide a good reason to prohibit drug use?

Again, it seems that one should not prohibit an activity on the grounds that it may indirectly cause some result, unless it would be appropriate to prohibit the direct bringing about of that result. Would it be appropriate, and within the legitimate functions of the state, to punish people for being unsympathetic and undutiful, or for behaving in an unsympathetic and undutiful way? Suppose that Howard—though not a drug user—doesn't sympathize with others. When people try to tell Howard their problems, he just tells them to quit whining. Friends and coworkers who ask Howard for favors are rudely rebuffed. Furthermore—though he does not harm others in ways that would be against our current laws—Howard has a poor sense of duty. He doesn't bother to show up for work on time, nor does he take any pride in his work; he doesn't donate to charity; he doesn't try to improve his community. All around, Howard is an ignoble and unpleasant individual. Should he be put in jail?

If not, then why should someone be put in jail merely for doing something that would have a *chance* of causing them to become like Howard? If it would be an abuse of governmental power to punish people for being jerks, then the fact that drug use may cause one to become a jerk is not a good reason to prohibit drug use.

II. DRUGS AND HARM TO OTHERS

Some argue that drug use must be outlawed because drug use harms the user's family, friends, and coworkers, and/or society in general. A report produced by the Office of National Drug Control Policy states:

> Democracies can flourish only when their citizens value their freedom and embrace personal responsibility. Drug use erodes the individual's capacity to pursue both ideals. It diminishes the individual's capacity to operate effectively in many of life's spheres—as a student, a parent, a spouse, an employee—even as a coworker or fellow motorist. And, while some claim it represents an expression of individual autonomy, drug use is in fact inimical to personal freedom, producing a reduced capacity to participate in the life of the community and the promise of America.[9]

At least one of these alleged harms—dangerous driving—*is* clearly the business of the state. For this reason, I entirely agree that people should be prohibited from driving while under the influence of drugs. But what about the rest of the alleged harms?

Return to our hypothetical citizen Howard. Imagine that Howard—again, for reasons having nothing to do with drugs—does not value freedom, nor does he embrace personal responsibility. It is unclear exactly what this means, but, for good measure, let us suppose that Howard embraces a totalitarian political ideology and denies the existence of free will. He constantly blames other people for his problems and tries to avoid making decisions. Howard is a college student with a part-time job. However, he is a terrible student and worker. He hardly ever studies and frequently misses assignments, as a result of which he gets poor grades. As mentioned earlier, Howard comes to work late and takes no pride in his work. Though he does nothing against our current laws, he is an inattentive and inconsiderate spouse and parent. Nor does he make any effort to participate in the life of his community, or the promise of America. He would rather lie around the house, watching television and cursing the rest of the world for his problems. In short, Howard does all the bad things to his family, friends, coworkers, and society that the ONDCP says *may* result from drug use. And most of this is voluntary.

Should Congress pass laws against what Howard is doing? Should the police then arrest him, and the district attorney prosecute him, for being a loser?

Once again, it seems absurd to suppose that we would arrest and jail someone for behaving in these ways, undesirable as they may be. Since drug use only has a *chance* of causing one to behave in each of these ways, it is even more absurd to suppose that we should arrest and jail people for drug use on the grounds that drug use has these potential effects.

III. THE INJUSTICE OF DRUG PROHIBITION

Philosopher Douglas Husak has characterized drug prohibition as the greatest injustice perpetrated in the United States since slavery.[10] This is no hyperbole. If the drug laws are unjust, then America has over half a million people unjustly imprisoned.[11]

Why think the drug laws are *unjust*? Husak's argument invokes a principle with which few could disagree: it is unjust for the state to punish people without having a good reason for doing so.[12] We have seen the failure of the most common proposed rationales for drug prohibition. If nothing better is forthcoming, then we must conclude that prohibitionists have no rational justification for punishing drug users. We have deprived hundreds of thousands of people of basic liberties and subjected them to severe hardship conditions, for no good reason.

This is bad enough. But I want to say something stronger: it is not merely that we are punishing people for no good reason. We are punishing people for exercising their natural rights. Individuals have a right to use drugs. This right is neither absolute nor exceptionless; suppose, for example, that there existed a drug which, once ingested, caused a significant proportion of users, without any further free choices on their part, to attack other people without provocation. I would think that stopping the use of this drug would be the business of the government. But no existing drug satisfies this description. Indeed, though I cannot take time to delve into the matter here, I think it is clear that the drug *laws* cause far more crime than drugs themselves do.

The idea of a right to use drugs derives from the idea that individuals own their own bodies. That is, a person has the right to exercise control over his own body—including the right to decide how it should be used, and to exclude others from using it—in a manner similar to the way one may exercise control over one's (other) property. This statement is somewhat vague; nevertheless, we can see the general idea embodied in common sense morality. Indeed, it seems that if there is *anything* one would have rights to, it would be one's own body. This explains why we think others may not physically attack you or kidnap you. It explains why we do not accept the use of unwilling human subjects for medical experiments, even if the experiments are beneficial to society—the rest of society may not decide to use your body for its own purposes without your permission. It explains why some believe that women have a right to an abortion—and why some others do not. The former believe that a woman has the right to do what she wants with her own body; the latter believe that the fetus is a distinct person, and a woman does not have the right to harm *its* body. Virtually no one disputes that, *if*

a fetus is merely a part of the woman's body, *then* a woman has a right to choose whether to have an abortion; just as virtually no one disputes that, *if* a fetus is a distinct person, then a woman lacks the right to destroy it. Almost no one disputes that persons have rights over their own bodies but not over others' bodies.

The right to control one's body cannot be interpreted as implying a right to use one's body in *every* conceivable way, any more than we have the right to use our property in every conceivable way. Most importantly, we may not use our bodies to harm others in certain ways, just as we may not use our property to harm others. But drug use seems to be a paradigm case of a legitimate exercise of the right to control one's own body. Drug consumption takes place in and immediately around the user's own body; the salient effects occur *inside* the user's body. If we consider drug use merely as altering the user's own body and mind, it is hard to see how anyone who believes in rights at all could deny that it is protected by a right, for: (a) it is hard to see how anyone who believes in rights could deny that individuals have rights over their own bodies and minds, and (b) it is hard to see how anyone who believes in such rights could deny that drug use, considered merely as altering the user's body and mind, is an example of the exercise of one's rights over one's own body and mind.

Consider two ways a prohibitionist might object to this argument. First, a prohibitionist might argue that drug use does not *merely* alter the user's own body and mind, but also harms the user's family, friends, co-workers, and society. I responded to this sort of argument in section II. Not just *any* way in which an action might be said to "harm" other people makes the action worthy of criminal sanctions. Here we need not try to state a general criterion for what sorts of harms make an action worthy of criminalization; it is enough to note that there are some kinds of "harms" that virtually no one would take to warrant criminal sanctions, and that these include the "harms" I cause to others by being a poor student, an incompetent worker, or an apathetic citizen.[13] That said, I agree with the prohibitionists at least this far: no one should be permitted to drive or operate heavy machinery while under the influence of drugs that impair their ability to do those things; nor should pregnant mothers be permitted to ingest drugs, if it can be proven that those drugs cause substantial risks to their babies (I leave open the question of what the threshold level of risk should be, as well as the empirical questions concerning the actual level of risk created by illegal drugs). But, in the great majority of cases, drug use does not harm anyone in any *relevant* ways—that is, ways that we normally take to merit criminal penalties—and should not be outlawed.

Second, a prohibitionist might argue that drug use fails to qualify as an exercise of the user's rights over his own body, because the individual is not truly acting freely in deciding to use drugs. Perhaps individuals only use drugs because they have fallen prey to some sort of psychological compulsion, because drugs exercise a siren-like allure that distorts users' perceptions, because users don't realize how bad drugs are, or something of that sort. The exact form of this objection doesn't matter; in any case, the prohibitionist faces a dilemma. If users do not freely choose to use drugs, then it is unjust to *punish* them for using drugs. For if users do not choose freely, then they are not morally responsible for their decision, and it is unjust to punish a person for something he is not responsible for. But if users *do* choose freely in deciding to use drugs, then this choice is an exercise of their rights over their own bodies.

I have tried to think of the best arguments prohibitionists could give, but in fact prohibitionists have remained puzzlingly silent on this issue. When a country goes to war, it tends to focus on how to win, sparing little thought for the rights of the victims in the enemy country. Similarly, one effect of America's declaring "war" on drug users seems to have been that prohibitionists have given almost no thought to the rights of drug users. Most either ignore the issue or mention it briefly only to dismiss it without argument.[14] In an effort to discredit legalizers, the Office of National Drug Control Policy produced the following caricature—

> The easy cynicism that has grown up around the drug issue is no accident. Sowing it has been the deliberate aim of a decades-long campaign by proponents of legalization, critics whose mantra is "nothing works," and whose central insight

appears to be that they can avoid having to propose the unmentionable—a world where drugs are ubiquitous and where use and addiction would skyrocket—if they can hide behind the bland management critique that drug control efforts are "unworkable."[15]

apparently denying the existence of the central issues I have discussed in this essay. It seems reasonable to assume that an account of the state's right to forcibly interfere with individuals' decisions regarding their own bodies is not forthcoming from these prohibitionists.

IV. CONCLUSION

Undoubtedly, the drug war has been disastrous in many ways that others can more ably describe—in terms of its effects on crime, on police corruption, and on other civil liberties, to name a few. But more than that, the drug war is morally outrageous in its very conception. If we are to call ours a free society, we cannot deploy force to deprive people of their liberty and property for whimsical reasons. The exercise of such coercion requires a powerful and clearly-stated rationale. Most of the reasons that have been proposed in the case of drug prohibition would be considered feeble if advanced in other contexts. Few would take seriously the suggestion that people should be imprisoned for harming their own health, being poor students, or failing to share in the American dream. It is still less credible that we should imprison people for an activity that only *may* lead to those consequences. Yet these and other, similarly weak arguments form the core of prohibition's defense.

Prohibitionists are likewise unable to answer the argument that individuals have a right to use drugs. Any such answer would have to deny either that persons have rights of control over their own bodies, or that consuming drugs constituted an exercise of those rights. We have seen that the sort of harms drug use allegedly causes to society do not make a case against its being an exercise of the user's rights over his own body. And the claim that drug users can't control their behavior or don't know what they are doing renders it even more mysterious why one would believe drug users deserve to be punished for what they are doing.

I will close by responding to a query posed by prohibition-advocate James Inciardi:

> The government of the United States is not going to legalize drugs anytime soon, if ever, and certainly not in this [the 20th] century. So why spend so much time, expense, and intellectual and emotional effort on a quixotic undertaking? . . . [W]e should know by now that neither politicians nor the polity respond positively to abrupt and drastic strategy alterations.[16]

The United States presently has 553,000 people unjustly imprisoned. Inciardi may—tragically—be correct that our government has no intention of stopping its flagrant violations of the rights of its people any time soon. Nevertheless, it remains the duty of citizens and of political and social theorists to identify the injustice, and not to tacitly assent to it. Imagine a slavery advocate, decades before the Civil War, arguing that abolitionists were wasting their breath and should move on to more productive activities, such as arguing for incremental changes in the way slaves are treated, since the southern states had no intention of ending slavery any time soon. The institution of slavery is a black mark on our nation's history, but our history would be even more shameful if no one at the time had spoken against the injustice.

Is this comparison overdrawn? I don't think so. The harm of being unjustly imprisoned is qualitatively comparable (though it usually ends sooner) to the harm of being enslaved. The increasingly popular scapegoating and stereotyping of drug users and sellers on the part of our nation's leaders is comparable to the racial prejudices of previous generations. Yet very few seem willing to speak on behalf of drug users. Perhaps the unwillingness of those in public life to defend drug users' rights stems from the negative image we have of drug users and the fear of being associated with them. Yet these attitudes remain baffling. I have used illegal drugs myself. I know of many decent and successful individuals who have used illegal drugs. Nearly half of all Americans over the age of 11 have used illegal drugs—including at least two United States Presidents, one Vice-President, one Speaker of the House, and one Supreme Court Justice.[17] But now

leave aside the absurdity of recommending criminal sanctions for all these people. My point is this: if we are convinced of the injustice of drug prohibition, then—even if our protests should fall on deaf ears—we cannot remain silent in the face of such a large-scale injustice in our own country. And, fortunately, radical social reforms *have* occurred, more than once in our history, in response to moral arguments.

NOTES

1. Douglas Husak (*Legalize This! The Case for Decriminalizing Drugs*, London: Verso, 2002, pages 7, 101–103) makes this sort of argument. I have added my own examples of harmful activities to his list.

2. Ali Mokdad, James Marks, Donna Stroup, and Julie Gerberding, "Actual Causes of Death in the United States, 2000," *Journal of the American Medical Association* 291, no. 10, 2004: 1238–45, p. 1242. The statistic includes estimated contributions of drug use to such causes of death as suicide, homicide, motor vehicle accidents, and HIV infection.

3. Mokdad et al., p. 1239; the statistic includes estimated effects of secondhand smoke. The Centers for Disease Control provides an estimate of 440,000 ("Annual Smoking-Attributable Mortality, Years of Potential Life Lost, and Economic Costs—United States, 1995–1999," *Morbidity and Mortality Weekly Report* 51, 2002: 300–303, http://www.cdc.gov/mmwr/PDF/wk/mm5114.pdf, page 300).

4. James Inciardi ("Against Legalization of Drugs" in Arnold Trebach and James Inciardi, *Legalize It? Debating American Drug Policy*, Washington, D.C.: American University Press, 1993, pp. 161, 165) makes this point, accusing drug legalizers of "sophism." He does not go on to calculate the number of deaths per user, however.

5. I include both current and former smokers among "at risk persons." The calculation for tobacco is based on Mokdad et al.'s report (p. 1239) that 22.2% of the adult population were smokers and 24.4% were former smokers in 2000, and the U.S. Census Bureau's estimate of an adult population of 209 million in the year 2000 ("Table 2: Annual Estimates

of the Population by Sex and Selected Age Groups for the United States: April 1, 2000 to July 1, 2007 [NC-EST2007-02]," release date May 1, 2008, http://www.census.gov/popest/national/asrh/NC-EST2007/NC-EST2007-02.xls). The calculation for illicit drugs is based on the report of the Office of National Drug Control Policy (hereafter, ONDCP) that, in the year 2000, 11% of persons aged 12 and older had used illegal drugs in the previous year ("Drug Use Trends," October 2002, http://www.whitehousedrugpolicy.gov/publications/factsht/druguse/), and the U.S. Census Bureau's report of a population of about 233 million Americans aged 12 and over in 2000 ("Table 1: Annual Estimates of the Population by Sex and Five-Year Age Groups for the United States: April 1, 2000 to July 1, 2007 [NC-EST2007-01]," release date May 1, 2008, http://www.census.gov/popest/national/asrh/NC-EST2007/NC-EST2007-02.xls). Interpolation was applied to the Census Bureau's "10 to 14" age category to estimate the number of persons aged 12 to 14. In the case of drugs, if "at risk persons" are considered to include only those who admit to having used illegal drugs in the past month, then the death rate is 1.2 per 1000 at-risk persons.

6. Based on 112,000 premature deaths caused by obesity in 2000 (Katherine Flegal, Barry Graubard, David Williamson, and Mitchell Gail, "Excess Deaths Associated With Underweight, Overweight, and Obesity," *Journal of the American Medical Association* 293, no. 15, 2005: 1861–7), a 30.5% obesity rate among U.S. adults in 2000 (Allison Hedley, Cynthia Ogden, Clifford Johnson, Margaret Carroll, Lester Curtin, and Katherine Flegal, "Prevalence of Overweight and Obesity Among U.S. Children, Adolescents, and Adults, 1999–2002," *Journal of the American Medical Association* 291, no. 23, 2004: 2847–2850) and a U.S. adult population of 209 million in 2000 (U.S. Census Bureau, "Table 2," *op. cit.*).

7. Inciardi, pp. 167, 172.

8. James Q. Wilson, "Against the Legalization of Drugs," *Commentary* 89, 1990: 21–8, p. 26.

9. NDCP, *National Drug Control Strategy 2002*, Washington, D.C.: Government Printing Office, http://www.whitehousedrugpolicy.gov/publications/policy/03ndcs/, pp. 1–2.

10. Husak, *Legalize This!*, p. 2.

11. In 2006, there were approximately 553,000 people in American prisons and jails whose most serious offense was a drug offense. This included 93,751 federal inmates (U.S. Department of Justice, "Prisoners in 2006," December 2007, http://www.ojp.usdoj.gov/bjs/pub/pdf/p06.pdf, p. 9). State prisons held another 269,596 drug inmates, based on the 2006 state prison population of 1,377,815 ("Prisoners in 2006," p. 2) and the 2004 rate of 19.57% of state prisoners held on drug charges ("Prisoners in 2006," p. 24). Local jails held another 189,204 drug inmates, based on the 2006 local jail population of 766,010 ("Prisoners in 2006," p. 3) and the 2002 rate of 24.7% of local inmates held on drug charges (U.S. Department of Justice, "Profile of Jail Inmates 2002," published July 2004, revised October 12, 2004, http://www.ojp.usdoj.gov/bjs/pub/pdf/pji02.pdf, p. 1). In all cases, I have used the latest statistics available as of this writing.

12. Husak, *Legalize This!*, p. 15. See his chapter 2 for an extended discussion of various proposed rationales for drug prohibition, including many issues that I lack space to discuss here.

13. Husak (*Drugs and Rights*, Cambridge University Press, 1992, pp. 166–168), similarly, argues that no one has a *right* that I be a good neighbor, proficient student, and so on, and that only harms that violate rights can justify criminal sanctions.

14. See Inciardi for an instance of ignoring and Daniel Lungren ("Legalization Would Be a Mistake" in Timothy Lynch, ed., *After Prohibition*, Washington, D.C.: Cato Institute, 2000, page 180) for an instance of unargued dismissal. Wilson (p. 24) addresses the issue, if at all, only by arguing that drug use makes users worse parents, spouses, employers, and co-workers. This fails to refute the contention that individuals have a right to use drugs.

15. ONDCP, *National Drug Control Strategy 2002*, p. 3.

16. Inciardi, p. 205.

17. In 2006, 45% of Americans aged 12 and over reported having used at least one illegal drug (U.S. Department of Health and Human Services, "National Survey on Drug Use and Health,"

2006, Table 1.1B, http://www.oas.samhsa.gov/
NSDUH/2k6NSDUH/tabs/Sect1peTabs1to46.
htm). Bill Clinton, Al Gore, Newt Gingrich and
Clarence Thomas have all acknowledged past
drug use (reported by David Phinney, "Dodging
the Drug Question," ABC News, August 19, 1999,
http://abcnews.go.com/sections/politics/Daily-
News/prez_questions990819.html). George W.
Bush has refused to state whether he has ever used
illegal drugs. Barack Obama has admitted to cocaine and marijuana use (*Dreams from My Father*,
New York: Random House, 2004, p. 93).

Michael Huemer: America's Unjust Drug War

1. Huemer admits that using drugs can be harmful to the user, but points out that alcohol,
   tobacco, unhealthy food, and unsafe sex can
   also be harmful. Is there any morally relevant
   difference between the harms caused by drugs
   and the harms caused by these other activities?

2. Huemer invokes the following principle: "if it
   would be wrong to punish people for *directly
   bringing about* some result, then it would also
   be wrong to punish people for doing some
   other action on the grounds that the action
   has a *chance* of bringing about that result indirectly." Do you find this principle plausible?
   Why or why not?

3. Consider Huemer's case involving Howard.
   Should Howard be punished for acting the
   way he does? If not, does it follow that we
   should not punish drug users?

4. Do individuals have a right to use drugs?
   What is Huemer's argument for thinking that
   they do? Do you find it convincing?

5. Suppose that we accept Huemer's contention
   that we ought to legalize recreational drug
   use. Does it follow that all of those currently
   in prison for drug-related offenses have been
   unjustly imprisoned?

Permissible Paternalism: Saving Smokers from Themselves

Robert E. Goodin

Paternalism involves the frustration of an individual's choices for her own good. Paternalism is usually thought by political liberals (those who place great value on personal
liberty) to be unjustifiable, since they believe that the only basis for restricting a person's liberty is to prevent the violation of rights. Self-regarding behavior—behavior
that affects only oneself—cannot violate rights, or so it is thought. And so such behavior should not, by the liberal's lights, be legally regulated at all.

Goodin disagrees. He begins his case by making a distinction between objective
and subjective interests. The latter are those that are endorsed by the person herself;
the former are what makes a person's life go better for her even if she disagrees.
Goodin claims that paternalism is justified only if it protects or advances a person's
subjective interests. In other words, permissible paternalistic interference must be
based on "some warrant in that person's own value judgments." Further, paternalism is morally acceptable only for life's big decisions—those where the stakes are
high and the potential harms one might suffer from one's choices are substantially
irreversible.

The strongest case for paternalistic legislation arises when all four of the following conditions are met. First, one's preferences have been formed as a result of misinformation or false belief. Second, one's preferences are limited to a certain time of life and run counter to preferences one has at other times. Third, one prefers not to have the preference that is thwarted by paternalistic legislation. Finally, one's preferences are inauthentic, having been shaped by influences that sidestep one's judgment. Goodin illustrates each condition with the example of a smoker, Rose Cipollone, whose preference for smoking resulted in part from misleading advertisements, ran contrary to preferences she had later in life, was one she wished she didn't have, and was formed by taking in the subliminal messages conveyed by advertising.

Paternalism is desperately out of fashion. Nowadays notions of "children's rights" severely limit what even parents may do to their own offspring, in their children's interests but against their will. What public officials may properly do to adult citizens, in their interests but against their will, is presumably even more tightly circumscribed. So the project I have set for myself—carving out a substantial sphere of morally permissible paternalism—might seem simply preposterous in present political and philosophical circumstances.

Here I shall say no more about the paternalism of parents toward their own children. My focus will instead be upon ways in which certain public policies designed to promote people's interests might be morally justifiable even if those people were themselves opposed to such policies.

Neither shall I say much more about notions of rights. But in focusing upon people's interests rather than their rights, I shall arguably be sticking closely to the sorts of concerns that motivate rights theorists. Of course, what it is to have a right is itself philosophically disputed; and on at least one account (the so-called "interest theory") to have a right is nothing more than to have a legally protected interest. But on the rival account (the so-called "choice theory") the whole point of rights is to have a legally protected choice. There, the point of having a right is that your choice in the matter will be respected, even if that choice actually runs contrary to your own best interests.

It is that understanding of rights which leads us to suppose that paternalism and rights are necessarily at odds, and there are strict limits in the extent to which we might reconcile the two positions. Still, there is some substantial scope for compromise between the two positions.

Those theorists who see rights as protecting people's choices rather than promoting their interests would be most at odds with paternalists who were proposing to impose upon people what is judged to be *objectively* good for them. That is to say, they would be most at odds if paternalists were proposing to impose upon people outcomes which are judged to be good for those people, whether or not there were any grounds for that conclusion in those people's own subjective judgments of their own good.

Rights theorists and paternalists would still be at odds, but less at odds, if paternalists refrained from talking about interests in so starkly objective a way. Then, just as rights command respect for people's choices, so too would paternalists be insisting that we respect choices that people themselves have or would have made. The two are not quite the same, to be sure, but they are much more nearly the same than the ordinary contrast between paternalists and rights theorists would seem to suggest.

That is precisely the sort of conciliatory gesture that I shall here be proposing. In paternalistically justifying some course of action on the grounds that it is in someone's interests, I shall always be searching for some warrant in that person's own

From Robert E. Goodin, "Permissible Paternalism: Saving Smokers from Themselves," *The Responsive Community* 1 (Summer 1991), pp. 42–51.

value judgments for saying that it is in that person's interests.

"Some warrant" is a loose constraint, to be sure. Occasionally will we find genuine cases of what philosophers call "weakness of will": people being possessed of a powerful, conscious present desire to do something that they nonetheless just cannot bring themselves to do. Then public policy forcing them to realize their own desire, though arguably paternalistic, is transparently justifiable even in terms of people's own subjective values. More often, though, the subjective value to which we are appealing is one which is present only in an inchoate form, or will only arise later, or can be appreciated only in retrospect.

Paternalism is clearly paternalistic in imposing those more weakly-held subjective values upon people in preference to their more strongly held ones. But, equally clearly, it is less offensively paternalistic thanks to this crucial fact: at least it deals strictly in terms of values that are or will be subjectively present, at some point or another and to some extent or another, in the person concerned.

I. THE SCOPE OF PATERNALISM

When we are talking about public policies (and maybe even when we are talking of private, familial relations), paternalism surely can only be justified for the "big decisions" in people's lives. No one, except possibly parents and perhaps not even they, would propose to stop you from buying candy bars on a whim, under the influence of seductive advertising and at some marginal cost to your dental health.

So far as public policy is concerned, certainly, to be a fitting subject for public paternalism a decision must first of all involve high stakes. Life-and-death issues most conspicuously qualify. But so do those that substantially shape your subsequent life prospects. Decisions to drop out of school or to begin taking drugs involve high stakes of roughly that sort. If the decision is also substantially irreversible—returning to school is unlikely, the drug is addictive—then that further bolsters the case for paternalistic intervention.

The point in both cases is that people would not have a chance to benefit by learning from their mistakes. If the stakes are so high that losing the gamble once will kill you, then there is no opportunity for subsequent learning. Similarly, if the decision is irreversible, you might know better next time but be unable to benefit from your new wisdom.

II. EVALUATING PREFERENCES

The case for paternalism, as I have cast it, is that the public officials might better respect your own preferences than you would have done through your own actions. That is to say that public officials are engaged in evaluating your (surface) preferences, judging them according to some standard of your own (deeper) preferences. Public officials should refrain from paternalistic interference, and allow you to act without state interference, only if they are convinced that you are acting on:

- *relevant* preferences;
- *settled* preferences;
- *preferred* preferences; and, perhaps,
- *your own* preferences.

In what follows, I shall consider each of those requirements in turn. My running example will be the problem of smoking and policies to control it. Nothing turns on the peculiarities of that example, though. There are many others like it in relevant respects.

It often helps, in arguments like this, to apply generalities to particular cases. So, in what follows, I shall further focus in on the case of one particular smoker, Rose Cipollone. Her situation is nowise unique—in all the respects that matter here, she might be considered the prototypical smoker. All that makes her case special is that she (or more precisely her heir) was the first to win a court case against the tobacco companies whose products killed her.

In summarizing the evidence presented at that trial, the judge described the facts of the case as follows.

Rose . . . Cipollone . . . began to smoke at age 16, . . . while she was still in high school. She testified that she began to smoke because she saw people smoking in the movies, in advertisements, and looked upon it as something "cool, glamorous and grown-up" to do. She began smoking Chesterfields . . . primarily because of advertising of "pretty girls and movie stars." and because Chesterfields were described as "mild.". . .

Mrs. Cipollone attempted to quit smoking while pregnant with her first child . . . , but even then she would sneak cigarettes. While she was in labor she smoked an entire pack of cigarettes, provided to her at her request by her doctor, and after the birth . . . she resumed smoking. She smoked a minimum of a pack a day and as much as two packs a day.

In 1955, she switched . . . to L&M cigarettes . . . because . . . she believed that the filter would trap whatever was "bad" for her in cigarette smoking. She relied upon advertisements which supported that contention. She . . . switched to Virginia Slims . . . because the cigarettes were glamorous and long, and were associated with beautiful women— and the liberated woman. . . .

Because she developed a smoker's cough and heard reports that smoking caused cancer, she tried to cut down her smoking. These attempts were unsuccessful. . . .

Mrs. Cipollone switched to lower tar and nicotine cigarettes based upon advertising from which she concluded that those cigarettes were safe or safer . . . [and] upon the recommendation of her family physician. In 1981 her cancer was diagnosed, and even though her doctors advised her to stop she was unable to do so. She even told her doctors and her husband that she had quit when she had not, and she continued to smoke until June of 1982 when her lung was removed. Even thereafter she smoked occasionally—in hiding. She stopped smoking in 1983 when her cancer had metastasized and she was diagnosed as fatally ill.

This sad history contains many of the features that I shall be arguing make paternalism most permissible.

Relevant Preferences

The case against paternalism consists in the simple proposition that, morally, we ought to respect people's own choices in matters that affect themselves and by-and-large only themselves. But there are many questions we first might legitimately ask about those preferences, without in any way questioning this fundamental principle of respecting people's autonomy.

One is simply whether the preferences in play are genuinely *relevant* to the decision at hand. Often they are not. Laymen often make purely factual mistakes in their means-ends reasoning. They think— or indeed, as in the case of Rose Cipollone, are led by false advertising to suppose—that an activity is safe when it is not. They think that an activity like smoking is glamorous, when the true facts of the matter are that smoking may well cause circulatory problems requiring the distinctly unglamorous amputation of an arm or leg.

When people make purely factual mistakes like that, we might legitimately override their surface preferences (the preference to smoke) in the name of their own deeper preferences (to stay alive and bodily intact). Public policies designed to prevent youngsters from taking up smoking when they want to, or to make it harder (more expensive or inconvenient) for existing smokers to continue smoking when they want to, may be paternalistic in the sense of running contrary to people's own manifest choices in the matter. But this overriding of their choices is grounded in their own deeper preferences, so such paternalism would be minimally offensive from a moral point of view.

Settled Preferences

We might ask, further, whether the preferences being manifested are "settled" preferences or whether they are merely transitory phases people are going through. It may be morally permissible to let people commit euthanasia voluntarily, if we are sure they really want to die. But if we think that they may subsequently change their minds, then we have good grounds for supposing that we should stop them.

The same may well be true with smoking policy. While Rose Cipollone herself thought smoking was both glamorous and safe, youngsters beginning to smoke today typically know better. But many of them still say that they would prefer a shorter but more glamorous life, and that they are therefore more than happy to accept the risks that smoking entails. Say what they may at age sixteen, though, we cannot help supposing that they will think differently when pigeons eventually come home to roost. The risk-courting preferences of youth are a characteristic product of a peculiarly dare-devil phase that virtually all of them will, like their predecessors, certainly grow out of.

Insofar as people's preferences are not settled—insofar as they choose one option now, yet at some later time may wish that they had chosen another—we have another ground for permissible paternalism. Policy-makers dedicated to respecting people's own choices have, in effect, two of the person's own choices to choose between. How such conflicts should be settled is hard to say. We might weigh the strength or duration of the preferences, how well they fit with the person's other preferences, and so on.

Whatever else we do, though, we clearly ought not privilege one preference over another just because it got there first. Morally, it is permissible for policymakers to ignore one of a person's present preferences (to smoke, for example) in deference to another that is virtually certain later to emerge (as was Rose Cipollone's wish to live, once she had cancer).

Preferred Preferences

A third case for permissible paternalism turns on the observation that people have not only multiple and conflicting preferences but also preferences for preferences. Rose Cipollone wanted to smoke. But, judging from her frequent (albeit failed) attempts to quit, she also wanted *not to want* to smoke.

In this respect, it might be said, Rose Cipollone's history is representative of smokers more generally. The US Surgeon General reports that some 90 percent of regular smokers have tried and failed to quit. That recidivism rate has led the World Health Organization to rank nicotine as an addictive substance on a par with heroin itself.

That classification is richly confirmed by the stories that smokers themselves tell about their failed attempts to quit. Rose Cipollone tried to quit while pregnant, only to end up smoking an entire pack in the delivery room. She tried to quit once her cancer was diagnosed, and once again after her lung was taken out, even then only to end up sneaking an occasional smoke.

In cases like this—where people want to stop some activity, try to stop it but find that they cannot stop—public policy that helps them do so can hardly be said to be paternalistic in any morally offensive respect. It overrides people's preferences, to be sure. But the preferences which it overrides are ones which people themselves wish they did not have.

The preferences which it respects—the preferences to stop smoking (like preferences of reformed alcoholics to stay off drink, or of the obese to lose weight)—are, in contrast, preferences that the people concerned themselves prefer. They would themselves rank those preferences above their own occasional inclinations to backslide. In helping them to implement their own preferred preferences, we are only respecting people's own priorities.

Your Own Preferences

Finally, before automatically respecting people's choices, we ought to make sure that they are really their *own* choices. We respect people's choices because in that way we manifest respect for them as persons. But if the choices in question were literally someone else's—the results of a post-hypnotic suggestion, for example—then clearly there that logic would provide no reason for our respecting those preferences.

Some people say that the effects of advertising are rather like that. No doubt there is a certain informational content to advertising. But that is not all there is in it. When Rose Cipollone read the tar and nicotine content in advertisments, what she was getting was information. What she was getting when looking at the accompanying pictures of movie stars and glamorous, liberated women was something else altogether.

Using the power of subliminal suggestion, advertising implants preferences in people in a way that largely or wholly bypasses their judgment. Insofar as it does so, the resulting preferences are not authentically that person's own. And those implanted preferences are not entitled to the respect that is rightly reserved for a person's authentic preferences, in consequence.

Such thoughts might lead some to say that we should therefore ignore altogether advertising-induced preferences in framing our public policy. I demur. There is just too much force in the rejoinder that, "Wherever those preferences came from in the first instance, they are mine now." If we want our policies to respect people by (among other things) respecting their preferences, then we will have to respect all of those preferences with which people now associate themselves.

Even admitting the force of that rejoinder, though, there is much that still might be done to curb the preference-shaping activities of, for example, the tobacco industry. Even those who say "they're my preferences now" would presumably have preferred, ahead of time, to make up their own minds in the matter. So there we have a case, couched in terms of people's own (past) preferences, for severely restricting the advertising and promotion of products—especially ones which people will later regret having grown to like, but which they will later be unable to resist.

III. CONCLUSIONS

What, in practical policy terms, follows from all that? Well, in the case of smoking, which has served as my running example, we might ban the sale of tobacco altogether or turn it into a drug available only on prescription to registered users. Or, less dramatically, we might make cigarettes difficult and expensive to obtain—especially for youngsters, whose purchases are particularly price-sensitive. We might ban all promotional advertising of tobacco products, designed as it is to attract new users. We might prohibit smoking in all offices, restaurants, and other public places, thus making it harder for smokers to find a place to partake and providing a further inducement for them to quit.

All of those policies would be good for smokers themselves. They would enjoy a longer life expectancy and a higher quality of life if they stopped smoking. But that is to talk the language of interests rather than of rights and choices. In those latter terms, all those policies clearly go against smokers' manifest preferences, in one sense or another. Smokers want to keep smoking. They do not want to pay more or drive further to get their cigarettes. They want to be able to take comfort in advertisements constantly telling them how glamorous their smoking is.

In other more important senses, though, such policies can be justified even in terms of the preferences of smokers themselves. They do not want to die, as a quarter of them eventually will (and ten to fifteen years before their time) of smoking-related diseases; it is only false beliefs or wishful thinking that make smokers think that continued smoking is consistent with that desire not to avoid a premature death. At the moment they may think that the benefits of smoking outweigh the costs, but they will almost certainly revise that view once those costs are eventually sheeted home. The vast majority of smokers would like to stop smoking but, being addicted, find it very hard now to do so.

Like Rose Cipollone, certainly in her dying days and intermittently even from her early adulthood, most smokers themselves would say that they would have been better off never starting. Many even agree that they would welcome anything (like a workplace ban on smoking) that might now make them stop. Given the internally conflicting preferences here in play, smokers also harbor at one and the same time preferences pointing in the opposite direction; that is what might make helping them to stop seem unacceptably paternalistic. But in terms of other of their preferences—and ones that deserve clear precedence, at that—doing so is perfectly well warranted.

Smoking is unusual, perhaps, in presenting a case for permissible paternalism on all four of the fronts here canvassed. Most activities might qualify under only one or two of the headings. However, that may well be enough. My point here is not that paternalism is always permissible but merely that it may always be.

In the discourse of liberal democracies, the charge of paternalism is typically taken to be a knock-down objection to any policy. If I am right, that knee-jerk response is wrong. When confronted with the charge of paternalism, it should always be open to us to say, "Sure, this proposal is paternalistic—but is the paternalism in view permissible or impermissible, good or bad?" More often than not, I think we will find, paternalism might prove perfectly defensible along the lines sketched here.

Robert E. Goodin: Permissible Paternalism: Saving Smokers from Themselves

1. What is the "conciliatory gesture" that Goodin speaks of? Do you find it plausible?
2. Goodin believes that paternalism can be justified only for life's "big decisions." Do you agree? Consider, for instance, some municipal policies that sought to ban the sale of large sodas, with the aim of improving health. Can such a policy be justified? Why or why not?

3. What should the default be with regard to government paternalism? Are governments presumptively justified in restricting their citizens' choices, for their own good? Or are citizens presumptively immune from such restrictions?
4. What is the best case you can put together for the idea that paternalism is sometimes morally justified in order to protect a person's *objective* interests?
5. Can we distinguish, in theory and in practice, between authentic and inauthentic preferences? If so, how? If not, how does this affect the case for paternalism?

CHAPTER 22

Genetic Engineering

JUST THE FACTS

Genetic engineering is the direct manipulation of an organism's DNA to alter its characteristics. When this manipulation is undertaken to improve a human's form or functioning beyond the level necessary for health, it's called **genetic enhancement**. **Genetically modified organisms** (GMOs) are those whose DNA has been directly manipulated.

Genetic engineering is distinct from other methods of manipulating an organism's DNA. Such manipulation might be done, for instance, by **artificial selection**—the process by which humans develop desirable traits in plants or animals by selecting which males or females will reproduce together. Farmers, scientists, and breeders have done this for ages, selectively breeding prized fruits, vegetables, livestock, and sport and show animals. Artificial selection is limited to naturally occurring variations within species.[1] By contrast, when an organism is genetically engineered, its DNA is directly manipulated. This can be done through changing a base pair, deleting a section of DNA, introducing a copy of a gene, or even inserting DNA extracted from a different organism (sometimes from a different species).[2] Both **germline cells**, which are reproductive, and **somatic cells**, which are not, can be manipulated. The former type of genetic engineering is more controversial when applied to humans, since changes made in germline cells will be passed on to the next generation.[3]

The first organism to be genetically engineered was a bacterium, in 1973. In 1974, scientists genetically engineered a mouse. By 1994, similar methods were applied to plants, and GMOs became a commercial product available to consumers.[4] Scientists have now engineered tomatoes that resist freezing temperatures by inserting genetic material from a fish—the winter flounder. They've created potatoes that don't bruise and apples that don't brown.[5]

The promise of GMOs is tremendous: genetic engineering is used to make crops more resilient, more nutritious, and faster growing. It can make certain crops immune to certain pesticides—it can even make pesticides unnecessary, in some cases. It's not hard to see how this could produce huge benefits: farmers will produce better crops, lose fewer of them to weather or insects, and they can perform the whole process faster and in some cases with less intervention. This would all mean higher efficiency, which means more food at lower cost. It might also allow foods to be grown in regions that have previously been hard to farm in. This could not only make the lives of average Americans better, but could help to solve the global famine problem as well.

---

1. https://www.nature.com/scitable/topicpage/genetically-modified-organisms-gmos-transgenic-crops-and-732

2. https://www.yourgenome.org/facts/what-is-genetic-engineering

3. https://www.yourgenome.org/facts/what-is-crispr-cas9

4. https://www.yourgenome.org/facts/what-is-genetic-engineering

5. https://www.livescience.com/40895-gmo-facts.html

Genetic engineering of human and nonhuman animals promises huge benefits as well. In one instance, scientists took DNA from a spider and engineered a goat that produces silk in its milk, allowing for production of an incredibly strong silk fabric.[6] Sheep have been engineered whose milk can be used to treat cystic fibrosis. Worms that have been manipulated to glow in the dark can be used to learn about Alzheimer's. Yeast and bacteria have even been used to produce insulin, which then is used to treat people with Type 1 diabetes.[7] Directly manipulating the human genome might bring yet greater advances: we might someday eliminate genetic disease—everything from color blindness to Down syndrome. It may even help cure cancer.[8]

Genetic enhancement offers the promise of yet further benefits. By altering a human's genes, it's possible that we could increase our intelligence, make us more attractive, and improve our memory. Perhaps we could make someone more musically adept, require less sleep, and live longer. We might even be able to improve our reasoning capacity and make ourselves more altruistic.[9] Some have even suggested that genetic engineering could make humans have less of a negative impact on the environment: for example, we could make human eyes that need less light.[10]

While much of this is still in the future, **CRISPR-cas9** (usually referred to just as "CRISPR"—short for clustered regularly interspaced short palindromic repeats) has started to bridge the gap between science fiction and science fact. CRISPR is a gene-editing tool that allows scientists to target specific sequences of DNA and either alter or delete them, or insert new genetic material altogether. For a long time, scientists had to rely on imprecise methods involving chemicals or radiation to cause random mutations in genes. They couldn't control where in the genome those changes occurred. CRISPR changed all that. It was developed out of a naturally occurring feature of some bacteria: they keep parts of the DNA of viruses that infect them.[11]

Genetic engineering is not without its critics. Some argue that widespread cultivation of GMOs could result in "super-insects" and "super-weeds" that are resistant to pesticides. The worry is that farmers will overuse certain pesticides, since they don't hurt the crops, and that insects and weeds will adapt to these pesticides, creating the need for even stronger pesticides to yield the same benefits. Others are concerned that the pesticide use that GMOs encourage will harm beneficial insect species, or even upend an ecosystem by spreading genetic material into non-GMO plants. Many worry that we don't have enough evidence that GMOs are truly safe—for all we know, GMOs may cause horrible damage to humans or to the environment.[12]

Concerns about human genetic engineering and genetic enhancement run even deeper. According to the Pew Research Center, 68 percent of US adults are worried about using genetic engineering even when it comes to reducing the risk of disease to human babies.[13] Again, many

6. http://www.bbc.com/news/av/science-environment-16,554,357/the-goats-with-spider-genes-and-silk-in-their-milk

7. https://www.yourgenome.org/facts/what-is-genetic-engineering

8. http://www.asgct.org/general-public/educational-resources/gene-therapy-and-cell-therapy-for-diseases/cancer-gene-and-cell-therapy

9. https://www.psychologytoday.com/blog/how-do-life/201604/human-genetic-enhancement

10. https://www.theatlantic.com/technology/archive/2012/03/how-engineering-the-human-body-could-combat-climate-change/253981/

11. https://www.yourgenome.org/facts/what-is-crispr-cas9

12. http://www.popsci.com/article/science/core-truths-10-common-gmo-claims-debunked

13. http://www.pewinternet.org/2016/07/26/u-s-public-wary-of-biomedical-technologies-to-enhance-human-abilities/ps_2016-07-26_human-enhancement-survey_0-01/

worry that we simply can't see far enough down the road to know what the effects of genetic engineering will be. Some worry that we will end up eliminating genetic disorders, such as high-functioning autism, that have huge benefits to society.[14] Another potential problem is that the benefits of genetic enhancement may very well accrue disproportionately to the wealthy. After all, genetic enhancements will be very expensive when they first become available to the public. In the United States and many other countries, this could serve to deepen the already large inequalities between the rich and the poor—or even between the rich and the middle class.[15]

It might seem as well that while genetic engineering is a tool that could be used for good, it could end up being used for nefarious purposes. One such purpose is **eugenics**, the attempt to use science to eliminate "undesirable" qualities from a human population.[16] Eugenics movements in the United States led to the forced sterilization of various already marginalized populations—between 1907 and 1931, thirty states enacted such laws, leading to the forced sterilization of more than 64,000 people, almost all of whom were poor and undereducated.[17] Though we look back on that episode as a deeply misguided one, critics of human genetic engineering worry that the association of "inferior" traits with members of marginalized communities is still with us, and that allowing genetic engineering will invariably lead to practices that marginalize them yet further.

---

14. https://www.psychologytoday.com/blog/how-do-life/201604/human-genetic-enhancement

15. https://www.genome.gov/10004767/genetic-enhancement/

16. https://www.washingtonpost.com/news/in-theory/wp/2016/02/22/whats-the-difference-between-genetic-engineering-and-eugenics/?utm_term=.0b02dcc56ed6

17. https://www.nature.com/scitable/forums/genetics-generation/america-s-hidden-history-the-eugenics-movement-123,919,444

ARGUMENT ANALYSIS

Though genetic engineering can take many forms, here we will restrict our focus to just two of them: the genetic enhancements of human beings, and the production of GMOs. As we will see, a few of the arguments we consider can be applied with equal force to both kinds of genetic engineering. Let's start with one of these arguments, which cites (in part) the promise of great benefits as a basis for the moral legitimacy of genetic engineering:

The Benefits Argument

1. If a practice provides great benefits to many people and violates no one's rights, then it is morally legitimate.
2. Genetic enhancement and the production of GMOs provide great benefits to many people and violate no one's rights.

Therefore,

3. Genetic enhancement and the production of GMOs are morally legitimate.

The benefits referred to in premise 2 are real—see the Just the Facts section earlier for details. But does genetic engineering also avoid violating people's rights? This is a difficult question whose full answer would require a lot more space than we have here, so let me make just a few brief remarks, first about genetic enhancement and then about GMOs.

Genetic enhancement would make individuals who receive it better off—more attractive, smarter, faster, and so on. This doesn't violate *their* rights. And it doesn't seem to violate the rights of others, either. True, it can give the recipients of genetic enhancement an advantage over those who do not have it. But it's not clear that this violates the rights of the "unenhanced."

Suppose that others are better looking than I am because they were more fortunate in the "natural lottery"—they were born with great genes. That doesn't violate my rights. Now suppose that others are better looking than I am because they paid for "cosmetic enhancement"—plastic surgery that involves no genetic manipulation, but leaves them looking way better than I do. That doesn't seem to violate my rights, either. But then it's unclear why obtaining this social advantage via genetic manipulation, rather than good fortune or cosmetic surgery, would violate my rights. And things don't appear to be any different when we are talking, not about good looks, but about cognitive or athletic or personality advantages that might be obtained through genetic enhancement.

There is an exception here: competitions that forbid contestants who have been enhanced. If the rules of a beauty pageant exclude entrants who have been surgically or genetically enhanced, then if some such contestant sneaks into the competition, that *does* violate the rights of the other participants. But this is because such behavior amounts to cheating—deliberately breaking the agreed-on rules so as to gain an unfair advantage. Most genetic enhancements are not forms of cheating, however. And so we don't as yet have reason to believe that genetic enhancements violate the rights of others.

When it comes to GMOs, they too can provide great benefits to human beings. Further, since we are not forced to use GMOs, it is difficult to see how their production or sale violates anyone's rights. One might think that we have a right that others refrain from genetically modifying organisms, but the basis of such a right is unclear, as we shall see later. At this point, then, since both genetic enhancements and GMOs yield substantial benefits, and since they don't appear to violate rights (except when they constitute cheating), premise 2 of the Benefits Argument seems fairly plausible.

We have already considered a variation of premise 1 (see the Social Harm Argument in Chapter 21). It combines a consequentialist element—the emphasis on generating excellent results—with a nonconsequentialist focus on individual rights. While this combination has a lot of appeal, it also has at least one vulnerability.

Imagine a practice that generates lots of good results and violates no rights. Still, that practice might produce lots of *terrible* results, too. Those might be enough to outweigh the benefits and to sink the claim to moral legitimacy.

Unsurprisingly, reasonable opponents of genetic engineering allow that it may yield real benefits. But their concern is with its potential harms, which they see as substantial. Though genetic enhancements are only in their infancy, and GMOs have not yet been shown to have caused substantial harms, it is relatively early days for these practices. Critics have worried that once these forms of genetic engineering become more widespread, significant harms are bound to arise. This worry provides the basis for

The Conservative Argument

1. We should legalize risky social policies only if we have excellent evidence that they will not lead to disaster.
2. We lack such evidence when it comes to genetic enhancements and GMOs.

Therefore,

3. We should not legalize genetic enhancements or GMOs.

The name of this argument has nothing to do with various right-wing causes. Rather, as traditionally understood, a **conservative** position is one that either seeks to preserve the status quo, or claims that we ought to change the traditional ways of doing things only if there is compelling evidence that doing so would be an improvement. In short, conservatives want to *conserve* what is already in place; their default setting is to resist change.

It's not clear what to say about premise 2. First of all, we have not yet experienced any disastrous results from GMOs or from genetic enhancement. So that might seem to undermine this premise. But the absence of evidence is not evidence of absence. Because genetic enhancements are still in their infancy, we lack evidence about whether they will cause long-term harms. The lack of evidence about their long-term effects does not amount to evidence that they are safe. GMOs have been widely on the market for a little more than two decades. Critics of genetic engineering claim that we won't be in a position to assess its long-term results for many years to come. But defenders of GMOs argue that since two decades is ample time to record the many benefits that GMOs have provided, then that span is long enough to gather evidence about whether GMOs have had disastrous effects. As a result, they claim that there is now excellent evidence that GMOs are safe. Rather than try to resolve the matter here, we should note only that, as a general matter, it is difficult to identify a neutral standpoint for determining what counts as *enough* time to gather evidence about the potentially disastrous results of some innovative social policy.

Premise 1 does a good job of expressing the core conservative idea. Reasonable conservatives will not reject all social innovations. They will just insist that these innovations be thoroughly tested before being introduced on a broad scale. When innovations carry not only the chance of great benefit but also great harm, we need to ensure that we can avoid those harms before authorizing the social experiment.

While this sounds very plausible, there is a Catch-22 problem here. Premise 1 allows us to legalize social innovations only if we have good evidence of their safety. But we can acquire such evidence only if we are allowed to implement those innovations and see how they do! In other words, premise 1 assigns a necessary condition for legalizing social innovations (namely, gathering evidence of their safety) and then forbids any action that would enable us to meet that necessary condition.

Actually, things are not quite so bad for premise 1. We might be able to get evidence that a new practice avoids terrible results by looking to *other* societies that have implemented the practice. But there are two difficulties here.

First, such evidence is available only because those other societies have violated premise 1. If they had obeyed the conservative principle, they would not have allowed those innovations to be tested in the first place. The second difficulty is what we might call the **extrapolation problem**. This is the difficulty of concluding that outcomes in one context will carry over to a different context. There are lots of extrapolation problems with animal experimentation, for instance—there are many cases in which a drug found to be helpful when tested on animals has proven ineffective or harmful when used on humans. In the present case, the extrapolation problem arises because social innovations that work well in one culture may prove to be quite harmful in another (and vice versa).

Careful readers will have noticed the similarity between the Conservative Argument and the slippery slope arguments that we have discussed in other chapters (see Chapters 15 and 19). Slippery slope arguments predict that disaster will occur if we allow a social innovation, and argue, on consequentialist grounds, that we should therefore ban that innovation. The difference between the two arguments is this: the Conservative Argument issues no predictions about the likely results of the relevant innovation, while the Slippery Slope Argument does precisely that. In effect, the Conservative Argument says that we ought to ban a social innovation until we have a solid basis for predicting its safety, whereas the Slippery Slope Argument says that we ought to ban an innovation because it is likely to have unsafe results. It is easy to craft a slippery slope argument against genetic engineering—just specify the terrible results you anticipate from genetic enhancement or GMOs, and add the claim that we ought to ban practices that are likely to yield terrible results. The trick, of course, is to see whether it is possible to substantiate such predictions.

I leave that as an exercise for you. In the meantime, let's look at another argument against genetic engineering that incorporates an interesting mix of consequentialist and fairness-based considerations. This argument says that genetic engineering will have a specific kind of bad outcome—namely, an increase in *inequality* between the "haves," who can afford to receive genetic enhancement, and the "have-nots," who can't. Those who are wealthier will become even better looking, will become immune to various diseases, and will be able to enhance their intelligence through genetic engineering, thereby increasing the already very wide gap between the life prospects of the wealthy and the less well-to-do. This worry serves as the basis of

The Inequality Argument

1. If a social policy is very likely to increase inequality by improving the lives of the better-off and leaving the worse-off behind, then that social policy is immoral.
2. Allowing genetic engineering is very likely to increase inequality by improving the lives of the better-off and leaving the worse-off behind.

Therefore,

3. Allowing genetic engineering is an immoral social policy.

Premise 2 is probably true, at least in the short run. A typical pattern with social innovation is that the wealthy and powerful reap the bulk of the initial advantages. In some cases, that is the end of the story. But in many others, the less-well-off also benefit, as the innovations become more commonplace and less expensive. (Think of TVs, cars, or computers—all initially within the reach of just a few, but widely accessible to middle and many lower income families in a relatively short amount of time.) It's not clear whether the distribution of the benefits of genetic engineering would follow the first path or the second. That said, innovations in genetic engineering need not increase inequality. We *could* design social policies so that the poorer among us receive subsidized genetic enhancements and free access to GMOs (should they want it). If we chose to do that, premise 2 would be false.

There is a lot to say about premise 1. But we have already said a good deal—see the Argument Analysis section in Chapter 16, which is almost entirely devoted to discussing the morality of social policies that allow or promote specifically economic inequalities. Though the inequalities we are considering in this chapter range more broadly, to cover appearance, intelligence, character traits, and physical skills, the underlying basis for most of the arguments in Chapter 16 can be easily carried over to discussions of these broader inequalities. As a result, I leave it to you to apply those arguments in the context of genetic engineering, in order to determine whether social policies that result in unequal distributions of benefits are always or usually immoral.

Each of the arguments we have looked at so far highlights the anticipated results of genetic engineering. Let's shift our attention to arguments that focus instead on its nature. These arguments are largely critical, and claim that there is something wrong, in itself, with genetic enhancements or with GMOs. These arguments allow that genetic engineering might have excellent results. But according to those who advance these arguments, there is something intrinsically immoral about genetic engineering.

The first of these criticisms is focused on genetic enhancements, not GMOs, and says that such enhancements rob us of our true selves. To be genetically enhanced is to lose our authenticity, to change us from who we really are to some artificial substitute:

The Authenticity Argument

1. If a practice undermines our authenticity, then it is immoral.
2. Genetic enhancement undermines our authenticity.

Therefore,

3. Genetic enhancement is immoral.

On behalf of premise 2, some argue that part of the human condition is to be limited in various ways and to be forced to face challenges based on one's limitations. An achievement is truly your own only if you gain it via effort that utilizes your own traits. Genetic enhancement is a shortcut that makes your elevated level of appearance, performance, or aptitude not truly your own. Defenders of genetic enhancement, though, say that part of our authentic self is the ability to choose how to move forward in our lives, how to change ourselves in desirable ways. Choosing to become better through enhancement may be an authentic choice—informed, freely selected, and expressive of our deepest commitments. These critics of premise 2 will say that if an outcome is a result of an authentic choice, then the outcome itself is authentic.

Regarding premise 1: there are certainly some practices that undermine our authenticity and are immoral. Think of cases where totalitarian government officials lobotomize political prisoners, or administer personality-altering drugs in an effort to neutralize the prisoner's opposition to the regime. These ways of undermining our authenticity are immoral, however, because they are done without the victim's consent. What about cases in which people voluntarily seek to change who they are in a very significant way?

Sometimes such changes are for the worse. Imagine an admittedly strange case—one in which a person is bored with who she is and decides to become a drug addict. She succeeds. We might call her decision unwise or imprudent; it's not clear, though, that she has done something immoral. (One reason for this, explored in the Legal Punishment Requires Immorality Argument in Chapter 21, is that it is unclear whether self-harm per se is ever immoral.) If she has done something wrong—say, because she is now neglecting her children—the immorality most clearly consists in that neglect, rather than in becoming a different sort of person. After all, sometimes we can engage in transformative change for the better. We can leave at least a significant part of our old selves behind, and become more compassionate, more open-minded, more hopeful, kinder, and wiser. These sorts of fundamental changes in personality or character do not seem to be immoral.

This last point gives us some reason to think that changing who we are is not in itself immoral. A lot depends on the sort of change we are talking about—if it is an improvement, then all seems to be morally OK. And enhancements are, by definition, improvements. So it seems that enhancing oneself is not immoral, contrary to premise 1.

Critics will claim that there is a fundamental difference between improving oneself through hard work, on the one hand, and genetic enhancement, on the other. It matters whether your better self emerges from your own extended efforts or whether it comes from paying someone else to perform a medical procedure. I think this is right. You deserve much more credit in the first case. But this is not enough to show that you have acted immorally if you go the easier, second route. Some people who effectively purchase their improvements may not deserve any credit for doing so, but that is different from showing that their actions have been immoral.

The last two arguments we'll consider target both genetic enhancement and GMOs. The first of these arguments comes from the core idea that inspires the natural law theory (see Chapter 8): what is natural is good or right, and what is unnatural is bad or wrong. Genetic engineering is designed to alter nature—our own, when it comes to genetic enhancements, or the nature of the food we eat, when it comes to GMOs. The worry here is not that tinkering with nature will lead to disastrous results down the road—that is the focus of a slippery slope or conservative argument. Rather, the idea is that there is something problematic, in and of itself, with acting contrary to nature:

The Unnaturalness Argument

1. Unnatural actions are immoral.
2. Genetic engineering is unnatural.

Therefore,

3. Genetic engineering is immoral.

The apparent simplicity of this argument is deceptive. That's because the notion of *being unnatural* is ambiguous—it has more than one meaning. As a result, defenders of the Unnaturalness Argument need to be very clear about which understanding of "unnatural" they have in mind when pressing their case against genetic engineering.

Perhaps the best way to assess the premises of this argument is just to run through the most common definitions of being natural or unnatural. We've already done this in Chapter 8, though, and the upshot is that premise 1 is deeply problematic on all four readings of "natural" that we discussed there. For ease of reference: "natural" could refer to what we share with other animals, what is innate, what all things of a given kind have in common, or what something is designed to be or do. Rather than repeat that discussion, let's consider two more understandings of what it is to be natural or unnatural. These are the ones that are likely to work best for the opponent of genetic engineering.

On the first view, to be natural is to be unchanged by human manipulation or intervention. Natural traits are opposed to acquired ones; unnatural activities are those that involve changing something or someone from a pristine, unmodified state. Genetic engineering is unnatural in this sense, because both genetic enhancement and GMO manufacture involve human intervention to modify someone or something from its "natural" state. In this sense, though, premise (1) is mistaken, because many human interventions that change things from their natural state are improvements. We act unnaturally in this sense when we educate children, modifying their understanding of the world, or when a furniture maker takes a piece of wood and transforms it into an elegant table. Contrary to premise 1, though, such activities are not immoral.

On the second understanding, natural activities are defined as those that *preserve* something's essence; unnatural activities are ones that change it. GMOs are unnatural in this sense, since they involve altering the genetic essence of crops or other foodstuffs. So premise 2 of the Unnaturalness Argument is true as applied to GMOs. But it's not so clear when it comes to genetic enhancements. Some cases—changing someone's eye color or height, for instance—seem more superficial, and don't involve modifying a person's essence. Premise 2 is false when it comes to such changes, and so this argument would not justify condemning this sort of genetic enhancement. Other genetic changes, though, do seem to go "deeper," and involve a transformation of who the person is at a more fundamental level. Premise 2 would be true of these instances.

Even with regard to these more essential changes, however, premise 1 remains problematic. It's not clear why changing something's nature need be immoral. For instance, by genetically modifying the germline of the anopheles mosquito—the insect responsible for transmitting malaria—scientists might be able to save the lives of millions of people over the course of the next few decades. Or by developing a new type of apple the old-fashioned way—through conventional, non-GMO means—farmers have modified the essence of the old species, but don't seem to have done anything immoral thereby. When it comes to human beings, things may be more controversial, but a large part of the explanation here has to do with doubts about whether humans have natures. If they don't, then genetic enhancements cannot be unnatural (on this last understanding of what it is to be unnatural). But suppose that people do have natures. In that case, is it always immoral to change them?

It doesn't seem so. After all, some such natures may be bad. Suppose that someone recognizes that he has a deeply flawed nature and wants to improve it. He sets out to do so—he goes to therapy, reads self-help books, and seeks religious counseling. Imagine that this combination is successful; he really does become a much better person, in part by removing the flaws that used to define him. The current understanding makes this sort of transformation unnatural. But contrary to premise 1, there doesn't seem to be anything immoral about it.

We've now canvassed six understandings of what it is to be natural or unnatural. None of these six definitions yields the result that premise 1 is true. This doesn't show that the Unnaturalness Argument is unsound, however, for there may be a seventh understanding that does the trick. If you're a fan of this argument, then, your job is to identify that further definition and to defend the claim that both premise 1 and premise 2 are true when utilizing that definition.

Let's now consider a final argument about the morality of genetic engineering. This one is based on the thought that such activity expresses a kind of arrogance. It is presumptuous of humans to assume that we are entitled to change nature to suit our tastes and preferences. In effect, when we set out to tinker with the genetic make-up of things, we are playing God:

The Playing God Argument

1. We are morally forbidden from playing God.
2. Engaging in genetic engineering amounts to playing God.

Therefore,

3. We are morally forbidden from engaging in genetic engineering.

In order to make sense of this argument, we need to unpack the metaphor of *playing God* in such a way that premise 2 comes out as true. We can then investigate whether playing God is, as premise 1 declares, really such a bad thing.

We can set aside the vexed question of whether God exists and ask instead about what God's role would be *if* God were to exist.

There are many answers to this question, but perhaps the most relevant is this: God is the creator of all things and has the final say about life and death. God decides when it is appropriate to end a life, when it is right to sustain or create it, and when it is acceptable to render a fundamental change in the nature of His creation. We play God when we take unto ourselves the authority to do these things.

On this understanding of what it is to play God, premise 2 is usually true. GMO production creates new life forms. Genetic enhancement would in many (though not all) cases render a fundamental change in the nature of those who receive it. But premise 1 is problematic. Parents who intend to conceive a child are playing God, on the current understanding, but need not be doing anything immoral thereby. Soldiers who sacrifice themselves to save their comrades are also playing God in this sense, as are emergency room doctors who are making life-and-death decisions. But such soldiers need not be acting immorally; the same can be said of these doctors. And as we've seen in the previous discussion, regarding the last of the definitions of "unnatural," there needn't be anything wrong in seeking to change something's fundamental nature.

The notion of playing God, like the notion of being unnatural, admits of many different understandings. I've selected the one that I think has the best shot at getting critics of genetic engineering what they want. As we've seen, this understanding does not succeed. But perhaps another one will. As before, the task for opponents of genetic enhancements and GMOs is to identify that different understanding and then to defend the premises that incorporate it.

CONCLUSION

While there is relatively little controversy about the morality of developing genetic *therapies*—procedures designed to restore health to the sick—there is substantial disagreement about whether genetic enhancements and GMOs

STAT SHOT

1. More than 90 percent of all soybean and corn acreage in the United States is used to grow GMOs.[1]

2. The United States, Brazil, and Argentina are the top GMO producers, accounting for 76.3 percent of all GMO crops (Figure 22.1).

3. According to a Harvard poll, 65 percent of US adults think that it should be illegal to genetically modify unborn babies. Eighty-three percent said it should be illegal to engage in genetic enhancement to enhance intelligence or physical attributes.[2]

4. Most countries in Europe have laws requiring that GMOs be labeled. Most countries in North America don't (Figure 22.2).

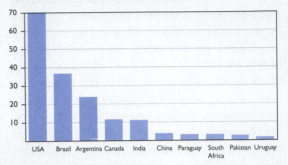

Top GMO crop–growing countries, in million hectares (2012)

Figure 22.1

Source: http://www.gmoinside.org/gmos-in-animal-feed/

1. http://time.com/3840073/gmo-food-charts/

2. https://cdn1.sph.harvard.edu/wp-content/uploads/sites/94/2016/01/STAT-Harvard-Poll-Jan-2016-Genetic-Technology.pdf

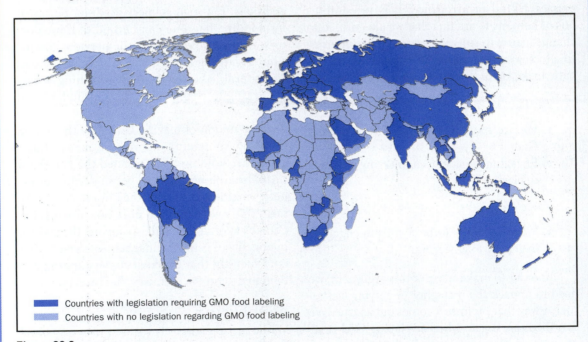

■ Countries with legislation requiring GMO food labeling
■ Countries with no legislation regarding GMO food labeling

Figure 22.2.
GMO labeling laws worldwide (2013).
Source: http://familywellnesshq.com/what-do-us-canada-and-most-of-the-third-world-countries-have-in-common-gmo-food/

are morally acceptable. The main reason in support of such efforts is that they promise to do so much good, without violating anyone's rights. But conservative and slippery slope critics argue that we should put the brakes on such research until we have good evidence of its safety, while other critics argue that these forms of genetic engineering will only increase social inequality.

Other objections to genetic engineering focus on its intrinsic nature, rather than on its expected results. Such criticisms claim that genetic enhancements are inauthentic, or that such enhancements and GMOs are unnatural or are instances of playing God. As we've seen, these critiques are not yet well-supported, though the jury is still out as to whether critics are able to identify other notions of unnaturalness or playing God that can serve their purposes.

ESSENTIAL CONCEPTS

Artificial selection: the process by which humans develop desirable traits in plants or animals by selecting which males or females will reproduce together. It's sometimes called "selective breeding."

Conservative: a position that either seeks to preserve the status quo or claims that we ought to change the traditional ways of doing things only if there is compelling evidence that doing so would be better.

CRISPR-cas9: a gene-editing tool that allows scientists to target specific sequences of DNA and either alter or delete them, or insert new genetic material altogether.

Eugenics: the use of selective breeding to develop desirable traits in human beings, or the use of sterilization to eradicate undesirable traits in human beings.

Extrapolation problem: the difficulty of concluding that outcomes in one context will carry over to a different context.

Genetic engineering: the direct manipulation of an organism's DNA to alter its characteristics.

Genetic enhancement: the direct manipulation of an organism's DNA to improve its form or functioning beyond the level necessary for health.

Genetically modified organism (GMO): organism whose DNA has been directly altered for human purposes.

Germline cells: reproductive cells.

Somatic cells: nonreproductive cells.

Cases for Critical Thinking

Growth Hormones: Just for the Deficient?

Some children have a hormone deficiency that causes them to be much shorter than average. In the 1980s, human growth hormone was approved for addressing their situation. Prescribing this hormone to such children allowed them to enjoy all the benefits of a typical height: for example, they could often compete in basketball, whereas otherwise they couldn't. However, in the 1990s, doctors started to prescribe growth hormone to children who didn't have a hormone deficiency, but whose short stature was due to their parents' height. By 1996, this kind of use accounted for 40 percent of human growth hormone prescriptions.[1]

Questions

1. Is normal height a benefit for people? If so, what makes it beneficial?
2. Is there any relevant difference between those children whose height resulted from a hormone deficiency and those whose height resulted from having inherited their

---

1. https://www.theatlantic.com/magazine/archive/2004/04/the-case-against-perfection/302927/

parents' genes, such that it is permissible to prescribe growth hormones to the former but not the latter?

3. Suppose Jack is of a typical height for boys his age and, given his family history, can expect to be roughly the average height for US males. But Jack has always dreamed of playing professional basketball. If we can permissibly prescribe growth hormones to those whose height is owing to their genetic inheritance, is it also permissible for Jack's doctor to prescribe them to him?

GMO Labeling Laws

In 2012, California voters decided against Proposition 37, which would have required that foods containing GMOs be labeled as such. (It also would have prohibited labeling them as "natural" or "certified organic," along with some other labels.) However, in June 2016, President Obama signed into law a bill requiring that foods with GMOs be labeled as such.[1] Many other countries have similar laws, including Australia, Japan, Russia, China, and twenty-eight countries in the European Union. [2]

Questions

1. Ought we to have such laws, or is it permissible for us not to have them? Why?

2. Suppose we did enough research to know that GMOs—or at least the ones available to consumers—had no adverse health consequences. Would labeling laws be morally advisable in that case? Why or why not?

3. In the United States, all processed foods must contain nutritional information. And tobacco products are required to display the Surgeon General's warning about the adverse health effects of tobacco use. Are these requirements justified? If not, why not? If so, do the arguments used to justify them also justify a requirement that GMOs be labeled as such?

Doping and Genetic Enhancement

Lance Armstrong won the Tour de France a record seven straight times. Those victories were voided when it was discovered that he was using performance-enhancing drugs. Similar episodes have plagued most major sports: Jon Jones, for example, the UFC light heavyweight champion and believed by many to be the greatest UFC fighter ever, was stripped of his title in 2017 when both of his urine samples came back positive for a banned substance. In March 2016, tennis star Maria Sharapova was banned from professional tennis for over a year as a result of having failed a drug test conducted during the Australian Open two months earlier.

Questions

1. Do you think that performance-enhancing drugs ought to be banned from professional sports? Why or why not?

2. Suppose performance-enhancing drugs ought to be banned from professional sports. Many individuals naturally have higher levels of hormones, such as testosterone, that give them athletic advantages. Should we also ban such people from competing, since they get the same kind of unearned advantage as those who use performance-enhancing drugs?

3. Suppose, as is currently the case, that we shouldn't ban competitors who have naturally higher levels of advantageous hormones. Does it follow that we should allow competitors who have had genetic enhancements? If not, what's the relevant difference between the two types of advantage?

[1] http://www.foodsafetynews.com/2016/09/the-new-gmo-labeling-law-a-matter-of-perspective/#.WcwF38iGPIU

[2] http://www.justlabelit.org/right-to-know-center/labeling-around-the-world/

READINGS

The Case Against Perfection

Michael Sandel

Michael Sandel argues against genetic enhancement and engineering by asking us to focus on what he calls "the gifted character of human powers and achievements." By this he means that our talents and our abilities are not entirely a product of our efforts. And this, he argues, is a very good thing. That much of what is important in a life is effectively outside of our control should encourage in us a degree of humility about our accomplishments. Genetic enhancement and engineering are an effort to control the key elements of our appearance, fitness, and personality in a way that supports pride and arrogance rather than humility. Further, we expand our human sympathies and sense of social solidarity if we recognize that the problems and difficulties confronted by others are not always of their own making.

Sandel draws a parallel between genetic engineering and the kind of "hyperparenting" in which parents obsessively attend to every detail of their children's lives. In both cases, a quest for perfection "represents the anxious excess of mastery and dominion that misses the sense of life as a gift." Recognizing a child's limitations and vulnerabilities not only helps a parent to develop important moral virtues such as compassion, sympathy, and empathy, but also provides an opportunity to appreciate the frailty and imperfections that come in every life.

Another worry about genetic engineering is that it is really no different from the eugenics programs of old. Those state-run programs forcibly sterilized or compelled abortions of members of unpopular minority groups in the name of creating a finer "race" of human beings. Although the state coercion at the heart of such programs is certainly morally troubling, Sandel argues that the impulse to genetically engineer a more perfect next generation is still morally problematic, even if we imagine that such engineering is done without any coercion at all.

. . .It is commonly said that genetic enhancements undermine our humanity by threatening our capacity to act freely, to succeed by our own efforts, and to consider ourselves responsible—worthy of praise or blame—for the things we do and for the way we are. It is one thing to hit seventy home runs as the result of disciplined training and effort, and something else, something less, to hit them with the help of steroids or genetically enhanced muscles. Of course, the roles of effort and enhancement will be a matter of degree. But as the role of enhancement increases, our admiration for the achievement fades—or, rather, our admiration for the achievement shifts from the player to his pharmacist. This suggests that our moral response to enhancement is a response to the diminished agency of the person whose achievement is enhanced.

Though there is much to be said for this argument, I do not think the main problem with enhancement and genetic engineering is that they undermine effort and erode human agency. The

From Michael J. Sandel, "The Case Against Perfection," *Atlantic Monthly* (April 2004), pp. 56–62. https://www.theatlantic.com/magazine/archive/2004/04/the-case-against-perfection/302927/

deeper danger is that they represent a kind of hyperagency—a Promethean aspiration to remake nature, including human nature, to serve our purposes and satisfy our desires. The problem is not the drift to mechanism but the drive to mastery. And what the drive to mastery misses and may even destroy is an appreciation of the gifted character of human powers and achievements.

To acknowledge the giftedness of life is to recognize that our talents and powers are not wholly our own doing, despite the effort we expend to develop and to exercise them. It is also to recognize that not everything in the world is open to whatever use we may desire or devise. Appreciating the gifted quality of life constrains the Promethean project and conduces to a certain humility. It is in part a religious sensibility. But its resonance reaches beyond religion.

It is difficult to account for what we admire about human activity and achievement without drawing upon some version of this idea. Consider two types of athletic achievement. We appreciate players like Pete Rose, who are not blessed with great natural gifts but who manage, through striving, grit, and determination, to excel in their sport. But we also admire players like Joe DiMaggio, who display natural gifts with grace and effortlessness. Now, suppose we learned that both players took performance-enhancing drugs. Whose turn to drugs would we find more deeply disillusioning? Which aspect of the athletic ideal—effort or gift—would be more deeply offended?

Some might say effort: the problem with drugs is that they provide a shortcut, a way to win without striving. But striving is not the point of sports; excellence is. And excellence consists at least partly in the display of natural talents and gifts that are no doing of the athlete who possesses them. This is an uncomfortable fact for democratic societies. We want to believe that success, in sports and in life, is something we earn, not something we inherit. Natural gifts, and the admiration they inspire, embarrass the meritocratic faith; they cast doubt on the conviction that praise and rewards flow from effort alone. In the face of this embarrassment we inflate the moral significance of striving, and depreciate giftedness. This distortion can be seen, for example, in network-television coverage of the Olympics, which focuses less on the feats the athletes perform than on heartrending stories of the hardships they have overcome and the struggles they have waged to triumph over an injury or a difficult upbringing or political turmoil in their native land.

But effort isn't everything. No one believes that a mediocre basketball player who works and trains even harder than Michael Jordan deserves greater acclaim or a bigger contract. The real problem with genetically altered athletes is that they corrupt athletic competition as a human activity that honors the cultivation and display of natural talents. From this standpoint, enhancement can be seen as the ultimate expression of the ethic of effort and willfulness—a kind of high-tech striving. The ethic of willfulness and the biotechnological powers it now enlists are arrayed against the claims of giftedness.

The ethic of giftedness, under siege in sports, persists in the practice of parenting. But here, too, bioengineering and genetic enhancement threaten to dislodge it. To appreciate children as gifts is to accept them as they come, not as objects of our design or products of our will or instruments of our ambition. Parental love is not contingent on the talents and attributes a child happens to have. We choose our friends and spouses at least partly on the basis of qualities we find attractive. But we do not choose our children. Their qualities are unpredictable, and even the most conscientious parents cannot be held wholly responsible for the kind of children they have. That is why parenthood, more than other human relationships, teaches what the theologian William F. May calls an "openness to the unbidden."

May's resonant phrase helps us see that the deepest moral objection to enhancement lies less in the perfection it seeks than in the human disposition it expresses and promotes. The problem is not that parents usurp the autonomy of a child they design. The problem lies in the hubris of the designing parents, in their drive to master the mystery of birth. Even if this disposition did not make parents tyrants to their children, it would disfigure the relation between parent and child, and deprive the parent of the humility and enlarged human sympathies that an openness to the unbidden can cultivate.

To appreciate children as gifts or blessings is not, of course, to be passive in the face of illness or disease. Medical intervention to cure or prevent illness or restore the injured to health does not desecrate nature but honors it. Healing sickness or injury does not override a child's natural capacities but permits them to flourish.

Nor does the sense of life as a gift mean that parents must shrink from shaping and directing the development of their child. Just as athletes and artists have an obligation to cultivate their talents, so parents have an obligation to cultivate their children, to help them discover and develop their talents and gifts. As May points out, parents give their children two kinds of love: accepting love and transforming love. Accepting love affirms the being of the child, whereas transforming love seeks the well-being of the child. Each aspect corrects the excesses of the other, he writes: "Attachment becomes too quietistic if it slackens into mere acceptance of the child as he is." Parents have a duty to promote their children's excellence.

These days, however, overly ambitious parents are prone to get carried away with transforming love—promoting and demanding all manner of accomplishments from their children, seeking perfection. "Parents find it difficult to maintain an equilibrium between the two sides of love," May observes. "Accepting love, without transforming love, slides into indulgence and finally neglect. Transforming love, without accepting love, badgers and finally rejects." May finds in these competing impulses a parallel with modern science: it, too, engages us in beholding the given world, studying and savoring it, and also in molding the world, transforming and perfecting it.

The mandate to mold our children, to cultivate and improve them, complicates the case against enhancement. We usually admire parents who seek the best for their children, who spare no effort to help them achieve happiness and success. Some parents confer advantages on their children by enrolling them in expensive schools, hiring private tutors, sending them to tennis camp, providing them with piano lessons, ballet lessons, swimming lessons, SAT-prep courses, and so on. If it is permissible and even admirable for parents to help their children in these ways, why isn't it equally admirable for parents to use whatever genetic technologies may emerge (provided they are safe) to enhance their children's intelligence, musical ability, or athletic prowess?

The defenders of enhancement are right to this extent: improving children through genetic engineering is similar in spirit to the heavily managed, high-pressure child-rearing that is now common. But this similarity does not vindicate genetic enhancement. On the contrary, it highlights a problem with the trend toward hyperparenting. One conspicuous example of this trend is sports-crazed parents bent on making champions of their children. Another is the frenzied drive of overbearing parents to mold and manage their children's academic careers.

As the pressure for performance increases, so does the need to help distractible children concentrate on the task at hand. This may be why diagnoses of attention deficit and hyperactivity disorder have increased so sharply. Lawrence Diller, a pediatrician and the author of *Running on Ritalin*, estimates that five to six percent of American children under eighteen (a total of four to five million kids) are currently prescribed Ritalin, Adderall, and other stimulants, the treatment of choice for ADHD. (Stimulants counteract hyperactivity by making it easier to focus and sustain attention.) The number of Ritalin prescriptions for children and adolescents has tripled over the past decade, but not all users suffer from attention disorders or hyperactivity. High school and college students have learned that prescription stimulants improve concentration for those with normal attention spans, and some buy or borrow their classmates' drugs to enhance their performance on the SAT or other exams. Since stimulants work for both medical and nonmedical purposes, they raise the same moral questions posed by other technologies of enhancement.

However those questions are resolved, the debate reveals the cultural distance we have traveled since the debate over marijuana, LSD, and other drugs a generation ago. Unlike the drugs of the 1960s and 1970s, Ritalin and Adderall are not for checking out but for buckling down, not for beholding the world and taking it in but for molding the world and fitting in. We used to speak of nonmedical drug use as "recreational." That term no longer applies. The steroids and stimulants that figure in the enhancement debate are not a source of recreation but a bid for compliance—a way of answering a competitive society's demand to improve our performance and perfect our nature. This demand for performance and perfection animates the impulse to rail against the given. It is the deepest source of the moral trouble with enhancement.

Some see a clear line between genetic enhancement and other ways that people seek improvement in their children and themselves. Genetic manipulation seems somehow worse—more intrusive, more sinister—than other ways of enhancing performance and seeking success. But morally speaking, the difference is less significant than it seems. Bioengineering gives us reason to question the low-tech, high-pressure child-rearing practices we commonly accept. The hyperparenting familiar in our time represents an anxious excess of mastery and dominion that misses the sense of life as a gift. This draws it disturbingly close to eugenics.

The shadow of eugenics hangs over today's debates about genetic engineering and enhancement. Critics of genetic engineering argue that human cloning, enhancement, and the quest for designer children are nothing more than "privatized" or "free-market" eugenics. Defenders of enhancement reply that genetic choices freely made are not really eugenic—at least not in the pejorative sense. To remove the coercion, they argue, is to remove the very thing that makes eugenic policies repugnant.

Sorting out the lesson of eugenics is another way of wrestling with the ethics of enhancement. The Nazis gave eugenics a bad name. But what, precisely, was wrong with it? Was the old eugenics objectionable only insofar as it was coercive? Or is there something inherently wrong with the resolve to deliberately design our progeny's traits?

James Watson, the biologist who, with Francis Crick, discovered the structure of DNA, sees nothing wrong with genetic engineering and enhancement, provided they are freely chosen rather than state-imposed. And yet Watson's language contains more than a whiff of the old eugenic sensibility. "If you really are stupid, I would call that a disease," he recently told *The Times* of London. "The lower 10 percent who really have difficulty, even in elementary school, what's the cause of it? A lot of people would like to say, 'Well, poverty, things like that.' It probably isn't. So I'd like to get rid of that, to help the lower 10 percent." A few years ago Watson stirred controversy by saying that if a gene for homosexuality were discovered, a woman should be free to abort a fetus that carried it. When his remark provoked an uproar, he replied that he was not singling out gays but asserting a principle: women should be free to abort fetuses for any reason of genetic preference—for example, if the child would be dyslexic, or lacking musical talent, or too short to play basketball.

Watson's scenarios are clearly objectionable to those for whom all abortion is an unspeakable crime. But for those who do not subscribe to the pro-life position, these scenarios raise a hard question: If it is morally troubling to contemplate abortion to avoid a gay child or a dyslexic one, doesn't this suggest that something is wrong with acting on any eugenic preference, even when no state coercion is involved?

Consider the market in eggs and sperm. The advent of artificial insemination allows prospective parents to shop for gametes with the genetic traits they desire in their offspring. It is a less predictable way to design children than cloning or pre-implantation genetic screening, but it offers a good example of a procreative practice in which the old eugenics meets the new consumerism. A few years ago some Ivy League newspapers ran an ad seeking an egg from a woman who was at least five feet ten inches tall and athletic, had no major family medical problems, and had a combined SAT score of 1400 or above. The ad offered $50,000 for an egg from a donor with these traits. More recently a Web site was launched claiming to auction eggs from fashion models whose photos appeared on the site, at starting bids of $15,000 to $150,000.

On what grounds, if any, is the egg market morally objectionable? Since no one is forced to buy or sell, it cannot be wrong for reasons of coercion. Some might worry that hefty prices would exploit poor women by presenting them with an offer they couldn't refuse. But the designer eggs that fetch the highest prices are likely to be sought from the privileged, not the poor. If the market for premium eggs gives us moral qualms, this, too, shows that concerns about eugenics are not put to rest by freedom of choice.

A tale of two sperm banks helps explain why. The Repository for Germinal Choice, one of America's first sperm banks, was not a commercial enterprise. It was opened in 1980 by Robert Graham, a philanthropist dedicated to improving the world's "germ plasm" and counteracting the rise of "retrograde humans." His plan was to collect the sperm of Nobel Prize-winning scientists and make it available to women of high intelligence, in hopes of breeding supersmart babies. But Graham had trouble persuading Nobel laureates to donate their sperm for his bizarre scheme, and so settled for sperm from young scientists of high promise. His sperm bank closed in 1999.

In contrast, California Cryobank, one of the world's leading sperm banks, is a for-profit company with no overt eugenic mission. Cappy Rothman, M.D., a co-founder of the firm, has nothing but disdain for Graham's eugenics, although the standards Cryobank imposes on the sperm it recruits are exacting. Cryobank has offices in Cambridge, Massachusetts, between Harvard and MIT, and in Palo Alto, California, near Stanford. It advertises for donors in campus newspapers (compensation up to $900 a month), and accepts less than five percent of the men who apply. Cryobank's marketing materials play up the prestigious source of its sperm. Its catalogue provides detailed information about the physical characteristics of each donor, along with his ethnic origin and college major. For an extra fee prospective customers can buy the results of a test that assesses the donor's temperament and character type. Rothman reports that Cryobank's ideal sperm donor is six feet tall, with brown eyes, blond hair, and dimples, and has a college degree—not because the company wants to propagate those traits, but because those are the traits his customers want: "If our customers wanted high school dropouts, we would give them high school dropouts."

Not everyone objects to marketing sperm. But anyone who is troubled by the eugenic aspect of the Nobel Prize sperm bank should be equally troubled by Cryobank, consumer-driven though it be. What,

after all, is the moral difference between designing children according to an explicit eugenic purpose and designing children according to the dictates of the market? Whether the aim is to improve humanity's "germ plasm" or to cater to consumer preferences, both practices are eugenic insofar as both make children into products of deliberate design.

A number of political philosophers call for a new "liberal eugenics." They argue that a moral distinction can be drawn between the old eugenic policies and genetic enhancements that do not restrict the autonomy of the child. "While old-fashioned authoritarian eugenicists sought to produce citizens out of a single centrally designed mould," writes Nicholas Agar, "the distinguishing mark of the new liberal eugenics is state neutrality." Government may not tell parents what sort of children to design, and parents may engineer in their children only those traits that improve their capacities without biasing their choice of life plans. A recent text on genetics and justice, written by the bioethicists Allen Buchanan, Dan W. Brock, Norman Daniels, and Daniel Wikler, offers a similar view. The "bad reputation of eugenics," they write, is due to practices that "might be avoidable in a future eugenic program." The problem with the old eugenics was that its burdens fell disproportionately on the weak and the poor, who were unjustly sterilized and segregated. But provided that the benefits and burdens of genetic improvement are fairly distributed, these bioethicists argue, eugenic measures are unobjectionable and may even be morally required.

The libertarian philosopher Robert Nozick proposed a "genetic supermarket" that would enable parents to order children by design without imposing a single design on the society as a whole: "This supermarket system has the great virtue that it involves no centralized decision fixing the future human type(s)."

Even the leading philosopher of American liberalism, John Rawls, in his classic *A Theory of Justice* (1971), offered a brief endorsement of noncoercive eugenics. Even in a society that agrees to share the benefits and burdens of the genetic lottery, it is "in the interest of each to have greater natural assets," Rawls wrote. "This enables him to pursue a preferred plan of life." The parties to the social contract "want to insure for their descendants the best genetic endowment (assuming their own to be fixed)." Eugenic policies are therefore not only permissible but required as a matter of justice. "Thus over time a society is to take steps at least to preserve the general level of natural abilities and to prevent the diffusion of serious defects."

But removing the coercion does not vindicate eugenics. The problem with eugenics and genetic engineering is that they represent the one-sided triumph of willfulness over giftedness, of dominion over reverence, of molding over beholding. Why, we may wonder, should we worry about this triumph? Why not shake off our unease about genetic enhancement as so much superstition? What would be lost if biotechnology dissolved our sense of giftedness?

From a religious standpoint the answer is clear: To believe that our talents and powers are wholly our own doing is to misunderstand our place in creation, to confuse our role with God's. Religion is not the only source of reasons to care about giftedness, however. The moral stakes can also be described in secular terms. If bioengineering made the myth of the "self-made man" come true, it would be difficult to view our talents as gifts for which we are indebted, rather than as achievements for which we are responsible. This would transform three key features of our moral landscape: humility, responsibility, and solidarity.

In a social world that prizes mastery and control, parenthood is a school for humility. That we care deeply about our children and yet cannot choose the kind we want teaches parents to be open to the unbidden. Such openness is a disposition worth affirming, not only within families but in the wider world as well. It invites us to abide the unexpected, to live with dissonance, to rein in the impulse to control. A *Gattaca*-like world in which parents became accustomed to specifying the sex and genetic traits of their children would be a world inhospitable to the unbidden, a gated community writ large. The awareness that our talents and abilities are not wholly our own doing restrains our tendency toward hubris.

Though some maintain that genetic enhancement erodes human agency by overriding effort, the real problem is the explosion, not the erosion, of responsibility. As humility gives way, responsibility expands to daunting proportions. We attribute less to chance and more to choice. Parents become responsible for choosing, or failing to choose, the right traits for their children. Athletes become responsible for acquiring, or failing to acquire, the talents that will help their teams win.

One of the blessings of seeing ourselves as creatures of nature, God, or fortune is that we are not wholly responsible for the way we are. The more we become masters of our genetic endowments, the greater the burden we bear for the talents we have and the way we perform. Today when a basketball player misses a rebound, his coach can blame him for being out of position. Tomorrow the coach may blame him for being too short. Even now the use of performance-enhancing drugs in professional sports is subtly transforming the expectations players have for one another; on some teams players who take the field free from amphetamines or other stimulants are criticized for "playing naked."

The more alive we are to the chanced nature of our lot, the more reason we have to share our fate with others. Consider insurance. Since people do not know whether or when various ills will befall them, they pool their risk by buying health insurance and life insurance. As life plays itself out, the healthy wind up subsidizing the unhealthy, and those who live to a ripe old age wind up subsidizing the families of those who die before their time. Even without a sense of mutual obligation, people pool their risks and resources and share one another's fate.

But insurance markets mimic solidarity only insofar as people do not know or control their own risk factors. Suppose genetic testing advanced to the point where it could reliably predict each person's medical future and life expectancy. Those confident of good health and long life would opt out of the pool, causing other people's premiums to skyrocket. The solidarity of insurance would disappear as those with good genes fled the actuarial company of those with bad ones.

The fear that insurance companies would use genetic data to assess risks and set premiums recently led the Senate to vote to prohibit genetic discrimination in health insurance. But the bigger danger, admittedly more speculative, is that genetic enhancement, if routinely practiced, would make it harder to foster the moral sentiments that social solidarity requires.

Why, after all, do the successful owe anything to the least-advantaged members of society? The best answer to this question leans heavily on the notion of giftedness. The natural talents that enable the successful to flourish are not their own doing but, rather, their good fortune—a result of the genetic lottery. If our genetic endowments are gifts, rather than achievements for which we can claim credit, it is a mistake and a conceit to assume that we are entitled to the full measure of the bounty they reap in a market economy. We therefore have an obligation to share this bounty with those who, through no fault of their own, lack comparable gifts.

A lively sense of the contingency of our gifts—a consciousness that none of us is wholly responsible for his or her success—saves a meritocratic society from sliding into the smug assumption that the rich are rich because they are more deserving than the poor. Without this, the successful would become even more likely than they are now to view themselves as self-made and self-sufficient, and hence wholly responsible for their success. Those at the bottom of society would be viewed not as disadvantaged, and thus worthy of a measure of compensation, but as simply unfit, and thus worthy of eugenic repair. The meritocracy, less chastened by chance, would become harder, less forgiving. As perfect genetic knowledge would end the simulacrum of solidarity in insurance markets, so perfect genetic control would erode the actual solidarity that arises when men and women reflect on the contingency of their talents and fortunes.

Thirty-five years ago Robert L. Sinsheimer, a molecular biologist at the California Institute of Technology, glimpsed the shape of things to come. In an article titled "The Prospect of Designed Genetic Change" he argued that freedom of choice would vindicate the new genetics, and set it apart from the discredited eugenics of old.

> To implement the older eugenics. . . .
> would have required a massive social

programme carried out over many generations. Such a programme could not have been initiated without the consent and co-operation of a major fraction of the population, and would have been continuously subject to social control. In contrast, the new eugenics could, at least in principle, be implemented on a quite individual basis, in one generation, and subject to no existing restrictions.

According to Sinsheimer, the new eugenics would be voluntary rather than coerced, and also more humane. Rather than segregating and eliminating the unfit, it would improve them. "The old eugenics would have required a continual selection for breeding of the fit, and a culling of the unfit," he wrote. "The new eugenics would permit in principle the conversion of all the unfit to the highest genetic level."

Sinsheimer's paean to genetic engineering caught the heady, Promethean self-image of the age. He wrote hopefully of rescuing "the losers in that chromosomal lottery that so firmly channels our human destinies," including not only those born with genetic defects but also "the 50,000,000 'normal' Americans with an IQ of less than 90." But he also saw that something bigger than improving on nature's "mindless, age-old throw of dice" was at stake. Implicit in technologies of genetic intervention was a more exalted place for human beings in the cosmos. "As we enlarge man's freedom, we diminish his constraints and that which he must accept as given," he wrote. Copernicus and Darwin had "demoted man from his bright glory at the focal point of the universe," but the new biology would restore his central role. In the mirror of our genetic knowledge we would see ourselves as more than a link in the chain of evolution: "We can be the agent of transition to a whole new pitch of evolution. This is a cosmic event."

There is something appealing, even intoxicating, about a vision of human freedom unfettered by the given. It may even be the case that the allure of that vision played a part in summoning the genomic age into being. It is often assumed that the powers of enhancement we now possess arose as an inadvertent by-product of biomedical progress—the genetic revolution came, so to speak, to cure disease, and stayed to tempt us with the prospect of enhancing our performance, designing our children, and perfecting our nature. That may have the story backwards. It is more plausible to view genetic engineering as the ultimate expression of our resolve to see ourselves astride the world, the masters of our nature. But that promise of mastery is flawed. It threatens to banish our appreciation of life as a gift, and to leave us with nothing to affirm or behold outside our own will.

Michael Sandel: The Case Against Perfectionism

1. Explain the difference between "accepting love" and "transforming love." To illustrate, give an example of each. Why does Sandel think both are important and how does he think they should be balanced? According to Sandel, what implications does this have for how parents should treat their children? Do you agree? Why or why not?

2. Explain how "liberal eugenics" differs from "old-fashioned authoritarian eugenics." Under what conditions do the proponents of "liberal eugenics" think that genetic engineering is morally permissible? Do you think that these conditions could ever be met? If they could be met, do you agree that in such circumstances genetic engineering would be morally permissible? Why or why not?

3. What does Sandel think the point of sports is? Explain the distinction between talent and striving, and how each contributes to our assessments of athletes and athletic performances. How do these considerations mirror those relevant to the moral permissibility of human enhancement? What lesson does Sandel draw from his consideration of athletics?

4. Sandel thinks that the practice of bioengineering will "[dissolve] our sense of giftedness," which in turn will "transform three key features of our moral landscape." Identify these three features and explain how Sandel thinks bioengineering would transform them. Do you agree with his assessment? Do you think the likely effects of bioengineering are a good reason to reject it? Defend your answer.

5. What does Sandel mean by "the ethic of giftedness"? What obligations does it impose upon us? What kind of obligations do we have that conflict with giftedness? According to Sandel, what implications does the ethic of giftedness have for the moral permissibility of human enhancement? Do you agree with this assessment? Why or why not?

Genetic Interventions and the Ethics of Enhancement of Human Beings

Julian Savulescu

Julian Savulescu offers three arguments in defense of the genetic enhancement of human beings.

First, suppose that parents could greatly improve their child's intelligence by altering the child's diet. They are lazy and fail to do this. We would condemn the parents for their laziness. Things are no different when it comes to genetic enhancements. If parents have the opportunity to greatly benefit their children, but deliberately or negligently fail to do so, then they have acted wrongly. It doesn't matter whether the benefit is conferred by enhanced diet or by introducing genetic changes.

Second, consistency requires that we treat "environmental" and biological enhancements in the same way. We train our children to be cooperative, intelligent, and well behaved. Such parental "interventions" alter a child's brain structure in irreversible but highly beneficial ways. This is exactly what many genetic interventions do.

Instilling useful and enjoyable traits in one's child is morally required. Genetic enhancement helps parents to meet this requirement.

Third, if we accept the treatment and prevention of disease as an important goal, then we should accept genetic interventions. Diseases undermine health, which in turn undermines a person's well-being and quality of life. Failure to prevent diseases by the use of genetic intervention is just as bad as failure to prevent them by the use of available drugs or surgeries.

Savulescu then replies to various objections that have been leveled against genetic enhancement. (1) Such practices amount to "playing God." Reply: we rightly make life-or-death decisions all the time, and many are permissible. (2) Genetic interventions will have discriminatory results. Reply: many people are born with serious biological handicaps, and genetic intervention can level the playing field and thus erase much existing disparity between those who were favored in the "natural lottery" and those who weren't. (3) Genetic engineering will lead to a single model of a desired child, and a sterile world where the surprise and mystery of life would disappear. Reply: manipulating genes will never erase differences among people and will still leave huge elements of our lives subject to chance. (4) Genetic enhancement is contrary to human nature. Reply: our nature as human beings is to be rational, and that requires us to use our reason to determine how best to improve our lives. Genetic engineering will do just that. (5) Genetic enhancement is self-defeating; its goal of making some people superior—more beautiful, intelligent, hard-working than others—will fail if everyone is genetically enhanced. Reply: critics have mistaken the goal of such enhancement: it is not to create or reinforce social divisions, but rather to improve people's lives.

Should we use science and medical technology not just to prevent or treat disease, but to intervene at the most basic biological levels to improve biology and enhance people's lives? By "enhance," I mean help them to live a longer and/or better life than normal. There are various ways in which we can enhance people but I want to focus on biological enhancement, especially genetic enhancement.

THE ETHICS OF ENHANCEMENT

I will now give three arguments in favour of enhancement and then consider several objections.

First Argument for Enhancement: Choosing Not to Enhance Is Wrong

Consider the case of the Neglectful Parents. The Neglectful Parents give birth to a child with a

From Julian Savulescu, "Genetic Interventions and the Ethics of Enhancement of Human Beings," in *The Oxford Handbook of Bioethics*, ed. Bonnie Steinbock (Oxford University Press, 2007), pp. 516–535. By permission of Oxford University Press.

special condition. The child has a stunning intellect but requires a simple, readily available, cheap dietary supplement to sustain his intellect. But they neglect the diet of this child and this results in a child with a stunning intellect becoming normal. This is clearly wrong.

But now consider the case of the Lazy Parents. They have a child who has a normal intellect but if they introduced the same dietary supplement, the child's intellect would rise to the same level as the child of the Neglectful Parent. They can't be bothered with improving the child's diet so the child remains with a normal intellect. Failure to institute dietary supplementation means a normal child fails to achieve a stunning intellect. The inaction of the Lazy Parents is as wrong as the inaction of the Neglectful Parents. It has exactly the same consequence: a child exists who could have had a stunning intellect but is instead normal.

Some argue that it is not wrong to fail to bring about the best state of affairs. This may or may not be the case. But in these kinds of case, when there are no other relevant moral considerations, the failure to introduce a diet that sustains a more desirable state is as wrong as the failure to introduce a diet that brings about a more desirable state. The costs of inaction are the same, as are the parental obligations.

If we substitute "biological intervention" for "diet," we see that in order not to wrong our children, we should enhance them. Unless there is something special and optimal about our children's physical, psychological, or cognitive abilities, or something different about other biological interventions, it would be wrong not to enhance them.

Second Argument: Consistency

Some will object that, while we do have an obligation to institute better diets, biological interventions like genetic interventions are different from dietary supplementation. I will argue that there is no difference between these interventions.

In general, we accept environmental interventions to improve our children. Education, diet, and training are all used to make our children better people and increase their opportunities in life. We train children to be well behaved, cooperative, and intelligent. Indeed, researchers are looking at ways to make the environment more stimulating for young children to maximize their intellectual development. But in the study of the rat model of Huntington's Chorea, the stimulating environment acted to change the brain structure of the rats. The drug Prozac acted in just the same way. These environmental manipulations do not act mysteriously. They alter our biology.

The most striking example of this is a study of rats that were extensively mothered and rats that were not mothered. The mothered rats showed genetic changes (changes in the methylation of the DNA) that were passed on to the next generation. . . . More generally, environmental manipulations can profoundly affect biology. Maternal care and stress have been associated with abnormal brain (hippocampal) development, involving altered nerve growth factors and cognitive, psychological, and immune deficits later in life.

Some argue that genetic manipulations are different because they are irreversible. But environmental interventions can equally be irreversible. Child neglect or abuse can scar a person for life. It may be impossible to unlearn the skill of playing the piano or riding a bike, once learnt. One may be wobbly, but one is a novice only once. Just as the example of mothering of rats shows that environmental interventions can cause biological changes that are passed onto the next generation, so too can environmental interventions be irreversible, or very difficult to reverse, within one generation.

Why should we allow environmental manipulations that alter our biology but not direct biological manipulations? What is the moral difference between producing a smarter child by immersing that child in a stimulating environment, giving the child a drug, or directly altering the child's brain or genes?

One example of a drug that alters brain chemistry is Prozac, which is a serotonin reuptake inhibitor. Early in life it acts as a nerve growth factor, but it may also alter the brain early in life to make it more prone to stress and anxiety later in life by altering receptor development. . . . Drugs like Prozac and maternal deprivation may have the same biological effects.

If the outcome is the same, why treat biological manipulation differently from environmental manipulation? Not only may a favourable environment improve a child's biology and increase a child's opportunities, so too may direct biological interventions. Couples should maximize the genetic opportunity of their children to lead a good life and a productive, cooperative social existence. There is no relevant moral difference between environmental and genetic intervention.

Third Argument: No Difference from Treating Disease

If we accept the treatment and prevention of disease, we should accept enhancement. The goodness of health is what drives a moral obligation to treat or prevent disease. But health is not what ultimately matters—health enables us to live well; disease prevents us from doing what we want and what is good. Health is instrumentally valuable—valuable as a resource that allows us to do what really matters, that is, lead a good life.

What constitutes a good life is a deep philosophical question. According to hedonistic theories, what is good is having pleasant experiences and being happy. According to desire fulfilment theories, and economics, what matters is having our preferences satisfied. According to objective theories, certain activities are good for people: developing deep personal relationships, developing talents, understanding oneself and the world, gaining knowledge, being a part of a family, and so on. We need not decide on which of these theories is correct in order to understand what is bad about ill health. Disease is important because it causes pain, is not what we want, and stops us engaging in those activities that give meaning to life. Sometimes people trade health for well-being: mountain climbers take on risk to achieve, smokers sometimes believe that the pleasures outweigh the risks of smoking, and so on. Life is about managing risk to health and life to promote well-being.

Beneficence—the moral obligation to benefit people—provides a strong reason to enhance people in so far as the biological enhancement increases their chance of having a better life. But can biological enhancements increase people's opportunities for well-being? There are reasons to believe that they might.

Many of our biological and psychological characteristics profoundly affect how well our lives go. In the 1960s Walter Mischel conducted impulse control experiments in which 4-year-old children were left in a room with one marshmallow, after being told that if they did not eat the marshmallow, they could later have two. Some children would eat it as soon as the researcher left; others would use a variety of strategies to help control their behaviour and ignore the temptation of the single marshmallow. A decade later they reinterviewed the children and found that those who were better at delaying gratification had more friends, better academic performance, and more motivation to succeed. Whether the child had grabbed for the marshmallow had a much stronger bearing on their SAT scores than did their IQ (Mischel et al. 1988).

Impulse control has also been linked to socioeconomic control and avoiding conflict with the law. The problems of a hot and uncontrollable temper can be profound.

Shyness too can greatly restrict a life. I remember one newspaper story about a woman who blushed violet every time she went into a social situation. This led her to a hermitic, miserable existence. She eventually had the autonomic nerves to her face surgically cut. This revolutionized her life and had a greater effect on her well-being than the treatment of many diseases.

Buchanan and colleagues have discussed the value of "all purpose goods" (Buchanan et al. 2000). These are traits that are valuable regardless of the kind of life a person chooses to live. They give us greater all-round capacities to live a vast array of lives. Examples include intelligence, memory, self-discipline, patience, empathy, a sense of humour, optimism, and just having a sunny temperament. All of these characteristics—sometimes described as virtues—may have some biological and psychological basis capable of manipulation using technology.

Technology might even be used to improve our *moral character*. We certainly seek through good instruction and example, discipline, and other methods to make better children. It may be possible to alter biology to make people predisposed to be more moral by promoting empathy, imagination, sympathy, fairness, honesty, etc.

In so far as these characteristics have some genetic basis, genetic manipulation could benefit us. There is reason to believe that complex virtues like fair-mindedness may have a biological basis. In one famous experiment a monkey was trained to perform a task and rewarded with either a grape or a piece of cucumber. He preferred the grape. On one occasion he performed the task successfully and was given a piece of cucumber. He watched as another monkey who had not performed the task was given a grape and he became very angry. This shows that even monkeys have a sense of fairness and desert—or at least self-interest!

At the other end, there are characteristics that we believe do not make for a good and happy life. One Dutch family illustrates the extreme end of the spectrum. For over thirty years this family recognized that there were a disproportionate number of male family members who exhibited aggressive and criminal behaviour (Morell 1993). This was characterized by aggressive outbursts resulting in arson, attempted rape, and exhibitionism. When a family tree was constructed, the pattern of inheritance was clearly X-linked recessive. This means, roughly, that women can carry the gene without being affected; 50 percent of men at risk of inheriting the gene get the gene and are affected by the disease.

Genetic analysis suggested that the likely defective gene was a part of the X chromosome known as the monoamine oxidase region. This region codes for two enzymes that assist in the breakdown of neurotransmitters. Neurotransmitters are substances that play a key role in the conduction of nerve impulses in our brain. Enzymes like the monoamine oxidases are required to degrade the neurotransmitters after they have performed their desired task. It was suggested that the monoamine oxidase activity might be disturbed in the affected individuals. Urine analysis showed a higher than normal amount of neurotransmitters being excreted in the urine of affected males (Morell 1993). These results were consistent with a reduction in the functioning of one of the enzymes (monoamine oxidase A).

How can such a mutation result in violent and antisocial behaviour? A deficiency of the enzyme results in a build-up of neurotransmitters. These abnormal levels of neurotransmitters result in excessive, and even violent, reactions to stress. This hypothesis was further supported by the finding that genetically modified mice that lack this enzyme are more aggressive.

This family is an extreme example of how genes can influence behaviour: it is the only family in which this mutation has been isolated. Most genetic contributions to behaviour will be weaker predispositions, but there may be some association between genes and behaviour that results in criminal and other antisocial behaviour.

How could information such as this be used? Some criminals have attempted a "genetic defence" in the United States, stating that their genes caused them to commit the crime, but this has never succeeded. However, it is clear that couples should be allowed to test to select offspring who do not have the mutation that predisposes them to act in this way, and if interventions were available, it might be rational to correct it since children without the mutation have a better chance of a good life.

"Genes, Not Men, May Hold the Key to Female Pleasure" ran the title of one recent newspaper article (*The Age* 2005), which reported the results of a large study of female identical twins in Britain and Australia. It found that "genes accounted for 31 per cent of the chance of having an orgasm during intercourse and 51 per cent during masturbation." It concluded that the "ability to gain sexual satisfaction is largely inherited" and went on to speculate that "The genes involved could be linked to physical differences in sex organs and hormone levels or factors such as mood and anxiety."

Our biology profoundly affects how our lives go. If we can increase sexual satisfaction by modifying biology, we should. Indeed, vast numbers of men attempt to do this already through the use of Viagra.

Summary: The Case for Enhancement

What matters is human well-being, not just treatment and prevention of disease. Our biology affects our opportunities to live well. The biological route to improvement is no different from the environmental. Biological manipulation to increase opportunity is ethical. If we have an obligation to treat and prevent disease, we have an obligation to try to manipulate these characteristics to give an individual the best opportunity of the best life.

HOW DO WE DECIDE?

If we are to enhance certain qualities, how should we decide which to choose? Eugenics was the movement early in the last century that aimed to use selective breeding to prevent degeneration of the gene pool by weeding out criminals, those with mental illness, and the poor, on the false belief that these conditions were simple genetic disorders. The eugenics movement had its inglorious peak when the Nazis moved beyond sterilization to extermination of the genetically unfit.

What was objectionable about the eugenics movement, besides its shoddy scientific basis, was that it involved the imposition of a state vision for a healthy population and aimed to achieve this through coercion. The movement was aimed not at what was good for individuals, but rather at what benefited society. Modern eugenics in the form of testing for disorders, such as Down syndrome, occurs very commonly but is acceptable because it is voluntary, gives couples a choice of what kind of child to have, and enables them to have a child with the greatest opportunity for a good life.

There are four possible ways in which our genes and biology will be decided:

1. nature or God;
2. "experts" (philosophers, bioethicists, psychologists, scientists);
3. "authorities" (government, doctors);
4. people themselves: liberty and autonomy.

It is a basic principle of liberal states like the United Kingdom that the state be "neutral" to different conceptions of the good life. This means that we allow individuals to lead the life that they believe is best for themselves, implying respect for their personal autonomy or capacity for self-rule. The sole ground for interference is when that individual choice may harm others. Advice, persuasion, information, dialogue are permissible. But coercion and infringement of liberty are impermissible.

There are limits to what a liberal state should provide:

1. safety: the intervention should be reasonably safe;
2. harm to others: the intervention (like some manipulation that increases uncontrollable aggressiveness) should not result in harm. Such harm should not be direct or indirect, for example, by causing some unfair competitive advantage;
3. distributive justice: the interventions should be distributed according to principles of justice.

The situation is more complex with young children, embryos, and fetuses, who are incompetent. These human beings are not autonomous and cannot make choices themselves about whether a putative enhancement is a benefit or a harm. If a proposed intervention can be delayed until that human reaches maturity and can decide for himself or herself, then the intervention should be delayed.

However, many genetic interventions will have to be performed very early in life if they are to have an effect. Decisions about such interventions should be left to parents, according to a principle of procreative liberty and autonomy. This states that parents have the freedom to choose when to have children, how many children to have, and arguably what kind of children to have.

Just as parents have wide scope to decide on the conditions of the upbringing of their children, including schooling and religious education, they should have similar freedom over their children's genes. Procreative autonomy or liberty should be extended to enhancement for two reasons. First, reproduction: bearing and raising children is a very private matter. Parents must bear much of the burden of having children, and they have a legitimate stake in the nature of the child they must invest so much of their lives raising.

But there is a second reason. John Stuart Mill argued that when our actions only affect ourselves, we should be free to construct and act on our own conception of what is the best life for us. Mill was not a libertarian. He did not believe that such freedom is valuable solely for its own sake. He believed that freedom is important in order for people to discover for themselves what kind of life is best for themselves. It is only through "experiments in living" that people discover what works for them and others come to see the richness and variety of lives that can be good. Mill strongly praised "originality" and variety in choice as being essential to discovering which lives are best for human beings.

Importantly, Mill believed that some lives are worse than others. Famously, he said that it is better to be Socrates dissatisfied than a fool satisfied. He distinguished between "higher pleasures" of "feelings and imagination" and "lower pleasures" of "mere sensation" (Mill 1910: 7). He criticized "ape-like imitation," subjugation of oneself to custom and fashion, indifference to individuality, and lack of originality (1910: 119–20, 123). Nonetheless, he was the champion of people's right to live their lives as they choose.

I have said that it is important to give the freest scope possible to uncustomary things, in order that it may appear in time which of these are fit to be converted into customs. But independence of action, and disregard of custom, are not solely deserving of encouragement for the chance they afford that better modes of action, and customs more worthy of general adoption, may be struck out; nor is it only persons of decided mental superiority who have a just claim to carry on their lives in their own way. There is no reason that all human existence should be constructed on some one or small number of patterns. If a person possesses any tolerable amount of common sense and experience, his own mode of laying out his existence is the best, not because it is the best in itself, but because it is his own mode (Mill 1910:125).

I believe that reproduction should be about having children with the best prospects. But to discover what are the best prospects, we must give individual couples the freedom to act on their own value judgement of what constitutes a life with good prospects. "Experiments in reproduction" are as important as "experiments in living" (as long as they don't harm the children who are produced). For this reason, procreative freedom is important.

There is one important limit to procreative autonomy that is different from the limits to personal autonomy. The limits to procreative autonomy should be:

1. safety;
2. harm to others;
3. distributive justice;
4. such that the parent's choices are based on a plausible conception of well-being and a better life for the child;
5. consistent with development of autonomy in the child and a reasonable range of future life plans.

These last two limits are important. It makes for a higher standard of "proof" that an intervention will be an enhancement because the parents are making choices for their child, not themselves. The critical question to ask in considering whether to alter some gene related to complex behaviour is: Would the change be better for the individual? Is it better for the individual to have a tendency to be lazy or hardworking, monogamous or polygamous? These questions are difficult to answer. While we might let

adults choose to be monogamous or polygamous, we would not let parents decide on their child's predispositions unless we were reasonably clear that some trait was better for the child.

There will be cases where some intervention is plausibly in a child's interests: increased empathy with other people, better capacity to understand oneself and the world around, or improved memory. One quality is especially associated with socio-economic success and staying out of prison: impulse control. If it were possible to correct poor impulse control, we should correct it. Whether we should remove impulsiveness altogether is another question.

Joel Feinberg has described a child's right to an open future (Feinberg 1980). An open future is one in which a child has a reasonable range of possible lives to choose from and an opportunity to choose what kind of person to be; that is, to develop autonomy. Some critics of enhancement have argued that genetic interventions are inconsistent with a child's right to an open future (Davis 1997). Far from restricting a child's future, however, some biological interventions may increase the possible futures or at least their quality. It is hard to see how improved memory or empathy would restrict a child's future. Many worthwhile possibilities would be open. But it is true that parental choice should not restrict the development of autonomy or reasonable range of possible futures open to a child. In general, fewer enhancements will be permitted in children than in adults. Some interventions, however, may still be clearly enhancements for our children, and so just like vaccinations or other preventative health care.

OBJECTIONS

Playing God or Against Nature

This objection has various forms. Some people in society believe that children are a gift, of God or of nature, and that we should not interfere in human nature. Most people implicitly reject this view: we screen embryos and fetuses for diseases, even mild correctable diseases. We interfere in nature or God's will when we vaccinate, provide pain relief to women in labour (despite objections of some earlier Christians that these practices thwarted God's will), and treat cancer. No one would object to the treatment of disability in a child if it were possible. Why, then, not treat the embryo with genetic therapy if that intervention is safe? This is no more thwarting God's will than giving antibiotics.

Another variant of this objection is that we are arrogant if we assume we could have sufficient knowledge to meddle with human nature. Some people object that we cannot know the complexity of the human system, which is like an unknowable magnificent symphony. To attempt to enhance one characteristic may have other unknown, unforeseen effects elsewhere in the system. We should not play God since, unlike God, we are not omnipotent or omniscient. We should be humble and recognize the limitations of our knowledge.

A related objection is that genes are pleiotropic—which means they have different effects in different environments. The gene or genes that predispose to manic depression may also be responsible for heightened creativity and productivity.

One response to both of these objections is to limit intervention, until our knowledge grows, to selecting between different embryos, and not intervening to enhance particular embryos or people. Since we would be choosing between complete systems on the basis of their type, we would not be interfering with the internal machinery. In this way, selection is less risky than enhancement.

But such a precaution could also be misplaced when considering biological interventions. When benefits are on offer, such objections remind us to refrain from hubris and over-confidence. We must do adequate research before intervening. And because the benefits may be fewer than when we treat or prevent disease, we may require the standards of safety to be higher than for medical interventions. But we must weigh the risks against the benefits. If confidence is justifiably high, and benefits outweigh harms, we should enhance.

Once technology affords us the power to enhance our own and our children's lives, to fail to do so would be to be responsible for the consequences. To fail to treat our children's diseases is to wrong them. To fail to prevent them from getting depression is to wrong them. To fail to improve their physical, musical, psychological, and other capacities is to wrong them, just as it would be to harm them if we gave them a toxic substance that stunted or reduced these capacities.

Another variant of the "Playing God" objection is that there is a special value in the balance and diversity that natural variation affords, and enhancement will reduce this. But in so far as we are products of evolution, we are merely random chance variations of genetic traits selected for our capacity to survive long enough to reproduce. There is no design to evolution. Evolution selects genes, according to environment, that confer the greatest chance of survival and reproduction. Evolution would select a tribe that was highly fertile but suffered great pain the whole of their lives over another tribe that was less fertile but suffered less pain. Medicine has changed evolution: we can now select individuals who experience less pain and disease. The next stage of human evolution will be rational evolution, according to which we select children who not only have the greatest chance of surviving, reproducing, and being free of disease, but who have the greatest opportunities to have the best lives in their likely environment. Evolution was indifferent to how well our lives went; we are not. We want to retire, play golf, read, and watch our grandchildren have children.

"Enhancement" is a misnomer. It suggests luxury. But enhancement is no luxury. In so far as it promotes well-being, it is the very essence of what is necessary for a good human life. There is no moral reason to preserve some traits—such as uncontrollable aggressiveness, a sociopathic personality, or extreme deviousness. Tell the victim of rape and murder that we must preserve diversity and the natural balance.

Genetic Discrimination

Some people fear the creation of a two-tier society of the enhanced and the unenhanced, where the inferior, unenhanced are discriminated against and disadvantaged all through life.

We must remember that nature allots advantage and disadvantage with no gesture to fairness. Some are born horribly disadvantaged, destined to die after short and miserable lives. Some suffer great genetic disadvantage while others are born gifted, physically, musically, or intellectually. There is no secret that there are "gifted" children naturally. Allowing choice to change our biology will, if anything, be more egalitarian, allowing the ungifted to approach the gifted. There is nothing fair about the natural lottery: allowing enhancement may be fairer.

But more importantly, how well the lives of those who are disadvantaged go depends not on whether enhancement is permitted, but on the social institutions we have in place to protect the least well off and provide everyone with a fair chance. People have disease and disability: egalitarian social institutions and laws against discrimination are designed to make sure everyone, regardless of natural inequality, has a decent chance of a decent life. This would be no different if enhancement were permitted. There is no necessary connection between enhancement and discrimination, just as there is no necessary connection between curing disability and discrimination against people with disability.

The Perfect Child, Sterility, and Loss of the Mystery of Life

If we engineered perfect children, this objection goes, the world would be a sterile, monotonous place where everyone was the same, and the mystery and surprise of life would be gone.

It is impossible to create perfect children. We can only attempt to create children with better opportunities of a better life. There will necessarily be difference. Even in the case of screening for disability, like Down syndrome, 10 percent of people choose not to abort a pregnancy known to be affected by Down syndrome. People value different things. There will never be complete convergence. Moreover, there will remain massive challenges for individuals to meet in their personal relationships and in the hurdles our unpredictable environment presents. There will remain much mystery and challenge—we will just be better able to deal with these. We will still have to work to achieve, but our achievements may have greater value.

Against Human Nature

One of the major objections to enhancement is that it is against human nature. Common alternative phrasings are that enhancement is tampering with our nature or an affront to human dignity. I believe that what separates us from other animals is our rationality, our capacity to make normative judgements and act on the basis of reasons. When we make decisions to improve our lives by biological and other manipulations, we express our rationality and express what is fundamentally important about our nature. And if those manipulations improve our capacity to make rational and normative judgements, they further improve what is fundamentally human. Far from being against the human spirit, such improvements express the human spirit. To be human is to be better.

Enhancements Are Self-Defeating

Another familiar objection to enhancement is that enhancements will have self-defeating or other adverse social effects. A typical example is increase in height. If height is socially desired, then everyone will try to enhance the height of their children at great cost to themselves and the environment (as taller people consume more resources), with no advantage in the end since there will be no relative gain.

If a purported manipulation does not improve well-being or opportunity, there is no argument in favour of it. In this case, the manipulation is not an enhancement. In other cases, such as enhancement of intelligence, the enhancement of one individual may increase that individual's opportunities only at the expense of another. So-called positional goods are goods only in a relative sense.

But many enhancements will have both positional and non-positional qualities. Intelligence is good not just because it allows an individual to be more competitive for complex jobs, but because it allows an individual to process information more rapidly in her own life, and to develop greater understanding of herself and others. These non-positional effects should not be ignored. Moreover, even in the case of so-called purely positional goods, such as height, there may be important non-positional values. It is better to be taller if you are a basketball player, but being tall is a disadvantage in balance sports such as gymnastics, skiing, and surfing.

Nonetheless, if there are significant social consequences of enhancement, this is of course a valid objection. But it is not particular to enhancement: there is an old question about how far individuals in society can pursue their own self-interest at a cost to others. It applies to education, health care, and virtually all areas of life.

Not all enhancements will be ethical. The critical issue is that the intervention is expected to bring about more benefits than harms to the individual. It must be safe and there must be a reasonable expectation of improvement. Some of the other features of ethical enhancements are summarized below.

WHAT IS AN ETHICAL ENHANCEMENT?

An ethical enhancement:

1. is in the person's interests;
2. is reasonably safe;
3. increases the opportunity to have the best life;
4. promotes or does not unreasonably restrict the range of possible lives open to that person;
5. does not unreasonably harm others directly through excessive costs in making it freely available;
6. does not place that individual at an unfair competitive advantage with respect to others, e.g. mind-reading;
7. is such that the person retains significant control or responsibility for her achievements and self that cannot be wholly or directly attributed to the enhancement;
8. does not unreasonably reinforce or increase unjust inequality and discrimination—economic inequality, racism.

What Is an Ethical Enhancement for a Child or Incompetent Human Being?

Such an ethical enhancement is all the above, but in addition:

1. the intervention cannot be delayed until the child can make its own decision;
2. the intervention is plausibly in the child's interests;
3. the intervention is compatible with the development of autonomy.

CONCLUSION

Enhancement is already occurring. In sport, human erythropoietin boosts red blood cells. Steroids and growth hormone improve muscle strength. Many people seek cognitive enhancement through nicotine, Ritalin, Modavigil, or caffeine. Prozac, recreational drugs, and alcohol all enhance mood. Viagra is used to improve sexual performance.

And of course mobile phones and aeroplanes are examples of external enhancing technologies. In the future, genetic technology, nanotechnology, and artificial intelligence may profoundly affect our capacities.

Will the future be better or just disease-free? We need to shift our frame of reference from health to life enhancement. What matters is how we live. Technology can now improve that. We have two options:

1. Intervention:

   - treating disease;
   - preventing disease;
   - supra-prevention of disease—preventing disease in a radically unprecedented way;
   - protection of well-being;
   - enhancement of well-being.

2. No intervention, and to remain in a state of nature—no treatment or prevention of disease, no technological enhancement.

I believe that to be human is to be better. Or, at least, to strive to be better. We should be here for a *good* time, not just a *long* time. Enhancement, far from being merely permissible, is something we should aspire to achieve.

REFERENCES

Buchanan, A., Brock, D., Daniels, N., and Wikler, D. (2000), *From Chance to Choice* (Cambridge: Cambridge University Press).

Davis, D. (1997), "Genetic Dilemmas and the Child's Right to an Open Future," *Hastings Center Report*, 27/2 (Mar.–Apr.), 7–15.

Feinberg, J. (1980), "The Child's Right to an Open Future," in W. Aiken and H. LaFollette (eds.), *Whose Child? Parental Rights, Parental Authority and State Power* (Totowa, NJ: Rowman and Littlefield), 124–53.

Mill, J. S. (1910), *On Liberty* (London: J. M. Dent).

Mischel, W., Shoda, Y., and Peake, P. K. (1988), "The Nature of Adolescent Competencies Predicted by Preschool Delay of Gratification," *Journal of Personality and Social Psychology*, 54/4:687–96.

Morell, V. (1993), "Evidence Found for a Possible "Aggression Gene," *Science*, 260: 1722–3.

Julian Savulescu: Genetic Interventions and the Ethics of Enhancement of Human Beings

1. What limits does Savulescu place on procreative autonomy over and above the limits placed on personal autonomy? Why does he think these limits are important? Do you think these limits are enough to protect the rights of children? Explain and defend your answer.

2. Explain Savulescu's consistency argument. What do you think the most powerful objection to this argument is? How do you think Savulescu would respond? Do you think this objection is ultimately successful? Why or why not?

3. Explain why eugenics might pose a problem for Savulescu's view. According to Savulescu, who should decide when and how to enhance certain qualities? Do you think his account is enough to neutralize the eugenics worry? Defend your response.

4. Savulescu considers a number of objections to his account. Reconstruct one of the objections as a valid argument. Then, explain how Savulescu responds to this argument by saying which premise he rejects and why. Do you think his response is successful? Why or why not?

5. Savulescu defends genetic enhancement by arguing that it is analogous to treating disease. Explain this argument. Then discuss the potential differences between treating disease and genetic enhancement. Is Savulescu right to say that there is *morally relevant* difference between the two? Defend your response.

6. Explain the principle of procreative liberty and autonomy. Then, explain the two reasons Savulescu cites for applying this principle to human enhancement. Do you think that this is enough to show that parents should have some freedom in determining their children's genes? Why or why not?

Transhumanist Values

Nick Bostrom

This selection is something of a manifesto for transhumanism, authored by one of the movement's founders, philosopher Nick Bostrom. In his words, human nature is "a work-in-progress, a half-baked beginning that we can learn to remold in desirable ways." Transhumanists seek to rely on scientific and technological means to improve our species in very significant ways—so much so that the individuals emerging from such transformations will rightly be regarded as "posthuman," rather than as members of the species *Homo sapiens*.

A large part of the transhumanist philosophy is dedicated to radical exercises of the imagination. Rather than focus on small, piecemeal improvements we can make with current technologies, transhumanists try to imagine what a vastly improved version of ourselves might look like, and what sorts of social structures, possibly quite different from those of today, might be best suited to enhancing our well-being.

Transhumanists begin their thinking by focusing on the limitations that currently beset our species. We live at most about 120 years; our intellectual capacities are imperfect in a great many ways; our bodies are vulnerable to any number of breakdowns; our mood can often be improved and our self-control is not always what it could be. While most of us take these limitations for granted, transhumanists encourage us to think of how, with adequate technological solutions, we might someday transcend them. Transhumanists emphasize the need to devote great resources to the sort of research required to bring about these changes. They also believe that we must ensure global security in order to make such transformations possible. They are also aware of potential issues of justice—for instance, having enhancement technologies available only to the wealthy, thereby allowing them to leave the rest of us mere mortals behind. For that reason transhumanists also maintain an ideal of wide access for these enhancement technologies.

I. WHAT IS TRANSHUMANISM?

Transhumanism is a loosely defined movement that has developed gradually over the past two decades.[1] It promotes an interdisciplinary approach to understanding and evaluating the opportunities for enhancing the human condition and the human organism opened up by the advancement of technology. Attention is given to both present technologies, like genetic engineering and information technology, and anticipated future ones, such as molecular nanotechnology and artificial intelligence.

The enhancement options being discussed include radical extension of human health-span, eradication of disease, elimination of unnecessary suffering, and augmentation of human intellectual, physical, and emotional capacities. Other transhumanist themes include space colonization and the possibility of creating superintelligent machines, along with other potential developments that could profoundly alter the human condition. The ambit is not limited to gadgets and medicine, but encompasses also economic, social, institutional designs, cultural development, and psychological skills and techniques.

Transhumanists view human nature as a work-in-progress, a half-baked beginning that we can learn to remold in desirable ways. Current humanity need not be the endpoint of evolution. Transhumanists hope that by responsible use of science, technology, and other rational means we shall eventually manage to become posthuman, beings with vastly greater capacities than present human beings have.

Some transhumanists take active steps to increase the probability that they personally will survive long enough to become posthuman, for example by choosing a healthy lifestyle or by making provisions for having themselves cryonically suspended in case of de-animation.[2] In contrast to many other ethical outlooks, which in practice often reflect a reactionary attitude to new technologies, the transhumanist view is guided by an evolving vision to take a more proactive approach to technology policy. This vision, in broad strokes, is to create the opportunity to live much longer and healthier lives, to enhance our memory and other intellectual faculties, to refine our emotional experiences and increase our subjective sense of well-being, and generally to achieve a greater degree of control over our own lives. This affirmation of human potential is offered as an alternative to customary injunctions against playing God, messing with nature, tampering with our human essence, or displaying punishable hubris.

Transhumanism does not entail technological optimism. While future technological capabilities carry immense potential for beneficial deployments, they also could be misused to cause enormous harm, ranging all the way to the extreme possibility of intelligent life becoming extinct. Other potential negative outcomes include widening social inequalities or a gradual erosion of the hard-to-quantify assets that we care deeply about but tend to neglect in our daily struggle for material gain, such as meaningful human relationships and ecological diversity. Such risks must be taken very seriously, as thoughtful transhumanists fully acknowledge.[3]

Transhumanism has roots in secular humanist thinking, yet is more radical in that it promotes not only traditional means of improving human nature, such as education and cultural refinement, but also direct application of medicine and technology to overcome some of our basic biological limits.

2. HUMAN LIMITATIONS

The range of thoughts, feelings, experiences, and activities accessible to human organisms presumably constitute only a tiny part of what is possible. There is no reason to think that the human mode of being is any more free of limitations imposed by our biological nature than are those of other animals. In much the same way as Chimpanzees lack the cognitive wherewithal to understand what it is like to be human—the ambitions we humans have, our philosophies, the complexities of human society, or the subtleties of our relationships with one another, so we humans may lack the capacity to form a realistic intuitive understanding of what it would be like to be a radically enhanced human (a "posthuman") and of the thoughts, concerns, aspirations, and social relations that such humans may have.

Our own current mode of being, therefore, spans but a minute subspace of what is possible or permitted by the physical constraints of the universe (see Figure 1). It is not farfetched to suppose that there are parts of this larger space that represent extremely valuable ways of living, relating, feeling, and thinking.

The limitations of the human mode of being are so pervasive and familiar that we often fail to notice them, and to question them requires manifesting

an almost childlike naiveté. Let's consider some of the more basic ones.

Lifespan. Because of the precarious conditions in which our Pleistocene ancestors lived, the human lifespan has evolved to be a paltry seven or eight decades. This is, from many perspectives, a rather short period of time. Even tortoises do better than that.

We don't have to use geological or cosmological comparisons to highlight the meagerness of our allotted time budgets. To get a sense that we might be missing out on something important by our tendency to die early, we only have to bring to mind some of the worthwhile things that we could have done or attempted to do if we had had more time. For gardeners, educators, scholars, artists, city planners, and those who simply relish observing and participating in the cultural or political variety shows of life, three scores and ten is often insufficient for seeing even one major project through to completion, let alone for undertaking many such projects in sequence.

Human character development is also cut short by aging and death. Imagine what might have become of a Beethoven or a Goethe if they had still been with us today. Maybe they would have developed into rigid old grumps interested exclusively in conversing about the achievements of their youth. But maybe, if they had continued to enjoy health and youthful vitality, they would have continued to grow as men and artists, to reach levels of maturity that we can barely imagine. We certainly cannot rule that out based on what we know today. Therefore, there is at least a serious possibility of there being something very precious outside the human sphere. This constitutes a reason to pursue the means that will let us go there and find out.

Intellectual capacity. We have all had moments when we wished we were a little smarter. The three-pound, cheese-like thinking machine that we lug around in our skulls can do some neat tricks, but it also has significant shortcomings. Some of these—such as forgetting to buy milk or failing to attain native fluency in languages you learn as an adult—are obvious and require no elaboration. These shortcomings are inconveniences but hardly fundamental barriers to human development.

Yet there is a more profound sense in the constraints of our intellectual apparatus limit our modes

The Space of Possible Modes of Being

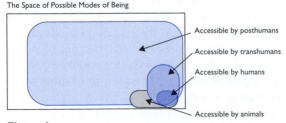

Accessible by posthumans

Accessible by transhumans

Accessible by humans

Accessible by animals

Figure 1.

of our mentation. I mentioned the Chimpanzee analogy earlier: just as is the case for the great apes, our own cognitive makeup may foreclose whole strata of understanding and mental activity. The point here is not about any logical or metaphysical impossibility: we need not suppose that posthumans would not be Turing computable or that they would have concepts that could not be expressed by any finite sentences in our language, or anything of that sort. The impossibility that I am referring to is more like the impossibility for us current humans to visualize a 200-dimensional hypersphere or to read, with perfect recollection and understanding, every book in the Library of Congress. These things are impossible for us because, simply put, we lack the brainpower. In the same way, may lack the ability to intuitively understand what being a posthuman would be like or to grok the playing field of posthuman concerns.

Further, our human brains may cap our ability to discover philosophical and scientific truths. It is possible that failure of philosophical research to arrive at solid, generally accepted answers to many of the traditional big philosophical questions could be due to the fact that we are not smart enough to be successful in this kind of enquiry. Our cognitive limitations may be confining us in a Platonic cave, where the best we can do is theorize about "shadows," that is, representations that are sufficiently oversimplified and dumbed-down to fit inside a human brain.

Bodily functionality. We enhance our natural immune systems by getting vaccinations, and we can imagine further enhancements to our bodies that would protect us from disease or help us shape our bodies according to our desires (e.g. by letting us control our bodies' metabolic rate). Such enhancements could improve the quality of our lives.

A more radical kind of upgrade might be possible if we suppose a computational view of the mind. It may then be possible to upload a human mind to a computer, by replicating *in silico* the detailed computational processes that would normally take place in a particular human brain.[4] Being an upload would have many potential advantages, such as the ability to make back-up copies of oneself (favorably impacting on one's life-expectancy) and the ability to transmit oneself as information at the speed of light. Uploads might live either in virtual reality or directly in physical reality by controlling a robot proxy.

Sensory modalities, special faculties and sensibilities. The current human sensory modalities are not the only possible ones, and they are certainly not as highly developed as they could be. Some animals have sonar, magnetic orientation, or sensors for electricity and vibration; many have a much keener sense of smell, sharper eyesight, etc. The range of possible sensory modalities is not limited to those we find in the animal kingdom. There is no fundamental block to adding say a capacity to see infrared radiation or to perceive radio signals and perhaps to add some kind of telepathic sense by augmenting our brains with suitably interfaced radio transmitters.

Humans also enjoy a variety of special faculties, such as appreciation of music and a sense of humor, and sensibilities such as the capacity for sexual arousal in response to erotic stimuli. Again, there is no reason to think that what we have exhausts the range of the possible, and we can certainly imagine higher levels of sensitivity and responsiveness.

Mood, energy, and self-control. Despite our best efforts, we often fail to feel as happy as we would like. Our chronic levels of subjective well-being seem to be largely genetically determined. Life-events have little long-term impact; the crests and troughs of fortune push us up and bring us down, but there is little long-term effect on self-reported well-being. Lasting joy remains elusive except for those of us who are lucky enough to have been born with a temperament that plays in a major key.

In addition to being at the mercy of a genetically determined setpoint for our levels of well-being, we are limited in regard to energy, will-power, and ability to shape our own character in accordance with our ideals. Even such "simple" goals as losing weight or quitting smoking prove unattainable to many.

Some subset of these kinds of problems might be necessary rather than contingent upon our current nature. For example, we cannot both have the ability easily to break any habit and the ability to form stable, hard-to-break habits. (In this regard, the best one can hope for may be the ability to easily get rid of habits we didn't deliberately choose for ourselves in the first place, and perhaps a more versatile habit-formation system that would let us choose with more precision when to acquire a habit and how much effort it should cost to break it.)

3. THE CORE TRANSHUMANIST VALUE: EXPLORING THE POSTHUMAN REALM

The conjecture that there are greater values than we can currently fathom does not imply that values are not defined in terms of our current dispositions. Take, for example, a dispositional theory of value such as the one described by David Lewis.[5] According to Lewis's theory, something is a value for you if and only if you would want to want it if you were perfectly acquainted with it and you were thinking and deliberating as clearly as possible about it. On this view, there may be values that we do not currently want, and that we do not even currently want to want, because we may not be perfectly acquainted with them or because we are not ideal deliberators. Some values pertaining to certain forms of posthuman existence may well be of this sort; they may be values for us now, and they may be so in virtue of our current dispositions, and yet we may not be able to fully appreciate them with our current limited deliberative capacities and our lack of the receptive faculties required for full acquaintance with them. This point is important because it shows that the transhumanist view that we ought to explore the realm of posthuman values does not entail that we should forego our current values. The posthuman values can be our current values, albeit ones that we have not yet clearly comprehended. Transhumanism does not require us to say that we should favor posthuman beings over human beings, but that the right way of favoring human beings is by enabling us to realize our ideals better and that some of our ideals may well be located outside the space of modes of being that are accessible to us with our current biological constitution.

We can overcome many of our biological limitations. It is possible that there are some limitations that are impossible for us to transcend, not only because of technological difficulties but on metaphysical grounds. Depending on what our views are about what constitutes personal identity, it could be that certain modes of being, while possible, are not possible for us, because any being of such a kind would be so different from us that they could not be us. Concerns of this kind are familiar from theological discussions of the afterlife. In Christian theology, some souls will be allowed by God to go to heaven after their time as corporal creatures is over. Before being admitted to heaven, the souls would undergo a purification process in which they would lose many of their previous bodily attributes. Skeptics may doubt that the resulting minds would be sufficiently similar to our current minds for it to be possible for them to be the same person. A similar predicament arises within transhumanism: if the mode of being of a posthuman being is radically different from that of a human being, then we may doubt whether a posthuman being could be the same person as a human being, even if the posthuman being originated from a human being.

We can, however, envision many enhancements that would not make it impossible for the post-transformation someone to be the same person as the pre-transformation person. A person could obtain quite a bit of increased life expectancy, intelligence, health, memory, and emotional sensitivity, without ceasing to exist in the process. A person's intellectual life can be transformed radically by getting an education. A person's life expectancy can be extended substantially by being unexpectedly cured from a lethal disease. Yet these developments are not viewed as spelling the end of the original person. In particular, it seems that modifications that add to a person's capacities can be more substantial than modifications that subtract, such as brain damage. If most of someone currently is, including her most important memories, activities, and feelings, is preserved, then adding extra capacities on top of that would not easily cause the person to cease to exist.

Preservation of personal identity, especially if this notion is given a narrow construal, is not everything. We can value other things than ourselves, or we might regard it as satisfactory if some parts or aspects of ourselves survive and flourish, even if that entails giving up some parts of ourselves such that we no longer count as being the same person. Which parts of ourselves we might be willing to sacrifice may not become clear until we are more fully acquainted with the full meaning of the options. A careful, incremental exploration of the posthuman realm may be indispensable for acquiring such an understanding, although we may also be able to learn from each other's experiences and from works of the imagination.

Additionally, we may favor future people being posthuman rather than human, if the posthumans would lead lives more worthwhile than the alternative humans would. Any reasons stemming from such considerations would not depend on the assumption that we ourselves could become posthuman beings.

Transhumanism promotes the quest to develop further so that we can explore hitherto inaccessible realms of value. Technological enhancement of human organisms is a means that we ought to pursue to this end. There are limits to how much can be achieved by low-tech means such as education, philosophical contemplation, moral self-scrutiny and other such methods proposed by classical philosophers with perfectionist leanings, including Plato, Aristotle, and Nietzsche, or by means of creating a fairer and better society, as envisioned by social reformists such as Marx or Martin Luther King. This is not to denigrate what we can do with the tools we have today. Yet ultimately, transhumanists hope to go further.

4. BASIC CONDITIONS FOR REALIZING THE TRANSHUMANIST PROJECT

If this is the grand vision, what are the more particular objectives that it translates into when considered as a guide to policy?

What is needed for the realization of the transhumanist dream is that technological means necessary for venturing into the posthuman space are made available to those who wish to use them, and that society be organized in such a manner that such explorations can be undertaken without causing unacceptable damage to the social fabric and without imposing unacceptable existential risks.

Global security. While disasters and setbacks are inevitable in the implementation of the transhumanist project (just as they are if the transhumanist project is not pursued), there is one kind of catastrophe that must be avoided at any cost:

Existential risk—one where an adverse outcome would either annihilate Earth-originating intelligent life or permanently and drastically curtail its potential.[6]

Several recent discussions have argued that the combined probability of the existential risks is very substantial.[7] The relevance of the condition of existential safety to the transhumanist vision is obvious: if we go extinct or permanently destroy our potential to develop further, then the transhumanist core value will not be realized. Global security is the most fundamental and nonnegotiable requirement of the transhumanist project.

Technological progress. That technological progress is generally desirable from a transhumanist point of view is also self-evident. Many of our biological shortcomings (aging, disease, feeble memories and intellects, a limited emotional repertoire and inadequate capacity for sustained well-being) are difficult to overcome, and to do so will require advanced tools. Developing these tools is a gargantuan challenge for the collective problem-solving capacities of our species. Since technological progress is closely linked to economic development, economic growth—or more precisely, productivity growth—can in some cases serve as a proxy for technological progress. (Productivity growth is, of course, only an imperfect measure of the relevant form of technological progress, which, in turn, is an imperfect measure of overall improvement, since it omits such factors as equity of distribution, ecological diversity, and quality of human relationships.)

The history of economic and technological development, and the concomitant growth of civilization, is appropriately regarded with awe, as humanity's most glorious achievement. Thanks to the gradual accumulation of improvements over the past several thousand years, large portions of humanity have been freed from illiteracy, life-expectancies of twenty years, alarming infant-mortality rates, horrible diseases endured without palliatives, and periodic starvation and water shortages. Technology, in this context, is not just gadgets but includes all instrumentally useful objects and systems that have been deliberately created. This broad definition encompasses practices and institutions, such as double-entry accounting, scientific peer-review, legal systems, and the applied sciences.

Wide access. It is not enough that the posthuman realm be explored by someone. The full realization of the core transhumanist value requires that, ideally, everybody should have the opportunity to become posthuman. It would be sub-optimal if the opportunity to become posthuman were restricted to a tiny elite.

There are many reasons for supporting wide access: to reduce inequality; because it would be a fairer arrangement; to express solidarity and respect for fellow humans; to help gain support for the transhumanist project; to increase the chances that you will get the opportunity to become posthuman; to increase the chances that those you care about can become posthuman; because it might increase the range of the posthuman realm that gets explored; and to alleviate human suffering on as wide a scale as possible.

The wide access requirement underlies the *moral urgency* of the transhumanist vision. Wide access does not argue for holding back. On the contrary, other things being equal, it is an argument for moving forward as quickly as possible. 150,000 human beings on our planet die every day, without having had any access to the anticipated enhancement technologies that will make it possible to become posthuman. The sooner this technology develops, the fewer people will have died without access.

Consider a hypothetical case in which there is a choice between (a) allowing the current human population to continue to exist, and (b) having it instantaneously and painlessly killed and replaced by six billion new human beings who are very similar but non-identical to the people that exist today. Such a replacement ought to be strongly resisted on moral grounds, for it would entail the involuntary death of six billion people. The fact that they would be replaced by six billion newly created similar people does not make the substitution acceptable. Human beings are not disposable. For analogous reasons, it is important that the opportunity be become posthuman is made available to as many humans as possible, rather than having the existing population merely supplemented (or worse, replaced) by a new set of posthuman people. The transhumanist ideal will be maximally realized only if the benefits of technologies are widely shared and if they are made available as soon as possible, preferably within our lifetime.

5. DERIVATIVE VALUES

From these specific requirements flow a number of derivative transhumanist values that translate the transhumanist vision into practice. (Some of these values may also have independent justifications, and transhumanism does not imply that that the list of values provided below is exhaustive.)

To start with, transhumanists typically place emphasis on individual freedom and individual choice in the area of enhancement technologies. Humans differ widely in their conceptions of what their own perfection or improvement would consist in. Some want to develop in one direction, others in different directions, and some prefer to stay the way they are. It would neither be morally unacceptable for anybody to impose a single standard to which we would all have to conform. People should have the right to choose which enhancement technologies, if any, they want to use. In cases where individual choices impact substantially on other people, this general principle may need to be restricted, but the mere fact that somebody may be disgusted or morally affronted by somebody else's using technology to modify herself would not normally a legitimate ground for coercive interference. Furthermore, the poor track record of centrally planned efforts to create better people (e.g. the eugenics movement and Soviet totalitarianism) shows that we need to be wary of collective decision-making in the field of human modification.

Another transhumanist priority is to put ourselves in a better position to make wise choices about where we are going. We will need all the wisdom we can get when negotiating the posthuman transition. Transhumanists place a high value on improvements in our individual and collective powers of understanding and in our ability to implement responsible decisions. Collectively, we might get smarter and more informed through such means as scientific research, public debate and open discussion of the future, information markets,[8] collaborative information filtering.[9] On an individual level, we can benefit from education, critical thinking, open-mindedness, study techniques, information technology, and perhaps memory- or attention-enhancing drugs and other cognitive enhancement technologies. Our ability to implement responsible decisions can be improved by expanding the rule of law and democracy on the international plane. Additionally, artificial intelligence, especially if and when it reaches human-equivalence or greater, could give an enormous boost to the quest for knowledge and wisdom.

Given the limitations of our current wisdom, a certain epistemic tentativeness is appropriate, along with a readiness to continually reassess our assumptions as more information becomes available. We cannot take for granted that our old habits and beliefs will prove adequate in navigating our new circumstances.

Global security can be improved by promoting international peace and cooperation, and by strongly counteracting the proliferation of weapons of mass destruction. Improvements in surveillance technology may make it easier to detect illicit weapons programs. Other security measures might also be appropriate to counteract various existential risks. More studies on such risks would help us get a better understanding of the long-term threats to human flourishing and of what can be done to reduce them.

Since technological development is necessary to realize the transhumanist vision, entrepreneurship, science, and the engineering spirit are to be promoted. More generally, transhumanists favor a pragmatic attitude and a constructive, problem-solving approach to challenges, preferring methods that experience tells us give good results. They think it better to take the initiative to "do something about it" rather than sit around complaining. This is one sense in which transhumanism is optimistic. (It is not optimistic in the sense of advocating an inflated belief in the probability of success or in the Panglossian sense of inventing excuses for the shortcomings of the status quo.)

Transhumanism advocates the well-being of all sentience, whether in artificial intellects, humans, and non-human animals (including extraterrestrial species, if there are any). Racism, sexism, speciesism, belligerent nationalism and religious intolerance are unacceptable. In addition to the usual grounds for deeming such practices objectionable, there is also a specifically transhumanist motivation for this. In order to prepare for a time when the human species may start branching out in various directions, we need to start now to strongly encourage the development of moral sentiments that are broad enough encompass within the sphere of moral concern sentiences that are constituted differently from ourselves.

Finally, transhumanism stresses the moral urgency of saving lives, or, more precisely, of preventing involuntary deaths among people whose lives are worth living. In the developed world, aging is currently the number one killer. Aging is also biggest cause of illness, disability and dementia. (Even if all heart disease and cancer could be cured, life expectancy would increase by merely six to seven years.) Anti-aging medicine is therefore a key transhumanist priority. The goal, of course, is to radically extent people's active health-spans, not to add a few extra years on a ventilator at the end of life.

Since we are still far from being able to halt or reverse aging, cryonic suspension of the dead should be made available as an option for those who desire it. It is possible that future technologies will make it possible to reanimate people who have cryonically suspended.[10] While cryonics might be a long shot, it definitely carries better odds than cremation or burial.

The table below summarizes the transhumanist values that we have discussed.

REFERENCES

Bostrom, N. (2002). "Existential Risks: Analyzing Human Extinction Scenarios and Related Hazards." *Journal of Evolution and Technology*, 9.

Bostrom, N. (2003). "Human Genetic Enhancements: A Transhumanist Perspective." *Journal of Value Inquiry*, Forthcoming.

Bostrom, N., et al. (1999). The Transhumanist FAQ. http://www.nickbostrom.com/views/transhumt.pdf

Chislenko, A. (1997). Automated Collaborative Filtering and Semantic Transports. http://www.lucifer.com/~sasha/articles/ACF.html

Drexler, K. E. *Engines of Creation: The Coming Era of Nanotechnology*. (Anchor Books: New York, 1986).

Ettinger, R. *The Prospect of Immortality*. (Doubleday: New York, 1964).

Hanson, R. (1995). "Could Gambling Save Science? Encouraging an Honest Consensus." *Social Epistemology*, 9:1: 3-33.

Hughes, J. (2001). "The Future of Death: Cryonics and the Telos of Liberal Individualism." *Journal of Evolution and Technology*, 6.

Leslie, J. *The End of the World: The Science and Ethics of Human Extinction.* (Routledge: London, 1996).

Lewis, D. (1989). "Dispositional Theories of Value." *Proceedings of the Aristotelian Society Supp.*, 63: 113-37.

Merkle, R. (1994). "The Molecular Repair of the Brain." *Cryonics*, 15(1 and 2).

Moravec, H. *Mind Children.* (Harvard University Press: Harvard, 1989).

Rees, M. *Our Final Hour: A Scientist's Warning.* (Basic Books: New York, 2003).

NOTES

1. Bostrom et al. 1999; Bostrom 2003
2. Ettinger 1964; Hughes 2001
3. Bostrom 2002
4. Drexler 1986; Moravec 1989
5. Lewis 1989
6. Bostrom 2002
7. Leslie 1996; Bostrom 2002; Rees 2003
8. Hanson 1995
9. Chislenko 1997
10. Ettinger 1964; Drexler 1986; Merkle 1994

Nick Bostrom: Transhumanist Values

1. What (if anything) do you find attractive about the transhumanist program? What (if anything) strikes you as problematic about it? Do the pros outweigh the cons?

2. Many would object to the transhumanist program by declaring that its advocates are playing God or wrongfully tampering with nature. What do you make of such criticisms?

3. Many transhumanist ideals, such as prolonging our lives indefinitely, are only very remote possibilities. How (if at all) is the improbability of achieving success relevant to assessing transhumanist ideals and values?

4. Enhancement technologies, like most technological innovations, are likely to be very expensive when first introduced. This creates the possibility that the wealthy will enjoy any benefits of such technology before the less well-off have a chance to do so. Is this a good reason to halt the development of such technologies?

5. Would the basic moral code for posthumans be the same or different from the basic moral code that governs us at present? If you think there are likely to be differences, what would they be?

Paternalism in the Age of Cognitive Enhancement: Do Civil Liberties Presuppose Roughly Equal Mental Ability?

Daniel Wikler

Using genetic modifications and biotechnology to make us smarter, more rational, more intelligent—what could be wrong with that? Plenty, according to Daniel Wikler. He does not argue that there is something wrong, in and of itself, with such enhancements. He doesn't, for instance, argue that they are somehow unnatural, or that they involve our wrongly playing God. Instead, he focuses on the likely scenario that such enhancements will be distributed unequally in a population. In that situation, some of those whose intelligence now qualifies as normal would become classified as having an abnormally low intelligence level. And that would almost certainly lead to violations of their civil liberties.

The key issue that Wikler addresses is that of determining when we are competent to make our own decisions, free from well-meaning but intrusive interference by others. Nowadays most adults are at liberty to choose their friends, job, or local address, because their intelligence level is suitable to such tasks. But what if a group within society became so cognitively enhanced that they became way better than the rest of us at making such decisions? Wikler believes that in such a scenario the unenhanced might well be judged to be so intellectually incompetent as to justify limiting their (our) liberty to make such decisions.

Wikler considers a natural reply—though the unenhanced are far less sharp than the enhanced, those who are currently within the normal range of cognitive abilities can still recognize when they are falling short, and can ask their enhanced fellow citizens for assistance. So there is no case for restricting the liberty of the unenhanced. But as Wikler notes, the enhanced are likely to know much sooner and better than the rest of us when we need help. In a new environment, where there is a class of people way smarter than the rest of us, we ordinary folks may not be aware that we need help in the first place. In that respect we may be in just the same boat as those who are currently mentally handicapped, and whose cognitive impairment prevents them from realizing that they are ill-equipped to make certain decisions for themselves. As a result, Wikler believes, a population where only some portion is cognitively enhanced is likely to lead to creating a group of second-class citizens whose liberties are infringed for their own good.

I. INTRODUCTION

Advances in genetics and biotechnology may enable scientists to augment our cognitive powers. If this does become feasible, it is virtually certain that many people will want this kind of intervention for their children, or indeed if it proves feasible, for themselves.

Perhaps the maximum enhancement will be minor, say a 5 to 10 percent increase in memory capacity, ability to concentrate, or speed of calculation. Some of us can achieve performance enhancements of this magnitude now, with training, coffee, or a good night's sleep. If many people achieved these gains, they might be more productive, and perhaps fewer accidents would occur. The aggregate benefit might be impressive. But their effect on our social institutions and relationships would be minor or non-existent.

But what if science will enable human beings, or at least some human beings, to be vastly smarter, passing by Einstein toward presently unimaginable heights. We would certainly notice these changes.

It would make a difference if everyone in that future society were much more intelligent than we are, or if only some were. I would like to focus on a society in which only some people achieve this enhancement. Perhaps the enhancement is expensive, and not all can afford it; or perhaps the technique for enhancing intelligence doesn't work with every candidate. Whatever the reason for making substantial cognitive enhancement less than universal, we should be prepared to face a difficult social problem; a potential threat to civil liberties. What once was "normal" intelligence might not be sufficient to navigate the society that the cognitively-enhanced create for themselves. The implications of this development for self-determination on the part of the un-enhanced may be dire.

2. A BRIEF LOOK BACKWARD: THE EUGENICISTS' CONCERNS ABOUT INTELLIGENCE

A neo-Nazi writer named Roger Pearson followed the Human Genome Program with great interest. Pearson understood the Human Genome project to vindicate his racist and eugenic vision of society and social problems. The Genome Project would

Daniel Wikler, "Paternalism in the Age of Cognitive Enhancement," in *Human Enhancement*, ed. Nick Bostrom and Julian Savulescu (Oxford University Press, 2009), pp. 341–354.

finally demonstrate, he thought, that people are *not* created equal, that some are much more gifted than others, and that the substrate for these differences are inherited (he also believed that they clustered along racial lines). And he took this to be an unanswerable refutation of egalitarianism.

Pearson's argument has a glaring flaw; egalitarians need not, and do not, assume or argue that everyone has the same intellectual capacity. The point of egalitarianism is to ensure that people do equally well, or have the same opportunities to do well, given the talents they are born with and those that they can acquire.

So of what interest is Pearson, or rather the kind of view he espouses, after all?

One reason is that if it becomes possible to increase the intelligence of appreciable numbers of our fellow-citizens, this development will inevitably bring to mind the old eugenics movement and the calamities it brought about, and we will need to think whether this precedent has anything to teach us in our new venture. Indeed the Human Genome Project has already proven to be a stimulus for this kind of reflection.

Eugenics was not one movement, but many, and eugenicists varied considerably in both their methods and their goals.

For all the disagreements over both means and ends within the eugenics movement, the historical record reveals a continuing preoccupation with one theme, and that is low intelligence (or "feeblemindedness," to use their stock phrase). The inherited stupidity of the genetic underclass led these people, by one pathway or another, to their multiple antisocial transgressions. These people were "shiftless," lazy, immoral, menacing, and lecherous (and, partly as a result, unusually fertile). Not all eugenicists blamed every social problem and individual failing on cognitive deficits, but this hardy theme has survived even into recent times. The authors of the neo-eugenic tome, *The Bell Curve*,[1] intimated that the reason that the genetic underclass in America did not adopt proper middle-class morals was that

morality is not easy to grasp and they simply did not have the mental capacity for it.

What follows from this understanding of the problem—whatever "problem" it was that for which eugenics was supposed to be the answer—was that this country badly needed a smarter population. The eugenicists, of course, could not dream of intervening at the level of molecular biology. Their interventions were crude and barely effective, as the best-educated and candid eugenicists acknowledged. All they could do was to ask the fit to mate more often, preferably with each other, and try to prevent the unfit from mating at all. Worse, they had no way of identifying who might be carrying recessive genes that would poison the next generation, and who were presumably much more numerous than the people who failed the newly-devised IQ test and who, thus identified as genetically compromised, could be handed over to authorities for sterilization. The prospect of direct intervention on genes to increase intelligence would, we can speculate, have put them into orbit—unless all the talk of eugenics was just a cover story for committing violence on a class of people they did not like.

We take comfort in being far more enlightened than these pseudoscientific zealots. We know that social problems stem largely from social failings and that the link between genes and behavior is in most cases indirect, complex, mediated, and nonspecific. But in fact some of the old controversy animates us. In debates over race, nothing is as germane and as incendiary as the belief, spoken or unspoken, that blacks are not as smart as whites. As we consider the prospects for intervening on the biochemical substrate of intelligence, especially if the resulting enhancement of that will be heritable, we might restimulate some of these controversies. This is especially the case if the enhancements will be extended, even if only at first, on a less than universal basis.

3. INTELLIGENCE AND CIVIL LIBERTIES IN THE PRE-GENOMIC AND POST-ENHANCEMENT ERAS

While distancing ourselves from Pearson's insistence that egalitarianism will crumble once we learn that people are not born equal, it should not

---

1. Richard Herrnstein and Charles Murray, *The Bell Curve: Intelligence and Class Structure in American Life* (Glencoe: Free Press. 1994).

escape our notice that there is at least one important respect in which unequal social status—a social fact—does seem to track unequal biological capacity for intelligence. We routinely restrict the freedom of people who are judged to be insufficiently intelligent to handle their own affairs. These are people who are classified as moderately retarded and who are found to be incompetent in respect to essential skills. In a humane society, their needs are met by caring family members or guardians, supported by government. Enlighted competency laws selectively permit the restriction of rights and liberties to be keyed to the abilities and challenges each faces as an individual rather than across the board. A person might, for example, have the right to buy her own clothes, but not to make long-term financial decisions.

We are used to this practice and it is uncontroversial, but I believe we can learn something by asking for its justification. In a paper I published some time ago,[2] I asked the reader to choose between two quite different accounts. These corresponded to two different notions of competence. A "relativist" account of competence points to the relative difference in intellectual ability between average people and the moderately retarded and to the corresponding (probable) difference in favorable outcomes of key decisions when made by the two categories of people.

A second view, I argued, saw competence as a property that is possessed in equal measure by all who possessed it. According to this view, what determines that one person is incompetent and the other competent is not the relative difference between them in respect to intelligence, but rather on which side of an absolute threshold their intellectual capacities fell. In this perspective, what matters is that one has the kinds of abilities typical of a person with, say, approximately 90 IQ points and who is otherwise sane and well balanced. I re-emphasize that the threshold should be expected to vary with the task, and a person judged competent for one task might be judged to require guardianship for another. Still, in respect to each of these competencies,

there would, in this view, have to be a threshold. Above the thresholds, all are equally competent.

Each of these views has both problems and advantages. To summarize a fairly complex matter, the relativist view needs fewer suppositions and assumptions about the somewhat mysterious threshold of competence; it points to relative differences, each measurable in an objective, standard (if disputed) way. But it is vulnerable to a follow-up question: if the relative difference between average people and the mildly or moderately retarded person justifies steps by the former to curtail the liberties of the latter—for his or her own good, of course—would the same consideration not justify similar action by a much smarter-than-average person vis-à-vis the average person? This would not necessarily be a pure hypothetical, if the gap in question is merely the least perceivable difference, i.e. two standard deviations in IQ. But even if the gap would have to be much greater, the hypothetical is troubling. Is this all that it take to justify lifting our rights to control our lives—just the assumption that a much smarter person could do a better job of it than we are doing?

The conception of competence as a threshold property has complementary attributes. It would not make paternalism so easy to justify, as the relativist view seems to do. We prize our powers to make decisions, come what may, even though others might do a better job. On this absolute understanding of competence we would retain these rights even if we encountered people so very bright that they would likely do a much better job than we are now doing, even assuming that they took our interests to heart. Of course, we would be at liberty to consult with them, and to ask them for their advice, but in the end it would be our decision whether to follow it. And if we come to grief because we reject the advice of people more intelligent than we are, then this is an eventuality tor which we take full responsibility, without regret.

So far so good for the absolute view. But what, considerations make it reasonable for us to insist on making key life decisions on our own? An adequate answer to this question cannot be given (if at all) in passing, but we can consider some of the standard candidates. First, no one else has the right to intervene, whether for good reasons or otherwise.

---

2. Daniel Wikler, "Paternalism and the Mildly Retarded," *Philosophy and Public Affairs*, 8(4): 377–92. 1979.

Second, we learn—not only practical lessons but also what life is all about—from the mistakes we make, and it Big Brother keeps intervening to keep us out of harm's way, we cannot mature, improve, and deepen. Third, Big Brothers have proven to be not so wise after all, and certainly not consistently beneficent. In particular, it does not follow from the fact that one person is intellectually superior to another that the former would make decisions on behalf of the latter that would be better for the latter. Good decisions require not only insight but also compassion, sensitivity, maturity, and practicality—all of which may be lacking in an exceptionally smart person, as readers of this chapter no doubt know from personal experience.

Do these considerations, singly or in combination, justify our insistence on remaining free to err? The first asserts a right, but it does not provide the rationale for insisting on this right. Perhaps we assert a right against well-intentioned intervention because, in our own experience, we have done better than such intervenors, either personally or collectively. Perhaps in a brave new world of the cognitively enhanced (save for our small band of previously normal, now subnormal unenhanced ones), these rights seem less self-evident; perhaps they seem less to indicate sound political philosophy than flaws in judgment and character. Perhaps the second defense—that we learn by error—should be understood as our advice to the cognitively enhanced on what kind of intervention is most likely to benefit us. If we're right, they will grasp this and we will be permitted some opportunities to err, just as wise parents refrain from being overprotective while maintaining a discreet safety net under their young children. In this light, this second consideration counts as advice on how the cognitively enhanced should intervene, not as a defense against their doing so. The third consideration—the sorry record of those who insisted that they knew better what was good for adults who had the cognitive capacities that our minority retains in the new society of the cognitively-enhanced—fails for obvious reasons. These are not the bumbling do-gooders and bureaucrats of old, but greatly enhanced supermen who really are much smarter than we are. And even if, collectively, they are no more likely to exceed in non-cognitive dimensions of good decision-making, their intellectual superiority gives them a crucial advantage.

Before the age of cognitive enhancement, we "normals" are used to thinking that we generally do fairly well for ourselves. It is the moderately retarded—those who have enough capacity to formulate and assert preferences but who lack the mental equipment to guide their lives without coming to grief—who need help. But perhaps this sense of confidence is wishful thinking. We need only to look around us to see how much improvement there could be over the way that average, or even somewhat better than average people ran things. Marriages fail, people do not save for their retirement, and voters elect manifestly inferior candidates. The recent flourishing of behavioral economics as a field research stems from abundant evidence of the gap between the ideal rationality of *homo economicus* and real human consumers and other decision-makers. If there were people much brighter than we, who had our interests at heart, things could go much better were they to make our decisions for us.

It might appear that we "normals" could retreat just a bit and still win the argument by claiming that the cognitive level of our newly-subnormal minority was and remains sufficient for us to know when we need help and advice from experts. We needn't know everything or be supreme geniuses to get by if we have knowledgeable geniuses to call upon for advice and help. In this view, our relative cognitive deficit vis-à-vis the newly enhanced does not render us incompetent. Indeed, precisely the opposite: the advent of techniques for enhancing cognition may have been denied to us, but it placed in our midst beings whose advice and assistance will prove to be more valuable than that of the accountants, marriage counselors, and psychotherapists we had been used to consulting. Like computers or the internet, the cognitively-enhanced thus enhance our own cognitive powers, even though our inherent cognitive abilities remain unchanged. We may be less clever than our newly-enhanced fellow-citizens, but we have sufficient cognitive capacity to manage our own affairs. If we mess things up, it will not be because of a lack of insight, or insufficient memory, or slow data processing—each a symptom of our cognitive inferiority. The problem is more likely to be arrogance or pride, if these vices result in our refusing to consult experts or to comply with their advice. Or perhaps we fail because we are rash, or immature, or self-destructive. We are just as prone to these vices as our cognitively-enhanced superiors. All of us, brilliant and dull alike, can be brought low through defects of character. The only advantage that our enhanced fellow-citizens have over us normals, according to this defense of civil liberties for the unenhanced, is that they need not seek out consultants. Assuming that we normals will get help when we need it and ask for it, our capacity to make good choices will remain in the same league as our smarter neighbors, and we need not cede any of our liberties to them in order to protect our own wellbeing.

This defense against paternalistic intervention by the cognitively-enhanced contains some truths (the unenhanced *would* have more expert experts to consult) but it does not succeed. If we always knew when we needed help or advice, then having experts around might suffice. Unfortunately, it takes insight to know when you don't know. Those who do not understand how little they understand are the most obvious of fools. The cognitively-enhanced would realize much sooner than we would that we were out of our depth and required their help. True, temperament is also a factor: some will gladly seek advice and follow it, while others spurn help at their peril. But these personality traits come into play only when we come to appreciate that we are in need of advice. If we are blissfully ignorant of the fact (when it is a fact) that we are ignorant, then it is pointless to invoke flaws of character in explaining our insistence of keeping our own counsel.

4. THE FAIRNESS AND THE UTILITY OF INCOMPETENCE

The argument thus far stems from an initial distinction between two accounts of mental competence: a relativist view that likens our position vis-à-vis the cognitively enhanced to the position of the moderately retarded living among us; and a threshold view according to which the amount of cognitive capacity that most of us possess in the pre-enhancement age is sufficient for each sane adult to insist on a right to make key life decisions free of intervention

from others. These seem to point to different justifications of the rights we assert in this, our current, pre-enhancement era, to make our most important decisions with no more help from others than we solicit. It is not clear that either could sustain this stance in an era in which most of our neighbors become cognitively enhanced. Thus far, neither seems to offer a secure foundation for a right to be left alone. But the worst is yet to come. Through further reflection on the social context in which ascriptions of mental competence are used to counter paternalism, a deeper problem comes into view. Liberty for the unenhanced would place a burden on their more clever fellow-citizens, one that might not be fair to them:

To see this, let us recall the notion of mental competence as a threshold (RSC) property. Some tasks can be handled equally well, or almost so, by people of widely divergent abilities. Grocery stores, for example, use bags that hold only so many products; the vast majority of people can walk away with two of these without difficulty. Building codes require that risers on stairs be no more than a certain height, again matching human capabilities at something like low-average capacity. Very strong people, or people with a long gait, can carry the grocery bags and climb the stairs, but, in ordinary circumstances, not with noticeably less difficulty than average people. We make bags and staircases with these facts in mind. Indeed, much of our social environment is created to achieve some kind of desirable balance between utility—a multiplicity of tiny grocery bags would be a nuisance to everyone except tiny or very weak people, and the same is true for stairs with one-inch risers—and inclusion. By requiring only so much capacity, we make our society accessible to the vast majority of its members. We sacrifice some utility, especially for those with excess capability, i.e., talent that is not used because we place the bar so low. But efficiency is not our only goal.

Something of the same story can be told about intellectual demands, too. The original idea behind Form 1040 of the United States Internal Revenue Service—an idea now lost in the mists of time, unfortunately—was that one did not have to be a genius or an accountant to use it to determine how much one owed by way of taxes. Directions on a power saw or even a bottle of pills are supposed to be simple enough for nearly everyone to read them with sufficient comprehension to avoid injury. The sum of the outcomes of these attempts to balance utility for the majority with protection for the less-able yields a social definition of competence.

Seen in this light, both the relative and the absolute conceptions of competence capture part of the truth. At the lowest end of the spectrum of cognitive abilities, there is indeed an absolute threshold. Those incapable of language, for example, cannot comprehend the options between which they would have to choose. But there is considerable space above that line in which a person's status as competent or not depends on social arrangements. Those whose intellectual capacities put them in this zone could be made competent if society set its demands low enough. Here the relative difference between a dull or not-very-bright minority and the majority who are just below average, or better, becomes important, and as that majority arranges society to suit themselves, their less-bright peers become incompetent. When they do, then in respect to a host of tasks that are central to everyday living, everyone but the less-bright people are fully competent. Those who are rendered incompetent in this manner need supervision, and in order to protect them in that now-dangerous environment, their rights are taken away. Humane regimes strive to protect as much of their range of free choice as possible, consistent with the need to protect them from serious or irremediable harm (and to protect others), but there is no supposition that everyone has a natural, inalienable right to self-determination that would rule out all configurations of the social and physical environment that are disadvantageous to the less-talented. Those who are made incompetent, so that society can be organized by rules and other conventions that have great utility but require high ability, do not have the full status of free citizens, sovereign in their own affairs and sharing equally in general governance.

5. WHEN INTELLIGENCE DIVERGES

Robert Nozick posed the hypothetical question: what if a super-smart race or tribe arrived on the scene?[3] And this is our question, too, put to

---

3. *Anarchy, State, and Utopia* (New York: Basic Books).

a different use. Suppose that half, or two thirds, of the population moves into the passing lane in intellectual capacity, becoming geniuses (by current standards) and upping the ante in the requirements for civic participation? What becomes of the citizenship, the liberties, the status as equals, of those of us who are merely average? Or even those considered fairly clever by the standards of the *ancien regime?*

Before applying the foregoing discussion to this predicament, here are two observations in passing to link the imagined future of enhanced cognition to the present and the past:

- There are important disparities in cognitive functioning even today, in every country. In many cases these stem from different experience with respect to such determinants as nutrition, environmental pollution, and very different cultural and educational opportunities. These determinants do not track class differences precisely—which is why Harvard's students are brighter now that academic potential is the chief criterion for admission, rather than being a descendant of previous Harvard graduates—but they do have consequences for one's eventual placement in the socioeconomic hierarchy. Our concern over the advantages provided by superior education is the motivation for Head Start, the early-intervention program for less-privileged children. Absent a convincing argument that shows that postnatal IQ boosts for the privileged are more objectionable than prenatal IQ boosts for the privileged, the latter should be judged similarly. Good education for all is fine, but good education only for the well-to-do is not.

- As remarked earlier, Pearson was just wrong about egalitarianism's assumptions. It requires no claim, true or false as the case may be, that we all have approximately equal intellectual or other capacities. It is equality of civil status that we're after, and this is consistent with—even celebrates to some extent—the evident fact of human differences. Why, then do egalitarians get so upset about allegations of innate differences in cognitive capacity? Because they are what *in*egalitarians and racists point to, to justify social class differences, to blame social miseries on the poor, and to deny learning opportunities to those who need them most. Eugenicists in the UK and US believed that the sufferings of the poor and the disadvantage of stigmatized racial and ethnic groups was a result of their inherited cognitive deficits; and for that reason society would do well to ensure that they reproduced less. Sterilization and worse were, in time, the regrettable result. For the eugenicists, it did not matter that the hereditarian explanation of the miseries of the lower classes invoked brute luck; that bad luck is what earned them their stigma. Though we would like to think that we live in a more enlightened age, we cannot know whether the cognitively enhanced, in the technologically-advanced society we are imagining, would regard their unenhanced, newly-subnormal brethren with kind concern or with contempt. As Thomas Scanlon noted in his "The Significance of Choice,"[4] the right to make one's own choices is a badge of full and equal status in a society like ours. Even if the cognitively-enhanced intervened in the personal affairs of those of us who remained unenhanced, our social status could be undermined.

What, then, would be the effect of selective enhancement of intellectual capacity—that is, enhancement for some, but not all—for the social and political world that we "normals" would inhabit? Would it erode the foundations of egalitarianism, undermining the claims of many who now hold title as citizens to that equal status? Would those made or engineered to be born smart be within their rights to deprive the rest of us of our rights, presumably with humanitarian intent?

In a word: yes. Or, at least, that is what my earlier argument implies, so far as I can see. It would depend in part on circumstances and in part on moral issues:

- First: How many people would get the boost in intellectual capacity? If only a few do, nothing will or should change. But suppose it is a majority.
- Second: Would raising the intellectual bar over our heads (speaking of "we" as people like those writing and reading this chapter) have very substantial benefits for this new majority, while admitting of the possibility of protecting the rest of us through some form of guardianship?
- Third, it depends on our view of distributive justice. If we gave absolute priority to the worst-off, intellectually speaking, we would keep the bar low so that we would be equally competent relative the new intellectual elite. The tasks would be easy enough for us to handle them. Otherwise, if there would be much to gain (for most people, but not all) by raising the bar high, it looks like the arrangement that would most closely mirror our own would be a regime in which we would be excluded from equal citizenship.

That prospect is unpleasant to contemplate. Perhaps I've taken a wrong turn. Is there a threshold of competence that I have not sighted, one that justifies our claim to be autonomous beings, captains of our own fates, regardless of how well some newly-enhanced fellow citizens might do if made our guardians? Do I have the calculation of benefits and burdens wrong? Should we be eternally vigilant and suspicious of people who appoint themselves "guardians," profess humanitarian motives, and then take over our lives?

Or do the shoes just hurt because they would be on *our* feet?

Daniel Wikler: Paternalism in the Age of Cognitive Enhancement: Do Civil Liberties Presuppose Roughly Equal Mental Ability?

1. Wikler doesn't argue that there is anything intrinsically wrong with cognitive enhancement produced through biotechnology or genetic

---

4. Thomas Scanlon, "The Significance of Choice," *The Tanner Lectures on Human Values*, ed. Sterling M. McMurrin (Salt Lake City: University of Utah Press), 151–216, 1988.

engineering. Do you think there is? Craft an argument in support of your view.

2. Wikler distinguishes between a relativist and a threshold view of mental competence. What are these two views, and what implications for civil liberties result from the difference between them?

3. Wikler devotes some time to presenting a history of the eugenics movement. Do you think that the development of cognitive enhancement programs would lead to similar results? Why or why not?

4. Suppose that a society wasn't able to provide all of its citizens with bioengineered cognitive enhancements, and only the wealthy ended up being able to afford them. Is it better to allow some people the opportunity to enhance their lives, even if others lack that opportunity?

5. Wikler asks, "Suppose that half, or two-thirds, of the population moves into the passing lane in intellectual capacity, becoming geniuses (by current standards). . . . What becomes of the citizenship, the liberties, the status as equals, of those of us who are merely average?" What's your answer to his question? What ethical implications do you draw from your answer?

CHAPTER 23

Sexual Morality

JUST THE FACTS

Questions of sexual morality are questions about the moral status of various sexual acts and sexual relationships, including, by extension, marital relationships. When we talk about sex, we sometimes mean sexual intercourse specifically, and sometimes mean sexual acts more generally. Sexual relationships are relationships that are defined in part by their general inclusion of a sexual component. Because marital relationships and other romantic relationships generally include such a component, they will also be discussed in this chapter.

Many questions about sexual morality ask whether or not it is morally acceptable to engage in certain kinds of sexual acts. Many kinds of sexual acts are defined by *who* is engaging in them. For example, heterosexual sex is sex between two people of the opposite sex, whereas homosexual sex is sex between two people of the same sex. **Premarital sex** is sex between two people who have not been married. **Casual sex** is sex between people who have expressed no commitment to each other. **Incest** is sex between two family members.

In many societies, traditional views about what kinds of sex are acceptable have been very restrictive. Such views often restrict permissible sex to heterosexual, marital sex and condemn all other sexual acts. In the United States, traditional attitudes about sexual morality have become less universal, but are still widespread. For example, the General Social Survey compiled by the National Opinion Research Center found that the percentage of Americans who answered that homosexual sex was "always wrong"

decreased from 70 percent in 1973 to 43.4 percent in 2012.[1] Recent research by the Pew Center suggests that roughly 60 percent of Americans believe that society should accept homosexuality.[2] Attitudes in other Western countries are even more liberal, with 80 percent of Canadians and 76 percent of Britons believing that society should accept homosexuality.[3] However, in many non-Western countries, traditional views about homosexuality are still accepted by almost everyone—in countries such as Pakistan, Indonesia, Egypt, Turkey, and Nigeria, fewer than 10 percent thought that homosexuality should be accepted.[4]

In the United States, attitudes about premarital sex have also become more liberal over time. The General Social Survey found that the percentage of Americans who answered that sex before marriage was "not wrong at all" increased from 26.5 percent in 1972 to 56 percent in 2012.[5] Such statistics suggest that sexual mores are trending away from the traditional view of sexual morality. But there are exceptions: between 1973 and 2012, the percentage of respondents who said that sex with someone other than one's spouse was "always wrong" *increased* from

---

1. http://www.norc.org/PDFs/sexmoralfinal_06-21_FINAL.PDF

2. http://www.pewglobal.org/2013/06/04/the-global-divide-on-homosexuality/

3. Ibid.

4. Ibid.

5. http://www.norc.org/PDFs/sexmoralfinal_06-21_FINAL.PDF

69.3 percent to 80.8 percent, and the percentage of respondents who said that sex between children under sixteen was "always wrong" remained around 66 percent. Furthermore, while statistics about attitudes toward incest and nonconsensual sex are hard to come by, we can infer that questions about them are not included on surveys like the General Social Survey because it is assumed that they would be almost universally condemned.

Though the aforementioned data suggest that homosexual sex and premarital sex have come to be considered much more morally acceptable than they used to be, they remain controversial. In the United States, a sizable minority of the population still considers homosexual sex and premarital sex to be immoral. With regard to homosexuality, there are controversial issues surrounding not just the moral status of homosexual sex, but also the status of same-sex marriage. In the history of the United States, legal recognition of same-sex relationships is a relatively recent phenomenon. State marriage laws have differed over time as to whether they explicitly define marriage as between a man and a woman, but until recently, marriage was de facto reserved for opposite-sex couples. For example, in 1970, a same-sex couple in Minnesota applied for a marriage license and was denied on the grounds that they were both men. Their appeal of the ruling went to the Minnesota Supreme Court, who ruled in *Baker* v. *Nelson* that the state did not recognize same-sex marriages.[6] In 1996, President Bill Clinton signed the Defense of Marriage Act, which defined marriage for federal purposes as between a man and a woman, and allowed states that had defined marriage as such to refuse to recognize same-sex marriages performed in other states.[7] However, in 2014, the Supreme Court struck down the Defense of Marriage Act, ruling

that states cannot ban same-sex marriage, and making same-sex marriage legal throughout the United States.[8] Same-sex marriage has also been legally recognized in Canada and much of Europe and Latin America.[9]

This shift toward legal recognition of same-sex marriage has corresponded with a dramatic shift in attitudes toward same-sex marriage. In 2001, the Pew Research Center found that Americans opposed the legalization of same-sex marriage by a margin of 57 percent to 35 percent. In 2017, Pew found that Americans supported the legalization of same-sex marriage by a margin of 62 percent to 32 percent.[10] However, it is important to note that, based on the data cited earlier, both remain significantly controversial in the United States. While acceptance of homosexuality continues to gain traction, it is still far from universal.

Issues about homosexuality are not the only issues of sexual morality where moral and legal questions intersect. For example, there are also questions about the moral and legal status of **polyamory**. Polyamorous relationships are sexual, romantic, or marital relationships between more than two people. Historically, many such relationships have been **polygamous** relationships, in which a man has more than one wife at the same time. However, there are also **polyandrous** relationships, in which a woman has more than one husband, as well as polyamorous relationships that are neither polygamous nor polyandrous. In the United States (and most other countries), polyamorous marriages are not legally recognized.[11] Furthermore, the practice of marrying more than one person is criminalized

6. Baker *v.* Nelson 291 Minn. 310, 191 N.W.2d 185 (1971)

7. https://www.govtrack.us/congress/bills/104/hr3396/summary

8. https://www.supremecourt.gov/opinions/14pdf/14-556_3204.pdf

9. http://www.pewforum.org/2017/08/08/gay-marriage-around-the-world-2013/

10. http://www.pewforum.org/fact-sheet/changing-attitudes-on-gay-marriage/

11. https://metro.co.uk/2015/06/22/where-exactly-is-polygamy-legal-5257418/

in the United States.[12] Polyamorous marriage has often been prohibited because of the prevalence of oppressive and exploitative polygamous relationships. For example, the United Nations Human Rights Committee has reported that the practice of polyamory, ostensibly because it is almost always polygamous, "violates the dignity of women" and "should be definitely abolished wherever it continues to exist."[13] Unfortunately, statistics about the acceptance of polyamory are hard to come by. However, questions about its moral and legal status have recently attracted increased public interest.[14]

Yet other questions of sexual morality are raised by **prostitution**, which is the act or practice of having sex in exchange for money. There are some practices, such as child prostitution and sex slavery, that are unquestionably immoral. However, the moral and legal status of prostitution by consenting adults is more controversial. Recent data on attitudes toward the morality of prostitution are sparse, but in data from 1996, 67 percent disagreed at least somewhat with the statement: "There is nothing inherently wrong with prostitution, so long as the health risks can be minimized. If consenting adults agree to exchange money for sex, that is their business."[15] More recent data are available on the question of whether or not to legalize prostitution. A 2016 Marist poll found that 49 percent thought that prostitution between consenting adults should be legalized, while 44 percent thought it should not be.[16] In the United States, prostitution is currently illegal in every state except for Nevada.

12. http://memory.loc.gov/cgi-bin/ampage?collId= llsl&fileName=012/llsl012.db&recNum=0532

13. http://hrlibrary.umn.edu/gencomm/hrcom28.htm

14. https://www.usatoday.com/story/news/ nation/2015/08/10/polyamorous-relationships-become-more-visible/31439123/

15. https://gssdataexplorer.norc.org/variables/1871/vshow

16. http://www.pbs.org/wgbh/point-taken/blog/marist-should-prostitution-be-legalized/

ARGUMENT ANALYSIS

When you think about it, there are *a lot* of prohibitions—conventional, moral, and legal—surrounding sexual behavior. The list of "don'ts" is extensive: don't have sex outside of marriage; don't masturbate; don't have nonconsensual sex; don't have sex with people your friends are romantically interested in; don't have sex with family members, with animals, minors, or co-workers. And this is just a partial list.

Do these prohibitions have any rational basis, or are they outdated taboos? Though each of these prohibitions deserves its own consideration, our focus must be limited, as usual. Still, we can make substantial headway by considering what we might call the **liberal position regarding sexual morality**: the view that sex is morally permissible if and only if it is engaged in by consenting adults.

This position is liberal in the classical sense—namely, as describing a view that places supreme importance on personal liberty. The core idea is given in the first premise of

The Liberal Argument

1. We are morally permitted to do what we want with our fellow human beings, so long as they provide informed consent to our treatment.
2. Every type of sexual activity among humans, except rape and sex with children, can be performed by those giving informed consent.

Therefore,

3. Every type of sexual activity among humans, except rape and sex with children, can be morally permissible, so long as their participants have given informed consent.

Premise 2 is plausible. Rape is defined as nonconsensual sex. And a child is someone who is defined, in part, as incapable of offering informed consent to engaging in sexual relations. In other words, if (say) a seventeen-year-old is mature enough to provide informed consent to having sex, then that seventeen-year-old is no longer a child. These cases aside, the Liberal Argument implies that other kinds of sexual relations that have been the target of moral criticism—for example, polygamy, prostitution, and incest—have been wrongly condemned, so long as their participants have provided informed consent.

Of course, many of those who have had these sorts of sexual relations have *not* offered their informed consent in doing so. Polygamy often preys on young females and contributes to their oppression. A great many prostitutes are effectively slaves, "owned" by pimps and threatened with harm if they fail to comply with the pimp's demands. Incest is usually rape. The Liberal Argument does not permit such behavior. What it says is that when those engaged in polygamy, prostitution and incest give their informed consent—this might be rare but it is not impossible—then (and only then) are such behaviors morally OK.

Premise 1 expresses a core liberal idea. It can be defended in at least two different ways. The first is by rule consequentialism (see Chapter 5). The thought is that if everyone were to follow the liberal idea, and behave toward others in ways they consented to, then the overall results would be terrific. Of course people are sometimes disappointed at how things turn out after having given their consent, but, the thought goes, they have no moral complaint in such cases. You'll be sad if you make a risky investment and it falls through, but you won't have any basis for morally criticizing your investment advisor if she warned you in advance of all the risks.

The second way to defend premise 1 is by a Kantian appeal to the importance of autonomy. We are able to decide for ourselves how best to live our life, and this ability gives each of us a moral right to do just that—so long as we respect the rights of others to live their life, too. Your ability to set your own goals, determine which principles you will live by, and commit to a way of life is an exalted thing. This ability

accounts for why human beings are so valuable. And that value needs protection, which moral rights offer—they protect our autonomy. To my mind, the toughest challenge to premise 1 is provided by a case I read about several years ago.[17] A German computer technician, Armin Meiwes, posted an ad seeking a willing volunteer for "slaughter and consumption." He apparently found one, a man named Bernd Brandes, who answered the ad and allowed himself to be killed and eaten by Meiwes. Though there was difficulty in determining whether Brandes really did consent to his death, let us suppose that the evidence clearly indicated that he did. Even so, most of us would recoil at the claim that what Meiwes did was morally acceptable.

The liberal has just two options—to argue that such consent can never be informed, or to allow that it can be, and that in such a case it is morally acceptable to kill and eat another human being. You might be tempted by the first option, thinking that Brandes could not be informed about the choice to be killed, since he had never had that experience. But that is too demanding a standard for informed consent. You can't know what it's truly like to skydive, have sex, or drive a car until you've actually done it. And yet first-timers are able to offer their informed consent to engage in each of these activities. True, the more dangerous the activity, the more information we require in order to judge that someone has given his informed consent to undertake it. So we are right to require that anyone who volunteers to be killed—whether fighting for one's country, say, or indulging a very unusual desire for self-destruction—be very well aware of what he is getting himself into. But it's not clear why we should think that meeting this standard is impossible.

The alternative for the liberal is to bite the bullet and allow that in very rare cases, people are morally permitted to kill others who ask for

---

17. http://www.nbcnews.com/id/11909486/ns/world_news/t/german-court-sentences-cannibal-life-jail/#.Wa2zQNGQw2w.

death. This is the position taken, for instance, by those who endorse the morality of active euthanasia (see Chapter 15). The difference here is that Brandes was not suffering from a terminal illness and that he was asking to be cannibalized. These are important differences, to be sure. The liberal will say, however, that so long as Brandes knew what he was getting into, and gave his consent accordingly, then Meiwes did not act immorally. Liberals know we probably are not going to like that. But they will say that our revulsion in this case is on par with the disgust so many people have felt at homosexual sex or masturbation—quite real, but also quite groundless.

Is the liberal verdict here correct? Let's focus on homosexual sex as a test case. Liberals argue that when such sex is consensual, there is nothing immoral about it. Despite greater acceptance of homosexuality in some societies nowadays, the liberal position has long been a minority view, and even now, in some societies, people are socially ruined or even killed if they are discovered to have engaged in sexual relations with others of the same sex.

Perhaps the most common defense of the view that homosexual sex is immoral is the argument from unnaturalness—unnatural actions are immoral; homosexual sex is unnatural; therefore, such sex is immoral. We won't pause to assess this argument here, since we have already considered (in Chapters 8 and 22) the six most prominent interpretations of what it is to be unnatural, none of which support the claim that unnatural actions per se are immoral. We can also set to one side another popular argument, already examined in Chapter 6, which says that homosexual sex is immoral because if everyone engaged in such behavior, then disastrous results would follow. Instead, let's focus on

The Family Values Argument

1. If a practice is contrary to family values, then it is immoral.

2. Homosexual relations are contrary to family values.

Therefore,

3. Homosexual relations are immoral.

Without a well-defined notion of what is meant by "family values," it's not clear what to say about premise 1. When I think of such values, I think of love, honesty, loyalty, and devotion. On this reading of family values, however, premise 2 is false, since homosexual couples can exhibit these values just as well as heterosexual ones. If honoring family values implies, in addition, that one has sex only when one intends to or is able to have children, then premise 2 is true. But then premise 1 is false, since it is not immoral for postmenopausal women to have sex. The same holds for men who have had a vasectomy, women who have had a hysterectomy, or men or women who are infertile for other reasons.

Many have argued that homosexual sex is immoral because God forbids it. This view presupposes the divine command theory (discussed in Chapter 1.E), which says that God is the author of the moral law. We won't rehearse the details of that discussion here, except to note its important upshot: if God really exists and is all-wise and all-good, then God will not issue arbitrary commands. God's commands will be backed by the very best reasons there are. So if God really does forbid homosexual sex, then there must be excellent reasons to oppose it. But what are those reasons? Such sex can be highly pleasurable and consensual. It doesn't harm others. It doesn't violate the rights of others. In many cases it is the expression of deeply felt love; in others, it stems from an urgent physical desire or passion. Though the image of same-sex couples having sex evokes disgust among many people, it fails to do so in many others, and in any event, disgust that arises from imagining sexual acts is not a morally reliable emotion. (Evidence: imagine your parents or grandparents having sex.)

As a glance at the Liberal Argument confirms, it does not pronounce a verdict just on the morality of sex among same-sex partners. It also has implications for the morality of prostitution and of casual sex—the focus of two of our readings in this chapter. So long as prostitutes are adults who are informed about the risks of their activities and consent to having sex for money, then, says the liberal, there is nothing immoral about their doing so. The same conditions apply to the morality of casual sex. According to the liberal, there is nothing intrinsically immoral about having sex just for the fun of it, even if such sex expresses only lust, not love, and even if it is clear that there is no expectation of any long-term relationship.

The liberal need not be blind to social reality. Many criticize prostitution because they claim, rightly, that a great many prostitutes are effectively sexual slaves, recruited under false pretenses and then forced against their will to engage in sex. And when it comes to casual sex, some of it certainly fails to be consensual; even when partners do consent, this is not always informed, as people sometimes withhold crucial information (e.g., that they have a sexually transmitted disease) from their sexual partners. Liberals, though, are in an especially good position to both acknowledge and explain why such behaviors are indeed morally wrong: when sexual activity among adults lacks informed consent, then it is immoral. But in those cases in which prostitutes or casual sex partners know what they are getting into and freely choose to engage in sexual activity, then, says the liberal, there is nothing immoral about doing so.

Some argue that prostitutes never give informed consent to having sex for money, because they do not truly consent to it: they are effectively coerced by their circumstances (of being poor, or undereducated, or abused) into becoming prostitutes. This is the basis of

The Prostitution Argument

1. Prostitution is morally acceptable only if the prostitute provides informed consent to selling sexual services.
2. Adult prostitutes do not provide informed consent to selling sexual services.

Therefore,

3. Adult prostitution is not morally acceptable.

The focus here is on adults, because child prostitution is unquestionably immoral, given a child's inability to provide informed consent to having sex.

Premise 1 states a plausible necessary condition on the moral acceptability of prostitution. But premise 2 needs further scrutiny. Assessing it requires being sensitive to two legitimate points. The first is that adults are presumed to be capable of making informed, autonomous decisions—one of which, for all we know, can be to receive money in exchange for sexual services. The second point is that prostitutes rarely have better options; they are often in positions of great insecurity (economic and otherwise), and it can seem that prostitution is essentially exploitative—taking advantage of a person's vulnerability to get her to do things she wouldn't otherwise agree to do.

Regarding the first point: as already indicated, many prostitutes do *not* consent to selling sexual services, but instead have been forced into doing so. Still, what of those who say that they know what they are doing and are not being coerced into it? Are they all mistaken?

Answering yes to this question runs the danger of treating adults—usually, but not always, adult women—as if they are incapable of knowing their own mind. Of course we do sometimes mistake our own motives, and we also sometimes say things we don't really mean. But it is presumptuous to insist, ahead of time, that no sex worker can offer informed consent when on the job. Those who do insist on this assume that such prostitutes must be either lying or ignorant (of their own motives). Such a position thus threatens to discredit the views of those who are already marginalized—something that is far too easy to do, and therefore something that we should be very cautious about.

Of course it's true that almost no one grows up hoping to become a prostitute. This (and much else) is evidence that prostitution is usually a last resort, something that is far from intrinsically attractive. But the same can be said of a great many other things—being a trash collector, a migrant field worker, or a latrine cleaner, for instance. It's possible for workers in such fields to give their informed consent to doing these jobs, unappealing as they are. For all we know, the same might be said of some sex workers. The upshot of these reflections is that while premise 2 is certainly true in many cases, because many sex workers have indeed been forced to engage in prostitution, this premise may be false in a number of others.

In addition to inquiring about the morality of various forms of sexual activity, we can also ask about the morality of laws that prohibit such behavior. For example, even if one agrees with the liberal in thinking that homosexual sex, prostitution, or incest among adults is morally acceptable when informed and consensual, one might reject the idea that we should legalize such behavior.

As a general matter, the burden is very high on those who want to criminalize morally acceptable behavior. That's because, as we discussed in Chapter 20, legal punishment involves the expression of moral condemnation, which makes little sense if the behavior being punished is acknowledged to be morally acceptable. Still, there are some now-familiar arguments—slippery slope arguments, for instance (surveyed in Chapters 15 and 19), or conservative arguments (reviewed in Chapter 22)—that can allow

an action to be morally permissible even while seeking to show that such actions ought to be legally forbidden.

Rather than assessing such arguments once again, only in this case as applied to various forms of consensual sex, let's consider some new arguments. As it happens, these are specific to same-sex marriage. For reasons we haven't yet encountered, one might think that while sexual relations among same-sex couples are morally OK, still, we should not legalize same-sex marriage. One reason for thinking this is

The Definition of Marriage Argument

1. If marriage is, by definition, a relation between a man and a woman, then a homosexual relationship can never qualify as a marriage.
2. Marriage is, by definition, a relation between a man and a woman.

Therefore,

3. A homosexual relationship can never qualify as a marriage.

Premise 1 is true. But premise 2 is problematic. The basic reason is this: we can't solve serious moral issues just by means of a definition. We can define our terms in many ways just to suit our own viewpoints, without doing anything to resolve the underlying moral question. For example, we could define marriage as a relation between adults *of the same race*. That was very widely accepted, and standard practice, for many decades. But the definition doesn't settle the moral question of whether blacks and whites should be allowed to marry one another. Even if you want to define "marriage" as a relation between a man and a woman, one can still ask: should there be legal recognition of relations that are exactly like heterosexual marriage, only between members of the same sex? That moral question won't be solved by means of a definition.

Another popular argument against same-sex marriage is more challenging. It seeks to show that consistency requires supporters of same-sex marriage to support polygamy as well. After all, if homosexuals ought to be allowed to marry one another because they can give their informed consent to doing so, then presumably those engaged in polygamy should be able to be married, since they, too, can offer such consent. This is the basis for

The Polygamy Argument

1. If same-sex marriage should be legalized, then we should also legalize polygamy.
2. We shouldn't legalize polygamy.

Therefore,

3. We shouldn't legalize same-sex marriage.

Some will claim that premise 2 is false; they will say that if a man and multiple women each give their informed consent to be married, then they should be allowed to do that. Perhaps that's right. If so, then this argument is unsound.

But suppose that isn't right, and we *should* outlaw polygamy. Why would that be? One answer is that polygamy is immoral. It certainly is if, as it has often been practiced, a man's wives include young girls who are unable to give consent that is genuinely informed. But laws might be enacted to ensure that such things don't occur. Other arguments for the immorality of polygamy follow the same basic structure as arguments for the immorality of homosexuality—polygamy is unnatural, God has forbidden it, and so on. Perhaps the most promising argument for the immorality of polygamy starts with a recognition that polygamy strongly contributes to the oppression of women. Societies that allow polygamy are ones in which men are likely to enjoy far greater economic and political status, and much greater household authority, than women. This doesn't seem to be an accident; there seems to be a causal relation, not just a correlation, between legalized polygamy and women's subservient status.

If this is right, then this provides a reason for rejecting premise 1. The thought here is that there is a relevant difference between same-sex marriage and polygamy, so that legalizing the former need not justify legalizing the latter. Allowing same-sex marriage actually works to *combat* oppression, since it confers legal status on relationships for people who have traditionally been social outcasts. It raises the status of homosexuals without downgrading the status of anyone else. Polygamy, by contrast, helps to reinforce the second-class status of women in society; if anything, it raises the status of men, who are already, as a class, at the top of the heap, and makes it yet more difficult for women to achieve social, political, economic, and domestic equality.

Those who endorse the Polygamy Argument usually assume that same-sex marriage can be justified only on the basis of the liberal claim that all informed, consensual conduct should be legalized, unless it violates anyone's rights. Since both same-sex and polygamous relations can meet these conditions, premise 1 seems to follow. But there are two potential problems with this line of reasoning.

First, one might claim that even if polygamy does not itself violate anyone's rights, its legalization is highly likely to do so, by contributing to oppression of the sort just discussed. If that were so, it would be similar to a case described in Chapter 21, in which someone takes a drug that reliably leads to violence on the part of users. Though taking the drug does not itself violate anyone's rights, its tendency to cause its users to violate the rights of others is a plausible basis for preventing its legalization.

But perhaps you are more skeptical than I am about the claim that polygamy is very likely to enforce oppression against women, or that oppression involves the violation of rights.

Still, there is a second difficulty with the line of reasoning sketched earlier, namely, that supporters of same-sex marriage do not in fact have to rely on the liberal assumption that we should legalize all consensual conduct. Such supporters could instead rely on this principle of equality: the government is morally required to provide all of its citizens with equal legal rights, unless there is a compelling reason for the government not to do so. The defender of same-sex marriage could then argue, along at least some of the lines discussed earlier, that there is no compelling reason for withholding marital rights to homosexuals when granting them to heterosexuals. If you disagree with this verdict, here's your assignment: identify a relevant difference between same-sex marriage and opposite-sex marriage that also provides a very strong reason to oppose the former while allowing the latter.

CONCLUSION

The liberal position regarding sexual morality judges all informed, consensual sexual activity to be morally permissible. This view is in obvious tension with some elements of traditional morality, which condemns such sexual activity as prostitution, homosexual sex, premarital sex, or incest among adults. The emphasis on informed consent as a necessary condition of morally acceptable sexual behavior is common ground between liberals and their critics. Where they part ways is in their view about whether such consent is a sufficient condition of morally acceptable behavior.

The liberal endorses this sufficient condition, and so affirms the morality of casual sex and prostitution, when their participants are informed and consenting. That said, liberals, like others, recognize that many instances of casual sex and sex work fail to qualify as informed or consensual, in which case liberals join their opponents in refusing to approve of such behavior.

Even if the liberal position about sexual morality is correct, we might still ask about the wisdom of legalizing all forms of informed, consensual sex. There are slippery slope and conservative arguments against doing so, but there are also novel arguments against same-sex marriage that can allow that intimate homosexual relations may be morally acceptable. One such argument, which relies on defining marriage as a relation between a man and a woman, is not a very good one. Another is more challenging, and seeks to show that consistency requires defenders of same-sex marriage to support polygamy as well. As we've seen, there may be good reason to resist this argument, either because polygamy contributes to oppression while same-sex marriages do not, or because the ultimate justification for same-sex marriage derives from a principle of equality, rather than from a liberal principle that endorses the legalization of all behavior that violates no rights.

ESSENTIAL CONCEPTS

Casual sex: sex between people who have expressed no commitment to each other.

Incest: a sexual relationship between family members.

Liberal position regarding sexual morality: the view that sex is morally permissible if and only if it is engaged in by consenting adults.

Polyamory: sexual, romantic, or marital relationships among more than two people.

Polyandrous: relating to a social practice in which a woman has more than one husband at the same time.

Polygamous: relating to a social practice in which a man has more than one wife at the same time.

Premarital sex: sex between two people who have not been married.

Prostitution: having sex in exchange for payment.

STAT SHOT

1. Attitudes about whether society should accept homosexuality differ throughout the world. Canada and Western Europe are the most accepting of homosexuality (74–88 percent), followed by the United States (60 percent). The Middle East and Africa are on average the least accepting of homosexuality (in many countries less than 10 percent).[1]

2. From 1972 to 2012, the attitudes of US adults toward premarital sex have become increasingly less traditional (Figure 23.1).

3. In a 2016 poll, 49 percent thought that prostitution between consenting adults should be legalized, while 44 percent thought it should not be.[2]

4. It is estimated that the world spends $186 billion per year on prostitution, including $14.6 billion in the United States, and that there are at least 13 million prostitutes around the world, including at least 1 million in the United States.[3]

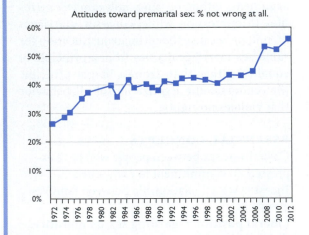

Attitudes toward premarital sex: % not wrong at all.

1. http://www.pewglobal.org/2013/06/04/the-global-divide-on-homosexuality/

2. http://www.pbs.org/wgbh/point-taken/blog/marist-should-prostitution-be-legalized/

3. http://www.havocscope.com/prostitution-statistics/

Figure 23.1
Source: https://www.norc.org/PDFs/GSS%20Reports/Trends%20in%20Sexual%20Moraility_Final.pdf

Cases for Critical Thinking

Polyamorous Relationships

In a column in the online magazine *Slate* about polyamory, writer Jillian Keenan tells a story about Richard, Vicki, Jim, and Maria, four people who ended up in a polyamorous relationship with one another.[1] The story begins with Richard meeting Vicki at a party—as the two describe it, they fell in love at first sight. Vicki had been married to Jim for nearly twenty years, but Jim and Vicki had an open relationship in which they were both permitted to have sexual relations with others. Vicki and Richard started dating, and Vicki and Jim continued their marriage happily. Nine months later, Jim met a woman named Maria, and they began dating as well. Eventually, the four of them, Richard, Vicki, Jim, and Maria, were in a polyamorous relationship together, describing themselves as "a family."

Richard, Vicki, Jim, and Maria's relationship is a relationship including two men and two women, all of whom ostensibly have more or less equal status. In light of this, modern-day polyamorists like this foursome balk at their relationships being compared to the more traditional polyamorous relationships, which are polygamous and likely to enforce oppression against women. They claim that far from being motivated by patriarchy or religious fundamentalism, they are simply doing what feels natural and healthy for them, and that their relationship is no less consensual and equal than a monogamous relationship would be.

Questions

1. Should defenders of the liberal position regarding sexual morality be just as accepting of polyamorous relationships as they are of homosexual relationships?

2. Should polyamorous relationships like the one described here be eligible for legal recognition? Why or why not?

3. When thinking about the moral status of a sexual relationship, how much, if at all, should we take into account whether relationships of that kind have been unequal or oppressive in the past?

4. When thinking about the moral status of different kinds of relationships, how specific should we be about what kinds we are thinking about? Should we separate questions about the morality of polyamory from questions about the morality of polygamy or polyandry?

Incestuous Relationships

In 2016, *Vice* magazine published a human interest story about a pair of half-siblings who were in a consensual relationship.[1] Katherine, who was adopted at birth, didn't know she had a half-brother until Scott recognized her last name on Facebook and got in touch with her. During their correspondence, Katherine and Scott established that they were half-siblings. But they also found that they were both highly attracted

1. http://www.slate.com/articles/double_x/doublex/2013/
06/polyamory_should_be_legal_it_s_consensual_and_
fine_for_children.html

to each other. They were aware that any sexual relationship between them would be incest, and that it would be both illegal and socially unacceptable, but they decided to pursue it anyway. "Sometimes it's reciprocated and sometimes it's not, but it's perfectly normal when you haven't grown up with that person," Katherine told the interviewer about her relationship with Scott. "Knowing that, we felt a lot better about how we felt about each other, so we just kind of decided to let nature run its course."

Within two years, Katherine had moved across the country to live with Scott. Their friends and family members think that they're merely living together as siblings, and they're careful about maintaining this ruse. They keep their curtains drawn at home and never display their relationship in public. If Katherine and Scott were found out, they would face both social and legal consequences. "It's kind of sad when we go out in public. I'd like to be able to hold his hand sometimes or be able to give him a kiss when I'm happy," Katherine said about their relationship. "That's very sad to me, because we did not grow up together. If I had met him on the street and not known we were related, I think I would have still been attracted to him."

Questions

1. Does this case, and others like it, make you suspicious of the liberal position regarding sexual morality? Why or why not?

2. When thinking about the moral status of incest, should we take into consideration only the biological relationship between family members, or also (or instead) the social relationship between family members?

3. When thinking about the moral status of cases of consensual incest, how much, if at all, should we take into account the fact that most cases of incest have been nonconsensual?

4. How relevant is the kind of familial relationship (sibling, parent–child, etc.) to the moral status of an incestuous relationship?

What Is Consent?

It is uncontroversial that nonconsensual sex is morally unacceptable. But it's more controversial what *counts* as informed consent. The legal treatment of consent has often operated under the assumption that encounters are consensual by default, that is, consensual unless there was some clear indication given by one of the parties that consent was not being given. For example, in many states, it has long been the case that a sex act is considered rape only if one of the parties physically resisted it.

However, this standard for consent has been heavily criticized over the last few decades. The slogan "No Means No," first coined by the Canadian Federation of Students, became a rallying cry for sexual assault activists. The idea behind "No Means No" is that a lack of physical resistance does not imply consent, because verbal resistance is sufficient to constitute a lack of consent. According to this standard, if one of the involved parties verbally resists a sex act, by saying "No" or something similar to it, then that act is not consensual. In light of this, many states have been revising their rape laws to reflect the thought that verbal resistance is enough to withdraw the presumption of consent. [1]

While the "No Means No" standard raises the bar for consent, it still operates under the assumption that sex is consensual unless it is resisted in some way; it simply broadens what forms of resistance are counted as constituting a lack of consent. Recently, this assumption has also been called into question. The slogan "No Means No" has been replaced by activists with "Yes Means Yes." [2] The idea behind "Yes Means Yes" is that a lack of resistance isn't enough for consent. Instead, sexual consent must be "affirmative," in the sense that there is some explicit indication from all parties that they're willing to engage in it, rather than just a lack of resistance. [3] The standard of affirmative consent throws out the idea that sexual acts are by default consensual and instead holds that sexual acts are by default *nonconsensual*; they only become consensual once consent is explicitly given. In 2014, California passed a law that requires universities to adopt affirmative consent policies toward campus sexual assault. [4] However, questions remain as to the specifics of how affirmative consent works, such as what counts as explicitly giving consent and how explicit consent has to be.

NOTES

1. https://www.washingtonpost.com/local/md-politics/no-means-no-measure-on-sexual-assault-becomes-law-in-maryland/2017/04/18/10e1428e-244e-11e7-bb9d-8cd6118e1409_story.html
2. http://www.pbs.org/newshour/rundown/means-enough-college-campuses/
3. http://system.suny.edu/sexual-violence-prevention-workgroup/policies/affirmative-consent/
4. https://leginfo.legislature.ca.gov/faces/billNavClient.xhtml?bill_id=201320140SB967

Questions

1. Should sex be considered consensual by default?
2. Which slogan more accurately describes what makes sex consensual, "No Means No" or "Yes Means Yes"?
3. Is a sex act rape if explicit, affirmative consent was not given by all parties?
4. Should our standards for what makes sex consensual be higher than our standards for what makes other activities consensual? Why or why not?

Why Shouldn't Tommy and Jim Have Sex? A Defense of Homosexuality

John Corvino

In this article, John Corvino considers and rejects each of the four most popular kinds of arguments that seek to establish the immorality of homosexuality. The first of these arguments claims that homosexuality is unnatural and therefore immoral. Corvino distinguishes five different senses in which things can be unnatural and concludes, for each of these meanings, that homosexuality is either perfectly natural or, if unnatural, is not unnatural in a way that makes it immoral.

The second kind of argument against homosexuality is that it is harmful, either to homosexuals themselves or to third parties. Corvino thinks that the harm-to-others charge would be very serious if it could be sustained. But he argues that it fails, as does the claim that partners in homosexual relations are likelier to harm other people than those involved in heterosexual relations.

The third argument is one based on biblical teaching. The Hebrew scriptures appear to contain explicit condemnations of male homosexual conduct, and both Jewish and Christian traditions have long condemned homosexuality. Corvino argues that a plausible interpretive principle for ancient texts enables us to justify a position, within these religious frameworks, that puts these condemnations in context and enables believers, in good faith, to emerge with a view that finds homosexuality morally acceptable.

The last argument takes the form of a slippery slope: If homosexuality is morally permitted, then so, too, are bestiality and polygamy. But these are immoral, and therefore so, too, is homosexuality. Corvino thinks that we can resist the slippery slope, because (as he argues) there are special reasons to condemn bestiality and polygamy that do not apply to the case of homosexuality.

Tommy and Jim are a homosexual couple I know. Tommy is an accountant; Jim is a botany professor. They are in their forties and have been together fourteen years, the last five of which they've lived in a Victorian house that they've lovingly restored. Although their relationship has had its challenges, each has made sacrifices for the sake of the other's happiness and the relationship's long-term success.

I assume that Tommy and Jim have sex with each other (although I've never bothered to ask).

Furthermore, I contend that they probably *should* have sex with each other. For one thing, sex is pleasurable. But it is also much more than that: a sexual relationship can unite two people in a way that virtually nothing else can. It can be an avenue of growth, of communication, and of lasting interpersonal fulfillment. These are reasons why most heterosexual couples have sex even if they don't want children, don't want children yet, or don't want additional children. And if these reasons are good enough for most heterosexual couples, then they should be good enough for Tommy and Jim.

Of course, having a reason to do something does not preclude there being an even better reason for not doing it. Tommy might have a good reason for

From John Corvino, "Why Shouldn't Tommy and Jim Have Sex?" in John Corvino, ed., *Same Sex: Debating the Ethics, Science and Culture of Homosexuality* (Totowa, NJ: Rowman and Littlefield, 1997), pp. 3–16.

drinking orange juice (it's tasty and nutritious) but an even better reason for not doing so (he's allergic). The point is that one would need a pretty good reason for denying a sexual relationship to Tommy and Jim, given the intense benefits widely associated with such relationships. The question I shall consider in this paper is thus quite simple: Why shouldn't Tommy and Jim have sex?

HOMOSEXUAL SEX IS "UNNATURAL"

Many contend that homosexual sex is "unnatural." But what does that mean? Many things that people value—clothing, houses, medicine, and government, for example—are unnatural in some sense. On the other hand, many things that people detest—disease, suffering, and death, for example—are "natural" in the sense that they occur "in nature." If the unnaturalness charge is to be more than empty rhetorical flourish, those who levy it must specify what they mean. Borrowing from Burton Leiser, I will examine several possible meanings of "unnatural."[1]

What Is Unusual or Abnormal Is Unnatural

One meaning of "unnatural" refers to that which deviates from the norm, that is, from what most people do. Obviously, most people engage in heterosexual relationships. But does it follow that it is wrong to engage in homosexual relationships? Relatively few people read Sanskrit, pilot ships, play the mandolin, breed goats, or write with both hands, yet none of these activities is immoral simply because it is unusual. As the Ramsey Colloquium, a group of Jewish and Christian scholars who oppose homosexuality, writes, "The statistical frequency of an act does not determine its moral status."[2] So while homosexuality might be unnatural in the sense of being unusual, that fact is morally irrelevant.

What Is Not Practiced by Other Animals Is Unnatural

Some people argue, "Even animals know better than to behave homosexually; homosexuality must be wrong." This argument is doubly flawed. First it rests on a false premise. Numerous studies—including Anne Perkins's study of "gay" sheep

and George and Molly Hunt's study of "lesbian" seagulls—have shown that some animals do form homosexual pair-bonds. Second, even if animals did not behave homosexually, that fact would not prove that homosexuality is immoral. After all, animals don't cook their food, brush their teeth, participate in religious worship, or attend college; human beings do all of these without moral censure. Indeed, the idea that animals could provide us with our standards—especially our sexual standards—is simply amusing.

What Does Not Proceed from Innate Desires Is Unnatural

Recent studies suggesting a biological basis for homosexuality have resulted in two popular positions. One side proposes that homosexual people are "born that way" and that it is therefore natural (and thus good) for them to form homosexual relationships. The other side maintains that homosexuality is a lifestyle choice, which is therefore unnatural (and thus wrong). Both sides assume a connection between the origin of homosexual orientation, on the one hand, and the moral value of homosexual activity, on the other. And insofar as they share that assumption, both sides are wrong.

Consider first the pro-homosexual side: "They are born that way; therefore it's natural and good." This inference assumes that all innate desires are good ones (i.e., that they should be acted upon). But that assumption is clearly false. Research suggests that some people are born with a predisposition toward violence, but such people have no more right to strangle their neighbors than anyone else. So while people like Tommy and Jim may be born with homosexual tendencies, it doesn't follow that they ought to act on them. Nor does it follow that they ought *not* to act on them, even if the tendencies are not innate. I probably do not have any innate tendency to write with my left hand (since I, like everyone else in my family, have always been right-handed), but it doesn't follow that it would be immoral for me to do so. So simply asserting that homosexuality is a lifestyle choice will not show that it is an immoral lifestyle choice.

Do people "choose" to be homosexual? People certainly don't seem to choose their sexual *feelings*, at least not in any direct or obvious way. (Do you? Think about it.) Rather, they find certain people attractive and certain activities arousing, whether they "decide" to or not. Indeed, most people at some point in their lives wish that they could control their feelings more—for example, in situations of unrequited love—and find it frustrating that they cannot. What they *can* control to a considerable degree is how and when they act upon those feelings. In that sense, both homosexuality and heterosexuality involve lifestyle choices. But in either case, determining the origin of the feelings will not determine whether it is moral to act on them.

What Violates an Organ's Principal Purpose Is Unnatural

Perhaps when people claim that homosexual sex is unnatural they mean that it cannot result in procreation. The idea behind the argument is that human organs have various natural purposes: eyes are for seeing, ears are for hearing, genitals are for procreating. According to this argument, it is immoral to use an organ in a way that violates its particular purpose.

Many of our organs, however, have multiple purposes. Tommy can use his mouth for talking, eating, breathing, licking stamps, chewing gum, kissing women, or kissing Jim; and it seems rather arbitrary to claim that all but the last use are "natural." (And if we say that some of the other uses are "unnatural, but not immoral," we have failed to specify a morally relevant sense of the term "natural.")

Just because people can and do use their sexual organs to procreate, it does not follow that they should not use them for other purposes. Sexual organs seem very well suited for expressing love, for giving and receiving pleasure, and for celebrating, replenishing, and enhancing a relationship—even when procreation is not a factor. Unless opponents of homosexuality are prepared to condemn heterosexual couples who use contraception or individuals who masturbate, they must abandon this version of the unnaturalness argument. Indeed, even the Roman Catholic Church, which forbids

contraception and masturbation, approves of sex for sterile couples and of sex during pregnancy, neither of which can lead to procreation. The Church concedes here that intimacy and pleasure are morally legitimate purposes for sex, even in cases where procreation is impossible. But since homosexual sex can achieve these purposes as well, it is inconsistent for the Church to condemn it on the grounds that it is not procreative.

One might object that sterile heterosexual couples do not *intentionally* turn away from procreation, whereas homosexual couples do. But this distinction doesn't hold. It is no more possible for Tommy to procreate with a woman whose uterus has been removed than it is for him to procreate with Jim. By having sex with either one, he is intentionally engaging in a non-procreative sexual act.

Yet one might press the objection further and insist that Tommy and the woman *could* produce children if the woman were fertile: whereas homosexual relationships are essentially infertile, heterosexual relationships are only incidentally so. But what does that prove? Granted, it might require less of a miracle for a woman without a uterus to become pregnant than for Jim to become pregnant, but it would require a miracle nonetheless. Thus it seems that the real difference here is not that one couple is fertile and the other not, nor that one couple "could" be fertile (with the help of a miracle) and the other not, but rather that one couple is male-female and the other male-male. In other words, sex between Tommy and Jim is wrong because it's male-male—i.e., because it's homosexual. But that, of course, is no argument at all.

What Is Disgusting or Offensive Is Unnatural

It often seems that when people call homosexuality "unnatural" they really just mean that it's disgusting. But plenty of morally neutral activities—handling snakes, eating snails, performing autopsies, cleaning toilets, and so on—disgust people. Indeed, for centuries, most people found interracial relationships disgusting, yet that feeling—which has by no means disappeared—hardly proves that such relationships are wrong. In sum, the charge that homosexuality is unnatural, at least in its most common forms, is longer on rhetorical flourish than on philosophical cogency. At best it expresses an aesthetic judgment, not a moral judgment.

HOMOSEXUAL SEX IS HARMFUL

One might instead argue that homosexuality is harmful. The Ramsey Colloquium, for instance, argues that homosexuality leads to the breakdown of the family and, ultimately, of human society, and it points to the "alarming rates of sexual promiscuity, depression, and suicide and the ominous presence of AIDS within the homosexual subculture."[3] Thomas Schmidt marshals copious statistics to show that homosexual activity undermines physical and psychological health.[4] Such charges, if correct, would seem to provide strong evidence against homosexuality. But are the charges correct? And do they prove what they purport to prove?

One obvious (and obviously problematic) way to answer the first question is to ask people like Tommy and Jim. It would appear that no one is in a better position to judge the homosexual lifestyle than those who know it firsthand. Yet it is unlikely that critics would trust their testimony. Indeed, the more homosexual people try to explain their lives, the more critics accuse them of deceitfully promoting an agenda. (It's like trying to prove that you're not crazy. The more you object, the more people think, "That's exactly what a crazy person would say.")

One might instead turn to statistics. An obvious problem with this tack is that both sides of the debate bring forth extensive statistics and "expert" testimony, leaving the average observer confused. There is a more subtle problem as well. Because of widespread antigay sentiment, many homosexual people won't acknowledge their romantic feelings to themselves, much less to researchers. I have known a number of gay men who did not "come out" until their forties and fifties, and no amount of professional competence on the part of interviewers would have been likely to open their closets sooner. Such problems compound the usual difficulties of finding representative population samples for statistical study.

Yet even if the statistical claims of gay rights opponents were true, they would not prove what they purport to prove, for several reasons. First, as any good statistician realizes, correlation does not equal cause. Even if homosexual people were more likely to commit suicide, be promiscuous, or contract AIDS than the general population, it would not follow that their homosexuality causes them to do these things. An alternative—and very plausible—explanation is that these phenomena, like the disproportionately high crime rates among African Americans, are at least partly a function of society's treatment of the group in question. Suppose you were told from a very early age that the romantic feelings that you experienced were sick, unnatural, and disgusting. Suppose further that expressing these feelings put you at risk of social ostracism or, worse yet, physical violence. Is it not plausible that you would, for instance, be more inclined to depression than you would be without such obstacles? And that such depression could, in its extreme forms, lead to suicide or other self-destructive behaviors? (It is indeed remarkable that couples like Tommy and Jim continue to flourish in the face of such obstacles.)

A similar explanation can be given for the alleged promiscuity of homosexuals. The denial of legal marriage, the pressure to remain in the closet, and the overt hostility toward homosexual relationships are all more conducive to transient, clandestine encounters than they are to long-term unions. As a result, that which is challenging enough for heterosexual couples—settling down and building a life together—becomes far more challenging for homosexual couples. . . .

But what about AIDS? Opponents of homosexuality sometimes claim that even if homosexual sex is not, strictly speaking, immoral, it is still a bad idea, since it puts people at risk for AIDS and other sexually transmitted diseases. But that claim is misleading: it is infinitely more risky for Tommy to have sex with a woman who is HIV-positive than with Jim, who is HIV-negative. Obviously, it's not homosexuality that's harmful, it's the virus; and the virus may be carried by both heterosexual and homosexual people.

Now it may be true (in the United States, at least) that homosexual males are statistically more likely to carry the virus than heterosexual females and thus that homosexual sex is *statistically* more risky than heterosexual sex (in cases where the partner's HIV status is unknown). But opponents of homosexuality need something stronger than this statistical claim. For if it is wrong for men to have sex with men because their doing so puts them at a higher AIDS risk than heterosexual sex, then it is also wrong for women to have sex with men because their doing so puts them at a higher AIDS risk than homosexual sex (lesbians as a group have the lowest incidence of AIDS). Purely from the standpoint of AIDS risk, women ought to prefer lesbian sex.

If this response seems silly, it is because there is obviously more to choosing a romantic or sexual partner than determining AIDS risk. And a major part of the decision, one that opponents of homosexuality consistently overlook, is considering whether one can have a mutually fulfilling relationship with the partner. For many people like Tommy and Jim, such fulfillment—which most heterosexuals recognize to be an important component of human flourishing—is only possible with members of the same sex. . . .

In sum, there is nothing *inherently* risky about sex between persons of the same gender. It is only risky under certain conditions: for instance, if they exchange diseased bodily fluids or if they engage in certain "rough" forms of sex that could cause tearing of delicate tissue. Heterosexual sex is equally risky under such conditions. Thus, even if statistical claims like those of Schmidt and the Ramsey Colloquium were true, they would not prove that homosexuality is immoral. At best, they would prove that homosexual people—like everyone else—ought to take great care when deciding to become sexually active.

Of course, there's more to a flourishing life than avoiding harm. One might argue that even if Tommy and Jim are not harming each other by their relationship, they are still failing to achieve the higher level of fulfillment possible in a heterosexual relationship, which is rooted in the complementarity of male and female. But this argument just ignores the facts: Tommy and Jim are homosexual *precisely because* they find relationships with men (and, in particular, with each other) more fulfilling than relationships with

women. Even evangelicals (who have long advocated "faith healing" for homosexuals) are beginning to acknowledge that the choice for most homosexual people is not between homosexual relationships and heterosexual relationships, but rather between homosexual relationships and celibacy. What the critics need to show, therefore, is that no matter how loving, committed, mutual, generous, and fulfilling the relationship may be, Tommy and Jim would flourish more if they were celibate. Given the evidence of their lives (and of others like them), this is a formidable task indeed.

Thus far I have focused on the allegation that homosexuality harms those who engage in it. But what about the allegation that homosexuality harms other, nonconsenting parties? Here I will briefly consider two claims: that homosexuality threatens children and that it threatens society.

Those who argue that homosexuality threatens children may mean one of two things. First, they may mean that homosexual people are child molesters. Statistically, the vast majority of reported cases of child sexual abuse involve young girls and their fathers, stepfathers, or other familiar (and presumably heterosexual) adult males. But opponents of homosexuality argue that when one adjusts for relative percentage in the population, homosexual males appear more likely than heterosexual males to be child molesters. As I argued above, the problems with obtaining reliable statistics on homosexuality render such calculations difficult. Fortunately, they are also unnecessary.

Child abuse is a terrible thing. But when a heterosexual male molests a child (or rapes a woman or commits assault), the act does not reflect upon all heterosexuals. Similarly, when a homosexual male molests a child, there is no reason why that act should reflect upon all homosexuals. Sex with adults of the same sex is one thing; sex with *children* of the same sex is quite another. Conflating the two not only slanders innocent people, it also misdirects resources intended to protect children. Furthermore, many men convicted of molesting young boys are sexually attracted to adult women and report no attraction to adult men. To call such men "homosexual," or even "bisexual," is probably to stretch such terms too far.

Alternatively, those who charge that homosexuality threatens children might mean that the increasing visibility of homosexual relationships makes children more likely to become homosexual. The argument for this view is patently circular. One cannot prove that doing X is bad by arguing that it causes other people to do X, which is bad. One must first establish independently that X is bad. That said, there is not a shred of evidence to demonstrate that exposure to homosexuality leads children to become homosexual.

But doesn't homosexuality threaten society? A Roman Catholic priest once put the argument to me as follows: "Of course homosexuality is bad for society. If everyone were homosexual, there would be no society." Perhaps it is true that if everyone were homosexual, there would be no society. But if everyone were a celibate priest, society would collapse just as surely, and my friend the priest didn't seem to think that he was doing anything wrong simply by failing to procreate. . . .

I have argued that Tommy and Jim's sexual relationship harms neither them nor society. On the contrary, it benefits both. It benefits them because it makes them happier—not merely in a short-term, hedonistic sense, but in a long-term, "big picture" sort of way. And, in turn, it benefits society, since it makes Tommy and Jim more stable, more productive, and more generous than they would otherwise be. In short, their relationship—including its sexual component—provides the same kinds of benefits that infertile heterosexual relationships provide (and perhaps other benefits as well). Nor should we fear that accepting their relationship and others like it will cause people to flee in droves from the institution of heterosexual marriage. After all . . . the usual response to a gay person is not "How come *he* gets to be gay and I don't?"

HOMOSEXUALITY VIOLATES BIBLICAL TEACHING

At this point in the discussion, many people turn to religion. "If the secular arguments fail to prove that homosexuality is wrong," they say, "so much the worse for secular ethics. This failure only proves that we need God for morality." Since people often justify their moral beliefs by appeal to religion, I will briefly consider the biblical position.

At first glance, the Bible's condemnation of homosexual activity seems unequivocal. Consider, for example, the following two passages, one from the "Old" Testament and one from the "New":

> You shall not lie with a male as with a woman; it is an abomination. (Lev. 18:22)

> For this reason God gave them up to degrading passions. Their women exchanged natural intercourse for unnatural, and in the same way also the men, giving up natural intercourse with women, were consumed with passion for one another. Men committed shameless acts with men and received in their own persons the due penalty for their error. (Rom. 1:26–27)

Note, however, that these passages are surrounded by other passages that relatively few people consider binding. For example, Leviticus also declares,

> The pig . . . is unclean for you. Of their flesh you shall not eat, and their carcasses you shall not touch; they are unclean for you. (11:7–8)

Taken literally, this passage not only prohibits eating pork, but also playing football, since footballs are made of pigskin. (Can you believe that the University of Notre Dame so flagrantly violates Levitical teaching?)

Similarly, St. Paul, author of the Romans passage, also writes, "Slaves, obey your earthly masters with fear and trembling, in singleness of heart, as you obey Christ" (Eph. 6:5)—morally problematic advice if there ever were any. Should we interpret this passage (as Southern plantation owners once did) as implying that it is immoral for slaves to escape? After all, God himself says in Leviticus,

> [Y]ou may acquire male and female slaves . . . from among the aliens residing with you, and from their families that are with you, who have

been born in your land; and they may be your property. You may keep them as a possession for your children after you, for them to inherit as property. (25:44–46)

How can people maintain the inerrancy of the Bible in light of such passages? The answer, I think, is that they learn to interpret the passages *in their historical context.*

Consider the Bible's position on usury, the lending of money for interest (for *any* interest, not just excessive interest). The Bible condemns this practice in no uncertain terms. In Exodus God says that "if you lend money to my people, to the poor among you, you shall not exact interest from them" (22:25). Psalm 15 says that those who lend at interest may not abide in the Lord's tent or dwell on his holy hill (1–5). Ezekiel calls usury "abominable"; compares it to adultery, robbery, idolatry, and bribery; and states that anyone who "takes advanced or accrued interest . . . shall surely die; his blood shall be upon himself" (18:13).

Should believers therefore close their savings accounts? Not necessarily. According to orthodox Christian teaching, the biblical prohibition against usury no longer applies. The reason is that economic conditions have changed substantially since biblical times, such that usury no longer has the same negative consequences it had when the prohibitions were issued. Thus, the practice that was condemned by the Bible differs from contemporary interest banking in morally relevant ways.

Yet are we not in a similar position regarding homosexuality? Virtually all scholars agree that homosexual relations during biblical times were vastly different from relationships like Tommy and Jim's. Often such relations were integral to pagan practices. In Greek society, they typically involved older men and younger boys. If those are the kinds of features that the biblical authors had in mind when they issued their condemnations, and such features are no longer typical, then the biblical condemnations no longer apply. As with usury, substantial changes in cultural context have altered the meaning and consequences—and thus the moral value—of the practice in question.

Put another way, using the Bible's condemnations of homosexuality against contemporary homosexuality is like using its condemnations of usury against contemporary banking.

Let me be clear about what I am *not* claiming here. First, I am not claiming that the Bible has been wrong before and therefore may be wrong this time. The Bible may indeed by wrong on some matters, but for the purpose of this argument I am assuming its infallibility. Nor am I claiming that the Bible's age renders it entirely inapplicable to today's issues. Rather, I am claiming that when we do apply it, *we must pay attention to morally relevant cultural differences between biblical times and today.* Such attention will help us distinguish between specific time-bound prohibitions (for example, laws against usury or homosexual relations) and the enduring moral values they represent (for example, generosity or respect for persons). And as the above argument shows, my claim is not very controversial. Indeed, to deny it is to commit oneself to some rather strange views on slavery, usury, women's roles, astronomy, evolution, and the like.

Here, one might also make an appeal to religious pluralism. Given the wide variety of religious beliefs (e.g., the Muslim belief that women should cover their faces, the Orthodox Jewish belief against working on Saturday, the Hindu belief that cows are sacred and should not be eaten), each of us inevitably violates the religious beliefs of others. But we normally don't view such violations as occasions for moral censure, since we distinguish between beliefs that depend on particular revelations and beliefs that can be justified independently (e.g., that stealing is wrong). Without an independent justification for condemning homosexuality, the best one can say is, "My religion says so." But in a society that cherishes religious freedom, that reason alone does not normally provide grounds for moral or legal sanctions. That people still fall back on that reason in discussions of homosexuality suggests that they may not have much of a case otherwise.

CONCLUSION

As a last resort, opponents of homosexuality typically change the subject: "But what about incest, polygamy, and bestiality? If we accept Tommy and Jim's sexual relationship, why shouldn't we accept those as well?" Opponents of interracial marriage used a similar slippery-slope argument in the 1960s when the Supreme Court struck down antimiscegenation laws.[5] It was a bad argument then, and it is a bad argument now.

Just because there are no good reasons to oppose interracial or homosexual relationships, it does not follow that there are no good reasons to oppose incestuous, polygamous, or bestial relationships. One might argue, for instance, that incestuous relationships threaten delicate familial bonds, or that polygamous relationships result in unhealthy jealousies (and sexism), or that bestial relationships—do I need to say it?—aren't really "relationships" at all, at least not in the sense we've been discussing. Perhaps even better arguments could be offered (given much more space than I have here). The point is that there is no logical connection between homosexuality, on the one hand, and incest, polygamy, and bestiality, on the other.

Why, then, do critics continue to push this objection? Perhaps it's because accepting homosexuality requires them to give up one of their favorite arguments: "It's wrong because we've always been taught that it's wrong." This argument—call it the argument from tradition—has an obvious appeal: people reasonably favor tried-and-true ideas over unfamiliar ones, and they recognize the foolishness of trying to invent morality from scratch. But the argument from tradition is also a dangerous argument, as any honest look at history will reveal.

I conclude that Tommy and Jim's relationship, far from being a moral abomination, is exactly what it appears to be to those who know them: a morally positive influence on their lives and on others. Accepting this conclusion takes courage, since it entails that our moral traditions are fallible. But when these traditions interfere with people's happiness for no sound reason, they defeat what is arguably the very point of morality: promoting individual and communal well-being. To put the argument simply, Tommy and Jim's relationship makes them better people. And that's not just good for Tommy and Jim: that's good for everyone.

NOTES

1. Burton M. Leiser, *Liberty, Justice, and Morals: Contemporary Value Conflicts* (New York: Macmillan, 1986), pp. 51–57.
2. The Ramsey Colloquium, "The Homosexual Movement," *First Things* (March 1994), pp. 15–20.
3. The Ramsey Colloquium, "Homosexual Movement," p. 19.
4. Thomas Schmidt, "The Price of Love" in *Straight and Narrow? Compassion and Clarity in the Homosexuality Debate* (Downers Grove, IL: InterVarsity Press, 1995), chap. 6.
5. *Loving v. Virginia*, 388 U.S. 1967.

John Corvino: Why Shouldn't Tommy and Jim Have Sex? A Defense of Homosexuality

1. What reasons do Tommy and Jim have for having sex? Do you agree with Corvino that these are the same reasons that many heterosexual couples have for having sex?
2. What does it mean to say that an activity is "unnatural"? Is the fact that something is unnatural ever a good reason for concluding that it is morally wrong?
3. Is homosexual sex harmful or risky to those who engage in it, in a way that heterosexual sex is not? If so, is this a good reason to think that it is morally wrong?
4. Some people argue that public acceptance of homosexual relationships would make children more likely to become homosexual. Why doesn't Corvino think this is a good argument against homosexual relationships? Do you agree with him?
5. How does Corvino respond to religious arguments against homosexuality? Do you find his responses convincing?
6. What is a "slippery slope" argument? Why does Corvino think that slippery slope arguments against homosexuality are bad arguments? Do you agree with him?

The Harms of Consensual Sex
Robin West

The title is surprising: while we immediately understand the harms of nonconsensual sex, a common thought is that there can be nothing wrong with an act if you give your consent to it. Many acts that are ordinarily wrong—sticking sharp needles into someone, entering their home without permission, punching them repeatedly—become morally OK when you give your consent to a vaccination, permit someone to cross your threshold, or voluntarily engage in a licensed boxing match. The thought is that if you really give someone consent to treat you in a given way, then you have no moral complaint if he does just that.

But we need to distinguish harms from wrongs. If a grown woman freely consents to having sex with a man, then there is no wrong done (so long as he does not proceed to act in a way that violates her consent). The woman's rights are not violated. But if Robin West is correct, there are many cases in which fully consensual heterosexual sex nevertheless *harms* the women who participate in it. Their interests are thwarted; their well-being is set back; they are at least in some respects worse off than they'd otherwise be.

The key to West's position is the recognition that many women consent to sex even though they do not desire it or expect any pleasure from it. She cites many reasons that explain this, and claims that such behavior may well be rational, since many women reasonably believe that refusing the sexual advances of the men in their lives will cause them even greater harm.

The harms of consensual sex include damage to a woman's capacity for self-assertion, her sense of self-possession, her autonomy, and her integrity. What's worse, the more frequently she engages in undesired and unpleasant sex, the more self-reinforcing these harms become. The harm is compounded in such a way that, in many cases, a woman will no longer recognize the kind or degree of harm she has undergone.

West concludes her article by diagnosing the ways in which the arguments of both liberal and radical feminists threaten to obscure the harms of consensual sex.

Are consensual, non-coercive, non-criminal, and even non-tortious, heterosexual transactions ever harmful to women? I want to argue briefly that many (not all) consensual sexual transactions are, and that accordingly we should open a dialogue about what those harms might be. Then I want to suggest some reasons those harms may be difficult to discern, even by the women sustaining them, and lastly two ways in which the logic of feminist legal theory and practice itself might undermine their recognition.

Let me assume what many women who are or have been heterosexually active surely know to be true from their own experience, and that is that some women occasionally, and many women quite frequently, consent to sex even when they do not desire the sex itself, and accordingly have a good

From Robin West, "The Harms of Consensual Sex, *The American Philosophical Association Newsletter on Feminism* 94, no. 2 (1995), pp. 52–55.

deal of sex that, although consensual, is in no way pleasurable. Why might a woman consent to sex she does not desire? There are, of course, many reasons. A woman might consent to sex she does not want because she or her children are dependent upon her male partner for economic sustenance, and she must accordingly remain in his good graces. A woman might consent to sex she does not want because she rightly fears that if she does not her partner will be put into a foul humor, and she simply decides that tolerating the undesired sex is less burdensome than tolerating the foul humor. A woman might consent to sex she does not want because she has been taught and has come to believe that it is her lot in life to do so, and that she has no reasonable expectation of attaining her own pleasure through sex. A woman might consent to sex she does not want because she rightly fears that her refusal to do so will lead to an outburst of violent behavior some time following—only if the violence or overt threat of violence is *very* close to the sexual act will this arguably constitute a rape. A woman may consent to sex she does not desire because she *does* desire a friendly man's protection against the very real threat of non-consensual violent rape by other more dangerous men, and she correctly perceives, or intuits, that to gain the friendly man's protection, she needs to give him in exchange for that protection, the means to his own sexual pleasure. A woman, particularly a young woman or teenager, may consent to sex she does not want because of peer expectations that she be sexually active, or because she cannot bring herself to hurt her partner's pride, or because she is uncomfortable with the prospect of the argument that might ensue, should she refuse.

These transactions may well be rational—indeed in some sense they all are. The women involved all trade sex for something they value more than they value what they have given up. But that doesn't mean that they are not harmed. Women who engage in unpleasurable, undesired, but consensual sex may sustain real injuries to their sense of selfhood, in at least four distinct ways. First, they may sustain injuries to their capacities for self-assertion: the "psychic connection," so to speak, between pleasure, desire, motivation, and action is weakened or severed. *Acting* on the basis of our own felt pleasures and pains is an important

component of forging our own way in the world—of "asserting" our "selves." Consenting to *unpleasurable* sex—acting in spite of displeasure—threatens that means of self-assertion. Second, women who consent to undesired sex may injure their sense of *self-possession*. When we consent to undesired penetration of our physical bodies we have in a quite literal way constituted ourselves as what I have elsewhere called "giving selves"—selves who cannot be violated, because they have been defined as (and define themselves as) being "for others." Our bodies to that extent no longer belong to ourselves. Third, when women consent to undesired and unpleasurable sex because of their felt or actual dependency upon a partner's affection or economic status, they injure their sense of autonomy: they have thereby neglected to take whatever steps would be requisite to achieving the self-sustenance necessary to their independence. And fourth, to the extent that these unpleasurable and undesired sexual acts are followed by contrary to fact claims that they enjoyed the whole thing—what might be called "hedonic lies"—women who engage in them do considerable damage to their sense of integrity.

These harms—particularly if multiplied over years or indeed over an entire adulthood—may be quite profound, and they certainly may be serious enough to outweigh the momentary or day-to-day benefits garnered by each individual transaction. Most debilitating, though, is their circular, self-reinforcing character: the more thorough the harm—the deeper the injury to self-assertiveness, self-possession, autonomy and integrity—the greater the likelihood that the woman involved will indeed *not* experience these harms as harmful, or as painful. A woman utterly lacking in self-assertiveness, self-possession, a sense of autonomy, or integrity will not experience the activities in which she engages that reinforce or constitute those qualities *as harmful*, because she, to that degree, lacks a self-asserting, self-possessed self who *could* experience those activities as a threat to her selfhood. But the fact that she does not experience these activities as harms certainly does not mean that they are not harmful. Indeed, that they are not felt as harmful is a consequence of the harm they have already caused. This phenomenon, of course, renders the "rationality" of these transactions tremendously and even tragically misleading. Although these women may be making rational calculations in the context of the particular decision facing them, they are by making those calculations, sustaining deeper and to some degree unfelt harms that undermine the very qualities that constitute the capacity for rationality being exercised.

Let me quickly suggest some reasons that these harms go so frequently unnoticed—or are simply not taken seriously—and then suggest in slightly more detail some ways that feminist legal theory and practice may have undermined their recognition. The first reason is cultural. There is a deep-seated U.S. cultural tendency to equate the legal with the good, or harmless: we are, for better or worse, an anti-moralistic, anti-authoritarian, and anti-communitarian people. When combined with the sexual revolution of the 1960s, this provides a powerful cultural explanation for our tendency to shy away from a sustained critique of the harms of consensual sex. Any suggestion that legal transactions to which individuals freely consent may be harmful, and hence *bad,* will invariably be met with skepticism—*particularly* where those transactions are sexual in nature. This tendency is even further underscored by more contemporary postmodern skeptical responses to claims asserting the pernicious consequences of false consciousness.

Second, at least our legal-academic discourses, and no doubt academic political discourses as well, have been deeply transformed by the "exchange theory of value," according to which, if I exchange A for B voluntarily, then I simply must be better off after the exchange than before, having, after all, agreed to it. If these exchanges *are* the source of value, then it is of course impossible to ground a *value* judgment that some voluntary exchanges are harmful. Although stated baldly this theory of value surely has more critics than believers, it nevertheless in some way perfectly captures the modern zeitgeist. It is certainly, for example, the starting and ending point of normative analysis for many, and perhaps most, law students. Obviously, given an exchange theory of value, the harms caused by consensual sexual transactions simply fade away into definitional oblivion.

Third, the exchange theory of value is underscored, rather than significantly challenged, by the continuing significance of liberal theory and ideology in academic life. To the degree that liberalism still rules the day, we continue to valorize individual choice against virtually anything with which it might seem to be in conflict, from communitarian dialogue to political critique, and continue to perceive these challenges to individual primacy as somehow on a par with threats posed by totalitarian statist regimes.

Fourth, and perhaps most obvious, the considerable harms women sustain from consensual but undesired sex must be downplayed if the considerable pleasure men reap from heterosexual transactions is morally justified—*whatever* the relevant moral theory. Men do have a psychosexual stake in insisting that voluntariness alone ought to be sufficient to ward off serious moral or political inquiry into the value of consensual sexual transactions.

Let me comment in a bit more detail on a further reason why these harms seem to be underacknowledged, and that has to do with the logic of feminist legal theory, and the efforts of feminist practitioners, in the area of rape law reform. My claim is that the theoretical conceptualizations of sex, rape, force, and violence that underscore both liberal and radical legal feminism undermine the effort to articulate the harms that might be caused by consensual sexuality. I will begin with liberal feminism and then turn to radical feminism.

First, and entirely to their credit, liberal feminist rape law reformers have been on the forefront of efforts to stiffen enforcement of the existing criminal sanction against rape, and to extend that sanction to include non-consensual sex which presently is not cognizable legally as rape but surely should be. This effort is to be applauded, but it has the *almost* inevitable consequence of valorizing, celebrating, or, to use the critical term, "legitimating" consensual sexual transactions. If rape is bad *because* it is non-consensual—which is increasingly the dominant liberal-feminist position on the badness of rape—then it seems to follow that *consensual* sex must be good because it is consensual. But appearances can be misleading, and this one certainly is. That non-consensual transactions—rape, theft, slavery—are bad because non-consensual, does *not* imply the value, worth or goodness of their consensual counterparts—sex, property, or work. It only follows that consensual sex, property, or work are not bad in the ways that non-consensual transactions are bad; they surely may be bad for some other reason. We need to explore, in the case of sex (as well as property and work), what those other reasons might be. Non-consensuality does not exhaust the types of harm we inflict on each other in social interactions, nor does consensuality exhaust the list of benefits.

That the liberal-feminist argument for extending the criminal sanction against rape to include non-consensual sex *seems* to imply the positive value of consensual sex is no doubt in part simply a reflection of the powers of the forces enumerated above—the cultural, economic, and liberal valorization of individualism against communal and authoritarian controls. Liberal feminists can obviously not be faulted for that phenomenon. What I want to caution against, is simply the ever present temptation to *trade on* those cultural and academic forces in putting forward arguments for reform of rape law. We need not trumpet the glories of consensual sex *in order to* make out a case for strengthening the criminal sanction against coercive sex. Coercion, violence, and the fear under which women live because of the threat of rape are sufficient evils to sustain the case for strengthening and extending the criminal law against those harms. We need not and should not supplement the argument with the unnecessary and unwarranted celebration of consensual sex—which whatever the harms caused by coercion, does indeed carry its own harms.

Ironically, radical feminist rhetoric—which *is* aimed at highlighting the damage and harm done to women by ordinary, "normal" heterosexual transactions—*also* indirectly burdens the attempt to articulate the harms done to women by consensual heterosexual transactions, although it does so in a very different way. Consider the claim, implicit in a good deal of radical feminist writing, explicit in some, that "all sex is rape," and compare it for a moment with the rhetorical Marxist claim that "all property is theft." Both claims are intended to push the reader or listener to a reexamination of the ordinary, and both do so by blurring the distinction between consent and coercion. Both seem to share the underlying premise that which is coerced—and perhaps *only* that which is coerced—is bad, or as a

strategic matter, is going to be perceived as bad. Both want us to reexamine the value of that which we normally think of as good or at least unproblematic because of its apparent consensuality—heterosexual transactions in the first case, property transactions in the second—and both do so by putting into doubt the reality of that apparent consensuality.

But there is a very real difference in the historical context and hence the practical consequences of these two rhetorical claims. More specifically, there are two pernicious, or at least counter-productive consequences of the feminist claim which are not shared, at least to the same degree, by the Marxist. First, and as any number of liberal feminists have noted, the radical feminist equation of sex and rape runs the risk of undermining parallel feminist efforts in a way not shared by the Marxist equation of property and theft. Marxists are for the most part not engaged in the project of attempting to extend the existing laws against *theft* so as to embrace non-consensual market transactions that are currently not covered by the laws against larceny and embezzlement. Feminists, however, *are* engaged in a parallel effort to extend the existing laws against rape to include all non-consensual sex, and as a result, the radical feminist equation of rape and sex is indeed undermining. The claim that all sex is in effect non-consensual runs the real risk of "trivializing," or at least confusing, the feminist effort at rape reform so as to include all truly non-consensual sexual transactions.

There is, though, a second cost to the radical feminist rhetorical claim, which I hope these comments have by now made clear. The radical feminist equation of rape and sex, no less than the liberal rape reform movement, gets its rhetorical force by trading on the liberal, normative-economic, and cultural assumptions that whatever is coercive is bad, and whatever is non-coercive is morally non-problematic. It has the effect, then, of further burdening the articulation of harms caused by consensual sex by forcing the characterization of those harms into a sort of "descriptive funnel" of non-consensuality. It requires us to say, in other words, that consensual sex is harmful, if it is, only because or to the extent that it shares in the attributes of non- consensual sex. But this might not be true—the harms caused by consensual sex might be just as important, just as serious, but nevertheless *different* from the harms caused by non-consensual sex. If so, then women are disserved, rather than served, by the equation of rape and sex, even were that equation to have the rhetorical effect its espousers clearly desire.

Liberal feminist rape reform efforts and radical feminist theory both, then, in different ways, undermine the effort to articulate the distinctive harms of consensual sex; the first by indirectly celebrating the value of consensual sex, and the latter by at least rhetorically denying the existence of the category. Both, then, in different ways, underscore the legitimation of consensual sex effectuated by non-feminist cultural and academic forces. My conclusion is simply that feminists could counter these trends in part by focusing attention on the harms caused women by consensual sexuality.

Robin West: The Harms of Consensual Sex

1. "If you've consented to X, then X can't harm you." How does West respond to such a claim? Do you find her replies plausible?

2. West claims that in many cases consensual sex leads to damage to a woman's capacity for self-assertion, self-possession, autonomy, and integrity. Explain each of these harms. Do you agree with West's claim that these are the sorts of harms that can result from consensual sex? Are there other harms that West has not listed?

3. West focuses just on the harms of consensual sex undergone by women in heterosexual relationships. What (if anything) justifies this restricted focus? Can her points be applied to other forms of sexual relationships? Why or why not?

4. West criticizes some liberal feminist thinkers for arguing along the following lines: "If non-consensual sex is bad, then consensual sex is good. Non-consensual sex is indeed bad. So consensual sex is good." West rejects the initial premise. Do you find her critique plausible? Defend your answer.

5. What flaws does West find in the thinking of those radical feminists who equate all sex, whether consensual or not, with rape? Do you find her criticisms compelling? Why or why not?

Sex, Lies, and Consent
Tom Dougherty

Many people believe what author Tom Dougherty calls "The Lenient Thesis": It is only a minor wrong to deceive another person into sex by misleading her or him about certain personal features such as natural hair color, occupation, or romantic intentions. Dougherty's aim is to convince you that the Lenient Thesis is false.

Dougherty believes that deceiving another person into sex—whether the content of deception concerns small details such as those just mentioned, or larger ones—involves having sex with that person while lacking her morally valid consent. And having sex with someone without having her morally valid consent is seriously wrong. So deceiving someone into sex is seriously wrong.

Dougherty offers two arguments for the claim that having sex with someone who does not validly consent is seriously wrong. The first argument is that we have very stringent rights to sexual autonomy that are violated if someone has sex without our valid consent. The second argument is what philosophers call an "inference to the best explanation." Arguments of this type support a given claim by showing that it provides the best explanation of key data points that need to be accounted for. In this case,

Dougherty argues that there are two relevant data—namely, that sex by means of extreme deception, and sex with an unwilling unconscious person, are each seriously immoral. What explains these data? If he is correct, it is the claim that in both types of case the victim did not validly consent to having sex, and that this lack of consent is what makes those sexual acts seriously immoral.

Dougherty then defends the claim that someone who has sex under false pretenses (even when deception involves only minor details) does not give her morally valid consent to sex. He argues that someone is wrongfully deceived into sex when the deception concerns what he calls a "deal-breaker"—a feature of the sexual encounter that makes a decisive difference to the victim's choice to have sex. And even apparently minor details (such as a person's natural hair color or his GPA or the town he grew up in) can, for some, amount to a deal breaker. When a person deceives another about a deal-breaking matter, then the deceived person does not give her morally valid consent to having sex, even if she says that she is consenting, and even if she feels no pressure to have sex. If Dougherty is correct, such deception is a serious moral wrong.

I. DECEITFUL SEDUCTION

According to a popular dating website, both men and women, on average, say that they are two inches taller and earn $20,000 more than one would expect. Now it may be that these are innocent errors although expensive ones for tax returns, or that rich and tall people find it particularly hard to meet partners in person. But in our more cynical moments, we may suspect that this is intentional deception. Why the tangled webs? Some may only want conversation over cappuccino, or a warm arm next to theirs in the movie theater. But others' aims will include sex. We might say that these people are "lying to get laid," if we wanted a snappy phrase. But it would be an inexact phrase insofar as the relevant moral phenomenon is deception, and some lies, understood as false assertions, do not deceive. In a notorious pickup joint where never a true word has been said, the regulars will not be fooled by tall tales, sweet nothings, and puffery. Indeed, in circumstances where lies are expected, telling the truth would itself be deceptive. Similarly, when certain expectations are in place, silence itself can be a form of communication and hence deceive.

Deceiving someone into sex is wrong. No surprise here: mother told us as much. But *how* wrong? I speculate that most people think that the wrongness depends on the type of deception involved. Impersonating someone's spouse is seriously wrong but not so with run-of-the-mill falsehoods like "I'm not fussed about mess," "I'm 27 years old," "I went to Harvard," "I haven't had implants," "I *don't* want a relationship," "I *do* want a relationship," and even the simple "I like you." As Alan Wertheimer notes, "prevailing moral norms" are quite "permissive" with respect to sexual deception, and so while people "may think it sleazy if a male lies about his marital status, affections, or intentions in order to get a woman into bed, . . . many do not think this is a particularly serious matter." . . . I will attempt to persuade you that much more severe criticisms are in order, arguing against the following thesis:

> **Lenient Thesis.** It is only a minor wrong to deceive another person into sex by misleading her or him about certain personal features such as natural hair color, occupation, or romantic intentions.

We should understand this thesis as the claim that there are some trivial aspects of one's identity, about which it is not seriously wrong to deceive someone in order to get them into bed. Examples of this run-of-the-mill deception might include deception

Tom Dougherty, "Sex, Lies, and Consent," *Ethics* 123 (2013), pp. 717–744.

about one's sexual history, one's attitudes toward pets, or even how funny one finds the other person. Against the Lenient Thesis, I will argue that even with run-of-the-mill deception, culpably *deceiving another person into sex* is seriously wrong . . .

My argument is based on the fact that not only coercion can vitiate consent; deception can do so too. Since coercion and deception are Kant's paradigms of "treating someone as a mere means," I think of this as a Kantian insight, though one that is acceptable to friends of other moral theories. . . . I will argue that when someone is deceived into sex, the deception vitiates the victim's sexual consent. Since it is seriously wrong to have sex with someone without her morally valid consent, deceiving someone into sex is seriously wrong. Thus, my main argument runs:

1. Having sex with someone, while lacking her morally valid consent, is seriously wrong.
2. Deceiving another person into sex involves having sex with that person, while lacking her morally valid consent.
3. Therefore, deceiving someone into sex is seriously wrong.

. . .

II. WHY NONCONSENSUAL SEX IS SERIOUSLY WRONG

I will begin with the less controversial premise of my main argument—that having sex with someone who does not validly consent is seriously wrong. To be fully clear, the premise concerns only morally valid consent. This is defined as the consent that someone must have in order not to wrong the consenter by violating a right of hers. Consequently, it is the consent that makes permissible some actions that would otherwise be impermissible. Morally valid consent requires more than mere agreement. For example, agreement must be freely given, and so highly intoxicated agreement would not count as morally valid consent. Now I imagine many readers will be sympathetic to the claim that it is seriously wrong to have sex with someone while lacking her morally valid consent. . . . Still the thesis requires defense. Moreover, defending the premise will make clear the argumentative burden that will fall

on my second premise—that someone does not give her morally valid consent to sex when she is deceived into sex.

The Rights-Based Argument

To introduce my first subargument, consider Joan McGregor's observation that the "moral wrongness of rape consists in violating an individual's autonomy right to control one's own body and one's sexual self-determination and the seriousness of rape derives from the special importance we attach to sexual autonomy."[1] Here McGregor has in mind coercive sex, but I am confident she would agree that her rationale extends to all forms of nonconsensual sex. In arguing for this claim, I make the following assumptions that are standard within rights theory. We have moral claim-rights (henceforth "rights") over our persons and property. These include so-called negative rights against interference: the moral default is that others may not lay hands on, nor damage, our persons or property. These rights over our persons and property consist in more specific rights against particular actions by particular individuals. We move away from the default by giving other people our morally valid consent, thereby waiving some specific rights. For example, a customer may waive her rights against a hairdresser touching her hair but not other parts of her body. These waivers are typically revocable—at any point, the customer can take back her consent and reimpose her rights.

The moral significance of these rights is that typically it is morally impermissible for someone to wrong another person by infringing her rights. How wrong it would be to violate a right depends on its stringency. The stringency of a right against a form of behavior depends on the importance to us of someone engaging in this behavior against our will. Now controlling the sexual contact that others have with us is centrally important to us. This is not to say that sex has to be an active, emotionally meaningful part of someone's lifestyle. But it is crucially important

---

1. Joan McGregor, "Force, Consent, and the Reasonable Woman," in Jules Coleman and Allen Buchanan, eds., *In Harm's Way: Essays in Honor of Joel Feinberg*. Oxford University Press, 1994, p. 236.

that her sexual choices determine how her sex life goes.... And we can accept this point while leaving open the grounds of this importance—whether we contingently find sexual autonomy important, whether we are biologically hard wired to find it important, or whether it has an objective importance, even if we fail to recognize this importance. This importance of sexual control explains the stringency of their sexual rights. In light of this stringency, it is seriously wrong to violate someone's sexual rights. One would violate these rights unless one has her morally valid consent to sex.

The Argument from Serious Sexual Wrongs

My second subargument operates by inference to the best explanation. The explananda [i.e., things to be explained] in question are the following two data. The first datum is that it is seriously wrong to have sex with someone by means of disguising the sexual nature of the encounter or by impersonating her spouse. Consider the following fictional examples. When naive and uneducated Dewey Dell arrived at a physician's seeking an abortion, it was seriously wrong for the assistant to cajole her into sex by telling her that the appropriate medical procedure was for him to penetrate her. When Milady mistook D'Artagnan for her lover in her ill-lit boudoir, it was seriously wrong of D'Artagnan knowingly to take advantage of her mistake to have sex with her. The second datum is that it is seriously wrong to have sex with an unconscious person against her will. For example, in Pedro Almodóvar's *Hable Con Ella*, it was seriously wrong for the caregiver, Benigno, to have sex with the chronically comatose patient, Alicia. I maintain that the best explanation of each of these data, considered in isolation from the other, is that the offenders lacked their victim's morally valid consent. I will call this the "Consent Explanation":

> **Consent Explanation.** The seriousness of the wrongs both of sex by means of egregious deception and of sex with an unwilling unconscious person is explained by the fact that the victim did not validly consent to the sex.

Since it is uncontroversial that Alicia, Dewey Dell, and Milady did not offer morally valid consent to sex, the Consent Explanation correctly predicts that Benigno, the assistant, and D'Artagnan acted seriously wrongly. Are other explanations at least as good? ... [T]he main alternative is the view I call "Harm Explanation":

> **Harm Explanation.** The seriousness of the wrongs both of sex by means of egregious deception and of sex with an unwilling unconscious person is explained by the harm suffered by the victim.

Thus stated, the explanation includes the view that the wrongness of a sexual offense depends only on harm; and it also includes the view that a sexual act can be wrong simply because it is nonconsensual, but the seriousness of the wrong is determined by the amount of harm.

The Harm Explanation is particularly attractive with respect to coercive sex, which is typically conceived of as sex obtained by physical force or threats of physical harm. We cannot offer a proper account of the full extent of the wrong of violent rape, unless we mention the harms suffered by victims. This would appear to provide a strong motivation for the Harm Explanation.

However, the Harm Explanation is inadequate when it comes to explaining the serious wrongness of sex with the unconscious or by egregious forms of deception. The reason why is simple: ... there need be no harm involved. The sex itself may not be physically damaging. Since the victims are unaware of having nonconsensual sex, they do not suffer experiential harms. And if these crimes remain undetected, then the victims will not suffer psychological harms later. Nonetheless, even when entirely harmless, sex with the unconscious and sex by means by egregious forms of deception are still seriously wrong....

Moreover, the Consent Explanation can accommodate the initial motivation for the Harm Explanation—the virtual platitude that harm is an important part of the explanation of why physically coercive sex is so bad. One can consistently hold that the nonconsensuality of physically coercive sex is sufficient for its being seriously wrong, while maintaining both that its particularly harmful nature is also sufficient for the action to be seriously wrong and that harm makes nonconsensual sex even worse. Indeed, as a fully general pattern, harm makes an action worse, even though its non-consensuality is itself sufficient for the action's wrongness. If a stranger trespasses in your garden, then her action is wrong in virtue of the fact that she lacks your consent. But it is worse if she thereby ruins the flower beds. The Consent Explanation that I advocate here does not claim that harm never makes a moral difference. It merely maintains that if a sexual encounter is nonconsensual, then this feature makes it seriously wrong.

III. WHY THE DECEIVED DO NOT CONSENT

. . . . I have so far argued for the claim that having nonconsensual sex with someone is seriously wrong. By "nonconsensual sex," I intended sex without the victim's morally valid consent. In doing so, I postponed much of the heavy lifting of the main argument to the defense of my second prem-ise. This means that in this section I must make the case that the deceived party does not give her mor-ally valid consent to sex. Moreover, I suspect that few would agree, since [the Lenient Thesis] seems right to many. And I speculate that people hold this view because they think that the deceiver would have the victim's morally valid consent. I will offer three subarguments to the contrary.

The Argument Against Sexual Moralism

My first subargument aims to remove a key source of opposition to my second premise, by arguing that the Lenient Thesis cannot be grounded on an acceptable account of morally valid consent. To focus our discussion on run-of-the-mill deception, suppose that Chloe meets a hippie, Victoria, on a night out. Victoria makes it clear that she wants to have sex only with someone who shares her love of nature and peace. Consequently, Chloe falsely claims to have spent time in a war zone as a human-itarian, when in fact she was there on military ser-vice. When Victoria asks whether she likes animals, Chloe omits the truth—"only to eat or to hunt"—and pretends to love petting them and watching them in the wild. As a result of this deception, the two spent a night together. My claim is that Victoria did not validly consent to sex with Chloe. I expect

that most friends of the Lenient Thesis will insist that Victoria did validly consent to sex, even if they disapprove of Chloe's deception on other grounds.

What account of morally valid consent could support the Lenient Thesis? A natural first thought is that Victoria consented because she was will-ing to have sex and indicated as much by means of speech or behavior. On this simpleminded account, if a competent person freely agrees to sex, then she consents. But this simpleminded account is implau-sible. For everyone should agree that Milady did not properly give her morally valid consent to the noc-turnal poseur, D'Artagnan. To separate the cases of Milady and Victoria, the Lenient Thesis can only plausibly be based on a more sophisticated account of consent that makes a fundamental distinction between different features of a sexual encounter. On this view, someone does not validly consent to a sexual encounter when deceived about its "core" features, such as the interaction's not being a gen-uine medical procedure or the other person's not being one's usual romantic partner. When some-one is misled about these core features, then her will is not sufficiently implicated in the act for it to be consensual. But on the other hand, someone may validly consent even when misled about the encounter's peripheral features, such as the other person's natural hair color, occupation, or romantic intentions.

We can see the problem with this account of consent by starting to investigate how to draw the distinction between the core and periphery. There are some controversial borderline cases. A Cuban spy, masquerading as a dissident, marries a Florida woman but leaves her when his operational orders dictate. A British undercover policeman starts a re-lationship with an environmentalist in order to in-filtrate her activist group. A Palestinian man pleads guilty to seducing an Israeli woman by falsely telling her that he was unmarried and Jewish. And the list goes on. Now I do not suppose that adherents of the Lenient Thesis will have uniform intuitions about whether the deceived person validly consents in each of these cases. People can agree that there is an important distinction between different features of a sexual encounter while disagreeing about how to draw this distinction. But what is important, for our purposes, is the nature of the debate about whether someone's religion, ethnicity, or political values count as a core feature of the sexual encounter. This is a debate about which features of a sexual encounter are objectively important enough to count as one of its core features. The lack of uniformity in people's intuitions about the cases simply reflects their differing views about the objective importance of religion, ethnicity, or political views or sex.

As such, the Lenient Thesis rests on an objectionably moralized conception of sex. It assumes that some features of a sexual encounter are morally more important than others. In this way, our moral norms about sexual morality are skewed because of common assumptions that some reasons are good reasons for deciding not to have sex, but other reasons are not. . . . It is up to each individual to determine which features of a sexual encounter are particularly important to her. The religion of a sexual partner is an important part of a sexual encounter for someone if and only if that person decides that it is. Similarly, whether or not a partner's views about peace and animals are an important part of Victoria's sexual encounters is down to Victoria. . . .

[S]omeone is deceived into sex when she forms a false belief about a *deal breaker*: the deception conceals a feature of the sexual encounter that makes a decisive difference to the victim's decision to have sex. To put this point in terms of our earlier example: the fact that Chloe is a soldier would count as a core feature of the sexual encounter precisely because this feature of Chloe is important enough to Victoria to make the difference between whether or not she is willing to have sex with her.

The Argument from the Case of the Chihuahua

To introduce my second subargument, let us set aside sex for a moment and consider a different example. Suppose that Aisha asks me to let her dog into my apartment. Knowing that I loathe Chihuahuas, Aisha falsely says that it is a Great Dane, and I hand over my key. Imagine my surprise and fright, then, to come home to find a Chihuahua scuttling around my floor like an overgrown furry cockroach. I say to Aisha, reasonably enough, that

this Chihuahua is not the agreed upon Great Dane. Aisha acknowledges the difference is undeniable. But she replies that I had consented to the arrangement since I had agreed to let her dog into my home. Aisha's reply will not do, I am afraid. Aisha has effectively trespassed upon my property. The fact that I agreed to admit *some dog* does not mean that I agreed to admit *that dog*. What I consented to let into my home was a Great Dane, and that dog was not a Great Dane.

There are superficial differences between the cases—an apartment is not the same as a body and a dog's entrance is not the same as sexual contact. But the soldier and dog-owner cases are alike in all morally relevant respects, which are as follows. The victim has a right to control others' behavior within her personal space. The deceiver would act impermissibly if she invades the personal space without the victim's morally valid consent. The victim's will is opposed to what the deceiver in fact intends. The deceiver manages to sidestep this obstacle to her plan by means of deception. This deception means that the victim's agreement does not count as morally valid consent. My aim here is to use the case of Aisha to illustrate this pattern, so that once we are primed, we will see it in the case of Chloe as well.

This is particularly clear if the deceived person explicitly thinks of, and voices, the restrictions on her consent. Suppose I say to Aisha, "You may bring in your dog as long as it isn't a Chihuahua— I won't stand to have such an unpredictable dog where I live." If I have thought and said this, then it is clear that I have not consented to her bringing in her Chihuahua. I have insisted on my moral right against having a Chihuahua in my apartment, and so Aisha would violate this right by bringing one in. Similarly, suppose that Victoria had explicitly said to Chloe, "I'm willing to have sex with you on the assumption that you love animals and have never been in the military; but I am unwilling to do so otherwise. You're an animal-lover and not a soldier, aren't you?" Since Chloe knows she is a soldier who is, at best, indifferent to animals' welfare, she cannot reasonably consider herself to have Victoria's morally valid consent if she deceives Victoria on these points. Victoria has insisted on her right against sexual contact with a soldier who is indifferent to animals, and so Chloe would violate this right by making such contact with her. But if this is right, then we must reject the view that someone consents to sex when she is deceived into sex by means of run-of-the-mill deception. . . .

Of course, knowledge of another person's deal breakers is hard to come by, particularly in light of the fact that someone's reasons for having sex can be opaque even to herself. But this knowledge also is unnecessary for a deceiver to lack a victim's valid consent. For suppose that Aisha is uncertain about whether I am against Chihuahuas in my apartment; still, she decides to deceive me about the breed of her dog in case I might refuse to admit a Chihuahua. Since her deception is aimed at the possibility that I am unwilling to admit a Chihuahua, and she knows this possibility actually obtains, she cannot reasonably consider herself to have my valid consent to admitting such a dog. And once more, when we are sensitive to this moral pattern, we will see the same is true with respect to sexual consent. Since Chloe deceives Victoria with the purpose of preventing Victoria's deal breakers getting in the way of sex, she cannot reasonably take herself to have Victoria's morally valid consent.

The Argument from a Substantive Account of Consent

My third subargument is the most controversial since it relies on a substantive account of consent. (But should you end up unpersuaded of this account, let me stress that the previous two subarguments do not rely on any particular substantive account of consent and are consistent with a less demanding account than the one I proceed to offer.)

I wish to motivate my account by leaning on the theory of rights I introduced earlier. We saw that we have (moral claim) rights over our persons and our property, and we can waive specific rights against particular interactions with particular individuals. So what fixes the set of rights that we waive? I suggest the following answer:

Intentions Thesis. The rights that we waive are the rights that we intend to waive.

The animating thought behind this thesis is the familiar one that rights are intimately linked to our autonomy and agency. They mark out personal realms over which we have exclusive control, and our decisions determine exactly what may permissibly happen within these realms. Having these personal realms is crucial to our leading our lives in the ways that we should like. Fundamentally, this generates duties in other people to respect our wills: they must respect the choices that we make about what shall happen within these realms. If our choices are to maximally determine the permissibility of others' actions, then the rights that we waive must be the rights that we intend to waive. Only this arrangement leaves us fully sovereign over these realms.

. . . . [W]e should observe that our intentions about waivers are typically both restrictive and extensive. Our intentions are restrictive insofar as we want to permit certain forms of behavior but not others. For example, we let hairdressers cut our hair but not stroke our hands. Meanwhile, our intentions are *extensive* insofar as there are always multiple courses of action that could realize the permitted behavior. There are countless permutations of snips that fall within any hairdresser's permitted range. Now, in general, the restrictions on our intentions are both explicit and implicit. Consider an intention unconnected to consent. Suppose Aisha intends to buy a puppy. She may explicitly have restricted herself to dogs in a shelter. But there will also be implicit restrictions on her intention. If she is like most prospective dog owners, then Aisha will not have considered the possibility that puppies can have rabies. Despite this, unless she is quite the eccentric, she does not intend to buy a rabid puppy. This restriction on her intention is entirely implicit. This is a general feature of intentions, which is thus shared by our intentions for rights-waivers: these typically have both implicit and explicit restrictions. For example, when I intend to waive my rights against Aisha bringing around her dog, I do not intend to permit her to bring around a rabid dog, even if I do not explicitly consider or mention rabies.

These points about intentions, in conjunction with the independently attractive Intentions Thesis, lead us to the following account of consent. In consenting, we intend to allow a restricted range of possibilities, where these restrictions are both implicit and explicit. Any actual interaction with our persons or property is consensual only if this interaction falls within this restricted range of permitted possibilities. On this account of consent, if we object to events in virtue of any feature of them, then they lie outside the restricted range of possibilities to which we are consenting. . . . A consequence of this account is that it is not always transparent to people whether they are giving their morally valid consent to particular events in the world. But this is simply a consequence of the fact that the features of particular events are sometimes opaque to agents. And this is a welcome consequence: any account of consent must predict that Milady did not give her morally valid consent to sex with D'Artagnan even though at the time she thought she was properly consenting to what happened.

Applying this general account of consent to sex, people validly consent to sexual encounters only if they are willing to engage in these encounters, given all the features that these encounters have. Thus, this account of consent implies that when someone is deceived into sex, the sex is nonconsensual. For the deception has concealed a deal-breaking feature of the sexual encounter. As a result, the sexual encounter lies outside the range of possibilities that the victim intends to consent to. Therefore, whenever someone is deceived into sex, she does not validly consent to the sex, even in the case of run-of-the-mill deception, for example, about her partner's attitudes concerning peace and animals.

. . . I would find it worrying if my account of consent has overly strong implications for the way consent functions in other aspects of our lives, and these implications contradicted relevant considered judgments of ours. Consider other aspects of our lives besides sex. Suppose Candace asks to store antique skis in Courtney's basement, and Courtney agrees. Unbeknownst to both parties, the skis were once owned by Josef Stalin. If Courtney had known about their former owner, then she would not have let Candace store them. Despite her opposition to this feature of the skis, are we really to say that Courtney did not validly consent to their presence in her basement?

I take this to be the most troubling challenge to my account of consent. I fully accept that this account implies that Courtney does not properly consent, and it is clear that Candace behaved blamelessly. As a result, we might be tempted to say that the reason why is that Candace had Courtney's morally valid consent. But we must be cautious about jumping to conclusions too hastily, for the correct analysis of this case is more subtle. The feature that is priming us to judge Candace innocent is not the existence of Courtney's consent. Rather, it is the fact that Candace is justifiably ignorant of the skis' history. As such, she would have a full excuse for acting in the way she did. And we can see that it is this excuse that is guiding our intuitions, by imagining instead that Candace does know both of the skis' history and of Courtney's unwillingness to store sporting equipment once owned by bloodthirsty dictators. By making these modifications to the case, it structurally resembles the case in which Aisha tries to sneak her Chihuahua into my apartment. As such, I hope you agree that in this version of the case Candace does not have Courtney's valid consent, and that this explains why Candace acts wrongfully in storing the skis. Now whether Courtney validly consents depends on facts about Courtney—it depends on the nature of her mental attitudes or utterances. Whether Courtney validly consents does not depend on Candace's epistemic state. Since Courtney does not consent when Candace knows the skis were Stalin's, equally she does not consent when Candace is ignorant of this fact. As a result, we can see that Courtney does fail to properly consent in the original case, and our intuitions about Candace's innocence are explained fully by Candace's justifiable ignorance. . . .

IV. BENIGN DECEPTION, CULPABILITY, AND THE SERIOUSNESS OF THE WRONG

So far I have defended both premises of my main argument, which together entail my conclusion that culpably deceiving someone into sex is seriously wrong. . . . Having completed my argument, I wish now to discuss three points about my conclusion.

First, let me stress that the serious wrong here is the nonconsensual sex, rather than the deception in itself. Indeed, deception sometimes plays benign, and even desirable, roles in attraction and sexual relationships. . . . Someone may harmlessly misrepresent how interested she is in her date's tales, and often one does best to conceal one's love until it is reciprocated. . . .

[N]o matter how benign the deception in other respects, if it vitiates someone's sexual consent, then this leads to seriously wrong misconduct. The possible benefits of romance and relationships would not justify having nonconsensual sex with someone. So if someone deceives another person for the sake of their mutually falling in love, then the price she will have to pay is abstinence until she is sufficiently confident that the false beliefs are not part of the other person's reasons for having sex. Moreover, I speculate that much of the harmless or welcome subterfuge that features in attraction and relationships does not hide deal breakers and hence does not lead to deceiving people into sex. If someone would still choose to have sex with another person, were the veil of ignorance lifted, then her sexual consent is unaffected by the deception.

Second, in addition to the serious wrongness of acts, there is the further issue of agents' culpability for performing wrong acts. . . . Someone is culpable for serious wrongdoing if she deliberately aims to deceive another person into sex, if she foresees that her actions will lead to her deceiving another person into sex, and if she recklessly takes an excessive risk of deceiving someone into sex. . . . Suppose that Chloe lied about her career simply to avoid the conversation taking an awkward turn that might disrupt her smooth pickup technique. Still, Chloe should realize that she was taking a risk that Victoria's belief that Chloe was an animal loving humanitarian ends up a crucial part of her reason for consenting to sex. Indeed, when sexual partners deceive each other about themselves, there is frequently some risk, however small, of this deception leading to nonconsensual sex. This is because of the epistemic limitations people face. It is hard for people to know what other people's reasons are for deciding to have sex . . . Whether taking these risks counts as recklessness depends on how much risk

it is acceptable to take. So how much of a risk may we take of deceiving another into sex? . . . given the seriousness of the moral wrong, I suspect that we will often judge that people have strenuous duties to reduce the risk of deceiving another into sex . . .

Third, a comparison between deceiving someone into sex and having sex with an unconscious person is enlightening because they are wrong for the same reason. Suppose that someone took highly effective precautions to ensure that his chronically comatose victim suffered no physical harm and never found out about his having sex with her. Why is his action wrong? My answer is twofold: the victim has a stringent right against sexual contact, which is based in the importance of her sexual autonomy, and he has violated this right by having nonconsensual sex with her. I have argued that these features are present when someone deceives another into sex. And so to avoid equating these cases, one would have to find a sufficiently morally important disanalogy. What could this be?

. . . . There is at least one morally important difference between the two types of nonconsensual sex. Victims of unconscious sex are likely to suffer a greater dignitary harm than victims of deceptive sex, insofar as the former victims are likely to feel that they have been more violated than the latter victims. However, I suggest that this is simply a consequence of the fact that the latter victims mistakenly accept the Lenient Thesis. Many people who are deceived into sex do not consider themselves to have suffered a serious moral wrong. In light of this, they do not consider themselves to be gravely disrespected. However, if it were more widely realized that the Lenient Thesis is false, then this difference between unconscious and deceptive sex would disappear. Both sets of victims would then realize that they have suffered a grave affront to their sexual autonomy.

V. CONCLUSION

To summarize, I have argued that deceiving someone into sex vitiates her consent to sex, and it is seriously wrong to have sex without someone's valid consent to sex. Therefore, deceiving someone into sex is seriously wrong. The seriousness of this wrong is widely recognized when the deception involves, say, spousal impersonation. But it is wrongly overlooked in the case of run-of-the-mill deception.

... Since deceiving someone into sex involves disrespecting her sexual choices, my thesis calls for more autonomy in our sex lives. As such, we should not see it as a prudish or reactionary thesis but a liberating one.

Tom Dougherty: Sex, Lies, and Consent

1. What might a supporter of the Lenient Thesis say on its behalf? Do you think that Dougherty's rejection of that thesis is adequately supported? Why or why not?

2. Reconstruct Dougherty's inference to the best explanation argument. Is his claim—that it's seriously wrong to have sex with someone who does not validly consent—the best explanation of the data he cites? Are there other data regarding immoral sexual conduct that might be better explained by the Lenient Thesis?

3. What information about a potential sexual partner do we have a right to know before we give our morally valid consent to having sex with that person?

4. Dougherty claims that "the Lenient Thesis rests on an objectionably moralized conception of sex." Why does he say this? Do you find his reasons compelling? Support your answer.

5. Many believe that if a person, without being coerced, tells a potential sex partner that she is willing to have sex with him, then she has given her morally valid consent to doing so. On what grounds does Dougherty disagree? Do you find his case plausible? Why or why not?

Is "Loving More" Better? The Values of Polyamory
Elizabeth Brake

In this selection Elizabeth Brake makes the ethical case for polyamory—the practice of maintaining multiple loving and sexual relationships that are guided by the values of radical honesty, open communication, nonpossessiveness, the rejection of jealousy, and a rejection of the conventional gender roles that so often structure monogamous relationships. If, as most believe, love and sex add value to a life, then perhaps a life with more of both goods is in this respect better than a life lived monogamously.

Brake is well aware that her proposals conflict with traditional relationship norms and devotes a good deal of her essay to addressing potential objections. These fall into two camps. Some critics of polyamory believe that it is immoral by nature—that loving and sexual relations are morally required to be exclusive. Other critics argue that the practice of polyamory, even if not wrong in and of itself, is nevertheless immoral because it is bound to lead to bad results. Brake carefully considers a variety of each type of objection and argues that none of them succeed. Indeed, she argues that polyamory is in many ways ethically better—both by nature and in the good results it may bring about—than romantic relationships governed by traditional ideals of romantic and sexual exclusivity.

Most people think that love and sex are good. And having more of a good thing is usually better than having less. So why isn't polyamory, which its practitioners claim involves having more love and sex than monogamy, more widely accepted and practiced? (*Loving More* is in fact the name of the major polyamory support organization and magazine.) Indeed, why isn't polyamory the *rational* choice for someone who values love and sex, because it—reportedly—increases those goods?

One common response is that polyamory is immoral, according to an objective standard of morality. Others have argued that polyamory does not truly involve love at all—as romantic or sexual love is necessarily exclusive, for only one person at a time—or that the love it involves is in some way less valuable than exclusive love. Others suggest that, given the prevalence of responses such as jealousy or risks of unfairness, polyamory is likely to be less satisfying than monogamy.

On the other hand, polyamory incorporates ethical values of its own—indeed, a case could be made that it is the *superior* approach to relationships. Some polyamorists claim to value love and sex more than exclusivity and possessiveness—indeed, in other areas of life, exclusivity and possessiveness are not usually good things. It could even be argued that we should all aspire to polyamory. This prompts the deeper question of whether one approach to relationships is better for everyone or whether there are simply different preferences.

This chapter explores the nature, ethics, and, to some extent, the politics of polyamory. I begin with a short discussion of its definition. I then explore arguments that it is impermissible or less valuable than monogamy, before turning to polyamory as an ideal. Finally, I briefly address its status under law.

WHAT IS POLYAMORY?

The etymology of *polyamory* is "many loves." This distinguishes it from *polygamy*, which means "many marriages," and its two subsets *polyandry* ("many husbands") and *polygyny* ("many wives"). Unlike polygamy, polyamorous relationships are

not predicated on a traditional form of marriage (legal or substantive) or spousal roles—thus, they need not involve the gendered spousal roles often associated with polygamy, in which husbands and wives take on very different sets of responsibilities and powers.

Polyamory, in the simplest definition, involves multiple love and sex relationships. Polyamorous relationships can be same-sex or different-sex, and polyamorists can be straight, gay, bisexual, or, more generally, queer. Polyamory is not defined by a particular form of relationship (as the monogamous dyad is). For example, it could involve an individual pursuing more than one simultaneous sexual relationship, in an open and forthright way, with varying degrees of love or commitment. Polyamory can also be practiced by a dyadic couple in an open relationship, in which partners agree to pursue independent romantic and sexual relationships. Polyamory can also take the form of a group relationship of more than two people.

Group relationships also take multiple forms. A group of three is referred to as a triad, and four as a quad. If group members only have sexual relationships within the group, it is "polyfidelity" (polyfidelity could in fact be seen as multiple monogamy, as opposed to an open and fluid relationship). A group could consist of three or more people who all have sex with each other, but each member in a polyamorous group need not have sex with every other member.

Polyamory is not defined by the formal structure of its relationships, nor is it best defined as a sexual orientation. While it may be that some people find monogamy more onerous than others, and so could perhaps be said to have a polyamorous orientation, this does not seem essential to being polyamorous. Rather, polyamory is best characterized as adopting, and consequently practicing, a certain set of attitudes toward monogamy, exclusivity, love, and sex. In my view, a core constituent of being polyamorous, or in a polyamorous relationship, is commitment to some of the values of polyamory. Being poly or identifying as poly, or having a polyamorous relationship, is not just a set of behaviors: it also requires adopting a core set of polyamorous beliefs or attitudes, as articulated in texts such as Dossie Easton and Catherine Liszt's *The Ethical Slut* and Deborah Anapol's *Polyamory in the 21st Century.*[1]

Thus, someone openly having multiple sexual relationships is not necessarily polyamorous. Polyamorous dating can be distinguished from simply dating multiple partners in that polyamorists are not aiming at eventually "settling down" in a monogamous relationship; polyamory typically involves intentionally living without exclusive, monogamous commitment. Likewise, polyamorous open relationships can be distinguished from "swinging," in which couples swap partners or seek out extra partners for sexual excitement and variety; by contrast, polyamory focuses on emotional relationships as well as sex (there is some dispute over this classification).

Polyamorous values center on non-possessiveness, communication, honesty, and critical reflection on the norms of monogamy, as well as love and sex. Polyamory is typically a choice made *against* marriage, possessiveness, and gendered spousal roles. Polyamorists claim that, unlike many married couples, they are deeply honest with their partners regarding their sexual desires and experiences outside the marriage. Such honesty is part of the consciously adopted ethical rules of polyamorists. While they can cheat on one another, polyamorists typically agree on rules of engagement, such as whether they will tell their partner(s) about every lover, what means of contraception and protection against STDs they will take, whether one partner has priority, and what that priority entails. Cheating within polyamory would consist of breaking these rules.

Polyamory is not an organized and monolithic movement, and hence there are disputes among polyamorists about the core tenets of polyamorous practice. One issue is whether polyamory primarily involves sex, love, or both. It seems that polyamory must involve sex, as otherwise polyamorous relationships would simply be affectionate relationships like friendships. (But complications arise, such as when group relationships involve sexual relationships between some, but not all, group members, and when the parties to the relationships are romantic asexuals.) They must also involve romantic love, otherwise polyamory would simply be promiscuous or "swinging" relationships. In general, then, polyamorous relationships involve sex and romantic love or affection.

Before turning to ethical issues, it is worthwhile addressing one objection to the claim that polyamory involves multiple romantic love relationships. Numerous philosophers of love have argued against the very possibility of polyamorous love, arguing that we cannot love more than one person at a time, at least in the sense of romantic or sexual love (for clearly we can love more than one parent, sibling, child, or friend at a time). If we cannot love more than one person at a time, then polyamory cannot involve multiple love relationships. Carrie Jenkins has called the view that it is conceptually impossible to love more than one person at a time "modal monogamy."[2]

As Jenkins points out, many philosophers of love have defended modal monogamy, taking exclusivity to be a defining feature of romantic love relationships. That is, they assume that romantic love necessarily focuses exclusively on one other person. But Jenkins offers reasons against modal monogamy. First, many people report loving more than one person at a time—not only polyamorists but also people who are torn between two lovers. Jenkins writes, "Unless all such people are either confused or lying, Modal Monogamy is false. And I know of no reason to suppose that all such people are either confused or lying." Second, other forms of love, such as love for friends or children, are not exclusive; why should romantic love be uniquely exclusive?

Additionally, Jenkins Warns that conceptual analysis of the nature of love may conflate culturally dominant norms with what is true *by definition* of the concept under examination. Given that monogamous romantic love is indeed a dominant

---

1. See Dossie Easton and Catherine Liszt, *The Ethical Slut: A Guide to Infinite Sexual Possibilities* (Emeryville, Calif.: Greenery Press, 1997), and Deborah Anapol, *Polyamory in the 21st Century: Love and Intimacy with Many Partners* (Lanham, MD: Rowman & Littlefield, 2010).

2. Carrie Jenkins, "Modal Monogamy," *Ergo* 2:8 (2015).

cultural conception, there is reason to think that cultural paradigms have shaped the intuitions of philosophers undertaking conceptual analysis of love. In other words, while it may seem as if exclusivity is essential to romantic love, this may simply reflect the cultural practice of our society—and it might be mentioned here that many societies have practiced polygamy or some form of institutionalized extramarital sex.

But precisely because of these cultural paradigms, it might be *psychologically* (as opposed to conceptually) impossible to love more than one person at a time. Just as our philosophical intuitions have been shaped culturally, our psychology has also been shaped culturally. Indeed, many people report that when in love with someone, they cannot be in love with someone else, at least during the initial passionate stages of love. The early stages of romantic love can bring an overwhelming and narrow focus on the love object which Sigmund Freud compared to "a neurotic compulsion"! However, it is clearly possible to love multiple people at one time *in different ways:* so while one might be in a state of limerence (early love) with one person, they might also love another person, in a companionate way— just as we do not cease loving friends and family when we fall into romantic love. An underlying assumption of modal monogamy is that romantic love involves being in love in the same way at the same time with one's love objects, but even within monogamy, the nature of romantic love for a single object can change over time—from limerence to companionate pair bonding.

THE ETHICS

While honesty and non-possessiveness are central to the "ethics" of polyamory, is polyamory really ethical? To those who see monogamy as the only permissible form of sexual relationships, it cannot be ethical. But what is the reason for such judgments?

Perhaps it is best to start with the following question: What is the ethical status of polyamorous relationships? We can distinguish worries about wrongs, harms, or deficiencies intrinsic to the practice (those which cannot be separated from it) from concerns about side effects likely to accompany

polyamory. To take a parallel example, some people argue that assisted suicide is inherently wrong, because it violates human dignity; it is wrong in itself. Others argue that it is not inherently wrong, but that permitting it would likely have bad side effects, such as leading hospitals or families to pressure elderly members to agree to be euthanized. If such side effects are sufficiently serious and widespread, they provide reason against a practice. But if such side effects are contingent on the social context, this would allow the practice to be ethical in some contexts or societies but not in others.

I will first look at the concerns that polyamory is inherently wrong. Then I will look at arguments that the practice of polyamory risks harmful side effects. I conclude by looking at the ethical values of polyamory and asking whether polyamory may be ethically *preferable* to monogamy.

1. Is Polyamory Inherently Wrong?

A first set of possible concerns about the nature of polyamory should be set aside. This is the assumption that polyamory—like many instances of extramarital sex—involves deception and promise-breaking. Extramarital sex (or sex outside committed relationships) may involve lies about the sex itself, as well as smaller lies concerning where spouses or partners have been, with whom, and so on. When spouses (or partners) have promised sexual exclusivity, sex outside the relationship also involves promise-breaking. However, such promise-breaking can be found in all types of relationships, not just in polyamorous ones (indeed, they might be less frequent in polyamorous than in monogamous relationships given that each partner has access to more than one sexual partner). Moreover, as we have seen, polyamorists aspire to avoid dishonesty and promise-breaking by engaging in radical honesty and only promising to obey rules which they believe they can keep.

More subtly, it might be suggested that because many people expect and want romantic love to be monogamous, offering non-monogamous love disappoints their expectations. This, however, could be guarded against through honest disclosure. People can have many expectations about their romantic partners (that they be employed, or healthy, etc.);

generally, disappointing such expectations is wrong only when there is an intention to deceive or when the expectations involve reasonable assumptions.

Thus, although polyamorists can be dishonest or break their promises, monogamists can do so also. The point is that these moral wrongs are not *intrinsic* to polyamory. They are moral failures by many polyamorists' own lights. We can then set aside concerns about cheating, deception, and promise-breaking because they are no more inherent to polyamory than to monogamy.

This cautions against idealizing or demonizing either monogamy or polyamory. Such overgeneralizations make fair comparisons impossible. Claims such as "monogamy is stable, loyal, and loving," "polyamory involves radical honesty and openness," or "monogamy leads to deceptive extramarital sex" all involve overgeneralizations, to the extent that they are not true in all cases. To assess either practice, we should keep in mind both the ideals to which it aspires and the reality of human beings imperfectly practicing such ideals. The fact that some polyamorists do not live up to their ideals of honesty and openness does not show that polyamory is inherently flawed, just as the fact that some monogamists do not live up to their ideals of exclusivity and loyalty does not show that monogamy is inherently flawed.

Some sexual ethicists, though, argue that even in its ideal form polyamory is inherently wrong, because sex outside a monogamous relationship (even stronger: outside *marriage*) is immoral. The philosopher Immanuel Kant, for example, held that sex involved giving oneself up to another, to be used for their pleasure, and this could be avoided only when the sex is between a couple who are in a monogamous (legal) marriage.

On Kant's view, respect for humanity requires always treating others as valuable in themselves, and not as a mere means for one's own purposes. Treating someone as a mere means to one's purposes is thus a grave wrong, violating their moral rights. Kant found many moral problems with sex. Indeed, he thought that in sex or masturbation we use our own bodies as mere means for pleasure. But he focused on the concern that sexual use of another treats them as a mere means for the purpose of sexual pleasure. Kant thought that our bodies are an essential part of our personhood, which morally demands respect as "beyond all price." Hence, respect for our personhood must extend to any use of our bodies. Even selling our hair or teeth, according to Kant, contravenes the respect we owe ourselves. When we offer up our bodies to another person for their pleasure, it is not like allowing them to use a tool that we own but rather allowing them to use as a mere means what must always be treated with respect. Kant's solution to this involved both parties reciprocally giving themselves up to each other in marriage: when both give themselves up wholly to each other, each in essence gets themselves back.

Kant's view involves some mysterious metaphysics, but we can attempt a sympathetic reconstruction of his views on polygamy. Kant explained what is wrong with multiple sexual relationships as follows (he focused on polygamy, but his reasoning would also extend to polyamory): when a man is involved with two women (say), each woman gives all of herself, but she receives only half of the man in return. Not only is this unfair and lopsided, but since the solution to the moral problem of sex requires that partners give themselves up to each other wholly and reciprocally, the man in this scenario is using each woman as a mere means to his sexual pleasure (and they are allowing themselves to be used).

There are problems with this account. First, it is difficult to see how Kant's view precludes three people giving themselves to each other wholly and reciprocally in polyfidelity. Members of a small group can give themselves up to the group, and thus get themselves back, just as members of a couple can. Second, it is difficult to see why consensual polyamory would inevitably treat the person as a mere means. In most cases, informed consent is sufficient to render treatment of others respectful; Kant's view that, in sex, both consent and reciprocal exchange of exclusive rights over each other are needed adds an unusual requirement, one found only in the context of sex. But we can use one another's bodies for pleasure in other ways—massage, partner yoga, dancing, cuddling—where consent does seem sufficient for the interaction to be permissible.

The difficulty for Kant's account is to explain why special moral requirements apply to sex. On a less stringent standard of sexual ethics—one requiring only respect, consent, honesty, and affection and concern for the other—it is hard to see how polyamory could be judged inherently wrong. After all, polyamory can involve respect, consent, honesty, affection, and concern for the others.

But it might be thought that although polyamory is not inherently wrong, polyamorous relationships inherently have less value than monogamous relationships—less intimacy or emotional depth, less of whatever makes romantic relationships valuable. For example, Chris Bennett has argued that being the "only one" for someone else confirms a sense of specialness. On his view, exclusive (although not necessarily sexually exclusive) dyadic love relationships uniquely support our autonomy by providing "reassurance about our own value."[3] Bennett writes:

> In conjugal love another person chooses to assume responsibility for you as a whole, because they value the detail of your life. They choose *you*. Furthermore, they choose you *and not anyone else*. The evaluation of you that is expressed in the choice, and in the very form of the relationship and its structures of responsibility, singles you out. You have been chosen over everyone else. This should not make you think that you are more special than everyone else. But it does quite rightly back up your sense that you are special in your own right. Being special for someone else affirms and recognises your sense that the things that make you a particular individual are valuable, because someone has chosen you *for* those things.[4]

Being special for someone else does likely bolster our sense of our own value. But our specialness is not only confirmed in monogamous love relationships. Imagine, for example, a triad in which members pledge mutual fidelity. A member of this triad may feel that the others have chosen her for just who she is and feel confirmed in her specialness by their

regard. And polyamorist couples can also commit to one another above everyone else—for example, they might draw a distinction between partners, who take priority, and companions.

A related objection might be that in polyamory, each partner shares their partner with another who competes for attention and so receives less love, affection, intimacy, or even sex than they would in a monogamous relationship. But this assumes, that relations of love, affection, intimacy, and sex are a zero-sum game—that is, a situation in which there must be winners and losers, as opposed to a situation in which everyone can achieve more by cooperating than they could on their own. The argument assumes that if one's partner loves someone else, one therefore must receive less love. But we don't think this way in relation to parental love or love for friends. There may well be a point at which someone simply lacks the time and psychological capacity to love and care for more children, friends, or partners equally, so each additional person will detract from what the others receive. But there is no reason to think that this point is reached at "more than one," and it plausibly differs from person to person.

Another problem with arguing that polyamorous relationships have less value than monogamous relationships—that they have "second-rate" love and sex—is that not everyone seeks the same qualities in a relationship. Some prize stability over spontaneity, closeness over independence, while others do not. So even if polyamory falls short of some monogamous ideal of priority or intimacy, polyamorists might respond, "Yes, but it's more important to me to have love and sex with more people than more exclusive or intimate love and sex if 'exclusivity' and 'intimacy' mean 'between only two people.'" At this point, to respond to the polyamorist's claim that relationships might involve multiple values requiring trade-offs and that such trade-offs are a matter of subjective preference, the critic must show that polyamory lacks something of objective value, such as something crucial to human flourishing or welfare. That is, the argument must show that polyamory falls short of an objective standard of value that the polyamorist cannot or should not opt out of. But this is a high argumentative standard

---

3. Christopher Bennett, "Liberalism, Autonomy, and Conjugal Love," *Res Publica* 9:3 (2003), 285–301, at 291.

4. Bennett, "Liberalism, Autonomy, and Conjugal Love," 297–98.

to meet, especially given the diversity of people's emotional needs and capacities.

Indeed, even if most people do prefer monogamy, the polyamorist can go on the offensive and claim that polyamory is the ideal that most of us are unable to meet. After all, "one and only," "exclusive," and other language surrounding romantic love suggests selfishness and possessiveness. Before examining this point, I'll consider harms which are "side effects" of the practice, not inherent to it.

2. Is It Harmful?

The foregoing concerns are about the alleged inherent wrongness of polyamory. But many objections to polyamory are about its likely side effects given contingent facts about society or facts of human psychology and biology. These concerns hold that even if polyamory is permissible in principle, it is likely to be harmful, and this generates reasons to refrain from it.

One concern often voiced regarding polyamory is the side effects on children of polyamorous parents. Critics worry that children will be confused, or, that polyamorous parents will serve as poor moral role models. There is little research on such children to make a strong empirical case either way. Literature concerning polygamous families is unlikely to be representative due to demographic differences between typical polygamists and typical polyamorists. While polygamy in the United States and Canada tends to be practiced in small, isolated religious communities where access to education is restricted, polyamorists tend to be well-educated urban professionals.[5]

In fact, there may be little research on polyamorous families because they tend to be closeted. Polyamorists have no legal protections against employment and housing discrimination. Polyamorists fearing loss of jobs, homes, or children have reason to be closeted.

Elizabeth Sheff has recently published the first study on polyamorous families, "a fifteen-year longitudinal, ethnographic study of polyamorous people and their children," which includes interviews with twenty-two children.[6] Sheff's analysis of the data focuses on two themes: first, having multiple, biologically unrelated parties in parental roles is not distinctive of polyamory. Both serial monogamy and some assisted reproductive technologies (involving gamete donation or contract pregnancy) create families with more than two parents, not all of whom are biologically related to the child. So the challenges of polyamorous families—in particular, identifying the adults responsible for a child—are already posed by other family forms.

Second, polyamorists argue that "multiple parenting" benefits children, and Sheff's data appear to suggest that benefits, as well as disadvantages, exist for children of polyamorous parents. The benefits include practical benefits such as more rides and more money, as well as the love and supervision of more parents, and a greater variety of parenting styles (due to the multiplicity of adults involved in a parental way with the child). While these benefits might also accrue to children in stepfamilies, some benefits are unique to polyamory: an emphasis on honesty and choice regarding sexual experience, and on maintaining friendly relations among former partners when sexual relationships end. These must be balanced with disadvantages such as the loss of parents' partners when relationships end (again, also found in monogamous divorce) and overcrowding in the home. Other disadvantages arise from social stigma and the unfamiliarity of such family forms.

A different objection concerns the gender politics of polyamory. Some critics suggest that polyamory, while potentially egalitarian, mainly takes the form of gender-structured polygyny-like relationships—one male and multiple females. Given significant gender inequality in income, wealth, and social power, it is reasonable to worry that women who are financially dependent on their male partners may be pressured into polyamory. Of course, the

---

5. For discussion of the demographics of polygamists, see British Columbia Supreme Court, *Reference re: Section 293 of the Criminal Code of Canada*. On polyamorists, see Mark Goldfeder and Elisabeth Sheff, "Children of Polyamorous Families: A First Empirical Look," *Journal of Law and Social Deviance* 5 (2013), 150–243, at 193.

6. Goldfeder and Sheff, "Children of Polyamorous Families," 189, 172–6.

concern that structural inequality between men and women may result in unequal decision-making power, even subtle coercion, also applies to monogamy. But critics could suggest that, within polyamory, competition between women might increase the opportunity for exploitation. On the other hand, some polyamorists are explicitly feminist, rejecting monogamous norms that they see as patriarchal, and advocates of polyamory argue that it allows the division of household work and childcare between more people—benefiting women, who typically take on a greater share of such work.

It might also be objected that the practical challenges of polyamory introduce risks and potential unfairness. One set of risks is sexual: possible transmission of STDs or unplanned pregnancy. These risks suggest the importance for polyamorists of creating explicit agreements regarding their practices, such as using protection and regularly taking STD tests (as, in fact, monogamists might be less likely to do). But polyamorists might point out that because their relationships are more open and involve access to multiple sexual partners, there is less temptation to cheat (by breaking the rules) and partners are aware of the risks, as they are not in a monogamous relationship in which one partner secretly cheats.

Another risk is that of unfair treatment. Polyamorists may experience sexual or romantic jealousy, and while partners may agree on prioritizing a primary relationship, with the expectation that secondary companions respect the primary relationship, this might not work in practice. One of the biggest reported challenges for polyamorists is simply making time for multiple relationships. The potential conflict between different partners, particularly in time spent together, might lead to forms of unequal treatment. Polyamorists, however, might respond that because communication is a core tenet of polyamorist practice, discussions of fairness and priority will be central to polyamorist practice—and monogamists might also benefit from embracing such discussions. While polyamorists might create hierarchies—between, for instance, a primary partner and a secondary companion—these hierarchies are both acknowledged and, to some extent, dynamic. Explicit attention to the hierarchies in relationships and openness to their fluidity could be better conditions for identifying and changing unfair hierarchies than the static hierarchies which emerge without discussion in some monogamous relationships. Finally, unfair treatment and jealousy are possible in monogamous relationships in which a partner might devote time or attention to non-romantic passions such as work, hobbies, friendships, or addictions.

Polyamorists, whether in open or in group relationships, can define their own rules, and doing so is essential given the risks and logistical challenges of polyamory. For example, an open couple might limit their contact with third parties to anonymous sexual encounters, or they might permit the formation of independent emotional relationships. A triad might agree to polyfidelity or agree to practice only safe sex with non-group members. Partners may find it important to establish rules setting out the priority of their relationship. For example, a couple in an open relationship might agree that partners have veto power over each other's lovers, or that partners will limit the time spent with secondary companions. Once again, polyamory does not mean that anything goes—infidelity can exist in an open relationship as much as in a closed one, if one partner breaks the agreed-upon rules.

3. The Values of Polyamory

As Luke Brunning writes in a recent essay, some polyamorists have tended to defend polyamory by comparing it to monogamy, focusing on similarities between the practices. But Brunning suggests a full understanding of the value of polyamory lies in its distinctiveness. Because of the potential for conflict it involves, it requires partners to practice communication, self- and other-awareness, and emotional work, thus making it, he argues, more emotionally challenging but also more emotionally rich than monogamy.[7] Indeed, critical reflection on the norms of monogamy is partly constitutive of polyamory, suggesting a crucial distance between the practices.

---

7. Luke Brunning, "The Distinctiveness of Polyamory," *Journal of Applied Philosophy Online* First (2016): DOI: 10.1111/japp. l2240; accessed December 28, 2016.

Polyamorists have articulated a range of values according to which polyamory could be seen as an improvement on monogamy. Honest communication is a foundational rule for polyamorous relationships. The ideal of "radical honesty," or openness about sexual desires, feelings, and encounters that monogamists typically conceal from their partners, could create greater intimacy and prompt partners to confront and work through negative feelings of jealousy. Not all polyamorists espouse the extreme of radical honesty; they may prefer a "don't ask, don't tell" policy, for example. But such a choice is still based on honest communication, rather than deception.

The ideal of non-possessiveness rejects relationship norms that treat partners as possessions who can be controlled. Monogamist norms resemble property norms (particularly when we examine the historical law of coverture in marriage): partners exclude all others from their holdings. The critic of capitalism John McMurtry, for instance, saw monogamy as an ideological tool of capitalism, disposing individuals to see the world—including their sexual partners—in terms of ownership and exclusion.[8] And of course such possessiveness has, historically, been gendered: thus the rejection of possessiveness is sometimes an explicitly feminist repudiation of traditional marriage norms which treated wives as tantamount to their husbands' property and limited women's value to their status as wives and mothers. Dossie Easton, the self-described "ethical slut," became a principled polyamorist after escaping an abusive relationship with a sexually possessive man. In part, she rejected monogamy so that she would gain self-knowledge, as opposed to losing her identity and independence in a relationship: "I resented those cultural values that said that my sense of security and self-worth were contingent on the status of whatever man I managed to attract to me, as if I had no status of my own. So I vowed to discover a security in myself, the stable ground of my very own being, something to do . . . with self-respect and self-acceptance."[9]

But polyamorists also aspire to a positive emotional ideal of non-possessiveness, talking delight in their partner's sexual and romantic experiences. Deborah Anapol describes the emotion of "compersion," which is "the opposite of jealousy," as feeling "joy and delight when one's beloved loves or is being loved by another."[10] This expands empathy to one's sexual partner, against cultural norms and feelings of sexual jealousy. From a polyamorous standpoint, such jealousy is irrational (though challenging): love and sex are good, and we should wish for our loved ones to have good things. For similar reasons, new partners are generally expected to respect the autonomy of existing relationships.

We can consider polyamory as an ideal by asking what it would be like if we lived in a society where polyamory (with its ideals of honesty, communication, and non-possessiveness) was the norm. We can imagine, as Easton suggests, that marital status would no longer be a marker to determine one's value or a symbol of adulthood. Marriage or being "coupled" is one of the primary means we now use to categorize ourselves and others socially. But in a polyamorous world these markers would be less clear-cut. Relationships would be more fluid, so the distinction between being in and out of a relationship would no longer be so important. This would allow romantic asexuals and friendships to flourish without being marginalized by cultural norms of coupledom; if being in a relationship of a certain form became less culturally important, it could become more acceptable to choose to opt out of romantic or sexual relationships altogether. A polyamorous society would be a post-monogamous society, in a way parallel to ideals of post-racial or post-gender societies: different sexual identities would not carry arbitrary penalties, and sexual identity itself might become more fluid.[11]

---

8. John McMurtry, "Monogamy: A Critique," *The Monist* 56:4 (1972), 587–99.
9. Easton and Liszt, *The Ethical Slut*, 11–12.

10. Anapol, *Polyamory in the 21st Century*, 22, 121.
11. Here, one might object that just as strong social norms with corresponding social exclusions develop under monogamy, so too a polyamorous society could stigmatize or marginalize monogamists. However, because polyamory involves negotiation and fluidity, it might be more difficult for stark discriminations of this kind to emerge.

A polyamorous hegemony might also have wider social, economic, and environmental effects. Communal living might become more common, with environmental benefits; and all the time spent on communication and pursuing relationships might lead toward a less consumerist society where people were more entranced by relationships—and conversations about how to conduct them—than the latest consumer items or celebrity gossip. It might even be a more fun society, in which flirtation and sexual possibility were more widespread, without the threat of disrupting existing relationships or requiring messy deceptions. At the same time, because sexuality was more open and polyamorous desires allowed open expression, popular culture might become less sexualized. People might come to better knowledge of themselves and others through the "emotional work" of polyamory. And as sex wouldn't carry the burden of uniting oneself with one monogamous partner, people who are currently disadvantaged on "mating markets"— perhaps those with less income, worse social skills, or unconventional looks—might have more access to sexual and romantic relationships.

There is also the tempting, albeit somewhat controversial, thought—which I will not pursue here— that polyamory is more suited to human nature (let's set aside doubts about the existence of such a thing as human nature): at least as far as sex is concerned, we might not be sexually monogamous by nature, and human sexual desire might target multiple sexual partners. (In a society that values monogamy, this could be one important reason why cheating is rampant and why polyamorists value honesty.) If so, polyamory might be truer to who we are than sexual monogamy.

For all these reasons, people might be more sexually and romantically fulfilled in a polyamorous world.

LAW AND POLITICS

While some forms of plural marriage or bigamy are illegal, polyamory as such is not criminalized in Western countries. In a liberal society, sexual freedom protects one's right to have sex with multiple partners (and freedom of association grants a right to interact with those whom one chooses, so long as they consent). But (at least in the United States) polyamorists have no protections against discrimination in housing and employment.

Polyamorists have not—yet—sought marriage equality. This may be because many reject the possessiveness and gender norms associated with traditional marriage. Moreover, legislating group marriage poses challenges not associated with recognizing same-sex marriage: How will marital rights and responsibilities be divided among three people, for example? And whose legal consent would be required to add another party to the relationship? But some form of legal recognition for groups or network relationships might be possible—and perhaps required for equal treatment.

Some legal theorists have considered whether being polyamorous should be construed as a minority sexual orientation such as being gay or lesbian, and hence arguably eligible for legal protection against discrimination. One concern with such a strategy is that almost everyone who is not asexual can be considered polyamorous in orientation, if that simply means desiring more than one person sexually. But it might be argued that polyamory is sufficiently embedded—deeply entwined with identity and pursued in the face of significant risks—to be legally classified as an orientation.

In a tolerant, liberal society, the state has no reason to discriminate among its citizens' different approaches to love, sex, and intimacy, as long as their choices do not harm unconsenting or incompetent others. The vibrant coexistence of polyamory alongside monogamy could benefit monogamists too, by encouraging the adoption of values such as radical honesty, communication, and more attention to needs for love and sex.

Elizabeth Brake: Is "Loving More" Better? The Values of Polyamory

1. What do you think is the strongest argument on behalf of exclusive, monogamous relationships? What is the best criticism of that argument? Can it be adequately answered?
2. Is there anything inherently wrong—wrong, in and of itself—with polyamorous relationships? If so, what?

3. Is Brake right to be as optimistic as she is about the consequences of polyamory? Are there likely to be problematic side-effects that she has not considered?

4. Suppose that we are "hard-wired" to be sexually attracted to many people at once. What implications—if any—would this have for the morality of being monogamous or polyamorous?

5. Suppose that polyamory is morally permissible. On that assumption, what legal protections—if any—should be granted to individuals who wish to participate in polygamous marriages?

"Whether from Reason or Prejudice": Taking Money for Bodily Services

Martha C. Nussbaum

In this article, Martha C. Nussbaum makes the case for the legalization of prostitution. Her central argument relies on an analogy between prostitution and other professions in which people take money for bodily services. She argues that if these other unproblematic professions ought to be legal, then so should prostitution.

Nussbaum considers several objections to the legalization of prostitution. One is that prostitution ought to be made illegal because it subjects women to health risks and risks of violence. Nussbaum argues that if the fact that a profession subjects its practitioners to health risks and violence were a sufficient reason to outlaw it, then we ought to outlaw boxing. Few prostitutes are subjected to the kind of violence that boxers are, and few suffer from the sort of health problems that boxers endure after a career of being punched in the head. And yet few advocate for the criminalization of boxing.

Others think that prostitution ought to be illegal because working prostitutes have little or no say about the work they do. Their work activities are controlled by others—namely, their clients. Nussbaum argues that this does not distinguish prostitution from many other kinds of bodily services performed by working-class women. For instance, few domestic servants have a say about what their day-to-day work looks like. The same is true of factory workers. And yet no one argues (nor should they) that we ought to outlaw domestic servitude or factory jobs.

Among the other objections that Nussbaum considers is the objection that prostitution involves the invasion of one's intimate bodily space, that it makes it difficult for prostitutes to have intimate relationships with others, and that it turns prostitutes into a commodity. Nussbaum argues that each objection fails, because there are other professions in which people offer their bodies in these ways and yet we do not, and should not, outlaw those activities.

. . . My aim in this article will be to investigate the question of sexual "commodification" by focusing on the example of "prostitution." I shall argue that

From Martha C. Nussbaum, "'Whether from Reason or Prejudice': Taking Money for Bodily Services," *Journal of Legal Studies* 27 (1998), pp. 693–724. Notes have been abridged.

a fruitful debate about the morality and legality of prostitution should begin from a twofold starting point: from a broader analysis of our beliefs and practices with regard to taking pay for the use of the body and from a broader awareness of the options and choices available to poor working women. The former inquiry suggests that at least some of our beliefs about prostitution are irrational; it will therefore help us to identify the elements in prostitution that are genuinely problematic. Most, though not all, of the genuinely problematic elements turn out to be common to a wide range of activities engaged in by poor working women, and the second inquiry will suggest that many of women's employment choices are so heavily constrained by poor options that they are hardly choices at all. I think that this should bother us and that the fact that a woman with plenty of choices becomes a prostitute should not bother us, provided that there are sufficient safeguards against abuse and disease, safeguards of a type that legalization would make possible.

It will therefore be my conclusion that the most urgent issue raised by prostitution is that of employment opportunities for working women and their control over the conditions of their employment. The legalization of prostitution, far from promoting the demise of love, is likely to make things a little better for women who have too few options to begin with. The really helpful thing for feminists to ponder if they deplore the nature of these options will be how to promote expansion in the option set through education, skills training, and job creation. These unsexy topics are insufficiently addressed by feminist philosophers in the United States, but they are inevitable in any practical project dealing with real-life prostitutes and their female children. This suggests that at least some of our feminist theory may be insufficiently grounded in the reality of working-class lives and too focused on sexuality as an issue in its own right, as if it could be extricated from the fabric of poor people's attempts to survive. . . .

Pervasive stigma itself does not appear to provide a good reason for the continued criminalization of prostitution, any more than it does for the illegality of interracial marriage. Nor does the stigma in question even appear to ground a sound *moral* argument against prostitution. This is not, however, the end of the issue: for there are a number of other significant arguments that have been made to support criminalization. Let us now turn to those arguments.

   1. *Prostitution Involves Health Risks and Risks of Violence.* To this we can make two replies. First, insofar as this is true, as it clearly is, the problem is made much worse by the illegality of prostitution, which prevents adequate supervision, encourages the control of pimps, and discourages health checking. As Corbin shows, regimes of legal but regulated prostitution have not always done well by women: the health checkups of the *filles soumises* were ludicrously brief and inadequate. But there is no reason why one cannot focus on the goal of adequate health checks, and some European nations have done reasonably well in this area. The legal brothels in Nevada have had no reported cases of AIDS. Certainly risks of violence can be far better controlled when the police is the prostitute's ally rather than her oppressor.

To the extent to which risks remain an inevitable part of the way of life, we must now ask what general view of the legality of risky undertakings we wish to defend. Do we ever want to rule out risky bargains simply because they harm the agent? Or do we require a showing of harm to others (as might be possible in the case of gambling, for example)? Whatever position we take on this complicated question, we will almost certainly be led to conclude that prostitution lies well within the domain of the legally acceptable: for it is probably less risky than boxing, another activity in which working-class people try to survive and flourish by subjecting their bodies to some risk of harm. There is a stronger case for paternalistic regulation of boxing than of prostitution, and externalities (the glorification of violence as example to the young) make boxing at least as morally problematic, probably more so. And yet I would not defend the criminalization of boxing, and I doubt that very many Americans would either. Sensible regulation of both prostitution and boxing, by contrast, seems reasonable and compatible with personal liberty.

In the international arena, many problems of this type stem from the use of force and fraud to induce women to enter prostitution, frequently at a very young age and in a strange country where they have no civil rights. An especially common destination, for example, is Thailand, and an especially common source is Burma, where the devastation of the rural economy has left many young women an easy mark for promises of domestic service elsewhere. Driven by customers' fears of HIV, the trade has focused on increasingly young girls from increasingly remote regions. Human rights interviewers have concluded that large numbers of these women were unaware of what they would be doing when they left their country and are kept there through both economic and physical coercion. (In many cases, family members have received payments, which then become a "debt" that the girl has to pay off.) These circumstances, terrible in themselves, set the stage for other forms of risk and violence. Fifty percent to seventy percent of the women and girls interviewed by Human Rights Watch were HIV positive; discriminatory arrests and deportations are frequently accompanied by abuse in police custody. All these problems are magnified by the punitive attitude of the police and government toward these women as prostitutes or illegal aliens or both, although under both national and international law trafficking victims are exempt from legal penalty and are guaranteed safe repatriation to their country of origin. This situation clearly deserves both moral condemnation and international legal pressure; but, it is made worse by the illegality of prostitution itself.

2. *The Prostitute Has No Autonomy; Her Activities Are Controlled by Others.* This argument does not serve to distinguish prostitution from very many types of bodily service performed by working-class women. The factory worker does worse on the scale of autonomy, and the domestic servant no better. I think this point expresses a legitimate moral concern: a person's life seems deficient in flourishing if it consists only of a form of work that is totally out of the control and direction of the person herself. Karl Marx rightly associated that kind of labor with a deficient realization of full humanity and (invoking Aristotle) persuasively argued that a flourishing human life probably requires some kind of use of one's own reasoning in the planning and execution of one's own work. But that is a pervasive problem of labor in the modern world, not a problem peculiar to prostitution as such. It certainly does not help the problem to criminalize prostitution—any more than it would be to criminalize factory work or domestic service.

A woman will not exactly achieve more control and "truly human functioning" by becoming unemployed. What we should instead think about are ways to promote more control over choice of activities, more variety, and more general humanity in the types of work that are actually available to people with little education and few options. That would be a lot more helpful than removing one of the options they actually have.

3. *Prostitution Involves the Invasion of One's Intimate Bodily Space.* This argument does not seem to support the legal regulation of prostitution so long as the invasion in question is consensual—that is, that the prostitute is not kidnapped, fraudulently enticed, a child beneath the age of consent, or under duress against leaving if she should choose to leave. In this sense, prostitution is quite unlike sexual harassment and rape and far more like the activity of the colonoscopy artist*—not to everyone's taste, and involving a surrender of bodily privacy that some will find repellant, but not for that reason necessarily bad, either for self or others. The argument does not even appear to support a moral criticism of prostitution, unless one is prepared to make a moral criticism of all sexual contact that does not involve love or marriage.

4. *Prostitution Makes It Harder for People to Form Relationships of Intimacy and Commitment.* This argument is prominently made by Elizabeth Anderson in defense of the criminalization of prostitution.[1] The first question we should ask is, Is this true? People still appear to fall in love in the Netherlands and Germany and Sweden; they also fell in love in ancient Athens, where prostitution was not only legal but also, probably, publicly subsidized. One type of relationship does not, in fact, appear to remove the need for the other—any more than a Jackie

---

* [In material omitted here, Nussbaum introduces the colonoscopy artist as one who receives payment in exchange for voluntarily having her colon examined with the latest medical instruments, in order to test out their range and capability.—ed.]

1. https://broadly.vice.com/en_us/article/wjeq44/why-cant-i-consent-to-sex-with-my-brother-on-genetic-sexual-attraction

Collins novel removes the desire to read Proust. Proust has a specific type of value that is by no means found in Jackie Collins, so people who want that value will continue to seek out Proust, and there is no reason to think that the presence of Jackie Collins on the bookstand will confuse Proust lovers into thinking that Proust is really like Jackie Collins. So too, one supposes, with love in the Netherlands: people who want relationships of intimacy and commitment continue to seek them out for the special value they provide, and they do not have much trouble telling the difference between one sort of relationship and another, despite the availability of both.

Second, one should ask which women Anderson has in mind. Is she saying that the criminalization of prostitution would facilitate the formation of love relationships on the part of the women who were (or would have been) prostitutes? Or is she saying that the unavailability of prostitution as an option for working-class women would make it easier for romantic middle-class women to have the relationships they desire? The former claim is implausible, since it is hard to see how reinforcing the stigma against prostitutes or preventing some poor women from taking one of the few employment options they might have would be likely to improve their human relations. The latter claim might possibly be true (though it is hardly obvious), but it seems a repugnant idea, which I am sure Anderson would not endorse, that we should make poor women poorer so that middle-class women can find love. Third, one should ask Anderson whether she is prepared to endorse the large number of arguments of this form that might plausibly be made in the realm of popular culture and, if not, whether she has any way of showing how she could reject those as involving an unacceptable infringement of liberty and yet allowing the argument about prostitution that she endorses. For it seems plausible that making rock music illegal would increase the likelihood that people would listen to Mozart and Beethoven, that making Jackie Collins illegal would make it more likely that people would turn to Joyce Carol Oates, that making commercial advertising illegal would make it more likely that we

would appraise products with high-minded ideas of value in our minds, and that making television illegal would improve children's reading skills. What is certain, however, is that we would and do utterly reject those ideas (we do not even seriously entertain them) because we do not want to live in Plato's *Republic*, with our cultural options dictated by a group of wise guardians, however genuinely sound their judgments may be.

5. *The Prostitute Alienates Her Sexuality on the Market; She Turns Her Sexual Organs and Acts into Commodities.* Is this true? It seems implausible to claim that the prostitute alienates her sexuality just on the grounds that she provides sexual services to a client for a fee. Does the singer alienate her voice, or the professor her mind? The prostitute still has her sexuality; she can use it on her own, apart from the relationship with the client, just as the domestic servant may cook for her family and clean her own house. She can also cease to be a prostitute, and her sexuality will still be with her, and hers, if she does. So she has not even given anyone a monopoly on those services, far less given them over into someone else's hands. The real issue that separates her from the professor and the singer seems to be the degree of choice she exercises over the acts she performs. But is even this a special issue for the prostitute, any more than it is for the factory worker or the domestic servant or the colonoscopy artist—all of whom choose to enter trades in which they will not have a great deal of say over what they do or (within limits) how they do it? Freedom to choose how one works is a luxury, highly desirable indeed, but a feature of few jobs that nonaffluent people perform.

As for the claim that the prostitute turns her sexuality into a commodity, we must ask what that means. If it means only that she accepts a fee for sexual services, then that is obvious; but nothing further has been said that would show us why this is a bad thing. The professor, the singer, the symphony musician—all accept a fee, and it seems plausible that this is a good state of affairs, creating spheres of freedom. Professors are more free to pursue their own thoughts now, as moneymakers, than they were in the days when they were supported by monastic orders; symphony musicians playing under the contract secured by the musicians union have more free time than nonunionized musicians and more opportunities to engage in experimental and solo work that will enhance their art. In neither case should we conclude that the existence of a contract has converted the abilities into things to be exchanged and traded separately from the body of the producer; they remain human creative abilities, securely housed in their possessor. So if, on the one hand, to "commodify" means merely to accept a fee, we have been given no reason to think that this is bad.

If, on the other hand, we try to interpret the claim of "commodification" using the narrow technical definition of "commodity" used by the Uniform Commercial Code, the claim is plainly false. For that definition stresses the "fungible" nature of the goods in question, and "fungible" goods are, in turn, defined as goods "of which any unit is, by nature or usage of trade, the equivalent of any other like unit." While we may not think that the soul or inner world of a prostitute is of deep concern to the customer, she is usually not regarded as simply a set of units fully interchangeable with other units. Prostitutes are probably somewhat more fungible than bassoon players, but not totally so. (Corbin reports that all *maisons de tolérance* standardly had a repertory of different types of women, to suit different tastes, and this should not surprise us.) What seems to be the real issue is that the woman is not attended to as an individual, not considered as a special unique being. But that is true of many ways people treat one another in many areas of life, and it seems implausible that we should use that kind of disregard as a basis for criminalization. It may not even be immoral: for surely we cannot deeply know all the people with whom we have dealings in life, and many of those dealings are just fine without deep knowledge. So our moral question boils down to the question, Is sex without deep personal knowledge always immoral? It seems to me officious and presuming to use one's own experience to give an affirmative answer to this question, given that people have such varied experiences of sexuality.

In general, then, there appears to be nothing baneful or value-debasing about taking money for a service, even when that service expresses something intimate about the self. Professors take a salary, artists work on commission under contract—frequently producing works of high intellectual and spiritual value. To take money for a production does not turn either the activity or the product (for example, the article, the painting) into a commodity in the baneful sense in which that implies fungibility. If this is so, there is no reason to think that a prostitute's acceptance of money for her services necessarily involves a baneful conversion of an intimate act into a commodity in that sense. If the prostitute's acts are, as they are, less intimate than many other sexual acts people perform, that does not seem to have a great deal to do with the fact that she receives money, given that people engage in many intimate activities (painting, singing, writing) for money all the time without loss of expressive value. Her activity is less intimate because that is its whole point; and it is problematic, to the extent that it is, neither because of the money involved nor because of the nonintimacy (which, as I have said, it seems to me officious to declare bad in all cases) but because of features of her working conditions and the way she is treated by others. . . .

6. *The Prostitute's Activity Is Shaped by, and in Turn Perpetuates, Male Dominance of Women.* The institution of prostitution as it has most often existed is certainly shaped by aspects of male domination of women. As I have argued, it is shaped by the perception that female sexuality is dangerous and needs careful regulation, that male sexuality is rapacious and needs a "safe" outlet, that sex is dirty and degrading, and that only a degraded woman is an appropriate sexual object. Nor have prostitutes standardly been treated with respect or been given the dignity one might think proper to a fellow human being. They share this with working-class people of many types in many ages; but, there is no doubt that there are particular features of the disrespect that derive from male supremacy and the desire to lord it over women—as well as from a tendency to link sex to (female) defilement that is common in the history of Western European culture. The physical abuse of prostitutes, and the control of their earnings by pimps—as well as the pervasive use of force and fraud in international markets—are features of male dominance that are extremely harmful and that do not have direct parallels in other types of low-paid work. Some of these forms of conduct may be largely an outgrowth of the illegality of the industry and closely comparable to the threatening behavior of drug wholesalers to their—usually male—retailers. So there remains a question about how far male dominance as such explains the violence involved. But in the international arena, where regulations against these forms of misconduct are usually treated as a joke, illegality is not a sufficient explanation for them.

Prostitution is hardly alone in being shaped by, and in reinforcing, male dominance. Systems of patrilineal property and exogamous marriage, for example, certainly do more to perpetuate not only male dominance but also female mistreatment and even death. There probably is a strong case for making the giving of dowry illegal, as has been done since 1961 in India and since 1980 in Bangladesh (though with little success): for it can be convincingly shown that the institution of dowry is directly linked with extortion and threats of bodily harm and ultimately with the deaths of large numbers of women. It is also obvious that the dowry system pervasively conditions the perception of the worth of girl children: they are a big expense, and they will not be around to protect one in one's old age. This structure is directly linked with female malnutrition, neglect, noneducation, even infanticide, harms that have caused the deaths of many millions of women in the world. It is perfectly understandable that the governments of India, Bangladesh, and Pakistan are very concerned about the dowry system, since it seems very difficult to improve the very bad economic and physical condition of women without some structural changes. (Pakistan has recently adopted a somewhat quixotic remedy, making it illegal to serve food at weddings—thus driving many caterers into poverty.) Dowry is an institution affecting millions of women, determining

the course of almost all girl children's lives pervasively and from the start. Prostitution as such usually does not have either such dire or such widespread implications. (Indeed, it is frequently the produce of the dowry system, when parents take payment for prostituting a female child for whom they would otherwise have to pay dowry.) The case for making it illegal on grounds of subordination seems weaker than the case for making dowry, or even wedding feasts, illegal; and yet these laws are themselves of dubious merit and would probably be rightly regarded as involving undue infringement of liberty under our constitutional tradition. (It is significant that Human Rights Watch, which has so aggressively pursued the issue of forced prostitution, takes no stand one way or the other on the legality of prostitution itself.)

More generally, one might argue that the institution of marriage as has most frequently been practiced both expresses and reinforces male dominance. It would be right to use law to change the most iniquitous features of that institution—protecting women from domestic violence and marital rape, giving women equal property and custody rights, and improving their exit options by intelligent shaping of the divorce law. But to rule that marriage as such should be illegal on the grounds that it reinforces male dominance would be an excessive intrusion on liberty, even if one should believe marriage irredeemably unequal. So too, I think, with prostitution: what seems right is to use law to protect the bodily safety of prostitutes from assault, to protect their rights to their incomes against the extortionate behavior of pimps, to protect poor women in developing countries from forced trafficking and fraudulent offers, and to guarantee their full civil rights in the countries where they end up—to make them, in general, equals under the law, both civil and criminal. But the criminalization of prostitution seems to pose a major obstacle to that equality.

Efforts on behalf of the dignity and self-respect of prostitutes have tended to push in exactly the opposite direction. In the United States, prostitutes have long been organized to demand greater respect, though their efforts are hampered by prostitution's continued illegality. In India, the National Federation of Women has adopted various strategies to give prostitutes more dignity in the public eye. For example, on National Women's Day, they selected a prostitute to put a garland on the head of the Prime Minister. In a similar manner, UNICEF in India's Andhra Pradesh has been fighting to get prostitutes officially classified as "working women" so that they can enjoy the child-care benefits local government extends to that class. As with domestic service, so here: giving workers greater dignity and control can gradually change both the perception and the fact of dominance.

7. *Prostitution Is a Trade That People Do Not Enter by Choice; Therefore the Bargains People Make Within It Should Not Be Regarded as Real Bargains.* Here we must distinguish three cases. First is the case where the woman's entry into prostitution is caused by some type of conduct that would otherwise be criminal: kidnapping, assault, drugging, rape, statutory rape, blackmail, a fraudulent offer. Here we may certainly judge that the woman's choice is not a real choice and that the law should take a hand in punishing her coercer. This is a terrible problem currently in developing countries; international human rights organizations are right to make it a major focus.

Closely related is the case of child prostitution. Child prostitution is frequently accompanied by kidnapping and forcible detention; even when children are not stolen from home, their parents have frequently sold them without their own consent. But even where it is not, we should judge that there is an impermissible infringement of autonomy and liberty. A child (and because of clients' fears of HIV, brothels now often focus on girls as young as ten) cannot give consent to a life in prostitution; not only lack of information and of economic options (if parents collude in the deal) but also absence of adult political rights makes such a "choice" no choice at all.

Different is the case of an adult woman who enters prostitution because of bad economic options: because it seems a better alternative than the chicken factory, because there is no other employment available to her, and so forth. This too, we should insist, is a case where autonomy has been infringed, but in a different way. Consider Joseph Raz's vivid example of "the hounded woman," a woman on a desert island who is constantly pursued by a man-eating animal.[2] In one sense, this woman is free to go anywhere on the island and do anything she likes. In another sense, of course, she is quite unfree. If she wants not to be eaten, she has to spend all her time and calculate all her movements in order to avoid the beast. Raz's point is that many poor people's lives are nonautonomous in just this way. They may fulfill internal conditions of autonomy, being capable of making bargains, reflecting about what to do, and so forth. But none of this counts for a great deal if in fact the struggle for survival gives them just one unpleasant option or a small set of (in various ways) unpleasant options.

This seems to me the truly important issue raised by prostitution. Like work in the chicken factory, it is not an option many women choose with alacrity when many other options are on their plate. This might not be so in some hypothetical culture in which prostitutes have legal protection, dignity, and respect and the status of skilled practitioner, rather like the masseuse. But it is true now in most societies, given the reality of the (albeit irrational) stigma attaching to prostitution. But the important thing to realize is that this is not an issue that permits us to focus on prostitution in isolation from the economic situation of women in a society generally. Certainly it will not be ameliorated by the criminalization of prostitution, which reduces poor women's options still further. We may grant that poor women do not have enough options and that society has been unjust to them in not extending more options, while nonetheless respecting and honoring the choices they actually make in reduced circumstances.

How could it possibly be ameliorated? Here are some things that have actually been done in India, where prostitution is a common last-ditch option for women who lack other employment opportunities. First, both government and private groups have focused on the provision of education to women, to equip them with skills that will enhance their options. One group I recently visited in Bombay focuses in particular on skills training for the children of prostitutes, who are at especially high risk of becoming prostitutes themselves unless some action increases their options. Second, nongovernmental organizations have increasingly focused on the provision of credit to women in order to enhance their employment options and give them a chance to "upgrade" in the domain of their employment. One such project that has justly won international renown is the Self-Employed Women's Association (SEWA), centered in Ahmedabad in Gujerat, which provides loans to women pursuing a variety of informal-sector occupations, from tailoring to hawking and vending to cigarette rolling to agricultural labor. With loans they can get wholesale rather than retail supplies, upgrade their animals or equipment, and so forth. They also get skills training and, frequently, the chance to move into leadership roles in the organization itself. Such women are far less likely to need to turn to prostitution to supplement their income. Third, they can form labor organizations to protect women employed in low-income jobs and to bargain for better working conditions—once again making this work a better source of income and diminishing the likelihood that prostitution will need to be selected. (This is the other primary objective of SEWA, which is now organizing hawkers and vendors internationally.) Fourth, they can form groups to diminish the isolation and enhance the self-respect of working women in low-paying jobs; this was a ubiquitous feature of both government and nongovernment programs I visited in India, and a crucial element of helping women deliberate about their options if they wish to avoid prostitution for themselves or their daughters.

These four steps are the real issue, I think, in addressing the problem of prostitution. Feminist philosophers do not talk a lot about credit and employment; they should do so far more. Indeed, it seems a dead end to consider prostitution in isolation from the other realities of working life of which it is a part, and one suspects that this has happened because prostitution is a sexy issue and getting a loan for a sewing machine appears not to be. But philosophers had better talk more about getting loans, learning to read, and so forth if they want to be relevant to the choices that are actually faced by working women and to the programs that are actually doing a lot to improve such women's options.

VI.

The stigma traditionally attached to prostitution is based on a collage of beliefs, most of which are not rationally defensible and which should be especially vehemently rejected by feminists: beliefs about the evil character of female sexuality, the rapacious character of male sexuality, the essentially marital and reproductive character of "good" women and "good" sex. Worries about subordination more recently raised by feminists are much more serious concerns, but they apply to many types of work poor women do. Concerns about force and fraud should be extremely urgent concerns of the international women's movement. Where these conditions do not obtain, feminists should view prostitutes as (usually) poor working women with few options, not as threats to the intimacy and commitment that many women and men (including, no doubt, many prostitutes) seek. This does not mean that we should not be concerned about ways in which prostitution as currently practiced, even in the absence of force and fraud, undermines the dignity of women, just as domestic service in the past undermined the dignity of members of a given race or class. But the correct response to this problem seems to be to work to enhance the economic autonomy and the personal dignity of members of that class, not to rule off-limits an option that may be the only livelihood for many poor women and to further stigmatize women who already make their living this way.

In grappling further with these issues, we should begin from the realization that there is nothing per se wrong with taking money for the use of one's body. That is the way most of us live, and formal recognition of that fact through contract is usually a good thing for people, protecting their security and their employment conditions. What seems wrong is that relatively few people in the world have the option to use their body, in their work, in what Marx would call a "truly human" manner of functioning, by which he meant (among other things) having some choices about the work to be performed, some reasonable measure of control over its conditions and outcome, and also the chance to use thought and skill rather than just to function as a cog in a machine. Women in many parts of the world are especially likely to be stuck at a low level of mechanical functioning, whether as agricultural laborers, factory workers, or prostitutes. The real question to be faced is how to expand the options and opportunities such workers face, how to increase the humanity inherent in their work, and how to guarantee that workers of all sorts are treated with dignity. In the further pursuit of these questions, we need, on balance, more studies of women's credit unions and fewer studies of prostitution.

NOTES

1. See Anderson, *Value in Ethics and Economics* (Harvard University Press, 1993), 150–158.

2. Joseph Raz, *The Morality of Freedom*, 374 (1986).

Martha C. Nussbaum: "Whether from Reason or Prejudice": Taking Money for Bodily Services

1. Nussbaum notes that prostitution is a highly stigmatized profession. Why do you think prostitution is so stigmatized? Is the stigma justified? Why or why not?

2. Nussbaum argues that criminalizing prostitution makes it more dangerous for prostitutes than if prostitution were legal. Why does she think this? Do you agree? Why or why not?

3. Which of the arguments for making prostitution illegal that Nussbaum considers did you find most compelling? How does Nussbaum respond? Do you find her response convincing?

4. Nussbaum's responses to the objections to legalizing prostitution depend on a strong analogy between prostitution and the other perfectly legal professions to which she compares prostitution. Were there any analogies that you thought didn't stand up to scrutiny? If so, why do you think her analogy wasn't quite apt?

5. Nussbaum's strategy for arguing for the legalization of prostitution is to show that prostitution shares much in common with other, already legal, professions. Can you think of any other professions or activities that are currently illegal, but that ought to be legal if Nussbaum's strategy is sound?

The Truth about Philosophy Majors

Here's the inaccurate, old-school way of thinking:

- Philosophy majors have no marketable skills; they are unemployable.
- They are unprepared for professional careers in anything but teaching philosophy.
- They are useless in an economy built on exploding tech, speed-of-light innovation, and market-wrenching globalization.
- They are destined to earn low salaries.

Here's the new reality: All these assumptions are FALSE.

CAREERS

A wide range of data suggest that philosophy majors are not just highly employable; they are thriving in many careers that used to be considered unsuitable for those holding "impractical" philosophy degrees. The unemployment rate for recent BA philosophy graduates is 4.3 percent, lower than the national average and lower than that for majors in biology, chemical engineering, graphic design, mathematics, and economics.[1]

Nowadays most philosophy majors don't get PhDs in philosophy; they instead land jobs in many fields outside academia. They work in business consulting firms, guide investors on Wall Street, lead teams of innovators in Silicon Valley, do humanitarian work for nongovernment organizations, go into politics, and cover the world as journalists. They teach, write, design, publish, create. They go to medical school, law school, and graduate school in everything from art and architecture to education, business, and computer science. (Of course, besides majoring in philosophy, students can also minor in it, combining a philosophy BA with other BA programs, or take philosophy courses to round out other majors or minors.)

Many successful companies—especially those in the tech world—don't see a philosophy degree as impractical at all. To be competitive, they want more than just engineers, scientists, and mathematicians. They also want people with broader, big-picture skills—people who can think critically, question assumptions, formulate and defend ideas, develop unique perspectives, devise and evaluate arguments, write effectively, and analyze and simplify complicated problems. And these competencies are abundant in people with a philosophy background.

Plenty of successful business and tech leaders say so. Speaking of her undergraduate studies, Carly Fiorina, philosophy major and eventual chief executive of Hewlett-Packard, says, "I learned how to separate the wheat from the chaff, essential from just interesting, and I think that's a particularly critical skill now when there is a ton of interesting but ultimately irrelevant information floating around."[2]

Flickr and Slack cofounder Stewart Butterfield, who has both bachelor's and master's degrees in philosophy, says, "I think if you have a good background in what it is to be human, an understanding of life, culture and society, it gives you a good perspective on starting a business, instead of an education purely in business. You can always pick up how to read a balance sheet and how to figure out profit and loss, but it's harder to pick up the other stuff on the fly."[3]

Sheila Bair got her philosophy degree from the University of Kansas and went on to become chair of the Federal Deposit Insurance Corporation from 2006 to 2011. She says that philosophy "helps you break things down to their simplest elements. My philosophy training really helps me with that intellectual rigor of simplifying things and finding out what's important."[4]

Photo 1: Carly Fiorina, businessperson and political figure
Photo 2: Stewart Butterfield, cofounder of Flickr and Slack
Photo 3: Sheila Bair, nineteenth chair of the FDIC
Photo 4: Katy Tur, author and broadcast journalist for NBC News
Photo 5: Damon Horowitz, entrepreneur and in-house philosopher at Google

Philosophy: A Natural Segue to Law and Medicine

Law schools will tell you that a major in philosophy provides excellent preparation for law school and a career in law. Philosophy excels as a pre-law major because it teaches you the very proficiencies that law schools require: developing and evaluating arguments, writing carefully and clearly, applying principles and rules to specific cases, sorting out evidence, and understanding ethical and political norms. Philosophy majors do very well on the LSAT (Law School Admission Test), typically scoring higher than the vast majority of other majors.

Philosophy has also proven itself to be good preparation for medical school. Critical reasoning is as important in medicine as it is in law, but the study and practice of medicine requires something else—expertise in grappling with the vast array of moral questions that now confront doctors, nurses, medical scientists, administrators, and government officials. These are, at their core, philosophy questions.

David Silbersweig, a Harvard Medical School professor, makes a good case for philosophy (and all the liberal arts) as an essential part of a well-rounded medical education. As he says,

If you can get through a one-sentence paragraph of Kant, holding all of its ideas and clauses in juxtaposition in your mind, you can think through most anything. . . . I discovered that a philosophical stance and approach could identify and inform core issues associated with everything from scientific advances to healing and biomedical ethics.[5]

Philosophy major and NBC journalist Katy Tur says, "I would argue that for the vast majority of people, an education of teaching you to think critically about the world you are in and what you know and what you don't know is useful for absolutely everything that you could possibly do in the future."[6]

It's little wonder, then, that the top ranks of leaders and innovators in business and technology have their share of philosophy majors, a fair number of whom credit their success to their philosophy background. The list is long, and it includes:[7]

Patrick Byrne, entrepreneur, e-commerce pioneer, founder and CEO of Overstock.com
Damon Horowitz, entrepreneur, in-house philosopher at Google
Carl Icahn, businessman, investor, philanthropist. . . .
Larry Sanger, Internet project developer, cofounder of Wikipedia
George Soros, investor, business magnate, philanthropist
Peter Thiel, entrepreneur, venture capitalist, cofounder of PayPal
Jeff Weiner, CEO of LinkedIn

Of course, there are also many with a philosophy background who are famous for their achievements outside the business world. This list is even longer and includes:

Wes Anderson, filmmaker, screenwriter (*The Royal Tenenbaums*, *The Grand Budapest Hotel*)
Stephen Breyer, Supreme Court justice
Mary Higgins Clark, novelist (*All by Myself, Alone*)
Ethan Coen, filmmaker, director
Stephen Colbert, comedian, TV host
Angela Davis, social activist
Lana Del Rey, singer, songwriter
Dessa, rapper, singer, poet
Ken Follett, author (*Eye of the Needle*, *Pillars of the Earth*)
Harrison Ford, actor
Ricky Gervais, comedian, creator of *The Office*
Philip Glass, composer
Rebecca Newberger Goldstein, author (*Plato at the Googleplex*)
Matt Groening, creator of *The Simpsons* and *Futurama*
Chris Hayes, MSNBC host
Kazuo Ishiguro, Nobel Prize–winning author (*The Remains of the Day*)
Phil Jackson, NBA coach
Thomas Jefferson, US president
Charles R. Johnson, novelist (*Middle Passage*)
Rashida Jones, actor
Martin Luther King Jr., civil rights leader
John Lewis, civil rights activist, congressman
Terrence Malick, filmmaker, director (*The Thin Red Line*)
Yann Martel, author (*Life of Pi*)

Photo 6: Larry Sanger, Internet project developer, cofounder of Wikipedia
Photo 7: Stephen Breyer, Supreme Court justice
Photo 8: Stephen Colbert, comedian, TV host
Photo 9: Angela Davis, social activist
Photo 10: Lana Del Rey, singer and songwriter
Photo 11: Chris Hayes, MSNBC host

Deepa Mehta, director, screenwriter (*Fire, Water*)
Iris Murdoch, author (*Under the Net*)
Robert Parris Moses, educator, civil rights leader
Stone Phillips, broadcaster
Susan Sarandon, actor
Susan Sontag, author (*Against Interpretation*), MacArthur Fellow
David Souter, Supreme Court justice
Alex Trebek, host of *Jeopardy!*
George F. Will, journalist, author (*Men at Work: The Craft of Baseball*)
Juan Williams, journalist

Philosophy Majors and the GRE

Philosophy majors score higher than *all other majors* on the Verbal Reasoning and Analytical Writing sections of the GRE (Graduate Record Examinations).

	Verbal Reasoning	Quantitative Reasoning	Analytic Writing
Philosophy	160	154	4.3
Average	149.97	152.57	3.48

Educational Testing Service, 2017 GRE Scores, between July 1, 2013, and June 30, 2016.

Photo 13: Martin Luther King Jr., civil rights leader

Photo 14 John Lewis, civil rights activist, congressman

Photo 12: Rashida Jones, actor

Photo 15: Terrence Malick, film-maker, director

Photo 16: Yann Martel, author (*Life of Pi*)

Photo 17: Deepa Mehta, director, screenwriter (*Fire*)

Photo 18: Susan Sontag, author, MacArthur Fellow

SALARIES

According to recent surveys by PayScale, a major source of college salary information, philosophy majors can expect to earn a median starting salary of $44,800 and a median mid-career salary of $85,100. As you might expect, most of the higher salaries go to STEM graduates (those with degrees in science, technology, engineering, or mathematics). But in a surprising number of cases, salaries for philosophy majors are comparable to those of STEM graduates. For example, while the philosophy graduate earns $85,100 at mid-career, the mid-career salary for biotechnology is $82,500; for civil engineering, $83,700; for chemistry, $88,000; for industrial technology, $86,600; and for applied computer science, $88,800. Median end-of-career salaries for philosophy majors (10–19 years' experience) is $92,665—not the highest pay among college graduates, but far higher than many philosophy-is-useless critics would expect.[8]

Another factor to consider is the increase in salaries over time. On this score, philosophy majors rank in the top ten of all majors with the highest salary increase from start to mid-career at 101 percent. The major with the highest increase: government, at 118 percent. Molecular biology is the fifth highest at 105 percent.[9]

And among liberal arts majors, philosophy salaries are near the top of the list. All liberal arts majors except economics earn lower starting and mid-career pay than philosophy does.

Salary Potential for Liberal Arts Bachelor's Degrees

Major	Median Early Pay (0–5 yrs. work experience)	Median Mid-Career Pay (10+ yrs. work experience)
Economics	$54,100	$103,200
Philosophy	$44,800	$85,100
Political Science	$44,600	$82,000
Modern Languages	$43,900	$77,400
Geography	$43,600	$72,700
History	$42,200	$75,700
English Literature	$41,400	$76,300
Anthropology	$40,500	$63,200
Creative Writing	$40,200	$68,500
Theatre	$39,700	$63,500
Psychology	$38,700	$65,300
Fine Art	$38,200	$62,200

PayScale, "Highest Paying Bachelor Degrees by Salary Potential," *2017–2018 College Salary Report*, https://www.payscale.com/college-salary-report/majors-that-pay-you-back/bachelors.

Salary Potential for Bachelor's Degrees

Major	Median Early Pay (0–5 yrs. work experience)	Median Mid-Career Pay (10+ yrs. work experience)
Mechanical Engineering	$58,000	$90,000
Applied Computer Science	$53,100	$88,800
Information Technology	$52,300	$86,300
Civil Engineering	$51,300	$83,700
Business and Finance	$48,800	$91,100
Biotechnology	$46,100	$82,500
Business Marketing	$45,700	$78,700
Philosophy	$44,800	$85,100
History	$42,200	$75,700
Advertising	$41,800	$84,200
General Science	$41,600	$75,200
Telecommunications	$41,500	$83,700
English Literature	$41,400	$76,300
Marine Biology	$37,200	$76,000

PayScale, "Highest Paying Bachelor Degrees by Salary Potential," *2017–2018 College Salary Report*, https://www.payscale.com/college-salary-report/majors-that-pay-you-back/bachelors.

MEANING

In all this talk about careers, salaries, and superior test scores, we should not forget that for many students, the most important reason for majoring in philosophy is the meaning it can add to their lives. They know that philosophy, after two-and-one-half millennia, is still alive and relevant and influential. It is not only for studying but also for living—for guiding our lives toward what's true and real and valuable. They would insist that philosophy, even with its ancient lineage and seemingly remote concerns, applies to your life and your times and your world. The world is full of students and teachers who can attest to these claims. Perhaps you will eventually decide to join them.

RESOURCES

American Philosophical Association, "Who Studies Philosophy?" http://www.apaonline.org/?whostudiesphilosophy.

BestColleges.com, "Best Careers for Philosophy Majors," 2017, http://www.bestcolleges.com/careers/philosophy-majors/.

George Anders, "That 'Useless' Liberal Arts Degree Has Become Tech's Hottest Ticket," *Forbes*, July 29, 2015, https://www.forbes.com/sites/georgeanders/2015/07/29/liberal-arts-degree-tech/#5fb6d740745d.

Laura Tucker, "What Can I Do with a Philosophy Degree?", TopUniversities.com, March 2, 2015, https://www.topuniversities.com/student-info/careers-advice/what-can-you-do-philosophy-degree

University of California, San Diego, Department of Philosophy, "What Can I Do with a Philosophy Degree?" https://philosophy.ucsd.edu/undergraduate/careers.html.

University of Maryland, Department of Philosophy, "Careers for Philosophy Majors," http://www.philosophy.umd.edu/undergraduate/careers.

The University of North Carolina at Chapel Hill, Department of Philosophy, "Why Major in Philosophy?" http://philosophy.unc.edu/undergraduate/the-major/why-major-in-philosophy/.

NOTES

1. Federal Reserve Bank of New York, "The Labor Market for Recent College Graduates," January 11, 2017, https://www.newyorkfed.org/research/college-labor-market/college-labor-market_compare-majors.html.

2. T. Rees Shapiro, "For Philosophy Majors, the Question after Graduation Is: What Next?" *Washington Post*, June 20, 2017.

3. Carolyn Gregoire, "The Unexpected Way Philosophy Majors Are Changing the World of Business," *Huffpost*, March 5, 2014, https://www.huffingtonpost.com/2014/03/05/why-philosophy-majors-rule_n_4891404.html.

4. Shapiro, "For Philosophy Majors."

5. David Silbersweig, "A Harvard Medical School Professor Makes a Case for the Liberal Arts and Philosophy," *Washington Post*, December 24, 2015.

6. Shapiro, "For Philosophy Majors."

7. American Philosophical Association, "Who Studies Philosophy?" (accessed November 14, 2017), http://www.apaonline.org/?whostudiesphilosophy.

8. PayScale, "Highest Paying Bachelor Degrees by Salary Potential," *2017–2018 College Salary Report*, https://www.payscale.com/college-salary-report/majors-that-pay-you-back/bachelors.

9. PayScale; reported by Rachel Gillett and Jacquelyn Smith, "People with These College Majors Get the Biggest Raises," *Business Insider*, January 6, 2016, http://www.businessinsider.com/college-majors-that-lead-to-the-biggest-pay-raises-2016-1/#20-physics-1.

Abolitionists those who believe that the death penalty is not morally justified (and so seek to abolish it where it exists); those who seek to abolish laws that criminalize drug use.

Abortion the deliberate termination of a pregnancy.

Absolute moral rules are absolute if and only if it is never permitted to break them.

Absolute rule a moral rule that may never permissibly be broken.

Absolutist theories those that endorse the idea that there are absolute moral rules (those that are never permissibly broken).

Act utilitarianism the moral theory that says that an action is morally required just because it does more to improve overall well-being than any other action one could have taken in the circumstances.

Active euthanasia euthanasia that occurs as the intentional termination of a patient's life that involves taking means to hasten her death.

Active surveillance any form of surveillance that is carried about by an actual person such that, when it is successful, the information collected on the target(s) of surveillance is immediately made known to the person conducting the surveillance.

Ad hominem fallacy trying to undermine the truth of a position by attacking the person who is advancing it.

Advance directive a document detailing a person's wishes about medical treatment in the event that that person can no longer communicate those wishes to a doctor.

Affirmative action a social policy that increases the chances of hiring or admissions on the basis of an applicant's status as a member of a group that has suffered extensive discrimination.

Aggravated murder a murder that is made even more severe by especially violent or harmful circumstances in connection with the murder.

Aggravating conditions features of a crime that increase its severity or harmful consequences.

Altruism the motivation to benefit others for their own sake.

Ambiguous having more than one meaning.

Anarchist someone who rejects the legitimacy of all governments and thinks that government ought to be abolished.

Antecedent the 'if' clause of a conditional; the clause that specifies a sufficient condition of the conditional's consequent.

Anthropogenic originated by human beings.

Appeal to authority an informal fallacy that involves relying on authority figures to substantiate a position outside of their area of expertise.

Appeal to ignorance an informal fallacy, also known as *ignoratio elenchi*, that can take one of two forms. In the first, one believes a claim to be true because it hasn't been proven false. In the second, one believes that a claim is false because it hasn't been proven true.

Appeal to irrelevant emotions an effort to convince you of a claim by playing on your emotions, rather than by offering facts and evidence that bear on the truth of the claim.

Arbitrary capricious, unprincipled, without a discernible rationale.

Argument a chain of thought in which reasons are offered in support of a particular conclusion.

Argument from analogy a type of argument that draws a parallel between two things that share several features, concluding that they are likely to share some further feature as well.

Artificial created or modified by human activity.

Artificial selection the process by which humans develop desirable traits in plants or animals by selecting which males or females will reproduce together. It's sometimes called "selective breeding."

Atheism the view that God does not exist.

Atheists those who believe that God does not exist.

Autonomy the power to guide our life through our own free choices.

Battery cages small wire cages housing chickens that can be lined up and stacked in a barn so that thousands of chickens can be stored in a very small space.

Begging the question assuming the truth of the conclusion that one's argument is meant to support.

Biconditional a claim that supplies a condition that is both necessary and sufficient for something; an 'if and only if' sentence.

Binge drinks consumes an excessive amount of alcohol in a short period of time to become severely intoxicated.

Biocentric focused on all living things and their interests and denying the greater intrinsic importance of human beings vis-à-vis other life forms.

Capital offenses those crimes that carry the death penalty as a possible punishment.

Capital punishment the death penalty.

Carbon sink a large system (e.g., an ocean, a forest) that absorbs and stores carbon dioxide from the atmosphere.

Casual sex sex between people who have expressed no commitment to each other.

Categorical imperative a command of reason that requires us to act in a certain way regardless of whether doing so will get us anything we care about.

Categorical reasons reasons that apply to us regardless of whether acting on them will get us what we want.

Cesarean section an operation that involves a surgical incision through the abdomen and uterus to remove the fetus from the womb, while seeking to preserve its life.

Climate change a change in weather patterns that lasts for a long time (e.g., thousands or millions of years).

Coercion the act of forcing someone to act in a particular way such that her autonomy is compromised.

Compensation the means of restoring those who have been harmed to the condition they were in prior to the harm having occurred. Compensation does not require a wrongdoer, and it need not be paid by the perpetrator of the harm.

Conception the point at which a sperm fertilizes an egg and a zygote is formed.

Conditional an 'if-then' sentence.

Consequent the 'then' clause of a conditional; it specifies a necessary condition of the conditional's antecedent.

Consequentialism the family of moral theories that say that an action or a policy is morally required just because it produces the best overall results.

Conservative a position that either seeks to preserve the status quo, or claims that we ought to change the traditional ways of doing things only if there is compelling evidence that doing so would be better.

Continent the feature of being able to manage to do the right thing, though with little or no pleasure, by suppressing very strong contrary desires.

Contradiction when one and the same claim is said to be both true and false.

Conventional morality the system of widely accepted rules and principles that members of a culture or society use to govern their own lives and to assess the actions and the motivations of others.

Counterfactual question a question that asks what would have occurred if, contrary to fact, something else had not taken place.

CRISPR-cas9 a gene-editing tool that allows scientists to target specific sequences of DNA and either alter or delete them, or insert new genetic material altogether.

Critical morality a set of moral norms that (1) does not have its origin in social agreements; (2) is untainted by mistaken beliefs, irrationality, or popular prejudices; and (3) can serve as the true standard for determining when conventional morality has got it right and when it has fallen into error.

De facto equality equality in real, lived experience.

De jure equality equality in the content of the law.

Death row the part of a prison with cells for people sentenced to death.

Decision procedure a method for reliably guiding our decisions, so that when we use it well, we make decisions as we ought to.

Deforestation the destruction of the forest to make land available for other uses (e.g., agriculture).

Desire satisfaction theory the view that something is intrinsically good for you *if* it satisfies your desires, *only if* it satisfies your desires, and *because* it satisfies your desires.

Deterrence theory the view that punishment is justified if, only if, and because it is an efficient way of preventing crime.

Difference principle the principle that says that when distributing resources and opportunities, societies are required to give the greatest priority to the interests of the worst-off among us.

Discriminatory marked by unjustified bias for or against a particular group.

Distributive justice justice in the social distribution of resources and opportunities.

Divine command theory the view that an act is morally required just because it is commanded by God, and immoral just because God forbids it.

Doctrine of double effect the principle that says that if your goal is worthwhile, you are sometimes permitted to act in ways that foreseeably cause certain types of harm, though you must never intend to cause such harms.

Drug addiction a chronic disease characterized by drug seeking and use that is compulsive, or difficult to control, despite harmful consequences.

Drugs chemicals that, when introduced into the bloodstream, predictably alter the way we feel.

Economic egalitarianism the view that it is morally important to distribute wealth and income equally.

Economic inequality the difference in economic well-being between different groups or between individuals within a group.

Embryo the growing offspring that was once a zygote; the embryonic period of gestation lasts from roughly two weeks to eight weeks after conception.

Error theory the view that says that (1) there are no moral features in this world; (2) no moral judgments are true; (3) our sincere moral judgments try, and always fail, to describe the moral features of things; and, as a result, (4) there is no moral knowledge.

Estate tax a tax paid by the estate of a person who has died.

Ethical egoism the ethical theory that says that an action is morally right if and only if it maximizes one's self-interest.

Ethical pluralism the view that there is more than one ultimate, fundamental moral principle.

Ethical vegetarians those who refrain from eating animals out of a moral concern for the rights or welfare of animals.

Ethics of care a moral perspective that emphasizes the centrality of care as the model of admirable moral relations.

Eugenics the use of selective breeding to develop desirable traits in human beings, or the use of sterilization to eradicate undesirable traits in human beings.

Euthanasia the practice of assisting in a patient's death, where such assistance is motivated by the hope of benefitting the patient.

Extrapolation problem the difficulty of concluding that outcomes in one context will carry over to a different context.

Factory farm a large industrial complex where large volumes of animals are packed into a small space to make raising and slaughtering them (or collecting their eggs) maximally efficient.

Fallacious the feature of exhibiting or having committed a fallacy.

Fallacy a kind of poor reasoning. A formal fallacy is an argument form all of whose instances are invalid. Informal fallacies are other kinds of mistakes in reasoning.

Fallacy of affirming the consequent any argument of the form if P, then Q; Q is true; therefore, P is true.

Fallacy of denying the antecedent any argument of the form if P, then Q; P is false; therefore, Q is false.

Feminist ethics a family of moral theories committed to four central claims (1) women are the moral equals of men; (2) the experiences of women deserve our respect and are vital to a full and accurate understanding of morality; (3) traits that have traditionally been associated with women are at least as morally important as traditionally masculine traits; (4) traditionally feminine ways of moral reasoning are often superior to traditionally masculine ways of reasoning.

Fetus the growing offspring that was once an embryo; the fetal period begins at about the eighth week and lasts for the duration of the pregnancy.

Fitness a being's success at survival and reproduction.

General deterrence using the threat of punishment to prevent crimes that might be committed by those other than the criminal himself.

Genetic engineering the direct manipulation of an organism's DNA to alter its characteristics.

Genetic enhancement the direct manipulation of an organism's DNA to improve its form or functioning beyond the level necessary for health.

Genetically modified organism (GMO) organisms whose DNA has been directly altered for human purposes.

Germline cells reproductive cells.

Gestation crates strong metal cages, barely larger than a pig, used to house breeding pigs.

Global warming a rise in average atmospheric temperatures across the world.

Golden Rule the moral principle that requires you to treat others as you would like to be treated.

Government surveillance surveillance carried out by the state or by orders of the state.

Greenhouse effect warming that results when greenhouse gases in the atmosphere (e.g., carbon dioxide, methane) trap heat radiating from the Earth's surface toward outer space.

Hasty generalization illicitly drawing a general lesson from only a small handful of cases.

Hedonism the view that a life is good to the extent that it is filled with pleasure and is free of pain.

Hypothetical imperative a command of reason that tells us to do whatever is needed in order to get what we care about.

Hypothetical syllogism an argument of the form if P, then Q; if Q, then R; therefore, if P, then R.

Iconoclast a person whose views are deeply opposed to conventional wisdom.

Implicit bias prejudice that we do not realize we have.

Incest a sexual relationship between family members.

Infallible incapable of making a mistake.

Inheritance tax a tax paid by the recipients who have inherited the wealth of the deceased.

Innate traits that we have from birth.

Innocence in general, the absence of guilt. In the context of terrorism, innocence denotes the absence of responsibility for the wrongful harms that terrorists are responding to.

Instrumental goods things that are valuable because of the good things they bring about.

Instrumentally valuable something good because of the other good things it makes possible.

Internment camps barbed-wire-enclosed living quarters where thousands of Japanese and Japanese American people were forced to live for two and half years during World War II.

Intrinsically good valuable in and of itself, and worth having for its own sake.

Intrinsically valuable worth pursuing for its own sake; valuable in its own right.

Involuntary euthanasia euthanasia that occurs when a person makes a voluntary choice to remain alive, but someone else overrides that choice and seeks to end the person's life, for his own good.

Jim Crow laws state and local laws passed in the 1880s, in the southern United States, enforcing segregation between white and black people in public places such as schools, restrooms, and restaurants.

Just deserts what a person deserves.

Legal moralism the doctrine that we can legally prohibit behavior that violates no one's rights, so long as that behavior is immoral.

Legal paternalism the doctrine that we can legally prohibit a person's behavior for her own good, even if that behavior is autonomous and violates no one's rights.

Lethal injection a method of executing a person by introducing deadly poison into his bloodstream.

Level down to decrease the resources or benefits of the better-off.

Lex talionis literally, the law of retaliation, which requires that one treat criminals in just the way they treated their victims.

Liberal position regarding sexual morality the view that sex is morally permissible if and only if it is engaged in by consenting adults.

Logical validity the feature of an argument that guarantees the truth of its conclusion, on the assumption that its premises are true.

Lone wolf attacks terrorist attacks undertaken by single individuals, rather than through the coordinated efforts of members of a terrorist group.

Maxim a principle of action you give yourself when you are about to do something.

Maximin principle a principle of rational choice that tells us to survey all of the options, determine the worst-case scenario in each of them, and pick the option that has the best of the worst-case scenarios.

Mere means to treat another as a mere means to the achievement of one's own goals is to treat her in ways that fail to respect her rationality and autonomy, as if she had no intrinsic importance.

Modus ponens an argument of the form: if P, then Q; P; therefore, Q.

Modus tollens an argument of the form: if P, then Q; Q is false; therefore, P is false.

Monistic theories those that endorse the idea that there is just a single ultimate moral rule.

Moral agent a being capable of understanding right and wrong and then conforming its behavior to that understanding; those who bear responsibility for their actions, and who are fit for praise or blame, because they can control their behavior through reasoning.

Moral community the group of those who possess independent moral importance—those who are valuable in and of themselves, regardless of how useful they are.

Moral exemplar a moral role model; someone who exhibits the moral virtues to a great degree.

Moral rights moral entitlements or liberties that protect our interests and choices.

Natural neither created nor altered by humans.

Natural law theory the view that actions are right just because they are natural, and wrong just because they are unnatural. And people are good or bad to the extent that they fulfill their true nature—the more they fulfill their true nature, the better they are.

Necessary condition a requirement, a prerequisite, a precondition.

Net worth a measure of wealth calculated by subtracting liabilities (i.e., debts or financial obligations) from assets (i.e., holdings regarded as having economic value).

Nonvoluntary euthanasia euthanasia that occurs when patients are incapable of making voluntary choices.

Normative system a set of norms, that is, a set of standards for how we ought to behave, ideals to aim for, rules that we should not break.

Norms standards that we ought to live up to.

Objective moral standards those that apply to everyone, even if people don't believe that they do, even if people are indifferent to them, and even if obeying them fails to satisfy anyone's desires.

Omniscient all-knowing.

Oppression a system of unjust and unequal social forces that systematically limit opportunities and impose other harms on members of a given population.

Optimific producing the best results.

Optimific social rule a social rule which, if nearly everyone accepted it, would yield better results than any competing social rule.

Original position John Rawls's term for the situation in which imaginary negotiators, stripped of all knowledge of the features that distinguish them from one another, come together to decide on social principles that will govern them.

Overdose a dangerously excessive and sometimes lethal amount of a drug.

Pacifism the view that peace is a paramount value and that violence (including war) is immoral.

Partiality showing greater concern for, or assigning greater importance to, some beings rather than others.

Passive euthanasia euthanasia that occurs when we "let nature take its course," allowing someone's terminal condition to worsen with the awareness that she will die as a result, all the while intending to make her as comfortable as possible.

Paternalism the practice of limiting someone's liberty, against his will, for his own good.

Passive surveillance any form of surveillance that is not carried out by an actual person such that the information collected on the target(s) of surveillance is not immediately made known to anyone.

Persons beings who are rational; can think, feel emotions, feel pain and pleasure; reflect on the value of their experiences; and communicate in original, sophisticated ways with one another.

Physician-assisted suicide a suicide performed with the help of a medical professional whose role is usually to prescribe and to oversee the administration of (but not to administer) lethal drugs.

Polyamory sexual, romantic, or marital relationships among more than two people.

Polyandrous relating to a social practice in which a woman has more than one husband at the same time.

Polygamous relating to a social practice in which a man has more than one wife at the same time.

Premarital sex sex between two people who have not been married.

Premeditated planned or thought out in advance.

Premises the reasons within an argument that, taken together, are meant to support the argument's conclusion.

Prima facie duty an excellent, nonabsolute, permanent reason to do (or refrain from) something.

Principle of humanity always treat a human being (yourself included) as an end, and never as a mere means.

Principle of merit positions should be awarded on the basis of qualifications.

Principle of universalizability an act is morally acceptable if, and only if, its maxim is universalizable.

Principle of utility the central doctrine of act utilitarianism.

Prisoner's dilemma a situation in which the pursuit of self-interest by all parties leads to a worse outcome than if each were to compromise.

Privacy the level of accessibility of one's personal information to others.

Prostitution having sex in exchange for payment.

Psychological egoism the psychological theory that says that the ultimate motivation behind every human action is the pursuit of self-interest.

Public safety the level of protection citizens and social institutions have against threats to their well-being.

Racism the belief that members of a given race are inferior by virtue of their racial identity.

Ratchet effect an exponential increase of a population over time, occurring in poor communities confronted with scarce resources.

Redlining the practice of denying services to residents of certain areas based on their racial or ethnic identities.

Relativism the view that there are no objective moral standards, and that all correct moral standards hold only relative to each person or each society.

Reparations repairing a wrong one has done to a victim. This requires acknowledgment that one has done wrong, and requires that the wrongdoer provide the victim with the needed repair.

Retributivism the view that punishment is justified if, only if, and because it gives a criminal his just deserts.

Right to life the right not to be killed.

Rule consequentialism the view that an action is morally right just because it is required by an optimific social rule.

Sentience the capacity to have sense experiences (e.g., feelings of pleasure or pain).

Shared privacy one person sharing private information only with some select second party, where that second party ensures that the information remains known only by the two parties.

Slash and burn agriculture a process in which a subsistence farmer cuts down the trees on a small parcel of land and then burns their stumps, so as to create an area suitable for agriculture.

Slippery slope argument an argument designed to criticize certain social innovations on the grounds that allowing them will lead to terrible results in the long run.

Somatic cells nonreproductive cells.

Sorites a form of argument that relies on the difficulty of drawing a principled line between two things that exist along a spectrum.

Soundness the feature that arguments have when they are logically valid and all of their premises are true.

Special deterrence using the threat of punishment to deter the criminal himself.

Speciesism the view that humans, just by virtue of their species membership, are morally more important than nonhuman animals.

Standard of rightness a principle that tells us the conditions under which actions are morally right.

State of nature anarchy; a situation in which there is no government, no central authority, and no group with the exclusive power to enforce its will on others.

Straw man fallacy a form of reasoning that depicts a position in a way that makes it easy to refute, thereby diverting attention from the real position being advanced.

Subjective experience the sort of experience one has when one is conscious and occupying a perspective on the world.

Sufficient condition a guarantee.

Supererogation action that is "above and beyond the call of duty."

Supererogatory praiseworthy action that is above and beyond the call of duty.

Supreme moral rule a moral rule that is both absolute and fundamental.

Surveillance any action that involves monitoring someone with the aim of collecting information about them.

Terrorism the deliberate use of violence on innocent victims, with the intent to intimidate a population, for the purpose of advancing some political goal.

Theists those who believe that God exists.

Tolerance the effect that occurs when the brain adjusts to a pattern of drug use, in which the high that users feel, compared to the high they felt when they first started taking a drug, is reduced.

Trimester one of three three-month stages of a full-term pregnancy.

Unconstitutional not permitted by, or in violation of, a country's political constitution.

Universalizable a maxim is universalizable if and only if the goal that it specifies can be achieved in a world in which everyone is acting on that maxim.

Vegans those who refrain from the purchase and consumption of all animals products.

Vegetarian a person who refrains from eating meat.

Veil of ignorance an imaginary device that erases all knowledge of your distinctive traits in preparation for selecting principles of justice or morality.

Viability the point at which a fetus can survive outside of the mother's womb.

Vicarious punishment punishment that targets innocent people as a way to deter the guilty.

Virtue an admirable character trait that helps to define a person.

Voluntary euthanasia euthanasia that occurs when patients voluntarily consent to end their lives and seek the assistance of others to do so.

Wealth inequality a difference in wealth between groups or individuals within a group.

White privilege the set of social, political, and economic advantages enjoyed by white people in Western countries that are not enjoyed by other racial or ethnic groups in those countries.

Wrongs violations of rights.

Zygote the fertilized egg that marks conception and begins pregnancy.

INDEX